Canadian Fifth Edition

Volume

Horngren | Harrison | Bamber | Lemon | Norwood

Accounting

Charles T. Horngren
Stanford University

Walter T. Harrison, Jr.
Baylor University

Linda Smith Bamber
University of Georgia

W. Morley Lemon
University of Waterloo

Peter R. Norwood
Langara College

Prentice
Hall

Toronto

Canadian Cataloguing in Publication Data

Main entry under title:

Accounting

Canadian 5th ed.
Canadian ed. published under title: Accounting/Charles T. Horngren,
Walter T. Harrison, W. Morley Lemon; with Carol E. Dilworth.
Contents: v. 1. Chapters 1–11—v. 2. Chapters 12–18—v. 3. Chapters 19–26.
ISBN 0-13-089693-4 (v. 1) ISBN 0-13-089694-2 (v. 2) ISBN 0-13-089695-0 (v. 3)

1. Accounting. 2. Managerial accounting. I. Horngren, Charles T., 1926-   .

HF5635.H8125 2002   657'.044   C00.933091-7

0-13-089693-4

Vice President, Editorial Director: Michael Young
Acquisitions Editor: Samantha Scully
Marketing Manager: James Buchanan
Developmental Editor/Copy Editor: Anita Smale, CA
Production Editor: Mary Ann McCutcheon
Production Coordinator: Deborah Starks
Page Layout: Bill Renaud
Permissions/Photo Research: Susan Wallace-Cox
Art Director: Mary Opper
Interior Design: Alex Li
Cover Design: Alex Li
Cover Image: Jim Krantz/Stone

1 2 3 4 5   06 05 04 03 02

Printed and bound in U.S.A.

BRIEF Contents

Contents

*In each chapter, Assignment Material includes Questions, Exercises, Beyond the Numbers, an Ethical Issue, and
     Problems (Group A and B, and Challenge Problems).
**Extending Your Knowledge includes Decision Problems and a Financial Statement Problem.

About the Authors

Charles T. Horngren is the Edmund W. Littlefield Professor of Accounting, Emeritus, at Stanford University. A graduate of Marquette University, he received his MBA from Harvard University and his Ph.D. from the University of Chicago. He is also the recipient of honourary doctorates from Marquette University and DePaul University.

A Certified Public Accountant, Horngren served on the Accounting Principles Board for six years, the Financial Accounting Standards Board Advisory Council for five years, and the Council of the American Institute of Certified Public Accountants for three years. For six years, he served as a trustee of the Financial Accounting Foundation, which oversees the Financial Accounting Standards Board and the Government Accounting Standards Board.

Horngren is a member of the Accounting Hall of Fame.

A member of the American Accounting Association, Horngren has been its President and its Director of Research. He received its first annual Outstanding Accounting Educator Award.

The California Certified Public Accountants Foundation gave Horngren its Faculty Excellence Award and its Distinguished Professor Award. He is the first person to have received both awards.

The American Institute of Certified Public Accountants presented its first Outstanding Educator Award to Horngren.

Horngren was named Accountant of the Year, Education, by the national professional accounting fraternity, Beta Alpha Psi.

Professor Horngren is also a member of the Institute of Management Accountants, where he has received its Distinguished Service Award. He was a member of the Institute's Board of Regents, which administers the Certified Management Accountant examinations.

Horngren is the author of other accounting books published by Prentice-Hall and Pearson Education: *Cost Accounting: A Managerial Emphasis*, Second Canadian Edition, 2000 (with George Foster, Srikant Datar and Howard D. Teall); *Introduction to Financial Accounting*, Third Canadian Edition, 2001 (with Gary L. Sundem, John A. Elliot and Howard D. Teall); *Management Accounting*, Fourth Canadian Edition, 2002, (with Gary L. Sundem, William O. Stratton, and Howard D. Teall); and *Financial Accounting*, Fourth Edition, 2001 (with Walter T. Harrison, Jr.).

Horngren is the Consulting Editor for the Charles T. Horngren Series in Accounting.

Walter T. Harrison, Jr. is Professor of Accounting at the Hankamer School of Business, Baylor University. He received his B.B.A. degree from Baylor University, his M.S. from Oklahoma State University, and his Ph.D. from Michigan State University.

Professor Harrison, recipient of numerous teaching awards from student groups as well as from university administrators, has also taught at Cleveland State Community College, Michigan State University, the University of Texas, and Stanford University.

A member of the American Accounting Association and the American Institute of Certified Public Accountants, Professor Harrison has served as Chairman of the Financial Accounting Standards Committee of the American Accounting Association, on the Teaching/Curriculum Development Award Committee, on the Program Advisory Committee for Accounting Education and Teaching, and on the Notable Contributions to Accounting Literature Committee.

Professor Harrison has lectured in several foreign countries and published articles in numerous journals, including *The Accounting Review, Journal of Accounting*

Research, Journal of Accountancy, Journal of Accounting and Public Policy, Economic Consequences of Financial Accounting Standards, Accounting Horizons, Issues in Accounting Education, and *Journal of Law and Commerce.* He is coauthor of *Financial Accounting, Fourth Edition,* 2001 (with Charles T. Horngren) and *Accounting, Fifth Edition* (with Charles T. Horngren and Linda S. Bamber) published by Prentice Hall. Professor Harrison has received scholarships, fellowships, research grants, or awards from Price Waterhouse & Co., Deloitte & Touche, the Ernst & Young Foundation, and the KMPG Peat Marwick Foundation.

Linda Smith Bamber is Professor of Accounting at the J.M. Tull School of Accounting at the University of Georgia. She graduated summa cum laude from Wake Forest University, where she was a member of Phi Beta Kappa. She is a certified public accountant. For her performance on the CPA examination, Professor Bamber received the Elijah Watt Sells Award in addition to the North Carolina Bronze Medal. Before returning to graduate school, she worked in cost accounting at RJR Foods. She then earned an MBA from Arizona State University, and a Ph.D. from The Ohio State University.

Professor Bamber has received numerous teaching awards from The Ohio State University, the University of Florida, and the University of Georgia, including selection as Teacher of the Year at the University of Florida's Fisher School of Accounting.

She has lectured in Canada and Australia in addition to the U.S., and her research has appeared in numerous journals, including *The Accounting Review, Journal of Accounting Research, Journal of Accounting and Economics, Journal of Finance, Contemporary Accounting Research, Auditing: A Journal of Practice and Theory, Accounting Horizons, Issues in Accounting Education,* and *CPA Journal.* She provided the annotations for the *Annotated Instructor's Edition* of Horngren, Foster, and Datar's *Cost Accounting: A Managerial Emphasis,* Seventh, Eighth, and Ninth Editions.

A member of the Institute of Management Accounting, the American Accounting Association (AAA), and the AAA's Management Accounting Section and Financial Accounting and Reporting Section, Professor Bamber has chaired the AAA New Faculty Consortium Committee, served on the AAA Council, the AAA Research Advisory Committee, the AAA Corporate Accounting Policy Seminar Committee, the AAA Wildman Medal Award Committee, the AAA Nominations Committee, and has chaired the Management Accounting Section's Membership Outreach Committee. She served as Associate Editor of *Accounting Horizons,* and is serving as editor of *The Accounting Review* from 1999 to 2002.

W. Morley Lemon is the PricewaterhouseCoopers Professor of Auditing and the Director of the School of Accountancy at the University of Waterloo. He obtained his BA from the University of Western Ontario, his MBA from the University of Toronto, and his PhD from the University of Texas at Austin. Professor Lemon obtained his CA in Ontario. In 1985 he was honoured by that Institute, which elected him a Fellow. He received his CPA in Texas.

Professor Lemon was awarded the University of Waterloo Distinguished Teacher Award at the 1998 convocation at the University.

Professor Lemon is coauthor, with Arens, Loebbecke, and Splettstoesser, of *Auditing and Other Assurance Services,* Canadian Edition, published by Prentice Hall Canada, and coauthored four previous Canadian editions of that text. He is also coauthor, with Horngren, Harrison, Bamber, and Norwood, of *Accounting,* Canadian Fifth Edition, published by Pearson Education Canada. He coathored the four previous Canadian editions of that text.

He was a member of the Canadian Institute of Chartered Accountants' Assurance Standards Board. He has also served on the Institute of Chartered Accountants of Ontario Council, as well as a number of committees for both bodies. He has chaired and served on a number of committees of the Canadian Academic Accounting Association. Professor Lemon has served on Council and chaired and served on a number of committees of the American Accounting Association.

Professor Lemon has presented lectures and papers at a number of universities and academic and professional conferences and symposia in Canada and the United States. He has chaired and organized six audit symposia held at the University of Waterloo. He has served on the editorial board of and reviewed papers for a number of academic journals including *The Accounting Review, Contemporary Accounting Research, Issues in Accounting Education, Auditing: A Journal of Practice and Theory, Advances in Accounting, Journal of Accounting and Public Policy,* and *CA Magazine.* Professor Lemon has coauthored two monographs and has had papers published in *Contemporary Accounting Research, Research on Accounting Ethics, Journal of Accounting, Auditing and Finance, The Chartered Accountant in Australia, The Journal of Business Ethics,* and *CA Magazine.* He has had papers published in the following collections: *Educating the Profession of Accountancy in the Twenty-First Century, Comparative International Accounting Education Standards, Comparative International Auditing Standards,* and *The Impact of Inflation on Accounting: A Global View.* Professor Lemon served as a judge for *CA Magazine's* Walter J. Macdonald Award.

Professor Lemon has received a number of research grants and has served as the Director of the Centre for Accounting Ethics, School of Accountancy, University of Waterloo. He has written a number of ethics cases published by the Centre.

Peter R. Norwood is an instructor in accounting and the Chair of the Financial Management Department in the School of Business at Langara College. A graduate of the University of Alberta, he received his MBA from the University of Western Ontario. He is a Chartered Accountant and a Certified Management Accountant.

Before entering the academic community, Mr. Norwood worked in public practice and industry for over fifteen years. He is a member of the Board of Examiners of the Canadian Institute of Chartered Accountants and is the Chair of the Professional Development Management Committee of the Institute of Chartered Accountants of British Columbia. In addition, he has been involved in program development for the Certified Management Accountants of British Columbia and the Chartered Accountants' School of Business. Mr. Norwood has lectured at the University of British Columbia and is the Chair of the Langara Foundation.

Photo Credits

2 Dick Hemmingway; **52** Trudy Woodcock's Image Network Inc./Randy Lincks; **108** Trudy Woodcock's Image Network Inc./Joseph Borrelli; **163** The Canadian Press/AP Photo/*St. Louis Post Dispatch,* Larry Williams; **216** The Forzani Group; **293** Dick Hemmingway; **348** Prentice Hall Archives; **407** The Canadian Press/ *Kitchener-Waterloo Record*/ Rich Koza; **456** Photo Disc; **506** IPSCO Inc.; **557** Dick Hemmingway

To the Student

On behalf of the authors, we would like to welcome you to introductory accounting. Whether you plan to major in accounting or are taking this course for interest, rest assured that a basic understanding of accounting is fundamental to the world of business. Many of the principles you will learn in this course will be useful in whatever career you choose to pursue.

As you will discover in this course, accounting is more than bookkeeeping. Accounting requires that you understand issues conceptually in addition to developing the technical ability to record, summarize, report, and interpret financial data. If you devote your efforts to understanding both of these aspects of accounting, you will be taking a large step towards developing a greater understanding of business fundamentals.

To maximize the benefit of this course and this text, there are certain responsibilities that you need to accept. As instructors, we know the volume of material covered in introductory accounting can be overwhelming. On a daily basis, you will learn new principles and techniques. In order to fully comprehend the new material, you should consider the following suggestions:

Read the textbook material in advance.   If you have had a chance to review the chapter before it is covered in class, you will find it much easier to grasp the material when it is presented in class.

Use the end-of-chapter material.   We have provided a multitude of exercises and problems at the end of each chapter. They range from single-objective, basic questions to comprehensive, multi-objective problems. These exercises and problems are designed to help provide a good understanding of the accounting issues you have covered in class. Check Figures for Problems have been provided at the end of the text to help you check your progress.

Use the resources available.   In addition to this text, there are several valuable resources available to help you understand accounting. The most important resource, of course, is your instructor. Other resources created to accompany this text are described below.

Accounting's **Companion Website**, with its on-line **Study Guide**, offers a number of opportunities to test your understanding of the material. Multiple-choice, true-and-false, fill-in-the-blanks, and short-answer questions are scored automatically by the computer, providing you with instant feedback. CBC videos and related cases are provided on-screen. Hot links are given for the companies mentioned in each chapter of the text allowing you instant access to these companies. Message board and chat areas let you contact other accounting students.

Study Guide with Demonstration Problems and Excel Templates provides you with a number of tools to master accounting. Each chapter provides a chapter review, Excel problems with templates on a disk, a Test Yourself section containing matching, multiple-choice, completion questions, exercises, and comprehensive demonstration problems. Solutions are provided for all *Study Guide* activities. A *Study Guide* to accompany Volume I and another to accompany Volume II are available from your bookstore.

Working Papers is a set of tear-out forms you can use to solve all the exercises and problems in Volume I and Volume II. Because the forms you need are already created, you avoid time-consuming set-up and focus on the accounting right away. The *Working Papers* are available from your bookstore.

Don't forget this text! Please look at the next few pages for all the features in the text that will help you succeed in accounting.

Features in *Accounting*

LEARNING accounting can be a bit overwhelming, especially if you have little business or accounting experience. But with a good text and instructor, you will succeed. To help you, we provide features in every chapter of this text to make accounting as easy to understand as possible. Please read through the next few pages to learn more about *Accounting* and the many ways it will help you understand, learn, and apply accounting concepts.

Chapter Objectives are listed on the first page of each chapter. This "roadmap" shows you what will be covered and what is especially important. Each objective is repeated in the margin where the material is first covered. The objectives are summarized at the end of the chapter.

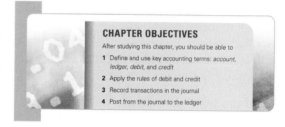

Chapter openers present a story about a real company or a real business situation, and show why the topics in the chapter are important to real companies. Some of the companies you'll read about include Research In Motion, Air Canada, IPSCO Inc., General Motors, and Intrawest. Students tell us that using real companies makes it easier for them to learn and remember accounting concepts.

Weblinks in the margin give you the internet address for the companies mentioned in the text. If you want to learn more about a company, use these handy references.

Objectives in the margin signal the beginning of the section that covers the objective topic. Look for this feature when you are studying and want to review a particular objective.

Student-to-Student boxes appear in every chapter. We asked real students to tell us which concepts or ideas they found particularly challenging and which feature or item in *Accounting* helped them overcome the challenge. One student said, "I think that the Student-to-Student boxes are great...they help students realize that other students have read and maybe even struggled with the same concepts that they are struggling with and they give them encouragement to continue."

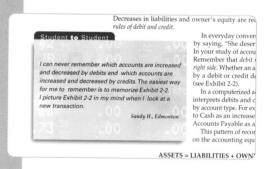

Learning Tips in the margin are suggestions for learning or remembering concepts that you might find difficult.

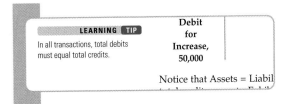

Exhibits are provided in full colour to make the concepts easier to understand and easier to remember.

Stop and Think boxes are "speed bumps" that allow you to slow down for a moment, review and apply to a decision situation material just covered in the text. These serve as an excellent way to check your progress because the answers are provided in the same box.

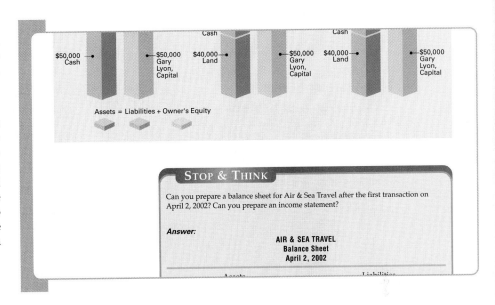

Assets = Liabilities + Owner's Equity

STOP & THINK

Can you prepare a balance sheet for Air & Sea Travel after the first transaction on April 2, 2002? Can you prepare an income statement?

Answer:

AIR & SEA TRAVEL
Balance Sheet
April 2, 2002

DON'T FORGET

the material in the margins! Some of these items allow you to pause and make sure you understand the material covered in the text. Others are excellent study aids because they help you find material you are looking for quickly. We already mentioned the Objectives, the Weblinks, and the Learning Tips in the margins. Here are some other margin items.

Working It Out are short calculation questions that appear throughout the chapter. Answers are provided to give you immediate feedback. You can use these questions to check your progress and to prepare for exams.

Thinking It Over are short questions about concepts just covered in the text. Answers are provided to give you immediate feedback. Like the Working It Out questions, you can use Thinking It Over questions to check your progress and to prepare for exams.

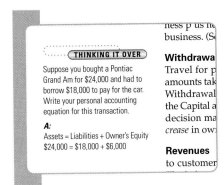

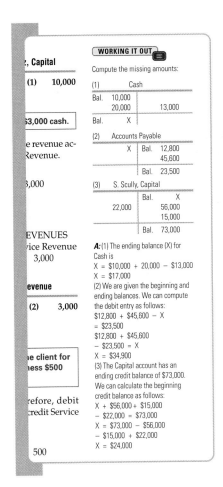

Key Points in the margin highlight important details from the text. These are good review tools for when you prepare for tests or exams.

Mid-Chapter Summary Problem for Your Review gives you another chance to review your understanding of the material covered in the first half of the chapter. A full solution is provided so you can judge whether you should look at the material again or proceed to the last half of the chapter.

Accounting and the E-World
or
Accounting Around the Globe
appears in each chapter. These boxes illustrate either how the world of e-commerce is influencing accounting or how accounting differs around the world. These boxes offer interesting views of accounting that might make you think about accounting in different ways.

(Right side)
Credit

e **debit** side, and the right side is called the can be confusing because they are new. To y remember this:

   left side
   right side

> **KEY POINT**
>
> The accounting equation must balance after every transaction. But verifying that total assets = total liabilities + owner's equity is no longer necessary after every transaction. The equation will balance as long as the debits in each transaction equal the credits in the transaction.

Mid-Chapter Summary Problem
for Your Review

On August 1, 2003, Mary Woo opens Woo Computer Consulting. During the business's first ten days of operations, it completes the following transactions:

a. To begin operations, Mary Woo deposits $40,000 of personal funds in a bank account entitled Woo Computer Consulting. The business receives the cash and gives Woo capital (owner's equity).
b. Woo Computer Consulting pays $20,000 cash for a small house to be used as an office and $10,000 for the land on which the house is located.
c. The business purchases office supplies for $500 on account.
d. The business pays $6,000 cash for office furniture.
e. The business pays $150 on the account payable created in Transaction (c).
f. Woo withdraws $1,000 cash for personal use.

Required

1. Prepare the journal entries to record these transactions. Key the journal entries by letter.
2. Post the entries to T-accounts and calculate the ending balance.
3. Prepare the trial balance of Woo Computer Consulting at August 10, 2003.

Solution to Review Problem

Requirement 1

Accounts and Explanation	Ref.	Debit	Credit
a. Cash		40,000	
Mary Woo, Capital			40,000
Record initial investment from owner.			
b. Building		20,000	
Land		10,000	
Cash			30,000
Purchased building for an office and land.			
c. Office Supplies		500	
Accounts Payable			500
Purchased office supplies on account.			

Accounting and the *e*-World

Using Computers and the Internet to Be Successful

Computers and the internet are two reasons that companies have been able to grow to sizes unimaginable a decade ago and to spread throughout the world. Computers process vast amounts of data quickly and the internet allows companies to maintain constant contact with far-flung operations.

Bombardier Inc. (**http://www.bombardier.com**) has operations in twelve countries on three continents covering four major lines of business. Imagine the difficulty that Bombardier would have in gathering together all the company's financial data to prepare its 2000 financial statements if it did not have computers and world-wide data linkage through the internet.

Magna International (**http://www.magna.com**) employs 59,000 people at 174 manufacturing divisions and 33 product development and engineering centres in 19 countries—and Magna is able to produce its annual financial statements within five weeks of its December 31 year end. Magna can do this because of its extensive use of computers and because all its world-wide operations are connected by means of an electronic network.

Both of these companies are successful because they produce excellent products and are world leaders at what they do. Their success is based on their ability to make good decisions, and they are able to do this because they have excellent information technology working for them. Their accounting systems around the world are compatible with each other. Management is confident that the information they receive daily is both accurate and current. Computers and the internet provide this accurate information for decision making in real time.

Decision Guidelines show how the accounting concepts covered in the chapter are used by business people to make business decisions. This feature shows why accounting principles and concepts are important in a broader business context, not just to accountants. The Decision Guidelines also serve as an excellent summary of the chapter topics.

Summary Problem for Your Review pulls together the chapter concepts with an extensive and challenging review problem. Full solutions are given so that you can check your progress.

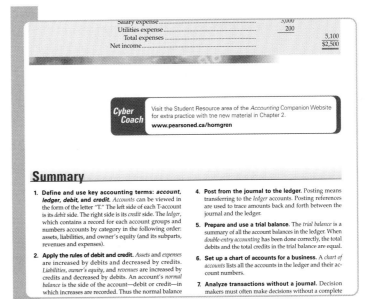

Summary Problem
for Your Review

The trial balance of Tommassini Computer Service Centre on March 1, 2003, lists the company's assets, liabilities, and owner's equity on that date.

	Balance	
Account Titles	**Debit**	**Credit**
Cash	$26,000	
Accounts receivable	4,500	
Accounts payable		$ 2,000
John Tomassini, Capital		28,500
Total	$30,500	$30,500

During March the business engaged in the following transactions:

a. Borrowed $45,000 from the bank and signed a note payable in the name of the business.

b. Paid cash of $40,000 to a real estate company to acquire land.

c. Performed service for a customer and received cash of $5,000.

d. Purchased supplies on account, $300.

Cyber Coach appears after both the Mid-Chapter Summary Problem for Your Review and the Summary Problem for Your Review. It is a reminder to visit the *Accounting* Companion Website's Online Study Guide and other student resources for extra practice with the new material introduced in the chapter.

	Salary expense		3,000	
	Utilities expense		200	
	Total expenses			5,100
	Net income			$2,500

Cyber Coach — Visit the Student Resource area of the *Accounting* Companion Website for extra practice with the new material in Chapter 2.
www.pearsoned.ca/horngren

Summary appears at the end of each chapter. It gives a concise description of the material covered in the chapter and is organized by objective. Use this summary as a starting point for organizing your review when studying for a test or exam.

Summary

1. **Define and use key accounting terms: *account*, *ledger*, *debit*, and *credit*.** *Accounts* can be viewed in the form of the letter "T." The left side of each T-account is its *debit* side. The right side is its *credit* side. The *ledger*, which contains a record for each account groups and numbers accounts by category in the following order: assets, liabilities, and owner's equity (and its subparts, revenues and expenses).

2. **Apply the rules of debit and credit.** *Assets* and *expenses* are increased by debits and decreased by credits. *Liabilities*, *owner's equity*, and *revenues* are increased by credits and decreased by debits. An account's *normal balance* is the side of the account—debit or credit—in which increases are recorded. Thus the normal balance

4. **Post from the journal to the ledger.** Posting means transferring to the *ledger* accounts. Posting references are used to trace amounts back and forth between the journal and the ledger.

5. **Prepare and use a trial balance.** The *trial balance* is a summary of all the account balances in the ledger. When *double-entry accounting* has been done correctly, the total debits and the total credits in the trial balance are equal.

6. **Set up a chart of accounts for a business.** A *chart of accounts* lists all the accounts in the ledger and their account numbers.

7. **Analyze transactions without a journal.** Decision makers must often make decisions without a complete

Self-Study Questions allow you to test your understanding of the chapter on your own. Page references are given for each of these multiple-choice questions so that you can review a section quickly if you miss an answer. The answers are provided after the Similar Accounting Terms (see below) so you can check your progress.

Accounting Vocabulary lists all the terms that were defined and appeared in bold type in the chapter. The page references are given so you can review the meanings of the terms. These terms are also collected and defined in the Glossary at the end of the text.

Similar Accounting Terms links the accounting terms used in the chapter to similar terms you might have heard outside your accounting class, in the media, in other courses, or in day-to-day business dealings. Knowing similar terms should make it easier to remember the accounting terms.

These are the Answers to the Self-Study Questions, mentioned above.

Self-Study Questions

Test your understanding of the chapter by marking the correct answer for each of the following questions:

1. An account has two sides called the *(p. 55)*
   a. Debit and credit   c. Revenue and expense
   b. Asset and liability d. Journal and ledger
2. Increases in liabilities are recorded by *(p. 56)*
   a. Debits   b. Credits
3. Why do accountants record transactions in the journal? *(p. 58)*
   a. To ensure that all transactions are posted to the ledger
   b. To ensure that total debits equal total credits
   c. To have a chronological record of all transactions
   d. To help prepare the financial statements
4. Posting is the process of transferring information from the *(p. 60)*
   a. Journal to the trial balance
   b. Ledger to the trial balance
   c. Ledger to the financial statements
   d. Journal to the ledger
5. The purchase of land for cash is recorded by a *(p. 61)*
   a. Debit to Cash and a credit to Land
   b. Debit to Cash and a debit to Land
   c. Debit to Land and a credit to Cash
   d. Credit to Cash and a credit to Land
6. The purpose of the trial balance is to *(p. 64)*
   a. List all accounts with their balances
   b. Ensure that all transactions have been recorded

   c. Speed the collection of cash receipts from customers
   d. Increase assets and owner's equity
7. What is the normal balance of the Accounts Receivable, Office Supplies, and Rent Expense accounts? *(p. 71)*
   a. Debit   b. Credit
8. A business has Cash of $3,000, Notes Payable of $2,500, Accounts Payable of $4,300, Service Revenue of $7,000 and Rent Expense of $1,800. Based on these data, how much are its total liabilities? *(p. 74)*
   a. $5,500   c. $9,800
   b. $6,800   d. $13,800
9. Smale Transport earned revenue on account. The earning of revenue on account is recorded by a *(pp. 74–78)*
   a. Debit to Cash and a credit to Revenue
   b. Debit to Accounts Receivable and a credit to Revenue
   c. Debit to Accounts Payable and a credit to Revenue
   d. Debit to Revenue and a credit to Accounts Receivable
10. The account credited for a receipt of cash on account is *(p. 77)*
    a. Cash   c. Service Revenue
    b. Accounts Payable d. Accounts Receivable

Answers to the Self-Study Questions follow the Similar Accounting Terms.

Accounting Vocabulary

Account *(p. 52)*	Journal *(p. 58)*
Chart of accounts *(p. 70)*	Ledger *(p. 52)*
Credit *(p. 55)*	Posting *(p. 60)*
Debit *(p. 55)*	Trial balance *(p. 64)*

Similar Accounting Terms

Cr	Credit; right
Dr	Debit; left
The Ledger	The Books; the General Ledger
Entering the transaction in a journal	Making the journal entry; journalizing the transaction
Withdrawals by owner(s)	In a *proprietorship* or *partnership*, distributions from a company to its owner(s).

Answers to Self-Study Questions				
1. a	3. c	5. c	7. a	9. b
2. b	4. d	6. a	8. b ($6,800 = $2,500 + $4,300)	10. d

THE END-OF-CHAPTER Assignment Material is
extensive because often the best way to make sure you grasp new accounting concepts is to practice, practice, practice! The number and variety of questions, exercises, and problems give you every opportunity to test your understanding of the chapter's concepts.

Questions require short, written answers or short calculations, often on a single topic.

Exercises on a single or a small number of topics require you to "do the accounting" and, often, to consider the implications of the result in the same way that real companies would. The objectives covered by each exercise are listed after the brief description of the concepts covered.

Serial Exercise in Chapters 2 to 5 follows one company and builds in complexity with each chapter, providing an excellent review of the accounting cycle.

Challenge Exercises provide a challenge for those students who have mastered the Exercises.

Beyond the Numbers exercises require analytical thinking and written responses about the topics presented in the chapter.

Ethical Issues are thought-provoking situations that help you recognize when ethics should affect an accounting decision.

Problems are presented in two groups that mirror each other, "A" and "B." Many instructors work through problems from Group A in class to demonstrate accounting concepts, then assign problems from Group B for homework or extra practice. The objectives covered by each problem are listed after the brief description of the concepts covered.

Challenge Problems encourage you to consider the effect of accounting information and apply it to decision situations.

THE EXTENDING Your Knowledge section contains
Decision Problems and a Financial Statement Problem.

Decision Problems allow you to prepare and interpret accounting information and then make recommendations to a business based on this information.

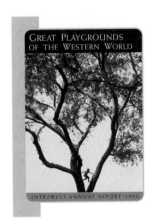

Financial Statement Problem allows you to use real financial information from Intrawest Corporation, the successful Canadian ski and resort company, to answer the problem. Selected information from Intrawest's 2000 Annual Report appears in Appendix A of Volume I and Volume II of *Accounting*.

A purple disk icon appears beside selected Exercises and Problems to remind you that Excel spreadsheets have been created to answer these questions. The spreadsheets are part of the *Study Guide with Excel Templates* that you can purchase from your bookstore. You don't have to use the spreadsheets to answer the questions but you may find they help to organize your answers.

In addition to the features above that appear in each chapter, two additional features appear at the end of each part of Volume I and Volume II.

Comprehensive Problem covers the content addressed in the book so far. This is a relatively long problem that provides an excellent review of all of the topics covered in the chapters in that part. See your instructor for the solution to this problem.

CBC **CBC Video Cases** appear at the end of each of the Parts in Volumes I and II. A CBC video of these interesting *Venture* and *Market Place* segments is also available to your instructor to accompany these cases. The videos demonstrate the importance of accounting concepts to real businesses and real entrepreneurs in a truly interesting way.

To the Instructor

Welcome to *Accounting*! *Accounting*, Canadian Fifth Edition, provides full introductory coverage of financial and management accounting in a three-volume, full-colour format. Volumes I and II cover financial accounting topics, and Volume III covers management accounting topics. The three-volume format gives *Accounting* the flexibility to be used in a one-, two-, or three-semester introductory accounting course.

Instructors have told us their greatest challenges are effectively teaching students with very different business and accounting backgrounds, and motivating students to give accounting the study time and attention it deserves. *Accounting*'s approach and features were designed to help you address and overcome these challenges. The keys are a supportive text and supplements package, and motivated students.

Accounting continues its tradition of complete and comprehensive coverage of the most widely used accounting theory and practices. We have always believed that it is better to provide instructors with comprehensive coverage that could be trimmed if necessary rather than reduced coverage that might require instructor supplementation. This gives instructors the flexibility to tailor their presentations and coverage to their students' experience level.

Accounting continues to use the easy-to-understand writing style that sets it apart from other accounting texts. Instuctors have told us time and again that if students miss an accounting class, the instructor knows that students can keep up by reading the text. This should help students feel less overwhelmed by the thought of missing a class and having to catch up.

Accounting principles and procedures are illustrated using examples from real Canadian companies. This real-world business context runs throughout the chapters and assignment material, motivating students to think about companies and situations they know, which can help make difficult concepts easier to grasp. Familiar companies enliven the material and illustrate the role of accounting in business. In those situations where "live" data drawn from real companies would complicate the material for introductory students, we illustrate the accounting with realistic examples from generic companies to give students the clearest examples possible.

Changes in the Canadian Fifth Edition of *Accounting*

The most obvious change in this new edition is the attractive, inviting full-colour presentation of the material. Students have said they find concepts easier to understand when key material and exhibits are presented in colour. However, colour is only the beginning—colour cannot make weak features stronger. The features have to stand on their own.

A number of well-received features were introduced in the previous edition of *Accounting*, and most of these features remain in this edition, including Decision Guidelines, Similar Accounting Terms, Working It Out, and Thinking It Over items. A number of new features have been added to this edition—they are described below. For detailed descriptions of all of the features in this text, please refer to the To the Student section earlier in this Preface.

The most significant change in this edition of *Accounting* is the focus on proprietorships in Volume I, especially in Chapters 1 to 5. This change was made after considerable discussion with many instructors from across the country. While most instructors agreed that corporations, large and small, are increasing in number in Canada, the majority of instructors felt that students grasp owner's equity concepts more easily by learning about proprietorships before learning about corporations. However, for those instructors who prefer a corporate focus in Chapters 1 to 5, we will offer a website containing a parallel presentation of Chapters 1 to 5 with a corporate focus in the same full-colour layout as the text.

New **Student-to-Student** boxes appear in every chapter. We asked students to tell us which concepts or ideas they found particularly challenging and which feature or item in *Accounting* helped them overcome the challenge. One student said, "I think that the Student-to-Student boxes are great...they help students realize that other students have read and maybe even struggled with the same concepts that they are struggling with and they give them encouragement to continue."

A new **Accounting and the E-World** or **Accounting Around the Globe** box appears in each chapter. These boxes illustrate how the world of e-commerce is influencing accounting or how accounting differs around the world. These boxes offer interesting views of accounting that motivate students to think about accounting in different ways.

A new **Cyber Coach** box appears after both the Mid-Chapter Summary Problem for Your Review and the Summary Problem for Your Review. It is a reminder to students to visit the *Accounting* Companion Website's Online Study Guide and other student resources for extra practice with the new material introduced in the chapter.

A new **Management Accounting for a Small Business** box appears in every chapter in Volume III. It shows how the management accounting concepts covered in the chapter, which are typically illustrated using large manufacturers, are used by real, small businesses.

Cash flow statements are introduced in Chapter 1 and covered fully in Chapter 17. To reduce possible student confusion, chapter-by-chapter introductions to portions of the cash flow statement have been eliminated in this edition.

The "generic" Financial Statement Problems in Chapters 1 to 18 have been moved from the text to the Companion Website and the *Instructor's Resource Manual and Video Guide*. However, the Intrawest Corporation Financial Statement Problems are still presented in the text.

What has *not* changed is the quantity, quality, and variety of exercises, questions, and problems presented in the text. All problems have been updated and revised, but the flexibility provided to instructors by the extensive assignment material remains.

Supplements

Accounting is supported by a variety of online course management solutions designed to meet the full range of instructor and student needs, including a Companion Website (see the following page to learn more about this supplement), a WebCT course, a BlackBoard course, and Pearson Education Canada's proprietary Course Compass course. For more information about any of these solutions, please contact your Pearson Education Canada Sales and Editorial Representative, or visit **www.pearsoned.com/dl**.

Also ask about the other supplements that accompany *Accounting:*

Instructor's Solutions Manual, Vol I: 013-093176-4; Vol II: 013-093177-2;
      Vol III: 013-093178-0
Instructor's Manual and Media Guide, Vol I: 013-093190-X; Vol II: 013-093201-9;
      Vol III: 013-093202-7
Test Item File, Vol I: 013-093193-4; Vol II: 013-093194-2;
      Vol III: 013-093195-0
Test Manager (Computerized Test Item File) for Volume I, II, III: 013-093276-0
CBC/Pearson Education Canada Video Library, 013-093270-1
Solutions Acetates, Vol I: 013-093275-2; Vol II: 013-093277-9;
      Vol III: 013-093279-5
Electronic Transparencies in PowerPoint, 013-093273-6
Adapting Your Lecture Notes if Using Larson et al., *Fundamental Accounting Principles*,
      9/C/E, 013-064588-5
Adapting Your Lecture Notes if Using Weygandt et al., *Accounting Principles*,
      Canadian Edition, 013-064589-3

Your Internet companion to the most exciting, state-of-the-art educational tools on the Web!

T

he Pearson Education Canada Companion Website is easy to navigate and is organized to correspond to the chapters in this textbook. The Companion Website comprises these distinct, functional features:

Customized Online Resources

Online Interactive Study Guide

Interactivities

Communication

Table of Contents

Explore these areas in this Companion Website. Students and distance learners will discover resources for indepth study, research, and communication, empowering them in their quest for greater knowledge and maximizing their potential for success in the course.

A NEW WAY TO DELIVER EDUCATIONAL CONTENT

Course Management

Our Companion Websites provide instructors and students with the ability to access, exchange, and interact with material specially created for our individual textbooks.

- Syllabus Manager provides instructors with the option of creating online classes and constructing an online syllabus linked to specific modules in the Companion Website.

- Grader allows the student to take a test that is automatically marked by the program. The results of the test can be e-mailed to the instructor and then added to the student's record.

- Help includes an evaluation of the user's system and a tune-up area that makes updating browsers and plug-ins easier. This new feature will facilitate the use of our Companion Websites.

Instructor Resources

This section features modules with additional teaching material organized by chapter for instructors. Downloadable PowerPoint Presentations, Electronic Transparencies, and an Instructor's Manual are just some of the materials that may be available in this section. Where appropriate, this section will be password protected. To get a password, simply contact your Pearson Education Canada representative or call Faculty Sales and Services at 1-800-850-5813.

General Resources

This section contains information that is related to the entire book and that will be of interest to all users of the site. A Table of Contents and a Glossary are just two examples of the kind of information you may find in this section.

The General Resources section may also feature Communication facilities that provide a key element for distributed learning environments:

- Message Board – This module takes advantage of browser technology to provide the users of each Companion Website with a national newsgroup to post and reply to relevant course topics.

- Chat Room – This module enables instructors to lead group activities in real time. Using our chat client, instructors can display website content while students participate in the discussion.

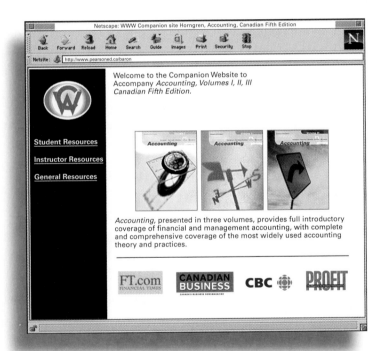

Acknowledgements for the Canadian Fifth Edition

We would like to thank Chuck Horngren, Tom Harrison, and Linda Bamber for their encouragement and support.

Particular thanks are due to the following people for reviewing the manuscript for this new edition, writing the supplements, and offering many useful suggestions:

Cécile Ashman, Algonquin College
Dave Bopara, Toronto School of Business
Nada Borden, College of the North Atlantic
Wayne Bridgeman, formerly with CGA-Canada
Chris Burnley, Malaspina University College
Maisie Caines, College of the North Atlantic
K. Suzanne Coombs, Kwantlen University College
Robert Dearden, Red River Community College
Vincent Durant, St. Lawrence College
Dave Fleming, George Brown College
Augusta Ford, College of the North Atlantic
Donna Grace, Sheridan College
Larry Howe, University College of the Fraser Valley
Stephanie Ibach, Northern Alberta Institute of Technology
Rick Martin, College of the North Atlantic
Penny Parker, Fanshawe College
Carson Rappell, Dawson College
David Sale, Kwantlen University College
Scott Sinclair, British Columbia Institute of Technology
Bob Sproule, University of Waterloo
Gregg Tranter, Southern Alberta Institute of Technology
H. Barrie Yackness, British Columbia Institute of Technology
Elizabeth Zaleschuk, Douglas College

We are also grateful to the instructors across the country who took the time to respond to surveys conducted during the planning stages of this edition. The thoughts and opinions of these instructors were a valuable guide as we mapped out a strategy for improving this new edition:

Cécile Ashman, Algonquin College
James E. Chambers, St. Clair College
K. Suzanne Coombs, Kwantlen University College
Richard Farrar, Conestoga College
Albert M. Ferris, University of Prince Edward Island
Reiner Frisch, Georgian College
Donna Grace, Sheridan College
Elizabeth Hicks, Douglas College
Wayne Irvine, Mount Royal College
Connie Johl, Douglas College
Allen McQueen, Grant MacEwan Community College
Ann MacGillivary, Mount Saint Vincent University
Tariq Nizami, Champlain Regional College CEGEP
Penny Parker, Fanshawe College
Gabriela Schneider, Grant MacEwan Community College
Scott Sinclair, British Columbia Institute of Technology
Bob Sproule, University of Waterloo
Elizabeth Zaleschuk, Douglas College

We especially want to thank those students who have generously and eloquently contributed Student to Student comments to the text and companion website. Our thanks go to those at the following schools who participated in this project. The students' and instructors' enthusiasm was greatly appreciated.

> Assiniboine Community College
> College of the North Atlantic
> Conestoga College
> Douglas College
> Humber College
> Langara College
> Malaspina University College
> McGill University
> University College of the Fraser Valley
> University of Waterloo

Thanks are extended to Intrawest Corporation for permission to use its annual report in Volumes I and II of the text. Thanks are extended to JVC Canada Inc. for permission to use its invoice in Chapter 5. Thanks are extended to the Canadian Institute of Chartered Accountants for permission to use materials published by the Institute. We acknowledge the support provided by *The Globe and Mail's Report on Business*, the *Financial Post*, and by the annual reports of a large number of public companies.

We would like to acknowledge the people of Pearson Education Canada, in particular Vice President, Editorial Director Michael Young and Acquisitions Editor Samantha Scully. We would also like to acknowledge especially the editorial and technical support of Anita Smale, CA.

I would like to thank my wife Sandra for her support and encouragement.

W. Morley Lemon

I would like to thank my wife, Helen, and my family very much for their support, assistance, and encouragement.

Peter R. Norwood

The Accounting Profession: Career Opportunities

The accounting profession offers exciting career opportunities because every organization uses accounting. The corner grocery store keeps accounting records to measure its success in selling groceries. The largest corporations need accounting to monitor their locations and transactions. And the dot.coms must account for their transactions. Why is accounting so important? Because it helps an organization understand its business in the same way a model helps an architect construct a building. Accounting helps a manager understand the organization as a whole without drowning in its details.

The Work of Accountants

Positions in the field of accounting may be divided into several areas. Two general classifications are *public accounting* and *private accounting*.

Canadian Institute of Chartered Accountants
www.cica.ca

Certified General Accountants Association of Canada
www.cga-canada.org

Society of Management Accountants of Canada
www.cma-canada.org

In Canada, most accountants, both public and private, belong to one of three accounting bodies, which set the standards for admission of members and deal with matters like the rules of professional conduct followed by their members: The Canadian Institute of Chartered Accountants (CICA), whose members are called *Chartered Accountants (CA)*; the Certified General Accountants Association of Canada (CGAAC), whose members are called *Certified General Accountants (CGA)*; and the Society of Management Accountants of Canada (SMAC), whose members are called *Certified Management Accountants (CMA)*. The role and activities of each of these bodies are discussed below.

Private accountants work for a single business, such as a local department store, the St-Hubert restaurant chain, or ATCO Ltd. Charitable organizations, educational institutions, and government agencies also employ private accountants. The chief accounting officer usually has the title of controller, treasurer, or chief financial officer. Whatever the title, this person often carries the status of vice-president.

Public accountants are those who serve the general public and collect professional fees for their work, much as doctors and lawyers do. Their work includes auditing, income tax planning and preparation of returns, management consulting, and various accounting services. These specialized accounting services are discussed in the next section. Public accountants represent about a quarter of all professional accountants.

Some public accountants pool their talents and work together within a single firm. Public accounting firms are called CA firms, CGA firms, or CMA firms, depending on the accounting body from which the partners of the firm come. Public accounting firms vary greatly in size. Some are small businesses, and others are medium-sized partnerships. The largest firms are worldwide partnerships with over 2,000 partners. The five largest accounting firms in the world are often called the Big Five. They represent the first four and sixth largest CA firms in Canada and are, in alphabetical order:

Arthur Andersen LLP
www.arthurandersen.com

Deloitte & Touche LLP
www.deloitte.com

Ernst & Young LLP
www.eyi.com

KPMG International LLP
www.kpmg.com

PricewaterhouseCoopers LLP
www.pwcglobal.com

Arthur Andersen	Ernst & Young
Deloitte & Touche (Samson Belair/ Deloitte & Touche in Quebec)	KPMG
	PricewaterhouseCoopers

Although these firms employ less than 25 percent of the more than 60,000 CAs in Canada, they audit most of the 1,000 largest corporations in Canada. The top partners in large accounting firms earn about the same amount as the top managers of other large businesses.

Exhibit 1 shows the accounting positions within public accounting firms and other organizations. Of special interest in the exhibit is the upward movement of accounting personnel, as the arrows show. In particular, note how accountants may move from positions in public accounting firms to similar or higher positions in industry and government. This is a frequently travelled career path. Because accounting deals with all facets of an organization—such as purchasing, manufacturing, marketing, and distribution—it provides an excellent basis for gaining broad business experience.

Accounting Organizations and Designations

The position of accounting in today's business world has created the need for control over the professional, educational, and ethical standards of accountants. Through statutes passed by provincial legislatures, the three accounting organizations in Canada have received the authority to set educational requirements and professional standards for their members and to discipline members who fail to adhere to their codes of conduct. The acts make them self-regulating bodies, just as provincial associations of doctors and lawyers are.

The *Canadian Institute of Chartered Accountants (CICA)*, whose members are chartered accountants or CAs, is the oldest accounting organization in Canada. Experience and education requirements for becoming a CA vary among the provinces. Generally, the educational requirement includes a university degree. All the provincial institutes, require is that an individual, to qualify as a CA, pass a national four-day uniform final examination administered by the CICA and meet articling requirements. The provincial institutes grant the right to use the professional designation CA.

CAs in Canada generally must earn their practical experience by working for a public accounting firm; subsequently, about half the CAs in Canada leave public practice for jobs in industry, government, or education. A small number of CAs meet their experience requirements working for the federal or provincial governments. CAs in public accounting have the right to perform audits and issue opinions on the audited financial statements in all provinces in Canada.

CAs belong to a provincial institute (*Ordre* in Quebec) and through that body to the CICA. The provincial institutes have the responsibility for developing and enforcing the code of professional conduct that guides the actions of the CAs in that province.

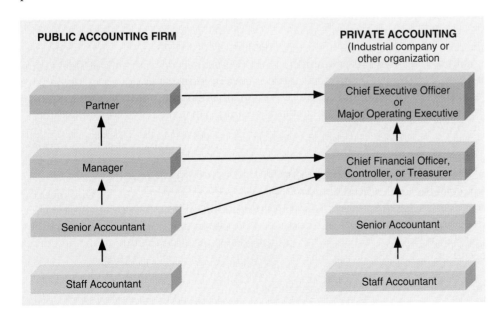

EXHIBIT 1

Accounting Positions within Organizations

The CICA, through the Accounting Standards Board and the Assurance Standards Board respectively, issues accounting standards or GAAP (discussed in Chapter 1) and auditing standards (Generally Accepted Auditing Standards or GAAS). These standards are collected in the *CICA Handbook*. Specific standards are italicized and called *Recommendations*. Accounting Recommendations are the standards or regulations that govern the preparation of financial statements in Canada. The Accounting Standards Board and the Assurance Standards Board publish Accounting Guidelines and Assurance and Related Services Guidelines respectively; these do not have the force of Recommendations, but simply provide guidance on specific issues.

The Emerging Issues Committee (EIC), another committee of the CICA, publishes Abstracts of Issues Discussed, which rank below Accounting Guidelines in terms of authority. A fourth body, the Public Sector Accounting Board (PSAB), issues standards pertaining to public sector accounting.

The CICA supports and publishes research relating primarily to financial reporting and auditing. The CICA publishes a monthly professional journal entitled *CA Magazine*.

The *Certified General Accountants Association of Canada (CGAAC)* is also regulated by provincial law. The experience and education requirements for becoming a CGA vary from province to province, but in all provinces the individual must either pass national examinations administered by the CGAAC in the various subject areas or gain exemption by taking specified university, college, and association courses. Certain subjects may only be passed by taking a national examination. CGA students require a university degree in order to obtain their designation; they do not need to have the degree to enroll as a student.

CGAs may gain their practical experience through work in public accounting, industry, or government. They are employed in public practice, industry, and government. Some provinces license CGAs in public practice, which gives them the right to conduct audits and issue opinions on financial statements, while some other provinces do not require a licence for them to perform audits.

The association supports research in various areas pertaining to accounting through the Canadian CGA Research Foundation. CGAAC publishes a professional journal entitled *CGA Magazine*.

The *Society of Management Accountants of Canada (SMAC)* administers the Certified Management Accountant program that leads to the Certified Management Accountant (CMA) designation. The use of this designation is similarly controlled by provincial law. Students generally must have a university degree. The SMAC administers an admission or entrance examination that students must pass before embarking on a two-year professional program and completing two years of required work experience. After completing the professional program and the work experience, they write a final examination and make a presentation to a SMAC committee, based on the professional program administered by the SMAC, in order to obtain the CMA designation. The SMAC also administers the professional program and the final examination. CMAs earn their practical experience in industry or government, and are generally employed in industry or government, although some CMAs are in public accounting. The Society issues standards relating to management accounting through the SMAC. The SMAC conducts and publishes research relating primarily to management accounting. The SMAC publishes a professional journal entitled *Cost and Management*.

The *Financial Executives Institute (FEI)* is an organization composed of senior financial executives from many of the large corporations in Canada, who meet on a regular basis with a view to sharing information on how they can better manage their organizations. Most of these executives have one of the three designations just discussed. The FEI supports and publishes research relating to management accounting. The FEI also publishes a journal, the *Financial Executive*.

The *Institute of Internal Auditors (IIA)* is a world-wide organization of internal auditors. It administers the examinations leading to and grants the Certified Internal

CA Magazine
www.cica.ca/magazine/
e_index.htm

CGA Magazine
www.cga-canada
org/index.html

CMA Magazine
www.cma-canada.org/
english/cma10.html

Financial Executives Institute
www.fei.org

Internal Auditor
www.rutgers.edu/
Accounting/raw/iia/period/
ia.htm

Auditor (CIA) designation. Internal auditors are employees of an organization whose job is to review the operations, including financial operations, of the organization with a view to making it more economical, efficient, and effective. Many Canadian internal auditors are members of Canadian chapters of the IIA. The IIA supports and publishes research and conducts courses related to internal auditing. The IIA journal is *The Internal Auditor*.

The *Canadian Academic Accounting Association (CAAA)* directs its attention toward the academic and research aspects of accounting. A high percentage of its members are professors. The CAAA publishes a journal devoted to research in accounting and auditing, *Contemporary Accounting Research*.

While it is not an accounting organization or designation, *Canada Customs and Revenue Agency (CCRA)* enforces the tax laws and collects the revenue needed to finance the federal government.

Canadian Academic Accounting Association
www.stmarys.ca/
partners/caaa/caaa.htm

Canada Customs and Revenue Agency
www.ccra-adrc.gc.ca

Specialized Accounting Services

As accounting affects so many people in so many different fields, public accounting and private accounting include specialized services.

Public Accounting

Auditing is one of the accounting profession's most significant services to the public. An audit is the independent examination that ensures the reliability of the reports that management prepares and submits to investors, creditors, and others outside the business. In carrying out an audit, public accountants from outside a business examine the business's financial statements. If the public accountants believe that these documents are a fair presentation of the business's operations, they offer a professional opinion stating that the firm's financial statements have been prepared in accordance with generally accepted accounting principles, or, if generally accepted accounting principles are not applicable, with an appropriate disclosed basis of accounting. Why is the audit so important? Creditors considering loans want assurance that the facts and figures the borrower submits are reliable. Shareholders, who have invested in the business, need to know that the financial picture management shows them is complete. Government agencies need information from businesses. All want information that is unbiased.

Tax accounting has two aims: complying with the tax laws and minimizing taxes to be paid. Because combined federal and provincial income tax rates range as high as 53 percent for individuals and 46 percent for corporations, reducing income tax is an important management consideration. Tax work by accountants consists of preparing tax returns and planning business transactions to minimize taxes. In addition, since the imposition of the Goods and Services Tax (GST), public accountants have been involved in advising their clients how to properly collect and account for GST. Public accountants advise individuals on what types of investments to make, and on how to structure their transactions. Accountants in corporations provide tax planning and preparation services as well.

Management consulting is the term that describes the wide scope of advice public accountants provide to help managers run a business. As they conduct audits, public accountants look deep into a business's operations. With the insight they gain, they often make suggestions for improvements in the business's management structure and accounting systems. Management consulting is the fastest-growing service provided by accountants.

Accounting services is also a catchall term used to describe the wide range of services related to accounting provided by public accountants. These services include bookkeeping and preparation of financial statements on a monthly or annual basis. Some small companies have all their accounting done by a public accounting firm.

Private Accounting

Cost accounting analyzes a business's costs to help managers control expenses or set selling prices. Good cost accounting records guide managers in pricing their products to achieve greater profits. Also, cost accounting information shows management when a product is not profitable and should be dropped from a product line.

Budgeting sets sales and profit goals, and develops detailed plans—called budgets—for achieving those goals. Some of the most successful companies in Canada have been pioneers in the field of budgeting, for example, Schneider Corporation, the food company.

Information systems design identifies the organization's information needs, both internal and external. Using flow charts and manuals, designers develop and implement the system to meet those needs.

Internal auditing is performed by a business's own audit staff. Many large organizations, Ontario Power Generation Inc., Hudson's Bay Co., and The Bank of Nova Scotia among them, maintain a staff of internal auditors. These accountants evaluate the firm's own accounting and management systems to improve operating efficiency, and to ensure that employees follow management's policies.

Exhibit 2 summarizes these accounting specializations.

As you work through *Accounting* you will learn how to use accounting to make business decisions. With the exciting career opportunities accounting offers, consider a career in accounting.

EXHIBIT 2

Specialization in Public and Private Accounting

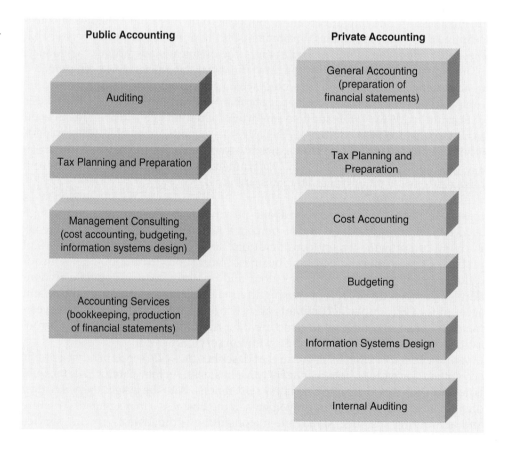

Public Accounting

- Auditing
- Tax Planning and Preparation
- Management Consulting (cost accounting, budgeting, information systems design)
- Accounting Services (bookkeeping, production of financial statements)

Private Accounting

- General Accounting (preparation of financial statements)
- Tax Planning and Preparation
- Cost Accounting
- Budgeting
- Information Systems Design
- Internal Auditing

1

Accounting and the Business Environment

CHAPTER OBJECTIVES

After studying this chapter, you should be able to

1   Use accounting vocabulary for decision making

2   Apply accounting concepts and principles to business situations

3   Use the accounting equation to describe an organization's financial position

4   Use the accounting equation to analyze business transactions

5   Prepare and use the financial statements

6   Evaluate the performance of a business

B riana Weill, a business student at the British Columbia Institute of Technology in Vancouver, wanted to earn some money to help pay for her education and a trip to the Yukon next summer. She had only $75 with the school year ahead.

Briana's father was a do-it-yourself person, and Briana often helped him as he finished the basement of the Weill home, built a deck at the back of the house, and constructed bookcases and all the other furniture in her room. Briana decided to use her experience to do light repair jobs for customers and named her company "Weill Do It For You." She purchased needed materials and provided them to customers at cost plus 20 percent for handling. She also charged $15 per hour for her time. Briana used her mother's van and paid only for the cost of the gas used. Her father loaned her his tools. She spent $30 on advertising leaflets, which she distributed herself.

Briana started her business in September 2001 and by April 2002 Briana had worked on 12 jobs and had been paid $1,550. She had paid her mother $125 for gas and had spent $230 for additional tools and supplies. After paying for leaflets, gas, tools, and supplies, Briana had $1,165 plus her original $75 left to pay for her schooling and trip and had gained valuable business experience. Prospective employers like to see experience like Briana's on a résumé.

How well did Briana Weill's business perform? In common language, we might say that, during the period September to April, Briana Weill "made" $1,165. This means that for the eight-month period, Briana earned a profit of $1,165 after all expenses were subtracted from all revenues she was paid. *Earnings, profit, revenues,* and *expenses* are key accounting terms. This chapter covers these and other terms and introduces the financial statements that businesses use to report their financial affairs.

W HAT role does accounting play in this situation? Briana Weill had to decide how to organize her company. Weill Do It For You is a proprietorship—a single-owner company—with Weill as the owner. As her business grows, she may consider joining forces with a fellow student to form a partnership. If she wants to expand the business after graduation, she could choose to incorporate—that is, to form a corporation. In this chapter, we discuss all three forms of business organization: proprietorships, partnerships, and corporations.

You may already know various accounting terms and relationships, because accounting affects people's behaviour in many ways. This first accounting course will sharpen your focus by explaining how accounting works. As you progress through this course, you will see how accounting helps people like Briana Weill—and you—achieve business goals.

Accounting:
The Basis for Business Decisions

OBJECTIVE 1
Use accounting vocabulary for decision making

Accounting is the information system that measures business financial activities, processes that information into reports, and communicates the results to decision makers. For this reason it is called "the language of business." The better you understand the language, the better your decisions will be, and the better you can manage the financial aspects of living. A recent survey indicates that business managers believe it is more important for college students to learn accounting than any other business subject. Decisions concerning personal financial planning, education expenses, loans, car payments, income taxes, and investments are based on the *information system* that we call accounting. Financial statements, a key product of an accounting system, provide information that helps people make informed business decisions. **Financial statements** report on a business in monetary amounts, providing information to help people make informed business decisions.

Is my business making a profit? Should I hire assistants? Am I earning enough money to pay my rent? Answers to business questions like these are based on accounting information.

Please don't mistake bookkeeping for accounting. *Bookkeeping* is a procedural element of accounting, just as arithmetic is a procedural element of mathematics. Increasingly, people are using computers to do detailed bookkeeping—in households, businesses, and organizations of all types. Exhibit 1-1 illustrates the role of accounting in business. The process starts and ends with people making decisions.

Users of Accounting Information: Decision Makers

Decision makers need information. The more important the decision, the greater the need for information. Virtually all businesses and most individuals keep accounting records to aid decision making. The following sections discuss some of the people and groups who use accounting information.

Individuals   People such as you use accounting information in day-to-day affairs to manage bank accounts, evaluate job prospects, make investments, and decide whether to rent or buy a house.

Businesses   Managers of businesses use accounting information to set goals for their organizations, evaluate their progress toward those goals, and take corrective action if necessary. Decisions based on accounting information may include which building to purchase, how much merchandise inventory to keep on hand, and how much cash to borrow. Briana Weill needed to know how much she could spend on advertising and on tools and supplies for her construction business.

Investors   Investors provide the money a business needs to begin operations. Briana Weill was able to begin operations by investing only $75 in her business. To decide whether to invest in a new venture, potential investors evaluate what return they can reasonably expect on their investment. This means analyzing the financial statements of the business and keeping up with developments in the business press, for example, *The Financial Post* (a part of *The National Post*) and *Report on Business* published by *The Globe and Mail*.

Creditors   Before making a loan, creditors (lenders) such as banks determine the borrower's ability to meet scheduled payments. This evaluation includes a report

EXHIBIT 1-1

The Flow of Information in an Accounting System

1. People make decisions.
2. Business transactions occur.
3. Businesses prepare reports to show the results of their operations.

of the borrower's financial position and a prediction of future operations, both of which are based on accounting information.

Government Regulatory Agencies   Most organizations face government regulation. For example, the provincial securities commissions in British Columbia, Alberta, Saskatchewan, Manitoba, Ontario, and Quebec see that businesses that sell their shares to or borrow money from the public disclose certain financial information to the investing public.

Taxing Authorities   Local, provincial, and federal governments levy taxes on individuals and businesses. Income tax is calculated using accounting information. Businesses determine their goods and services tax and sales tax based on their accounting records that show how much they have sold.

Nonprofit Organizations   Nonprofit organizations such as churches, hospitals, government agencies, and colleges, which operate for purposes other than to earn a profit, use accounting information in much the same way that profit-oriented businesses do.

Other Users   Employees and labour unions may make wage demands based on the accounting information that shows their employer's reported income. Consumer groups and the general public are also interested in the amount of income that businesses earn. And newspapers may report "an improved profit picture" of a major company as it emerges from economic difficulties. Such news, based on accounting information, is related to the company's health.

Financial Accounting and Management Accounting

Users of accounting information are a diverse population, but they may be categorized as external users or internal users. This distinction allows us to classify accounting into fields—financial accounting and management accounting.

Financial accounting provides information to people outside the firm. Creditors and outside investors, for example, are not part of the day-to-day management of the company. Likewise, government agencies and the general public are external users of a firm's accounting information. Chapters 2 through 18 in Volumes I and II of this book deal primarily with financial accounting.

Management accounting generates information for internal decision makers, such as top executives, department heads, college deans, and hospital administrators. Volume III of this book covers management accounting.

The History and Development of Accounting

Accounting has a long history. Some scholars claim that writing arose in order to record accounting information. Account records date back to the ancient civilizations of China, Babylonia, Greece, and Egypt. The rulers of these civilizations used accounting to keep track of the cost of labour and materials used in building structures like the great pyramids. The need for accounting has existed as long as there has been business activity.

Accounting developed further as a result of the information needs of merchants in the city-states of Italy during the 1400s. In that busy commercial climate, the monk Luca Pacioli, a mathematician and friend of Leonardo da Vinci, published the first known description of double-entry bookkeeping in 1494.

In the Industrial Revolution of the nineteenth century, the growth of corporations spurred the development of accounting. The corporation owners—the shareholders—were no longer necessarily the managers of their business. Managers had to create accounting systems to report to the owners how well their businesses were doing. Because managers want their performance to look good, society needs a way to ensure that the business information provided is reliable.

In Canada, the *Accounting Standards Board (AcSB)* of the Canadian Institute of Chartered Accountants (CICA) determines how financial accounting is practised. The AcSB is made up of Chartered Accountants (CAs) from public accounting, industry, government, and academe, plus individuals nominated by the Canadian Council of Financial Analysts, the Financial Executives Institute of Canada, the Canadian Academic Accounting Association, the Certified General Accountants Association of Canada, and the Society of Management Accountants of Canada. As described in the Appendix following Chapter 1, the federal and provincial legislatures through the various companies' acts and the various provincial securities commissions have given the standards or *generally accepted accounting principles (GAAP)* issued by the AcSB their legal status.

Like other segments of society, accounting must be practised in an ethical manner. We look next at the ethical dimension of accounting.

Ethical Considerations in Accounting and Business

Ethical considerations pervade all areas of accounting and business. Consider a situation that challenges the ethical conduct of the accountant.

A company is being sued by a competitor for allegedly copying the competitor's process. Loss of the lawsuit will impose significant financial hardship on the company, jeopardize the company's relationships with its customers and creditors, and likely cause the price of the company's stock to fall. Should the company disclose this sensitive information in its financial statements? Generally accepted accounting principles require the company to describe the lawsuit in its financial statements and the company's auditor to indicate if he or she thinks the company's disclosure is inadequate.

Of the 200 companies surveyed in the CICA's 1999 edition of *Financial Reporting in Canada, Twenty-Fourth Edition*, 102 reported information about lawsuits or possible judgments against the company in the notes to their financial statements.[1]

By what criteria do accountants address questions that challenge their ethical conduct? The three accounting bodies described below all have rules of conduct that govern their members' professional behaviour. Many companies have codes of conduct that bind their management and employees to high levels of ethical conduct.

The Professional Accounting Bodies and Their Standards of Professional Conduct

Chartered Accountants (CAs), Certified General Accountants (CGAs), and Certified Management Accountants (CMAs) are all governed by rules of conduct created by their respective organizations. Many of the rules apply whether the members are public accountants working in public practice or private accountants working in industry or government, while other rules are applicable only to those members in public practice.

The rules of conduct serve both the members of the accounting bodies and the public. The rules serve members by setting standards that they must meet, and providing a benchmark against which they will be measured by their peers. The public is served because the rules of conduct provide it with a list of the standards to which the members of the body adhere. This helps the public determine its

---

[1]Byrd, C., I. Chen, and H. Chapman, *Financial Reporting in Canada 1999*, Twenty-fourth Edition. (Toronto: Canadian Institute of Chartered Accountants, 1999), p. 360.

expectations of members' behaviour. However, the rules of conduct should be considered a minimum standard of performance; ideally, the members should continually strive to exceed them.

There are certain rules that are fundamental to the practice of accounting and common to the rules of conduct of all three bodies. They concern the confidentiality of information the accountant is privy to, maintenance of the reputation of the profession, the need to perform their work with integrity and due care, competence, refusal to be associated with false and misleading information, and compliance by the accountant with professional standards such as the accounting standards found in the *CICA Handbook*.

There are other rules that are fundamental to the practice of public accounting. They deal with the public accountant's need for independence, and with the rules governing advertising, the seeking of clients, and the conduct of practice.

Codes of Business Conduct of Companies

Many companies have codes of conduct that apply to their employees in their dealings with each other and with the companies' suppliers and customers. Some of these companies mention their code in the report of management section of the annual report. For example, the Schneider Corporation 1999 annual report stated:

> The Corporation communicates throughout the organization the responsibility for employees to maintain high ethical standards in their conduct of the Corporation's affairs. This responsibility is characterized in the Code of Conduct signed by each management employee which provides for compliance with laws of each jurisdiction in which the Corporation operates and for observance of rules of ethical business conduct.

The company indicates to its employees how management expects employees to behave.

Types of Business Organizations

A business takes one of three forms of organization, and in some cases accounting procedures depend on the organizational form. Therefore, you should understand the differences among the three types of business organizations: proprietorships, partnerships, and corporations.

Proprietorships   A **proprietorship** has a single owner, called the proprietor, who is usually also the manager. Briana Weill's business is a proprietorship. Proprietorships tend to be small retail establishments and individual professional businesses, such as those of physicians, lawyers, and accountants, but also can be very large. From the accounting viewpoint, each proprietorship is distinct from its proprietor. Thus the accounting records of the proprietorship do *not* include the proprietor's personal accounting records.

Partnerships   A **partnership** joins two or more individuals together as co-owners. Each owner is a partner. Briana Weill's business would be a partnership when she took on a partner. Many retail establishments, as well as some professional organizations of physicians, lawyers, and accountants, are partnerships. Most partnerships are small and medium-sized, but some are quite large; there are public accounting firms in Canada with more than 500 partners and law firms with more than 100 partners. Accounting treats the partnership as a separate organization distinct from the personal affairs of each partner.

Corporations   A **corporation** is a business owned by **shareholders**, people or other corporations who own stock in or shares of ownership in the business. The corporation is the dominant form of business organization in Canada. Although

KEY POINT

A proprietorship and a partnership (Ch. 12) are not legal entities separate from their owners, so the income from proprietorships and partnerships is taxable to their owners, not to the business. But in accounting, the owner and the business are considered separate entities, and separate records are kept for each. A corporation (Ch. 13) is a separate legal entity. The corporation is taxed on its income, and the owners are taxed on any income they receive from the corporation.

proprietorships and partnerships are more numerous, corporations enact more business and are generally larger in terms of total assets, income, and number of employees. Most well-known companies, such as Bombardier Inc., McCain Foods Ltd., and National Bank of Canada, are corporations. In Canada, generally corporations must have *Ltd.* or *Limited, Inc.* or *Incorporated,* or *Corp.* or *Corporation* in their legal name to indicate that they are incorporated. Corporations need not be large; a business with only a few assets and employees could be organized as a corporation.

A business becomes a corporation when the federal or a provincial government approves its articles of incorporation. From a legal perspective, a corporation is a distinct entity. The corporation operates as an "artificial person" that exists apart from its owners and that conducts business in its own name. The corporation has many of the rights that a person has. For example, a corporation may buy, own, and sell property. The corporation may enter into contracts and sue and be sued. Like the proprietorship and the partnership, the corporation is an organization with an existence separate from its owners.

Corporations differ significantly from proprietorships and partnerships in one important way. If a proprietorship or partnership cannot pay its debts, lenders can take the owners' personal assets—cash and belongings—to satisfy the business's obligations. But if a corporation goes bankrupt, lenders cannot take the personal assets of the shareholders. The *limited personal liability* of shareholders for corporate debts explains why corporations are the dominant form of business organization. People can invest in corporations with limited personal risk.

Another factor in corporate growth is the division of ownership into individual shares. Companies such as BCE, Inc., the Bank of Nova Scotia, and Canadian Pacific Limited have issued millions of shares of stock and have tens of thousands of shareholders. An investor with no personal relationship either to the corporation or to any other shareholder can become an owner by buying 30, 100, 5,000, or any number of shares of its stock. For most corporations, the investor may sell the shares at any time. It is usually harder to sell one's investment in a proprietorship or a partnership than to sell one's investment in a corporation.

Exhibit 1-2 shows how the three types of business organizations compare.

Accounting for corporations includes some unique complexities. For this reason, we initially focus on proprietorships. We cover partnerships in Chapter 12 and begin our discussion of corporations in Chapter 13.

Accounting Concepts and Principles

Accounting practices follow certain guidelines. The rules that govern how accountants measure, process, and communicate financial information fall under the heading GAAP, which stands for **generally accepted accounting principles**.

EXHIBIT 1-2

Comparison of the Three Forms of Business Organization

	Proprietorship	Partnership	Corporation
1. Owner(s)	Proprietor—one owner	Partners—two or more owners	Shareholders—generally many owners
2. Life of organization	Limited by owner's choice or death	Limited by owners' choices or death	Indefinite
3. Personal liability of owner(s) for business debts	Proprietor is personally liable	Partners are personally liable	Shareholders are not personally liable
4. Accounting status	The proprietorship is separate from the proprietor	The partnership is separate from the partners	The corporation is separate from the shareholders

Accounting principles draw their authority from their acceptance in the business community. They are generally accepted by those people and organizations who need guidelines in accounting for their financial undertakings.

GAAP in Canada rests on Section 1000, "Financial Statement Concepts," of the *CICA Handbook. The primary objective of financial reporting is to provide information useful for making investment and lending decisions and for assessing management's stewardship.* Decision makers who require useful accounting information include investors, creditors, members (in the case of not-for-profit organizations such as cooperatives), contributors (in the case of not-for-profit organizations such as charities), and other users, including management. The objective of financial statements appears at the top of the hierarchy shown in Exhibit 1-3.

To be useful, information must be *understandable, relevant,* and *reliable,* as well as *comparable* and *consistent.* The information must be *understandable* to users if they are to be able to use it. *Relevant* information influences decisions and is useful for making predictions and for evaluating past performance. *Reliable* information is free from error and the bias of a particular viewpoint; it is in agreement with the underlying events and transactions. *Comparable* information is information that is produced by organizations using the same accounting principles and policies, and allows comparison between the organizations. *Consistent* application of these

EXHIBIT 1-3

A Hierarchy of Qualities that Increase the Value of Information for Decision Making

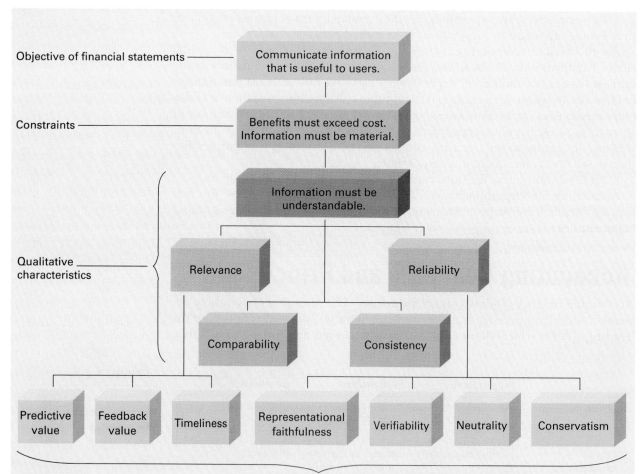

Factors that increase the quality of information*

*Section 1000 of the *CICA Handbook* describes these factors as attributes that make accounting information relevant or reliable.
Predictive value: the information can be used to make predictions. *Feedback value*: the information can be used to confirm the accuracy or inaccuracy of earlier predictions. *Timeliness*: the information must be received in time to make decisions. *Representational faithfulness*: the information presented agrees with the underlying transactions. *Verifiability*: the information can be confirmed by reference to other sources. *Neutrality*: the information is free of bias that would influence users' decisions. *Conservatism*: the assets, revenues, and gains are not overstated; the liabilities, expenses, and losses are not understated.

principles over time allows year-to-year comparisons. Exhibit 1-3 summarizes these qualitative characteristics that increase the value of accounting information.

There are two constraints to providing information to users that is understandable, relevant, reliable, comparable, and consistent. The first constraint is that the benefits of the information produced should exceed the costs of producing the information, as stated in Paragraph 1000.16 in the *CICA Handbook*. For example, it may be very costly to produce detailed information beyond that required by GAAP for a forestry company's lumber inventory. If the cost of providing this information exceeds the benefits to decision makers of receiving this information, the detailed information should not be provided.

The second constraint is *materiality*, as stated in Paragraph 1000.17; a piece of information is material if it would affect a decision maker's decision. Materiality is not defined in the standards but is a matter of the information preparer's judgment. For example, information about inventory is important to users of Canadian Tire's financial statements, since a change in inventory could change a decision maker's decision about investing in Canadian Tire or selling products to Canadian Tire. Thus, such information would be provided to decision makers. However, information about the supplies inventory at Vancouver City Savings Credit Union would not likely change the investment decision of a member of the credit union, so details of such information are not provided. Both of these constraints are reflected in Exhibit 1-3.

The characteristics presented in Exhibit 1-3 combine to shape the concepts and principles that make up GAAP. This course will expose you to the generally accepted methods of accounting. We begin the discussion of GAAP in this section and introduce additional concepts and principles as needed throughout the book. Appendix B at the end of Volume I and Volume II summarizes the major elements of generally accepted accounting principles.

The Entity Concept

The most basic concept in accounting is that of the **entity**. An accounting entity is an organization or a section of an organization that stands apart from other organizations and individuals as a separate economic unit. From an accounting perspective, sharp boundaries are drawn around each entity so as not to confuse its affairs with those of other entities.

Suppose Briana Weill's bank account showed a $2,000 balance at the end of the year. Suppose only $700 of that amount grew from the business's operations. The other $1,300 arose from a gift from her parents. If Briana follows the entity concept, she will keep separate the money generated by the business—one economic unit—from the money generated by the gift from her family—a second economic unit. This separation makes it possible to view the business's operating result clearly.

Suppose Briana disregarded the entity concept and treated the full $2,000 amount as income from her business operations. She would be misled into believing that the business produced more cash than it did. Any steps needed to make the business more successful might not be taken.

Consider Petro-Canada, a giant company with oil exploration, oil-refining, and retail gasoline sales operations (see Exhibit 1-4). Petro-Canada accounts for each of these divisions separately in order to know which part of the business is earning a profit, which needs to borrow money, and so on. If sales in the retail gasoline division were dropping drastically, Petro-Canada would do well to identify the reason. But if sales figures from all divisions were analyzed as a single amount, then management would not even know that the company was selling less gasoline. Thus the entity concept also applies to the parts of a large organization—in fact, *to any entity that needs to be evaluated separately*. When a company is preparing its financial statements for external users, all of these entities are consolidated into a single entity. Thus the divisions of Petro-Canada are combined and reported in the consolidated financial statements of Petro-Canada.

Petro-Canada Corporation
www.petro-canada.ca

EXHIBIT 1-4

The Entity Petro-Canada

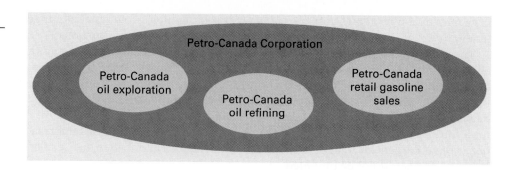

The entity concept also applies to nonprofit organizations such as churches, synagogues, and government agencies. A hospital, for example, may have an emergency room, a pediatrics unit, and a surgery unit. The accounting system of the hospital should account for each separately to allow the managers to evaluate the progress of each unit.

In summary, the transactions of different entities making up the whole organization should not be accounted for together. Each entity should be accounted for separately.

The Reliability (Objectivity) Principle

Accounting records and statements are based on the most reliable data available so that they will be as accurate and useful as possible. This guideline is the **reliability principle**, also called the **objectivity principle**. Reliable data are verifiable. They may be confirmed by any independent observer. For example, Briana Weill's purchase of tools and supplies for $230 is supported by paid invoices. This is objective evidence of her cost of the tools and supplies. Ideally, accounting records are based on information that flows from activities that are documented using objective evidence. Without the reliability principle, accounting records would be based on whims and opinions and would be subject to dispute.

Suppose you want to open a stereo shop. To have a place for operations, you transfer a small building to the business. You believe the building is worth $155,000. To confirm its value, you hire two real-estate professionals, who appraise the building at $147,000. Is $155,000 or $147,000 the more reliable estimate of the building's value? The real-estate appraisal of $147,000 is, because it is supported by independent, objective observation. The business should record the building cost as $147,000.

The Cost Principle

The **cost principle** states that acquired assets and services should be recorded at their actual cost (also called *historical cost*). Even though the purchaser may believe the price paid is a bargain, the item is recorded at the price paid in the transaction and not at the "expected" cost. Suppose your stereo shop purchased some stereo equipment from a supplier who was going out of business. Assume you got a good deal on this purchase and paid only $2,000 for merchandise that would have cost you $3,000 elsewhere. The cost principle requires you to record this merchandise at its actual cost of $2,000, not the $3,000 that you believe the equipment to be worth.

The cost principle also holds that the accounting records should maintain the historical cost of an asset for as long as the business holds the asset. Why? Because cost is a reliable measure. Suppose your store holds the stereo equipment for six months. During that time, stereo prices increase, and the equipment can be sold for $3,500. Should its accounting value—the figure "on the books"—be the actual cost of $2,000 or the current market value of $3,500? According to the cost principle, the accounting value of the equipment remains at actual cost, $2,000.

The Going-Concern Concept

Another reason for measuring assets at historical cost is the **going-concern concept**, which holds that the entity will remain in operation for the forseeable future. Most assets—that is, the firm's resources, such as supplies, land, buildings, and equipment—are acquired to use rather than to sell. Under the going-concern concept, accountants assume the business will remain in operation long enough to use existing assets for their intended purpose.

To understand the going-concern concept, consider the alternative, which is to go out of business. A store that is holding a Going Out of Business Sale is trying to sell all its assets. In that case, the relevant measure of the assets is their current market value. Going out of business, however, is the exception rather than the rule.

The Stable-Monetary-Unit Concept

We think of a loaf of bread and a month's apartment rent in terms of their dollar value. In Canada, accountants record transactions in dollars because the dollar is the medium of exchange. French accountants record transactions in francs, and Japanese accountants record transactions in yen.

Unlike a litre, a kilometre, or a tonne, the value of a dollar or a British pound sterling changes over time. A rise in the general level of prices is called *inflation*. During inflation a dollar will purchase less milk, less toothpaste, and less of other goods. When prices are relatively stable—when there is little inflation—a dollar's purchasing power is also stable.

Accountants assume that the dollar's purchasing power is relatively stable. The **stable-monetary-unit concept** is the basis for ignoring the effect of inflation in the accounting records. It allows accountants to add and subtract dollar amounts as though each dollar has the same purchasing power as any other dollar at any other time. In certain countries in South America, where inflation rates are often high, accountants make adjustments to report monetary amounts in units of current buying power—a very different concept.

The Accounting Equation

Financial statements tell us how a business is performing and where it stands. They are the final product of the accounting process. But how do we arrive at the items and amounts that make up the financial statements? The most basic tool of the accountant is the **accounting equation**. This equation presents the resources of the business and the claims to those resources.

> ### STOP & THINK
>
> Suppose you are considering the purchase of land for future expansion. The seller is asking $50,000 for land that cost her $35,000. An appraisal shows the land has a value of $47,000. You first offer $44,000. The seller counteroffers with $48,000. Finally, you and the seller agree on a price of $46,000. What dollar amount for this land is reported on your financial statements? Which accounting concept or principle guides your answer?
>
> **Answer:** According to the *cost principle*, goods and services should be recorded at their actual cost. You paid $46,000 for the land. Therefore $46,000 is the cost to report on your financial statements.

EXHIBIT 1-5

The Accounting Equation

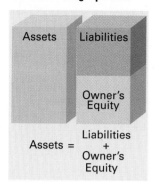

Assets and Liabilities

Assets are the economic resources owned by a business that are expected to be of benefit to the business in the future. Cash, office supplies, merchandise, furniture, land, and buildings are examples.

Claims to those assets come from two sources. **Liabilities** are *outsider* claims, which are economic obligations—debts— payable to outsiders. These outside parties are called *creditors*. For example, a creditor who has loaned money to a business has a claim—a legal right—to a part of the assets until the business pays the debt. *Insider* claims to the business assets are called **owner's equity** or **capital**. These are the claims held by the owners of the business. An owner has a claim to the entity's assets because he or she has invested in the business. The $75 Briana Weill invested in her home repair business is an example. Owner's equity is measured by subtracting liabilities from assets.

The accounting equation in Exhibit 1-5 shows the relationship among assets, liabilities, and owner's equity. Assets appear on the left-hand side of the equation. The legal and economic claims against the assets—the liabilities and owner's equity—appear on the right-hand side of the equation. As Exhibit 1-5 shows, the two sides must be equal:

Economic Resources   *Claims to Economic Resources*

ASSETS = LIABILITIES + OWNER'S EQUITY

Let us take a closer look at the elements that make up the accounting equation. Suppose you own Top Cut Meats, which supplies beef to Harvey's and other restaurants. Some customers may pay you in cash when you deliver the meat. Cash is an asset. Other customers may buy on credit and promise to pay you within a certain time after delivery. This promise is also an asset because it is an economic resource that will benefit you in the future when you receive cash from the customer. To Top Cut Meats Company, this promise is called an **account receivable**. A written promise that entitles you to receive cash in the future is called a **note receivable**.

Harvey's promise to pay Top Cut Meats Company in the future for the meat it purchases on credit creates a debt for Harvey's. This liability is an **account payable** of Harvey's—the debt is not written out. Instead it is supported by the reputation and credit standing of Harvey's. A written promise of future payment is called a **note payable**.

Owner's Equity

Owner's equity is the amount of an entity's assets that remains after the liabilities are subtracted. For this reason, owner's equity is often referred to as *net assets*. We often write the accounting equation to show that the owner's claim to business assets is a residual; something that is left over after subtracting the liabilities.

ASSETS – LIABILITIES = OWNER'S EQUITY

The purpose of business is to increase owner's equity through **revenues**, which are amounts earned by delivering goods or services to customers. Revenues increase owner's equity because they increase the business's assets but not its liabilities. As a result, the owner's share of business assets increases. Exhibit 1-6 shows that owner investments and revenues increase the owner's equity of the business.

Exhibit 1-6 also indicates the types of transactions that decrease owner's equity. **Owner withdrawals** are those amounts removed from the business by the owner. Withdrawals are the opposite of owner investments. **Expenses** are decreases in owner's equity that occur from using assets or increasing liabilities in the course of delivering goods and services to customers. Expenses are the cost of doing business and are the opposite of revenues. Expenses include office rent, interest payments, salaries of employees, insurance, newspaper advertisements, property taxes, utility payments for water, electricity, gas, and so forth.

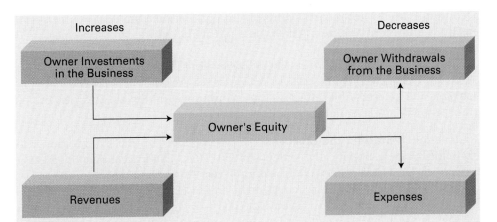

EXHIBIT 1-6

Transactions that Increase or Decrease Owner's Equity

Accounting and the *e*-World

Using the Internet to Increase Income

At the beginning of this chapter, you read about Briana Weill and her home repair business Weill Do It For You. Briana needed to tell people about her business and how she could solve their light repair problems. She followed the conventional route, printing and distributing leaflets to a large number of homes in her neighbourhood.

While some calls and some repair jobs were a result of the leaflets, Briana realized she could increase her income by reaching a wider market. She felt that by providing more information to more prospective customers, she would be able to obtain more repair jobs and, therefore, more income. Briana discussed this idea with her brother John, a computer science student at the University of British Columbia. He suggested she create a web page that explained her business.

Briana loved the idea and, with her brother's help, created a web page that listed her services, gave sample prices for certain jobs, and showed photos of some of her work. She then approached Mr. Donner, who owned the local hardware store where she and her father bought materials and tools. He agreed to link Briana's web page to his store's website. She also linked her web page to the business section of her city's website.

Briana discovered that about one-third of her customers learned about Weill Do It For You from the web page; these customers had not seen her leaflets. She calculated that the increase in income as a result of the web page was much greater than the time and expense involved in creating it. She now recommends using the Internet to anyone thinking of starting a business.

Accounting for Business Transactions

In accounting terms, a **transaction** is any event that *both* affects the financial position of the business entity *and* can be reliably recorded. Many events may affect a company, including (1) elections, (2) economic booms and recessions, (3) purchases and sales of merchandise inventory, (4) payment of rent, (5) collection of cash from customers, and so on. But, an accountant records only events with effects that can be measured reliably as transactions.

Which of the above five events would the accountant record? The answer is events (3), (4), and (5) because their dollar amounts can be measured reliably. The

OBJECTIVE 4
Use the accounting equation to analyze business transactions

accountant would not record events (1) and (2) because the dollar effects that elections and economic trends have on a particular entity cannot be measured reliably.

To illustrate accounting for business transactions, let's assume that Gary Lyon opens a travel agency that he calls Air & Sea Travel. We now consider 11 events and analyze each in terms of its effect on the accounting equation of Air & Sea Travel. Transaction analysis is the essence of accounting.

Transaction 1: Starting the Business Gary Lyon invests $50,000 of his money to begin the business. Specifically, he deposits $50,000 in a bank account entitled Air & Sea Travel. The travel agency offers service in two ways. Some customers phone or email Air & Sea Travel. Other customers do business with the travel agency strictly on-line. On-line customers plan and pay for their trips through the Air & Sea Travel website. The website is linked to airlines, hotels, and cruise lines, so clients can obtain the latest information at any time. The website allows Air & Sea Travel to transact more business and to operate with fewer employees, leading to lower operating costs. The travel agency passes the cost savings to customers by charging them lower commissions, making this a favourable situation for the business and the customer.

The effect of this transaction on the accounting equation of the Air & Sea Travel business entity is

	Assets	} = {	Liabilities	+	Owner's Equity	Type of Owner's Equity Transaction
	Cash				Gary Lyon, Capital	
(1)	+50,000				+50,000	*Owner investment*

For every transaction, the amount on the left side of the equation must equal the amount on the right side. The first transaction increases both the assets (in this case, Cash) and the owner's equity of the business (Gary Lyon, Capital). The transaction involves no liabilities of the business because it creates no obligation for Air & Sea Travel to pay an outside party. To the right of the transaction we write "Owner investment" to keep track of the reason for the effect on owner's equity. This transaction is identical to Briana Weill's investment of $75 to start her business.

Transaction 2: Purchase of Land Air & Sea Travel purchases land for a future office location, paying cash of $40,000. The effect of this transaction on the accounting equation is

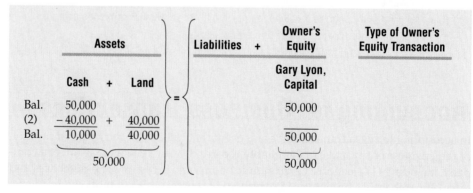

	Assets			} = {	Liabilities	+	Owner's Equity	Type of Owner's Equity Transaction
	Cash	+	Land				Gary Lyon, Capital	
Bal.	50,000						50,000	
(2)	−40,000	+	40,000					
Bal.	10,000		40,000				50,000	
		50,000					50,000	

The cash purchase of land increases one asset, Land, and decreases another asset, Cash, by the same amount. After the transaction is completed, Air & Sea Travel has cash of $10,000, land of $40,000, no liabilities, and owner's equity of $50,000.

Transaction 3: Purchase of Office Supplies Air & Sea Travel buys stationery and other office supplies, agreeing to pay $500 within 30 days. This transaction increases both the assets and the liabilities of the company. Its effect on the accounting equation is

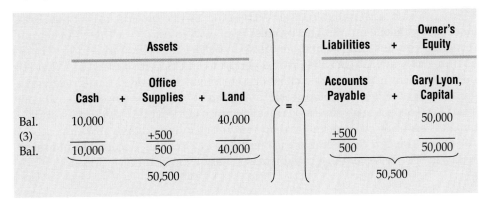

	Assets				Liabilities	+	Owner's Equity
	Cash	+	Office Supplies	+ Land		Accounts Payable	+	Gary Lyon, Capital
Bal.	10,000			40,000	=		50,000
(3)			+500			+500	
Bal.	10,000		500	40,000		500	50,000
		50,500					50,500

The asset affected is Office Supplies, and the liability is called an account payable. The term *payable* signifies a liability. Because Air & Sea Travel is obligated to pay $500 in the future but signs no formal promissory note, we record the liability as an Account Payable, not as a Note Payable.

Transaction 4: Earning of Service Revenue Air & Sea Travel earns service revenue by providing travel arrangement services for clients. Assume the business earns $5,500 and collects this amount in cash. The effect on the accounting equation is an increase in the asset Cash and an increase in Gary Lyon, Capital, as follows:

	Assets			Liabilities	+	Owner's Equity	Type of Owner's Equity Transaction
	Cash	+ Office Supplies	+ Land	Accounts Payable	+	Gary Lyon, Capital	
Bal.	10,000	500	40,000	500		50,000	
(4)	+ 5,500					+ 5,500	*Service revenue*
Bal.	15,500	500	40,000	500		55,500	
		56,000			56,000		

This revenue transaction caused the business to grow, as shown by the increase in total assets and in the sum of total liabilities plus owner's equity. A company that sells goods to customers is a merchandising business. Its revenue is called *sales revenue*. In contrast, Air & Sea Travel and Briana Weill perform services for clients; their revenue is called *service revenue*.

Transaction 5: Earning of Service Revenue on Account   Air & Sea Travel performs services for clients who do not pay immediately. In return for the services, Air & Sea Travel issues an invoice and receives the clients' promise to pay the $3,000 amount within one month. This promise is an asset to Air & Sea Travel, an account receivable because the business expects to collect the cash in the future. In accounting, we say that Air & Sea Travel performed this service *on account*. When the business performs service for a client or a customer, the business earns revenue regardless of whether it receives cash immediately or expects to collect cash later. This $3,000 of service revenue is as real an increase in the wealth of Air & Sea Travel's business as the $5,500 of revenue that was collected immediately in Transaction 4. Air & Sea Travel records an increase in the asset Accounts Receivable and an increase in Service Revenue, which increases Gary Lyon, Capital, as follows:

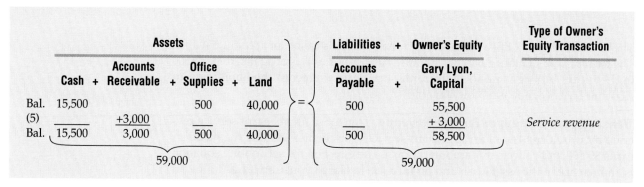

Transaction 6: Payment of Expenses   During the month, Air & Sea Travel pays $2,700 in cash expenses: office rent, $1,100; employee salary $1,200 (for a part-time assistant); and total utilities, $400. The effects on the accounting equation are

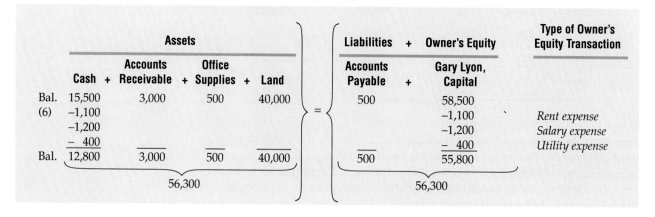

Because expenses have the opposite effect of revenues, they cause the business to shrink, as shown by the smaller amounts of total assets and total liabilities and owner's equity.

Each expense should be recorded in a separate transaction. Here, for simplicity, they are listed together. Alternatively, we could record the cash payment in a single amount for the sum of those three expenses, $2,700 ($1,100 + $1,200 + $400). In either case, the "balance" of the equation holds, as we know it must.

Businesspeople, Gary Lyon and Briana Weill included, run their businesses with the objective of having more revenues than expenses. An excess of total revenues over total expenses is called **net income**, **net earnings**, or **net profit**. If total expenses exceed total revenues, the result is called a **net loss**.

Transaction 7: Payment on Account   Air & Sea Travel pays $400 to the store from which it purchased $500 worth of office supplies in Transaction 3. In accounting, we say that the business pays $400 *on account*. The effect on the accounting equation is a decrease in the asset Cash and a decrease in the liability Accounts Payable as follows:

	Assets						Liabilities	+	Owner's Equity
	Cash +	Accounts Receivable +	Office Supplies +	Land		=	Accounts Payable	+	Gary Lyon, Capital
Bal.	12,800	3,000	500	40,000			500		55,800
(7)	– 400						– 400		
Bal.	12,400	3,000	500	40,000			100		55,800
		55,900						55,900	

The payment of cash on account has no effect on the asset Office Supplies because the payment does not increase or decrease the supplies available to the business.

Transaction 8: Personal Transaction   Gary Lyon remodels his home at a cost of $30,000, paying cash from personal funds. This event is *not* a transaction of Air & Sea Travel. It has no effect on Air & Sea Travel's business affairs and therefore is not recorded by the business. It is a transaction of the Gary Lyon personal entity, not the Air & Sea Travel business entity. We are focusing now solely on the *business* entity, and this event does not affect it. This transaction illustrates the application of the *entity concept*.

Transaction 9: Collection on Account   In Transaction 5, Air & Sea Travel performed services for clients on account. The business now collects $1,000 from a client. We say that it collects the cash *on account*. It will record an increase in the asset Cash. Should it also record an increase in service revenue? No, because Air & Sea Travel already recorded the revenue when it performed the service in Transaction 5. The phrase "collect cash on account" means to record an increase in Cash and a decrease in the asset Accounts Receivable. The effect on the accounting equation is

	Assets						Liabilities	+	Owner's Equity
	Cash +	Accounts Receivable +	Office Supplies +	Land		=	Accounts Payable	+	Gary Lyon, Capital
Bal.	12,400	3,000	500	40,000			100		55,800
(9)	+ 1,000	–1,000							
Bal.	13,400	2,000	500	40,000			100		55,800
		55,900						55,900	

Total assets are unchanged from the preceding transaction's total. Why? Because Air & Sea Travel merely exchanged one asset for another. Also, the total of liabilities and owner's equity is unchanged.

Transaction 10: Sale of Land   An individual approaches Gary Lyon about selling a parcel of land owned by the Air & Sea Travel entity. Gary Lyon and the other person agree to a sale price of $22,000, which is equal to the business's cost of the land. Air & Sea Travel sells the land and receives $22,000 cash, and the effect on the accounting equation is

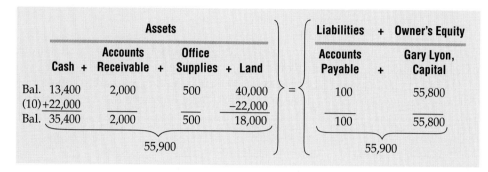

	Assets				=	Liabilities	+	Owner's Equity
	Cash +	Accounts Receivable +	Office Supplies +	Land		Accounts Payable	+	Gary Lyon, Capital
Bal.	13,400	2,000	500	40,000		100		55,800
(10)	+22,000			−22,000				
Bal.	35,400	2,000	500	18,000		100		55,800
		55,900					55,900	

Transaction 11: Withdrawing of Cash   Gary Lyon withdraws $2,100 cash for his personal use. The effect on the accounting equation is

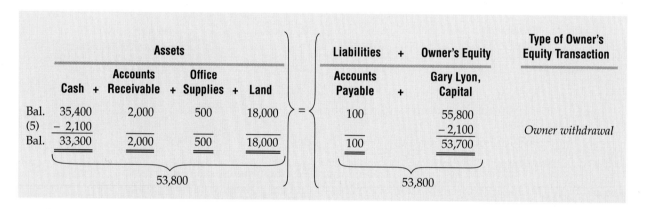

	Assets				=	Liabilities	+	Owner's Equity	Type of Owner's Equity Transaction
	Cash +	Accounts Receivable +	Office Supplies +	Land		Accounts Payable	+	Gary Lyon, Capital	
Bal.	35,400	2,000	500	18,000		100		55,800	
(5)	− 2,100							− 2,100	*Owner withdrawal*
Bal.	33,300	2,000	500	18,000		100		53,700	
		53,800					53,800		

Gary Lyon's withdrawal of $2,100 cash decreases the asset Cash and also the owner's equity of the business.

The withdrawal does not represent a business expense because the cash is used for personal affairs unrelated to the business. We record this decrease in owner's equity as Withdrawals or Drawings. The double underlines below each column indicate a final total.

STOP & THINK

Why does Gary Lyon, or anyone else, go into business? If you could identify only one reason, what would it be? How will accounting serve to meet this need?

Answer: Gary Lyon went into business to earn a profit—and thereby to make a living. He hopes Air & Sea Travel's accounting revenues exceed its expenses to provide an excess—a net income. Accounting tells Gary Lyon how much income the business has earned, how much cash and other assets the business has, and how much in liabilities the business owes.

Evaluating Business Transactions

Exhibit 1-7 summarizes the 11 preceding transactions. Panel A of the exhibit lists the details of the transactions, and Panel B presents the analysis. As you study the exhibit, note that every transaction maintains the equality

ASSETS = LIABILITIES + OWNER'S EQUITY

EXHIBIT 1-7

Analysis of Transactions of Air & Sea Travel

Panel A: Details of Transactions

(1) The business recorded the $50,000 cash investment made by Gary Lyon.
(2) Paid $40,000 cash for land.
(3) Bought $500 of office supplies on account.
(4) Received $5,500 cash from clients for service revenue earned.
(5) Performed services for clients on account, $3,000.
(6) Paid cash expenses: rent, $1,100; employee salary, $1,200; utilities, $400.
(7) Paid $400 on the account payable created in Transaction 3.
(8) Remodelled his personal residence. This is *not* a transaction of the business.
(9) Collected $1,000 on the account receivable created in Transaction 5.
(10) Sold land for cash equal to its cost of $22,000.
(11) The business paid $2,100 cash to Gary Lyon as a withdrawal.

Panel B: Analysis of Transactions

	Assets					Liabilities +	Owner's Equity	Type of Owner's Equity Transaction
	Cash +	Accounts Receivable +	Office Supplies +	Land		Accounts Payable +	Gary Lyon, Capital	
(1)	+50,000						+50,000	Owner investment
Bal.	50,000						50,000	
(2)	−40,000			+40,000				
Bal.	10,000			40,000			50,000	
(3)			+500			+ 500		
Bal.	10,000		500	40,000		500	50,000	
(4)	+ 5,500						+ 5,500	Service revenue
Bal.	15,500		500	40,000		500	55,500	
(5)		+3,000					+ 3,000	Service revenue
Bal.	15,500	3,000	500	40,000	=	500	58,500	
(6)	− 1,100						− 1,100	Rent expense
	− 1,200						− 1,200	Salary expense
	− 400						− 400	Utilities expense
Bal.	12,800	3,000	500	40,000		500	55,800	
(7)	− 400					− 400		
Bal.	12,400	3,000	500	40,000		100	55,800	
(8)	Not a transaction of the business							
(9)	+ 1,000	−1,000						
Bal.	13,400	2,000	500	40,000		100	55,800	
(10)	+22,000			−22,000				
Bal.	35,400	2,000	500	18,000		100	55,800	
(11)	− 2,100						− 2,100	Owner withdrawal
Bal.	33,300	2,000	500	18,000		100	53,700	

53,800   53,800

The Financial Statements

Once the analysis of the transactions is complete, what is the next step in the accounting process? How does a business present the results of the analysis? We now look at the *financial statements*, which are the formal reports of an entity's financial information. The primary financial statements are the (1) income statement, (2) statement of owner's equity, (3) balance sheet, and (4) cash flow statement.

Income Statement The **income statement** presents a summary of the *revenues* and *expenses* of an entity for a specific period of time, such as a month or a year. The income statement, also called the **statement of earnings** or **statement of operations**, is like a video of the entity's operations—it presents a moving financial picture of business operations during the period. The income statement holds perhaps the most important single piece of information about a business—its *net income*, revenues minus expenses. If expenses exceed revenues, a net loss results for the period.

Statement of Owner's Equity The **statement of owner's equity** presents a summary of the changes that occurred in the entity's *owner's equity* during a specific period of time, such as a month or a year. Increases in owner's equity arise from investments by the owner and from net income earned during the period. Decreases result from a net loss for the period or from owner withdrawals. Net income or net loss comes directly from the income statement. Owner investments and withdrawals are capital transactions between the business and its owner, so they do not affect the income statement.

Balance Sheet The **balance sheet** lists all the assets, liabilities, and owner's equity of an entity as of a specific date, usually the end of a month or a year. The balance sheet is like a snapshot of the entity. For this reason, it is also called the **statement of financial position**.

Cash Flow Statement The **cash flow statement** reports the amount of cash coming in (*cash receipts*) and the amount of cash going out (*cash payments* or *disbursements*) during a period. Business activities result in a net cash inflow (receipts greater than payments) or a net cash outflow (payments greater than receipts). The cash flow statement shows the net increase or decrease in cash during the period and the cash balance at the end of the period. We will cover the cash flow statement in greater depth in Chapter 17.

Computers and software programs have had a significant impact on the preparation of the financial statements. Financial statements can be produced instantaneously after the data from the financial records are entered into the computer. Of course, any errors that exist in the financial records will be passed on to the financial statements. For this reason, the person responsible for analyzing the accounting data is critical to the accuracy of the financial statements.

Financial Statement Headings

Each financial statement has a heading, which gives the name of the business (in our discussion Air & Sea Travel), the name of the particular statement, and the date or time period covered by the statement. A balance sheet taken at the end of year 2002 would be dated December 31, 2002. A balance sheet prepared at the end of March 2003 is dated March 31, 2003.

An income statement or a statement of owner's equity covering an annual period ending on December 31, 2002 is dated "For the Year Ended December 31, 2002." A monthly income statement or statement of owner's equity for September 2003 has in its heading "For the Month Ended September 30, 2003" or simply "For the Month of September 2003." Income is meaningless unless identified with a particular time period.

Relationships among the Financial Statements

OBJECTIVE 6
Evaluate the performance of a business

Exhibit 1-8 on page 22 illustrates all four statements. Their data come from the transaction analysis in Exhibit 1-7. We are assuming the transactions occurred during the month of April 2002. Study the exhibit carefully, because it shows the relationships among the four financial statements.

Observe the following in Exhibit 1-8:

1. The *income statement* for the month ended April 30, 2002
   a. Reports all *revenues* and all *expenses* during the period. Expenses are often listed alphabetically.
   b. Reports *net income* of the period if total revenues exceed total expenses, as in the case of Air & Sea Travel's operations for April. If total expenses exceed total revenues, a *net loss* is reported instead.

2. The *statement of owner's equity* for the month ended April 30, 2002
   a. Opens with the owner's capital balance at the beginning of the period.
   b. Adds *investment by the owner* and adds *net income* (or subtracts *net loss*, as the case may be). Net income (or net loss) comes directly from the income statement (see arrow ① in Exhibit 1-8).
   c. Subtracts *withdrawals by the owner*. The parentheses around an amount indicate a subtraction.
   d. Ends with the owner's equity balance at the end of the period.

3. The *balance sheet* at April 30, 2002, the end of the period
   a. Reports all *assets*, all *liabilities*, and *owner's equity* of the business at the end of the period.
   b. Reports that total assets equal the sum of total liabilities plus total owner's equity.
   c. Reports the owner's ending capital balance, taken directly from the statement of owner's equity (see arrow ②).

4. The *cash flow statement* for the month ended April 30, 2002
   a. Reports cash flows from three types of business activities (*operating, investing,* and *financing* activities) during the month.
      - *Operating activities* bring in revenues and the related cash collections from customers. They also include the payment of expenses.
      - *Investing activities* are the purchase and sale of assets that the business uses for its operations.
      - *Financing activities* are the receipts of cash from people or companies that finance the business and also payments back to those people or companies. Each category of cash-flow activities includes both cash receipts, which are positive amounts, and cash payments, which are negative amounts (denoted by parentheses). Each category results in a net cash inflow or a net cash outflow for the period. We discuss these categories in detail in Chapter 17.
   b. Reports a net increase in cash during the month and ends with the cash balance at April 30, 2002. This is the amount of cash to report on the balance sheet (see arrow ③).

> **Student to Student**
>
> *I had trouble understanding the relationships between all of the financial statements and why they need to be done in a particular order. Exhibit 1-8 on page 22 shows you the order to do your statements in. The guiding arrows tell you where some of the figures on those statements come from.*
>
> Jonny M., Kitchener

EXHIBIT 1-8

Financial Statements of Air & Sea Travel

AIR & SEA TRAVEL
Income Statement
For the Month Ended April 30, 2002

Revenue:		
Service revenue		$8,500
Expenses:		
Salary expense	$1,200	
Rent expense	1,100	
Utilities expense	400	
Total expenses		2,700
Net income		$5,800

$\qquad$ ① $\qquad$

AIR & SEA TRAVEL
Statement of Owner's Equity
For the Month Ended April 30, 2002

Gary Lyon, Capital, April 1, 2002	$ 0
Add: Investment by owner	50,000
Net income for the month	5,800
	55,800
Less: Withdrawals by owner	(2,100)
Gary Lyon, Capital, April 30, 2002	$53,700

②

AIR & SEA TRAVEL
Balance Sheet
April 30, 2002

Assets		Liabilities	
Cash	$33,300	Accounts payable	$ 100
Accounts receivable	2,000		
Office supplies	500	**Owner's Equity**	
Land	18,000	Gary Lyon, Capital	53,700
		Total liabilities and	
Total assets	$53,800	owner's equity	$53,800

③

AIR & SEA TRAVEL
Cash Flow Statement*
For the Month Ended April 30, 2002

Cash flows from operating activities		
Cash collections from customers**		$ 6,500
Cash payments to suppliers***	$(1,900)	
Cash payments to employees	(1,200)	(3,100)
Net cash inflow from operating activities		3,400
Cash flows from investing activities		
Acquisition of land	$(40,000)	
Proceeds from sale of land	22,000	
Net cash outflow from investing activities		(18,000)
Cash flows from financing activities		
Investment by owner	$50,000	
Withdrawal by owner	(2,100)	
Net cash inflow from financing activities		47,900
Net increase in cash		$33,300
Cash balance, April 1, 2002		0
Cash balance, April 30, 2002		$33,300

* Chapter 17 explains how to prepare this statement.
** $5,500 + $1,000 = $6,500
*** $1,100 + $400 + $400 = $1,900

Study Exhibit 1-8, which gives the financial statements for Air & Sea Travel at April 30, 2002, the end of the first month of operations. Answer these questions for Air & Sea Travel to evaluate the business's results.

1. What was the business's result of operations for the month of April—a net income (profit) or a net loss, and how much? Which financial statement provides this information?

2. How much revenue did the business earn during April? What was the business's largest expense? How much were total expenses?

3. Is the income statement dated at the last day of the period or for the entire period? Why?

4. How much owner capital did the company have at the beginning of April? At the end of April? Identify all the items that changed owner capital during the month, along with their amounts. Which financial statement provides this information?

5. How much cash does the company have as it moves into the next month—that is, May 2002? Which financial statement provides this information?

6. How much do clients owe Air & Sea Travel at April 30? Is this an asset or a liability for the business? What does the business call this item?

7. How much does the business owe outsiders at April 30? Is this an asset or a liability for the business? What does the business call this item?

8. How is the balance sheet dated? Why is it dated this way? Why does the balance sheet's date differ from the date on the income statement?

Answers:

1. Net income = $5,800. The income statement provides this information.

2. From the income statement: Total revenue = $8,500. Salary was the largest expense, at $1,200. Total expenses = $2,700.

3. The income statement is dated "For the Month Ended April 30, 2002." The income statement is dated for the entire period because the revenues and the expenses occurred *during* the month, not at the end of the month. The income statement reports on the business's operations during the whole span of the period.

4. From the statement of owner's equity:

   Beginning owner capital = $0   Ending owner capital = $53,700

   Increases: Investment by owner = $50,000; Net income for the month = $5,800

   Decrease: Withdrawal by owner = $2,100

5. Cash = $33,300. The balance sheet or cash flow statement provides this information.

6. Clients owe the business $2,000, which is an *asset* called Accounts Receivable.

7. The business owes outsiders $100, for a *liability* called Accounts Payable.

8. The balance sheet is dated April 30, 2002, which means at midnight on April 30, 2002. The balance sheet is dated at a single moment in time (in this case, April 30, 2002) to show the amount of assets, liabilities, and owner's equity the business had on that date. The balance sheet is like a snapshot, while the income statement provides a moving picture of the business through time.

The Decision Guidelines feature below summarizes the chapter by examining some decisions that businesspeople must make. A Decision Guidelines feature appears in each chapter of this book. The Decision Guidelines serve as useful summaries of the decision-making process and its foundation in accounting information.

DECISION GUIDELINES — *Major Business Decisions*

Decision	Guidelines
How to organize the business?	If a single owner, but not incorporated—a *proprietorship*.
	If two or more owners, but not incorporated—a *partnership*.
	If the business issues shares of stock to shareholders—a *corporation*.
What to account for?	Account for the business, which is a separate entity apart from its owner (*Entity concept*).
	Account for transactions and events that affect the business and can be measured objectively. (*Reliability principle*).
How much to record for assets and liabilities?	Actual historical amount (*Cost principle*).
How to organize the various effects of a transaction?	The accounting equation:
	ASSETS = LIABILITIES + OWNER'S EQUITY
	Note: Owner's equity is called shareholders' equity if the entity is a corporation.
How to measure profits and losses?	Income statement:
	REVENUES − EXPENSES = NET INCOME (or NET LOSS)
Did owner's equity increase or decrease?	Statement of owner's equity
	Beginning capital + Owner investments + Net income (or − Net loss) − Owner withdrawals ————————— = Ending capital
Where does the business stand financially?	Balance sheet (accounting equation):
	ASSETS = LIABILITIES + OWNER'S EQUITY
Where did the business's cash come from? Where did the cash go?	Cash flow statement: *Operating activities:* Net cash inflow (or outflow) + *Investing activities:* Net cash inflow (or outflow) + *Financing activities:* Net cash inflow (or outflow) ————————— = Net increase (decrease) in cash

Jill Smith opens an apartment-locator business in Regina. She is the sole owner of the proprietorship, which she names Fast Apartment Locators. During the first month of operations, July 2002, the following transactions occurred:

a. Smith invests $35,000 of personal funds to start the business.

b. The business purchases, on account, office supplies costing $350.

c. Fast Apartment Locators pays cash of $30,000 to acquire a parcel of land. The business intends to use the land as a future building site for its business office.

d. The business locates apartments for clients and receives cash of $1,900.

e. The business pays $100 on the account payable created in Transaction (b).

f. Jill Smith pays $2,000 of personal funds for a vacation for her family.

g. The business pays cash expenses for office rent, $400, and utilities, $100.

h. The business returns to the supplier office supplies that cost $150. The wrong supplies were shipped.

i. Jill Smith withdraws $1,200 cash for personal use.

Required

1. Analyze the preceding transactions in terms of their effects on the accounting equation of Fast Apartment Locators. Use Exhibit 1-7 as a guide but show balances only after the last transaction.

2. Prepare the income statement, statement of owner's equity, and balance sheet of Fast Apartment Locators after recording the transactions. Use Exhibit 1-8 as a guide.

Solution to Review Problem

1. **Panel A: Details of Transactions**

a. Smith invested $35,000 cash to start the business.

b. Purchased $350 in office supplies on account.

c. Paid $30,000 to acquire land as a future building site.

d. Earned service revenue and received cash of $1,900.

e. Paid $100 on account.

f. Paid for a personal vacation, which is not a transaction of the business.

g. Paid cash expenses for rent, $400, and utilities, $100.

h. Returned office supplies that cost $150.

i. Withdrew $1,200 for personal use.

Cyber Coach

Visit the Student Resources area of the *Accounting* Companion Website for extra practice with the new material in Chapter 1.

www.pearsoned.ca/horngren

	Assets				Liabilities	+	Owner's Equity	Type of Owner's Equity Transaction
	Cash	+	Office Supplies	+ Land	Accounts Payable	+	Jill Smith, Capital	
(a)	+35,000						+35,000	*Owner investment*
(b)			+ 350		+ 350			
(c)	−30,000			+30,000				
(d)	+ 1,900						+ 1,900	*Service revenue*
(e)	− 100				− 100			
(f)	Not a business transaction							
(g)	− 400						− 400	*Rent expense*
	− 100						− 100	*Utilities expense*
(h)			− 150		− 150			
(i)	− 1,200						− 1,200	*Owner withdrawal*
Bal.	5,100		200	30,000	100		35,200	

35,300

35,300

2. Financial Statements of Fast Apartment Locators

FAST APARTMENT LOCATORS
Income Statement
For the Month Ended July 31, 2002

Revenue:		
Service revenue		$1,900
Expenses:		
Rent expense	$400	
Utilities expense	100	
Total expenses		500
Net Income		$1,400

FAST APARTMENT LOCATORS
Statement of Owner's Equity
For the Month Ended July 31, 2002

Jill Smith, Capital, July 1, 2002	$ 0
Add: Investment by owner	35,000
Net income for July	1,400
	36,400
Less: Withdrawal by owner	1,200
Jill Smith, Capital, July 31, 2002	$35,200

FAST APARTMENT LOCATORS
Balance Sheet
July 31, 2002

Assets		Liabilities	
Cash	$ 5,100	Accounts payable	$ 100
Office supplies	200	**Owner's Equity**	
Land	30,000	Jill Smith, Capital	35, 200
		Total liabilities and	
Total assets	$35,300	owner's equity	$35,300

Summary

1. **Use accounting vocabulary for decision-making.** Accounting is an information system for measuring, processing, and communicating financial information. As the "language of business," accounting helps a wide range of decision makers.

2. **Apply accounting concepts and principles to analyze business situations.** *Generally accepted accounting principles (GAAP)* guide accountants in their work. The three basic forms of business organization are the proprietorship, the partnership, and the corporation. Whatever the form, accountants use the *entity concept* to keep the business's records separate from other economic units. Other important guidelines are the *reliability principle*, the *cost principle*, the *going-concern concept*, and the *stable-monetary-unit concept.*

3. **Use the accounting equation to describe an organization's financial position.** In its most common form, the accounting equation is

Assets = Liabilities + Owner's Equity

4. **Use the accounting equation to analyze business transactions.** A transaction is an event that both affects the financial position of an entity and can be reliably recorded. Transactions affect a business's assets, liabilities, and owner's equity. Therefore transactions are often analyzed in terms of their effect on the accounting equation.

5. **Prepare and use the financial statements.** The *financial statements* communicate information for decision-making by an entity's managers, owners, creditors, by government agencies, and by other users. The *income statement* summarizes the entity's operations in terms of revenues earned and expenses incurred during a specific period. Total revenues minus total expenses equal net income. The *statement of owner's equity* reports the changes in owner's equity during the period. The *balance sheet* lists the entity's assets, liabilities, and owner's equity at a specific time. The *cash flow statement* reports the cash coming in and the cash going out during the period.

6. **Evaluate the performance of a business.** High net income indicates success in business; net loss indicates a lack of success in business.

Self-Study Questions

Test your understanding of the chapter by marking the correct answer for each of the following questions:

1. The organization that formulates generally accepted accounting principles is (*p. 5*)
   a. Ontario Securities Commission
   b. Public Accountants Council of Canada
   c. Canadian Institute of Chartered Accountants (CICA)
   d. Canada Customs and Revenue Agency

2. Which of the following forms of business organization is an "artificial person" and must obtain legal approval from the federal government or a province to conduct business? (*p. 7*)
   a. Law firm   c. Partnership
   b. Proprietorship   d. Corporation

3. You have purchased some T-shirts for $1,000 and can sell them immediately for $1,500. What accounting concept or principle governs the amount at which to record the goods you purchased? (*p. 10*)
   a. Entity concept
   b. Reliability principle
   c. Cost principle
   d. Going-concern concept

4. The economic resources of a business are called (*p. 12*)
   a. Assets   c. Owner's equity
   b. Liabilities   d. Accounts payable

5. A business has assets of $140,000 and liabilities of $60,000. How much is its owner's equity? (*p. 12*)
   a. $0   c. $140,000
   b. $80,000   d. $200,000

6. The purchase of office supplies on account will (*p. 15*)
   a. Increase an asset and increase a liability
   b. Increase an asset and increase owner's equity
   c. Increase one asset and decrease another asset
   d. Increase an asset and decrease a liability

7. The performance of service for a customer or client and immediate receipt of cash will (*p. 15*)
   a. Increase one asset and decrease another asset
   b. Increase an asset and increase owner's equity
   c. Decrease an asset and decrease a liability
   d. Increase an asset and increase a liability

8. The payment of an account payable will (*p. 17*)
   a. Increase one asset and decrease another asset
   b. Decrease an asset and decrease owner's equity
   c. Decrease an asset and decrease a liability
   d. Increase an asset and increase a liability

9. The report of assets, liabilities, and owner's equity is called the (*p. 20*)
   a. Cash flow statement   c. Income statement
   b. Balance sheet   d. Statement of owner's equity

10. The financial statements that are dated for a time

period (rather than a specific point in time) are the (pp. 21–22)

a. Balance sheet and income statement
b. Balance sheet and statement of owner's equity
c. Income statement, statement of owner's equity, and cash flow statement
d. All financial statements are dated for a time period.

Answers to the Self-Study Questions follow the Similar Accounting Terms.

Accounting Vocabulary

Like many other subjects, accounting has a special vocabulary. It is important that you understand the following terms. They are explained in the chapter and also in the glossary at the end of the book.

account payable (p. 12)
account receivable (p. 12)
accounting (p. 2)
accounting equation (p. 11)
asset (p. 12)
balance sheet (p. 20)
capital (p. 12)
cash flow statement (p. 20)
corporation (p. 6)
cost principle (p. 10)
entity (p. 9)
expense (p. 12)
financial accounting (p. 4)
financial statements (p. 3)

generally accepted accounting principles (GAAP) (pp. 7, 47)
going-concern concept (p. 11)
income statement (p. 20)
liability (p. 12)
management accounting (p. 4)
net earnings (p. 17)
net income (p. 17)
net loss (p. 17)
net profit (p. 17)
note payable (p. 12)
note receivable (p. 12)
objectivity principle (p. 10)
owner's equity (p. 12)
owner withdrawals (p. 12)

partnership (p. 6)
proprietorship (p. 6)
reliability principle (p. 10)
revenue (p. 12)
shareholder (p. 6)
stable-monetary-unit concept (p. 11)
statement of earnings (p. 20)
statement of financial position (p. 20)
statement of operations (p. 20)
statement of owner's equity (p. 20)
transaction (p. 13)

Similar Accounting Terms

Accounting equation	Assets = Liabilities + Owner's Equity
Balance Sheet	Statement of Financial Position
Income Statement	Statement of Operations; Statement of Earnings
Net Income	Net Earnings; Net Profit

Answers to Self-Study Questions

1. c	3. c	5. b	7. b	9. b
2. d	4. a	6. a	8. c	10. c

Assignment Material

Questions

1. Distinguish between accounting and bookkeeping.
2. Identify five users of accounting information and explain how they use it.
3. Name two important reasons for the development of accounting.
4. Name three professional designations of accountants. Also give their abbreviations.
5. What organization formulates generally accepted accounting principles? Is this organization a government agency?
6. Name the four principal types of services provided by public accounting firms.
7. Identify the owner(s) of a proprietorship, a partnership, and a corporation.
8. Why do ethical standards exist in accounting? Which professional organizations direct their standards more toward independent auditors? Which organizations direct their standards more toward management accountants?
9. Why is the entity concept so important to accounting?

10. Give four examples of accounting entities.

11. Briefly describe the reliability principle.

12. What role does the cost principle play in accounting?

13. If assets = liabilities + owner's equity, then how can liabilities be expressed?

14. Explain the difference between an account receivable and an account payable.

15. What role do transactions play in accounting?

16. Give a more descriptive title for the balance sheet.

17. What feature of the balance sheet gives this financial statement its name?

18. Give another title for the income statement.

19. Which financial statement is like a snapshot of the entity at a specific time? Which financial statement is like a video of the entity's operation during a period of time?

20. What information does the statement of owner's equity report?

21. Give a synonym for the owner's equity of a proprietorship.

22. What piece of information flows from the income statement to the statement of owner's equity? What information flows from the statement of owner's equity to the balance sheet? What balance sheet item is explained by the cash flow statement?

Exercises

Exercise 1-1 *Explaining assets, liabilities, owner's equity* **(Obj. 1)**

Shortly after starting Red River Express Company you realize the company needs a bank loan to purchase office equipment. In evaluating the loan request, the banker asks about the assets and liabilities of the business. In particular, she wants to know the amount of the owner's equity. In your own words define *assets*, *liabilities*, and *owner's equity*. What is the *relationship* among assets, liabilities, and owner's equity?

Exercise 1-2 *Explaining the income statement and the balance sheet* **(Obj. 1)**

Felix and Charlotte Jiminez want to open a Mexican restaurant in Calgary. In need of cash, they ask the Bank of Nova Scotia for a loan. The bank's procedures require borrowers to submit financial statements to show likely results of operations for the first year and likely financial position at the end of the first year. With little knowledge of accounting, Felix and Charlotte don't know how to proceed. Explain to them the information provided by the income statement (the statement of operations) and the balance sheet (the statement of financial position). Indicate why a lender would require this information.

Exercise 1-3 *Business situations* **(Obj. 2)**

For each of the following items, give an example of a business transaction that has the described effect on the accounting equation:

a. Increase an asset and increase a liability.

b. Increase one asset and decrease another asset.

c. Decrease an asset and decrease owner's equity.

d. Decrease an asset and decrease a liability.

e. Increase an asset and increase owner's equity.

Exercise 1-4 *Transaction analysis* **(Obj. 2)**

Lam Enterprises, a business owned by Annie Lam, experienced the following events. State whether each event (1) increased, (2) decreased, or (3) had no effect on the total assets of the business. Identify any specific asset affected.

a. Annie Lam increased her cash investment in the business.

b. Paid cash on accounts payable.

c. Purchased office equipment; signed a promissory note in payment.

d. Performed service for a customer on account.

e. Annie Lam withdrew cash for personal expenses.

f. Received cash from a customer on account receivable.

g. Annie Lam used personal funds to purchase a swimming pool for her home.

h. Sold undesirable land for a price equal to the cost of the land; received cash.

i. Borrowed money from the bank.

j. Cash purchase of desirable land for a future building site.

Exercise 1-5   *Accounting equation   (Obj. 3)*

Compute the missing amount in the accounting equation of each of the following three entities:

	Assets	Liabilities	Owner's Equity
Business A	$?	$61,800	$84,400
Business B	45,900	?	34,000
Business C	81,700	59,800	?

Exercise 1-6   *Using the accounting equation   (Obj. 3)*

Chuck McElravy owns Common Grounds Coffee House, near the campus of Northern College. The company has cash of $2,000 and furniture that cost $12,000. Debts include accounts payable of $1,000 and a $7,000 note payable. What is the owner's equity of the company? Write the accounting equation of Common Grounds Coffee House.

Exercise 1-7   *Accounting equation   (Obj. 3)*

Dia Met Minerals Ltd., a mineral exploration and development company in Vancouver, had total assets of $330 million and total liabilities of $278 million at January 31, 1999. At the company's year end on January 31, 2000, Dia Met Minerals Ltd.'s total assets were $328 million and total liabilities were $232 million.

Required

1. Did the shareholders' equity (which is the owner's equity of a corporation) of Dia Met Minerals Ltd. increase during the period February 1, 1999, to January 31, 2000? By how much?

2. Identify two possible reasons for the change in shareholders' equity of Dia Met Minerals Ltd. during the period February 1, 1999, to January 31, 2000.

Exercise 1-8   *Transaction analysis   (Obj. 4)*

Indicate the effects of the following business transactions on the accounting equation of a proprietorship. Transaction *a* is answered as a guide.

a. Received $35,000 cash from the owners.

   Answer: Increase asset (Cash)
            Increase owner's equity (Owner, Capital)

b. Paid the current month's office rent of $500.

c. Paid $700 cash to purchase office supplies.

d. Performed engineering service for a client on account, $2,000.

e. Purchased on account office furniture at a cost of $500.

f. Received cash on account, $900.

g. Paid cash on account, $250.

h. Sold land for $12,000, which was the business's cost of the land.

i. Performed engineering services for a client and received cash of $780.

Exercise 1-9   *Transaction analysis, accounting equation*   **(Obj. 2, 4)**

Milos Scopis D.V.M. opens an animal hospital to specialize in small animals. During his first month of operation, January, his hospital, entitled Milos Scopis Veterinarian Services, experienced the following events:

Jan.	6	Scopis invested $80,000 in the hospital by opening a bank account in the name of Milos Scopis Veterinarian Services.
	9	Milos Scopis Veterinarian Services paid cash for land costing $75,000. There are plans to build a clinic on the land.
	12	The business purchased medical supplies for $2,000 on account.
	15	On January 15, Milos Scopis Veterinarian Services officially opened for business.
	15–31	During the rest of the month the business earned professional fees of $8,000 and received cash immediately.
	15–31	The business paid cash expenses: employee salaries, $1,400; office rent, $1,000; utilities, $300.
	28	The business sold supplies to another animal hospital at cost for $500.
	31	The business paid $1,500 on account.

Required

Analyze the effects of these events on the accounting equation of the animal hospital, Milos Scopis Veterinarian Services. Use a format similar to that of Exhibit 1-7, Panel B in the chapter with headings for: Cash; Medical Supplies; Land; Accounts Payable; and Milos Scopis, Capital.

Exercise 1-10   *Business organization, transactions, and net income*
(Obj. 2, 3, 4)

The analysis of the transactions that Danko Equipment Rental engaged in during its first month of operations follows. The business buys electronic equipment that it rents out to earn rental revenue. The owner of the business, Ken Danko, made only one investment to start the business and made no withdrawals from Danko Equipment Rental.

	Cash	+	Accounts Receivable	+	Rental Equipment	=	Accounts Payable	+	K.Danko, Capital
a.	+50,000								+50,000
b.	+ 750								+ 750
c.					+120,000		+120,000		
d.			+800						+ 800
e.	− 1,000								−1,000
f.	+ 5,600								+5,600
g.	+ 150		−150						
h.	− 12,000						− 12,000		

Required

1. Describe each transaction of Danko Equipment Rental.

2. If these transactions fully describe the operations of Danko Equipment Rental during the month, what was the amount of net income or net loss?

Exercise 1-11   *Business organization, balance sheet*   **(Obj. 2, 5)**

Presented below are the balances of the assets and liabilities of Onax Logistics as of September 30, 2002. Also included are the revenue and expense account balances of the business for September. Darlene Nixon, the owner, invested $6,000 when the business was formed.

Delivery service revenue	$9,100	Delivery equipment	$15,500
Accounts receivable	4,900	Supplies	1,600
Accounts payable	1,750	Note payable	8,000
Salary expense	2,000	Rent expense	700
D. Nixon, Capital	?	Cash	750

Required

1. What type of business organization is Onax Logistics? How can you tell?

2. Prepare the balance sheet of Onax Logistics as of September 30, 2002.

3. What does the balance sheet report—financial position or operating results? Which financial statement reports the other information?

Exercise 1-12 *Preparing the financial statements* **(Obj. 5)**

Examine Exhibit 1-7 on page 19. The exhibit summarizes the transactions of Air & Sea Travel for the month of April 2002. Suppose the business completed transactions 1 to 7 and needed a bank loan on April 21, 2002. The vice-president of the bank requires financial statements to support all loan requests.

Required

Prepare the income statement, statement of owner's equity, and balance sheet that Air & Sea Travel would present to the banker on April 21, 2002, after completing the first seven transactions. Exhibit 1-8, page 22, shows the format of these financial statements.

Exercise 1-13 *Income statement for a proprietorship* **(Obj. 2, 5)**

The assets, liabilities, owner's equity, revenue and expenses of Douglas Company, a proprietorship, have the following balances at December 31, 2003, the end of its first year of business. During the year the proprietor, Kristen Douglas, invested $15,000 in the business.

Note payable	$ 21,000	Office furniture	$ 35,000
Utilities expense	6,800	Rent expense	18,000
Accounts payable	3,300	Cash	3,600
K. Douglas, capital	21,000	Office supplies	4,800
Service revenue	181,200	Salary expense	65,000
Accounts receivable	9,000	Salary payable	2,000
Supplies expense	8,000	Business tax expense	1,400
Equipment	10,000	K. Douglas, withdrawals	?

Required

1. Prepare the income statement of Douglas Company for the year ended December 31, 2003. What is Douglas Company's net income or net loss for 2003?

2. What was the amount of each of Kristen Douglas's withdrawals during the year?

Exercise 1-14 *Evaluating the performance of a real company* **(Obj. 7)**

The 2000 annual report of Bombardier Inc. reported sales revenue of $13,619 million. Total expenses for the year were $12,900 million. Bombardier ended the year with total assets of $17,034 million and total liabilities of $13,422 million.

During the preceding year, 1999, Bombardier earned net income of $554 million. At year end 1999, Bombardier reported total assets of $14,278 million and total liabilities of $10,789 million.

Required

1. Compute Bombardier's net income for 2000. Did net income increase or decrease from 1999 to 2000? By how much?

2. Did Bombardier's shareholders' equity increase or decrease during 2000? By how much?

3. Bombardier's management strives for a steady increase in net income and shareholders' equity. How would you rate Bombardier's performance for 2000—excellent, fair, or poor? Give your reason.

Challenge Exercise

Exercise 1-15   *Using the financial statements*   *(Obj. 5)*

Compute the missing amounts for each of the following businesses.

	Purple Co.	White Co.	Orange Co.
Beginning:			
Assets	$110,000	$ 50,000	$ 90,000
Liabilities	50,000	20,000	60,000
Ending:			
Assets	$160,000	$ 70,000	$?
Liabilities	70,000	35,000	80,000
Owner's equity:			
Investments by owner	$?	$ 0	$ 10,000
Withdrawals by owner	110,000	40,000	70,000
Income Statement:			
Revenues	$440,000	$210,000	$400,000
Expenses	320,000	?	300,000

Beyond the Numbers

Beyond the Numbers 1-1   *Analyzing a loan request*   *(Obj. 1, 3)*

As an analyst for Scotiabank, it is your job to write recommendations to the bank's loan committee. Dixon Engineering Co., a client of the bank, has submitted these summary data to support the company's request for a $400,000 loan:

Income Statement Data	2004	2003	2002
Total revenues	$890,000	$830,000	$820,000
Total expenses	640,000	570,000	540,000
Net income	$250,000	$260,000	$280,000

Statement of Owner's Equity Data	2004	2003	2002
Beginning capital	$380,000	$400,000	$390,000
Add: Net income	250,000	260,000	280,000
	$630,000	$660,000	$670,000
Less: Withdrawals	(290,000)	(280,000)	(270,000)
Ending capital	$340,000	$380,000	$400,000

Balance Sheet Data	2004	2003	2002
Total assets	$730,000	$720,000	$660,000
Total liabilities	$390,000	$340,000	$260,000
Total owner's equity	340,000	380,000	400,000
Total liabilities and owner's equity	$730,000	$720,000	$660,000

Required

Analyze these financial statement data to decide whether the bank should lend $400,000 to Dixon Engineering Co. Consider the trends in net income and owner's equity and the change in total liabilities in making your decision. Write a one-paragraph recommendation to the bank's loan committee.

Beyond the Numbers 1-2 *Transaction analysis, effects on financial statements* *(Obj. 4)*

Camp Presquile conducts summer camps for children with disabilities. Because of the nature of its business, Camp Presquile experiences many unusual transactions. Evaluate each of the following transactions in terms of its effect on Camp Presquile's income statement and balance sheet.

a. A camper suffered a dental injury that was not covered by insurance. Camp Presquile paid $400 for the child's dental care. How does this transaction affect the income statement and the balance sheet?

b. One camper's mother is a physician. Camp Presquile allows this child to attend camp in return for the mother's serving part-time in the camp infirmary for the two-week term. The standard fee for a camp term is $700. The physician's salary for this part-time work would be $700. How should Camp Presquile account for this arrangement?

c. Lightning during a storm damaged the camp dining hall. The cost to repair the damage will be $6,400 over and above what the insurance company will pay.

Ethical Issues

Ethical Issue 1

The oil spill of the Exxon *Valdez* tanker off the coast of Alaska continues to plague Exxon, the giant petroleum company. More than ten years later, Exxon's financial statements still report the accident's effects on the company. At the time of the accident, it appeared that the damage to Exxon could be gigantic. Generally accepted accounting principles require companies to report in their financial statements the effects of potential losses that the company might suffer as a result of past events.

Required

1. Suppose you are the chief financial officer (CFO) responsible for the financial statements of Exxon Corporation. What ethical issue would you face as you consider what to report in Exxon's annual report about the *Valdez* oil spill? What is the ethical course of action for the Exxon's CFO to take in this situation?

2. What are some of the negative consequences to Exxon of not telling the truth? What are some of the negative consequences to Exxon of telling the truth?

Ethical Issue 2

The board of directors of Darien Ltd. is meeting to discuss the past year's results before releasing financial statements to the public. The discussion includes this exchange:

> Sue Darien, company president: "Well, this has not been a good year! Revenue is down and expenses are up—way up. If we don't do some fancy stepping, we'll report a loss for the third year in a row. I can temporarily transfer some land that I own into the company's name, and that will beef up our balance sheet. Rob, can you shave $500,000 from expenses? Then we can probably get the bank loan that we need."

> Rob Ling, company chief accountant: "Sue, you are asking too much. Generally accepted accounting principles are designed to keep this sort of thing from happening."

Required

1. What is the fundamental ethical issue in this situation?

2. Discuss how Sue Darien's proposals violate generally accepted accounting principles. Identify the specific concept or principle involved.

Problems (Group A)

Problem 1-1A *Entity concept, transaction analysis, accounting equation* **(Obj. 2, 4)**

Raj Imani was an environmental consultant and partner in a large firm, a partnership, for five years after graduating from university. Recently he resigned his position to open his own consultancy practice, which he operates as a sole proprietorship. The name of the new company is Environmental Consultants.

Imani recorded the following events during the organizing phase of his new business and its first month of operations. Some of the events were personal and did not affect his consultancy practice. Others were business transactions and should be accounted for by the business.

May	4	Imani received $70,000 cash from his former partners in the consulting firm from which he resigned.
	5	Imani invested $70,000 cash in his business, Environmental Consultants.
	5	The business paid office rent expense for the month of May, $1,200.
	6	The business paid $300 cash for letterhead stationery for the office.
	7	The business purchased office furniture for the office and will pay the account payable, $8,000, within six months.
	10	Imani sold 750 shares of Dofasco stock, which he and his wife had owned for several years, receiving $18,000 cash from his stockbroker.
	11	Imani deposited the $18,000 cash from sale of the Dofasco stock in his personal bank account.
	12	A representative of a large forestry company telephoned Imani and told him of the company's intention to transfer its consulting business to Environmental Consultants.
	29	The business finished an environmental assessment for a client and submitted the bill for services, $5,000. The business expected to collect from this client within two weeks.
	31	Imani withdrew $1,000 cash from the business.

Required

1. Classify each of the preceding events as one of the following:
   a. A business transaction to be accounted for by the business, Environmental Consultants.
   b. A business-related event but not a transaction to be accounted for by Environmental Consultants.
   c. A personal transaction not to be accounted for by Environmental Consultants.
2. Analyze the effects of the above events on the accounting equation of Environmental Consultants. Use a format similar to Exhibit 1-7, Panel B.

Problem 1-2A *Balance sheet for a sole proprietorship* **(Obj. 2, 5)**

The bookkeeper of Kwok Services Co., a sole proprietorship, prepared the balance sheet of the company while the accountant was ill. The balance sheet contains numerous errors. In particular, the bookkeeper knew that the balance sheet should balance, so he plugged in the owner's equity amount needed to achieve this balance. The owner's equity amount, however, is not correct. All other amounts are accurate.

KWOK SERVICES CO.
Balance Sheet
For the Month Ended July 31, 2003

Assets		Liabilities	
Cash..	$12,000	Service revenue	72,000
Office supplies	1,000	Note payable..............................	6,000
Land	44,000	Accounts payable.......................	8,000
Advertising expense....................	2,500		
Office furniture...........................	10,000	**Owner's Equity**	
Accounts receivable....................	13,000	K. Kwok, capital.........................	4,500
Rent expense...............................	8,000	Total liabilities and	
Total assets	$90,500	owners' equity.......................	$90,500

Required

1. Prepare the correct balance sheet, and date it correctly. Compute total assets, total liabilities, and owner's equity.

2. Identify the accounts listed above that should *not* be presented on the balance sheet and state why you excluded them from the correct balance sheet you prepared for Requirement 1.

Problem 1-3A *Balance sheet for a sole proprietorship, entity concept* (Obj. 2, 3, 5)

Luci Vachon is a realtor. She buys and sells properties on her own, and she also earns commission revenue as a real estate agent. She organized her business as a sole proprietorship on November 24, 2002. Consider the following facts as of November 30, 2002:

a. Vachon owed $55,000 on a note payable for some undeveloped land. This land had been acquired by the business for a total price of $100,000.

b. Vachon's business had spent $25,000 for a Re/Max Ltd. real estate franchise, which entitled her to represent herself as a Re/Max agent. Re/Max is a national affiliation of independent real estate agents. This franchise is a business asset.

c. Vachon owed $80,000 on a personal mortgage on her personal residence, which she acquired in 1998 for a total price of $170,000.

d. Vachon had $10,000 in her personal bank account and $17,000 in her business bank account.

e. Vachon owed $600 on a personal charge account with The Bay.

f. The business acquired business furniture for $17,000 on November 25. Of this amount, the company owed $6,000 on account at November 30.

g. The real estate office had $1,000 of office supplies on hand on November 30.

Required

1. Prepare the balance sheet of the real estate business of Luci Vachon, Realtor, at November 30, 2002.

2. Identify the personal items given in the preceding facts that would not be reported on the balance sheet of the business.

Problem 1-4A *Business transactions and analysis* (Obj. 4)

Tofino Suppliers was recently formed. The balance of each item in the business's accounting equation is shown below for May 21 and for each of the nine following business days.

	Cash	Accounts Receivable	Supplies	Land	Accounts Payable	Owner's Equity
May 21	$ 8,000	$ 4,000	$1,000	$ 8,000	$4,000	$17,000
22	13,000	4,000	1,000	8,000	4,000	22,000
23	6,000	4,000	1,000	15,000	4,000	22,000
24	6,000	4,000	4,000	15,000	7,000	22,000
25	5,000	4,000	4,000	15,000	6,000	22,000
26	7,000	2,000	4,000	15,000	6,000	22,000
27	14,000	2,000	4,000	15,000	6,000	29,000
28	11,000	2,000	4,000	15,000	3,000	29,000
29	9,000	2,000	6,000	15,000	3,000	29,000
30	2,000	2,000	6,000	15,000	3,000	22,000

Required

Assuming that a single transaction took place on each day, describe briefly the transaction that was most likely to have occurred, beginning with May 22. Indicate which accounts were affected and by what amount. No revenue or expense transactions occurred on these dates.

Problem 1-5A *Income statement, statement of owner's equity, balance sheet* (Obj. 5)

Presented below are the amounts of (a) the assets and liabilities of Spectrum Sounds as of December 31 and (b) the revenues and expenses of the company for the year ended on that date. The items are listed in alphabetical order.

Accounts payable	$ 36,000	Insurance expense	$ 2,000
Accounts receivable	22,000	Interest expense	9,000
Advertising expense	13,000	Note payable	125,000
Building	170,000	Rent expense	23,000
Cash	10,000	Salary expense	120,000
Consulting expense	18,000	Salary payable	9,000
Electronic equipment	110,000	Service revenue	255,000
Furniture	20,000	Supplies	3,000

The opening balance of owner's equity was $150,000. At year end, after the calculation of net income, the owner, Pavel Rabinovitch, withdrew $55,000.

Required

1. Prepare the business's income statement for the year ended December 31 of the current year.

2. Prepare the statement of owner's equity of the business for the year ended December 31.

3. Prepare the balance sheet of the business at December 31.

4. Answer these questions about the business:

   a. Was the result of operations for the year a profit or a loss? How much was it?

   b. Did the business's owner's equity increase or decrease during the year? How would this affect the business's ability to borrow money from a bank in the future?

   c. How much in total economic resources does the business have at December 31 as it moves into the new year? How much does the business owe? What is the dollar amount of the owner's portion of the business at December 31?

Problem 1-6A *Transaction analysis, accounting equation, financial statements* (Obj. 4, 5)

Janet Kap is proprietor of a career counselling and employee search business, Kap Personnel Services. The following amounts summarize the financial position of the business on August 31, 2002:

	Assets				=	Liabilities	+	Owner's Equity
		Accounts		Furniture and		Accounts		J. Kap,
	Cash +	Receivable +	Supplies +	Computers	=	Payable	+	Capital
Bal.	1,250	1,500		12,000		4,000		10,750

During September 2002, the following company transactions occurred:

a. Kap deposited $20,000 cash in the business bank account.

b. Performed services for a client and received cash of $900.

c. Paid off the August 31, 2002, balance of accounts payable.

d. Purchased supplies on account, $1,000.

e. Collected cash from a customer on account, $1,000.

f. Consulted on a large downsizing by a major corporation and billed the client for services rendered, $8,000.

g. Recorded the following business expenses for the month:

   (1) Paid office rent for August 2002—$900.

   (2) Paid advertising—$100.

h. Sold supplies to another business for $150 cash, which was the cost of the supplies.

i. Janet Kap withdrew $4,000 cash.

Required

1. Analyze the effects of the above transactions on the accounting equation of Kap Personnel Services. Adapt the format of Exhibit 1-7, Panel B.
2. Prepare the income statement of Kap Personnel Services for the month ended September 30, 2002. List expenses in decreasing order by amount.
3. Prepare the business's statement of owner's equity for the month ended September 30, 2002.
4. Prepare the balance sheet of Kap Personnel Services at September 30, 2002.

Problem 1-7A *Accounting concepts/principles* *(Obj. 2)*

Michael Bakal had been operating his law practice in Burnaby under the name Michael Bakal, Lawyer, for two years and had the following business assets and liabilities (at their historical costs) on April 30, 2000:

Cash	$ 6,000
Accounts receivable	3,000
Supplies	400
Furniture and computers	14,000
Accounts payable	2,000

The following business transactions took place during the month of May 2000:

May 1 Bakal deposited $20,000 cash into the business bank account.

3 Bakal completed legal work for a home builder. He charged the builder $1,000, not the $1,800 the work was worth, in order to promote business from the builder.

5 The business bought furniture from Arthur Wolff for $4,000, paying $1,000 cash and promising to pay $500 a month at the beginning of each month starting June 1, 2000 for six months.

10 The company signed a lease to rent additional space at a cost of $900 per month. Michael Bakal will occupy the premises effective June 1, 2000.

18 Determining that the business would need more cash in June, Bakal went to the bank and borrowed $10,000 on a personal loan and transferred the money to the company.

22 The company did legal work for CBB Co. for $6,000. CBB Co. agreed to pay $3,000 in 30 days and $3,000 in 90 days.

25 Bakal purchased a painting for his home from one of his clients. He paid for the $300 purchase with his personal credit card.

28 Bakal withdrew $3,000 from the business. He used $1,000 of the money to repay a portion of the loan arranged on May 18.

31 The business did legal work with a value of $4,000 for Apex Computers Ltd. Apex paid for the work by giving the company computer equipment with a selling price of $8,000.

Required

Identify the accounting concept or principle that would be applicable to each of the transactions and discuss the effects it would have on the financial statements of Michael Bakal, Lawyer.

Problem 1-8A *Accounting concepts/principles, transaction analysis, accounting equation, financial statements, evaluation* *(Obj. 2, 4, 5, 6)*

Boards R Us was started on December 31, 2002, by Jay Carter with an investment of $15,000 cash. It has been operating for one year. Carter has made additional investments of $10,000 but he has not withdrawn any funds. The company rents snowboards and related gear out of a small store. The balance sheet accounts at November 30, 2003, are as follows:

Cash	$ 1,000
Accounts receivable	9,000
Rental gear	18,000
Rental snowboards	34,000
Store equipment	13,000
Accounts payable	12,000

The following transactions took place during the month of December 2003:

Dec. 1 Carter borrowed $15,000 from his family and invested $6,000 in the business. The other $9,000 was intended for Carter's living expenses.

1 The business paid $3,000 for the month's rent on the store space.

4 The business signed a one-year lease for the rental of additional store space at a cost of $2,000 per month. The lease is effective January 1. The business will pay the first month's rent in January.

6 Rental fees for the week were: Gear, $6,000; Boards, $14,000. Half the fees were paid in cash and half on account.

10 The business paid the accounts payable from November 30, 2003.

12 The business purchased gear for $9,000 and boards for $16,000, all on account.

13 Rental fees for the week were: Gear, $3,000; Boards, $6,000. All the fees were paid in cash.

15 The company received payment for the accounts receivable owing at November 30, 2003.

18 The company purchased computer equipment for $4,000 by paying $1,000 cash with the balance due in 60 days.

20 Rental fees for the week were: Gear, $4,000; Boards, $10,000. Half the fees were paid in cash and half on account.

24 The company paid the balance owing for the purchases made on December 12.

27 Rental fees for the week were: Gear, $2,000; Boards, $8,000. All the fees were paid in cash.

27 The company received payment for rental fees on account from December 6.

Required

1. What is the total net income earned by the business over the period of December 31, 2002 to November 30, 2003?

2. Analyze the effects of the December 2003 transactions on the accounting equation of Boards R Us. Include the account balances from November 30, 2003.

3. Prepare the income statement for Boards R Us for the month ended December 31, 2003.

4. Prepare the statement of owner's equity for Boards R Us for the month ended December 31, 2003.

5. Prepare the balance sheet for Boards R Us at December 31, 2003.

6. Carter has expressed concern that although the business seems to be profitable and growing, he constantly seems to be investing additional money into it and has been unable to make any withdrawals for the work he has put into it. Prepare a reply to his concerns.

Problems (Group B)

Problem 1-1B *Entity concept, transaction analysis, accounting equation* *(Obj. 2, 4)*

Lisa D'Amato was an architect and partner with a large firm, a partnership, for ten years after graduating from university. Recently she resigned her position to open her own architecture office, which she operates as a proprietorship. The name of the new entity is D'Amato Design.

D'Amato recorded the following events during the organizing phase of her new business and its first month of operations. Some of the events were personal and did not affect the practice of architecture. Others were business transactions and should be accounted for by the business.

May 1   Lisa D'Amato sold 1,100 shares of Bank of Montreal stock, which she had owned for several years, receiving $55,000 cash from her stockbroker.

2   Lisa D'Amato deposited the $55,000 cash from sale of the Bank of Montreal stock in her personal bank account.

3   Lisa D'Amato received $150,000 cash from her former partners in the architecture firm from which she resigned.

5   Lisa D'Amato deposited $100,000 into a bank account in the name of D'Amato Design.

5   The business paid office rent for the month of May, $1,900.

6   A representative of a large real estate company telephoned Lisa D'Amato and told her of the company's intention to transfer its design business to her business, D'Amato Design.

7   The business paid $550 cash for letterhead stationery.

9   The business purchased office furniture for the office, on account, for $9,500, promising to pay in three months.

23   The business finished design work for a client and submitted the bill for design services, $3,000. It expects to collect from this client within one month.

31   Lisa D'Amato withdrew $1,000 for personal expenses.

Required

1. Classify each of the preceding events as one of the following:

   a. A business transaction to be accounted for by the business, D'Amato Design.

   b. A business-related event but not a transaction to be accounted for by D'Amato Design.

   c. A personal transaction not to be accounted for by D'Amato Design.

2. Analyze the effects of the above events on the accounting equation of D'Amato Design. Use a format similar to Exhibit 1-7, Panel B.

Problem 1-2B   *Balance sheet*   *(Obj. 2, 5)*

The bookkeeper of Firman Insurance Agency prepared the balance sheet of the company while the accountant was ill. The balance sheet contains numerous errors. In particular, the bookkeeper knew that the balance sheet should balance, so she "plugged in" the owner's equity amount needed to achieve this balance. The owner's equity amount, however, is not correct. All other amounts are accurate.

FIRMAN INSURANCE AGENCY
Balance Sheet
For the Month Ended October 31, 2002

Assets		Liabilities	
Cash...	$ 3,400	Premium revenue	$72,000
Insurance expense.......................	300	Accounts payable......................	3,000
Land	21,500	Note payable..............................	21,000
Salary expense	3,300		
Office furniture...........................	5,700		
Accounts receivable....................	12,600	**Owner's Equity**	
Utilities expense	2,100	J. Firman, capital	(43,100)
Notes receivable	4,000	Total liabilities and	
Total assets	$52,900	owner's equity	$52,900

Required

1. Prepare the correct balance sheet, and date it correctly. Compute total assets, total liabilities, and owner's equity.

2. Identify the accounts listed above that should *not* be presented on the balance sheet and state why you excluded them from the correct balance sheet you prepared for Requirement 1.

Problem 1-3B   *Balance sheet, entity concept*   **(Obj. 2, 3, 5)**

Jai Shah is a realtor. He buys and sells properties on his own, and he also earns commission revenue as a real estate agent. He invested $60,000 on March 10, 2003, in the business, Jai Shah Realty. Consider the following facts as of March 31, 2003:

a. Shah had $10,000 in his personal bank account and $16,000 in the business bank account.

b. The real estate office had $1,000 of office supplies on hand on March 31, 2003.

c. Jai Shah Realty had spent $15,000 for a Realty World Canada franchise, which entitled the company to represent itself as a Realty World Canada member firm. This franchise is a business asset.

d. The company owed $37,000 on a note payable for some undeveloped land that had been acquired by the company for a total price of $64,000.

e. Shah owed $110,000 on a personal mortgage on his personal residence, which he acquired in 2001 for a total price of $240,000.

f. Shah owed $950 on a personal charge account with The Bay.

g. The company acquired business furniture for $14,000 on March 26. Of this amount, Jai Shah Realty owed $8,000 on account at March 31, 2003.

Required

1. Prepare the balance sheet of the real estate business of Jai Shah Realty at March 31, 2003.

2. Identify the personal items given in the preceding facts that would not be reported on the balance sheet of the business.

Problem 1-4B   *Business transactions and analysis*   **(Obj. 4)**

Recently, Tammy Smiljanic formed a management accounting practice as a sole proprietorship. The balance of each item in the proprietorship accounting equation follows for April 2 and for each of the nine business days given:

	Cash	Accounts Receivable	Office Supplies	Land	Accounts Payable	Owner's Equity
Apr. 2	$3,000	$7,000	$ 800	$11,000	$3,800	$18,000
9	6,000	4,000	800	11,000	3,800	18,000
14	4,000	4,000	800	11,000	1,800	18,000
17	4,000	4,000	1,100	11,000	2,100	18,000
19	6,000	4,000	1,100	11,000	2,100	20,000
20	4,900	4,000	1,100	11,000	1,000	20,000
22	10,900	4,000	1,100	5,000	1,000	20,000
25	10,900	4,200	900	5,000	1,000	20,000
26	10,700	4,200	1,100	5,000	1,000	20,000
30	6,600	4,200	1,100	5,000	1,000	15,900

Required

Assuming that a single transaction took place on each day, describe briefly the transaction that was most likely to have occurred beginning with April 9. Indicate which accounts were affected and by what amount. No revenues or expense transactions occurred on these dates.

Problem 1-5B   *Income statement, statement of owner's equity, balance sheet*   **(Obj. 5)**

The amounts of (a) the assets and liabilities of Inkjet Office Cleaning as of December 31 of the current year and (b) the revenues and expenses of the company for the year ended on that date appear below. The items are listed in alphabetical order.

Accounts payable	$17,000	Land	$ 28,000	
Accounts receivable	3,000	Note payable	36,000	
Building	51,000	Property tax expense	2,000	
Cash	1,000	Rent expense	12,000	
Equipment	21,000	Salary expense	42,000	
Interest expense	5,000	Service revenue	104,000	
Interest payable	1,000	Supplies	22,000	
		Utilities expense	3,000	

The beginning amount of owner's equity was $61,000. During the year, the owner, Cathy Reynolds, withdrew $29,000.

Required

1. Prepare the income statement of Inkjet Office Cleaning for the year ended December 31 of the current year.

2. Prepare the statement of owner's equity of the business for the year ended December 31.

3. Prepare the balance sheet of the business at December 31.

4. Answer these questions about Inkjet Office Cleaning.

   a. Was the result of operations for the year a profit or a loss? How much was it?

   b. Did the business's owner's equity increase or decrease during the year? How would this affect the business's ability to borrow money from a bank in the future?

   c. How much in total economic resources does the company have at December 31 as it moves into the new year? How much does the company owe? What is the dollar amount of the owner's portion of the business at December 31?

Problem 1-6B *Transaction analysis, accounting equation, financial statements* *(Obj. 4, 5)*

Regina Bagnoli operates an interior design studio called Regina Design Studio. The following amounts summarize the financial position of the business on April 30, 2002:

	Assets				=	Liabilities	+	Owner's Equity
		Accounts				Accounts		R. Bagnoli,
Cash	+	Receivable	+ Supplies	+ Land	=	Payable	+	Capital
Bal. 1,720		2,240		24,100		5,400		22,660

During May 2002 the company did the following:

a. Bagnoli received $14,000 as a gift and deposited the cash in the business bank account.

b. Paid the beginning balance of accounts payable.

c. Performed services for a client and received cash of $1,100.

d. Collected cash from a customer on account, $900.

e. Purchased supplies on account, $720.

f. Consulted on the interior design of a major office building and billed the client for services rendered, $6,000.

g. Recorded the following business expenses for the month:

   (1) Paid office rent for May 2002—$1,200.

   (2) Paid advertising—$660.

h. Sold supplies to another interior designer for $80 cash, which was the cost of the supplies.

i. Withdrew $1,400 cash for personal use.

Required

1. Analyze the effects of the above transactions on the accounting equation of Regina Design Studio. Adapt the format of Exhibit 1-7, Panel B.

2. Prepare the income statement of Regina Design Studio for the month ended May 31, 2002. List expenses in decreasing order by amount.

3. Prepare the statement of owner's equity of Regina Design Studio for the month ended May 31, 2002.

4. Prepare the balance sheet of Regina Design Studio at May 31, 2002.

Problem 1-7B   *Accounting concepts/principles*   **(Obj. 2)**

Paul Lim has been operating a plumbing business as a sole proprietorship (Paul Lim Plumbing) for four years and had the following business assets and liabilities (at their historical costs) on May 31, 2003:

Cash	$10,000
Accounts receivable	5,000
Shop supplies	2,000
Shop equipment	15,000
Accounts payable	5,000

The following transactions took place during the month of June 2003:

June 1   Paul's brother, John, had been in a similar business in the same city and moved to England. He sold Paul his equipment for $9,000. The equipment had cost $17,000 and had a replacement cost of $11,000.

       3   The business did some plumbing repairs for Sheldon Kantor, a customer. The business would normally have charged $200 for the work, but had agreed to do it for $150 cash in order to promote more business from the client.

      10   The business signed a lease to rent additional shop space for the business at a cost of $800 per month. The business will occupy the premises effective July 1, 2003.

      18   Finding he was low on cash, Lim went to the bank and borrowed $1,500 on a personal loan.

      22   The company did repairs to the plumbing of Mary's Fine Foods for $7,000. Mary's Fine Foods paid $5,000 cash and agreed to pay $2,000 in 90 days.

      28   Paul Lim withdrew $2,000 from the business and used $1,500 to repay the bank loan of June 18.

Required
Identify the accounting concept or principle that would be applicable to each of the transactions and discuss the effects it would have on the financial statements of Paul Lim Plumbing.

Problem 1-8B   *Accounting concepts/principles, transaction analysis, accounting equation, financial statements, evaluation*   **(Obj. 2, 4, 5, 6)**

Saskatoon Computer Concepts, a sole proprietorship owned by Melanie Palm, was started on January 1, 2000, by Melanie Palm with an investment of $10,000 cash. It has been operating for three years. Palm has made additional investments of $22,000 but has not made any withdrawals. The company prepares marketing plans for clients and has seen business grow from a small business using rented equipment and having only two customers to one with the following balances as of December 31, 2002:

Cash	$ 4,000
Accounts receivable	8,000
Software	6,000
Office furniture	24,000
Computer equipment	36,000
Accounts payable	13,000
Owner's equity	65,000

The following transactions took place during the month of January 2003:

Jan. 2 Palm invested $5,000 in the business.

2 The business paid $1,000 for the month's rent on the office space.

4 The business signed a lease for the rental of additional office space at a cost of $800 per month. The lease is effective February 1. The business will pay the first month's rent in February.

6 The business developed a systems design for Arc Ltd. and received $900 now plus additional $500 payments to be received on the 15th of the month for the next three months.

10 The business paid $50 to a courier service.

12 Palm signed an agreement to provide design work to Borax Inc. for $10,000 to be paid upon completion of the work.

14 The company purchased $1,500 of software that will be required for the Borax assignment. The company paid $1,000 and promised to pay the balance by the end of the month.

15 The company received $500 as the monthly payment from Arc Ltd. of January 6.

18 The company purchased computer equipment for $5,000 by paying $1,500 cash with the balance due in 60 days.

23 The company completed a network design for Carlo Ltd., which promised to pay $6,000 by the end of the month.

29 The company paid the balance owing for the software purchased on January 14.

Required

1. What is the total net income earned by the business over the period of January 1, 2000, to December 31, 2002?

2. Analyze the effects of the January 2003 transactions on the accounting equation of Saskatoon Computer Concepts. Be sure to include the account balances from December 31, 2002.

3. Prepare the income statement for Saskatoon Computer Concepts for the month ended January 31, 2003.

4. Prepare the statement of owner's equity for Saskatoon Computer Concepts for the month ended January 31, 2003.

5. Prepare the balance sheet for Saskatoon Computer Concepts at January 31, 2003.

6. Palm has expressed concern that although the business seems to be profitable and growing, she constantly seems to be investing additional money into it and has been unable to make any withdrawals for the work she has put into it. Prepare a reply to her concerns.

Challenge Problems

Problem 1-1C   *Understanding the going-concern concept*   *(Obj. 2)*

The going-concern concept is becoming an increasing source of concern for users of financial statements. There are instances of companies filing for bankruptcy several months after issuing their annual audited financial statements. The question is: why didn't the financial statements predict the problem?

A friend has just arrived on your doorstep; you realize she is very angry. After calming her down, you ask what the problem is. She tells you that she had inherited $5,000 from an uncle and invested the money in the common stock of Always Good Yogurt Corp. She had carefully examined Always Good Yogurt's financial statements for the year ended six months previously and concluded that the company was financially sound. This morning, she had read in the local paper that the company had gone bankrupt and her investment was worthless. She asks you why the financial statements valued the assets at values that are in excess of those the Trustee in Bankruptcy expects to realize from liquidating the assets. Why have the assets suddenly lost so much of the value they had six months ago?

Required

Explain to your friend why assets are valued on a going-concern basis in the financial statements and why they are usually worth less when the company goes out of business. Use inventory and accounts receivable as examples.

Problem 1-2C   *Accounting for business transactions*   *(Obj. 4)*

You and three friends have decided to go into the lawn care business for the summer to earn money to pay for your schooling in the fall. Your first step was to sign up customers to satisfy yourselves that the business had the potential to be profitable. Next, you planned to go to the bank to borrow money to buy the equipment you would need.

After considerable effort, your group obtained contracts from customers for 200 lawns for the summer. One of your partners wants to prepare a balance sheet showing the value of the contracts as an asset. She is sure that you will have no trouble with borrowing the necessary funds from the bank on the basis of the proposed balance sheet.

Required

Explain to your friend why the commitments (signed contracts) from customers cannot be recognized as assets. What suggestions do you have that might assist your group in borrowing the necessary funds?

Extending Your Knowledge

Decision Problems

1. *Using financial statements to evaluate a request for a loan (Obj. 1, 3, 7)*

Two businesses, Tim's Cycle World and Jake's Party Pantry, have sought business loans from you. To decide whether to make the loans, you have requested their balance sheets.

TIM'S CYCLE WORLD
Balance Sheet
December 31, 2003

Assets		Liabilities	
Cash..............................	$ 9,000	Accounts payable.....................	$ 12,000
Accounts receivable	14,000	Note payable............................	118,000
Merchandise inventory	85,000	Total liabilities..........................	130,000
Store supplies............................	500		
Furniture and fixtures	9,000	**Owner's Equity**	
Building......................................	82,000	T. Jones, Capital........................	83,500
Land	14,000	Total liabilities and	
Total assets	$213,500	owner's equity......................	$213,500

JAKE'S PARTY PANTRY
Balance Sheet
December 31, 2003

Assets		Liabilities	
Cash..	$ 10,000	Accounts payable	$ 3,000
Accounts receivable	4,000	Note payable	68,000
Office supplies	2,000	Total liabilities..........................	71,000
Inventory	20,000		
Office furniture	5,000	**Owner's Equity**	
Investments*.............................	200,000	J. Smith, Capital.......................	170,000
		Total liabilities and	
Total assets................................	$241,000	owner's equity	$241,000

*The investments of $200,000 can be sold today
  for $280,000.

Required

1. Based solely on these balance sheets, which entity would you be more comfortable loaning money to? Explain fully, citing specific items and amounts from the balance sheets.
2. In addition to the balance sheet data, what other financial statement information would you require? Be specific.

2. Using accounting information (Obj. 1, 2, 3, 4, 5)

A friend learns that you are taking an accounting course. Knowing that you do not plan a career in accounting, the friend asks why you are "wasting your time." Explain to the friend:

1. Why you are taking the course.
2. How accounting information is used or will be used:
   a. In your personal life.
   b. In the business life of your friend, who plans to be a farmer.
   c. In the business life of another friend, who plans a career in sales.

Financial Statement Problem

Identifying items from a company's financial statements (Obj. 4)

This and similar problems in later chapters focus on the financial statements of a real, Canadian company—Intrawest Corporation, a developer and operator of such well-known mountain resorts as Whistler/Blackcomb, Panorama, Tremblant, Mont Ste. Marie and Blue Mountain in Canada, and Mammoth, Copper, Stratten, and Showshoe in the United States, as well as resorts in France and a golf course resort in Florida. As you study each financial statement problem, you will gradually build the confidence that you can understand and use actual financial statements.

Refer to the Intrawest Corporation financial statements in Appendix A. Notice that Intrawest reports financial results in U.S. dollars.

Required

1. How much cash and short-term deposits did Intrawest Corporation have at June 30, 2000?
2. What were total assets at June 30, 2000? At June 30, 1999?
3. Write the company's accounting equation at June 30, 2000, by filling in the dollar amounts:

ASSETS = LIABILITIES + SHAREHOLDERS' EQUITY

4. Identify total revenue for the year ended June 30, 2000. Do the same for the year ended June 30, 1999. Did revenue increase or decrease in 2000?
5. How much net income or net loss did Intrawest Corporation experience for the year ended June 30, 2000? Was 2000 a good year or bad year compared to 1999?

Appendix

The History and Development of Accounting

Every technical area seems to have professional associations and regulatory bodies that govern its practice. Accounting is no exception. In Canada, the Canadian Institute of Chartered Accountants (CICA) has had the responsibility for issuing accounting standards that form the basis of **generally accepted accounting principles** or GAAP. GAAP is like the law of accounting—rules for conducting behaviour in a way acceptable to the majority of people. The rules that govern how accountants measure, process, and communicate financial information fall under the heading GAAP.

Responsibility for Setting the Standards

Initially, from 1946, when the first accounting standard was issued by the CICA's Accounting and Auditing Research Committee, until 1972, the CICA assumed for itself the responsibility for issuing accounting standards.[1]

Then in 1972, the Canadian Securities Administrators, a body composed of officials appointed by the provincial governments with securities exchanges to set securities law, issued National Policy Statement 27 (NP 27) designating the *CICA Handbook* as generally accepted accounting principles (GAAP). In 1975, the *Canada Business Corporations Act* did likewise. The *Ontario Securities Act* in 1978 also designated the *CICA Handbook* as GAAP (Exhibit A1-1). In these ways, the CICA became the official promulgator of generally accepted accounting principles. Exhibit A1-1 illustrates how the authority for setting GAAP is delegated to the CICA by the federal and provincial governments and the Securities Administrators.

From the date of the first accounting standard in 1946 until 1968, some 26 "Bulletins" were issued by the Accounting and Auditing Research Committee. In 1968, the CICA changed the format of pronouncements; from that date they became *Recommendations* and were the italicized portions of a looseleaf binder entitled the *CICA Handbook*. Sections 1000 to 4999 of the *Handbook* are concerned with accounting, while Sections 5000 to 9200 are concerned with assurance. The Recommendations are standards or regulations that must be followed, except in those rare cases where a particular Recommendation or Recommendations would not lead to fair presentation. In those cases, the accountant should, using professional judgment, select the appropriate accounting principle. An accountant who determines that the *Handbook* is not appropriate and selects some other basis of accounting must be prepared to defend that decision. The *Handbook* also includes *Accounting Guidelines* and *Assurance Guidelines*. They do not have the force of Recommendations and are issued simply to suggest methods for dealing with issues that are not covered by Recommendations. Frequently, they become replaced eventually by Recommendations on the issues.

In 1972, the Accounting and Auditing Research Committee was split into two committees—the Accounting Research Committee (ARC), renamed in 1982, the Accounting Standards Committee (AcSC) and the Auditing Standards Committee (AuSC). In 1992, the two committees were renamed the Accounting Standards Board and the Auditing Standards Board respectively. The Auditing Standards Board

---

[1]This material is from George J. Murphy, "A Chronology of the Development of Corporate Financial Reporting in Canada: 1850 to 1983." *The Accounting Historians Journal*, Spring, 1986.

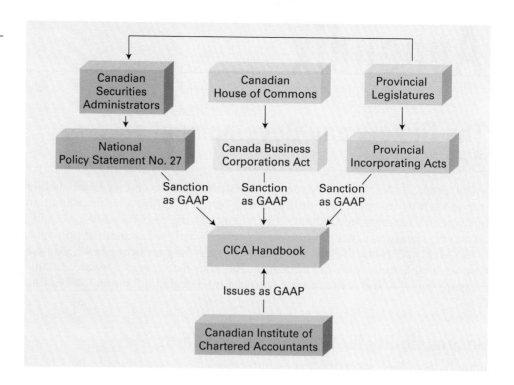

became the Assurance Standards Board in 1998. The former has the responsibility for establishing accounting standards, while the latter has the responsibility for establishing assurance standards.

The CICA established another standards committee in 1981, the Public Sector Accounting and Auditing Standards Committee (PSAAC), and a new handbook to contain the standards issued by that body. The PSAAC, renamed the Public Sector Accounting Standards Board (PSAB) in 1998, issues standards dealing with accounting by public sector entities, such as Transport Canada, provincial liquor commissions, municipalities, hospitals, and school boards. The Recommendations issued by PSAB have the same force as standards issued by the Accounting Standards Board except that they apply only to public sector entities. The CICA formed the Criteria of Control Board in 1992 and the Assurance Services Development Board in 1998.

Each new accounting Recommendation issued by the Accounting Standards Board becomes part of GAAP, the "accounting law of the land." In the same way that our laws draw authority from their acceptance by the people, GAAP depends on the general acceptance by the business community. Throughout this book, we refer to GAAP as the proper way to do accounting.

The Standard-Setting Process

Setting accounting standards is a complex process. The *Accounting Standards Board* determines how accounting is practised. The AcSB is made up of CAs from public accounting, industry, government, and academe, plus individuals nominated by the Canadian Council of Financial Analysts, the Financial Executives Institute of Canada, the Canadian Academic Accounting Association, the Certified General Accountants Association of Canada, and the Society of Management Accountants of Canada. The Accounting Standards Board does research on a particular issue, for example, the proper accounting for a lease. A document called an exposure draft is issued; it is a draft of the proposed new *Handbook* material. The exposure draft is distributed by the Accounting Standards Board to all interested parties, who are asked to make comments by a specified date. The Accounting Standards Board considers the responses to the exposure draft and issues a new Recommendation,

**Canadian Institute of Chartered
Accountants**
www.cica.ca

which becomes part of the *Handbook*. Occasionally, the proposed *Handbook* section is redrafted and re-exposed as a re-exposure draft to get additional comments before it is incorporated into the *Handbook*.

In 1988, the CICA set up the *Emerging Issues Committee* (EIC) to develop appropriate accounting standards for emerging accounting issues on a timely basis. The abstracts of issues published by the EIC are considered to be an authoritative source of GAAP in the absence of an accounting Recommendation. At the time of this writing, 112 abstracts of issues had been published by the EIC.

Individuals and companies often exert pressure on the Accounting Standards Board in their efforts to shape accounting decisions to their advantage. Occasionally governmental bodies have exerted pressure when they perceived that a proposed standard was not in harmony with government policy. Accountants also try to influence accounting decisions.

We will see that GAAP guides companies in their financial statement preparation. Independent auditing firms of public accountants hold the responsibility for making sure companies do indeed follow GAAP.

Sources of Generally Accepted Accounting Principles

While the primary source of GAAP is the Recommendations in the *CICA Handbook*, they cannot possibly cover all situations that accountants encounter. When situations not covered by the Recommendations in the *CICA Handbook* arise, Section 1000.60 of the *Handbook* suggests that the accountant should use other accounting principles that are

1. Generally accepted by virtue of being general practice (accounting principles that have general acceptance even though they are not codified); or of being industry practice (some industries, such as the Canadian Institute of Public Real Estate Companies, or CIPREC, have developed and enunciated principles for their industry); or

2. In the professional judgment of the accountant, consistent with the Recommendations in the *Handbook*, and developed through consultation with or reference to one or more of the following sources:

   a. Other parts of the *Handbook*

   b. General practice

   c. Accounting Guidelines. The Accounting Standards Board issues Guidelines, which are that body's interpretations of Recommendations or opinions on issues that are not yet codified as Recommendations.

   d. Abstracts of Issues by the Emerging Issues Committee (discussed earlier).

   e. International Accounting Standards. The Canadian Institute of Chartered Accountants, along with the Certified General Accountants Association of Canada and the Society of Management Accountants of Canada, are charter members of the International Federation of Accountants. This body, which includes as members professional accounting organizations in more than 91 countries, is attempting through the International Accounting Standards Committee to harmonize GAAP in those countries by issuing *international accounting standards* (IASs). Other members include the United Kingdom, the United States, the member countries of the European Community, Japan, and Australia. Section 1501 of the *Handbook* lists the 35 international accounting standards that have been issued to date. IASs do not override Canadian GAAP as set forth in the *Handbook*, which has precedence as local regulation. The Accounting Standards Board is attempting, where possible, to harmonize the Recommendations in the *CICA Handbook* with the IASs.

   f. Authoritative pronouncements from other jurisdictions. The Financial

International Federation of Accountants
www.ifac.org

International Accounting Standards Committee
www.iasc.org.uk

International Accounting Standards
www.iasc.org.uk/frame/cen2.htm

Accounting Standards Board (FASB), the body responsible for setting accounting standards in the United States, has issued a number of accounting standards in areas where there may not be a pronouncement from the CICA.

g. CICA research studies. The CICA has issued a number of research studies, such as *Financial Statements for Pension Plan Participants*, that provide guidance to accountants. In addition, the Certified General Accountants Association of Canada and the Society of Management Accountants of Canada publish research studies dealing with accounting issues.

h. Accounting texts and professional journals such as *CA magazine* and the *Journal of Accountancy* (published in the U.S. by the AICPA).

If confronted with an accounting issue that is not dealt with by the *CICA Handbook*, accountants should consider these sources and select the most appropriate treatment, that is, the one that provides the most informative disclosure.

Recording Business Transactions

CHAPTER OBJECTIVES

After studying this chapter, you should be able to

1 Define and use key accounting terms: *account*, *ledger*, *debit*, and *credit*

2 Apply the rules of debit and credit

3 Record transactions in the journal

4 Post from the journal to the ledger

5 Prepare and use a trial balance

6 Set up a chart of accounts for a business

7 Analyze transactions without a journal

"Because we are diversified across numerous locations in North America, we needed to put the right information systems in place. We've done that. We can now review on a moment's notice the status of any one of the dozens of real estate projects we are developing across the continent. Similar systems are now in place in our ski operations and this year we will have daily financial operating results for each resort available in Vancouver by 10 o'clock the following morning. This information intelligence has made our path of growth both clear and predictable." (Joe S. Houssian, Chairman, President and Chief Executive Officer of Intrawest Corporation.)

The 2000 Intrawest Annual Report describes Intrawest, headquartered in Vancouver, British Columbia, as "the leading developer and operator of mountain resorts across North America." The company owns year-round resorts at Whistler/Blackcomb and Panorama in British Columbia, Tremblant and Mont Ste. Marie in Quebec, Blue Mountain in Ontario, Copper in Colorado, Stratten in Vermont, Snowshoe in West Virginia, Mammoth in California, and Mountain Creek in New Jersey. The company also has an investment in Compagnie des Alpes, France, the largest ski company in the world, and a golf resort, Sandestin, in Florida.

Like all other companies, Intrawest represents itself to outsiders through its financial statements. But the accounting information is also used internally. Intrawest managers at all levels use financial statement data for decision making. They keep track of the revenue and expenses at the company's many resort properties by using accounting records like those we illustrate in this chapter. Accounting helps to measure profits and losses for each resort and for the company as a whole.

Intrawest Corporation
www.intrawest.com

Vancouver Grizzlies
www.nba.com/grizzlies/index.html

Hudson's Bay Company
www.hbc.com/english.asp

Zellers
www.hbc.com/zellers/default.htm

CHAPTER 1

introduced transaction analysis and the financial statements. But that chapter did not show how the financial statements are prepared. Chapters 2, 3, and 4 cover the accounting process that results in the financial statements.

Chapter 2 discusses the processing of accounting information as it is actually done in practice. Throughout this chapter and the next two, we continue to illustrate accounting procedure with service businesses, such as Air & Sea Travel, a systems design engineering company, or a sports franchise like the Vancouver Grizzlies. In Chapter 5 we move into merchandising businesses such as The Bay and Zellers. All these businesses use the basic accounting system that we illustrate in this book.

By learning how accounting information is processed, you will understand where the facts and figures reported in the financial statements come from. This knowledge will increase your confidence as you make decisions. It will also speed your progress in your business career.

OBJECTIVE 1
Define and use key accounting terms: *account, ledger, debit,* and *credit*

The Account

The basic summary device of accounting is the **account**, the detailed record of the changes that have occurred in a particular asset, liability, or item of owner's equity during a period of time. For convenient access to the information, accounts are grouped together in a record called the **ledger**. In the phrases "keeping the books" and "auditing the books," *books* refers to the ledger. Today the ledger usually takes the form of a computer listing.

Accounts are grouped in three broad categories, according to the accounting equation:

$$\text{ASSETS} = \text{LIABILITIES} + \text{OWNER'S EQUITY}$$

Recall that in Chapter 1, page 11, we learned that the accounting equation is the most basic tool of the accountant. It measures the assets of the business and the claims to those assets.

Assets

Assets are the economic resources that benefit the business and will continue to do so in the future. Most firms use the following asset accounts.

Cash   The Cash account shows the cash effects of a business's transactions. Cash means money and any medium of exchange that a bank accepts at face value, such as bank account balances, paper currency, coins, certificates of deposit, and cheques. Successful companies such as Intrawest usually have plenty of cash. Most business failures result from a shortage of cash.

Accounts Receivable   A business may sell its goods or services in exchange for an oral or implied promise of future cash receipts. Such sales are made on credit ("on account"). The Accounts Receivable account contains these amounts. Most sales in Canada and in other developed countries are made on account.

Notes Receivable   A business may sell its goods or services in exchange for a *promissory note*, which is a written pledge that the customer will pay the business a fixed amount of money by a certain date. The Notes Receivable account is a record of the promissory notes that the business expects to collect in cash. A note receivable offers more security for collection than a mere account receivable does.

Prepaid Expenses   A business often pays certain expenses in advance. A *prepaid expense* is an asset because it provides future benefits to the business. The business avoids having to pay cash in the future for the specified expense. The ledger holds a separate asset account for each prepaid expense. Prepaid Rent, Prepaid Insurance, and Office Supplies are accounted for as prepaid expenses.

Land   The Land account is a record of the cost of land a business owns and uses in its operations. Land held for sale is accounted for separately—in an investment account.

Building   The cost of a business's buildings—office, warehouse, garage, and the like—appear in the Building account. Intrawest owns buildings at Whistler, Tremblant, and its other resorts. Buildings held for sale are separate assets accounted for as investments. Intrawest builds condominiums at its resorts and sells them. These condominiums would, therefore, *not* be included in the Building account; they would be a part of inventory, discussed in Chapter 5.

Equipment, Furniture, and Fixtures   A business has a separate asset account for each type of equipment—Computer Equipment, Office Equipment, and Store Equipment, for example. The Furniture and Fixtures account shows the cost of these assets.

We will discuss other asset categories and accounts as needed. For example, many businesses have an Investments account for their investments in the stocks and bonds of other companies.

Liabilities

Recall that a *liability* is a debt. A business generally has fewer liability accounts than asset accounts because a business's liabilities can be summarized under relatively few categories.

Accounts Payable   This account is the opposite of the Accounts Receivable account. The oral or implied promise to pay off debts arising from credit purchases appears in the Accounts Payable account. Such purchases are said to be made on account. All companies, including Intrawest, have accounts payable.

Notes Payable   The Notes Payable account is the opposite of the Notes Receivable account. Notes Payable represents the amounts that the business must pay because it signed a promissory note to borrow money to purchase goods or services.

Accrued Liabilities   Liability categories and accounts are added as needed. Utilities Payable, Interest Payable, and Salary Payable are liability accounts used by most companies.

Owner's Equity

THINKING IT OVER

Name two things that (1) increase owner's equity;
(2) decrease owner's equity.

A: (1) Investments by owner and net income (revenue greater than expenses).
(2) Withdrawals and net loss (expenses greater than revenue).

The owner's claims to the assets of a business are called *owner's equity*. In a proprietorship, like that of Briana Weill or Gary Lyon, described in Chapter 1, or a partnership, owner's equity is often split into separate accounts for the owner's capital balance and for the owner's withdrawals. In a partnership, each partner would have a capital balance and a withdrawal account.

Capital   The Capital account shows the owner's claim to the assets of the business, whether it is Briana Weill or Gary Lyon of Air & Sea Travel. After total liabilities are subtracted from total assets, the remainder is the owner's capital. Amounts received from the owner's investment in the business are recorded directly in the Capital account. The Capital balance equals the owner's investments in the business plus net income minus net losses and owner withdrawals over the life of the business. (See the statement of owner's equity in Chapter 1.)

Withdrawals   When Gary Lyon withdraws cash or other assets from Air & Sea Travel for personal use, the business's assets and owner's equity decrease. The amounts taken out of the business appear in a separate account entitled Gary Lyon, Withdrawals, or Gary Lyon, Drawings. If withdrawals were recorded directly in the Capital account, the amount of owner withdrawals would not be highlighted and decision making would be more difficult. The Withdrawals account shows a *decrease* in owner's equity.

THINKING IT OVER

Suppose you bought a Pontiac Grand Am for $24,000 and had to borrow $18,000 to pay for the car. Write your personal accounting equation for this transaction.

A:
Assets = Liabilities + Owner's Equity
$24,000 = $18,000 + $6,000

Revenues   The increase in owner's equity created by delivering goods or services to customers or clients is called *revenue*. The ledger contains as many revenue accounts as needed. Air & Sea Travel would have a Service Revenue account for amounts earned by providing services for clients. If a business loans money to an outsider, it will need an Interest Revenue account for the interest earned on the loan. If the business rents a building to a tenant, it will need a Rent Revenue account.

Expenses   Expenses use up assets or create liabilities in the course of operating a business. Expenses have the opposite effect of revenues; they decrease owner's equity. A business needs a separate account for each type of expense, such as Salary Expense, Rent Expense, Advertising Expense, and Utilities Expense. Businesses strive to minimize their expenses in order to maximize net income whether they are Briana Weill, Air & Sea Travel, or Intrawest.

Exhibit 2-1 shows how asset, liability, and owner's equity accounts can be grouped into the ledger.

Double-Entry Accounting

Accounting is based on a *double-entry system*, which means that we record the *dual effects* of a business transaction. *Each transaction affects at least two accounts.* For example, in Chapter 1, Gary Lyon's $50,000 cash investment in his travel agency increased both the Cash account and the Capital account of the business. It would be incomplete to record only the increase in the entity's cash without recording the increase in its owner's equity.

Consider a cash purchase of supplies. What are the dual effects of this transaction?

Exhibit 2-1

The Ledger (Asset, Liability, and Owner's Equity Accounts)

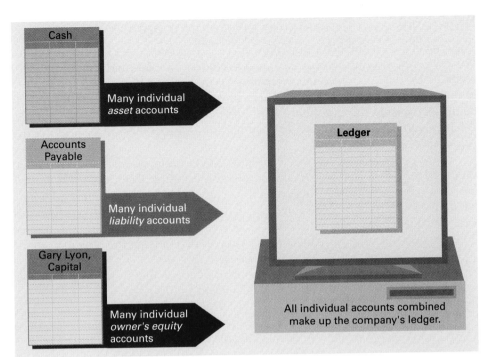

The purchase (1) decreases cash and (2) increases supplies. A purchase of supplies on credit (1) increases supplies and (2) increases accounts payable. A cash payment on account (1) decreases cash and (2) decreases accounts payable. All transactions have at least two effects on the accounts of the entity.

The T-Account

How do we record transactions? The account format used for most illustrations in this book is called the *T-account* because it takes the form of the capital letter "T." The vertical line in the letter divides the account into its left and right sides. The account title rests on the horizontal line. For example, the Cash account of a business appears in the following T-account format:

Cash

(Left side)	(Right side)
Debit	*Credit*

The left side of the account is called the **debit** side, and the right side is called the **credit** side. The words *debit* and *credit* can be confusing because they are new. To become comfortable using them, simply remember this:

debit = left side
credit = right side

Even though *left side* and *right side* may be more convenient, *debit* and *credit* are deeply entrenched in business.[1] Debit and credit are abbreviated as follows:

* Dr = Debit
* Cr = Credit

> **KEY POINT**
>
> A T-account is a quick way to show the effect of transactions on a particular account—a useful shortcut in accounting.

> **KEY POINT**
>
> The accounting equation must balance after every transaction. But verifying that total assets = total liabilities + owner's equity is no longer necessary after every transaction. The equation will balance as long as the debits in each transaction equal the credits in the transaction.

---

[1] The words *debit* and *credit* have a Latin origin (*debitum* and *creditum*). Pacioli, the Italian monk who wrote about accounting in the fifteenth century, used these terms.

Increases and Decreases in the Accounts

The type of an account determines how increases and decreases in it are recorded. For any given account, all increases are recorded on one side, and all decreases are recorded on the other side. Increases in *assets* are recorded in the left (debit) side of the account. Decreases in assets are recorded in the right (credit) side of the account. Conversely, increases in *liabilities* and *owner's equity* are recorded by *credits*. Decreases in liabilities and owner's equity are recorded by *debits*. These are the *rules of debit and credit.*

In everyday conversation, we may praise someone by saying, "She deserves credit for her good work." In your study of accounting forget this general usage. Remember that *debit means left side* and *credit means right side*. Whether an account is increased or decreased by a debit or credit depends on the type of account (see Exhibit 2-2).

In a computerized accounting system, the computer interprets debits and credits as increases or decreases by account type. For example, a computer reads a debit to Cash as an increase to that account and a credit to Accounts Payable as an increase to that account.

This pattern of recording debits and credits is based on the accounting equation:

$$\text{ASSETS} = \text{LIABILITIES} + \text{OWNER'S EQUITY}$$

Assets are on the opposite side from liabilities and owner's equity. Therefore, increases and decreases in assets are recorded in the opposite manner from liabilities and owner's equity. And liabilities and owner's equity, which are on the same side of the equal sign, are treated in the same way. Exhibit 2-2 shows the relationship between the accounting equation and the rules of debit and credit.

To illustrate the ideas diagrammed in Exhibit 2-2, reconsider the first transaction from Chapter 1. Gary Lyon invested $50,000 in cash to begin the travel agency. The company received $50,000 cash from Lyon and gave him the owner's equity. We are accounting for the business entity, Air & Sea Travel. What accounts of Air & Sea Travel are affected? By what amounts? On what side (debit or credit)? The answer is that Assets and Capital would increase by $50,000, as the following T-accounts show:

ASSETS	=	LIABILITIES	+	OWNER'S EQUITY
Cash				**Gary Lyon, Capital**

| Debit for Increase, 50,000 | | | | Credit for Increase, 50,000 |

Notice that Assets = Liabilities + Owner's Equity *and* that total debit amounts = total credit amounts. Exhibit 2-3 on page 58 illustrates the accounting equation and Air & Sea Travel's first three transactions.

EXHIBIT 2-2

The Accounting Equation and the Rules of Debit and Credit (The Effects of Debits and Credits on Assets, Liabilities, and Owner's Equity)

Accounting Equation:	Assets	=	Liabilities	+	Owner's Equity	
Rule of Debit and Credit:	Debit +	Credit −	Debit −	Credit +	Debit −	Credit +

The amount remaining in an account is called its *balance*. This initial transaction gives Cash a $50,000 debit balance, and Gary Lyon, Capital a $50,000 credit balance.

The second transaction is a $40,000 cash purchase of land. This transaction affects two assets: Cash and Land. It decreases (credits) Cash and increases (debits) Land, as shown in the T-accounts:

ASSETS	=	LIABILITIES	+	OWNER'S EQUITY

Cash

Balance 50,000	Credit for Decrease, 40,000
Balance 10,000	

Land

Debit for Increase, 40,000	
Balance 40,000	

Gary Lyon, Capital

	Balance 50,000

After this transaction, Cash has a $10,000 debit balance ($50,000 debit balance reduced by the $40,000 credit amount), Land has a debit balance of $40,000, and Gary Lyon, Capital has a $50,000 credit balance as shown in the middle section of Exhibit 2-3 (labelled Transaction 2).

Transaction 3 is a $500 purchase of office supplies on account. This transaction increases the asset Office Supplies and the liability Accounts Payable, as shown in the following accounts and in the right side of Exhibit 2-3 (labelled Transaction 3):

ASSETS	=	LIABILITIES	+	OWNER'S EQUITY

Cash

Balance 10,000	

Office Supplies

Debit for Increase, 500	
Balance 500	

Land

Balance 40,000	

Accounts Payable

	Credit for Increase, 500
	Balance 500

Gary Lyon, Capital

	Balance 50,000

We can create accounts as they are needed. The process of creating a new T-account in preparation for recording a transaction is called *opening the account*. For Transaction 1, we opened the Cash account and the Gary Lyon, Capital account. For Transaction 2, we opened the Land account, and for Transaction 3, Office Supplies and Accounts Payable.

We could record all transactions directly in the accounts as we have shown for the first three transactions. However, that way of accounting does not leave a clear record of each transaction. You may have to search through all the accounts to find both sides of a particular transaction. To save time, accountants keep a record of each transaction in a *journal* and then transfer this information from the journal into the accounts.

EXHIBIT 2-3

The Accounting Equation and the First Three Transactions of Air & Sea Travel

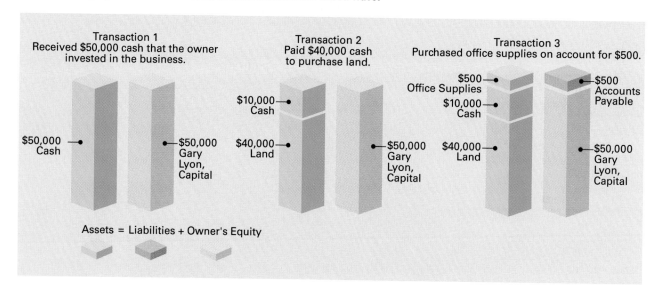

STOP & THINK

Can you prepare a balance sheet for Air & Sea Travel after the first transaction on April 2, 2002? Can you prepare an income statement?

Answer:

AIR & SEA TRAVEL
Balance Sheet
April 2, 2002

Assets		Liabilities	
Cash.............................	$50,000		$ 0
		Owner's Equity	
		Gary Lyon, Capital	$50,000
		Total liabilities and	
Total assets.............................	$50,000	owner's equity	$50,000

You could not yet prepare an income statement because the business has experienced no revenues or expenses.

Recording Transactions in Journals

In practice, accountants record transactions first in a **journal**, which is a chronological record of the entity's transactions. The journalizing process follows four steps:

1. Identify the transactions from source documents, such as bank deposit slips, sales invoices, or cheque stubs.

2. Specify each account affected by the transaction and classify it by type (asset, liability, or owner's equity).

3. Determine whether each account is increased or decreased by the transaction.

Using the rules of debit and credit, determine whether to debit or credit the account to record its increase or decrease.

4. Enter the transaction in the journal, including a brief explanation for the journal entry. The debit side of the entry is entered first and the credit side last.

Step 4, "Enter the transaction in the journal," means to record the transaction in the journal. This step is also called "making the journal entry" or "journalizing the transaction."

These four steps are completed in a computerized accounting system as well as in a manual system. In step 4, however, the journal entry is generally entered into the computer by account number, and the account name is then listed automatically. Most computer programs replace the explanation in the journal entry with some other means of tracing the entry back to its source documents.

Let's apply the four steps to journalize the first transaction of Air & Sea Travel—the business's receipt of Lyon's $50,000 cash investment in the business.

Step 1. The source documents are Air & Sea Travel's bank deposit slip and the $50,000 cheque, which is deposited in the business bank account.

Step 2. The accounts affected by the transaction are *Cash* and *Gary Lyon, Capital*. Cash is an asset account, and Gary Lyon, Capital is an owner's equity account.

Step 3. Both accounts increase by $50,000. Therefore, Cash, the asset account, is increased (debited), and Gary Lyon, Capital, the owner's equity account, is increased (credited).

Step 4. The journal entry is

Date	Accounts and Explanation	Debit	Credit
Apr. 2[a]	Cash[b]	50,000[d]	
	Gary Lyon, Capital[c]		50,000[e]
	Received initial investment from owner.[f]		

The journal entry includes (a) the date of the transaction, (b) the title of the account debited (placed flush left), (c) the title of the account credited (indented slightly), the dollar amounts of (d) the debit (left) and (e) the credit (right)—dollar signs are omitted in the money columns—and (f) a short explanation of the transaction.

The journal offers information that the ledger accounts do not provide. Each journal entry shows the complete effect of a business transaction. Consider Gary Lyon's initial investment. The Cash account shows a single figure, the $50,000 debit. We know that every transaction has a credit, so in what account will we find the corresponding $50,000 credit? In this illustration, we know that the Capital account holds this figure. But imagine the difficulties you would face trying to link debits and credits for hundreds of daily transactions—without a separate record of each transaction. The journal solves this problem and presents the full story for each transaction. Exhibit 2-4 shows how Journal page 1 looks after the first transaction is recorded.

KEY POINT

In a journal entry, such as Exhibit 2-4, the account debited is always written first (not indented). The account credited is indented on the line below, and the explanation is not indented on the next line. Journal entries should always be recorded in this format.

LEARNING TIP

When analyzing a transaction, first pinpoint the obvious effects on the accounts. For example, cash effects are easy to identify. Did cash increase or decrease? Then find its effect on other accounts.

	Journal			Page 1
Date	Accounts and Explanation	Ref.	Debit	Credit
Apr. 2	Cash		50,000	
	Gary Lyon, Capital			50,000
	Received initial investment from owner.			

EXHIBIT 2-4

The Journal

Regardless of the accounting system in use, an accountant must analyze every business transaction in the manner we are presenting in these opening chapters. Once the transaction has been analyzed, a computerized accounting package performs the same actions as accountants do in a manual system. For example, when a sales clerk runs your MasterCard through the credit card reader, the underlying accounting system records the store's sales revenue and receivable from MasterCard. The computer automatically records the transaction as a journal entry, but an accountant had to program the computer to do so. A computer's ability to perform routine tasks and mathematical operations quickly and without error frees accountants for decision making.

OBJECTIVE 4
Post from the journal to the ledger

Transferring Information (Posting) from the Journal to the Ledger

Posting means transferring the amounts from the journal to the accounts in the ledger. Debits in the journal are posted as debits in the ledger, and credits in the journal as credits in the ledger. The initial investment transaction of Air & Sea Travel is posted to the ledger as shown in Exhibit 2-5. Computers perform this tedious task quickly and without error. In these introductory discussions we temporarily ignore the date of each transaction in order to focus on the accounts and their dollar amounts.

The Flow of Accounting Data

Exhibit 2-6 summarizes the flow of accounting data from the business transaction all the way through the accounting system to the ledger. In the pages that follow, we continue the example of Air & Sea Travel and account for six of the business's early transactions. Keep in mind that we are accounting for the business entity, Air & Sea Travel. We are *not* accounting for Gary Lyon's *personal* transactions.

Transaction Analysis, Journalizing, and Posting to the Accounts

1.	Transaction:	Gary Lyons invested $50,000 cash to begin his travel business, Air & Sea Travel.

Analysis:	Lyon's investment in Air & Sea Travel increased its asset cash; to record this increase, debit Cash. The investment also increased its owner's equity; to record this increase, credit Gary Lyon, Capital.
Journal Entry:	Cash .... 50,000 Gary Lyon, Capital.............. 50,000 Received initial investment from owner.

Accounting Equation:	ASSETS	=	LIABILITIES	+	OWNER'S EQUITY
	Cash				Gary Lyon, Capital
	+50,000	=	0	+	50,000

The journal entry records the same information that you learned by using the accounting equation in Chapter 1. Both accounts—Cash and Gary Lyon, Capital—increased because the business received $50,000 cash and gave Lyon $50,000 of capital (owner's equity) in the business.

EXHIBIT 2-5

Journal Entry and Posting to
the Ledger

Panel A — Journal Entry

Date	Accounts and Explanation	Debit	Credit
April 2	Cash...	50,000	
	Gary Lyon, Capital......................................		50,000
	Received initial investment from owner.		

Panel B — Posting to Ledger

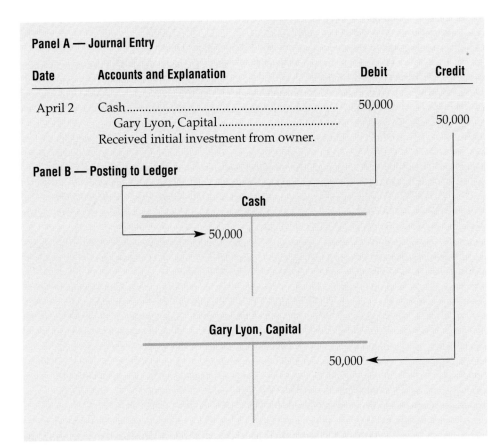

Cash

50,000

Gary Lyon, Capital

50,000

Prepare the journal entry to record
a $1,600 payment on account.
(1) Identify the accounts.
(2) Are these accounts increased
or decreased? Should they be
debited or credited?
(3) Make the journal entry, with an
explanation.
A: (1) The company paid $1,600 on
account. The accounts affected are
Cash and Accounts Payable.
(2) Cash (an asset) decreases by
$1,600. Accounts Payable (a
liability) decreases by the same
amount. To record a decrease in an
asset, we use a credit. To record a
decrease in a liability, we use a
debit. Review Exhibit 2-2.
(3) Accounts
　Payable...... 1,600
　　Cash ..... 　　1,600
　Made payment on
　account.

*Ledger
Accounts:*

Cash		Gary Lyon, Capital	
(1) 50,000			(1) 50,000

2.	*Transaction:*	**Air & Sea Travel paid $40,000 cash for land as a future office location.**

Analysis: The purchase decreased cash; therefore, credit Cash. The purchase increased the entity's asset land; to record this increase, debit Land.

Exhibit 2-6

Flow of Accounting Data

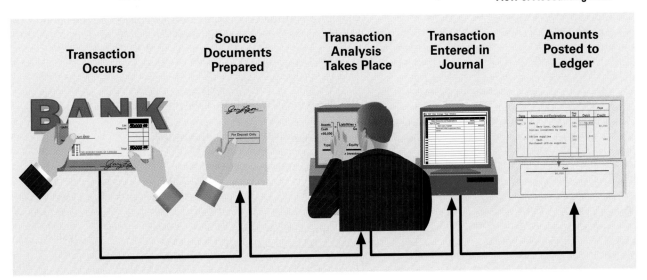

Transaction Occurs	Source Documents Prepared	Transaction Analysis Takes Place	Transaction Entered in Journal	Amounts Posted to Ledger

Journal Entry:

Land 40,000
     Cash 40,000
Paid cash for land.

Accounting Equation:

ASSETS		=	LIABILITIES	+	OWNER'S EQUITY
Cash	Land				
−40,000	+40,000	=	0	+	0

This transaction increased one asset, land, and decreased another asset, cash. The net effect on the business's total assets was zero, and there was no effect on liabilities or owner's equity. We use the term *net* in business to mean an amount after a subtraction.

Ledger Accounts:

Cash			Land	
(1) 50,000	(2) 40,000		(2) 40,000	

---

3. *Transaction:* **The business purchased office supplies for $500 on account payable.**

Analysis: The credit purchase of office supplies increased this asset, so we debit Office Supplies. The purchase also increased the liability accounts payable; to record this increase, credit Accounts Payable.

Journal Entry:

Office Supplies 500
    Accounts Payable 500
Purchased office supplies on account.

Accounting Equation:

ASSETS	=	LIABILITIES	+	OWNER'S EQUITY
Office Supplies		Accounts Payable		
+500	=	+500	+	0

Ledger Accounts:

Office Supplies		Accounts Payable	
(3) 500			(3) 500

4.	**Transaction:**	**The business paid $400 on the account payable created in Transaction 3.**

Analysis:	The payment decreased the asset cash; therefore, credit Cash. The payment also decreased the liability accounts payable, so we debit Accounts Payable.	

Journal Entry:

Accounts Payable 400
    Cash 400
Paid cash on account.

Accounting Equation:

ASSETS	=	LIABILITIES	+	OWNER'S EQUITY
Cash		Accounts Payable		
−400	=	−400	+	0

Ledger Accounts:

Cash				Accounts Payable			
(1)	50,000	(2)	40,000	**(4)**	**400**	(3)	500
		(4)	**400**				

5.	**Transaction:**	**Gary Lyon remodelled his personal residence with personal funds and a loan from their bank. This is not a business transaction of the travel business, so no journal entry is made.**

6.	**Transaction:**	**Gary Lyon withdrew $2,100 cash for personal living expenses.**

Analysis:	The withdrawal decreased the entity's cash; therefore, credit Cash. The transaction also decreased the owner's equity of the entity. Decreases in the owner's equity of a proprietorship that result from owner withdrawals are debited to a separate owner's equity account entitled Withdrawals. Therefore, debit Gary Lyon, Withdrawals.	

Journal Entry:

Gary Lyon, Withdrawals.............. 2,100
    Cash 2,100
Withdrawal of cash by owner.

Accounting Equation:

ASSETS	=	LIABILITIES	+	OWNER'S EQUITY
Cash				Gary Lyon, Withdrawals
−2,100	=	0		−2,100

Ledger Accounts:

Cash				Gary Lyon, Withdrawals		
(1)	50,000	(2)	40,000	**(6)**	**2,100**	
		(4)	400			
		(6)	**2,100**			

Each journal entry posted to the ledger is keyed by date or by transaction number. In this way any transaction can be traced from the journal to the ledger, and, if need be, back to the journal. This linking allows you to locate efficiently any information needed.

Accounts after Posting

We next illustrate how the accounts look when the amounts of the preceding transactions have been posted. The accounts are grouped under the accounting equation's headings.

Each account has a balance, denoted as *Bal.* This amount is the difference between the account's total debits and its total credits. For example, the balance in the Cash account is the difference between the debits, $50,000 and the credits, $42,500 (i.e., $40,000 + $400 + $2,100). Thus the cash balance is $7,500. The balances are residual amounts left over after the journal entries have been posted to the accounts. We set an account balance apart by horizontal lines. The final figure in an account below the horizontal line is the balance of the account after the transactions have been posted.

If the sum of an account's debits is greater than the sum of its credits, that account has a debit balance, as the Cash account does here. If the sum of its credits is greater, that account has a credit balance, as Accounts Payable does.

ASSETS		=	LIABILITIES		+	OWNER'S EQUITY	
Cash			**Accounts Payable**			**Gary Lyon, Capital**	
(1) 50,000	(2) 40,000		(4) 400	(3) 500			(1) 50,000
	(4) 400			Bal. 100			Bal. 50,000
	(6) 2,100						
Bal. 7,500							
Office Supplies						**Gary Lyon, Withdrawals**	
(3) 500						(6) 2,100	
Bal. 500						Bal. 2,100	
Land							
(2) 40,000							
Bal. 40,000							

OBJECTIVE 5
Prepare and use a trial balance

WORKING IT OUT

Assume that Gary Lyon, Withdrawals, $2,100, is erroneously listed as a credit amount on the trial balance in Exhibit 2-7.
(1) Recompute the trial balance totals.
(2) To find the mistake, calculate the difference between the column totals.
(3) Then divide the difference by two.
A: (1) Debit = $48,000;
Credit = $52,200.
(2) $52,200 − $48,000 = $4,200.
(3) $4,200 ÷ 2 = $2,100.

If you find that amount somewhere on the trial balance, you may have entered it in the wrong column. This is one easy way to find an error if your trial balance does not balance.

The Trial Balance

A **trial balance** is a list of all accounts with their balances—assets first, followed by liabilities and then owner's equity—taken from the ledger. Before computers, the trial balance provided a check on accuracy by showing whether the total debits equalled the total credits. The trial balance is still useful as a summary of all the accounts and their balances. A trial balance may be taken at any time the postings are up to date. The most common time is at the end of the accounting period. Exhibit 2-7 is the trial balance of the ledger of Air & Sea Travel after the six transactions have been journalized and posted.

Correcting Trial Balance Errors

In a trial balance, the total debits and total credits should be equal. If they are not equal, then accounting errors exist. Computerized accounting systems eliminate most recording errors by often prohibiting unbalanced journal entries from being recorded. Computerized accounting systems also post journal amounts precisely as they have been journalized. But computers cannot *eliminate* all errors because humans sometimes input the wrong data.

Many out-of-balance conditions can be detected by computing the difference between total debits and total credits on the trial balance. Then perform one or more of the following actions:

EXHIBIT 2-7

Trial Balance

AIR & SEA TRAVEL
Trial Balance
April 30, 2002

Account Titles	Balance	
	Debit	Credit
Cash	$ 7,500	
Office supplies..	500	
Land...	40,000	
Accounts payable..		$ 100
Gary Lyon, Capital		50,000
Gary Lyon, Withdrawals...	2,100	
Total	$50,100	$50,100

1. Search the trial balance for a missing account. For example, suppose the accountant omitted Gary Lyon, Withdrawals from the trial balance in Exhibit 2-7. The total amount of the debts would be $48,000 ($50,100 – $2,100). Trace each account and its balance from the ledger to the trial balance, and you will locate the missing account.

2. Search the journal for the amount of difference. For example, suppose the total credits on Air & Sea Travel's trial balance equal $50,100 and total debits equal $49,700. A $400 transaction may have been recorded incorrectly in the journal or posted incorrectly to the ledger. Search the journal for a $400 transaction.

3. Divide the difference between total debits and total credits by 2. A debit treated as a credit, or vice versa, doubles the amount of error. Suppose Air & Sea Travel debited $500 to Cash instead of crediting the Cash account, or assume the accountant posted a $500 credit as a debit. Total debits contain the $500, and total credits omit the $500. The out-of-balance amount is $1,000, and dividing by 2 identifies the $500 of the transaction. Then search the journal for a $500 transaction and trace to the account affected.

4. Divide the out-of-balance amount by 9. If the result is evenly divisible by 9, the error may be a *slide*, which is adding or deleting one or several zeroes in a figure (example: writing $61 as $610), or a *transposition* (example: treating $61 as $16). Suppose Air & Sea Travel listed the $2,100 Gary Lyon, Withdrawals balance as $21,000 on the trial balance—a slide-type error. Total debits would differ from total credits by $18,900 (i.e., $21,000 – $2,100 = $18,900). Dividing $18,900 by 9 yields $2,100, the correct amount of the withdrawals. Trace this amount through the ledger until you reach the Gary Lyon, Withdrawals account with a balance of $2,100. Computer-based systems avoid such errors.

A warning: Do not confuse the trial balance with the balance sheet. A trial balance is an internal document seen only by the company's owners, managers, and accountants. The company reports its financial position—both inside the business and to the public—on the balance sheet, a formal financial statement. And remember that the financial statements are the focal point of the accounting process. The trial balance is merely a step in the preparation of the financial statements.

On August 1, 2003, Mary Woo opens Woo Computer Consulting. During the business's first ten days of operations, it completes the following transactions:

a. To begin operations, Mary Woo deposits $40,000 of personal funds in a bank account entitled Woo Computer Consulting. The business receives the cash and gives Woo capital (owner's equity).

b. Woo Computer Consulting pays $20,000 cash for a small house to be used as an office and $10,000 for the land on which the house is located.

c. The business purchases office supplies for $500 on account.

d. The business pays $6,000 cash for office furniture.

e. The business pays $150 on the account payable created in Transaction (c).

f. Woo withdraws $1,000 cash for personal use.

Required

1. Prepare the journal entries to record these transactions. Key the journal entries by letter.

2. Post the entries to T-accounts and calculate the ending balance.

3. Prepare the trial balance of Woo Computer Consulting at August 10, 2003.

Solution to Review Problem

Requirement 1

Accounts and Explanation	Ref.	Debit	Credit
a. Cash		40,000	
Mary Woo, Capital			40,000
Record initial investment from owner.			
b. Building		20,000	
Land		10,000	
Cash			30,000
Purchased building for an office and land.			
c. Office Supplies		500	
Accounts Payable			500
Purchased office supplies on account.			
d. Office Furniture		6,000	
Cash			6,000
Purchased office furniture.			
e. Accounts Payable		150	
Cash			150
Paid cash on account.			
f. Mary Woo, Withdrawals		1,000	
Cash			1,000
Withdrew cash for personal use.			

Requirement 2

ASSETS

Cash

(a)	40,000	(b)	30,000
		(d)	6,000
		(e)	150
		(f)	1,000
Bal.	2,850		

Office Supplies

(c)	500	
Bal.	500	

Land

(b)	10,000	
Bal.	10,000	

Office Furniture

(d)	6,000	
Bal.	6,000	

Building

(b)	20,000	
Bal.	20,000	

LIABILITIES

Accounts Payable

(e)	150	(c)	500
		Bal.	350

OWNER'S EQUITY

Mary Woo, Capital

(a)	40,000	
Bal.	40,000	

Mary Woo, Withdrawals

(f)	1,000	
Bal.	1,000	

Requirement 3

WOO COMPUTER CONSULTING
Trial Balance
August 10, 2003

	Balance	
Account Titles	**Debit**	**Credit**
Cash	$ 2,850	
Office supplies	500	
Office furniture	6,000	
Building	20,000	
Land..	10,000	
Accounts payable		$ 350
Mary Woo, Capital....................................		40,000
Mary Woo, Withdrawals	1,000	
Total	$40,350	$40,350

Details of Journals and Ledgers

To focus on the main points of journalizing and posting, we purposely omitted certain essential data. In practice, the journal and the ledger provide additional details that create a "trail" through the accounting records for future reference. For example, a supplier may bill us twice for the same item we purchased on account. To prove we paid the bill, we would search the accounts payable records and work backward to the journal entry that recorded our payment. To see how this works, let's take a closer look at the journal and the ledger.

Details in the Journal   Exhibit 2-8, Panel B presents a widely used journal format. The journal page number appears in the upper-right corner. As the column headings indicate, the *journal* displays the following information:

1. The *date*, which indicates when the transaction occurred. The year appears only when the journal is started or when the year has changed. The date of the transaction is recorded for every transaction.

2. The *account title* and explanation of the transaction, as in Exhibit 2-4.

3. The *posting reference*, abbreviated Post. Ref. How this column helps the accountant becomes clear when we discuss the details of posting.

4. The *debit* column, which shows the amount debited.

5. The *credit* column, which shows the amount credited.

Details in the Ledger   Exhibit 2-8, Panel C presents the *ledger* in three-column format. The first two amount columns are for the debit and credit amounts posted from the journal. The third amount column is for the account's balance. This three-column format keeps a running balance in the account. The balance is usually indicated by the letters Dr or Cr (indicating a debit or credit respectively) appearing in the third amount column. Each account has its own record in the illustrative ledger. Our example shows Air & Sea Travel's Cash account, Office Supplies account, and Gary Lyon, Capital account. Each account in the ledger has its own identification number.

The column headings identify the ledger account's features:

1. The date.

2. The item column. This space is used for any special notation.

3. The journal reference column, abbreviated Jrnl. Ref. The importance of this column becomes clear when we discuss the mechanics of posting.

4. The debit column, with the amount debited.

5. The credit column, with the amount credited.

6. The balance column, with the debit or credit running balance.

Posting from the Journal to the Ledger

We know that posting means transferring information from the journal to the ledger accounts. But how do we handle the additional details that appear in the journal and the ledger formats that we have just seen? Exhibit 2-8 illustrates the steps in full detail. Panel A lists the first two transactions of the business entity Air & Sea Travel; Panel B presents the journal; and Panel C shows the ledger. The posting process includes four steps:

After recording the transaction in the journal:

Arrow ①—Copy (post) the transaction date from the journal to the ledger.

Arrow ②—Copy (post) the journal page number from the journal to the ledger. We use several abbreviations:

Jrnl. Ref. means Journal Reference. J. 1 refers to Journal page 1.

Exhibit 2-8

Details of Journalizing and Posting

Panel A: Two of Air & Sea's Transactions

Date	Transaction
Apr. 2, 2002	Gary Lyon invested $50,000 in travel agency. The business received cash and gave Lyon owner's equity in the business.
Apr. 3, 2002	Paid $500 cash for office supplies.

Panel B: The Journal

Page 1

Date	Accounts and Explanation	Post. Ref.	Debit	Credit
2002				
Apr. 2	Cash	1100	50,000	
	Gary Lyon, Capital	3000		50,000
	Received initial investment from owner.			
3	Office Supplies	1400	500	
	Cash	1100		500
	Purchased office supplies.			

① ② ③ ④

Panel C: The Ledger

Account: Cash   **Account No.** 1100

Date	Item	Jrnl. Ref.	Debit	Credit	Balance
2002					
Apr. 2		J.1	50,000		50,000 Dr
Apr. 3		J.1		500	49,500 Dr

1 Transfer the date of the transaction from the journal to the ledger.

2 Transfer the page number from the journal to the journal reference column of the ledger.

3 Post the debit figure from the journal as a debit figure in the ledger account.

4 Enter the account number in the posting reference column of the journal once the figure has been posted to the ledger.

Account: Office Supplies   **Account No.** 1400

Date	Item	Jrnl. Ref.	Debit	Credit	Balance
2002					
Apr. 3		J.1	500		500 Dr

Account: Gary Lyon, Capital   **Account No.** 3000

Date	Item	Jrnl. Ref.	Debit	Credit	Balance
2002					
Apr. 2		J.1		50,000	50,000 Cr

This step indicates where the information in the ledger came from: Journal page 1.

Arrow ③—Copy (post) the dollar amount of the debit ($50,000) from the journal as a debit to the same account (Cash) in the ledger. Likewise, post the dollar amount of the credit (also $50,000) from the journal to the appropriate account in the ledger. Now the ledger accounts have their correct amounts.

Arrow ④—Copy (post) the account number (1100) from the ledger back to the journal. This step indicates that the $50,000 debit to Cash has been posted to the Cash account in the ledger. Also, copy the account number (3000) for Gary Lyon, Capital back to the journal to show that the $50,000 amount of the credit has been posted to the ledger.

Post. Ref. is the abbreviation for Posting Reference.

After posting, you can prepare the trial balance, as we discussed earlier.

OBJECTIVE 6
Set up a chart of accounts for a business

Chart of Accounts in the Ledger

As you know, the ledger contains the business's accounts grouped under these headings:

1. Balance Sheet Accounts: Assets, Liabilities, and Owner's Equity
2. Income Statement Accounts: Revenues and Expenses.

To keep track of their accounts, organizations have a **chart of accounts**, which lists all the accounts in the ledger and their account numbers. These account numbers are used as posting references, as illustrated by Arrow 4 in Exhibit 2-8. This numbering system makes it easy to locate individual accounts in the ledger.

Accounts are identified by account numbers with two or more digits. Assets are often numbered beginning with 1, liabilities with 2, owner's equity with 3, revenues with 4, and expenses with 5. The second, third, and higher digits in an account number indicate the position of the individual account within the category. For example, Cash might be account number 1001, which is the first asset account. Accounts receivable may be account number 1101, the second asset account. Accounts payable may be number 2001, the first liability account. All accounts are numbered by this system.

Organizations with many accounts use lengthy account numbers; some may have more than 25 digits. The account number can provide much useful information. For example, the account number might indicate the type of account (for example, Petty Cash) and the location of the account within the organization (for example, the Yorkton branch). The chart of accounts of Brown and Hansell, a law partnership, (in Exhibit 2-9) uses a four-digit account number. The assignment material reflects the variety found in practice.

The chart of accounts for Air & Sea Travel appears in Exhibit 2-10. Notice the gap in account numbers between 1200 and 1400. Gary Lyon realizes that at some later date the business may need to add another category of receivables—for example, Notes Receivable, to be numbered 1210.

Appendix C at the end of Volume I and Volume II gives three expanded charts of accounts that you will find helpful as you work through this course. The first chart lists the typical accounts of a large *service* proprietorship. The second chart is for a *merchandising* corporation, one that sells a product rather than a service. The third chart lists some accounts a *manufacturing* company uses. These accounts will be used in connection with Chapters 19–26. Study the service proprietorship chart of accounts now, and refer to the other charts of accounts as needed later.

The expense accounts are listed in alphabetical order throughout this chapter.

Account Number	Account Name
1101	Petty Cash
1110	Cash in Bank
1201	Accounts Receivable
1300	Office Supplies
1601	Office Furniture
1701	Computers
2201	Accounts Payable
2250	Notes Payable
2300	Employee Withholdings Payable
3000	H. Brown, Capital
3001	B. Hansell, Capital
3100	H. Brown, Withdrawals
3101	B. Hansell, Withdrawals
4000	Fee Revenue
5001	Rent Expense
5101	Supplies Expense
5401	Wages Expense

EXHIBIT 2-10

Chart of Accounts—
Air & Sea Travel

Balance Sheet Accounts:

Assets		Liabilities		Owner's Equity	
1100	Cash	2100	Accounts Payable	3000	Gary Lyon, Capital
1200	Accounts Receivable	2300	Notes Payable	3100	Gary Lyon, Withdrawals
1400	Office Supplies				
1500	Office Furniture				
1900	Land				

Income Statement Accounts (part of Owner's Equity)

Revenues		Expenses	
4000	Service Revenue	5100	Rent Exp.
		5200	Salary Exp.
		5300	Utilities Exp.

Many businesses follow such a scheme for their records and financial statements since computer programs often list accounts alphabetically. The other ordering is by balance or size, with the accounts with the largest balances listed first; the service, merchandising, and manufacturing accounts shown in Appendix C are taken from the financial statements of real companies and are listed in the order used by those companies.

Normal Balance of an Account

An account's *normal balance* appears on the side of the account—debit or credit—where *increases* are recorded. That is, the normal balance is on the side that is positive. For example, Cash and other assets usually have a debit balance (the debit side is positive and the credit side negative), so the normal balance of assets is on the debit side, and assets are called *debit-balance accounts*. Conversely, liabilities and owner's equity usually have a credit balance, so their normal balances are on the

Accounting and the *e*-World

Using Computers and the Internet to Be Successful

Computers and the internet are two reasons that companies have been able to grow to sizes unimaginable a decade ago and to spread throughout the world. Computers process vast amounts of data quickly and the internet allows companies to maintain constant contact with far-flung operations.

Bombardier Inc. **(http://www.bombardier.com)** has operations in twelve countries on three continents covering four major lines of business. Imagine the difficulty that Bombardier would have in gathering together all the company's financial data to prepare its 2000 financial statements if it did not have computers and world-wide data linkage through the internet.

Magna International **(http://www.magna.com)** employs 59,000 people at 174 manufacturing divisions and 33 product development and engineering centres in 19 countries—and Magna is able to produce its annual financial statements within five weeks of its December 31 year end. Magna can do this because of its extensive use of computers and because all its world-wide operations are connected by means of an electronic network.

Both of these companies are successful because they produce excellent products and are world leaders at what they do. Their success is based on their ability to make good decisions, and they are able to do this because they have excellent information technology working for them. Their accounting systems around the world are compatible with each other. Management is confident that the information they receive daily is both accurate and current. Computers and the internet provide this accurate information for decision making in real time.

credit side, and they are called *credit-balance accounts*. Exhibit 2-11 illustrates the normal balances of assets, liabilities, and owner's equity.

An account that normally has a debit balance may occasionally have a credit balance, which indicates a negative amount of the item. For example, Cash will have a temporary credit balance if the entity overdraws its bank account. Similarly, the liability Accounts Payable—normally a credit balance account—will have a debit balance if the entity overpays its accounts payable. In other instances, the shift of a balance amount away from its normal column may indicate an accounting error. For example, a credit balance in Office Furniture or Buildings indicates an error because negative amounts of these assets cannot exist.

EXHIBIT 2-11

Normal Balances of Balance Sheet Accounts

Assets		=	Liabilities		+	Owner's Equity	
Normal Bal. Debit				Normal Bal. Credit			Normal Bal. Credit

As we saw earlier in the chapter, owner's equity usually contains several accounts. In total, these accounts show a normal credit balance. An individual owner's equity account with a normal credit balance represents an *increase* in owner's equity. An owner's equity account that has a normal debit balance represents a *decrease* in owner's equity.

Expanding the Accounting Equation to Account for Owner's Equity Accounts: Revenues and Expenses

KEY POINT

Because withdrawals reduce owner's equity, the Withdrawals account is sometimes referred to as a *contra equity* account, meaning that it has the opposite balance of owner's equity.

Owner's equity includes Revenues and Expenses because revenues and expenses make up net income or net loss, which flows into owner's equity. As we have discussed, *revenues* are increases in owner's equity that result from delivering goods and services to customers in the course of operating the business. *Expenses* are decreases in owner's equity that occur from using assets or increasing liabilities in the course of operating the business. Therefore, the accounting equation may be expanded as shown in Exhibit 2-12. Revenues and expenses appear in parentheses to highlight the fact that their net effect—revenues minus expenses—equals net income, which increases owner's equity. If expenses are greater than revenues, the net effect of operations is a net loss, which decreases owner's equity.

We can now express the rules of debit and credit in final form as shown in Panel A of Exhibit 2-13. Panel B shows the *normal* balances of the five types of accounts: *Assets*; *Liabilities*; and *Owner's Equity* and its subparts, *Revenue* and *Expenses*. All of accounting is based on these five types of accounts. **You should not proceed until you have learned the rules of debit and credit and the normal balances of the five types of accounts.**

Expanded Problem Including Revenues and Expenses

Let's account for the revenues and expenses of Sarah Gunz's law practice for the month of July 2003. We follow the same steps illustrated earlier in this chapter: Analyze the transaction, journalize, post to the ledger, and prepare the trial balance.

EXHIBIT 2-12

Expansion of the Accounting Equation

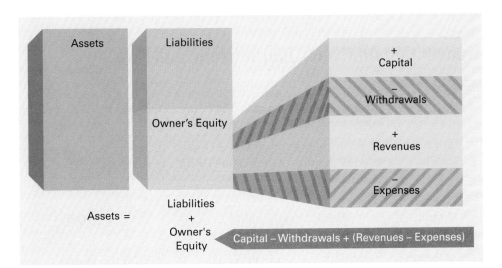

Panel A: Rules of Debit and Credit

Assets		=	Liabilities		+	Capital	
Debit for Increase	Credit for Decrease		Debit for Decrease	Credit for Increase		Debit for Decrease	Credit for Increase

Withdrawals

Debit for Increase	Credit for Decrease

Revenues

Debit for Decrease	Credit for Increase

Expenses

Debit for Increase	Credit for Decrease

Panel B: Normal Balances

Assets	Debit	
Liabilities		Credit
Owner's equity—overall		Credit
Capital		Credit
Withdrawals	Debit	
Revenue		Credit
Expenses	Debit	

Transaction Analysis, Journalizing, and Posting

1.	*Transaction:*	**Sarah Gunz invested $10,000 cash in a business bank account to open her law practice. The business received the cash and gave Gunz owner's equity.**

	Analysis:	The business asset cash is increased; therefore, debit Cash. The owner's equity of the business is increased, so credit Sarah Gunz, Capital.

	Journal Entry:	Cash 10,000
		Sarah Gunz, Capital 10,000
		Received investment from owner.

Accounting Equation:

ASSETS	=	LIABILITIES	+	OWNER'S EQUITY
Cash				Sarah Gunz, Capital
+10,000	=	0	+	10,000

Cash	Sarah Gunz, Capital
(1) 10,000	**(1) 10,000**

(1)   Cash

Bal. 10,000	
20,000	13,000
Bal. X	

2.   Transaction: Gun\provided legal services for a client and received $3,000 cash.

Analysis: The asset cash is increased; therefore, debit Cash. The revenue account service revenue is increased; credit Service Revenue.

Journal Entry:

Cash 3,000

    Service Revenue   3,000

Performed service and received cash.

(2)   Accounts Payable

X	Bal. 12,800
	45,600
	Bal. 23,500

Accounting Equation:

ASSETS	=	LIABILITIES	+	OWNER'S EQUITY	+	REVENUES
Cash						Service Revenue
+3,000	=	0			+	3,000

(3)   S. Scully, Capital

	Bal. X
22,000	56,000
	15,000
	Bal. 73,000

Ledger Accounts:

Cash	Service Revenue
(1) 10,000	**(2) 3,000**
(2) 3,000	

A: (1) The ending balance (X) for Cash is

X = $10,000 + 20,000 − $13,000

X = $17,000

(2) We are given the beginning and ending balances. We can compute the debit entry as follows:

$12,800 + $45,600 − X

= $23,500

$12,800 + $45,600

− $23,500 = X

X = $34,900

(3) The Capital account has an ending credit balance of $73,000. We can calculate the beginning credit balance as follows:

X + $56,000 + $15,000

− $22,000 = $73,000

X = $73,000 − $56,000

− $15,000 + $22,000

X = $24,000

3.   Transaction: Gunz provided legal services to JM Co. and billed the client for $500 on account. This means JM Co. owes the business $500 and Gunz expects to collect the $500 later.

Analysis: The asset accounts receivable is increased; therefore, debit Accounts Receivable. Service revenue is increased; credit Service Revenue.

Journal Entry:

Accounts Receivable 500

    Service Revenue   500

Performed service on account.

Accounting Equation:

ASSETS	=	LIABILITIES	+	OWNER'S EQUITY	+	REVENUES
Accounts Receivable						Service Revenue
+500	=	0			+	500

Ledger Accounts:

Accounts Receivable	Service Revenue
(3) 500	**(2) 3,000**
	(3) 500

4.   Transaction: Gunz provided and billed legal services of $700 to a doctor, who paid $300 cash immediately. Gunz billed the remaining $400 to the doctor on accounts receivable.

Analysis: The assets cash and accounts receivable are increased; therefore, debit both of these asset accounts. Service revenue is increased; credit Service Revenue for the sum of the two debit amounts.

Journal Entry:	Cash	300	
	Accounts Receivable	400	
	Service Revenue		700
	Performed service for cash and on account.		

Accounting Equation:

	ASSETS		=	LIABILITIES	+	OWNER'S EQUITY	+	REVENUES
		Accounts						Service
Cash		Receivable						Revenue
+300		+400	=	0			+	700

Note: Because this transaction affects more than two accounts at the same time, the entry is called a *compound entry*. **No matter how many accounts a compound entry affects—there may be any number—total debits must equal total credits.**

Ledger Accounts:

Cash

(1)	10,000	
(2)	3,000	
(4)	**300**	

Accounts Receivable

| (3) | 500 | |
| **(4)** | **400** | |

Service Revenue

		(2)	3,000
		(3)	500
		(4)	**700**

---

5. **Transaction:** **Gunz paid the following cash expenses: office rent, $900; employee salary, $1,500; and utilities, $500.**

Analysis: The asset cash is decreased; therefore, credit Cash for each of the three expense amounts. The following expenses are increased: Rent Expense, Salary Expense, and Utilities Expense. Each should be debited for the appropriate amount.

Journal Entry:	Rent Expense	900	
	Salary Expense	1,500	
	Utilities Expense	500	
	Cash		2,900
	Issued three cheques to pay cash expenses.		

Accounting Equation:

ASSETS	=	LIABILITIES	+	OWNER'S EQUITY	–	EXPENSES		
						Rent	Salary	Utilities
Cash						Expense	Expense	Expense
–2,900	=	0				–900	–1,500	–500

Note: In practice, the business would record these three transactions separately. To save space, we can record them together in a compound journal entry.

Ledger
Accounts:

Cash			
(1)	10,000	(5)	2,900
(2)	3,000		
(4)	300		

Rent Expense			
(5)	900		

Salary Expense			
(5)	1,500		

Utilities Expense			
(5)	500		

---

6. *Transaction:* **Gunz received a telephone bill for $120 and will pay this expense next week.**

Analysis: Utilities expense is increased; therefore, debit this expense. The liability accounts payable is increased, so credit Accounts Payable.

Journal Entry:
Utilities Expense 120
    Accounts Payable   120
Received utility bill.

Accounting Equation:

ASSETS	=	LIABILITIES	+	OWNER'S EQUITY	–	EXPENSES
		Accounts Payable				Utilities Expense
0	=	+120			–	120

Ledger Accounts:

Accounts Payable			
		(6)	120

Utilities Expense			
(5)	500		
(6)	120		

LEARNING TIP

Recording an expense does not necessarily involve a credit to cash. In Transaction 6 the expense is recorded now, but the cash will be paid later. Likewise, a debit to cash does not always reflect revenue. Transaction 7 records cash collected on a receivable (the revenue was recorded in Transaction 3).

7. *Transaction:* **Gunz received $200 cash from JM Co., the client discussed in Transaction 3.**

Analysis: The asset cash is increased; therefore, debit Cash. The asset accounts receivable is decreased; therefore, credit Accounts Receivable.

Journal Entry:
Cash 200
    Accounts Receivable   200
Received cash on account.

Accounting Equation:

ASSETS		=	LIABILITIES	+	OWNER'S EQUITY
Cash	Accounts Receivable				
+200	–200	=	0	+	0

Note: This transaction has no effect on revenue; the related revenue is accounted for in Transaction 3.

Ledger Accounts:

Cash			
(1)	10,000	(5)	2,900
(2)	3,000		
(4)	300		
(7)	200		

Accounts Receivable			
(3)	500	(7)	200
(4)	400		

Chapter Two Recording Business Transactions   **77**

8. Transaction: Gunz paid the telephone bill that was received and recorded in Transaction 6.

Analysis: The asset cash is decreased; credit Cash. The liability accounts payable is decreased; therefore, debit Accounts Payable.

Journal Entry:

Accounts Payable 120
    Cash 120
Paid cash on account.

Accounting Equation:

ASSETS	=	LIABILITIES	+	OWNER'S EQUITY
		Accounts		
Cash		Payable		
−120	=	−120	+	0

Note: This transaction has no effect on expense because the related expense was recorded in Transaction 6.

Ledger Accounts:

	Cash					Accounts Payable		
(1)	10,000	(5)	2,900		**(8)**	**120**	(6)	120
(2)	3,000	**(8)**	**120**					
(4)	300							
(7)	200							

---

9. Transaction: Gunz withdrew $1,100 cash for personal use.

Analysis: The asset cash decreased; credit Cash. The withdrawal decreased owner's equity; therefore, debit Sarah Gunz, Withdrawals.

Journal Entry:

Sarah Gunz, Withdrawals 1,100
    Cash 1,100
Withdrew cash for personal use.

Accounting Equation:

ASSETS	=	LIABILITIES	+	OWNER'S EQUITY
Cash				Sarah Gunz, Withdrawals
−1,100	=	0		−1,100

Ledger Accounts:

	Cash					Sarah Gunz, Withdrawals	
(1)	10,000	(5)	2,900		**(9)**	**1,100**	
(2)	3,000	(8)	120				
(4)	300	**(9)**	**1,100**				
(7)	200						

STOP & THINK

Review the chapter-opening story and concentrate on Intrawest's need for financial statement information. How will the procedures you have applied in this chapter help Intrawest convince potential investors that the business is financially stable?

Answer: The end product of the accounting process is a set of financial statements. Intrawest's accounting records will generate the income statement, cash flow statement, and balance sheet that potential investors require of companies before investing.

Ledger Accounts after Posting

ASSETS		LIABILITIES		OWNER'S EQUITY		REVENUE		EXPENSES	
Cash		**Accounts Payable**		**Sarah Gunz, Capital**		**Service Revenue**		**Rent Expense**	

Cash

(1) 10,000	(5) 2,900
(2) 3,000	(8) 120
(4) 300	(9) 1,100
(7) 200	
Bal. 9,380	

Accounts Payable

| (8) 120 | (6) 120 |
| | Bal. 0 |

Sarah Gunz, Capital

| | (1) 10,000 |
| | Bal. 10,000 |

Sarah Gunz, Withdrawals

| (9) 1,100 | |
| Bal. 1,100 | |

Service Revenue

	(2) 3,000
	(3) 500
	(4) 700
	Bal. 4,200

Rent Expense

| (5) 900 | |
| Bal. 900 | |

Salary Expense

| (5) 1,500 | |
| Bal. 1,500 | |

Accounts Receivable

(3) 500	(7) 200
(4) 400	
Bal. 700	

Utilities Expense

(5) 500	
(6) 120	
Bal. 620	

Trial Balance

To prepare the trial balance, we list and summarize the balances from the ledger accounts.

SARAH GUNZ, LAWYER
Trial Balance
July 31, 2003

Account Title	Balance	
	Debit	Credit
Cash	$ 9,380	
Accounts receivable	700	
Accounts payable		$ 0
Sarah Gunz, Capital		10,000
Sarah Gunz, Withdrawals	1,100	
Service revenue		4,200
Rent expense	900	
Salary expense	1,500	
Utilities expense	620	
Total	$14,200	$14,200

You have now seen how to record business transactions, post to the ledger accounts, and prepare a trial balance. Solidify your understanding of the accounting process by reviewing the Decision Guidelines feature, described on page 80.

> **THINKING IT OVER**
>
> Which side of the trial balance is affected by a debit to accounts payable?
>
> **A:** The credit side. (Students may want to say debit.) Illustration:
>
> **Accounts Payable**
>
> | | Bal. 6,000 |
>
> A debit to accounts payable reduces the *credit* balance of Accounts Payable.
>
> **Accounts Payable**
>
> | | Bal. 6,000 |
> | 1,000 | |
> | | Bal. 5,000 |

Use of Accounting Information for Quick Decision Making

> **OBJECTIVE 7**
> Analyze transactions without a journal

Often businesspeople make decisions without taking the time to follow all the steps in an accounting system. For example, suppose Intrawest, which owns a number of ski resorts, needs an additional ski lift at Blackcomb to meet skiers' demand. The company can either build an additional lift and increase revenues or not build the lift. The decision to build the lift will depend upon the different effects on the company.

DECISION GUIDELINES — *Analyzing and Recording Transactions*

Decision	Guidelines
Has a transaction occurred?	If the event affects the entity's financial position and can be reliably recorded—*Yes* If either condition is absent—*No*
Where to record the transaction?	In the *journal*, the chronological record of transactions
What to record for each transaction?	Increases and/or decreases in all the accounts affected by the transaction (at cost)

How to record an increase/decrease in a(an)

Rules of debit and credit:

	Increase	Decrease
Asset	Debit	Credit
Liability	Credit	Debit
Owner's equity	Credit	Debit
Revenue	Credit	Debit
Expense	Debit	Credit

Decision	Guidelines
Where to store all the information for each account?	In the *ledger*, the book of accounts and their balances
Where to list all the accounts and their balances?	In the *trial balance*
Where to report the Results of operations?	In the income statement (revenues − expenses = net income or net loss)
Financial position?	In the balance sheet (assets = liabilities + owner's equity)

Intrawest management does not need to record in the journal all the transactions that would be affected by its decision. After all, the company has not completed a transaction yet. But management does need to know how Intrawest will be affected by the decision. If the decision makers know accounting, they can skip the journal and go directly to the ledger accounts that would be affected. The following accounts summarize the immediate effects of building the lift and not building the lift.

BUILD THE LIFT

Cash	Revenue
1,000,000	300,000 per year for ten years

Expenses	
100,000 per year for ten years	

DO NOT BUILD THE LIFT

Cash	Revenue
No effect	No effect

Immediately Intrawest's management can see that building the additional lift will require more cash. But management can also see that Intrawest will generate more revenues if the lift is built. This may motivate Intrawest's management to use cash to build the lift.

Companies do not actually keep their records in this short-cut fashion. But a decision maker who needs information immediately can quickly analyze the effect of a set of transactions on the company's financial statements.

Summary Problem
for Your Review

The trial balance of Tomassini Computer Service Centre on March 1, 2003, lists the company's assets, liabilities, and owner's equity on that date.

Account Titles	Balance Debit	Balance Credit
Cash	$26,000	
Accounts receivable	4,500	
Accounts payable		$ 2,000
John Tomassini, Capital		28,500
Total	$30,500	$30,500

During March the business engaged in the following transactions:

a. Borrowed $45,000 from the bank and signed a note payable in the name of the business.

b. Paid cash of $40,000 to a real estate company to acquire land.

c. Performed service for a customer and received cash of $5,000.

d. Purchased supplies on account, $300.

e. Performed customer service and earned revenue on account, $2,600.

f. Paid $1,200 of the Accounts Payable at March 1, 2003.

g. Paid the following cash expenses: salaries, $3,000; rent, $1,500; and interest, $400.

h. Received $3,100 of the Accounts Receivable at March 1, 2003.

i. Received a $200 utility bill that will be paid next week.

j. Tomassini withdrew $1,800 for personal use.

Required

1. Open the following accounts, with the balances indicated, in the ledger of Tomassini Computer Service Centre. Use the T-account format.
   Assets: Cash, $26,000; Accounts Receivable, $4,500; Supplies, no balance; Land, no balance
   Liabilities: Accounts Payable, $2,000; Note Payable, no balance
   Owner's Equity: JohnTomassini, Capital, $28,500; JohnTomassini, Withdrawals, no balance
   Revenues: Service Revenue, no balance
   Expenses: (none have balances) Salary Expense, Rent Expense, Utilities Expense, Interest Expense

2. Journalize the preceding transactions. Key journal entries by transaction letter.

3. Post to the ledger.

4. Prepare the trial balance of Tomassini Computer Service Centre at March 31, 2003.

5. Compute the net income or net loss of the entity during the month of March by producing an income statement. List expenses in alphabetical order.

Solution to Review Problem

Requirement 1

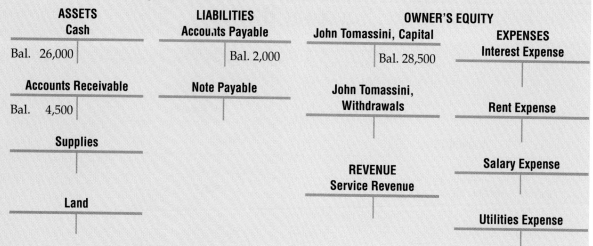

ASSETS

Cash

Bal. 26,000 |

Accounts Receivable

Bal. 4,500 |

Supplies

Land

LIABILITIES

Accounts Payable

| Bal. 2,000

Note Payable

OWNER'S EQUITY

John Tomassini, Capital

| Bal. 28,500

John Tomassini,
Withdrawals

REVENUE
Service Revenue

EXPENSES
Interest Expense

Rent Expense

Salary Expense

Utilities Expense

Requirement 2

	Accounts and Explanation	Debit	Credit
a.	Cash...	45,000	
	Note Payable		45,000
	Borrowed cash on note payable.		
b.	Land...	40,000	
	Cash		40,000
	Purchased land for cash.		
c.	Cash...	5,000	
	Service Revenue.................................		5,000
	Performed service and received cash.		
d.	Supplies..	300	
	Accounts Payable....................................		300
	Purchased supplies on account.		
e.	Accounts Receivable	2,600	
	Service Revenue....................................		2,600
	Performed service on account.		
f.	Accounts Payable	1,200	
	Cash		1,200
	Paid cash to reduce accounts payable.		
g.	Salary Expense..	3,000	
	Rent Expense..	1,500	
	Interest Expense	400	
	Cash		4,900
	Issued three cheques to pay cash expenses.		
h.	Cash...	3,100	
	Accounts Receivable................................		3,100
	Received cash on account.		
i.	Utilities Expense.......................................	200	
	Accounts Payable....................................		200
	Received utility bill.		
j.	John Tomassini, Withdrawals........................	1,800	
	Cash		1,800
	Withdrew cash for personal use.		

Requirement 3

ASSETS

Cash

Bal.	26,000	(b)	40,000
(a)	45,000	(f)	1,200
(c)	5,000	(g)	4,900
(h)	3,100	(j)	1,800
Bal.	31,200		

Accounts Receivable

Bal.	4,500	(h)	3,100
(e)	2,600		
Bal.	4,000		

Supplies

| (d) | 300 | | |
| Bal. | 300 | | |

Land

| (b) | 40,000 | | |
| Bal. | 40,000 | | |

LIABILITIES

Accounts Payable

(f)	1,200	Bal.	2,000
		(d)	300
		(i)	200
		Bal.	1,300

Note Payable

| | | (a) | 45,000 |
| | | Bal. | 45,000 |

OWNER'S EQUITY

John Tomassini, Capital

| | | Bal. | 28,500 |

John Tomassini, Withdrawals

| (j) | 1,800 | | |
| Bal. | 1,800 | | |

REVENUE

Service Revenue

		(c)	5,000
		(e)	2,600
		Bal.	7,600

EXPENSES

Interest Expense

| (g) | 400 | | |
| Bal. | 400 | | |

Rent Expense

| (g) | 1,500 | | |
| Bal. | 1,500 | | |

Salary Expense

| (g) | 3,000 | | |
| Bal. | 3,000 | | |

Utilities Expense

| (i) | 200 | | |
| Bal. | 200 | | |

Requirement 4

TOMASSINI COMPUTER SERVICE CENTRE
Trial Balance
March 31, 2003

Account Title	Balance	
	Debit	Credit
Cash	$31,200	
Accounts receivable	4,000	
Supplies	300	
Land	40,000	
Accounts payable		$ 1,300
Note payable		45,000
John Tomassini, capital		28,500
John Tomassini, withdrawals	1,800	
Service revenue		7,600
Interest expense	400	
Rent expense	1,500	
Salary expense	3,000	
Utilities expense	200	
Total	$82,400	$82,400

TOMASSINI COMPUTER SERVICE CENTRE
Income Statement
For the Month Ended March 31, 2003

Revenues		
Service revenue		$7,600
Expenses:		
Interest expense..	$ 400	
Rent expense...	1,500	
Salary expense...	3,000	
Utilities expense..	200	
Total expenses		5,100
Net income...		$2,500

Cyber Coach

Visit the Student Resource area of the *Accounting* Companion Website for extra practice with tne new material in Chapter 2.

www.pearsoned.ca/horngren

Summary

1. **Define and use key accounting terms:** *account,* *ledger, debit,* and *credit. Accounts* can be viewed in the form of the letter "T." The left side of each T-account is its *debit* side. The right side is its *credit* side. The *ledger,* which contains a record for each account groups and numbers accounts by category in the following order: assets, liabilities, and owner's equity (and its subparts, revenues and expenses).

2. **Apply the rules of debit and credit.** *Assets* and *expenses* are increased by debits and decreased by credits. *Liabilities, owner's equity,* and *revenues* are increased by credits and decreased by debits. An account's *normal balance* is the side of the account—debit or credit—in which increases are recorded. Thus the normal balance of assets and expenses is a debit, and the normal balance of liabilities, owner's equity, and revenues is a credit. The Withdrawals account, which decreases owner's equity, normally has a debit balance. *Revenues,* which are increases in owner's equity, have a normal credit balance. *Expenses,* which are decreases in owner's equity, have a normal debit balance.

3. **Record transactions in the journal.** The accountant begins the recording process by entering the transaction's information in the *journal,* a chronological list of all the entity's transactions.

4. **Post from the journal to the ledger.** Posting means transferring to the *ledger* accounts. Posting references are used to trace amounts back and forth between the journal and the ledger.

5. **Prepare and use a trial balance.** The *trial balance* is a summary of all the account balances in the ledger. When *double-entry accounting* has been done correctly, the total debits and the total credits in the trial balance are equal.

6. **Set up a chart of accounts for a business.** A *chart of accounts* lists all the accounts in the ledger and their account numbers.

7. **Analyze transactions without a journal.** Decision makers must often make decisions without a complete accounting system. They can analyze the transactions without a journal.

We can now trace the flow of accounting information through these steps:

Business Transaction ⟶ Source Documents

⟶ Journal Entry ⟶ Posting to Ledger

⟶ Trial Balance

Self-Study Questions

Test your understanding of the chapter by marking the correct answer for each of the following questions:

1. An account has two sides called the (p. 55)
   a. Debit and credit
   b. Asset and liability
   c. Revenue and expense
   d. Journal and ledger

2. Increases in liabilities are recorded by (p. 56)
   a. Debits
   b. Credits

3. Why do accountants record transactions in the journal? (p. 58)
   a. To ensure that all transactions are posted to the ledger
   b. To ensure that total debits equal total credits
   c. To have a chronological record of all transactions
   d. To help prepare the financial statements

4. Posting is the process of transferring information from the (p. 60)
   a. Journal to the trial balance
   b. Ledger to the trial balance
   c. Ledger to the financial statements
   d. Journal to the ledger

5. The purchase of land for cash is recorded by a (p. 61)
   a. Debit to Cash and a credit to Land
   b. Debit to Cash and a debit to Land
   c. Debit to Land and a credit to Cash
   d. Credit to Cash and a credit to Land

6. The purpose of the trial balance is to (p. 64)
   a. List all accounts with their balances
   b. Ensure that all transactions have been recorded

   c. Speed the collection of cash receipts from customers
   d. Increase assets and owner's equity

7. What is the normal balance of the Accounts Receivable, Office Supplies, and Rent Expense accounts? (p. 71)
   a. Debit
   b. Credit

8. A business has Cash of $3,000, Notes Payable of $2,500, Accounts Payable of $4,300, Service Revenue of $7,000 and Rent Expense of $1,800. Based on these data, how much are its total liabilities? (p. 74)
   a. $5,500
   b. $6,800
   c. $9,800
   d. $13,800

9. Smale Transport earned revenue on account. The earning of revenue on account is recorded by a (pp. 74–78)
   a. Debit to Cash and a credit to Revenue
   b. Debit to Accounts Receivable and a credit to Revenue
   c. Debit to Accounts Payable and a credit to Revenue
   d. Debit to Revenue and a credit to Accounts Receivable

10. The account credited for a receipt of cash on account is (p. 77)
    a. Cash
    b. Accounts Payable
    c. Service Revenue
    d. Accounts Receivable

Answers to the Self-Study Questions follow the Similar Accounting Terms.

Accounting Vocabulary

Account (p. 52)
Chart of accounts (p. 70)
Credit (p. 55)
Debit (p. 55)

Journal (p. 58)
Ledger (p. 52)
Posting (p. 60)
Trial balance (p. 64)

Similar Accounting Terms

Cr	Credit; right
Dr	Debit; left
The Ledger	The Books; the General Ledger
Entering the transaction in a journal	Making the journal entry; journalizing the transaction
Withdrawals by owner(s)	In a *proprietorship* or *partnership*, distributions from a company to its owner(s).

Answers to Self-Study Questions
1. a   3. c   5. c   7. a   9. b
2. b   4. d   6. a   8. b ($6,800 = $2,500 + $4,300)   10. d

Assignment Material

Questions

1. Name the basic summary device of accounting. What letter of the alphabet does it resemble? Name its two sides.

2. Is the following statement true or false? Debit means decrease and credit means increase. Explain your answer.

3. Write two sentences that use the term *debit* differently.

4. What are the three *basic* types of accounts? Name two additional types of accounts. To which one of the three basic types are these two additional types of accounts most closely related?

5. Suppose you are the accountant for Smith Courier Service. Keeping in mind double-entry book-keeping, identify the *dual effects* of Mary Smith's investment of $10,000 cash in her business.

6. Briefly describe the flow of accounting information.

7. To what does the *normal balance* of an account refer?

8. Indicate the normal balance of the five types of accounts.

Account Type	Normal Balance
Assets	_____
Liabilities	_____
Owner's equity	_____
Revenues	_____
Expenses	_____

9. What does posting accomplish? Why is it important? Does it come before or after journalizing?

10. Label each of the following transactions as increasing owner's equity (+), decreasing owner's equity (–), or as having no effect on owner's equity (0). Write the appropriate symbol in the space provided.

    ____ Investment by owner
    ____ Bill customer for services
    ____ Purchase of supplies on credit
    ____ Pay expenses
    ____ Cash payment on account
    ____ Withdrawal by owner
    ____ Borrowing money on a note payable
    ____ Sale of services on account

11. What four steps does posting include? Which step is the fundamental purpose of posting?

12. Rearrange the following accounts in their logical sequence in the chart of accounts:

Notes Payable	Cash
Accounts Receivable	Jane East, Capital
Sales Revenue	Salary Expense

13. What is the meaning of the statement, Accounts Payable has a credit balance of $1,700?

14. Jack Brown Campus Cleaners launders the shirts of customer Bobby Baylor, who has a charge account at the cleaners. When Bobby picks up his clothes and is short of cash, he charges it. Later, when he receives his monthly statement from the cleaners, Bobby writes a cheque on his bank account and mails the cheque to the cleaners. Identify the two business transactions described here. Which transaction increases the business's owner's equity? Which transaction increases Jack Brown Campus Cleaners' cash?

15. Explain the difference between the ledger and the chart of accounts.

16. Why do accountants prepare a trial balance?

17. What is a compound journal entry?

18. The accountant for Bower Construction mistakenly recorded a $500 purchase of supplies on account as $5,000. He debited Supplies and credited Accounts Payable for $5,000. Does this error cause the trial balance to be out of balance? Explain your answer.

19. What is the effect on total assets of collecting cash on account from customers?

20. What is the advantage of analyzing and recording transactions without the use of a journal? Describe how this "journal-less" analysis works.

21. Briefly summarize the similarities and differences between manual and computer-based accounting systems in terms of journalizing, posting, and preparing a trial balance.

Exercises

Exercise 2-1 *Using accounting vocabulary* *(Obj. 1)*

Your employer, OceanTours, has just hired an office manager who does not understand accounting. The Ocean Tours' trial balance lists Cash of $43,900. Write a short memo to the office manager, explaining the accounting process that produced this listing on the trial balance. Mention *debits, credits, journal, ledger, posting,* and *trial balance.*

Exercise 2-2 *Using debits and credits with the accounting equation* *(Obj. 1, 2)*

Link Back to Chapter 1 (Accounting Equation). Canadian National Railway Company (CN) is one of North America's leading railroads. At the end of 1999, CN had total assets of $16.4 billion and total liabilities of $10.3 billion.

Required

1. Write the company's accounting equation, and label each element as a debit amount or a credit amount.
2. CN's total revenues for 1999 were $5.2 billion, and total expenses for the year were $4.4 billion. How much was CN's net income (or net loss) for 1999? Write the equation to compute CN's net income, and indicate which element is a debit amount and which element is a credit amount. Does net income represent a net debit or a net credit? Does net loss represent a net debit or a net credit? Review Exhibit 1-8, page 22, if needed.
3. During 1999, the owners of CN were paid $118 million in the form of dividends (this is the same as owner's withdrawals). Did the dividends represent a debit amount or a credit amount?
4. Considering both CN's net income (or net loss) and dividends for 1999, by how much did the company's owner's equity increase or decrease during 1999? Was the increase in owner's equity a debit amount or a credit amount?

Exercise 2-3 *Analyzing and journalizing transactions* *(Obj. 2, 3)*

Analyze the following transactions in the manner shown for the December 1 transaction of Rotman Strategic Consulting. Also, record each transaction in the journal.

Dec. 1 Paid monthly utilities expense of $700. (Analysis: The expense, utilities expense, is increased; therefore, debit Utilities Expense. The asset, cash, is decreased; therefore, credit Cash.)

1	Utilities Expense	700	
	Cash		700

4 Borrowed $8,000 cash, signing a note payable.
8 Performed service on account for a customer, $1,600.
12 Purchased office furniture on account, $1,000.
19 Sold for $74,000 land that had cost this same amount.
24 Purchased building for $140,000; signed a note payable.
27 Paid the liability created on December 12.

Exercise 2-4 *Applying the rules of debit and credit* *(Obj. 2)*

Refer to Exercise 2-3 for the transactions of Rotman Strategic Consulting.

Required

1. Open the following T-accounts with their December 1 balances: Cash, debit balance $6,000; Land, debit balance $74,000; S. Rotman, Capital, credit balance $80,000.

2. Record the transactions of Exercise 2-3 directly in the T-accounts affected. Use dates as posting references in the T-accounts. Journal entries are not required.

3. Compute the December 31 balance for each account, and prove that total debits equal total credits.

Exercise 2-5   *Journalizing transactions*   *(Obj. 3)*

Wellness Health Club engaged in the following transactions during March 2002, its first month of operations:

Mar.	1	The business received $45,000 cash investment from Louise Chen to start the Wellness Health Club.
	2	Purchased supplies for $500 on account.
	4	Paid $40,000 cash for building to use as an office.
	6	Presented a wellness seminar for a corporate customer and received cash, $2,500.
	9	Paid $100 on accounts payable.
	17	Performed wellness assessments for customers on account, $1,000.
	23	Received $800 cash from a customer on account.
	31	Paid the following expenses: salary, $1,200; rent, $500.

Required

Record the preceding transactions in the journal of Wellness Health Club. Key transactions by date and include an explanation for each entry, as illustrated in the chapter and Exhibit 2-4. Use the following accounts: Cash; Accounts Receivable; Office Supplies; Building; Accounts Payable; L. Chen, Capital; Service Revenue; Salary Expense; Rent Expense.

Exercise 2-6   *Posting to the ledger and preparing a trial balance*   *(Obj. 4, 5)*

Refer to Exercise 2-5 for the transactions of Wellness Health Club.

Required

1. After journalizing the transactions of Exercise 2-5, post the entries to the ledger, using T-account format. Key transactions by date. Date the ending balance of each account Mar. 31.

2. Prepare the trial balance of Wellness Health Club at March 31, 2002.

Exercise 2-7   *Describing transactions and posting*   *(Obj. 3, 4)*

The journal of Mountain Snowboards for August 2003 is on page 89.

Required

1. Describe each transaction.

2. Post the transactions to the ledger using the following account numbers: Cash, 1000; Accounts Receivable, 1200; Supplies, 1400; Accounts Payable, 2000; Note Payable, 2100; Karli Rees, Capital, 3000; Sales Revenue, 4000; Advertising Expense, 5100; Rent Expense, 5600; Utilities Expense, 5800. Use dates, journal references, and posting references as illustrated in Exhibit 2-8. You may write the account numbers as posting references directly in your book unless directed otherwise by your instructor.

3. Compute the balance in each account after posting. Prepare Mountain Snowboard's trial balance at August 31, 2003.

Date	Accounts and Explanation	Post Ref.	Debit	Credit
Aug. 2	Cash		18,000	
	Karli Rees, Capital			18,000
5	Cash		15,000	
	Note Payable			15,000
9	Supplies..		270	
	Accounts Payable...............................			270
11	Accounts Receivable..................................		8,100	
	Sales Revenue.....................................			8,100
14	Rent Expense		2,000	
	Cash			2,000
22	Cash		1,400	
	Accounts Receivable..........................			1,400
25	Advertising Expense		350	
	Cash			350
27	Accounts Payable......................................		270	
	Cash			270
31	Utilities Expense		320	
	Accounts Payable...............................			320

Exercise 2-8   *Journalizing transactions*   *(Obj. 3)*

The first five transactions of Dale Hoch Archery School have been posted to the company's accounts as shown below:

Cash

(1)	60,000	(3)	42,000
(4)	11,000	(5)	6,000

Supplies

(2)	600

Archery Equipment

(5)	6,000

Land

(3)	42,000

Accounts Payable

(2)	600

Note Payable

(4)	11,000

D. Hoch, Capital

(1)	60,000

Required

Prepare the journal entries that served as the sources for the five transactions. Date each entry April 30, 2002, and include an explanation for each entry as illustrated in the chapter.

Exercise 2-9   *Preparing a trial balance*   *(Obj. 5)*

Prepare the trial balance of Dale Hoch Archery School at April 30, 2002, using the account data from Exercise 2-8.

Exercise 2-10   *Preparing a trial balance*   *(Obj. 5)*

The accounts of Klassen Consulting are listed on page 90 with their normal balances at October 31, 2002. The accounts are listed in no particular order.

Required

Prepare the company's trial balance at October 31, 2002, listing accounts in the sequence illustrated in the chapter. Supplies comes before Building and Land. List the expenses alphabetically.

Account	Balance
L. Klassen, Capital	$48,800
Advertising expense	1,650
Accounts payable	5,300
Services revenue	27,000
Land	29,000
Note payable	45,000
Cash	5,000
Salary expense	6,000
Building	65,000
Computer rental expense	7,000
L. Klassen, withdrawals	6,000
Utilities expense	400
Accounts receivable	5,500
Supplies expense	300
Supplies	250

Exercise 2-11 *Correcting errors in a trial balance* *(Obj. 5)*

The trial balance of Archway Travel at February 28, 2003, does not balance.

Cash	$ 4,200	
Accounts receivable	2,900	
Supplies	600	
Land	66,000	
Accounts payable		$23,000
B. Reynolds, capital		41,600
Service revenue		10,700
Rent expense	800	
Salary expense	1,800	
Utilities expense	300	
Total	$76,600	$75,300

Investigation of the accounting records reveals that the bookkeeper

a. Recorded a $400 cash revenue transaction by debiting Accounts Receivable. The credit entry was correct.

b. Posted a $1,000 credit to Accounts Payable as $100.

c. Did not record utilities expense or the related account payable in the amount of $200.

d. Understated B. Reynolds, Capital by $400.

Required

Prepare the correct trial balance at February 28, 2003 complete with a heading. Journal entries are not required.

Exercise 2-12 *Recording transactions without a journal* *(Obj. 7)*

Open the following T-accounts for Picard Pension Consulting at May 1, 2002: Cash; Accounts Receivable; Office Supplies; Office Furniture; Accounts Payable; Paule Picard, Capital; Paule Picard, Withdrawals; Service Revenue; Rent Expense; Salary Expense.

Record the following May transactions directly in the T-accounts of the business without using a journal. Use the letters to identify the transactions.

a. Paule Picard opened a pension consulting firm by investing $12,400 cash and office furniture valued at $5,400.

b. Paid monthly rent of $1,500.

c. Purchased office supplies on account, $600.

d. Paid employee salary, $1,000.

e. Paid $400 of the account payable credited in c.

f. Performed consulting service on account, $23,000.

g. Withdrew $2,000 for personal use.

Exercise 2-13 *Preparing a trial balance* **(Obj. 5)**

After recording the transactions in Exercise 2-12, prepare the trial balance of Picard Pension Consulting at May 31, 2002.

Exercise 2-14 *Analyzing transactions without a journal* **(Obj. 7)**

AltaVista Nursing Services began when Elaine Peugeot deposited $45,000 cash in the business bank account. During the first week, the business purchased supplies on credit for $5,000 and paid $8,000 cash for equipment. AltaVista later paid $3,000 on account.

Required

1. Open the following T-accounts: Cash; Supplies; Equipment; Accounts Payable; E. Peugeot, Capital.

2. Record the transactions described above directly in the T-accounts without using a journal.

3. Compute the balance in each account. Show that total debits equal total credits after you have recorded all the transactions.

Serial Exercise

Exercise 2-15 begins an accounting cycle that is completed in Chapter 5.

Exercise 2-15 *Recording transactions and preparing a trial balance* **(Obj. 2, 3, 4, 5)**

Anya Perreault Architects completed these transactions during early December 2002:

Dec. 2 Received $14,000 cash from Anya Perreault. The business gave owner's equity in the business to Perreault.

2 Paid monthly office rent, $500.

3 Paid cash for a Dell computer, $3,000. The computer is expected to remain in service for five years.

4 Purchased office furniture on account, $5,600. The furniture should last for five years.

5 Purchased supplies on account, $300.

9 Performed design services for a client and received cash for the full amount of $1,000.

12 Paid utility expenses, $200.

18 Performed design services for a client on account, $1,700.

Required

1. Open T-accounts in the ledger: Cash; Accounts Receivable; Supplies; Equipment; Furniture; Accounts Payable; Anya Perreault, Capital; Anya Perreault, Withdrawals; Service Revenue; Rent Expense; Salaries Expense; and Utilities Expense. (Some of these T-accounts will be used in later chapters.)

2. Journalize the transactions. Explanations are not required.

3. Post to the T-accounts. Key all items by date, and denote an account balance as *Bal*. Formal posting references are not required.

4. Prepare a trial balance at December 18, 2002. In the Serial Exercise of Chapter 3,

we will add transactions for the remainder of December and will require a trial balance at December 31, 2002.

Challenge Exercises

Exercise 2-16   *Computing financial statement amounts without a journal*   **(Obj. 7)**

The owner of Auch Technical Services is an engineer with little understanding of accounting. She needs to compute the following summary information from the accounting records:

a. Net income for the month of March.

b. Total cash paid during March.

c. Cash collections from customers during March.

d. Cash paid on a note payable during March.

The quickest way to compute these amounts is to analyze the following accounts:

Account	Balance Feb. 28	Balance Mar. 31	Additional Information for the Month of March
a. S. Auch, Capital	$ 9,000	$15,000	Withdrawals, $4,000
b. Cash..	5,000	4,000	Cash receipts, $67,000
c. Accounts Receivable	24,000	26,000	Sales on account, $63,500
d. Notes Payable	13,000	16,000	New note borrowing, $6,300

The net income for March can be computed as follows:

S. Auch, Capital

March Withdrawals	4,000	Feb. 28 Bal.	9,000
		March Net Income	x = $10,000
		March 31 Bal.	15,000

Use a similar approach to compute the other three items of summary information the shareholder needs.

Exercise 2-17   *Analyzing accounting errors*   **(Obj. 2, 3, 4, 5)**

Stan has trouble keeping his debits and credits equal. During a recent month he made the following errors:

a. In journalizing a cash receipt, Stan debited Cash for $1,000 instead of the correct amount of $1,900. He credited Service Revenue for $1,000, the incorrect amount.

b. Stan posted a $700 utility expense as $70. The credit posting to Cash was the correct amount of $700.

c. In preparing the trial balance, Stan omitted an $8,000 note payable.

d. Stan recorded a $120 purchase of supplies on account by debiting Supplies and crediting Accounts Payable for $210.

e. In recording a $700 payment on account, Stan debited Supplies and credited Accounts Payable.

Required

1. For each of these errors, state whether the total debits equal total credits on the trial balance.

2. Identify any accounts with misstated balances, and indicate the amount and direction of the error (account balance too high or too low).

Beyond the Numbers

Beyond the Numbers 2-1

Joan McMullen asks your advice in setting up the accounting records for her new business, Joan's Photo Shoppe. The business will be a photography studio and will operate in a rented building. Joan's Photo Shoppe will need office equipment and cameras. The business will borrow money on notes payable to buy the needed equipment. Joan's Photo Shoppe will purchase on account photographic supplies and office supplies. Each asset has a related expense account, some of which have not yet been discussed. For example, equipment wears out (amortizes) and thus needs an amortization account. As supplies are used up, the business must record a supplies expense.

The business will need an office manager. This person will be paid a weekly salary of $900. Other expenses will include advertising and insurance. Since Joan's Photo Shoppe will want to know which aspects of the business generate the most and the least revenue, it will use a separate service revenue account for portraits, school pictures, and weddings. Joan's Photo Shoppe's better customers will be allowed to open accounts receivable with the business.

Required

List all the accounts Joan's Photo Shoppe will need, starting with the assets and ending with the expenses. Indicate which accounts will be reported on the balance sheet and which accounts will appear on the income statement.

Ethical Issue

Associated Charities Inc., a charitable organization in Brandon, Manitoba, has a standing agreement with Prairie Trust. The agreement allows Associated Charities Inc. to overdraw its cash balance at the bank when donations are running low. In the past, Associated Charities Inc. managed funds wisely and rarely used this privilege. Greg Osadchuk has recently become the president of Associated Charities Inc. To expand operations, Osadchuk is acquiring office equipment and spending large amounts for fund-raising. During his presidency, Associated Charities Inc. has maintained a negative bank balance (a credit Cash balance) of approximately $14,000.

Required

What is the ethical issue in this situation? State why you approve or disapprove of Osadchuk's management of Associated Charities Inc.'s funds.

Problems (Group A)

Problem 2-1A   *Analyzing a trial balance*   *(Obj. 1)*

The owner of Drolet Logistics, Sean Drolet, is selling the business. He offers the trial balance shown on page 94 to prospective buyers.

Your best friend is considering buying Drolet Logistics. He seeks your advice in interpreting this information. Specifically, he asks whether this trial balance is the same as a balance sheet and an income statement. He also wonders whether Drolet Logistics is a sound company because all the accounts are in balance.

Required

Write a short note to answer your friend's questions. To aid his decision, state how he can use the information on the trial balance to compute the Drolet Logistics net income or net loss for the current period. State the amount of net income or net loss in your note.

DROLET LOGISTICS
Trial Balance
December 31, 2003

Cash	$ 12,000	
Accounts receivable	27,000	
Prepaid expenses	4,000	
Land for future expansion	76,000	
Accounts payable		$ 35,000
Note payable		32,000
Sean Drolet, Capital		30,000
Sean Drolet, Withdrawals	48,000	
Sales revenue		134,000
Advertising expense	3,000	
Rent expense	26,000	
Supplies expense	7,000	
Wage expense	28,000	
Totals	$231,000	$231,000

Problem 2-2A *Analyzing and journalizing transactions* *(Obj. 2, 3)*

Valleyfield Theatre Co. owns movie theatres in the shopping centres of a major metropolitan area. The business engaged in the following transactions in 2002:

Feb.	1	Received cash of $100,000 from the owner Mary Clark.
	1	Paid February rent on a theatre building, $2,000.
	2	Paid $50,000 cash to purchase land for a theatre site.
	5	Borrowed $220,000 from the bank to finance the first phase of construction of the new theatre. The business signed a note payable to the bank.
	7	Received $20,000 cash from ticket sales and deposited this amount in the bank. (Label the revenue as Sales Revenue.)
	10	Purchased theatre supplies on account, $1,700.
	15	Paid theatre employee salaries, $2,800.
	15	Paid property tax expense on a theatre building, $1,600.
	16	Paid $800 on account.
	17	The owner withdrew $6,500 for personal expenses.

Valleyfield Theatre Co. uses the following accounts: Cash; Supplies; Land; Accounts Payable; Notes Payable; Mary Clark, Capital; Mary Clark, Withdrawals; Sales Revenue; Property Tax Expense; Rent Expense; Salary Expense.

Required

1. Prepare an analysis of each business transaction of Valleyfield Theatre Co. as shown for the February 1 transaction:

    Feb. 1   The asset Cash is increased. Increases in assets are recorded by debits; therefore, debit Cash. The owner's equity of the entity is increased. Increases in owner's equity are recorded by credits; therefore, credit Mary Clark, Capital.

2. Record each transaction in the journal, using the account titles given. Key each transaction by date. Explanations are not required.

Problem 2-3A *Journalizing transactions, posting to T-accounts, and preparing a trial balance (Obj. 2, 3, 4, 5)*

L. da Vinci opened a renovation business called Renaissance Renovations on September 3, 2003. During the first month of operations, the business completed the following transactions:

Sept.	3	L. da Vinci deposited his cheque for $35,000 into the business bank account. The business gave da Vinci owner's equity in the business.
	4	Purchased supplies, $200, and furniture, $1,800, on account.
	5	Paid September rent expense, $500.
	6	Performed design services for a client and received $4,000 cash.
	7	Paid $15,000 cash to acquire land for a future office site.
	10	Designed a bathroom for a client, billed the client, and received her promise to pay the $1,000 within one week.
	14	Paid for the furniture purchased September 4 on account.
	15	Paid assistant's salary, $600.
	17	Received partial payment from client on account, $500.
	20	Prepared a recreation room design for a client on account, $1,800.
	28	Received $1,500 cash from a client for renovation of a cottage.
	30	Paid assistant's salary, $600.
	30	L. da Vinci withdrew $2,400 for personal use.

Required

Open the following T-accounts: Cash; Accounts Receivable; Supplies; Furniture; Land; Accounts Payable; L. da Vinci, Capital; L. da Vinci, Withdrawals; Service Revenue; Rent Expense; Salary Expense.

1. Record each transaction in the journal, using the account titles given. Key each transaction by date. Explanations are not required.

2. Post the transactions to the T-accounts, using transaction dates as posting references in the T-accounts. Label the balance of each account *Bal.*, as shown in the chapter.

3. Prepare the trial balance of Renaissance Renovations at September 30, 2003.

Problem 2-4A *Journalizing transactions, posting to ledger accounts, and preparing a trial balance* **(Obj. 2, 3, 4, 5)**

The trial balance of Sutherland Designs is dated February 14, 2003.

SUTHERLAND DESIGNS
Trial Balance
February 14, 2003

Account Number	Account	Debit	Credit
1100	Cash	$ 2,000	
1200	Accounts receivable	8,000	
1300	Supplies	800	
1600	Automobile	18,600	
2000	Accounts payable		$ 3,000
3000	H. Sutherland, Capital		25,000
3100	H. Sutherland, Withdrawals	1,200	
5000	Service revenue		7,200
6100	Rent expense	1,000	
6200	Salary expense	3,600	
	Total	$35,200	$35,200

During the remainder of February, Sutherland Designs completed the following transactions:

Feb.	15	Collected $3,000 cash from a client on account.
	16	Designed a system for a client on account, $2,900.
	20	Paid on account, $1,600.
	21	Purchased supplies on account, $100.
	21	H. Sutherland withdrew $1,000 for personal use.

Feb.	21	Received a verbal promise of a $10,000 contract.
	22	Received cash of $3,100 for consulting work just completed.
	28	Paid employees' salaries, $1,600.

Required

1. Record the transactions that occurred during February 15 through 28 in *Page 3* of the journal. Include an explanation for each entry.

2. Open the ledger accounts listed in the trial balance, together with their balances at February 14. Use the three-column account format illustrated in the chapter. Enter *Bal.* (for previous balance) in the Item column, and place a check mark (✓) in the journal reference column for the February 14 balance in each account.

   Post the transactions to the ledger, using dates, account numbers, journal references, and posting references.

3. Prepare the trial balance of Sutherland Designs at February 28, 2003.

Problem 2-5A   *Correcting errors in a trial balance*   *(Obj. 2, 5)*

Link Back to Chapter 1 (Income Statement). The following trial balance does not balance:

HAMMOND LANDSCAPE CONSULTING
Trial Balance
June 30, 2002

Cash..	$ 2,000	
Accounts receivable...	10,000	
Supplies..	900	
Office furniture..	3,600	
Land for future expansion......................................	47,000	
Accounts payable...		$ 3,800
Note payable..		23,000
K. Hammond, Capital...		31,600
K. Hammond, Withdrawals......................................	2,000	
Consulting service revenue.....................................		6,500
Advertising expense...	500	
Rent expense..	1,000	
Salary expense..	2,100	
Utilities expense...	400	
Total..	$69,500	$64,900

The following errors were detected:

a. The cash balance is understated by $900.

b. The cost of the land was $44,600, not $47,000.

c. A $400 purchase of supplies on account was neither journalized nor posted.

d. A $3,800 credit to Consulting Service Revenue was not posted.

e. Rent Expense of $200 was posted as a credit rather than a debit.

f. The balance of Advertising Expense is $600, but it was listed as $500 on the trial balance.

g. A $300 debit to Accounts Receivable was posted as $30. The credit to Consulting Service Revenue was correct.

h. The balance of Utilities Expense is overstated by $70.

i. A $900 debit to the K. Hammond, Withdrawals account was posted as a debit to K. Hammond, Capital.

Required

1. Prepare the correct trial balance at June 30, 2002. Journal entries are not required.

2. Prepare the company's income statement for the month ended June 30, 2002. Use it to determine the Hammond Landscape Consulting net income or net loss for the month.

Problem 2-6A   *Recording transactions directly in the ledger; preparing a trial balance (Obj. 2, 5, 7)*

Sharon Yee started an investment counselling business, Coast Partners, in Prince George, British Columbia on June 1, 2003. During the first month of operations, the business completed the following selected transactions:

a. Yee began the business with an investment of $20,000 cash, land valued at $20,000, and a building valued at $40,000. The business gave Yee owner's equity in the business for the value of the cash, land, and building.

b. Coast Partners borrowed $30,000 from the bank; signed a note payable.

c. Purchased office supplies on account, $1,300.

d. Paid $18,000 for office furniture.

e. Paid employee salary, $2,200.

f. Performed consulting service on account for client, $5,100.

g. Paid $800 of the account payable created in transaction c.

h. Received a $2,000 bill for advertising expense that will be paid in the near future.

i. Performed consulting services for customers and received cash, $5,600.

j. Received cash on account, $1,200.

k. Paid the following cash expenses:
   (1) Rent of photocopier, $700.
   (2) Utilities, $400.

l. Sharon Yee withdrew $2,500 for personal use.

Required

1. Open the following T-accounts: Cash; Accounts Receivable; Office Supplies; Office Furniture; Land; Building; Accounts Payable; Note Payable; Sharon Yee, Capital; Sharon Yee, Withdrawals; Service Revenue; Advertising Expense; Equipment Rental Expense; Salary Expense; Utilities Expense.

2. Record each transaction directly in the T-accounts without using a journal. Use the letters to identify the transactions.

3. Prepare the trial balance of Coast Partners at June 30, 2003.

Problem 2-7A   *Preparing the financial statements   (Obj. 5)*

Link Back to Chapter 1 (Income Statement, Statement of Owner's Equity, Balance Sheet). Refer to Problem 2-6A. After completing the trial balance in Problem 2-6A, prepare the following financial statements for Coast Partners:

1. Income statement for the month ended June 30, 2003.

2. Statement of owner's equity for the month ended June 30, 2003.

3. Balance sheet at June 30, 2003.

Draw arrows linking the financial statements. If needed, use Exhibit 1-8, page 22, as a guide for preparing the financial statements.

Problem 2-8A   *Applying the rules of debit and credit, and recording transactions in the journal   (Obj. 2, 3)*

Bobby Reynolds operated a fishing charter business, Atlantic Charters. The business had the following transactions in September, 2002:

Sept. 1 Reynolds invested $20,000 cash and his 10-metre power boat in the charter business. The business gave Reynolds owner's equity in the business. The boat had originally cost him $40,000, but had a fair market value of $25,000 on September 1, 2002.

3 Purchased a new boat by paying $7,000 cash and promising to pay another $14,000 in one week. Reynolds felt that this was an excellent bargain as the boat had a catalogue price of $30,000 and he knew it was worth at least $25,000.

4 Paid moorage fees of $1,400 for the month of September. These fees covered two moorage slips—one for each charter boat.

5 Hired a deckhand at a rate of $400 per week.

9 Took clients out on a charter for $1,300. They paid $600 and promised to pay the balance in 30 days.

10 Paid $1,000 of the amount owing on the boat purchased on September 3. Signed a promissory note for the balance as the company was unable to pay the full amount that day.

15 Purchased $5,000 of equipment from a supplier. To pay for the equipment, Atlantic Charters took the supplier and her employees out on a day charter and also paid the supplier $3,000 cash.

20 Received $300 from the clients of September 9 as payment on the charter.

26 Paid the deckhand for three weeks' work.

29 A client chartered the two boats for two days for $4,000. In payment, the client, the owner of a service station, provided Atlantic Charters with $2,000 of repair parts that can be used on the boats, and cash.

30 Used $400 of repair parts on each of the two boats.

Required

Record each transaction in the journal. Key each transaction by date. Explanations are not required.

Problem 2-9A *Applying the rules of debit and credit, and recording transactions (Obj. 2, 3, 4, 5)*

Reliable Movers had the following account balances, in random order, on December 15, 2002 (all accounts have their "normal" balances):

Moving fees earned	$ 87,200	Cash	$ 2,400	
Accounts receivable	5,800	Storage fees earned	19,300	
Rent expense	15,700	Notes receivable	15,000	
R. Sprott, Capital	50,000	Utilities expense	800	
Office supplies expense	700	Office supplies	3,200	
Mortgage payable	13,000	Accounts payable	11,000	
Salaries expense	53,700	Office equipment	4,100	
Insurance expense	2,100	Moving equipment	77,400	

The following events took place during the final days of the year:

Dec. 16 The accountant discovered that an error had been made in posting an entry to the Moving Fees Earned account. The entry was correctly journalized but $1,200 was accidentally posted as $2,100 in the account.

17 Moved a customer's goods to Reliable's rented warehouse for storage. The moving fees were $1,000. Storage fees are $200 per month and are due from the customer in 30 days.

18 Collected a $5,000 note owed to Reliable Movers and collected interest of $600.

21 Purchased storage racks for $4,000. Paid $1,200, provided moving services for $500, and promised to pay the balance in 60 days.

23 Collected $1,000; $750 of this was for moving goods on December 15 (recorded as an accounts receivable at that time) and the balance was for storage fees for the period of December 16 to 23.

24 Reliable Movers paid $6,000 owing on the mortgage.

27 Réal Sprott withdrew $2,000 for personal use.

29 Provided moving services to a lawyer for $800. The lawyer paid Reliable Movers $500 and provided legal work for the balance.

Dec. 31   Réal Sprott, the owner of Reliable Movers, sold 1,000 shares he held in Whitehorse
Haulage Inc. for $4,000.

Required

Where appropriate, record each transaction from December 16 to 31 in the journal.
Explanations are not required.

Problems (Group B)

Problem 2-1B   *Analyzing a trial balance*   *(Obj. 1)*

Link Back to Chapter 1 (Balance Sheet, Income Statement). Sylvie Fortin, the owner of
Fortin Designs, is selling the business. She offers the following trial balance to
prospective buyers:

FORTIN DESIGNS Trial Balance December 31, 2003		
Cash..........	$ 13,000	
Accounts receivable	15,000	
Prepaid expenses...........	2,000	
Land for future expansion	34,000	
Accounts payable.........		$ 31,000
Note payable........		22,000
Sylvie Fortin, Capital........		33,000
Sylvie Fortin, Withdrawals	15,000	
Service revenue........		70,000
Advertising expense	8,000	
Rent expense........	12,000	
Supplies expense.........	9,000	
Wage expense	48,000	
Total........	$156,000	$156,000

Your best friend is considering buying Fortin Designs. She seeks your advice in interpreting this information. Specifically, she asks whether this trial balance is the
same as a balance sheet and an income statement. She also wonders whether Fortin
Designs is a sound company. She thinks it must be because the accounts are in
balance.

Required

Write a short note to answer your friend's questions. To aid her decision, state how
she can use the information on the trial balance to compute the Fortin Designs net
income or net loss for the current period. State the amount of net income or net
loss in your note.

Problem 2-2B   *Analyzing and journalizing transactions*   *(Obj. 2, 3)*

Ray Tam practises civil engineering under the business title Ray Tam Consulting.
During April 2003 the company engaged in the following transactions:

Apr. 1   Tam deposited $35,000 cash in the business bank account. The business gave
Tam owner's equity in the business.

5   Paid monthly rent on drafting equipment, $700.

9   Paid $22,000 cash to purchase land for an office site.

10   Purchased supplies on account, $1,500.

19   Paid $1,000 on account for supplies purchased on April 10.

22   Borrowed $20,000 from the bank for business use. Tam signed a note payable to the
bank in the name of the business.

Apr. 30   Revenues earned during the month included $6,000 cash and $7,000 on
            account.
     30   Paid employee salaries of $2,400, office rent of $1,600, and utilities of $400.
     30   Ray Tam withdrew $4,000 from the business for personal use.

Ray Tam Consulting uses the following accounts: Cash; Accounts Receivable;
Supplies; Land; Accounts Payable; Notes Payable; R. Tam, Capital; R. Tam,
Withdrawals; Service Revenue; Rent Expense; Salary Expense; Utilities Expense.

Required

1. Prepare an analysis of each business transaction of Ray Tam Consulting, as shown
   for the April 1 transaction:

   Apr. 1   The asset Cash is increased. Increases in assets are recorded by debits;
               therefore, debit Cash. The owner's equity is increased. Increases in owner's
               equity are recorded by credits; therefore, credit R. Tam, Capital.

2. Record each transaction in the journal, using the account titles given. Key each
   transaction by date. Explanations are not required.

Problem 2-3B   *Journalizing transactions, posting to T-accounts, and preparing a trial
                   balance*   **(Obj. 2, 3, 4, 5)**

Marie Goyette opened a translation business on January 2, 2002. During the first
month of operations the business completed the following transactions:

Jan.   2   The business received $40,000 cash from Marie Goyette, which was in a business
             bank account entitled Marie Goyette Translation Service.
       3   Purchased supplies, $500, and furniture, $4,200, on account.
       3   Paid January rent expense, $900.
       4   Performed translation services for a client and received cash, $1,500.
       7   Paid $22,000 cash to acquire land for a future office site.
      11   Translated a brochure for a client and billed the client $800.
      15   Paid secretary salary, $650.
      16   Paid for the furniture purchased January 3 on account.
      18   Received partial payment from client on account, $400.
      19   Translated legal documents for a client on account, $900.
      22   Paid the water and electricity bills, $230.
      29   Received $1,800 cash for translation for a client in an overseas business transaction.
      31   Paid secretary salary, $650.
      31   Marie Goyette withdrew $1,500 for personal use.

Required

Open the following T-accounts: Cash; Accounts Receivable; Supplies; Furniture;
Land; Accounts Payable; Marie Goyette, Capital; Marie Goyette, Withdrawals;
Translation Revenue; Rent Expense; Salary Expense; Utilities Expense.

1. Record each transaction in the journal, using the account titles given. Key each
   transaction by date. Explanations are not required.

2. Post the transactions to the ledger using T-accounts, using transaction dates in the
   ledger. Label the balance of each account *Bal.* as shown in the chapter.

3. Prepare the trial balance of Marie Goyette Translation Service at January 31, 2002.

4. How will what you have learned in this problem help you manage a business?

Problem 2-4B   *Journalizing transactions, posting to ledger accounts, and preparing a trial
                   balance*   **(Obj. 2, 3, 4, 5)**

The trial balance of the desktop publishing business of Steven Chang at November 15,
2003, is shown on page 101.

STEVEN CHANG PUBLISHING
Trial Balance
November 15, 2003

Account Number	Account	Debit	Credit
1100	Cash..	$ 3,000	
1200	Accounts receivable	8,000	
1300	Supplies..	600	
1900	Land..	35,000	
2100	Accounts payable		$ 4,600
4000	S. Chang, Capital		40,000
4100	S. Chang, Withdrawals	2,300	
5000	Service revenue.............................		7,100
6000	Rent expense	1,000	
6100	Salary expense...............................	1,800	
	Total..	$51,700	$51,700

During the remainder of November, the business completed the following transactions:

Nov. 16 Collected $4,000 cash from a client on account.
17 Performed publishing services for a client on account, $2,100.
21 Paid on account, $2,600.
22 Purchased supplies on account, $600.
23 Steven Chang withdrew $2,100 for personal use.
24 Was advised that Desk Top Inc. was prepared to buy all of Steven Chang Publishing for $60,000.
26 Received $1,900 cash for design work just completed.
30 Paid employees' salaries, $2,400.

Required

1. Record the transactions that occurred during November 16 through 30 in *Page 6* of the journal. Include an explanation for each entry.

2. Post the transactions to the ledger, using dates, account numbers, journal references and posting references. Open the ledger accounts listed in the trial balance together with their balances at November 15. Use the three-column account format illustrated in the chapter. Enter *Bal.* (for previous balance) in the Item column, and place a check mark (✓) in the journal reference column for the November 15 balance of each account.

3. Prepare the trial balance of Steven Chang Publishing at November 30, 2003.

Problem 2-5B *Correcting errors in a trial balance* **(Obj. 2, 5)**

Link Back to Chapter 1 (Income Statement). The trial balance for Lethbridge Copy Centre shown below, does not balance. The following errors were detected:

a. The cash balance is overstated by $400.

b. Rent expense of $200 was posted as a credit rather than a debit.

c. The balance of Advertising Expense is $300, but it is listed as $400 on the trial balance.

d. A $600 debit to Accounts Receivable was posted as $60.

e. The balance of Utilities Expense is understated by $60.

f. A $1,300 debit to the S. Scotty, Withdrawals account was posted as a debit to S. Scotty, Capital.

g. A $100 purchase of supplies on account was neither journalized nor posted.

h. A $5,800 credit to Service Revenue was not posted.

i. Office furniture should be listed in the amount of $1,300.

LETHBRIDGE COPY CENTRE
Trial Balance
October 31, 2002

Cash...	$ 3,800	
Accounts receivable	2,000	
Supplies	500	
Office furniture..	2,300	
Land	46,000	
Accounts payable...		$ 2,000
Note payable..		18,300
S. Scotty, Capital		29,500
S. Scotty, Withdrawals	3,700	
Service revenue..		4,900
Salary expense	1,500	
Rent expense	600	
Advertising expense...	400	
Utilities expense	200	
Total...	$61,000	$54,700

Required

1. Prepare the correct trial balance at October 31, 2002. Journal entries are not required.

2. Prepare Lethbridge Copy Centre's income statement for the month ended October 31, 2002. Determine the company's net income or net loss for the month. Refer to Exhibit 1-8, page 22 if necessary.

Problem 2-6B *Recording transactions directly in the ledger; preparing a trial balance (Obj. 2, 5, 7)*

George Tatulis started a catering service called Tatulis Catering in the province of New Brunswick. During the first month of operations, January, 2002, the business completed the following selected transactions:

a. Tatulis began the company with an investment of $15,000 cash and a van (automobile) valued at $13,000. The business gave Tatulis owner's equity in the business.

b. Borrowed $25,000 from the bank; signed a note payable.

c. Paid $3,000 for food service equipment.

d. Purchased supplies on account, $2,400.

e. Paid employee salary, $1,300.

f. Received $2,000 for a catering job.

g. Performed services at a wedding on account, $3,300.

h. Paid $1,000 of the account payable created in transaction d.

i. Received an $800 bill for advertising expense that will be paid in the near future.

j. Received cash on account, $1,100.

k. Paid the following cash expenses:

   (1) Rent, $1,000.

   (2) Insurance, $800.

l. George Tatulis withdrew $1,000 for personal use.

Required

1. Open the following T-accounts: Cash; Accounts Receivable; Supplies; Food Service Equipment; Automobile; Accounts Payable; Note Payable; G. Tatulis, Capital; G. Tatulis, Withdrawals; Service Revenue; Advertising Expense; Insurance Expense; Rent Expense; Salary Expense.

2. Record the transactions directly in the T-accounts without using a journal. Use the letters to identify the transactions.

3. Prepare the trial balance of Tatulis Catering at January 31, 2002.

Problem 2-7B *Preparing the financial statements (Obj. 5)*

Link Back to Chapter 1 (Income Statement, Statement of Owner's Equity, Balance Sheet). Refer to Problem 2-6B. After completing the trial balance in Problem 2-6B, prepare the following financial statements for Tatulis Catering.

1. Income statement for the month ended January 31, 2002.

2. Statement of owner's equity for the month ended January 31, 2002.

3. Balance sheet at January 31, 2002.

Draw arrows linking the financial statements. If needed, use Exhibit 1-8, page 22, as a guide for preparing the financial statements.

Problem 2-8B *Applying the rules of debit and credit, recording transactions in the journal (Obj. 2, 3)*

Arnold Ziffle operates a heavy equipment transport company, Red Deer Transport. The company had the following transactions for the month of August, 2002:

Aug. 1 Red Deer Transport received $15,000 cash and a truck and trailer from Ziffle. The truck had originally cost Ziffle $150,000, but had a fair market value of $115,000 on August 1. The trailer had a fair market value of $15,000.

   3 Purchased a new trailer by paying $8,000 cash and promising to pay another $30,000 in one week. The trailer had a list price of $47,000 and Ziffle knew it was worth at least $43,000.

   4 Paid parking space rental fees of $900 for the month of August. These fees covered three spaces—two for the trailers and one for the truck.

   5 Hired an assistant at a rate of $500 per week.

   9 Transported equipment for clients for $1,600. They paid $800 and promised to pay the balance in 30 days.

   10 Paid $6,000 of the amount owing on the trailer purchase on August 3. Signed a promissory note for the balance as the company was unable to pay the full amount that day.

   20 Received $800 from the clients of August 9 as payment on the haulage.

   26 Paid the assistant for three weeks' work.

   29 Billed a client $2,500 for hauling equipment from Red Deer to Edmonton. The client, who was the owner of a service station, paid the bill by providing the company with $2,500 of repair parts that can be used on the truck.

   30 Used $300 of repair parts on the truck.

Required

Record each transaction in the journal. Key each transaction by date. Explanations are not required.

Problem 2-9B *Applying the rules of debit and credit, recording transactions, posting to the ledger, preparing a trial balance (Obj. 2, 3, 4, 5)*

Ocean Rest, owned by Larry LaRue, had the following account balances, in random order, on December 15, 2002 (all accounts have their "normal" balances):

Guest revenue	$104,500	Furniture	$28,900
Accounts receivable	4,400	Cash	1,900
Equipment rental expense	5,900	Notes receivable	13,000
L. LaRue, Capital	46,900	Utilities expense	500
Supplies expense	1,400	Supplies inventory	2,900
Mortgage payable	15,000	Accounts payable	6,000
Salaries expense	40,500	Office equipment	5,100
Insurance expense	3,400	Boating equipment	48,400

The following events also took place during the final days of the year:

Dec. 16 The accountant discovered that an error had been made in posting an entry to the Guest Revenue account. The entry was correctly journalized but $2,100 was accidentally posted as $1,200 in the account.

17 Agreed to let a retired professor move in in the off season for a long stay, beginning today. The monthly rate will be $1,600.

18 Collected a $6,000 note owed to Ocean Rest and collected interest of $600.

21 Purchased boating equipment for $7,000 from Boats Unlimited. Ocean Rest paid $1,500, provided room rentals for $800 to Boats Unlimited and promised to pay the balance in 60 days.

23 Collected $1,200 for rooms for a conference held from December 16 to 23.

24 Ocean Rest paid $2,000 owing on the mortgage.

27 Larry LaRue withdrew $3,500 for personal use.

29 Provided meeting rooms to a lawyer for $1,000. The lawyer paid Ocean Rest $600 and provided legal work for the balance.

Required

Where appropriate, record each transaction from December 16 to 31 in the journal. Explanations are not required.

Challenge Problems

Problem 2-1C   *Understanding the rules of debit and credit*   *(Obj. 2)*

Some individuals, for whatever reason, do not pay income tax or pay less than they should. Often their business transactions are cash transactions so there is no paper trail to prove how much or how little they actually earned. Canada Customs and Revenue Agency, however, has a way of dealing with these individuals; they use a model (based on the accounting equation), to calculate how much the individual must have earned.

Canada Customs and Revenue Agency is about to audit Cathy Mackenzie for the period January 1, 2001, to December 31, 2001. Cathy buys and sells used cars for cash; the purchaser is responsible for having the car certified so it can be licensed and insured. Cathy had $2,000 cash, and no other assets or liabilities at January 1, 2001.

Required

1. Use the accounting equation to explain how the Canada Customs and Revenue Agency model will be used to audit Cathy.

2. What do you think are the accounting concepts underlying the model?

Problem 2-2C   *Using a formal accounting system.*   *(Obj. 3, 4, 6)*

Over the years you have become friendly with a farmer, Kay Hudson, who raises crops, which she sells, and has small herds of beef cattle and sheep. Kay maintains her basic herds and markets the calves and lambs each fall. Her accounting system is quite simple; all her transactions are in cash. Kay pays tax each year on her income, which she estimates. She indicated to you once that she must be doing it right because Canada Customs and Revenue Agency audited her recently and assessed no additional tax.

You are taking your first accounting course and are quite impressed with the information one can gain from a formal accounting system.

Required
Explain to Kay Hudson why it would be to her advantage to have a more formal accounting system with accounts, ledgers, and journals.

Extending Your Knowledge

Decision Problems

1. Recording transactions directly in the ledger, preparing a trial balance, and measuring net income or loss   (Obj. 2, 5, 7)

Your friend, Charles Lee, has asked your advice about the effects that certain business transactions will have on his business. His business, Car Finders, finds the best deals on automobiles for clients. Time is short, so you cannot journalize transactions. Instead, you must analyze the transactions without the use of a journal. Lee will continue in the business only if he can expect to earn monthly net income of $4,000. The business had the following transactions during March 2002:

a. Lee deposited $10,000 cash in a business bank account.

b. The business borrowed $4,000 cash from the bank and issued a note payable due within one year.

c. Paid $300 cash for supplies.

d. Paid cash for advertising in the local newspaper, $600.

e. Paid the following cash expenses for one month: secretary (part-time) salary, $1,200; office rent, $400; utilities, $300; interest, $100.

f. Earned revenue on account, $5,300.

g. Earned $2,500 revenue and received cash.

h. Collected cash from customers on account, $1,200.

Required
1. Open the following T-accounts: Cash; Accounts Receivable; Supplies; Notes Payable; Charles Lee, Capital; Service Revenue; Advertising Expense; Interest Expense; Rent Expense; Salary Expense; Utilities Expense.

2. Record the transactions directly in the T- accounts without using a journal. Key each transaction by letter.

3. Prepare a trial balance at March 31, 2002. List expenses alphabetically.

4. Compute the amount of net income or net loss for this first month of operations. Would you recommend Lee continue in business?

2. Using the accounting equation   (Obj. 2)

Although all the following questions deal with the accounting equation, they are not related:

1. Explain the advantages of double-entry bookkeeping to a friend who is opening a used-book store.

2. When you deposit money in your bank account, the bank credits your account. Is the bank misusing the word *credit* in this context? Why does the bank use the term *credit* to refer to your deposit, and not *debit*?

3. Your friend asks, "When revenues increase assets and expenses decrease assets, why are revenues credits and expenses debits and not the other way around?" Explain to your friend why revenues are credits and expenses are debits.

Financial Statement Problems

Journalizing transactions   (Obj. 2, 3)

This problem helps to develop journalizing skill by using an actual company's account titles. Refer to the Intrawest Corporation financial statements (reported in U.S. dollars) in Appendix A. Assume Intrawest completed the following selected transactions during November 2000:

Nov. 5 Earned ski and resort operations revenues on account, $6,000,000.

9 Borrowed $8,000,000 by signing a note payable (long-term other indebtedness).

12 Purchased ski and resort operations equipment on account, $9,000,000.

17 Paid $1,200,000, which represents payment of $1,000,000 on long-term debt plus interest expense of $200,000.

19 Earned resort revenues and immediately received cash of $500,000.

22 Collected the cash on account that was earned on November 5.

29 Received an electricity bill for $10,000 for Whistler and Blackcomb resorts, which will be paid in December. (This is a ski and resort operations expense.)

29 Paid half the account payable created on November 12.

Required

Journalize these transactions using the following account titles taken from the financial statements of Intrawest Corporation: Cash; Amounts Receivable; Ski and Resort Operations Assets; Amounts Payable; Long-Term Bank and Other Indebtedness; Ski and Resort Operations Revenue; Ski and Resort Operations Expenses; Interest. Explanations are not required.

Measuring Business Income: The Adjusting Process

CHAPTER OBJECTIVES

After studying this chapter, you should be able to

1 Distinguish accrual-basis accounting from cash-basis accounting

2 Apply the revenue and matching principles

3 Make adjusting entries at the end of the accounting period

4 Prepare an adjusted trial balance

5 Prepare the financial statements from the adjusted trial balance

A1 Account for a prepaid expense recorded initially as an expense

A2 Account for an unearned (deferred) revenue recorded initially as a revenue

"**D**aniel Jarvis, the Executive Vice President at Intrawest, said that the company is able to beat analyst revenue and earnings projections because it has succeeded in diversifying its operations geographically." (*The Financial Post*, May 16, 2000)

Business publications in Canada, such as *The Financial Post* (a part of *The National Post*) and *The Globe and Mail*'s *Report on Business*, publish articles on particular companies in addition to more general business news, daily stock prices, sales of stock on North American stock exchanges, commodity prices, and exchange rates. As well, many companies that provide services to investors have developed websites where investors and potential investors can browse information about publicly listed companies (which are companies whose shares of stock are traded on the stock market).

In May 2000, *The Financial Post* published an article about Intrawest Corporation, the company we explore in the end-of-chapter Financial Statement Problems. Intrawest's financial statements for the year ended June 30, 2000, are in Appendix A of this text.

The Financial Post's article discusses the performance of Intrawest's common stock, which is listed and traded on the Toronto, New York, and Canadian Venture stock exchanges. The article reports that Intrawest's third quarter (January 2000 to March 2000) earnings in fiscal 2000 were 33% higher than in January to March of the previous year—U.S. $48.1 million compared to U.S. $35.9 million. Because this increase in earnings was greater than the rate predicted by analysts, Intrawest's stock price increased when the third-quarter earnings were reported.

Source: John Schreiner, "Intrawest Earnings Rebound to 33% Jump in Third Quarter," *The Financial Post*, May 16, 2000, via National Post Online, www.nationalpost.com.

Financial Post
www.nationalpost.com

Globe and Mail
www.globeandmail.com

Report on Business
www.robmagazine.com

Toronto Stock Exchange
www.tse.com

Canadian Venture Exchange
www.cdnx.ca

New York Stock Exchange
www.nyse.com

THINKING IT OVER

All parts of the financial statements are important in describing the financial condition of a business. Which financial statement would be most helpful to Intrawest's management in evaluating the company's performance for the past year?

A: The income statement, because it reports how profitable the company has been for that period.

WHAT do we mean when we say that Intrawest earned U.S. $48.1 million in the third quarter of the year ended June 30, 2000? The business earned net income, or profit, of U.S. $48.1 million in the quarter as reported on its income statement. Intrawest's revenues consist of ski and resort revenue and real estate sales and rentals of U.S. $208 million. What are Intrawest's expenses? Advertising, salaries, costs of running the lifts, administrative and other office costs, snow grooming, and many others. Intrawest operates in much the same way, except on a much larger scale, as Air & Sea Travel, the travel business we studied in Chapters 1 and 2.

Whether the business is Intrawest Corporation or Air & Sea Travel, the profit motive increases the owners' drive to carry on the business. As you study this chapter, consider how important net income is to a business.

At the end of each accounting period, the entity prepares its financial statements. The period may be a month, three months, six months, or a full year. Intrawest is typical. The company reports on a quarterly basis—at the end of every three months, with audited financial statements at the end of its year.

Whatever the length of the period, the end accounting product is the financial statements. And the most important single amount in these statements is the net income or net loss—the profit or loss—for the period. Net income captures much information: total revenues minus total expenses for the period. A business that consistently earns net income adds value to its owners, its employees, its customers, and society.

An important step in financial statement preparation is the trial balance. The trial balance, introduced in Chapter 2 on page 64, lists the ledger accounts and their balances. The account balances in the trial balance include the effects of the transactions that occurred during the period—cash collections, purchases of assets, payments of bills, sales of assets, and so on. To measure its income, however, a business must do some additional accounting at the end of the period to bring the records up to date before preparing the financial statements. This process is called *adjusting the books* and it consists of making special entries called *adjusting entries*. This chapter focuses on these adjusting entries to show how to measure business income.

The accounting profession has concepts and principles to guide the measurement of business income. Chief among these are the concepts of accrual accounting, the accounting period, the revenue principle, and the matching principle. In this chapter, we apply these (and other) concepts and principles to measure the income and prepare the financial statements of Air & Sea Travel for the month of April.

Accrual-Basis Accounting versus Cash-Basis Accounting

OBJECTIVE 1
Distinguish accrual-basis accounting from cash-basis accounting

There are two ways to do accounting:

- **Accrual-basis accounting** records the effect of every business transaction as it occurs. Most businesses use the accrual basis, and that is the method covered in this book.

- **Cash-basis accounting** records only cash receipts and cash payments. It ignores receivables, payables, and amortization. Only very small businesses tend to use cash-basis accounting.

Suppose Drugstore.com purchased $2,000 of supplies on account from Johnson & Johnson, the health-care products company. On the accrual basis, Drugstore.com records the asset Supplies and the liability Accounts Payable as follows:

Supplies..	2,000	
Accounts Payable................................		2,000
Purchased supplies on account.		

Under the accrual basis, Drugstore.com's balance sheet reports the asset Supplies and the liability Accounts Payable.

In contrast, cash-basis accounting ignores this transaction because Drugstore.com paid no cash. The cash basis records only cash receipts and cash payments. *Cash receipts are treated as revenues, and cash payments are handled as expenses.* Therefore, under the cash basis, Drugstore.com would record the $2,000 cash payment as an expense rather than as an asset. This is faulty accounting: Drugstore.com acquired supplies, which are assets because they provide future benefit to the company.

Now let's see how differently the accrual basis and the cash basis account for a revenue. Suppose Drugstore.com sold goods on account. Under the accrual basis, Drugstore.com records a $10,000 sale as follows:

Accounts Receivable.....................................	10,000	
Sales Revenue		10,000
Sold goods on account.		

The balance sheet then reports the asset Accounts Receivable, and the income statement reports Sales Revenue. We have a complete picture of the transaction.

Under the cash basis, Drugstore.com would not record a sale *on account* because there is no cash receipt. Instead, it would wait until cash is received and then record the cash as revenue. As a result, cash-basis accounting never reports accounts receivable from customers. It shows the revenue in the wrong accounting period, when cash is received. Revenue should be recorded when it is earned, and that is how the accrual basis operates.

Exhibit 3-1 illustrates the difference between the

Student to Student

I found the adjusting process to be a challenging topic in this chapter. What I found helpful was the Working It Out questions in the side margins. The explanations and examples helped me see exactly what was going on in the adjusting process.

Brock N., Vancouver

EXHIBIT 3-1

Accrual-Basis Accounting
versus Cash-Basis
Accounting

Panel A (a revenue)—Collect $3,000 cash on January 1. The $3,000 of revenue is to be earned evenly during January, February, and March.

		Jan.	Feb.	Mar.
Accrual-basis Accounting	Service revenue..............	$1,000	$1,000	$1,000
Cash-basis Accounting	Service revenue..............	$3,000		

Panel B (an expense)—Prepay $6,000 for TV advertising to be run during October, November, and December.

		Oct.	Nov.	Dec.
Accrual-basis Accounting	Advertising expense	$2,000	$2,000	$2,000
Cash-basis Accounting	Advertising expense	$6,000		

LEARNING TIP

You can distinguish cash-basis and accrual-basis accounting this way:

Cash basis: Record revenue when you receive cash, regardless of when the service was performed or the sale made. Record expenses when you pay cash, regardless of when the expense was incurred or the item used. There are no accounts receivable and no accounts payable.

Accrual basis: Forget cash flow. Record revenue when you make a sale or perform a service. Record expenses when the business uses goods or services. Revenues and expenses may not coincide with cash flows.

THINKING IT OVER

A client pays Air & Sea Travel $900 on March 15 for service to be performed April 1 to June 30. Has Air & Sea Travel earned revenue on March 15?

A: No. Air & Sea Travel has received the cash but will not perform the service until later. Under the accrual method, Air & Sea Travel will record Unearned Service Revenue on March 15. It is a liability because Air & Sea Travel has an obligation to perform a service in the future.

OBJECTIVE 2
Apply the revenue and matching principles

accrual basis and the cash basis. Keep in mind that the accrual basis is the correct way to do accounting. As we saw in Exhibit 1-3 on page 8, the objective of financial statements is to communicate information that is useful to users. Clearly, accrual-basis accounting provides more complete information than does cash-basis accounting. This difference is important because the more complete the data, the better equipped decision makers are to reach accurate conclusions about the firm's financial health and future prospects. Four concepts used in accrual accounting are the accounting period, the revenue principle, the matching principle, and the time-period concept.

The Accounting Period

The only way to know for certain how successfully a business has operated is to close its doors, sell all its assets, pay the liabilities, and return any leftover cash to the owner. This process, called *liquidation*, is the same as going out of business. Obviously, it is not practical for accountants to measure business income in this manner. Instead, businesses need periodic reports on their progress. Accountants slice time into small segments and prepare financial statements for specific periods.

The most basic accounting period is one year, and virtually all businesses prepare annual financial statements. For about 60 percent of companies in a recent Canadian survey, the annual accounting period runs the calendar year from January 1 through December 31. The other companies in the survey use a *fiscal year* ending on some date other than December 31. The year-end date is usually the low point in business activity for the year. Retailers are a notable example. Traditionally, they have used a fiscal year ending on January 31, because the low point in their business activity has followed the after-Christmas sales during January; Mark's Work Wearhouse and Hudson's Bay Co. are two examples. Eight percent of the companies in the survey mentioned above have a January 31 year-end date like Mark's Work Wearhouse.

Managers and investors cannot wait until the end of the year to gauge a company's progress. Companies therefore prepare financial statements for *interim* periods, which are less than a year. Managers want financial information more often so monthly financial statements are common. A series of monthly statements can be combined for quarterly and semiannual periods. Most of the discussions in this book are based on an annual accounting period but the procedures and statements can also be applied to interim periods as well.

Revenue Principle

The **revenue principle** tells accountants (1) *when* to record revenue, and (2) the *amount* of revenue to record. Revenue, defined in Chapter 1, page 12, is the increase in owner's equity from delivering goods and services to customers in the course of operating a business. When we speak of "recording" something in accounting, we mean to make an entry in the journal. That is where the accounting process starts.

The general principle guiding *when* to record revenue is that revenue should be recorded as it has been earned—but not before. In *most* cases, revenue is earned when the business has delivered a completed good or service to the customer. The business has done everything required by the agreement, including transferring the item to the customer. Exhibit 3-2 shows two situations that provide guidance on when to record revenue. The first situation illustrates when *not* to record revenue, because the client merely states her plans. Situation 2 illustrates when revenue should be recorded—after Air & Sea Travel has performed the service for the client.

The general principle guiding the *amount* of revenue to record is record revenue equal to the cash value of the goods or the service transferred to the customer. Suppose that in order to obtain a new client, Air & Sea Travel performs travel service for the price of $500. Ordinarily, the business would have charged $600 for this service. How much revenue should the business record? The answer is $500 because that was the cash value of the transaction. Air & Sea Travel will not receive the full value of $600, so that is not the amount of revenue to record. The business will receive only $500 cash, and that pinpoints the amount of revenue earned.

The Matching Principle

The **matching principle** is the basis for recording expenses. Recall that expenses—such as rent, utilities, and advertising—are the costs of assets and services that are consumed in the earning of revenue. The matching principle directs accountants to (1) identify all expenses incurred during the accounting period, (2) measure the expenses, and (3) match the expenses against the revenues earned during that same span of time. To match expenses against revenues means to subtract the expenses from the revenues in order to compute net income or net loss. Exhibit 3-3 illustrates the matching principle.

There is a natural link between revenues and some types of expenses. Accountants follow the matching principle by first identifying the revenues of a period and then the expenses that can be linked to particular revenues. For example, a business that pays sales commissions to its sales persons will have commission expense if the employees make sales. If they make no sales, the business has no commission expense. *Cost of goods sold* is another example. If there are no sales of Sea-Doos, Bombardier reports no cost of goods sold.

Other expenses are not so easy to link with particular sales. Monthly rent expense occurs, for example, regardless of the revenues earned during the period. The matching principle directs accountants to identify these types of expenses with a particular time period, such as a month or a year. If Air & Sea Travel employs a secretary at a monthly salary of $1,900, the business will record salary expense of $1,900 each month.

..... **THINKING IT OVER**

Air & Sea Travel pays $4,500 on July 31 for office rent for the next three months. Has Air & Sea Travel incurred an expense on July 31?

A: No. Air & Sea Travel has paid cash, but the rent will not expire, or be used up, for three months. Under the accrual method, Air & Sea Travel will record Prepaid Rent on July 31. It is an asset because Air & Sea Travel has paid in advance for the use of an office in the future.

EXHIBIT 3-2

Recording Revenue

No transaction has occurred.
Situation 1—Do Not Record Revenue

I plan to have you make my travel arrangements.

Air & Sea Travel
MARCH 12

Travel Itinerary
Depart ___
Arrive ___

The client has taken a trip arranged by Air & Sea Travel.
Situation 2—Record Revenue

Air & Sea Travel
APRIL 2

EXHIBIT 3-3

The Matching Principle

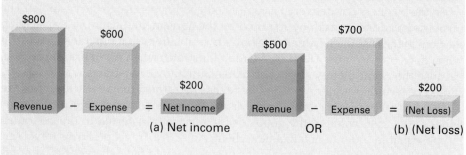

Match the expense of a period against the revenue earned during the period. To "match" an expense means to subtract the expense from the revenue to measure net income or net loss.

$800 Revenue − $600 Expense = $200 Net Income
(a) Net income

OR

$500 Revenue − $700 Expense = $200 (Net Loss)
(b) (Net loss)

Air & Sea Travel prepares a monthly statement for the business at April 30. How does the company account for a transaction that begins in April but ends in May? How does it bring the accounts up to date for preparing the financial statements? To answer these questions, accountants use the time-period concept.

Time-Period Concept

Managers, investors, and creditors make decisions daily and need periodic readings on the business's progress. Therefore, accountants prepare financial statements at regular intervals.

The **time-period concept** ensures that accounting information is reported at regular intervals. It interacts with the accounting period, revenue principle, and matching principle to underlie the use of accruals. To measure income accurately, companies update the revenue and expense accounts immediately prior to the end of the period. For example, Finning Ltd., which sells Caterpillar earthmoving equipment, provides a real example of an expense accrual. Finning Ltd. has a December 31 year end. When December 31 falls during a pay period (say, December 31, 2003, which is on a Wednesday, and Finning pays its employees weekly on Friday), the company must record the employee compensation owed to the workers for unpaid services performed up to and including December 31. Assume weekly salary and wages expense for Finning's B.C. Division is $2,300,000; the entry to accrue the expense would be ($\frac{3}{5} \times \$2,300,000 = \$1,380,000$):

Finning Ltd.
www.finning.co.uk

Caterpillar
www.caterpillar.com

```
2003
Dec. 31   Salary and Wages Expense.....................................   1,380,000
                      Salary and Wages Payable ..........................                 1,380,000
          Accrued salary and wages expense for December 28 to 31, 2003.
```

This entry serves two purposes. First, it assigns the expense to the proper period. Without the accrual entry at December 31, total expenses for 2003 would be understated, and as a result, net income would be overstated. Incorrectly, the expense would fall in the 2004 fiscal year when Finning makes the next payroll disbursement. Second, the accrual entry also records the liability for reporting on the balance sheet at December 31, 2003. Without the accrual entry, total liabilities would be understated.

At the end of the accounting period, companies also accrue revenues that have been earned but not collected. The remainder of the chapter discusses how to make the adjusting entries to bring the accounts up to date.

OBJECTIVE 3
Make adjusting entries at the end of the accounting period

Adjusting the Accounts

At the end of the period, the accountant prepares the financial statements. This end-of-the-period process begins with the trial balance that lists the accounts and their balances after the period's transactions have been recorded in the journal and posted to the accounts in the ledger. We prepared trial balances in Chapter 2.

Exhibit 3-4 is the trial balance of Air & Sea Travel at April 30, 2003. (Accounts and balances differ from those in Chapter 2. Assume the company has been in business for one year.) This *unadjusted trial balance* includes some new accounts that will be explained here. It lists most, but not all, of the revenue accounts and the expenses of the travel agency for the month of April. These trial balance amounts are incomplete because they omit certain revenue and expense transactions that affect more than one accounting period. That is why the trial balance is *unadjusted*. In most cases, however, we refer to it simply as the trial balance, without the label "unadjusted."

Under the cash basis of accounting, there would be no need for adjustments to the accounts because all April cash transactions would have been recorded. However, the accrual basis requires adjusting entries at the end of the period in order to produce correct balances for the financial statements. To see why, consider the Supplies account in Exhibit 3-4.

Air & Sea Travel uses supplies in providing travel services for clients during the month. This use reduces the quantity of supplies on hand and thus constitutes an expense, just like salary expense or rent expense. The business does not bother to record this expense daily, and it is not worth the effort to record supplies expense more than once a month. It is time-consuming to make hourly, daily, or even weekly journal entries to record the expense incurred by the use of supplies. So how does the business account for supplies expense?

By the end of the month, the Supplies balance of $700 on the unadjusted trial balance (Exhibit 3-4) is not correct. The unadjusted balance represents the amount of supplies on hand at the start of the month plus any supplies purchased during the month. This balance fails to take into account the supplies used (*supplies expense*) during the accounting period. It is necessary, then, to subtract the month's expenses from the amount of supplies listed on the trial balance. The resulting new adjusted balance measures the cost of supplies that are still on hand at April 30, say $400, based on a physical count of supplies remaining on hand. This is the correct amount of supplies to report on the balance sheet—$400. The adjusting entry will, in this way, bring the supplies accounts up to date.

Adjusting entries assign revenues to the period in which they are earned and expenses to the period in which they are incurred. Adjusting entries also update the asset and liability accounts. They are needed to (1) measure properly the period's income on the income statement, and (2) bring related asset and liability accounts to correct balances for the balance sheet. For example, an adjusting entry is needed to transfer the amount of supplies used during the period from the asset account

EXHIBIT 3-4

Unadjusted Trial Balance

AIR & SEA TRAVEL Unadjusted Trial Balance April 30, 2003		
Cash	$24,800	
Accounts receivable	2,250	
Supplies	700	
Prepaid rent	3,000	
Furniture	16,500	
Accounts payable		$13,100
Unearned service revenue		450
Gary Lyon, capital		31,250
Gary Lyon, withdrawals	3,200	
Service revenue		7,000
Salary expense	950	
Utilities expense	400	
Total	$51,800	$51,800

Supplies to the expense account Supplies Expense. The adjusting entry updates both the Supplies asset account and the Supplies Expense account. This achieves accurate measures of assets and expenses. Adjusting entries, which are the key to accrual-basis accounting, are made before the financial statements are prepared. The end-of-period process of updating the accounts is called *adjusting the accounts*, *making the adjusting entries*, or *adjusting the books*.

A large company would use accounting software to print out a trial balance. For example, at Nexen Inc., a multidivisional company that locates, produces, and transports oil and natural gas, each division has its own accounting software that prints a monthly trial balance. The accountants then analyze the amounts on the trial balance. This analysis results in the adjusting entries. Nexen posts the adjusting entries to update its ledger accounts. The trial balance has now become the company's *adjusted* trial balance. At Nexen, the adjusted trial balances from all divisions are consolidated, or grouped. This chapter shows the adjusting process as it moves from the trial balance to the adjusted trial balance.

Two basic types of adjustments are *prepaids* and *accruals*.

Nexen Inc.
www.nexeninc.com

Prepaids (Deferrals) and Accruals

In a *prepaid*-type adjustment, the cash transaction occurs before the related expense or revenue is recorded. Prepaids are also called *deferrals* because the recording of the expense or the revenue is deferred until after cash is paid or received. *Accrual*-type adjustments are the opposite of prepaids. For accruals we record the expense or revenue before the related cash is paid or received.

Adjusting entries can be further divided into five categories:

1. Prepaid expenses
2. Amortization of capital assets
3. Accrued expenses
4. Accrued revenues
5. Unearned revenues

The core of this chapter is the discussion of these five types of adjusting entries on pages 114–123. Study this material carefully because it is the most challenging topic in all of introductory accounting.

Prepaid Expenses

LEARNING TIP

Prepaid expenses are assets, not expenses.

Prepaid expenses are advance payments of expense. The category includes miscellaneous assets that typically expire or are used up in the near future. Prepaid rent and prepaid insurance are examples of prepaid expenses. They are called "prepaid" expenses because they are expenses that are paid in advance. Salary expense and utilities expense, among others, are typically *not* prepaid expenses because they are not paid in advance. All companies, large and small, must make adjustments regarding prepaid expenses. For example, Swiss Chalet must contend with such prepayments as rents, packaging supplies, and insurance.

Prepaid Rent   Landlords usually require tenants to pay rent in advance. This prepayment creates an asset for the tenant, because that person has purchased the future benefit of using the rented item. Suppose Air & Sea Travel prepays three months' rent on April 1, 2003, after negotiating a lease for the business office. If the lease specifies monthly rental amounts of $1,000 each, the entry to record the payment for three months is a debit to the asset account, Prepaid Rent, as follows:

Apr. 1	Prepaid Rent	3,000	
	Cash		3,000
	Paid three months' rent in advance ($1,000 × 3).		

After posting, Prepaid Rent appears as follows:

ASSETS
Prepaid Rent

Apr. 1	3,000

The trial balance at April 30, 2003 lists Prepaid Rent as an asset with a debit balance of $3,000. Throughout April, the Prepaid Rent account maintains this beginning balance, as shown in Exhibit 3-4. But $3,000 is *not* the amount to report for Prepaid Rent on Air & Sea Travel's balance sheet at April 30. Why?

At April 30, Prepaid Rent should be adjusted to remove from its balance the amount of the asset that has been used up, which is one month's worth of the prepayment. By definition, the amount of an asset that has been used, or has expired, is *expense*. The adjusting entry transfers one-third, or $1,000 ($3,000 × ⅓), of the debit balance from Prepaid Rent to Rent Expense. The debit side of the entry records an increase in Rent Expense and the credit records a decrease in the asset Prepaid Rent.

Apr. 30	Rent Expense...	1,000	
	Prepaid Rent...		1,000
	To record rent expense ($3,000 × ⅓).		

After posting, Prepaid Rent and Rent Expense appear as follows:

ASSETS					**EXPENSES**		
Prepaid Rent					**Rent Expense**		
Apr. 1	3,000	Apr. 30	1,000		Apr. 30	1,000	
Bal.	2,000				Bal.	1,000	

Correct asset amount, $2,000 → Total accounted for, $3,000 ← Correct expense amount, $1,000

The full $3,000 has been accounted for. Two-thirds measures the asset, and one-third measures the expense. Recording this expense illustrates the matching principle.

The same analysis applies to a prepayment of three months' insurance premiums. The only difference is in the account titles, which would be Prepaid Insurance and Insurance Expense instead of Prepaid Rent and Rent Expense. In a computerized system, the adjusting entry crediting the prepaid account and debiting the expense account could be established to recur automatically in each subsequent accounting period until the prepaid account has a zero balance.

The chapter appendix shows an alternate treatment of prepaid expenses. The end result on the financial statements is the same as that for the method given here.

Supplies Supplies are accounted for the same way as prepaid expenses. On April 2, Air & Sea Travel paid cash of $700 for office supplies.

Apr. 2	Supplies..	700	
	Cash..		700
	Paid cash for supplies.		

Assume that the business purchased no additional supplies during April. The April 30 trial balance, therefore, lists Supplies with a $700 debit balance as shown in Exhibit 3-4. But Air & Sea Travel's April 30 balance sheet should *not* report supplies of $700. Why?

During April, Air & Sea Travel used supplies in performing services for clients. The cost of the supplies used is the measure of *supplies expense* for the month. To measure the business's supplies expense during April, Gary Lyon counts the supplies on hand at the end of the month. This is the amount of the asset still available to the business. Assume the count indicates that supplies costing $400 remain. Subtracting the entity's $400 of supplies on hand at the end of April from the cost of supplies available during April ($700) measures supplies expense during the month ($300).

Cost of asset available during the period	−	Cost of asset on hand at the end of the period	=	Cost of asset used (expense) during the period
$700	−	$400	=	$300

The April 30 adjusting entry to update the Supplies account and to record the supplies expense for the month debits the expense and credits the asset:

Apr. 30	Supplies Expense..	300	
	Supplies		300
	To record supplies expense ($700 – $400).		

After posting, the Supplies and Supplies Expense accounts appear as follows:

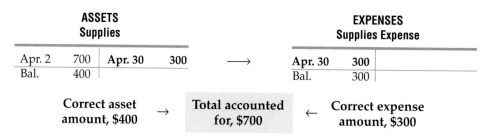

The Supplies account enters the month of May with a $400 balance, and the adjustment process is repeated each month.

Amortization of Capital Assets

The logic of the accrual basis is best illustrated by how businesses account for capital assets. **Capital assets** are long-lived tangible assets, such as land, buildings, furniture, machinery, and equipment. As one accountant said, "All assets but land are on a march to the junkyard." That is, all capital assets but land decline in usefulness as they age. This decline is an *expense* to the business. Accountants systematically spread the cost of each capital asset, except land, over the years of its useful life. The *CICA Handbook* calls this process of allocating the cost of a long-lived or capital asset to expense over its life **amortization**. Another term in common usage is *depreciation*.

Similarity to Prepaid Expenses The concept underlying accounting for capital assets and amortization expense is the same as for prepaid expenses. In a sense, capital assets are large prepaid expenses that expire over a number of periods. For both prepaid expenses and capital assets, the business purchases an asset that wears out or is used up. As the asset is used, more and more of its cost is transferred from the asset account to the expense account. The major difference between prepaid expenses and capital assets is the length of time it takes for the asset to lose its usefulness (or expire). Prepaid expenses usually expire within a year, whereas most capital assets remain useful for a number of years.

Consider Air & Sea Travel's operations. Suppose on April 3, the business purchased furniture on account for $16,500 and made this journal entry:

Apr. 3	Furniture..	16,500	
	Accounts Payable...		16,500
	Purchased office furniture on account.		

After posting, the Furniture account appears as follows:

ASSETS
Furniture

Apr. 3	16,500

In accrual-basis accounting, an asset is recorded when the furniture is acquired. Then, a portion of the asset's cost is transferred from the asset account to Amortization Expense each period that the asset is used. This method matches the asset's expense to the revenue of the period, which is an application of the matching principle. In many computerized systems, the adjusting entry for amortization is programmed to occur automatically each month for the duration of the asset's life.

Gary Lyon believes the furniture will remain useful for five years and be virtually worthless at the end of its life. One way to compute the amount of amortization for each year is to divide the cost of the asset ($16,500 in our example) by its useful life (5 years). This procedure—called the straight-line method—gives annual amortization of $3,300 ($16,500/5 years = $3,300 per year). Amortization for the month of April is $275 ($3,300/12 months = $275 per month).

The Accumulated Amortization Account Amortization expense for April is recorded by the following entry:

Apr. 30	Amortization Expense—Furniture	275	
	Accumulated Amortization—Furniture		275
	To record monthly amortization expense on furniture.		

Accumulated Amortization is credited instead of Furniture, because the original cost of the capital asset should remain in the asset account as long as the business uses the asset. Accountants and managers may refer to the Furniture account to see how much the asset cost. This information is useful in a decision about whether to replace the furniture and the amount to pay.

The amount of amortization, however, is an *estimate*. Accountants use the **Accumulated Amortization** account to show the cumulative sum of all amortization expense from the date of acquiring the asset. Therefore, the balance in this account increases over the life of the asset.

Accumulated Amortization is a *contra asset* account, which means an asset account with a normal credit balance. [Recall from Chapter 2, page 71, that the normal balance on an account marks the side of the account where increases are recorded.] A **contra account** has two distinguishing characteristics:

- A contra account has a companion account.

- A contra account's normal balance (debit or credit) is opposite that of the companion account.

In this case, Accumulated Amortization is the contra account that accompanies Furniture. It appears in the ledger directly after Furniture. Furniture has a debit balance, and therefore Accumulated Amortization, a contra asset, has a credit balance. *All contra asset accounts have credit balances.*

A business carries an accumulated amortization or depreciation account for each depreciable asset. If a business has a building and a machine, for example, it will carry the accounts Accumulated Amortization—Building, and Accumulated Amortization—Machine.

After the amortization entry has been posted, the Furniture, Accumulated Amortization—Furniture, and Amortization Expense accounts of Air & Sea Travel are

KEY POINT

Use a separate Amortization Expense account and Accumulated Amortization account for each type of asset (Amortization Expense—Furniture, Amortization Expense—Buildings, and so on). You must know the amount of amortization recorded for each asset.

THINKING IT OVER

Describe one similarity and one difference between
(1) prepaid expenses and
(2) capital assets and the related amortization.

A: Similarity: For both prepaid expenses and capital assets, the business first records the purchase as an asset. The business then records the expense later. Difference: Prepaid expenses cover a shorter time period than capital assets and the related amortization.

ASSETS Furniture		CONTRA ASSET Accumulated Amortization— Furniture		EXPENSES Amortization Expense— Furniture	
Apr. 3 16,500			Apr. 30 275	Apr. 30 275	
Bal. 16,500			Bal. 275	Bal. 275	

Carrying Value The balance sheet shows the relationship between Furniture and Accumulated Amortization—Furniture. The balance of Accumulated Amortization—Furniture is subtracted from the balance of Furniture. This net amount of a capital asset (cost minus accumulated amortization) is called its **carrying value**, or *net carrying value*, or *book value*, as shown below for Furniture:

Furniture...	$16,500
Less: Accumulated Amortization—Furniture	275
Carrying Value	$16,225

Suppose the travel agency owns a building that cost $48,000, on which annual amortization is $2,400. The amount of amortization for one month would be $200 ($2,400/12), and the following entry records amortization for April.

Apr. 30	Amortization Expense—Building	200	
	Accumulated Amortization—Building................		200
	To record monthly amortization on building.		

The balance sheet at April 30 would report Air & Sea Travel's capital assets as shown in Exhibit 3-5.

Exhibit 3-6 shows how Inco—producers of nickel, copper, alloys, and other primary metal products—displayed capital assets in a recent annual report. Inco has mines and mining plants located around the world; they are displayed in line 1 of Exhibit 3-6. Lines 2, 3, 4, and 6 list the costs of processing facilities and other buildings used for offices, production, and research as well as air conditioners, computers, plumbing, and so on, in those facilities and buildings. In addition, trucks, automobiles, and other such vehicles would be included. Note that Inco uses the

WORKING IT OUT

(1) What is the carrying value of Air & Sea Travel's furniture at the end of May?
(2) Is that what the furniture could be sold for at the end of May?
(3) What is the asset's carrying value at the end of its useful life?

A: (1) $16,500 − $275 − $275 = $15,950.
(2) Not necessarily. *Carrying value* represents the part of the asset's *cost* that has not yet been amortized.
(3) $0.

Inco
www.inco.com

EXHIBIT 3-5

Capital Assets on the Balance Sheet of Air & Sea Travel (April 30)

Capital Assets		
Furniture...	$16,500	
Less: Accumulated Amortization—Furniture...............	275	$16,225
Building	48,000	
Less: Accumulated Amortization—Building.................	200	47,800
Capital Assets, Net...		$64,025

EXHIBIT 3-6

Inco's Reporting of Capital Assets (Amounts in Millions)

(1) Mines and mining plants	$2,606
(2) Processing facilities	3,205
(3) Voisey's Bay project	3,490
(4) Other	469
(5) Primary metals facilities	9,770
(6) Other facilities	73
(7) Total capital assets, at cost	9,843
(8) Accumulated depreciation	2,654
(9) Accumulated depletion	939
(10) Total accumulated depreciation and depletion	3,593
(11) Capital assets, net	$6,250

terms *depreciation* and *depletion* in lines 9 and 10; they are other words for amortization. Amortization is discussed more fully in Chapter 10.

Let's now return to Air & Sea Travel's situation.

Accrued Expenses

Businesses incur many expenses before they pay cash. Payment is not due until later. Consider an employee's salary. The employer's salary expense and salary payable grow as the employee works, so the liability is said to *accrue*. Another example is interest expense on a note payable. Interest accrues as time passes. The term **accrued expense** refers to an expense that the business has incurred but has not yet paid. Therefore, accrued expenses can be viewed as the opposite of prepaid expenses.

It is time-consuming to make hourly, daily, or even weekly journal entries to accrue expenses. Consequently, the accountant waits until the end of the period. Then an adjusting entry brings each expense (and related liability) up to date just before the financial statements are prepared.

Salary Expense Most companies pay their employees at predetermined times. Suppose Air & Sea Travel pays its employee a monthly salary of $1,900, half on the 15th and half on the last day of the month. Here is a calendar for April with the two paydays circled:

			APRIL			
S	M	T	W	T	F	S
					1	2
3	4	5	6	7	8	9
10	11	12	13	14	(15)	16
17	18	19	20	21	22	23
24	25	26	27	28	29	(30)

Assume that if either payday falls on a weekend, Air & Sea Travel pays the employee on the following Monday. During April, the travel agency paid its employee's first half-month salary of $950 on Friday, April 15, and recorded the following entry:

Apr. 15	Salary Expense...	950	
	Cash...		950
	To pay salary.		

After posting, the Salary Expense account is

EXPENSES
Salary Expense

| Apr. 15 | 950 | |

The trial balance at April 30 (Exhibit 3-4) includes Salary Expense, with its debit balance of $950. Because April 30, the second payday of the month, falls on a Saturday, the second half-month amount of $950 will be paid on Monday, May 2. Without an adjusting entry, this second $950 amount is not included in the April 30 trial balance amount for Salary Expense. Therefore, at April 30, the business adjusts for additional *salary expense* and *salary payable* of $950 by recording an increase in each of these accounts as follows:

Apr. 30	Salary Expense	950	
	Salary Payable		950
	To accrue salary expense.		

After posting, the Salary Expense and Salary Payable accounts are updated to April 30:

EXPENSES				LIABILITIES		
Salary Expense				**Salary Payable**		
Apr.15	950				Apr. 30	950
Apr. 30	**950**				Bal.	950
Bal.	1,900					

The accounts at April 30 now contain the complete salary information for the month of April. The expense account has a full month's salary, and the liability account shows the portion that the business still owes at April 30. Air & Sea Travel will record the payment of this liability on Monday, May 2.

This payment entry does not affect April or May expenses because the April expense was recorded on April 15 and April 30. May expense will be recorded in a like manner, starting on May 15. All accrued expenses are recorded with similar entries—a debit to the appropriate expense account and a credit to the related liability account.

Many computerized systems contain a payroll module. The adjusting entry for accrued weekly and monthly salaries is automatically journalized and posted at the end of each accounting period.

Accrued Revenues

Businesses often earn revenue before they collect the cash. Collection occurs later. A revenue that has been earned but not yet collected is called an **accrued revenue**.

Assume Air & Sea Travel is hired on April 15 by Guerrero Tours Co. to make travel arrangements on a monthly basis. Under this agreement, Guerrero will pay Air & Sea Travel $500 monthly, with the first payment on May 15. During April, Air & Sea Travel will earn half a month's fee, $250, for work performed April 15 through April 30. On April 30, Air & Sea Travel makes the following adjusting entry to record an increase in Accounts Receivable and Service Revenue:

Apr. 30	Accounts Receivable	250	
	Service Revenue		250
	To accrue service revenue ($500 × ½).		

We see from the unadjusted trial balance in Exhibit 3-4 that Accounts Receivable has an unadjusted balance of $2,250. The Service Revenue unadjusted balance is $7,000. Posting the April 30 adjustment has the following effects on these two accounts:

ASSETS				REVENUES		
Accounts Receivable				**Service Revenue**		
	2,250					7,000
Apr. 30	**250**				**Apr. 30**	**250**
Bal.	2,500				Bal.	7,250

This adjusting entry illustrates the revenue principle. Without the adjustment, the travel agency's financial statements would be misleading—they would understate Accounts Receivable and Service Revenue by $250 each. All accrued revenues are accounted for similarly—by debiting a receivable and crediting a revenue.

We now turn to a different category of adjusting entries.

Suppose Air & Sea Travel holds a note receivable from a client. At the end of April, Air & Sea Travel has earned $125 of interest revenue on the note.

1. Which accounts need to be adjusted at April 30?

2. Make the adjusting entry.

Answers:

1. Earlier we saw that Air & Sea Travel debits Accounts Receivable when it earns revenue that it has not yet received in cash. Here, Air & Sea Travel is not earning service revenue. Rather, it is earning interest revenue; so we debit another account, *Interest Receivable*. We will credit another revenue account called *Interest Revenue*.

2. Interest Receivable 125
      Interest Revenue 125
   To accrue interest revenue.

Unearned Revenues

Some businesses collect cash from customers in advance of doing work for them. Receiving cash in advance creates a liability called **unearned revenue** or **deferred revenue**. This obligation arises from receiving cash in advance of providing a product or service. Only when the job is completed will the business have earned the revenue.

Suppose Baldwin Investments engages Air & Sea Travel's services, agreeing to pay the travel agency $450 monthly, beginning immediately. Suppose Baldwin makes the first payment on April 20. Air & Sea Travel records the cash receipt and the related increase in the business's liabilities as follows:

Apr. 20	Cash..	450	
	Unearned Service Revenue		450
	Received revenue in advance.		

After posting, the liability account appears as follows:

LIABILITIES
Unearned Service Revenue

| | Apr. 20 | 450 |

Unearned Service Revenue is a liability because it represents Air & Sea Travel's obligation to perform service for the client. The April 30 unadjusted trial balance (Exhibit 3-4) lists Unearned Service Revenue with a $450 credit balance prior to the adjusting entries. During the last 10 days of the month—April 21 through April 30—the travel agency will have *earned* one-third (10 days divided by April's total 30 days) of the $450, or $150. Therefore, the accountant makes the following adjustment to decrease the liability, Unearned Service Revenue, and to record an increase in Service Revenue as follows:

Apr. 30	Unearned Service Revenue	150	
	Service Revenue		150
	To record service revenue that was collected in advance ($450 × $\frac{1}{3}$).		

This adjusting entry shifts $150 of the total amount of unearned service revenue from the liability account to the revenue account. After posting, the balance of Service Revenue is increased by $150 and the balance of Unearned Service Revenue has been reduced by $150 to $300. Now, both accounts have their correct balances at April 30, as follows:

LIABILITIES			REVENUES		
Unearned Service Revenue			**Service Revenue**		
Apr. 30	150	Apr. 20 450			7,000
		Bal. 300		Apr. 30	250
				Apr. 30	**150**
				Bal.	7,400

Correct liability amount, $300 → Total accounted for, $450 ← Correct revenue amount, $150

All types of revenues that are collected in advance are accounted for similarly.

An unearned revenue to one company can be a prepaid expense to the company that made the payment. For example, suppose that two months in advance Xerox Canada Inc. paid Air Canada $1,800 for the airfare of Xerox executives. To Xerox, the payment is Prepaid Travel Expense. To Air Canada, the receipt of cash creates Unearned Service Revenue. After the executives take the trip, Air Canada records the revenue by reducing Unearned Service Revenue.

Exhibit 3-7 diagrams the timing of prepaid-type and accrual-type adjusting entries. The chapter appendix shows an alternate treatment of unearned revenues and prepaid expenses.

Xerox Canada
www.xerox.ca

EXHIBIT 3-7

Prepaid-Type and Accrual-Type Adjustments*

PREPAIDS—The cash transaction occurs initially.

	Initially		Later	
Prepaid expenses	Pay cash and record an asset: Prepaid Expense............................ XXX Cash..		→	Record an expense and decrease the asset: Expense.. XXX Prepaid Expense.........................
			XXX	XXX
Unearned revenues	Receive cash and record unearned revenue: Cash... XXX Unearned Revenue.................		→	Record a revenue and decrease unearned revenue: Unearned Revenue........................... XXX Revenue.......................................
		XXX		XXX

ACCRUALS—The cash transaction occurs later.

	Initially		Later	
Accrued expenses	Record (accrue) an expense and the related payable: Expense.. XXX Payable.....................................		→	Pay cash and decrease the payable: Payable.. XXX Cash...
		XXX		XXX
Accrued revenues	Record (accrue) a revenue and the related receivable: Receivable...................................... XXX Revenue		→	Receive cash and decrease the receivable: Cash... XXX Receivable...................................
		XXX		XXX

The authors thank Darrel Davis and Alfonso Oddo for suggesting this exhibit.

*See the Appendix of this chapter for an alternate treatment of accounting for prepaids and accruals.

STOP & THINK

Consider the tuition you pay. Assume that one semester's tuition costs $1,200 and that you make a single payment at the start of the term. Can you make the journal entries to record the tuition transaction on your own books and on the books of your college or university?

Answer:

Start of semester:

Your Entries			Your College's Entries		
Prepaid Tuition	1,200		Cash	1,200	
Cash		1,200	Unearned Tuition Revenue		1,200
Paid semester tuition.			Received revenue in advance.		

End of semester:

Tuition Expense	1,200		Unearned Tuition Revenue	1,200	
Prepaid Tuition		1,200	Tuition Revenue		1,200
To record tuition expense.			To record unearned tuition revenue that has been earned.		

Summary of the Adjusting Process

One purpose of the adjusting process is to measure business income accurately. The other purpose of the adjusting process is to update the balance sheet accounts. All adjusting entries debit or credit:

- At least one *income statement* account, either a **Revenue** or an **Expense**

and

- At least one *balance sheet* account, either an **Asset** or a **Liability**

No adjusting entry debits or credits Cash because the cash transactions are recorded at other times. (The exception to this rule is when an adjusting entry is made to correct an error involving Cash.) Exhibit 3-8 summarizes the adjusting entries.

Exhibit 3-9 on page 124 summarizes the adjusting entries of Air & Sea Travel at April 30. Panel A of the exhibit briefly describes the data for each adjustment, Panel B gives the adjusting entries, and Panel C shows the accounts after they have been posted. (Recall from Chapter 2, page 60, that posting is the process of transferring amounts from the journal to the ledger.) The adjustments are keyed by letter.

EXHIBIT 3-8

Summary of Adjusting Entries

	Type of Account	
Category of Adjusting Entry	**Debited**	**Credited**
Prepaid expense	Expense	Asset
Amortization	Expense	Contra asset
Accrued expense	Expense	Liability
Accrued revenue	Asset	Revenue
Unearned revenue	Liability	Revenue

Adapted from material provided by Beverly Terry.

EXHIBIT 3-9

Journalizing and Posting the Adjusting Entries

Panel A: Information for Adjustments at April 30, 2003

a. Prepaid rent expired during April, $1,000.
b. Supplies remaining on hand at April 30, 2003, $400.
c. Amortization on furniture for the month of April, $275.
d. Accrued salary expense, $950.
e. Accrued service revenue, $250.
f. Amount of unearned service revenue that was earned during April, $150.

Panel B: Adjusting Entries

a. Rent Expense 1,000
    Prepaid Rent 1,000
  To record rent expense.

b. Supplies Expense 300
    Supplies... 300
  To record supplies used.

c. Amortization Expense—Furniture.. 275
    Accumulated Amortization—Furniture.. 275
  To record amortization on furniture.

d. Salary Expense 950
    Salary Payable 950
  To accrue salary expense.

e. Accounts Receivable 250
    Service Revenue 250
  To accrue service revenue.

f. Unearned Service Revenue.. 150
    Service Revenue 150
  To record unearned revenue that has been earned.

Panel C: Ledger Accounts

ASSETS	LIABILITIES	OWNER'S EQUITY	EXPENSES

ASSETS

Cash
Bal. 24,800

Accounts Receivable
Bal. 2,250
(e) 250
Bal. 2,500

Supplies
Bal. 700 | (b) 300
Bal. 400

Prepaid Rent
Bal. 3,000 | (a) 1,000
Bal. 2,000

Furniture
Bal. 16,500

Accumulated Amortization—Furniture
| (c) 275
| Bal. 275

LIABILITIES

Accounts Payable
| Bal. 13,100

Salary Payable
| (d) 950
| Bal. 950

Unearned Service Revenue
(f) 150 | Bal. 450
| Bal. 300

OWNER'S EQUITY

Gary Lyon, Capital
| Bal. 31,250

Gary Lyon, Withdrawals
Bal. 3,200

REVENUES

Service Revenue
| Bal. 7,000
| (e) 250
| (f) 150
| Bal. 7,400

EXPENSES

Rent Expense
(a) 1,000
Bal. 1,000

Salary Expense
Bal. 950
(d) 950
Bal. 1,900

Supplies Expense
(b) 300
Bal. 300

Amortization Expense—Furniture
(c) 275
Bal. 275

Utilities Expense
Bal. 400

"Grossing Up" the Revenue: Priceline.com and Ventro

Suppose you plan to travel to Australia. You want a cheap airline ticket, and Priceline.com lets you "name your price" for airline tickets and hotel rooms. Your bid of $975 is accepted. Priceline.com makes a profit by keeping the difference between your price and the amount that Priceline.com pays the airline. What should Priceline.com claim as revenue—the fee Priceline.com earns or the entire price of your ticket?

Priceline.com and other Internet service companies are recording as revenue the entire value of the products sold through their sites. In the U.S., the Securities and Exchange Commission (SEC) and the Financial Accounting Standards Board (FASB) call this practice "grossing up" revenue. The practice helps to attract investors and increase the stock price. Grossing up may be legal, but the SEC and the FASB are considering placing restrictions on this practice.

One company that would be adversely affected by a restriction is Ventro, which handles the sale of specialty medical products over the Internet. Ventro's $29 million in grossed-up revenue for 1999 was expected to more than quadruple to $140 million in 2000. Ventro argues that its accounting method is sound since the company assumes various revenue risks: reimbursing cash if a product is returned, bearing credit risk if the customer won't pay, and taking title to the products sold. Yet Ventro never takes actual products into its own inventory and only takes title to the products during the time it takes to ship them. Ventro's suppliers are willing to absorb refund costs and Ventro's blue-chip customers rarely pose credit problems.

If the accounting rulemakers decide that grossing-up is legal, expect to see the value of business-to-business sites like Ventro soar. These cyber deal-makers handle sales for high-ticket items like heavy equipment and chemicals. Currently, most are only booking the fees they get as revenue, but they would certainly claim the entire sale price as revenue if they could.

Based on: Elizabeth McDonald, "Plump from Web Sales, Some Dot-Coms Face Crash Diet of Restriction on Booking Revenue," *Wall Street Journal*, February 28, 2000, p. C4. Jeremy Kahn, "Presto Chango! Sales Are Huge!" *Fortune*, March 20, 2000, pp. 90-96.

The Adjusted Trial Balance

OBJECTIVE 4
Prepare an adjusted trial balance

This chapter began with the trial balance before any adjusting entries—the unadjusted trial balance (Exhibit 3-4). After the adjustments are journalized and posted, the accounts appear as shown in Exhibit 3-9, Panel C. A useful step in preparing the financial statements is to list the accounts, along with their adjusted balances, on an **adjusted trial balance**. This document has the advantage of listing all the accounts and their adjusted balances in a single place. Exhibit 3-10 on page 126 shows the preparation of the adjusted trial balance.

Exhibit 3-10 shows the first six columns of a *work sheet*. We will consider the complete work sheet in Chapter 4. For now, simply note how clearly this format presents the data. The information in the Account Title column and in the Trial Balance columns is drawn directly from the ledger. The two Adjustments columns list the debit and credit adjustments directly across from the appropriate account title. Each adjusting debit is identified by a letter in parentheses that refers to the adjusting entry. For example, the debit labelled (a) on the work sheet refers to the debit adjusting entry of $1,000 to Rent Expense in Panel B of Exhibit 3-9. Likewise for credit adjusting entries, the corresponding credit—labelled (a)—refers to the $1,000 credit to Prepaid Rent.

KEY POINT

The differences between the amounts in the trial balance in Exhibit 3-4 and in the adjusted trial balance of Exhibit 3-10 result from the adjusting entries. If the adjusting entries were not given, you could determine them by computing the differences between the adjusted and unadjusted amounts.

EXHIBIT 3-10

Preparation of Adjusted Trial Balance

AIR & SEA TRAVEL
Preparation of Adjusted Trial Balance
April 30, 2003

Account Title	Trial Balance Debit	Trial Balance Credit	Adjustments Debit	Adjustments Credit	Adjusted Trial Balance Debit	Adjusted Trial Balance Credit
Cash	24,800				24,800	
Accounts receivable	2,250		(e) 250		2,500	
Supplies	700			(b) 300	400	
Prepaid rent	3,000			(a) 1,000	2,000	
Furniture	16,500				16,500	
Accumulated amortization				(c) 275		275
Accounts payable		13,100				13,100
Salary payable				(d) 950		950
Unearned service revenue		450	(f) 150			300
Gary Lyon, capital		31,250				31,250
Gary Lyon, withdrawals	3,200				3,200	
Service revenue		7,000		(e) 250		7,400
				(f) 150		
Rent expense			(a) 1,000		1,000	
Salary expense	950		(d) 950		1,900	
Supplies expense			(b) 300		300	
Amortization expense			(c) 275		275	
Utilities expense	400				400	
	51,800	51,800	2,925	2,925	53,275	53,275

EXHIBIT 3-11

Preparing the Financial Statements of Air & Sea Travel from the Adjusted Trial Balance

Account Title	Adjusted Trial Balance Debit	Adjusted Trial Balance Credit	
Cash	24,800		
Accounts receivable	2,500		
Supplies	400		
Prepaid rent	2,000		
Furniture	16,500		
Accumulated amortization		275	Balance Sheet (Exhibit 3-14)
Accounts payable		13,100	
Salary payable		950	
Unearned service revenue		300	
Gary Lyon, Capital		31,250	Statement of Owner's Equity (Exhibit 3-13)
Gary Lyon, Withdrawals	3,200		
Service revenue		7,400	
Rent expense	1,000		
Salary expense	1,900		
Supplies expense	300		Income Statement (Exhibit 3-12)
Amortization expense	275		
Utilities expense	400		
	53,275	53,275	

The Adjusted Trial Balance columns give the adjusted account balances. Each amount on the adjusted trial balance of Exhibit 3-10 is computed by combining the amounts from the unadjusted trial balance plus or minus the adjustments. For example, Accounts Receivable starts with a debit balance of $2,250. Adding the $250 debit amount from adjusting entry (e) gives Accounts Receivable an adjusted balance of $2,500. As we discussed at the outset of the chapter, Supplies begins with a debit balance of $700. After the $300 credit adjustment, its adjusted balance is $400. More than one entry may affect a single account, as is the case for Service Revenue. If an account is unaffected by the adjustments, it will show the same amount on both the adjusted and unadjusted trial balances. This is true for the Cash, Furniture, Accounts Payable, and Gary Lyon, Withdrawals accounts, to name a few.

Preparing the Financial Statements from the Adjusted Trial Balance

OBJECTIVE 5
Prepare the financial statements from the adjusted trial balance

The April financial statements of Air & Sea Travel can be prepared from the adjusted trial balance. Exhibit 3-11 shows how the accounts are distributed from the adjusted trial balance to three of the four main financial statements. The income statement (Exhibit 3-12) comes from the revenue and expense accounts. The statement of owner's equity (Exhibit 3-13) shows the reasons for the change in the owner's capital account during the period. The balance sheet (Exhibit 3-14) reports the assets, liabilities, and owner's equity. You learned these relationships in Chapter 1.

The financial statements are best prepared in the order shown: the income statement first, followed by the statement of owner's equity and then, the balance sheet. The essential features of all financial statements are:

Heading:
- Name of the entity
- Title of the statement
- Date, or period, covered by the statement

Body of the statement

It is customary to list expenses in descending order by amount, as shown in Exhibit 3-12, or in alphabetical order. However, Miscellaneous Expense, a catch-all account for expenses that do not fit another category, is usually reported last. Miscellaneous Expense should be a relatively low dollar amount. If it is not, new expense accounts should be created.

Relationships among the Three Financial Statements

The arrows in Exhibits 3-12, 3-13, and 3-14, illustrate the relationship among the income statement, the statement of owner's equity, and the balance sheet. (The relationships among the financial statements were introduced in Chapter 1, page 21.) Consider why the income statement is prepared first and the balance sheet last.

1. The income statement reports net income or net loss, calculated by subtracting expenses from revenues. Because revenues and expenses are owner's equity accounts, their net figure is then transferred to the statement of owner's equity. Note that net income in Exhibit 3-12, $3,525, increases owner's equity in Exhibit 3-13. A net loss would decrease owner's equity.

2. Capital is a balance sheet account, so the ending balance in the statement of owner's equity is transferred to the balance sheet. This amount is the final balancing element of the balance sheet. To solidify your understanding of this relationship, trace the $31,575 figure from Exhibit 3-13 to Exhibit 3-14.

EXHIBIT 3-12

Income Statement

AIR & SEA TRAVEL Income Statement For the Month Ended April 30, 2003		
Revenue:		
Service revenue		$7,400
Expenses:		
Salary expense	$1,900	
Rent expense	1,000	
Utilities expense	400	
Supplies expense	300	
Amortization expense	275	
Total expenses		3,875
Net income		$3,525

EXHIBIT 3-13

Statement of Owner's Equity

AIR & SEA TRAVEL Statement of Owner's Equity For the Month Ended April 30, 2003	
Gary Lyon, capital, April 1, 2003	$31,250
Add: Net income	3,525
	34,775
Less: Withdrawals	3,200
Gary Lyon, capital, April 30, 2003	$31,575

1

EXHIBIT 3-14

Balance Sheet

AIR & SEA TRAVEL Balance Sheet April 30, 2003				
Assets			**Liabilities**	
Cash		$24,800	Accounts payable	$13,100
Accounts receivable		2,500	Salary payable	950
Supplies		400	Unearned service	
Prepaid rent		2,000	revenue	300
Furniture	$16,500		Total liabilities	14,350
Less: Accumulated				
amortization	275	16,225	**Owner's Equity**	
			Gary Lyon, capital	31,575
			Total liabilities and	
Total assets		$45,925	owner's equity	$45,925

2

You may be wondering why the total assets on the balance sheet ($45,925 in Exhibit 3-14) do not equal the total debits on the adjusted trial balance ($53,275 in Exhibit 3-11). Likewise, the total liabilities and owner's equity do not equal the total credits on the adjusted trial balance ($53,275 in Exhibit 3-11). The reason for these differences is that Accumulated Amortization and Gary Lyon, Withdrawals are contra accounts. Recall that contra accounts are *subtracted* from their companion accounts on the balance sheet. However, on the adjusted trial balance, contra accounts are *added* as a debit or credit in their respective columns.

Ethical Issues in Accrual Accounting

Like most other aspects of life, accounting poses ethical challenges. At the most basic level, accountants must be honest in their work. Only with honest and complete information, including accounting data, can people expect to make wise decisions. An example will illustrate the importance of ethics in accrual accounting.

Futons Unlimited is a small business started three years ago by Andrea McGinty and Marcia Lamb in Regina. The company sells futons and related bedding products; its target market is college and university students. The company has been quite successful and so the two owners decide to open a branch in Saskatoon. They need to borrow $100,000 for inventory and for prepaid rent on a store they have found. Assume that Futons Unlimited understated expenses purposely in order to inflate net income as reported on the company's income statement. A banker could be tricked into lending money to Futons Unlimited. Then if Futons Unlimited could not repay the loan, the bank would lose money—all because the banker relied on incorrect accounting information.

Accrual accounting provides several opportunities for unethical accounting. Recall from earlier in this chapter that amortization expense is an estimated figure. No business can foresee exactly how long its buildings and equipment will last, so accountants must estimate these assets' useful lives. Accountants then record amortization on capital assets over their *estimated* useful lives. A dishonest proprietor could buy a five-year asset and amortize it over 10 years. For each of the first five years, the company will report less amortization expense, and more net income, than it should. People who rely on the company's financial statements, such as bank lenders, can be deceived into doing business with the company. You may reply, "But the company will be recording amortization for the full 10 years, including the last five years after the asset is worn out. Net income will be lower in the last five years, and this lower net income will offset the higher net income reported during the first five years." This is true, but the damage to the company's reputation from reporting too much net income too quickly will remain. Accounting information must be honest and complete—completely ethical—to serve its intended purpose. As you progress through introductory accounting, you will see other situations that challenge the ethics of accountants.

The cash basis of accounting poses fewer ethical challenges because cash is not an estimated figure. Either the company has the cash, or it does not. Therefore, the amount of cash a company reports is rarely disputed. By contrast, adjusting entries for accrued expenses, accrued revenues, and amortization often must be estimated. Whenever there is an estimate, the accountant must often deal with pressure from managers or owners of the business to use the adjusting process to make the company look different from its true condition. The rules of conduct of the various professional accounting associations (discussed in Chapter 1) prohibit accountants from being associated with false or misleading financial information. Even with added ethical challenges, the accrual basis provides more complete accounting information than the cash basis. That is why accounting rests on the accrual basis.

The Decision Guidelines feature provides a map of the adjusting process that leads up to the adjusted trial balance.

DECISION GUIDELINES | **Measuring Business Income: The Adjusting Process**

Decision	Guidelines
Which basis of accounting better measures income (revenues – expenses)?	*Accrual basis*, because it provides more complete reports of operating performance
How to measure Revenues? Expenses?	Revenue principle Matching principle
Where to start with the measurement of income at the end of the period?	Unadjusted trial balance, usually referred to simply as the *trial balance*
How to update the accounts for preparation of the financial statements?	*Adjusting entries* at the end of the accounting period
What are the categories of adjusting entries?	Prepaid expenses Amortization of capital assets Accrued expenses Accrued revenues Unearned revenues
How do the adjusting entries differ from other journal entries?	1. Adjusting entries are usually made at the end of the accounting period. 2. Adjusting entries never affect cash (except to correct errors). 3. All adjusting entries debit or credit • At least one *income statement* account (a **Revenue** or an **Expense**) and • At least one *balance sheet* account (an **Asset** or a **Liability**)
Where are the accounts with their adjusted balances summarized?	*Adjusted trial balance*, which becomes the basis for preparing the financial statements

for Your Review

The trial balance of O'Malley's Service Company pertains to December 31, 2003, which is the end of its year-long accounting period.

O'MALLEY'S SERVICE COMPANY
Trial Balance
December 31, 2003

Cash	$ 198,000	
Accounts receivable	370,000	
Supplies	6,000	
Furniture and fixtures	100,000	
Accumulated amortization—furniture and fixtures		$ 40,000
Building	210,000	
Accumulated amortization—building		130,000
Land	50,000	
Accounts payable		380,000
Salary payable		
Unearned service revenue		45,000
Terry O'Malley, capital		293,000
Terry O'Malley, withdrawals	65,000	
Service revenue		286,000
Salary expense	172,000	
Supplies expense		
Amortization expense—furniture and fixtures		
Amortization expense—building		
Miscellaneous expense	3,000	
Total	$1,174,000	$1,174,000

Data needed for the adjusting entries include:

a. A count of supplies shows $2,000 of unused supplies on hand on December 31.

b. Amortization for the year on furniture and fixtures, $20,000.

c. Amortization for the year on building, $10,000.

d. Salaries owed but not yet paid, $5,000.

e. Accrued service revenue, $12,000.

f. Of the $45,000 balance of unearned service revenue, $32,000 was earned during the year.

Required

1. Open the ledger accounts with their unadjusted balances using T-account format.

2. Journalize O'Malley's Service Company's adjusting entries at December 31, 2003. Key entries by letter as in Exhibit 3-9.

3. Post the adjusting entries into the T-accounts.

4. Write the trial balance on a work sheet, enter the adjusting entries, and prepare an adjusted trial balance, as shown in Exhibit 3-10.

5. Prepare the income statement, the statement of owner's equity, and the balance sheet. Draw the arrows linking these three statements.

Solution to Review Problem

Requirements 1 and 3

ASSETS

Cash

| Bal. 198,000 | |

Accounts Receivable

Bal. 370,000	
(e) 12,000	
Bal. 382,000	

Supplies

| Bal. 6,000 | (a) 4,000 |
| Bal. 2,000 | |

Furniture and Fixtures

| Bal. 100,000 | |

Accumulated Amortization—Furniture and Fixtures

	Bal. 40,000
	(b) 20,000
	Bal. 60,000

Building

| Bal. 210,000 | |

Accumulated Amortization—Building

	Bal. 130,000
	(c) 10,000
	Bal. 140,000

Land

| Bal. 50,000 | |

LIABILITIES

Accounts Payable

| | Bal. 380,000 |

Salary Payable

| | (d) 5,000 |
| | Bal. 5,000 |

Unearned Service Revenue

| (f) 32,000 | Bal. 45,000 |
| | Bal. 13,000 |

OWNER'S EQUITY

Terry O'Malley, Capital

| | Bal. 293,000 |

Terry O'Malley, Withdrawals

| Bal. 65,000 | |

REVENUE

Service Revenue

	Bal. 286,000
	(e) 12,000
	(f) 32,000
	Bal. 330,000

EXPENSES

Salary Expense

Bal. 172,000	
(d) 5,000	
Bal. 177,000	

Supplies Expense

| (a) 4,000 | |
| Bal. 4,000 | |

Amortization Expense—Furniture and Fixtures

| (b) 20,000 | |
| Bal. 20,000 | |

Amortization Expense—Building

| (c) 10,000 | |
| Bal. 10,000 | |

Miscellaneous Expense

| Bal. 3,000 | |

Requirement 2

2003

a. Dec. 31 Supplies Expense.. 4,000
     Supplies...   4,000
     To record supplies used ($6,000 – $2,000).

b. Dec. 31 Amortization Expense—Furniture and Fixtures 20,000
     Accumulated Amortization—Furniture
     and Fixtures...   20,000
     To record amortization expense on furniture and
     fixtures.

c. Dec. 31 Amortization Expense—Building 10,000
     Accumulated Amortization—Building   10,000
     To record amortization expense on building.

d. Dec. 31 Salary Expense 5,000
     Salary Payable...   5,000
     To accrue salary expense.

e. Dec. 31 Accounts Receivable 12,000
     Service Revenue..   12,000
     To accrue service revenue.

f. Dec. 31 Unearned Service Revenue 32,000
     Service Revenue..   32,000
     To record unearned service revenue that has been
     earned.

Requirement 4

O'MALLEY'S SERVICE COMPANY
Preparation of Adjusted Trial Balance
December 31, 2003

Account Title	Trial Balance Debit	Trial Balance Credit	Adjustments Debit	Adjustments Credit	Adjusted Trial Balance Debit	Adjusted Trial Balance Credit
Cash	198,000				198,000	
Accounts receivable	370,000		(e) 12,000		382,000	
Supplies	6,000			(a) 4,000	2,000	
Furniture and fixtures	100,000				100,000	
Accumulated amortization —furniture and fixtures		40,000		(b) 20,000		60,000
Building	210,000				210,000	
Accumulated amortization —building		130,000		(c) 10,000		140,000
Land	50,000				50,000	
Accounts payable		380,000				380,000
Salary payable				(d) 5,000		5,000
Unearned service revenue		45,000	(f) 32,000			13,000
Terry O'Malley, capital		293,000				293,000
Terry O'Malley, withdrawals	65,000				65,000	
Service revenue		286,000		(e) 12,000 (f) 32,000		330,000
Salary expense	172,000		(d) 5,000		177,000	
Supplies expense			(a) 4,000		4,000	
Amortization expense —furniture and fixtures			(b) 20,000		20,000	
Amortization expense —building			(c) 10,000		10,000	
Miscellaneous expense	3,000				3,000	
	1,174,000	1,174,000	83,000	83,000	1,221,000	1,221,000

Requirement 5

O'MALLEY'S SERVICE COMPANY
Income Statement
For the Year Ended December 31, 2003

Revenues:		
Service revenue...		$330,000
Expenses:		
Salary expense	$177,000	
Amortization expense—furniture and fixtures	20,000	
Amortization expense—building	10,000	
Supplies expense	4,000	
Miscellaneous expense	3,000	
Total expenses...		214,000
Net income		$116,000

(1)

O'MALLEY'S SERVICE COMPANY
Statement of Owner's Equity
For the Year Ended December 31, 2003

Terry O'Malley, capital, January 1, 2003...	$293,000
Add: Net income	116,000
	409,000
Less: Withdrawals	65,000
Terry O'Malley, capital, December 31, 2003..	$344,000

O'MALLEY'S SERVICE COMPANY
Balance Sheet
December 31, 2003

(2)

Assets			**Liabilities**		
Cash.............................		$198,000	Accounts payable		$380,000
Accounts			Salary payable...........................		5,000
receivable..................		382,000	Unearned service revenue		13,000
Supplies		2,000	Total liabilities.......................		398,000
Furniture					
and fixtures	$100,000		**Owner's Equity**		
Less: Accumulated			Terry O'Malley, capital		344,000
amortization	60,000	40,000			
Building	$210,000				
Less: Accumulated					
amortization	140,000	70,000			
Land		50,000			
			Total liabilities and		
Total assets		$742,000	owner's equity.....................		$742,000

Summary

1. **Distinguish accrual-basis accounting from cash-basis accounting.** In *accrual-basis accounting*, business events are recorded as they occur. In *cash-basis accounting*, only those events that affect cash are recorded. The cash basis omits important events such as purchases and sales of assets on account. It also distorts the financial statements by labelling as expenses those cash payments that have long-term effects, such as the purchases of buildings and equipment. Some small organizations use cash-basis accounting, but the generally accepted method is the accrual basis.

2. **Apply the revenue and matching principles.** Businesses divide time into definite periods—such as a month, a quarter, and a year—to report the entity's financial statements. The year is the basic *accounting period*, but companies prepare financial statements as often as they need the information. Accountants have developed the *revenue principle* to determine when to record revenue and the amount of revenue to record. The *matching principle* guides the accounting for expenses. It directs accountants to match expenses against the revenues earned during a particular period of time.

3. **Make adjusting entries at the end of the accounting period.** *Adjusting entries* are a result of the accrual basis of accounting. Made at the end of the period, these entries update the accounts for preparation of the financial statements. Adjusting entries can be divided into five categories: *prepaid expenses, amortization, accrued expenses, accrued revenues,* and *unearned revenues.*

4. **Prepare an adjusted trial balance.** To prepare the *adjusted trial balance,* enter the adjusting entries next to the *unadjusted trial balance* and compute each account's balance.

5. **Prepare the financial statements from the adjusted trial balance.** The adjusted trial balance can be used to prepare the financial statements. The three financial statements are related as follows: Income, shown on the *income statement,* increases the owner's capital, which also appears on the *statement of owner's equity.* The ending balance of capital is the last amount reported on the *balance sheet.*

Self-Study Questions

Test your understanding of the chapter by marking the correct answer for each of the following questions:

1. Accrual-basis accounting (*pp. 109–110*)
   a. Results in higher income than cash-basis accounting
   b. Leads to the reporting of more complete information than does cash-basis accounting
   c. Is not acceptable under GAAP
   d. Omits adjusting entries at the end of the period

2. Under the revenue principle, revenue is recorded (*p. 110*)
   a. At the earliest acceptable time
   b. At the latest acceptable time
   c. After it has been earned, but not before
   d. At the end of the accounting period

3. The matching principle provides guidance in accounting for (*pp. 111–112*)
   a. Expenses   c. Assets
   b. Owner's equity   d. Liabilities

4. Adjusting entries (*pp. 112–114*)
   a. Assign revenues to the period in which they are earned
   b. Help to properly measure the period's net income or net loss
   c. Bring asset and liability accounts to correct balances
   d. All of the above

5. A building-cleaning firm began November with supplies of $160. During the month, the firm purchased supplies of $290. At November 30, supplies on hand total $210. Supplies expense for the period is (*pp. 115–116*)
   a. $210   c. $290
   b. $240   d. $450

6. A building that cost $120,000 has accumulated amortization of $50,000. The carrying value of the building is (*pp. 118–119*)
   a. $50,000   c. $120,000
   b. $70,000   d. $170,000

7. The adjusting entry to accrue salary expense (*pp. 119–120*)
   a. Debits Salary Expense and credits Cash
   b. Debits Salary Payable and credits Salary Expense
   c. Debits Salary Payable and credits Cash
   d. Debits Salary Expense and credits Salary Payable

8. A business received cash of $3,000 in advance for service that will be provided later. The cash receipt entry debited Cash and credited Unearned Revenue for $3,000. At the end of the period, $1,100 is still unearned. The adjusting entry for this situation will (*pp. 121–122*)
   a. Debit Unearned Revenue and credit Revenue for $1,900
   b. Debit Unearned Revenue and credit Revenue for $1,100
   c. Debit Revenue and credit Unearned Revenue for $1,900
   d. Debit Revenue and credit Unearned Revenue for $1,100

9. The links among the financial statements are (pp. 127–129)
   a. Net income from the income statement to the statement of owner's equity
   b. Ending capital from the statement of owner's equity to the balance sheet
   c. Both a and b above
   d. None of the above

10. Accumulated Amortization is reported on the (p. 128)
    a. Balance sheet
    b. Income statement
    c. Statement of owner's equity
    d. Both a and b

Answers to the Self-Study Questions follow the Similar Accounting Terms.

Accounting Vocabulary

Accrual-basis accounting (p. 109)
Accrued expense (p. 119)
Accrued revenue (p. 120)
Accumulated amortization (p. 117)
Adjusted trial balance (p. 125)
Adjusting entry (p. 113)
Amortization (p. 116)
Capital asset (p. 116)
Carrying value (of a capital asset) (p. 118)

Cash-basis accounting (p. 109)
Contra account (p. 117)
Deferred revenue (p. 121)
Matching principle (p. 111)
Prepaid expense (p. 114)
Revenue principle (p. 110)
Time-period concept (p. 112)
Unearned revenue (p. 121)

Similar Accounting Terms

Amortization	Depreciation; depletion
Capital asset	Plant asset; fixed asset
Carrying value	Book value
Deferred	Unearned

Assignment Material

Questions

1. Distinguish accrual-basis accounting from cash-basis accounting.

2. How long is the basic accounting period? What is a fiscal year? What is an interim period?

3. What two questions does the revenue principle help answer?

4. Briefly explain the matching principle.

5. What is the purpose of making adjusting entries?

6. Why are adjusting entries usually made at the end of the accounting period, not during the period?

7. Name five categories of adjusting entries and give an example of each.

8. Do all adjusting entries affect the net income or net loss of the period? Include the definition of an adjusting entry.

9. Why must the balance of Supplies be adjusted at the end of the period?

10. Manning Supply Company pays $3,600 for an insurance policy that covers three years. At the end of the first year, the balance of its Prepaid Insurance account contains two elements. What are the two elements, and what is the correct amount of each?

11. The title Prepaid Expense suggests that this type of account is an expense. If so, explain why. If it is not, what type of account is it?

12. What is a contra account? Identify the contra

account introduced in this chapter, along with the account's normal balance.

13. The manager of Quickie-Pickie, a convenience store, presents the company's balance sheet to a banker to obtain a loan. The balance sheet reports that the company's capital assets have a carrying value of $135,000 and accumulated amortization of $65,000. What does *carrying value* of a capital asset mean? What was the cost of the capital assets?

14. Give the entry to record accrued interest revenue of $800.

15. Why is an unearned revenue a liability? Give an example.

16. Identify the types of accounts (assets, liabilities, and so on) debited and credited for each of the five types of adjusting entries.

17. What purposes does the adjusted trial balance serve?

18. Explain the relationship among the income statement, the statement of owner's equity, and the balance sheet.

19. Bellevue Company failed to record the following adjusting entries at December 31, the end of its fiscal year: (a) accrued expenses, $1,000; (b) accrued revenues, $1,700; and (c) amortization, $2,000. Did these omissions cause net income for the year to be understated or overstated and by what overall amount?

Exercises

Exercise 3-1 *Cash-basis versus accrual-basis accounting* **(Obj. 1)**

Como Lake Lodge had the following selected transactions during January:

Jan.		
	1	Paid cash for rent for January, February, and March, $3,900.
	5	Paid electricity expenses, $600.
	9	Received cash for the day's room rentals, $2,100.
	14	Paid cash for six television sets, $4,500. They will last three years.
	23	Served a banquet, receiving a note receivable, $1,800.
	31	Made an adjusting entry for January's rent (from January 1).
	31	Accrued salary expense, $1,350.

Show how each transaction would be handled using the cash basis and the accrual basis of accounting. Under each column give the amount of revenue or expense for January. Journal entries are not required. Use the following format for your answer, and show your computations:

Como Lake Lodge —Amount of Revenue or Expense for January

Date	Cash Basis	Accrual Basis

Exercise 3-2 *Applying accounting concepts and principles* **(Obj. 2)**

Identify the accounting concept or principle that gives the most direction on how to account for each of the following situations:

a. Expenses of the period total $6,000. This amount should be subtracted from revenue to compute the period's income.

b. Expenses of $2,000 must be accrued at the end of the period to measure income properly.

c. A customer states her intention to switch travel agencies. Should the new travel agency record revenue based on this intention?

d. The owner of a business desires monthly financial statements to measure the financial progress of the entity on an ongoing basis.

Exercise 3-3 *Applying the revenue and matching principles; accrual basis versus cash basis* **(Obj. 1, 2)**

U-Stor-It Co. operates approximately 250 miniwarehouses across Canada. The company's headquarters are in Burnaby, B.C. During 2003, U-Stor-It earned rental revenue of $15.0 million and collected cash of $16.0 million from customers. Total expenses for 2003 were $9.0 million, of which U-Stor-It paid $8.5 million.

Required

1. Apply the revenue principle and the matching principle to compute U-Stor-It Co.'s net income for 2003.
2. Identify the information that you did not use to compute U-Stor-It Co.'s net income. Give the reason for not using the information.

Exercise 3-4   *Applying accounting concepts   (Obj. 2)*

Write a memo to your supervisor explaining in your own words the concept of amortization as it is used in accounting. Use the following format:

Date:	(fill in)
To:	Supervisor
From:	(Student Name)
Subject:	The concept of amortization

Exercise 3-5   *Allocating prepaid expense to the asset and expense   (Obj. 2, 3)*

Compute the amounts indicated by question marks for each of the following Prepaid Insurance situations. For situations 1 and 2, journalize the needed entry. Consider each situation separately.

	Situation			
	1	2	3	4
Beginning Prepaid Insurance	$ 600	$1,000	$1,800	$1,200
Payments for Prepaid Insurance during the year	2,800	?	2,200	?
Total amount to account for	?	?	4,000	2,600
Ending Prepaid Insurance	400	800	?	1,000
Insurance Expense	$?	$1,400	$2,800	$1,600

Exercise 3-6   *Journalizing adjusting entries   (Obj. 3)*

Journalize the entries for the following adjustments at December 31, the end of the accounting period:

a. Employee salaries owed for Monday and Tuesday of a five-day workweek; weekly payroll, $15,000.

b. Prepaid insurance expired, $600.

c. Interest revenue accrued, $4,000.

d. Unearned service revenue that becomes earned, $1,600.

e. Amortization, $4,800.

Exercise 3-7   *Analyzing the effects of adjustments on net income   (Obj. 3)*

Suppose the adjustments required in Exercise 3-6 were not made. Compute the overall overstatement or understatement of net income as a result of the omission of these adjustments.

Exercise 3-8   *Journalizing adjusting entries*   *(Obj. 3)*

Journalize the adjusting entry needed at December 31 for each of the following in-dependent situations.

a. On July 1, when we collected $12,000 rent in advance, we debited Cash and cred-ited Unearned Rent Revenue. The tenant was paying for one year's rent in advance.

b. The business owes interest expense of $1,800 that it will pay early in the next period.

c. Interest revenue of $1,400 has been earned but not yet received on a $20,000 note receivable held by the business.

d. Salary expense is $2,000 per day—Monday through Friday—and the business pays employees each Friday. This year December 31 falls on a Wednesday.

e. The unadjusted balance of the Supplies account is $4,500. The total cost of sup-plies remaining on hand on December 31 is $1,500.

f. Equipment was purchased last year at a cost of $50,000. The equipment's useful life is four years. It will have no value after four years.

g. On September 1, when we paid $1,800 for a one-year insurance policy, we deb-ited Prepaid Insurance and credited Cash.

Exercise 3-9   *Recording adjustments in T-accounts*   *(Obj. 3)*

The accounting records of Conference Planners include the following unadjusted bal-ances at May 31: Accounts Receivable, $1,800; Supplies, $900; Salary Payable, $0; Unearned Service Revenue, $800; Service Revenue, $29,400; Salary Expense, $2,400; and Supplies Expense, $0.

   The company's accountant develops the following data for the May 31 adjusting entries:

a. Supplies on hand, $150.

b. Salary owed to employee, $900.

c. Service revenue accrued, $525.

d. Unearned service revenue that has been earned, $300.

Open T-accounts as needed and record the adjustments directly in the accounts, keying each adjustment amount by letter. Show each account's adjusted balance. Journal entries are not required.

Exercise 3-10   *Explaining unearned revenues*   *(Obj. 3)*

Write a paragraph to explain why unearned revenues are liabilities rather than rev-enues. In your explanation use the following actual example: *Maclean's Magazine* collects cash from subscribers in advance and later mails the magazines to sub-scribers over a one-year period. Explain what happens to the unearned subscription revenue over the course of a year as the magazines are mailed to subscribers. Into what other account does the unearned subscription revenue go? Give the adjusting entry that *Maclean's Magazine* would make to record the earning of $20,000 of Subscription Revenue. Include an explanation for the entry.

Exercise 3-11   *Adjusting the accounts*   *(Obj. 3, 4)*

The adjusted trial balance of Total Express Service is incomplete. Enter the adjust-ment amounts directly in the adjustment columns of the text. Service Revenue is the only account affected by more than one adjustment.

	TOTAL EXPRESS SERVICE Preparation of Adjusted Trial Balance May 31, 2003					
	Trial Balance		Adjustments		Adjusted Trial Balance	
Account Title	**Debit**	**Credit**	**Debit**	**Credit**	**Debit**	**Credit**
Cash	6,000				6,000	
Accounts receivable	13,000				14,200	
Supplies	2,080				1,600	
Office furniture	64,600				64,600	
Accumulated amortization		28,080				28,800
Salary payable						1,800
Unearned revenue		1,800				1,380
T. Owner, capital		52,720				52,720
T. Owner, withdrawals	12,000				12,000	
Service revenue		23,260				24,880
Salary expense	5,380				7,180	
Rent expense	2,800				2,800	
Amortization expense					720	
Supplies expense					480	
	105,860	105,860			109,580	109,580

Exercise 3-12   *Journalizing adjustments*   **(Obj. 3, 4)**

Make journal entries for the adjustments that would complete the preparation of the adjusted trial balance in Exercise 3-11. Date the entries and include explanations.

Exercise 3-13   *Explaining the adjusted trial balance*   **(Obj. 4)**

Write a business memorandum to your supervisor explaining the difference between the unadjusted amounts and the adjusted amounts in Exhibit 3-10, page 126. Use Accounts Receivable in your explanation. If necessary, refer back to the discussion of Accrued Revenues that begins on page 120.

Business memos are formatted as follows:

Date: (fill in)

To: Supervisor

From: (Student Name)

Subject: Difference between the *unadjusted* and the *adjusted* amounts on an adjusted trial balance.

Exercise 3-14   *Preparing the financial statements*   **(Obj. 5)**

Refer to the adjusted trial balance in Exercise 3-11. Prepare Total Express Service's income statement and statement of owner's equity for the month ended May 31, 2003, and its balance sheet on that date. Draw the arrows linking the three statements.

Exercise 3-15   *Preparing the financial statements*   **(Obj. 5)**

The accountant for Bernice Ma's business, Ma IT Knowledgeworks has posted adjusting entries (a) through (e) to the accounts at December 31, 2003. Selected balance sheet accounts and all the revenues and expenses of the entity follow in T-account form:

Accounts Receivable		Supplies		Accumulated Amortization —Furniture	
69,000		12,000	(a) 3,000		15,000
(e) 13,500				(b) 6,000

Accumulated Amortization —Electronic Equipment		Salaries Payable		Service Revenue	
	99,000		(d) 4,500		405,000
	(c) 15,000				(e) 13,500

Salary Expense		Supplies Expense		Amortization Expense— Furniture		Amortization Expense— Electronic Equipment	
84,000		(a) 3,000		(b) 6,000		(c) 15,000	
(d) 4,500							

Required

1. Prepare the income statement of Ma IT Knowledgeworks for the year ended December 31, 2003. List expenses in order from the largest to the smallest.
2. Were the company's 2003 operations successful? Give the reason for your answer.

Exercise 3-16 *Preparing the statement of owner's equity* *(Obj. 5)*

24-Hour Copy Centre began the year on January 1, 2003, with capital of $105,000. On July 12, 2003, Eric Greer (the owner) invested $12,000 cash in the business. On September 26, 2003, he transferred to the company land valued at $70,000. The income statement for the year ended December 31, 2003, reported a net loss of $28,000. During this fiscal year, Greer withdrew $1,500 monthly for personal use.

Required

1. Prepare the copy centre's statement of owner's equity for the year ended December 31, 2003.
2. Did the owner's equity of the business increase or decrease during the year? What caused this change?

Serial Exercise

Exercise 3-17 continues the Anya Perreault Architects situation begun in Exercise 2-15 of Chapter 2.

Exercise 3-17 *Adjusting the accounts, preparing an adjusted trial balance, and preparing the financial statements* *(Obj. 3, 4, 5)*

Refer to Exercise 2-15 of Chapter 2. Start from the trial balance and the posted T-accounts that Anya Perreault Architects prepared for her architectural practice at December 18. Make sure the account balances in your trial balance and T-accounts match those in the trial balance at December 18, 2002, shown on the next page.

ANYA PERREAULT ARCHITECTS
Trial Balance
December 18, 2002

Cash	$11,300	
Accounts receivable	1,700	
Supplies	300	
Equipment	3,000	
Furniture	5,600	
Accounts payable		$ 5,900
Anya Perreault, capital		14,000
Anya Perreault, withdrawals		
Service revenue		2,700
Rent expense	500	
Utilities expense	200	
Salary expense		
Total	$22,600	$22,600

Later in December, the business completed these transactions:

Dec. 21 Received $1,200 in advance for architectural work to be performed evenly over the next 30 days.
   21 Hired a secretary to be paid $2,100 salary on the 21st day of each month.
   26 Paid for the supplies purchased on December 5.
   28 Collected $600 from the consulting client of December 18.
   30 Anya Perreault withdrew $1,600 cash for personal use.

Required

1. Open these T-accounts: Accumulated Amortization—Equipment; Accumulated Amortization—Furniture; Salary Payable; Unearned Service Revenue; Amortization Expense—Equipment; Amortization Expense—Furniture; Supplies Expense.

2. Journalize the transactions of December 21 through 30.

3. Post to the T-accounts, keying all items by date.

4. Prepare a trial balance at December 31. Also set up columns for the adjustments and for the adjusted trial balance, as illustrated in Exhibit 3-10.

5. At December 31, the company gathers the following information for the adjusting entries:

   a. Accrued service revenue, $600.

   b. Earned a portion of the service revenue collected in advance on December 21.

   c. Supplies remaining on hand at December 31, $100.

   d. Amortization expense—equipment, $50; furniture, $60.

   e. Accrued expense for secretary salary.

   Make these adjustments directly in the adjustments columns, and complete the adjusted trial balance at December 31.

6. Journalize and post the adjusting entries. Denote each adjusting amount as *Adj.* and an account balance as *Bal.*

7. Prepare the income statement and statement of owner's equity of Anya Perreault Architects for the month ended December 31, 2002 and prepare the balance sheet at that date.

Challenge Exercises

Exercise 3-18 *Computing the amount of revenue* **(Obj. 3)**

Lei Ma Enterprises aids Singaporean students upon their arrival in Canada. Paid by the Singaporean government, Lei Ma collects some service revenue in advance. In other cases Lei Ma Enterprises receives cash after performing relocation services. At the end of August—a particularly busy period—Lei Ma's books show the following:

	July 31	August 31
Accounts receivable	$4,400	$5,000
Unearned service revenue	2,400	800

During August, Lei Ma Enterprises received cash of $8,000 from the Singaporean government. How much service revenue did the business earn during August? Show your work.

Exercise 3-19 *Computing cash amounts* **(Obj. 3)**

For the situation of Exercise 3-18, assume the service revenue of Lei Ma Enterprises was $11,800 during August. How much cash did the business collect from the Singaporean government that month? Show your work.

Beyond the Numbers

Beyond the Numbers 3-1

Suppose a new management team is in charge of Cool Waters Inc., a micro-brewery. Assume Cool Waters Inc.'s new top executives rose through the company ranks in the sales and marketing departments and have little appreciation for the details of accounting. Consider the following conversation between two executives:

Lee Stice, President: "I want to avoid the hassle of adjusting the books every time we need financial statements. Sooner or later we receive cash for all our revenues, and we pay cash for all our expenses. I can understand cash transactions, but all these accruals confuse me. If I cannot understand *our own* accounting, I'm fairly certain the average person who invests in our company cannot understand it either. Let's start recording only our cash transactions. I bet it won't make any difference to anyone."

Jan Bond, Chief Financial Officer: "Sounds good to me. This will save me lots of headaches. I'll implement the new policy immediately."

Write a business memo to the company president giving your response to the new policy. Identify at least five individual items (such as specific accounts) in the financial statements that will be reported incorrectly. Will outside investors care? Use the format of a business memo given with Exercise 3-13 on page 140.

Ethical Issue

The net income of Adkin's, a specialty store, decreased sharply during 2003. Mary Adkin, owner of the store, anticipates the need for a bank loan in 2004. Late in 2003, she instructed the accountant to record a $12,300 sale of furniture to the Adkin family, even though the goods will not be shipped from the manufacturer until January 2004. Adkin also told the accountant not to make the following December 31, 2003 adjusting entries:

Salaries owed to employees	$13,500
Prepaid insurance that has expired	600

Required

1. Compute the overall effect of these transactions on the store's reported income for 2003.

2. Why did Adkin take this action? Is this action ethical? Give your reason, identifying the parties helped and the parties harmed by Adkin's action.

3. As a personal friend, what advice would you give *the accountant*?

Problems (Group A)

Problem 3-1A   *Cash basis versus accrual basis*   **(Obj. 1, 2)**

Armitage Office Design had the following selected transactions during October:

Oct.		
	1	Paid for insurance for October through December, $900.
	4	Performed design service on account, $1,500.
	5	Purchased office furniture on account, $225.
	8	Paid advertising expense, $450.
	11	Purchased office equipment for cash, $1,200.
	19	Performed design services and received cash, $1,050.
	24	Collected $600 on account for the October 4 service.
	26	Paid account payable from October 5.
	29	Paid salary expense, $1,550.
	31	Recorded adjusting entry for October insurance expense (see Oct. 1).
	31	Debited unearned revenue and credited revenue to adjust these accounts, $900.

Required

1. Show how each transaction would be accounted for using the cash basis and the accrual basis. Under each column give the amount of revenue or expense for October. Journal entries are not required. Use the following format for your answer, and show your computations:

Armitage Office Design—Amount of Revenue or Expense for October

Date	Cash Basis	Accrual Basis

2. Compute October net income or net loss under each method.

3. Indicate which measure of net income or net loss is preferable. Give your reason.

Problem 3-2A   *Applying accounting principles*   **(Obj. 2, 3)**

As the controller of Wang Security Systems, you have hired a new bookkeeper, whom you must train. She objects to making an adjusting entry for accrued salaries at the end of the period. She reasons, "We will pay the salaries soon. Why not wait until payment to record the expense? In the end, the result will be the same." Write a business memo to explain to the bookkeeper why the adjusting entry for accrued salary expense is needed.

This is the format of the business memo:

Date: (fill in) _____

To: New Bookkeeper

From: (Student Name) _____

Subject: Why the adjusting entry for salary expense is needed

Problem 3-3A   *Journalizing adjusting entries*   *(Obj. 3)*

Journalize the adjusting entry needed on December 31, the end of the current accounting period, for each of the following independent cases affecting Bruce Telecommunications:

a. Each Friday the company pays its employees for the current week's work. The amount of the payroll is $12,000 for a five-day workweek. The current accounting period ends on Thursday.

b. Bruce Telecommunications has received notes receivable from some clients for professional services. During the current year, Bruce Telecommunications has earned interest revenue of $510, which will be received next year.

c. The beginning balance of Supplies was $5,400. During the year the company purchased supplies costing $7,590, and at December 31 the inventory of supplies remaining on hand is $2,910.

d. The company is developing a wireless communication system for a large company, and the client paid Bruce $108,000 at the start of the project. Bruce recorded this amount as Unearned Consulting Revenue. The development will take several months to complete. Bruce executives estimate that the company has earned three-fourths of the total fee during the current year.

e. Amortization for the current year includes: Office Furniture, $16,500 and Design Equipment, $19,080. Make a compound entry.

f. Details of Prepaid Insurance are shown in the account:

Prepaid Insurance

Jan. 1	Bal.	900
Apr. 30		1,350
Oct. 31		1,350

Bruce Telecommunications pays semiannual insurance premiums (the payment for insurance coverage is called a *premium*) on April 30 and October 31. At December 31, part of the last payment is still available to cover January to April of the next year.

Problem 3-4A   *Analyzing and journalizing adjustments*   *(Obj. 3)*

Nizar Consulting's unadjusted and adjusted trial balances at December 31, 2004, appear at the top of page 146.

Required
Journalize the adjusting entries that account for the differences between the two trial balances.

Problem 3-5A   *Journalizing and posting adjustments to T-accounts; preparing and using the adjusted trial balance and the financial statements*   *(Obj. 3, 4)*

The trial balance of Lam Laser Printing at December 31, 2003, appears at the bottom of page 146. The data needed for the month-end adjustments appear below.

Adjustment data:

a. Unearned revenue still remaining to be earned at December 31, $2,505.

b. Prepaid rent still available at December 31, $930.

c. Supplies used during the month, $1,050.

d. Amortization for the month, $600.

e. Accrued advertising expense at December 31, $915. (Credit Accounts Payable.)

f. Accrued salary expense at December 31, $825.

NIZAR CONSULTING
Adjusted Trial Balance
December 31, 2004

Account Title	Trial Balance Debit	Trial Balance Credit	Adjusted Trial Balance Debit	Adjusted Trial Balance Credit
Cash	21,980		21,980	
Accounts receivable	16,520		28,180	
Supplies	2,180		560	
Prepaid insurance	5,200		4,660	
Office furniture	43,260		43,260	
Accumulated amortization— office furniture		16,440		21,000
Accounts payable		12,620		12,620
Salary payable				1,920
Interest payable				960
Note payable		24,000		24,000
Unearned consulting revenue		3,680		2,320
N. Nizar, capital		27,020		27,020
N. Nizar, withdrawals	45,000		45,000	
Consulting revenue		139,780		152,800
Amortization expense—furniture			4,560	
Supplies expense			1,620	
Utilities expense	9,920		9,920	
Salary expense	53,320		55,240	
Rent expense	24,400		24,400	
Interest expense	1,760		2,720	
Insurance expense			540	
	223,540	223,540	242,640	242,640

LAM LASER PRINTING
Trial Balance
December 31, 2003

	Debit	Credit
Cash	$10,650	
Accounts receivable	35,670	
Prepaid rent	3,630	
Supplies	1,770	
Furniture and equipment	29,610	
Accumulated amortization— furniture and equipment		$ 5,445
Accounts payable		4,965
Salary payable		
Unearned revenue		4,185
C. Lam, capital		59,265
C. Lam, withdrawals	8,025	
Revenue		23,550
Salary expense	5,700	
Rent expense		
Amortization expense— furniture and equipment		
Advertising expense	2,355	
Supplies expense		
Total	$97,410	$97,410

Required

1. Open T-accounts for the accounts listed in the trial balance, inserting their December 31 unadjusted balances.

2. Journalize the adjusting entries on December 31, and post them to the T-accounts. Key the journal entries and posted amounts by letter.

3. Prepare the adjusted trial balance.

4. How will the company use the adjusted trial balance?

Problem 3-6A *Preparing the financial statements from an adjusted trial balance (Obj. 3, 4, 5)*

The adjusted trial balance of Clement Antique Auctioneers at the end of its year, December 31, 2004, is shown below.

Required

1. Prepare Clement Antique Auctioneer's 2004 income statement, statement of owner's equity, and balance sheet. List expenses in decreasing order on the income statement and show total liabilities on the balance sheet. If your three financial statements appear on one page, draw the arrows linking the three financial statements. If they are on separate pages, write a short paragraph describing how the three financial statements are linked. How will what you have learned in this problem help you manage a business?

2. a. Which financial statement reports Clement's results of operations? Were 2004 operations successful? Cite specifics from the financial statements to support your evaluation.

   b. Which statement reports the company's financial position? Does Clement's financial position look strong or weak? Give the reason for your evaluation.

CLEMENT ANTIQUE AUCTIONEERS
Adjusted Trial Balance
December 31, 2004

Cash	$ 4,680	
Accounts receivable	82,980	
Prepaid rent	2,700	
Supplies	1,940	
Equipment	151,380	
Accumulated amortization—equipment		$ 44,480
Office furniture	48,200	
Accumulated amortization—office furniture		7,340
Accounts payable		27,200
Unearned service revenue		9,040
Interest payable		4,260
Salary payable		1,860
Note payable		90,000
A. Clement, capital		64,760
A. Clement, withdrawals	96,000	
Service revenue		391,580
Amortization expense—equipment	22,600	
Amortization expense—office furniture	4,820	
Salary expense	175,600	
Rent expense	24,000	
Interest expense	8,400	
Utilities expense	7,540	
Insurance expense	6,300	
Supplies expense	3,380	
Total	$640,520	$640,520

Problem 3-7A *Preparing an adjusted trial balance and the financial statements*
(Obj. 3, 4, 5)

Consider the unadjusted trial balance of TMS Landscaping at October 31, 2003, and the related month-end adjustment data.

TMS LANDSCAPING
Trial Balance
October 31, 2003

Cash..	$ 9,450	
Accounts receivable	12,000	
Prepaid rent..	6,000	
Supplies	900	
Equipment..	40,500	
Accumulated amortization—		
equipment		$ 4,500
Accounts payable...		4,200
Salary payable...		
T. Mack, capital...		54,000
T. Mack, withdrawals	5,400	
Landscaping design revenue...............................		14,100
Salary expense	2,100	
Rent Expense...		
Utilities expense	450	
Amortization expense—		
equipment		
Supplies expense...		
Total...	$76,800	$76,800

Adjustment data:

a. Accrued landscaping design revenue at October 31, $3,000.

b. Some of the prepaid rent had expired during the month. The unadjusted prepaid balance of $6,000 relates to the period October 1, 2003, through January 31, 2004.

c. Supplies remaining on hand at October 31, $300.

d. Amortization on equipment for the month. The equipment's expected useful life is five years; it will have no value at the end of its useful life, and the straight-line method of amortization is used.

e. Accrued salary expense at October 31 should be for one day only. The five-day weekly payroll is $3,000.

Required

1. Recopy the trial balance using the format in Exhibit 3-10, and prepare the adjusted trial balance of TMS Landscaping at October 31, 2003. Key each adjusting entry by letter.

2. Prepare the income statement, the statement of owner's equity, and the balance sheet. Draw the arrows linking the three financial statements, or write a short description of how they are linked.

Problem 3-8A *Applying the revenue and matching principles, making adjusting entries, preparing an adjusted trial balance and income statement* *(Obj. 2, 3, 4, 5)*

Friendly Employment Counsellors provides counselling services to employees of companies that are downsizing. On December 31, 2003, the end of its first year of operations, the business had the following account balances (in alphabetical order):

Accounts payable	$ 39,000
Accounts receivable	8,400
Accumulated amortization—building	0
Accumulated amortization—computer equipment	0
Building	120,000
Cash	3,600
Computer equipment	28,800
Consulting revenue	153,000
K. Mazza, capital	138,000
K. Mazza, withdrawals	33,000
Land	60,000
Prepaid consulting expense	4,800
Salaries expense	50,400
Supplies	2,100
Supplies expense	10,200
Utilities expense	8,700

The following information was available on December 31, 2003:

a. A physical count shows $3,600 of supplies remaining on hand on December 31.

b. The building has an expected useful life of 10 years, with no expected value after 10 years. The building was purchased on January 2, and the straight-line method of amortization is used.

c. The computer equipment, purchased on January 2, is expected to be used for four years with no expected value after four years. The straight-line method of amortization is used.

d. On November 1, the company hired a pension consultant and agreed to pay her $1,200 per month. The company paid her for four months' work, in advance.

e. The company's assistant, who earns $200 per day, worked the last six days of the year and will be paid on January 4, 2004.

f. On December 29, the company provided counselling services to a customer for $6,000, to be paid in 30 days.

Required

1. Journalize the adjusting entries required on December 31, 2003.
2. Prepare, with accounts in the correct sequence, an adjusted trial balance on December 31, 2003.
3. Prepare an income statement for the year ended December 31, 2003.

Problems (Group B)

Problem 3-1B   *Cash-basis versus accrual-basis accounting*   *(Obj. 1, 2)*

Mayfair Speech and Hearing Clinic experienced the following selected transactions during March:

Mar.	1	Paid for insurance for March through May, $1,800.
	4	Paid gas bill, $800.
	5	Performed services on account, $2,000.
	9	Purchased office equipment for cash, $2,800.
	12	Received cash for services performed, $1,800.
	14	Purchased office equipment on account, $600.
	28	Collected $1,000 on account from March 5.
	31	Paid salary expense, $2,200.
	31	Paid account payable from March 14.
	31	Recorded adjusting entry for March insurance expense (see March 1)
	31	Debited unearned revenue and credited revenue to adjust these accounts, $1,400.

Required

1. Show how each transaction would be accounted for using the cash basis and the accrual basis. Under each column give the amount of revenue or expense for March. Journal entries are not required. Use the following format for your answer, and show your computations:

Mayfair Speech and Hearing Clinic—Amount of Revenue or Expense for March

Date	Cash Basis	Accrual Basis

2. Compute March net income or net loss under each method.

3. Indicate which measure of net income or net loss is preferable. Give your reason.

Problem 3-2B *Applying accounting principles* **(Obj. 1, 2)**

Write a business memo to a new bookkeeper to explain the difference between the cash basis of accounting and the accrual basis. Mention the roles of the revenue principle and the matching principle in accrual-basis accounting.

This is the format of a business memo:

Date:	(fill in)
To:	New Bookkeeper
From:	(Student Name)
Subject:	Difference between cash-basis and accrual-basis accounting

Problem 3-3B *Journalizing adjusting entries* **(Obj. 3)**

Journalize the adjusting entry needed on December 31, the end of the current accounting period, for each of the following independent cases affecting Wilkinson Cable Contractors:

a. Details of Prepaid Rent are shown in the account:

Prepaid Rent

Jan.	1	Bal. 2,000
Mar.	31	4,000
Sept.	30	4,000

Wilkinson Cable pays office rent semiannually on March 31 and September 30. At December 31, part of the last payment is still available to cover January to March of the next year.

b. Wilkinson Cable pays its employees each Friday. The amount of the weekly payroll is $8,000 for a five-day workweek, and the daily salary amounts are equal. The current accounting period ends on Monday.

c. Wilkinson Cable has loaned money to help employees find housing, receiving notes receivable in return. During the current year the entity has earned interest revenue of $1,500, which it will receive next year.

d. The beginning balance of Supplies was $4,020. During the year the company purchased supplies costing $12,360, and at December 31 the inventory of supplies remaining on hand is $4,300.

e. Wilkinson Cable is installing cable in a large building, and the owner of the building paid Wilkinson Cable $25,000 as the annual service fee. Wilkinson Cable recorded this amount as Unearned Service Revenue. Robin Zweig, the general manager, estimates that the company has earned one-fourth of the total fee during the current year.

f. Amortization for the current year includes: Equipment, $7,700; and Trucks, $20,640. Make a compound entry.

Problem 3-4B *Analyzing and journalizing adjustments* *(Obj. 3)*

Napoli Construction's unadjusted and adjusted trial balances at April 30, 2003, are as follows:

NAPOLI CONSTRUCTION
Adjusted Trial Balance
April 30, 2003

Account Title	Trial Balance		Adjusted Trial Balance	
	Debit	Credit	Debit	Credit
Cash	12,360		12,360	
Accounts receivable	12,720		13,400	
Interest receivable			400	
Note receivable	8,200		8,200	
Supplies	1,960		580	
Prepaid rent	4,960		1,440	
Equipment	132,900		132,900	
Accumulated amortization— equipment		32,020		34,580
Accounts payable		13,840		13,840
Wages payable				640
Unearned service revenue		1,340		220
H. Owner, capital		117,580		117,580
H. Owner, withdrawals	7,200		7,200	
Service revenue		19,880		21,680
Interest revenue				400
Wage expense	3,200		3,840	
Rent expense			3,520	
Amortization expense— equipment			2,560	
Insurance expense	740		740	
Supplies expense			1,380	
Utilities expense	420		420	
	184,660	184,660	188,940	188,940

Required

Journalize the adjusting entries that account for the differences between the two trial balances.

Problem 3-5B *Journalizing and posting adjustments to T-accounts; preparing the adjusted trial balance* *(Obj. 3, 4)*

The trial balance of Chiliwack Realty at October 31, 2004, appears on the next page. The data needed for the month-end adjustments follow:

Adjustment data:

a. Prepaid rent still available at October 31, $600.

b. Supplies used during the month, $960.

c. Amortization for the month, $1,350.

d. Accrued advertising expense at October 31, $480. (Credit Accounts Payable.)

e. Accrued salary expense at October 31, $270.

f. Unearned commission revenue still remaining to be earned at October 31, $3,000.

CHILIWACK REALTY
Trial Balance
October 31, 2004

Cash	$ 6,650	
Accounts receivable	22,125	
Prepaid rent	4,650	
Supplies	1,170	
Furniture	34,065	
Accumulated amortization—furniture		$17,460
Accounts payable		2,910
Salary payable		
Unearned commission revenue		3,435
S. Jones, capital		37,590
S. Jones, withdrawals	1,000	
Commission revenue		12,600
Salary expense	3,240	
Rent expense		
Amortization expense—furniture		
Advertising expense	1,095	
Supplies expense		
Total	$73,995	$73,995

Required

1. Open T-accounts for the accounts listed in the trial balance, inserting their October 31 unadjusted balances.

2. Journalize the adjusting entries and post them to the T-accounts. Key the journal entries and the posted amounts by letter.

3. Prepare the adjusted trial balance.

4. How will the company use the adjusted trial balance?

Problem 3-6B *Preparing the financial statements from an adjusted trial balance* **(Obj. 5)**

The adjusted trial balance of Thompson Systems at December 31, 2003, follows on the next page:

Required

1. Prepare Thompson Systems' 2003 income statement, statement of owner's equity, and balance sheet. List expenses in decreasing order on the income statement and show total liabilities on the balance sheet. If your three financial statements appear on one page, draw the arrows linking the three financial statements. If they are on separate pages, write a short paragraph describing how the three financial statements are linked. How will what you have learned in this problem help you manage a business?

2. a. Which financial statement reports Thompson Systems' results of operations? Were operations successful during 2003? Cite specifics from the financial statements to support your evaluation.

   b. Which statement reports the company's financial position? Does Thompson Systems' financial position look strong or weak? Give the reason for your evaluation.

THOMPSON SYSTEMS
Adjusted Trial Balance
December 31, 2003

Cash	$ 2,640	
Accounts receivable	17,840	
Supplies	4,600	
Prepaid rent	3,200	
Equipment	40,360	
Accumulated amortization —equipment		$ 8,700
Office furniture	75,420	
Accumulated amortization —office furniture		9,740
Accounts payable		9,480
Interest payable		1,660
Unearned service revenue		1,240
Note payable		27,000
L. Thompson, capital		52,180
L. Thompson, withdrawals	58,000	
Service revenue		249,820
Amortization expense—equipment	13,360	
Amortization expense—office furniture	4,740	
Salary expense	79,800	
Rent expense	34,800	
Interest expense	6,200	
Utilities expense	5,340	
Insurance expense	7,620	
Supplies expense	5,900	
Total	$359,820	$359,820

Problem 3-7B *Preparing an adjusted trial balance and the financial statements*
(Obj. 3, 4, 5)

The unadjusted trial balance of Dataquest at July 31, 2004, and the related month-end adjustment data appear below:

DATAQUEST
Trial Balance
July 31, 2004

Cash	$ 8,400	
Accounts receivable	17,400	
Prepaid rent	5,400	
Supplies	1,200	
Furniture	43,200	
Accumulated amortization—furniture		$ 5,250
Accounts payable		5,175
Salary payable		
K. Fortin, capital		57,975
K. Fortin, withdrawals	6,000	
Consulting revenue		17,625
Salary expense	3,600	
Rent expense		
Utilities expense	825	
Amortization expense—furniture		
Supplies expense		
Total	$86,025	$86,025

Adjustment data:

a. Accrued consulting revenue at July 31, $1,350.

b. Prepaid rent had expired during the month. The unadjusted prepaid balance of $5,400 relates to the period July through October.

c. Supplies remaining on hand at July 31, $600.

d. Amortization on furniture for the month. The estimated useful life of the furniture is four years, it will have no value at the end of the four years, and the straight-line method of amortization is used.

e. Accrued salary expense at July 31 for one day only. The five-day weekly payroll is $1,500.

Required

1. Using Exhibit 3-10 as an example, recopy the trial balance and prepare the adjusted trial balance of Dataquest at July 31, 2004. Key each adjusting entry by letter.

2. Prepare the income statement, the statement of owner's equity, and the balance sheet. Draw the arrows linking the three financial statements, or write a short description of how they are linked.

Problem 3-8B *Applying the revenue and matching principles, making adjusting entries, preparing an adjusted trial balance and income statement* **(Obj. 2, 3, 4, 5)**

Bradshaw Communications provides telecommunications consulting services. On December 31, 2004, the end of its first year of operations, the business had the following account balances (in alphabetical order):

Accounts payable	$ 8,000
Accounts receivable	7,600
Accumulated amortization—equipment	0
Accumulated amortization—furniture	0
Cash	4,000
Computer equipment	24,000
Consulting revenue	142,000
Furniture	80,000
R. Bradshaw, capital	64,000
R. Bradshaw, withdrawals	30,000
Travel expense	17,200
Prepaid consulting expense	5,000
Salaries expense	36,600
Supplies	1,800
Supplies expense	7,800

The following information was available on December 31, 2004:

a. A physical count shows $2,000 of supplies remaining on hand on December 31.

b. The computer equipment has an expected useful life of four years, with no expected value after four years. The computers were purchased on January 2, and the straight-line method of amortization is used.

c. The furniture, purchased on January 2, is expected to be used for 10 years, with no expected value after 10 years. The straight-line method of amortization is used.

d. On October 1, Bradshaw Communications hired a consultant to prepare a business plan and agreed to pay her $1,000 per month. The business paid her for five months' work in advance.

e. The company's office manager, who earns $200 per day, worked the last five days of the year and will be paid on January 5, 2005.

f. On December 30, Bradshaw Communications provided consulting for a client for $2,000 to be paid in 30 days.

Required

1. Journalize the adjusting entries required on December 31, 2004. Key the journal entries by letter.
2. Prepare, with accounts in the correct sequence, an adjusted trial balance on December 31, 2004.
3. Prepare an income statement for the year ended December 31, 2004.

Challenge Problems

Problem 3-1C   *Understanding accrual-basis accounting*   *(Obj. 1, 2, 3)*

The basic accounting period is one year and all organizations report on an annual basis. It is common for large companies to report on an annual basis and some even report monthly. Interim reporting has a cost, however.

You are working part-time as an accounting clerk for Delray Corp. The company was private and only prepared annual financial statements for its shareholders. Delray has gone public and now must report quarterly. Mary Miller, your supervisor in the accounting department, is concerned about all the additional work that will be required to produce the quarterly statements.

Required

What does Mary mean when she talks about "additional work"?

Problem 3-2C   *Application of the matching principle*   *(Obj. 2)*

The matching principle is well established as a basis for recording expenses.

Required

1. New accountants sometimes state the principle as matching revenues against expenses. Explain to a new accountant why matching revenues against expenses is incorrect.
2. It has been suggested that not-for-profit organizations, such as churches and hospitals, should flip their income statements and show revenues as a deduction from expenses. Why do you think that the suggestion has been made?

Extending Your Knowledge

Decision Problems

1. Valuing a business on the basis of its net income   *(Obj. 4, 5)*

Pat Ghent has owned and operated BC Biomedical Systems, a management consulting firm for physicians, since its beginning 10 years ago. From all appearances the business has prospered. Ghent lives in the fast lane—flashy car, home located in an expensive suburb, frequent trips abroad, and other signs of wealth. In the past few years, you have become friends with her and her husband through weekly rounds of golf at the country club. Recently, she mentioned that she has lost her zest for the business and would consider selling it for the right price. She claims that her clientele is firmly established, and that the business "runs on its own." According to Ghent, the consulting procedures are fairly simple, and anyone could perform the work.

Assume you are interested in buying this business. You obtain its most recent monthly trial balance, which follows. Assume that revenues and expenses vary little from month to month and April is a typical month.

Your investigation reveals that the trial balance does not include the effects of monthly revenues of $1,650 and expenses totalling $3,150. If you were to buy BC Biomedical Systems, you would hire a manager so you could devote your time to other duties. Assume that this person would require a monthly salary of $3,000.

BC BIOMEDICAL SYSTEMS **Trial Balance** **April 30, 2004**		
Cash...	$ 14,550	
Accounts receivable.....................................	22,350	
Prepaid expenses	3,900	
Capital assets	361,950	
Accumulated amortization.............................		$284,400
Land for future expansion	72,000	
Accounts payable...		20,700
Salary payable...		
Unearned consulting revenue......................		85,050
P. Ghent, capital..		86,100
P. Ghent, withdrawals	13,500	
Consulting revenue......................................		18,450
Salary expense	5,100	
Rent expense...		
Utilities expense	1,350	
Amortization expense		
Supplies expense...		
Total..	$494,700	$494,700

Required

1. Is this an unadjusted or adjusted trial balance? How can you tell?
2. Assume that the most you would pay for the business is 40 times the monthly net income you could expect to earn from it. Compute this possible price.
3. Ghent states that the lowest price she will accept for the business is $225,000 plus the balance in owner's equity on April 30. Compute this amount.
4. Under these conditions, how much should you offer Ghent? Give your reasons.

2. Understanding the concepts underlying the accrual basis of accounting (Obj. 1, 2)

The following independent questions relate to the accrual basis of accounting:

1. It has been said that the only time a company's financial position is known for certain is when the company is wound up and its only asset is cash. Why is this statement true?
2. A friend suggests that the purpose of adjusting entries is to correct errors in the accounts. Is your friend's statement true? What is the purpose of adjusting entries if the statement is wrong?
3. The text suggested that furniture (and each other capital asset that is amortized) is a form of prepaid expense. Do you agree? Why do you think some accountants view capital assets this way?

Financial Statement Problems

1. Journalizing and posting transactions, and tracing account balances to the financial statements (Obj. 3, 4, 5)

Intrawest Corporation—like all other businesses—makes adjusting entries prior to year end in order to measure assets, liabilities, revenues, and expenses properly.

Examine Intrawest's balance sheet and pay particular attention to Prepaid Expenses and Other (Hint: Note 7(a)) and Amounts Payable (which includes Salary Payable and Interest Payable) and Deferred Revenue (another name for unearned revenue).

Required

1. Open T-accounts for: Prepaid Expenses and Other; Amounts Payable; and Season Pass Revenue (see Deferred Revenue and include current and long-term). Insert Intrawest's balances (in thousands) at June 30, 1999.

2. Journalize the following for the current year, ended June 30, 2000. Key entries by letter. Explanations are not required.

   Cash transactions (amounts in thousands of U.S. dollars):

   a. Paid prepaid expenses, $8,898.

   b. Paid the June 30, 1999, accounts payable.

   c. Received $11,236 cash for customers' advance season's pass payments.

   Adjustments at June 30, 2000 (amounts in thousands of U.S. dollars):

   d. Prepaid expenses expired, $6,500. (Debit Ski and Resort Operations Expense.)

   e. Amounts Payable, $146,648. (Debit Ski and Resort Operations Expense.)

   f. Earned sales revenue for which cash has been received from customers in advance for season's passes, $5,881.

3. After these entries are posted, show that the balance in the Prepaid Expenses and Other account agrees with the corresponding amount reported in the June 30, 2000, balance sheet.

Appendix

OBJECTIVE A1
Account for a prepaid expense
recorded initially as an expense

Alternate Treatment of Accounting for Prepaid Expenses and Unearned Revenues

Chapters 1 through 3 illustrate the most popular way to account for prepaid expenses and unearned revenues. This appendix illustrates an alternate—equally appropriate—approach to handling prepaid expenses and unearned revenues.

·············
······ **THINKING IT OVER**

How does a business record
(1) prepayment of monthy rent in
an expense account;
(2) utilities expense;
(3) the prepayment of three
months' rent?

A:

(1) Rent Expense   XX
    Cash   XX
(2) Utilities Expense   XX
    Cash   XX
(3) Rent Expense   XX
    Cash   XX

It is easier to record the payment
as an expense than as an asset,
like most payments.

Prepaid Expenses

Prepaid expenses are advance payments of expenses. Prepaid Insurance, Prepaid Rent, Prepaid Advertising, and Prepaid Legal Cost are prepaid expenses. Supplies that will be used up in the current period or within one year are also accounted for as prepaid expenses.

When a business prepays an expense—rent, for example—it can debit an *asset* account (Prepaid Rent) as illustrated on page 114 as follows:

Aug. 1	Prepaid Rent	XXX	
	Cash		XXX

Alternatively, it can debit an *expense* account in the entry to record this cash payment:

Aug. 1	Rent Expense	XXX	
	Cash		XXX

Regardless of the account debited, the business must adjust the accounts at the end of the period to report the correct amounts of the expense and the asset.

Prepaid Expense Recorded Initially as an Expense

Prepaying an expense creates an asset, as explained under the "Prepaid Rent" heading on page 114. However, the asset may be so short-lived that it will expire in the current accounting period—within one year or less. Thus the accountant may decide to debit the prepayment to an expense account at the time of payment. A $6,000 cash payment for rent (one year, in advance) on August 1, 2003, may be debited to Rent Expense:

2003			
Aug. 1	Rent Expense	6,000	
	Cash		6,000

At December 31, 2003, only five months' prepayment has expired, leaving seven months' rent still prepaid. In this case, the accountant must transfer $7/12$ of the original prepayment of $6,000, or $3,500, to Prepaid Rent. At December 31, 2003, the business still has the benefit of the prepayment for January through July of 2004. The December 31 adjusting entry is

Adjusting Entries

2003			
Dec. 31	Prepaid Rent	3,500	
	Rent Expense		3,500
	Prepaid rent is $3,500 ($6,000 × $7/12$).		

After posting, the two accounts appear as follows:

ASSETS Prepaid Rent		**EXPENSES** Rent Expense	
2003		2003	2003
Dec. 31 Adj. 3,500		Aug. 1 CP 6,000	Dec. 31 Adj. 3,500
Dec. 31 Bal. 3,500		Dec. 31 Bal. 2,500	

CP = Cash payment entry   Adj. = Adjusting entry

The balance sheet for 2003 reports Prepaid Rent of $3,500, and the income statement for 2003 reports Rent Expense of $2,500, regardless of whether the business initially debits the prepayment to an asset account or to an expense account.

Unearned (Deferred) Revenues

Unearned (deferred) revenues arise when a business collects cash in advance of earning the revenue. The recognition of revenue is *deferred* until later when it is earned. Unearned revenues are liabilities because the business that receives cash owes the other party goods or services to be delivered later.

Unearned (Deferred) Revenue Recorded Initially as a Revenue

OBJECTIVE A2
Account for an unearned (deferred) revenue recorded initially as a revenue

Receipt of cash in advance of earning the revenue creates a liability, as recorded on page 121. Another way to account for the initial transaction is to credit a *revenue* account. If the business has earned all the revenue within the period during which it received the cash, no adjusting entry is needed at the end of the period. However, if the business earns only a part of the revenue during the period, it must make adjusting entries.

Suppose on October 1, 2004, a consulting firm records the receipt of cash for a nine-month advance fee of $7,200 as revenue. The cash receipt entry is

2004			
Oct. 1	Cash	7,200	
	Consulting Revenue.........................		7,200

At December 31 the firm has earned only $3/9$ of the $7,200, or $2,400. Accordingly, the firm makes an adjusting entry to transfer the unearned portion ($6/9$ of $7,200, or $4,800) from the revenue account to a liability account as follows:

Adjusting Entries

2004			
Dec. 31	Consulting Revenue..............................	4,800	
	Unearned Consulting Revenue......		4,800
	Consulting revenue earned in advance.		

The adjusting entry leaves the unearned portion ($6/9$, or $4,800) of the original amount in the liability account because the consulting firm still owes consulting service to the client during January through June of 2005. After posting, the total amount ($7,200) is properly divided between the liability account ($4,800) and the revenue account ($2,400), as follows:

LIABILITIES Unearned Consulting Revenue		**REVENUE** Consulting Revenue	
	2004	2004	2004
	Dec. 31 Adj. 4,800	Dec. 31 Adj. 4,800	Oct. 1 CR 7,200
	Dec. 31 Bal. 4,800		Dec. 31 Bal. 2,400

CR = Cash receipt entry   Adj. = Adjusting entry

THINKING IT OVER

The required adjusting entry depends on the way the transaction was originally recorded.
(1) If the receipt of cash is recorded as a liability before it is earned, what adjusting entry is required?
(2) If the receipt of cash is originally recorded as revenue, what adjusting entry is required?

A:
(1) Unearned Revenue XX
        Revenue   XX
(2) Revenue   XX
        Unearned Revenue   XX
These entries are not interchangeable.

The firm's 2004 income statement reports consulting revenue of $2,400, and the balance sheet at December 31, 2004, reports as a liability the unearned consulting revenue of $4,800, regardless of whether the business initially credits a liability account or a revenue account.

Appendix Exercises

Exercise 3A-1 *Recording supplies transactions two ways* **(Obj. A1)**

At the beginning of the year, supplies of $1,690 were on hand. During the year, the business paid $5,400 cash for supplies. At the end of the year, the count of supplies indicates the ending balance is $1,360.

Required

1. Assume that the business records supplies by initially debiting an *asset* account. Therefore, place the beginning balance in the Supplies T-account, and record the above entries directly in the accounts without using a journal.

2. Assume that the business records supplies by initially debiting an *expense* account. Therefore, place the beginning balance in the Supplies Expense T-account, and record the above entries directly in the accounts without using a journal.

3. Compare the ending account balances under both approaches. Are they the same? Explain.

Exercise 3A-2 *Recording unearned revenues two ways* *(Obj. A2)*

At the beginning of the year, the company owed customers $2,750 for unearned service revenue collected in advance. During the year, the business received advance cash receipts of $10,000. At year end, the unearned revenue liability is $3,700.

Required

1. Assume that the company records unearned revenues by initially crediting a *liability* account. Open T-accounts for Unearned Service Revenue and Service Revenue, and place the beginning balance in Unearned Service Revenue. Journalize the cash collection and adjusting entries, and post their dollar amounts. As references in the T-accounts, denote a balance by *Bal.*, a cash receipt by *CR*, and an adjustment by *Adj*.

2. Assume that the company records unearned revenues by initially crediting a *revenue* account. Open T-accounts for Unearned Service Revenue and Service Revenue, and place the beginning balance in Service Revenue. Journalize the cash collection and adjusting entries, and post their dollar amounts. As references in the T-accounts, denote a balance by *Bal.*, a cash receipt by *CR*, and an adjustment by *Adj*.

3. Compare the ending balances in the two accounts. Explain why they are the same or different.

Appendix Problems

Problem 3A-1 *Recording prepaid rent and rent revenue collected in advance two ways* *(Obj. A1, A2)*

Diebolt Sales and Service completed the following transactions during 2003:

Aug. 31 Paid $3,000 store rent covering the six-month period ending February 28, 2004.
Dec. 1 Collected $3,200 cash in advance from customers. The service revenue will be earned $800 each month over the period ending March 31, 2004.

Required

1. Journalize these entries by debiting an asset account for Prepaid Rent and by crediting a liability account for Unearned Service Revenue. Explanations are not required.

2. Journalize the related adjustments at December 31, 2003.

3. Post the entries to the ledger accounts, and show their balances at December 31, 2003. Posting references are not required.

4. Repeat Requirements 1 through 3. This time debit Rent Expense for the rent payment and credit Service Revenue for the collection of revenue in advance.

5. Compare the account balances in Requirements 3 and 4. They should be equal.

Problem 3A-2 *Applying the revenue and matching principles, making adjusting entries, accounting for prepaid expenses recorded initially as an expense, accounting for unearned revenue recorded initially as a revenue* **(Obj. 2, 3, A1, A2)**

The Solutions Company develops custom software for clients in the construction business. Solutions Company had the following information available at the close of its first year of business, June 30, 2003:

1. Insurance payments during the year were debited to Insurance Expense. An examination of the policies showed the following:
   - Policy 1: a two-year policy purchased on March 31, 2003, for $2,400.
   - Policy 2: a one-year policy purchased on July 2, 2002, for $600.

2. On July 2, 2002, the company purchased $500 of supplies and recorded the purchase as a debit to Supplies Expense. Throughout the year the company purchased additional supplies for $1,200, recording the purchase the same way. An inventory count on June 30, 2003, showed that $800 of supplies remained on hand.

3. Computer equipment was purchased on January 2, 2003 for $16,000. The equipment was expected to be used for four years and then discarded.

4. The six employees each earn an average of $300 per day for a five-day week and are paid each Thursday. June 30, 2003, was a Friday.

5. An examination of the contracts signed with clients showed the following:
   - Customer A signed a contract on September 1, 2002 and paid $24,000 to Solutions Company. The contract was for software that was to be completed in twelve months from the date of signing.
   - Customer B signed a contract on October 30, 2002, and was to make progress payments of $1,000 each month commencing November 1. The contract was for 30 months. Revenue was recognized on a monthly basis.

   All money received to date on the two contracts was credited to Development Fees Earned. Any change to the contract amount will be made at the end of the contract.

Required

1. Journalize the adjusting entries on June 30, 2003.

2. Give the journal entry required to record the payment of wages on July 6, 2003. Since all employees are paid for the July 1 holiday, each was paid for five working days on July 6.

3. Calculate the *total effects* of the adjusting entries (parts 1 to 5) on each of the:
   a. Income statement
   b. Balance sheet.

Completing the Accounting Cycle

CHAPTER OBJECTIVES

After studying this chapter, you should be able to

1. Prepare an accounting work sheet

2. Use the work sheet to complete the accounting cycle

3. Close the revenue, expense, and withdrawal accounts

4. Correct typical accounting errors

5. Classify assets and liabilities as current or long-term

6. Use the current and debt ratios to evaluate a business's ability to pay its debts

"**G**eneral Motors profits rose 1%, to US$1.75 billion in the second quarter, as continued strong sales were offset in part by development costs for new vehicles" (*National Post*, July 19, 2000)

Shareholders of companies, both public and private, eagerly await the quarterly and annual reports issued by the companies whose shares they own. Judging by the article above, shareholders do not have to wait long. General Motors reported its earnings for the second quarter of 2000 just *19 days* after the end of the quarter on June 30. Why the hurry?

Shareholders make decisions about whether to buy, sell, or hold stock based, in part, on the financial results of companies. Investors may also use information or opinions expressed by stock-market analysts to make investment decisions. Stock-market analysts predict what a company's results will be and then eagerly await the actual results. If the financial results are available sooner,

investors and analysts can make decisions sooner. (In the case of General Motors, analysts had predicted income in the second quarter to be lower than it actually was. General Motors' stock price rose as a result.)

To compete in a swiftly changing world, then, companies like General Motors must provide financial data to decision makers quickly and at low cost. Companies accomplish these goals by rapidly *closing their accounts* or *closing their books*—the process of preparing the accounts at the end of each period for recording the transactions of the next period. Closing the books quickly is important to both internal decision makers, such as managers, and external decision makers, such as shareholders and lenders, since it allows more time for analysis and planning.

Source: "Sales Surge Lifts GM Profit to $1.75B in Quarter," *National Post*, July 19, 2000, via National Post Online, www.nationalpost.com.

IN CHAPTER 3

we prepared the financial statements from an adjusted trial balance. That approach works well for quick decision making, but organizations of all sizes take the accounting process a step further. Whether it's General Motors or Air & Sea Travel, the closing process follows the basic pattern outlined in this chapter. It marks the end of the *accounting cycle* for a given period.

The accounting process often uses a document known as the accountant's *work sheet*. There are many different types of work sheets in business—as many as there are needs for summary data. Work sheets are valuable because they aid decision making.

General Motors
www.gm.com

The Accounting Cycle

The **accounting cycle** is the process by which companies produce their financial statements for a specific period of time. For a new business, the cycle begins with setting up (opening) the ledger accounts. Gary Lyon started Air & Sea Travel on April 1, 2002, so the first step in the cycle was to open the accounts. After a business has operated for one period, however, the account balances carry over from period to period. Therefore, the accounting cycle usually starts with the account balances at the beginning of the period. Exhibit 4-1 outlines the complete accounting cycle. The boldface items in Panel A indicate the new steps that we will be discussing in this chapter.

The accounting cycle includes work performed at two different times:

- During the period—Journalizing transactions
  Posting to the ledger
- End of the period—Adjusting the accounts, including journalizing and posting the adjusting entries

Closing the accounts, including journalizing and posting the closing entries

Preparing the financial statements (income statement, statement of owner's equity, and balance sheet)

The end-of-period work also readies the accounts for the next period. In Chapters 3 and 4, we cover the end-of-period accounting for a service business such as Air & Sea Travel. Chapter 5 then shows how a merchandising entity adjusts and closes its books.

Companies prepare financial statements on a monthly or a quarterly basis, and steps 1 to 6a in Exhibit 4-1 are adequate for statement preparation. Steps 6b through 7 can be performed monthly or quarterly but are necessary only at the end of the year.

OBJECTIVE 1
Prepare an accounting work sheet

The Work Sheet

Accountants often use a **work sheet**, a document with many columns, to help move data from the trial balance to the financial statements. The work sheet summarizes the data for the statements. Listing all the accounts and their unadjusted balances helps identify the accounts that need adjustment. The work sheet aids the closing process by listing the ending adjusted balances of all the accounts.

The work sheet is not part of the ledger or the journal, nor is it a financial statement. Therefore, it is not part of the formal accounting system. Instead, it is a summary device that exists for the accountant's convenience.

Exhibits 4-2 through 4-6 illustrate the development of a typical work sheet for Air & Sea Travel. The heading at the top names the business, identifies the document, and states the accounting period. A step-by-step description of its preparation follows.

Steps introduced in Chapter 3 to prepare the adjusted trial balance:

1. Print the account titles and their unadjusted ending balances in the Trial Balance columns of the work sheet, and total the amounts (Exhibit 4-2).

2. Enter the adjustments in the Adjustments columns, and total the amounts (Exhibit 4-3).

3. Compute each account's adjusted balance by combining the trial balance and adjustment figures. Enter the adjusted amounts in the Adjusted Trial Balance columns (Exhibit 4-4).

New steps introduced in this chapter:

4. Extend the asset, liability, and owner's equity amounts from the Adjusted Trial Balance to the Balance Sheet columns. Extend the revenue and expense amounts to the Income Statement columns. Total the statement columns (Exhibit 4-5).

5. Compute net income or net loss as the difference between total revenues and total expenses on the income statement. Enter net income or net loss as a balancing amount on the income statement and the balance sheet, and compute the adjusted column totals (Exhibit 4-6).

Let's examine these steps in greater detail.

1. Print the account titles and their unadjusted ending balances in the Trial Balance columns of the work sheet, and total the amounts. Total debits must equal total credits as shown in Exhibit 4-2. The account titles and balances come directly from the ledger accounts before the adjusting entries are prepared. Accounts are grouped on the work sheet by category (assets, liabilities, owner's equity, revenues, expenses) and are usually listed in the order they appear in the ledger (Cash first, Accounts Receivable second, and so on).

Accounts may have zero balances (for example, Amortization Expense). All

Exhibit 4-1

The Accounting Cycle

PANEL A

During the Period	End of the Period

During the Period

1. Start with the account balances in the ledger at the beginning of the period.
2. Analyze and journalize transactions as they occur.
3. Post journal entries to the ledger accounts.

End of the Period

4. Compute the unadjusted balance in each account at the end of the period.
5. **Enter the trial balance on the work sheet, and complete the work sheet. (Optional)**
6. Using the adjusted trial balance or the full work sheet as a guide,
   a. Prepare the financial statements.
   b. Journalize and post the adjusting entries.
   c. **Journalize and post the closing entries.**
7. **Prepare the postclosing trial balance. This trial balance becomes step 1 for the next period.**

PANEL B

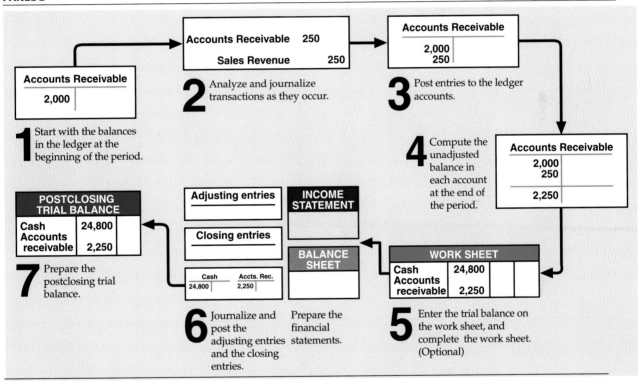

accounts are listed on the trial balance because they appear in the ledger. Electronically prepared work sheets list all the accounts, not just those with a balance.

2. Enter the adjusting entries in the Adjustments columns, and total the amounts. Exhibit 4-3 includes the April adjusting entries. These are the same adjustments as those we used in Chapter 3 to prepare the adjusted trial balance.

We can identify the accounts that need to be adjusted by scanning the trial balance. Cash needs no adjustment because all cash transactions are recorded as they occur during the period. Consequently, Cash's balance is up to date.

Accounts Receivable is listed next. Has Air & Sea Travel earned revenue that it has not yet recorded? The answer is yes. At April 30, the business has earned $250, which must be accrued because the cash will be received during May. Air & Sea Travel debits Accounts Receivable and credits Service Revenue on the work sheet in Exhibit 4-3. A letter is used to link the debit and the credit of each adjusting entry.

EXHIBIT 4-2

Trial Balance

	AIR & SEA TRAVEL Accounting Work Sheet For the Month Ended April 30, 2003										
	Trial Balance		Adjustments		Adjusted Trial Balance		Income Statement		Balance Sheet	
Account Title	Dr.	Cr.	Dr.	Cr.	Dr.	Cr.	Dr.	Cr.	Dr.	Cr.
Cash	24,800									
Accounts receivable	2,250									
Supplies	700									
Prepaid rent	3,000									
Furniture	16,500									
Accumulated amortization										
Accounts payable		13,100								
Salary payable										
Unearned service revenue		450								
Gary Lyon, capital		31,250								
Gary Lyon, withdrawals	3,200									
Service revenue		7,000								
Rent expense										
Salary expense	950									
Supplies expense										
Amortization expense										
Utilities expense	400									
	51,800	51,800								

Net income

{
Print the account
titles and their un-
adjusted ending
balances in the
Trial Balance
columns of the
work sheet, and
total the amounts.

By moving down the trial balance, the accountant identifies the remaining accounts that need adjustment. Supplies is next. The business has used supplies during April, so it debits Supplies Expense and credits Supplies. The other adjustments are analyzed and entered on the work sheet as you learned in Chapter 3.

Listing the accounts in their proper sequence aids the process of identifying accounts that need to be adjusted. But suppose that one or more accounts is omitted from the trial balance. This account can always be written below the first column totals—$51,800. Assume that Supplies Expense was accidentally omitted and thus did not appear on the trial balance. When the accountant identifies the need to update the Supplies account, he or she knows that the debit in the adjusting entry is to Supplies Expense. In this case, the accountant can write Supplies Expense on the line beneath the amount totals and enter the debit adjustment—$300—on the Supplies Expense line. Keep in mind that the work sheet is not the finished version of the financial statements, so the order of the accounts on the work sheet is not critical. Supplies Expense can be listed in its proper sequence on the income statement. After the adjustments are entered on the work sheet, the amount columns are totalled.

3. Compute each account's adjusted balance by combining the trial balance and adjustment figures. Enter the adjusted amounts in the Adjusted Trial Balance columns. Exhibit 4-4 shows the work sheet with the adjusted trial balance columns completed. Accountants perform this step as illustrated in Chapter 3. For example, the Cash balance is up to date, so it receives no adjustment. Accounts Receivable's adjusted balance of $2,500 is computed by adding the trial balance amount of $2,250 to the $250 debit adjustment. Supplies' adjusted balance of $400 is determined by subtracting the $300 credit adjustment from the unadjusted debit balance of $700. An account may receive more than one adjustment, as does Service Revenue. The column totals must maintain the equality of debits and credits.

4. Extend (that is, transfer) the asset, liability and owner's equity amounts from the Adjusted Trial Balance to the Balance Sheet columns. Extend the revenue and expense amounts to the Income Statement columns. Total the statement columns. Every account is either a balance sheet account or an income statement account. The asset, liability, and owner's equity accounts go to the balance sheet, and the revenues and expenses go to the income statement. Debits on the adjusted trial balance remain debits in the statement columns, and credits remain credits. Generally, each account's adjusted balance should appear in only one statement column, as shown in Exhibit 4-5.

Total the *income statement columns first*, as follows:

Income Statement
- Debits (Dr.) Total expenses = $3,875 ⎤
                                         ⎥ Difference
                                         ⎥ = $3,525
- Credits (Cr.) Total revenues = $7,400 ⎦

Then total the *balance sheet* columns:

Balance Sheet
- Debits (Dr.) Total assets = $49,400 ⎤
                                         ⎥ Difference
                                         ⎥ = $3,525
- Credits (Cr.) Total liabilities
                 and owner's equity = $45,875 ⎦

5. Compute net income or net loss as the difference between total revenues and total expenses on the income statement. Enter net income as a debit balancing amount on the income statement and as a credit amount on the balance sheet. Then compute the adjusted column totals. Exhibit 4-6 presents the completed accounting work sheet, which shows net income of $3,525, computed as follows:

KEY POINT

Remember, from Chapter 3, how posting references help track data from the journal to the ledger. These identifiers are equally important for organizing the adjusting entries on the work sheet.

KEY POINT

Net income is the difference between the debit and credit Income Statement columns.

Revenue (total credits on the income statement)	$7,400
Expenses (total debits on the income statement)	3,875
Net income	$3,525

Net income of $3,525 is entered in the debit column of the income statement, to balance with the credit column of the income statement, which totals at $7,400. The net income amount is then extended to the credit column of the balance sheet because an excess of revenues over expenses increases capital, and increases in capital are recorded by a credit. In the closing process, net income will find its way into the Capital account, as we shall soon see. After completion, total debits equal total credits in the Income Statement columns and in the Balance Sheet columns. The balance sheet columns are totalled at $49,400.

If expenses exceed revenues, the result is a net loss. In that event, *Net loss* is printed on the work sheet. The loss amount should be entered in the *credit* column of the income statement and in the *debit* column of the balance sheet, because an excess of expenses over revenue decreases capital, and decreases in capital are recorded by a debit.

Mid-Chapter Summary Problem
for Your Review

The trial balance of O'Malley's Service Company at December 31, 2003, the end of its fiscal year, is presented below:

O'MALLEY'S SERVICE COMPANY
Trial Balance
December 31, 2003

Cash	$ 198,000	
Accounts receivable.......................................	370,000	
Supplies...	6,000	
Furniture and fixtures	100,000	
Accumulated amortization —furniture and fixtures		$ 40,000
Building..	210,000	
Accumulated amortization—building.........		130,000
Land...	50,000	
Accounts payable...		380,000
Salary payable		
Unearned service revenue		45,000
Terry O'Malley, capital		293,000
Terry O'Malley, withdrawals	65,000	
Service revenues..		286,000
Salary expense...	172,000	
Supplies expense...		
Amortization expense —furniture and fixtures............................		
Amortization expense—building...............		
Miscellaneous expense..................................	3,000	
Total	$1,174,000	$1,174,000

Data needed for the adjusting entries include:

a. Supplies remaining on hand at year end, $2,000

b. Amortization on furniture and fixtures, $20,000

c. Amortization on building, $10,000

d. Salaries owed but not yet paid, $5,000

e. Service revenues to be accrued, $12,000

f. Of the $45,000 balance of Unearned Service Revenue, $32,000 was earned during 2003.

Required

Prepare the work sheet of O'Malley's Service Company for the year ended December 31, 2003. Key each adjusting entry by the letter corresponding to the data given.

Solution to Review Problem

O'MALLEY'S SERVICE COMPANY
Work Sheet
For the Year Ended December 31, 2003

Account Title	Trial Balance Debit	Trial Balance Credit	Adjustments Debit	Adjustments Credit	Adjusted Trial Balance Debit	Adjusted Trial Balance Credit	Income Statement Debit	Income Statement Credit	Balance Sheet Debit	Balance Sheet Credit
Cash	198,000				198,000				198,000	
Accounts receivable	370,000		(e) 12,000		382,000				382,000	
Supplies	6,000			(a) 4,000	2,000				2,000	
Furniture and fixtures	100,000				100,000				100,000	
Accumulated amortization —furniture and fixtures		40,000		(b) 20,000		60,000				60,000
Building	210,000				210,000				210,000	
Accumulated amortization —building		130,000		(c) 10,000		140,000				140,000
Land	50,000				50,000				50,000	
Accounts payable		380,000				380,000				380,000
Salary payable				(d) 5,000		5,000				5,000
Unearned service revenue		45,000	(f) 32,000			13,000				13,000
Terry O'Malley, capital		293,000				293,000				293,000
Terry O'Malley, withdrawals	65,000				65,000				65,000	
Service revenues		286,000		(e) 12,000 (f) 32,000		330,000		330,000		
Salary expense	172,000		(d) 5,000		177,000		177,000			
Supplies expense			(a) 4,000		4,000		4,000			
Amortization expense —furniture and fixtures			(b) 20,000		20,000		20,000			
Amortization expense—building			(c) 10,000		10,000		10,000			
Miscellaneous expense	3,000				3,000		3,000			
	1,174,000	1,174,000	83,000	83,000	1,221,000	1,221,000	214,000	330,000	1,007,000	891,000
Net income							116,000			116,000
							330,000	330,000	1,007,000	1,007,000

OBJECTIVE 2
Use the work sheet to complete the accounting cycle

Completing the Accounting Cycle

The work sheet helps organize accounting data and compute the net income or net loss for the period. It also aids in preparing the financial statements, recording the adjusting entries, and closing the accounts.

Preparing the Financial Statements

The work sheet shows the amount of net income or net loss for the period, but it is still necessary to prepare the financial statements. (The financial statements can be prepared directly from the adjusted trial balance; see page 126. This is why completion of the work sheet is optional.) The sorting of accounts to the balance sheet and income statement eases the preparation of the statements. The work sheet also provides the data for the statement of owner's equity. Exhibit 4-7 presents the April financial statements for Air & Sea Travel (based on the data from the work sheet in Exhibit 4-6).

Recording the Adjusting Entries

The adjusting entries are a key element of accrual-basis accounting. The work sheet helps identify the accounts that need adjustments. But, actual adjustment of the accounts requires journal entries that are posted to the ledger accounts; see Panel A of Exhibit 4-8. Panel B shows the postings to the accounts, with "Adj." denoting an amount posted from an adjusting entry. Only the revenue and expense accounts are presented in the exhibit in order to focus on the closing process, which is discussed in the next section.

The adjusting entries can be recorded in the journal as they are entered on the work sheet, but it is not necessary to journalize them at the same time. Most accountants prepare the financial statements immediately after completing the work sheet. They can wait to journalize and post the adjusting entries before they make the closing entries.

Delaying the journalizing and posting of the adjusting entries illustrates another use of the work sheet. Many companies journalize and post the adjusting entries—as in Exhibit 4-8—only once annually—at the end of the year. The need for monthly and quarterly financial statements, however, requires a tool like the work sheet. The entity can use the work sheet to aid in preparing interim statements without journalizing and posting the adjusting entries.

OBJECTIVE 3
Close the revenue, expense, and withdrawal accounts

Closing the Accounts

Closing the accounts refers to the step at the end of the period that prepares the accounts for recording the transactions of the next period. Closing the accounts consists of journalizing and posting the closing entries. Closing results in the balances of the revenue and expense accounts becoming zero in order to clearly measure the net income of each period separately from all other periods.

Recall that the income statement reports only one period's income. For example, net income for Air Canada Corporation for the year ended December 31, 2003, relates exclusively to the twelve months ended on that date. At December 31, 2003, Air Canada accountants close the company's revenues and expense accounts for that year. Because these accounts' balances relate to a particular accounting period

Air Canada
www.aircanada.ca

EXHIBIT 4-7

April Financial Statements of
Air & Sea Travel

AIR & SEA TRAVEL
Income Statement
For the Month Ended April 30, 2003

Revenues:		
Service revenue		$7,400
Expenses:		
Salary expense	$1,900	
Rent expense	1,000	
Utilities expense	400	
Supplies expense	300	
Amortization expense—furniture	275	
Total expenses		3,875
Net income		$3,525

AIR & SEA TRAVEL
Statement of Owner's Equity
For the Month Ended April 30, 2003

Gary Lyon, capital, April 1, 2003	$31,250
Add: Net income	3,525
	34,775
Less: Withdrawals	3,200
Gary Lyon, capital, April 30, 2003	$31,575

AIR & SEA TRAVEL
Balance Sheet
April 30, 2003

Assets			Liabilities	
Cash		$24,800	Accounts payable	$13,100
Accounts receivable		2,500	Salary payable	950
Supplies		400	Unearned service revenue	300
Prepaid rent		2,000	Total liabilities	14,350
Furniture	$16,500			
Less: Accumulated			**Owner's Equity**	
amortization	275	16,225	Gary Lyon, capital	31,575
			Total liabilities and	
Total assets		$45,925	owner's equity	$45,925

(2003 in this case) and are therefore closed at the end of the period (December 31, 2003), the revenue and expense accounts are called **temporary (nominal) accounts**. For example, assume Air & Sea Travel's year end is April 30, 2003. The balance of Service Revenue at April 30, 2003, is $7,400. This balance relates exclusively to the month of April and must be zeroed out before Air & Sea Travel starts accounting for the revenue the business will earn during the next year, beginning May 1, 2003.

The Withdrawals account—although not a revenue or an expense—is also a temporary account, because it measures withdrawals taken during a specific period. The closing process applies only to temporary accounts.

To better understand the closing process, contrast the nature of the temporary accounts with the nature of the **permanent (real) accounts**—the asset, liability, and owner's capital accounts. The asset, liability, and owner's capital accounts are *not*

EXHIBIT 4-8

Journalizing and Posting the
Adjusting Entries

Panel A: Journalizing Adjusting Entries   Page 4

Apr. 30	Accounts Receivable...	250	
	Service Revenue		250
30	Supplies Expense...	300	
	Supplies		300
30	Rent Expense...	1,000	
	Prepaid Rent		1,000
30	Amortization Expense—Furniture	275	
	Accumulated Amortization—Furniture		275
30	Salary Expense...	950	
	Salary Payable...		950
30	Unearned Service Revenue.............................	150	
	Service Revenue		150

Panel B: Posting the Adjustments to the Revenue and Expense Accounts

REVENUE		EXPENSES			
Service Revenue		**Rent Expense**		**Salary Expense**	
	7,000	Adj. 1,000			950
Adj.	250	Bal. 1,000		Adj. 950	
Adj.	150			Bal. 1,900	
Bal.	7,400				

Amortization Expense—Furniture		**Utilities Expense**	
Adj.	275		400
Bal.	275	Bal. 400	

Supplies Expense	
Adj.	300
Bal.	300

Adj. = Amount posted from an adjusting entry   Bal. = Balance

....
THINKING IT OVER

Where is each account
extended—Income Statement,
debit column; Income Statement,
credit column; Balance Sheet,
debit column; or Balance Sheet,
credit column?

1. Cash.
   A: Balance Sheet, debit

2. Supplies.
   A: Balance Sheet, debit

3. Supplies Expense.
   A: Income Statement, debit

4. Unearned Revenue.
   A: Balance Sheet, credit

5. Service Revenue.
   A: Income Statement, credit

6. Owner's Equity.
   A: Balance Sheet, credit

closed at the end of the period because their balances are not used to measure income. Consider Cash, Accounts Receivable, Supplies, Buildings, Accounts Payable, Notes Payable, and Capital. These accounts do not represent *business activity* for a single period as do revenues and expenses, which relate exclusively to one accounting period. Instead the permanent accounts represent assets, liabilities, and capital that are on hand at a specific time. This is why their balances at the end of one accounting period carry over to become the beginning balances of the next period. For example, the Cash balance at December 31, 2002 is also the beginning balance for 2003.

Closing entries transfer the revenue, expense, and withdrawal balances from their respective accounts to the Capital account. As you know,

REVENUES   *increase*   owner's equity

EXPENSES
and   *decrease*   owner's equity
WITHDRAWALS

It is when we post the closing entries that the Capital account absorbs the impact of the balances in the temporary accounts.

As an intermediate step, however, the revenues and the expenses are transferred first to an account entitled **Income Summary**, which collects in one place the total debit for the sum of all expenses and the total credit for the sum of all revenues of the period. The Income Summary account is like a temporary "holding tank" that is used only in the closing process. Then the balance of Income Summary is transferred to the Capital account. The steps in closing the accounts of a corporation like Air & Sea Travel are as follows (the circled numbers are keyed to Exhibit 4–9):

① Debit each *revenue* account for the amount of its credit balance. Credit Income Summary for the sum of the revenues. This entry transfers the sum of the revenues to the *credit* side of the Income Summary.

② Credit each *expense* account for the amount of its debit balance. Debit Income Summary for the sum of the expenses. This entry transfers the sum of the expenses to the *debit* side of the Income Summary. It is not necessary to make a separate closing entry for each expense. In one closing entry, record one debit to Income Summary and a separate credit to each expense account.

③ To close net income, debit Income Summary for the amount of its *credit balance* (*net income* equals revenues minus expenses) and credit the Capital account. If there is a *net loss*, Income Summary has a *debit balance*. In that case, credit Income Summary for this amount and debit Capital. This entry transfers the net income or loss from Income Summary to the Capital account.

④ Credit the *Withdrawals* account for the amount of its debit balance. Debit the Capital account. This entry transfers the Withdrawals amount to the *debit* side of the Capital account. Withdrawals are not expenses and do not affect net income or net loss.

These steps are best illustrated with an example. Suppose Air & Sea Travel closes the books at the end of April. Exhibit 4-9 presents the complete closing process for the business. Panel A gives the closing journal entries, and Panel B shows the accounts after the closing entries have been posted.

The amount in the debit side of each expense account is its adjusted balance. For example, Rent Expense has a $1,000 debit balance. Also note that Service Revenue has a credit balance of $7,400 before closing. These amounts come directly from the adjusted balances in Exhibit 4-8, Panel B.

- Closing entry ① , denoted in the Service Revenue account by *Clo.*, transfers Service Revenue's balance to the Income Summary account. This entry zeroes out Service Revenue for April and places the revenue on the credit side of Income Summary.

- Closing entry ② zeroes out the expenses and moves their total ($3,875) to the debit side of Income Summary. At this point, Income Summary contains the impact of April's revenues and expenses; hence Income Summary's balance is the month's net income ($3,525).

- Closing entry ③ closes the Income Summary account by transferring net income to the credit side of Gary Lyon, Capital.[1]

- The last closing entry, ④ , moves the owner withdrawals to the debit side of Gary Lyon, Capital, leaving a zero balance in the Gary Lyon, Withdrawals account.

The closing entries set all the revenues, the expenses, and the Withdrawals account back to zero. Now the Capital account includes the full effects of the April revenues, expenses, and withdrawals. These amounts, combined with the beginning

---

[1] The Income Summary account is a convenience for combining the effects of the revenues and expenses prior to transferring their income effect to Capital. It is not necessary to use the Income Summary account in the closing process. Another way of closing the revenues and expenses makes no use of this account. In this alternative procedure, the revenues and expenses are closed directly to Capital.

Exhibit 4-9

Journalizing and Posting the Closing Entries

Panel A: Journalizing

Closing Entries   Page 5

①Apr. 30   Service Revenue 7,400

           Income Summary..............................   7,400

           To close the revenue account and
create the Income Summary account.

②   30   Income Summary 3,875

           Rent Expense   1,000

           Salary Expense   1,900

           Supplies Expense   300

           Amortization Expense.....................   275

           Utilities Expense   400

           To close the expense accounts.

③   30   Income Summary 3,525

           Gary Lyon, Capital   3,525

           To close the Income Summary
account and transfer net income to
the Capital account.
(Income Summary balance
= $7,400 – $3,875).

④   30   Gary Lyon, Capital............................... 3,200

           Gary Lyon, Withdrawals.................   3,200

           To close the Withdrawals account and
transfer the Withdrawals amount to
the Capital account.

Panel B: Posting

Rent Expense

Adj.	1,000		
Bal.	1,000	Clo.	1,000

Salary Expense

	950		
Adj.	950		
Bal.	1,900	Clo.	1,900

Supplies Expense

Adj.	300		
Bal.	300	Clo.	300

Amortization Expense

Adj.	275		
Bal.	275	Clo.	275

Utilities Expense

	400		
Bal.	400	Clo.	400

Income Summary

Clo.	3,875	Clo.	7,400
Clo.	3,525	Bal.	3,525

Service Revenue

			7,000
		Adj.	250
		Adj.	150
Clo.	7,400	Bal.	7,400

Gary Lyon, Withdrawals

Bal.	3,200	Clo.	3,200

Gary Lyon, Capital

Clo.	3,200		31,250
		Clo.	3,525
		Bal.	31,575

Adj. = Amount posted from an adjusting entry   Clo. = Amount posted from a closing entry   Bal. = Balance

Capital's balance, give the Capital account an ending balance of $31,575. Trace this ending Capital balance to the statement of owner's equity and also to the balance sheet in Exhibit 4-7.

Closing a Net Loss   What would the closing entries be if Air & Sea Travel had suffered a net *loss* during April? Suppose April expenses totalled $7,700 and all other factors were unchanged. Only closing entries ② and ③ would change. Closing entry ② would transfer expenses of $7,700 to Income Summary, as follows:

Income Summary

Clo.	7,700	Clo.	7,400
Bal.	300		

Closing entry ③ would then credit Income Summary to close its debit balance and to transfer the net loss to Gary Lyon, Capital:

③   Apr. 30   Gary Lyon, Capital...   300
            Income Summary   300

After posting, these two accounts would appear as follows:

Income Summary

Clo.	7,700	Clo.	7,400
Bal.	300	Clo.	300

Gary Lyon, Capital

Clo.	300	31,250

KEY POINT

The double line in an account means that the account has a zero balance; nothing more will be posted to it in the current period. The double line is drawn immediately after the closing entry is posted. In the general ledger, the account has a zero balance.

Finally, the Withdrawals balance would be closed to Capital, as before. The double line in an account means that the account has a zero balance; nothing more will be posted to it in the current period.

The closing process is fundamentally mechanical and is completely automated in a computerized system. Accounts are identified as either temporary or permanent. The temporary accounts are closed automatically by selecting that option from the software's menu. Posting also occurs automatically.

Student to Student

One of the most effective pages in this chapter is Exhibit 4-1 on page 164a—it's a great breakdown of the accounting cycle. Panel B makes it easy to remember what the process looks like. Exhibit 4-2 is also a great learning tool. Using transparencies to display the step-by-step process is excellent.

Matt H., Kitchener

Postclosing Trial Balance

The accounting cycle ends with the **postclosing trial balance** (Exhibit 4-10). The postclosing trial balance is the final check on the accuracy of journalizing and posting the adjusting and closing entries. It lists the ledger's accounts and their adjusted balances after closing. This step shows where the business stands as it moves into the next accounting period. The postclosing trial balance is dated as of the end of the period for which the statements have been prepared.

The postclosing trial balance resembles the balance sheet. It contains the ending balances of the permanent accounts—the balance sheet accounts: the assets, liabilities, and owner's equity. No temporary accounts—revenues, expenses, or withdrawal accounts—are included because their balances have been closed. The ledger is up to date and ready for the next period's transactions.

Correcting Journal Entries

In Chapter 2 we discussed errors that affect the trial balance: treating a debit as a credit and vice versa; transpositions; and slides. Here we show how to correct errors in journal entries.

When a journal entry contains an error and the error is detected before posting, the entry can be corrected.

OBJECTIVE 4
Correct typical accounting errors

EXHIBIT 4-10

Postclosing Trial Balance

AIR & SEA TRAVEL
Postclosing Trial Balance
April 30, 2003

Cash...	$24,800	
Accounts receivable.....................................	2,500	
Supplies..	400	
Prepaid rent	2,000	
Furniture...	16,500	
Accumulated amortization—Furniture..........		$ 275
Accounts payable..		13,100
Salary payable		950
Unearned service revenue		300
Gary Lyon, Capital..		31,575
Total	$46,200	$46,200

If the error is detected after posting, the accountant makes a *correcting entry*. Suppose Air & Sea Travel paid $5,000 cash for furniture and erroneously debited Supplies as follows:

Incorrect Entry

May 13	Supplies..	5,000	
	Cash..		5,000
	Bought supplies.		

The debit to Supplies is incorrect, so it is necessary to make the following correcting entry:

Correcting Entry

May 15	Furniture..	5,000	
	Supplies..		5,000
	To correct May 13 entry.		

The credit to Supplies in the second entry offsets the incorrect debit of the first entry. The debit to Furniture in the correcting entry places the furniture's cost in the correct account. Now both Supplies and Furniture are correct. Cash was unaffected by the error because Cash was credited correctly in the entry to purchase the furniture.

WORKING IT OUT

(1) Ann Firth recorded the collection of a $1,000 receivable as a debit to Cash and a credit to Service Revenue for $1,000. Prepare the correcting entry.
(2) If Firth's net income before the correction was $26,000, how much is the corrected net income?

A:
(1) Service Rev.   1,000
        Accounts Rec.   1,000
(2) $25,000
      ($26,000 – $1,000)

OBJECTIVE 5
Classify assets and liabilities as current or long-term

Classification of Assets and Liabilities

On the balance sheet, assets and liabilities are classified as either *current* or *long-term* to indicate their relative liquidity. **Liquidity** is a measure of how quickly an item can be converted to cash. Cash is the most liquid asset. Accounts receivable is a relatively liquid asset because the business expects to collect the amount in cash in the near future. Supplies are less liquid than accounts receivable, and furniture and buildings are even less so.

Users of financial statements are interested in liquidity because business difficulties often arise due to a shortage of cash. How quickly can the business convert an asset to cash and pay a debt? How soon must a liability be paid? These are questions of liquidity. Balance sheets list assets and liabilities in the order of their relative liquidity.

Assets

Current Assets   **Current assets** are assets that are expected to be converted to cash, sold, or consumed during the next 12 months or within the business's normal operating cycle if longer than a year. The **operating cycle** is the time span during which (1) cash is used to acquire goods and services, and (2) those goods and services are sold to customers, who in turn pay for their purchases with cash. For most businesses, the operating cycle is a few months. A few types of business have operating cycles longer than a year. Cash, Accounts Receivable, Notes Receivable due within a year or less, and Prepaid Expenses are current assets. Merchandising entities such as The Bay and Zellers, and manufacturing entities such as Magna and Bombardier, have an additional current asset, Inventory. This account shows the cost of goods that are held for sale to customers.

Magna
www.magnaint.com

Bombardier
www.bombardier.com

The Hudson's Bay Company
www.hbc.com

Long-Term Assets   **Long-term assets** are all assets other than current assets. One category of long-term assets is **capital assets**. Land, Buildings, Furniture and Fixtures, and Equipment are capital assets. Of these, Air & Sea Travel has only Furniture.

Other categories of long-term assets include Investments and Other Assets (a catchall category for assets that are not classified more precisely). We discuss these categories in more detail in later chapters.

Liabilities

Financial statement users (such as creditors) are interested in the due dates of an entity's liabilities. Liabilities that must be paid the soonest create the greatest strain on cash. Therefore, the balance sheet lists liabilities in the order in which they are due to be paid. Knowing how many of a business's liabilities are current and how many are long-term helps creditors assess the likelihood of collecting from the entity. Balance sheets usually have at least two liability classifications, *current liabilities* and *long-term liabilities*.

Current Liabilities   **Current liabilities** are debts that are due to be paid within one year or one of the entity's operating cycles if the cycle is longer than a year. Accounts Payable, Notes Payable due within one year, Salaries Payable, Unearned Revenue, Goods and Services Tax Payable, and Interest Payable owed on notes payable are current liabilities.

Long-Term Liabilities   All liabilities that are not current are classified as **long-term liabilities**. Many notes payable are long-term—payable after the longer of one year or the entity's operating cycle. Some notes payable are paid in installments, with the first installment due within one year, the second installment due the second year, and so on. In this case, the first installment would be a current liability and the remainder long-term liabilities. For example, a $100,000 note payable to be paid $10,000 per year over ten years would include a current liability of $10,000 for next year's payment and a long-term liability of $90,000.

Thus far in this book we have presented the *unclassified* balance sheet of Air & Sea Travel. Our purpose was to focus on the main points of assets, liabilities, and owner's equity without the details of *current* assets, *current* liabilities, and so on. Exhibit 4-11 presents Air & Sea Travel's classified balance sheet. (Notice that Air & Sea Travel has no long-term liabilities. Suppose the company had incurred a debt for its furniture and the debt would not be repaid during the coming year. This debt would have appeared as a long-term liability on the Balance Sheet.)

Compare Air & Sea Travel's *classified* balance sheet in Exhibit 4-11 with the *unclassified* balance sheet in Exhibit 4-7. The classified balance sheet reports totals for current assets and current liabilities, which do not appear on the unclassified balance sheet. Also, Air & Sea Travel has no long-term liabilities, so there are none to report on either balance sheet.

The classified balance sheet of AS Products Company, a fictitious company, is shown in Exhibit 4-12. It shows how a company with many different accounts could present its data on a classified balance sheet.

Now let's examine an actual company's classified balance sheet.

Exhibit 4-11

Classified Balance Sheet of
Air & Sea Travel

AIR & SEA TRAVEL
Balance Sheet
April 30, 2003

Assets		Liabilities	
Current assets:		**Current liabilities:**	
Cash	$24,800	Accounts payable	$13,100
Accounts receivable	2,500	Salary payable	950
Supplies	400	Unearned service revenue	300
Prepaid rent	2,000	Total current liabilities	14,350
Total current assets	$29,700		
		Owner's Equity	
Capital assets:		Gary Lyon, capital	31,575
Furniture $16,500			
Less: Accumulated			
amortization 275			
Total capital assets	16,225	Total liabilities and	
Total assets	$45,925	owner's equity	$45,925

STOP & THINK

Why is the classified balance sheet in Exhibit 4-11 more useful than an unclassified balance sheet (Exhibit 4-7) to a banker considering whether to lend $10,000 to Air & Sea Travel?

Answer: A classified balance sheet indicates

- which of Air & Sea Travel's liabilities, and the dollar amounts, that the company must pay within the next year.
- which of Air & Sea Travel's assets are the most liquid and thus available to pay the liabilities.
- which assets and liabilities (and amounts) are long-term.

An Actual Classified Balance Sheet

Exhibit 4-13 is an adapted classified balance sheet of Noranda Inc., a Canadian mining company. The statement is labelled Consolidated because it reports the accounts of Noranda and its component companies as well. Dollar amounts are reported in millions to avoid clutter. Noranda Inc.'s year end is December 31, 1999. It is customary to present two or more years' statements together to allow people to compare one year with the other—1999 and 1998 in this case.

You should be familiar with all but a few of Noranda Inc.'s account titles. Titles you might not be familiar with are Deferred Credits, Minority Interest in Subsidiaries, and Shareholders' Equity. In Noranda Inc.'s case, Deferred Credits include the accrued costs of closing down mines owned by the company and the accrued costs of future pensions payable. *Minority Interest in Subsidiaries* includes the preferred and common shares of stock of companies in which Noranda Inc. has a significant investment. *Shareholders' Equity* is the owners' equity of a corporation, and includes shareholders' investment in shares of Noranda Inc. stock and the results of ongoing operations.

Note that Noranda Inc. provides labels only for current assets and current liabilities; the remaining assets and liabilities are long-term because they are not labelled "current."

Noranda Inc.
www.noranda.com

EXHIBIT 4-12

Classified Balance Sheet of
AS Products Company

AS PRODUCTS COMPANY
Balance Sheet
June 30, 2004

Assets

Current assets:

Cash	$ 13,200	
Investments	28,500	
Accounts receivable	117,500	
Interest receivable	13,400	
Current portion of note receivable	25,800	
Inventory	423,900	
Prepaid insurance	12,300	
Prepaid rent	13,500	
Supplies	2,600	
Total current assets		$650,700

Capital assets:

Equipment	$ 30,000		
Less: accumulated amortization	9,000	21,000	
Furniture and fixtures	35,000		
Less: accumulated amortization	15,000	20,000	
Buildings	120,000		
Less: accumulated amortization	80,000	40,000	
Land		35,000	
Total capital assets			116,000

Other assets:

Note receivable	50,000	
Less: Current portion of note receivable	25,800	
Total other assets		24,200
Total assets		$790,900

Liabilities

Current liabilities:

Accounts payable	$178,500	
Salaries and wages payable	11,200	
Interest payable	12,300	
Current portion of notes payable	30,000	
Goods and services tax payable	32,300	
Current portion of mortgage payable	36,100	
Other current liabilities	11,800	
Total current liabilities		$312,200

Long-term liabilities:

Notes payable	$170,000		
Less current portion of notes payable	30,000	140,000	
Mortgage payable	110,000		
Less current portion of mortgage payable	36,100	73,900	
Total long-term liabilities			213,900
Total liabilities			526,100

Owner's Equity

A. Sommerfeld, capital	264,800
Total liabilities and owner's equity	$790,900

EXHIBIT 4-13

Consolidated Balance Sheet

NORANDA INC.
Consolidated Balance Sheet
December 31, 1999

($ millions)	1999	1998
ASSETS		
Current assets		
Cash and short-term notes...	$ 727	$ 1,296
Accounts receivable	1,520	1,242
Inventories..	1,510	1,491
	3,757	4,029
Capital assets	7,234	6,806
Investment and other assets	388	340
	$11,379	$11,175
LIABILITIES AND SHAREHOLDERS' EQUITY		
Current liabilities		
Bank advances and short-term notes	$ 86	$ 76
Accounts and taxes payable	1,644	1,202
Debt due within one year	225	143
	1,955	1,421
Long-term debt..	2,952	3,274
Deferred credits..	917	937
Minority interest in subsidiaries..	1,388	1,356
Shareholders' equity...	4,167	4,187
	$11,379	$11,175

Canada Business Corporations Act
www.cbsc.org/fedbis

Formats of Balance Sheets

The balance sheets of AS Products Company shown in Exhibit 4-12 and of Noranda Inc. shown in Exhibit 4-13 list the assets at the top, with the liabilities and owner's equity below. This is the *report format*. The balance sheet of Air & Sea Travel presented in Exhibit 4-7 lists the assets at the left, with the liabilities and the owner's equity at the right. That is the *account format*.

Either format is acceptable. The report format is more extensively used by Canadian companies.

OBJECTIVE 6
Use the current and debt ratios to evaluate a business's ability to pay its debts

Accounting Ratios

The purpose of accounting is to provide information for decision making. Chief users of accounting information include managers, investors, and creditors. A creditor considering lending money must predict whether the borrower can repay the loan. If the borrower already has a large amount of debt, the probability of repayment is lower than if the borrower has a small amount of liabilities. To assess financial position, decision makers use ratios computed from a company's financial statements.

Current Ratio

One of the most common ratios is the **current ratio**, which is the ratio of an entity's current assets to its current liabilities:

$$\text{Current Ratio} = \frac{\text{Total current assets}}{\text{Total current liabilities}}$$

The current ratio measures the ability to pay current liabilities with current assets. A company prefers a high current ratio, which means the business has sufficient current assets to pay current liabilities when they come due, plus a cushion of additional current assets. An increasing current ratio from period to period generally indicates improvement in financial position.

A rule of thumb: A strong current ratio would be in the range of 2.00; it would indicate that the company has approximately $2.00 in current assets for every $1.00 in current liabilities. A company with a current ratio of 2.00 would probably have little trouble paying its current liabilities. Most successful businesses operate with current ratios between 1.30 and 2.00. A current ratio of 1.00 is considered quite low. Lenders and investors would view a company with a current ratio of 1.50 to 2.00 as substantially less risky. Such a company could probably borrow money on better terms and also attract more investors.

Debt Ratio

A second aid to decision making is the **debt ratio**, which is the ratio of total liabilities to total assets:

$$\text{Debt ratio} = \frac{\text{Total liabilities}}{\text{Total assets}}$$

The debt ratio indicates the proportion of a company's assets that are financed with debt. This ratio measures a company's ability to pay both current and long-term debts—total liabilities.

A low debt ratio is safer than a high debt ratio. Why?

Because a company with a small amount of liabilities has low required payments. Such a company is unlikely to get into financial difficulty. By contrast, a company with a high debt ratio may have trouble paying its liabilities, especially when sales are low and cash is scarce. When a company fails to pay its debts on a timely basis, the creditors can take the business away from its owners. The largest retail bankruptcy in history, Federated Department Stores (owned at the time by the Canadian company Campeau Corporation) was due largely to high debt during a retail-industry recession. Campeau was unable to weather the downturn and had to declare bankruptcy.

Managing Both the Current Ratio and the Debt Ratio In general, a *high* current ratio is preferred over a low current ratio. *Increases* in the current ratio indicate improving financial position. By contrast, a *low* debt ratio is preferred over a high debt ratio. Improvement is indicated by a *decrease* in the debt ratio.

A rule of thumb: A debt ratio below 0.60, or 60%, is considered safe for most businesses. A debt ratio above 0.80, or 80%, borders on high risk. Most companies have debt ratios in the range of 0.60 to 0.80.

Financial ratios are an important aid to decision makers. However, it is unwise to place too much confidence in a single ratio or group of ratios. For example, a company may have a high current ratio, which indicates financial strength. It may also have a high debt ratio, which suggests weakness. Which ratio gives the more reliable signal about the company? Experienced managers, lenders and investors evaluate a company by examining a large number of ratios over several years to spot trends and turning points. These people also consider other facts, such as the company's cash position and its trend in net income. No single ratio gives the whole picture about a company.

As you progress through the study of accounting, we will introduce key ratios used for decision making. Chapter 18 then summarizes all the ratios discussed in this book and provides a good overview of ratios used in decision making.

THINKING IT OVER

A company has current assets of $100,000 and current liabilities of $50,000. How will the payment of a $10,000 account payable affect the current ratio?

A: The payment of an account payable would cause both cash and accounts payable to decrease and thus would increase the current ratio from 2.00 to 2.25. In other words, payment of the liability would make the company look better.

REAL WORLD EXAMPLE

Schneider Corporation has a current ratio of 1.38 (1.38 = $123,642,000/$89,542,000). While the ratio is at the lower end of the range discussed in the text, it is positive, and Schneider has operated successfully with a similar ratio for a number of years.

REAL WORLD EXAMPLE

Schneider Corporation has a debt ratio of 0.64 (0.64 = $206,479,000/$321,675,000). This ratio is virtually unchanged from previous years.

Schneider Corporation
www.schneider.ca

Decision	Guidline
How (where) to summarize the effects of all the company's transactions and adjustments throughout the period?	Accountant's *work sheet* with columns for: • Trial balance • Adjustments • Adjusted trial balance • Income statement • Balance sheet
What is the last *major* step in the accounting cycle?	*Closing entries* for the *temporary accounts:* Revenues Expenses $\Big\}$ Income statement accounts Owner's withdrawals
Why close revenues, expenses, and owner withdrawals?	Because the *temporary accounts* have balances that relate only to one accounting period (fiscal year) and do *not* carry over to the next accounting period (fiscal year).
Which accounts do not get closed?	*Permanent (balance sheet) accounts:* • Assets • Liabilities • Owner's capital The balances of these accounts *do* carry over to the next accounting period.
How do businesses classify their assets and liabilities for reporting on the balance sheet?	*Current* (within one year or the company's operating cycle if longer than a year) or *Long-term* (not current)
How do decision makers evaluate a company?	There are many ways, such as the company's net income or net loss on the income statement. Another way to evaluate a company is based on the company's *financial ratios.* Two key ratios: Current ratio $\quad = \quad \dfrac{\text{Total current assets}}{\text{Total current liabilities}}$ The current ratio measures the company's ability to pay its current liabilities with its current assets. Debt ratio $\quad = \quad \dfrac{\text{Total liabilities}}{\text{Total assets}}$ The debt ratio shows the proportion of the entity's assets that are financed with debt. The debt ratio measures the entity's overall ability to pay its liabilities.

Accounting Around the Globe

A Forced Debt Ratio for South Korea's Companies

Samsung. Daewoo. Hyundai. Just five years ago, these companies were the economic engines driving South Korea's economy. Today they are deeply in debt. When the Asian currency crisis began in 1997, investors moved their investments elsewhere and South Korean companies had to borrow money to continue to grow. The bigger the company, the more debt they had to take on. Since most large South Korean companies are *chaebol*, or family-controlled companies, it became risky for lenders to loan such large amounts to these companies.

According to the reformist government of President Kim Dae Jung, the only way for the chaebol to keep the levels of debt reasonable and thus, to move toward financial stability, is to meet a strict debt ratio target of 200%. This means forcing chaebol to loosen their strict family control, and sell off assets and whole subsidiaries to generate cash and reduce their debts. For instance, car-making giant Daewoo was struggling to meet payments on $47 billion in debt—equivalent to the entire national debt of Poland or Malaysia—so the government guided a plan to dismember the company and sell off the pieces.

This kind of drastic action has created many critics of the government's reform plan. Some say that the measures companies must take to meet the 200% debt ratio target—withdrawing cash deposits and selling off assets—may cause a loss of liquidity and trigger financial crises. Other critics fault the plan for trying to use a one-size-fits-all debt-ratio target, regardless of the economic conditions faced by each of the chaebol. For instance, carmakers like Hyundai, which make huge purchases of plant and equipment, will have naturally high debt ratios. So, while President Kim's reform plan may save some companies from bankruptcy, it may weaken otherwise sound firms.

Based on: Howard W. French, "Dismantling of Yesterday's Economic Engines," *New York Times*, September 3, 1999, p. C1. Jane L. Lee, "Korea Moves Anew to Reform Top 5 Chaebols; This Time, Control by Families Could Diminish," *Wall Street Journal*, August 26, 1999, p. A13. Anonymous, "Government Under Fire for Strict Debt Ratio Target," *Business Korea*, December 1999, pp. 18–19.

Summary Problem
for Your Review

Refer to the data in the Mid-Chapter Summary Problem for Your Review, presented on pages 166–167.

Required

1. Journalize and post the adjusting entries. (Before posting to the accounts, enter into each account its balance as shown in the trial balance. For example, enter the $370,000 balance in the Accounts Receivable account before posting its adjusting entry.) Key adjusting entries by *letter*, as shown in the work sheet solution to the mid-chapter review problem. You can take the adjusting entries straight from the work sheet on p. 167. Explanations are not required. Find the ending balances of the permanent accounts.

2. Journalize and post the closing entries. (Each account should carry its balance as shown in the adjusted trial balance.) Provide explanations. To distinguish closing entries from adjusting entries, key the closing entries by *number*. Draw the arrows to illustrate the flow of data, as shown in Exhibit 4-9, page 172. Indicate the balance of the Capital account after the closing entries are posted.

3. Prepare the income statement for the year ended December 31, 2003. List Miscellaneous Expense last among the expenses, a common practice.

4. Prepare the statement of owner's equity for the year ended December 31, 2003. Draw the arrow that links the income statement to the statement of owner's equity, if both statements are on the same page. Otherwise, explain how they are linked.

5. Prepare the classified balance sheet at December 31, 2003. Use the report form. All liabilities are current. Draw the arrow that links the statement of owner's equity to the balance sheet, if both statements are on the same page. Otherwise, explain how they are linked.

Solution to Review Problem

Requirement 1

a. Dec. 31	Supplies Expense	4,000	
	Supplies		4,000
b. Dec. 31	Amortization Expense—Furniture and Fixtures	20,000	
	Accumulated Amortization		
	—Furniture and Fixtures		20,000
c. Dec. 31	Amortization Expense—Building	10,000	
	Accumulated Amortization—Building		10,000
d. Dec. 31	Salary Expense	5,000	
	Salary Payable		5,000
e. Dec. 31	Accounts Receivable	12,000	
	Service Revenue		12,000
f. Dec. 31	Unearned Service Revenue	32,000	
	Service Revenue		32,000

Accounts Receivable	
370,000	
(e) 12,000	
Bal. 382,000	

Supplies	
6,000	(a) 4,000
Bal. 2,000	

Accumulated Amortization—Furniture and Fixtures	
	40,000
	(b) 20,000
	Bal. 60,000

Accumulated Amortization—Building	
	130,000
	(c) 10,000
	Bal. 140,000

Salary Payable	
	(d) 5,000
	Bal. 5,000

Unearned Service Revenue	
(f) 32,000	45,000
	Bal. 13,000

Service Revenue	
	286,000
	(e) 12,000
	(f) 32,000
	Bal. 330,000

Salary Expense	
172,000	
(d) 5,000	
Bal. 177,000	

Supplies Expense	
(a) 4,000	
Bal. 4,000	

Amortization Expense—Furniture and Fixtures	
(b) 20,000	
Bal. 20,000	

Amortization Expense—Building	
(c) 10,000	
Bal. 10,000	

Requirement 2

a. Dec. 31	Service Revenue..	330,000			
	Income Summary			330,000	
	To close the revenue account and create the				
	Income Summary account.				
b. Dec. 31	Income Summary	214,000			
	Salary Expense..			177,000	
	Supplies Expense...			4,000	
	Amortization Expense				
	—Furniture and Fixtures.........................			20,000	
	Amortization Expense—Building..............			10,000	
	Miscellaneous Expense...............................			3,000	
	To close the expense accounts.				
c. Dec. 31	Income Summary	116,000			
	Terry O'Malley, Capital			116,000	
	To close the Income Summary account.				
	(Income Summary balance				
	= $330,000 – $224,000).				
d. Dec. 31	Terry O'Malley, Capital	65,000			
	Terry O'Malley, Withdrawals....................			65,000	
	To close the Withdrawals account and transfer				
	the Withdrawals amount to the Capital				
	account.				

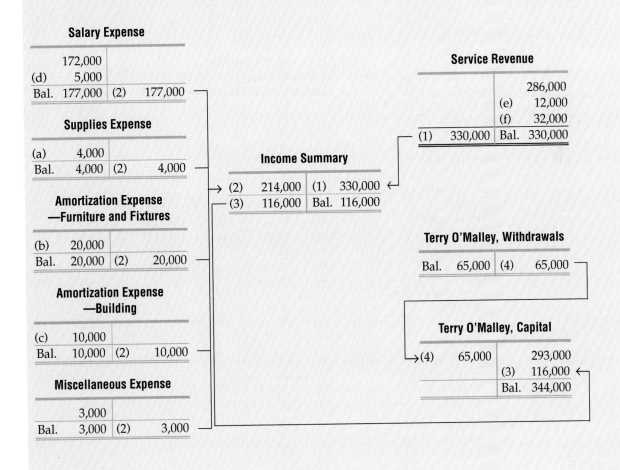

Requirement 3

O'MALLEY'S SERVICE COMPANY
Income Statement
For the Year Ended December 31, 2003

Revenues:		
Service revenue		$330,000
Expenses:		
Salary expense	$177,000	
Amortization expense—furniture and fixtures	20,000	
Amortization expense—building	10,000	
Supplies expense	4,000	
Miscellaneous expense	3,000	
Total expenses		214,000
Net Income		$116,000

Requirement 4

O'MALLEY'S SERVICE COMPANY
Statement of Owner's Equity
For the Year Ended December 31, 2003

Terry O'Malley, Capital, January 1, 2003	$293,000
Add: Net income	116,000
	409,000
Less: Withdrawals	65,000
Terry O'Malley, Capital, December 31, 2003	$344,000

Requirement 5

O'MALLEY'S SERVICE COMPANY
Balance Sheet
December 31, 2003

Assets

Current assets:		
Cash		$198,000
Accounts receivable		382,000
Supplies		2,000
Total current assets		582,000
Capital assets:		
Furniture and fixtures	$100,000	
Less: Accumulated amortization	60,000	40,000
Building	210,000	
Less: Accumulated amortization	140,000	70,000
Land		50,000
Total capital assets		160,000
Total assets		$742,000

Liabilities

Current liabilities:		
Accounts payable		$380,000
Unearned service revenue		13,000
Salary payable		5,000
Total current liabilities		398,000

Owner's Equity

Terry O'Malley, capital		344,000
Total liabilities and owner's equity		$742,000

Summary

1. **Prepare an accounting work sheet.** The *accounting cycle* is the process by which accountants produce the financial statements for a specific period of time. The cycle starts with the beginning account balances. During the period, the business journalizes transactions and posts them to the ledger accounts. At the end of the period, the trial balance is prepared, and the accounts are adjusted in order to measure the period's net income or net loss. Completion of the accounting cycle is aided by use of a *work sheet*. This multicolumned document summarizes the effects of all the period's activity.

2. **Use the work sheet to complete the accounting cycle.** The work sheet is neither a journal nor a ledger but merely a convenient device for completing the accounting cycle. It has columns for the trial balance, the adjustments, the adjusted trial balance, the income statement, and the balance sheet. It aids the adjusting process, and it is the place where the period's net income or net loss is first computed. The work sheet also provides the data for the financial statements and the *closing entries*. It is not, however, a necessity. The accounting cycle can be completed from the less elaborate adjusted trial balance.

3. **Close the revenue, expense, and withdrawal accounts.** Revenues, expenses, and withdrawals represent increases and decreases in the capital account for a specific period. At the end of the period, their balances are closed out to zero, and, for this reason, they are called *temporary accounts*. Assets, liabilities, and capital accounts are not closed because they are the *permanent accounts*. Their balances at the end of one period become the beginning balances of the next period. The final accuracy check of the period is the *postclosing trial balance*.

4. **Correct typical accounting errors.** Accountants correct errors by making correcting journal entries.

5. **Classify assets and liabilities as current or long-term.** The balance sheet reports *current* and *long-term assets* and *current* and *long-term liabilities*. It can be presented in *report format* or *account format*.

6. **Use the current and debt ratios to evaluate a business's ability to pay its debts.** Two decision-making aids are the *current ratio* (total current assets divided by total current liabilities) and the *debt ratio* (total liabilities divided by total assets).

Self-Study Questions

Test your understanding of the chapter by marking the correct answer to each of the following questions:

1. The focal point of the accounting cycle is the (*p. 163*)
   a. Financial statements   c. Adjusted trial balance
   b. Trial balance   d. Work sheet

2. Arrange the following accounting cycle steps in their proper order (*p. 164a*)
   a. Complete the work sheet
   b. Journalize and post adjusting entries
   c. Prepare the postclosing trial balance
   d. Journalize and post cash transactions
   e. Prepare the financial statements
   f. Journalize and post closing entries

3. The work sheet is a (*p. 164*)
   a. Journal   c. Financial statement
   b. Ledger   d. Convenient device for completing the accounting cycle

4. The usefulness of the work sheet is (*pp. 164–164a*)
   a. Identifying the accounts that need to be adjusted

   b. Summarizing the effects of all the transactions of the period
   c. Aiding the preparation of the financial statements
   d. All of the above

5. Which of the following accounts is not closed? (*pp. 168–171*)
   a. Supplies Expense   c. Interest Revenue
   b. Prepaid Insurance d. Withdrawals

6. The closing entry for Salary Expense, with a balance of $322,000, is (*pp. 168–171*)

   a. Salary Expense   322,000
         Income Summary   322,000
   b. Salary Expense   322,000
         Salary Payable   322,000
   c. Income Summary   322,000
         Salary Expense   322,000
   d. Salary Payable   322,000
         Salary Expense   322,000

7. The purpose of the postclosing trial balance is to (*p. 173*)
   a. Provide the account balances for preparation of the balance sheet
   b. Ensure that the ledger is in balance for the start of the next period
   c. Aid the journalizing and posting of the closing entries
   d. Ensure that the ledger is in balance for completion of the work sheet

8. A payment on account was recorded by debiting Supplies and crediting Cash. This entry was posted. The correcting entry is (*pp. 173–174*)
   a. Accounts Payable   X
       Supplies   X
   b. Supplies   X
       Accounts Payable   X
   c. Cash   X
       Accounts Payable   X
   d. Cash   X
       Supplies   X

9. The classification of assets and liabilities as current or long-term depends on (*p. 174*)
   a. Their order of listing in the ledger
   b. Whether they appear on the balance sheet or the income statement
   c. The relative liquidity of the item
   d. The format of the balance sheet—account format or report format

10. Suppose in 2003, Air & Sea Travel debited Amortization Expense for the cost of a computer used in the business. For 2003, this error (*pp. 173–174*)
    a. Overstated net income
    b. Understated net income
    c. Either a or b, depending on the circumstances
    d. Had no effect on net income

Answers to the Self-Study Questions follow the Similar Accounting Terms.

Accounting Vocabulary

Accounting cycle (*p. 163*)
Capital asset (*p. 175*)
Closing entries (*p. 170*)
Closing the accounts (*p. 168*)
Current asset (*p. 174*)
Current liability (*p. 175*)
Current ratio (*p. 178*)
Debt ratio (*p. 179*)
Income Summary (*p. 171*)
Liquidity (*p. 174*)

Long-term asset (*p. 175*)
Long-term liability (*p. 175*)
Nominal account (*p. 169*)
Operating cycle (*p. 175*)
Permanent account (*p. 169*)
Postclosing trial balance (*p. 173*)
Real account (*p. 169*)
Reversing entry (*p. 212*)
Temporary account (*p. 169*)
Work sheet (*p. 164*)

Similar Accounting Terms

Capital assets	Fixed assets; Plant and equipment; Property, plant, and equipment; Plant assets
Current ratio	Working capital ratio
Permanent account	Real account
Temporary account	Nominal account

Answers to Self-Study Questions

1. a	3. d	5. b	7. b	9. c
2. d, a, e, b, f, c	4. d	6. c	8. a	10. b

Assignment Material

Questions

1. Identify the steps in the accounting cycle; distinguish those that occur during the period from those that are performed at the end of the period.

2. Why is the work sheet a valuable accounting tool?

3. Name two advantages the work sheet has over the adjusted trial balance.

4. Why must the adjusting entries be journalized and posted if they have already been entered on the work sheet?

5. Why should the adjusting entries be journalized and posted before the closing entries are made?

6. Which types of accounts are closed?

7. What purpose is served by closing the accounts?

8. State how the work sheet helps with recording the closing entries.

9. Distinguish between permanent accounts and temporary accounts; indicate which type is closed at the end of the period. Give five examples of each type of account.

10. Is Income Summary a permanent account or a temporary account? When and how is it used?

11. Give the closing entries for the following accounts (balances in parentheses): Service Revenue ($4,700), Salary Expense ($1,100), Income Summary (credit balance of $2,000), Withdrawals ($2,300).

12. Why are assets classified as current or long-term?

On what basis are they classified? Where do the classified amounts appear?

13. Indicate which of the following accounts are current assets and which are long-term assets: Prepaid Rent, Building, Furniture, Accounts Receivable, Merchandise Inventory, Cash, Note Receivable (due within one year), Note Receivable (due after one year).

14. In what order are assets and liabilities listed on the balance sheet?

15. Name an outside party that is interested in whether a liability is current or long-term. Why would this party be interested in this information?

16. A friend tells you that the difference between a current liability and a long-term liability is that they are payable to different types of creditors. Is your friend correct? Include in your answer the definitions of these two categories of liabilities.

17. Show how to compute the current ratio and the debt ratio. Indicate what ability each ratio measures, and state whether a high value or a low value is safer for each.

18. Capp Company purchased supplies of $120 on account. The accountant debited Inventory and credited Accounts Payable for $120. A week later, after this entry has been posted to the ledger, the accountant discovers the error. How should he correct the error?

Exercises

Exercise 4-1. *Preparing a work sheet* **(Obj. 1)**

The trial balance of Psutka Testing Services appears on the following page.

Additional information at September 30, 2004:

a. Accrued service revenue, $210.

b. Amortization, $40.

c. Accrued salary expense, $500.

d. Prepaid rent expired, $600.

e. Supplies used, $1,650.

PSUTKA TESTING SERVICES
Trial Balance
September 30, 2004

Cash	$ 3,560	
Accounts receivable	3,440	
Prepaid rent	1,200	
Supplies	3,390	
Equipment	32,600	
Accumulated amortization		$ 2,840
Accounts payable		1,600
Salary payable		
B. Psutka, capital		36,030
B. Psutka, withdrawals	3,000	
Service revenue		9,300
Amortization expense		
Salary expense	1,800	
Rent expense		
Utilities expense	780	
Supplies expense		
Total	$49,770	$49,770

Required

Complete Psutka Testing Services work sheet for September 2004.

Exercise 4-2   *Journalizing adjusting and closing entries*   *(Obj. 2)*

Journalize the adjusting and closing entries for the company in Exercise 4-1.

Exercise 4-3   *Posting adjusting and closing entries*   *(Obj. 2)*

Set up T-accounts for those accounts affected by the adjusting and closing entries in Exercise 4-1. Post the adjusting and closing entries to the accounts, denoting adjustment amounts by *Adj.*, closing amounts by *Clo.*, and balances by *Bal.* Double underline the accounts with zero balances after you close them and show the ending balance in each account.

Exercise 4-4   *Preparing a postclosing trial balance*   *(Obj. 2)*

Prepare the postclosing trial balance for the company in Exercise 4-1.

Exercise 4-5   *Identifying and journalizing closing entries*   *(Obj. 3)*

Bombardier Inc., the transporation, motorized consumer products, aerospace, and financial and real estate services company, reported the following items adapted from a recent financial report (amounts in millions):

Cash and term deposits	$ 896	Amortization expense	$ 166	
Revenues	7,976	Other assets	230	
Accounts payable	2,125	Interest expense	160	
Accounts receivable	358	Long-term liabilities	1,355	

Prepare Bombardier Inc.'s closing entries for the above accounts.

Exercise 4-6   *Identifying and journalizing closing entries*   *(Obj. 3)*

From the following selected accounts that Tri-County Printers reported in its June 30, 2003, annual financial statements, prepare the company's closing entries.

Capital	$ 91,200	Interest expense	$ 4,400
Service revenue	168,200	Accounts receivable	28,000
Unearned revenues	2,700	Salary payable	1,700
Salary expense	25,000	Amortization expense	20,400
Accumulated amortization	70,000	Rent expense	11,800
Supplies expense	3,400	Withdrawals	60,000
Interest revenue	1,400	Supplies	2,800

Exercise 4-7 *Identifying and journalizing closing entries* (Obj. 4)

The accountant for Mendez Environmental Consulting has posted adjusting entries (a) through (e) to the accounts at December 31, 2004. All the revenue, expense, and owner's equity accounts of the entity are listed here in T-account form.

Accounts Receivable

13,000	
(a) 1,750	

Supplies

2,000	(b) 1,000

Accumulated Amortization —Furniture

	3,000
	(c) 550

Accumulated Amortization —Building

	16,500
	(d) 3,000

Salary Payable

	(e) 350

R. Mendez, Capital

	26,200

R. Mendez, Withdrawals

30,700	

Service Revenue

	55,500
	(a) 1,750

Salary Expense

13,000	
(e) 350	

Supplies Expense

(b) 1,000	

Amortization Expense —Furniture

(c) 550	

Amortization Expense —Building

(d) 3,000	

Required

1. Journalize Mendez Environmental Consulting's closing entries at December 31, 2004.
2. Determine Mendez Environmental Consulting's ending capital balance at December 31, 2004.

Exercise 4-8 *Preparing a statement of owner's equity* (Obj. 3)

From the following accounts of Eastern Logistics prepare the entity's statement of owner's equity for the year ended December 31, 2004.

L. Kew, Capital

Dec. 31 16,000	Jan. 1 18,000		
	Dec. 31 21,500		

L. Kew, Withdrawals

Mar. 31 4,500	Dec. 31 16,000		
Jun. 30 3,500			
Sept. 30 4,500			
Dec. 31 3,500			

Income Summary

Dec. 31 42,500	Dec. 31 64,000
Dec. 31 21,500	

Exercise 4-9 *Identifying and recording adjusting and closing entries* **(Obj. 2, 3)**

The trial balance and income statement amounts from the March work sheet of Domm Systems follow:

Account Title	Trial Balance		Income Statement	
Cash	$ 6,200			
Supplies	4,800			
Prepaid rent	2,200			
Office equipment	100,200			
Accumulated amortization		$ 12,400		
Accounts payable		9,200		
Salary payable				
Unearned service revenue		8,800		
B. Domm, capital		71,600		
B. Domm, withdrawals	2,000			
Service revenue		23,400		$26,000
Salary expense	6,000		$ 7,600	
Rent expense	2,400		2,800	
Amortization expense			600	
Supplies expense			800	
Utilities expense	1,600		1,600	
	$125,400	$125,400	$13,400	$26,000
Net income			12,600	
			$26,000	$26,000

Required

Journalize the adjusting and closing entries of Domm Systems at March 31.

Exercise 4-10 *Making correcting entries* **(Obj. 4)**

1. Suppose Air & Sea Travel paid an account payable of $600 and erroneously debited Supplies. Make the journal entry to correct this error.

2. Suppose Air & Sea Travel made the following adjusting entry to record amortization at April 30:

Amortization Expense	550	
Furniture		550

Make the journal entry to correct this error.

3. Suppose, in closing the books, Air & Sea Travel made this closing entry:

Income Summary	14,800	
Service Revenue		14,800

Make the journal entry to correct this error.

Exercise 4-11 *Preparing a classified balance sheet* **(Obj. 5, 6)**

Refer to Exercise 4-9.

Required

1. After solving Exercise 4-9, use the data in that exercise to prepare Domm Systems' classified balance sheet at March 31, 2004. Use the report format.

2. Compute Domm Systems' current ratio and debt ratio at March 31, 2004. One year ago, the current ratio was 1.20 and the debt ratio was 0.30. Indicate whether Domm Systems' ability to pay its debts has improved or deteriorated during the current year.

Exercise 4-12 *Correcting accounting errors* *(Obj. 4)*

Prepare a correcting entry for each of the following accounting errors:

a. Debited Supplies and credited Accounts Payable for a $1,500 purchase of office equipment on account.

b. Accrued interest revenue of $500 by a debit to Accounts Receivable and a credit to Interest Revenue.

c. Adjusted prepaid rent by debiting Prepaid Rent and crediting Rent Expense for $1,000. This adjusting entry should have debited Rent Expense and credited Prepaid Rent for $1,000.

d. Debited Salary Expense and credited Accounts Payable to accrue salary expense of $2,000.

e. Recorded the earning of $1,300 service revenue collected in advance by debiting Accounts Receivable and crediting Service Revenue.

Exercise 4-13 *Classifying assets and liabilities as current or long-term* *(Obj. 5)*

Merit Corporation had sales of $1,700 million during 2003, and total assets of $400 million at December 31, 2003, the end of the company's fiscal year. Merit Corporation's financial statements reported the following (all amounts in millions):

Sales revenue	$1,200	Prepaid expenses	$15
Inventory	150	Land and buildings	80
Long-term debt	1	Accounts payable	85
Receivables	9	Operating expenses	500
Interest expense	1	Accumulated amortization	75
Equipment	200	Accrued liabilities	
		(such as Salary payable)	30

While some of these account titles may be new to you, they are similar to those you have seen already.

Required

1. Identify the assets (including contra assets) and liabilities.
2. Classify each asset and each liability as current or long-term.

Serial Exercise

This exercise continues the Anya Perreault Architects situation begun in Exercise 2-15 of Chapter 2 and extended to Exercise 3-17 of Chapter 3.

Exercise 4-14 *Closing the books, preparing a classified balance sheet, and evaluating a business* *(Obj. 3, 5, 6)*

Refer to Exercise 3-17 of Chapter 3. Start from the posted T-accounts and the adjusted trial balance on the next page that Anya Perreault Architects prepared at December 31.

Required

1. Journalize and post the closing entries at December 31, 2002. Denote each closing amount as *Clo.* and an account balance as *Bal.*

2. Prepare a classified balance sheet at December 31, 2002.

3. Compute the current ratio and the debt ratio of Anya Perreault Architects and evaluate these ratio values as indicative of a strong or weak financial position.

4. If your instructor assigns it, complete the accounting work sheet at December 31, 2002.

ANYA PERREAULT ARCHITECTS
Adjusted Trial Balance
December 31, 2002

Cash	$11,200	
Accounts receivable	1,700	
Supplies	100	
Equipment	3,000	
Accumulated amortization—equipment		$ 50
Furniture	5,600	
Accumulated amortization—furniture		60
Accounts payable		5,600
Salary payable		700
Unearned service revenue		800
Anya Perreault, capital		14,000
Anya Perreault, withdrawals	1,600	
Service revenue		3,700
Rent expense	500	
Utilities expense	200	
Salary expense	700	
Amortization expense—equipment	50	
Amortization expense—furniture	60	
Supplies expense	200	
Total	$24,910	$24,910

Challenge Exercise

Exercise 4-15   *Computing financial statement amounts*   **(Obj. 2, 5)**

The unadjusted accounts balance of Chan Consulting follow:

Cash	$ 3,800	Unearned service revenue	$10,600
Accounts receivable	14,400	Stephanie Chan, capital	180,400
Supplies	2,200	Stephanie Chan, withdrawals	92,400
Prepaid Insurance	4,400	Service revenue	187,200
Furniture	16,800	Salary expense	65,400
Accumulated amortization—		Amortization expense—	
furniture	2,600	furniture	
Building	115,600	Amortization expense—	
Accumulated amortization—		building	
building	29,800	Supplies expense	
Land	102,400	Insurance expense	
Accounts payable	12,200	Utilities expense	5,400
Salary payable			

Adjusting data at the end of the year included the following:

a. Unearned service revenue that has been earned, $7,200.

b. Accrued service revenue, $3,400.

c. Supplies used in operations, $1,200.

d. Accrued salary expense, $2,800.

e. Insurance expense, $3,600.

f. Amortization expense—furniture, $1,600; building, $4,200.

Stephanie Chan, the proprietor of Chan Consulting has received an offer to sell her company. She needs to know the following information as soon as possible:

1. Net income for the year covered by these data.

2. Total assets.

3. Total liabilities.

4. Total owner's equity.

5. Proof that total assets equal total liabilities plus total owner's equity after all items are updated.

Required

Without opening any accounts, making any journal entries, or using a work sheet, provide Stephanie Chan with the requested information. Show all computations.

Ethical Issue

Cash & Carry Carpets wishes to expand its business and has borrowed $100,000 from The Toronto-Dominion Bank. As a condition for making this loan, the bank required Cash & Carry Carpets to maintain a current ratio of at least 1.50 and a debt ratio of no more than 0.50, and to submit annual financial statements to the bank.

Business during the third year has been good but not great. Expansion costs have brought the current ratio down to 1.40 and the debt ratio up to 0.51 at December 15. The managers of Cash & Carry Carpets are considering the implication of reporting this current ratio to The Toronto-Dominion Bank. One course of action that the managers are considering is to record in December of the third year some revenue on account that Cash & Carry Carpets will earn in January of next year. The contract for this job has been signed, and Cash & Carry Carpets will deliver the carpet during January.

Required

1. Journalize the revenue transaction using your own numbers, and indicate how recording this revenue in December would affect the current ratio and the debt ratio.

2. State whether it is ethical to record the revenue transaction in December. Identify the accounting principle relevant to this situation.

3. Propose an ethical course of action for Cash & Carry Carpets.

Problems (Group A)

Problem 4-1A   *Preparing a work sheet*   *(Obj. 1)*

The trial balance of Kenora Construction at July 31, 2004, appears on page 194.

Additional data at July 31, 2004:

a. Amortization: equipment, $680; building, $740.

b. Accrued wage expense, $480.

c. A count of supplies showed that unused supplies amounted to $29,480.

d. During July, $1,000 of prepaid insurance coverage expired.

e. Accrued interest expense, $360.

f. Of the $21,120 balance of Unearned Service Revenue, $9,940 was earned during July.

g. Accrued advertising expense, $200. (Credit Accounts Payable.)

h. Accrued service revenue, $2,200.

Required

Complete Kenora Construction's work sheet for July.

KENORA CONSTRUCTION
Trial Balance
July 31, 2004

Cash	$ 42,400	
Accounts receivable	75,640	
Supplies	35,320	
Prepaid insurance	4,600	
Equipment	65,380	
Accumulated amortization—equipment		$ 52,480
Building	85,780	
Accumulated amortization—building		21,000
Land	56,600	
Accounts payable		45,380
Interest payable		
Wages payable		
Unearned service revenue		21,120
Note payable, long-term		44,800
T. Jackson, capital		158,260
T. Jackson, withdrawals	8,400	
Service revenue		40,380
Amortization expense—equipment		
Amortization expense—building		
Wages expense	6,400	
Insurance expense		
Interest expense		
Utilities expense	2,220	
Advertising expense	680	
Supplies expense		
Total	$383,420	$383,420

Problem 4-2A *Preparing financial statements from an adjusted trial balance; journalizing adjusting and closing entries; evaluating a business* **(Obj. 2, 5, 6)**

The *adjusted* trial balance of Full Spectrum Design at June 30, 2004, the end of the company's fiscal year, appears on the following page.

Adjusting data at June 30, 2004, which *have been incorporated* into the trial balance figures on page 195, consist of:

a. Amortization for the year: equipment, $4,380; building, $2,382.
b. Supplies used during the year, $2,148.
c. During the year, $1,860 of prepaid insurance coverage expired.
d. Accrued interest expense, $414.
e. Accrued service revenue, $564.
f. Of the balance of Unearned Service Revenue at the beginning of the year, $4,674 was earned during the year.
g. Accrued wage expense, $462.

Required

1. Journalize the adjusting entries that would lead to the adjusted trial balance shown here. Also journalize the closing entries.

2. Prepare Full Spectrum Design's income statement and statement of owner's equity for the year ended June 30, 2004, and the classified balance sheet on that date. Use the account format for the balance sheet.

3. Compute Full Spectrum Design's current ratio and debt ratio at June 30, 2004. One

year ago, the current ratio stood at 1.01, and the debt ratio was 0.71. Did Full Spectrum Design's ability to pay debts improve or deteriorate during the year?

FULL SPECTRUM DESIGN
Adjusted Trial Balance
June 30, 2004

Cash	$ 11,610	
Accounts receivable	15,882	
Supplies	18,774	
Prepaid insurance	1,920	
Equipment	33,480	
Accumulated amortization—equipment		$ 9,888
Building	68,940	
Accumulated amortization—building		10,110
Land	18,000	
Accounts payable		23,040
Interest payable		894
Wages payable		462
Unearned service revenue		1,380
Note payable, long-term		58,200
L. Rainville, capital		41,034
L. Rainville, withdrawals	27,180	
Service revenue		83,916
Amortization expense—equipment	4,380	
Amortization expense—building	2,382	
Wages expense	12,882	
Insurance expense	1,860	
Interest expense	6,906	
Utilities expense	2,580	
Supplies expense	2,148	
Total	$228,924	$228,924

Problem 4-3A *Taking the accounting cycle through the closing entries* *(Obj. 2, 3)*

The unadjusted T-accounts of Wong Software Solutions at December 31, 2004, and the related year-end adjustment data appear on the next page.

Adjustment data at December 31, 2004, include:

a. Of the $10,000 balance of Unearned Service Revenue at the beginning of the year, all of it was earned during the year.

b. Supplies still unused at year end, $2,000.

c. Amortization for the year, $18,000.

d. Accrued salary expense, $2,000.

e. Accrued service revenue, $4,000.

Required

1. Write the trial balance on a work sheet, and complete the work sheet. Key each adjusting entry by the letter corresponding to the data given.

2. Prepare the income statement, the statement of owner's equity, and the classified balance sheet in account format.

3. Journalize the adjusting and closing entries.

4. Did Wong Software Solutions have a profitable year or a bad year during 2004? Give the reason for your answer.

Cash		Accounts Receivable		Supplies	
Bal. 10,000		Bal. 72,000		Bal. 18,000	

Equipment		Accumulated Amortization		Accounts Payable	
Bal. 198,000			Bal. 72,000		Bal. 12,000

Salary Payable		Unearned Service Revenue		Note Payable, Long-Term	
			Bal. 10,000		Bal. 120,000

N. Wong, Capital		N. Wong, Withdrawals		Supplies Expense	
	Bal. 72,000	Bal. 124,000			

Service Revenue		Salary Expense		Rent Expense	
	Bal. 298,000	Bal. 106,000		Bal. 30,000	

Amortization Expense		Interest Expense	
		Bal. 12,000	

Insurance Expense	
Bal. 14,000	

Problem 4-4A   *Completing the accounting cycle*   *(Obj. 2, 3)*

This problem should be used only in conjunction with Problem 4-3A. It completes the accounting cycle by posting to T-accounts and preparing the postclosing trial balance.

Required

1. Using the Problem 4-3A data, post the adjusting and closing entries to the T-accounts, denoting adjusting amounts by *Adj.*, closing amounts by *Clo.*, and account balances by *Bal.*, as shown in Exhibit 4-9. Double underline all accounts with a zero ending balance.
2. Prepare the postclosing trial balance.

Problem 4-5A   *Completing the accounting cycle*   *(Obj. 2, 3, 5)*

The trial balance of Baines Insurance Agency at August 31, 2004, appears on page 197. The data needed for the month-end adjustments follow.

Adjustment data:

a. Commission revenue received in advance that had not been earned at August 31, $10,125.

b. Rent still prepaid at August 31, $1,575.

c. Supplies used during the month, $510.

d. Amortization on furniture for the month, $555.

e. Amortization on building for the month, $195.

f. Accrued salary expense at August 31, $690.

BAINES INSURANCE AGENCY
Trial Balance
August 31, 2004

Account Number	Account Title	Debit	Credit
110	Cash..	$ 35,700	
120	Accounts receivable	23,340	
130	Prepaid rent	1,935	
140	Supplies	1,350	
150	Furniture...	23,025	
151	Accumulated amortization—furniture....................		$ 19,200
170	Building	112,350	
171	Accumulated amortization—building......................		42,900
180	Land	22,500	
210	Accounts payable...		6,360
220	Salary payable..		
230	Unearned commission revenue		13,350
300	B. Baines, capital...		107,880
330	B. Baines, withdrawals	7,200	
400	Commission revenue..		40,950
510	Salary expense	1,650	
520	Rent expense..		
530	Utilities expense	615	
540	Amortization expense—furniture		
550	Amortization expense—building		
560	Advertising expense...	975	
570	Supplies expense..		
	Total...	$230,640	$230,640

Required

1. Open the accounts listed in the trial balance and insert their August 31 unadjusted balances. Also open the Income Summary account, number 340. Date the balances of the following accounts as of August 1: Prepaid Rent, Supplies, Furniture, Accumulated Amortization—Furniture, Building, Accumulated Amortization—Building, Unearned Commission Revenue, and B. Baines, Capital.

2. Write the trial balance on a work sheet and complete the work sheet of Baines Insurance Agency for the month ended August 31, 2004.

3. Using the completed work sheet, prepare the income statement, the statement of owner's equity, and the classified balance sheet in report format.

4. Using the work sheet data, journalize and post the adjusting and closing entries. Use dates and posting references. Use page 7 as the number of the journal page.

5. Prepare a postclosing trial balance.

Problem 4-6A *Preparing a classified balance sheet in report format; evaluating a business (Obj. 5, 6)*

The accounts of Mogan Travel at December 31, 2004, are listed in alphabetical order on the following page.

Required

1. *All adjustments have been journalized and posted, but the closing entries have not yet been made.* Prepare the company's classified balance sheet in report format at December 31, 2004. Use captions for total assets, total liabilities, and owner's equity.

2. Compute Mogan Travel's current ratio and debt ratio at December 31, 2004. At December 31, 2003, the current ratio was 1.52 and the debt ratio was 0.37. Did Mogan Travel's ability to pay debts improve or deteriorate during 2004?

Accounts payable	$10,200	Interest payable	$ 1,200
Accounts receivable	13,200	Interest receivable	400
Accumulated amortization		Land	40,000
—building	75,600	Note payable, long-term	55,600
Accumulated amortization		Note receivable, long-term	8,000
—furniture	23,200	Other assets	7,200
Advertising expense	4,400	Other current liabilities	9,400
Amortization expense	2,600	Prepaid insurance	2,200
Building	208,800	Prepaid rent	13,200
Cash	13,000	Salary expense	49,200
Commission revenue	187,000	Salary payable	7,800
E. Mogan, capital	139,600	Supplies	5,000
E. Mogan, withdrawals	94,800	Supplies expense	11,400
Furniture	45,400	Unearned commission	
Insurance expense	1,600	revenue	10,800

Problem 4-7A *Analyzing and journalizing corrections, adjustments, and closing entries*
(Obj. 3, 4)

Link Bank to Chapter 2 (Accounting Errors).

Accountants for Taurus Catering Service encountered the following situations while adjusting and closing the books at December 31. Consider each situation independently.

a. The company bookkeeper made the following entry to record a $3,000 credit purchase of office equipment:

Nov. 12	Office Supplies	3,000	
	Accounts Payable		3,000

Prepare the correcting entry, dated December 31.

b. A $1,500 credit to Cash was posted as a debit.

(1) At what stage of the accounting cycle will this error be detected?

(2) Describe the technique for identifying the amount of the error.

c. The $59,000 balance of Equipment was entered as $5,900 on the trial balance.

(1) What is the name of this type of error?

(2) Assume this is the only error in the trial balance. Which will be greater, the total debits or the total credits, and by how much?

(3) How can this type of error be identified?

d. The accountant failed to make the following adjusting entries at December 31:

(1) Accrued property tax expense, $400.

(2) Supplies expense, $2,180.

(3) Accrued interest revenue on a note receivable, $1,300.

(4) Amortization of equipment, $8,000.

(5) Earned service revenue that had been collected in advance, $10,200.

Compute the overall net income effect of these omissions.

e. Record each of the adjusting entries identified in item d.

f. The revenue and expense accounts, *after* the adjusting entries had been posted, were Service Revenue, $38,400; Interest Revenue, $1,000; Salary Expense, $8,460; Rent Expense, $2,550; and Amortization Expense, $2,775. Two balances prior to closing were Capital, $24,300, and Withdrawals, $15,000. Journalize the closing entries.

Problem 4-8A *Preparing a work sheet, journalizing the adjustments, closing the accounts*
(Obj. 1, 3)

Master Fleet Services performs overhauls and repairs to trucks on the road and at the customer's location. The company's trial balance for the year ended March 31, 2003 is shown below.

MASTER FLEET SERVICES
Trial Balance
March 31, 2003

Cash..	$ 5,100	
Accounts receivable	31,800	
Repair supplies..	13,350	
Prepaid insurance	5,850	
Equipment...	105,000	
Accumulated amortization—equipment.........		$ 42,000
Building	141,000	
Accumulated amortization—building.............		28,200
Land	97,500	
Accounts payable...		10,800
Unearned repair revenues		2,250
Employee withholdings payable		3,000
Notes payable, long-term..................................		12,000
Mortgage payable		90,000
D. Crew, capital		143,550
D. Crew, withdrawals...	13,500	
Repair fees earned..		141,450
Wages expense...	47,100	
Utilities expense	1,650	
Travel expenses..	11,400	
Total..	$473,250	$473,250

Additional information:

a. On March 31, supplies costing $1,950 were still on hand.

b. An examination of the insurance policies showed $3,150 of insurance coverage had expired during the year ended March 31, 2003.

c. An examination of the equipment and the building showed the following:

	Equipment	*Building*
Estimated useful life	5 years	10 years
Estimated value at the end of the useful life	$0	$0

Amortization is calculated on a straight-line basis over the asset's life.

d. The company had performed $1,200 of services for a client who had paid $2,250 in advance.

e. Accrued interest on the mortgage at March 31, $900.

f. Accrued wages at March 31, $1,350.

Required

1. Complete a work sheet for the year ended March 31, 2003.

2. Journalize the adjusting required on March 31, 2003.

3. Journalize the closing entries that would be required on March 31, 2003.

4. Prepare a postclosing trial balance for March 31, 2003.

Problem 4-9A   *Preparing a work sheet, closing the accounts, classifying the assets and liabilities, evaluating the current and debt ratios*   **(Obj. 1, 3, 4, 6)**

Kim Woeller, the accountant for Gallagher Logistics had prepared the work sheet shown on the next page on a computer spreadsheet but has lost much of the data. The only particular item Woeller can recall is that there was an adjustment made to correct an error made where $800 of supplies, purchased on credit, had been incorrectly recorded as $8,000 of equipment.

Required:

1. Complete the work sheet by filling in the missing data.
2. Journalize the closing entries that would be required on December 31, 2004.
3. Prepare the company's classified balance sheet at December 31, 2004.
4. Compute Gallagher Logistics' current ratio and debt ratio for December 31, 2004. On December 31, 2003, the current ratio was 2.14 and the debt ratio was 0.47. Comment on the changes in the ratios.

Problems   (Group B)

Problem 4-1B   *Preparing a work sheet*   **(Obj. 1)**

The trial balance of Mandy White Productions at May 31, 2003, follows:

MANDY WHITE PRODUCTIONS Trial Balance May 31, 2003		
Cash	$ 17,340	
Notes receivable	20,260	
Interest receivable		
Supplies	1,120	
Prepaid insurance	3,580	
Furniture	54,820	
Accumulated amortization—furniture		$ 2,960
Building	107,800	
Accumulated amortization—building		69,120
Land	37,400	
Accounts payable		29,460
Interest payable		
Salary payable		
Unearned production services revenue		17,600
Note payable, long-term		37,400
Mandy White, capital		68,580
Mandy White, withdrawals	7,600	
Production services revenue		33,940
Interest revenue		
Amortization expense—furniture		
Amortization expense—building		
Salary expense	4,340	
Insurance expense		
Interest expense		
Utilities expense	2,260	
Advertising expense	2,120	
Supplies expense		
Total	$259,060	$259,060

GALLAGHER LOGISTICS
Accounting Work Sheet
For the Year Ended December 31, 2004

Account Title	Trial Balance Debit	Trial Balance Credit	Adjustments Debit	Adjustments Credit	Adjusted Trial Balance Debit	Adjusted Trial Balance Credit	Income Statement Debit	Income Statement Credit	Balance Sheet Debit	Balance Sheet Credit
Cash	22,000								22,000	
Accounts receivable	27,200				27,600					
Supplies	3,800			(b) 1,600						
Prepaid insurance	4,000				3,200					
Equipment	55,000				47,000					
Accumulated amortization—equipment		4,800				7,200				
Building	120,000				120,000					
Accumulated amortization—building		8,000		(e) 4,000						
Land	60,000				60,000					
Accounts payable		10,000								
Interest payable		6,000								
Wages payable		2,400		(f) 1,200						
Unearned revenues		7,000	(g) 1,000							
Mortgage payable		100,000								100,000
T. Gallagher, capital		82,000								82,000
T. Gallagher, withdrawals	12,000				12,000				12,000	
Consulting fees earned		166,600						168,000		
Wages expense	67,000				68,200					
Insurance expense	8,800									
Interest expense	6,000									
Utilities expense	1,000				1,000					
Supplies expense			(b) 1,600				1,600			
Amortization expense—equipment			(d) 2,400				2,400			
Amortization expense—building										
Totals	386,800	386,800								

Additional data at May 31, 2003:

a. Amortization: furniture, $960; building, $920.

b. Accrued salary expense, $1,200.

c. A count of supplies showed that unused supplies amounted to $820.

d. During May, $780 of prepaid insurance coverage expired.

e. Accrued interest expense, $440.

f. Of the $17,600 balance of Unearned Revenue, $8,800 was earned during May.

g. Accrued advertising expense, $120. (Credit Accounts Payable.)

h. Accrued interest revenue, $340.

Required

Complete Mandy White Productions' work sheet for May.

Problem 4-2B *Preparing financial statements from an adjusted trial balance; journalizing adjusting and closing entries; evaluating a business* **(Obj. 2, 5, 6)**

The adjusted trial balance of Vernon Golf School at April 30, 2004, the end of the company's fiscal year, follows:

VERNON GOLF SCHOOL
Adjusted Trial Balance
April 30, 2004

Cash	$ 2,740	
Accounts receivable	87,480	
Supplies	7,380	
Prepaid insurance	4,580	
Equipment	127,860	
Accumulated amortization—equipment		$ 56,860
Building	148,660	
Accumulated amortization—building		36,520
Land	40,000	
Accounts payable		39,100
Interest payable		4,560
Wages payable		1,660
Unearned teaching revenue		7,320
Note payable, long-term		139,800
P. Vernon, capital		128,400
P. Vernon, withdrawals	55,000	
Teaching revenue		197,100
Amortization expense—equipment	13,800	
Amortization expense—building	7,420	
Wages expense	65,620	
Insurance expense	10,740	
Interest expense	16,340	
Utilities expense	9,940	
Supplies expense	13,760	
Total	$611,320	$611,320

Adjusting data at April 30, 2004, which have all been incorporated into the trial balance figures above, consist of:

a. Of the balance of Unearned Teaching Revenue at the beginning of the year, $8,360 was earned during the year.

b. Supplies used during the year, $11,760.

c. During the year, $10,740 of prepaid insurance coverage expired.

d. Accrued interest expense, $2,560.

e. Accrued teaching revenue, $4,400.

f. Amortization for the year: equipment, $13,800; building, $7,420.

g. Accrued wages expense, $1,660.

Required

1. Journalize the adjusting entries that would lead to the adjusted trial balance shown here. Also journalize the closing entries.

2. Prepare Vernon Golf School's income statement and statement of owner's equity for the year ended April 30, 2004, and the classified balance sheet on that date. Use the account format for the balance sheet.

3. Compute Vernon Golf School's current ratio and debt ratio at April 30, 2004. One year ago, the current ratio stood at 1.21, and the debt ratio was 0.82. Did Vernon Golf School's ability to pay debts improve or deteriorate during 2004?

Problem 4-3B *Taking the accounting cycle through the closing entries* **(Obj. 2, 3)**

The unadjusted T-accounts of Ainsworth Media at December 31, 2003, and the related year-end adjustment data follow:

Cash		Accounts Receivable		Supplies	
Bal. 58,000		Bal. 88,000		Bal. 12,000	

Equipment		Accumulated Amortization		Accounts Payable	
Bal. 114,000			Bal. 24,000		Bal. 32,000

Salary Payable		Unearned Service Revenue		Note Payable, Long-Term	
			Bal. 4,000		Bal. 80,000

W. Ainsworth, Capital		W. Ainsworth, Withdrawals		Service Revenue	
	Bal. 82,000	Bal. 108,000			Bal. 260,000

Supplies Expense		Salary Expense		Insurance Expense	
		Bal. 72,000		Bal. 20,000	

Amortization Expense		Interest Expense	
		Bal. 10,000	

Adjustment data at December 31, 2003, include:

a. Amortization for the year, $10,000.

b. Supplies still unused at the year end, $4,000.

c. Accrued service revenue, $8,000.

d. Of the $4,000 balance of Unearned Service Revenue at the beginning of the year, the entire amount was earned during the year.

e. Accrued salary expense, $8,000.

Required

1. Write the trial balance on a work sheet and complete the work sheet. Key each adjusting entry by the letter corresponding to the data given.
2. Prepare the income statement, the statement of owner's equity, and the classified balance sheet in account format.
3. Journalize the adjusting and closing entries.
4. Did Ainsworth Media have a profitable year or a bad year during 2003? Give the reason for your answer.

Problem 4-4B *Completing the accounting cycle (Obj. 2, 3)*

This problem should be used only in conjunction with Problem 4-3B. It completes the accounting cycle by posting to T-accounts and preparing the postclosing trial balance.

Required

1. Using the Problem 4-3B data, post the adjusting and closing entries to the T-accounts, denoting adjusting amounts by *Adj.*, closing amounts by *Clo.*, and account balances by *Bal.*, as shown in Exhibit 4-9. Double underline all accounts with a zero ending balance.
2. Prepare the postclosing trial balance.

Problem 4-5B *Completing the accounting cycle (Obj. 2, 3, 5)*

The trial balance of Environmental Protection Services at October 31, 2004, and the data needed for the month-end adjustments are as follows:

ENVIRONMENTAL PROTECTION SERVICES
Trial Balance
October 31, 2004

Account Number	Account Title	Debit	Credit
110	Cash	$ 7,350	
120	Accounts receivable	22,965	
130	Prepaid rent	3,300	
140	Supplies	1,260	
150	Furniture	40,245	
151	Accumulated amortization—furniture		$ 5,100
160	Building	102,450	
161	Accumulated amortization—building		18,150
180	Land	27,000	
210	Accounts payable		10,935
220	Salary payable		
230	Unearned consulting revenue		7,950
300	K. Jones, capital		153,735
330	K. Jones, withdrawals	5,850	
400	Consulting revenue		18,840
510	Salary expense	2,760	
520	Rent expense		
530	Utilities expense	1,530	
540	Amortization expense—furniture		
550	Amortization expense—building		
570	Supplies expense		
	Total	$214,710	$214,710

The data needed for the month-end adjustments are as follows:

a. Unearned consulting revenue that still had not been earned at October 31, $7,350.

b. Rent still prepaid at October 31, $3,000.

c. Supplies used during the month, $1,155.

d. Amortization on furniture for the month, $375.

e. Amortization on building for the month, $870.

f. Accrued salary expense at October 31, $465.

Required

1. Open ledgers for the accounts listed in the trial balance, inserting their October 31 unadjusted balances. Also open the Income Summary ledger account, number 340. Date the balances of the following accounts October 1: Prepaid Rent, Supplies, Building, Accumulated Amortization—Building, Furniture, Accumulated Amortization—Furniture, Unearned Consulting Revenue, and K. Jones, capital.

2. Write the trial balance on a work sheet and complete the work sheet of Environmental Protection Services for the month ended October 31, 2004.

3. Using the completed work sheet, prepare the income statement, the statement of owner's equity, and the classified balance sheet in report format.

4. Using the work sheet data, journalize and post the adjusting and closing entries. Use dates and posting references. Use 12 as the number of the journal page.

5. Prepare a postclosing trial balance.

Problem 4-6B *Preparing a classified balance sheet in report format; evaluating a business (Obj. 5, 6)*

The accounts of Leaf Financial Services at March 31, 2003, are listed in alphabetical order.

Accounts payable	$7,350	Interest receivable	$ 450
Accounts receivable	5,750	Land	5,000
Accumulated amortization		Note payable, long-term	1,600
—building	23,650	Note receivable, long-term	3,450
Accumulated amortization		Other assets	1,150
—furniture	3,850	Other current liabilities	550
Advertising expense	450	Prepaid insurance	300
Amortization expense	950	Prepaid rent	2,350
Building	27,950	Salary expense	8,900
Cash	1,700	Salary payable	1,200
Cathy Maple, capital	25,350	Service revenue	35,550
Cathy Maple, withdrawals	15,600	Supplies	1,900
Furniture	21,600	Supplies expense	2,300
Insurance expense	300	Unearned service revenue	850
Interest payable	150		

Required

1. *All adjustments have been journalized and posted, but the closing entries have not yet been made.* Prepare the company's classified balance sheet in report format at March 31, 2003. Use captions for total assets, total liabilities, and total liabilities and owner's equity.

2. Compute Leaf Financial Services' current ratio and debt ratio at March 31, 2003. At March 31, 2002, the current ratio was 1.28, and the debt ratio was 0.32. Did Leaf Financial Services' ability to pay debts improve or deteriorate during 2003?

Problem 4-7B *Analyzing and journalizing corrections, adjustments, and closing entries (Obj. 3, 4)*

Link Back to Chapter 2 (Accounting Errors).

The auditors of Smirnov Printing encountered the following situations while adjusting and closing the books at February 28. Consider each situation independently.

a. The company bookkeeper made the following entry to record a $310 credit purchase of supplies:

| Feb. 26 | Equipment | 310 | |
| | Accounts Payable | | 310 |

Prepare the correcting entry, dated February 28.

b. A $450 debit to Accounts Receivable was posted as $540.
   (1) At what stage of the accounting cycle will this error be detected?
   (2) Describe the technique for identifying the amount of the error.

c. The $1,620 balance of Utilities Expense was entered as $16,200 on the trial balance.
   (1) What is the name of this type of error?
   (2) Assume this is the only error in the trial balance. Which will be greater, the total debits or the total credits, and by how much?
   (3) How can this type of error be identified?

d. The accountant failed to make the following adjusting entries at February 28:
   (1) Accrued service revenue, $1,800.
   (2) Insurance expense, $720.
   (3) Accrued interest expense on a note payable, $1,040.
   (4) Amortization of equipment, $7,400.
   (5) Earned service revenue that had been collected in advance, $5,400.

   Compute the overall net income effect of these omissions.

e. Record each of the adjusting entries identified in item d.

f. The revenue and expense accounts *after* the adjusting entries had been posted were Service Revenue, $154,995; Wage Expense, $53,325; Amortization Expense, $9,270; and Insurance Expense, $960. Two balances prior to closing were Capital, $112,725, and Withdrawals, $66,000. Journalize the closing entries.

Problem 4-8B *Preparing a work sheet, journalizing adjusting entries, closing the accounts (Obj. 1, 3)*

Alexander Brothers Marina performs overhauls and repairs to boats and motors at the marina and at the customer's location. The company's trial balance for the year ended June 30, 2004, appears on page 207.

Additional information:

a. On June 30, repair supplies costing $4,400 were still on hand.

b. An examination of the insurance policies showed $5,800 of insurance coverage had expired in the year ended June 30, 2004.

c. An examination of the equipment and the building showed the following:

	Equipment	Building
Estimated useful life	5 years	10 years
Estimated value at the end of the useful life	$0	$0

Amortization is calculated on a straight-line basis over the asset's life.

d. The company had performed $2,000 of services for a client who had paid $4,000 in advance.

e. Accrued interest on the mortgage at June 30, $1,600.

f. Accrued wages at June 30, $2,400.

ALEXANDER BROTHERS MARINA
Trial Balance
June 30, 2004

Cash	$ 4,600	
Accounts receivable	24,400	
Repair supplies	39,600	
Prepaid insurance....................................	9,400	
Equipment	120,000	
Accumulated amortization—equipment		$ 48,000
Building...	176,000	
Accumulated amortization—building		35,200
Land..	110,000	
Accounts payable......................................		13,000
Unearned repair revenues........................		4,000
Property taxes payable..............................		2,000
Notes payable, long-term		18,000
Mortgage payable.....................................		120,000
J. Alexander, capital..................................		115,200
J. Alexander, withdrawals	94,000	
Repair fees earned		345,000
Wages expense	89,200	
Utilities expense.......................................	1,600	
Travel expenses	31,600	
Total	$700,400	$700,400

Required

1. Complete a work sheet for the year ended June 30, 2004.

2. Journalize the adjusting required on June 30, 2004.

3. Journalize the closing entries that would be required on June 30, 2004.

4. Prepare a postclosing trial balance for June 30, 2004.

Problem 4-9B *Preparing a work sheet, closing the accounts, classifying the assets and liabilities, evaluating the current and debt ratios* **(Obj. 1, 3, 4, 6)**

Erin Klump, the accountant for Forsey Design had prepared the work sheet shown on the next page on a computer spreadsheet but has lost much of the data. The only particular item the accountant can recall is that there was an adjustment made to correct an error made where $300 of supplies, purchased on credit, had been incorrectly recorded as $3,000 of equipment.

Required

1. Complete the work sheet by filling in the missing data.

2. Journalize the closing entries that would be required on December 31, 2003.

3. Prepare the company's classified balance sheet as of December 31, 2003.

4. Compute Forsey Design's current ratio and debt ratio for December 31, 2003. On December 31, 2002, the current ratio was 2.25 and the debt ratio was 0.41. Comment on the changes in the ratios.

FORSEY DESIGN
Accounting Work Sheet
For the Year Ended December 31, 2003

Account Title	Trial Balance Debit	Trial Balance Credit	Adjustments Debit	Adjustments Credit	Adjusted Trial Balance Debit	Adjusted Trial Balance Credit	Income Statement Debit	Income Statement Credit	Balance Sheet Debit	Balance Sheet Credit
Cash	1,000								1,000	
Accounts receivable	11,350				11,400					
Supplies	700			(b) 350	700					
Prepaid insurance	800				700					
Equipment	13,000				11,500					
Accumulated amortization—equipment		1,500				2,250				
Building	43,000				43,000					
Accumulated amortization—building		12,300		(e) 1,150						
Land	12,000				12,000					
Accounts payable		8,000								
Wages payable		450								
Interest payable		1,000		(f) 200						
Unearned revenues		1,350	(g) 200							
Mortgage payable		20,000								20,000
B. Forsey, capital		29,500								29,500
B. Forsey, withdrawals	9,000				9,000				9,000	
Design fees earned		47,550						47,800		
Wages expense	28,350				28,550					
Insurance expense	1,100									
Interest expense	1,000									
Utilities expense	350				350					
	121,650	121,650								
Supplies expense			(b) 350				350			
Amortization expense—equipment			(d) 750				750			
Amortization expense—building										
Totals										

Challenge Problems

Problem 4-1C   *Closing the revenue and expense accounts*   *(Obj. 3)*

Small businesses used to use a simplified journal called a "synoptic" journal to account for their businesses. The synoptic journal usually had columns for cash, accounts receivable, other assets, accounts payable, revenues, expenses, and so on. It required double-entry bookkeeping and the columns were usually totalled every month. None of the accounts in the synoptic journal were ever closed; each year flowed into the next year. The column totals for revenues and expenses grew ever larger.

Required

1. Explain why the synoptic journal was used by small businesses. What was the advantage it provided?
2. What do you think was the principal disadvantage of the synoptic journal? Why is it a disadvantage?

Problem 4-2C   *Understanding the current ratio*   *(Obj. 6)*

It is July 15, 2004. A friend, who works in the office of a local company that has four fast-food restaurants, has come to you with a question. He knows you are studying accounting and asks if you could help him sort something out. He acknowledges that although he has worked for the company for three years as a general clerk, he really does not understand the accounting work he is doing.

The company has a large bank loan and, as your friend understands it, the company has agreed with the bank to maintain a current ratio (he thinks that is what it is called) of 1.8 to 1 (1.8:1). The company's year end is June 30. The owner came to him on July 7, 2004, and asked him to issue a batch of cheques to suppliers but to date them June 30. Your friend recognizes that the cheques will have an effect on the June 30, 2004, financial statements but doesn't think the effect will be too serious.

Required

Explain to your friend what the effect of paying invoices after June 30 but dating the cheques prior to June 30 has on the current ratio. Provide an example to illustrate your explanation.

Extending Your Knowledge

Decision Problems

1. Completing the accounting cycle to develop the information for a bank loan (Obj. 4, 6)

One year ago, your friend Michel Cote founded Computer Solutions. The business has prospered. Cote, who remembers that you took an accounting course while in college, comes to you for advice. He wishes to know how much net income his business earned during the past year. He also wants to know what the entity's total assets, liabilities, and owner's equity are. The accounting records consist of the T-accounts of the company's ledger, which were prepared by a bookkeeper who moved to another city. The ledger at December 31 of the current year appears as follows:

Cash		Accounts Receivable		Prepaid Rent	
Dec. 31 11,660		Dec. 31 24,720		Jan. 2 5,600	

Supplies		Computer Equipment		Accumulated Amortization	
Jan. 2 5,200		Jan. 2 87,200			

Accounts Payable		Unearned Service Revenue		Salary Payable	
	Dec. 31 37,080		Dec. 31 8,260		

M. Cote, Capital		M. Cote, Withdrawals		Service Revenue	
	Jan. 2 50,000	Dec. 31 86,840			Dec. 31 161,480

Amortization Expense		Salary Expense		Supplies Expense	
		Dec. 31 34,000			

Rent Expense		Utilities Expense	
		Dec. 31 1,600	

Cote indicates that at the year's end customers owe the company $3,200 accrued service revenue, which he expects to collect early next year. These revenues have not been recorded. During the year the company collected $8,260 service revenue in advance from customers, but the company earned only $1,200 of that amount. Rent expense for the year was $4,800, and the company used up $4,200 in supplies. Cote estimates that amortization on the equipment was $11,800 for the year. At December 31, Computer Solutions owes an employee $2,400 accrued salary.

Cote expresses concern that his withdrawals during the year might have exceeded the business's net income. To get a loan to expand the business, Cote must show the bank that Computer Solutions' owner's equity has grown from its original $50,000 balance. Has it? You and Cote agree that you will meet again in one week. You perform the analysis and prepare the financial statements to answer his questions.

2. Finding an error in the work sheets   (Obj. 1, 4)

You are preparing the financial statements for the year ended October 31, 2003, for Argus Publishing Company, a weekly newspaper. You began with the trial balance of the ledger, which balanced, and then made the required adjusting entries. To save time, you omitted preparing an adjusted trial balance. After making the adjustments on the work sheet, you extended the balances from the trial balance, adjusted for the adjusting entries, and computed amounts for the income statement and balance sheet columns.

a. When you added the debits and credits on the income statement columns, you found that the credits exceeded the debits by $20,000. According to your finding, did Argus Publishing Company have a profit or a loss?

b. You took the balancing amount from the income statement columns to the debit column of the balance sheet and found that the total debits exceeded the total credits in the balance sheet. The difference between the total debits and the total credits on the balance sheet is $40,000, which is two times the amount of the difference you calculated for the income statement columns. What is the cause of this difference? (Except for these errors, everything else is correct.)

Financial Statement Problem

Using an actual balance sheet (Obj. 6)

This problem, based on Intrawest Corporation's balance sheet in Appendix A, will familiarize you with some of the assets and liabilities of this actual company. Answer these questions, using Intrawest's balance sheet:

a. Which balance sheet format does Intrawest use?

b. What currency does Intrawest use to report financial results in its financial statements?

c. Name the company's largest current asset and largest current liability at June 30, 2000.

d. How much were total current assets and total current liabilities at June 30, 1999? Which had changed by the greater percentage during the year ended June 30, 2000: total current assets or total current liabilities? What were the percent changes?

e. Compute Intrawest Corporation's current ratio at June 30, 2000, and June 30, 1999. Also compute the debt ratios at these dates. Did the ratio values improve or deteriorate during 2000?

f. What is the cost of the company's capital assets at June 30, 2000? What is the book value of these assets? To answer this question, refer to the Properties note.

Appendix

Reversing Entries: An Optional Step

Reversing entries are special types of entries that ease the burden of accounting after adjusting and closing entries have been made at the end of a period. Reversing entries are used most often in conjunction with accrual-type adjustments such as an accrued salary expense and accrued service revenue. Reversing entries are *not* used for adjustments to record amortization and prepayments. *GAAP do not require reversing entries. They are used only for convenience and to save time.*

Accounting for Accrued Expenses   To see how reversing entries work, return to Air & Sea Travel's unadjusted trial balance at April 30, 2003 (Exhibit 4-2, page 164b). Salary Expense has a debit balance of $950 from salaries paid during April. At April 30, the company owes employees an additional $950 for the last part of the month.

Assume for this illustration that on May 5, the next payroll date, Air & Sea Travel will pay $950 of accrued salary plus $100 in salary that the employee has earned in the first few days of May. Air & Sea Travel's next payroll payment will be $1,050 ($950 + $100). But Air & Sea Travel must include the $950 in salary expense for April. To do so, Air & Sea Travel makes the following adjusting entry on April 30:

Adjusting Entries

April 30	Salary Expense	950	
	Salary Payable		950

After posting, the Salary Payable and Salary Expense accounts appear as follows:[2]

Salary Payable

	Apr. 30 Adj.[2] 950
	Apr. 30 Bal. 950

Salary Expense

Paid
during
April   CP   950
Apr. 30 Adj.   950
Apr. 30 Bal. 1,900

After the adjusting entry,
- The April income statement reports salary expense of $1,900.
- The April 30 balance sheet reports salary payable of $950.

The $1,900 debit balance of Salary Expense is eliminated by this closing entry at April 30, 2003, as follows:

Closing Entries

April 30	Income Summary	1,900	
	Salary Expense		1,900

---

[2] Entry explanations used throughout this discussion are
  Adj. = Adjusting entry   CP = Cash payment entry—includes a credit to Cash
  Bal. = Balance   CR = Cash receipt entry—includes a debit to Cash
  Clo. = Closing entry   Rev. = Reversing entry

After posting, Salary Expense has a zero balance as follows:

Salary Expense

Paid during April	CP	950		
Apr. 30 Adj.		950		
Apr. 30 Bal.		1,900	Apr. 30 Clo.	1,900

Accounting without a Reversing Entry   On May 5, the next payday, Air & Sea Travel pays the payroll of $1,050 and makes this journal entry:

May 5	Salary Payable	950	
	Salary Expense	100	
	Cash		1,050

This method of recording the cash payment is correct. However, it wastes time because the company's accountant must refer to the adjusting entries of April 30. Otherwise, Air & Sea Travel does not know the amount of the debit to Salary Payable (in this example, $950). Searching the preceding period's adjusting entries takes time and, in business, time is money. To save time, accountants use reversing entries.

Making a Reversing Entry   A *reversing entry* switches the debit and the credit of a previous adjusting entry. *A reversing entry, then, is the exact opposite of a prior adjusting entry.* The reversing entry is dated the first day of the period following the adjusting entry.

To illustrate reversing entries recall that on April 30, 2003, Air & Sea Travel made the following adjusting entry to accrue Salary Payable:

Adjusting Entries

Apr. 30	Salary Expense	950	
	Salary Payable		950

The reversing entry simply reverses the position of the debit and the credit:

Reversing Entries

May 1	Salary Payable..	950	
	Salary Expense		950

Observe that the reversing entry is dated the first day of the new period. It is the exact opposite of the April 30 adjusting entry. Ordinarily, the accountant who makes the adjusting entry also prepares the reversing entry at the same time. Air & Sea Travel dates the reversing entry as of the first day of the next period, however, so that it affects only the new period. Note how the accounts appear after the company posts the reversing entry:

Salary Payable

May 1 Rev.	950	Apr. 30 Bal.	950
	Zero balance		

Salary Expense

Apr. 30 Bal.	1,900	Apr. 30 Clo.	1,900
	Zero balance		
		May 1 **Rev.**	950

WORKING IT OUT

A company pays its employees $1,500 every Friday, the end of a 5-day workweek. What journal entry is made each Friday?

Salary Expense	1,500	
Cash		1,500

If December 31 falls on a Tuesday, what would be the adjusting entry?

Salary Expense	600	
Salary Payable		600

What would be the reversing entry on January 1?

Salary Payable	600	
Salary Expense		600

What would be the entry to record the payroll the next Friday?

Salary Expense	1,500	
Cash		1,500

The arrow shows the transfer of the $950 credit balance from Salary Payable to Salary Expense. This credit balance in Salary Expense does not mean that the entity has negative salary expense, as you might think. Instead, the odd credit balance is merely a temporary result of the reversing entry. The credit balance is eliminated on May 5 when the $1,050 cash payment for salaries is debited to Salary Expense in the customary manner:

May 5	Salary Expense	1,050	
	Cash		1,050

Then this cash payment entry is posted as follows:

Salary Expense

May 5	CP	1,050	May 1	Rev.	950
May 5	Bal.	100			

Now Salary Expense has its correct debit balance of $100, which is the amount of salary expense incurred thus far in May. The $1,050 cash disbursement also pays the liability for Salary Payable so that Salary Payable has a zero balance, which is correct.

Accounting for Accrued Revenues   While most reversing entries are made to accrue expenses, reversing entries may be made to accrue revenues. For example, if Air and Sea Travel had completed some consulting work for a client, an entry would be made to debit Fees Receivable and credit Fee Revenue at April 30, 2003. Fee Revenue would be closed to the Income Summary in the usual way. A reversing entry on May 1, 2003, would reduce the Fee Receivable and temporarily create a debit balance in the Fee Revenue account. When the payment is received, the accountant would debit Cash and credit Fee Revenue.

Appendix Problem

Problem 4A-1   *Using reversing entries*

Refer to the data in Problem 4-5A, pages 196–197.

Required

1. Open ledger accounts for Salary Payable and Salary Expense. Insert their unadjusted balances at August 31, 2004.

2. Journalize adjusting entry *f* and the closing entry for Salary Expense at August 31. Post to the accounts.

3. On September 5, Baines Insurance paid the next payroll amount of $870. Journalize this cash payment, and post to the accounts. Show the balance in each account.

4. Repeat Requirements 1 through 3 using a reversing entry. Compare the balances of Salary Payable and Salary Expense computed by using a reversing entry with those balances computed without using a reversing entry (as appear in your answer to Requirement 3).

CHAPTER

5

Merchandising Operations and the Accounting Cycle

CHAPTER OBJECTIVES

After studying this chapter, you should be able to

1. Use sales and gross margin to evaluate a company

2. Account for the purchase and sale of inventory under the perpetual inventory system

3. Adjust and close the accounts of a merchandising business under the perpetual inventory system

4. Prepare a merchandiser's financial statements under the perpetual inventory system

5. Use the gross margin percentage and the inventory turnover ratio to evaluate a business

6. Compute the cost of goods sold under the periodic inventory system

Supplement Learning Objectives

S2. Account for the purchase and sale of inventory under the periodic inventory system

S3. Compute the cost of goods sold under the periodic inventory system

S4. Adjust and close the accounts of a merchandising business under the periodic inventory system

S5. Prepare a merchandiser's financial statements under the periodic inventory system

The Forzani Group Ltd. (FGL) is Canada's largest-selling retailer of sporting goods. The company operates its retail stores under four different banners: SportChek, Sports Experts, Forzani's, and Coast Mountain Sports.

"FGL has redefined the concept of sporting goods retailing by migrating the experience to one focussed on an active lifestyle." Indeed, the company recovered from near-bankruptcy in the mid-1990s to become one of the most successful retailers in the country. The company operates over 130 corporate stores and 165 franchised stores with over 46,000 product items available. FGL has defined its target markets and is taking strategic initiatives to ensure success.

One such initiative is to deliver the "customer experience" at the lowest possible cost. To achieve this initiative, the company must successfully manage its inventory, which accounted for 55 percent of its total assets in fiscal year 2000. Inventory management for retailers, like FGL, is critical to their success. SportChek wants to ensure that it has enough inventory on hand and the "right" products to meet the needs of its customers. At the same time, too much inventory or the "wrong" products in inventory can cause cashflow problems. Advances in computer systems have helped companies manage their inventory by providing up-to-date inventory data in real time.

FGL recognizes the potential changes in buying habits that the internet will bring. To this end, FGL is creating its own website to take advantage of e-commerce retailing.

Source: The Forzani Group Ltd. 2000 Annual Report.

The Forzani Group Ltd.
www.forzanigroup.com

The Bay
www.hbc.com

Canadian Tire
www.canadiantire.com

Petro-Canada
www.petro-canada.ca

Molson Breweries
www.molson.com

WHAT comes to mind when you think of *merchandising?* You probably think of the clothing that you purchase from a department store, the bread you buy at the grocery store, or the gas you purchase at your local service station. In addition to SportChek and Sports Experts stores, other merchandisers include Zellers, The Bay, Canadian Tire, Petro-Canada, and Shoppers Drug Mart.

How do the operations of The Forzani Group Ltd. and other merchandisers differ from those of the businesses we have studied so far? In the first four chapters, Air & Sea Travel provided an illustration of a business that earns revenue by selling its services. Service enterprises include Four Seasons Hotels, Air Canada, physicians, lawyers, public accountants, the Vancouver Canucks hockey club, and the twelve-year-old who cuts lawns in your neighbourhood. A *merchandising entity* earns its revenue by selling products, called *merchandise inventory* or, simply, *inventory.*

This chapter demonstrates the central role of inventory in a business that sells merchandise. **Inventory** includes all goods that the company owns and expects to sell in the normal course of operations. Some businesses, such as Zellers department stores, Petro-Canada gas stations, and Safeway grocery stores, buy their inventory in finished form ready for sale to customers. Others, such as Bombardier and Molson Breweries, manufacture their own products. Both groups sell products rather than services.

We illustrate accounting for the purchase and sale of inventory, how to adjust and close the books of a merchandiser and how to prepare financial statements for a merchandiser. The chapter illustrates both the perpetual and periodic inventory methods. The chapter covers two ratios that investors and creditors use to evaluate companies.

Before launching into merchandising, let's compare service entities, with which you are familiar, to merchandising companies. The following summarized financial statements will show how the two types of companies are similar and different:

SERVICE CO.* Income Statement For the Year Ended June 30, 2002		MERCHANDISING CO.** Income Statement For the Year Ended June 30, 2002	
Service revenue	$XXX	*Sales* revenue............................	$XXX
Expenses		*Cost of goods sold*	X
Salary expense	X	Gross margin	XX
Amortization expense	X	Operating *expenses*	
Net income.............................	$ X	Salary expense	X
		Amortization expense	X
		Income tax expense.............	X
		Net income.............................	$ X

SERVICE CO. Balance Sheet June 30, 2002		MERCHANDISING CO. Balance Sheet June 30, 2002	
Assets		**Assets**	
Current assets:		Current assets:	
Cash......................................	$X	Cash......................................	$X
Short-term investments......	X	Short-term investments......	X
Accounts receivable, net.....	X	Accounts receivable, net.....	X
Prepaid expenses................	X	*Inventory*...............................	X
		Prepaid expenses................	X

* Such as Air & Sea Travel

** Such as The Forzani Group Ltd., a corporation

What Are Merchandising Operations?

OBJECTIVE 1
Use sales and gross margin to evaluate a company

Exhibit 5-1 shows the income statement of The Forzani Group Ltd. (FGL) for two recent years. FGL generates revenue in two different ways. Corporate revenue is revenue earned by selling merchandise through company-owned stores. Franchise revenue is revenue earned from selling merchandise to franchise stores, which are stores that belong to other owners that are allowed to use FGL's store names, advertising, and selling expertise. In return, the franchise stores agree to purchase all inventory from FGL. FGL's income statement differs from those of the service business discussed in previous chapters. For comparison, Exhibit 5-1 also provides the income statement for Air & Sea Travel. The highlighted items in the FGL statement are unique to merchandising operations.

The selling price of merchandise sold by a business is called **sales revenue**, often abbreviated as **sales**. (**Net sales** equals sales revenue minus any sales returns and sales discounts.) The major revenue of a merchandising entity, sales revenue, results in an increase in capital from delivering inventory to customers. The major expense of a merchandiser is **cost of goods sold**, also called **cost of sales**. It represents the entity's cost of the goods (the inventory) it sold to customers. While inventory is held by a business, the inventory is an asset because the goods are an economic resource with future value to the company. When the inventory is sold, however, the inventory's cost becomes an expense to the seller because the goods are no longer available. When one of FGL's SportChek stores sells equipment to a customer, the equipment's cost is expensed as cost of goods sold on SportChek's books.

THE FORZANI GROUP LTD.
Consolidated Statements of Income (adapted)
For the Years Ended January 30, 2000, and January 31, 1999

	(In thousands of dollars)	
	2000	1999
Revenue		
Corporate	$325,041	$275,293
Franchise	129,060	103,355
	454,101	378,648
Cost of sales	310,816	253,679
Gross margin	143,285	124,969
Operating and administrative expenses		
Store operating	84,828	76,826
General and administrative	33,008	29,358
	117,836	106,184
Operating income before undernoted items	25,449	18,785
Amortization	8,564	6,514
Interest	2,542	4,147
	11,106	10,661
Net earnings	$ 14,343	$ 8,124

AIR & SEA TRAVEL
Income Statement
For the Year Ended December 31, 2003

Service revenue	$113,000
Expenses (listed individually)	42,000
Net earnings	$ 71,000

Net sales revenue minus cost of goods sold is called **gross margin** or **gross profit**.

Net sales revenue (sometimes abbreviated as Sales)	–	Cost of goods sold (same as Cost of sales)	=	Gross margin (same as Gross profit)

or, more simply,

Sales	–	Cost of sales	=	Gross profit

Gross margin is a measure of business success. A sufficiently high gross margin is vital to a merchandiser, since all other expenses of the company are deducted from this gross margin. FGL's operations were more successful during the year ended January 30, 2000 because net income increased.

The following example will clarify the nature of gross margin. Suppose SportChek's cost for a certain piece of hockey equipment is $50 and SportChek sells the equipment to a customer in Halifax for $90. SportChek's gross margin on the equipment is $40 ($90 – $50). The gross margin reported on FGL's income statement, $143,285,000, is the sum of the gross margins on all the products the company sold during its 2000 fiscal year.

What Goes into Inventory Cost?

The $113,827,000 cost of inventory on The Forzani Group Ltd.'s (FGL) balance sheet represents all the costs FGL incurred to bring the merchandise to the point of sale.

Suppose FGL's Sports Experts stores purchase soccer balls from a manufacturer in Hong Kong. Sports Experts' cost of a soccer ball would include

- Cost of the ball—say $4.00 per ball.
- Customs duties paid to the Canadian government in order to import the soccer balls—say $0.35, added to the cost of each ball.
- Shipping cost from the manufacturer in Hong Kong to Sports Experts' location in Ontario. This cost is called *freight* or *freight in*. Assume freight adds $0.50 to each soccer ball.
- Insurance on the soccer balls while in transit—say $0.15 per ball.

In total, Sports Experts' cost of a soccer ball totals $5.00 ($4.00 + $0.35 + $0.50 + $0.15). The cost principle applies to all assets, as follows:

**The cost of any asset is the sum of all the costs
incurred to bring the asset to its intended use.**

For merchandise inventory, the intended use is readiness for sale. After the goods are offered for sale, then other costs, such as advertising, display, and sales commissions, are expensed. Thus these costs are *not* included as the cost of inventory.

The Operating Cycle for a Merchandising Business

Some merchandising entities buy inventory, sell the inventory to their customers, and use the cash to purchase more inventory to repeat the cycle. Other merchandisers, like microbreweries such as Sleeman's or companies like Magna International Inc., manufacture their products and sell them to customers. The balance of this chapter considers the first group of merchandisers that buy products and resell them. Exhibit 5-2 diagrams the operating cycle for *cash sales* and for *sales on account*. For a cash sale—Panel A—the cycle is from cash to inventory, which is purchased for resale and back to cash. For a sale on account—Panel B—the cycle is from cash to inventory to accounts receivable and back to cash. In all lines of business, managers strive to shorten the cycle in order to keep assets active. The faster the sale of inventory and the collection of cash, the higher the profits, assuming cost and selling price stay the same.

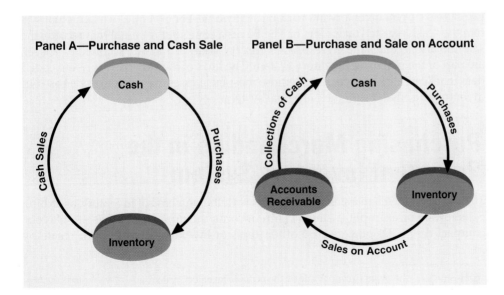

EXHIBIT 5-2

Operating Cycle of a Merchandiser

Inventory Systems: Perpetual and Periodic

There are two main types of inventory accounting systems: the periodic system and the perpetual system.

The **periodic inventory system** is used by businesses that sell relatively inexpensive goods. A very small grocery store without an optical-scanning cash register to read UPC codes does not keep a daily running record of every loaf of bread and package of bacon that it buys and sells. The cost of record keeping would be overwhelming. Instead, grocers count their inventory periodically—at least once a year—to determine the quantities on hand. The inventory amounts are used to prepare the annual financial statements. Businesses such as restaurants and small retail stores also use the periodic inventory system. The end-of-chapter supplement covers the periodic inventory system. That system is being used less and less as more businesses keep their inventory records by computer.

Under the **perpetual inventory system**, the business maintains a running record of inventory and cost of goods sold. This system achieves control over expensive goods such as automobiles, jewellery, and furniture. Recently, the low cost of computer information systems has increased the use of perpetual systems. Computers reduce the time required to manage inventory and thus increase a company's ability to control its merchandise. But even under a perpetual system the business counts the inventory on hand at least once a year. The physical count establishes the correct amount of ending inventory, which may have been affected by pilferage or spoilage, and serves as a check on the perpetual records.

The following chart compares the perpetual and periodic systems:

Perpetual Inventory System	Periodic Inventory System
• Keeps a running record of all goods bought and sold (units and price).	• Does *not* keep a running record of all goods bought and sold.
• Inventory counted at least once a year.	• Inventory counted at least once a year.
• Used for all types of goods.	• Used for *inexpensive* goods.

Computerized Inventory Systems

A computerized inventory system can keep accurate, up-to-date records of the number and cost of units purchased, the number and cost of units sold, and the quantities and cost on hand. Inventory systems are often integrated with accounts receivable and sales. The computer can keep up-to-the-minute records, so managers can call up current inventory information at any time. For example, in a perpetual system the "cash register" at Zellers or The Bay is a computer terminal that records the sale and also updates the inventory records. Bar codes, which are scanned by a laser, are part of the perpetual inventory system. The lines of the bar code represent coded data that keep track of each item. Because most businesses use bar codes, we base our inventory discussions on the perpetual system.[1]

OBJECTIVE 2
Account for the purchase and sale of inventory under the perpetual inventory system

Purchasing Merchandise in the Perpetual Inventory System

The cycle of a merchandising entity begins with the purchase of inventory, as Exhibit 5-2 shows. For example, a stereo centre records the purchase of cassette players, compact disc (CD) players, and other items of inventory acquired for resale by

---

[1]For instructors who prefer to concentrate on the periodic inventory system, an overview starts on page 241 and a comprehensive treatment of that system begins on p. 273. Follow Chapter Objectives S2 through S5 instead of 2 through 4.

debiting the Inventory account. A $500 purchase on account is recorded as follows:

June 14   Inventory 500
              Accounts payable...................................... 500
           Purchased inventory on account.

The Purchase Invoice: A Basic Business Document

Business documents are the tangible evidence of transactions. In this section, we trace the steps that Austin Sound Centre, in Kingston, Ontario, takes to order, receive, and pay for inventory. Many companies buy and sell their goods electronically—with no invoices, no cheques, and so on. Here we use actual documents to illustrate what takes place behind the scenes.

1. Suppose Austin Sound Centre wants to stock JVC brand CD players, cassette decks, and speakers. Austin prepares a *purchase order* and mails it, faxes it, or transmits it via computer to JVC Canada Inc.

2. On receipt of the purchase order, JVC searches its warehouse for the inventory that Austin Sound Centre ordered. JVC ships the equipment and sends the invoice to Austin Sound on the same day. The **invoice** is the seller's request for payment from the purchaser. It is also called the *bill*.

3. Often the purchaser receives the invoice before the inventory arrives. Austin Sound does not pay immediately. Instead, Austin waits until the inventory arrives in order to ensure that it is the correct type and quantity ordered, and in good condition. After the inventory is inspected and approved, Austin Sound pays JVC the invoice amount according to the terms of payment previously negotiated.

Exhibit 5-3 is a copy of an invoice from JVC Canada Inc. to Austin Sound Centre. From Austin Sound's perspective, this document is a *purchase invoice* (it is being used to purchase goods). To JVC it is a *sales invoice* (it is being used to sell goods).

JVC Canada Inc.
www.jvc.ca

Discounts from Purchase Prices

There are two major types of discounts from purchase prices: quantity discounts and cash discounts (called *purchase discounts*).

Quantity Discounts   A *quantity discount* works this way. The larger the quantity purchased, the lower the price per item. For example, JVC may offer no quantity discount for the purchase of only one or two CD players, and charge the *list* price—the full price—of $200 per unit. However, JVC may offer the following quantity discount terms in order to persuade customers to buy more CD players:

Quantity	Quantity Discount	Net Price Per Unit
Buy minimum quantity, 3 CD players	5%	$190 [$200 − 0.05($200)]
Buy 4–9 CD players	10%	$180 [$200 − 0.10($200)]
Buy more than 9 CD players	20%	$160 [$200 − 0.20($200)]

Suppose Austin Sound Centre purchases five CD players from this manufacturer. The cost of each CD player is, therefore, $180. Purchase of five units on account would be recorded by debiting Inventory and crediting Accounts Payable for the total price of $900 ($180 per unit × 5 items purchased).

There is no Quantity Discount account and no special accounting entry for a quantity discount. Instead, all accounting entries are based on the net price of a purchase after the quantity discount has been subtracted, as shown on the invoice.

Purchase Discounts   Many businesses also offer purchase discounts to their customers. A purchase discount is totally different from a quantity discount. A *purchase discount* is a reward for prompt payment. If a quantity discount is also offered, the purchase discount is computed on the net purchase amount after the quantity discount has been subtracted, further reducing the cost of the inventory to the purchaser.

EXHIBIT 5-3

Business Invoice

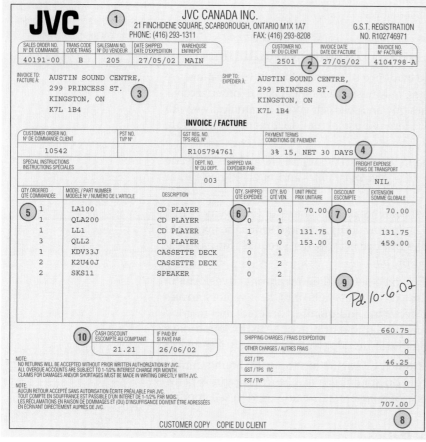

The annotations to the right of the invoice:

1. The seller.

2. The invoice date, needed for determining whether the purchaser gets a discount for prompt payment (see 4).

3. The purchaser. This inventory is invoiced (billed) and shipped to the same address.

4. Credit terms of the transaction: If it pays within 15 days of the invoice date, Austin Sound may deduct 3% of the total amount. Otherwise, the full amount—net—is due in 30 days.*

5. Austin ordered 6 CD players, 3 cassette decks, and 2 speakers.

6. JVC shipped 5 CD players, no cassette decks, and no speakers.

7. Quantity discount offered by JVC.

8. Total invoice amount.

9. Austin's payment date. How much did Austin pay? (See 10.)

10. Payment occurred 14 days after the invoice date—within the discount period—so Austin paid $685.79 ($707 – 3% discount). We will disregard GST for now.

*A full discussion of discounts appears in the next section.

WORKING IT OUT

Austin Sound Centre purchases $1,000 of merchandise on account, terms 2/10, n/30 on September 15; $100 of merchandise is returned for credit on September 20. Payment in full is made on September 25. Journalize the transactions.

A:

Sept. 15
Inventory   1,000
   Accts. Pay.   1,000

Sept. 20
Accts. Pay.   100
   Inventory   100

Sept. 25
Accts. Pay.   900
   Inventory   18
   Cash   882
Discount is $18 (2% × $900). No discount is given on the merchandise returned.

JVC's credit terms of 3% 15, NET 30 DAYS can also be expressed as 3/15 n/30. This means that Austin Sound Centre may deduct 3 percent of the total amount due if Austin pays within 15 days of the invoice date. Otherwise, the full amount—NET—is due in 30 days. Terms of simply n/30 indicate that no discount is offered, and that payment is due 30 days after the invoice date. Terms of *eom* mean that payment is due by the end of the current month. However, a purchase after the 25th of the current month on terms of *eom* can be paid at the end of the next month.

Many businesses that have computerized accounting systems program their system to flag invoices as the date for taking the discount approaches so the business can take advantage of the purchase discount.

Let's use the Exhibit 5-3 transaction to illustrate accounting for a purchase discount. For the moment, disregard GST and use the invoice total of $707.00 when recording purchases and purchase discounts. GST is discussed on page 228. Austin Sound Centre records the purchase on account as follows:

May 27	Inventory	707.00	
	Accounts Payable		707.00
	Purchased inventory on account.		

The accounting equation shows that a credit purchase of inventory increases both assets (Inventory) and liabilities (Accounts Payable), as follows:

ASSETS	=	LIABILITIES	+	OWNER'S EQUITY
Inventory	=	Accounts Payable		
$707	=	$707	+	0

Austin paid within the discount period so its cash payment entry is

June 10	Accounts Payable	707.00	
	Cash		685.79
	Inventory...		21.21
	Paid on account within discount period.		
	The discount is $21.21 [707.00 × 0.03]		

After paying the account, Austin Sound's assets and liabilities both decrease, as follows:

ASSETS			=	LIABILITIES	+	OWNER'S EQUITY
Cash	+	Inventory	=	Accounts Payable		
–$685.29		–$21.21	=	–$707	+	0

–$707

Note the credit to Inventory. After Austin Sound has taken its discount, Austin Sound must adjust the Inventory account to reflect its true cost of the goods. In effect, this inventory cost Austin Sound $685.79 ($707.00 minus the purchase discount of $21.21 [3% of $707.00]), as shown in the following Inventory account:

Inventory

May 27	707.00	June 10	21.21
Bal.	685.79		

However, if Austin Sound pays this invoice after the discount period, it must pay the full invoice amount. In this case, the payment entry is

June 29	Accounts Payable	707.00	
	Cash		707.00
	Paid on account after discount period.		

Without the discount, Austin Sound's cost of the inventory is the full amount of $707, as shown in the following T-account:

Inventory

May 27	707.00	

Purchase Returns and Allowances

Most businesses allow their customers to *return* merchandise that is defective, damaged in shipment, or otherwise unsuitable. Or if the buyer chooses to keep damaged goods, the seller may deduct an *allowance* from the amount the buyer owes. Both purchase returns and purchase allowances decrease the amount that the buyer must pay the seller.

Suppose the $70 CD player (model LA100) purchased by Austin Sound Centre (in Exhibit 5-3) was not the CD player ordered. Austin Sound returns the merchandise to the seller and records the purchase return as follows:

June 3	Accounts Payable	70.00	
	Inventory..		70.00
	Returned inventory to seller.		

Now assume that one of the JVC CD players was damaged in shipment to Austin Sound Centre. The damage is minor, and Austin decides to keep the CD player in exchange for a $10 allowance from JVC. To record this purchase allowance, Austin Sound Centre makes this entry:

June 4	Accounts Payable	10.00	
	Inventory..		10.00
	Received a purchase allowance.		

The return and the allowance had two effects:

(1) They decreased Austin Sound's liability, which is why we debit Accounts Payable.

(2) They decreased the net cost of the inventory, which is why we credit Inventory.

Assume that Austin Sound has not yet paid its liability to JVC. After these return ($70) and allowance ($10) transactions are posted, Austin Sound's accounts will show these balances:

Inventory					Accounts Payable			
May 27	707.00	June 3	70.00		June 3	70.00	May 27	707.00
		June 4	10.00		June 4	10.00		
Bal.	627.00						Bal.	627.00

Austin Sound's cost of *inventory* is $627, and Austin Sound owes JVC $627 on *account payable*. If Austin Sound pays within the discount period, 3 percent will be deducted from the $627.00 balance.

Transportation Costs: Who Pays?

The transportation cost of moving inventory from seller to buyer can be significant. The purchase agreement specifies FOB terms to indicate who pays the shipping charges. *FOB* means *free on board*. FOB governs

(1) when legal title passes from the seller to buyer, and

(2) who pays the freight.

- Under FOB *shipping point* terms, title passes when the inventory leaves the seller's place of business—the shipping point. The buyer owns the goods while they are in transit, and therefore the buyer pays the transportation cost.

- Under FOB *destination* terms, title passes when the goods reach the destination, so the seller pays transportation cost.

Exhibit 5-4 summarizes FOB.

Freight In FOB shipping point terms are the most common, so the buyer generally pays the shipping cost. A freight cost that the buyer pays on an inventory purchase is called *freight in*. In accounting, the cost of an asset includes all costs incurred to bring the asset to its intended use. For inventory, cost therefore includes the

- *Net cost* after all discounts, returns, and allowances have been subtracted, plus

- *Freight* (transportation, or shipping) costs to be paid

To record the payment for freight in, the buyer debits Inventory and credits Cash or Accounts Payable for the amount. Suppose Austin Sound receives a $60 shipping bill directly from the freight company. Austin's entry to record payment of the freight charge is:

June 1	Inventory	60	
	Cash		60
	Paid a freight bill.		

EXHIBIT 5-4

FOB Terms

	FOB Shipping Point	FOB Destination
When does title pass to buyer?	At the shipping point	At the destination
Who pays transportation cost?	Buyer	Seller

The freight charge increases the cost of the inventory to $687.00 as follows:

Inventory

(Purchase)	May 27	707.00	June 3	70.00	(Return)
(Freight)	June 1	60.00	June 4	10.00	(Allowance)
(Net cost)	Bal.	687.00			

Any discounts would be computed only on the account payable to the seller, not on the transportation costs, because the freight company usually offers no discount.

Under FOB shipping point terms, the seller sometimes prepays the transportation cost as a convenience, and adds this cost on the invoice. The buyer can debit Inventory for the combined cost of the inventory and the shipping cost because both costs apply to the merchandise. A $5,000 purchase of goods, coupled with a related freight charge of $400, would be recorded as follows:

March 12	Inventory	5,400	
	Accounts Payable		5,400
	Purchased inventory on account, including freight of $400.		

If the buyer pays within the discount period, the discount will be computed on the $5,000 merchandise cost, not on the $5,400. No discount is offered on transportation cost.

Freight Out   The cost of freight charges paid to ship goods sold to customers is called *freight out*. Freight out is a delivery expense, which is paid by the seller, not the purchaser. Delivery expense is an operating expense for the seller. It is debited to the Delivery Expense account.

Selling Inventory and Recording Cost of Goods Sold

After a company buys inventory, the next step in the operating cycle is to sell the goods. We shift now to the selling side and follow Austin Sound Centre through a sequence of selling transactions. A sale earns a reward, Sales Revenue. A sale also requires a sacrifice in the form of an expense, Cost of Goods Sold, as the seller gives up the asset Inventory.

After making a sale on account, Austin Sound Centre may experience any of the following:

- A sales return: The customer may return goods to Austin Sound.

- A sales allowance: For one reason or another, Austin Sound may grant a sales allowance to reduce the amount of cash collected from the customer.

- A sales discount: If the customer pays within the discount period—under terms such as 2/10 n/30—Austin Sound collects the discounted amount.
- Freight out: Austin Sound may have to pay Delivery Expense to transport the goods to the buyer's location.

The sale of inventory may be for cash or on account, as Exhibit 5-2 shows.

Cash Sale   Sales of retailers, such as grocery stores and restaurants, are often for cash. Cash sales of $3,000 would be recorded by debiting Cash and crediting Sales Revenue as follows:

Jan. 9	Cash...	3,000	
	Sales Revenue		3,000
	Cash sale.		

To update the inventory records, the business also must decrease the Inventory balance. Suppose these goods cost the seller $1,900. An accompanying entry is needed to transfer the $1,900 cost of the goods—*not their selling price of $3,000*—from the Inventory account to the Cost of Goods Sold account as follows:

Jan . 9	Cost of Goods Sold...	1,900	
	Inventory..		1,900
	Recorded the cost of goods sold.		

Cost of goods sold (also called cost of sales) is the largest single expense of most businesses that sell merchandise, such as Bombardier, JVC, and Austin Sound. It is the cost of the inventory that the business has sold to customers. The Cost of Goods Sold account keeps a current balance as transactions are journalized and posted.

After posting, the Cost of Goods Sold account holds the cost of the merchandise sold ($1,900 in this case):

Inventory				Cost of Goods Sold		
Purchases	50,000	Jan. 9	1,900	Jan. 9	1,900	
(amount						
assumed)						

The computer automatically records this entry when the cashier keys in the code number of the inventory that is sold. Optical scanners at cash registers perform this task in most stores.

Sale on Account   Most sales in Canada are made on account (on credit) using either the seller's credit facility or a credit card such as Visa or MasterCard. To simplify the discussion, we will assume the seller records the receivable as a regular account receivable rather than a special receivable from the credit card company. A $5,000 sale on account is recorded by a debit to Accounts Receivable and a credit to Sales Revenue, as follows:

Jan. 11	Accounts Receivable..	5,000	
	Sales Revenue		5,000
	Sale on account.		

If we assume that these goods cost the seller $2,900, the accompanying cost of goods sold and inventory entry is

Jan . 11	Cost of Goods Sold...	2,900	
	Inventory..		2,900
	Recorded the cost of goods sold.		

After recording the January 9 and 11 transactions, sales revenue is $8,000 ($3,000 + $5,000). Cost of goods sold totals $4,800 ($1,900 + $2,900).

The seller records the related cash receipt on account as follows:

Jan . 19	Cash...	5,000	
	Accounts Receivable...		5,000
	Collection on account.		

Offering Sales Discounts and Sales Returns and Allowances

We just saw that purchase discounts and purchase returns and allowances decrease the cost of inventory purchases. In the same way, **sales discounts** and **sales returns and allowances**, which are contra accounts to Sales Revenue, decrease the revenue earned on sales.

Credit-balance account — Debit-balance accounts — Credit subtotal (*not* a separate account)

Sales Revenue − Sales Discounts − Sales Returns and Allowances = Net sales revenue*

*Often abbreviated as Net sales.

This equation calculates net sales. Note that sales discounts can be given on both goods and services.

Companies keep close watch on their customers' paying habits and on their own sales of defective and unsuitable merchandise. They maintain separate accounts for Sales Discounts and Sales Returns and Allowances. Let's examine a sequence of the sale transactions of JVC. Assume JVC is selling to Austin Sound Centre.

On July 7, JVC sells stereo components for $7,200 on credit terms of 3/15 n/30. These goods cost JVC $4,700. JVC's entries to record this credit sale and the related cost of goods sold are:

July 7	Accounts Receivable	$7,200	
	Sales Revenue		$7,200
	Sale on account.		

July 7	Cost of Goods Sold	$4,700	
	Inventory		$4,700
	Recorded the cost of goods sold.		

Assume the buyer, Austin Sound Centre, returns goods that were sold by JVC for $600. These goods are not damaged and can be resold. JVC records the sales return and the related decrease in Accounts Receivable as follows:

July 12	Sales Returns and Allowances	600	
	Accounts Receivable		600
	Received returned goods.		

JVC receives the returned merchandise and updates the inventory records. JVC must also decrease cost of goods sold as follows (these goods cost JVC $400):

July 12	Inventory	400	
	Cost of Goods Sold		400
	Returned goods to inventory.		

Suppose JVC grants to the buyer a $100 sales allowance for damaged goods. Austin Sound then subtracts $100 from the amount it will pay JVC. JVC journalizes this transaction by debiting Sales Returns and Allowances and crediting Accounts Receivable as follows:

July 15	Sales Returns and Allowances..................................	100	
	Accounts Receivable..		100
	Granted a sales allowance for damaged goods.		

No inventory entry is needed for a sales allowance transaction because the seller, JVC, receives no returned goods from the customer. Instead, JVC will simply receive less cash from the customer.

After the preceding entries are posted, all the accounts have up-to-date balances. JVC's Accounts Receivable has a $6,500 debit balance, as follows:

Accounts Receivable

(Sale)	July 7	7,200	July 12	600	(Return)
			15	100	(Allowance)
	Bal.	6,500			

WORKING IT OUT

Best Company sold $2,000 of merchandise to Super Sales Co. on March 1, 2003, and granted a 5% quantity discount off that list price. Super Sales returned merchandise on March 4, and Best granted Super Sales a sales allowance of $200. Best Company collected the balance on March 9, after subtracting a 2% sales discount. Record Best's collection of cash on March 9.

A:

Cash	1,666[1]	
Sales Discounts	34[2]	
Accounts Receivable		1,700[3]

[1]$2,000 − 0.05($2,000) = $1,900
$1,900 − $200 = $1,700
$1,700 − 0.02($1,700) = $1,666
[2]$1,700 × 0.02 = $34
[3]$2,000 − 0.05 ($2000) − 200 = $1,700

On July 22, the last day of the discount period, JVC collects $4,000 of this accounts receivable. Assume JVC allows customers to take discounts on all amounts JVC receives within the discount period. JVC's cash receipt is $3,880 [calculated as $4,000 − (0.03 × $4,000)], and the collection entry is

July 22	Cash..	3,880	
	Sales Discounts.	120	
	Accounts Receivable..		4,000
	Cash collection within the discount period.		
	Sales discount is $120 (0.03 × $4,000).		

Suppose JVC collects the remainder of $2,500 on July 28. That date is after the discount period, so there is no sales discount. To record this collection on account, JVC debits Cash and credits Accounts Receivable for the same amount, as follows:

July 28	Cash..	2,500	
	Accounts Receivable..		2,500
	Cash collection after the discount period.		

In Exhibit 5-1, The Forzani Group Ltd.—like most other businesses—reports to the public only the net sales figure. But FGL managers use the return and allowance data to track customer satisfaction and product quality.

Goods and Services Tax

This topic is introduced here to make you aware of the goods and services tax because most goods and services sold today in Canada have the Goods and Services Tax (GST) levied on them by the federal government at the time of sale. However, it was decided to omit consideration of the GST from the discussion and examples in the early chapters to avoid making the material overly complicated. The following discussion provides a brief introduction to the topic; GST is dealt with more fully in Chapter 11.

The manufacturer, wholesaler, and retailer pay the GST on the cost of their purchases, and then pass it on to the next link in the economic chain by charging and collecting it on their respective sales. The consumer, the last link in the chain, pays the final tax. Each entity that collects the GST remits the tax collected to the Receiver General at the Canada Customs and Revenue Agency (CCRA).

The GST is designed to be a consumption tax and, as was suggested above, the entity ultimately paying the tax is the final purchaser of the product or service. Earlier links in the chain (for example, the retailer) pay tax on their purchases, but are then allowed to deduct that tax from the tax they themselves collect on their sales. Therefore the GST paid on purchases does not really affect the cost of the purchase. For example, Austin Sound Centre paid the GST of 7 percent, or $4.90 ($70 × 0.07), on the LA100 purchased on Exhibit 5-3. The entry to record the purchase of the single CD player would have been:

May 27	Inventory	70.00	
	GST Payable	4.90	
	Accounts Payable..		74.90
	Purchased JVC LA100 CD player on account.		

Assume Austin Sound sold the JVC LA100 CD player for $110.00 to a customer; the GST on the sale would be $7.70 ($110.00 × 0.07). The entry to record the sale would be

June 10	Cash	117.70	
	GST Payable...		7.70
	Sales		110.00
	Sold JVC LA100 CD player for cash.		

Subsequently, Austin Sound would have to remit to the Receiver General at the CCRA the difference between the GST paid and the GST collected, the net GST. The entry would be

July 31	GST Payable..	2.80	
	Cash		2.80
	Payment of GST collected net of GST paid		
	on purchases ($7.70 – $4.90).		

The discussion of GST above is greatly simplified for the purposes of this text. The actual GST is more complicated than as presented for two major reasons:

1. Supplies and services are divided into three classes and each class is taxed differently. The three classes are (1) Taxable supplies and services; (2) Zero-rated supplies and services; (3) Exempt supplies and services.

2. Some provinces (Quebec, Nova Scotia, New Brunswick, and Newfoundland and Labrador) have harmonized, or combined, their provincial sales tax with the GST to some degree.

Discussion of the GST beyond the level above is beyond the scope of this chapter.

Mid-Chapter Summary Problem
for Your Review

Brun Sales Company engaged in the following transactions during June of the current year:

June	3	Purchased inventory on credit terms of 1/10 net eom, $1,610.
	9	Returned 40 percent of the inventory purchased on June 3. It was defective.
	12	Sold goods for cash, $920 (cost, $550).
	15	Purchased goods of $5,100, less a $100 quantity discount. Credit terms were 3/15 n/30.
	16	Paid a $260 freight bill on goods purchased.
	18	Sold inventory for $2,000 on credit terms of 2/10 n/30 (cost, $1,180).

June	22	Received merchandise returned from the customer from the June 18 sale, $800 (cost, $480). Merchandise was the wrong size.
	24	Borrowed money from the bank to take advantage of the discount offered on the June 15 purchase. Signed a note payable to the bank for the net amount.
	24	Paid supplier for goods purchased on June 15, less all discounts.
	28	Received cash in full settlement of the account from the customer who purchased inventory on June 18.
	29	Paid the amount owed on account from the purchase of June 3, less the June 9 return.
	30	Purchased inventory for cash, $900, less a quantity discount of $35.

Required

1. Journalize the transactions above. Explanations are not required.

2. Set up T-accounts and post the journal entries to show the ending balances in the Inventory and Cost of Goods Sold accounts.

3. Assume that the note payable signed on June 24 requires the payment of $95 interest expense. Was the decision to borrow funds to take advantage of the cash discount wise or unwise?

Solution to Review Problem

Requirement 1

Note: To save space, calculations have been included in the journal entries. Normally, they would be included in the explanations and space would be left between each journal entry.

June	3	Inventory...	1,610	
		Accounts Payable		1,610
	9	Accounts Payable ($1,610 × 0.40)	644	
		Inventory		644
	12	Cash..	920	
		Sales Revenue..		920
	12	Cost of Goods Sold...	550	
		Inventory		550
	15	Inventory ($5,100 − $100)	5,000	
		Accounts Payable		5,000
	16	Inventory	260	
		Cash...		260
	18	Accounts Receivable	2,000	
		Sales Revenue..		2,000
	18	Cost of Goods Sold...	1,180	
		Inventory		1,180
	22	Sales Returns and Allowances	800	
		Accounts Receivable		800
	22	Inventory...	480	
		Cost of Goods Sold..		480
	24	Cash [$5,000 − 0.03($5,000)]	4,850	
		Note Payable..		4,850
	24	Accounts Payable..	5,000	
		Inventory ($5,000 × 0.03)		150
		Cash ($5,000 × 0.97)		4,850
	28	Cash [($2,000 − $800) × 0.98]	1,176	
		Sales Discounts [($2,000 − $800) × 0.02]	24	
		Accounts Receivable ($2,000 − $800)....................		1,200
	29	Accounts Payable ($1,610 − $644)	966	
		Cash...		966
	30	Inventory ($900 − $35)	865	
		Cash...		865

Inventory				Cost of Goods Sold			
June 3	1,610	June 9	644	June 12	550	June 22	480
15	5,000	12	550	18	1,180		
16	260	18	1,180	Bal.	1,250		
22	480	24	150				
30	865						
Bal.	5,691						

Requirement 3

The decision to borrow funds was wise, because the discount ($150) exceeded the interest paid on the amount borrowed ($95). Thus the entity was $55 better off as a result of its decision.

Cyber Coach

Visit the Student Resource area of the *Accounting* Companion Website for extra practice with the new material in Chapter 5.

www.pearsoned.ca/horngren

Adjusting and Closing the Accounts of a Merchandiser

> **OBJECTIVE 3**
> Adjust and close the accounts of a merchandising business under the perpetual inventory system

A merchandising business adjusts and closes the accounts the same way a service entity does. If a work sheet is used, the trial balance is entered and the work sheet is completed to determine net income or net loss. The work sheet provides the data for journalizing the adjusting and closing entries and for preparing the financial statements.

Adjusting Inventory Based on a Physical Count

In theory, the Inventory account remains up to date at all times. However, the actual amount of inventory on hand may differ from what the books show. Losses due to theft and damage can be significant. Also, accounting errors can cause Inventory's balance to need adjustment either upwards or, more often, downwards. For this reason virtually all businesses, such as the grocery chain Loblaws, take a physical count of inventory at least once each year. The most common time for a business to count its inventory is at the end of the fiscal year, before the financial statements are prepared. The business then adjusts the Inventory account to the correct amount on the basis of the physical count.

Exhibit 5-5, Austin Sound Centre's trial balance at December 31, 2004, lists a $40,500 balance for inventory. With no shrinkage—due to theft or error—the business should have on hand inventory costing $40,500. But on December 31, when Frank Ernest, the owner of Austin Sound, counts the merchandise in the store, the total cost of the goods on hand comes to only $40,200. Austin Sound would record the inventory shrinkage of $300 (which is $40,500 − $40,200) with this adjusting entry:

> **KEY POINT**
> If book inventory exceeds physical inventory, book inventory would be adjusted downwards. As a result of this inventory adjustment, cost of goods sold is higher and gross margin is lower. The cost associated with buying these missing units is not accompanied by the revenue from a sale. Therefore gross margin shrinks by this amount (cost).

EXHIBIT 5-5

Trial Balance

AUSTIN SOUND CENTRE
Trial Balance
December 31, 2004

Cash	$ 2,850	
Accounts receivable	4,600	
Note receivable, current	8,000	
Interest receivable		
Inventory	**40,500**	
Supplies	650	
Prepaid insurance	1,200	
Furniture and fixtures	33,200	
Accumulated amortization		$ 2,400
Accounts payable		47,000
Unearned sales revenue		2,000
Wages payable		
Interest payable		
Note payable, long-term		12,600
Frank Ernest, capital		25,900
Frank Ernest, withdrawals	54,100	
Sales revenue		**168,000**
Sales discounts	**1,400**	
Sales returns and allowances	**2,000**	
Interest revenue		600
Cost of goods sold	**90,500**	
Wages expense	9,800	
Rent expense	8,400	
Amortization expense		
Insurance expense		
Supplies expense		
Interest expense	1,300	
Total	$258,500	$258,500

Additional data at December 31, 2004:

a. Interest revenue earned but not yet collected, $400.

b. Inventory on hand, $40,200.

c. Supplies on hand, $100.

d. Prepaid insurance expired during the year, $1,000.

e. Amortization, $600.

f. Unearned sales revenue earned during the year, $1,300.

g. Accrued wage expense, $400.

h. Accrued interest expense, $200.

Dec. 31	Cost of Goods Sold	300	
	Inventory		300

This entry brings Inventory and Cost of Goods Sold to their correct balances. Austin Sound's December 31, 2004, adjustment data, including this inventory information [item (b)], are given at the bottom of Exhibit 5-5.

The physical count can indicate that more inventory is present than the books show. A search of the records may reveal that Austin Sound received inventory but did not record the corresponding purchase entry. This would be entered the standard way: debit Inventory and credit Cash or Accounts Payable. If the reason for the excess inventory could not be identified, the business adjusts the accounts by debiting Inventory and crediting Cost of Goods Sold. To illustrate a merchandiser's adjusting and closing process, let's use Austin Sound's December 31, 2004, trial balance in

Exhibit 5-5. All the new accounts—Inventory, Cost of Goods Sold, and the contra accounts—are highlighted for emphasis. The additional data item (b) gives the ending inventory figure as $40,200.

Preparing and Using the Work Sheet of a Merchandising Business

The Exhibit 5-6 work sheet is similar to the work sheets we have seen so far, but there are a few differences. This work sheet does not include adjusted trial balance columns. In most accounting systems, a single operation combines trial balance amounts with the adjustments and extends the adjusted balances directly to the income statement and balance sheet columns. Therefore, to reduce clutter, the adjusted trial balance columns are omitted so that the work sheet contains four pairs of columns, not five.

Account Title Columns   The trial balance lists a number of accounts without balances. Ordinarily, these accounts are affected by the adjusting process. Examples include Interest Receivable, Wages Payable, and Amortization Expense. The accounts are listed in order by account number, the order they appear in the ledger. If additional accounts are needed, they can be written in at the bottom of the work sheet above the net income amount.

Trial Balance Columns   Examine the Inventory account in the Trial Balance. Inventory has a balance of $40,500 before the physical count at the end of the year. Cost of Goods Sold's balance is $90,500 before any adjustment based on the physical count. We shall assume that any difference between the Inventory amount on the trial balance ($40,500) and the correct amount based on the physical count ($40,200) is unexplained and should be debited or credited directly to Cost of Goods Sold.

Adjustments Columns   The adjustments are similar to those discussed in Chapters 3 and 4. They may be entered in any order desired. The debit amount of each entry should equal the credit amount, and total debits should equal total credits. You should review the adjusting data in Exhibit 5-5 to reassure yourself that the adjustments are correct.

Income Statement Columns   The income statement columns contain adjusted amounts for the revenues and expenses. Sales Revenue, for example, has an adjusted balance of $169,300.

The *income statement* column subtotals indicate whether the business had a net income or a net loss.

- Net income: Total credits > Total debits
- Net loss: Total debits > Total credits

Austin Sound's total credits of $170,300 exceed the total debits of $116,450, so the company earned a net income.

Insert the net *income* amount in the debit column to bring total debits into agreement with total credits. Insert a net *loss* amount in the credit column to equalize total debits and total credits. Net income or net loss is then extended to the opposite column of the balance sheet, so that total debits equal total credits.

Balance Sheet Columns   The only new item on the balance sheet is Inventory. The balance listed in Exhibit 5-6 is the ending amount of $40,200, as determined by the physical count of goods on hand at the end of the period.

KEY POINT

If you were preparing a work sheet, you could omit the adjusted trial balance columns. Once you understand the mechanics of the work sheet, you can take a trial balance amount, add or subtract the adjustments, and extend the new amount to either the income statement or balance sheet columns.

EXHIBIT 5-6

Work Sheet

AUSTIN SOUND CENTRE
Accounting Work Sheet
For the Year Ended December 31, 2004

Account Title	Trial Balance Debit	Trial Balance Credit	Adjustments Debit	Adjustments Credit	Income Statement Debit	Income Statement Credit	Balance Sheet Debit	Balance Sheet Credit
Cash	2,850						2,850	
Accounts receivable	4,600						4,600	
Note receivable, current	8,000						8,000	
Interest receivable			(a) 400				400	
Inventory	40,500			(b) 300			40,200	
Supplies	650			(c) 550			100	
Prepaid insurance	1,200			(d)1,000			200	
Furniture and fixtures	33,200						33,200	
Accumulated amortization		2,400		(e) 600				3,000
Accounts payable		47,000						47,000
Unearned sales revenue		2,000	(f) 1,300					700
Wages payable				(g) 400				400
Interest payable				(h) 200				200
Note payable, long-term		12,600						12,600
Frank Ernest, capital		25,900						25,900
Frank Ernest, withdrawals	54,100						54,100	
Sales revenue		168,000		(f) 1,300		169,300		
Sales discounts	1,400				1,400			
Sales returns and allowances	2,000				2,000			
Interest revenue		600		(a) 400		1,000		
Cost of goods sold	90,500		(b) 300		90,800			
Wages expense	9,800		(g) 400		10,200			
Rent expense	8,400				8,400			
Amortization expense			(e) 600		600			
Insurance expense			(d)1,000		1,000			
Supplies expense			(c) 550		550			
Interest expense	1,300		(h) 200		1,500			
	258,500	258,500	4,750	4,750	116,450	170,300	143,650	89,800
Net income					53,850			53,850
					170,300	170,300	143,650	143,650

Preparing the Financial Statements of a Merchandiser

Exhibit 5-7 presents Austin Sound Centre's financial statements.

To solidify your understanding of how the financial statements are prepared, you should trace the amounts in the work sheet (Exhibit 5-6) to the financial statements in Exhibit 5-7.

Income Statement   The income statement reports **operating expenses**, which are those expenses other than cost of goods sold incurred in the entity's major line of business—merchandising. Austin Sound's operating expenses include wages expense, rent, insurance, amortization of furniture and fixtures, and supplies expense. In Exhibit 5-1, The Forzani Group Ltd.'s total operating expenses are $117,836,000 for the year ended January 30, 2000.

Many companies report their operating expenses in two categories:

EXHIBIT 5-7

Financial Statements of Austin Sound Centre

AUSTIN SOUND CENTRE
Income Statement
For the Year Ended December 31, 2004

Sales revenue...		$169,300	
Less: Sales discounts...	$1,400		
Sales returns and allowances...................	2,000	3,400	
Net sales revenue			$165,900
Cost of goods sold			90,800
Gross margin...			75,100
Operating expenses:			
Wages expense..		10,200	
Rent expense...		8,400	
Insurance expense....................................		1,000	
Amortization expense		600	
Supplies expense......................................		550	20,750
Income from operations			54,350
Other revenue and (expense):			
Interest revenue.......................................		1,000	
Interest expense.......................................		(1,500)	(500)
Net income			$ 53,850

AUSTIN SOUND CENTRE
Statement of Owner's Equity
For the Year Ended December 31, 2004

Frank Ernest, capital, January 1, 2004...	$25,900
Add: Net income..	53,850
	79,750
Less: Withdrawals	54,100
Frank Ernest, capital, December 31, 2004...	$25,650

AUSTIN SOUND CENTRE
Balance Sheet
December 31, 2004

Assets

Current assets:

Cash.......................................	$ 2,850	
Accounts receivable............	4,600	
Note receivable	8,000	
Interest receivable...............	400	
Inventory	40,200	
Prepaid insurance...............	200	
Supplies................................	100	
Total current assets	56,350	

Capital assets:

Furniture and fixtures........	$33,200		
Less: Accumulated amortization	3,000	30,200	
Total assets		$86,550	

Liabilities

Current liabilities:

Accounts payable	$47,000
Unearned sales revenue	700
Wages payable	400
Interest payable.............................	200
Total current liabilities	48,300
Long-term liability:	
Note payable	12,600
Total liabilities	60,900

Owner's Equity

F. Ernest, capital	25,650
Total liabilities and owner's equity..............................	$86,550

- *Selling expenses* are those expenses related to marketing the company's products—sales salaries; sales commissions; advertising; amortization, rent, utilities, and property taxes on store buildings; amortization on store furniture; delivery expense; and so on.
- *General expenses* include office expenses, such as the salaries of the company president and office employees; amortization, rent, utilities, property taxes on the home office building; and office supplies.

The Forzani Group Ltd. (Exhibit 5-1) separates store operating (selling) and general and administrative expenses for reporting on the income statement.

Gross margin minus operating expenses equals **income from operations**, or **operating income**. Many people view operating income as an important indicator of a business's performance because it measures the results of the entity's major ongoing activities.

The last section of Austin Sound's income statement is **other revenue and expense**. This category reports revenues and expenses that are outside the main operations of the business. Examples include gains and losses on the sale of capital assets (not inventory) and gains and losses on lawsuits. Accountants have traditionally viewed Interest Revenue and Interest Expense as "other" items, because they arise from loaning money and borrowing money. These are financing activities that are outside the operating scope of selling merchandise. The Forzani Group Ltd.'s income statement in Exhibit 5-1 shows interest expense and amortization expense as separate expenses.

The bottom line of the income statement is net income:

Net income = Total revenues and gains – Total expenses and losses

We often hear the term *bottom line* used to refer to a final result. *Bottom line* originated in the position of net income on the income statement.

Statement of Owner's Equity   A merchandiser's statement of owner's equity looks exactly like that of a service business. In fact, you cannot determine whether the entity sells merchandise or services from looking at the statement of owner's equity.

Balance Sheet   If the business is a merchandiser, the balance sheet shows inventory as a major current asset. In contrast, service businesses usually have no inventory at all or minor amounts of inventory.

LEARNING TIP

The adjusting and closing entries here are very similar to those discussed in Chapter 4, pages 168–173. The closing entries also clear the Cost of Goods Sold expense account for accumulating costs in the next period.

Journalizing the Adjusting and Closing Entries for a Merchandising Business

Exhibit 5-8 presents Austin Sound Centre's adjusting entries, which are similar to those you have seen previously, except for the inventory adjustment [entry (b)]. The closing entries in the exhibit also follow the pattern illustrated in Chapter 4.

The *first closing entry* debits the revenue accounts for their ending balances. The offsetting credit of $170,300 transfers their sum to Income Summary. This amount comes directly from the credit column of the income statement on the work sheet (Exhibit 5-6).

The *second closing entry* includes credits to Cost of Goods Sold, to the contra revenue accounts (Sales Discounts, Sales Returns and Allowances), and to the expense accounts. The offsetting $116,450 debit to Income Summary represents the amount of total expenses plus the contra revenue accounts, which come from the debit column of the income statement on the work sheet.

The *last two closing entries* close net income from Income Summary and also close the owner withdrawals into the Capital account.

Study Exhibits 5-6, 5-7, and 5-8 carefully because they illustrate the entire end-of-period process that leads to the financial statements. As you progress through this book, you may want to refer to these exhibits to refresh your understanding of the adjusting and closing process for a merchandising business.

EXHIBIT 5-8

Adjusting and Closing Entries for a Merchandiser

Journal

Adjusting Entries

a.	Dec. 31	Interest receivable	400	
		Interest revenue		400
b.	Dec. 31	Cost of goods sold..	300	
		Inventory..		300
c.	Dec. 31	Supplies expense ($650 – $100)	550	
		Supplies..		550
d.	Dec. 31	Insurance expense..	1,000	
		Prepaid insurance...		1,000
e.	Dec. 31	Amortization expense	600	
		Accumulated amortization		600
f.	Dec. 31	Unearned sales revenue	1,300	
		Sales revenue..		1,300
g.	Dec. 31	Wages expense..	400	
		Wages payable...		400
h.	Dec. 31	Interest expense..	200	
		Interest payable..		200

Closing Entries

Dec. 31	Sales revenue	169,300	
	Interest revenue	1,000	
	Income summary		170,300
Dec. 31	Income summary..	116,450	
	Cost of goods sold...		90,800
	Sales discounts..		1,400
	Sales returns and allowances......................		2,000
	Wages expense...		10,200
	Rent expense..		8,400
	Amortization expense		600
	Insurance expense...		1,000
	Supplies expense		550
	Interest expense..		1,500
Dec. 31	Income summary ($170,300 – $116,450)	53,850	
	Frank Ernest, Capital...................................		53,850
Dec. 31	Capital...	54,100	
	Frank Ernest, Withdrawals		54,100

Learning Tip   Here is an easy way to remember the closing process. First, look at the work sheet. Then:

1. Debit all income statement accounts with a credit balance. Credit Income Summary for the total of all these debits.
2. Credit all income statement accounts with a debit balance. Debit Income Summary for the total of all these credits.
3. Take the balance in the Income Summary account. If the account has a debit balance, there is a net loss; credit Income Summary for that amount, and debit Capital. If Income Summary has a credit balance, there is a net income; debit Income Summary for that amount, and credit Capital.
4. Look at the debit balance of Withdrawals in the balance sheet column. Credit Withdrawals for its balance, and debit Capital for the same amount.

Income Statement Formats: Multi-Step and Single-Step

We have seen that the balance sheet appears in two formats: the report format (assets on top, owner's equity at the bottom) and the account format (assets at left,

For a review of balance sheet formats see Chapter 4, page 177.

liabilities and owner's equity at right). There are also two basic formats for the income statement: *multi-step* and *single-step*. A recent survey indicated the multi-step format was used by more than 90 percent of the companies surveyed; the remainder used the single-step format.[2]

Multi-Step Income Statement

The **multi-step format** shows subtotals to highlight significant relationships. In addition to net income, it also presents gross margin and operating income, or income from operations. This format communicates a merchandiser's results of operations especially well, because gross margin and income from operations are two key measures of operating performance. Schneider Corporation (maker of Schneider's meat products) uses the multi-step format. The income statements presented thus far in this chapter have been multi-step income statements. Austin Sound Centre's multi-step income statement for the year ended December 31, 2004, appears in Exhibit 5-7.

Single-Step Income Statement

Gulf Canada Resources
www.gulf.ca

The **single-step format** groups all revenues together, and then lists and deducts all expenses together without drawing any subtotals. Gulf Canada Resources uses this format. The single-step format has the advantage of listing all revenues together and all expenses together, as shown in Exhibit 5-9. Thus it clearly distinguishes revenues from expenses. The income statements in Chapters 1 through 4 were single-step. This format works well for service entities because they have no gross margin to report or for companies that have several types of revenues.

Most published financial statements are highly condensed. Appendix A at the end of the book gives the income statement for Intrawest Corporation. Of course, condensed statements can be supplemented with desired details in the notes to the financial statements.

EXHIBIT 5-9

Single-Step Income
Statement

AUSTIN SOUND CENTRE	
Income Statement	
For the Year Ended December 31, 2004	
Revenues:	
Net sales (net of sales discounts, $1,400, and returns and allowances, $2,000)	$165,900
Interest revenue	1,000
Total revenues	166,900
Expenses:	
Cost of goods sold	$ 90,800
Wages expense	10,200
Rent expense	8,400
Interest expense	1,500
Insurance expense	1,000
Amortization expense	600
Supplies expense	550
Total expenses	113,050
Net income	$ 53,850

---

[2]Byrd, C., I. Chen, and H. Chapman, *Financial Reporting in Canada 1999*, Twenty-fourth Edition. (Toronto: Canadian Institute of Chartered Accountants, 1999), p. 28.

Two Key Ratios for Decision Making

OBJECTIVE 5
Use the gross margin percentage and the inventory turnover ratio to evaluate a business

Merchandise inventory is the most important asset to a merchandising business because it captures the essence of the entity. To manage the business, owners and managers focus on the best way to sell the inventory. They use several ratios to evaluate operations, among them *gross margin percentage* and *rate of inventory turnover*.

The Gross Margin Percentage

A key decision tool for a merchandiser is related to gross margin, which is net sales minus cost of goods sold. Merchandisers strive to increase the **gross margin percentage**, which is computed as follows:

For Austin Sound Centre (Exhibit 5-7)

$$\text{Gross margin percentage} = \frac{\text{Gross margin}}{\text{Net sales revenue}} = \frac{\$75,100}{\$165,900} = 0.453 = 45.3\%$$

The gross margin percentage (also called the *gross profit percentage*) is one of the most carefully watched measures of profitability. A 45-percent gross margin means that each dollar of sales generates 45 cents of gross profit. On average, the goods cost the seller 55 cents. A small increase in the gross margin percentage may signal an important rise in income, and vice versa for a decrease.

Exhibit 5-10 compares Austin Sound Centre's gross margin to Wal-Mart's gross margin.

The Rate of Inventory Turnover

Owners and managers strive to sell inventory as quickly as possible because it generates no profit until it is sold. The faster the sales occur, the higher the income. The slower the sales, the lower the income. Ideally, a business could operate with zero inventory. Most businesses, however, including retailers such as Austin Sound Centre, must keep goods on hand for customers. Successful merchandisers purchase carefully to keep the goods moving through the business at a rapid pace. **Inventory turnover**, the ratio of cost of goods sold to average inventory, indicates how rapidly inventory is sold. Its computation follows:

For Austin Sound Centre (Exhibit 5-7)

$$\frac{\text{Inventory}}{\text{turnover}} = \frac{\text{Cost of goods sold}}{\text{Average inventory}} = \frac{\text{Cost of goods sold}}{(\text{Beginning inventory} + \text{ending inventory})/2} = \frac{\$90,800}{(\$38,600^* + \$40,200)/2}$$

$$= \textbf{2.3 times per year (about every 159 days)}$$

*Taken from the balance sheet at the end of the preceding period.

Inventory turnover is usually computed for an annual period, and the relevant cost-of-goods sold figure is the amount from the entire year. Average inventory is computed from the beginning and ending balances of the annual period. Austin Sound Centre's beginning inventory would be taken from the business's balance sheet at the end of the preceding year. The resulting inventory turnover statistic shows how many times the average level of inventory was sold during the year. A high rate of turnover is preferable to a low turnover rate. An increase in turnover rate usually means higher profits, but may sometimes lead to a shortage of inventory to sell.

WORKING IT OUT

Cavey Company reports sales revenue of $3,000,000 and cost of goods sold of $1,800,000 for the 2002 fiscal year. Calculate (1) Cavey's gross margin percentage for 2002, and (2) Cost of goods sold as a percentage of sales for 2002. (3) What do these percentages mean to Cavey management?

A:

(1) Gross margin = $3,000,000 − $1,800,000 = $1,200,000
Gross margin percentage = $1,200,000/$3,000,000 = 40%
(2) $1,800,000/$3,000,000 = 60%
(3) Per dollar of sales, Cavey spends (on average) $0.60 to acquire or manufacture its products and it earns (on average) $0.40 of gross margin per dollar of sales revenue.

Wal-Mart
www.wal-mart.com

EXHIBIT 5-10

Gross Margin on $1.00 of Sales for Two Merchandisers

	Wal-Mart	Austin Sound Centre
Gross profit	$0.21	$0.45
Cost of goods sold	$0.79	$0.55

Varsitybooks.com: A Textbook Case on the Fulfillment Cost Issue

If you were to order this edition of *Accounting* from Varsitybooks.com, the company arranges for Baker & Taylor, a book distributor, to ship it to you immediately. Varsitybooks.com does not have a warehouse or any inventory, but it does have to pay Baker & Taylor to deliver the texts from the publishers to you. How does Varsitybooks.com, a fledgling company, account for these significant fulfillment costs?

E-commerce has revolutionized business and has "bent" certain accounting rules in the process. One such rule is that the cost of goods sold to customers is reported on the Cost of Goods Sold line on the income statement. Yet, online companies like Amazon.com and Etoys Inc report some of this cost as Sales and Marketing Expenses because the companies never own the inventory. By including these fulfillment costs on the Marketing Expenses line, these companies do not subtract the considerable costs from their gross margin.

Varsitybooks.com wanted to follow this practice, arguing that mail-order companies have always done this. Also, investors would understand that increased marketing costs are necessary for start-up companies to build a solid customer base. This practice would also protect already-thin gross margins. For instance, if Amazon.com accounts for fulfillment costs on the Cost of Goods Sold line, gross margins for the last quarter of 1999 would go from 15% to -3%. The company's sales and net profit or net loss amounts would remain the same, but analysts and investors look at the gross margin figure to see how well a company can make money from basic business operations.

This approach is controversial. The auditors of Varsitybooks.com advised that fulfillment costs be reported as cost of goods sold, and Varsitybooks.com finally followed their advice.

Based on: Shannon Henry, "An E-Tail Identity Crisis," *The Washington Post*, May 4, 2000, p. E01. Anonymous, "Web Retailers' 'Gross Profit' Questioned; The SEC may make some firms account for distribution costs, possibly turning their profits into losses," *The Los Angeles Times*, February 19, 2000, p. 2.

WORKING IT OUT

Calculate inventory turnover from the following data:

Beginning inventory	$2,350
Ending inventory	1,980
Cost of goods sold	15,310

A:

Inventory turnover =

$$\frac{\text{Cost of goods sold}}{(\text{Beginning inventory} + \text{Ending inventory})/2}$$

Inventory turnover is

$$\frac{\$15,310}{(\$2,350 + \$1,980)/2}$$

$$= \frac{\$15,310}{\$2,165}$$

= 7.1 times per year

Inventory turnover varies from industry to industry. Grocery stores, for example, turn their goods over faster than automobile dealers do. Drug stores have a higher turnover than furniture stores do. Retailers of electronic products, such as Austin Sound Centre, have an average turnover of 3.6 times per year. Austin Sound's turnover rate of 2.3 times per year suggests that Austin Sound is not very successful. Exhibit 5-11 compares the inventory turnover rate of Austin Sound and Wal-Mart Stores, Inc.

Exhibits 5-10 and 5-11 tell an interesting story. Wal-Mart sells lots of inventory at a relatively low gross profit margin. Wal-Mart earns its profits by turning its inventory over rapidly—7.0 times during the year. Austin Sound Centre, a small business, prices inventory to earn a higher gross margin on each dollar of sales and only turns over its inventory 2.3 times during the year.

Gross margin percentage and rate of inventory turnover do not provide enough information to yield an overall conclusion about a merchandiser, but this example showed how owners and managers may use accounting information to evaluate a company.

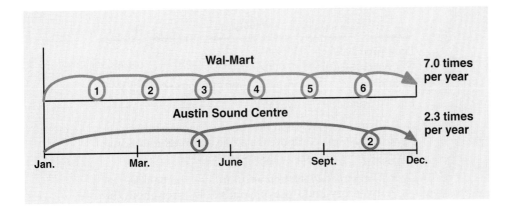

Exhibit 5-11

Rate of Inventory Turnover for Two Merchandisers

 **REAL WORLD EXAMPLE**

Many business use the gross margin percentage (also known as the markup percentage) as a means of determining how well inventory is selling. If too much inventory is purchased and it must be marked down, the gross margin percentage will decline. By monitoring the gross margin percentage, problems can be corrected quickly.

OBJECTIVE 6
Compute the cost of goods sold under the periodic inventory system

Measuring Cost of Goods Sold and Inventory Purchases in the Periodic Inventory System

The perpetual inventory accounting system that we have illustrated is designed to produce up-to-date records of inventory and cost of goods sold. That system provides the data for many day-to-day decisions and for preparation of the financial statements. However, managers have other information needs that the perpetual inventory system does not meet. For example, the buyers for The Forzani Group Ltd. and Austin Sound Centre must know how much inventory to purchase in order to reach their sales goals.

Another computation of cost of goods sold—from the periodic inventory system—helps managers plan their purchases of inventory. This alternative computation of cost of goods sold is used so often in accounting that your education would be incomplete without it. (The supplement at the end of the chapter covers the periodic inventory system in more detail.)

Exhibit 5-12 gives the alternative computation of Austin Sound Centre's cost of goods sold for 2004. Austin Sound began the year with inventory of $38,600. During the year, Austin Sound purchased more goods, also paying freight charges. The sum of these amounts make up Austin Sound's cost of goods available for sale. Note that **net purchases** equals purchases minus purchase discounts and purchase returns

WORKING IT OUT

Calculate inventory turnover given the following data:
Beg. inventory.............$ 2,350
End. inventory.................1,980
Purchases 14,550
Freight in............................390

A: Cost of goods sold/Avg. inv.
Inv. turn. = $15,310*/ $2,165**
= 7.1 times
*$2,350 + $14,550 + $390 − $1,980
= $15,310
**($2,350 + $1,980)/2 = $2,165

EXHIBIT 5-12

Measuring Cost of Goods Sold in the Periodic Inventory System

Beginning inventory.......................................	$ 38,600
+ **Net purchases**	87,200*
+ Freight in...	5,200
= Cost of goods available for sale	131,000
− Ending inventory......................................	(40,200)
= Cost of goods sold...................................	$ 90,800
*Computation of **Net purchases**:	
Purchases...	$ 91,400
− Purchase discounts	(3,000)
− Purchase returns and allowances	(1,200)
= Net purchases..	$ 87,200

EXHIBIT 5-13

**Relationship Between the
Inventory Account and Cost
of Goods Sold in the Periodic
Inventory System (Amounts
for Austin Sound Centre)**

Inventory

Beginning balance	38,600		
Net purchases	87,200		
Freight in	5,200	Cost of goods sold	90,800
Ending balance	40,200		

This T-account shows that the *perpetual* and the *periodic* inventory systems compute the same amounts for ending inventory and for cost of goods sold:

- The *perpetual* system accumulates the balances of Inventory and Cost of Goods Sold throughout the period.
- The *periodic* system determines the correct amounts for Inventory and Cost of Goods Sold only at the end of the period.

The authors thank Betsy Willis for suggesting this exhibit.

and allowances. Subtract ending inventory, and the result is cost of goods sold for the period. Exhibit 5-13 diagrams the alternative computation of cost of goods sold, with Austin Sound Centre amounts used for the illustration.

The Decision Guidelines feature summarizes some key decisions of a merchandising business. One key decision is how much inventory the business should purchase in order to achieve its goals.

Here is how Frank Ernest, the owner of Austin Sound Centre, would decide how much inventory to buy (all numbers based on Exhibit 5-13):

1. Owner predicts Cost of goods sold for the period...................... $ 90,800
2. Owner predicts Ending inventory at the end of the period 40,200
3. Cost of goods available for sale = Sum of Ending inventory + Cost of goods sold... 131,000
4. Subtract the period's beginning inventory .... (38,600)
5. The difference is the amount of inventory to purchase (including Freight in) during the coming year........................... $ 92,400

Decision	Guidelines

Decision | **Guidelines**

How do merchandising operations differ from service operations?

- Merchandisers buy and sell *merchandise inventory* (often called inventory, or goods).
- Service entities perform a *service*.

How do a merchandiser's financial statements differ from the financial statements of a service business?

Balance sheet:
- Merchandiser has *inventory*, an asset.
- Service business has no inventory.

Income statement:

Merchandiser

	Sales revenue	$XXX
−	Cost of goods sold	(X)
=	Gross margin	$ XX
−	Operating expenses	(X)
=	Net income	$ X

Service Business

	Service revenue	$XX
−	Operating expense	(X)
=	Net income	$ X

Statements of owner's equity:
No difference

What types of inventory systems are there?

- *Perpetual system* shows the amount of inventory on hand (the asset) and the cost of goods sold (the expense) at all times.
- *Periodic system* shows the correct balances of inventory and cost of goods sold only after a physical count of the inventory and adjustment of the books to reflect that count, which occurs at least once each year.

How do the adjusting and closing processes of merchandisers and service entities differ?

Very little. The merchandiser may have to *adjust* the Inventory account for spoilage and theft. The merchandiser must *close* the Cost of Goods Sold account. Service entities have no inventory to adjust or cost of goods sold to close.

How to format the merchandiser's income statement?

Multi-step format

	Sales revenue	$XXX
−	Cost of goods sold	(X)
=	Gross margin	$ XX
−	Operating expenses	(X)
+	Other revenues	X
=	Net income	$ XX

Single-step format

Revenues:	
Sales revenue	$ XXX
Other revenues	X
Total revenues	$ XXX
Expenses:	
Cost of goods sold	(X)
Operating expenses	(X)
Total expenses	$ XX
Net income	$ XX

How to evaluate inventory operations?

Two key ratios:

$$\text{Gross margin percentage*} = \frac{\text{Gross margin}}{\text{Net sales revenue}}$$

$$\text{Inventory turnover*} = \frac{\text{Cost of goods sold}}{\text{Average inventory}}$$

*In most cases—the higher, the better

How to determine the amount of cost of goods sold?

Can use the *cost of goods sold* model from the periodic system (assumed amounts):

	Beginning inventory	$100
+	Net purchases and freight in	800
=	Cost of goods available	900
−	Ending inventory	(200)
=	Cost of goods sold	$700

Cost of goods sold is computed automatically in the perpetual inventory system.

The following trial balance and additional data are related to Jan King Distributing Company.

JAN KING DISTRIBUTING COMPANY
Trial Balance
December 31, 2003

Cash	$ 5,670	
Accounts receivable	37,100	
Inventory	60,500	
Supplies	3,930	
Prepaid rent	6,000	
Furniture and fixtures	26,500	
Accumulated amortization		$ 21,200
Accounts payable		46,340
Salary payable		
Interest payable		
Unearned sales revenue		3,500
Note payable, long-term		35,000
Jan King, capital		23,680
Jan King, withdrawals	48,000	
Sales revenue		346,700
Sales discounts	10,300	
Sales returns and allowances	8,200	
Cost of goods sold	171,770	
Salary expense	82,750	
Rent expense	7,000	
Amortization expense		
Utilities expense	5,800	
Supplies expense		
Interest expense	2,900	
Total	$476,420	$476,420

Additional data at December 31, 2003:

a. Supplies used during the year, $2,580.

b. Prepaid rent remaining in force, $1,000.

c. Unearned sales revenue still not earned, $2,400. The company expects to earn this amount during the next few months.

d. Amortization. The furniture and fixtures' estimated useful life is ten years, and they are expected to have no value when they are retired from service.

e. Accrued salaries, $1,300.

f. Accrued interest expense, $600.

g. Inventory still remaining on hand, $65,800.

Required

1. Enter the trial balance on a work sheet and complete the work sheet.

2. Journalize the adjusting and closing entries at December 31, 2003. Post to the Income Summary account as an accuracy check on the entries affecting that account. The credit balance closed out of Income Summary should equal net income computed on the work sheet.

3. Prepare the company's multi-step income statement, statement of owner's equity, and balance sheet in account format. Draw arrows connecting the statements, or state how the statements are linked.

4. Compute the inventory turnover for 2003. Inventory at December 31, 2002, was $59,500. Turnover for 2002 was 2.1 times. Would you expect Jan King Distributing Company to be more or less profitable in 2003 than in 2002? Give your reason.

Solution to Review Problem

Requirement 1

JAN KING DISTRIBUTING COMPANY
Work Sheet
For the Year Ended December 31, 2003

Account Title	Trial Balance Debit	Trial Balance Credit	Adjustments Debit	Adjustments Credit	Income Statement Debit	Income Statement Credit	Balance Sheet Debit	Balance Sheet Credit
Cash	5,670						5,670	
Accounts receivable	37,100						37,100	
Inventory	60,500		(g)5,300				65,800	
Supplies	3,930			(a) 2,580			1,350	
Prepaid rent	6,000			(b) 5,000			1,000	
Furniture and fixtures	26,500						26,500	
Accumulated amortization		21,200		(d)2,650				23,850
Accounts payable		46,340						46,340
Salary payable				(e) 1,300				1,300
Interest payable				(f) 600				600
Unearned sales revenue		3,500	(c)1,100					2,400
Note payable, long-term		35,000						35,000
Jan King, capital		23,680						23,680
Jan King, withdrawals	48,000						48,000	
Sales revenue		346,700		(c) 1,100		347,800		
Sales discounts	10,300				10,300			
Sales returns and allowances	8,200				8,200			
Cost of goods sold	171,770			(g) 5,300	166,470			
Salary expense	82,750		(e)1,300		84,050			
Rent expense	7,000		(b)5,000		12,000			
Amortization expense			(d)2,650		2,650			
Utilities expense	5,800				5,800			
Supplies expense			(a)2,580		2,580			
Interest expense	2,900		(f) 600		3,500			
	476,420	476,420	18,530	18,530	295,550	347,800	185,420	133,170
Net income					52,250			52,250
					347,800	347,800	185,420	185,420

Requirement 2

Adjusting entries

2003

Dec. 31	Supplies expense..	2,580	
	Supplies..		2,580
Dec. 31	Rent expense...	5,000	
	Prepaid rent		5,000
Dec. 31	Unearned sales revenue ($3,500 – $2,400)	1,100	
	Sales revenue...		1,100
Dec. 31	Amortization expense ($26,500/10)...................	2,650	
	Accumulated amortization		2,650
Dec. 31	Salary expense..	1,300	
	Salary payable		1,300
Dec. 31	Interest expense	600	
	Interest payable...		600
Dec. 31	Inventory ($65,800 – $60,500)............................	5,300*	
	Cost of goods sold		5,300

Closing entries

2003

Dec. 31	Sales revenue	347,800	
	Income summary..		347,800
Dec. 31	Income summary	295,550	
	Cost of goods sold		166,470
	Sales discounts..		10,300
	Sales returns and allowances......................		8,200
	Salary expense...		84,050
	Rent expense		12,000
	Amortization expense......................................		2,650
	Utilities expense...		5,800
	Supplies expense		2,580
	Interest expense		3,500
Dec. 31	Income summary ($347,800 – $295,550)	52,250	
	Jan King, Capital...		52,250
Dec. 31	Jan King, Capital...	48,000	
	Jan King, Withdrawals...................................		48,000

Income Summary

Clo.	295,550	Clo.	347,800
Clo.	52,250	Bal.	52,250

---

*Excess of inventory on hand over the balance in the Inventory account. This adjustment brings Inventory to its correct balance.

JAN KING DISTRIBUTING COMPANY
Income Statement
For the Year Ended December 31, 2003

Sales revenue		$347,800	
Less: Sales discounts	$10,300		
Sales returns and allowances	8,200	18,500	
Net sales revenue			$329,300
Cost of goods sold			166,470
Gross margin			162,830
Operating expenses:			
Salary expense		84,050	
Rent expense		12,000	
Utilities expense		5,800	
Amortization expense		2,650	
Supplies expense		2,580	107,080
Income from operations			55,750
Other expense:			
Interest expense			3,500
Net income			$ 52,250

JAN KING DISTRIBUTING COMPANY
Statement of Owner's Equity
For the Year Ended December 31, 2003

Jan King, capital, January 1, 2003	$23,680
Add: Net income	52,250
	75,930
Less: Withdrawals	48,000
Jan King, capital, December 31, 2003	$27,930

JAN KING DISTRIBUTING COMPANY
Balance Sheet
December 31, 2003

Assets

Current assets:		
Cash		$ 5,670
Accounts receivable		37,100
Inventory		65,800
Supplies		1,350
Prepaid Rent		1,000
Total current assets		110,920
Capital assets:		
Furniture and fixtures	$26,500	
Less: Accumulated amortization	23,850	2,650
Total assets		$113,570

Liabilities

Current liabilities:	
Accounts payable	$ 46,340
Salary payable	1,300
Interest payable	600
Unearned sales revenue	2,400
Total current liabilities	50,640
Long-term liabilities	
Note payable	35,000
Total liabilities	85,640

Owner's Equity

Jan King, capital	27,930
Total liabilities and owner's equity	$113,570

$$\text{Inventory turnover} = \frac{\text{Cost of goods sold}}{\text{Average inventory}} = \frac{\$166,470}{(\$59,500 + \$65,800)/2} = 2.7 \text{ times}$$

The increase in the rate of inventory turnover from 2.1 to 2.7 *suggests* higher profits in 2003 than in 2002. However, gross margin and expenses for both years must be checked to verify this suggestion.

Cyber Coach

Visit the Student Resource area of the *Accounting* Companion Website for extra practice with the new material in Chapter 5.

www.pearsoned.ca/horngren

Summary

1. **Use sales and gross margin to evaluate a company.** The major revenue of a merchandising business is *sales revenue*, or *net sales*. The major expense is *cost of goods sold*. Net sales minus cost of goods sold is called *gross margin*, or *gross profit*. This amount measures the business's success or failure in selling its products at a higher price than it paid for them.

2. **Account for the purchase and sale of inventory.** The merchandiser's major asset is *inventory*. In a merchandising entity the accounting cycle is from cash to inventory as the inventory is purchased for resale, and back to cash as the inventory is sold. The *invoice* is the business document generated by a purchase or sale transaction. Most merchandising entities offer *discounts* to their customers and allow them to *return* unsuitable merchandise. They also grant *allowances* for damaged goods that the buyer chooses to keep. Sales Discounts and Returns and Allowances are contra accounts to Sales Revenue.

3. **Adjust and close the accounts of a merchandising business.** The end-of-period adjusting and closing process of a merchandising business is similar to that of a service business. In addition, a merchandiser adjusts inventory for theft losses, damage, and accounting errors.

4. **Prepare a merchandiser's financial statements.** The income statement may appear in the *single-step format* or the *multi-step format*. A single-step income statement has only two sections—one for revenues and the other for expenses—and a single income amount for net income. A multi-step income statement has subtotals for gross margin and income from operations. The multi-step format is the most widely used format.

5. **Use the gross margin percentage and the inventory turnover ratio to evaluate a business.** Two key decision aids for a merchandiser are the *gross margin percentage* (gross margin/net sales revenue) and the *rate of inventory turnover* (cost of goods sold/average inventory). Increases in these measures usually signal an increase in profits.

6. **Compute cost of goods sold.** *Cost of goods sold* is the cost of the inventory that the business has sold. It is the largest single expense of most merchandising businesses. Cost of goods sold is the sum of the cost of goods sold amounts recorded during the period. In a periodic inventory system, Cost of goods sold = Beginning inventory + Purchases (net of any contra accounts) + Freight in − Ending inventory.

Self-Study Questions

Test your understanding of the chapter by marking the correct answer for each of the following questions:

1. The major expense of a merchandising business is (*p. 217*)
   a. Cost of goods sold   c. Rent
   b. Amortization   d. Interest

2. Sales total $440,000, cost of goods sold is $210,000, and operating expenses are $160,000. How much is gross margin? (*p. 218*)
   a. $440,000   c. $210,000
   b. $230,000   d. $70,000

3. A purchase discount results from (*p. 221*)
   a. Returning goods to the seller
   b. Receiving a purchase allowance from the seller

c. Buying a large enough quantity of merchandise to get the discount

d. Paying within the discount period

4. Which one of the following pairs includes items that are the most similar? (*p. 227*)
   a. Purchase discounts and purchase returns
   b. Cost of goods sold and inventory
   c. Net sales and sales discounts
   d. Sales returns and sales allowances

5. Which of the following is *not* an account? (*p. 217*)
   a. Sales revenue   c. Inventory
   b. Net sales   d. Supplies expense

6. Cost of goods sold is computed by adding beginning inventory and net purchases and subtracting X. What is X? (*p. 241*)
   a. Net sales   c. Ending inventory
   b. Sales discounts   d. Net purchases

7. Which account causes the main difference between a merchandiser's adjusting and closing process and that of a service business? (*p. 236*)
   a. Advertising expense   c. Cost of goods sold
   b. Interest revenue   d. Accounts receivable

8. The major item on a merchandiser's income statement that a service business does not have is (*p. 236*)
   a. Cost of goods sold   c. Salary expense
   b. Inventory   d. Total revenue

9. The closing entry for Sales Discounts includes (*pp. 236–237*)
   a. Sales Discounts
       Income Summary
   b. Sales Discounts
       Sales Revenue
   c. Income Summary
       Sales Discounts
   d. Not used: Sales Discounts is a permanent account, which is not closed.

10. Which income statement format reports income from operations? (*p. 238*)
    a. Account format   c. Single-step format
    b. Report format   d. Multi-step format

Answers to the Self-Study Questions follow the Similar Accounting Terms.

Accounting Vocabulary

Cost of goods sold (*p. 217*)
Cost of sales (*p. 217*)
Gross margin (*p. 218*)
Gross margin percentage (*p. 239*)
Gross profit (*p. 218*)
Income from operations (*p. 236*)
Inventory (*p. 216*)
Inventory turnover (*p. 239*)
Invoice (*p. 221*)

Multi-step income statement (*p. 238*)
Net purchases (*p. 241*)
Net sales (*p. 217*)
Operating expense (*p. 234*)
Operating income (*p. 236*)
Other expense (*p. 236*)
Other revenue (*p. 236*)
Periodic inventory system (*p. 220*)

Perpetual inventory system (*p. 220*)
Sales (*p. 217*)
Sales discount (*p. 227*)
Sales returns and allowances (*p. 227*)
Sales revenue (*p. 217*)
Single-step income statement (*p. 238*)

Similar Accounting Terms

Freight	Freight in; Transportation costs; Shipping costs
Gross margin	Gross profit
Income from operations	Operating income
Invoice	Bill
List price	Full price; Price with no discounts deducted
Purchase discount	Cash discount; Discount given to reward prompt payment
Quantity discount	Trade discount; Discount given to reward purchase of more than one of a particular item
Sales revenue	Sales
Cost of goods sold	Cost of sales

Answers to Self-Study Questions

1. a	4. d	7. c	10. d
2. b ($440,000 – $210,000 = $230,000)	5. b	8. a	
3. d	6. c	9. c	

Assignment Material

Questions

1. Gross margin is often mentioned in the business press as an important measure of success. What does gross margin measure, and why is it important?

2. Describe the operating cycle for (a) the purchase and cash sale of inventory, and (b) the purchase and sale of inventory on account.

3. Identify ten items of information on an invoice.

4. Indicate which accounts are debited and credited under the perpetual inventory system for (a) a credit purchase of inventory and the subsequent cash payment, and (b) a credit sale of inventory and the subsequent cash collection. Assume no discounts, returns, allowances, or freight.

5. Inventory costing $1,000 is purchased and invoiced on July 28 under terms of 3/10 n/30. Compute the payment amount on August 6. How much would the payment be on August 9? What explains the difference? What is the latest acceptable payment date under the terms of sale?

6. Inventory listed at $35,000 is sold subject to a quantity discount of $3,000 and under payment terms of 2/15 n/45. What is the net sales revenue on this sale if the customer pays within 15 days?

7. Name the new contra accounts introduced in this chapter.

8. Briefly discuss the similarity in computing supplies expense and computing cost of goods sold by the method shown in Exhibit 5-12 on page 241.

9. Why is the title of Cost of Goods Sold especially descriptive? What type of account is Cost of Goods Sold?

10. Beginning inventory is $5,000, net purchases total $30,000, and freight in is $1,000. If ending inventory is $8,000, what is cost of goods sold?

11. You are evaluating two companies as possible investments. One entity sells its services; the other entity is a merchandiser. How can you identify the merchandiser by examining the two entities' balance sheets and income statements?

12. You are beginning the adjusting and closing process at the end of your company's fiscal year. Does the trial balance carry the final ending amount of inventory? Why or why not?

13. Give the adjusting entry for inventory if shrinkage is $9,100.

14. What is the identifying characteristic of the "other" category of revenues and expenses? Give an example of each.

15. Name and describe formats for the two income statements and identify the type of business to which each format best applies.

16. List eight different operating expenses.

17. Which financial statement reports sales discounts and sales returns and allowances? Show how they are reported, using any reasonable amounts in your illustration.

18. Does a merchandiser prefer a high or low rate of inventory turnover? Explain.

19. In general, what does a decreasing gross margin percentage, coupled with an increasing rate of inventory turnover, suggest about a business's pricing strategy?

Exercises

Exercise 5-1 *Evaluating a company's revenues, gross margin, operating income, and net income* *(Obj. 1)*

The Toy Store reported the information shown on page 251:

Required

1. Is The Toy Store a merchandising entity, a service business, or both? How can you tell? List the items in The Toy Store financial statements that influence your answer.

2. Compute The Toy Store's gross margin for fiscal years 2004 and 2003. Did the gross margin increase or decrease in 2004? Is this a good sign or a bad sign about the company?

3. Write a brief memo to the owner advising her of The Toy Store's trend of sales, gross margin, and net income. Indicate whether the outlook for The Toy Store is favourable or unfavourable, based on this trend. Use the following memo format:

<table>
<tr><td>Date:</td><td>_____</td></tr>
<tr><td>To:</td><td>The Owner</td></tr>
<tr><td>From:</td><td>Student Name</td></tr>
<tr><td>Subject:</td><td>Trend of sales, gross margin, and net income for The Toy Store</td></tr>
</table>

THE TOY STORE
Income Statements
(Dollars in thousands)

	Fiscal Year Ended	
	January 31, 2004	January 31, 2003
Net sales	$10,000	$9,500
Costs and expenses:		
Cost of sales	7,000	6,700
Selling, advertising, general, and administrative	2,030	1,900
Amortization	206	192
Other charges	60	397
Interest expense	99	103
Interest and other income	(17)	(17)
	9,378	9,275
Earnings before taxes on income	622	225
Taxes on income	249	90
Net earnings	$ 373	$ 135

THE TOY STORE
Balance Sheets (partial)
(Dollars in thousands)

	January 31, 2004	January 31, 2003
Assets		
Current assets:		
Cash	$765	$205
Accounts and other receivables	145	130
Merchandise inventories	2,215	2,000
Prepaid expenses and other current assets	42	88
Total current assets	$3,167	$2,423

Exercise 5-2 *Recording purchase transactions under the perpetual inventory system*
 (Obj. 2)

Suppose The Bay purchases $50,000 of women's sportswear on account from Liz Claiborne, Inc. Credit terms are 2/10 net 30. The Bay pays electronically, and Liz Claiborne receives the money on the tenth day.

Journalize The Bay's (a) purchase and (b) cash payment transactions. What was The Bay's net cost of this inventory?
Note: Exercise 5-3 covers this same situation for the seller.

Exercise 5-3 *Recording sales, cost of goods sold, and cash collections under the perpetual inventory system* *(Obj. 2)*

Liz Claiborne, Inc. sells $50,000 of women's sportswear to The Bay under credit terms of 2/10 net 30. Liz Claiborne's cost of the goods is $32,000, and it receives the appropriate amount of cash from The Bay on the tenth day.

Journalize Liz Claiborne's (a) sale, (b) cost of goods sold, and (c) cash receipt. How much gross margin did Liz Claiborne earn on this sale?

Note: Exercise 5-2 covers the same situation for the buyer.

Exercise 5-4 *Journalizing purchase and sale transactions under the perpetual inventory system* **(Obj. 2)**

Journalize, without explanations, the following transactions of Pinetree Fashions during the month of June 2004:

June 3 Purchased $1,400 of inventory under terms of 2/10 n/eom and FOB shipping point.
      7 Returned $600 of defective merchandise purchased on June 3.
      9 Paid freight bill of $220 on June 3 purchase.
     10 Sold inventory for $4,400, collecting cash of $800. Payment terms on the remainder were 2/15 n/30. The goods cost Pinetree Fashions $2,600.
     12 Paid amount owed on credit purchase of June 3, less the discount and the return.
     16 Granted a sales allowance of $1,600 on the June 10 sale.
     23 Received cash from June 10 customer in full settlement of her debt, less the allowance and the discount.

Exercise 5-5 *Journalizing transactions from a purchase invoice under the perpetual inventory system* **(Obj. 2)**

As the proprietor of Kendrick Tire, you receive the invoice below from a supplier (GST has been disregarded).

Required

1. Record the May 14 purchase on account.

ABC TIRE WHOLESALE DISTRIBUTORS
2600 Victoria Avenue
Regina, Saskatchewan S4P 1B3

Invoice date: May 14, 2003   **Payment terms:** 2/10 n/30

Sold to: Kendrick Tire
            4219 Cumberland Avenue
            Saskatoon, SK S7M 1X3

Quantity Ordered	Description	Quantity Shipped	Price	Amount
6	P135-X4 Radials.........	6	$55.71	$334.26
8	L912 Belted-bias........	8	61.98	495.84
14	R39 Truck tires.........	10	75.03	750.30
	Total..			$1,580.40

Due date: **Amount:**
May 24, 2003 $1,548.79
May 25 through June 13, 2003 $1,580.40

Paid:

---

2. The R39 truck tires were ordered by mistake and therefore were returned to ABC. Journalize the return on May 19.

3. Record the May 22 payment of the amount owed.

Exercise 5-6   *Journalizing purchase transactions under the perpetual inventory system (Obj. 2)*

On April 30, Mavis Jewellers purchased inventory of $7,500 on account from La Roche Fine Gems Ltd., a jewellery importer. Terms were 3/15 n/45. On receiving the goods Mavis checked the order and found $1,200 worth of items that were not ordered. Therefore, Mavis returned this amount of merchandise to La Roche on May 4.

To pay the remaining amount owing on the invoice, Mavis had to borrow from the bank. On May 14 Mavis signed a short-term note payable to the bank and immediately paid La Roche Fine Gems Ltd. with the borrowed funds. On June 14, Mavis paid the bank the net amount of the invoice, which Mavis had borrowed, plus 1 percent interest monthly (round to the nearest dollar).

Required

Record the indicated transactions in the journal of Mavis Jewellers. Explanations are not required.

Exercise 5-7   *Journalizing sale transactions under the perpetual inventory system   (Obj. 2)*

Refer to the business situation in Exercise 5-6. Journalize the transactions of La Roche Fine Gems Ltd. La Roche's gross margin is 40 percent so cost of goods sold is 60 percent of sales. Explanations are not required.

Exercise 5-8   *Making closing entries under a perpetual inventory system   (Obj. 3)*

An independent hardware store's accounting records carried the following accounts at January 31, 2002:

Accounts receivable	$ 6,520	Selling expense	$ 55,680
Interest revenue	400	Sales revenue	309,400
Accounts payable	16,500	Interest expense	80
Other expense	10,320	Merchandise inventories	43,600
Cost of goods sold	223,700	General and administrative	
Withdrawals	13,600	expense	5,380

Required

Note: For simplicity, all operating expenses have been summarized in the accounts Selling Expense and General and Administrative Expenses.

1. Journalize all of this company's closing entries at January 31, 2002.

2. Set up T-accounts for the Income Summary account and the Capital account. Post to these accounts and calculate their ending balances. One year earlier, at January 31, 2001, the Capital balance was $6,884.

Exercise 5-9   *Using work sheet data make the closing entries under the perpetual inventory system   (Obj. 3)*

The trial balance and adjustments columns of the work sheet of First Choice Paint Centre include the accounts and balances at March 31, 2003 (on page 254).

Required

Journalize First Choice Paint Centre's closing entries at March 31, 2003.

Account Title	Trial Balance		Adjustments	
	Debit	Credit	Debit	Credit
Cash	$ 1,000			
Accounts receivable	8,500		(a) 3,100	
Inventory	37,100			(b) 1,170
Supplies	13,000			(c) 9,600
Store fixtures	42,470			
Accumulated amortization		$ 11,250		(d) 2,250
Accounts payable		8,300		
Salary payable				(e) 1,200
Note payable, long-term		7,500		
P. Lang, capital		33,920		
P. Lang, withdrawals	45,000			
Sales revenue		234,000		(a) 3,100
Sales discounts	2,000			
Cost of goods sold	111,600		(b) 1,170	
Selling expense	21,050		(c) 5,700	
			(e) 1,200	
General expense	10,500		(c) 3,900	
			(d) 2,250	
Interest expense	2,750			
Total	$294,970	$294,970	$17,320	$17,320

Exercise 5-10 *Preparing a multi-step income statement under the perpetual inventory system* *(Obj. 4)*

Use the data in Exercise 5-9 to prepare the multi-step income statement of First Choice Paint Centre for the year ended March 31, 2003.

Exercise 5-11 *Using the gross margin percentage and the rate of inventory turnover to evaluate profitability* *(Obj. 5)*

Refer to Exercise 5-10. After completing First Choice Paint Centre's income statement for the year ended March 31, 2003, compute these ratios to evaluate First Choice Paint Centre's performance:

- Gross margin percentage
- Inventory turnover (Ending inventory one year earlier, at March 31, 2002, was $30,500.)

Compare your figures with the 2002 gross margin percentage of 49 percent and the inventory turnover rate of 3.16 times for 2002. Does the two-year trend suggest that First Choice Paint Centre's profits are increasing or decreasing?

Exercise 5-12 *Preparing a merchandiser's multi-step income statement under the perpetual inventory system to evaluate the business* *(Obj. 4, 5)*

Selected accounts of Handy Hand, a hardware store, are listed in alphabetical order.

Accounts receivable	$ 8,100	R. Brown, capital	$ 63,035
Accumulated amortization	9,350	Sales discounts	4,500
Cost of goods sold	45,650	Sales returns	2,300
General expenses	11,750	Sales revenue	100,500
Interest revenue	750	Selling expense	18,900
Inventory, Dec. 31, 2003	10,500	Unearned sales revenue	3,250
Inventory, Dec. 31, 2004	9,700		

Required

1. Prepare the business's multi-step income statement for the year ended December 31, 2004.

2. Compute the rate of inventory turnover for the year. Last year the turnover was 3.8 times. Does this two-year trend suggest improvement or deterioration in profitability?

Exercise 5-13   *Preparing a single-step income statement for a merchandising business under the perpetual inventory system*   *(Obj. 4, 5)*

Prepare Handy Hand's single-step income statement for 2004, using the data from Exercise 5-12. Compute the gross margin percentage, and compare it to last year's value of 58 percent for Handy Hand. Does this two-year trend suggest better or worse profitability during the current year?

Exercise 5-14   *Computing cost of goods sold in a periodic inventory system*   *(Obj. 6)*

The periodic inventory records of Handy Hand include these accounts at December 31, 2004:

Purchases of inventory	$45,300
Purchase discounts	1,500
Purchase returns and allowances	1,000
Freight in	2,050
Inventory	9,700

One year ago, at December 31, 2003, Handy Hand's inventory balance stood at $10,500.

Required

Compute Handy Hand's cost of goods sold for 2004. (Note: Your answer should be the same as the amount given in Exercise 5-12.)

Exercise 5-15   *Computing inventory and cost of goods sold under the periodic inventory system*   *(Obj. 6)*

Supply the missing income statement amounts in each of the following situations:

Sales	Sales Discounts	Net Sales	Beginning Inventory	Net Purchases	Ending Inventory	Cost of Goods Sold	Gross Margin
$96,300	(a)	$93,500	$35,500	$66,700	$39,400	(b)	$30,700
82,400	$2,100	(c)	25,750	43,000	(d)	$44,100	(e)
93,500	1,800	91,700	(f)	44,900	22,600	59,400	(g)
(h)	3,000	(i)	40,700	(j)	48,230	72,500	38,600

Exercise 5-16   *Computing cost of goods sold under the periodic inventory system*   *(Obj. 6)*

For the year ended December 31, 2003, House of Fabrics, a retailer of home-related products, reported net sales of $338,000 and cost of goods sold of $154,000. The company's balance sheet at December 31, 2002 and 2003, reported inventories of $133,000 and $129,000, respectively. What were House of Fabrics' net purchases during 2003?

Exercise 5-17   *Computing inventory purchases*   *(Obj. 6)*

The Gap, Inc. reported Cost of Goods Sold totalling $3,285 million. Ending inventory was $578 million, and beginning inventory was $483 million. How much inventory did The Gap purchase during the year?

Serial Exercise

This exercise completes the Anya Perreault Architects situation begun in Exercise 2-15 of Chapter 2 and extended to Exercise 3-17 of Chapter 3 and Exercise 4-14 of Chapter 4.

Exercise 5-18   *Accounting for both merchandising and service transactions under the perpetual inventory system*   **(Obj. 2, 3, 4)**

The architecture practice of Anya Perreault now includes a great deal of systems consulting business. In conjunction with the consulting, the business has begun selling design software. During January the business completed these transactions:

Jan. 2 Completed a consulting engagement and received cash of $8,700.
  2 Prepaid three months' office rent, $2,250.
  7 Purchased design software on account for merchandise inventory, $6,000.
  16 Paid employee salary, $2,100.
  18 Sold design software on account, $1,650 (cost $1,050).
  19 Consulted with a client for a fee of $1,350 on account.
  21 Paid on account, $3,000.
  24 Paid utilities, $450.
  28 Sold design software for cash, $900 (cost $600).
  31 Recorded these adjusting entries:
      Accrued salary expense, $2,100.
      Accounted for expiration of prepaid rent.
      Amortization of office furniture, $300.

Required

1. Open the following T-accounts in the ledger: Cash, Accounts Receivable, Design Software Inventory, Prepaid Rent, Accumulated Amortization—Office Furniture, Accounts Payable, Salary Payable, Anya Perreault, Capital, Income Summary, Service Revenue, Sales Revenue, Cost of Goods Sold, Salary Expense, Rent Expense, Utilities Expense, and Amortization Expense—Office Furniture.

2. Journalize and post the January transactions. Key all items by date. Compute each account balance, and denote the balance as *Bal.* Journalize and post the closing entries. Denote each closing amount as *Clo.* After posting, prove the equality of debits and credits in the ledger.

3. Prepare the January 2003 income statement of Anya Perreault Architects. Use the single-step format.

Beyond the Numbers

Beyond the Numbers 5-1   *Evaluating a company's profitability*   **(Obj. 1, 5)**

Chadwick Pharmaceuticals is a leading provider of pharmaceutical products. The company recently reported the figures on the following page.

Required

Evaluate Chadwick Pharmaceuticals' operations during 2004 in comparison with 2003. Consider sales, gross margin, operating income, and net income. Track the gross margin percentage and inventory turnover in both years. Chadwick Pharmaceuticals' inventories at December 31, 2004, 2003, and 2002, were $7,700,

$12,160, and $10,180 thousands, respectively. In the annual report Chadwick Pharmaceuticals' management describes the restructuring charges in 2004, the costs of down-sizing the company, as a one-time event. How does this additional information affect your evaluation?

CHADWICK PHARMACEUTICALS Consolidated Statements of Operations (Adapted) For the Years Ended July 31, 2004 and 2003		
	Amounts in Thousands	
	2004	**2003**
Sales...	$110,000	$82,000
Cost of sales..	80,000	61,000
Gross margin...	30,000	21,000
Cost and expenses:		
Selling, general, and administrative.............	22,000	17,000
Amortization...	2,000	900
Restructuring charges...............................	7,000	—
	31,000	17,900
Operating income (loss)............................	(1,000)	3,100
Other items (summarized)...............................	(600)	(1,300)
Net income (loss).......................................	$ (1,600)	$ 1,800

Ethical Issue

Delta Belting Company makes all sales of industrial conveyor belts under terms of FOB shipping point. The company usually receives orders for sales approximately one week before shipping inventory to customers. For orders received late in December, Meg Barnes, the owner, decides when to ship the goods. If profits are already at an acceptable level, the company delays shipment until January. If profits are lagging behind expectations, the company ships the goods during December.

Required

1. Under Delta Belting Company's FOB policy, when should the company record a sale?

2. Do you approve or disapprove of Delta Belting Company's means of deciding when to ship goods to customers? If you approve, give your reason. If you disapprove, identify a better way to decide when to ship goods. (There is no accounting rule against Delta Belting Company's practice.)

Problems (Group A)

Problem 5-1A *Explaining the perpetual inventory system* *(Obj. 2)*

The Bay is one of the largest retailers in Canada. The women's sportswear department of The Bay purchases clothing from many well-known manufacturers. The Bay uses a sophisticated perpetual inventory system.

Required

You are the manager of a Bay store in Calgary. Write a memo to a new employee in the women's sportswear department that explains how the company accounts for the purchase and sale of merchandise inventory.

  Use the following heading for your memo:

<table>
<tr><td colspan="2">Date: _____</td></tr>
<tr><td>To:</td><td>New Employee</td></tr>
<tr><td>From:</td><td>Store Manager</td></tr>
<tr><td>Subject:</td><td>The Bay's accounting system for inventories</td></tr>
</table>

Problem 5-2A *Accounting for the purchase and sale of inventory under the perpetual inventory system* **(Obj. 2)**

The following transactions occurred between Merck Frosst Canada Inc. and Drug Trading Company during February of the current year.

Feb. 6 Merck Frosst sold $12,600 worth of merchandise to Drug Trading on terms of 2/10 n/30, FOB shipping point. Merck Frosst prepaid freight charges of $500 and included this amount in the invoice total. (Merck Frosst's entry to record the freight payment debits Accounts Receivable and credits Cash.) These goods cost Merck Frosst $8,200.

10 Drug Trading returned $1,800 of the merchandise purchased on February 6. Merck Frosst issued a credit memo for this amount and returned the goods to inventory (cost, $1,180).

15 Drug Trading paid $6,000 of the invoice amount owed to Merck Frosst for the February 6 purchase. This payment included none of the freight charge.

27 Drug Trading paid the remaining amount owed to Merck Frosst for the February 6 purchase.

Required

Journalize these transactions, first on the books of Drug Trading Company, and second on the books of Merck Frosst Canada Inc.

Problem 5-3A *Journalizing purchase and sale transactions under the perpetual inventory system* **(Obj. 2)**

Salimi Distributing Company engaged in the following transactions during May of the current year:

May 3 Purchased office supplies for cash, $900.

7 Purchased inventory on credit terms of 3/10 net eom, $6,000.

8 Returned half the inventory purchased on May 7. It was not the inventory ordered.

10 Sold goods for cash, $1,350 (cost, $750).

13 Sold inventory on credit terms of 2/15 n/45, for $11,700, less $1,800 quantity discount offered to customers who purchased in large quantities (cost, $5,400).

16 Paid the amount owed on account from the purchase of May 7, less the discount and the return.

17 Received wrong-sized inventory as a sales return from May 13 sale, $2,700, which is the net amount after the quantity discount. Salimi 's cost of the inventory received was $1,800.

18 Purchased inventory of $12,000 on account. Payment terms were 2/10 net 30.

26 Borrowed $11,760 from the bank to take advantage of the discount offered on the May 18 purchase. Signed a note payable to the bank for this amount.

26 Paid supplier for goods purchased on May 18, less the discount.

28 Received cash in full settlement of the account from the customer who purchased inventory on May 13, less the discount and the return.

29 Purchased inventory for cash, $6,000, less a quantity discount of $1,200, plus freight charges of $480.

Required

1. Journalize the preceding transactions on the books of Salimi Distributing Company.

2. The note payable signed on May 26 requires Salimi to pay $90 interest expense. Was the decision to borrow funds to take advantage of the cash discount wise or unwise? Support your answer by comparing the discount to the interest paid.

Problem 5-4A *Preparing a merchandiser's work sheet under the perpetual inventory system* **(Obj. 3)**

The trial balance of Monica's Jewellery pertains to December 31, 2004.

MONICA'S JEWELLERY
Trial Balance
December 31, 2004

Cash..	$ 2,540	
Accounts receivable...............................	8,860	
Inventory...	147,800	
Prepaid rent	8,800	
Jewellery-making equipment.................	44,200	
Accumulated amortization.....................		$ 16,760
Accounts payable...................................		12,580
Salary payable		
Interest payable		
Note payable, long-term		36,000
Monica Jones, capital............................		111,840
Monica Jones, withdrawals	79,100	
Sales revenue		340,300
Cost of goods sold.................................	135,740	
Salary expense.......................................	49,400	
Rent expense..	15,400	
Advertising expense...............................	9,020	
Utilities expense	7,760	
Amortization expense		
Insurance expense..................................	5,540	
Interest expense.....................................	3,320	
Total...	$517,480	$517,480

Additional data at December 31, 2004:

a. Rent expense for the year, $20,400.
b. Jewellery-making equipment has an estimated useful life of ten years and is expected to have no value when it is retired from service.
c. Accrued salaries at December 31, $1,800.
d. Accrued interest expense at December 31, $720.
e. Inventory based on the inventory count on December 31, $146,400.

Required

Complete Monica's Jewellery's work sheet for the year ended December 31, 2004.

Problem 5-5A *Journalizing the adjusting and closing entries of a merchandising business under the perpetual inventory system* **(Obj. 3)**

Refer to the data in Problem 5-4A.

Required

1. Journalize the adjusting and closing entries.
2. Determine the December 31, 2004, balance of Capital for Monica's Jewellery.

Problem 5-6A   Preparing a multi-step income statement and a classified balance sheet under the perpetual inventory system   *(Obj. 4)*

Link Back to Chapter 4 (Classified Balance Sheet). Items from the accounts of Ste. Rose Dairy at May 31, 2004, follow, listed in alphabetical order. The General Expenses account summarizes all operating expenses.

Accounts payable....................	$ 20,000	Interest payable.....................	$ 1,100	
Accounts receivable...............	50,000	Inventory: May 31, 2004......	65,500	
Accumulated amortization		Note payable, long-term......	45,000	
—equipment........................	38,000	Salary payable	2,800	
Cash	7,800	Sales discounts	10,400	
Cecil Ste. Rose, capital............	57,500	Sales returns and		
Cecil Ste. Rose,		allowances..........................	18,000	
withdrawals.........................	9,000	Sales revenue	781,000	
Cost of goods sold	387,000	Selling expenses	140,000	
Equipment	146,000	Supplies..................................	5,100	
General expenses	120,000	Unearned sales revenue.......	13,800	
Interest expense......................	400			

Required

1. Prepare the business's multi-step income statement for the month ended May 31, 2004.

2. Prepare Ste. Rose Dairy's classified balance sheet in *report format* at May 31, 2004. Show your computation of the May 31, 2004, balance of Capital.

Problem 5-7A   Preparing a single-step income statement and a balance sheet under the perpetual inventory system   *(Obj. 4)*

Link Back to Chapter 4 (Classified Balance Sheet).

1. Use the data of Problem 5-6A to prepare Ste. Rose Dairy's *single-step* income statement for the month ended May 31, 2004. In addition to the data in Problem 5-6A, Ste. Rose Dairy had interest revenue of $200.

2. Prepare Ste. Rose Dairy's classified balance sheet in report format at May 31, 2004. Show your computation of the May 31 balance of Capital. For this problem, withdrawals totalled $9,200.

Problem 5-8A   Using work sheet data to prepare financial statements and evaluate the business under the perpetual inventory system; multi-step income statement   *(Obj. 4, 5)*

The trial balance and adjustments columns of the work sheet of Brandon Products include the accounts and balances at November 30, 2003 shown on the following page.

Required

1. Inventory on hand at November 30, 2002, is $32,000. Without entering the preceding data on a formal work sheet, prepare the company's multi-step income statement for the year ended November 30, 2003.

2. Compute the gross margin percentage and the rate of inventory turnover for 2003. For 2002, Brandon Product's gross margin percentage was 58 percent, and inventory turnover was 1.8 times during the year. Does the two-year trend in these ratios suggest improvement or deterioration in profitability?

Account Title	Trial Balance Debit	Trial Balance Credit	Adjustments Debit	Adjustments Credit
Cash...	$ 24,000			
Accounts receivable	14,500		(a) 6,000	
Inventory	35,000		(b) 1,000	
Supplies...	2,800			(c) 2,000
Furniture...	39,600			
Accumulated amortization		$ 4,900		(d) 2,450
Accounts payable		12,600		
Salary payable..................................				(f) 1,000
Unearned sales revenue		13,570	(e) 7,000	
Note payable, long-term.................		15,000		
W. Leduc, capital		55,130		
W. Leduc, withdrawals....................	42,000			
Sales revenue...................................		180,000		(a) 6,000
				(e) 7,000
Sales returns	6,800			
Cost of goods sold	73,000			(b) 1,000
Selling expense................................	29,000		(f) 1,000	
General expense...............................	13,000		(c) 2,000	
			(d) 2,450	
Interest expense	1,500			
Total...	$281,200	$281,200	$19,450	$19,450

Problem 5-9A *Computing cost of goods sold and gross margin in a periodic inventory system; evaluating the business* (**Obj. 5, 6**)

Selected accounts from the accounting records of Smith Security had the balances shown below at November 30, 2003.

Purchases of inventory	$66,000
Selling expenses...	4,400
Furniture and fixtures..	18,600
Purchase returns and allowances..	450
Salary payable...	150
S. Smith, capital..	26,400
Sales revenue..	97,300
Sales returns and allowances	1,600
Inventory: November 30, 2002...	20,850
November 30, 2003...	20,750
Accounts payable..	4,750
Cash	1,850
Freight in..	800
Accumulated amortization—furniture and fixtures	6,800
Purchase discounts...	300
Sales discounts	1,050
General expenses..	9,650

Required

1. Show the computation of Smith Security's net sales, cost of goods sold, and gross margin for the year ended November 30, 2003.

2. Sandra Smith, the proprietor of Smith Security, strives to earn a gross margin percentage of 25 percent. Did she achieve this goal?

3. Did the rate of inventory turnover reach the industry average of 3.4 times per year?

Problem 5-10A

Under the perpetual inventory system, accounting for the purchase and sale of inventory, computing cost of goods sold and gross margin, using the gross margin percentage to evaluate a business **(Obj. 2, 5, 6)**

Software Warehouse uses the perpetual inventory method in tracking its inventory purchases and sales. All sales that result in a return, allowance, or discount are tracked in separate accounts in order to give management the proper information to control operations. The following information is available for the month of April 2004:

April 1   Inventory on hand at the beginning of the month was $27,600.

     2   Purchased $10,000 of merchandise from Microsoft, terms 2/10 n/30. The goods were expected to be resold for $22,000.

     4   Sold merchandise for $14,000 to Coast Logistics Inc., terms 2/10 n/60. The goods had a cost of $8,000 to Software Warehouse.

     6   Software Warehouse returned $4,000 of defective merchandise purchased from Microsoft on April 2.

     8   Sold merchandise for $16,000 cash; the goods had a cost of $12,000.

     9   Purchased $18,000 of merchandise from Corel, terms 2/10 n/30.

    10   Software Warehouse paid the balance owing to Microsoft.

    12   Software Warehouse accepted the return of half of the merchandise sold on April 8 as it was not compatible with the customer's needs. The goods were returned to inventory and a cash refund paid.

    18   Paid the balance owing to Corel from the purchase of April 9.

    20   Sold merchandise for $8,000 to Robertson Personnel Services Ltd., terms 2/10 n/60. The goods had cost $6,000.

    22   Robertson Personnel Services Ltd. complained about the quality of goods it received and Software Warehouse gave an allowance of $1,000.

    25   Purchased $12,000 of merchandise for cash and paid $1,000 for freight.

    29   Software Warehouse sold merchandise for $12,000 to Burnaby Design Studio, terms 2/10 n/30. The goods had cost $6,000. The terms of the sale where FOB shipping point, but, as a convenience, Software Warehouse prepaid $800 of freight for Burnaby Design Studio.

    30   Collected the balance owing from Robertson Personnel Services Ltd.

Required

1. Record any journal entries required for the above transactions.

2. What is the inventory balance on April 30, 2004?

3. Prepare a multi-step income statement, to the point of gross margin, for the month of April 2004.

4. The average gross margin percentage for the industry is 50 percent; how does Software Warehouse compare to the industry?

Problem 5-11A

Under the perpetual inventory system, computing cost of goods sold and gross margin, adjusting and closing the accounts of a merchandising company, preparing a merchandiser's financial statements **(Obj. 3, 4, 6)**

Rapid Kayaks has the following account balances (in alphabetical order) on July 31, 2003:

Accounts payable	$ 1,450
Accounts receivable	1,550
Accumulated amortization—equipment	4,300
Cash	500
Cathy Zappa, capital	24,250
Cathy Zappa, withdrawals	1,000
Cost of goods sold	45,650
Equipment	12,000
Interest earned	400
Inventory	9,350
Operating expenses	24,100

Sales discounts..	550
Sales returns and allowances..	3,800
Sales revenues...	69,000
Supplies	1,900
Unearned sales revenue	1,000

Note: For simplicity, all operating expenses have been summarized in the account Operating Expenses.

Additional data at July 31, 2003:

a. A physical count of items showed $200 of supplies on hand.

b. An inventory count showed inventory on hand at July 31, 2003, $9,850.

c. The equipment has an estimated useful life of eight years and is expected to have no value at the end of its life.

d. Unearned sales revenues of $350 were earned by July 31, 2003.

Required

1. Record all adjustments and closing entries that would be required on July 31, 2003.

2. Prepare the financial statements of Rapid Kayaks for the year ended July 31, 2003.

Problems (Group B)

Problem 5-1B   *Explaining the perpetual inventory system   (Obj. 2)*

Claire Vision is a regional chain of optical shops in Manitoba. The company offers a large selection of eyeglass frames, and Claire Vision stores provide while-you-wait service. Claire Vision has launched a vigourous advertising campaign promoting its two-for-the-price-of-one frame sale.

Required

Claire Vision expects to grow rapidly and increase its level of inventory. As chief accountant of the company, you wish to install a perpetual inventory system. Write a memo to the company president to explain how the system would work.

Use the following heading for your memo:

Date:	_____
To:	Company President
From:	Chief Accountant
Subject:	How a perpetual inventory system works

Problem 5-2B   *Accounting for the purchase and sale of inventory under the perpetual inventory system   (Obj. 2)*

The following transactions occurred between Shoppers Drug Mart and Johnson & Johnson Inc. during June of the current year.

June   8   Johnson & Johnson sold $9,800 worth of merchandise to Shoppers Drug Mart on terms of 2/10 n/30, FOB shipping point. These goods cost Johnson & Johnson $4,200. Johnson & Johnson prepaid freight charges of $200 and included this amount in the invoice total. (Johnson & Johnson's entry to record the freight payment debits Accounts Receivable and credits Cash.)

      11   Shoppers Drug Mart returned $1,200 of the merchandise purchased on June 8.

Johnson & Johnson issued a credit memo for this amount and returned the goods, in excellent condition, to inventory (cost $500).

June 17 Shoppers Drug Mart paid $4,000 of the invoice amount owed to Johnson & Johnson for the June 8 purchase. This payment included none of the freight charge. Shopper's took the purchase discount on the partial payment.

26 Shoppers Drug Mart paid the remaining amount owed to Johnson & Johnson for the June 8 purchase.

Required

Journalize these transactions, first on the books of Shoppers Drug Mart, and second on the books of Johnson & Johnson.

Problem 5-3B *Journalizing purchase and sale transactions under the perpetual inventory system (Obj. 2)*

Segal Furniture Company engaged in the following transactions during July of the current year:

July 2 Purchased inventory for cash, $1,200, less a quantity discount of $225.
5 Purchased store supplies on credit terms of net eom, $675.
8 Purchased inventory of $4,500 less a quantity discount of 10%, plus freight charges of $230. Credit terms are 3/15 n/30.
9 Sold goods for cash, $1,800. Segal's cost of these goods was $1,050.
11 Returned $300 (net amount after the quantity discount) of the inventory purchased on July 8. It was damaged in shipment.
12 Purchased inventory on credit terms of 3/10 n/30, $5,000.
14 Sold inventory on credit terms of 2/10 n/30, for $14,400, less a $900 quantity discount (cost, $7,500).
16 Received and paid the electricity and water bills, $400.
20 Received returned inventory from the July 14 sale, $600 (net amount after the quantity discount). Segal shipped the wrong goods by mistake. Segal's cost of the inventory received was $375.
21 Borrowed the amount owed on the July 8 purchase. Signed a note payable to the bank for $3,867.50, which takes into account the return of inventory on July 11.
21 Paid supplier for goods purchased on July 8 less the discount and the return.
23 Received $10,290 cash in partial settlement of the account from the customer who purchased inventory on July 14. Granted the customer a 2% discount and credited his account receivable for $10,500.
30 Paid for the store supplies purchased on July 5.

Required

1. Journalize the preceding transactions on the books of Segal Furniture Company.

2. Compute the amount of the receivable at July 31 from the customer to whom Segal sold inventory on July 14. What amount of cash discount applies to this receivable at July 31?

Problem 5-4B *Preparing a merchandiser's work sheet under the perpetual inventory system (Obj. 3)*

Prairie Produce Company's trial balance on page 265 pertains to December 31, 2003.

Additional data at December 31, 2003:

a. Insurance expense for the year should total $12,180.

b. Store fixtures have an estimated useful life of ten years and are expected to have no value when they are retired from service.

c. Accrued salaries at December 31, $2,520.

d. Accrued interest expense at December 31, $1,740.

e. Store supplies on hand at December 31, $1,520.

f. Inventory based on the inventory count on December 31, $199,300.

PRAIRIE PRODUCE COMPANY
Trial Balance
December 31, 2003

Cash	$ 5,820	
Accounts receivable	13,120	
Inventory	203,520	
Store supplies	3,980	
Prepaid insurance	6,400	
Store fixtures	127,800	
Accumulated amortization		$ 75,280
Accounts payable		59,540
Salary payable		
Interest payable		
Note payable, long-term		74,400
D. Champ, capital		126,240
D. Champ, withdrawals	72,600	
Sales revenue		572,740
Cost of goods sold	322,180	
Salary expense	93,160	
Rent expense	29,260	
Utilities expense	13,560	
Amortization expense		
Insurance expense	10,600	
Store supplies expense		
Interest expense	6,200	
Total	$908,200	$908,200

Required

Complete Prairie Produce Company's work sheet for the year ended December 31, 2003. Key adjustments by letter.

Problem 5-5B *Journalizing the adjusting and closing entries of a merchandising business under the perpetual inventory system* **(Obj. 4)**

Refer to the data in Problem 5-4A.

Required

1. Journalize the adjusting and closing entries of Prairie Produce Company.
2. Determine the December 31, 2003, balance in the Capital account.

Problem 5-6B *Preparing a multi-step income statement and a classified balance sheet under the perpetual inventory system* **(Obj. 3, 4)**

Link Back to Chapter 4 (Classified Balance Sheet) For simplicity, all operating expenses are summarized in the accounts Selling Expenses and General Expenses. Selected accounts of Saturna Home Entertainment, at July 31, 2003, are listed in alphabetical order on page 266.

Required

1. Prepare the entity's multi-step income statement for the month ended July 31, 2003.
2. Prepare Saturna's classified balance sheet in *report format* at July 31, 2003. Show separately your computation of the July 31, 2003, balance of B. Saturna, Capital.

Accounts payable	$63,650	Inventory: July 31, 2003	$93,650
Accounts receivable	15,600	Note payable, long-term	80,000
Accumulated amortization		Salary payable	3,050
—store equipment	8,200	Sales discounts	4,150
B. Saturna, capital	33,550	Sales returns and	
B. Saturna, withdrawals	5,500	allowances	8,950
Cash	6,150	Sales revenue	265,800
Cost of goods sold	180,450	Selling expenses	42,300
General expenses	37,900	Store equipment	63,000
Interest expense	600	Supplies	2,150
Interest payable	1,500	Unearned sales revenue	4,650

Problem 5-7B *Preparing a single-step income statement and a classified balance sheet under the perpetual inventory system* **(Obj. 4)**

Link Back to Chapter 4 (Classified Balance Sheet).

1. Use the data of Problem 5-6B to prepare Saturna Home Entertainment's *single-step* income statement for July 31, 2003. In addition to the data given in Problem 5-6B, Saturna had interest revenue of $150.

2. Prepare Saturna 's classified balance sheet in *report format* at July 31, 2003. Show your computation of the July 31 balance of Capital. For this problem, withdrawals were $5,650.

Problem 5-8B *Using work sheet data to prepare financial statements and evaluate the business under the perpetual inventory system; multi-step income statement* **(Obj. 4, 5, 6)**

The trial balance and adjustments columns of the work sheet of Yellowknife Trading Company include the following accounts and balances at September 30, 2003:

	Trial Balance		Adjustments	
Account Title	**Debit**	**Credit**	**Debit**	**Credit**
Cash	$ 7,900			
Accounts receivable	4,360		(a) 2,000	
Inventory	9,630		(b) 2,100	
Supplies	13,000			(c) 9,600
Equipment	99,450			
Accumulated amortization		$ 29,800		(d) 9,900
Accounts payable		15,800		
Salary payable				(f) 200
Unearned sales revenue		3,780	(e) 3,000	
Note payable, long-term		10,000		
L. Miller, capital		43,060		
L. Miller, withdrawals	35,000			
Sales revenue		240,000		(a) 2,000
				(e) 3,000
Sales returns	3,100			
Cost of goods sold	108,000			(b) 2,100
Selling expense	40,000		(c) 9,600	
			(f) 200	
General expense	21,000		(d) 9,900	
Interest expense	1,000			
Total	$342,440	$342,440	$26,800	$26,800

Required

1. Inventory on hand at September 30, 2002, was $11,000. Without completing a formal accounting work sheet, prepare the company's multi-step income statement for the year ended September 30, 2003.

2. Compute the gross margin percentage and the inventory turnover for 2003. For 2002, Yellowknife Trading Company's gross margin percentage was 60 percent and the inventory turnover rate was 9.8 times. Does the two-year trend in these ratios suggest improvement or deterioration in profitability?

Problem 5-9B *Computing cost of goods sold and gross margin in a periodic system; evaluating the business* *(Obj. 5, 6)*

Selected accounts from the accounting records of PEI Products at June 30, 2004, are shown below.

Cash	$ 6,800
Purchases of inventory	49,050
Freight in	2,150
Sales revenue	89,550
Purchases returns and allowances	700
Salary payable	900
Jake Bradshaw, capital	18,000
Sales returns and allowances	6,050
Inventory: June 30, 2003	11,900
June 30, 2004	14,250
Selling expenses	14,900
Equipment	22,350
Purchase discounts	650
Accumulated amortization—equipment	3,450
Sales discounts	1,700
General expenses	8,150
Accounts payable	11,900

Required

1. Show the computation of PEI Products' net sales, cost of goods sold, and gross margin for the year ended June 30, 2004.

2. Jake Bradshaw, owner of PEI Products, strives to earn a gross margin percentage of 40 percent. Did he achieve this goal?

3. Did the rate of inventory turnover reach the industry average of 3.4 times per year?

Problem 5-10B *Under the perpetual inventory system, accounting for the purchase and sale of inventory, computing cost of goods sold and gross margin, using the gross margin percentage to evaluate a business* *(Obj. 2, 5, 6)*

Century Life Products uses the perpetual inventory method in tracking its inventory purchases and sales. All sales that result in a return, allowance, or discount are tracked in separate accounts in order to give management the proper information to control operations. The following information is available for the month of April 2004:

April 1 The balance of inventory on hand at the beginning of the month was $53,250.
2 Purchased $6,000 of merchandise from Muzac Corp., terms 2/10 n/30. The goods were expected to be resold for $13,500.
4 Sold merchandise for $9,000 to Delta Fitness Club Ltd., terms 2/10 n/60. The goods had a cost of $4,500 to Century.

April 6 Century Life Products returned $1,500 of defective merchandise purchased from Muzac Corp. on April 2.
8 Sold merchandise for $13,500 cash; the goods had a cost of $9,000.
9 Purchased $12,000 of merchandise from Keiser Corp., terms 2/10 n/30.
10 Century Life Products paid the balance owing to Muzac Corp.
12 Century Life Products accepted the return of half of the merchandise sold on April 8 as it was not compatible with the customer's needs. The goods were returned to stock and a cash refund paid.
18 Paid the balance owing to Keiser Corp. from the purchase of April 9.
20 Sold merchandise for $7,500 to Clearbrook Health Clubs Ltd., terms 2/10 n/60. The goods had cost $5,250.
22 Clearbrook Health Clubs Ltd. complained about the quality of goods it received and Century Life Products gave an allowance of $900.
25 Purchased $10,500 of merchandise for cash and paid $600 for freight.
29 Century Life Products sold merchandise for $7,500 to England Fitness Ltd., terms 2/10 n/30. The goods had cost $4,500. The terms of the sale were FOB shipping point, but as a convenience, Century Life Products prepaid $450 of freight for England Fitness Ltd. and included the charge on its invoice.
30 Collected the balance owing from Clearbrook Health Clubs Ltd.

Required

1. Record any journal entries required for the above transactions.

2. What is the inventory balance on April 30, 2004?

3. Prepare a multi-step income statement, to the point of gross margin, for the month of April 2004.

4. The average gross margin percentage for the industry is 48 percent; how does Century Life Products compare to the industry?

Problem 5-11B *Under the perpetual inventory system, computing cost of goods sold and gross margin, adjusting and closing the accounts of a merchandising company, preparing a merchandiser's financial statements* **(Obj. 3, 4, 6)**

Saskatoon Skate Products has the following account balances (in alphabetical order) on August 31, 2004:

Accounts payable	$ 11,600
Accounts receivable	12,400
Accumulated amortization—equipment	34,400
Cash	4,000
C. Dewar, capital	126,000
C. Dewar, withdrawals	8,000
Cost of goods sold	221,200
Equipment	86,000
Interest earned	3,200
Inventory	74,800
Operating expenses	156,800
Sales discounts	4,400
Sales returns and allowances	30,400
Sales revenues	430,000
Supplies	15,200
Unearned sales revenue	8,000

Note: For simplicity, all operating expenses have been summarized in the account Operating Expenses.

Additional data at August 31, 2004:

a. A physical count of items showed $260 of supplies were on hand.

b. An inventory count showed inventory on hand at August 31, 2004, $72,000.

c. The equipment is expected to last five years and have no value at the end of five years.

d. Unearned sales of $2,000 were earned by August 31, 2004.

Required

1. Record all adjustments and closing entries that would be required on August 31, 2004.

2. Prepare the financial statements of Saskatoon Skate Products for the year ended August 31, 2004.

Challenge Problems

Problem 5-1C *Understanding purchasing and gross margin* **(Obj. 1, 2, 5)**

You have been recently hired as an accountant by AllSave Stores, a small chain of discount stores. One of your first activities is to review the accounting system for AllSave.

In your review, you discover that the company determines selling prices by adding a standard markup on cost of 10 percent (i.e., cost plus 10 percent of cost) to the cost of all products. The company uses a perpetual inventory system. You also discover that your predecessor, a bookkeeper, had set up the accounting system so that all purchase discounts and purchase returns and allowances were accumulated in an account that was treated as "other income" for financial statement purposes because he believed that they were financing items and not related to operations.

Marion Farouk, owner of AllSave, has an MBA and uses modern decision-making techniques in running AllSave. Two ratios she particularly favours are the gross margin percentage and inventory turnover ratio.

Required

1. What is a possible effect of the accounting system described on the pricing of products and thus operations of AllSave Stores?

2. What is the effect of the accounting system instituted by your predecessor on the two ratios Ms. Farouk favours?

Problem 5-2C *Using an inventory system for control* **(Obj. 1)**

Arthur Leung is concerned about theft by shoplifters in his chain of three electronics stores and has come to your public accounting firm for advice. Specifically, he has several questions he would like you to answer.

a. He wonders if there is any inventory system he can use that will allow him to keep track of products that leave his stores as legitimate purchases and merchandise that is stolen?

b. He realizes that carrying inventory is expensive and wants to know if you have any suggestions as to how he can keep close tabs on his inventory at the three stores so he can be sure that the stores don't run out of product.

c. The space in the stores is limited. Arthur also wants to install an inventory system that will tell him when a product is slow-moving or obsolete so he can clear it out and replace it with a potentially faster-moving product.

Required

Indicate whether a perpetual inventory system or a periodic inventory system will provide Arthur with answers to the three questions he has asked. Explain how the inventory system indicated will provide the specific information he has requested.

Extending Your Knowledge

Decision Problems

1. Using financial statements to decide on a business expansion   *(Obj. 4, 5)*

Link Back to Chapter 4 (Classified Balance Sheet, Current Ratio, Debt Ratio). David Garner owns Heights Pharmacy, which has prospered during its second year of operation. In deciding whether to open another pharmacy in the area, Garner's bookkeeper has prepared the current financial statements of the business.

HEIGHTS PHARMACY
Income Statement
For the Year Ended December 31, 2003

Sales revenue		$180,000
Interest revenue		24,600
Total revenue		204,600
Cost of goods sold		87,000
Gross margin		117,600
Operating expenses:		
Salary expense	20,000	
Rent expense	12,000	
Interest expense	6,000	
Amortization expense	4,900	
Utilities expense	2,330	
Supplies expense	1,500	
Total operating expenses		46,730
Income from operations		70,870
Other expense:		
Sales discounts ($3,600) and returns ($7,100)		10,700
Net income		$60,170

HEIGHTS PHARMACY
Statement of Owner's Equity
For the Year Ended December 31, 2003

David Garner, capital, January 1, 2003	$30,000
Add: Net income	60,170
David Garner, capital, December 31, 2003	$90,170

HEIGHTS PHARMACY
Balance Sheet
December 31, 2003

Assets

Current assets:
Cash	$ 5,320
Accounts receivable	10,710
Inventory	30,100
Supplies	2,800
Store fixtures	63,000
Total current assets	111,930

Other asset:
Withdrawals	45,000
Total assets	$156,930

Liabilities

Current liabilities:
Accumulated amortization—store fixtures	$ 6,300
Accounts payable	9,560
Salary payable	900
Total current liabilities	16,760

Other liability:
Note payable due in 90 days	50,000
Total liabilities	66,760

Owner's Equity

David Garner, capital	90,170
Total liabilities and owner's equity	$156,930

David Garner recently read in an industry trade journal that a successful pharmacy meets all of these criteria:

a. Gross margin is at least 50 percent.

b. Current ratio is at least 2.0.

c. Debt ratio is no higher than 0.50.

d. Inventory turnover is at least 3.40 times per year. (Heights Pharmacy's inventory at December 31, 2003, was $19,200.)

Basing his opinion on the entity's financial statement data, David Garner believes the business meets all four criteria. He plans to go ahead with the expansion plan, and asks your advice on preparing the pharmacy's financial statements in accordance with generally accepted accounting principles. He assures you that all amounts are correct.

Required

1. Compute the four ratios based on the Heights Pharmacy financial statements prepared by Garner's bookkeeper. Does the business appear to be ready for expansion?

2. Prepare a correct multi-step income statement, a statement of owner's equity, and a classified balance sheet in report format.

3. On the basis of the corrected financial statements, compute correct measures of the four criteria listed in the trade journal.

4. Make a recommendation about whether to undertake the expansion at this time.

2. Understanding the operating cycle of a merchandiser *(Obj. 1, 3)*

Gayle Yip-Chuck has come to you for advice. Earlier this year, she opened a record store in a plaza near the university she had attended. The store sells compact discs at very low prices and on special credit for students. Many of the students at the university are co-op students who alternate school and work terms. Gayle allows co-op students to buy on credit while they are on a school term, with the understanding that they will pay their account shortly after starting a work term.

Business has been very good. Gayle is sure it is because of her competitive prices and the unique credit terms she offers. Her problem is that she is short of cash, and her loan with the bank has grown significantly. The bank manager has indicated that he wishes to reduce Yip-Chuck's line of credit because he is worried that she will get into financial difficulties.

Required

1. Explain to Yip-Chuck why you think she is short of cash.
2. Yip-Chuck has asked you to explain her problem to the bank manager and to assist in asking for more credit. What might you say to the bank manager to assist Yip-Chuck?

3. Correcting an inventory error *(Obj. 6)*

The employees of Northern Tech Company made an error when they performed the periodic inventory count at year end, October 31, 2003. Part of one warehouse was not counted and therefore was not included in inventory.

Required

1. Indicate the effect of the inventory error on cost of goods sold, gross margin, and net income for the year ended October 31, 2003.
2. Will the error affect cost of goods sold, gross margin, and net income in 2004? If so, what will be the effect?

Financial Statement Problem

Closing entries for a corporation that sells merchandise; evaluating ratio data *(Obj. 3, 5)*

This problem uses both the income statement (consolidated statement of operations) and the balance sheet of Intrawest Corporation in Appendix A. It will aid your understanding of the closing process of a business.

1. Journalize Intrawest's closing entries for the year ended June 30, 2000. You will be unfamiliar with certain revenues and expenses, but you should treat them all similarly. Make "General and administrative" the final expense you close. Instead of closing to a Capital account, close to the Retained Earnings account (since Intrawest is a corporation, not a proprietorship).
2. What amount was closed to Retained Earnings? What were dividends in 2000?
3. Intrawest is not a typical merchandiser but it does have two types of inventory: (1) Inventory related to ski operations (Note 7 in the financial statements); (2) Inventory of properties under development and held for sale (Note 5). The company develops resort properties for resale, some of which will be sold in the current year and are classified as current assets. The remainder of the properties will be sold in future years and are classified as long-term assets. What balances are reported as current assets on the *balance sheet* for the two types of inventory at June 30, 2000? At June 30, 1999?

Supplement to Chapter 5

Accounting for Merchandise in a Periodic Inventory System

Purchasing Merchandise in the Periodic Inventory System

Some businesses find it uneconomical to invest in a computerized (perpetual) inventory system that keeps up-to-the-minute records of merchandise on hand and cost of goods sold.

Recording Purchases of Inventory

All inventory systems use the Inventory account. But in a periodic inventory system, purchases, purchase discounts, purchase returns and allowances, and transportation costs are recorded in separate expense accounts bearing these titles. Let's account for Austin Sound Centre's purchase of the JVC goods in Exhibit 5S-1. For the moment, disregard GST and use the invoice total of $707.00 when recording purchases and purchase discounts. GST is discussed on page 228. The following entries record the purchase and payment on account within the discount period:

OBJECTIVE S2
Account for the purchase and sale of inventory under the periodic inventory system

May 27	Purchases..	707.00	
	Accounts Payable...............................		707.00
	Purchased inventory on account.		
June 10	Accounts Payable..	707.00	
	Cash..		685.79
	Purchase Discounts ($707.00 × 0.03)		21.21
	Paid for inventory on account within discount period.		
	The discount is $21.21.		

Recording Purchase Returns and Allowances

Suppose instead that prior to payment, Austin Sound returned to JVC goods costing $70 and also received from JVC a purchase allowance of $10. Austin Sound would record these transactions as follows:

June 3	Accounts Payable	70.00	
	Purchase Returns and Allowances		70.00
	Returned inventory to seller.		
June 4	Accounts Payable	10.00	
	Purchase Returns and Allowances		10.00
	Received a purchase allowance.		

KEY POINT

A contra account always has a companion account with the opposite balance. Thus both Purchase Discounts and Purchase Returns and Allowances (credit balances) are reported with Purchases (debit balance) on the income statement.

During the period, the business records the cost of all inventory bought in the Purchases account. The balance of Purchases is a *gross* amount because it does not include subtractions for purchase discounts, returns, or allowances. **Net purchases** is the remainder computed by subtracting the contra accounts from Purchases:

> **Purchase (*debit* balance account)**
> – **Purchase Discounts (*credit* balance account)**
> – **Purchase Returns and Allowances (*credit* balance account)**
> = **Net purchases (a *debit* subtotal, not a separate account)**

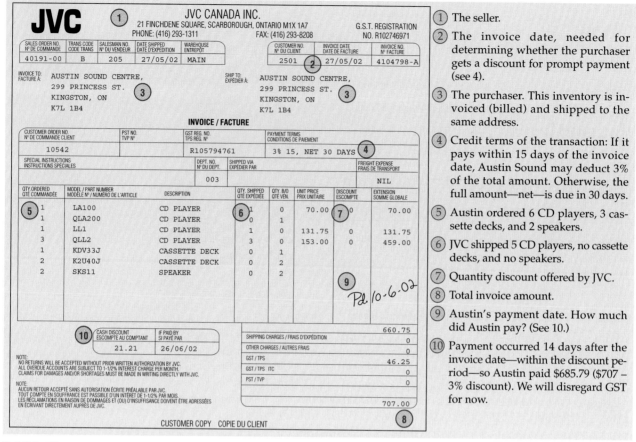

The numbered annotations on the right side of the invoice:

1. The seller.

2. The invoice date, needed for determining whether the purchaser gets a discount for prompt payment (see 4).

3. The purchaser. This inventory is invoiced (billed) and shipped to the same address.

4. Credit terms of the transaction: If it pays within 15 days of the invoice date, Austin Sound may deduct 3% of the total amount. Otherwise, the full amount—net—is due in 30 days.

5. Austin ordered 6 CD players, 3 cassette decks, and 2 speakers.

6. JVC shipped 5 CD players, no cassette decks, and no speakers.

7. Quantity discount offered by JVC.

8. Total invoice amount.

9. Austin's payment date. How much did Austin pay? (See 10.)

10. Payment occurred 14 days after the invoice date—within the discount period—so Austin paid $685.79 ($707 – 3% discount). We will disregard GST for now.

Exhibit 5S-1

An Invoice

Recording Transportation Costs

Under the periodic system, costs to transport purchased inventory from seller to buyer are debited to a separate expense account, as shown for payment of a $60 freight bill:

June 1	Freight In	60.00	
	Cash..		60.00
	Paid a freight bill.		

Recording the Sale of Inventory

Recording sales is streamlined in the periodic system. With no running record of inventory to maintain, we can record a $3,000 sale as follows:

June 5	Accounts Receivable	3,000	
	Sales Revenue		3,000
	Sale on account.		

No accompanying entry to Inventory and Cost of Goods Sold is required. Also, sales discounts and sales returns and allowances are recorded as shown for the perpetual system on page 227, but with no entry to Inventory and Cost of Goods Sold.

OBJECTIVE 3
Compute the cost of goods sold under the periodic inventory system

Cost of Goods Sold

Cost of goods sold (also called **cost of sales**) is the largest single expense of most businesses that sell merchandise, such as SportChek and Austin Sound. It is the cost of the inventory that the business has sold to customers. In a periodic system, cost of goods sold must be computed as in Exhibit 5S-2 and is *not* a ledger account.

Panel A

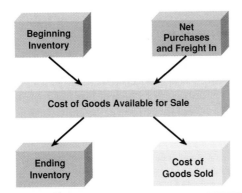

$$
\begin{aligned}
&\text{Beginning inventory} \\
&+ \text{Net purchases} \longleftarrow \\
&+ \text{Freight in}
\end{aligned}
\quad
\left\{
\begin{aligned}
&\text{Purchases of inventory} \\
&- \text{Purchase discounts} \\
&- \text{Purchase returns and allowances} \\
&= \text{Net purchases}
\end{aligned}
\right.
$$

= Cost of goods available for sale
– Ending inventory

= Cost of goods sold

Panel B

[Flowchart: Beginning Inventory and Net Purchases and Freight In flow into Cost of Goods Available for Sale, which flows into Ending Inventory and Cost of Goods Sold]

It is the residual left when we subtract ending inventory from the cost of goods available for sale.

Exhibit 5S-3 summarizes the first half of this Supplement by showing Austin Sound's net sales revenue, cost of goods sold—including net purchases and freight in—and gross margin on the income statement for the periodic system. (All amounts are assumed.)

EXHIBIT 5S-2

Measuring Cost of Goods Sold in the Periodic Inventory System

(WORKING IT OUT)

Assume:

Purchases	$265,000
Sales	463,000
Gross Margin	200,000
Purchase Returns and Allowances	2,600
Beginning Inventory	12,000
Sales Returns and Allowances	4,500
Purchase Discounts	2,400
Ending Inventory	?
Sales Discounts	8,500

How much is Ending Inventory?

A: $22,000. (Net sales: $463,000 – $4,500 – $8,500 = $450,000; Cost of goods sold: $450,000 – $200,000 = $250,000; Ending inventory: $12,000 + $265,000 – $2,600 – $2,400 – $250,000 = $22,000).

EXHIBIT 5S-3

Partial Income Statement

AUSTIN SOUND CENTRE
Income Statement
For the Year Ended December 31, 2004

PANEL A—Detailed Gross Margin Section—Often Required by Management

Sales revenue			$169,300
Less: Sales discounts		$ 1,400	
Sales returns and allowances		2,000	3,400
Net sales			$165,900
Cost of goods sold:			
Beginning inventory			38,600
Purchases		91,400	
Less: Purchase discounts	$3,000		
Purchase returns and allowances	1,200	4,200	
Net purchases			87,200
Freight in			5,200
Cost of goods available for sale			131,000
Less: Ending inventory			40,200
Cost of goods sold			90,800
Gross margin			$ 75,100

PANEL B—Summary Gross Margin Section—Most Common in Annual Reports to Outsiders

Net sales	$165,900
Cost of goods sold	90,800
Gross margin	$ 75,100

Adjusting and Closing the Accounts in a Periodic Inventory System

A merchandising business adjusts and closes the accounts much as a service entity does. The steps of this end-of-period process are the same: If a work sheet is used, the trial balance is entered and the work sheet completed to determine net income or net loss. The work sheet provides the data for journalizing the adjusting and closing entries and for preparing the financial statements.

At the end of the period, before any adjusting or closing entries, the Inventory account balance is still the cost of the inventory that was on hand at the end of the preceding period. It is necessary to remove this beginning balance and replace it with the cost of the inventory on hand at the end of the period. Various techniques may be used to bring the inventory records up to date.

To illustrate a merchandiser's adjusting and closing process under the periodic inventory system, let's use Austin Sound's December 31, 2004, trial balance in Exhibit 5S-4. All the new accounts—Inventory, Purchases, Freight In, and the contra accounts—are highlighted for emphasis. Inventory is the only account that is affected by the new closing procedures. The additional data item (h) gives the ending inventory figure $40,200.

Preparing and Using the Work Sheet in a Periodic Inventory System

The Exhibit 5S-5 work sheet on page 278 is similar to the work sheets we have seen so far, but a few differences appear. This work sheet is slightly different from the one you saw in Chapter 4; it does not include adjusted trial balance columns. In most accounting systems, a single operation combines trial balance amounts with the adjustments and extends the adjusted balances directly to the income statement and balance sheet columns. Therefore, to reduce clutter, the adjusted trial balance columns are omitted so that the work sheet contains four pairs of columns, not five.

Account Title Columns   The trial balance lists a number of accounts without balances. Ordinarily, these accounts are affected by the adjusting process. Examples include Interest Receivable, Interest Payable, and Amortization Expense. The accounts are listed in the order they appear in the ledger. If additional accounts are needed, they can be written in at the bottom, above net income.

Trial Balance Columns   Examine the Inventory account, $38,600 in the trial balance. This $38,600 is the cost of the beginning inventory. The work sheet is designed to replace this outdated amount with the new ending balance, which in our example is $40,200 [additional data item (h) in Exhibit 5S-4]. As we shall see, this task is accomplished later in the columns for the income statement and the balance sheet.

Adjustments Columns   The adjustments are similar to those discussed in Chapters 3 and 4. They may be entered in any order desired. The debit amount of each entry should equal the credit amount, and total debits should equal total credits. You should review the adjusting data in Exhibit 5S-5 to reassure yourself that the adjustments are correct.

Income Statement Columns   The income statement columns contain adjusted amounts for the revenues and the expenses. Sales Revenue, for example, is $169,300, which includes the $1,300 adjustment.

You may be wondering why the two inventory amounts appear in the income statement columns. The reason is that both beginning inventory and ending inventory enter the computation of cost of goods sold. *Placement of beginning inventory ($38,600) in the work sheet's income statement debit column has the effect of adding*

KEY POINT

Recall that Purchases (not Inventory) was debited for merchandise purchased. In the periodic system, no entries are made to the Inventory account for purchases or sales. Beginning inventory remains on the books and on the trial balance until ending inventory replaces it at the end of the period.

KEY POINT

If you were preparing a work sheet, you could omit the adjusted trial balance columns. Once you understand the mechanics of the work sheet, you can take a trial balance amount, add or subtract the adjustments, and extend the new amount to either the income statement or balance sheet column.

AUSTIN SOUND CENTRE
Trial Balance
December 31, 2004

Cash	$ 2,850	
Accounts receivable	4,600	
Note receivable, current	8,000	
Interest receivable		
Inventory	**38,600**	
Supplies	650	
Prepaid insurance	1,200	
Furniture and fixtures	33,200	
Accumulated amortization		$ 2,400
Accounts payable		47,000
Unearned sales revenue		2,000
Wages payable		
Interest payable		
Note payable, long-term		12,600
Frank Ernest, capital		25,900
Frank Ernest, withdrawals	54,100	
Sales revenue		168,000
Sales discounts	1,400	
Sales returns and allowances	2,000	
Interest revenue		600
Purchases	**91,400**	
Purchase discounts		**3,000**
Purchase returns and allowances		**1,200**
Freight in	**5,200**	
Wages expense	9,800	
Rent expense	8,400	
Amortization expense		
Insurance expense		
Supplies expense		
Interest expense	1,300	
Total	$262,700	$262,700

Additional data at December 31, 2004:

a. Interest revenue earned but not yet collected, $400.

b. Supplies on hand, $100.

c. Prepaid insurance expired during the year, $1,000.

d. Amortization for the year, $600.

e. Unearned sales revenue earned during the year, $1,300.

f. Accrued wage expense, $400.

g. Accrued interest expense, $200.

h. Inventory on hand based on inventory count, $40,200.

beginning inventory in computing cost of goods sold. Placing ending inventory ($40,200) in the credit column decreases cost of goods sold.

Purchases and Freight In appear in the debit column because they are added in computing cost of goods sold. Purchase Discounts and Purchase Returns and Allowances appear as credits because they are subtracted in computing cost of goods sold—$90,800 on the income statement in Exhibit 5S-6 on page 279.

The income statement column subtotals on the work sheet indicate whether the business earned net income or incurred a net loss. If total credits are greater, the result is net income, as shown in Exhibit 5S-5. If total debits are greater, a net loss has occurred.

AUSTIN SOUND CENTRE
Accounting Work Sheet
For the Year Ended December 31, 2004

Account Title	Trial Balance Debit	Trial Balance Credit	Adjustments Debit	Adjustments Credit	Income Statement Debit	Income Statement Credit	Balance Sheet Debit	Balance Sheet Credit
Cash	2,850						2,850	
Accounts receivable	4,600						4,600	
Note receivable, current	8,000						8,000	
Interest receivable			(a) 400				400	
Inventory	**38,600**				**38,600**	**40,200**	**40,200**	
Supplies	650			(b) 550			100	
Prepaid insurance	1,200			(c) 1,000			200	
Furniture and fixtures	33,200						33,200	
Accumulated amortization		2,400		(d) 600				3,000
Accounts payable		47,000						47,000
Unearned sales revenue		2,000	(e) 1,300					700
Wages payable				(f) 400				400
Interest payable				(g) 200				200
Note payable, long-term		12,600						12,600
Frank Ernest, capital		25,900						25,900
Frank Ernest, withdrawals	54,100						54,100	
Sales revenue		168,000		(e) 1,300		169,300		
Sales discounts	1,400				1,400			
Sales returns and allowances	2,000				2,000			
Interest revenue		600		(a) 400		1,000		
Purchases	**91,400**				91,400			
Purchase discounts		**3,000**				3,000		
Purchase returns and allowances		**1,200**				1,200		
Freight in	**5,200**				5,200			
Wages expense	9,800		(f) 400		10,200			
Rent expense	8,400				8,400			
Amortization expense			(d) 600		600			
Insurance expense			(c) 1,000		1,000			
Supplies expense			(b) 550		550			
Interest expense	1,300		(g) 200		1,500			
	262,700	262,700	4,450	4,450	160,850	214,700	143,650	89,800
Net income					53,850			53,850
					214,700	214,700	143,650	143,650

Balance Sheet Columns The only new item on the balance sheet is inventory. The balance listed is the ending amount of $40,200, which is determined by a physical count of inventory on hand at the end of the period.

OBJECTIVE S5
Prepare a merchandiser's financial statements under the periodic inventory system

Preparing the Financial Statements of a Merchandiser

Exhibit 5S-6 presents Austin Sound's financial statements. The *income statement* through gross margin repeats Exhibit 5S-3. This information is followed by the **operating expenses**, expenses other than cost of goods sold that are incurred in the entity's major line of business—merchandising. Wages expense is Austin Sound's cost of employing workers. Rent is the cost of obtaining store space. Insurance helps to protect the inventory. Store furniture and fixtures wear out; the expense is amortization. Supplies expense is the cost of stationery, mailing, and the like, used in operations.

AUSTIN SOUND CENTRE
Income Statement
For the Year Ended December 31, 2004

Sales revenue			$169,300
Less: Sales discounts		$ 1,400	
Sales returns and allowances		2,000	3,400
Net sales revenue			$165,900
Cost of goods sold:			
Beginning inventory		38,600	
Purchases		91,400	
Less: Purchase discounts	$ 3,000		
Purchase returns and allowances	1,200	4,200	
Net purchases		87,200	
Freight in		5,200	
Cost of goods available for sale		131,000	
Less: Ending inventory		40,200	
Cost of goods sold			90,800
Gross margin			75,100
Operating expenses:			
Wages expense		10,200	
Rent expense		8,400	
Insurance expense		1,000	
Amortization expense		600	
Supplies expense		550	20,750
Income from operations			54,350
Other revenue and (expense):			
Interest revenue		1,000	
Interest expense		(1,500)	(500)
Net income			$ 53,850

AUSTIN SOUND CENTRE
Statement of Owner's Equity
For the Year Ended December 31, 2004

Frank Ernest, capital, January 1, 2004	$25,900
Add: Net income	53,850
	79,750
Less: Withdrawals	54,100
Frank Ernest, capital, December 31, 2004	$25,650

AUSTIN SOUND CENTRE
Balance Sheet
December 31, 2004

Assets

Current assets:		
Cash		$ 2,850
Accounts receivable		4,600
Note receivable		8,000
Interest receivable		400
Inventory		40,200
Prepaid insurance		200
Supplies		100
Total current assets		56,350
Capital assets:		
Furniture and fixtures	$33,200	
Less: Accumulated amortization	3,000	30,200
Total assets		$86,550

Liabilities

Current liabilities:		
Accounts payable		$47,000
Unearned sales revenue		700
Wages payable		400
Interest payable		200
Total current liabilities		48,300
Long-term liability:		
Note payable		12,600
Total liabilities		60,900

Owner's Equity

F. Ernest, capital		25,650
Total liabilities and owner's equity		$86,550

Many companies report their operating expenses in two categories.

- *Selling expenses* are those expenses related to marketing the company's products—sales salaries; sales commissions; advertising; amortization, rent, utilities, and property taxes on store buildings; amortization on store furniture; delivery expense; and so on.
- *General expenses* include office expenses, such as the salaries of office employees; and amortization, rent, utilities, and property taxes on the home office building.

Gross margin minus operating expenses and plus any other operating revenues equals **operating income**, or **income from operations**. Many businesspeople view operating income as the most reliable indicator of a business's success because it measures the entity's major ongoing activities.

The last section of Austin Sound's income statement is **other revenue and expenses**, which is handled the same way in both inventory systems. This category reports revenues and expenses that are outside the company's main line of business.

Journalizing the Adjusting and Closing Entries in the Periodic Inventory System

Exhibit 5S-7 on page 281 presents Austin Sound's adjusting entries. These entries follow the same pattern illustrated in Chapter 4 for a service entry.

The exhibit also gives Austin Sound's closing entries. The first closing entry closes the revenue accounts. Closing entries 2 and 3 are new. Entry 2 closes the beginning balance of the Inventory account ($38,600), along with Purchases and Freight In, into the temporary Cost of Goods Sold account. Entry 3 sets up the ending balance of Inventory ($40,200) with a debit and also closes the Purchases contra accounts to the temporary Cost of Goods Sold account.[1] Now Inventory and the temporary Cost of Goods Sold account have their correct ending balances as shown below.

Inventory			
Jan. 1	Bal. 38,600	Dec. 31	Clo. 38,600
Dec. 31	Clo. 40,200		
Dec. 31	Bal. 40,200		

Cost of Goods Sold (temporary)			
Beg. inv.	38,600	Pur. discts.	3,000
Purchases	91,400	Pur. ret. and	
Freight in	5,200	allowances	1,200
		End. inventory	40,200
Bal.	90,800		

The entries to the Inventory account deserve additional explanation. Recall that before the closing process Inventory still has the period's beginning balance. At the end of the period, this balance is one year old and must be replaced with the ending balance in order to prepare the financial statements at December 31, 2004. The closing entries give Inventory its correct ending balance of $40,200.

---

[1]Some accountants make the inventory entries as adjustments rather than as part of the closing process. The adjusting-entry approach adds these adjustments (shifted out of the closing entries):

Adjusting Entries

Dec. 31	Income Summary	38,600	
	Inventory (beginning balance)		38,600
Dec. 31	Inventory (ending balance)..............................	40,200	
	Income Summary		40,200

When these entries are posted, the Inventory account will look exactly as shown above, except that the journal references will be "Adj." instead of "Clo." The financial statements are unaffected by the approach used for these inventory entries.

Journal

Adjusting Entries

a. Dec. 31	Interest receivable		400	
	Interest revenue			400
b. Dec. 31	Supplies expense ($650 – $100)		550	
	Supplies			550
c. Dec. 31	Insurance expense		1,000	
	Prepaid insurance			1,000
d. Dec. 31	Amortization expense		600	
	Accumulated amortization			600
e. Dec. 31	Unearned sales revenue		1,300	
	Sales revenue			1,300
f. Dec. 31	Wages expense		400	
	Wages payable			400
g. Dec. 31	Interest expense		200	
	Interest payable			200

Closing Entries

1. Dec. 31	Sales revenue		169,300	
	Interest revenue		1,000	
	Income summary			170,300
2. Dec. 31	Cost of goods sold		135,200	
	Inventory (beginning balance)			38,600
	Purchases			91,400
	Freight in			5,200
3. Dec. 31	Inventory (ending balance)		40,200	
	Purchase discounts		3,000	
	Purchase returns and allowances		1,200	
	Cost of goods sold			44,400
4. Dec. 31	Income summary		116,450	
	Sales discounts			1,400
	Sales returns and allowances			2,000
	Cost of goods sold ($135,200 – $44,400)			90,800
	Wages expense			10,200
	Rent expense			8,400
	Amortization expense			600
	Insurance expense			1,000
	Supplies expense			550
	Interest expense			1,500
5. Dec. 31	Income summary ($170,300 – $116,450)		53,850	
	Frank Ernest, capital			53,850
6. Dec. 31	Frank Ernest, capital		54,100	
	Frank Ernest, withdrawals			54,100

Closing entry 4 then closes the Sales contra accounts and the temporary Cost of Goods Sold account along with the other expense accounts into Income Summary. Closing entries 5 and 6 complete the closing process. All data for the closing entries are taken from the income statement columns of the work sheet. (Note that some companies close the accounts in closing entries 2 and 3 into the Income Summary account, instead of the temporary Cost of Goods Sold account. This has the same result overall. However, as mentioned above, Inventory and Cost of Goods Sold have their correct account balances before being closed to the Income summary account if they are closed to the temporary Cost of Goods Sold account first.)

Study Exhibits 5S-5, 5S-6, and 5S-7 carefully because they illustrate the entire end-of-period process that leads to the financial statements. As you progress through this book, you may want to refer to these exhibits to refresh your understanding of the adjusting and closing process for a merchandising business.

Net sales, cost of goods sold, operating income, and net income are unaffected by the choice of inventory system. You can prove this by comparing Austin Sound's financial statements given in Exhibit 5S-6 with the corresponding statements in Exhibit 5-7 on page 235. The only differences appear in the cost-of-goods-sold section of the income statement, and those differences are unimportant. In fact, virtually all companies report cost of goods sold in streamlined fashion, as shown for The Forzani Group Ltd. in Exhibit 5-1 and for Austin Sound in Exhibit 5-7.

Learning Tip   Here is an easy way to remember the closing process. First look at the work sheet. Then:

1. Debit all income statement accounts with a credit balance. Credit Income Summary for the sum of all these debits.
2. Credit all income statement accounts with a debit balance. Debit Income Summary for the sum of all these credits.
3. Credit the inventory account for the amount of opening inventory and debit inventory for the amount of ending inventory obtained from the year-end physical count.
4. Take the balance in the Income Summary account. If the account has a debit balance, there is a net loss; credit Income Summary for that amount, and debit Capital. If Income Summary has a credit balance, there is a net income for the period; debit Income Summary for that amount, and credit Capital.
5. Look at the debit balance of Withdrawals in the balance-sheet column. Credit Withdrawals for its balance, and debit Capital for the same amount.

Summary Problem
for Your Review

The following trial balance pertains to Jan King Distributing Company.

JAN KING DISTRIBUTING COMPANY
Trial Balance
December 31, 2003

Cash	$ 5,670	
Accounts receivable	37,100	
Inventory	60,500	
Supplies	3,930	
Prepaid rent	6,000	
Furniture and fixtures	26,500	
Accumulated amortization		$ 21,200
Accounts payable		46,340
Salary payable		
Interest payable		
Unearned sales revenue		3,500
Note payable, long-term		35,000
Jan King, capital		23,680
Jan King, withdrawals	48,000	
Sales revenue		346,700
Sales discounts	10,300	
Sales returns and allowances	8,200	
Purchases	175,900	
Purchase discounts		6,000
Purchase returns and allowances		7,430
Freight in	9,300	
Salary expense	82,750	
Rent expense	7,000	
Amortization expense		
Utilities expense	5,800	
Supplies expense		
Interest expense	2,900	
Total	$489,850	$489,850

Additional data at December 31, 2003:

a. Supplies used during the year, $2,580.

b. Prepaid rent remaining in force, $1,000.

c. Unearned sales revenue still not earned, $2,400. The company expects to earn this amount during the next few months.

d. Amortization. The furniture and fixtures' estimated useful life is ten years, and they are expected to have no value when they are retired from service.

e. Accrued salaries, $1,300.

f. Accrued interest expense, $600.

g. Inventory on hand based on an inventory count, $65,800.

Required

1. Enter the trial balance on a work sheet and complete the work sheet.

2. Journalize the adjusting and closing entries at December 31, 2003. Post to the Income Summary account as an accuracy check on the entries affecting that account. The credit balance closed out of Income Summary should equal net income computed on the work sheet.

3. Prepare the company's multi-step income statement, statement of owner's equity, and balance sheet in account format. Draw arrows connecting the statements, or state how the statements are linked.

4. Compute the inventory turnover for 2003. Turnover for 2002 was 2.1 times. Would you expect Jan King Distributing Company to be more or less profitable in 2003 than in 2002? Give your reason.

Solution to Review Problem

Requirement 1

JAN KING DISTRIBUTING COMPANY
Work Sheet
For the Year Ended December 31, 2003

Account Title	Trial Balance Debit	Trial Balance Credit	Adjustments Debit	Adjustments Credit	Income Statement Debit	Income Statement Credit	Balance Sheet Debit	Balance Sheet Credit
Cash	5,670						5,670	
Accounts receivable	37,100						37,100	
Inventory	60,500				60,500	65,800	65,800	
Supplies	3,930			(a) 2,580			1,350	
Prepaid rent	6,000			(b) 5,000			1,000	
Furniture and fixtures	26,500						26,500	
Accumulated amortization		21,200		(d) 2,650				23,850
Accounts payable		46,340						46,340
Salary payable				(e) 1,300				1,300
Interest payable				(f) 600				600
Unearned sales revenue		3,500	(c) 1,100					2,400
Note payable, long-term		35,000						35,000
Jan King, capital		23,680						23,680
Jan King, withdrawals	48,000						48,000	
Sales revenue		346,700		(c) 1,100		347,800		
Sales discounts	10,300				10,300			
Sales returns and allowances	8,200				8,200			
Purchases	175,900				175,900			
Purchase discounts		6,000				6,000		
Purchase returns and allowances		7,430				7,430		
Freight in	9,300				9,300			
Salary expense	82,750		(e) 1,300		84,050			
Rent expense	7,000		(b) 5,000		12,000			
Amortization expense			(d) 2,650		2,650			
Utilities expense	5,800				5,800			
Supplies expense			(a) 2,580		2,580			
Interest expense	2,900		(f) 600		3,500			
	489,850	489,850	13,230	13,230	374,780	427,030	185,420	133,170
Net income					52,250			52,250
					427,030	427,030	185,420	185,420

Requirement 2

Adjusting Entries

2003

Dec. 31	Supplies expense..	2,580	
	Supplies..		2,580
Dec. 31	Rent expense...	5,000	
	Prepaid rent		5,000
Dec. 31	Unearned sales revenue ($3,500 – $2,400)	1,100	
	Sales revenue..		1,100
Dec. 31	Amortization expense ($26,500/10)..................	2,650	
	Accumulated amortization		2,650
Dec. 31	Salary expense...	1,300	
	Salary payable		1,300
Dec. 31	Interest expense	600	
	Interest payable..		600

Closing Entries

2003

Dec. 31	Sales revenue	347,800	
	Income summary...		347,800
Dec. 31	Cost of goods sold	245,700	
	Inventory (beginning balance)		60,500
	Purchases		175,900
	Freight in..		9,300
Dec. 31	Inventory (ending balance)	65,800	
	Purchase discounts	6,000	
	Purchase returns and allowances....................	7,430	
	Cost of goods sold		79,230
Dec. 31	Income summary	295,550	
	Sales discounts..		10,300
	Sales returns and allowances......................		8,200
	Cost of goods sold		
	($245,700 – $79,230)		166,470
	Salary expense...		84,050
	Rent expense		12,000
	Amortization expense..................................		2,650
	Utilities expense...		5,800
	Supplies expense		2,580
	Interest expense		3,500
Dec. 31	Income summary ($347,800 – $295,550)	52,250	
	Jan King, capital..		52,250
Dec. 31	Jan King, capital	48,000	
	Jan King, withdrawals		48,000

Income Summary

Clo.	295,550	Clo.	347,800
Clo.	52,250	Bal.	52,250

Requirement 3

JAN KING DISTRIBUTING COMPANY
Income Statement
For the Year Ended December 31, 2003

Sales revenue...			$347,800
Less: Sales discounts...		$ 10,300	
Sales returns and allowances..................		8,200	18,500
Net sales revenue			$329,300
Cost of goods sold:			
Beginning inventory			60,500
Purchases...		175,900	
Less: Purchase discounts.............................	$6,000		
Purchase returns and allowances...........	7,430	13,430	
Net purchases			162,470
Freight in			9,300
Cost of goods available for sale			232,270
Less: Ending inventory.................................			65,800
Cost of goods sold........................			166,470
Gross margin...........................			162,830
Operating expenses:			
Salary expense		84,050	
Rent expense		12,000	
Utilities expense		5,800	
Amortization expense		2,650	
Supplies expense.......................................		2,580	107,080
Income from operations			55,750
Other expense:			
Interest expense..................................			3,500
Net income			$ 52,250

JAN KING DISTRIBUTING COMPANY
Statement of Owner's Equity
For the Year Ended December 31, 2003

Jan King, capital, January 1, 2003	$23,680
Add: Net income..	52,250
	75,930
Less: Withdrawals	48,000
Jan King, capital, December 31, 2003	$27,930

JAN KING DISTRIBUTING COMPANY
Balance Sheet
December 31, 2003

Assets			**Liabilities**		
Current assets:			Current liabilities:		
Cash..............................		$ 5,670	Accounts payable..................		$ 46,340
Accounts receivable.....		37,100	Salary payable		1,300
Inventory......................		65,800	Interest payable......................		600
Supplies.........................		1,350	Unearned sales revenue........		2,400
Prepaid rent		1,000	Total current liabilities.......		50,640
Total current assets....		110,920	Long-term note payable.............		35,000
Capital assets:			Total liabilities................		85,640
Furniture and					
fixtures.....................	$26,500		**Owner's Equity**		
Less: Accumulated			Jan King, capital		27,930
amortization	23,850	2,650			
			Total liabilities and		
Total assets.........................		$113,570	owner's equity		$113,570

$$\text{Inventory turnover} = \frac{\text{Cost of goods sold}}{\text{Average inventory}} = \frac{\$166,470}{(\$60,500 + \$65,800)/2} = 2.6 \text{ times per year}$$

The increase in the rate of inventory turnover from 2.1 to 2.6 times suggests higher profits in 2003 than in 2002.

Supplement Exercises

Exercise 5S-1 *Journalizing purchase and sale transactions under the periodic inventory system (Obj. S2)*

Journalize, without explanations, the following transactions of Pinetree Fashions during the month of June 2004:

June 3   Purchased $1,400 of inventory under terms of 2/10 n/eom (end of month) and FOB shipping point.
7   Returned $600 of defective merchandise purchased on June 3.
9   Paid freight bill of $110 on June 3 purchase.
10   Sold inventory for $4,400, collecting cash of $800. Payment terms on the remainder were 2/15 n/30.
12   Paid amount owed on credit purchase of June 3, less the discount and the return.
16   Granted a sales allowance of $1,600 on the June 10 sale.
23   Received cash from June 10 customer in full settlement of her debt, less the allowance and the discount.

Exercise 5-S2 *Journalizing transactions from a purchase invoice under the periodic inventory system (Obj. S2)*

As the proprietor of Kendrick Tire, you receive the invoice on page 288 from a supplier (GST has been disregarded):

Required

1. Record the May 14 purchase on account.

2. The R39 truck tires were ordered by mistake and therefore were returned to ABC. Journalize the return on May 19.

3. Record the May 22 payment of the amount owed.

Exercise 5S-3 *Journalizing purchase transactions under the periodic inventory system (Obj. S2)*

On April 30, Mavis Jewellers purchased inventory of $7,500 on account from La Roche Fine Gems Ltd., a jewellery importer. Terms were 3/15 net 45. On receiving the goods Mavis checked the order and found $1,200 of unsuitable merchandise. Therefore, Mavis returned $1,200 of merchandise to La Roche on May 4.

To pay the remaining amount owed, Mavis had to borrow from the bank. On May 14 Mavis signed a short-term note payable to the bank and immediately paid the borrowed funds to La Roche. On June 14, Mavis paid the bank the net amount of the invoice, which Mavis had borrowed, plus 1% interest monthly (round to the nearest dollar).

```
                    ABC TIRE WHOLESALE DISTRIBUTORS
                            2600 Victoria Avenue
                          Regina, Saskatchewan S4P 1B3

    Invoice date: May 14, 2003              Payment terms: 2/10 n/30

    Sold to: Kendrick Tire
             4219 Cumberland Avenue
             Saskatoon, SK S7M 1X3


    Quantity                        Quantity
    Ordered         Description      Shipped      Price        Amount

       6      P135-X4 Radials.........    6       $55.71       $334.26
       8      L912 Belted-bias........    8        61.98        495.84
      14      R39 Truck tires.........   10        75.03        750.30

                                                              _____
              Total..........................................$1,580.40


    Due date:                              Amount:
      May 24, 2003                           $1,548.79
      May 25 through June 13, 2003           $1,580.40

    Paid:
```

Required

Record the required transactions in the journal of Mavis Jewellers. Explanations are not required.

Exercise 5S-4   *Journalizing sale transactions under the periodic inventory system* **(Obj. S2)**

Refer to the business situation in Exercise 5S-3. Journalize the transactions of La Roche Fine Gems Ltd. Explanations are not required.

Note: Exercise 5-14 (page 255), 5-15 (page 255), and 5-16 (page 255) also pertain to the periodic inventory system.

Supplement Problems

Problem 5S-1   *Accounting for the purchase and sale of inventory under the periodic system*   **(Obj. S2)**

The following transactions occurred between Merck Frosst Canada Inc. and Drug Trading Co. during February of the current year.

Feb. 6   Merck Frosst sold $12,600 worth of merchandise to Drug Trading on terms of 2/10 n/30, FOB shipping point. Merck Frosst prepaid freight charges of $500 and included this amount in the invoice total. (Merck Frosst's entry to record the freight payment debits Accounts Receivable and credits Cash.)

    10   Drug Trading returned $1,800 of the merchandise purchased on February 6. Merck Frosst issued a credit memo for this amount.

    15   Drug Trading paid $6,000 of the invoice amount owed to Merck Frosst for the February 6 purchase. This payment included none of the freight charge.

    27   Drug Trading paid the remaining amount owed to Merck Frosst for the February 6 purchase.

Required

Journalize these transactions, first on the books of Drug Trading Co. and second on the books of Merck Frosst Canada Inc.

Problem 5S-2 *Journalizing purchase and sale transactions under the periodic inventory system (Obj. S2)*

Salimi Distributing Company engaged in the following transactions during May of the current year:

May	3	Purchased office supplies for cash, $900.
	7	Purchased inventory on credit terms of 3/10 net eom, $6,000.
	8	Returned half the inventory purchased on May 7. It was not the inventory ordered.
	10	Sold goods for cash, $1,350.
	13	Sold inventory on credit terms of 2/15 n/45 for $11,700, less $1,800 quantity discount offered to customers who purchased in large quantities.
	16	Paid the amount owed on account from the purchase of May 7, less the discount and the return.
	17	Received wrong-sized inventory returned from May 13 sale, $2,700, which is the net amount after the quantity discount.
	18	Purchased inventory of $12,000 on account. Payment terms were 2/10 net 30.
	26	Borrowed $11,760 from the bank to take advantage of the discount offered on the May 18 purchase. Signed a note payable to the bank for this amount.
	26	Paid supplier for goods purchased on May 18, less the discount.
	28	Received cash in full settlement of the account from the customer who purchased inventory on May 13, less the discount and the return.
	29	Purchased inventory for cash, $6,000, less a quantity discount of $1,200, plus freight charges of $480.

Required

1. Journalize the preceding transactions on the books of Salimi Distributing Company.

2. The note payable signed on May 26 requires Salimi to pay $90 interest expense. Was the decision to borrow funds to take advantage of the cash discount wise or unwise? Support your answer by comparing the discount to the interest paid.

Problem 5S-3 *Journalizing purchase and sale transactions under the periodic inventory system (Obj. S2)*

Segal Furniture Company engaged in the following transactions during July of the current year:

July	2	Purchased inventory for cash, $1,200, less a quantity discount of $225.
	5	Purchased store supplies on credit terms of net eom, $675.
	8	Purchased inventory of $4,500, less a quantity discount of 10%, plus freight charges of $230. Credit terms are 3/15 n/30.
	9	Sold goods for cash, $1,800.
	11	Returned $300 (net amount after the quantity discount) of the inventory purchased on July 8. It was damaged in shipment.
	12	Purchased inventory on credit terms of 3/10 n/30, $5,000.
	14	Sold inventory on credit terms of 2/10 n/30, for $14,400, less a $900 quantity discount.
	16	Paid the electricity bill, $400.
	20	Received returned inventory from the July 14 sale, $600 (net amount after the quantity discount). Segal shipped the wrong goods by mistake.
	21	Borrowed the amount owed on the July 8 purchase. Signed a note payable to the bank for $3,867.50, which takes into account the return of inventory on July 11.
	21	Paid supplier for goods purchased on July 8 less the discount and the return.

July   23   Received $10,290 cash in partial settlement of the account from the customer who purchased inventory on July 14. Granted the customer a 2% discount and credited his account receivable for $10,500.
        30   Paid for the store supplies purchased on July 5.

Required

1. Journalize the preceding transactions on the books of Segal Furniture Company.

2. Compute the amount of the receivable at July 31 from the customer to whom Segal sold inventory on July 14. What amount of cash discount applies to this receivable at July 31?

Problem 5S-4   *Preparing a merchandiser's accounting work sheet, financial statements, and adjusting and closing entries under the periodic system*   **(Obj. S3, S4, S5)**

The year-end trial balance of Bliss Sales Company on the following page pertains to March 31, 2004.

Additional data at March 31, 2004:

a. Accrued interest revenue, $1,030.
b. Insurance expense for the year, $3,000.
c. Furniture has an estimated useful life of six years. It is expected to have no value when it is retired from service.
d. Unearned sales revenue still not earned, $8,200.
e. Accrued salaries, $1,200.
f. Accrued sales commissions, $1,700.
g. Inventory on hand based on inventory count, $133,200.

Required

1. Enter the trial balance on an accounting work sheet, and complete the work sheet for the year ended March 31, 2004.

2. Prepare the company's multi-step income statement and statement of owner's equity for the year ended March 31, 2004. Also prepare its balance sheet at that date. Long-term notes receivable should be reported on the balance sheet between current assets and capital assets in a separate section labelled Investments.

3. Journalize the adjusting and closing entries at March 31, 2004.

4. Post to the W. Bliss, Capital account and to the Income Summary account as an accuracy check on the adjusting and closing process.

BLISS SALES COMPANY
Trial Balance
March 31, 2004

Cash..	$ 7,880	
Notes receivable, current	12,400	
Interest receivable		
Inventory..	130,050	
Prepaid insurance	3,600	
Notes receivable, long-term...........................	62,000	
Furniture..	6,000	
Accumulated amortization.............................		$ 4,000
Accounts payable...		12,220
Sales commission payable		
Salary payable		
Unearned sales revenue		9,610
W. Bliss, capital...		172,780
W. Bliss, withdrawals	66,040	
Sales revenue		440,000
Sales discounts	4,800	
Sales returns and allowances	11,300	
Interest revenue...		8,600
Purchases..	233,000	
Purchase discounts		3,100
Purchase returns and allowances		7,600
Freight in	10,000	
Sales commission expense..............................	78,300	
Salary expense...	24,700	
Rent expense...	6,000	
Utilities expense	1,840	
Amortization expense		
Insurance expense..		
Total...	$657,910	$657,910

Note: Problems 5-9A (p. 261) and 5-9B (p. 267) also pertain to the periodic inventory system.

6

Accounting Information Systems

CHAPTER OBJECTIVES

After studying this chapter, you should be able to

1 Describe the features of an effective accounting information system

2 Understand how computerized and manual accounting systems work

3 Understand how spreadsheets are used in accounting

4 Use the sales journal, the cash receipts journal, and the accounts receivable subsidiary ledger

5 Use the purchases journal, the cash payments journal, and the accounts payable subsidiary ledger

With the introduction over the past decade of accounting software applications that are relatively simple to use, you would think accountants would be worried about the future. Why hire an accountant when the software does the accounting? Programs such as ACCPAC®, Peachtree®, MYOB®, and QuickBooks® have made the cost of recording and generating accounting information more affordable for large and small businesses. However, instead of reducing the need for accountants, these programs have changed the role of the accountant from a processor of data to an advisor.

Ken Gelhorn is a chartered accountant in Vancouver. Ken acts as a software consultant for businesses. Specifically, he advises companies about the type of accounting information systems they require for their business. He helps companies implement the hardware and software required and provides training for users. Once a successful implementation has been achieved, Ken then offers advice to a company's management, primarily in the areas of financial statement analysis and taxation.

EVERY organization needs an accounting system. An **accounting information system** is the combination of personnel, records, and procedures that a business uses to meet its needs for financial data. We have already been using an accounting information system in this text. It consists of two basic components:

- A general journal
- A general ledger

Every accounting system has these components, but this simple system can efficiently handle only a few transactions per accounting period. Businesses cope with heavy transaction loads in two ways: computerization and specialization. We *computerize* to do the accounting faster and more reliably. *Specialization* comes when we group similar transactions to speed the process. We explore special journals in the second half of this chapter.

Effective Accounting Information Systems

OBJECTIVE 1
Describe the features of an effective accounting information system

Good personnel are critical to the success of any operation. Employees must be both competent and honest. And several design features make accounting systems run efficiently. A good system—whether computerized or manual—includes four features: control, compatibility, flexibility, and a favourable cost/benefit relationship.

Features

Control Managers need *control* over operations. *Internal controls* are the methods and procedures used to authorize transactions, to ensure adherence to management policy, to safeguard assets and records, to prevent and detect error and fraud, and to ensure that information produced is accurate and timely.

For example, in companies such as Intrawest, McCain Foods, and Kinko's, managers control cash disbursements to avoid theft through unauthorized payments. VISA, MasterCard, Diners Club/en Route, and other credit-card companies keep accurate records of their accounts receivable to ensure that customers are billed and collections are received on time.

McCain Foods
www.mccain. com

Kinko's
www.kinkos. com

Compatibility   A *compatible* system is one that works smoothly with the business's operations, personnel, and organizational structure. An example is The Bank of Nova Scotia, which is organized as a network of branch offices. The bank's top managers want to know how much revenue was generated in each region where the bank does business. They also want to analyze the bank's loans in different geographic regions. If revenues and loans in Alberta or Nova Scotia are lagging, the managers can concentrate their collection efforts in that region. They may relocate some branch offices, open new branches, or hire new personnel to increase their revenues and net income. A compatible accounting *information* system conforms to the particular needs of the business.

Flexibility   Organizations evolve. They develop new products, sell off unprofitable operations and acquire new ones, and adjust employee pay scales. Changes in the business often call for changes in the accounting system. A well-designed system is *flexible* if it accommodates changes without needing a complete overhaul. Consider Bombardier's acquisition of Canadair, the aircraft manufacturer. Bombardier's accounting system had the flexibility to fold Canadair's financial statements into those of Bombardier, the parent company.

Favourable Cost/Benefit Relationship   Achieving control, compatibility, and flexibility costs money. Managers strive for a system that offers maximum benefits at a minimum cost—that is, a favourable *cost/benefit relationship*. Most small companies, such as Westmount Drugs, an independent pharmacy near Montreal, use off-the-shelf computerized accounting packages. Such packages include ACCPAC®, Simply Accounting®, MYOB®, and Peachtree®. The very smallest businesses might not computerize at all. But large companies, such as the brokerage firm Scotia McLeod, have specialized needs for information. For them, customized programming is a must because the benefits—in terms of information tailored to the company's needs—far outweigh the cost of the system. The result? Better decisions.

Components of a Computerized Accounting System

Three components form the heart of a computerized accounting system: hardware, software, and company personnel. Each component is critical to the system's success.

   Hardware is the electronic equipment that includes computers, disk drives, monitors, printers, and the network that connects them. Most modern accounting systems require a **network** (often a local area network, or LAN), the system of electronic linkages that allows different computers to share the same information. In a networked system many computers can be connected to the main computer, or **server**, which stores programs and data. With the right communications hardware and software, a Deloitte & Touche auditor in Vancouver can access the data of a client located in Sydney, Australia. The result is a speedier audit for the client, often at lower cost than if the auditor had to perform all the work on site in Sydney.

   Software is the set of programs that cause the computer to perform the work desired. Accounting software accepts, edits (alters), and stores transaction data and generates the reports managers use to run the business. Many accounting software packages operate independently from the other computing activities of the system. Most accounting packages have been created so that a business can purchase only the programs it needs for its particular stage of growth. Other packages can be added later. For example, a company that is only partly computerized may use software programs to account for employee payrolls, and sales and accounts receivable. The other parts of the accounting system may not be fully computerized.

   For large enterprises, such as TransCanada PipeLines and McCain Foods, the accounting software is integrated within the overall company **database**, or computerized storehouse of information. Many business databases, or *management information systems*, include both accounting and nonaccounting data. For example, CN Railroad, in negotiating a union contract, often needs to examine the relationship between the employment history and salary levels of company employees. CN's data-

ACCPAC International
www.accpac.com

Peachtree Software
www.peachtree.com

MYOB
www.myob.com

Simply Accounting
www.accpac.com

....
(THINKING IT OVER)

How might a business, such as The Bay, save money with a computerized information system?

A: Personnel time saved from collecting sales data manually and stocking excess inventories; revenue saved from avoiding deep discounts on slow-moving goods; costs saved by avoiding errors.

TransCanada
www.transcanada.com

base provides the data that managers need to negotiate effectively with their labour unions. During negotiations, both parties carry laptop computers so that they can access the database and analyze the effects of decisions on the spot.

Personnel who operate the system must be properly trained. Properly trained staff are critical to the success of any accounting information system. Modern accounting systems give nonaccounting personnel access to parts (but not all) of the system. For example, an Old Dutch Food Co. Ltd. marketing manager (a nonaccountant) may use a microcomputer and regional sales data (accounting information) to identify the territory that needs a promotional campaign. Management of a computerized accounting system requires careful consideration of data security and screening of the people in the organization who will have access to the data. Security is usually achieved with *passwords*, codes that restrict access to computerized records.

How Computerized and Manual Accounting Systems Work

Computerized accounting systems have replaced manual systems in many organizations—even small businesses such as Westmount Drugs. As we discuss the stages of data processing, observe the differences between a computerized system and a manual system. The relationship among the three stages of data processing (inputs, processing, outputs) is shown in Exhibit 6-1.

Inputs represents data from source documents, such as sales receipts and bank deposit slips, and electronically generated data from fax orders and other telecommunications. Inputs are usually grouped by type. For example, a firm would enter cash sale transactions separately from credit sales and purchase transactions.

In a manual system, *processing* includes journalizing transactions, posting to the accounts, and preparing the financial statements. A computerized system also processes, but without the intermediate steps (journal, ledger, and trial balance).

Outputs are the reports used for decision making, including the financial statements (income statement, balance sheet, and so on). Business owners are making better decisions—and prospering—because of the reports produced by the company's accounting system. In a computerized accounting system, a trial balance is a report (an output). But a manual system would treat the trial balance as a *processing* step leading to the preparation of financial statements. Exhibit 6-2 is an overview of a computerized accounting system.

Designing an Accounting System: The Chart of Accounts

Design of the accounting system begins with the chart of accounts. Recall from Chapter 2, page 70, that the chart of accounts lists all accounts and their account numbers in the general ledger. In the accounting system of a company such as Southam Inc., the account numbers take on added importance. It is efficient to

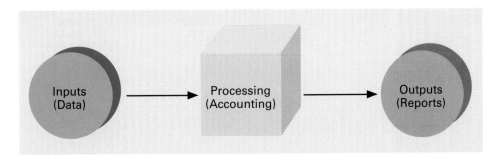

EXHIBIT 6-1

The Three Stages of Data Processing

EXHIBIT 6-2

Overview of a Computerized Accounting System

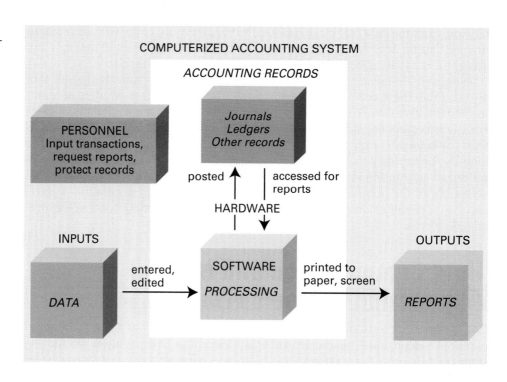

COMPUTERIZED ACCOUNTING SYSTEM

Businesses use account numbers to input transactions. The account numbers can be chosen to provide additional data. For example, account numbers for the housewares department might end with the digit 2. Thus, a departmental income statement could easily be prepared for the housewares department by selecting all revenue and expense accounts that end in "2".

represent a complex account title, such as Accumulated Amortization—Photographic Equipment, with a concise account number (for example, 16570).

Recall the asset accounts generally begin with the digit 1, liabilities with the digit 2, owner's equity accounts with the digit 3, revenues with 4, and expenses with 5. Exhibit 6-3 diagrams one structure for computerized accounts. Assets are divided into current assets, capital assets (property, plant, and equipment), and other assets. Among the current assets we illustrate only three general ledger accounts: Cash in Bank (Account No. 111), Accounts Receivable (No. 112), and Prepaid

EXHIBIT 6-3

Structure for Computerized Accounts

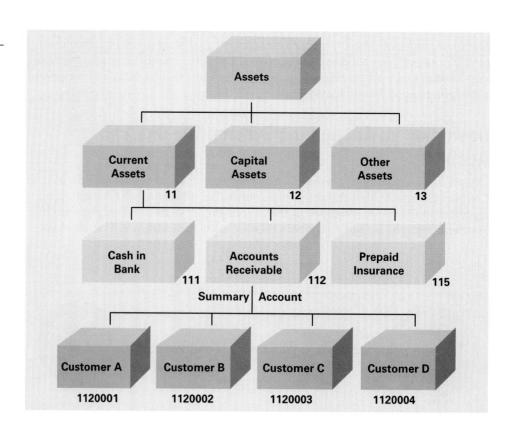

Insurance (No. 115). Accounts Receivable holds the *total* dollar amount receivable from all customers.

The account numbers in Exhibit 6-3 get more detailed as you move from top to bottom. For example, Customer A's account number is 1120001, in which 112 represents Accounts Receivable and 0001 refers to Customer A.

The importance of a well-structured chart of accounts cannot be over-emphasized. This is because the reporting component of a computerized accounting system relies on *account number ranges* to translate accounts and their balances into properly organized financial statements and other reports. For example, the accounts numbered 101–399 (assets, liabilities, and owner's equity) are sorted to the balance sheet, and the accounts numbered 401–599 (revenues and expenses) go to the income statement.

Processing Transactions: Manual Menu-Driven Accounting Systems

Recording transactions in an actual accounting system requires an additional step that we have skipped thus far. A business of any size *classifies* transactions by type for efficient handling. In a manual system, credit sales, purchases on account, cash receipts, and cash payments are treated as four separate categories, with each type entered into its own special journal. (We discuss these journals in detail later in this chapter.) For example:

- Credit sales of merchandise are recorded in a special journal called a *sales journal*.
- Cash receipts are entered into a *cash receipts journal*.
- Credit purchases of inventory and other assets are recorded in a *purchases journal*.
- Cash payments are entered in a *cash payments journal*.
- Payroll payments are recorded in the *payroll journal*.
- Transactions that do not fit any of the special journals, such as the adjusting and closing entries at the end of the period, are recorded in the *general journal*, which serves as the "journal of last resort."

> **KEY POINT**
>
> The general journal will have the fewest entries. Most transactions fall into one of these four categories: credit sales, cash receipts, credit purchases, or cash payments.

Computerized systems are organized by function, or task. Access to functions is arranged in terms of menus. A **menu** is a list of options for choosing computer functions. In such a *menu-driven* system, you first access the most general group of functions, called the *main menu*. You then choose from one or more submenus until you finally reach the function you want.

Exhibit 6-4 illustrates one type of menu structure. The row at the top of the exhibit shows the main menu. The computer operator (or accountant) had chosen the General option (short for General Ledger), as shown by the highlighting. This action opened a submenu of four items—Transactions, Posting, Account Maintenance, and Closing. The Transactions option was then chosen (highlighted).

Posting in a computerized system can be performed continuously as transac-

EXHIBIT 6-4

**Main Menu of a
Computerized Accounting
System**

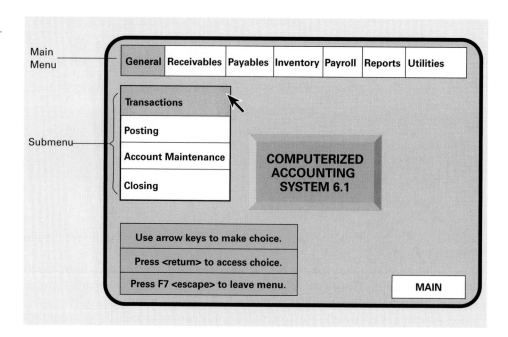

tions are being recorded (**on-line** or **real-time processing**) or later for a group of similar transactions (**batch processing**). In either case, posting is automatic. Batch processing of accounting data allows accountants to check the entries for accuracy before posting them. In effect, the transaction data are "parked" or stored in the computer to await posting, which simply updates the account balances. Outputs—accounting reports—are the final stage of data processing. In a computerized system, the financial statements can be printed automatically. For example, the Reports option in the main menu gives the operator various report choices, which are expanded in the Reports submenu of Exhibit 6-5. In the exhibit, the operator is working with the financial statements, specifically the balance sheet, as shown by the highlighting.

Exhibit 6-6 summarizes the accounting cycle in a computerized system and in a manual system. As you study the exhibit, compare and contrast the two types of systems.

EXHIBIT 6-5

**Reports Submenu of a
Computerized Accounting
System**

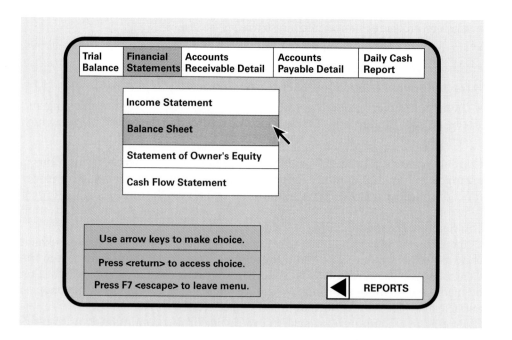

Computerized System	Manual System
1. Start with the account balances in the ledger at the beginning of the period.	1. Same.
2. Analyze and classify business transactions by type. Access appropriate menus for data entry.	2. Analyze and journalize transactions as they occur.
3. Computer automatically posts transactions as a batch or when entered on-line.	3. Post journal entries to the ledger accounts.
4. The unadjusted balances are available immediately after each posting.	4. Compute the unadjusted balance in each account at the end of the period.
5. The trial balance, if needed, can be accessed as a report.	5. Enter the trial balance on the work sheet, and complete the work sheet (optional).
6. Enter and post adjusting entries. Print the financial statements. Run automatic closing procedures after backing up the period's accounting records.	6. Prepare the financial statements. Journalize and post the adjusting entries. Journalize and post the closing entries.
7. The next period's opening balances are created automatically as a result of closing.	7. Prepare the postclosing trial balance. This trial balance becomes step 1 for the next period.

Comparison of the Accounting Cycle in a Computerized and a Manual System

---

KEY POINT

You may think a computer skips steps when data are entered because the computer performs some of the steps internally. However, a computerized system performs all the steps a manual system does, except for the work sheet. Even if you never keep a manual set of books, you still need to understand the entire accounting system.

Accounting and the *e*-World

Accounting Pioneers on the Virtual Frontier

As you saw in the chapter-opening story, computer and Internet technology are remaking the bookkeeping and tax aspects of accounting. Now there are "virtual" or "online" accountants who serve clients via the Internet. Companies with slogans like "Real Accounting in a Virtual World" and "Outsourced Accounting Services for a Wired World" are advertising services like basic bookkeeping, full-service outsourcing, real-time accounting, and 24-hour access to accounting data.

The Accounting Department (TAD), a business founded by Lance and Deanna Gildea in San Diego, is one such service currently operating in the United States. TAD has clients scan their invoices, bank statements, and other documents into the computer; TAD even provides the scanner free-of-charge to some clients. The scanned documents are then transmitted to TAD, and within minutes, TAD updates the client's accounts. Clients then use a Web browser to sign in to their home page (prepared by TAD), where clients can view, print, and download reports, cheques, and other information. Soon clients will be able to get real-time access to their accounting data through a new Web-based service.

For clients—typically small- to mid-sized businesses—the key benefits of hiring TAD to do their accounting are price, reliability, and access. In some cases, TAD's monthly fees are half of what it would cost to hire a bookkeeper—and TAD never calls in sick or takes vacations. In Canada, companies in remote areas can gain access to accounting expertise that might be unavailable to them otherwise. A big plus for the "virtual accountants" is being able to live wherever they please, regardless of where clients are located.

Adapted from Antoinette Alexander, "Pioneers on the Virtual Frontier," *Accounting Technology*, Jan/Feb 2000, pp. 18–24.

Chapter Six Accounting Information Systems   **299**

OBJECTIVE 3
Understand how spreadsheets
are used in accounting

Integrated Accounting Software:
Spreadsheets

Computerized accounting packages are organized by **modules**, separate but integrated units that are compatible and that function together. Changes affecting one module will affect others. For example, entering and posting a credit-sales transaction will update two modules: Accounts Receivable/Sales and Inventory/Cost of Goods Sold. Accounting packages, such as ACCPAC Plus Accounting, Business Works™, Peachtree™, DacEasy™, One-Write Plus™, and RealWorld® Accounting, come as a complete set of accounting modules to form an integrated system.

You may have been preparing homework assignments manually. Imagine preparing a work sheet for Bombardier. Each adjustment changes the company's financial statement totals. Consider computing Bombardier's revenue amounts by hand. The task would be overwhelming. For even a small business with only a few departments, the computations are tedious, time-consuming, and therefore expensive. Also, errors are more likely.

Spreadsheets are computer programs that link data by means of formulas and functions. These electronic work sheets were invented to update budgets. Spreadsheets are organized as a rectangular grid composed of grid points called *cells*, each defined by a column number and a row number. A cell can contain words (called labels), numbers, or formulas (relationships among cells). The *cursor*, or electronic highlighter, indicates which cell is active, and it can be moved around the spreadsheet. When the cursor is placed over any cell, information can be entered there for processing.

Exhibit 6-7 shows a simple income statement on a spreadsheet screen. The labels were entered in cells A1 through A4. The dollar amount of revenues was entered in cell B2 and expenses in cell B3. A formula was placed in B4 as follows: =B2–B3. This formula subtracts expenses from revenues to compute net income in cell B4. If revenues in cell B2 increase to $220,000, net income in B4 automatically increases to $100,000. No other cells will change.

Spreadsheets are ideally suited to preparing a budget, which summarizes the financial goals of a business. Consider Canada's Procter & Gamble Inc., whose

**Business Works
(20-20 Software)**
www.20-20.com/index.htm

DacEasy
www.daceasy.com

One-Write Plus
www.onewrite.com

RealWorld
www.realworld.com

EXHIBIT 6-7

A Spreadsheet Screen

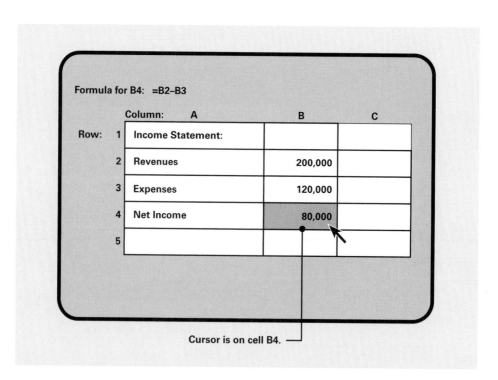

Health-Care Sector has an annual advertising budget of $30–$40 million. Suppose Procter & Gamble allocates $4–5 million for its Crest Complete toothbrush and $500,000 for a new stand-up tube for Crest toothpaste. Procter & Gamble's advertising expenses will increase in both cases. The company will also forecast an increase in sales revenue, cost of goods sold, and other expenses. A spreadsheet computes all these changes automatically in response to the advertising. The spreadsheet lets Procter & Gamble's managers track relative profitability of each product. Armed with current data, the managers can make informed decisions. The result is higher profits.

We can add or delete whole rows and columns of data and move blocks of numbers and words on a spreadsheet. The power and versatility of spreadsheets are apparent when enormous amounts of data are entered on the spreadsheet with formula relationships. Change only one number, and you save hours of manual recalculation. Exhibit 6-8 shows the basic arithmetic operations in some popular spreadsheet programs such as Excel.

Special Journals

KEY POINT

Transactions are recorded in either the general journal or a special journal, but not in both.

Exhibit 6-9 diagrams a typical accounting system for a merchandising business. The remainder of this chapter describes some of the more important aspects of that system.

Special Accounting Journals

The journal entries illustrated so far in this book have been made in the **general journal**. The general journal is used to record all transactions that do not fit one of the special journals. In practice, it is not efficient to record all transactions in the general journal, so we use special journals. A **special journal** is an accounting journal designed to record one specific type of transaction.

Both manual systems and computerized systems organize transaction entries by type using special journals and accounting modules. In a computerized system, accountants input data through various modules, such as the Accounts Receivable module for credit sales. In a manual system, they enter transaction data in special journals. But the underlying accounting principles are the same in both manual and computerized systems.

In all likelihood, you will be working with a computerized system. We would rather you *not* view the process as a black box. To help you understand the basic accounting, over the next several pages, we go through the steps in a manual system.

Most of a business's transactions fall into one of five categories, so accountants

> **Student to Student**
>
> *I found the Cash Receipts Journal and the posting of its entries challenging. I thought that posting to the accounts receivable ledger and the general ledger would result in more work and double counting of certain accounts. I found Exhibit 6-11 on page 307 to be very helpful in overcoming this challenge. This visual helped me understand that the account is not counted twice even though it is posted twice.*
>
> *Adrian B., Montreal*

Operation	Symbol
Addition	+
Subtraction	−
Multiplication	*
Division	/
Addition of a range of cells	=SUM(beginning cell:ending cell)
Examples:	
Add the contents of cells A2 through A9	=SUM(A2:A9)
Divide the contents of cell C2 by the contents of cell D1	=C2/D1

EXHIBIT 6-8

Basic Arithmetic Operations in Excel Spreadsheets

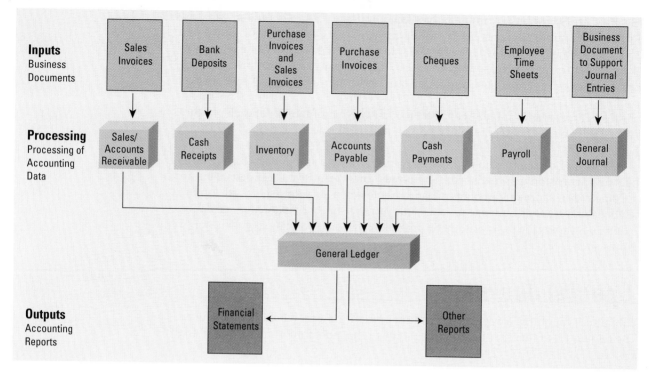

EXHIBIT 6-9

Overview of an Accounting System with Special Journals for a Merchandising Business

use five different journals to record these transactions. This system reduces the time and cost otherwise spent journalizing, as we will see. The five categories of transactions, the related special journal, and the posting abbreviations are as follows:

Transaction	Special Journal	Posting Abbreviation
1. Sale of merchandise on account	Sales journal	S
2. Cash receipt	Cash receipts journal	CR
3. Purchase on account	Purchases journal	P
4. Cash payment*	Cash payments journal	CP
5. All others	General journal	J

*Some companies also use a Payroll Journal for payroll transactions, which is a part of the companies' *payroll system*. Payroll systems are covered in Chapter 11.

Adjusting and closing entries are entered in the general journal. Transactions are recorded in either the general journal or a special journal, but not in both.

OBJECTIVE 4
Use the sales journal, the cash receipts journal, and the accounts receivable subsidiary ledger

KEY POINT

Only credit sales of merchandise are recorded in the sales journal.

Using the Sales Journal

Most merchandisers sell at least some of their inventory on account. These *credit sales* are recorded in the **sales journal**. Credit sales of assets other than inventory—for example, buildings—occur infrequently and may be recorded in the general journal.

Exhibit 6-10 illustrates a sales journal (Panel A) and the related posting to the ledgers (Panel B) of Austin Sound Centre, the stereo shop we introduced in Chapter 5. Each entry in the Accounts Receivable/Sales Revenue column of the sales journal in Exhibit 6-10 is a debit (Dr.) to Accounts Receivable and a credit (Cr.) to Sales Revenue, as the heading above this column indicates. For each transaction, the accountant enters the date, invoice number, customer account, and transaction amount. This streamlined way of recording sales on account saves a vast amount of time that, in a manual system, would be spent entering account titles and dollar amounts in the general journal.

Panel A: Sales Journal

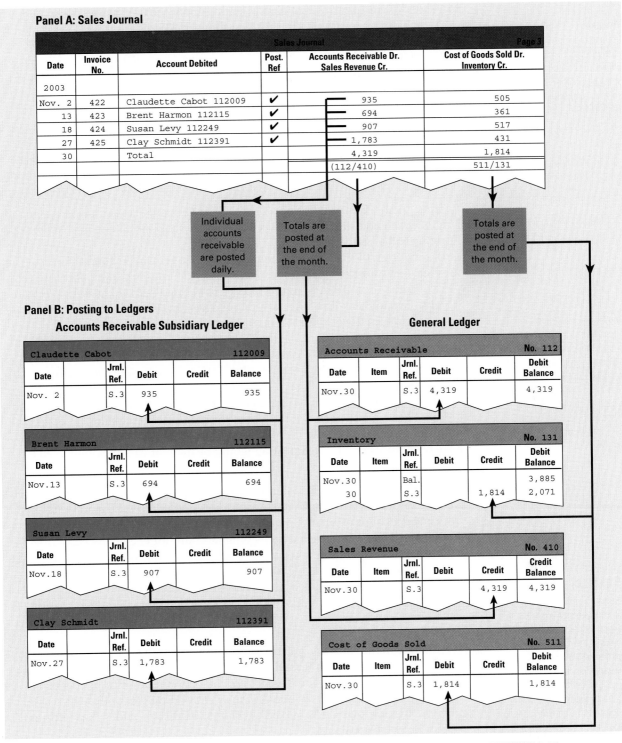

Date	Invoice No.	Account Debited	Post. Ref	Accounts Receivable Dr. Sales Revenue Cr.	Cost of Goods Sold Dr. Inventory Cr.
2003					
Nov. 2	422	Claudette Cabot 112009	✔	935	505
13	423	Brent Harmon 112115	✔	694	361
18	424	Susan Levy 112249	✔	907	517
27	425	Clay Schmidt 112391	✔	1,783	431
30		Total		4,319	1,814
				(112/410)	511/131

Individual accounts receivable are posted daily.

Totals are posted at the end of the month.

Totals are posted at the end of the month.

Panel B: Posting to Ledgers

Accounts Receivable Subsidiary Ledger

Claudette Cabot   112009

Date		Jrnl. Ref.	Debit	Credit	Balance
Nov. 2		S.3	935		935

Brent Harmon   112115

Date		Jrnl. Ref.	Debit	Credit	Balance
Nov.13		S.3	694		694

Susan Levy   112249

Date		Jrnl. Ref.	Debit	Credit	Balance
Nov.18		S.3	907		907

Clay Schmidt   112391

Date		Jrnl. Ref.	Debit	Credit	Balance
Nov.27		S.3	1,783		1,783

General Ledger

Accounts Receivable   No. 112

Date	Item	Jrnl. Ref.	Debit	Credit	Debit Balance
Nov.30		S.3	4,319		4,319

Inventory   No. 131

Date	Item	Jrnl. Ref.	Debit	Credit	Debit Balance
Nov.30		Bal.			3,885
30		S.3		1,814	2,071

Sales Revenue   No. 410

Date	Item	Jrnl. Ref.	Debit	Credit	Credit Balance
Nov.30		S.3		4,319	4,319

Cost of Goods Sold   No. 511

Date	Item	Jrnl. Ref.	Debit	Credit	Debit Balance
Nov.30		S.3	1,814		1,814

EXHIBIT 6-10

Sales Journal (Panel A) and Posting to Ledgers (Panel B) under the Perpetual Inventory System

In recording credit sales in the previous chapter, we did not keep a record of the names of credit-sale customers. In practice the business must know the amount receivable from each customer. How else can the company identify who owes it money, when payment is due, and how much?

Consider the first transaction in Panel A. On November 2, Austin Sound sold stereo equipment on account to Claudette Cabot for $935. The invoice number is 422. All this information appears on a single line in the sales journal. No explanation is necessary. The transaction's presence in the sales journal means that it is a credit sale, debited to Accounts Receivable—Claudette Cabot and credited to Sales

Revenue. To gain any additional information about the transaction, we would look at the actual invoice (which in this case shows a $35 discount will be granted for prompt payment).

Recall from Chapter 5 that Austin Sound uses a *perpetual* inventory system. At the time of recording the sale, Austin Sound also records the cost of goods sold and the decrease in inventory. Many computerized accounting systems are programmed to read both the sales amount (from the bar code on the package of the item sold) and the cost of goods sold. A separate column of the sales journal holds the cost of goods sold and inventory amount—$505 for the sale to Claudette Cabot. If Austin Sound used a *periodic* inventory system, it would not record cost of goods sold and the decrease in inventory at the time of sale. The sales journal would need only one column to debit Accounts Receivable and to credit Sales Revenue for the amount of the sale.

Posting to the General Ledger

The ledger we have used so far is the **general ledger**, which holds the accounts reported in the financial statements. We will soon introduce other ledgers.

Posting from the sales journal to the general ledger can be done at any time, but for efficiency, most companies post only once each month. In Exhibit 6-10 (Panel A), November's credit sales total $4,319. This column has two headings, Accounts Receivable and Sales Revenue. In a manual system, when the $4,319 is posted to these accounts in the general ledger, their account numbers are written beneath the total in the sales journal. In Panel B of Exhibit 6-10, the account number for Accounts Receivable is 112 and the account number for Sales Revenue is 410. Printing these account numbers beneath the credit sales total in the sales journal signifies that the $4,319 has been posted to the two accounts.

The debit to Cost of Goods Sold and the credit to Inventory for the monthly total of $1,814 is normally posted at the end of the month. After posting, these accounts' numbers are entered beneath the total to show that Cost of Goods Sold and Inventory have been updated. No such posting would be made if Austin Sound used a periodic inventory system.

Posting to the Accounts Receivable Subsidiary Ledger

The $4,319 sum of the November debits to Accounts Receivable does not identify the amount receivable from any specific customer. A business may have thousands of customers. For example, *MacLean's Magazine* has a customer account for each of its subscribers.

To streamline operations, businesses place the accounts of their individual credit customers in a subsidiary ledger, called the Accounts Receivable Subsidiary ledger. A **subsidiary ledger** is a book or file of accounts that provides supporting details on individual balances, the total of which appears in a general ledger account. The customer accounts usually are arranged in alphabetical order and often have a customer number.

Amounts in the sales journal are posted to the subsidiary ledger *daily* to keep a current record of the amount receivable from each customer. The amounts are debits. Daily posting allows the business to answer customer inquiries promptly. Suppose Claudette Cabot telephones Austin Sound on November 11 to ask how much money she owes. The subsidiary ledger readily provides that information, $935 in Exhibit 6-10, Panel B.

When each transaction amount is posted to the subsidiary ledger in a manual system, a check mark or some other notation is entered in the posting reference column of the sales journal (see Exhibit 6-10, Panel A). This is because subsidiary ledger accounts are not part of the general ledger, and, thus, have no general ledger account numbers.

Journal References in the Ledgers

When amounts are posted to the ledgers, the journal page number is written in the account to identify the source of the data. All transaction data in Exhibit 6-10 originated on page 3 of the sales journal so all posting references in the ledger accounts are S.3. The "S." indicates sales journal.

Trace all the postings in Exhibit 6-10. The most effective way to learn about accounting systems and special journals is to study the flow of data. The arrows indicate the direction of the information. The arrows show the links between the individual customer accounts in the subsidiary ledger and the Accounts Receivable account. (The arrows are for illustration only—they do not appear in the accounting records.) The Accounts Receivable debit balance in the general ledger should equal the sum of the individual customer balances in the subsidiary ledger, as follows:

General Ledger	
Accounts Receivable debit balance.........................	$4,319

Subsidiary Ledger: Customer Accounts Receivable	
Customer	**Balance**
Claudette Cabot 112009	$ 935
Brent Harmon 112115..	694
Susan Levy 112249..	907
Clay Schmidt 112391	1,783
Total accounts receivable...	$4,319

Accounts Receivable in the general ledger is a **control account**. Its balance equals the sum of the balances of a group of related accounts in a subsidiary ledger. The individual customer accounts are subsidiary accounts. They are said to be "controlled" by the Accounts Receivable account in the general ledger.

Additional data can be recorded in the sales journal. For example, a company may add a column to record sale terms, such as 2/10 n/30. The design of the journal depends on the managers' needs for information. Special journals are flexible—they can be tailored to meet any special needs of a business.

Using Documents as Journals in a Manual Accounting System

Many small businesses streamline their accounting systems by using their business documents as the journals. This practice avoids the need to keep special journals and thereby saves money. For example, Austin Sound could keep sales invoices in a looseleaf binder and let the invoices themselves serve as the sales journal. At the end of the period, the accountant simply totals the sales on account and posts the total as a debit to Accounts Receivable and a credit to Sales Revenue. Also, the accountant can post directly from invoices to customer accounts in the accounts receivable subsidiary ledger.

STOP & THINK

Suppose Austin Sound had 400 credit sales for the month. How many postings to the general ledger would be made from the sales journal? (Ignore Cost of Goods Sold and Inventory.) How many would there be if all sales transactions were routed through the general journal?

Answer: There are only two postings from the sales journal to the general ledger: one to Accounts Receivable and one to Sales Revenue. There would be 800 postings from the general journal: 400 to Accounts Receivable and 400 to Sales Revenue. This difference clearly shows the benefit of using a sales journal.

Using the Cash Receipts Journal

Cash transactions are common in most businesses because cash receipts from customers are the lifeblood of business. To record repetitive cash receipt transactions, accountants use the **cash receipts journal**.

Exhibit 6-11, Panel A, illustrates the cash receipts journal. The related posting to the ledgers is shown in Panel B. The exhibit illustrates November transactions for Austin Sound Centre.

Every transaction recorded in this journal is a cash receipt, so the first column is for debits to the Cash account. The next column is for debits to Sales Discounts on collections from customers. In a typical merchandising business, the main sources of cash are collections on account, and cash sales.

The cash receipts journal has credit columns for Accounts Receivable and Sales Revenue. The journal also has a credit column for Other Accounts, which lists sources of cash other than cash sales and collections on account. This Other Accounts column is also used to record the names of customers from whom cash is received on account.

In Exhibit 6-11, cash sales occurred on November 6, 19, and 28. Observe the debits to Cash and the credits to Sales Revenue ($517, $853, and $1,802). Each sale entry is accompanied by an entry that debits Cost of Goods Sold and credits Inventory for the cost of the merchandise sold, since the perpetual inventory system is being used. The column for this entry is at the far right side of the cash receipts journal. No such entry would be made if Austin Sound used a periodic inventory system.

On November 11, Austin Sound borrowed $1,000 from Scotiabank. Cash is debited, and Note Payable to Scotiabank is credited in the Other Accounts column because it is a rare transaction and no specific credit column is set up to account for borrowings. For this transaction, we enter the account title, Note Payable to Scotiabank, in the Other Accounts/Account Title column. This entry records the source of cash.

On November 25, Austin Sound collected $762 of interest revenue. The account credited, Interest Revenue, must be written in the Other Accounts column. The November 11 and 25 transactions illustrate a key fact about business. Different entities have different types of transactions, and they design their special journals to meet their particular needs for information. In this case, the Other Accounts Credit column is the catch-all that is used to record all nonroutine cash receipt transactions.

On November 14, Austin Sound collected $900 from Claudette Cabot. Referring back to Exhibit 6-10, we see that on November 2 Austin Sound sold merchandise for $935 to Claudette Cabot. The terms of sale allowed a $35 discount for prompt payment and she paid within the discount period. Austin's cash receipt is recorded by debiting Cash for $900 and Sales Discounts for $35 and by crediting Accounts Receivable for $935. The customer's name appears in the Other Accounts/Account Title column.

Total debits must equal total credits in the cash receipts journal. This equality holds for each transaction and for the monthly totals. For the month, total debits ($6,134 + $35 = $6,169) equal total credits ($1,235 + $3,172 + $1,762 = $6,169). The debit to Cost of Goods Sold and the credit to Inventory are separate, and only apply to the perpetual inventory system.

Posting to the General Ledger   The column totals are usually posted monthly. To indicate their posting, the account number is written below the column total in the cash receipts journal. Note the account number for Cash (101) below the column total $6,134, and trace the posting to Cash in the general ledger. Likewise, the Sales Discounts, Accounts Receivable, and Sales Revenue column totals also are posted to the general ledger.

The column total for *Other Accounts* is *not* posted. Instead, these credits are posted individually. In Exhibit 6-11, the November 11 transaction reads "Note Payable to Scotiabank." This account's number (222) in the Post. Ref. column indicates that the transaction amount was posted individually. The check mark, instead of an

EXHIBIT 6-11

Cash Receipts Journal (Panel A) and Posting to the Ledgers (Panel B) under the Perpetual Inventory System

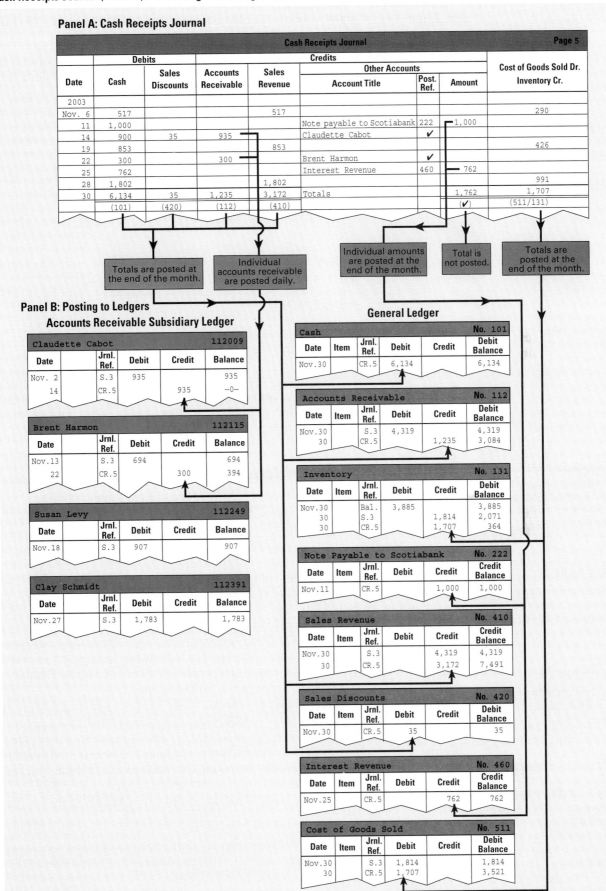

THINKING IT OVER

If Austin Sound did not use an accounts receivable subsidiary ledger and Claudette Cabot asked you for her account balance, could you answer her?

A: It would be difficult! A subsidiary ledger is needed for ready access to the data for each customer. The alternative is to look through all transactions in the general journal for the ones involving Claudette Cabot. (This would be a very inefficient and error-prone alternative.)

account number, below the column total indicates that the column total was not posted. The November 25 collection of interest revenue is also posted individually. These amounts can be posted to the general ledger at the end of the month. But their date in the ledger accounts should be their actual date in the journal to make it easy to trace each amount back to the cash receipts journal.

Posting to the Subsidiary Ledger Amounts from the cash receipts journal are posted to the subsidiary accounts receivable ledger daily to keep the individual balances up to date. The postings to the accounts receivable ledger are credits. Trace the $935 posting to Claudette Cabot's account. It reduces the balance in her account to zero. The $300 receipt from Brent Harmon reduces his accounts receivable balance to $394.

After posting, the sum of the individual balances that remain in the accounts receivable ledger equals the general ledger balance in Accounts Receivable.

General Ledger	
Accounts Receivable debit balance	$3,084

Subsidiary Ledger: Customer Accounts Receivable	
Customer	**Balance**
Brent Harmon 112115...	$ 394
Susan Levy 112249..	907
Clay Schmidt 112391	1,783
Total accounts receivable..	$3,084

Austin Sound's list of account balances from the subsidiary ledger helps it follow up on slow-paying customers. Good accounts receivable records help a business manage its cash.

Using the Purchases Journal

OBJECTIVE 5
Use the purchases journal, the cash payments journal, and the accounts payable subsidiary ledger

A merchandising business purchases inventory and supplies frequently. Such purchases are usually made on account. The **purchases journal** is designed to account for all purchases of inventory, supplies, and other assets *on account*. It can also be used to record expenses incurred on account. Cash purchases are recorded in the cash payments journal.

KEY POINT

The source document for entries in the purchases journal is the supplier's (creditor's) invoice.

Exhibit 6-12 illustrates Austin Sound's purchases journal (Panel A) and posting to the ledgers (Panel B).[1] The purchases journal in Exhibit 6-12 has amount columns for credits to Accounts Payable and debits to Inventory, Supplies, and Other Accounts. A periodic inventory system would replace the Inventory column with a column entitled "Purchases." The Other Accounts columns accommodate purchases of assets other than inventory and supplies. Each business designs its purchases journal to meet its own needs for information and efficiency. Accounts Payable is credited for all transactions recorded in the purchases journal.

KEY POINT

Every transaction in the purchases journal will include a credit to Accounts Payable.

On November 2, Austin Sound purchased stereo inventory costing $700 from JVC Canada Inc. The creditor's name (JVC Canada Inc.) is entered in the Account Credited column. The purchase terms of 3/15 n/30 are also entered to help identify the due date and the discount available. Accounts Payable is credited and Inventory is debited for the transaction amount. On November 19, a credit purchase of supplies is entered as a debit to Supplies and a credit to Accounts Payable.

Note the November 9 purchase of fixtures from City Office Supply Co. The

REAL WORLD EXAMPLE

Companies design journals to meet their special needs. A repair service might not use a Supplies column but might need a Small Tools column for frequent purchases of tools.

---

[1]This is the only special journal that we illustrate with the credit column usually placed to the left and the debit columns to the right. This arrangement of columns focuses on Accounts Payable, which is credited for each entry to this journal, and on the individual supplier to be paid.

EXHIBIT 6-12

Purchases Journal (Panel A) and Posting to the Ledgers (Panel B) under the Perpetual Inventory System

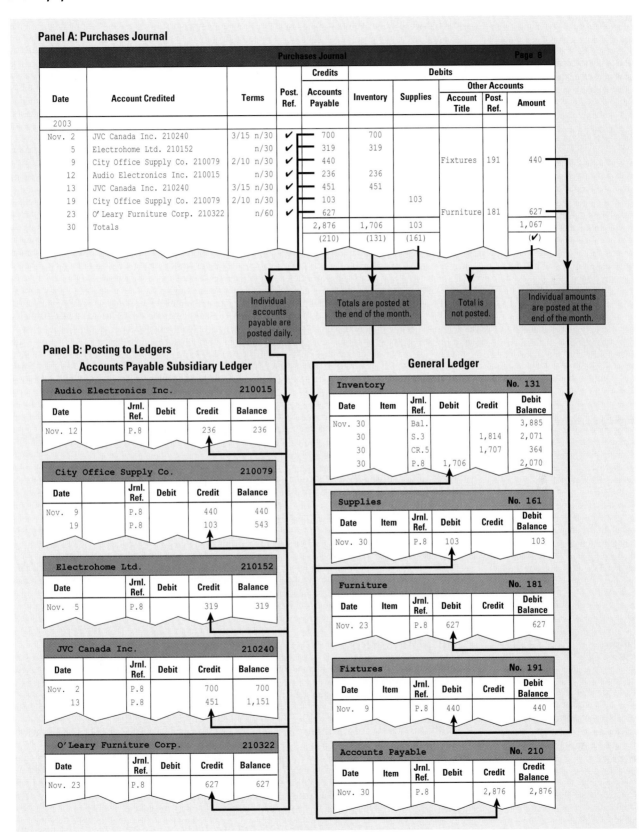

Panel A: Purchases Journal

				Credits	Debits				
							Other Accounts		
Date	Account Credited	Terms	Post. Ref.	Accounts Payable	Inventory	Supplies	Account Title	Post. Ref.	Amount
2003									
Nov. 2	JVC Canada Inc. 210240	3/15 n/30	✔	700	700				
5	Electrohome Ltd. 210152	n/30	✔	319	319				
9	City Office Supply Co. 210079	2/10 n/30	✔	440			Fixtures	191	440
12	Audio Electronics Inc. 210015	n/30	✔	236	236				
13	JVC Canada Inc. 210240	3/15 n/30	✔	451	451				
19	City Office Supply Co. 210079	2/10 n/30	✔	103		103			
23	O'Leary Furniture Corp. 210322	n/60	✔	627			Furniture	181	627
30	Totals			2,876	1,706	103			1,067
				(210)	(131)	(161)			(✔)

Purchases Journal — Page 8

Individual accounts payable are posted daily.

Totals are posted at the end of the month.

Total is not posted.

Individual amounts are posted at the end of the month.

Panel B: Posting to Ledgers

Accounts Payable Subsidiary Ledger

Audio Electronics Inc. 210015

Date		Jrnl. Ref.	Debit	Credit	Balance
Nov. 12		P.8		236	236

City Office Supply Co. 210079

Date		Jrnl. Ref.	Debit	Credit	Balance
Nov. 9		P.8		440	440
19		P.8		103	543

Electrohome Ltd. 210152

Date		Jrnl. Ref.	Debit	Credit	Balance
Nov. 5		P.8		319	319

JVC Canada Inc. 210240

Date		Jrnl. Ref.	Debit	Credit	Balance
Nov. 2		P.8		700	700
13		P.8		451	1,151

O'Leary Furniture Corp. 210322

Date		Jrnl. Ref.	Debit	Credit	Balance
Nov. 23		P.8		627	627

General Ledger

Inventory No. 131

Date	Item	Jrnl. Ref.	Debit	Credit	Debit Balance
Nov. 30		Bal.			3,885
30		S.3		1,814	2,071
30		CR.5		1,707	364
30		P.8	1,706		2,070

Supplies No. 161

Date	Item	Jrnl. Ref.	Debit	Credit	Debit Balance
Nov. 30		P.8	103		103

Furniture No. 181

Date	Item	Jrnl. Ref.	Debit	Credit	Debit Balance
Nov. 23		P.8	627		627

Fixtures No. 191

Date	Item	Jrnl. Ref.	Debit	Credit	Debit Balance
Nov. 9		P.8	440		440

Accounts Payable No. 210

Date	Item	Jrnl. Ref.	Debit	Credit	Credit Balance
Nov. 30		P.8		2,876	2,876

purchases journal contains no column for fixtures, so the Other Accounts debit column is used. Because this was a credit purchase, the accountant enters the creditor name (City Office Supply Co.) in the Account Credited column and writes "Fixtures" in the Other Accounts/Account Title column.

The total credits in the purchases journal ($2,876) equal to the total debits ($1,706 + $103 + $1,067 = $2,876). This equality proves the accuracy of the entries in the purchases journal.

KEY POINT

The posting procedure is the same as for the other special journals: column totals can be posted to the general ledger at the end of the month; other accounts are posted individually to the general ledger; and individual accounts payable amounts are posted daily to the subsidiary ledger.

Accounts Payable Subsidiary Ledger   To pay debts efficiently, a company must know how much it owes particular creditors. The Accounts Payable account in the general ledger shows only a single total for the amount owed on account. It does not indicate the amount owed to each creditor. Companies keep an accounts payable subsidiary ledger that is similar to the accounts receivable subsidiary ledger that we used in conjunction with credit sales.

The accounts payable subsidiary ledger lists the creditors in alphabetical order, often by account number, along with the amounts owed to them. Exhibit 6-12, Panel B, shows Austin Sound's accounts payable subsidiary ledger, which includes accounts for Audio Electronics Inc., City Office Supply Co., and others. After the daily and period-end postings are done, the total of the individual balances in the subsidiary ledger equals the balance in the Accounts Payable control account in the general ledger.

Posting from the Purchases Journal   Posting from the purchases journal is similar to posting from the sales journal and the cash receipts journal. Exhibit 6-12, Panel B, illustrates the posting process.

Individual accounts payable in the purchases journal are posted daily to the *accounts payable subsidiary ledger*, and column totals and other amounts are usually posted to the *general ledger* at the end of the month. The column total for *Other Accounts* is not posted. Each account's number in the Post. Ref. column indicates the transaction amount was posted individually. The check mark below the column total indicates the column total was *not* posted. In the ledger accounts, P.8 indicates the source of the posted amounts—that is, page 8 of the purchases journal.

STOP & THINK

Contrast the number of general ledger postings from the purchases journal in Exhibit 6-12 with the number that would be required if the general journal were used to record the same seven transactions.

Answer: Use of the purchases journal requires only five general ledger postings—$2,876 to Accounts Payable, $1,706 to Inventory, $103 to Supplies, $440 to Fixtures, and $627 to Furniture. Without the purchases journal, there would have been 14 postings, two for each of the seven transactions.

REAL WORLD EXAMPLE

Businesses make most cash payments by cheque to control their cash. Imagine the confusion and the opportunity for theft if all employees could take cash from the cash register to pay for purchases.

Using the Cash Payments Journal

Businesses make most cash disbursements by cheque. All payments by cheque are recorded in the **cash payments journal**. Other titles of this special journal are the *cheque register* and the *cash disbursements journal*. Like the other special journals, it has multiple columns for recording cash payments that occur frequently.

Exhibit 6-13, Panel A, illustrates the cash payments journal, and Panel B shows the postings to the ledgers of Austin Sound. This cash payments journal has two debit columns—for Other Accounts and Accounts Payable. It has two credit columns—one for purchase discounts, which are credited to the Inventory account in a perpetual inventory system, and one for Cash. This special journal also has columns for the date, cheque number, and payee of each cash payment.

The cash payments journal for a company using a periodic inventory system

EXHIBIT 6-13

Cash Payments Journal (Panel A) and Posting to the Ledgers (Panel B) under the Perpetual Inventory System

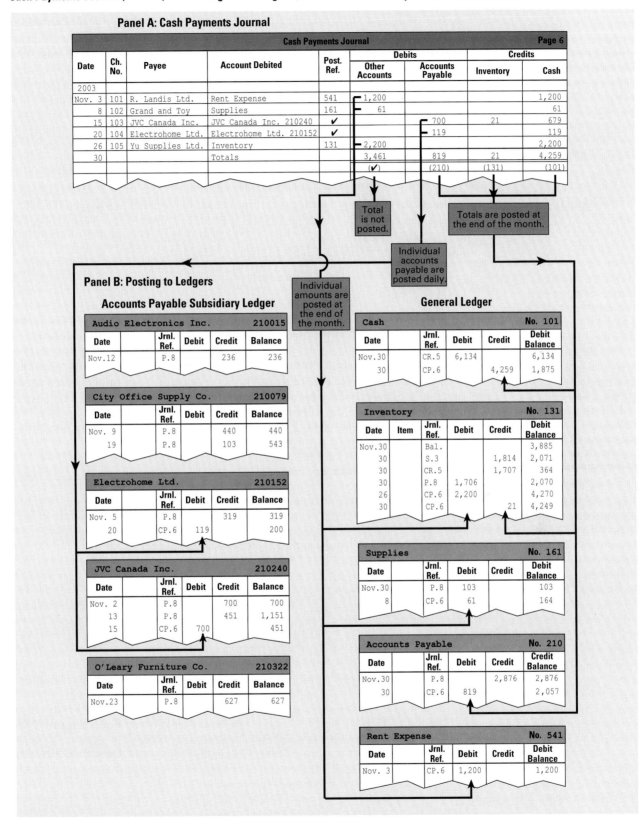

Panel A: Cash Payments Journal

Panel B: Posting to Ledgers

would have the same two debit columns as those shown in Exhibit 6-13, Panel A—Other Accounts and Accounts Payable—and three credit columns—for Purchase Discounts, Purchase Returns and Allowances, and Cash.

Suppose a business makes numerous cash purchases of inventory and uses the perpetual inventory system. What additional column would its cash payments journal need to be most useful? A column for Inventory, which would appear under the Debits heading, would streamline record keeping in the cash payments journal.

All entries in the cash payments journal include a credit to Cash. Payments on account are debits to Accounts Payable. On November 15, Austin Sound paid JVC Canada Inc. on account, with credit terms of 3/15 n/30 (for details, see the first transaction in Exhibit 6-12). Therefore, Austin took the 3 percent discount and paid $679 ($700 less the $21 discount). The discount is credited to the Inventory account.

The Other Accounts column is used to record debits to accounts for which no special column exists. For example, on November 3, Austin Sound paid rent expense of $1,200.

As with all other journals, the total debits ($3,461 + $819 = $4,280) must equal the total credits ($21 + $4,259 = $4,280).

Posting from the Cash Payments Journal   Posting from the cash payments journal is similar to posting from the cash receipts journal. Individual creditor amounts are posted daily. Column totals and Other Accounts are usually posted at the end of the month. Exhibit 6-13, Panel B, illustrates the posting process.

Observe the effect of posting to the Accounts Payable account in the general ledger. The first posted amount in the Accounts Payable account (credit $2,876) originated in the purchases journal, page 8 (P.8). The second posted amount (debit $819) came from the cash payments journal, page 6 (CP.6). The resulting credit balance in Accounts Payable is $2,057. Also, see the Cash account. After posting, its debit balance is $1,875.

Amounts in the Other Accounts column are posted individually (for example, Rent Expense—debit $1,200). When each Other Accounts amount is posted to the general ledger, the account number is written in the Post. Ref. column of the journal. The check mark below the column total signifies that the total is *not* posted.

To review their accounts payable, companies list the individual creditor balances in the accounts payable subsidiary ledger:

General Ledger	
Accounts Payable credit balance	$2,057

Subsidiary Ledger: Creditor Accounts Payable	
Creditor	**Balance**
Audio Electronics Inc. 210015.............................	$ 236
City Office Supply Co. 210079...........................	543
Electrohome Ltd. 210152	200
JVC Canada Inc. 210240......................................	451
O'Leary Furniture Co. 210322	627
Total accounts payable..	$2,057

This total agrees with the Accounts Payable balance in Exhibit 6-13. Agreement of the two amounts indicates that the resulting account balances are correct.

The payroll register is a special form of cash payments journal and is discussed in Chapter 11.

The General Journal's Role in an Accounting Information System

Special journals save much time in recording repetitive transactions and posting to the ledgers. But some transactions do not fit into any of the special journals.

Examples include the amortization of buildings and equipment, the expiration of prepaid insurance, and the accrual of salary payable at the end of the period. Therefore, *even the most sophisticated accounting system needs a general journal. The adjusting entries and the closing entries that we illustrated in Chapters 3 through 5 are recorded in the general journal.*

Accountants also record other transactions in the general journal. Many companies record their sales returns and allowances and their purchase returns in the general journal. Let's examine the *credit memorandum*, the document that leads to the entries for sales returns and allowances.

The Credit Memorandum—The Document for Recording Sales Returns and Allowances

As we saw in Chapter 5, customers sometimes return merchandise to the seller, and sellers grant sales allowances to customers because of product defects and for other reasons. The effect of sales returns and sales allowances is the same—both decrease net sales in the same way a sales discount does. The document issued by the seller for a credit to the customer's Account Receivable is called a **credit memorandum**, or **credit memo**, because the company gives the customer credit for the returned merchandise. When a company issues a credit memo, it debits Sales Returns and Allowances and credits Accounts Receivable.

On November 27, Austin Sound sold four stereo speakers for $1,783 on account to Clay Schmidt. Later, Schmidt discovered a defect and returned the speakers. Austin Sound then issued to Schmidt a credit memo like the one in Exhibit 6-14.

To record the *sale return* and receipt of the defective speakers from the customer, Clay Schmidt, Austin Sound would make the following entries in the general journal:

KEY POINT

Receipt of a "credit" memo does not indicate that you should "credit" Accounts Receivable. The originator of the credit memo is "crediting" Accounts Receivable. The receiver of the credit memo debits Accounts Payable.

General Journal				Page 9
Date	**Accounts**	**Post Ref.**	**Debit**	**Credit**
Dec. 1	Sales Returns and Allowances..	430	1,783	
	Accounts Receivable—Clay Schmidt 112391	112/✓		1,783
	Credit memo no. 27.			
Dec. 1	Inventory	131	431	
	Cost of Goods Sold..	511		431
	Received defective goods from customer.			

Focus on the first entry. The debit side of the entry is posted to Sales Returns and Allowances. Its account number (430) is written in the posting reference column when $1,783 is posted. The credit side of the entry requires two $1,783 postings, one to Accounts Receivable, the *control account* in the general ledger (account number 112), and the other to Clay Schmidt's *individual account* in the accounts receivable subsidiary ledger, account number 112391. These credit postings explain why the document is called a *credit memo*.

Observe that the posting reference of the credit includes two notations. The account number (112) denotes the posting to Accounts Receivable in the general ledger. The check mark (✓) denotes the posting to Schmidt's account in the subsidiary ledger. Why are two postings needed? Because this is the general journal. Without specially designed columns, it is necessary to write both posting preferences on the same line.

A business with a high volume of sales returns, such as a department store chain, may use a special journal for sales returns and allowances.

The second entry records Austin Sound's receipt of the defective inventory from the customer. The speakers cost Austin Sound $431, and Austin Sound, like all other merchandisers, records its inventory at cost. Now let's see how Austin Sound records the return of the defective speakers to JVC, from which Austin Sound purchased them.

WORKING IT OUT

Brown Sales Co. sold $500 of merchandise on account to Lee Smith, terms 2/10 n/30. Smith later returned $40 of the goods and received a credit memo from Brown Sales Co. What is the balance in Smith's account before payment and how much will Smith pay if she pays within the discount period?

A: Smith's balance is $460 and she will pay $450.80 [$460 − (0.02 × $460)]. (Note that Brown Sales Co. must make an entry to debit Inventory for the original cost of the goods when the goods are returned.)

EXHIBIT 6-14

Credit Memorandum

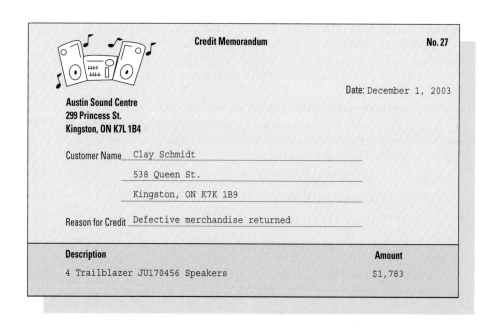

The Debit Memorandum—The Business Document for Recording Purchase Returns and Allowances

Purchase returns occur when a business returns goods to the seller. The procedures for handling purchase returns are similar to those dealing with sales returns. The purchaser gives the merchandise back to the seller and receives either a cash refund or replacement goods.

When a business returns merchandise to the seller, it may also send a business document known as a **debit memorandum**, or **debit memo**. This document states that the buyer no longer owes the seller for the amount of the returned purchases. The buyer debits the Accounts Payable to the seller and credits Inventory for the cost of the goods returned to the seller.

Many businesses record their purchase returns in the general journal. Austin Sound would record its return of defective speakers to JVC as follows:

	General Journal			Page 9
Date	**Accounts**	**Post Ref.**	**Debit**	**Credit**
Dec. 2	Accounts Payable—JVC Corp. 210240	210/✓	431	
	Inventory	131		431
	Debit memo no. 16.			

Balancing the Ledgers

At the end of the period, after all postings have been made, equality should exist between:

1. *General ledger:*

Total debits = Total credits, of all account balances

2. *General ledger and Accounts receivable subsidiary ledger:*

Balance of   Sum of individual customer account
Accounts Receivable = balances in the accounts receivable
control account   subsidiary ledger

3. *General ledger and Accounts payable subsidiary ledger:*

Balance of
Accounts Payable = Sum of individual creditor account balances in the accounts payable
control account subsidiary ledger

This process of ensuring that these equalities exist is called *balancing the ledgers, reconciling the ledgers,* or *proving the ledgers.* It is an important control procedure because it helps ensure the accuracy of the accounting records.

Blending Computers and Special Journals in an Accounting Information System

Computerizing special journals to create accounting modules requires no drastic change in the accounting system's design. Systems designers create a special screen for each accounting application (module)—credit sales, cash receipts, credit purchases, payroll, and cash payments. The special screen for credit sales would prompt the operator entering the data, for example, on a terminal or a cash register, to type in the following information: date, customer number, customer name, invoice number, and the dollar amount of the sale. These data can generate debits to the subsidiary accounts receivable, and files from which are generated monthly customer statements that show activity and ending balance. For purchases on account, additional computer files keep the subsidiary ledger information on individual vendors.

The Decision Guidelines feature on the next page provides guidelines for some of the major decisions that accountants must make as they use an information system.

Sales Tax

In Chapter 5, the federal Goods and Services Tax (GST) was discussed; recall that the GST is collected at each level of transaction right down to the consumer, the final level. The discussion that follows relates to consumption or sales taxes levied by all the provinces except Alberta. The Yukon, the Northwest Territories, and Nunavut also do not have a sales tax. Sellers must add the tax to the sale amount, then pay or remit the tax to the provincial government. In most jurisdictions, sales tax is levied only on final consumers, so retail businesses usually do not pay sales tax on the goods they purchase for resale. For example, Gunz Stereo Company would not pay sales tax on a purchase of equipment from JVC Canada Inc., a wholesaler. However, when retailers like Gunz Stereo make sales, they must collect sales tax from the consumer. In effect, retailers serve as collecting agents for the taxing authorities. The amount of tax depends on the total sales and the provincial tax rate.

Retailers set up procedures to collect the sales tax, account for it, and pay it on time. Invoices may be preprinted with a place for entering the sales tax amount, and the general ledger has a liability account entitled Sales Tax Payable. The sales journal may include a special column for sales tax, such as the one illustrated in Exhibit 6-15. The sales tax rate in the exhibit is 7 percent, the rate of sales tax in British Columbia and Manitoba.

Note that the amount debited to Accounts Receivable ($3,783.66) is the sum of the credits to Sales Tax Payable ($232.33), GST Payable ($232.33), and Sales Revenue ($3,319.00). This is so because the customers' payments, the Accounts Receivable figures, are partly for the purchase of merchandise (Sales Revenue) and partly for taxes charged on the sale. The check marks in the Posting Reference column show that individual amounts have been posted to the customer accounts. The absence of account numbers under the column totals shows that the total amounts have not yet been posted.

Most companies that use cash registers have them programmed to calculate separate totals, as sales are being rung in, of taxable items and nontaxable items; the register then calculates the relevant taxes—sales tax, if applicable, and GST—and

REAL WORLD EXAMPLE

Periodically, a list (print-out) is prepared that shows each customer's name and account balance. The total of the individual balances must equal Accounts Receivable (control) in the general ledger. This process is called *balancing*, or proving, the ledgers. Likewise, the total of the creditor balances from the accounts payable subsidiary ledger must equal the balance of Accounts Payable (control) in the general ledger.

Decision	Guidelines
What are the main components of an accounting system?	**Journals** • General journal • Special journals **Ledgers** • General ledger • Subsidiary ledgers
Where to record • Sales of merchandise on account? • Cash receipts? • Purchases on account? • Cash payments? • All other transactions?	Journals: Sales journal Cash receipts journal Purchases journal Cash payments journal General journal

How does the general ledger relate to the subsidiary ledgers?

GENERAL LEDGER

Accounts Receivable	Accounts Payable
X,XXX	XX

SUBSIDIARY LEDGERS

ACCOUNTS RECEIVABLE FROM: **ACCOUNTS PAYABLE TO:**

Arnold	Barnes	Agnew	Black
XX	XX	X	X

When to post from the journals to
• General ledger?
• Subsidiary ledgers?

—Monthly (or more often, if needed)
—Daily

How to achieve control over
• Accounts receivable?
• Accounts payable?

Balance the ledgers, as follows:

General Ledger		Subsidiary Ledger
Accounts receivable	=	Sum of individual *customer* account balances
Accounts payable	=	Sum of individual *creditor* account balances

computes the total owing. Provincial sales tax and the federal GST are not applicable to all items. (For example, food and prescription medicines are excluded from both; reading material is excluded from most sales taxes but not from the GST.) Most businesses calculate sales tax and GST at the time of sale.

A business whose sales are all taxable may use a simplified approach to account for sales tax as follows. The business enters a single amount, which is the sum of sales revenue and sales tax, in the Sales Revenue account. This amount is what the customer pays the retailer. At the end of the accounting period, the business computes the tax collected and transfers that amount from Sales Revenue to Sales Tax Payable through a general journal entry. This procedure eliminates the need for a special multicolumn sales journal.

Suppose a retailer's Sales Revenue account shows a $10,600 balance at the end of July. This retailer chooses to enter the full amount of each sale—the actual sales revenue and the sales tax—as Sales Revenue. How does the retailer divide the total amount into its two parts?

To compute the actual sales revenue, the Sales Revenue balance is divided by 1

EXHIBIT 6-15

Sales Journal Designed to
Account for Sales Tax

Sales Journal							**Page 4**
Date	Inv. No.	Account Debited	Post. Ref.	Accounts Receivable Dr.	Sales Tax Payable Cr.	GST Payable Cr.	Sales Revenue Cr.
2003							
Nov. 2	422	Anne Fortin	✔	1,065.90	65.45	65.45	935.00
Nov. 13	423	Brent Mooney	✔	791.16	48.58	48.58	694.00
Nov. 18	424	Debby Levy	✔	1,033.98	63.49	63.49	907.00
Nov. 27	425	Dan Girardi	✔	892.62	54.81	54.81	783.00
Nov. 30		Totals		3,783.66	232.33	232.33	3,319.00

plus the tax rate. Assume that sales tax is 6 percent, the sales tax rate in Saskatchewan. Thus the retailer divides $10,600 by 1.06 (1 + 0.06), which yields $10,000. Subtracting the actual sales revenue, the $10,000, from the $10,600 total yields $600, the sales tax. The retailer makes the following entry in the general journal:

General Journal				**Page 9**
Date	Accounts	Post Ref.	Debit	Credit
July 31	Sales Revenue	41	600	
	Sales Tax Payable..	28		600
	To transfer sales tax to the liability account.			

Sales tax and GST are discussed more fully in Chapter 11.

Summary Problem
for Your Review

Riggs Company completed the following selected transactions during March:

Mar. 4   Received $500 from a cash sale to a customer (cost $319).
6   Received $60 on account from Brady Lee. The full invoice amount was $65, but Lee paid within the discount period to earn the $5 discount.
9   Received $1,080 on a note receivable from Lesley Mann. This amount includes the $1,000 note receivable plus $80 of interest revenue.
15   Received $800 from a cash sale to a customer (cost $522).
24   Borrowed $2,200 by signing a note payable to the Bank of Nova Scotia.
27   Received $1,200 on account from Lance Au. Payment was received after the discount period lapsed.

The general ledger showed the following balances at February 28: Cash, $1,117; Accounts Receivable, $2,790; Note Receivable—Lesley Mann, $1,000; Inventory, $1,819. The accounts receivable subsidiary ledger at February 28 contained debit balances as follows: Lance Au, $1,840; Melinda Fultz, $885; Brady Lee, $65.

Required

1. Record the transactions in the cash receipts journal, page 7. Riggs Company uses a perpetual inventory system.

2. Compute column totals at March 31. Show that total debits equal total credits in the cash receipts journal.

3. Post to the general ledger and the accounts receivable subsidiary ledger. Use complete posting references, including the following account numbers: Cash, 11; Accounts Receivable, 12; Note Receivable—Lesley Mann, 13; Inventory, 14; Note Payable—Bank of British Columbia, 22; Sales Revenue, 41; Sales Discounts, 42; Interest Revenue, 46; and Cost of Goods Sold, 51. Insert Bal. in the posting reference column (Jrnl. Ref.) for each February 28 account balance.

4. Show that the total of the balances in the subsidiary ledger equals the general ledger balance in Accounts Receivable.

Solution to Review Problem

Requirements 1 and 2

Cash Receipts Journal   Page 7

| | Debits | | Credits | | | | | Cost of Goods Sold Dr. Inventory Cr. |
| | Cash | Sales Discounts | Accounts Receivable | Sales Revenue | Other Accounts | | | |
Date					Account Title	Post. Ref.	Amount	
Mar. 4	500			500				319
6	60	5	65		Brady Lee	✔		
9	1,080				Note Receivable			
					— Lesley Mann	13	1,000	
					Interest Revenue	46	80	
15	800			800				522
24	2,200				Note Payable—			
					Bank of			
					Nova Scotia	22	2,200	
27	1,200		1,200		Lance Au	✔		
31	5,840	5	1,265	1,300	Total		3,280	841
	(11)	(42)	(12)	(41)			(✔)	(51/14)

Total Dr. = 5,845   Total Cr. = 5,845

Requirement 3

Accounts Receivable Subsidiary Ledger
Lance Au

Date	Item	Jrnl. Ref.	Debit	Credit	Balance
Feb. 28		Bal.			1,840
Mar. 27		CR. 7		1,200	640

Melinda Fultz

Date	Item	Jrnl. Ref.	Debit	Credit	Balance
Feb. 28		Bal.			885

Brady Lee

Date	Item	Jrnl. Ref.	Debit	Credit	Balance
Feb. 28		Bal.			65
Mar. 6		CR. 7		65	—

General Ledger
Cash — No. 11

Date	Item	Jrnl. Ref.	Debit	Credit	Debit Balance
Feb. 28		Bal.			1,117
Mar. 31		CR. 7	5,840		6,957

Accounts Receivable — No. 12

Date	Item	Jrnl. Ref.	Debit	Credit	Debit Balance
Feb. 28		Bal.			2,790
Mar. 31		CR. 7		1,265	1,525

Note Receivable—Lesley Mann — No. 13

Date	Item	Jrnl. Ref.	Debit	Credit	Debit Balance
Feb. 28		Bal.			1,000
Mar. 9		CR. 7		1,000	—

Inventory — No. 14

Date	Item	Jrnl. Ref.	Debit	Credit	Balance
Mar. 31		Bal.			1,819
31		CR.7		841	978

Note Payable—Bank of Nova Scotia — No. 22

Date	Item	Jrnl. Ref.	Debit	Credit	Credit Balance
Mar. 24		CR. 7		2,200	2,200

Sales Revenue — No. 41

Date	Item	Jrnl. Ref.	Debit	Credit	Credit Balance
Mar. 31		CR. 7		1,300	1,300

Sales Discounts — No. 42

Date	Item	Jrnl. Ref.	Debit	Credit	Debit Balance
Mar. 31		CR. 7	5		5

Interest Revenue — No. 46

Date	Item	Jrnl. Ref.	Debit	Credit	Credit Balance
Mar. 9		CR. 7		80	80

Cost of Goods Sold — No. 51

Date	Item	Jrnl. Ref.	Debit	Credit	Debit Balance
Mar. 31		CR. 7	841		841

Requirement 4

General Ledger	
Accounts Receivable debit balance..................................	$1,525

Accounts Receivable Subsidiary Ledger: Customer Accounts Receivable	
Customer	**Balance**
Lance Au...	$ 640
Melinda Fultz..	885
Total accounts receivable....................................	$1,525

Note: If Riggs Company had used the periodic inventory system, account No. 51, Cost of Goods Sold, would not exist, so there would be no Cost of Goods Sold column in the cash receipts journal. As well, there would be no $841 credit posting to Inventory.

Cyber Coach

Visit the Student Resource area of the *Accounting* Companion Website for extra practice with the new material in Chapter 6.

www.pearsoned.ca/horngren

Summary

1. **Describe the features of an effective accounting information system.** An effective *accounting information system* captures and summarizes transactions quickly, accurately, and usefully. The four major aspects of a good accounting system are (1) control over operations, (2) compatibility with the particular features of the business, (3) flexibility in response to changes in the business, (4) a favourable cost/benefit relationship, with benefits outweighing costs.

2. **Understand how computerized and manual accounting systems work.** Computerized accounting systems process inputs faster than do manual systems and can generate more types of reports. The key components of a computerized accounting system are *hardware, software*, and *company personnel*. Account numbers play a bigger role in the operation of computerized systems than they do in manual systems, because computers classify accounts by account numbers. Both computerized and manual accounting systems require transactions to be classified by type.

    Computerized systems use a *menu* structure to organize accounting functions. Posting, trial balances, financial statements, and closing procedures are usually carried out automatically in a computerized accounting system. Computerized accounting systems are integrated so that the different *modules* of the system are updated together.

3. **Understand how spreadsheets are used in accounting.**

Spreadsheets are electronic work sheets whose grid points, or cells, are linked by means of formulas. The numerical relationships in the spreadsheet are maintained whenever changes are made to the spreadsheet. Spreadsheets are ideally suited to detailed computations, as in budgeting.

4. **Use the sales journal, the cash receipts journal, and the accounts receivable subsidiary ledger.** Many accounting systems use *special journals* to record transactions by category. Credit sales are recorded in a *sales journal*, and cash receipts in a *cash receipts journal*. Posting from these journals is to the *general ledger* and from the sales journal to the accounts receivable *subsidiary ledger*, which lists each customer and the amount receivable from that customer. The accounts receivable subsidiary ledger is the main device for ensuring that the company collects from customers.

5. **Use the purchases journal, the cash payments journal, and the accounts payable subsidiary ledger.** Credit purchases are recorded in a *purchases journal*, and cash payments in a *cash payments journal*. Posting from these journals is to the general ledger and to the accounts payable subsidiary ledger. The accounts payable subsidiary ledger helps the company stay current in payments to suppliers and take advantage of purchase discounts.

Self-Study Questions

Test your understanding of the chapter by marking the correct answer for each of the following questions:

1. Why does a jewellery store need an accounting system different from that which a physician uses? (*p. 293*)
   a. They have different kinds of employees.
   b. They have different kinds of journals and ledgers.
   c. They have different kinds of business transactions.
   d. They work different hours.

2. Which feature of an effective information system is most concerned with safeguarding assets? (*p. 293*)
   a. Control
   b. Compatibility
   c. Flexibility
   d. Favourable cost/benefit relationship

3. The account number 211031 most likely refers to (*p. 297*)
   a. Liabilities
   b. Current liabilities
   c. Accounts payable
   d. An individual vendor

4. If the amount of total revenues is in cell E7 of a spreadsheet and the amount for total expenses is in cell E20, then net income would be computed by the formula (*p. 300*)
   a. =E7+E20
   b. =E7–E20
   c. =E20–E7
   d. None of the above formulas will work

5. Special journals help most by (*p. 301*)
   a. Limiting the number of transactions that have to be recorded
   b. Reducing the cost of operating the accounting system
   c. Improving accuracy in posting to subsidiary ledgers
   d. Easing the preparation of the financial statements

6. Galvan Company recorded 523 credit sale transactions in the sales journal. Ignoring Cost of Goods Sold and Inventory, how many postings would be required if these transactions were recorded in the general journal? (*p. 305*)
   a. 523
   b. 1,046
   c. 1,569
   d. 2,092

7. Which two dollar-amount columns in the cash receipts journal will be used the most by a department store that makes half of its sales for cash and half on credit? (*pp. 306–307*)
   a. Cash Debit and Sales Discounts Debit
   b. Cash Debit and Accounts Receivable Credit
   c. Cash Debit and Other Accounts Credit
   d. Accounts Receivable Debit and Sales Revenue Credit

8. Entries in the purchases journal are posted to the (*pp. 308–310*)
   a. General ledger only
   b. General ledger and the accounts payable subsidiary ledger
   c. General ledger and the accounts receivable subsidiary ledger
   d. Accounts receivable subsidiary ledger and the accounts payable subsidiary ledger

9. Every entry in the cash payments journal includes a (*pp. 310–312*)
   a. Debit to Accounts Payable
   b. Debit to an Other Account
   c. Credit to Inventory
   d. Credit to Cash

10. Balancing the ledgers at the end of the period is most closely related to (*p. 314*)
    a. Control
    b. Compatibility
    c. Flexibility
    d. Favourable cost/benefit relationship

Answers to the Self-Study Questions follow the Similar Accounting Terms.

Accounting Vocabulary

Accounting information system (*p. 293*)
Batch processing (*p. 298*)
Cash payments journal (*p. 310*)
Cash receipts journal (*p. 306*)
Control account (*p. 305*)
Credit memorandum or credit memo (*p. 313*)
Database (*p. 294*)
Debit memorandum or debit memo (*p. 314*)
General journal (*p. 301*)
General ledger (*p. 304*)
Hardware (*p. 294*)
Menu (*p. 297*)

Module (*p. 300*)
Network (*p. 294*)
On-line processing (*p. 298*)
Purchases journal (*p. 308*)
Real-time processing (*p. 298*)
Sales journal (*p. 302*)
Server (*p. 294*)
Software (*p. 294*)
Special journal (*p. 301*)
Spreadsheet (*p. 300*)
Subsidiary ledger (*p. 304*)

Similar Accounting Terms

Accounts payable subsidiary ledger	Accounts payable ledger
Accounts receivable subsidiary ledger	Accounts receivable ledger
Balancing the ledgers	Proving the ledgers, reconciling the ledgers
Cash payments journal	Cash disbursements journal
Credit memorandum	Credit memo
Database	Management information system
Debit memorandum	Debit memo
On-line processing	Real-time processing

Assignment Material

Questions

1. Describe the four criteria of an effective accounting system.

2. Distinguish batch computer processing from online computer processing.

3. What accounting categories correspond to the account numbers 1, 2, 3, 4, and 5 in the chart of accounts in a typical computerized accounting system?

4. Why might the number 112 be assigned to Accounts Receivable and the number 1120708 to Carl Erickson, a customer?

5. Describe the function of menus in a computerized accounting system.

6. How do formulas in spreadsheets speed the process of budget preparation and revision?

7. Name four special journals used in accounting systems. For what type of transaction is each designed?

8. Describe the two advantages that special journals have over recording all transactions in the general journal.

9. What is a control account, and how is it related to a subsidiary ledger? Name two common control accounts.

10. Graff Company's sales journal has one amount column headed Accounts Receivable Dr. and Sales Revenue Cr. In this journal, 86 transactions are recorded. How many posting references appear in the journal? State what each posting reference represents.

11. The accountant for Bannister Co. posted all amounts correctly from the cash receipts journal to the general ledger. However, she failed to post three credits to customer accounts in the accounts receivable subsidiary ledger. How would this error be detected?

12. At what two times is posting done from a special journal? What items are posted at each time?

13. Describe two ways to account for sales tax collected from customers.

14. What is the purpose of balancing the ledgers?

15. Posting from the journals of McKedrick Realty is complete. But the total of the individual balances in the accounts payable subsidiary ledger does not equal the balance in the Accounts Payable control account in the general ledger. Does this necessarily indicate that the trial balance is out of balance? Explain.

16. Assume that posting is completed. The trial balance shows no errors, but the sum of the individual accounts payable does not equal the Accounts Payable control balance in the general ledger. What two errors could cause this problem?

Exercises

Exercise 6-1 *Features of an effective information system (Obj. 1)*

Suppose you have just invested your life savings in a company that prints rubber-ized logos on T-shirts. The business is growing fast, and you need a better ac-counting information system. Consider the features of an effective system, as discussed on pages 293–294. Which features do you regard as most important? Why? Which feature must you consider if your financial resources are limited?

Exercise 6-2 *Assigning account numbers (Obj. 2)*

Assign account numbers (from the list that follows) to the accounts of LP Gas Co. Identify the headings, which are *not* accounts and would not be assigned an ac-count number.

Assets	Capital
Current Assets	Withdrawals
Capital Assets	Revenues
Accounts Payable	Selling Expenses

Numbers from which to choose:

1	12	32
2	16	33
3	17	53
4	21	121
5	28	131
11	31	411

Exercise 6-3 *Setting up a chart of accounts (Obj. 2)*

Use account numbers 11 through 16, 21, 22, 31, 32, 41, 51, and 52 to correspond to the following selected accounts from the general ledger of Mountainview Gift Shop. List the accounts and their account numbers in proper order, starting with the most liquid current asset.

Capital	Amortization expense
Cost of goods sold	Cash
Accounts payable	Withdrawals
Inventory	Prepaid insurance
Sales revenue	Accumulated amortization
Store fixtures	Accounts receivable
Note payable, long-term	

Exercise 6-4 *Using a trial balance (Obj. 2)*

The following accounts and sums of accounts in the computerized accounting system of Daxton Supplies show some of the company's adjusted balances before closing:

Total assets	?
Current assets	11,200
Capital assets	26,800
Total liabilities	?
Current liabilities	2,200
Long-term liabilities	?
Capital	27,200
Withdrawals	10,000
Total revenues	36,000
Total expenses	22,000

Compute the missing amounts.

Exercise 6-5   Using a spreadsheet to compute amortization *(Obj. 3)*

A capital asset listed on a spreadsheet has a cost of $60,000; this amount is located in cell E7. The number of years of the asset's useful life is found in cell E9. Write the spreadsheet formula to express annual amortization expense for this asset. Assume the value at the end of the useful life will be zero.

Exercise 6-6   Using a spreadsheet *(Obj. 3)*

Refer to the spreadsheet screen in Exhibit 6-7, page 300. Suppose cells B1 through B4 are your business's actual income statement for the current year. You wish to develop your financial plan for the coming year. Assume that you expect revenues to increase by 10 percent and expenses to increase by 8 percent. Write the formulas in cells C2 through C4 to compute the amounts of expected revenues, expenses, and net income for the coming year.

Exercise 6-7   Computing financial statement amounts with a spreadsheet *(Obj. 3)*

Suppose the values of the following items are stored in the cells of Joe's Photos Co.'s spreadsheet:

Item	Cell
Total assets	E7
Current assets	E8
Capital assets	E9
Total liabilities	E10
Current liabilities	E11
Long-term liabilities	E12

Write the spreadsheet formula to calculate the store's:

a. Current ratio
b. Total owner's equity
c. Debt ratio

Exercise 6-8   Using the sales and cash receipts journals (perpetual inventory system) *(Obj. 4)*

The sales and cash receipts journals of Super Stereo include the following entries:

Sales Journal

Date	Invoice No.	Account Debited	Post. Ref.	Accounts Receivable Dr. Sales Revenue Cr.	Cost of Goods Sold Dr. Inventory Cr.
Oct. 7	671	C. Carlson	✔	1,395	825
10	672	T. Choi	✔	5,700	2,955
10	673	E. Lovell	✔	1,035	615
12	674	B. Goebel	✔	8,205	5,010
31		Total		16,335	9,405

Cash Receipts Journal

Date	Cash	Sales Discounts	Accounts Receivable	Sales Revenue	Account Title	Post. Ref.	Amount	Cost of Goods Sold Dr. Inventory Cr.
		Debits		**Credits**		**Other Accounts**		
Oct. 16					C. Carlson	✔		
19					E. Lovell	✔		
24	450			450				270
30					T. Choi	✔		

Super Stereo makes all sales on credit terms of 2/10 n/30. Complete the cash receipts journal for those transactions indicated. Also, total the journal and show that total debits equal total credits. Each cash receipt was for the full amount of the receivable.

Exercise 6-9 *Classifying postings from the cash receipts journal* **(Obj. 4)**

The cash receipts journal of Ice-Level Sports follows:

Cash Receipts Journal   Page 7

Date	Cash	Sales Discounts	Accounts Receivable	Sales Revenue	Account Title	Post. Ref.	Amount
	Debits			**Credits**		**Other Accounts**	
Dec. 2	1,588	32	1,620		Magna Corp.	(a)	
9	491		491		Kamm, Inc.	(b)	
14	3,904			3,904			
19	6,480				Note Receivable	(c)	6,000
					Interest Revenue	(d)	480
30	314	7	321		J. T. Kazarian	(e)	
31	4,235			4,235			
31	17,012	39	2,432	8,139	Totals		6,480
	(f)	(g)	(h)	(i)			(j)

Ice-Level Sport's chart of accounts (general ledger) includes the following selected accounts, along with their account numbers:

Number	Account	Number	Account
111	Cash	511	Sales revenue
112	Accounts receivable	512	Sales discounts
113	Note receivable	513	Sales returns
119	Land	521	Interest revenue

Required

Indicate whether each posting reference (a) through (j) should be a

- Check mark (✓) for a posting to a customer account in the accounts receivable subsidiary ledger.
- Account number for a posting to an account in the general ledger. If so, give the account number.
- Letter (x) for an amount not posted.

Exercise 6-10 *Identifying transactions from postings to the accounts receivable ledger* (*Obj. 4*)

An account in the accounts receivable subsidiary ledger of Battle River Office Supplies follows:

Lumby Lumber Inc.   112590

Date		Jrnl. Ref.	Dr.	Cr.	Debit Balance
May 1	....				806
6	....	S.5	2,360		3,166
19	....	J.8		382	2,784
21	....	CR.9		1,406	1,378

Required

Describe the three posted transactions.

Exercise 6-11 *Recording purchase transactions in the general journal and purchases journal* (*Obj. 5*)

During June, Max's Bakery completed the following credit purchase transactions:

June   4   Purchased inventory, $3,808, from McGraw Ltd. Max's Bakery uses a perpetual inventory system.
  7   Purchased supplies, $214, from Maine Co.
  19   Purchased equipment, $3,500, from Liston-Fry Corp.
  27   Purchased inventory, $4,420, from Milan, Inc.

Record these transactions first in the general journal—with explanations—and then in the purchases journal. Omit credit terms and posting references. Which procedure for recording transactions is quicker? Why?

Exercise 6-12 *Posting from the purchases journal; balancing the ledgers* (*Obj. 5*)

The purchases journal of Westboard Wave follows:

Purchases Journal   Page 7

								Other Accounts Dr.		
Date	Account Credited	Terms	Post. Ref.	Accounts Payable Cr.	Inventory Dr.	Supplies Dr.	Acct. Title	Post. Ref.	Amt. Dr.
Sept. 2	Brotherton, Inc.	n/30		2,600	2,600				
5	Rolf Office Supply	n/30		350		350			
13	Brotherton, Inc.	2/10 n/30		1,694	1,694				
26	Marks Equipment Company	n/30		1,832			Equipment		1,832
30	Totals			6,476	4,294	350			1,832

Required

1. Open general ledger accounts for Inventory, Supplies, Equipment, and Accounts Payable. Post to these accounts from the purchases journal. Use dates and posting references in the ledger accounts.

2. Open accounts in the accounts payable subsidiary ledger for Brotherton, Inc., Rolf Office Supply, and Marks Equipment Company. Post from the purchases journal. Use dates and journal references in the ledger accounts.

3. Balance the Accounts Payable control account in the general ledger with the total of the balances in the accounts payable subsidiary ledger.

4. Does Westboard Wave use a perpetual or a periodic inventory system?

Exercise 6-13 *Using the cash payments journal* **(Obj. 5)**

During February, McCoy Products had the following transactions:

Feb. 3 Paid $1,350 on account to Marquis Corp. net of a $12 discount for an earlier purchase of inventory.

6 Purchased inventory for cash, $1,900.

11 Paid $575 for supplies.

15 Purchased inventory on credit from Monroe Corporation, $774.

16 Paid $12,093 on account to LaGrange Ltd.; there was no discount.

21 Purchased furniture for cash, $1,440.

26 Paid $5,865 on account to Graff Software Ltd. for an earlier purchase of inventory. The purchase discount was $135.

28 Made a semiannual interest payment of $1,200 on a long-term note payable. The entire payment was for interest. (Assume none of the interest had been accrued previously.)

Required

1. Draw a cash payments journal similar to the one illustrated in this chapter. Omit the payee column.

2. Record the transactions in the journal. Which transaction should not be recorded in the cash payments journal? In what journal does it belong?

3. Total the amount columns of the journal. Determine that the total debits equal the total credits.

Exercise 6-14 *Using business documents to record transactions* **(Obj. 5)**

Link Back to Chapter 5 (Recording Purchases, Sales, and Returns). The following documents describe two business transactions:

Invoice		
Date: March 14, 2003		
Sold to: Eddie's Bicycle Shop		
Sold by: Schwinn Company		
Terms: 2/10 n/30		
Items Purchased Bicycles		
Quantity	Price	Total
8	$95	$760
2	70	140
10	60	600
Total $1,500		

Debit Memo		
Date: March 20, 2003		
Issued to: Schwinn Company		
Issued by: Eddie's Bicycle Shop		
Items Returneed Bicycles		
Quantity	Price	Total
2	$95	$190
2	70	140
Total $330		
Reason: Damaged in shipment		

Use the general journal to record these transactions and Eddie's Bicycle Shop's cash payment on March 21. Record the transactions first on the books of Eddie's Bicycle

Shop and, second, on the books of Schwinn Company, which makes and sells bicycles. Both Eddie's Bicycle Shop and Schwinn Company use a perpetual system as illustrated in Chapter 5. Schwinn Company's cost of the bicycles sold to Eddie's Bicycle Shop was $800. Schwinn Company's cost of the returned merchandise was $160. Round to the nearest dollar. Explanations are not required. Using the perpetual system of inventory, set up your answer in the following format:

Date	Eddie's Bicycle Shop Journal Entries	Schwinn Journal Entries

Challenge Exercise

Exercise 6-15   *Using the special journals* *(Obj. 4, 5)*

Link Back to Chapter 5 (Cost of goods sold, gross margin).

1. Austin Sound Centre's special journals in Exhibits 6-10 through 6-13 (pages 303–311) provide the manager with much of the data needed for preparation of the financial statements. Austin Sound uses the *perpetual* inventory system, so the amount of cost of goods sold is simply the ending balance in that account. The manager needs to know the business's gross margin for November. Compute the gross margin.

2. Suppose Austin Sound used the *periodic* inventory system. In that case, the business must compute cost of goods sold by the formula:

Cost of goods sold:
Beginning inventory	$	X*
+ Net purchases		XXX
= Cost of goods available for sale		X,XXX
− Ending inventory		(XX)
= Cost of goods sold	$	XX

*$0 for Austin Sound at November 1.

Perform this calculation of cost of goods sold for Austin Sound. Does this computation of cost of goods sold agree with your answer to requirement 1?

Beyond the Numbers

Beyond the Numbers 6-1   *Designing a special journal* *(Obj. 4, 5)*

Monarch Technology Associates creates and sells cutting-edge network software. Monarch's quality control officer estimates that 20 percent of the company's sales and purchases of inventory are returned for additional debugging. Monarch needs special journals for

- Sales returns and allowances
- Purchase returns and allowances

Required

1. Design the two special journals. For each journal, include a column for the appropriate business document.

2. Enter one transaction in each journal, using the Austin Sound transaction data illustrated on pages 313 and 314. Show all posting references, including those for column totals. In the purchase returns and allowances journal, assume debit memo number 14.

Ethical Issue

On a recent trip to Brazil, Carlo Degas, sales manager of Cyber Systems, took his wife along for a vacation and included her airfare and meals on his expense report, which he submitted for reimbursement. Chelsea Brindley, vice-president of sales and Degas' boss, thought his total travel and entertainment expenses seemed excessive. However, Brindley approved the reimbursement because she owed Degas a favour. Brindley, well aware that the company president routinely reviewed all expenses recorded in the cash payments journal, had the accountant record the expenses of Degas' wife in the general journal as follows:

Sales Promotion Expense	5,000	
Cash		5,000

Required

1. Does recording the transaction in the general journal rather than in the cash payments journal affect the amounts of cash and total expenses reported in the financial statements?

2. Why did Ms. Brindley want this transaction recorded in the general journal?

3. What is the ethical issue in this situation? What role does accounting play in the ethical issue?

Problems (Group A)

Problem 6-1A   *Using a spreadsheet to prepare an income statement and evaluate operations (Obj. 3)*

The following spreadsheet shows the income statement of Kirkham Wholesalers.

	A	B
5	Revenues:	
6	Service revenue	
7	Rent revenue	
8		————
9	Total revenue	
10		
11	Expenses	
12	Salary expense	
13	Supplies expense	
14	Rent expense	
15	Amortization expense	
16		————
17	Total expenses	
18		————
19	Net income	
20		════

Required

1. Write the word *number* in the cells (indicated by colour) where numbers will be entered.

2. Write the appropriate formula in each cell that will need a formula. Symbols from which to choose are:

```
+        add
−        subtract
*        multiply
/        divide
=SUM(beginning cell:ending cell)
```

3. Last year Kirkham Wholesalers used this spreadsheet to prepare the company's budgeted income statement—which shows the company's net income goal—for the current year. It is now one year later, and Kirkham has prepared its actual income statement for the year. State how the owner of the company can use this income statement in decision making.

Problem 6-2A *Using the sales, cash receipts, and general journals (with the perpetual inventory system)* **(Obj. 4)**

The general ledger of Raffan Distributors includes the following accounts, among others:

Cash	11	Sales Revenue	41
Accounts Receivable	12	Sales Discounts	42
Inventory	13	Sales Returns and Allowances	43
Notes Receivable	15	Interest Revenue	47
Supplies	16	Cost of Goods Sold	51
Land	18		

All credit sales are on the company's standard terms of 2/10 n/30. Transactions in May that affected sales and cash receipts were as follows:

May 2 Sold inventory on credit to Fortin Inc., $1,400. Raffan's cost of these goods was $800.
　　 4 As a favour to a competitor, sold supplies at cost, $170, receiving cash.
　　 7 Cash sales of merchandise for the week totalled $3,780 (cost, $3,280).
　　 9 Sold merchandise on account to A. L. Price, $14,640 (cost, $10,220).
　　 10 Sold land that cost $20,000 for cash of $20,000.
　　 11 Sold goods on account to Sloan Forge Ltd., $10,208 (cost, $7,040).
　　 12 Received cash from Fortin Inc. in full settlement of its account receivable from May 2.
　　 14 Cash sales of merchandise for the week were $4,212 (cost, $3,060).
　　 15 Sold inventory on credit to the partnership of Wilkie & Blinn, $7,300 (cost, $4,520).
　　 18 Received inventory sold on May 9 to A. L. Price for $1,200. The goods shipped were the wrong size. These goods cost Raffan $880.
　　 20 Sold merchandise on account to Sloan Forge Ltd., $1,258 (cost, $900).
　　 21 Cash sales of merchandise for the week were $1,980 (cost, $1,380).
　　 22 Received $8,000 cash from A. L. Price in partial settlement of his account receivable.
　　 25 Received cash from Wilkie & Blinn for its account receivable from May 15.
　　 25 Sold goods on account to Olsen, Inc., $3,040 (cost, $2,100).
　　 27 Collected $10,250 on a note receivable, of which $250 was interest.
　　 28 Cash sales of merchandise for the week were $7,548 (cost, $4,920).
　　 29 Sold inventory on account to R. O. Bankston Inc., $484 (cost, $340).
　　 30 Received goods sold on May 25 to Olsen, Inc. for $80. The wrong items were shipped. The cost of the goods was $50.
　　 31 Received $5,440 cash on account from A. L. Price.

Required

1. Raffan Distributors records sales returns and allowances in the general journal. Use the appropriate journal to record the above transactions in a sales journal (omit the Invoice No. column), a cash receipts journal, and a general journal.

2. Total each column of the cash receipts journal. Show that the total debits equal the total credits.

3. Show how postings would be made from the journals by writing the account numbers and check marks in the appropriate places in the journals.

Problem 6-3A *Correcting errors in the cash receipts journal (perpetual inventory system)* **(Obj. 4)**

The cash receipts journal below contains five entries. All five entries are for legitimate cash receipt transactions, but the journal contains some errors in recording the transactions. In fact, only one entry is correct, and each of the other four entries contains one error.

Cash Receipts Journal — Page 22

Date	Cash (Debits)	Sales Discounts (Debits)	Accounts Receivable (Credits)	Sales Revenue (Credits)	Account Title (Other Accounts)	Post. Ref.	Amount	Cost of Goods Sold Dr. Inventory Cr.
May 6		300		300				145
7	429	22			Marc Fortin	✔	451	
14	4,100				Note Receivable	13	3,850	
					Interest Revenue	45	250	
18				330				150
24	1,100		770					
	5,629	322	770	630	Totals		4,551	295
	(11)	(42)	(12)	(41)			(✔)	51/13

Total Dr. = $5,951   Total Cr. = $5,951

Required

1. Identify the correct entry.
2. Identify the error in each of the other four entries.
3. Using the following format, prepare a corrected cash receipts journal.

Cash Receipts Journal — Page 22

Date	Cash (Debits)	Sales Discounts (Debits)	Accounts Receivable (Credits)	Sales Revenue (Credits)	Account Title (Other Accounts)	Post. Ref.	Amount	Cost of Goods Sold Dr. Inventory Cr.
May 6								
7					Marc Fortin	✔		
14					Note Receivable	13		
					Interest Revenue	45		
18								
24								
	5,929	22	1,221	630	Totals		4,100	
	(11)	(42)	(12)	(41)			(✔)	

Total Dr. = $5,951   Total Cr. = $5,951

Problem 6-4A   *Using the purchases, cash payments, and general journals* **(Obj. 5)**

The general ledger of Suto Supplies includes the following accounts:

Cash	111	Furniture	187
Inventory	131	Accounts Payable	211
Prepaid Insurance	161	Rent Expense	564
Supplies	171	Utilities Expense	583

Transactions in August that affected purchases and cash payments were as follows:

Aug. 1 Purchased inventory on credit from Worth Corp., $3,800. Terms were 2/10 n/30.
1 Paid monthly rent, debiting Rent Expense for $4,000.
5 Purchased supplies on credit terms of 2/10 n/30 from Ross Supply Ltd., $900.
8 Paid electricity bill, $600.
9 Purchased furniture on account from Rite Office Supply, $8,200. Payment terms were net 30.
10 Returned the furniture to Rite Office Supply. It was the wrong colour.
11 Paid Worth Corp. the amount owed on the purchase of August 1.
12 Purchased inventory on account from Wynne, Inc., $8,800. Terms were 3/10 n/30.
13 Purchased inventory for cash, $1,310.
14 Paid a semiannual insurance premium, debiting Prepaid Insurance, $1,200.
15 Paid the account payable to Ross Supply Ltd., from August 5.
18 Paid gas and water bills, $200.
21 Purchased inventory on credit terms of 1/10 n/45 from Cyber Software, Ltd., $10,400.
21 Paid account payable to Wynne, Inc., from August 12.
22 Purchased supplies on account from Favron Sales, $548. Terms were net 30.
25 Returned $2,400 of the inventory purchased on August 21 to Cyber Software, Ltd.
31 Paid Cyber Software, Ltd. the net amount owed from August 21.

Required

1. Suto Supplies records purchase returns in the general journal. Use the appropriate journal to record the above transactions in a purchases journal, a cash payments journal (omit the Cheque No. column), and a general journal.

2. Total each column of the special journals. Show that the total debits equal the total credits in each special journal.

3. Show how postings would be made from the journals by writing the account numbers and check marks in the appropriate places in the journals.

Problem 6-5A   *Understanding how manual accounting systems are used; using the cash payments journal (perpetual inventory system)* **(Obj. 2, 4)**

Blue Quill Distributors had the following transactions for the month of April 2004:

April 1 Sold $1,000 of merchandise to James Inc., terms 2/10 n/30. Inventory had a cost of $445.

3 Purchased $9,500, of merchandise from MNO Suppliers Ltd., terms net 30.

6 Paid for the purchase of April 3 (MNO Suppliers Ltd.), cheque #12.

7 Paid $3,500 wages to employee, cheque #13.

9 Owner withdrew $5,000 for personal use, cheque #14.

11 Collected $490 from James Inc. (April 1) with the discount allowed and issued a credit memo for $250 allowance for damaged merchandise.

13 Purchased equipment from MB Machinery Ltd., $7,500, terms 2/10 n/30.

14 Issued a debit memo to MB Machinery Ltd. (April 13) for $500 of equipment returned as defective.

15 Sold $4,000 of merchandise to St. Boniface Supply Corp., receiving $500 and a promise to pay the balance in 30 days. Inventory cost, $2,500.

April 16 Paid the account owing to MB Machinery Ltd., cheque #15.

17 Purchased $12,500 of equipment from Dearing Equipment Inc., terms net 60.

22 Paid a $3,000 note due to the Commercial Bank, plus interest of $300, cheque #16.

24 Sold $750 of merchandise for cash; inventory cost was $500.

25 Paid $500 to Canada Customs and Revenue Agency for income taxes owing from December 31, 2003, cheque #17.

26 Returned $1,500 of the merchandise purchased from MNO Suppliers Ltd.

28 Purchased inventory for $2,000 from Artois Ltd., paying $500 down (cheque #18) and promising to pay the balance in 30 days.

30 Recorded the adjusting journal entries for the month of April.

Required

1. Indicate which journal would be used to record each of the transactions assuming Blue Quill Distributors uses a general journal, a sales journal, a cash receipts journal, a purchases journal, and a cash payments journal.

2. Record the appropriate transactions in the cash payments journal, using the cash payments journal format shown in this chapter.

3. Show how postings would be made from the cash payments journal by writing the account numbers and check marks in the appropriate place in the cash payments journal. Select your own three-digit account numbers.

Problem 6-6A *Using all the journals, posting, and balancing the ledgers* *(Obj. 4, 5)*

Lang Wholesaling, which uses the perpetual inventory system and makes all credit sales on terms of 2/10 n/30, completed the following transactions during July:

July 2 Issued invoice no. 913 for sale on account to N. J. Seiko Inc., $8,200. Lang's cost of this inventory was $3,600.

3 Purchased inventory on credit terms of 3/10 n/60 from Chicosky Corp., $4,934.

5 Sold inventory for cash, $2,154 (cost, $960).

5 Issued cheque no. 532 to purchase furniture for cash, $4,370.

8 Collected interest revenue of $3,550.

9 Issued invoice no. 914 for sale on account to Bell Ltd., $11,100 (cost, $4,620).

10 Purchased inventory for cash, $2,286, issuing cheque no. 533.

12 Received cash from N. J. Seiko Inc. in full settlement of its account receivable from the sale on July 2.

13 Issued cheque no. 534 to pay Chicosky Corp. the net amount owed from July 3. (Round to the nearest dollar.)

13 Purchased supplies on account from Manley, Inc., $882. Terms were net end of month.

15 Sold inventory on account to M. O. Brown, issuing invoice no. 915 for $1,330 (cost, $480).

17 Issued credit memo to M. O. Brown for $1,330 for merchandise sent in error and returned by Brown. Also accounted for receipt of the inventory.

18 Issued invoice no. 916 for credit sale to N. J. Seiko Inc., $714 (cost, $254).

19 Received $10,878 from Bell Ltd. in full settlement of its account receivable from July 9.

20 Purchased inventory on credit terms of net 30 from Sims Distributing Ltd., $4,094.

22 Purchased furniture on credit terms of 3/10 n/60 from Chicosky Corp., $1,290.

22 Issued cheque no. 535 to pay for insurance coverage, debiting Prepaid Insurance for $2,000.

24 Sold supplies to an employee for cash of $108, which was the cost of the supplies.

25 Issued cheque no. 536 to pay utilities, $906.

28 Purchased inventory on credit terms of 2/10 n/30 from Manley, Inc., $1,350.

29 Returned damaged inventory to Manley, Inc., issuing a debit memo for $1,350.

29 Sold goods on account to Bell Ltd., issuing invoice no. 917 for $992 (cost, $440).

30 Issued cheque no. 537 to pay Manley, Inc. in full on account from July 13.

July 31 Received cash in full on account from N. J. Seiko Inc.
31 Issued cheque no. 538 to pay monthly salaries of $4,694.

Required

1. For Lang Wholesaling, open the following general ledger accounts using the account numbers given:

Cash	111	Sales Revenue	411
Accounts Receivable	112	Sales Discounts	412
Supplies	116	Sales Returns and Allowances	413
Prepaid Insurance	117	Interest Revenue	419
Inventory	118	Cost of Goods Sold	511
Furniture	151	Salary Expense	531
Accounts Payable	211	Utilities Expense	541

2. Open these accounts in the subsidiary ledgers: Accounts receivable subsidiary ledger—Bell Ltd., M. O. Brown, and N. J. Seiko Inc.; accounts payable subsidiary ledger—Chicosky Corp., Manley, Inc., and Sims Distributing Ltd.

3. Enter the transactions in a sales journal (page 7), a cash receipts journal (page 5), a purchases journal (page 10), a cash payments journal (page 8), and a general journal (page 6), as appropriate.

4. Post daily to the accounts receivable subsidiary ledger and to the accounts payable subsidiary ledger. On July 31, post to the general ledger.

5. Total each column of the special journals. Show that the total debits equal the total credits in each special journal.

6. Balance the total of the customer account balances in the accounts receivable subsidiary ledger against Accounts Receivable in the general ledger. Do the same for the accounts payable subsidiary ledger and Accounts Payable in the general ledger.

Problems (Group B)

Problem 6-1B *Using a spreadsheet to prepare a partial balance sheet and evaluate financial positions* **(Obj. 3)**

The spreadsheet below shows the assets section of the Compu Products balance sheet:

	A	B
5	Assets:	
6	Current assets:	
7	Cash	
8	Receivables	
9	Inventory	
10		
11	Total current assets	
12		
13	Equipment	
14	Accumulated amortization	
15		
16	Equipment, net	
17		
18	Total assets	
19		

Required

1. Write the word *number* in the cells (indicated by colour) where numbers will be entered.

2. Write the appropriate formula in each cell that will need a formula. Symbols from which to choose are:

+	add	/	divide
–	subtract		=SUM(beginning cell:ending cell)
*	multiply		

3. Last year Compu Products used this spreadsheet to prepare the company's balance sheet for the current year. The budgeted balance sheet shows the company's goal for total current assets at the end of the year. It is now one year later, and Compu Products has prepared its actual year-end balance sheet. State how the company can use this balance sheet in decision making.

Problem 6-2B *Using the sales, cash receipts, and general journals (with the perpetual inventory system)* **(Obj. 4)**

The general ledger of Kravitz Systems Supply includes the following accounts:

Cash	111	Sales Revenue	411
Accounts Receivable........................	112	Sales Discounts	412
Notes Receivable.............................	115	Sales Returns and Allowances..........	413
Inventory...	131	Interest Revenue.................................	417
Equipment...	141	Gain on Sale of Land.........................	418
Land	142	Cost of Goods Sold............................	511

All credit sales are on the company's standard terms of 2/10 n/30. Transactions in February that affected sales and cash receipts were as follows:

Feb. 1 Sold inventory on credit to Ijiri Ltd., $2,000. Kravitz Systems Supply's cost of these goods was $1,114.

5 As a favour to another company, sold new equipment for its cost of $1,540, receiving cash in this amount.

6 Cash sales of merchandise for the week totalled $4,214 (cost, $2,724).

8 Sold merchandise on account to McNair Ltd., $5,560 (cost, $3,578).

9 Sold land that cost $22,000 for cash of $40,000.

11 Sold goods on account to Nickerson Builders Inc., $6,099 (cost, $3,853).

11 Received cash from Ijiri Ltd. in full settlement of its account receivable from February 1.

13 Cash sales of merchandise for the week were $3,990 (cost, $2,572).

15 Sold inventory on credit to Montez and Montez, a partnership, $1,600 (cost, $1,034).

18 Received inventory sold on February 8 to McNair Ltd. for $240. The goods shipped were the wrong colour. These goods cost Kravitz Systems Supply $146.

19 Sold merchandise on account to Nickerson Builders, $5,200 (cost, $3,927).

20 Cash sales of merchandise for the week were $4,660 (cost, $3,148).

21 Received $2,400 cash from McNair Ltd. in partial settlement of its account receivable.

22 Received payment in full from Montez and Montez for its account receivable from February 15.

22 Sold goods on account to Diamond, Inc., $4,044 (cost, $2,650).

25 Collected $4,200 on a note receivable, of which $200 was interest.

27 Cash sales of merchandise for the week totalled $4,455 (cost, $2,904).

27 Sold inventory on account to Littleton Corporation, $2,290 (cost, $1,434).

28 Received goods sold on February 22 to Diamond, Inc. for $1,360. The goods were shipped in error, so were returned to inventory. The cost of these goods was $960.

28 Received $3,020 cash on account from McNair Ltd.

Required

1. Use the appropriate journal to record the above transactions in a sales journal

(omit the Invoice No. column), a cash receipts journal, and a general journal. Kravitz Systems Supply records sales returns and allowances in the general journal.

2. Total each column of the cash receipts journal. Determine that the total debits equal the total credits.

3. Show how postings would be made from the journals by writing the account numbers and check marks in the appropriate places in the journals.

Problem 6-3B *Correcting errors in the cash receipts journal (perpetual inventory system)* **(Obj. 4)**

The Cash Receipts Journal (A) below contains five entries. All five entries are for legitimate cash receipt transactions, but the journal contains some errors in recording the transactions. In fact, only one entry is correct, and each of the other four entries contains one error.

(A)

Cash Receipts Journal Page 16

Date	Cash	Debits Sales Discounts	Accounts Receivable	Sales Revenue	Other Accounts Account Title	Post. Ref.	Amount	Cost of Goods Sold Dr. Inventory Cr.
Sept.								
3	1,422	68	1,490		Alcon Labs Ltd.	✔		
9			692	692	Carl Ryther	✔		
10	22,000			22,000	Land	19		
19	146							88
31	2,120			2,266				1,262
	25,688	68	2,182	24,958	Totals			1,350
	(11)	(42)	(12)	(41)			(✔)	51/13

Total Dr. = $25,756   Total Cr. = $27,140

(B)

Cash Receipts Journal Page 16

Date	Cash	Debits Sales Discounts	Accounts Receivable	Sales Revenue	Other Accounts Account Title	Post. Ref.	Amount	Cost of Goods Sold Dr. Inventory Cr.
Sept.								
3					Alcon Labs Ltd.	✔		
9					Carl Ryther	✔		
10					Land	19		
19								
31								
	26,380	68	2,182	2,266	Totals		22,000	
	(11)	(42)	(12)	(41)			(✔)	51/13

Total Dr. = $26,448   Total Cr. = $26,448

Required

1. Identify the correct entry in Cash Receipts Journal (A).

2. Identify the error in each of the other four entries in Cash Receipts Journal (A).

3. Using the Cash Receipts Journal (B) format, prepare a corrected cash receipts journal.

Problem 6-4B *Using the purchases, cash payments, and general journals* *(Obj. 5)*

The general ledger of Andino Luggage Company includes the following accounts:

Cash	111	Equipment	189
Inventory	131	Accounts Payable	211
Prepaid Insurance	161	Rent Expense	562
Supplies	171	Utilities Expense	565

Transactions in November that affected purchases and cash payments were as follows:

Nov.		
	1	Paid monthly rent, debiting Rent Expense for $675.
	3	Purchased inventory on credit from Sylvania Ltd., $1,000. Terms were 2/15 n/45.
	4	Purchased supplies on credit terms of 2/10 n/30 from Harmon Sales Ltd., $400.
	7	Paid gas and water bills, $203.
	10	Purchased equipment on account from Lancer Corp., $550. Payment terms were 2/10 n/30.
	11	Returned the equipment to Lancer Corp. It was defective.
	12	Paid Sylvania Ltd. the amount owed on the purchase of November 3.
	12	Purchased inventory on account from Lancer Corp., $550. Terms were 2/10 n/30.
	14	Purchased inventory for cash, $800.
	15	Paid an insurance premium, debiting Prepaid Insurance, $1,208.
	16	Paid the account payable to Harmon Sales Ltd. from November 4.
	17	Paid electricity bill, $100.
	20	Paid the November 12 account payable to Lancer Corp., less the purchase discount.
	21	Purchased supplies on account from Master Supply Ltd., $377, terms net 30.
	22	Purchased inventory on credit terms of 1/10 n/30 from Linz Brothers Inc., $1,700.
	26	Returned $250 of inventory purchased on November 22 to Linz Brothers Inc.
	30	Paid Linz Brothers Inc. the net amount owed.

Required

1. Use the appropriate journal to record the above transactions in a purchases journal, a cash payments journal (do not use the Ch. No. column), and a general journal. Andino Luggage Company records purchase returns in the general journal.

2. Total each column of the special journals. Show that the total debits equal the total credits in each special journal.

3. Show how postings would be made from the journals by writing the account numbers and check marks in the appropriate places in the journals.

Problem 6-5B *Understanding how manual accounting systems are used; using the cash payments journal (perpetual inventory system)* *(Obj. 2, 4)*

McKenzie Distributing had the following transactions for the month of June 2003:

June		
	1	Sold $4,000 of merchandise to Thoms Supply Ltd., terms 2/10 n/30. Inventory had a cost of $2,750.
	3	Purchased $3,000 of merchandise from STU Suppliers Inc., terms net 30.
	6	Paid for the purchase of June 3 (STU Suppliers Inc.), cheque #12.
	7	Paid $5,500 wages to employee, cheque #13.
	9	Owner withdrew $7,500 for personal use, cheque #14.
	11	Collected $980 from Thoms Supply Ltd. (June 1) with the discount allowed and issued a credit memo for $500 allowance for damaged merchandise.
	13	Purchased equipment from DE Machinery Inc., $5,000, terms 2/10 n/30.

June	14	Issued a debit memo to DE Machinery Inc. (June 13) for $1,000 of equipment returned as defective.
	15	Sold $2,500 of merchandise to DePloy Construction Ltd., receiving $1,000 and a promise to pay the balance in 30 days. Inventory had a cost of $1,500.
	16	Paid the account owing to DE Machinery Inc. (June 13, 14), cheque #15.
	17	Purchased $15,000 of equipment from Alfreds Equipment Inc., terms net 60.
	22	Paid a $5,000 note due to the Commercial Bank, plus interest of $500, cheque #16.
	24	Sold $1,750 of merchandise for cash; inventory cost was $1,000.
	25	Paid $750 to Canada Customs and Revenue Agency for income taxes owing for the year 2003, cheque #17.
	26	Returned $500 of the merchandise purchased from STU Suppliers Inc.
	28	Purchased inventory for $3,000 from Damon Ltd., paying $1,000 down (cheque #18) and promising to pay the balance in 30 days.
	30	Recorded the adjusting journal entries for the month of June.

Required

1. Indicate which journal would be used to record each of the transactions assuming McKenzie Distributing uses a general journal, a sales journal, a cash receipts journal, a purchases journal, and a cash payments journal.

2. Record the appropriate transactions in the cash payments journal, using the cash payments journal format shown in this chapter.

3. Show how postings would be made from the cash payments journal by writing the account numbers and check marks in the appropriate place in the cash payments journal. Select your own three-digit account numbers.

Problem 6-6B   *Using all the journals, posting, and balancing the ledgers*   *(Obj. 4, 5)*

King Sales Company, which uses the perpetual inventory system and makes all credit sales with terms 2/10 n/30, had these transactions during January:

Jan.	2	Issued invoice no. 191 for sale on account to Wooten Design Ltd., $4,700. King's cost of this inventory was $2,780.
	3	Purchased inventory on credit terms of 3/10 n/60 from Delwood Co., $11,800.
	4	Sold inventory for cash, $1,616 (cost, $1,020).
	5	Issued cheque no. 473 to purchase furniture for cash, $2,174.
	8	Collected interest revenue of $4,880.
	9	Issued invoice no. 192 for sale on account to Vachon Inc., $12,500 (cost, $6,600).
	10	Purchased inventory for cash, $1,552, issuing cheque no. 474.
	12	Received $4,606 cash from Wooten Design Ltd. in full settlement of its account receivable.
	13	Issued cheque no. 475 to pay Delwood Co. net amount owed from January 3.
	13	Purchased supplies on account from Havrilla Corp., $1,378. Terms were net end of month.
	15	Sold inventory on account to Wakeland Ltd., issuing invoice no. 193 for $1,486 (cost, $820).
	17	Issued credit memo to Wakeland Ltd. for $1,486 for merchandise sent in error and returned to King by Wakeland. Also accounted for receipt of the inventory.
	18	Issued invoice no. 194 for credit sale to Wooten Design Ltd., $3,650 (cost, $1,940).
	19	Received $12,250 from Vachon Inc. in full settlement of its account receivable from January 9.
	20	Purchased inventory on credit terms of net 30 from Jasper Sales Ltd., $4,300.
	22	Purchased furniture on credit terms of 3/10 n/60 from Delwood Co., $1,550.
	22	Issued cheque no. 476 to pay for insurance coverage, debiting Prepaid Insurance for $2,690.
	24	Sold supplies to an employee for cash of $172, which was the cost of the supplies.
	25	Issued cheque no. 477 to pay utilities, $776.
	28	Purchased inventory on credit terms of 2/10 n/30 from Havrilla Corp., $842.
	29	Returned damaged inventory to Havrilla Corp., issuing a debit memo for $842.

Jan. 29 Sold goods on account to Vachon Inc., issuing invoice no. 195 for $1,134 (cost, $628).

30 Issued cheque no. 478 to pay Havrilla Corp. on account from January 13.

31 Received cash in full on account from Wooten Design Ltd. for credit sale of January 18. There was no discount.

31 Issued cheque no. 479 to pay monthly salaries of $5,200.

Required

1. For King Sales Company, open the following general ledger accounts using the account numbers given:

Cash	111	Sales Discount	412
Accounts Receivable	112	Sales Returns and	
Supplies	116	Allowances	413
Prepaid Insurance	117	Interest Revenue	419
Inventory	118	Cost of Goods Sold	511
Furniture	151	Salary Expense	531
Accounts Payable	211	Utilities Expense	541
Sales Revenue	411		

2. Open these accounts in the subsidiary ledgers: Accounts receivable subsidiary ledger—Vachon Inc., Wakeland Ltd., and Wooten Design Ltd.; accounts payable subsidiary ledger—Delwood Co., Havrilla Corp., and Jasper Sales Ltd.

3. Enter the transactions in a sales journal (page 8), a cash receipts journal (page 3), a purchases journal (page 6), a cash payments journal (page 9), and a general journal (page 4), as appropriate.

4. Post daily to the accounts receivable subsidiary ledger and to the accounts payable subsidiary ledger. On January 31, post to the general ledger.

5. Total each column of the special journals. Show that the total debits equal the total credits in each special journal.

6. Balance the total of the customer account balances in the accounts receivable subsidiary ledger against Accounts Receivable in the general ledger. Do the same for the accounts payable subsidiary ledger and Accounts Payable in the general ledger.

Challenge Problems

Problem 6-1C *Advantage of an effective accounting system* *(Obj. 1)*

An accounting information system that provides timely, accurate information to management is an important asset of any organization. This is especially true as organizations become larger and move into different parts of the world. The integration of computers into many organizations' information systems has enhanced their usefulness to the organization.

Required

Assume your older sister is a pharmacist. She regards an information system as simply an accounting system that keeps track of her company's revenues and expenses. Explain to her how an effective accounting information system can make her a more effective pharmacist.

Problem 6-2C *Providing advice about a computerized accounting system* *(Obj. 2)*

Information technology is increasingly sophisticated and everyone wants the latest technology. Your brother has asked you about installing this "wonderful" computer system in his car dealership and auto repair business. The salesperson has promised your brother that the system "will do everything you want and then some." Your brother has come to you for advice about acquiring this new computerized accounting information system. At present he uses a manual accounting system.

Required

Provide the advice your brother wants, focusing on the costs of the new computerized accounting information system; your brother has been told all the positive aspects of purchasing the system.

Extending Your Knowledge

Decision Problems

1. *Reconstructing transactions from amounts posted to the accounts receivable ledger* (Obj. 4)

A fire destroyed some accounting records of Bloomfield Company. The owner, Jennifer Bloomfield, asks for your help in reconstructing the records. *She needs to know the beginning and ending balances of Accounts Receivable and the credit sales and cash receipts on account from customers during March.* All Bloomfield Company sales are on credit, with payment terms of 2/10 n/30. All cash receipts on account reached Bloomfield Company within the 10-day discount period, except as noted. The only accounting record preserved from the fire is the accounts receivable subsidiary ledger, which follows:

Adam Chi

Date		Jrnl. Ref.	Debit	Credit	Balance
Mar. 8		S.6	5,000		5,000
16		S.6	1,000		6,000
18		CR.8		5,000	1,000
19		J.5		200	800
27		CR.8		800	-0-

Anna Fowler

Date		Jrnl. Ref.	Debit	Credit	Balance
Mar. 1	Balance				1,100
5		CR.8		1,100	-0-
11		S.6	400		400
21		CR.8		400	-0-
24		S.6	4,000		4,000

Norris Associates Ltd.

Date		Jrnl. Ref.	Debit	Credit	Balance
Mar. 1	Balance				3,000
15		S.6	3,000		6,000
29		CR.8		2,900*	3,100

Robertson Inc.

Date		Jrnl. Ref.	Debit	Credit	Balance
Mar. 1	Balance				500
3		CR.8		500	-0-
25		S.6	4,000		4,000
29		S.6	1,200		5,200

*Cash receipt did not occur within the discount period.

2. Understanding an accounting system (Obj. 4, 5)

The external auditor must ensure that the amounts shown on the balance sheet for Accounts Receivable represent actual amounts that customers owe the company. Each customer account in the accounts receivable subsidiary ledger must represent an actual credit sale to the person or company indicated, and the customer's balance must not have been collected. This auditing concept is called *validity,* or *validating* the accounts receivable.

The auditor must also ensure that all amounts that the company owes are included in Accounts Payable and other liability accounts. For example, all credit purchases of inventory made by the company (and not yet paid) should be included in the balance of the Accounts Payable account. This auditing concept is called *completeness.*

Required

Suggest how an auditor might test a customer's account receivable balance for validity. Indicate how the auditor might test the balance of the Accounts Payable account for completeness.

Comprehensive Problems
for Part One

1. Completing a Merchandiser's Accounting Cycle

The end-of-month trial balance of Regina Building Materials at January 31, 2003, is shown on the next page.

Additional data at January 31, 2003:

a. Supplies consumed during the month, $1,500. One-half is selling expense, and the other half is general expense.

b. Amortization for the month: building, $4,000; fixtures, $4,800. One-fourth of amortization is selling expense, and three-fourths is general expense.

c. Unearned sales revenue still unearned, $1,200.

d. Accrued salaries, a general expense, $1,150.

e. Accrued interest expense, $780.

f. Inventory on hand, $63,720. Regina Building Materials uses the perpetual inventory system.

REGINA BUILDING MATERIALS
Trial Balance
January 31, 2003

Account Number	Account	Balance Debit	Balance Credit
110	Cash..	$ 16,430	
120	Accounts receivable	19,090	
130	Inventory	65,400	
140	Supplies	2,700	
150	Building	188,170	
151	Accumulated amortization—building.................		$ 36,000
160	Fixtures	45,600	
161	Accumulated amortization—fixtures..................		5,800
200	Accounts payable...		28,300
205	Salary payable..		
210	Interest payable		
240	Unearned sales revenue		6,560
250	Note payable, long-term		87,000
300	G. Regina, capital		144,980
311	G. Regina, withdrawals.....................................	9,200	
400	Sales revenue		187,970
402	Sales discounts..	7,300	
430	Sales returns and allowances..........................	8,140	
500	Cost of goods sold...	103,000	
600	Selling expense	21,520	
700	General expense	10,060	
705	Interest expense..		
	Total...	$496,610	$496,610

Required

1. Using three-column accounts, open the accounts listed on the trial balance, inserting their unadjusted balances. Date the balances of the following accounts January 1: Supplies; Building; Accumulated Amortization—Building; Fixtures; Accumulated Amortization—Fixtures; Unearned Sales Revenue; and G. Regina, Capital. Date the balance of G. Regina, Withdrawals, January 31.

2. Enter the trial balance on an accounting work sheet, and complete the work sheet for the month ended January 31, 2003. Regina Building Materials groups all operating expenses under two accounts, Selling Expense and General Expense. Leave two blank lines under Selling Expense and three blank lines under General Expense.

3. Prepare the company's multi-step income statement and statement of owner's equity for the month ended January 31, 2003. Also prepare the balance sheet at that date in report form.

4. Journalize the adjusting and closing entries at January 31, 2003, using page 3 of the general journal.

5. Post the adjusting and closing entries, using dates and posting references.

6. Compute Regina Building Materials' current ratio and debt ratio at January 31, 2003, and compare these values with the industry averages of 1.9 for the current ratio and 0.57 for the debt ratio. Compute the gross margin percentage and the rate of inventory turnover for the month (the inventory balance at the end of December 2002, was $63,720) and compare these ratio values with the industry averages of 0.36 for the gross margin ratio and 1.7 times for inventory turnover. Does Regina Building Materials appear to be stronger or weaker than the average company in the building materials industry?

2. Completing the Accounting Cycle for a Merchandising Entity

Note: This problem can be solved with or without special journals. See Requirement 2.
Canmore Distributors closes its books and prepares financial statements at the end of each month. Canmore uses the perpetual inventory system. The company completed the following transactions during August 2004.

Aug.
1   Issued cheque no. 682 for August office rent $2,000. (Debit Rent Expense.)

2   Issued cheque no. 683 to pay salaries of $1,240, which includes salary payable of $930 from July 31. Canmore does *not* use reversing entries.

2   Issued invoice no. 503 for sale on account to R. T. Loeb, $600. Canmore's cost of this merchandise was $190.*

3   Purchased inventory on credit terms of 1/15 n/60 from Grant Ltd., $1,400.

4   Received net amount of cash on account from Fullam Corp., $2,156, within the discount period.

4   Sold inventory for cash, $330 (cost, $104).

5   Received from Park-Hee, Inc. merchandise that had been sold earlier for $550 (cost, $174). The wrong merchandise had been sent.

5   Issued cheque no. 684 to purchase supplies for cash, $780.

6   Collected interest revenue of $1,100.

7   Issued invoice no. 504 for sale on account to K. D. Skipper Inc., $2,400 (cost, $759).

8   Issued cheque no. 685 to pay Fayda Corp. $2,600 of the amount owed at July 31. This payment occurred after the end of the discount period.

11   Issued cheque no. 686 to pay Grant Ltd. the net amount owed from August 3.

12   Received cash from R. T. Loeb in full settlement of her account receivable from August 2.

16   Issued cheque no. 687 to pay salary expense of $1,240.

19   Purchased inventory for cash, $850, issuing cheque no. 688.

22   Purchased furniture on credit terms of 3/15 n/60 from Beaver Corporation, $510.

23   Sold inventory on account to Fullam Corp., issuing invoice no. 505 for $9,966 (cost, $3,152).

24   Received half the July 31 amount receivable from K. D. Skipper Inc.—after the end of the discount period.

25   Issued cheque no. 689 to pay utilities, $432.

26   Purchased supplies on credit terms of 2/10 n/30 from Fayda Corp., $180.

30   Returned damaged inventory to company from whom Canmore made the cash purchase on August 19, receiving cash of $850.

30   Granted a sales allowance of $175 to K. D. Skipper Inc.

31   Purchased inventory on credit terms of 1/10 n/30 from Suncrest Supply Ltd., $8,330.

31   Issued cheque no. 690 to Jack West, owner of Canmore, for $1,700.

---

* On August 2, Canmore Distributors sold inventory to R. T. Loeb and collected in full on August 12. Upon learning that the shipment to Loeb was incomplete, Canmore plans to ship the goods to her during September. At August 31, $450 of unearned sales revenue needs to be recorded and the cost of this merchandise ($142) needs to be removed from Cost of Goods Sold and returned to Inventory.

Required

1. Open the following accounts with their account numbers and July 31 balances in the ledgers indicated.

General Ledger:

101	Cash	$ 4,490
102	Accounts Receivable	22,560
104	Interest Receivable	
105	Inventory	41,800
109	Supplies	1,340
117	Prepaid Insurance	2,200
140	Note Receivable, Long-term	11,000

160	Furniture	37,270
161	Accumulated Amortization—Furniture	10,550
201	Accounts Payable	12,600
204	Salary Payable	930
207	Interest Payable	320
208	Unearned Sales Revenue	
220	Note Payable, Long-term	42,000
301	Jack West, Capital	54,260
303	Jack West, Withdrawals	
400	Income Summary	
401	Sales Revenue	
402	Sales Discounts	
403	Sales Returns and Allowances	
410	Interest Revenue	
501	Cost of Goods Sold	
510	Salary Expense	
513	Rent Expense	
514	Amortization Expense—Furniture	
516	Insurance Expense	
517	Utilities Expense	
519	Supplies Expense	
523	Interest Expense	

Accounts Receivable Subsidiary Ledger: Fullam Corp., $2,200; R. T. Loeb; Park-Hee, Inc., $11,590; K. D. Skipper Inc., $8,770.

Accounts Payable Subsidiary Ledger: Beaver Corporation; Fayda Corp., $12,600; Grant Ltd.; Suncrest Supply Ltd.

2. Ask your professor for directions. Journalize the August transactions either in the general journal (page 9; explanations not required) or, as illustrated in Chapter 6, in a series of special journals: a sales journal (page 4), a cash receipts journal (page 11), a purchases journal (page 8), a cash payments journal (page 5), and a general journal (page 9). Canmore makes all credit sales on terms of 2/10 n/30.

3. Post daily to the accounts receivable subsidiary ledger and the accounts payable subsidiary ledger. On August 31, 2004, post to the general ledger.

4. Prepare a trial balance in the Trial Balance columns of a work sheet, and use the following information to complete the work sheet for the month ended August 31, 2004.

   a. Accrued interest revenue, $100.
   b. Supplies on hand, $990.
   c. Prepaid insurance expired, $550.
   d. Amortization expense, $230.
   e. Accrued salary expense, $1,030.
   f. Accrued interest expense, $320.
   g. Unearned sales revenue, $450.*
   h. Inventory on hand, $46,700.

5. Prepare Canmore's multi-step income statement and statement of owner's equity for August. Prepare the balance sheet at August 31, 2004.

6. Journalize and post the adjusting and closing entries.

7. Prepare a postclosing trial balance at August 31, 2004. Also, balance the total of the customer accounts in the accounts receivable subsidiary ledger against the Accounts Receivable balance in the general ledger. Do the same for the accounts payable subsidiary ledger and Accounts Payable in the general ledger.

Appendix

XBRL—The New Language of Business[1,2]

Accountants will be hearing more and more about XBRL (eXtensible Business Reporting Language), a language that will enable electronic business documents to be created and easily compared. XBRL is a variant of a language called XML (Extensible Markup Language), which is a variant of a language called SGML (Standard Generalized Markup Language) that defines the structure and content of electronic documents. Another well-known variant of SGML is HTML (HyperText Markup Language), which has been used extensively in creating items for the World Wide Web.

Both XML and HTML attach tags to the content of a document to describe the format of that content. For example, an electronic document created using HTML can contain a number as its content and use tags to indicate if the number should be formatted to be italic or bold. However, HTML's tags do not indicate what the number *represents*—the number could be a price or a product identification number. XML's advantage over HTML is that it *does* provide tags to capture a number's meaning— electronic document data can be tagged to describe what each item is. This means that computers receiving these electronic documents can use the tags to select particular data, such as prices or net income or anything else for which a tag exists. However, for XML tags to be useful, tags must be defined the same way by everyone. If this is not done, a "capital asset" tag might mean "original cost" for one user and "cost less amortization" for another user. This would mean that different documents would have different definitions for the same tags, making comparisons between companies misleading and transactions between companies difficult.

XBRL is the variant of XML being developed specifically to facilitate business communication and e-business over the Internet. A consortium is determining what tags are needed for business communication and creating common definitions for those tags. XBRL will be freely available for everyone to use, and will allow comparisons of like data and business transactions using these common definitions. For example, you will be able to download financial statements from several companies from the web and compare them easily in the ways suggested in Chapter 18, confident that you are comparing similar numbers. "Capital asset" will mean the same thing to all companies. Ultimately, you will be able to compare statements from all over the world electronically, with ease.

XBRL is *not* setting new accounting standards. It is a tool that facilitates communication in the current GAAP environment. XBRL uses XML-based data tags to describe financial statements for both public and private companies. The actual process of developing the tags is not complicated but is quite detailed and must be done precisely if XBRL is to be of value. XBRL's development is being led by the XBRL working group, which includes a constantly expanding number of organizations and companies, including the CICA, the AICPA, the large accounting firms, Microsoft, Oracle, SAP, IBM, and ACCPAC, in a number of countries, including Australia, Canada, England, Germany, Taiwan, the U.S., and Wales. The International Accounting Standards Committee is also involved.

To learn more about the ongoing development of XBRL, consult the references provided in Footnote 1.

---

[1] The interested reader is directed to the XML website at **http://www.w3.org** and the XBRL website at **www.xbrl.org**. A helpful article describing XBRL is Zarowin, Stanley, and Wayne E. Harding, "Finally, Business Talks the Same Language," *Journal of Accountancy*, August 2000, pp. 24-30.

[2] The authors would like to thank Professor Carla Carnaghan for her assistance and suggestions.

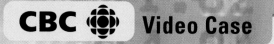
Earth Buddy to Spin Master:
The Role of Accounting in a New Business

Many young people dream of owning their own business. Four entrepreneurs started their own business after graduating from university in 1993. The product they produced and sold was a head-shaped object that sprouted hair (grass) when watered. The concept was very simple: a nylon stocking was filled with sawdust and some grass seed; the head was shaped and a face was painted on it; then, the head was placed in a printed box ready for shipping.

The company was successful with orders from Canadian Tire and Zellers. It then landed a possible order from KMart U.S. for 500,000 Earth Buddies. But the company must produce the 500,000 units quickly to get the order.

The partners are good at marketing and production. They were able to get the large order and produce the needed Earth Buddies. But successful companies need more than a product, marketing, and production skills. They also need accounting skills.

The company's accountant tells Anton Rabie, the president, that the owners regard the administration of the company as something they can do in their spare time. He tells Anton that the books are a mess. The owners have been too busy making money to keep track of it.

The partners think the company needs a large loan from the bank to finance the production of Earth Buddies for the KMart U.S. order. They go to their banker and are able to obtain a line of credit for the necessary funds. However, when the books are finally straightened out, the partners discover that the company had sufficient funds without the bank loan.

The order from KMart comes in and the company earned over $500,000 profit. The company was a success; Anton was asked to address a class at Ryerson Polytechnic University in Toronto about entrepreneurship.

Epilogue

Earth Buddy, now Spin Master Toys, continues to be a success story. Between 1993 and 2000, the partners expanded the product line, buying the marketing rights to products including the air-powered "Air Hogs," the new finger bike line, and the water rocket (the secret product behind the shower screen). Toys R Us, with its 700-plus stores in North America, has become a major partner. A number of other chains also want to sell Spin Master products, with the demand exceeding supply for many of the company's products.

The partners hired a number of senior people, including accountants, to guide and support the company's growth. They have become business professionals; when we first met them, they were enthusiastic but inexperienced.

Sales jumped from $10 million in 1998 to $50 million in 2000. In 2000, Financial Post selected the company as one of the 50 best-managed private companies in Canada.

CASE QUESTIONS

1. What do you think the partners in Earth Buddies would need "accounting skills" to do, based on the first video?

2. Why do you think Roys Я Us might be interested in the company's financial statements?

3. What are some potential problems that the books' "being in a mess" might cause?

4. What have you learned about accounting from this video case?

Sources: *Venture*, CBC 1994 and 2000; McDougall, Diane, "Putting a New Spin on Toys," *Financial Post*, December 13, 2000.

Internal Control, Managing Cash, and Making Ethical Judgments

CHAPTER OBJECTIVES

After studying this chapter, you should be able to

1 Define internal control

2 Identify the characteristics of an effective system of internal control

3 Prepare a bank reconciliation and the related journal entries

4 Apply internal controls to cash receipts

5 Apply internal controls to cash payments, including petty cash transactions

6 Use a budget to manage cash

7 Make ethical judgments in business

"If all employees were always accurate and ethical, internal controls would not be necessary. Our ineffective internal control system gave one dishonest employee the opportunity to embezzle cash over several years' time. From now on, we're going to make it a lot harder to steal anything!" Jan Larsen, President of Larsen & Company.

Jack Van Auken was a cashier at the brokerage firm Larsen & Company. Van Auken's problems began when an auto accident forced him to miss work. Only then did president Jan Larsen receive complaints from customers who had not received credit for their deposits. Larsen uncovered an embezzlement scheme that Van Auken had begun five years earlier.

The court found that Van Auken had stolen over $610,934 in a "rob-John-to-pay-Jim" scheme: Van Auken was transferring customer deposits into his own personal account and concealing the missing amounts with deposits from other customers. In this way, customer accounts always balanced as long as Van Auken could manipulate the computerized records. But while Van Auken was recovering in the hospital, his replacement was unable to explain the missing deposits. All the evidence pointed in the direction of the absent employee. Van Auken was sentenced to jail, and Jan Larsen then understood why her dedicated cashier never took a vacation. [Identifying details have been changed to protect the parties involved.]

WHAT went wrong at Larsen & Company? Jack Van Auken was able to control not only the cash received from customers but also part of his company's computerized accounting records. By manipulating the records he was able to hide his theft for several years. Evidently, no one checked his work on a regular basis. Several procedures that we discuss in this chapter will explain how Larsen & Company could have prevented this embezzlement. Such control systems cannot prevent all employee misconduct, but they can help to detect illegal behaviour and thereby to limit its effects.

The need for internal control procedures has received increased attention since the 1970s. During that time some illegal payments, embezzlements, and other criminal business practices became evident. Concerned citizens wanted to know why the companies' internal controls had failed to alert top management to these illegalities.

This chapter discusses *internal control*—the organizational plan that managers use to protect company assets. The chapter applies internal control techniques mainly to cash, the most liquid asset, and provides a framework for making ethical judgments in business. Later chapters discuss how managers control other assets.

Cash

Cash, including cash on hand in funds such as *petty cash funds*, cash on deposit in banks and trust companies, and cash equivalents, such as Treasury Bills, is the most liquid asset an organization has. Accordingly, it is usually the first item under the heading "Current Assets" on the balance sheet.

Cash's liquidity is a virtue because it is easily exchangeable for other assets. However, cash's liquidity is also a fault because it is the most easily stolen asset. The next section will explain how organizations strive to protect their cash by using internal controls.

Internal Control

One of a manager's key responsibilities is to control operations. The owners and the top managers set the entity's goals, the managers lead the way, and the employees carry out the plan. Good managers must decide where the organization is headed for the next several years. But unless they control operations today, they may not remain in business long enough to put lofty plans into effect.

The *CICA Handbook* states in paragraph 5200.03 that "**internal control** consists of the policies and procedures established and maintained by management to assist in achieving its objective of ensuring . . . the orderly and efficient conduct of [a company's] business." The *Handbook* indicates in paragraph 5200.06 and Appendix C to Sections 5200–5220 that management's internal control objectives are

1. Optimizing the use of resources by providing reliable information for decisions, and monitoring the implementation and compliance with management's business policies.
2. Preventing and detecting error and fraud.
3. Safeguarding assets and records.
4. Maintaining reliable control systems to provide reliable information for decision making.

Internal control is the organizational plan and all related measures adopted by an entity to meet management's internal control objectives. When determining internal control, top management should ask these questions:

1. Is our organization likely to achieve its objectives?
2. Is our organization resilient enough to learn and adapt amidst change?
3. Are we appropriately managing the risks facing the organization?
4. Are we appropriately recognizing opportunities and acting on them?[1]

A company's internal control consists of two elements: (1) the control environment, which in essence consists of the actions, policies, and procedures that reflect the attitudes of the owners and top management of a company about control and its importance to the entity; and (2) the control systems, which can be divided into two components—the accounting system and the control procedures. The accounting system refers to the policies and procedures that pertain to the collection, recording, and processing of data and reporting information, while the control procedures pertain to enhancing the reliability of the data and information.

Internal control is a management priority, not merely a part of the accounting system. Thus it is not only a responsibility of accountants but of managers as well. Internal controls are most effective when employees at all levels adopt the organization's goals and ethical standards. Top managers need to communicate these goals and standards to workers. Lee Iacocca, former president of Chrysler Corporation, instilled management's goals in Chrysler employees by spending time with assembly-line workers. (Japanese firms pioneered this style of participative management.) The result? Defects decreased dramatically, and Chrysler products became more competitive.

Exhibit 7-1 presents an excerpt from the 1999 Annual Report of IPSCO Inc., a major steel company whose head office is in Regina. IPSCO's top managers take responsibility for the financial statements and the related system of internal control. Another example of a statement of management's responsibility is that of Intrawest Corporation in Appendix A. Note that the management of Intrawest states "[Intrawest] maintains appropriate systems of internal control, policies and procedures which provide management with reasonable assurance that assets are safeguarded and that financial

REAL WORLD EXAMPLE

One of the auditor's first steps in auditing a business is to understand and evaluate its internal controls. If a company has good controls, then mistakes are minimized and are usually corrected before the financial statements are prepared. If the control system is weak, then mistakes can go undetected. The auditor determines the extent of testing of the accounting records on the basis of the strength of the company's internal control system.

REAL WORLD EXAMPLE

A recent survey by KPMG reported that 56% of fraud in the surveyed companies was a result of poor internal controls and that 59% of fraud was detected through internal controls already in place.

Chrysler
www.chryslercorp.com

---

[1] Criteria of Control Board, *Guidance on Assessing Control*. (Toronto: Canadian Institute of Chartered Accountants, 1995), p. 1.

Management's Responsibility for Financial Statements

The accompanying consolidated financial statements of IPSCO Inc., and all information in this report, were prepared by management, which is responsible for its integrity and objectivity.

The integrity and reliability of IPSCO's reporting systems are achieved through the use of formal policies and procedures, the careful selection of employees, and an appropriate division of responsibilities. Internal accounting controls are continually monitored by an internal audit staff through ongoing reviews and comprehensive audit programs. IPSCO regularly communicates throughout the organization the requirement for employees to maintain high ethical standards in their conduct of the company's affairs.

Roger Phillips
President and
Chief Executive Officer
24 January 2000

Edwin Tiefenbach
Senior Vice President and
Chief Financial Officer

records are reliable and form a proper basis for the preparation of the financial statements."

Let's examine in detail how businesses create the goals of an effective system of internal control.

An Effective System of Internal Control

Whether the business is Larsen & Company, IPSCO Inc., or a local department store, its system of internal controls, if effective, has the characteristics discussed below.

Competent, Reliable, and Ethical Personnel Employees should be *competent*, *reliable*, and *ethical*. Paying top salaries to attract top-quality employees, training them to do their job well, and supervising their work all help a company build a competent staff.

In a small business (or a small office of a large company), the owner/manager can ensure that assets are protected. In a larger business, internal controls can help protect assets by ensuring that policies are in place and are followed.

Assignment of Responsibilities In a business with a good internal control system, no important duty is overlooked. Each employee is assigned certain responsibilities. A model of such *assignment of responsibilities* appears in the corporate organizational chart in Exhibit 7-2. Notice that the corporation has a vice-president of finance and accounting. Two other officers, the treasurer and the controller, report to that vice-president. The treasurer is responsible for cash management. The **controller** is the chief accounting officer.

Within this organization, the controller may be responsible for approving invoices (bills) for payment and the treasurer may actually sign the cheques. Working under the controller, one accountant may be responsible for property taxes, a second for income taxes, and a third for sales tax and the Goods and Services Tax (GST). In sum, all duties should be clearly defined and assigned to individuals who bear responsibility for carrying them out.

Most banks and retail businesses assign each cashier a money tray and hold the cashier responsible if that fund is short at the end of the shift. This internal control device clearly assigns responsibility to each employee. Shortages or discrepancies can be traced to the person responsible.

Proper Authorization An organization generally has written rules that outline approved procedures. Any deviation from policy requires *proper authorization*. For example, managers or assistant managers of retail stores must approve customer

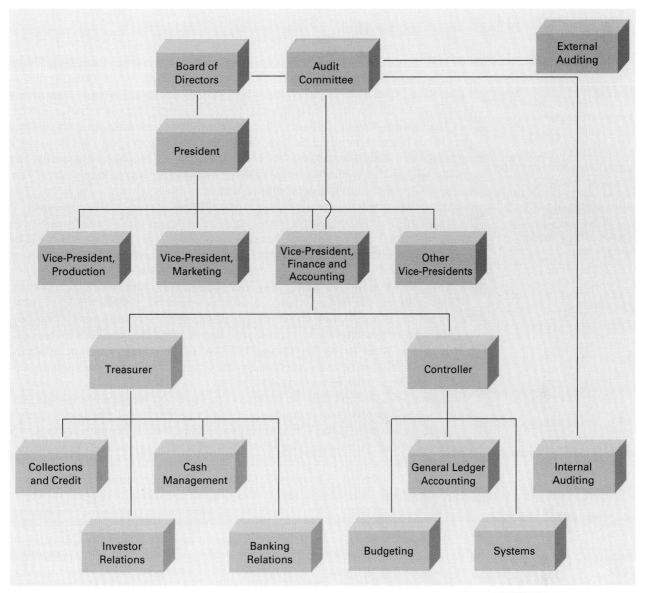

EXHIBIT 7-2

Organization Chart of a Corporation

cheques for amounts above the store's usual limit. Likewise, deans or heads of departments of colleges and universities must give the authorization for a first- or second-year student to enroll in courses otherwise restricted to upper-year students.

Separation of Duties   Smart management divides the responsibilities for transactions between two or more people or departments. *Separation of duties* (also called segregation of duties) limits the chances for fraud and promotes the accuracy of accounting records. The IPSCO Inc. management responsibility statement (Exhibit 7-1) mentions "an appropriate division of responsibilities." This crucial and often neglected component of internal control may be subdivided into four parts.

1. *Separation of operations from accounting.* The entire accounting function should be completely separate from operating departments, such as manufacturing or sales. This way reliable records may be kept. What would happen if the sales personnel had control over the company's revenue records? Sales figures would probably be inflated, and top managers would be unsure about exactly how much

the company actually sold. Observe the separation of accounting from marketing (sales) in Exhibit 7-2.

2. *Separation of the custody of assets from accounting.* Temptation and fraud are reduced if accountants do not handle cash and cashiers do not have access to the accounting records. If one employee had both cash-handling and accounting duties, that person can steal cash and conceal the theft by making a fictitious entry on the books. We see this component of internal control in the organization chart in Exhibit 7-2. The treasurer has custody of cash and the controller accounts for cash. Neither person has both responsibilities. Jack Van Auken was able to apply one customer's cash deposit to another customer's account at Larsen & Company. Apparently, Van Auken, the cashier, controlled some data entered into the accounting system. This is a serious violation of the separation of duties.

Warehouse employees with no accounting duties should control inventory. If they were allowed to account for the inventory, they could steal it and write it off as obsolete. A *write-off* is an entry that credits an asset account. This write-off could be recorded by debiting Loss on Inventory Obsolescence and crediting Inventory. A person with custody of assets should not have access to the computer programs. Similarly, the programmer should not have access to tempting assets such as cash.

3. *Separation of the authorization of transactions from the custody of related assets.* Persons who authorize transactions should not handle the related asset. For example, the same individual should not authorize the payment of a supplier's invoice and also sign the cheque to pay the invoice. With both duties, the person can authorize payments to him- or herself and then sign the cheques. When these duties are separated, only legitimate bills are paid.

4. *Separation of duties within the accounting function.* Different people should perform the various phases of accounting to minimize errors and the opportunities for fraud. For example, different accountants should be responsible for recording cash receipts and cash payments. The employees who process accounts payable and cheque requests should have nothing to do with the approval process.

Even small businesses should have internal controls and some separation of duties. For example, if the bookkeeper writes all cheques and keeps the general ledger records, the owner should sign all cheques and reconcile the monthly bank statement.

Internal and External Audits   To demonstrate to users and to satisfy management that the financial statements present fairly the financial position of an organization and the results of its operations, most companies have periodic audits. An **audit** is an examination of the organization's financial statements and the accounting systems, controls, and records that produced them.

It is not economically feasible for auditors to examine all the transactions during a period, so they must rely to some degree on the accounting system to produce accurate data. To evaluate the company's accounting system, auditors examine its system of internal controls. Auditors often spot weaknesses in internal control and recommend corrections. Auditors are *objective* or unbiased in their reports, while managers, immersed in operations, may overlook their own biases.

Audits can be internal or external. Exhibit 7-2 shows *internal auditors* as employees of the organization reporting directly to the audit committee. Some organizations have internal auditors report directly to a vice-president. Throughout the year, the internal auditors examine various segments of the organization to ensure that employees are following company policies and that operations are running efficiently.

External auditors are required to be independent of the organization. They are hired by an organization to determine that the organization's financial statements are prepared in accordance with generally accepted accounting principles.

An auditor may find that an employee has both cash-handling and cash-accounting duties, or may learn that a cash shortage has resulted from lax efforts to collect accounts receivable. In such cases, both internal and external auditors would suggest improvements that would help the business to run more efficiently.

Documents and Records Business *documents and records* vary considerably, from source documents such as sales invoices and purchase orders to special journals and subsidiary ledgers. Documents should be prenumbered. A gap in the numbered sequence calls attention to a missing document.

Prenumbering cash-sale receipts discourages theft by the cashier because the copy retained by the cashier lists the amount of the sale. These figures can be checked against the actual amount of cash received. If receipts are not prenumbered, the cashier can destroy the sale receipt copy and pocket the cash received. However, if receipts are prenumbered, the missing copy can easily be identified. In a computerized system, a permanent record of the sale is stored electronically when the transaction is completed.

In a bowling alley, for example, a key document is the score sheet. The manager can check on cashiers by comparing the number of games scored with the amount of cash received. By multiplying the number of games by the price per game and comparing the result with each day's cash receipts, the manager can see whether all the bowling revenue is being collected by the business. If cash received is low, the cashier might be stealing.

Electronic Devices and Computer Controls Businesses use electronic devices to protect assets and control operations. For example, retailers such as The Bay and Sears Canada control their inventories by attaching an *electronic sensor* to merchandise. The cashier removes the sensor when a sale is made. If a customer tries to remove from the store an item with the sensor attached, an alarm is activated. According to Checkpoint Systems, which manufactures electronic sensors, these devices reduce loss due to theft by as much as 50 percent.

Accounting systems are relying less and less on documents and more and more on digital storage devices. Computers produce accurate records and enhance operational efficiency, but that does not automatically safeguard assets or encourage employees to behave in accordance with company policies. What computers have done is shift the internal controls to the people who write the programs. Programmers carry out the plans of managers and accountants. All the controls that apply to accountants apply to computer programmers as well. Some companies now employ electronic data processing (EDP) auditors to ensure the integrity of their computer systems and databases.

Other Controls Businesses of all types keep cash and important business documents (such as titles to property) in *fireproof vaults*. They use *burglar alarms* and *fences* around properties to protect buildings and other property.

Retailers receive most of their cash from customers on the spot. To safeguard cash, they use *point-of-sale terminals* that serve as a cash register and also record each transaction as it is entered in the machine. In conjunction with Universal Product Codes (UPCs), point-of-sale terminals ensure correct selling prices are entered (customers cannot switch price tags, and keypunching errors are reduced) and perpetual inventory records can be maintained. Several times each day a supervisor removes the cash for deposit in the bank.

Employees who handle cash are in an especially tempting position. Many businesses purchase *fidelity bonds* on cashiers. The bond is an insurance policy that reimburses the company for any losses due to the employee's theft. Before issuing a fidelity bond, the insurance company investigates the employee's past record.

Mandatory vacations and *job rotation* require that employees be trained to do a variety of jobs. Some companies, such as General Electric Canada, move employees from job to job—often at six-month intervals. This improves morale by giving employees a broad view of the business and helps them decide where they want to specialize. Knowing that someone else will be doing their job next month also keeps employees honest. Had Larsen & Company moved Jack Van Auken from job to job and required him to take a vacation, his embezzlement would probably have been detected much earlier.

 **REAL WORLD EXAMPLE**

If a clerk in a retail store makes a mistake on the sales ticket, the ticket is not destroyed but is marked VOID. Most businesses use prenumbered sales receipts, so a missing receipt would be noted.

Internal Controls for E-Commerce

E-commerce creates some new risks. Buying and selling over the Internet can give computer hackers access to confidential information unavailable in face-to-face transactions. Confidentiality is a significant challenge for "dot.com" companies. Pitfalls include stolen credit-card numbers, computer viruses and Trojan horses, and impersonation of companies. To convince people to buy online, companies must ensure security of data.

Dangers *Stolen credit-card numbers.* Suppose you buy several CDs from Futureshop.ca. To make the purchase, your credit-card number must travel through cyberspace. In the U.S., amateur hacker Carlos Salgado, Jr. used his home computer to steal from an Internet service provider 100,000 credit-card numbers with a combined credit limit exceeding $1 billion. Salgado was caught when he tried to sell the credit-card numbers to an undercover FBI agent.

Computer viruses and Trojan horses. A **computer virus** is a malicious program that reproduces itself, gets included into program code without consent, and performs actions that can be destructive. A **Trojan horse** works like a computer virus, but it does not reproduce. Computer viruses can destroy or alter data, make bogus calculations, and infect word-processing and spreadsheet files. The International Computer Security Association reports that 99.3% of firms it surveyed found a virus somewhere in their organization.

Impersonation of companies. Computer hackers sometimes create bogus websites, which might attract a large number of web surfers, and solicit confidential data from unsuspecting people. The hackers then use the data for a variety of illicit purposes.

Firewalls and Encryption Information travelling *along* the Internet is secure. It is the server holding information that may be insecure. A server is a computer that performs a particular function (for example, data storage or printing) in a computer network. Two standard techniques companies use to secure e-commerce data are encryption and firewalls.

Encryption is the primary method of achieving confidentiality in e-commerce.

Plain-text messages are rearranged by some mathematical process. The encrypted message cannot be read by anyone who does not know the process. A simple accounting example is the use of check-sum digits for customer account numbers. Each account number is set up so that the last digit is the sum of the previous digits, for example Customer Number 2237, where 2 + 2 + 3 = 7. Any account number that fails this test triggers an error message.

Firewalls limit access to a local network. The intent is to keep intruders out. Often firewalls work between two networks, such as between a local network and the Internet. Firewalls enable members of the local network to access the Internet but keep nonmembers out of the network. Usually several firewalls are built into the local network so that hackers must work their way around more than one. At the point of entry of a network, passwords, personal identification numbers (PINs), fingerprints, and signatures are used to restrict entry. More sophisticated firewalls are used deeper in the network.

The Limitations of Internal Control

Unfortunately, most internal control measures can be circumvented or overcome. Two or more employees working as a team—*colluding*—can beat an internal con-

---

Accounting Around the Globe

The Barings Bank Debacle: What Your Internal Auditor Tells You Might Save You

Barings Bank was founded in 1763 and was the oldest merchant bank in London, England. Barings had helped the United States government finance the Louisiana Purchase from France and had helped the British government raise funds to fight Napoleon. The estimated value of Barings at the end of 1994 was £1 billion.

In 1992, Barings sent a young 28-year-old trader, Nick Leeson, to work in its Singapore office. Less than three years later, on February 26, 1995, as a result of Leeson's speculation on Japan's Nikkei stock market, Barings lost more than £830 million and the firm collapsed. Shortly thereafter, ING, a Dutch bank, paid £1 for Barings and assumed £200 million of Barings' debt.

It was clear that Leeson was responsible for the financial disaster. In December 1995 he was convicted by a court in Singapore and sentenced to six years in jail.

The question was asked how a lowly stock trader was able to lose so much money in such a short period of time. The answer was lack of internal controls. Stock brokerage firms have a "front office" that transacts the trades and a "back office" that does the record keeping and tracks who owes what to whom. In other words, the back office acts as a control on the front office. The front office has the power to commit the brokerage firm to risks that can, as in the case of Barings, amount to hundreds of millions of pounds. The back office acts as a check on that power.

In the case of the Singapore branch of Barings, Nick Leeson was a front office person, and he was also responsible for the back office. Barings' internal auditors and others in the firm warned senior management that allowing Leeson to have both functions was extremely risky. But Leeson was "apparently" making huge profits for the firm, so the advice was ignored.

The result was one of the largest financial disasters the world of finance has seen.

Source: Gapper, John and Nicholas Denton, *All that Glitters: The Fall of Barings*. (London: Hamish Hamilton Ltd., 1996).

---

trol system and defraud the firm. Consider the Big-Hit Theatre. Ralph and a fellow employee could put together a scheme in which the ticket seller pockets the cash from ten customers and the ticket taker admits ten customers without tickets. To prevent this situation, the manager must take additional control measures, such as counting the people in the theatre and matching that figure against the number of ticket stubs retained. But that would take time away from other duties. The stricter the internal control, the more expensive and time-consuming it becomes.

A system of internal control that is too complex may strangle the business with red tape. Efficiency and control are hurt rather than helped. Just how tight should internal control be? Managers must make sensible judgments. Investments in internal control must be judged in the light of the costs and benefits.

The Bank Account as a Control Device

Cash is the most liquid asset because it is the medium of exchange. But cash can also be intangible, often consisting of electronic impulses in a bank's accounting system with no accompanying paper cheques or deposit slips. Cash is easy to conceal, easy to move, and relatively easy to steal. As a result, most businesses create specific controls to safeguard cash.

Keeping cash in a *bank account* is important because banks have established practices for safeguarding cash. Banks also provide depositors with detailed records of their transactions. To take full advantage of these control features, the business must deposit all cash receipts in the bank account and make all cash payments through it (except petty cash payments, which we look at later in this chapter).

The documents used to control a bank account include the signature card, the deposit ticket, the cheque, the bank statement, and the bank reconciliation.

Signature Card Banks require each person authorized to transact business through an account in that bank to sign a *signature card*. The bank compares the signatures on documents against the signature card to protect the bank and the depositor against forgery.

Deposit Ticket Banks supply standard forms such as *deposit tickets* or *deposit slips*. The customer fills in the dollar amount and date of deposit. As proof of the transaction, the customer retains either (1) a duplicate copy of the deposit ticket or slip, or (2) a deposit receipt, depending on the bank's practice.

Cheque To draw money from an account, the depositor writes a **cheque**, which is a document that instructs the bank to pay the designated person or business the specified amount of money. There are three parties to a cheque: the *maker*, who signs the cheque; the *payee*, to whom the cheque is paid; and the *bank* on which the cheque is drawn.

Most cheques are serially numbered and preprinted with the name and address of the maker and the bank. The cheques have places for the date, the name of the payee, the signature of the maker, and the amount. The bank name and bank identification number, and the maker's account number are usually printed in magnetic ink for machine processing.

Exhibit 7-3 shows a cheque drawn on the bank account of Business Research. The cheque has two parts: the cheque itself and the *remittance advice*, an optional attachment that tells the payee the reason for payment. The maker (Business Research) retains a duplicate copy of the cheque for its recording in the cheque register (cash payments journal). Note that internal controls at Business Research require two signatures on cheques. (Other businesses might not use cheques with a duplicate copy. Instead, the necessary information might be recorded on the stub. The stub could be used as the source document.)

Bank Statement Banks send monthly bank statements to their depositors. A **bank statement** is the document the bank uses to report what it did with the

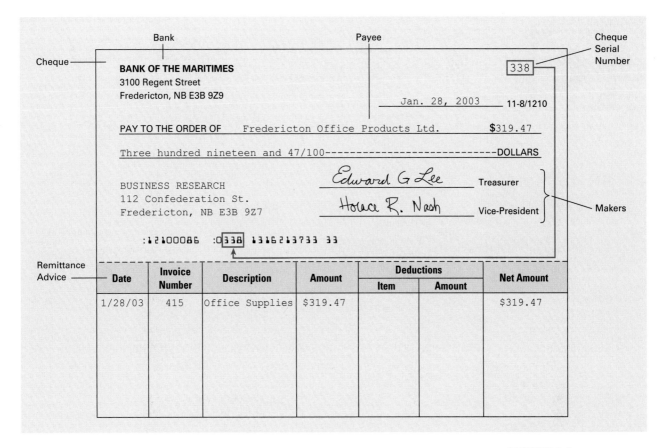

Labels on the image:
- Cheque
- Bank
- Payee
- Cheque Serial Number

BANK OF THE MARITIMES
3100 Regent Street
Fredericton, NB E3B 9Z9

338

Jan. 28, 2003   11-8/1210

PAY TO THE ORDER OF   Fredericton Office Products Ltd. $319.47

Three hundred nineteen and 47/100----------------------------DOLLARS

BUSINESS RESEARCH
112 Confederation St.
Fredericton, NB E3B 9Z7

Edward G Lee   Treasurer

Horace R. Nash   Vice-President

Makers

:12100086 :0338 1316213733 33

Remittance Advice

Date	Invoice Number	Description	Amount	Deductions		Net Amount
				Item	Amount	
1/28/03	415	Office Supplies	$319.47			$319.47

EXHIBIT 7-3

Cheque with Remittance Advice

depositor's cash. The statement shows the bank account's beginning and ending cash balances for the period and lists the month's cash transactions conducted through the bank. Included with the statement are the maker's *cancelled cheques*, those cheques that have been paid by the bank on behalf of the depositor. The bank statement also lists any deposits and other changes in the account. Deposits appear in chronological order, and cheques in a logical order (usually by cheque serial number or date of clearing the account), along with the date each cheque and deposit cleared the bank. Exhibit 7-4 is the bank statement of Business Research for the month ended January 31, 2003. Most businesses, like Business Research, receive their bank statement a few days following the end of each calendar month.

Electronic funds transfer (EFT) is a system that relies on electronic communications—not paper documents—to transfer cash. More and more businesses today rely on EFT for repetitive cash transactions. It is much cheaper for a company to pay employees by EFT (direct deposit) than by issuing hundreds of payroll cheques. Also, many people make mortgage, rent, and insurance payments by prior arrangement with their bank and never write cheques for those payments. The bank statement lists cash receipts by EFT among the deposits, and cash payments by EFT among the cheques and other bank charges.

One of the newest methods to transfer funds electronically is through the use of a *debit card*. When you make a purchase from a store and pay with a debit card, you authorize your bank to immediately withdraw the money for the purchase from your bank account and deposit it into the store's bank account. You will see the amount of the withdrawal on your monthly bank statement or passbook, and the store will see the amount of the deposit on its monthly bank statement. Debit cards, or bank cards, will be discussed more fully in Chapter 8.

BUSINESS ACCOUNT

The Generic Bank of Canada
KING SQUARE BRANCH
FREDERICTON, NEW BRUNSWICK
E3B 8Z1

1024/   0/   5

BUSINESS RESEARCH,
112 CONFEDERATION ST.
FREDERICTON, NB

E3B 9Z7

For Current Interest Rates:	Statement of Account		Statement From – To
CALL OUR INFOLINE 1-800-386-2093 QUEBEC 1-800-386-1600 TORONTO 987-7735	**Branch No.**	**Account No.**	JAN 1/03 JAN 31/03
	1024	1316213733	**Page** 1 **of** 1

BEGINNING BALANCE	TOTAL DEPOSITS	TOTAL WITHDRAWALS	SERVICE CHARGES	ENDING BALANCE
6556.12	4352.64	4963.00	39.25	5906.51

CHEQUING ACCOUNT TRANSACTIONS

DEPOSITS

DEPOSIT	01-04	1000.00
DEPOSIT	01-04	112.00
DEPOSIT	01-08	194.60
EFT COLLECTION OF RENT	01-17	904.03
BANK COLLECTION	01-26	2114.00
INTEREST	01-31	28.01

CHARGES

SERVICE CHARGES (INCLUDES NSF CHARGE, $25.00)	01-31	39.25

CHEQUES			CHEQUES			BALANCE	
NUMBER	DATE	AMOUNT	NUMBER	DATE	AMOUNT	DATE	BALANCE
332	01-12	3000.00	334	01-10	100.00	12-31	6556.12
656	01-06	100.00	335	01-06	100.00	01-04	7616.12
333	01-12	150.00	336	01-31	1100.00	01-06	7416.12
						01-08	7610.72
						01-10	7510.72
						01-12	4360.72
						01-17	5264.75
						01-20	4903.75
						01-26	7017.75
						01-31	5906.51

OTHER CHARGES	DATE	AMOUNT
NSF	01-04	52.00
EFT INSURANCE	01-20	361.00

MONTHLY SUMMARY

9 WITHDRAWALS   4360.72 MINIMUM BALANCE   6091.00 AVERAGE BALANCE

EXHIBIT 7-4

Bank Statement

Debits and Credits in Accounting and Banking

In this introductory accounting course, you have learned that

- Debit means the **left** side of an account
- Credit means the **right** side of an account

In banking

- Debits are bad (for you)
- Credits are good (for you)

Both perspectives are correct. To illustrate, let's consider two transactions: (1) your receipt of $1,000 cash, which you deposit in the bank, and (2) your payment of cash by writing a $600 cheque. Record these transactions, first on your own books, and then on the bank's books. You will understand debits and credits much better.

On *your* books, journalize (1) receipt of $1,000 cash for sales revenue (you immediately deposit the cash in your bank account), and (2) payment of $600 cash to purchase supplies (you write a cheque to an office supply store).

Answer:
Journal Entries on Your Books:

Cash	1,000	
Sales Revenue		1,000
Received cash for revenue earned.		
Supplies	600	
Cash		600
Purchased supplies.		

In these journal entries you correctly debit the Cash account for a receipt, and you credit Cash for a payment. Now let's see how the bank accounts for your cash.

When you deposit cash in your account, the amount of cash in the bank increases. Then when you write a cheque, the bank pays cash from your account. As a result, the amount of cash in the bank decreases. The critical thing to remember is this: *The bank owes your money to you because you can withdraw it or write cheques on it at any time. The bank thus has a Deposit Payable, a liability, for your cash on deposit.*

On the bank's books, journalize the same two transactions: (1) receipt of $1,000 cash from you (when you deposit cash in your account), and (2) payment of $600 cash for you.

Answer:
Journal Entries on the Bank's Books:

Cash	1,000	
Deposit Payable		1,000
Received cash from deposit customer.		
Deposit Payable	600	
Cash		600
Paid cash for deposit customer.		

In the first entry the bank debits Cash when it receives your deposit. The bank also credits Deposit Payable, a liability, to indicate that it owes you $1,000 whenever you wish to withdraw the money or write a cheque. This explains why a credit is "good" for you in a banking relationship. The bank has a liability for the amount of your money it has on deposit.

Now let's examine the bank's journal entry for the cash payment. The bank credits Cash when it pays your cheque. The bank debits Deposit Payable (to you) because the bank paid the $600 cheque that you wrote. As a result, the bank no longer owes you the $600. This explains why a debit is "bad" for you in a banking relationship: The bank has less liability to you.

The confusion about debits and credits in banking arises because many people view their own cash from the perspective of the bank. This is backwards, because:

- To the bank, your deposit account is a liability (a credit-balance account).
- To you, your cash is an asset (a debit-balance account).

The Bank Reconciliation There are two records of the business's cash: (1) its Cash account in its own general ledger, and (2) the bank statement, which tells the actual amount of cash the business has in the bank. The balance in the business's Cash account rarely equals the balance shown on the bank statement.

The books and the bank statement may show different amounts, but both are correct. The difference arises because of a time lag in recording certain transactions. When a firm writes a cheque, it immediately credits its Cash account. The bank, however, will not subtract the amount of the cheque until the cheque reaches it for payment. This may take days, even weeks, if the payee waits to cash the cheque. Likewise, the business immediately debits Cash for all cash receipts, and it may take a day or more for the bank to add this amount to the business's bank balance.

To ensure accuracy of the financial records, the firm's accountant must explain the reasons for the difference between the firm's records and bank statement figures on a certain date. The result of this process is a document called the **bank reconciliation**, which is prepared by the business (not the bank). Properly done, the bank reconciliation ensures that all cash transactions have been accounted for, and that bank and book records of cash are correct. Knowledge of where cash comes from, how it is spent, and the balance of cash available is vital to success in business.

Here are some common items that cause differences between the bank balance and the book balance.

1. Items recorded by the company but not yet recorded by the bank:
   a. **Deposits in transit** (outstanding deposits). The business has recorded these deposits, but the bank has not.
   b. **Outstanding cheques**. These cheques have been issued by the business and recorded on its books but the bank has not yet paid them.

2. Items recorded by the bank but not yet recorded by the business:
   a. **Bank collections**. Banks sometimes collect money on behalf of depositors. Many businesses have their customers pay directly to the business bank account. This practice, called a *lock-box system*, reduces the possibility of theft and places the business's cash in circulation faster than if the cash had to be collected and deposited by business personnel. An example is a bank's collecting cash on a note receivable and interest revenue for the depositor. The bank may notify the depositor of these bank collections on the bank's statement.
   b. *Electronic funds transfers*. The bank may receive or pay cash on behalf of the depositor. The bank statement will list the EFTs and may notify the depositor of these bank collections on the bank's statement.
   c. *Service charge*. This is the bank's fee for processing the depositor's transactions. Banks commonly base service charges on the balance in the account. The depositor learns the amount of service charge from the bank statement.
   d. *Interest revenue on chequing account*. Banks often pay interest to depositors who keep a large enough balance of cash in their account. This is sometimes true of business chequing accounts. The bank notifies the depositor of this interest on the bank statement.
   e. **NSF (nonsufficient funds) cheques** received from customers. To understand how to handle NSF cheques, (sometimes called *bounced cheques*) consider the route a cheque takes. The maker writes the cheque and gives the cheque to the payee, who deposits the cheque in his or her bank. The payee's bank adds the receipt amount to the payee's bank balance on the assumption that the cheque is good. A good cheque is returned to the maker's bank, which then

deducts the cheque amount from the maker's bank balance. NSF cheques are cash receipts that turn out to be worthless. If the maker's bank balance is insufficient to pay the cheque, the maker's bank refuses to pay the cheque and sends an NSF notice to the payee's bank. The payee's bank subtracts the cheque amount from the payee's bank balance and notifies the payee of this NSF action. This process may take from three to seven days. The payee's bank often charges a service charge for each NSF cheque, in this case $25.00. The payee may learn of NSF cheques through the bank statement, which lists the NSF cheque as a charge (subtraction), as shown near the bottom of Exhibit 7-4. Because an NSF cheque is worthless, the customer still owes Business Research $52 in Exhibit 7-4. As a result, Business Research has a receivable from the customer who wrote the NSF cheque.

LEARNING TIP

NSF cheques are customer cheques received by the business—not cheques the business has written.

f. *Cheques collected, deposited, and returned to the payee by the bank for reasons other than NSF.* Banks return cheques to the payee if (1) the maker's account has been closed, (2) the date is "stale" (the cheque has not been cashed within six month's of the cheque issue date and so is not honoured by the bank), (3) the signature is not authorized, (4) the cheque has been altered, or (5) the cheque form is improper (for example, a counterfeit). Accounting for all returned cheques is the same as for NSF cheques.

g. *The cost of printed cheques.* This charge against the company's bank account balance is handled like a service charge.

EXHIBIT 7-5

The Paths that Two Cheques Take

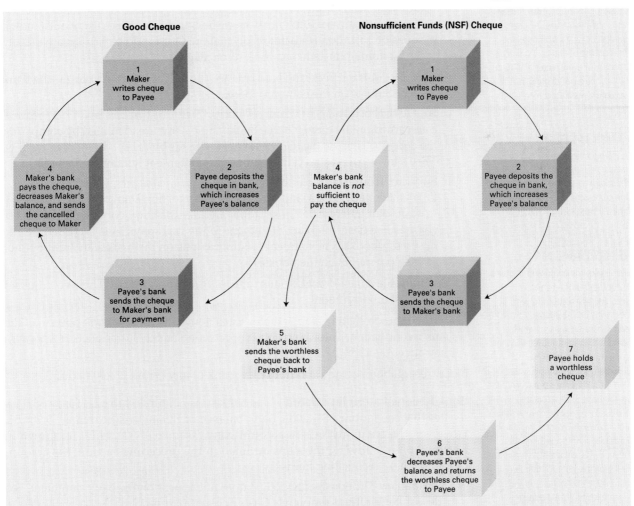

Good Cheque

Nonsufficient Funds (NSF) Cheque

1 Maker writes cheque to Payee

2 Payee deposits the cheque in bank, which increases Payee's balance

3 Payee's bank sends the cheque to Maker's bank for payment

4 Maker's bank pays the cheque, decreases Maker's balance, and sends the cancelled cheque to Maker

1 Maker writes cheque to Payee

2 Payee deposits the cheque in bank, which increases Payee's balance

3 Payee's bank sends the cheque to Maker's bank

4 Maker's bank balance is *not* sufficient to pay the cheque

5 Maker's bank sends the worthless cheque back to Payee's bank

6 Payee's bank decreases Payee's balance and returns the worthless cheque to Payee

7 Payee holds a worthless cheque

3. Errors by either the business or the bank. For example, a bank may improperly charge (decrease) the bank balance of Business Research for a cheque drawn by another business, perhaps Business Research Associates. Or a business may miscompute its bank balance on its own books. Computational errors are becoming less frequent with the widespread use of computers. Nevertheless, all errors must be corrected, and the corrections will be a part of the bank reconciliation.

OBJECTIVE 3
Prepare a bank reconciliation and the related journal entries

Preparing the Bank Reconciliation

The steps in preparing the bank reconciliation are as follows:

1. Start with two figures, the balance in the business's Cash account in the general ledger (*balance per books*) and the balance shown on the bank statement (*balance per bank*). These two amounts will probably disagree because of the timing differences discussed earlier.

2. Add to, or subtract from, the *bank* balance those items that appear correctly on the books but not on the bank statement.

   a. Add *deposits in transit* to the bank balance. Deposits in transit are identified by comparing the deposits listed on the bank statement to the business's list of cash receipts. They appear as cash receipts on the books but not as deposits on the bank statement.

   b. Subtract *outstanding cheques* from the bank balance. Outstanding cheques are identified by comparing the cancelled cheques returned with the bank statement to the business's list of cheques written for cash payment. Outstanding cheques appear as cash payments on the books but not as paid cheques on the bank statement. If cheques were outstanding on the bank reconciliation for the preceding month and have still not been cashed, add them to the list of outstanding cheques on this month's bank reconciliation. Outstanding cheques are usually the most numerous item on a bank reconciliation.

3. Add to, or subtract from, the *book* balance those items that appear on the bank statement but not on the company books.

   a. Add to the book balance (1) *bank collections*, (2) *EFT cash receipts*, and (3) *interest revenue* earned on the money in the bank. These items are identified by comparing the deposits listed on the bank statement with the business's list of cash receipts. They show up as cash receipts on the bank statement but not on the books.

   b. Subtract from the book balance (1) *EFT cash payments*, (2) *service charges*, (3) *cost of printed cheques*, and (4) *other bank charges* (for example, charges for NSF or stale-date cheques). These items are identified by comparing the other charges listed on the bank statement to the cash payments recorded on the business's books. They appear as subtractions on the bank statement but not as cash payments on the books.

4. Compute the *adjusted bank balance* and *adjusted book balance*. The two adjusted balances should be equal.

5. Journalize each item in step 3, that is, each item listed on the book portion of the bank reconciliation. These items must be recorded on the business's books because they affect cash.

6. Correct all book errors, and notify the bank of any errors it has made.

Bank Reconciliation Illustrated   The bank statement in Exhibit 7-4 (page 358) indicates that the January 31, 2003, bank balance of Business Research is $5,906.51. However, the company's Cash account has a balance of $3,294.21, as shown in Exhibit 7-6. In following the steps outlined in the preceding section, the accountant finds these reconciling items:

1. The January 31 deposit of $1,591.63 does not appear on the bank statement. See the last item in the Company's Cash Account (Exhibit 7-6).

KEY POINT

Errors can be made by the bank or on the books. The balance that is adjusted for the error depends on where the error occurred. If the bank makes the error, the bank statement balance is adjusted. If the error is on the books, the book balance is adjusted.

KEY POINT

Preparing the bank reconciliation does not change the Cash balance on the books; it just shows what the balance should be. An entry is needed for every reconciling item on the book side to bring the Cash account to its correct reconciled balance.

KEY POINT

A journal entry is needed for each reconciling item on the *book* side. There are no entries for items on the bank side. These items have already been recorded on the books.

KEY POINT

Remember the purpose of the bank reconciliaton. The bank has recorded transactions to your account, such as interest earned and service charges, of which you are unaware until you receive the bank statement. You have recorded transactions on your books that have not been recorded by the bank, such as outstanding cheques. The bank reconciliation determines the correct amount of cash that should appear on the financial statements. The amount will probably not be either the bank statement balance or the current ledger (book) balance.

General Ledger:

ACCOUNT Cash No. 1100

Date	Item	Jrn. Ref.	Debit	Credit	Balance
2003					
Jan. 1	Balance	✔			6,556.22 Dr
2	Cash receipt	CR. 9	1,112.00		7,668.22 Dr
7	Cash receipt	CR. 9	194.60		7,862.82 Dr
31	Cash payments	CP. 17		6,160.24	1,702.58 Dr
31	Cash receipt	CR. 10	1,591.63		3,294.21 Dr

Cash Payments:

Cheque No.	Amount
332	$3,000.00
333	510.00
334	100.00
335	100.10
336	1,100.00
337	286.00
338	319.47
339	83.00
340	203.14
341	458.53
Total	$6,160.24

EXHIBIT 7-6

Cash Records of Business Research

WORKING IT OUT

The bank statement balance is $4,500 and shows a service charge of $15, interest earned of $5, and an NSF cheque for $300. Deposits in transit total $1,200; outstanding cheques are $575. The bookkeeper recorded as $152 a cheque of $125 in payment of an account payable. (1) What was the book balance of cash before the reconciliation? (2) What is the adjusted book balance? (3) What is the adjusted bank balance?

A: (1) $5,408 ($4,500 + $1,200 − $575 + $15 + $300 − $27 − $5); (2) $5,125 ($5,408 + $27 − $15 + $5 − $300); (3) $5,125 ($4,500 + $1,200 − $575). The adjusted bank and book balances are the same. The answer can be determined by working backward from the adjusted balance.

2. The bank erroneously charged to the Business Research account a $100 cheque—number 656—written by Business Research Associates.

3. Five company cheques issued late in January and recorded in the cash payments journal have not been paid by the bank:

Cheque No.	Date	Amount
337	Jan. 17	$286.00
338	26	319.47
339	27	83.00
340	28	203.14
341	30	458.53

These cheques are listed under cash payments in Exhibit 7-6.

4. The bank received $904.03 by EFT on behalf of Business Research. The bank statement serves as initial notification of this receipt of monthly rent revenue on unused office space.

5. The bank collected on behalf of the company a note receivable, $2,114 (including interest revenue of $214). Business Research has not recorded this cash receipt.

6. The bank statement shows interest revenue of $28.01, which the company has earned on its cash balance.

7. Cheque number 333 for $150 paid to Brown Corp. on account was recorded as a cash payment of $510, creating a $360 understatement of the Cash balance in the books.

8. The bank service charges for the month were $39.25 ($14.25 + $25.00 NSF charge).

9. The bank statement shows an NSF cheque for $52, which was received from customer L. Ross.

KEY POINT

Each reconciling item is treated in the same way in every situation. Here is a summary:

Bank Balance—always
- *Add* deposits in transit
- *Subtract* outstanding cheques

Book Balance—always
- *Add* bank collection items, interest revenue, and EFT receipts
- *Subtract* service charges, NSF cheques, and EFT payments

Errors—adjust the side where the error was made

Journal Entries—only for items on the book side

10. Business Research pays insurance expense monthly by EFT. The company has not yet recorded this $361 payment.

Exhibit 7-7 on page 365 is the bank reconciliation based on the preceding data. Panel A lists the reconciling items, which are referenced by number to the reconciliation in Panel B. After the reconciliation, the adjusted bank balance equals the adjusted book balance. This equality is an accuracy check.

Journalizing for Transactions from the Reconciliation   The bank reconciliation does not directly affect the journals or ledgers. Like the work sheet, the reconciliation is an accountant's tool, separate from the company's books.

The bank reconciliation acts as a control device by signalling the company to record transactions listed as reconciling items in the books section because the company has not yet done so. For example, the bank collected the note receivable on behalf of the company, but the company has not yet recorded this cash receipt. In fact, the company learned of the cash receipt only when it received the bank statement.

On the basis of the reconciliation in Exhibit 7-7, Business Research makes the following entries. They are dated January 31 to bring the Cash account to the correct balance on that date. Numbers in parentheses correspond to the reconciling items listed in Exhibit 7-7, Panel A.

WORKING IT OUT

Prepare the adjusting journal entry(ies) for the previous Working It Out.

A:

Cash	27	
Acct. Payable		27
Bank Charges Exp.	15	
Cash		15
Acct. Receivable	300	
Cash		300
Cash	5	
Interest Rev.		5

(4)	Jan. 31	Cash	904.03	
		Rent revenue		904.03
		Receipt of monthly rent.		
(5)	Jan. 31	Cash	2,114.00	
		Notes receivable		1,900.00
		Interest revenue		214.00
		Note receivable collected by bank.		
(6)	Jan. 31	Cash	28.01	
		Interest revenue		28.01
		Interest earned on bank balance.		
(7)	Jan. 31	Cash	360.00	
		Accounts payable—Brown Corp.		360.00
		Correction of cheque no. 333.		
(8)	Jan. 31	Bank charges expense	39.25	
		Cash		39.25
		Bank service charges.		
(9)	Jan. 31	Accounts receivable—L. Ross	52.00	
		Cash		52.00
		NSF cheque returned by bank.		
(10)	Jan. 31	Insurance expense	361.00	
		Cash		361.00
		Payment of monthly insurance.		

These entries bring the business's books up to date.

The entry for the NSF cheque (entry 9) needs explanation. Upon learning that L. Ross's $52 cheque was not good, Business Research credits Cash to bring the Cash account up to date. Since Business Research still has a receivable from Ross, it debits Accounts Receivable—L. Ross and pursues collection from him.

On-Line and Telephone Banking   Canadian banks now permit on-line and telephone banking, where customers use their computer or telephone to effect trans-

> **STOP & THINK**
>
> Why does the company *not* need to record the reconciling items on the bank side of the reconciliation?
>
> **Answer:** Those items have already been recorded on the company books.

Panel A: Reconciling Items

1. Deposit in transit, $1,591.63.
2. Bank error; add $100 to bank balance.
3. Outstanding cheques: no. 337, $286.00; no. 338, $319.47; no. 339, $83.00; no. 340, $203.14; no. 341, $458.53.
4. EFT receipt of rent revenue, $904.03.
5. Bank collection of note receivable, $2,114, including interest revenue of $214.
6. Interest earned on bank balance, $28.01.
7. Book error; add $360 to book balance.
8. Bank service charges, $39.25.
9. NSF cheque from L. Ross, $52.00.
10. EFT payment of insurance expense, $361.00.

Panel B: Bank Reconciliation

BUSINESS RESEARCH
Bank Reconciliation
January 31, 2003

Bank			Books		
Balance, January 31, 2003		$5,906.51	Balance, January 31, 2003		$3,294.21
Add:			Add:		
1. Deposit of January 31 in transit		1,591.63	4. EFT receipt of rent revenue		904.03
2. Correction of bank error —Business Research Associates cheque erroneously charged against company account		100.00	5. Bank collection of note receivable, including interest revenue of $214		2,114.00
		$7,598.14	6. Interest revenue earned on bank balance		28.01
3. Less: outstanding cheques			7. Correction of book error—Overstated amount of cheque no. 333		360.00
No. 337	$286.00				6,700.25
No. 338	319.47		Less:		
No. 339	83.00		8. Service charges	$39.25	
No. 340	203.14		9. NSF cheque	52.00	
No. 341	458.53	(1,350.14)	10. EFT payment of insurance expense	361.00	(452.25)
Adjusted bank balance		$6,248.00	Adjusted book balance		$6,248.00

Amounts agree

EXHIBIT 7-7

Bank Reconciliation

actions such as paying bills, transferring money from one account to another, and arranging a loan. With telephone banking, the bank gives the customer a transaction number over the telephone when the transaction is completed; the transaction is confirmed by its appearance in the passbook or on a subsequent bank statement. There is no other "paper trail" as evidence of the transaction. Similarly, with on-line banking, customers use a computer and a modem or an Internet connection to effect transactions. The bank supplies a confirmation number on the customer's computer screen to show the transaction has occurred, and the transaction is confirmed by its appearance in the passbook or on a subsequent bank statement. Again, there is no other paper trail as evidence of the transaction.

Since bank statements are usually received monthly, a bank reconciliation is often performed only once a month. However, with on-line access to bank account information, you are able to print your bank account transaction data at any time. Thus, companies and individuals could prepare bank reconciliations more frequently than once a month.

How Owners and Managers Use the Bank Reconciliation

The bank reconciliation is a powerful control device in the hands of a business owner or manager, as the following example illustrates.

Randy Vaughn is a CA in Regina, Saskatchewan. He owns several small apartment complexes that are managed by his cousin. His accounting practice keeps him busy, so he has little time to devote to his apartment investments. Vaughn's cousin approves tenants, collects the monthly rent cheques, arranges custodial and maintenance work, hires and fires employees, writes the cheques, and performs the bank reconciliation. In short, she does it all. This concentration of duties in one person is terrible from an internal control standpoint. Vaughn's cousin could be stealing from him, and as a CA he is aware of this possibility.

Vaughn trusts his cousin because she is a member of the family. Nevertheless, he exercises some loose controls over her management of his apartments. Vaughn periodically drops by his properties to see whether the custodial/maintenance staff is keeping them in good condition.

To control cash, Vaughn uses the bank statement and the bank reconciliation. On an irregular basis, he examines the bank reconciliation that his cousin has performed. He matches every cheque that cleared the bank to the journal entry on the books. Vaughn would know immediately if his cousin is writing cheques to herself. Vaughn sometimes prepares his own bank reconciliation to see whether he agrees with his cousin's work. If his cousin is stealing cash and concealing it by manipulating the bank reconciliation, this would come to light. To keep his cousin on her toes, Vaughn lets her know that he periodically checks her work.

Vaughn has a simple method for controlling cash receipts. He knows the occupancy level of his apartments. He also knows the monthly rent he charges. He multiplies the number of apartments—say 20—by the monthly rent (which averages $500 per unit) to arrive at expected monthly rent revenue of $10,000. By tracing the $10,000 revenue to the bank statement, Vaughn can tell that his rent money went into his bank account.

Control activities such as these (often referred to as "executive controls") are critical in small businesses. With only a few employees, a separation of duties may not be feasible. The owner must oversee the operations of the business, or the assets will disappear, as they did for Larsen & Company in the chapter opening story on page 348.

Mid-Chapter Summary Problem
for Your Review

The cash account of Labelle Property Holdings at February 28, 2002 follows:

Cash

Feb.	1	Balance	3,995	Feb.	3	400
	6		800		12	3,100
	15		1,800		19	1,100
	23		1,100		25	500
	28		2,400		27	900
	28	Balance	4,095			

Labelle Property Holdings receives this bank statement on February 28, 2002, with the information shown below (negative amounts appear in parentheses):

Bank Statement for February 2002

Beginning balance		$3,995
Deposits:		
Feb. 7	$ 800	
15	1,800	
24	1,100	3,700
Cheques (total per day):		
Feb. 8	$ 400	
16	3,100	
23	1,100	(4,600)
Other items:		
Service charge		(10)
NSF cheque from M. E. Crown		(700)
Bank collection of note receivable for the company		1,000*
EFT—monthly rent expense		(330)
Interest on account balance		15
Ending balance		$3,070

*Includes interest of $119.

Additional data: Labelle Property Holdings deposits all cash receipts in the bank and makes all cash payments by cheque.

Required

1. Prepare the bank reconciliation of Labelle Property Holdings at February 28, 2002.

2. Record the entries based on the bank reconciliation.

Solution to Review Problem

Requirement 1

LABELLE PROPERTY HOLDINGS
Bank Reconciliation
February 28, 2002

Bank		
Balance, February 28, 2002		$3,070
Add: Deposit of February 28 in transit		2,400
		5,470
Less: Outstanding cheques issued on Feb. 25 ($500) and Feb. 27 ($900)		(1,400)
Adjusted bank balance, February 28, 2002		$4,070
Books		
Balance, February 28, 2002		$4,095
Add: Bank collection of note receivable, including interest of $119		1,000
Add: Interest earned on bank balance		15
		5,110
Less: Service charge	$ 10	
NSF cheque	700	
EFT—Rent expense	330	(1,040)
Adjusted book balance, February 28, 2002		$4,070

Requirement 2

Feb.	28	Cash		1,000	
		Note Receivable			881
		Interest Revenue			119
		Note receivable collected by bank ($1,000 – $119).			
Feb.	28	Cash		15	
		Interest Revenue			15
		Interest earned on bank balance.			
Feb.	28	Bank Charges Expense		10	
		Cash			10
		Bank service charge.			
Feb.	28	Accounts Receivable—M. E. Crown		700	
		Cash			700
		NSF cheque returned by bank.			
Feb.	28	Rent Expense		330	
		Cash			330
		Monthly rent expense.			

Cyber Coach

Visit the Student Resource area of the *Accounting* Companion Website for extra practice with the new material in Chapter 7.

www.pearsoned.ca/horngren

OBJECTIVE 4
Apply internal controls to cash receipts

Internal Control Over Cash Receipts

Internal control over cash receipts (the term includes cash, cheques, and other negotiable instruments) ensures that all cash receipts are deposited in the bank and the company's accounting records are correct. Many businesses receive cash over the counter and through the mail. Each source of cash receipts calls for its own security measures.

Cash Receipts Over the Counter   The point-of-sale terminal (cash register) offers management control over cash received in a store. Consider a Canadian Tire store. First, the terminal should be positioned so that customers can see the amounts the cashier enters into the terminal. No person willingly pays more than the marked price for an item, so the customer helps prevent the sales clerk from overcharging and pocketing the excess over actual prices. Company policy should require issuance of a receipt to make sure each sale is recorded in the terminal.

Second, the cash drawer opens only when the salesclerk enters an amount on the keypad, and a duplicate roll of tape locked inside the machine or the store's central computer records each sale and cash transaction. At the end of the day, a manager proves the cash by comparing the total amount in the cash drawer against the duplicate tape's total or the computer's total. This step helps prevent outright theft by the clerk. For security reasons, the clerk should not have access to the duplicate tape or the computer.

Third, pricing merchandise at "uneven" amounts—say, $3.95 instead of $4.00—means that the clerk generally must make change, which in turn means having to get into the cash drawer. This requires entering the amount of the sale on the keypad, which records the transaction on the register tape or central computer.

At the end of the day, the cashier or other employee with cash-handling duties deposits the cash in the bank. The cash register is usually reset to zero for the next day's sales. The accounting department uses the tape or the amount recorded in the central computer as the basis for an entry in the cash receipts journal. These security measures, coupled with periodic on-site inspection by a manager, discourage theft.

Cash Receipts by Mail   All incoming mail should be opened by a mail-room employee. This person should compare the amount of the cheque received with the attached remittance advice (the slip of paper that lists the amount of the cheque). If no advice was sent, the mail-room employee should prepare one and enter the amount of each receipt on a control tape. At the end of the day, this control tape is given to a responsible official, such as the controller, for verification. Cash receipts should be given to the cashier, who combines them with any cash received over the counter and prepares the bank deposit.

Having a mail-room employee handle postal cash receipts is another application of a good internal control procedure—in this case, separation of duties. If the accountants opened postal cash receipts, they could easily hide a theft.

The mail-room employee forwards the remittance advices to the accounting department. They provide the data for entries in the cash receipts journal and postings to customers' accounts in the accounts receivable ledger. As a final step, the controller compares the three records of the day's cash receipts: (1) the control tape total from the mail room, (2) the bank deposit amount from the cashier, and (3) the debit to Cash from the accounting department.

As was mentioned earlier, some companies use a lock-box system to separate cash duties and establish control over cash receipts. Customers send their cheques directly to an address that is essentially a bank account. Internal control over the cash is enhanced because company personnel do not handle the cash. The lock-box system improves efficiency because the cash is added to the bank account and goes to work for the company immediately.

Cash Short and Over   A difference may exist between actual cash receipts and the day's record of cash received. Usually the difference is small and results from honest errors. When the recorded cash balance exceeds cash on hand, we have a *cash short* situation. When the actual cash exceeds the recorded cash balance, we have a *cash over* situation. Suppose the tapes from a cash register at a Little Short Stop convenience store indicated sales revenue of $15,000, but the cash received was $14,980. To record the day's sales for that register, the store would make this entry:

Cash	14,980	
Cash Short and Over..	20	
Sales Revenue		15,000
Daily cash sales.		

As the entry shows, Cash Short and Over, an expense account, is debited when sales revenue exceeds cash receipts. This account is credited when cash receipts exceed sales. A debit balance in Cash Short and Over appears on the income statement as Miscellaneous Expense; a credit balance may be shown as Other Revenue.

The Cash Short and Over account's balance should be small. The debits and credits for cash shorts and overs collected over an accounting period tend to cancel each other out. A large balance signals the accountant to investigate. For example, too large a debit balance may mean an employee is stealing. Cash Short and Over, then, acts as an internal control device.

Exhibit 7-8 summarizes the controls over cash receipts.

EXHIBIT 7-8

Internal Controls over Cash Receipts

Element of Internal Control	Internal Controls over Cash Receipts
Competent, reliable, ethical personnel	Companies carefully screen employees for undesirable personality traits. They commit time and effort to training programs.
Assignment of responsibilities	Specific employees are designated as cashiers, supervisors of cashiers, or accountants for cash receipts.
Proper authorization	Only designated employees, such as department managers, can grant exceptions for customers, approve cheque receipts above a certain amount, allow customers to purchase on credit, and void sales.
Separation of duties	Cashiers and mail-room employees who handle cash do not have access to the accounting records. Accountants who record cash receipts have no opportunity to handle cash.
Internal and external audits	Internal auditors examine company transactions for agreement with management policies. External auditors examine the internal controls over cash receipts to determine whether the accounting system produces accurate amounts for revenues, receivables, and other items related to cash receipts.
Documents and records	Customers receive receipts as transaction records. Bank statement lists cash receipts for deposit. Customers who pay by mail include a remittance advice showing the amount of cash they sent to the company.
Electronic devices and computer control	Cash registers serve as transaction records. Each day's receipts are matched with customer remittance advices and with the day's deposit ticket with the bank.
Other Controls	Cashiers are bonded. Cash is stored in vaults and banks. Employees are rotated among jobs and are required to take vacations.

Internal Control Over Cash Payments

Exercising controls over cash payments (disbursements) is as important as controlling cash receipts.

Controls Over Payment by Cheque

Payment by cheque is an important control over cash payments. First, the cheque acts as a source document. Second, to be valid the cheque must be signed by an authorized official, so that each payment by cheque draws the attention of management. Before signing the cheque, the manager should study the evidence or documentation supporting the payment.

To illustrate the internal control over cash payments, let's suppose the business is buying inventory for sale to customers.

Controls Over Purchasing   The purchasing process—outlined in Exhibit 7-9—starts when the sales department identifies the need for merchandise and prepares a *purchase request* (or *requisition*). A separate purchasing department locates the goods and mails a *purchase order* to the supplier, the outside company that sells the needed goods. When the supplier ships the goods to the requesting business, the supplier also mails the *invoice*, or bill, as notification to pay. (We introduced purchase orders and invoices in Chapter 5, page 221.) As the goods arrive, the receiving department checks them for any damage and lists the merchandise received on a document called the *receiving report*. The accounting department attaches all the foregoing documents, checks them for accuracy and agreement, and forwards this payment packet with a completed cheque to designated officers for approval and payment.

EXHIBIT 7-9

Purchasing Process

Business Document	Prepared by	Sent to
Purchase request (requisition)	Sales department	Purchasing department
Purchase order	Purchasing department	Outside company that sells the needed merchandise (supplier or vendor)
Invoice (bill)	Outside company that sells the needed merchandise (supplier or vendor)	Accounting department
Receiving report	Receiving department	Accounting department
Payment packet	Accounting department	Officer who signs the cheque

The packet includes the invoice, receiving report, purchase order, and purchase request, as shown in Exhibit 7-10.

Controls Over Approval of Payments   Before approving the payment, the controller and the treasurer should examine a sample of transactions to determine that the accounting department has performed the following control steps:

1. The invoice is compared with a copy of the purchase order and purchase request to ensure that the business pays cash only for the goods that it ordered.
2. The invoice is compared with the receiving report to ensure that cash is paid only for the goods that are actually received.
3. The mathematical accuracy of the invoice is proved.

To avoid document alteration, some firms use machines that stamp the amount on the cheque in indelible ink. After payment, the cheque signer can punch a hole through the payment packet. This hole denotes that the invoice has been paid and makes it hard to run the documents through the system for a duplicate payment.

Technology is streamlining cash payment procedures in many businesses. Evaluated Receipts Settlement (ERS) compresses the approval process into a single step: compare the receiving report to the purchase order. If the two documents match, that proves, for example, that Kinko's received the paper it ordered. Then Kinko's pays Hammermill Paper, the supplier. ERS requires fewer employees and saves on accounting expense.

An even more streamlined process bypasses people and documents altogether. In Electronic Data Interchange (EDI), Canadian Tire's home office computers can communicate directly with the computers of suppliers like General Tire, Rubbermaid,

THINKING IT OVER

Two officers' signatures are required for cheques over $1,000. One officer is going on vacation and pre-signs several cheques so that the cheques will be available if needed while she is gone. The cheques are locked in the vault. What is the internal control feature in this scenario?

A: Proper authorization. Two signatures are required to ensure that no unauthorized expenditures are made. Pre-signing the cheques defeats the control and should be discouraged.

EXHIBIT 7-10

Payment Packet

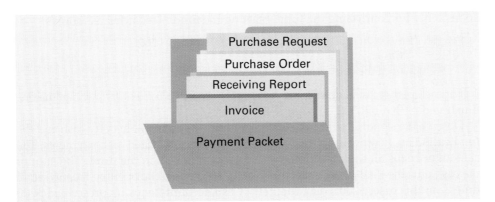

and Procter & Gamble. When Canadian Tire's auto tires reach a certain (low) level, the computer sends a purchase order to General Tire. General Tire ships the tires and invoices Canadian Tire electronically. Then an electronic fund transfer (EFT) sends the cash from Canadian Tire to General Tire.

These streamlined procedures depend on the mutual trust of the companies involved. They know each other well and operate in a highly ethical manner. They cannot afford to do otherwise. Exhibit 7-11 summarizes the internal controls over cash payments.

STOP & THINK

Talon Computer Concepts processes payroll cheques for small businesses. Clients give their employees' time cards to Talon each week, and Talon programmers write computer programs to meet the clients' payrolls. Talon computer operators process and deliver the cheques to the clients for distribution to employees. Identify two employee functions of Talon's cash payments system that should be separated. Give your reason.

Answer: The *programmers* should not also be computer *operators*. Any person who performed both functions could write the program to process cheques to himself or herself or to a fictitious employee and then pocket the printed cheques.

THINKING IT OVER

You manage a community performing arts centre. Customers pay for tickets through the mail as well as in person. You maintain a relatively large petty cash fund at all times. You have determined that your monthly petty cash needs are approximately $5,000. Each of your three employees has been with you for at least five years and has access to the petty cash fund. When you were reimbursing the fund at the end of the month, $2,000 was unaccounted for. How could you correct this problem?

A: Restrict access to the fund to only one person; replenish the fund more often so that less money is subject to theft and problems can be corrected more quickly; or give each employee his or her own fund.

Controlling Petty Cash Payments

It would be uneconomical for a business to write a separate cheque for an executive's taxi fare, a box of floppy disks needed right away, or the delivery of a special message across town. Therefore, companies keep a small amount of cash on hand to pay for such minor amounts. This fund is called **petty cash**.

Even though the individual amounts paid through the petty cash fund may be small, such expenses occur so often that the total amount over an accounting period may grow quite large. Thus the business needs to set up these controls over petty cash:

1. Designate an employee to administer the fund as its custodian.
2. Keep a specific amount of cash on hand.
3. Support all fund payments with a petty cash ticket.
4. Replenish the fund through normal cash payment procedures.

The petty cash fund is opened when a payment is approved for a predetermined amount and a cheque for this amount is issued to the petty cash custodian. Assume that on February 28 the business decides to establish a petty cash fund of $200. The custodian cashes the cheque and places the currency and coin in the fund, which may be a cash box, safe, or other device. The petty cash custodian is assigned the responsibility for controlling the fund. Starting the fund is recorded as follows:

Feb. 28	Petty Cash..	200	
	Cash...		200
	To open the petty cash fund.		

For each petty cash payment, the custodian prepares a *petty cash ticket* like the one illustrated in Exhibit 7-12 on page 374.

Observe the signatures (or initials) that identify the recipient of petty cash and the fund custodian. Requiring both signatures reduces unauthorized cash payments. The custodian keeps all the pre-numbered petty cash tickets in the fund. The sum of the cash plus the total of the ticket amounts should equal the opening balance at all times—in this case, $200. Also, the Petty Cash account keeps its prescribed $200

EXHIBIT 7-11

Internal Controls over Cash Payments

Element of Internal Control	Internal Controls over Cash Payments
Competent, reliable, ethical personnel	Cash payments are entrusted to high-level employees, with larger amounts paid by the treasurer or assistant treasurer.
Assignment of responsibility	Specific employees approve purchase documents for payment. Executives examine approvals, then sign cheques.
Proper authorization	Large expenditures must be authorized by the company owner or board of directors to ensure agreement with organizational goals.
Separation of duties	Computer operators and other employees who handle cheques have no access to the accounting records. Accountants who record cash payments have no opportunity to handle cash.
Internal and external audits	Internal auditors examine company transactions for agreement with management policies. External auditors examine the internal controls over cash payments to determine whether the accounting system produces accurate amounts for expenses, assets, and other items related to cash payments.
Documents and records	Suppliers issue invoices that document the need to pay cash. Bank statements list cash payments (cheques and EFT payments) for reconciliation with company records. Cheques are prenumbered and used in sequence to account for payments.
Electronic devices, computer controls and other controls	Blank cheques are stored in a vault and controlled by a responsible official with no accounting duties. Machines stamp the amount on a cheque in indelible ink. Paid invoices are punched or otherwise mutilated to avoid duplicate payment.

balance at all times. Maintaining the Petty Cash account at this balance, supported by the fund (cash plus tickets totalling the fund amount) is a characteristic of an **imprest system**. The control feature of an imprest system is that it clearly identifies the amount of cash for which the fund custodian is responsible.

Payments reduce the amount of cash in the fund, so periodically the fund must be replenished. Suppose that on March 31 the fund has $118 in cash and $82 in tickets. A cheque for $82 is issued, made payable to the petty cash custodian. The fund custodian cashes this cheque for currency and coins, and puts the money in the fund to return its actual cash to $200. The petty cash tickets identify the accounts to be debited: Office Supplies for $23, Delivery Expense for $17, and Miscellaneous Selling Expense for $42. The entry to record replenishment of the fund is

Mar. 31	Office Supplies	23	
	Delivery Expense	17	
	Selling Expense	42	
	Cash		82
	To replenish the petty cash fund.		

If this cash payment exceeds the sum of the tickets—that is, if the fund comes up short, Cash Short and Over is debited for the missing amount. If the sum of the tickets exceeds the payment, Cash Short and Over is credited. Replenishing the fund does *not* affect the Petty Cash account. Petty Cash keeps its $200 balance at all times.

> **KEY POINT**
>
> Access to the petty cash fund should be permitted only to the fund custodian. All petty cash tickets should be signed by both the custodian and the recipient of the petty cash.

> **KEY POINT**
>
> As petty cash is used and petty cash tickets are written, the sum of the cash remaining in the petty cash fund plus the tickets written should *always* equal the predetermined petty cash fund amount.

EXHIBIT 7-12

Petty Cash Ticket

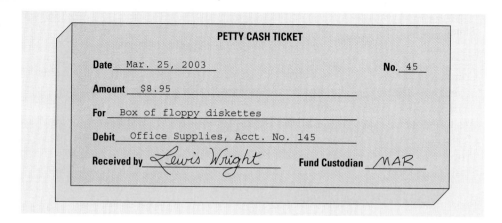

PETTY CASH TICKET	
Date Mar. 25, 2003	No. 45
Amount $8.95	
For Box of floppy diskettes	
Debit Office Supplies, Acct. No. 145	
Received by Lewis Wright	Fund Custodian MAR

KEY POINT

No journal entries are made for petty cash payments until the fund is replenished. At that time, all petty cash payments will be recorded in a summary entry. This procedure avoids the need to journalize many payments for small amounts.

KEY POINT

Attached to the petty cash ticket is a cash register receipt, invoice, or other documentation to support the payment.

OBJECTIVE 6
Use a budget to manage cash

Whenever petty cash runs low, the fund is replenished. It *must* be replenished on the balance sheet date. Otherwise, the reported balance for Petty Cash will be overstated by the amount of the tickets in the fund. The income statement will understate the expenses listed on these tickets.

The Petty Cash account in the General Ledger is debited only when the fund is started (see the February 28 entry) or when its amount is changed. In our illustration, suppose the business decides to raise the fund amount from $200 to $250 because of increased demand for petty cash. This step would require a $50 debit to the Petty Cash account.

Using a Budget to Manage Cash

Owners and managers control their organizations with the help of budgets. A **budget** is a quantitative expression of a plan that helps managers coordinate the entity's activities. Cash receives the most attention in the budgeting process because all transactions ultimately affect cash. In this section, we introduce *cash budgeting* as a way to manage this important asset. (We discuss budgeting in much greater detail in Chapters 23 and 24).

How does BCT. TELUS Communications Inc. decide when to invest in new telecommunications equipment? How will the company decide how much to spend? Will borrowing be needed, or can BCT. TELUS finance the purchase with internally generated cash? Similarly, by what process do you decide how much to spend on your education? On an automobile? On a house? All these decisions depend to some degree on the information that a cash budget provides.

> A cash budget helps a business manage its cash by expressing the plan for the receipt and payment of cash during a future period.

To prepare for the future, a company must determine how much cash it will need and then determine how to obtain the needed cash. Preparation of a cash budget proceeds in four steps:

1. Start with the entity's cash balance at the beginning of the period. The beginning balance tells how much cash is left over from the preceding period.

2. Add the budgeted cash receipts and subtract the budgeted cash payments. This is the most challenging part of the budgeting process because managers must predict the cash effects of all transactions of the budget period, including

   a. Revenue and expense transactions
   b. Asset acquisition and sale transactions
   c. Liability and owner's equity transactions

LEARNING TIP

The cash budget is entirely separate from net income or net loss on the income statement. For this reason, net income does not appear on the cash budget.

Foresight is imperfect, so the actual figure will not always turn out as expected. It is important to develop *realistic* estimates of the cash receipts and payments during the budget period.

3. The beginning balance plus the expected receipts minus the expected payments equals the expected cash balance at the end of the period.

4. Compare the expected cash balance to the desired, or *budgeted*, cash balance at the end of the period. Owners and managers know the minimum amount of cash they need (the budgeted balance) to keep the entity running. If there is excess cash, they can invest more than originally planned. If the expected cash balance falls below the budgeted balance, the company must obtain additional financing to reach the desired cash balance.

Let's consider the benefits of budgeting cash. Suppose the BCT. TELUS budget reveals a cash shortage during June of the coming year. The budget gives BCT. TELUS managers an early warning of the need for additional cash. Managers can arrange financing in advance and probably get a lower interest rate and better payment terms than if they are forced to borrow money under rushed conditions. In short, the cash budget helps managers make decisions in an orderly manner. A budget serves the same purpose for individuals.

Exhibit 7-13 shows a hypothetical cash budget for The Gap, Inc., for the year ended January 31, 2002. Study it carefully because at some point in your career or personal affairs you will use a cash budget.

The cash budget has sections for cash receipts and cash payments. The budget is prepared *before* the period's transactions and can take any form that helps people make decisions. The cash budget is an internal document, so it is not bound by generally accepted accounting principles.

The Gap's hypothetical budget in Exhibit 7-13 begins with the company's actual cash balance at the beginning of the period. At February 1, 2001, The Gap had cash of $203 million (line 1). The budgeted cash receipts and payments are expected to create a need for additional financing during the year (line 13).

Observe that the budget for expanding existing stores will require $206 million (line 7), and the opening of new stores is expected to cost the company $349 million

THINKING IT OVER

How can a business that reports net income benefit from cash budgeting?

A: (1) A company that is profitable will not necessarily have a good cash flow. The income statement is prepared using *accrual accounting*—that is, revenue and expenses are recorded when earned or incurred, not when the cash flow occurs. Amortization is an example of an expense that does not affect cash. (2) Even profitable companies may experience temporary cash shortages. Budgeting helps companies plan ahead so these cash shortages can be averted or managed properly. (3) *Actual* results can be compared to the budget. Problems often are pinpointed and then can be avoided in future periods.

Gap
www.gap.com

EXHIBIT 7-13

Cash Budget (Hypothetical)

THE GAP, INC. Cash Budget (Hypothetical) For the Year Ended January 31, 2002			
			(In millions)
(1)	Cash balance, February 1, 2001		$ 203
	Estimated cash receipts:		
(2)	Collections from customers	$ 2,858	
(3)	Interest and dividends on investments	6	
(4)	Sale of store fixtures	5	2,869
			3,072
	Estimated cash payments:		
(5)	Purchases of inventory	$(1,906)	
(6)	Operating expenses	(561)	
(7)	Expansions of existing stores	(206)	
(8)	Opening of new stores	(349)	
(9)	Payment of long-term debt	(145)	
(10)	Payment to owners of the business	(219)	(3,386)
(11)	Cash available (needed) before new financing		(314)
(12)	Budgeted cash balance, January 31, 2002		(200)
(13)	Cash available for additional investments, or (New financing needed)		$ (514)

WORKING IT OUT

Suppose line 11 of Exhibit 7-13 showed cash available of $250 million. What would The Gap do, borrow additional money or have an excess to invest?

A: The Gap would have an additional $50 million to invest ($250 million available – $200 million needed = excess of $50 million).

(line 8). Without these investing transactions, The Gap would not have needed additional cash. But long-term investments, such as new stores, keep the company competitive.

Assume that managers of The Gap wish to maintain a cash balance of at least $200 million (line 12). Because the year's activity is expected to leave the company with a *negative* cash balance of $314 million (line 11), The Gap's managers must arrange $514 million of financing (line 13). Line 11 of the cash budget identifies the amount of cash available or needed. Line 12 lists the minimum cash balance to maintain at all times. *Add* lines 11 and 12 to arrive at the amount of new financing needed. To meet this need for new financing, The Gap can either borrow or raise the money from outside investors.

Managers also use budgets to evaluate performance. As the year progresses, managers compare actual figures with the budgeted amounts. Suppose it is now April 15, 2001, and sales and collections from customers are lagging behind expectations for the first quarter of the year. Knowledge of the slowdown in sales alerts top management of The Gap to take action.

International transactions add to the complexity of managing cash. When a Canadian company buys goods internationally, it may pay cash in a foreign currency, such as U.S. dollars or Mexican pesos. Foreign currencies change in value from day to day. When paying for a transaction, a company may have a gain or a loss on its foreign-currency transactions. We show how to account for foreign-currency transactions in Chapter 16.

Reporting Cash on the Balance Sheet

Cash is the first current asset listed on the balance sheet of most companies. Even small businesses have several bank accounts and one or more petty cash funds, but companies usually combine all cash amounts into a single total called "Cash and Cash Equivalents" on the balance sheet.

Cash equivalents include liquid assets such as time deposits and certificates of deposit, which are interest-bearing accounts that can be withdrawn with no penalty after a short period of time. Although they are slightly less liquid than cash, they are sufficiently similar to be reported along with cash. For example, the balance sheet of Nortel Networks Corporation recently reported the following:

NORTEL NETWORKS CORPORATION Balance Sheet (Adapted) December 31, 1999	
(In millions of U.S. dollars)	
Assets	
Current assets:	
Cash and equivalents	$ 2,257
Accounts receivable	6,786
Material and supplies....................................	2,956
Other current assets	1,069
Total current assets...	$13,068
Source: Nortel Networks Corporation. 1999 Annual Report	

Nortel's cash balance means that $2,257 million is available for use as needed. Cash that is restricted and unavailable for immediate use should not be reported as a current asset if the company does not expect to spend the cash within a year or within the company's operating cycle, if longer than a year. For example, some banks require their depositors to maintain a *compensating balance* on deposit in the bank in order to borrow from the bank.

Ethics and Accounting

OBJECTIVE 7
Make ethical judgments in business

A *Wall Street Journal* article described a young Russian entrepreneur who claimed that he was getting ahead in business by breaking laws. He stated that "Older people have an ethics problem. By that I mean they *have* ethics." Conversely, Robert Schad, President and CEO of Husky Injection Molding Systems Ltd., in Bolton, Ontario, said, "Ethical practice is, quite simply, good business." Schad has been in business long enough to see the danger in unethical behaviour. Sooner or later unethical conduct comes to light, as was true in our chapter-opening story on page 348. Moreover, ethical behaviour wins out in the end because it is the right thing to do.

Corporate and Professional Codes of Ethics

Most large companies have a code of ethics to encourage employees to behave ethically and responsibly. However, a set of general guidelines may not be specific enough to identify misbehaviour and a list of do's and don'ts can lead to the false view that anything is okay if it's not specifically forbidden. But codes of ethics are not enough by themselves. Senior management must set a high ethical tone at the uppermost levels of the organization. They must make it clear that the company will not tolerate unethical conduct by employees.

Accountants have additional incentives to behave ethically. As professionals, they are expected to maintain higher standards than society in general. Their ability to attract business depends entirely on their reputation.

As you learned in Chapter 1, there are three bodies of professional accountants in Canada: the CAs; the CGAs; and the CMAs. Members of each of the bodies must adhere to the rules of professional conduct of their respective organizations. These documents set minimum standards of conduct for members. Unacceptable actions can result in expulsion from the organization, which makes it impossible for the person to remain a professional accountant.

Ethical Issues in Accounting

In many situations the ethical choice is easy. For example, stealing cash, as in the chapter-opening story, is illegal and unethical. The cashier's actions led to a jail sentence. In other cases, the choices are more difficult. But, in every instance, ethical judgments become a personal decision. What should I do in a given situation? Let's consider two ethical issues in accounting.

Situation 1   Sonja Kleberg is preparing the income tax return of a client who has had a particularly good year—higher income than expected. On January 2, the client pays for newspaper advertising to run in late January and asks Sonja to backdate the expense to the preceding year. The tax deduction would help the client more in the year just ended than in the current year. Backdating would decrease taxable income of the earlier year and postpone a few dollars in tax payments. After all, there is a difference of only two days between January 2 and December 31. This client is important to Kleberg. What should she do?

> **She should refuse the request because the transaction**
> **took place in January of the new year.**

What internal control device could prove that Kleberg behaved unethically if she backdated the transaction in the accounting records? A Canada Customs and Revenue Agency audit of the documents and records: The date of the cash payment and the running date of the ad prove that the expense occurred in January rather than in December.

Situation 2   Emilia Gomez, an accountant for Hoover Electronics Ltd., discovers that her supervisor, Myles Packer, made several errors last year. Overall, the errors

Wall Street Journal
info.wsj.com

Husky Injection Molding Systems Ltd.
www.husky.ca

REAL WORLD EXAMPLE

In a survey, 81 percent of companies had a corporate code of conduct. Another 7 percent planned to establish such a code.

overstated net income by 20 percent. It is not clear whether the errors were deliberate or accidental. Gomez is deciding what to do. She knows that Packer evaluates her job performance, and lately her work has been marginal. What should Gomez do?

The answer is uncertain.

To make her decision, Gomez should follow the framework outlined in the Decision Guidelines feature.

DECISION GUIDELINES *Framework for Making Ethical Judgments*

Weighing tough ethical judgments requires a decision framework. Consider these six questions as general guidelines:

Question	Decision Guidelines
1. What are the facts?	1. *Determine the facts.*
2. What is the ethical issue, if any?	2. *Identify the ethical issues.* The root word of ethical is *ethics*, which Webster's dictionary defines as "the discipline dealing with what is good and bad and with moral duty and obligation." Gomez's ethical dilemma is to decide what she should do with the information she has uncovered.
3. What are the alternatives?	3. *Specify the alternatives.* For Emilia Gomez, four reasonable alternatives include (a) reporting the errors to Packer, (b) reporting the errors to Packer's boss, (c) correcting the errors and saying nothing, and (d) doing nothing.
4. Who is involved in the situation?	4. *Identify the stakeholders, the people involved.* Individuals who could be affected inlude Gomez, Packer, Gomez's co-workers who observe her behaviour, Hoover Electronics Ltd., and the people who use Hoover Electronics Ltd.'s financial statements.
5. What are the possible consequences of each alternative in question 3?	5. *Assess the possible outcomes of each alternative.* (a) If Gomez reports the errors to Packer, he might penalize her, or he might reward her for careful work. Reporting the errors would preserve her integrity and probably would lead to restated financial statements. But Hoover Electronics Ltd. could suffer embarrassment if this situation were made public. (b) If Gomez reports to Packer's boss—"going over Packer's head"—her integrity would be preserved. Her relationship with Packer would surely be strained, and it might be difficult for them to work together in the future. Gomez might be rewarded for careful work. But if Packer's boss has colluded with Packer in recording the expenses, Gomez could be penalized. (c) If the error is corrected and outsiders notified, Hoover Electronics Ltd. would be embarrassed. Others observing this situation would be affected by the outcome. (d) If Gomez does nothing, she would avoid a confrontation with Packer or his boss. They might or might not discover the error. If they discover it, they might or might not correct it. All might criticize Gomez for not bringing the error to their attention. Colleagues might or might not learn of the situation. Gomez's conscience would likely bother her.
6. What shall I do?	6. *Make a decision.* The best choice is not obvious. Gomez must balance the likely effects on the various people against the dictates of her own conscience. Even though this framework does not provide an easy decision, it identifies the relevant factors. Gomez should report the errors. Ordinarily, Packer should be the first person contacted. If Packer fails to act in an honest way, then Gomez should inform Packer's boss. Senior management should always protect the messenger of accurate news, whether good or bad.

Ethics and External Controls

There is another dimension to most ethical issues: *external controls*, which refer to the discipline placed on business conduct by outsiders who interact with the company.

- In situation 1, for example, Sonja Kleberg could give in to the client's request to backdate the advertising expense. But this action would be both dishonest and illegal. These external controls arise from the business's interaction with the taxing authorities. A Canada Customs and Revenue Agency audit of Kleberg's client could uncover her action.

- The primary external control in situation 2 results from creditors and other outside users of Hoover Electronics Ltd.'s financial statements. If these users suffered a financial loss because they were deceived by Hoover's overstated income, they could file a lawsuit against Hoover. The legal system in Canada places the burden of proof on companies to show that their financial information is accurate. A lender or an investor who can demonstrate that a loss resulted from reliance on fraudulent information can recover damages against the company.

A shifting of income to one year usually causes a corresponding decrease in the income of a later year. Thus Hoover's reporting 20 percent too much income last year may cause the company to report 20 percent too little income the next year. The ethical implication is that companies that are caught manipulating their reported income lose their good reputations very quickly. This loss would make it difficult to attract investors and to borrow money on favourable terms. Honest errors can occur, and lenders and investors can be forgiving, but companies must work hard to keep their reputations clean. That is why they have codes of conduct and why, as Robert Schad put it, "Ethical practice is…good business."

STOP & THINK

Can you identify the external control in the chapter-opening story on page 348? How did it impose discipline on the cashier?

Answer: The external control was the monthly statement that Larsen & Company sends each client. When customers saw their account balances underreported on the monthly statements, they called in to ask why. Jack Van Auken must have spent half his time explaining the out-of-balance conditions of clients' accounts. Sooner or later he was bound to get caught. That's how external controls work.

Summary Problem
for Your Review

Grudnitski Systems Design established a $300 petty cash fund. James C. Brown is the fund custodian. At the end of the first week, the petty cash fund contains the following:

1. Cash: $171

2. Petty cash tickets

No.	Amount	Issued to	Signed by	Account Debited
44	$14	B. Jarvis	B. Jarvis and JCB	Office Supplies
45	9	S. Bell	S. Bell	Miscellaneous Expense
47	43	R. Tate	R. Tate and JCB	—
48	33	G. Blair	G. Blair and JCB	Travel Expense

Required

1. Identify the four internal control weaknesses revealed in the given data.
2. Prepare the general journal entries to record
   a. Establishment of the petty cash fund.
   b. Replenishment of the fund. Assume petty cash ticket no. 47 was issued for the purchase of office supplies.
3. What is the balance in the Petty Cash account immediately before replenishment? Immediately after replenishment?

Solution to the Review Problem

Requirement 1

The four internal control weaknesses are

a. Petty cash ticket no. 46 is missing. Coupled with weakness b, this omission raises questions about the administration of the petty cash fund and about how the petty cash funds were used.

b. The $171 cash balance means that $129 has been paid ($300 − $171 = $129). However, the total amount of the petty cash tickets is only $99 ($14 + $9 + $43 + $33). The fund, then, is $30 short of cash ($129 − $99 = $30). Was petty cash ticket no. 46 issued for $30? The data in the problem offer no hint that helps answer this question. In a real-world setting, management would investigate the problem.

c. The petty cash custodian (JCB) did not sign petty cash ticket no. 45. This omission may have been an oversight on his part. However, it raises the question of whether he authorized the payment. Both the fund custodian and recipient of cash should sign the ticket.

d. Petty cash ticket no. 47 does not indicate which account to debit. What did Tate do with the money, and what account should be debited? At worst, the funds have been stolen. At best, asking the custodian to reconstruct the transaction from memory is haphazard. Since we are instructed to assume petty cash ticket no. 47 was issued for the purchase of office supplies, debit Office Supplies.

Requirement 2

Petty cash journal entries

a. Entry to establish the petty cash fund

Petty Cash..	300	
Cash..		300
To open the petty cash fund.		

b. Entry to replenish the fund

Office Supplies ($14 + $43)..	57	
Miscellaneous Expense...	9	
Travel Expense..	33	
Cash Short and Over..	30	
Cash..		129
To replenish the petty cash fund.		

The balance in Petty Cash is *always* its specified balance, in this case $300, as shown by posting the above entries to the account.

Petty Cash

(a)	300

The entry to establish the fund—(entry a)—debits Petty Cash. The entry to replenish the fund—(entry b)—neither debits nor credits Petty Cash.

Cyber Coach

Visit the Student Resource area of the *Accounting* Companion Website for extra practice with the new material in Chapter 7.

www.pearsoned.ca/horngren

Summary

1. **Define internal control.** *Internal control* is the organizational plan and all related measures adopted by an entity to meet management's objectives of discharging statutory responsibilities, profitability, prevention and detection of fraud and error, safeguarding of assets, reliability of accounting records, and timely preparation of reliable financial information.

2. **Identify the characteristics of an effective system of internal control.** An effective internal control system includes these features: *competent, reliable and ethical personnel; clear assignment of responsibilities; proper authorization; separation of duties; internal and external audits; documents and records;* and *electronic devices and computer controls.* Many companies also make use of fireproof vaults, point-of-sale terminals, fidelity bonds, mandatory vacations, and job rotation. Effective computerized internal control systems must meet the same basic standards that good manual systems do.

3. **Prepare a bank reconciliation and the related journal entries.** The *bank account* helps to control and safeguard cash. Businesses use the *bank statement* and the *bank reconciliation* to account for banking transactions.

4. **Apply internal controls to cash receipts.** To control cash receipts over the counter, companies use point-of-sale terminals that customers can see, and require that cashiers provide customers with receipts. A duplicate tape inside the machine or a link to a central computer records each sale and cash transaction. Pricing with uneven amounts means that cashiers must open the drawer to make change, which requires the transaction to be recorded on tape.

To control cash receipts by mail, a mail-room employee should be assigned the responsibility for opening the mail, comparing the enclosed amount with the remittance advice, and preparing a control tape. This is an essential separation of duties—the accounting deparment should not open the mail. At the end of the day, the controller compares the three records of the day's cash receipts: the control tape total from the mail-room, the bank deposit amount from the cashier, and the debit to Cash from the accounting department.

5. **Apply internal controls to cash payments, including petty cash transactions.** To control payments by cheque, cheques should be issued and signed only when a *payment packet* including the purchase request, purchase order, invoice (bill), and receiving report (all with appropriate signatures) has been prepared. To control petty cash payments, the custodian of the fund should require a completed petty cash ticket for all payments.

6. **Use a budget to manage cash.** A budget is a quantitative expression of a plan that helps managers coordinate the entity's activities. To prepare for the future, first a company must determine how much cash it will need. Then it budgets cash receipts and payments for the upcoming period. By comparing the ending budgeted cash balance to the amount needed, managers can determine whether they need to borrow or will have extra cash to invest.

7. **Make ethical judgments in business.** To make ethical decisions, people should proceed in six steps: (1) Determine the facts. (2) Identify the ethical issues. (3) Specify the alternatives. (4) Identify the stakeholders, the people involved. (5) Assess the possible outcomes of each alternative. (6) Make the decision.

Self-Study Questions

Test your understanding of the chapter by marking the correct answer for each of the following questions:

1. Which of the following is an objective of internal control? (*p. 349*)

   a. Safeguarding assets
   b. Maintaining reliable control systems
   c. Optimizing the use of resources
   d. Preventing and detecting fraud and error
   e. All the above are objectives of internal control.

2. Which of the characteristics of an effective system of internal control is violated by allowing the employee who handles inventory to also account for inventory? (*pp. 350–352*)

   a. Competent and reliable personnel
   b. Assignment of responsibilities
   c. Proper authorization
   d. Separation of duties

3. What control function is performed by auditors? (*p. 352*)

   a. Objective opinion on the fair presentation of the financial statements
   b. Assurance that all transactions are accounted for correctly
   c. Communication of the results of the audit to regulatory agencies
   d. Guarantee that a proper separation of duties exists within the business

4. The bank account serves as a control device over (*pp. 356–359*)

   a. Cash receipts   c. Both of the above
   b. Cash payments   d. None of the above

5. Which of the following items appears on the bank side of a bank reconciliation? (*p. 362*)

   a. Book error
   b. Outstanding cheque
   c. NSF cheque
   d. Interest revenue earned on bank balance

6. Which of the following reconciling items requires a journal entry on the books of the company? (*p. 362*)

   a. Book error
   b. Outstanding cheque
   c. NSF cheque
   d. Interest revenue earned on bank balance
   e. All of the above, except (b)
   f. None of the above

7. What is the major internal control measure over the cash receipts of a Zellers store? (*pp. 368–369*)

   a. Reporting the day's cash receipts to the controller
   b. Preparing a petty cash ticket for all payments from the fund
   c. Pricing merchandise at uneven amounts, coupled with use of a cash register
   d. Channeling all cash receipts through the mail room, whose employees have no cash-accounting responsibilities

8. Before signing a cheque to pay for goods purchased, the company should determine that the (*pp. 370–372*)

   a. Invoice is for the goods ordered
   b. Merchandise was received
   c. Amount of the bill is correct
   d. All of the above are correct

9. The internal control feature that is specific to petty cash is (*p. 373*)

   a. Separation of duties
   b. Assignment of responsibility
   c. Proper authorization
   d. The imprest system

10. Ethical judgments in accounting and business (*pp. 377–378*)

    a. Require employees to break laws to get ahead
    b. Force decision makers to think about what is good and bad
    c. Always hurt someone
    d. Are affected by internal controls but not by external controls

Answers to the Self-Study Questions follow the Similar Accounting Terms.

Accounting Vocabulary

Audit (*p. 352*)
Bank collection (*p. 360*)
Bank reconciliation (*p. 360*)
Bank statement (*p. 356*)
Budget (*p. 374*)
Cheque (*p. 356*)
Computer virus (*p. 354*)
Controller (*p. 350*)
Deposit in transit (*p. 360*)

Electronic funds transfer (EFT) (*p. 357*)
Encryption (*p. 354*)
Firewall (*p. 355*)
Imprest system (*p. 373*)
Internal control (*p. 349*)
NSF (nonsufficient funds) cheque (*p. 360*)
Outstanding cheque (*p. 360*)
Petty cash (*p. 372*)
Trojan horse (*p. 354*)

Similar Accounting Terms

Cash receipts	Cash, cheques, and other negotiable instruments received
Separation of duties	Segregation of duties, division of duties
Purchase request	Requisition
Invoice	Bill

Assignment Material

Questions

1. Which of the features of effective internal control is the most fundamental? Why?

2. Which company employees bear primary responsibility for a company's financial statements and for maintaining the company's system of internal control? How do these persons carry out this responsibility?

3. Identify at least seven features of an effective system of internal control.

4. Separation of duties may be divided into four parts. What are they?

5. How can internal control systems be circumvented?

6. Are internal control systems designed to be foolproof and perfect? What is a fundamental constraint in planning and maintaining systems?

7. Briefly state how each of the following serves as an internal control measure over cash: bank account, signature card, deposit ticket, and bank statement.

8. What is the remittance advice portion of a cheque? What use does it serve?

9. Each of the items in the following list must be accounted for in the bank reconciliation. Next to each item, enter the appropriate letter from the following possible treatments: (a) bank side of reconciliation—add the item; (b) bank side of reconciliation—subtract the item; (c) book side of reconciliation—add the item; and (d) book side of reconciliation—subtract the item.

    _____ Outstanding cheque
    _____ NSF cheque
    _____ Bank service charge
    _____ Cost of printed cheques
    _____ EFT receipt
    _____ Bank error that decreased bank balance
    _____ Deposit in transit
    _____ Bank collection
    _____ EFT payment
    _____ Customer's cheque returned because of unauthorized signature
    _____ Book error that increased balance of Cash account

10. What purpose does a bank reconciliation serve?

11. Suppose a company has six bank accounts, two petty cash funds, and three certificates of deposit that can be withdrawn on demand. How many cash amounts would this company likely report separately on its balance sheet?

12. What role does a cash register play in an internal control system?

13. Describe internal control procedures for cash received by mail.

14. What documents make up the payment packet? Describe three procedures that use the payment packet to ensure that each payment is appropriate.

15. What balance does the Petty Cash account have at all times? Does this balance always equal the amount of cash in the fund? When are the two amounts equal? When are they unequal?

16. Describe how a budget helps a company manage its cash.

17. Suppose the cash budget indicates an excess of $20,000 cash receipts over cash payments and estimated cash requirements for the period. Will the business need additional financing? What is the business likely to do with the extra cash?

18. Why should accountants adhere to a higher standard of ethical conduct than many other members of society do?

19. "Our managers know that they are expected to meet budgeted profit figures. We don't want excuses. We want results." Discuss the ethical implications of this policy.

20. Why should the same employee not write the computer programs for cash payments, sign cheques, and mail the cheques to payees?

Exercises

Exercise 7-1 *Definition of internal control* *(Obj. 1)*

Internal controls are designed to safeguard assets and records, encourage employees to follow company policies, promote operational efficiency, and ensure accurate records. Which of these four goals of internal control is most important? Stated differently, which goal must the internal controls accomplish for the business to survive? Give your reason.

Exercise 7-2 *Correcting an internal control weakness* *(Obj. 2)*

Consider this excerpt from a recent business newspaper article:

> TOKYO—Sumitomo Corp., a Japanese trading company, said unauthorized trades by its former head of copper trading caused losses that may total $2.7 billion. Sumitomo said it learned of the damage when Yaduo Hamanaka called a superior and confessed to making unauthorized trades that led to the losses over a 10-year period. Mr. Hamanaka, according to a Sumitomo statement, admitted to concealing the losses by falsifying Sumitomo's books and records.

What internal control weaknesses at Sumitomo Corp. allowed this loss to grow so large? How could the company have avoided and/or limited the size of the loss?

Exercise 7-3 *Identifying internal control strengths and weaknesses* *(Obj. 2)*

The following situations suggest either a strength or weakness in internal control. Identify each as *strength* or *weakness* and give the reason for your answer.

a. Top managers delegate all internal control measures to the accounting department.

b. The accounting department orders merchandise and approves vouchers for payment.

c. Cash received by mail goes straight to the accountant, who debits Cash and credits Accounts Receivable from the customer.

d. The vice-president who signs cheques assumes the accounting department has matched the invoice with other supporting documents and therefore does not examine the payment packet.

e. The operator of the computer has no other accounting or cash-handling duties.

f. Cash received over the counter is controlled by the salesclerk, who rings up the sale and places the cash in the register. The salesclerk has access to the control tape stored in the register.

Exercise 7-4 *Identifying internal controls* *(Obj. 2)*

Identify the missing internal control characteristic in the following situations:

a. Business is slow at the White Water Park on Tuesday, Wednesday, and Thursday nights. To reduce expenses the owner decides not to use a ticket taker on those nights. The ticket seller (cashier) is told to keep the tickets as a record of the number sold.

b. When business is brisk, Beckers and many other retail stores deposit cash in the bank several times during the day. The manager at another convenience store wants to reduce the time spent by employees delivering cash to the bank, so he starts a new policy. Cash will build up over Saturdays and Sundays, and the total two-day amount will be deposited on Sunday evening.

c. In the course of auditing the records of a company, you find that the same employee orders merchandise and approves invoices for payment.

d. The manager of a discount store wants to speed the flow of customers through check-out. She decides to reduce the time spent by cashiers making change, so she prices merchandise at round dollar amounts—such as $8.00 and $15.00—instead of the customary amounts—$7.95 and $14.95.

e. Grocery stores such as Save-on-Foods and Great Canadian Superstore purchase large quantities of their merchandise from a few suppliers. At another grocery store the manager decides to reduce paperwork. He eliminates the requirement that a receiving department employee prepare a receiving report, which lists the quantities of items received from the supplier.

Exercise 7-5   *Explaining the role of internal control*   *(Obj. 2)*

The following questions pertain to internal control. Consider each situation separately.

1. Ling Company requires that all documents supporting a cheque be cancelled (stamped Paid) by the person who signs the cheque. Why do you think this practice is required? What might happen if it were not?

2. Separation of duties is an important consideration if a system of internal control is to be effective. Why is this so?

3. Cash may be a relatively small item on the financial statements. Nevertheless, internal control over cash is very important. Why is this true?

4. Many managers think that safeguarding assets is the most important objective of internal control systems, while auditors emphasize internal control's role in ensuring reliable accounting data. Explain why managers are more concerned about safeguarding assets and auditors are more concerned about the quality of the accounting records.

Exercise 7-6   *Classifying bank reconciliation items*   *(Obj. 3)*

The following seven items may appear on a bank reconciliation:

1. Bank collection of a note receivable on our behalf.

2. Book error: We debited Cash for $200. The correct debit was $2,000.

3. NSF cheque.

4. Service charge.

5. Deposits in transit.

6. Bank error: The bank charged our account for a cheque written by another customer.

7. Outstanding cheques.

Classify each item as (a) an addition to the bank balance, (b) a subtraction from the bank balance, (c) an addition to the book balance, or (d) a subtraction from the book balance.

Exercise 7-7   *Preparing a bank reconciliation*   *(Obj. 3)*

Ana Stuka's chequebook lists the entries shown on page 386:

Required
Prepare Ana Stuka's bank reconciliation at September 30, 2002.

Date	Cheque No.	Item	Cheque	Deposit	Balance
Sept.					
1					$ 525
4	622	Treats Gift Shop	$ 19		506
9		Dividends received		$ 240	746
13	623	BCT. TELUS	43		703
14	624	Petro-Canada	58		645
18	625	Cash	100		545
26	626	Canadian Cancer Society	25		520
28	627	Bent Tree Apartments	400		120
30		Paycheque		2,100	2,220

Stuka's September bank statement shows:

Balance..			$525
Add: Deposits..			240
Deduct cheques:	No.	Amount	
	622	$19	
	623	43	
	624	68*	
	625	100	(230)
Other charges			
Printed cheques..		$ 8	
Service charge		12	(20)
Balance			$515

* This is the correct amount of cheque number 624.

Exercise 7-8 *Preparing a bank reconciliation* *(Obj. 3)*

Pierre Vincelette operates two Petro-Canada stations. He has just received the monthly bank statement at October 31 from the Bank of Nova Scotia, and the statement shows an ending balance of $4,690. Listed on the statement are an EFT rent collection of $400, a service charge of $12, two NSF cheques totalling $71, and a $12 charge for printed cheques. In reviewing his cash records, Vincelette identifies outstanding cheques totalling $467 and an October 31 deposit in transit of $1,812. During October, he recorded a $290 cheque for the salary of a part-time employee by debiting Salary Expense and crediting Cash for $29. Vincelette's cash account shows an October 31 cash balance of $5,991. Prepare the bank reconciliation at October 31, 2003.

Exercise 7-9 *Making journal entries from a bank reconciliation* *(Obj. 3)*

Using the data from Exercise 7-8, record the entries that Vincelette should make in the general journal on October 31. Include an explanation for each of the entries.

Exercise 7-10 *Applying internal controls to the bank reconciliation* *(Obj. 2, 3)*

A jury convicted the treasurer of U-Need-A Taxi Company for stealing cash from the company. Over a three-year period the treasurer allegedly took almost $50,000 and attempted to cover the theft by manipulating the bank reconciliation.

Required

What is a likely way that a person would manipulate a bank reconciliation to cover a theft? Be specific. What internal control arrangement could have avoided this theft?

Exercise 7-11　*Evaluating internal control over cash receipts*　**(Obj. 4)**

A cash register is located in each department of Henry's Discount Store. The register shows the amount of each sale, the cash received from the customer, and any change returned to the customer. The machine also produces a customer receipt but keeps no record of transactions. At the end of the day, the clerk counts the cash in the register and gives it to the cashier for deposit in the company bank account.

Required

Write a memo to convince Henry Lett, the owner, that there is an internal control weakness over cash receipts. Identify the weakness that gives an employee the best opportunity to steal cash, and state how to prevent such a theft.

Exercise 7-12　*Petty cash, cash short and over*　**(Obj. 5)**

Record the following selected transactions of Kim's Fine Foods in general journal format (explanations are not required):

2002

April	1	Established a petty cash fund with a $300 balance.
	2	Journalized the day's cash sales. Cash register tapes show a $2,990 total, but the cash in the register is $3,010.
	10	The petty cash fund has $121 in cash and $161 in petty cash tickets issued to pay for Office Supplies ($111), Delivery Expense ($13) and Entertainment Expense ($37). Replenished the fund.

Exercise 7-13　*Accounting for petty cash*　**(Obj. 5)**

United Way of Regina, Saskatchewan, created a $500 imprest petty cash fund. During the first month of use, the fund custodian authorized and signed petty cash tickets as shown below.

Ticket No.	Item	Account Debited	Amount
1	Delivery of pledge cards to donors	Delivery Expense	$ 32.19
2	Stamp purchase	Postage Expense	52.80
3	Newsletter	Supplies Expense	134.14
4	Key to closet	Miscellaneous Expense	3.95
5	Waste basket	Miscellaneous Expense	13.78
6	Staples	Supplies Expense	7.37

Required

1. Make general journal entries for creation of the petty cash fund and its replenishment. Include explanations.
2. Describe the items in the fund immediately prior to replenishment.
3. Describe the items in the fund immediately after replenishment.

Exercise 7-14　*Preparing a cash budget*　**(Obj. 6)**

1. Return to The Gap's hypothetical cash budget in Exhibit 7-13, page 375. Suppose The Gap were to postpone the opening of new stores until later in 2003. In that case, how much additional financing would The Gap need for the year ended January 31, 2002?
2. Now suppose The Gap were to postpone both the expansions of existing stores and the opening of new stores until later in 2003. How much new financing would The Gap need, or how much cash would the company have available for additional investments during the year ended January 31, 2002?

Exercise 7-15 *Preparing a cash budget* **(Obj. 6)**

Planned Living is a major housing cooperative. Suppose the company begins 2003 with cash of $6 million. Planned Living estimates cash receipts during 2003 will total $153 million. Planned payments for the year will require cash of $160 million. To meet daily cash needs, Planned Living must maintain a cash balance of at least $7 million.

Prepare Planned Living's cash budget for 2003. Identify two ways Planned Living can obtain the new financing.

Exercise 7-16 *Preparing a cash budget* **(Obj. 6)**

Suppose Bell Mobility, the mobile telephone company, is preparing its cash budget for 2001. Suppose the company ended 2000 with $126 million, and top management foresees the need for a cash balance of at least $125 million for the coming year.

Collections from customers are expected to total $2,517 million during 2001, and payments for the cost of services and products should reach $1,080 million. Operating expense payments are budgeted at $544 million.

During 2001, Bell Mobility expects to invest $826 million in new equipment and to sell older assets for $26 million cash. Debt payments scheduled for 2001 will total $97 million. The company forecasts net income of $90 million for 2001 and plans to pay $38 million in cash dividends to its shareholders.

Required

Prepare Bell Mobility's cash budget for 2001. Will the budgeted level of cash receipts leave Bell Mobility with the desired ending cash balance of $125 million, or will the company need additional financing?

Exercise 7-17 *Evaluating the ethics of conduct by a manager* **(Obj. 7)**

You have a part-time job in a local supermarket, which is part of a chain of supermarkets. You received the job through your parent's friendship with Larry Gilbert, the store manager. The job is going well, but you are puzzled by the actions of Larry and his wife Dorothy. Each day, one or both of them fills a shopping cart with groceries and takes the cart to Larry's office. Later you notice Larry or Dorothy carrying bags of groceries to their car. You know the groceries were not rung through a checkout counter. When you ask a co-worker about the practice, you are told that Larry is the boss and can do as he wishes, and besides, many employees help themselves to the store's inventory.

Required

You have been given the assignment in a business ethics course to comment on the issue. Apply the decision guidelines for ethical judgments outlined in the Decision Guidelines feature on page 378 to decide whether a manager of a store should help himself to inventory on a regular basis and not pay for what he takes.

Exercise 7-18 *Preparing and using a cash budget* **(Obj. 6)**

Among its many products, Quebec Paper makes paper for shopping bags, the labels on canned foods, and various magazines. Marianne Vachon, the Chief Financial Officer, is responsible for Quebec Paper's cash budget for 2003. The budget will help Vachon determine the amount of long-term borrowing needed to end the year with a cash balance of $290 million. Vachon's assistants have assembled budget data for 2003, which the computer printed in alphabetical order. Not all of the following data items are used in preparing the cash budget.

Receipts are positive amounts, payments are in parentheses	(In thousands)
Acquisition of other companies	$ (1,168)
Actual cash balance, December 31, 2002	270
Borrowing	?
Budgeted total assets before borrowing	23,977
Budgeted total current assets before borrowing	5,873
Budgeted total current liabilities before borrowing	4,792
Budgeted total liabilities before borrowing	15,890
Budgeted total owner's equity before borrowing	7,797
Collections from customers	17,967
Withdrawals made by owners	(237)
Net income	1,153
New owner investment	516
Other cash receipts	161
Payment of long-term and short-term debt	(950)
Payment of operating expenses	(1,949)
Purchases of inventory	(13,145)
Purchase of property and equipment	(1,518)

Required

1. Prepare the cash budget to determine the amount of borrowing Quebec Paper needs during 2003.

2. *Link Back to Chapter 4 (Current Ratio and Debt Ratio).* Compute Quebec Paper's expected current ratio and debt ratio at December 31, 2003, both before and after borrowing on long-term debt. Assume you are the chief loan officer at a bank. Based on these figures, and on the budgeted levels of assets and liabilities, would you lend the requested amount to Quebec Paper? Give the reason for your decision.

Beyond the Numbers

Beyond the Numbers 7-1 *Correcting an internal control weakness*   **(Obj. 1, 5)**

This case is based on a situation experienced by one of the authors. Alpha Construction Company, headquartered in Chattanooga, Tennessee, built a Roadway Inn Motel in Cleveland, 35 kilometres east of Chattanooga. The construction foreman, whose name was Slim, moved into Cleveland in March to hire the 40 workers needed to complete the project. Slim hired the construction workers, had them fill out the necessary tax forms, and sent the employment documents to the home office, which opened a payroll file for each employee.

Work on the motel began on April 1 and ended September 1. Each Thursday evening, Slim filled out a time card that listed the hours worked by each employee during the five-day workweek ended at 5 p.m. on Thursday. Slim faxed the time sheets to the home office, which prepared the payroll cheques on Friday morning. Slim drove to the home office after lunch on Friday, picked up the payroll cheques, and returned to the construction site. At 5 p.m. on Friday, Slim distributed the payroll cheques to the workers.

a. Describe in detail the internal control weakness in this situation. Specify what negative result(s) could occur because of the internal control weakness.

b. Describe what you would do to correct the internal control weakness.

Ethical Issue

Mark Wiebe owns apartment buildings in British Columbia, Alberta, and Manitoba. Each property has a manager who collects rent, arranges for repairs, and runs advertisements in the local newspaper. The property managers transfer cash to Wiebe monthly and prepare their own bank reconciliations.

The manager in Alberta has been stealing large sums of money. To cover the theft, she understates the amount of outstanding cheques on the monthly bank reconciliation. As a result, each monthly bank reconciliation appears to balance. However, the balance sheet reports more cash than Wiebe actually has in the bank. In negotiating the sale of the Alberta property, Wiebe is showing the balance sheet to prospective investors.

Required

1. Identify two parties other than Wiebe who can be harmed by this theft. In what ways can they be harmed?
2. Discuss the role accounting plays in this situation.

Problems (Group A)

Problem 7-1A *Identifying the characteristics of an effective internal control system (Obj. 1,2)*

An employee of Midco Construction recently stole thousands of dollars of the company's cash. The company has decided to install a new system of internal controls.

Required

As controller of Midco Construction write a memo to the president, Jane Dausch, explaining how a separation of duties helps to safeguard assets.

Problem 7-2A *Identifying internal control weaknesses (Obj. 2, 4, 5)*

Each of the following situations has an internal control weakness:

a. Luann Sorelle employs three professional interior designers in her design studio. She is located in an area with a lot of new construction, and her business is booming. Ordinarily, Sorelle does all the purchasing of furniture, draperies, carpets, fabrics, sewing services, and other materials and labour needed to complete jobs. During the summer she takes a long vacation, and in her absence she allows each designer to purchase materials and labour. At her return, Sorelle reviews operations and notes that expenses are much higher and net income much lower than in the past.

b. Nepean Software Programs is a software company that specializes in computer programs with accounting applications. The company's most popular program prepares the general journal, cash receipts journal, voucher register, cheque register, accounts receivable subsidiary ledger, and general ledger. In the company's early days, the owner and eight employees wrote the computer programs, lined up manufacturers to produce the diskettes, sold the products to stores such as The Office Place and Grand & Toy, and performed the general management and accounting of the company. As the company has grown, the number of employees has increased dramatically. Recently, the development of a new software program stopped while the programmers redesigned Nepean Software Programs' accounting system. Nepean Software Programs' own accountants could have performed this task.

c. Sue Florio, a widow with no known sources of outside income, has been a trusted employee of Arch Designs for 15 years. She performs all cash handling and accounting duties, including opening the mail, preparing the bank deposit, accounting for all aspects of cash and accounts receivable, and preparing the bank reconciliation. She has just purchased a new Cadillac and a new home in an expensive suburb. Lu Archway, the owner of the company, wonders how she can afford these luxuries on her salary.

d. Discount stores such as Zellers receive a large portion of their sales revenue in cash, with the remainder in credit card sales. To reduce expenses, a store manager ceases purchasing fidelity bonds on the cashiers.

e. The office supply company from which Champs Sporting Goods purchases cash receipt forms recently notified Champs that the last shipped receipts were not prenumbered. Stephanie Champion, the owner, replied that she did not use the receipt numbers, so the omission is not important.

Required

1. Identify the missing internal control characteristic in each situation.

2. Identify the business's possible problem.

3. Propose a solution to the problem.

Problem 7-3A *Using the bank reconciliation as a control device* **(Obj. 3)**

The cash receipts and the cash payments of Xircom Resources for March 2003 are as follows:

Cash Receipts (Posting reference is CR)		Cash Payments (Posting reference is CP)	
Date	Cash Debit	Cheque No.	Cash Credit
Mar. 4	$2,716	1413	$ 1,465
9	544	1414	1,004
11	1,655	1415	450
14	896	1416	98
17	367	1417	775
25	890	1418	88
31	2,038	1419	4,126
Total	$9,106	1420	970
		1421	200
		1422	2,267
		Total	$11,443

The Cash account of Xircom Resources shows the following information on March 31, 2003:

Cash

Date	Item	Jrnl. Ref.	Debit	Credit	Balance
Mar. 1	Balance				15,188 Dr
31		CR. 10	9,106		24,294 Dr
31		CP. 16		11,443	12,851 Dr

On April 3, 2003, Xircom Resources received this bank statement:

Bank Statement for March 2003

Balance, March 1, 2003..		$15,188
Deposits and other Credits:		
Mar. 1	$ 775 EFT	
5	2,716	
10	544	
11	1,655	
15	896	
18	367	
25	890	
31	1,200 BC	9,043

Cheques and other Debits:

Mar. 8	$ 441 NSF	
9	1,465	
13	1,004	
14	450	
15	98	
19	340 EFT	
22	775	
29	88	
31	4,216	
31	25 SC	(8,902)
Balance, March 31, 2003..		$15,329

Explanations: BC—bank collection, EFT—electronic funds transfer,
NSF—nonsufficient funds cheque, SC—service charge.

Additional data for the bank reconciliation:

a. The EFT deposit was a receipt of monthly rent. The EFT debit was payment of monthly insurance.

b. The NSF cheque was received late in February from Jay Andrews.

c. The $1,200 bank collection of a note receivable on March 31 included $180 interest revenue.

d. The correct amount of cheque number 1419, a payment on account, is $4,216. (The Xircom Resources accountant mistakenly recorded the cheque for $4,126.)

Required

1. Prepare the bank reconciliation of Xircom Resources at March 31, 2003.

2. Describe how a bank account and the bank reconcilation help Xircom managers control the business's cash.

Problem 7-4A *Preparing a bank reconciliation and related journal entries* **(Obj. 3)**

The May 31, 2002 bank statement of Canmore College has just arrived from the Royal Bank. To prepare the Canmore College bank reconciliation, you gather the following data:

a. The May 31 bank balance is $19,530.82.

b. The bank statement includes two charges for returned cheques from students. One is an NSF cheque in the amount of $67.50 received from Harley Doherty, recorded on the books by a debit to Cash and deposited on May 19. The other is a $195.03 cheque received from Maria Gucci and deposited on May 21. It was returned by Ms. Gucci's bank with the imprint "Unauthorized Signature."

c. The following Canmore College cheques are outstanding at May 31:

Cheque No.	Amount
616	$403.00
802	74.25
806	36.60
809	161.38
810	229.05
811	512.00

d. A few students pay monthly fees by EFT. The May bank statement lists a $4,500 deposit for student fees.

e. The bank statement includes two special deposits: $899.14, which is the amount of dividend revenue the bank collected from BCE on behalf of Canmore College; and $16.86, the interest revenue Canmore College earned on its bank balance during May.

f. The bank statement lists a $27.50 subtraction for the bank service charge.

g. On May 31, the Canmore College treasurer deposited $381.14, but this deposit does not appear on the bank statement.

h. The bank statement includes a $375.00 deduction for a cheque drawn by Canmore Freight, Inc. Canmore College promptly notified the bank of its error.

i. Canmore College's Cash account shows a balance of $13,744.71 on May 31.

Required

1. Prepare the bank reconciliation for Canmore College at May 31, 2002.

2. Record in general journal form the entries necessary to bring the book balance of Cash into agreement with the adjusted book balance on the reconciliation. Include an explanation for each entry.

Problem 7-5A *Identifying internal control weakness in cash receipts* **(Obj. 4)**

Dot.com Systems makes all software sales on credit. Cash receipts arrive by mail, usually within 30 days of sale. Paule Desjarlais opens envelopes and separates the cheques from the accompanying remittance advices. Desjarlais forwards the cheques to another employee, who makes the daily bank deposit but has no access to the accounting records. Desjarlais sends the remittance advices, which show the amount of cash received, to the accounting department for entry in the accounts. Her only other duty is to grant sales allowances to customers. (Recall that a *sales allowance* decreases the amount that the customer must pay.) When she receives a customer cheque for less than the full amount of the invoice, she records the sales allowance and forwards the document to the accounting department.

Required

You are a new management employee of Dot.com Systems. Write a memo to the company president, Arthur Kinnear, identifying the internal control weakness in this situation. State how to correct the weakness.

Problem 7-6A *Applying internal controls to cash payments, including petty cash transactions* **(Obj. 5)**

Atlantic Marine Products is located in Gander, Newfoundland, with a sales territory covering the island.

The company has established a large petty cash fund to handle small cash payments and cash advances to the salespeople to cover frequent sales trips.

The controller, Mary Munn, has decided that two people (Susan White and Archie Courage) should be in charge of the fund as money is often needed when one person may be out for coffee or lunch. Munn also feels this will increase internal control, as the work of one person will serve as a check on that of the other.

Regular small cash payments are handled by either White or Courage, who make the payment and have the person receiving the money sign a sheet of paper listing the date and reason for the payment. Whenever a salesperson requires an advance for a trip, he or she simply signs a receipt for the money received. The salespeople later submit receipts for the cost of the trip to either White or Courage to offset the cash advance.

Munn is puzzled that the fund is almost always out of balance and either over or short.

Required

Comment on the internal control procedures of Atlantic Marine Products. Suggest changes that you think would improve the system.

Problem 7-7A   *Accounting for petty cash transactions*   *(Obj. 5)*

Suppose that on April 1, Union Energy opens a regional office in Sarnia and creates a petty cash fund with an imprest balance of $500. During April, Eleanor Zych, the fund custodian, signs the following petty cash tickets:

Ticket Number	Item	Amount
101	Office supplies	$86.89
102	Cab fare for executive	25.00
103	Delivery of package across town	18.00
104	Dinner money for sales manager entertaining a customer	80.00
105	Office Supplies	85.70
106	Water for cooler	36.00
107	Six boxes of computer disks	58.75

On April 30, prior to replenishment, the fund contains these tickets plus $113.66. The accounts affected by petty cash payments are Office Supplies Expense, Travel Expense, Delivery Expense, Entertainment Expense, and Water Cooler Expense.

Required

1. Explain the characteristics and internal control features of an imprest fund.
2. Make general journal entries to create the fund and to replenish it. Include explanations. Also, briefly describe what the custodian does on these dates.

Problem 7-8A   *Preparing a personal cash budget*   *(Obj. 6)*

Suppose you are preparing your personal cash budget for the year 2003. During 2003, assume that you can expect to earn $3,600 from your summer job and $1,200 for work as a tutor. Also, your family always gives you gifts totalling around $400 during the year. A scholarship from a local Kiwanis Club adds $1,000 each year while you are in college.

Assume your family pays your college costs except for room and board. Planned expenditures for 2003 include apartment rent of $150 per month for 12 months and annual food costs of $5,600. Transporation expenses usually run about $40 per month. You need to have a little fun, so entertainment will cost $100 per month.

You need to keep a little cash in reserve for travel and other emergencies, so you maintain a cash reserve of $500 at all times. To start 2003, you have this cash reserve plus $200.

Will you need a loan during 2003? To answer this question, prepare your personal cash budget for the year based on the data given.

Problem 7-9A   *Using cash-flow information to prepare a cash budget*   *(Obj. 6)*

Martha Dunlop, Chief Financial Officer of Markdale Farm Products, is responsible for the company's budgeting process. Suppose Dunlop's staff is preparing the Markdale Farm Products cash budget for 2003. A key input to the budgeting process is the previous year's cash flow statement, which provides the data on the next page for 2002. Cash receipts appear as positive amounts; cash payments are negative amounts, denoted within parentheses.

Required

1. Prepare the Markdale Farm Products cash budget for 2003. Date the budget simply "2003" and denote the beginning and ending cash balances as "beginning" and "ending." Assume the company expects 2003 to be similar to 2002, but with the following changes:

a. In 2003, the company expects a 12% increase in collections from customers and an 8% increase in purchases of inventory.

b. Dunlop plans to end the year with a cash balance of $500,000.

2. Based on the cash budget you prepared, how much additional cash does it appear that Markdale Farm Products will have available for additional investments during 2003?

MARKDALE FARM PRODUCTS
(Cash-Flow Data)

(In thousands)	2002
Collections from customers	$8,089
Interest revenue	24
Purchases of inventory	(5,597)
Operating expenses	(1,929)
Purchases of capital assets	(614)
Short-term borrowings	119
Long-term borrowings	41
Long-term debt repayments	22
Investments by owner	30
Withdrawals by owner	(183)
Cash and Cash Equivalents:	
Beginning of year 2002	$ 764
End of year 2002	$ 792

Problem 7-10A *Preparing a bank reconciliation and related journal entries* *(Obj. 3)*

Saskatoon Flooring Products had a computer failure on February 1, 2002, which resulted in the loss of data, including the balance of its cash account and its bank reconciliation from January 31, 2002. The accountant, Raoul Payette, has been able to obtain the following information from the records of the company and its bank:

a. An examination showed that two cheques (#131 for $180 and #144 for $325) had not been cashed as of February 1. Payette recalled that there was only one deposit in transit on the January 31 bank reconciliation, but was unable to recall the amount.

b. The cash receipts and cash payments journal contained the following entries for February 2002:

Cash Receipts:	Cash Payments:	
Amounts	Cheque #	Amount
$ 485	157	$ 105
680	158	165
1,510	159	230
920	160	435
270	161	215
$3,865	162	1,370
	163	void
	164	200
	165	460
		$3,180

c. The company's bank provided the following statement as of February 28, 2002:

Date	Cheques and Other Debits		Deposits and Other Credits		Balance
Feb. 1	#158	165.00		880.00	2,005.00
3	#144	325.00			1,680.00
5	#159	230.00			1,450.00
8				485.00	1,935.00
14	#157	105.00		640.00	2,290.00
17	EFT	210.00			2,080.00
19			EFT	160.00	2,240.00
21	#161	215.00		680.00	2,705.00
22	#162	1,730.00	EFT	410.00	1,385.00
24			EFT	175.00	1,560.00
26	NSF	235.00		1,510.00	2,835.00
27	SC	25.00			2,810.00
28	#165	460.00		920.00	3,270.00

d. The deposit made on February 14 was for the collection of a note receivable ($600) plus interest.

e. The electronic funds transfers (EFTs) had not yet been recorded by Saskatoon Flooring Products as the bank statement was the first notification of them.

- The February 17 EFT was for the monthly payment on an insurance policy for Saskatoon Flooring Products.
- The February 19 and 24 EFTs were collections on accounts receivable.
- The February 22 EFT was in error—the transfer should have been to Saskatoon Construction Corporation.

f. The NSF cheque on February 26 was received from a customer as payment for carpet purchased for $235 (cost to Saskatoon Flooring Products was $120).

g. Cheque #162 was correctly written for $1,730 for the purchase of office supplies, but incorrectly recorded by the cash payments clerk.

Required

1. Prepare a bank reconciliation as of February 28, 2002, including the calculation of the book balance of February 28, 2002.

2. Prepare all journal entries that would be required by the bank reconciliation.

Problem 7-11A *Making an ethical judgment* *(Obj. 7)*

The Canadian Imperial Bank of Commerce (CIBC) in Brandon, Manitoba, has a loan receivable from Magellan Manufacturing Corp. Magellan is six months late in making payments to the bank, and Lee Kowaleski, a CIBC vice-president, is assisting Magellan to restructure its debt. With unlimited access to Magellan's records Kowaleski learns that the company is depending on landing a manufacturing contract from Thibeault and Son Ltd., another CIBC client. Kowaleski also serves as the Thibeault and Son loan officer at the bank. In this capacity she is aware that Thibeault and Son is considering declaring bankruptcy. No one else outside Thibeault and Son knows this. Kowaleski has been a great help to Magellan Manufacturing, and Magellan's owner is counting on her expertise in loan workouts to carry the company through this difficult process. To help the bank collect on this large loan, Kowaleski has a strong motivation to help Magellan survive.

Required

Apply the ethical judgment framework outlined in the Decision Guidelines feature on page 378 to help Lee Kowaleski plan her next action.

Problems (Group B)

Problem 7-1B *Identifying the characteristics of an effective internal control system*
(Obj. 1, 2)

Chester Real Estate Development Company prospered during the lengthy economic expansion of the 1980s and 1990s. Business was so good that the company bothered with few internal controls. The recent decline in the local real estate market, however, has caused Chester to experience a shortage of cash. Jessie Fulcher, the company owner, is looking for ways to save money.

Required

As controller of the company, write a memorandum to convince Jessie Fulcher of the company's need for a system of internal control. Be specific in telling her how an internal control system could possibly lead to saving money. Include the definition of internal control, and briefly discuss each characteristic beginning with competent, reliable, and ethical personnel.

Problem 7-2B *Identifying internal control weaknesses*   *(Obj. 2, 4, 5)*

Each of the following situations has an internal control weakness:

a. In evaluating the internal control over cash payments, an auditor learns that the purchasing agent is responsible for purchasing platinum for use in the company's manufacturing process, approving the invoices for payment, and signing the cheques. No supervisor reviews the purchasing agent's work.

b. Mindy Bullen owns a firm that performs engineering services. Her staff consists of twelve professional engineers, and she manages the office. Often her work requires her to travel to meet with clients. During the past six months, she has observed that when she returns from a business trip, the engineering jobs in the office have not progressed satisfactorily. She learns that when she is away several of her senior employees take over office management and neglect their engineering duties. One employee could manage the office.

c. Amy Fariss has been an employee of Langstaff's Shoe Store for many years. Because the business is relatively small, Amy performs all accounting duties, including opening the mail, preparing the bank deposit, and preparing the bank reconciliation.

d. Most large companies have internal audit staffs that continuously evaluate the business's internal control. Part of the internal auditor's job is to evaluate how efficiently the company is running. For example, is the company purchasing inventory from the least expensive wholesaler? After a particularly bad year, Erb Logistics eliminates its internal audit department to reduce expenses.

e. Public accounting firms, law firms, and other professional organizations use paraprofessional employees to do some of their routine tasks. For example, an accounting paraprofessional might examine documents to assist a public accountant in conducting an audit. In the public accounting firm of Derby and Koch, Jeanette Derby, the senior partner, turns over a significant portion of her high-level audit work to her paraprofessional staff.

Required

1. Identify the missing internal control characteristic in each situation.
2. Identify the business's possible problem.
3. Propose a solution to the problem.

Problem 7-3B   *Using the bank reconciliation as a control device*   (*Obj. 3*)

The cash receipts and the cash payments of Fudders Designs for April 2002 are as follows:

Cash Receipts (Posting reference is CR)		Cash Payments (Posting reference is CP)	
Date	**Cash Debit**	**Cheque No.**	**Cash Credit**
Apr. 2	$ 4,174	3113	$ 891
8	407	3114	147
10	559	3115	1,930
16	2,187	3116	664
22	1,854	3117	1,472
29	1,060	3118	1,000
30	487	3119	632
Total	$10,728	3120	1,675
		3121	400
		3122	2,413
		Total	$11,224

Assume that the Cash account of Fudders Designs shows the following information at April 30, 2002:

Cash

Date	Item	Jrnl. Ref.	Debit	Credit	Balance
Apr. 1	Balance				7,911 Dr
30		CR. 6	10,728		18,639 Dr
30		CP. 11		11,224	7,415 Dr

Fudders Designs received this bank statement on April 30, 2002, shown below.

Bank Statement for April 2002

Beginning balance		$ 7,911
Deposits and other Credits:		
Apr. 1	$ 326 EFT	
4	4,174	
9	407	
12	559	
17	2,187	
22	1,368 BC	
23	1,854	10,875
Cheques and other Debits:		
Apr. 7	$ 891	
13	1,390	
14	903 US	
15	147	
18	664	
21	219 EFT	
26	1,472	
30	1,000	
30	35 SC	(6,721)
Ending balance		$12,065

Explanations: EFT—electronic funds transfer, BC—bank collection, US—unauthorized signature, SC—service charge.

Additional data for the bank reconciliation:

a. The EFT deposit was a receipt of monthly rent. The EFT debit was payment of monthly insurance.

b. The unauthorized-signature cheque was received from S.M. Holt.

c. The $1,368 bank collection of a note receivable on April 22 included $185 interest revenue.

d. The correct amount of cheque number 3115, a payment on account, is $1,390. (Fudders Designs' accountant mistakenly recorded the cheque for $1,930.)

Required

1. Prepare the Fudders Designs bank reconciliation at April 30, 2002.

2. Describe how a bank account and the bank reconciliation help the Fudders Designs managers control the business's cash.

Problem 7-4B *Preparing a bank reconciliation and the related journal entries* **(Obj. 3)**

The August 31, 2003, bank statement of Hurry Fine Clothes has just arrived from the Bank of Montreal. To prepare the Hurry Fine Clothes bank reconciliation, you gather the following data:

a. The Hurry Fine Clothes Cash account shows a balance of $4,121.14 on August 31.

b. The bank statement includes two charges for returned cheques from customers. One is a $395.00 cheque received from Shoreline Advertising and deposited on August 20, returned by Shoreline's bank with the imprint "Unauthorized Signature." The other is an NSF cheque in the amount of $146.67 received from Lipsey, Inc. This cheque had been deposited on August 17.

c. Hurry Fine Clothes pays rent ($850) and insurance ($290) each month by EFT.

d. The following Hurry Fine Clothes cheques are outstanding at August 31:

Cheque No.	Amount
237	$ 46.10
288	286.00
291	578.05
293	11.87
294	609.51
295	8.88
296	101.63

e. The bank statement includes a deposit of $1,191.17, collected by the bank on behalf of Hurry Fine Clothes. Of the total, $1,011.81 is collection of a note receivable, and the remainder is interest revenue.

f. The bank statement shows that Hurry Fine Clothes earned $38.19 in interest on its bank balance during August. This amount was added to the Hurry Fine Clothes account by the bank.

g. The bank statement lists a $10.50 subtraction for the bank service charge.

h. On August 31, the Hurry Fine Clothes treasurer deposited $316.15, but this deposit does not appear on the bank statement.

i. The bank statement includes a $500.00 deposit that Hurry Fine Clothes did not make. The bank had erroneously credited the Hurry Fine Clothes account for another bank customer's deposit.

j. The August 31 bank balance is $5,484.22.

Required

1. Prepare the bank reconciliation for Hurry Fine Clothes at August 31, 2003.

2. Record in general journal form the entries necessary to bring the book balance of Cash into agreement with the adjusted book balance on the reconciliation. Include an explanation for each entry.

Problem 7-5B *Identifying internal control weakness in cash receipts* **(Obj. 4)**

Par Buster makes all sales of its golf clubs to retailers on credit. Cash receipts arrive by mail, usually within 30 days of the sale. Lynn Tatum opens envelopes and separates the cheques from the accompanying remittance advices. Tatum forwards the cheques to another employee, who makes the daily bank deposit but has no access to the accounting records. Tatum sends the remittance advices, which show the amount of cash received, to the accounting department for entry in the accounts. Tatum's only other duty is to grant sales allowances to customers. (Recall that a *sales allowance* decreases the amount that the customer must pay.) When she receives a customer cheque for less than the full amount of the invoice, she records the sales allowance and forwards the document to the accounting department.

Required

You are a new management employee of Par Buster. Write a memo to the company president, Bobby Jones, identifying the internal control weakness in this situation. State how to correct the weakness.

Problem 7-6B *Applying internal controls to cash payments, including petty cash transactions* **(Obj. 5)**

Lee's Wholesale Greenhouses is located in White Rock, B.C., with a sales territory covering the lower mainland and Vancouver Island. Employees live on both the mainland and the island, but all report to work at the company's offices in White Rock.

The company has established a large petty cash fund to handle small cash payments and cash advances to its salespeople to cover frequent ferry trips to and from the island on sales trips.

The controller, Jane Simonic, has decided that two people (Marilyn Ling and Hugh Garner) should be in charge of the petty cash fund as money is often needed when one person may be out for coffee or lunch. Simonic also feels this will increase internal control, as the work of one person will serve as a check on that of the other.

Regular small cash payments are handled by either Ling or Garner, who make the payment and have the person receiving the money sign a sheet of paper listing the date and reason for the payment. Whenever a salesperson requires an advance for a trip to the island, they simply sign a receipt for the money received. The salespeople later submit receipts for the cost of the ferry ride to either Ling or Garner to offset the cash advance.

Simonic, a family friend, doesn't think the system is working and, knowing you are studying accounting, has asked for your advice.

Required

Write a memo to Jane Simonic commenting on the internal control procedures of Lee's Wholesale Greenhouses. Suggest changes that you think would improve the system.

Problem 7-7B *Accounting for petty cash transactions* **(Obj. 5)**

Suppose that on June 1, Laser Electronics opens a district office in Cornerbrook, Newfoundland, and creates a petty cash fund with an imprest balance of $400. During June, Sharon Dietz, the fund custodian, signs the following petty cash tickets (on page 401).

On June 30, prior to replenishment, the fund contains these tickets plus $191.51. The accounts affected by petty cash payments are Office Supplies Expense, Entertainment Expense, and Postage Expense.

Ticket Number	Item	Amount
1	Postage for package received	$ 18.40
2	Decorations and refreshments for office party	34.50
3	Two boxes of computer disks	20.82
4	Office Supplies	18.75
5	Dinner money for sales manager entertaining a customer	72.00

Required

1. Explain the characteristics and the internal control features of an imprest fund.

2. Make the general journal entries to create the fund and to replenish it. Include explanations. Also, briefly describe what the custodian does on these dates.

3. Make the entry on July 1 to increase the fund balance to $500. Include an explanation and briefly describe what the custodian does.

Problem 7-8B *Preparing a personal cash budget* *(Obj. 6)*

Suppose you are preparing your personal cash budget for 2003. During 2003, assume that you can expect to earn $3,000 from your summer job and $2,200 for work in the college cafeteria. Also, your family always gives you gifts totalling around $300 during the year. A scholarship from your local Rotary Club adds $750 each year while you are in college.

Assume your family pays your college costs except for room and board. Planned expenditures for 2003 include your share of apartment rent of $175 per month for 12 months and annual food costs of $5,000. Gas and other auto expenses usually run about $60 per month. You need to have a little fun, so entertainment will cost $125 per month.

You need to keep a little cash in reserve for auto repairs and other emergencies, so you maintain a cash reserve of $500 at all times. To start 2003, you have this cash reserve plus $100.

Will you need a loan during 2003? To answer this question, prepare your personal cash budget for the year based on the data given.

Problem 7-9B *Using cash-flow information to prepare a cash budget* *(Obj. 6)*

Louis Lipschitz, Chief Financial Officer of Toys "Я" Us, Inc., is responsible for the company's budgeting process. Suppose Lipschitz's staff is preparing the company's cash budget for 2002. A key input to the budgeting process is the previous year's cash flow statement, which provides the data on the following page for 2001. Cash receipts appear as positive amounts; cash payments are negative amounts, denoted within parentheses.

Required

1. Prepare the Toys "Я" Us cash budget for 2002. Date the budget simply "2002" and denote the beginning and ending cash balances as "beginning" and "ending." Assume the company expects 2002 to be similar to 2001, but with the following changes:

   a. In 2002, the company expects a 12% increase in collections from customers and a 10% increase in purchases of inventory.

   b. Lipschitz plans to end the year with a cash balance of $400 million.

2. Based on the cash budget you prepared, how much additional cash does it appear that Toys "Я" Us will need beyond the borrowings already scheduled for 2002?

TOYS "Я" US, INC.
(Cash-Flow Data)

(In millions)	2001
Collections from customers	$9,414
Interest revenue	23
Purchases of inventory	(6,750)
Operating expenses	(2,431)
Purchases of capital assets	(535)
Short-term borrowings	12
Long-term borrowings	290
Long-term debt repayments	(9)
Payments to shareholders	(200)
Cash and Cash Equivalents:	
Beginning of year 2001	$ 370
End of year 2001	$ 203

Problem 7-10B *Preparing a bank reconciliation and related journal entries* **(Obj. 3)**

Tower Scaffolding had a computer failure on April 1, 2002, which resulted in the loss of data including the balance of its cash account and its bank reconciliation from March 31, 2002. The accountant, Gemma Mendez, has been able to obtain the following information from the records of the company and its bank:

a. An examination showed that two cheques (#164 for $320 and #173 for $240) had not been cashed as of April 1. Mendez recalled that there was only one deposit in transit on the March 31 bank reconciliation, but was unable to recall the amount.

b. The cash receipts and cash payments journal contained the following entries for April 2002:

Cash Receipts: Amounts		Cash Payments: Cheque #	Amount
$ 845		182	$ 245
410		183	340
380		184	1,195
860		185	465
1,460		186	180
$3,955		187	475
		188	void
		189	290
		190	520
			$3,710

c. The bank provided the following statement as of April 30, 2002:

Date	Cheques and Other Debits		Deposits and Other Credits	Balance
April 1	#183	340.00	880.00	2,030.00
3	#173	240.00		1,790.00
5	#184	1,195.00		595.00
8			845.00	1,440.00
16	#182	245.00	440.00	1,635.00
17	EFT	320.00		1,315.00
19			EFT 420.00	1,735.00
21	#186	180.00	410.00	1,965.00
22	#187	745.00	EFT 190.00	1,410.00
24			EFT 145.00	1,555.00
26	NSF	570.00	380.00	1,365.00
27	SC	25.00		1,340.00
30	#190	520.00	860.00	1,680.00

d. The deposit made on April 16 was for the collection of a note receivable ($400) plus interest.

e. The electronic funds transfers (EFTs) had not yet been recorded by Tower Scaffolding as the bank statement was the first notification of them.

- The April 17 EFT was for the monthly payment on an insurance policy for Tower Scaffolding.
- The April 19 and 24 EFTs were collections on accounts receivable.
- The April 22 EFT was in error—the transfer should have been to Tower Construction Corporation.

f. The NSF cheque on April 26 was received from a customer as payment for ladders purchased for $570 (cost to Tower Scaffolding was $420).

g. Cheque #187 was correctly written for $745 for the purchase of office supplies, but incorrectly recorded by the cash payments clerk.

Required

1. Prepare a bank reconciliation as of April 30, 2002, including the calculation of the book balance of March 31, 2002.

2. Prepare all journal entries that would be required by the bank reconciliation.

Problem 7-11B   *Making an ethical judgment*   *(Obj. 5, 7)*

Lars Nelford is a vice-president of the Bank of Nova Scotia in Burnaby, B.C. Active in community affairs, Nelford serves on the board of directors of Zenith Steel Products. Zenith is expanding rapidly and is considering relocating its plant. At a recent meeting, board members decided to try to buy 15 hectares of land on the edge of town. The owner of the property is Mary Aldous, a customer of the Bank of Nova Scotia. Aldous is completing a bitter divorce. Nelford knows that Aldous is eager to sell her local property. In view of Aldous' anguished condition, Nelford believes she would accept almost any offer for the land. Realtors have appraised the property at $4 million.

Required

Apply the ethical judgment framework outlined in the Decision Guidelines feature on page 378 to help Lars Nelford decide what his role should be in Zenith's attempt to buy the land from Mary Aldous.

Challenge Problems

Problem 7-1C   *Management's role in internal control*   *(Obj. 1)*

Effective internal control must begin with top management. The "tone at the top" is a necessary condition if an organization is to have an effective system of internal control. These statements are becoming a more important part of internal control literature and thought.

The chapter lists a number of characteristics that are important for an effective system of internal control. Many of these characteristics have been part of the internal control literature for years.

Required

Explain why you think a commitment to good internal control by top management is fundamental to an effective system of internal control.

Problem 7-2C *Applying internal controls to cash transactions* **(Obj. 4, 5)**

Many companies require some person other than the person preparing the bank reconciliation to review the reconciliation. Organizations routinely require cheques over a certain amount to be signed by two signing officers. The purchasing department orders goods but the receiving department receives the goods.

Required

All of the above illustrations have a common thread. What is that common thread and why is it important?

Extending Your Knowledge

Decision Problems

1. Using the bank reconciliation to detect a theft   *(Obj. 3)*

ComTech Company has poor internal control over its cash transactions. Recently Cindy Fong, the owner, has suspected the cashier of stealing. Details of the business's cash position at September 30, 2003 follow:

1. The Cash account shows a balance of $21,602. This amount includes a September 30 deposit of $3,794 that does not appear on the September 30 bank statement.

2. The September 30 bank statement shows a balance of $18,924. The bank statement lists a $600 credit for a bank collection, an $8 debit for the service charge and a $36 debit for an NSF cheque. Helena Hunt, the ComTech accountant, has not recorded any of these items on the books.

3. At September 30 the following cheques are outstanding:

Cheque No.	Amount
154	$116
256	150
278	253
291	190
292	306
293	145

4. Tim Harris, the cashier, handles all incoming cash and makes bank deposits. He also reconciles the monthly bank statement. His September 30 reconciliation follows:

Balance per books, September 30......................		$21,602
Add: Outstanding cheques...............................		560
Bank collection		600
		22,762
Less: Deposits in transit	$3,794	
Service charge...	8	
NSF cheque..	36	3,838
Balance per bank, September 30		$18,924

Fong has requested that you determine whether Harris has stolen cash from the business and, if so, how much. Fong also asks you to identify how Harris has attempted to conceal the theft. To make this determination, you perform your own bank reconciliation using the format illustrated on page 365. There are no bank or book errors. Fong also asks you to evaluate the internal controls and recommend any changes needed to improve them.

2. The role of internal control   (Obj. 2)

The following questions are unrelated except that they all pertain to internal control:

1. Separation of duties is an important consideration if a system of internal control is to be effective. Why is this so?

2. Marvel Company requires that all documents supporting a cheque be cancelled by the person who signs the cheque. Why do you think this practice is required? What might happen if it were not required?

3. Many managers think that safeguarding assets is the most important objective of internal control systems, whereas auditors, on the other hand, emphasize reliable accounting data. Explain why auditors are more concerned about the quality of the accounting records and data.

4. Cash may be a relatively small item on the financial statements. Nevertheless, internal control over cash is very important. Why do you think this is true?

Financial Statement Problem

Audit opinion, management responsibility, internal controls and cash   (Obj. 1)

Study the management report (titled "Management's Responsibility") and the auditors' report on Intrawest Corporation's financial statements, given in Appendix A. Answer the following questions about Intrawest's internal controls and cash position:

1. What is the name of Intrawest's outside auditing firm? What office of this firm signed the auditor's report? How long after Intrawest's year end did the auditors issue their opinion?

2. Who bears primary responsibility for the financial statements? How can you tell?

3. Does it appear that Intrawest's internal controls are adequate? How can you tell?

4. What standard of auditing did the outside auditors use in examining Intrawest's financial statements? By what accounting standards were the statements evaluated?

5. By how much did Intrawest's cash position change during 2000? The cash flow statement, or statement of changes in financial position (discussed in detail in Chapter 17) tells why this change occurred. Which type of activity—operating, financing, or investing—contributed most to this change?

8

Accounts and Notes Receivable

CHAPTER OBJECTIVES

After studying this chapter, you should be able to

1. Design internal controls for receivables

2. Use the allowance method to account for uncollectibles and estimate uncollectibles by the percent of sales and the aging methods

3. Use the direct write-off method to account for uncollectibles

4. Account for credit-card and debit-card sales

5. Account for notes receivable

6. Report receivables on the balance sheet

7. Use the acid-test ratio and days' sales in receivables to evaluate a company's financial position

Research In Motion Ltd. (RIM) is an internationally recognized leader in wireless communications. The RIM wireless handheld 950 and 850 and the newer Blackberry, the world's leading wireless email solution and *Infoworld's* Product of the Year in 1999, have led RIM to a phenomenal rate of growth, especially over the past two years.

As a result of RIM's innovative and timely products, RIM's co-CEOs, Michael Lazaridis and James L. Balsillie, have been able to form alliances with such industry leaders as Nortel Networks, Bell South, Compaq Computer, Rogers AT&T Wireless, and Motient Corporation.

RIM's financial statements reflect the success of the wireless handhelds and the BlackBerry. Revenue has climbed from $20,901,000 in 1998 through $47,342,000 in 1999 to $84,967,000 in 2000 (all amounts in US dollars). At the same time, inventory has increased from $10,341,000 in 1998, $19,812,000 in 1999 to $36,852,000 in 2000. Accounts receivable has grown from $10,045,000 in 1998 through $12,515,000 in 1999 to $36,852,000 in 2000.

Companies like RIM that grow very quickly have to be concerned with their cash flow. They have to translate production into inventory, inventory into sales and receivables, and receivables into cash. A danger is that a company can be sales rich and cash poor. Well-managed companies like RIM monitor their increased accounts receivables and inventory. It is this attention to all aspects of their business that makes companies such as RIM the successes they are.

Sources: 2000 and 1999 Research In Motion Annual Reports; Olive David, "CEO Scorecard 2000," *National Post Business*, November 2000, pp. 104–105 and 112–113.

LIKE most other assets, accounts receivable can represent good news or bad news: Good news because receivables represent a claim to the customer's cash; bad news when the business fails to collect the cash. Fast-growing companies like Research In Motion (RIM) must manage their accounts receivable very carefully. They want to avoid having too much of their resources in accounts receivable—an asset that earns no income. If cash does not flow into the business quickly enough, companies like RIM may have to borrow money, and the related interest expense would reduce profits.

In this chapter we discuss the role of the credit department in deciding to which customers the business will sell on account. We explain receivables, including how to account for them when they appear to be uncollectible, and internal control over receivables. We also cover notes receivable and introduce several measures that help a business manage customer accounts, including *days' sales in receivables.*

A *receivable* arises when a business (or person) sells goods or services to a second business (or person) on credit. A receivable is the seller's claim against the buyer for the amount of the transaction. Each credit transaction involves at least two parties:

- The **creditor** sells a service or merchandise and obtains a receivable.

- The **debtor** makes the purchase and has a payable, which is a liability.

This chapter focuses on accounting for receivables by the seller (the creditor).

Receivables: An Introduction

The Types of Receivables

Receivables are monetary claims against businesses and individuals. The two major types of receivables are accounts receivable and notes receivable. A business's *accounts*

THINKING IT OVER

What are (1) the major advantages of selling on credit and (2) the major disadvantages of selling on credit?

A: (1) More sales, because it is easier for customers to buy and therefore net income will be higher.
(2) Some customers will pay late or not at all; also, credit sales are more costly because the company must maintain a credit department and a billing department.

Research In Motion Ltd.
www.rim.net

KEY POINT

Trade Accounts Receivable do not include amounts due from employees or officers (these are called Receivables from Employees or from Officers). Trade Accounts Receivable arise from selling goods or services to customers.

receivable are amounts owed by its customers. Accounts receivable, which are *current assets*, are sometimes called *trade receivables*.

As we saw in Chapter 6, the Accounts Receivable account in the general ledger serves as a *control account*. It summarizes the total amounts receivable from all customers. Companies also keep a *subsidiary ledger* of accounts receivable with a separate account for each customer, illustrated as follows:

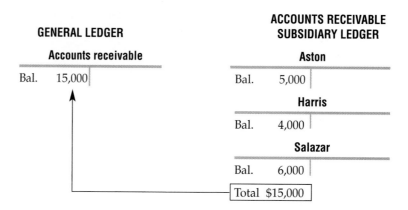

Notes receivable are more formal than accounts receivable. The debtor for a note receivable promises in writing to pay the creditor a definite sum at a definite future date—the *maturity* date. The terms of these notes usually extend for at least 60 days. A written document known as a *promissory note* serves as evidence of the receivable. The note may require the debtor to pledge *security* for the loan: This means that the borrower promises that the lender may claim certain assets if the borrower fails to pay the amount due at maturity.

Notes receivable due within one year, or operating cycle if longer than one year, are current assets. Notes due beyond one year are *long-term receivables*. Some notes receivable are collected in periodic instalments. The portion due within one year is a current asset, and the remaining amount a long-term asset. The Bank of Nova Scotia may hold a $6,000 note receivable from you, but only the $1,500 you owe on it this year is a current asset to the Bank of Nova Scotia.

Other receivables is a miscellaneous category that includes loans to employees and subsidiary companies. Usually these are long-term receivables, but they are current assets if receivable within one year or less. Long-term notes receivable and other receivables are often reported on the balance sheet after current assets and before capital assets, as shown in Exhibit 8-1. The receivables are highlighted for emphasis.

The Bank of Nova Scotia
www.scotiabank.com

Establishing Internal Control over the Collection of Receivables

Businesses that sell on credit receive most of their cash receipts by mail. Internal control over collections of cash on account is an important part of the overall internal control system (see Chapter 7). A critical element of internal control deserves emphasis here: the separation of cash-handling and cash-accounting duties. Consider the following case:

Butler Supply Co. is a family-owned office supply business that takes pride in the loyalty of its workers. Most company employees have been with Butler for at least five years. The company makes 90 percent of its sales on account.

The office staff consists of a bookkeeper and a supervisor. The bookkeeper maintains the general ledger and the accounts receivable subsidiary ledger. He also makes the daily bank deposit. The supervisor prepares monthly financial statements and any special reports Butler Supply Co. requires. She also takes sales orders from customers and serves as office manager.

EXAMPLE COMPANY
Balance Sheet
Date

Assets			Liabilities		
Current assets:			Current liabilities:		
Cash		$X,XXX	Accounts payable		$X,XXX
Accounts receivable...........	**X,XXX**		Notes payable, short-term.................		X,XXX
Less: Allowance for			Accrued current liabilities.................		X,XXX
uncollectible accounts..	**(XXX)**	**X,XXX**	Total current liabilities....................		X,XXX
Notes receivable, short-term................		**X,XXX**			
Inventories		X,XXX	Long-term liabilities:		
Prepaid expenses...................................		X,XXX	Notes payable, long-term..................		X,XXX
Total current assets..........................		X,XXX	Total liabilities.................................		$X,XXX
Investments and long-term receivables:					
Investments in other companies........		X,XXX			
Notes receivable, long-term		**X,XXX**			
Other receivables		**X,XXX**			
Total non-current assets..................		X,XXX			
Capital assets:			**Owner's Equity**		
Property, plant and equipment			Capital..		X,XXX
(net of amortization)		X,XXX	Total liabilities and owner's		
Total assets...		$X,XXX	equity		$X,XXX

EXHIBIT 8-1

Balance Sheet

Can you identify the internal control weakness here? The bookkeeper has access to the general ledger and the accounts receivable subsidiary ledger, and also has custody of the cash. The bookkeeper could steal a customer cheque and write off the customer's account as uncollectible.[1] Unless the supervisor or some other manager reviews the bookkeeper's work regularly, the theft may go undetected. In small businesses like Butler Supply Co., such a review may not be performed routinely.

How can this control weakness be corrected? The supervisor could open incoming mail and make the daily bank deposit. *The bookkeeper should not be allowed to handle cash.* Only the remittance advices would be forwarded to the bookkeeper to indicate which customer accounts to credit. By removing cash-handling duties from the bookkeeper and keeping the accounts receivable subsidiary ledger away from the supervisor, the company would separate duties and strengthen internal control. These actions would reduce an employee's opportunity to steal cash and then cover it up with a false credit to a customer account.

Using a bank lock box achieves the same separation of duties. Customers can be instructed to send their payments directly to Butler Supply Co.'s bank, which records the cash receipts and deposits the cash into the company's bank account. The bank then forwards the remittance advices to Butler Supply Co.'s bookkeeper, who credits the appropriate customer accounts. We examined the lock-box system in detail in Chapter 7, page 369.

---

[1]The bookkeeper would need to forge the endorsements of the cheques and deposit them in a bank account he controls.

Managing the Collection of Receivables: The Credit Department

Most companies have a department to evaluate customers who apply for credit. The extension of credit requires a "balancing act." The company does not want to lose sales to good customers who need time to pay. It also wants to avoid losses from selling to customers who are unlikely to pay.

A customer who uses a credit card to acquire goods or services is buying on account. This transaction creates a receivable for the seller. Most companies with a high proportion of sales on account (for example, Canadian Tire) have a separate credit department (or division or even company). This department evaluates customers who apply for credit cards by using standard formulas—which include the applicant's income and credit history, among other factors—for deciding which customers the company will sell to on account.

After approving a customer, the credit department monitors customer payment records. Customers with a history of paying on time may receive higher credit limits. Those who fail to pay on time have their limits reduced or eliminated. The goal is to collect from customers quickly enough to keep cash circulating. The credit department also assists the accounting department in measuring collection losses on customers who do not pay.

For good internal control over cash collections of receivables, it is critical that the credit department has no access to cash. For example, if a credit employee handles cash, he or she can pocket the money received from a customer. He or she can then label the customer's account as uncollectible, and the accounting department writes off the account receivable as discussed in the next section. The company stops billing the customer, and the credit employee has covered up the embezzlement, the pocketing of the money. If the customer places another order with the company, the credit employee can reinstate the account and repeat the cycle of theft. For this reason, a sharp separation of duties is important indeed.

The Decision Guidelines feature identifies the main issues in controlling, managing, and accounting for receivables. These guidelines serve as a framework for the remainder of the chapter.

DECISION GUIDELINES — Controlling, Managing, and Accounting for Receivables

The main issues in *controlling* and *managing* the collection of receivables, and the related plans of action, are as follows:

Issue	Action
Extend credit only to creditworthy customers, the ones most likely to pay us.	Run a credit check on prospective customers.
Separate cash-handling, credit, and accounting duties to keep employees from stealing the cash collected from customers.	Design the internal control system to separate duties.
Pursue collection from customers to maximize cash flow.	Keep a close eye on collections from customers.

The main issues in *accounting* for receivables, and the related plans of action, are as follows:

Issue	Action
Measure and report receivables on the balance sheet at their *net realizable value*, the amount we expect to collect. This is necessary to report assets accurately.	Estimate the amount of uncollectible receivables. Report receivables at their net realizable value (accounts receivable − allowance for uncollectible accounts).
Measure and report the expense associated with failure to collect receivables, which we call *uncollectible-account expense*, on the income statement. This helps report net income at a reasonable amount.	Measure the expense of failing to collect from our customers.

Accounting for Uncollectible Accounts (Bad Debts)

OBJECTIVE 2
Use the allowance method to account for uncollectibles and estimate uncollectibles by the percent of sales and aging methods

Selling on credit creates both a benefit and a cost.

- *The benefit:* The business increases sales revenues and profits by making sales to good customers who are unwilling or unable to pay cash immediately.
- *The cost:* The company will be unable to collect from some of its credit customers, and that creates an expense, which is called **uncollectible-account expense, doubtful-account expense,** or **bad-debt expense.**

KEY POINT

Selling on credit enables a company to generate more sales revenue. But there is a cost associated with selling on credit; bad-debt expense arises as a result of not collecting from some customers.

Uncollectible-account expense varies from company to company. In certain businesses, a six-month-old receivable of $1 is worth only 67 cents and a five-year-old receivable of $1 is worth only 4 cents. The older the receivable, the less valuable it is because of the increasing likelihood that the customer will not pay. Uncollectible-account expense depends on the credit risks that managers are willing to accept. At Albany Ladder Ltd., a $23 million construction-equipment and supply firm, 85 percent of company sales are on account. Albany Ladder Ltd.'s receivables grow in proportion to sales. Uncollectible accounts, or bad debts, cost Albany Ladder Ltd. about $100,000 a year, or about 1 to 1½ percent of total sales. Albany Ladder Ltd. undertakes careful credit screening and rigourous collection activity. It takes Albany Ladder Ltd. an average of 70 days to collect its receivables.

Many small retail businesses accept a higher level of risk than large stores such as The Bay. Why? Extending credit increases sales. Moreover, small businesses often have personal ties to customers who are more likely to pay their accounts when they know the proprietor personally.

For a firm that sells on credit, uncollectible-account expense is as much a part of doing business as salary expense and amortization expense. Uncollectible-Account Expense—an operating expense—must be measured, recorded, and reported. To do so, accountants use the allowance method or, in certain limited cases, the direct write-off method (which we discuss on page 415).

The Allowance Method To present the most accurate financial statements possible, accountants in firms with large credit sales use the **allowance method** to measure bad debts. This method records collection losses based on estimates instead of waiting to see which customers the business will not collect from. This is in keeping with the matching principle, which directs that all expenses relating to a sale be recorded in the same accounting period as the sale. Since it records collection losses on the basis of estimates, the allowance method can be viewed as in *indirect* approach.

Smart managers know that not every customer will pay in full. But at the time of sale, managers do not know which customers will not pay. If they did, they would not sell on credit to those customers.

Rather than try to guess which accounts will go bad, managers estimate the total uncollectible-account expense for the period on the basis of the company's collection experience. The business records Uncollectible-Account Expense for the estimated amount, and sets up **Allowance for Uncollectible Accounts** (or **Allowance for Doubtful Accounts**), a contra account related to Accounts Receivable. This allowance account shows the amount of receivables that the business expects *not* to collect.

Subtracting the uncollectible allowance amount from Accounts Receivable yields the net amount that the company does expect to collect, as shown here (using assumed numbers):

KEY POINT

The longer an account is outstanding, the less chance of collection. But even if a past-due account is collected in full, there is a cost associated with collecting an account late. Also, when an account is past due, the seller is essentially giving an interest-free loan to the buyer because the seller does not have the cash to use in the business. This increases the seller's cost of doing business.

Balance sheet (partial):

Accounts receivable	$10,000
Less Allowance for uncollectible accounts	(900)
Accounts receivable, net	$ 9,100

Customers owe this company $10,000, of which the business expects to collect $9,100. The company estimates that it will not collect $900 of its accounts receivable.

Another way to report these receivables follows the pattern used by Research In Motion Ltd., Rogers Communications Inc., and other companies, as follows;

Accounts receivable, net of allowance for uncollectible
accounts of $900 .... $9,100

The income statement reports Uncollectible-Account Expense among the operating expenses, as follows (using assumed figures):

Income statement (partial):

Expenses:
Uncollectible-account expense... $2,000

Estimating Uncollectibles

The more accurate the estimate of uncollectible accounts, the more reliable the information in the financial statements. How are bad-debt estimates made? The most logical way to estimate uncollectibles is to examine the business's past records. There are two basic ways to estimate uncollectibles:

- *Percent of sales method*
- *Aging of accounts receivable method*

Both approaches work under the allowance method.

Percent of Sales Method   The **percent of sales method** computes uncollectible-account expense as a percentage of net credit sales. This method is also called the **income-statement approach** because it focuses on the amount of expense to be reported on the income statement. Uncollectible-account expense is recorded by an adjusting entry at the end of the period. Assume it is December 31, 2003, and the accounts have these balances *before the year-end adjustments:*

Accounts Receivable	Allowance for Uncollectible Accounts
120,000	500

Customers owe the business $120,000, and the Allowance for Uncollectible Accounts is too low. The $500 balance in the Allowance account is left over from the preceding period. Prior to any adjustments, the net receivable amount is $119,500 ($120,000 − $500), which is more than the business expects to collect from customers.

Based on prior experience, the credit department estimates that uncollectible-account expense is 1.5 percent of net credit sales, which were $500,000 in 2003. The adjusting entry to record uncollectible-account expense for the year and to update the allowance is:

2003
Dec. 31   Uncollectible-Account Expense.............................. 7,500
                 Allowance for Uncollectible Accounts.............. 7,500
                 To record expense for the year ($500,000 × 0.015).

The accounting equation shows that the transaction to record the expense decreases the business's assets by the amount of the expense:

Assets	=	Liabilities	+	Owner's Equity	−	Expenses
−7,500	=	0			−	7,500

Notice that the $500 balance in Allowance for Uncollectible Accounts from the pre-

Rogers Communications Inc.
www.rogers.com

KEY POINT

The amount of uncollectible-account expense depends on the volume of credit sales, the effectiveness of the credit department, and the diligence of the collection department.

KEY POINT

Owners have to make a number of estimates of expenses when they calculate net income. In this case, estimating uncollectible-account expense actually makes net income more correct than if it were omitted. This is because reality is better reflected when uncollectible-account expense is included, based on past experience.

KEY POINT

The percent of sales approach is often referred to as the income-statement approach to estimating bad-debt expense because the entry is based on credit sales for the period (an income statement figure).

vious period has no effect on the entry to record uncollectible-account expense for the year. Now the accounts are ready for reporting in the 2003 financial statements.

Accounts Receivable		Allowance for Uncollectible Accounts	
120,000			500
		Adj.	7,500
			8,000

Customers still owe the business $120,000, but now the allowance for uncollectible accounts is realistic. The balance sheet will report accounts receivable at the net amount of $112,000 ($120,000 – $8,000). The income statement will report the period's uncollectible-account expense of $7,500, along with the operating expenses for the period.

Aging of Accounts Receivable   The second popular method for estimating uncollectible accounts is the **aging of accounts receivable method.** This method is also called the **balance-sheet approach** because it focuses on accounts receivable. In the aging method, individual accounts receivable from specific customers are analyzed according to the length of time they have been receivable from the customer.

Computerized accounting packages prepare a report for aging accounts receivable. The computer accesses customer data and sorts accounts by customer number and by date of invoice. For example, the credit department of Schmidt Builders Supply groups its accounts receivable into 30-day periods, as Exhibit 8-2 shows.

Schmidt's total balance of accounts receivable is $112,000. Of this amount, the aging schedule indicates that the company will *not* collect $3,769. Prior to the year-end adjustment, Schmidt's customers owed the company $112,000. The allowance for uncollectible accounts is not up-to-date. Schmidt Builders Supply's accounts appear as follows *before the year-end adjustment*:

Accounts Receivable		Allowance for Uncollectible Accounts	
112,000			1,100

The aging method is designed to bring the balance of the allowance account to the needed amount ($3,769) determined by the aging schedule in Exhibit 8-2 (see the lower right corner for the final result—a needed credit balance of $3,769.)

THINKING IT OVER

(1) What problems are encountered if a company records a sale in 2002 to a customer whose account will eventually be uncollectible, but does not record the doubtful-account expense until 2003?
(2) Is recording the expense in 2003 incorrect?

A: (1) Accounts Receivable for 2002 will be overstated and the matching principle is violated. (2) Yes. The question could be rephrased: When did the account become uncollectible? The account was uncollectible at the time of sale and should therefore be deducted from revenue in the period of sale (2002).

KEY POINT

The aging of accounts receivable approach is often referred to as the balance sheet approach to estimating bad debts because the computation focuses on Accounts Receivable (a balance sheet figure).

EXHIBIT 8-2

Aging the Accounts Receivable of Schmidt Builders Supply

Customer Name	Age of Account				
	1–30 Days	31–60 Days	61–90 Days	Over 90 Days	Total Balance
Baring Tools Co.	$20,000				$ 20,000
Calgary Pneumatic Parts Ltd.	10,000				10,000
Red Deer Pipe Corp.......		$13,000	$10,000		23,000
Seal Coatings, Inc.			3,000	$1,000	4,000
Other accounts*	39,000	12,000	2,000	2,000	55,000
Totals................................	$69,000	$25,000	$15,000	$3,000	$112,000
Estimated percent uncollectible.................	× 0.1%	× 1%	× 5%	× 90%	
Allowance for Uncollectible Accounts........................	$69	$250	$750	$2,700	$3,769

* Each of the "Other accounts" would appear individually.

To update the allowance, Schmidt makes this adjusting entry at the end of the period:

2003			
Dec. 31	Uncollectible-Account Expense............................	2,669	
	Allowance for Uncollectible Accounts		2,669
	To record expense for the year ($3,769 − $1,100).		

Again, the recording of the expense decreases the business's assets by the amount of the expenses. The accounting equation of the expense transaction is

Assets	=	Liabilities	+	Owner's Equity	−	Expenses
−2,669	=	0			−	2,669

Now the balance sheet can report the amount that Schmidt Builders Supply expects to collect from customers, $108,231 ($112,000 – $3,769), as follows:

Accounts Receivable		Allowance for Uncollectible Accounts		
112,000				1,100
			Adj.	2,669
				3,769

Net accounts receivable, $108,231

As with the percent of sales method, the income statement reports the uncollectible account expense.

The *net* amount of accounts receivable—$108,231 in this case—is called net realizable value because it is the amount Schmidt expects to realize (collect in cash) from the receivables.

Using the Percent of Sales and the Aging Methods Together   In practice, many companies use the percent of sales and the aging of accounts receivable methods together.

- For *interim statements* (monthly or quarterly), companies use the percent of sales method because it is easier to apply. The percent of sales method focuses on the amount of uncollectible-account *expense*. But that is not enough.

- At the end of the year, these companies use the aging method to ensure that Accounts Receivable is reported at *expected realizable value*—that is, the expected amount to be collected. The aging method focuses on the amount of the receivables—the *asset*—that is uncollectible.

- Using the two methods together provides good measures of both the expense and the asset. Exhibit 8-3 summarizes and compares the two methods.

Exhibit 8-3
———————————————
Comparing the Percent of Sales and Aging Methods for Estimating Uncollectibles

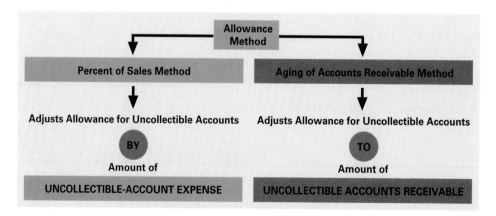

Writing Off Uncollectible Accounts

During 2004 Schmidt Builders Supply collects on most of its $112,000 accounts receivable and records the cash receipts as follows:

2004
Jan–Mar.   Cash...   92,000
      Accounts Receivable—
        Various Customers   92,000
      To record collections on account.

Cash increases, and Accounts Receivable decreases by the same amount. Total assets are unchanged.

Assets	=	Liabilities	+	Owner's Equity
+92,000 −92,000	=	0	+	0

Suppose that, after repeated attempts to collect from customers, Schmidt's credit department determines that Schmidt Builders Supply cannot collect a total of $1,200 from customers Abbott ($900) and Smith ($300). Schmidt's accountant writes off the company's receivables with the following entry:

2004
Mar. 31   Allowance for Uncollectible Accounts............   1,200
      Accounts Receivable—Abbott.......................   900
      Accounts Receivable—Smith   300
      To write off uncollectible accounts.

The accounting equation shows that the write-off of uncollectible accounts has no effect on total assets or any other account.

Assets	=	Liabilities	+	Owner's Equity
+1,200 −1,200	=	0	+	0

Study the write-off entry carefully. Because the write-off entry affects no expense account, it *does not affect net income*. The write-off has no effect on net receivables either, as shown for Schmidt Builders Supply in Exhibit 8-4.

The Direct Write-Off Method

There is an alternative way to account for uncollectible receivables. This method does *not* use an allowance account. Under the **direct write-off method** of accounting for uncollectible receivables, the company waits until it decides that a customer's account receivable is uncollectible. Then the accountant writes off the

THINKING IT OVER

If the write-off of specific uncollectible accounts affects neither an expense account nor the net amount of receivables, then why write off the uncollectible accounts of specific customers?

A: The business has decided that the uncollectible accounts are worthless. It is appropriate to eliminate these accounts from the accounts receivable records, which alerts the credit department not to waste time and money pursuing collections from these customers. The credit department stores their names in a database. If they later apply for credit, the credit department will carefully consider selling to them on account.

WORKING IT OUT

Given:
Accts. Rec. $90,000
– Allow. for Uncoll.
   Accts. ....   − 3,500
= Net Accts. Rec.
  (Net Realizable
  Value)............... $86,500

Give (1) the journal entry to record the write-off of a $700 Accounts Receivable for Kathy Brown and (2) the Net Accounts Receivable after the write-off.

A:
(1) Allow. for Uncoll.
   Accts........   700
     Accts. Rec.—
     K. Brown   700
(2) $86,500
   [($90,000 − 700)
   − (3,500 − 700)]

OBJECTIVE 3
Use the direct write-off method to account for uncollectibles

EXHIBIT 8-4

Net Receivables Are the Same Before and After the Write-off of Uncollectible Accounts

	Before Write-Off		After Write-Off
Accounts receivable ($112,000 – $92,000)	$20,000	($20,000 – $1,200)	$18,800
Less Allowance for uncollectible accounts	(3,769)	(($3,769) – $1,200)	(2,569)
Accounts receivable, net	$16,231 ←	—— same ——	→ $16,231

customer's account receivable by debiting Uncollectible-Account Expense and crediting the customer's Account Receivable, as follows (using assumed data):

```
2002
Jan. 2    Uncollectible-Account Expense....................    1,500
               Accounts Receivable—Kwan....................              1,500
          Wrote off an uncollectible account.
```

This method is defective for two reasons:

1. It does not set up an allowance for uncollectible accounts. As a result, it always reports the receivables at their full amount, which is more than the business expects to collect. Assets are therefore overstated on the balance sheet.

2. It may not match the uncollectible-account expense of each period against the revenue of the period in which the sale was made. In this example, the company made the sale to Kwan in 2001 and should have recorded the uncollectible-account expense during 2001 to measure net income properly. By recording the expense in 2002, the company overstates net income in 2001 and understates net income in 2002.

Do not confuse the direct write-off method with the allowance method. The two methods of accounting for uncollectible receivables are totally different, and a company adopts one method or the other. The direct write-off method is acceptable only when the amount of uncollectible receivables is very low. It works well for retailers such as Wal-Mart and the Gap, which carry almost no receivables.

STOP & THINK

1. How accurately does the direct write-off method measure income?

Answer: Following generally accepted accounting principles means matching each period's expenses against its revenues. The direct write-off method fails this test: In our example above, the full amount of sales revenue appears for 2001, but the uncollectible-account expense incurred to generate this revenue appears in 2002. Consequently, this method gives misleading income figures for both years. The $1,500 uncollectible-account expense should be matched against the sales revenue for 2001.

2. How accurately does the direct write-off method value accounts receivable?

Answer: The 2001 balance sheet shows accounts receivable at the full figure, say $100,000. But any businessperson knows that uncollectible accounts are unavoidable when selling on credit. There are always a few customers who will fail to pay the amount they owe. Is $100,000, then, the expected realizable value of the accounts? No, showing the full $100,000 in the balance sheet falsely implies that the $100,000 will be collected completely.

Recoveries of Uncollectible Accounts

When an account receivable is written off as uncollectible, the customer still has an obligation to pay. However, the company may stop pursuing collection and writes off the account as uncollectible. Some companies turn such accounts over to a lawyer or collection agency for collection in the hope of recovering part of the receivable. This is called the recovery of a bad account. Let's see how to record the recovery of an account that we wrote off earlier. Recall that on March 31, 2004, Schmidt Builders Supply wrote off the $900 receivable from customer Abbott (see page 415). Suppose it is now January 4, 2005, and the company unexpectedly receives $900 from Abbott. To account for this recovery, Schmidt makes two journal entries to (1) reverse the earlier write-off and (2) record the cash collection, as follows:

(1) Accounts Receivable—Abbott	900	
Allowance for Uncollectible Accounts		900
Reinstated Abbott's account receivable.		

(2) Cash	900	
Accounts Receivable—Abbott		900
Collected on account.		

If Abbott's account had been written off using the direct write-off method and is later collected, the journal entry to (1) reverse the earlier write-off and (2) record the cash collection would be

(1) Accounts Receivable—Abbott	900	
Uncollectible Account Expense		900
Reinstated Abbott's account receivable.		

(2) Cash	900	
Accounts Receivable—Abbott		900
Collected on account.		

Accounts Receivable—Abbott

| Sale | 900 | 900 | Write-off |
| Recovery | 900 | 900 | Collection |

Credit-Card and Debit-Card Sales

Credit-Card Sales

Credit-card sales are common in retailing. American Express, Diners Club enRoute, VISA, and MasterCard are popular. The customer presents the credit card as payment for purchases. The credit-card company then pays the seller the transaction amount less a fee and bills the customer, who then pays the credit-card company.

Credit cards offer consumers the convenience of buying without having to pay the cash immediately. A VISA customer receives a monthly statement from VISA, detailing each of the customer's credit-card transactions. The customer can write a single cheque to cover the entire month's credit-card purchases.

Retailers also benefit from credit-card sales. They do not have to check a customer's credit rating. The company that issues the card has already done so. Retailers do not have to keep an accounts receivable subsidiary ledger account for each customer, and they do not have to collect cash from customers. Further, retailers receive cash more quickly from the credit-card companies than they would from the customers themselves.

Of course, these services to the seller do not come free. The seller receives less than 100 percent of the face value of the invoice. The credit-card company takes a discount[2] on the sale to cover its services. Suppose a friend treats you and two others to lunch at Hy's Steak House (the seller) and pays the bill—$100—with a Diners Club enRoute card. The seller's entry to record the $100 Diners Club enRoute card sale, subject to the credit-card company's 2-percent discount, is

Accounts Receivable—Diners Club enRoute	98	
Credit-Card Discount Expense	2	
Sales Revenue		100

On collection of the discounted value, the seller records the following:

| Cash | 98 | |
| Accounts Receivable—Diners Club enRoute | | 98 |

---

[2] The rate varies among companies and over time.

Debit-Card Sales

Debit-card sales are common in retailing. A *debit card* allows a customer to pay for a purchase immediately without using cash. Most banks issue debit cards. The Toronto Dominion Bank's Personal Access Green Card is an example. When a business makes a sale, the customer "swipes" her debit card through an Interac card reader and enters her personal information number (PIN). The bank deducts the cost of the purchase, plus a fee for the service, from the customer's account and transfers the purchase amount, less a fee, into the business's account. For example, suppose you buy groceries at a Loblaws store for a total cost of $56.35. You swipe your debit card, enter your PIN, and Loblaws records the sale as follows:

Cash..	$55.85	
Debit Card Service Fee	0.50	
Sales Revenue		$56.35
To record a debit-card sale.		

Credit-Card and Debit-Card Risk   Both credit cards and debit cards bear a risk for the card holder, the issuer, and the business accepting the card. The cards can be lost, and stolen cards can be used to make purchases for which the card-issuer will not receive payment. All parties should recognize this risk when they use, issue, and accept credit and debit cards.

The Toronto-Dominion Bank
www.tdbank.ca

Accounting and the *e*-World

Merchant Beware: Online Sales Using Credit Cards Boom—But So Does Fraud

The advertisements are very seductive. Buying over the Web is so easy. You can buy books, stocks, cars, groceries, and even houses. Currently almost all Web transactions are paid for by credit card. As with bricks-and-mortar retailers such as Beaver Lumber, the "e-tailer" pays the credit-card company a fee (usually between 2 percent and 4 percent of the purchase price) for every transaction a customer has transacted by credit card with the e-tailer. Visa, MasterCard, Diners Club enRoute, American Express, and other credit-card companies receive millions of dollars in transaction fees every year.

When a fraudulent charge is made on a credit card in a transaction with a bricks-and-mortar retailer, for example a purchase on a Bank of Montreal MasterCard of service from Forbes Pontiac Buick Cadillac, the credit-card issuer, Bank of Montreal, bears the cost. Who bears the cost when customers deny that they made the credit-card charges that appear on their account and the amount is charged back to the e-tailer? Who bears the cost when someone commits "identity theft" and makes purchases with stolen credit cards? It is the online merchants, the e-tailers.

The lack of face-to-face transactions has led to an increase in charges back to e-tailers for online sales. The e-tailer never physically touches the card and the on-line purchaser never signs a credit-card ticket. The result is that there is no paper trail to prove the cardholder actually initiated the charge. Anonymity also makes it easier for identity theft to occur. There are many examples of e-tailers having to set aside money to reimburse the credit-card companies for fraud.

Companies that see their bad debt expenses rise due to online fraud are paying attention to "red flags" that may indicate a possible fraud. Orders with different "bill to" and "ship to" addresses arouse suspicion. Orders that come from free e-mail services and from countries other than Canada are also getting special attention.

Credit Balances in Accounts Receivable

Occasionally, customers overpay their accounts or return merchandise for which they have already paid. The result is a credit balance in the customer's accounts receivable. For example, Leather and Stuff's subsidiary ledger contains 213 accounts, with balances as shown:

210 accounts with *debit* balances totalling...	$185,000
3 accounts with *credit* balances totalling...	2,800
Net total of all balances..	$182,200

Leather and Stuff should *not* report the asset Accounts Receivable at the net amount—$182,200. Why not? The credit balance—$2,800—is a liability. Like any other liability, customer credit balances are debts of the business. A balance sheet that did not indicate this liability would be misleading. Therefore, Leather and Stuff would report on its balance sheet:

Assets		Liabilities	
Current:		Current:	
Accounts receivable	$185,000	Credit balances in	
		customer accounts	$2,800

Many companies would include this $2,800 with other accounts payable.

Mid-Chapter Summary Problem
for Your Review

Wolfville Lumber Company is a chain of hardware and building supply stores concentrated in the Maritimes. The company's year-end balance sheet for 2002 reported:

Accounts receivable	$7,455,648
Allowance for uncollectible accounts	(224,000)

Required

1. How much of the December 31, 2002, balance of accounts receivable did Wolfville Lumber Company expect to collect? Stated differently, what was the expected realizable value of these receivables?

2. Journalize, without explanations, year 2003 entries for Wolfville Lumber Company, assuming:
   a. Estimated Uncollectible-Account Expense of $225,000, based on the percent of sales method.
   b. Write-offs of accounts receivable totalled $290,000.
   c. December 31, 2003, aging of receivables, which indicates that $242,000 of the total receivables of $7,980,346 is uncollectible. Post all three entries to Allowance for Uncollectible Accounts.

3. Show how Wolfville Lumber Company's receivables and related allowance will appear on the December 31, 2003, balance sheet.

4. What is the expected realizable value of receivables at December 31, 2003? How much is uncollectible-account expense for 2003?

Solution to Review Problem

Requirements

1. Wolfville Lumber Company expected to collect $7,231,648 (i.e., $7,455,648 – $224,000).

2. a. Uncollectible-Account Expense 225,000
       Allowance for Uncollectible Accounts 225,000

   b. Allowance for Uncollectible Accounts............................ 290,000
       Accounts Receivable 290,000
   c. Uncollectible-Account Expense ($242,000 – $159,000) ... 83,000
       Allowance for Uncollectible Accounts 83,000

Allowance for Uncollectible Accounts

2003 Write-offs	290,000	Dec. 31, 2002, Bal.	224,000
		2003 Expense	225,000
		Bal. before Adj.	159,000
		Dec. 31, 2003, Adj.	83,000
		Dec. 31, 2003, Bal.	242,000

3. Accounts receivable... $7,980,346
      Less: Allowance for uncollectible accounts 242,000

4. Expected realizable value of receivables at
      December 31, 2003, ($7,980,346 – $242,000)..................... $7,738,346

   Uncollectible-account expense for 2003
      ($225,000 + $83,000) 308,000

Cyber Coach

Visit the Student Resource area of the *Accounting* Companion Website for extra practice with the new material in Chapter 8.

www.pearsoned.ca/horngren

Notes Receivable: An Overview

As we pointed out earlier in this chapter, notes receivable are more formal arrangements than accounts receivable. Often the debtor signs a promissory note, which serves as evidence of the debt. Let's define the special terms used to discuss notes receivable:

Promissory note. A written promise to pay a specified sum of money at a particular future date.

Maker of the note (**debtor**). The person or business that signs the note and promises to pay the amount required by the note agreement; the maker of the note is the *debtor*.

Payee of the note (**creditor**). The person or business to whom the maker promises future payment; the payee of the note is the *creditor*.

Principal amount or **principal**. The amount loaned out by the payee and borrowed by the maker of the note.

Interest. The revenue to the payee for loaning out the principal and the expense to the maker for borrowing the principal.

Interest period. The period of time during which interest is to be computed. It extends from the original date of the note to the maturity date. Also called the **note period**, **note term**, or simply **time**.

Interest rate. The percentage rate that is multiplied by the principal amount and time to compute the amount of interest on the note. Interest rates are almost always stated for a period of one year. Therefore, a 9-percent note means that the amount of interest for *one year* is 9 percent of the principal amount of the note.

Maturity date (also called **due date**). The date on which final payment of the note is due. Debts with a maturity date are permitted by law to be paid three days after their maturity or due date. These three days are called "days of grace."

Maturity value. The sum of principal and interest due at the maturity date of a note.

Exhibit 8-5 illustrates a promissory note. Study it carefully.

Identifying the Maturity Date of a Note

Some notes specify the maturity date of a note, as shown in Exhibit 8-5. Other notes state the period of the note, in days or months. When the period is given in months, the note's maturity date falls on the same day of the month as the date the note was issued. For example, a 6-month note dated February 16 matures on August 16. With the days of grace taken into account, the note must be repaid by August 19.

When the period is given in days, the maturity date is determined by counting the days from date of issue. A 120-day note dated September 14, 2002, matures on January 12, 2003, as shown below:

Month		Number of Days	Cumulative Total
Sept.	2002	16*	16
Oct.	2002	31	47
Nov.	2002	30	77
Dec.	2002	31	108
Jan.	2003	12	120

*30 − 14 = 16

The note would have to be *repaid* by January 15, 2003 (January 12 + 3 days of grace). In counting the days remaining for a note, remember to count the maturity date and to omit the date the note was issued. (From this point forward in this text, we will ignore the three days of grace when identifying the maturity date of a note.)

WORKING IT OUT

Calculate the maturity dates of these notes:

(1) A 90-day note dated January 4, 2002.
(2) A 150-day note dated September 30, 2002.
(3) A 45-day note dated May 15, 2003. Begin counting on the day following the date of the note, so that the due date on a 90-day note is day number 90.

A: (1) April 4, 2002
(2) February 27, 2003
(3) June 29, 2003

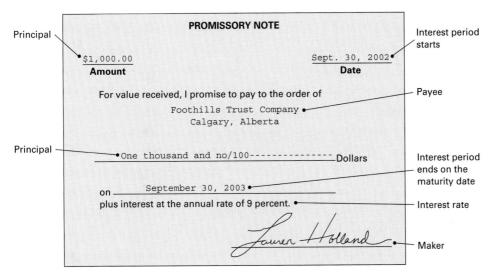

PROMISSORY NOTE

Principal — $1,000.00
Amount

Sept. 30, 2002 — Interest period starts
Date

For value received, I promise to pay to the order of

Foothills Trust Company — Payee
Calgary, Alberta

Principal — One thousand and no/100------------------ Dollars

Interest period ends on the maturity date

on ——— September 30, 2003 ———

plus interest at the annual rate of 9 percent. — Interest rate

Lauren Holland — Maker

Exhibit 8-5

A Promissory Note

Computing Interest on a Note

The formula for computing interest is

Principal × Interest Rate × Time = Amount of Interest

Using the data in Exhibit 8-5, Foothills Trust Company computes its interest revenue for one year on its note receivable as:

		Interest Rate		Time		Amount of Interest
Principal						
$1,000	×	0.09	×	1 (yr.)	=	$90

The maturity value of the note is $1,090 ($1,000 principal + $90 interest). The time element is one (1) because interest is computed over a one-year period.

When the interest period of a note is stated in months, we compute the interest based on the 12-month year. Interest on a $2,000 note at 15 percent for three months is computed as

		Interest Rate		Time		Amount of Interest
Principal						
$2,000	×	0.15	×	$3/12$	=	$75

When the interest period of a note is stated in days, we usually compute interest based on a 365-day year. The interest on a $5,000 note at 12 percent for 60 days is computed as

		Interest Rate		Time		Amount of Interest
Principal						
$5,000	×	0.12	×	$60/365$	=	$98.63

Interest rates are usually stated as an annual rate. Therefore, the time in the formula for computing interest should also be expressed in terms of a year.

> **KEY POINT**
>
> Here *rate* means interest rate and *time* means interest period.

> **WORKING IT OUT**
>
> Reed Furniture Mfg. loaned $6,000 to Doane Stores on a 90-day, 6% note. Compute (1) the interest and (2) the maturity value.
>
> **A:**
> (1) $88.77
> ($6,000 × 0.06 × $90/365$);
> (2) $6,088.77
> ($6,000 + $88.77)

> **WORKING IT OUT**
>
> Practise calculating interest:
>
> (1) $30,000, 12½%, 180-day note;
> (2) $8,500, 9%, 6-month note
>
> **A:** (1) ($30,000 × 0.125 × $180/365$) = $1,849.32;
> (2) ($8,500 × 0.09 × $6/12$) = $382.50

> **OBJECTIVE 5**
> Account for notes receivable

Accounting for Notes Receivable

Recording Notes Receivable

Consider the loan agreement shown in Exhibit 8-5. After Lauren Holland signs the note and presents it to the trust company, Foothills Trust Company gives her $1,000 cash. At maturity date, Holland pays the trust company $1,090 ($1,000 principal + $90 interest). The trust company's entries (assuming it has a September 30 year end) are

Sept. 30, 2002	Note Receivable—L. Holland.....................	1,000	
	Cash		1,000
	To lend money.		
Sept. 30, 2003	Cash..	1,090	
	Note Receivable—L. Holland		1,000
	Interest Revenue		90
	To record collection at maturity ($1,000 × 0.09 × 1).		

Some companies sell merchandise in exchange for notes receivable. This arrangement occurs often when the payment term extends beyond the customary accounts receivable period, which generally ranges from 30 to 60 days.

Suppose that on October 20, 2002, EMCO Ltd. sells plumbing supplies for $15,000 to Dorman Builders. Dorman signs a 90-day promissory note at 10 percent interest.

EMCO Limited
www.emco.ca

EMCO 's entries to record the sale and collection from Dorman (EMCO's year end is June 30) are

Oct. 20, 2002	Note Receivable		
	— Dorman Builders........................	15,000	
	Sales Revenue		15,000
	To record sale.		
Jan. 18, 2003	Cash..	15,370	
	Note Receivable		
	—Dorman Builders.....................		15,000
	Interest Revenue..............................		370

To record collection at maturity ($15,000 $\times$ 0.10 $\times$ $^{90}/_{365}$).

THINKING IT OVER

Do the journal entries for October 20, 2002, and January 18, 2003, resemble general journal entries to Accounts Receivable control and the subsidiary ledger?

A: Yes. Very often a company will set up a subsidiary ledger for Notes Receivable in the same manner. The subsidiary ledger is especially helpful if the business has many notes receivable.

A company may accept a note receivable from a trade customer who fails to pay an account receivable within the customary 30 to 60 days. The customer signs a promissory note—that is, becomes the maker of the note—and gives it to the creditor, who becomes the payee.

Suppose Maison Fortin sees that it will not be able to pay off its account payable to Hoffman Supply, which is due in 15 days. Hoffman Supply may accept a 12-month $2,400 note receivable, with 9 percent interest, from Maison Fortin on October 1, 2002. Hoffman Supply's entry is

Oct. 1, 2002	Note Receivable—Maison Fortin..........................	2,400	
	Accounts Receivable—		
	Maison Fortin..		2,400
	Received a note on account from a customer.		

Accruing Interest Revenue

Notes receivable may be outstanding at the end of the accounting period. The interest revenue earned on the note during the year is part of of that year's earnings. Recall that interest revenue is earned over time, not just when cash is received. We saw in Chapter 3 on page 120 that accrued revenue creates an asset for the amount that has been earned but not received.

Let's continue with the Hoffman Supply note receivable from Maison Fortin. Hoffman Supply's accounting period ends December 31. How much of the total interest revenue does Hoffman earn in 2002? How much in 2003?

Hoffman Supply will earn three months' interest in 2002—for October, November, and December. In 2003, Hoffman will earn nine months' interest—for January through September. Therefore, at December 31, 2002, Hoffman Supply will make the following adjusting entry to accrue interest revenue:

Dec. 31, 2002	Interest Receivable	54	
	Interest Revenue		54
	To accrue interest revenue earned in		
	2002 but not yet received ($2,400 $\times$ 0.09 $\times$ $^{3}/_{12}$).		

Then, on the maturity date Hoffman Supply records collection of principal and interest as follows:

WORKING IT OUT

Calculate interest accrued at Dec. 31 on an 11%, $3,500, 90-day note receivable dated Oct. 15.

A: $3,500 $\times$ 0.11 $\times$ $^{77}/_{365}$ = $81 (rounded)

Sept. 30, 2003	Cash	2,616	
	Note Receivable—Maison Fortin.........		2,400
	Interest Receivable................................		54
	Interest Revenue		162
	To collect note receivable on which interest		
	has been accrued previously. Interest		
	receivable is $54 ($2,400 $\times$ 0.09 $\times$ $^{3}/_{12}$) and		
	interest revenue is $162 ($2,400 $\times$ 0.09 $\times$ $^{9}/_{12}$).		

The entries to accrue interest revenue earned in 2002 and to record collection in 2003 assign the correct amount of interest to each year (or fiscal period), in keeping with the matching principal.

Dishonoured Notes Receivable

If the maker of a note does not pay a note receivable at maturity (plus the days of grace), the maker is said to **dishonour** or **default on** the note. Because the term of the note has expired, the note agreement is no longer in force, nor is the note negotiable. However, the payee still has a claim against the note's maker, and usually transfers the claim from the note receivable account to Accounts Receivable. The payee records interest revenue earned on the note and debits Accounts Receivable for full maturity value of the note.

Suppose Rubinstein Jewellers has a six-month, 10-percent note receivable for $1,200 from Dora Hatachi. On the February 3 maturity date, Hatachi defaults. Rubinstein Jewellers would record the default as follows:

Feb. 3	Accounts Receivable—Dora Hatachi......................	1,260	
	Note Receivable—Dora Hatachi		1,200
	Interest Revenue		60

To record dishonour of note receivable.
Accounts receivable is $1,260
[$1,200 + ($1,200 × 0.10 × ⁶⁄₁₂)] and interest
revenue is $60 ($1,200 × 0.10 × ⁶⁄₁₂).

Rubinstein Jewellers would pursue collection from Dora Hatachi as an account receivable. The company may treat accounts receivable such as this as a special category to highlight them for added collection efforts. If the account receivable later proves uncollectible, Rubenstein Jewellers would then write off the account against Allowance for Uncollectible Accounts in the manner previously discussed. Note that all notes receivable bear interest until they are proved to be uncollectible.

OBJECTIVE 6
Report receivables on the balance sheet

Reporting Receivables on the Balance Sheet: Actual Company Reports

Let's look at how some companies report their receivables and related allowances for uncollectibles on the balance sheet. The terminology and setup vary, but you can understand these actual presentations based on what you have learned in this chapter.

Paragraph 3020.01 in the *CICA Handbook* indicates that because "... it is ... assumed that adequate allowance for doubtful accounts has been made ... it is not considered necessary to refer to [the] allowance" in the financial statements. The 1999 edition of *Financial Reporting in Canada,* published by the CICA, indicates that only 19 percent of the 200 companies surveyed made reference, on the balance sheet or in the notes, to the allowance in 1999.[3]

One Canadian company that did provide information was Canadian National Railway Company (CN). In its 1999 annual report, CN reported (amounts in millions):

WORKING IT OUT

1. How much did customers owe CN?
2. How much did CN expect to collect?
3. How much did CN expect *not* to collect?

A: 1. $846 million = ($800 million net + $46 million provision for doubtful accounts)
2. $800 million
3. $46 million

	December	
	1999	**1998**
Current assets		
Accounts receivable (note 3)	$800	$399
Notes to the Consolidated Financial Statements		
3. Accounts receivable	$846	440
Provision for doubtful accounts	(46)	(41)
	$800	$399

While some companies like CN provide information about the allowance for doubtful accounts, as was suggested above, many companies in Canada such as Schneider Corporation, the food products company, and Loblaw Companies Limited,

---

[3]Byrd, C., I. Chen, and H. Chapman, *Financial Reporting in Canada 1999.* Twenty-fourth edition (Toronto: Canadian Institute of Chartered Accountants, 1999), p. 216.

the food retailer, tend to show only net accounts receivable. They do not show the allowance.

Bombardier Inc., the transportation, aerospace, consumer products, and financial services giant, lists accounts receivable of $570.7 million and asset-based financing items of $7,149.9 million at January 31, 2000. The latter account includes commercial loans, leases receivable, finance receivables, and others. The notes to the financial statements provide more complete information about the various receivables, including the allowances for credit losses of the asset-based financing items.

CN, like some other corporations, factors or sells its receivables to raise funds. The notes to the December 31, 1999, financial statements state

> ... At December 31, 1999, ... $147 million [Canadian] and U.S. $40 million (Canadian $58 million) had been sold on a limited recourse basis ...

In other words, as the seller, CN is contingently liable if the receivables sold are not paid to the financial institution when due.

Computers and Accounts Receivable

Accounting for receivables for a company like McCain Foods Ltd. requires tens of thousands of postings to customer accounts each month for credit sales and cash collections. Manual accounting methods cannot keep up.

As we saw in Chapter 6, Accounts Receivable can be set up on a computerized system. The order entry and shipping systems interface with the billing system, which credits Sales Revenue and debits Accounts Receivable. The computer then creates a sales invoice for each customer. At the same time, the computer generates records that lead to the printout of sales for the period. Finally, computerized posting to the general ledger and accounts receivable subsidiary ledger occurs.

Using Accounting Information for Decision Making

The balance sheet lists assets in their order of relative liquidity (closeness to cash):

- Cash comes first because it is the medium of exchange and can be used to purchase any item or pay any bill.
- Short-term investments (covered in a later chapter) come next because they can be sold for cash whenever the owner wishes.
- Current receivables are less liquid than short-term investments because the receivables must be collected.
- Merchandise inventory is less liquid than receivables because the goods must be sold.

A partial balance sheet of IPSCO Inc., a steelmaker whose head office is in Regina, Saskatchewan, provides an example in Exhibit 8-6.

Acid-Test (or Quick) Ratio

Owners and managers use ratios for decision making. In Chapter 4, for example, we discussed the current ratio, which indicates the ability to pay current liabilities with current assets. A more stringent measure of the ability to pay current liabilities is the **acid-test** (or **quick**) **ratio**. The acid-test ratio tells whether the entity could pay all its current liabilities if they came due immediately.

$$\text{Acid-test ratio} = \frac{\text{Cash + Short-term investments + Net current receivables}}{\text{Total current liabilities}}$$

For IPSCO Inc. (Exhibit 8-6) (Dollar amounts in thousands of U.S. dollars)

$$\frac{\$103,931 + \$0 + \$120,346}{\$196,671} = 1.14$$

OBJECTIVE 7
Use the acid-test ratio and days' sales in receivables to evaluate a company's financial position

🌍 **REAL WORLD EXAMPLE**

The average acid-test ratio in the computer industry is 1.20. For auto dealers, the average is 0.20, and for restaurants, 0.40.

WORKING IT OUT

Compute the current and acid-test ratios for the following selected accounts and their balances at Dec. 31:

Equipment	$4,000
Supplies	500
Interest Payable	600
Accounts Receivable	2,600
Accounts Payable	3,400
Accum. Amort.	1,200
Inventory	1,600
Cash	1,300

A: Current ratio = 1.5
($6,000*/$4,000†)
Acid-test ratio = 0.975
($3,900‡/$4,000)

* ($500 + $2,600 + $1,600 + $1,300 = $6,000)
† ($600 + $3,400 = $4,000)
‡ ($2,600 + $1,300 = $3,900)

Exhibit 8-6

An Actual Company's Partial
Balance Sheet

IPSCO Inc. Consolidated Statements of Financial Position (adapted) As at December 31, 1999		
(thousands of U.S. dollars)	1999	1998
CURRENT ASSETS		
Cash and cash equivalents.....................................	$103,931	$133,271
Accounts receivable		
Trade less allowances	111,343	90,333
Other..	9,003	26,084
Inventories	212,382	164,557
Prepaid expenses...	2,758	1,797
Other..	39,779	37,625
	$479,196	$453,667
CURRENT LIABILITIES		
Accounts payable and accrued charges................	132,754	100,670
Accrued payroll and related liabilities.................	18,330	18,567
Income and other taxes payable	7,157	—
Current portion of long-term debt	21,100	1,100
Other current liabilities	17,330	4,885
	$196,671	$125,222

WORKING IT OUT

Use the data in Exhibit 8-6 to
compute IPSCO Inc.'s current ratio
at December 31, 1999. Then
compare IPSCO Inc.'s current ratio
and acid-test ratio. Why is the
current ratio higher?

A: Current ratio

$= \dfrac{\text{Total current assets}}{\text{Total current liabilities}}$

$= \dfrac{\$479,196}{\$196,671}$

$= 2.44$

Acid-test ratio = 1.14

The current ratio is higher because
assets in the numerator include
inventory, prepayments, and other
current assets, which are excluded
from the acid-test ratio.

The higher the acid-test ratio, the better able the business is to pay its current liabilities. IPSCO's ratio was 1.14, showing good liquidity.

What is an acceptable acid-test ratio value? The answer depends on the industry. Automobile dealers can operate smoothly with an acid-test ratio of 0.20. Several things make this possible: Car dealers have almost no current receivables. The acid-test ratio for most department stores clusters about 0.80, while travel agencies average 1.10. In general, an acid-test ratio of 1.00 is considered safe.

Days' Sales in Receivables

After a business makes a credit sale, the next critical event in the business cycle is collection of the receivable. Several financial ratios centre on receivables. **Days' sales in receivables**, also called the **collection period**, indicates how many days it takes to collect the average level of receivables. The shorter the collection period, the more quickly the organization has cash to use for operations. The longer the collection period, the less cash is available to pay bills and expand. Days' sales in receivables can be computed in two steps, as follows:

WORKING IT OUT

Given:

Net Sales $48,000
Accts. Rec. (Jan. 1)...... 10,000
Accts. Rec. (Dec. 31) ... 14,000

What is the average
collection period?

A: One day's sales = $132
($48,000/365). Days' sales in
average accounts receivable
= 91 days ($12,000/$132)

1. One day's sales $= \dfrac{\text{Net sales}}{\text{365 days}}$

2. $\dfrac{\text{Days' sales in}}{\text{average accounts}} = \dfrac{\text{Average net accounts receivable}}{\text{One day's sales}} = \dfrac{\text{(Beginning net receivables} + \text{Ending net receivables)/2}}{\text{One day's sales}}$

THINKING IT OVER

Refer to the previous Working It
Out. If the company's credit sale
terms were 3/10 n/45, how would
you evaluate days' sales in
receivables?

A: Far too high; 91 days is more
than twice the allowable credit
period of 45 days.

For IPSCO Inc. (Exhibit 8-6) (Dollar amounts in thousands of U.S. dollars)

1. One day's sales $= \dfrac{\$808,251^*}{365} = \$2,214 \text{ per day}$

2. $\dfrac{\text{Days' sales in}}{\text{average accounts receivable}} = \dfrac{(\$111,343 + \$90,333)/2}{\$2,214} = 46 \text{ days}$

*Taken from IPSCO Inc.'s 1999 income statement, not reproduced here.

The length of the collection period depends on the credit terms of the company's sales. For example, sales on net 30 terms should be collected within approximately 30 days. When there is a discount, such as 2/10 net 30, the collection period may be shorter. We discussed sales discounts in Chapter 5, page 227. Terms of net 45 or net 60 will result in longer collection periods.

A company should watch its collection period closely. Whenever the collection period lengthens, the business must find other sources of financing, such as borrowing. During recessions, customers pay more slowly, and a longer collection period may be unavoidable.

This situation points to the challenge of financial analysis. Investors and creditors do not evaluate a company on the basis of one or two ratios. Instead they perform a thorough analysis of all the information available. They then stand back from the data and ask, "What is our overall impression of this business?" In Chapter 18, we discuss a wide range of ratios used for decision making.

DECISION GUIDELINES *Accounting for Receivables Transactions*

Decision	Guidelines
Accounts Receivable	
How much of our receivables will we collect?	Less than the full amount of the receivables because we will be unable to collect from some customers.
How to report receivables at their net realizable value?	1. Use the *allowance method* to account for uncollectible receivables. Set up the Allowance for Uncollectible Accounts.
	2. Estimate uncollectibles by the
	a. *Percent of sales method* (income-statement approach) (page 412)
	b. *Aging of receivables method* (balance-sheet approach) (page 413)
	3. Write off uncollectible receivables as they are deemed uncollectible (page 415).
	4. $\begin{array}{ccc}\text{Net accounts} \\ \text{receivable}\end{array} = \begin{array}{c}\text{Accounts} \\ \text{Receivable}\end{array} - \begin{array}{c}\text{Allowance for} \\ \text{Uncollectible Accounts}\end{array}$ (page 411)
Is there another way to account for uncollectible receivables?	The *direct write-off method* simply debits Uncollectible Accounts Expense and credits an individual customer's Account Receivable to write off an uncollectible account.
	This method uses no allowance for uncollectibles account and thus reports receivables at their full amount. This method is acceptable only when uncollectibles are insignificant.
Notes Receivable	Notes receivable, an asset, earns *interest revenue*.
What two other accounts are related to notes receivable?	• If the interest revenue has been collected in cash, then debit *Cash* and credit *Interest Revenue*.
	• If the interest revenue has not been collected, then it must be accrued. Debit *Interest Receivable* and credit *Interest Revenue*.
How to compute the interest on a note receivable?	Amount of Interest = Principal × Interest Rate × Time
	Interest is a function of time. If the time element is zero, there can be no interest on the note receivable.

continued

Decision	Guidelines

Receivables in General

What are the two key decision aids that use receivables to evaluate a company's financial position?

- Acid-test ratio $= \dfrac{\text{Cash} + \text{Short-term investments} + \text{Net current receivables}}{\text{Total current liabilities}}$

- $\dfrac{\text{Days' sales in}}{\text{average accounts receivable}} = \dfrac{\dfrac{\text{Average net accounts receivable}}{}}{\text{One day's sales}}$

How to report receivables on the balance sheet?

Accounts (or Notes) receivable	$XXX
Less: Allowances for uncollectible accounts	$ X
Net accounts (or notes) receivable	$ XX

Summary Problem
for Your Review

Suppose Petro-Canada engaged in the following transactions:

2002
Apr. 1   Loaned $8,000 to Phil Bland, a service station operator. Received a six-month, 10 percent note.
Oct. 1   Collected the Bland note at maturity.
Nov. 30   Loaned $6,000 to Réjean Houle, a regional distributor of Petro-Canada products, on a three-month, 11 percent note.
Dec. 31   Accrued interest revenue on the Houle note.

2003
Feb. 28   Collected the Houle note at maturity.

Petro-Canada's accounting period ends on December 31.

Required

Explanations are not needed.

1. Record the 2002 transactions on April 1, October 1, and November 30 on Petro-Canada's books.

2. Make the adjusting entry needed on December 31, 2002.

3. Record the February 28, 2003 collection of the Houle note.

Solution to Review Problem

Requirement 1

2002				
Apr. 1	Note Receivable—Phil Bland..........................	8,000		
	Cash..			8,000
Oct. 1	Cash..	8,400		
	Note Receivable—Phil Bland.................			8,000
	Interest Revenue ($8,000 × 0.10 × %₂)......			400
Nov. 30	Note Receivable—Réjean Houle	6,000		
	Cash..			6,000

Requirement 2

Adjusting Entry

2002			
Dec. 31	Interest Receivable	55	
	Interest Revenue		55
	Interest receivable is $55 ($6,000 × 0.11 × ½).		

Requirement 3

2003			
Feb. 28	Cash	6,165	
	Note Receivable—Réjean Houle.............		6,000
	Interest Receivable..................................		55
	Interest Revenue		110
	Interest revenue is $110 ($6,000 × 0.11 × ³₂).		
	Cash is $6,165 [$6,000 + ($6,000 × 0.11 × ³₂)].		

Cyber Coach

Visit the Student Resource area of the *Accounting* Companion Website for extra practice with the new material in Chapter 8.

www.pearsoned.ca/horngren

Summary

1. **Design internal controls for receivables.** Companies that sell on credit receive most customer collections in the mail. Good *internal control* over mailed-in cash receipts means separating cash-handling duties from cash-accounting duties.

2. **Use the allowance method to account for uncollectibles and estimate uncollectibles by the percent of sales and aging methods.** Uncollectible receivables are accounted for by the allowance method or the direct write-off method. The *allowance method* matches expenses to sales revenue and also results in a more realistic measure of net accounts receivable. The *percent of sales method* and the *aging of accounts receivable method* are the two main approaches to estimating bad debts under the allowance method.

3. **Use the direct write-off method to account for uncollectibles.** The *direct write-off method* is easy to apply, but it fails to match the uncollectible-account expense to the corresponding sales revenue. Also, Accounts Receivable are reported at their full amount, which is misleading because it suggests that the company expects to collect all its accounts receivable.

4. Account for credit-card and debit-card sales. When customers pay for their purchases using a *credit card* such as MasterCard, the credit-card company pays the vendor and collects from the customer. When a customer pays with a *debit card*, the issuer (usually a financial institution) removes the amount of the purchase from the customer's bank account and puts it into the vendor's account.

5. Account for notes receivable. *Notes receivable* are formal credit agreements. Interest earned by the creditor is computed by multiplying the note's principal amount by the interest rate times the length of the interest period.

6. Report receivables on the balance sheet. All accounts receivable, notes receivable, and allowance accounts appear in the balance sheet. However, companies use various formats and terms to report these assets.

7. Use the acid-test ratio and days' sales in receivables to evaluate a company's financial position. The *acid-test ratio* measures ability to pay current liabilities from the most liquid current assets. *Days' sales in receivables* indicates how long it takes to collect the average level of receivables.

Self-Study Questions

Test your understanding of the chapter by marking the correct answer for each of the following questions:

1. The party that holds a receivable is called the (*p. 407*)
   a. Creditor
   b. Debtor
   c. Maker
   d. Security holder

2. The function of the credit department is to (*p. 410*)
   a. Collect accounts receivable from customers
   b. Report bad credit risks to other companies
   c. Evaluate customers who apply for credit
   d. Write off uncollectible accounts receivable

3. Longview Rentals made the following entry related to uncollectibles:

   Uncollectible-Account Expense ...   1,900
      Allowance for Uncollectible
        Accounts   1,900

   The purpose of this entry is to (*pp. 411–414*)
   a. Write off uncollectibles
   b. Close the expense account
   c. Age the accounts receivable
   d. Record uncollectible-account expense

4. Longview Rentals also made this entry:

   Allowance for Uncollectible
      Accounts   2,110
        Accounts Receivable (detailed)   2,110

   The purpose of this entry is to (*p. 415*)
   a. Write off uncollectibles
   b. Close the expense account
   c. Age the accounts receivable
   d. Record uncollectible-account expense

5. Longview Rentals also made this entry:

   Accounts Receivable (detailed) ...   560
      Allowance for Uncollectible
        Accounts   560

   The purpose of this entry is to (*p. 416*)

   a. Write off uncollectibles
   b. Close the expense account
   c. Reverse the write-off of a receivable
   d. Record uncollectible-account expense

6. The credit balance in Allowance for Uncollectibles is $14,300 prior to the adjusting entries at the end of the period. The aging of the accounts indicates that an allowance of $78,900 is needed. The amount of expense to record is (*pp. 413–414*)
   a. $14,300
   b. $64,600
   c. $78,900
   d. $93,200

7. The most important internal control over cash receipts is (*p. 408*)
   a. Assigning an honest employee the responsibility for handling cash
   b. Separating the cash-handling and cash-accounting duties
   c. Ensuring that cash is deposited in the bank daily
   d. Centralizing the opening of incoming mail in a single location

8. A six-month, $30,000 note specifies interest of 9 percent. The full amount of interest on this note will be (*p. 422*)
   a. $450
   b. $900
   c. $1,350
   d. $2,700

9. The note in Self-Study Question 8 was issued on August 31, and the company's accounting year ends on December 31. The year-end balance sheet will report interest receivable of (*pp. 422–423*)
   a. $450
   b. $900
   c. $1,350
   d. $2,700

10. The best acid-test ratio is (*pp. 425–426*)
   a. 0.10
   b. 0.80
   c. 1.0
   d. 1.2

Answers to the Self-Study Questions follow the Similar Accounting Terms.

Accounting Vocabulary

Acid-test ratio *(p. 425)*
Aging of accounts receivable
    (p. 413)
Allowance for Doubtful
    Accounts *(p. 411)*
Allowance for Uncollectible
    Accounts *(p. 411)*
Allowance method *(p. 411)*
Bad-debt expense *(p. 411)*
Balance-sheet approach *(p. 413)*
Collection period *(p. 426)*
Contingent liability *(p. 452)*
Creditor *(pp. 407, 420)*
Days' sales in receivables *(p. 426)*
Debtor *(pp. 407, 420)*

Default on a note *(p. 424)*
Direct write-off method *(p. 415)*
Discounting a note receivable
    (p. 451)
Dishonour of a note *(p. 424)*
Doubtful-account expense *(p. 411)*
Due date *(p. 421)*
Income-statement approach
    (p. 412)
Interest *(p. 420)*
Interest period *(p. 421)*
Interest rate *(p. 421)*
Maker of a note *(p. 420)*

Maturity date *(p. 421)*
Maturity value *(p. 421)*
Note period *(p. 421)*
Note term *(p. 421)*
Payee of a note *(p. 420)*
Percent of sales method *(p. 412)*
Principal *(p. 420)*
Principal amount *(p. 420)*
Promissory note *(p. 420)*
Quick ratio *(p. 425)*
Receivable *(p. 407)*
Time *(p. 421)*
Uncollectible-account
    expense *(p. 411)*

Similar Accounting Terms

Acid-test ratio	Quick ratio
Aging of accounts receivable method (of estimating uncollectibles)	Balance-sheet approach (of estimating uncollectibles)
Allowance for Uncollectible Accounts	Allowance for Doubtful Accounts; Allowance for Bad Debts
Days' sales in receivables	Collection period
Dishonour a note	Default on a note
Interest period	Note period; Note term; Time
Maturity date	Due date
Percent of Sales Method (of estimating uncollectibles)	Income-statement approach (of estimating uncollectibles)
Uncollectible-account expense	Bad-debt expense; Doubtful-account expense

---

Answers to Self-Study Questions

1. a		6.	b ($78,900 – $14,300 = $64,600)
2. c		7.	b
3. d		8.	c ($30,000 × 0.09 × ⁶⁄₁₂ = $1,350)
4. a		9.	b ($30,000 × 0.09 × ⁴⁄₁₂ = $900)
5. c		10.	d

Assignment Material

Questions

1. Name the two parties to a receivable/payable transaction. Which party has the receivable? Which has the payable? The asset? The liability?

2. List three categories of receivables. State how each category is classified for reporting on the balance sheet.

3. Many businesses receive most of their cash on credit sales through the mail. Suppose you own a business so large that you must hire employees to handle cash receipts and perform the related accounting duties. What internal control feature should you use to ensure that cash received from customers is not taken by a dishonest employee?

4. Name the two methods of accounting for uncollectible receivables. Which method is easier to apply? Which method is consistent with generally accepted accounting principles?

5. Which of the two methods of accounting for

uncollectible accounts—the allowance method or the direct write-off method—is preferable? Why?

6. Identify the accounts debited and credited to account for uncollectibles under (a) the allowance method, and (b) the direct write-off method.

7. What is another term for Allowance for Uncollectible Accounts? What are two other terms for Uncollectible-Account Expense?

8. Which entry decreases net income under the allowance method of accounting for uncollectibles: the entry to record uncollectible-account expense, or the entry to write off an uncollectible account receivable?

9. Identify and briefly describe the two ways to estimate uncollectible-account expense and uncollectible accounts.

10. Briefly describe how a company may use both the percent of sales method and aging method to account for uncollectibles.

11. How does a credit balance arise in a customer's account receivable? How does the company report this credit balance on its balance sheet?

12. Use the terms *maker, payee, principal amount, maturity date, promissory note,* and *interest* in an appropriate sentence or two describing a note receivable.

13. Name three situations in which a company might receive a note receivable. For each situation, show the account debited and the account credited to record receipt of the note.

14. For each of the following notes receivable, compute the amount of interest revenue earned during 2002:

	Principal	Interest Rate	Interest Period	Maturity Date
a. Note 1	$ 10,000	9%	60 days	Nov. 30, 2002
b. Note 2	50,000	10%	3 months	Sept. 30, 2002
c. Note 3	100,000	8%	1 ½ years	Dec. 31, 2003
d. Note 4	15,000	12%	90 days	Jan. 15, 2003

15. When the maker of a note dishonours the note at maturity, what accounts does the payee debit and credit?

16. Why does the payee of a note receivable usually need to make adjusting entries for interest at the end of the accounting period?

17. Show three ways to report Accounts Receivable of $100,000 and Allowance for Uncollectible Accounts of $2,800 on the balance sheet or in the related notes.

18. Why is the acid-test ratio a more stringent measure of the ability to pay current liabilities than is the current ratio?

19. Which measure of days' sales in receivables is preferable, 30 or 40? Give your reason.

Exercises

Exercise 8-1   *Controlling cash receipts from customers* **(Obj. 1)**

As a recent college graduate, you land your first job in the customer collections department of Bakall and Seinfeld, a partnership. Robin Bakall, one of the partners, has asked you to propose a system to ensure that cash received by mail from customers is properly handled. Draft a short memorandum identifying the essential element in your proposed plan, and state why this element is important. Refer to Chapter 7 if necessary. Use this format for your memo:

Date: _____

To: Robin Bakall

From: Student Name

RE: Essential element of internal control over collections from customers

Exercise 8-2   *Identifying and correcting an internal control weakness* **(Obj. 1)**

Link Back to Chapter 7 (Internal Control Over Cash Receipts). Suppose Nestlé, the Swiss chocolate company, is opening a district office in Guelph, Ontario. Gunther Oswald, the office manager, is designing the internal control system for the office. Oswald proposes the following procedures for credit checks on new customers, sales on account, cash collections, and write-offs of uncollectible receivables:

• The credit department will run a credit check on all customers who apply for credit.

- Sales on account are the responsibility of the Nestlé salespersons. Credit sales above $50,000 (which is a reasonable limit) require the approval of the sales manager.

- Cash receipts come into the credit department, which separates the cash received from the customer remittance slips. The credit department lists all cash receipts by name of customer and the amount of cash received. The cash goes to the treasurer for deposit in the bank. The remittance slips go to the accounting department for posting to individual customer accounts in the accounts receivable subsidiary ledger. Each day's listing of cash receipts goes to the controller for her end-of-day comparison with the daily deposit slip and the day's listing of the total dollar amount posted to customer accounts from the accounting department. The three amounts must agree.

- The credit department reviews customer accounts receivable monthly. Late-paying customers are notified that their accounts are past due. After 90 days, the credit department turns over past-due accounts to a lawyer or collection agency for collection. After 180 days, the credit department writes off a customer account as uncollectible.

Identify the internal control weakness in this situation, and propose a way to strengthen the controls.

Exercise 8-3   *Using the allowance method (percent of sales) for bad debts (Obj. 2, 6)*

On September 30, Rainy River Camping Outfitters had a $38,000 debit balance in Accounts Receivable. During October, the company had sales of $112,000, which included $90,000 in credit sales. October collections were $91,000 and write-offs of uncollectible receivables totalled $1,070. Other data include:

a. September 30 credit balance in Allowance for Uncollectible Accounts, $1,900.

b. Uncollectible account expense, estimated as 2 percent of credit sales.

Required

1. Prepare journal entries to record sales, collections, uncollectible-account expense by the allowance method (using the percent of sales method), and write-offs of uncollectibles during October.

2. Show the ending balances in Accounts Receivable, Allowance for Uncollectible Accounts, and *net* accounts receivable at October 31. Does Rainy River expect to collect the net amount of the receivable?

3. Show how Rainy River will report Accounts Receivable on its October 31 balance sheet.

Exercise 8-4   *Using the aging approach to estimate bad debts (Obj. 2, 6)*

At December 31, 2003, the accounts receivable balance of Red Deer Lumber is $269,000. The allowance for doubtful accounts has a $3,910 credit balance. Accountants for Red Deer Lumber prepare the following aging schedule for its accounts receivable:

Total Balance	1–30 Days	31–60 Days	61–90 Days	Over 90 Days
	Age of Accounts			
$310,000	$137,000	$89,000	$69,000	$15,000
Estimated percent uncollectible	0.3%	1.5%	6.0%	50.0%

Required

1. Journalize the adjusting entry for doubtful accounts based on the aging schedule. Show the T-account for the allowance.

2. Show how Red Deer Lumber will report Accounts Receivable on its December 31, 2003, balance sheet.

Exercise 8-5 *Using the allowance method (aging of accounts receivable) to account for uncollectibles* *(Obj. 2)*

The Huehn Pool Services accounts include the following balances at December 31, 2003, before the year-end adjustments:

Accounts Receivable	Allowance for Uncollectible Accounts
89,000	2,010

The aging of accounts receivable yields these data:

	Age of Accounts Receivable				
	0–30 Days	31–60 Days	61–90 Days	Over 90 Days	Total Receivables
Amount receivable	$60,000	$15,000	$10,000	$4,000	$89,000
Percent uncollectible	× 1%	× 2%	× 4%	× 25%	

Required

1. Journalize Huehn Pool Services' entry to record uncollectible-account expense for the year and to adjust the allowance account to its correct balance at December 31, 2003.

2. What caused Allowance for Uncollectible Accounts to have the unadjusted debit balance that appears in the preceding T-account?

Exercise 8-6 *Reporting bad debts by the allowance method* *(Obj. 2, 6)*

At December 31, 2002, Gateway Supplies has an accounts receivable balance of $112,000. Sales revenue for 2002 is $950,000, including credit sales of $600,000. For each of the following situations, prepare the year-end adjusting entry to record uncollectible-account expense. Show how the accounts receivable and the allowance for uncollectible accounts are reported on the balance sheet.

a. Allowance for Uncollectible Accounts has a credit balance before adjustment of $2,300. Gateway Supplies estimates that uncollectible-account expense for the year is 0.5 percent of credit sales.

b. Allowance for Uncollectible Accounts has a debit balance before adjustment of $1,600. Gateway Supplies estimates that $4,200 of the accounts receivable will prove uncollectible.

Exercise 8-7 *Using the direct write-off method for bad debts* *(Obj. 3)*

Refer to the situation of Exercise 8-3.

Required

1. Record uncollectible account expense for October by the direct write-off method.

2. What amount of net accounts receivable would Rainy River Camping Outfitters report on its October 31 balance sheet under the direct write-off method? Does Rainy River Camping Outfitters expect to collect this much of the receivable? Give your reason.

Exercise 8-8 *Contrasting the allowance method and the direct write-off method of accounting for uncollectibles* **(Obj. 2, 3)**

Return to the Schmidt Builders Supply example of accounting for uncollectibles that begins under the heading "Writing Off Uncollectible Accounts" on page 415. Suppose Schmidt Builders Supply's past experience indicates that the company will fail to collect 2.5 percent of net credit sales, which totalled $100,000 during the three-month period January through March of 2004.

Record Schmidt Builders Supply's uncollectible-account expense for the three-month period January through March under

a. The allowance method

b. The direct write-off method (You need not identify individual customer accounts. Use the data given for Abbott and Smith on page 415.)

Which method of accounting for uncollectibles is better? What makes this preferred method better? Mention accounting principles in your answer.

Exercise 8-9 *Recording notes receivable and accruing interest revenue* **(Obj. 5)**

Record the following transactions in the journal of Prospect Property Management:

Nov. 1 Loaned $65,000 cash to Jean Tremblay on a one-year, 9 percent note.
Dec. 3 Sold goods to Lofland, Inc., receiving a 90-day, 12 percent note for $3,750.
     16 Received a $3,000, six-month, 12 percent note on account from EMC Ltd.
     31 Accrued interest revenue on all notes receivable.

Exercise 8-10 *Recording debit-card sales and a note receivable and accruing interest revenue* **(Obj. 4, 5)**

Record the following transactions in Postino Travel's journal:

2002
Feb. 12 Recorded Scotiabank debit-card sales of $45,000, less a 2 percent discount.
Apr. 1 Loaned $8,000 to Lee Franz on a one-year, 12 percent note.
Dec. 31 Accrued interest revenue on the Franz note.

2003
Apr. 1 Received the maturity value of the note from Franz.

Exercise 8-11 *Evaluating ratio data* **(Obj. 7)**

Sussman's Ltd., a department store, reported the amounts on the next page in its 2002 financial statements. The 2001 figures are given for comparison.

Required

1. Determine whether Sussman's Ltd.'s acid-test ratio improved or deteriorated from 2001 to 2002. How does Sussman's Ltd.'s acid-test ratio compare with the industry average of 0.90?

2. Compare the days' sales in receivables measure for 2002 with the company's credit terms of net 30. What action, if any, should Sussman's Ltd. take?

	2002		2001	
Current assets:				
Cash...		$ 6,000		$ 11,000
Short-term investments.............		23,000		0
Accounts receivable....................	$ 86,000		$77,000	
Less: Allowance for				
uncollectibles....................	7,000	79,000	5,000	72,000
Inventory......................................		192,000		189,000
Prepaid insurance.......................		2,000		2,000
Total current assets		302,000		274,000
Total current liabilities....................		126,000		107,000
Net sales...		705,000		732,000

Exercise 8-12   *Analyzing a real company's financial statements*   **(Obj. 6)**

Wal-Mart Stores, Inc. is the largest retailer in the world. Recently, Wal-Mart reported these figures, in millions of dollars:

	1999	1998
Net sales	$165,000	$138,000
Receivables at end of year	1,000	1,000

The Wal-Mart financial statements include no uncollectible-account expense or allowance for uncollectibles.

Required

1. Compute Wal-Mart's average collection period on receivables during 1999.
2. Why are Wal-Mart's receivables so low? How can Wal-Mart have $1 billion of receivables at January 31, 1999, and no significant allowance for uncollectibles?

Challenge Exercise

Exercise 8-13   *Evaluating debit-card sales for profitability* **(Obj. 4)**

Twin Pines Men's Store has sold on store credit and managed its own receivables. Average experience for the past three years has been:

	Cash	Credit	Total
Sales	$200,000	$150,000	$350,000
Cost of goods sold	120,000	90,000	210,000
Uncollectible-account expense	—	6,000	6,000
Other expenses	28,000	27,000	55,000

Ira Salomon, the owner, is considering whether to accept debit cards (using the Interac system). Typically, the availability of debit cards increases sales by 12 percent. But the Interac system charges approximately 1 percent of sales. If Salomon switches to debit cards, he can save $2,800 on accounting and other expenses. He figures that cash customers will continue buying in the same volume regardless of the type of credit the store offers.

Required

Should Twin Pines Men's Store start offering debit-card service using the Interac system? Show the computations of net income under the present plan and under the debit-card plan.

Beyond the Numbers

Beyond the Numbers 8-1 *Computing receivables amounts to report on the balance sheet* **(Obj. 6)**

Chatham Office Supply's cash flow statement reported the following *cash* receipts and *cash* payments (the amounts in brackets) for the year ended June 30, 2002:

CHATHAM OFFICE SUPPLY
Cash Flow Statement
For the Year Ended June 30, 2002

Cash flows from operating activities:	
Cash receipts from customers...	$350,000
Interest received...	7,000
Cash flows from investing activities:	
Loans made on notes receivable..	(60,000)
Collection of loans on notes receivable	50,000

Chatham's balance sheet one year earlier—at June 30, 2001—reported Accounts Receivable of $40,000 and Notes Receivable of $20,000. Credit sales for the year ended June 30, 2002, totalled $360,000, and the company collects all of its accounts receivable because uncollectibles rarely occur.

Chatham Office Supply needs a loan and the manager is preparing the company's balance sheet at June 30, 2002. To complete the balance sheet, the owner needs to know the balances of Accounts Receivable and Notes Receivable at June 30, 2002. Supply the needed information; T-accounts are helpful.

Ethical Issue

Provincial Finance Ltd. is in the consumer loan business. It borrows from banks, and loans out the money at higher interest rates. Provincial Finance Ltd.'s bank requires Provincial Finance Ltd. to submit quarterly financial statements in order to keep its line of credit. Provincial Finance Ltd.'s main asset is Notes Receivable. Therefore, Uncollectible-Account Expense and Allowance for Uncollectible Accounts are important accounts.

Provincial Finance Ltd.'s president, Marie Holton, likes net income to increase in a smooth pattern rather than to increase in some periods and decrease in other periods. To report smoothly increasing net income, Holton underestimates Uncollectible-Account Expense in some accounting periods. In other accounting periods, Holton overestimates the expense. She reasons that the income overstatements roughly offset the income understatements over time.

Required

Is Provincial Finance Ltd.'s practice of smoothing income ethical? Give your reasons, mentioning any accounting principles that might be violated.

Problems (Group A)

Problem 8-1A *Controlling cash receipts from customers* **(Obj. 1)**

Garner Hockey Equipment distributes merchandise to sporting goods stores. All sales are on credit, so virtually all cash receipts arrive in the mail. Graham Garner, the company owner, has just returned from a trade association meeting with new ideas for the business. Among other things, Garner plans to institute stronger internal controls over cash receipts from customers.

Required

Assume you are Graham Garner, the company owner. Write a memo to employees outlining a set of procedures to ensure that all cash receipts are deposited in the bank and that the total amounts of each day's cash receipts are posted as credits to customer accounts receivable. Use the memorandum format given in Exercise 8-1, page 432.

Problem 8-2A *Accounting for uncollectibles by the direct write-off and allowance methods (Obj. 2, 3, 6)*

On February 28, 2002, Dynatel had a $130,000 debit balance in Accounts Receivable. During March, the business had sales revenue of $509,000, which included $445,000 in credit sales. Other data for March include

a. Collections on account receivable, $446,600.

b. Write-offs of uncollectible receivables, $4,800.

Required

1. Record uncollectible-account expense for March by the direct write-off method. Show all March activity in Accounts Receivable and Uncollectible-Account Expense.

2. Record uncollectible-account expense and write-offs of customer accounts for March by the allowance method. Show all March activity in Accounts Receivable, Allowance for Uncollectible Accounts, and Uncollectible-Account Expense. The February 28 unadjusted balance in Allowance for Uncollectible Accounts was $800 (debit). Uncollectible-Account Expense was estimated at 3 percent of credit sales.

3. What amount of uncollectible account expense would Dynatel report on its March income statement under the two methods? Which amount better matches expense with revenue? Give your reason.

4. What amount of *net* accounts receivable would Dynatel report on its March 31 balance sheet under the two methods? Which amount is more realistic? Give your reason.

Problem 8-3A *Using the percent of sales and aging methods for uncollectibles (Obj. 2, 6)*

The June 30, 2002, balance sheet of Schully Paper Products reports the following:

Accounts Receivable..	$265,000
Allowance for Uncollectible Accounts (credit balance)	7,100

At the end of each quarter, Schully Paper Products estimates uncollectible-account expense to be 3 percent of credit sales. At the end of the year, the company ages its accounts receivable and adjusts the balance in Allowance for Uncollectible Accounts to correspond to the aging schedule. During the second half of 2002, Schully Paper Products completes the following selected transactions:

July 14 Made a compound entry to write off the following uncollectible accounts: C.H. Harris, $766; Graphics, Inc., $2,413; and Bev McQueen, $184.

Sept. 30 Recorded uncollectible-account expense based on credit sales of $141,400.

Nov. 22 Wrote off the following accounts receivable as uncollectible: Al Monet, $1,345; Blocker, Inc., $1,549; and M Street Plaza, $755.

Dec. 31 Recorded uncollectible-account expense based on the following summary of the aging of accounts receivable.

Total Balance	Age of Accounts			
	1-30 Days	31-60 Days	61-90 Days	Over 90 Days
$296,600	$161,500	$86,000	$34,000	$15,100
Estimated percent uncollectible	0.2%	0.5%	4.0%	40.0%

Required

1. Record the transactions in the journal.

2. Open the Allowance for Uncollectible Accounts, and post entries affecting that account. Keep a running balance.

3. Most companies report two-year comparative financial statements. If Schully Paper Products' Accounts Receivable balance was $271,400 and the Allowance for Uncollectible Accounts stood at $8,240 at December 31, 2001, show how the company will report its accounts receivable in a comparative balance sheet for 2002 and 2001.

Problem 8-4A *Using the percent of sales and aging approaches for uncollectibles (Obj. 2, 6)*

Link Back to Chapter 4 (Closing Entries). Torcel Co. completed the following transactions during 2002 and 2003:

2002
Dec. 31 Estimated that uncollectible account expense for the year was 1.50 percent of credit sales of $450,000 and recorded that amount as expense.
      31 Made the closing entry for uncollectible-account expense.

2003
Feb. 4 Sold inventory to Gerry Carter, $1,521, on credit terms of 2/10 n/30. Ignore cost of goods sold.
July 2 Wrote off Carter's account as uncollectible after repeated efforts to collect from him.
Oct. 19 Received $521 from Gerry Carter, along with a letter stating his intention to pay his debt in full within 30 days. Reinstated his account in full.
Nov. 15 Received the balance due from Carter.
Dec. 31 Made a compound entry to write off the following accounts as uncollectible: Kris Moore, $899; Marie Mandue, $530; and Grant Fryer, $476.
      31 Estimated that uncollectible account expense for the year was 1.50 percent on credit sales of $540,000 and recorded the expense.
      31 Made the closing entry for uncollectible-account expense.

Required

1. Open general ledger accounts for Allowance for Uncollectible Accounts and Uncollectible-Account Expense. Keep running balances.

2. Record the transactions in the general journal and post to the two ledger accounts.

3. The December 31, 2003, balance of Accounts Receivable is $164,500. Show how Accounts Receivable would be reported at that date.

4. This requirement is entirely independent of Requirements 1 through 3. Assume that Torcel Co. begins aging accounts receivable on December 31, 2003. The balance in Accounts Receivable is $164,500, the credit balance in Allowance for Uncollectible Accounts is $1,845, and the company estimates that $8,545 of its accounts receivable will prove uncollectible.
   a. Make the adjusting entry for uncollectibles.
   b. Show how Accounts Receivable will be reported on the December 31, 2003, balance sheet.

Problem 8-5A *Accounting for notes receivable, including accruing interest revenue*
(Obj. 5)

A company received the following notes during 2003:

Note	Date	Principal Amount	Interest Rate	Term
(a)	October 30	$ 7,000	12%	3 months
(b)	November 19	15,000	10%	60 days
(c)	December 1	18,000	9%	1 year

Required

Identify each note by letter, compute interest using a 365-day year for all notes, round all interest amounts to the nearest cent, and present entries in general journal form. Explanations are not required.

1. Determine the due date and maturity value of each note.
2. Journalize a single adjusting entry at December 31, 2003, to record accrued interest revenue on the notes.
3. Journalize the collection of principal and interest on note (a).

Problem 8-6A *Accounting for notes receivable, dishonoured notes, and accrued interest revenue (Obj. 5)*

Record the following selected transactions in the general ledger of Lindsay Business Products. Explanations are not required.

2002
Dec. 21 Received a $3,600, 30-day, 10% note from Myron Blake on account.
31 Made an adjusting entry to accrue interest on the Myron Blake note.
31 Made an adjusting entry to record uncollectible-account expense based on 1.25 percent of credit sales of $604,800.
31 Made a compound closing entry for interest revenue and uncollectible-account expense.

2003
Jan. 20 Collected the maturity value of the Myron Blake note.
Sept. 14 Loaned $3,000 cash to Baxter Home Products, receiving a three-month, 13 percent note.
30 Received a $1,675, 60-day, 16 percent note from Matt Kartz on his past-due account receivable.
Nov. 29 Matt Kartz dishonoured (failed to pay) his note at maturity; wrote off the account as uncollectible.
Dec. 14 Collected the maturity value of the Baxter Home Products note.
31 Wrote off as uncollectible the accounts receivable of Ty Larson, $800 and Marcus Gee, $345.

Problem 8-7A *Journalizing uncollectible notes receivable and accrued interest revenue (Obj. 5)*

Assume that Northern Paint & Varnish, a major paint manufacturer, completed the following selected transactions:

2002
Dec. 1 Sold goods to Central Paint Stores, receiving a $17,000, three-month, 10 percent note. Ignore cost of goods sold.
31 Made an adjusting entry to accrue interest on the Central Paint Stores note.
31 Made an adjusting entry to record uncollectible-account expense based on an aging of accounts receivable. The aging analysis indicates that $27,300 of accounts receivable will not be collected. Prior to this adjustment, the credit balance in Allowance for Uncollectible Accounts is $22,750.

2003

Mar. 1 Collected the maturity value of the Central Paint Stores note.

July 21 Sold merchandise to Alex Logos, receiving a 60-day, 9 percent note for $5,000. Ignore cost of goods sold.

Sept. 19 Alex Logos dishonoured (failed to pay) its note at maturity; converted the maturity value of the note to an account receivable.

Nov. 11 Sold merchandise to Kincardine Home Builders for $4,000, receiving a 90-day, 9 percent note. Ignore cost of goods sold.

Dec. 2 Collected in full from Alex Logos.

31 Accrued the interest on the Kincardine Home Builders note.

Required

Record the transactions in the journal. Explanations are not required.

Problem 8-8A   *Using ratio data to evaluate a company's position* **(Obj. 7)**

Link Back to Chapter 4 (Current Ratio). The comparative financial statements of Mercatur Company for 2002, 2001, and 2000 included the following selected data:

	2002	2001	2000
	(In millions)		
Balance Sheet			
Current assets:			
Cash..	$ 87	$ 26	$ 22
Short-term investments........................	73	101	69
Receivables, net of allowance for uncollectible accounts of $7, $6, and $4	146	164	127
Inventories...	408	383	341
Prepaid expenses...................................	32	31	25
Total current assets.........................	746	705	584
Total current liabilities.............................	470	482	414
Income Statement			
Sales revenue	$2,671	$2,505	$1,944
Cost of sales...	1,380	1,360	963

Required

1. Compute these ratios for 2002 and 2001:
   a. Current ratio
   b. Acid-test ratio
   c. Days' sales in receivables
2. Write a memo explaining to Marlene Mercatur, owner of Mercatur Company, which ratio values showed improvement from 2001 to 2002 and which ratio values deteriorated. Which item in the financial statements caused some ratio values to improve and others to deteriorate? Discuss whether this factor conveys a favourable or unfavourable sign about the company.

Problem 8-9A   *Using the allowance method of accounting for uncollectibles, estimating uncollectibles using the aging process, reporting receivables on the balance sheet*   **(Obj. 2, 6)**

Gander Outfitters started business on January 1, 2002. The company produced monthly financial statements and had total sales of $249,000 (of which $152,000 were on credit) during the first four months.

On April 30, the Accounts Receivable account had a balance of $62,040 (no accounts have been written off to date), which was made up of the following accounts aged as to the date of the sale:

		Month of Sale:		
Customer:	**January**	**February**	**March**	**April**
Alvin Jones	$ 500	$ 350	$ 780	$ 470
Connie Lawson............................	200	440	650	290
Star Hunting Camp.....................	1,560	1,250	3,440	1,890
Gordon Ullman............................	2,080	1,340	3,320	5,690
Other Accounts Receivable.........	4,800	7,240	11,500	14,250
	$9,140	$10,620	$19,690	$22,590

The following accounts receivable transactions took place in May 2002:

May 12 Decided the Connie Lawson account was uncollectible and wrote it off.
  15 Collected $1,630 from Alvin Jones for sales made in the first three months.
  21 Decided the Star Hunting Camp account was uncollectible and wrote it off.
  24 Collected $2,080 from Gordon Ullman for sales made in the month of January.
  26 Received a cheque from Star Hunting Camp for $5,140 plus four cheques, of $750 each, post-dated to June 26, July 26, August 26, and September 26.
  31 Total sales in the month were $140,000; 80 percent of these were on credit, and 70 percent of the credit sales were collected in the month.

Required

1. Gander Outfitters has heard that other companies in the industry use the allowance method of accounting for uncollectibles, with many of these estimating the uncollectibles through an aging of accounts receivable. Journalize the adjustments that would have to be made on April 30 (for the months of January through April) as well as the transactions of May 2002, and the month-end adjustment, assuming the following estimates of uncollectibles:

Age of Accounts Receivable:	**Percent Estimated to be Uncollectible:**
From current month's sales...	2%
From prior month's sales..	4%
From two months prior...	8%
From three months prior	25%
From four months prior...	40%

(Round your total estimate to the nearest whole dollar.)

2. For the method of accounting for the uncollectibles used above, show
 a. The balance sheet presentation of the accounts receivable.
 b. The overall effect of the credit sales and uncollectibles on the income statement for the month of May 2002.

Problem 8-10A *Using the allowance method of accounting for uncollectibles, estimating uncollectibles by the percent of sales and the aging approaches, accounting for notes receivable* **(Obj. 2, 5)**

Sapawe Supplies uses the allowance method in accounting for uncollectible accounts with the estimate based on an aging of accounts receivable. The company had the following account balances on May 31, 2002:

Accounts Receivable..	$257,500
Allowance for Uncollectible Accounts (credit balance)	33,900

The following transactions took place during June 2002:

June 2 Axel Ltd., which owes $26,000, is unable to pay on time and has given a 20-day, 10 percent note in settlement of the account.
  6 Determined the account receivable from Ely Rouch ($7,500) was uncollectible and wrote it off.
  9 Received notice that a customer (Hy Fogelman) has filed for bankruptcy. Fogelman owes $14,000 to Sapawe Supplies.

June	11	Determined the account receivable for Mary Kay ($5,500) was uncollectible and wrote it off.
	15	Ely Rouch, whose account was written off on July 6, has paid $4,000 on the account and promises to pay the balance in 30 days.
	18	Received a cheque from the courts in the amount of $8,400 as final settlement of Hy Fogelman's account.
	22	Axel Ltd. paid the note received on July 2.
	25	Determined the account receivable for Art Beynon ($3,900) was uncollectible and wrote it off.
	30	Sales for the month totalled $278,000 (of which 70 percent were on credit) and collections on account totalled $212,000.
	30	Sapawe Supplies did an aging of accounts receivable that indicated that $39,800 is expected to be uncollectible. The company recorded the appropriate adjustment.

Required

1. Record the above transactions in the general journal.

2. What would be the adjusting entry required on June 30 if the company used the percent of sales method with an estimate of uncollectibles equal to 10 percent of credit sales?

3. Which of the two methods of estimating uncollectible accounts would normally be more accurate? Why?

(Problems (Group B)

Problem 8-1B   *Controlling cash receipts from customers (Obj. 1)*

Creemore Laboratories provides laboratory testing for samples that veterinarians send in. All work is performed on account, with regular monthly billing to participating veterinarians. Alan Forsby, accountant for Creemore Laboratories, receives and opens the mail. Company procedure requires him to separate customer cheques from the remittance slips, which list the amounts he posts as credits to customer accounts receivable in the subsidiary ledger. Forsby deposits the cheques in the bank. He computes each day's total amount posted to customer accounts and agrees this total to the bank deposit slip. This is intended to ensure that all receipts are deposited in the bank.

Required

As the auditor of Creemore Laboratories, write a memo to Donna Creemore, the owner, to evaluate the company's internal controls over cash receipts from customers. If the system is effective, identify its strong features. If the system has flaws, propose a way to strengthen the controls.

Problem 8-2B   *Accounting for uncollectibles by the direct write-off and allowance methods (Obj. 2, 3, 6)*

On May 31, 2002, Chester Fishing Outfitters had a $219,000 debit balance in Accounts Receivable. During June, the company had sales revenue of $789,000, which included $660,000 in credit sales. Other data for June include:

a. Collections of accounts receivable, $581,400.

b. Write-offs of uncollectible receivables, $10,200.

Required

1. Record uncollectible account expense for June by the direct write-off method. Show all June activity in Accounts Receivable and Uncollectible-Account Expense.

2. Record uncollectible-account expense and write-offs of customer accounts for June by the allowance method. Show all June activity in Accounts Receivable,

Allowance for Uncollectible Accounts, and Uncollectible-Account Expense. The May 31 unadjusted balance in Allowance for Uncollectible Accounts was $2,800 (credit). Uncollectible-Account Expense was estimated at 2 percent of credit sales.

3. What amount of uncollectible-account expense would Chester Fishing Outfitters report on its June income statement under the two methods? Which amount better matches expense with revenue? Give your reason.

4. What amount of *net* accounts receivable would Chester Fishing Outfitters report on its June 30 balance sheet under the two methods? Which amount is more realistic? Give your reason.

Problem 8-3B *Using the percent of sales and aging methods for uncollectibles* **(Obj. 2, 6)**

The June 30, 2002, balance sheet of e.Logistics reports the following:

Accounts Receivable...	$143,000
Allowance for Uncollectible Accounts (credit balance)......................	3,200

At the end of each quarter, e.Logistics estimates uncollectible-account expense to be $1^1/_2$ percent of credit sales. At the end of the year, the company ages its accounts receivable and adjusts the balance in Allowance for Uncollectible Accounts to correspond to the aging schedule. During the second half of 2002, e.Logistics completes the following selected transactions:

Aug.	9	Made a compound entry to write off the following uncollectible accounts: H. Tam, $375; Matz Ltd., $188; and L. Norris, $706.
Sept.	30	Recorded uncollectible-account expense based on credit sales of $165,000.
Oct.	18	Wrote off as uncollectible the $767 account receivable from Bliss Ltd. and the $430 account receivable from Micro Data Corp.
Dec.	31	Recorded uncollectible-account expense based on the following summary of the aging of accounts receivable.

Total Balance	Age of Accounts			
	1-30 Days	31-60 Days	61-90 Days	Over 90 Days
$135,400	$74,600	$31,100	$14,000	$15,700
Estimated percent uncollectible	0.1%	0.4%	5.0%	30.0%

Required

1. Record the transactions in the journal.

2. Open the Allowance for Uncollectible Accounts, and post entries affecting that account. Keep a running balance.

3. Most companies report two-year comparative financial statements. If e.Logistics' Accounts Receivable balance was $118,000 and the Allowance for Uncollectible Accounts stood at $2,700 at December 31, 2001, show how the company will report its accounts receivable on a comparative balance sheet for 2002 and 2001.

Problem 8-4B *Using the percent of sales and aging approaches for uncollectibles* **(Obj. 2, 6)**

Link Back to Chapter 4 (Closing Entries). Seelinger's Linen Store completed the following selected transactions during 2001 and 2002:

2001
Dec.	31	Estimated that uncollectible-account expense for the year was 0.75 percent of credit sales of $300,000 and recorded that amount as expense.
	31	Made the closing entry for uncollectible-accounts expense.

2002

Jan. 17   Sold inventory to Mary Lee, $402, on credit terms of 2/10 n/30. Ignore the cost of goods sold.

June 29   Wrote off Mary Lee's account as uncollectible after repeated efforts to collect from the customer.

Aug. 6   Received $151 from Mary Lee, along with a letter stating her intention to pay her debt in full within 30 days. Reinstated the account in full.

Sept. 4   Received the balance due from Mary Lee.

Dec. 31   Made a compound entry to write off the following accounts as uncollectible: Bernard Klaus, $737; Mann Ltd., $348; and Linda Leslie, $622.

    31   Estimated that uncollectible account expense for the year was 0.66 percent of credit sales of $420,000 and recorded the expense.

    31   Made the closing entry for uncollectible-account expense.

Required

1. Open general ledger accounts for Allowance for Uncollectible Accounts and Uncollectible-Account Expense. Keep running balances.

2. Record the transactions in the general journal and post to the two ledger accounts.

3. The December 31, 2002, balance of Accounts Receivable is $139,000. Show how Accounts Receivable would be reported at that date.

4. This requirement is entirely independent of Requirements 1 through 3. Assume that Seelinger's Linen Store begins aging its accounts receivable on December 31, 2002. The balance in Accounts Receivable is $139,000; the credit balance in Allowance for Uncollectible Accounts is $543; and the company estimates that $2,800 of its accounts receivable will prove uncollectible.

    a. Make the adjusting entry for uncollectibles.

    b. Show how Accounts Receivable will be reported on the December 31, 2002, balance sheet.

Problem 8-5B   *Accounting for notes receivable, including accruing interest revenue* **(Obj. 5)**

Smart Financial Services received the following notes during 2003.

Note	Date	Principal Amount	Interest Rate	Term
(a)	November 30	$12,000	12%	6 months
(b)	December 7	6,000	10%	30 days
(c)	December 23	15,000	9%	1 year

Required

Identify each note by letter, compute interest using a 365-day year for all notes, round all interest amounts to the nearest cent, and present entries in general journal form. Explanations are not required.

1. Determine the due date and maturity value of each note.

2. Journalize a single adjusting entry at December 31, 2003, to record accrued interest revenue on all three notes.

3. Journalize the collection of principal and interest on note (b).

Problem 8-6B   *Accounting for notes receivable, dishonoured notes, and accrued interest revenue* **(Obj. 5)**

Record the following selected transactions in the general journal of Well Point Instrument Company. Explanations are not required.

2002

Dec. 19 Received a $3,500, 60-day, 12 percent note from Claude Bernard to settle his $3,500 account receivable balance.

31 Made an adjusting entry to accrue interest on the Claude Bernard note.

31 Made an adjusting entry to record uncollectible-account expense in the amount of 2 percent of credit sales of $474,500.

31 Made a compound closing entry for interest revenue and uncollectible-account expense.

2003

Feb. 17 Collected the maturity value of the Claude Bernard note.

June 1 Loaned $8,000 cash to Linz Ltd., receiving a six-month, 11 percent note.

Oct. 31 Received a $1,500, 60-day, 12 percent note from Ned Pierce on his past-due account receivable.

Dec. 1 Collected the maturity value of the Linz Ltd. note.

30 Ned Pierce dishonoured (failed to pay) his note at maturity; wrote off the receivable as uncollectible, debiting Allowance for Uncollectible Accounts.

31 Wrote off as uncollectible the account receivable of Al Bynum, $435, and Ray Sharp, $276.

Problem 8-7B *Journalizing uncollectibles, notes receivable, and accrued interest revenue (Obj. 5)*

Assume that McCain Foods Ltd., famous for its frozen foods, completed the following selected transactions:

2002

Nov. 1 Sold goods to Safeway Co., receiving a $10,000, three-month, 8 percent note. Ignore cost of goods sold.

Dec. 31 Made an adjusting entry to accrue interest on the Safeway Co. note.

31 Made an adjusting entry to record uncollectible-account expense based on an aging of accounts receivable. The aging analysis indicates that $197,400 of accounts receivable will not be collected. Prior to this adjustment, the credit balance in Allowance for Uncollectible Accounts is $176,400.

2003

Feb. 1 Collected the maturity value of the Safeway Co. note.

23 Received a 90-day, 15 percent, $4,000 note from Bliss Foods Ltd. on account.

June 23 Sold merchandise to Lankin Stores, receiving a 60-day, 10 percent note for $9,000. Ignore cost of goods sold.

Aug. 22 Lankin Stores dishonoured (failed to pay) its note at maturity; converted the maturity value of the note to an account receivable.

Nov. 16 Loaned $8,500 cash to McNeil Fine Foods, receiving a 90-day, 12 percent note.

Dec. 5 Collected in full from Lankin Stores.

31 Accrued the interest on the McNeil Fine Foods note.

Required

Record the transactions in the journal. Explanations are not required.

 Problem 8-8B *Using ratio data to evaluate a company's financial position (Obj. 7)*

The comparative financial statements of Pinnacle East for 2002, 2001, and 2000 included the selected data shown on page 447.

Required

1. Compute these ratios for 2002 and 2001:
   a. Current ratio
   b. Acid-test ratio
   c. Days' sales in receivables

2. Write a memo explaining to Walter Sawchuk, owner of Pinnacle East, which ratio values showed improvement from 2001 to 2002, and which ratio values

showed deterioration. Which item in the financial statements caused some ratio values to improve and others to deteriorate? Discuss whether this factor conveys a favourable or an unfavourable impression about the company.

	2002	2001	2000
	(In millions)		
Balance Sheet			
Current assets:			
Cash	$ 76	$ 80	$ 60
Short-term investments....................................	140	174	122
Receivables, net of allowance for uncollectible accounts of			
$6, $6, and $5...	284	265	218
Inventories	429	341	302
Prepaid expenses...	21	27	46
Total current assets	950	887	748
Total current liabilities...................................	503	528	413
Income statement			
Sales revenue..	$5,495	$5,010	$4,697
Cost of sales	2,734	2,636	2,418

Problem 8-9B *Using the allowance method of accounting for uncollectibles, estimating uncollectibles using the aging process, reporting receivables on the balance sheet* **(Obj. 2, 5)**

Fredericton Office Temps started business on January 1, 2002. The company produces monthly financial statements and had total sales of $180,000 (of which $150,000 were on credit) during the first four months.

On April 30, the Accounts Receivable account had a balance of $58,680 (no accounts have been written off to date), which was made up of the following accounts aged according to the date of the sale of the temp service:

		Month of Service:		
Customer	**January**	**February**	**March**	**April**
Eagle Tires.......................................	$ 700	$ 400	$ 650	$ 540
Noble Ltd...	400	270	490	1,320
Mary Royce	1,920	1,300	2,730	2,140
Mel Glass	1,840	990	4,610	5,430
Other Accounts Receivable.........	4,100	5,950	10,400	12,500
	$8,960	$8,910	$18,880	$21,930

The following accounts receivable transactions took place in May 2002:

May 12 Determined the account of Noble Ltd. was uncollectible and wrote it off.

15 Collected $1,750 from Eagle Tires for services in the first three months.

21 Decided the account of Mary Royce was uncollectible and wrote it off.

24 Collected $1,840 from Mel Glass for services in the month of January.

26 Received a cheque from Mary Royce for $2,090 plus two cheques, of $3,000 each, post-dated to July 10 and September 10.

31 Total sales of service in the month were $80,000; 75 percent of these were on credit and 80 percent of the credit sales were collected in the month.

Required

1. Fredericton Office Temps has heard that other companies in the industry use the allowance method of accounting for uncollectibles, with many of these estimating the uncollectibles through an aging of accounts receivable. Journalize the adjustments that would have to be made on April 30 (for the months of January through April) as well as the transactions of May 1999, and the month-end adjustment, assuming the following estimates of uncollectibles:

Age of Accounts Receivable	Estimated Percent to Be Uncollectible
From current month's sales of service	2%
From prior month's sales of service	4%
From two months prior..	8%
From three months prior	25%
From four months prior...	40%

(Round your total estimate to the nearest whole dollar.)

2. For the method of accounting for the uncollectibles used above, show
   a. the balance sheet presentation of the accounts receivable.
   b. the overall effect of the credit sales and uncollectibles on the income statement for May, 2002.

Problem 8-10B *Using the allowance method of accounting for uncollectibles, estimating uncollectibles by percent of sales and the aging approaches, accounting for notes receivable* **(Obj. 2, 5)**

Brandon Construction Co. uses the allowance method in accounting for uncollectible accounts with the estimate based on an aging of accounts receivable. The company had the following account balances on June 30, 2003:

Accounts Receivable...	$345,000
Allowance for Doubtful Accounts (credit balance)	41,000

The following transactions took place during the month of July 2003:

July   2   Andy Downs, who owes $35,000, is unable to pay on time and has given a 20-day, 12 percent note in settlement of the account.

6   Determined the account receivable for David Smith ($6,000) was uncollectible and wrote it off.

9   Received notice that a customer (Henry Lui) has filed for bankruptcy. Lui owes $18,000 to Brandon Constuction Co.

11   Determined the account receivable for Mary Kyle ($4,900) was uncollectible and wrote it off.

15   David Smith, whose account was written off on July 6, paid $3,000 on his account and promises to pay the balance in 30 days.

18   Received a cheque from the courts in the amount of $10,500 as final settlement of Henry Lui's account.

22   Andy Downs paid the note received on July 2.

25   Determined the account receivable for Ernest Moore ($4,700) was uncollectible and wrote it off.

31   Sales for the month totalled $576,000 (of which 90 percent were on credit) and collections on account totalled $371,000.

31   Brandon Constuction Co. did an aging of accounts receivable that indicated that $42,600 is expected to be uncollectible. The company recorded the appropriate adjustment.

Required

1. Record the above transactions in the general journal.

2. What would be the adjusting entry required on July 31 if the company used the percent of sales method with an estimate of uncollectibles equal to 8 percent of credit sales?

3. Which of the two methods of estimating uncollectible accounts would normally be more accurate? Why?

Challenge Problems

Problem 8-1C *Understanding accounts receivable management* **(Obj. 1, 2)**

Apex Electronics Company is a six-store chain of retail stores selling appliances and electronic equipment mainly on credit; the company has its own credit card and does not accept other cards. Apex Electronics Company had a tendency to institute policies that conflicted with each other. Management rarely became aware of these conflicts until they became serious.

Recently, the owner, Arnie Daw, who has been reading all the latest management texts, has instituted a new bonus plan. All managers are to be paid bonuses based on the success of their department. For example, for Jane Nash, the sales manager, her bonus is based on how much she can increase sales. For Sally Chang, the credit manager, her bonus is based on reducing the uncollectible-account expense.

Required

Describe the conflict that the bonus plan has created for the sales manager and the credit manager. How might the conflict be resolved?

Problem 8-2C *Explaining days' sales in accounts receivable* **(Obj. 2)**

Days' sales in receivables is a good measure of a company's ability to collect the amounts owing to it. You have owned shares in Dayco Office Supplies for some years and follow the company's progress by reading the annual report. You noticed the most recent report indicated that the days' sales in receivables had increased over the previous year, and are concerned.

Required

Suggest reasons that may have resulted in the increase in the number of days' sales in receivables.

Extending Your Knowledge

Decision Problems

1. Uncollectible accounts and evaluating a business   (Obj. 2, 3)

Singh Plumbing Mfg. sells its products either for cash or on notes receivable that earn interest. The business uses the direct write-off method to account for uncollectible accounts. Ray Singh, the owner, has prepared Singh Plumbing Mfg.'s financial statements. The most recent comparative income statements, for 2002 and 2001, are as follows:

	2002	2001
Total revenue	$220,000	$195,000
Total expenses	157,000	140,000
Net income	$ 63,000	$ 55,000

Based on the increase in net income, Singh seeks to expand the operations. He asks you to invest $50,000 in the business. You and Singh have several meetings, at which you learn that notes receivable from customers were $200,000 at the end of 2000, and $420,000 at the end of 2001. Also, total revenues for 2002 and 2001 include interest at 15 percent on the year's beginning notes receivable balance. Total expenses include doubtful-account expense of $2,000 each year, based on the direct write-off basis. Singh estimates that doubtful-account expense would be 5 percent of sales revenue if the allowance method were used.

Required

1. Prepare for Singh Plumbing Mfg. a comparative single-step income statement that identifies sales revenue, interest revenue, uncollectible-account expense, and other expenses, all computed in accordance with generally accepted accounting principles.

2. Is Singh Plumbing Mfg.'s future as promising as Singh's income statement makes it appear? Give the reason for your answer.

2. *Estimating the collectibility of accounts receivable* (Obj. 2)

Assume you work in the corporate loan department of the Bank of Nova Scotia. Stephanie Hudson, sole owner of SH Manufacturing, a manufacturer of wooden furniture, has come to you seeking a loan of $500,000 to buy new manufacturing equipment to expand her operations. She proposes to use her accounts receivable as collateral for the loan, and has provided you with the following information from her most recent audited financial statements:

(in thousands of dollars)	2002	2001	2000
Sales...	$1,475	$1,589	$1,502
Cost of goods sold..	876	947	905
Gross profit	599	642	597
Other expenses	518	487	453
Net profit before taxes.................................	$ 81	$ 155	$ 144
Accounts receivable......................................	458	387	374
Allowance for doubtful accounts.....................	20	32	29

Required

1. Analyze the information Hudson has provided. Would you grant the loan based on this information? Give your reason.

2. What additional information would you request from Hudson? Give your reason.

3. Assume Hudson provided you with the information requested in Requirement 2. What would make you change the decision you made in Requirement 1?

Financial Statement Problems

Accounts receivable and related uncollectibles (Obj. 2, 7)

Answer the following questions using the financial statements for Intrawest Corporation in Appendix A.

1. Analyze the Amounts Receivable account at June 30, 2000. What is the total receivable? How much of Intrawest Corporation's Amounts Receivable are due in the year ended June 30, 2001? In the year 2002?

2. How many days' sales are in Amounts Receivable from Ski and Resort Operations at June 30, 2000? How many days' sales are in Amounts Receivable from Sales of Real Estate at June 30, 2000? Why do you think the two numbers are different?

3. Certain Amounts Receivable have been pledged as security for borrowings. What are the assets pledged?

4. Which of the various categories of receivables have increased most from 1999 to 2000? Have any categories decreased from 1999 to 2000?

5. Compute Intrawest Corporation's acid-test ratio at June 30, 2000.

Appendix

Discounting (Selling) a Note Receivable

A payee of a note receivable (the person to whom the money is owed) may need the cash before the maturity date of the note. When this occurs, the payee may sell the note. A note receivable is a *negotiable instrument*, which means it is readily transferable from one party to another, and may be sold. Selling a note is called **discounting a note receivable**. This practice is common with long-term notes receivable secured by real estate as collateral. A bank that has lent money may discount the note receivable to another lender. The net result is that the banks and trust companies can quickly replenish their cash for lending.

Computers can be used to discount notes. A spreadsheet may handle the accounting (if the accounting software package does not include a special function for discounting). Companies that discount notes on a regular basis would have a standard program to compute the proceeds.

The price the purchaser of a discounted note pays for the note receivable depends mainly on the interest rate the purchaser seeks to earn on its investment. The purchaser pays cash now—at a discounted price—to receive a larger amount at a future date. This is the concept of *present value:* One dollar today grows to a larger sum in the future.

A payee may also discount a short-term note receivable, one with a maturity of one year or less. There are several ways to compute the price to be received. Fundamentally the price is determined by present-value concepts. We discuss these concepts in detail in Chapter 15. But the transaction between the seller and the buyer of the note can take any form agreeable to the two parties. Here we illustrate one procedure used for discounting short-term notes receivable. To receive cash immediately, the seller is willing to accept a lower price than the note's maturity value.

To illustrate discounting a note receivable, suppose EMCO Ltd. loaned $15,000 to Dorman Builders on October 20, 2002. The maturity date of the 90-day, 10 percent Dorman note is January 18, 2003. Suppose EMCO discounts the Dorman Builders note at the National Bank on December 9, 2002, when the note is 50 days old. The bank applies a 12 percent annual interest rate in computing the discounted value of the note. The bank will use a discount rate that is higher than the interest rate on the note in order to earn some interest on the transaction. EMCO may be willing to accept this higher rate in order to get cash quickly. The discounted value, called the *proceeds*, is the amount EMCO receives from the bank. The proceeds can be computed in five steps, as shown in Exhibit 8-1A. At maturity the bank collects $15,370 from the maker of the note and earns $202 interest revenue from holding the note.

EMCO Ltd. 's entry to record discounting (selling) the note on December 9, 2002, is

Dec. 9, 2002	Cash	15,168	
	Note Receivable		
	— Dorman Builders		15,000
	Interest Revenue		168
	To record discounting a note receivable.		

When the proceeds from discounting a note receivable are less than the principal amount of the note, the payee records a debit to Interest Expense for the amount of the difference. For example, EMCO could discount the note receivable for cash proceeds of $14,980. The entry to record this transaction is

Dec. 9, 2002	Cash	14,980	
	Interest Expense	20	
	Note Receivable—Dorman Builders		15,000

EXHIBIT 8-1A

Discounting (Selling) a Note Receivable: EMCO Ltd. Discounts the Dorman Builders Note

Step	Computation	
1. Compute the original amount of interest of the note receivable.	$15,000 x 0.10 x 90/365	= $ 370
2. Maturity value of note = principal + interest	$15,000 + $370	= $15,370
3. Determine the period (number of days, months, or years) the bank will hold the note (the discount period).	Dec. 9, 2002, to Jan. 18, 2003	= 40 days
4. Compute the bank's discount on the note. This is the bank's interest revenue from holding the note.	$15,370 x 0.12 x 40/365	= $ 202
5. Seller's proceeds from discounting the note receivable* = maturity value of note – bank's discount on the note	$15,370 – $202	= $15,168

*(Buyer's cost of purchasing)

The authors thank Doug Hamilton for suggesting this exhibit.

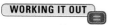

WORKING IT OUT

If a 60-day note dated April 16 is discounted on May 2, what is the discount period?

A: 44 days. Method: Compute the number of days the note was held prior to discounting (April 16 to May 2 is 16 days). Subtract the days held from the length of the note (60 − 16 = 44). This method eliminates the necessity of determining the maturity date and then having to count from the discount date to the maturity date.

In the discounting of the note receivable just described, interest revenue accrued from the original date of the note (October 20, 2002) to the date of discounting (December 9, 2002). Since the amount is not material, we will recognize this fact but disregard the interest revenue in the rest of this Appendix.

Contingent Liabilities on Discounted Notes Receivable

A **contingent liability** is a potential liability that will become an actual liability only if a potential event does occur. Discounting a note receivable creates a contingent liability for the endorser. If the maker of the note (Dorman Builders in our example) fails to pay the maturity value to the new payee (the bank), the original payee (EMCO Ltd., the note's endorser) legally must pay the bank the amount due.[4] Now we see why the liability is "potential." If Dorman Builders pays the bank, EMCO can forget the note. But if Dorman dishonours the note—fails to pay it—EMCO then has an actual liability.

EMCO's contingent liability exists from the time of endorsement to the note's maturity date. In our example, the contingent liability exists from December 9, 2002—when EMCO endorsed the note—to the January 18, 2003, maturity date.

Contingent liabilities are not included with actual liabilities on the balance sheet. After all, they are not real debts. However, financial statement users should be alerted that the business has incurred *potential* debts. Most businesses report contingent liabilities in a note to the financial statements. EMCO Ltd.'s end-of-period financial statement might carry this note:

> As of December 31, 2002, the Company is contingently liable for notes receivable discounted in the amount of $15,000.

[4]The discounting agreement between the endorser and the purchaser may be "without recourse," which means that the endorser has no liability if the note is dishonoured at maturity. Under such an arrangement there is no contingent liability.

Appendix Exercises

Exercise 8-1A General Telecom installs telephone systems and receives its pay in the form of notes receivable. General Telecom installed a system for the city of Red Deer, Alberta, receiving a nine-month, 8%, $500,000 note receivable on May 31, 2003. To obtain cash quickly, General Telecom discounted the note with the Bank of Montreal on June 30, 2003. The bank charged a discount rate of 9%.

Compute General Telecom's cash proceeds from discounting the note. Follow the five-step procedure outlined in Exhibit 8-1A, page 452.

Exercise 8-2A *Link Back to Chapter 5 (Recording a Sale).* Use your answers to Exercise 8-1A to journalize General Telecom's transactions as follows:

May 31 Sold a telecommunications system, receiving a 9-month, 8%, $500,000 note from the city of Red Deer. General Telecom's cost of the system was $450,000.
June 30 Received cash for interest revenue for one month.
June 30 Discounted the note to the Bank of Montreal at a discount rate of 9%.

Exercise 8-3A Saltspring Provisioners sells on account. When a customer account becomes three months old, Saltspring Provisioners converts the account to a note receivable and immediately discounts the note to a bank. During 2002, Saltspring Provisioners completed these transactions:

Aug. 29 Sold goods on account to Viv Moyer, $4,600.
Dec. 1 Received a $4,000, 60-day, 10 percent note and cash of $600 from Viv Moyer in satisfaction of her past-due account receivable.
1 Sold the Moyer note by discounting it to a bank for proceeds of $3,700.

Required

1. Record the transactions in Saltspring Provisioners' journal.
2. Write the financial statement note to disclose the contingent liability at December 31.

Appendix Problems

Problem 8-1A A company received the following notes during 2003. Notes (a), (b), and (c) were discounted on the dates and at the rates indicated.

Note	Date	Principal Amount	Interest Rate	Term	Date Discounted	Discount Rate
(a)	July 12	$10,000	10%	3 months	Aug. 12	15%
(b)	Aug. 4	9,000	11%	90 days	Aug. 30	13%
(c)	Oct. 21	8,000	15%	60 days	Nov. 3	18%

Required

Identify each note by letter, compute interest using a 365-day year for all notes, round all interest amounts to the nearest cent, and present entries in general journal form. Explanations are not required.

1. Determine the due date and maturity value of each note.
2. Determine the discount and proceeds from the sale (discounting) of each note.
3. Journalize the discounting of notes (a) and (b).

Problem 8-2A A company received the following notes during 2003. Notes (a), (b), and (c) were discounted on the dates and at the rates indicated.

Note	Date	Principal Amount	Interest Rate	Term	Date Discounted	Discount Rate
(a)	July 15	$ 6,000	10%	6 months	Oct. 15	12%
(b)	Aug. 19	9,000	12%	90 days	Aug. 30	14%
(c)	Sept. 1	10,000	15%	120 days	Nov. 2	20%

Required

Identify each note by letter, compute interest using a 365-day year for each note, round all interest amounts to the nearest cent, and present entries in general journal form. Explanations are not required.

1. Determine the due date and maturity value of each note.

2. Determine the discount and proceeds from the sale (discounting) of each note.

3. Journalize the discounting of notes (a) and (b).

Merchandise Inventory

CHAPTER OBJECTIVES

After studying this chapter, you should be able to

1 Account for inventory by the perpetual and periodic systems

2 Apply the inventory costing methods: specific unit cost, weighted-average cost, FIFO, and LIFO

3 Describe the income effects of the inventory costing methods

4 Apply the lower-of-cost-or-market rule to inventory

5 Determine the effects of inventory errors on cost of goods sold and net income

6 Estimate ending inventory by the gross margin method and the retail method

To a layperson, it might seem peculiar that three identical companies could have three very different net incomes or losses on the income statement and three different values for inventory on the balance sheet using accounting procedures that comply with generally accepted accounting principles. Yet this scenario is possible.

The *CICA Handbook* permits different methods of determining inventory cost, and as you will see as you read the chapter, they result in very different measurements of closing inventory and thus of net income. Management does have the latitude to select the method used, but, as the *Handbook* states, management should select that method that results in the most appropriate matching of inventory costs against revenues. And perhaps more importantly, management is required to report the method chosen in the financial statements.

The importance of inventory is demonstrated by the fact that 180 or 90 percent of the companies included in *Financial Reporting in Canada*, 1999, Twenty-Fourth Edition[1] reported a figure for inventory. Of those 180 companies, 147 disclosed the valuation method used: 40 percent used average cost exclusively, 33 percent used FIFO exclusively, 2 percent used LIFO exclusively, 22 percent used more than one method, while the rest used a variety of other methods.

Merchandise inventory is very important to a merchandising entity such as Mark's Work Wearhouse or The Bay.

---

[1]Source: Byrd, C., I. Chen, and H.Chapman, *Financial Reporting in Canada*, 1999, Twenty-Fourth Edition, Toronto: Canadian Institute of Chartered Accountants, 1999, pp. 229–231.

COMPANIES

such as Future Shop, Zellers, Canadian Tire, and Mountain Equipment Co-op are **merchandising companies**—companies that resell products they have previously purchased from suppliers. Merchandise inventory is the lifeblood of a merchandising entity—the entity's major current asset. What is the entity's major expense? It is *cost of goods sold* or *cost of sales*, the cost of the inventory that the business sold to its customers. For example, Wal-Mart Stores, Inc. reported cost of goods sold at U.S. $74.6 billion and operating, selling, and administrative expenses at U.S. $15.0 billion. For Wal-Mart and many other merchandising companies, cost of goods sold is greater than all other expenses combined.

We begin this chapter with the basic concept of accounting for inventories. Then we examine the different inventory systems (perpetual and periodic), the different inventory methods (FIFO, LIFO, and average cost), and several related topics.

REAL WORLD EXAMPLE

Inventories can vary in importance from industry to industry. For example, for soft drink manufacturers, inventories are 13.1% of total assets, while for wholesale groceries, inventories are 33.3% of total assets.

Mountain Equipment Co-op
www.mec.ca

Wal-Mart Stores, Inc.
www.walmart.com

The Brick
www.thebrick.com

Accounting for Inventory and Inventory Systems

Basic Concepts

The basic concept of accounting for inventory is straightforward. Suppose The Brick buys three chairs for $300 each, marks them up $200, and sells two chairs for the retail price of $500 each. The Brick's balance sheet reports the inventory that the company still has, and the income statement reports the cost of goods sold for the units sold, as follows (focus on the highlighted items):

Balance Sheet (partial):		Income Statement (partial):	
Current assets:		Sales revenue	
Cash...	$XXX	(2 chairs @ $500)	$1,000
Short-term investments..............	XXX	**Cost of goods sold**	
Accounts receivable	XXX	(2 chairs @ $300)	600
Inventory		Gross margin................................	$ 400
(1 chair @ $300)	300		
Prepaid expenses.........................	XXX		

As we saw in Chapter 5, **gross margin**, also called **gross profit**, is the excess of sales revenue over cost of goods sold. It is called *gross* margin because operating expenses have not yet been subtracted. Gross margin minus all the operating expenses equals *net* income. In practice, accounting for inventory is usually more complex than our simple example would suggest.

There are two main types of inventory accounting systems: the periodic system and the perpetual system. We described these methods briefly in Chapter 5, on page 220. The **periodic inventory system** is used by businesses that sell relatively inexpensive goods. Convenience stores without optical-scanning cash registers do not keep a daily running record of every loaf of bread and every can of pop they buy and sell. Instead, these stores count their inventory periodically—at least once a year—to determine the quantities on hand to calculate cost of goods sold and ending inventory, and prepare the annual financial statements.

Under the **perpetual inventory system**, the business maintains a running record of inventory on hand, usually on computer. This system achieves control over goods such as automobiles, jewellery, and furniture. The loss of one item would be significant, and this justifies the cost of a perpetual system. Because the cost of computers and accounting software has come down, even many small businesses now use perpetual inventory systems for all types of goods.

Under both systems, the business still counts the inventory on hand annually. The physical count establishes the correct amount of ending inventory and serves as a check on the inventory records. The following chart compares the periodic and perpetual systems.

Periodic Inventory System	Perpetual Inventory System
• Does not keep a running record of all goods bought, sold, and on hand	• Keeps a running record of all goods bought, sold, and on hand
• Used for inexpensive goods	• Used for all types of goods
• Inventory counted at least once a year	• Inventory counted at least once a year

Perpetual Inventory System

Perpetual inventory records can be a computer printout like the CompuSave record shown for a calculator, model RK 42, in Exhibit 9-1.

The quantities of goods on hand are updated daily, as inventory transactions occur. Many companies keep their perpetual records in terms of quantities only, as shown in Exhibit 9-1. Others keep perpetual inventory records both in quantities and dollar cost as shown in Exhibit 9-5, page 471.

Entries Under the Perpetual System In the perpetual system, the business records purchases of inventory by debiting the Inventory account. When the business makes a sale, two entries are needed: one to record the sale and the other to record the decrease in inventory on hand.

Exhibit 9-2 illustrates the accounting for inventory transactions in a perpetual system (and in a periodic system as well) at CompuSave. Focus on the left column of Exhibit 9-2, which shows the inventory transactions in a perpetual system. Panel A gives the journal entries and the T-accounts, and Panel B presents the income statement and balance-sheet effects. All amounts are assumed.

EXHIBIT 9-1

**Perpetual Inventory Record
(Quantities Only)—
CompuSave**

Item: Calculator Model RK42

Date	Quantity Received	Quantity Sold	Quantity on Hand
Nov. 1			10
5		6	4
7	10		14
12		9	5
26	17		22
30		14	8
Totals	27	29	8

In Exhibit 9-2, Panel A, the first entry to Inventory summarizes a lot of detail. The cost of the inventory, $560,000, is the *net* amount of the purchases, determined as follows (using assumed amounts):

Net Purchases	
Purchase price of the inventory from the seller (including freight in)	$600,000
–Purchase returns for damaged or otherwise unsuitable goods returned to the seller	(25,000)
–Purchase allowances granted by the seller	(5,000)
–Purchase discounts taken for early payment	(10,000)
=Net purchases of inventory	$560,000

Throughout the remainder of the book, we often refer to net purchases simply as Purchases, as in Exhibit 9-2. The terms will be used interchangeably.

The cost of the goods purchased by CompuSave during the year was $560,000. This is based on a general principle:

> The cost of an asset $=$ The sum of all the costs incurred to bring the asset to its intended purpose, after subtracting all discounts

Therefore, the buyer's cost of transporting goods from the supplier (freight in) is part of the purchase cost of the inventory. Freight in is *not* recorded as an expense.

The company records the sale in the usual manner—debits Cash or Accounts Receivable and credits Sales Revenue for the sale price of the goods. The company also debits Cost of Goods Sold (which is an expense account) and credits Inventory for cost. The debit to Inventory (for purchases) and the credit to Inventory (for sales) serve to keep an up-to-date record of the cost of inventory on hand. The Inventory account and the Cost of Goods Sold account carry an up-to-date balance throughout the period. Therefore, at the end of the period, no adjusting entries may be required, since both Inventory and Cost of Goods Sold are up to date. Adjusting entries may be required to record shrinkage from theft or spoilage.

Periodic Inventory System

In the periodic inventory system, the business does not keep a continuous record of the inventory on hand. Instead, at the end of the period, the business makes a physical count of the inventory on hand and applies the unit costs to determine the cost of ending inventory. This inventory figure appears on the balance sheet and is used to compute cost of goods sold.

EXHIBIT 9-2

Recording and Reporting Inventory Transactions of CompuSave—Perpetual and Periodic Systems (amounts assumed)

Panel A—Recording in the Journal and Posting to the T-accounts

Perpetual System	Periodic System

1. Credit purchases of $560,000:
Inventory 560,000
    Accounts Payable 560,000
	1. Credit purchases of $560,000:
	Purchases 560,000
	    Accounts Payable..................... 560,000

2. Credit sales of $900,000
(cost $540,000):
Accounts Receivable 900,000
    Sales Revenue 900,000
Cost of Goods Sold.................. 540,000
    Inventory 540,000
	2. Credit sales of $900,000:
	Accounts Receivable.................... 900,000
	    Sales Revenue........................... 900,000

3. End-of-period entries:
No entries required. Both
Inventory and Cost of Goods
Sold are up to date.
	3. End-of-period entries to update Inventory and
	record Cost of Goods Sold:
	a. Transfer the cost of beginning
	inventory ($100,000) to Cost
	of Goods Sold:
	Cost of Goods Sold 100,000
	    Inventory (beginning balance) 100,000
	b. Record the cost of ending
	inventory ($120,000) based
	on a physical count:
	Inventory (ending balance).... 120,000
	    Cost of Goods Sold 120,000
	c. Transfer the cost of purchases
	to Cost of Goods Sold:
	Cost of Goods Sold 560,000
	    Purchases............................... 560,000

Inventory and Cost of Goods Sold Accounts (Perpetual)

Inventory		Cost of Goods Sold	
100,000*	540,000	**540,000**	
560,000			
120,000			

*Beginning inventory was $100,000.

Inventory and Cost of Goods Sold Accounts (Periodic)

Inventory		Cost of Goods Sold	
100,000*	100,000	100,000	120,000
120,000		560,000	
		540,000	

*Beginning inventory was $100,000.

Panel B—Reporting in the Financial Statements

Perpetual System	Periodic System

Income Statement (partial):
Sales revenue $900,000
Cost of goods sold................... **540,000** ◄
Gross margin............................ $360,000
	Sales revenue $900,000
	Cost of goods sold:
	  Beginning inventory............... $100,000
	  Purchases 560,000
	  Cost of goods available
	    for sale 660,000
	  Less: Ending inventory............... (120,000)
	Cost of goods sold 540,000
	Gross margin................................. $360,000

Ending Balance Sheet (partial):
Current assets:
  Cash.. $ XXX
  Short-term investments........... XXX
  Accounts receivable XXX
  Inventories............................... **120,000** ◄
  Prepaid expenses..................... XXX
	Current Assets:
	  Cash.. $ XXX
	  Short-term investments........... XXX
	  Accounts receivable XXX
	  Inventories............................... **120,000**
	  Prepaid expenses..................... XXX

The periodic system is also called the *physical system* because it relies on the actual physical count of inventory. To use the periodic system effectively, the company's owner must be able to control inventory by visual inspection. For example, when a customer inquires about quantities on hand, the owner or manager should be able to estimate the goods in the store by looking on the shelves or in the storage area.

A company purchased $5,000 of merchandise on credit and sold $2,500 of it for $3,900. Prepare the general journal entries to record these transactions under both the perpetual and periodic systems.

Perpetual

To record purchase of inventory:

Inventory	5,000	
Accounts Payable		5,000

To record credit sales:

Accounts Receivable	3,900	
Sales Revenue		3,900
Cost of Goods Sold	2,500	
Inventory		2,500

Periodic

To record purchase of inventory:

Purchases	5,000	
Accounts Payable		5,000

To record credit sales:

Accounts Receivable	3,900	
Sales Revenue		3,900

Entries Under the Periodic System Exhibit 9-2, in the right column, illustrates the accounting for transactions in a periodic system at CompuSave. In the periodic system (Exhibit 9-2, Panel A), the business uses a Purchases account to record the purchase of inventory. Purchases is an expense account. Throughout the period, the Inventory account carries the beginning balance left over from the end of the preceding period. At the end of the period, the Inventory account is then updated for the financial statements. A journal entry removes the beginning balance, crediting Inventory and debiting Cost of Goods Sold. A second journal entry sets up the ending inventory balance, based on the physical count. The debit is to Inventory, and the credit to Cost of Goods Sold. The final entry in this sequence transfers the amount of Purchases as well as freight-in and any related contra accounts to Cost of Goods Sold. These end-of-period entries can be made during the closing process.

After the process is complete, Inventory has its correct balance of $120,000, and Cost of Goods Sold shows $540,000, regardless of which inventory system is used.

Comparing the Perpetual and Periodic Inventory Systems

Compare the entries under both inventory systems in Exhibit 9-2 step by step. First, study the perpetual system all the way through. On the income statement, the perpetual system reports cost of goods sold on a single line. Then study the periodic system, which reports a more detailed computation of cost of goods sold. Both inventory systems report the *same* amounts for inventory on the balance sheet, cost of goods sold on the income statement, and everything else.

THINKING IT OVER

Indicate which inventory system, perpetual or periodic, best fits each of the following statements.

1. Uses the Purchases account.
A: Periodic
2. Uses the Cost of Goods Sold account.
A: Perpetual (COGS will appear on the income statement under the periodic system, but it is derived by adding/subtracting several accounts.)
3. Inventory balance does not change all year until closing.
A: Periodic
4. Affords better inventory control.
A: Perpetual
5. Requires a physical inventory count at least once a year.
A: Both perpetual and periodic
6. Debits Inventory for goods purchased.
A: Perpetual

STOP & THINK

Answer the following questions about various features of the perpetual inventory system and the periodic inventory system.

1. Do the perpetual and periodic inventory systems result in the same or different dollar amounts for Inventory and Cost of Goods Sold to be reported in the financial statements? Explain.

2. a. Which inventory system records the cost of inventory purchased as an asset and then records the cost of inventory sold as expense?
   b. Which inventory system records the cost of inventory purchased as an expense (name the expense account) and then records the cost of inventory on hand at the end of the period as an asset?

3. Suppose your company produces microchips for use in manufacturing computer circuit boards. Technology is advancing rapidly, and you require monthly financial statements to remain competitive. Which inventory system should you use?

Answers:
1. Both inventory systems result in the same amounts for Inventory and Cost of Goods Sold because the facts are the same regardless of the inventory system.

2. a. The *perpetual inventory system* records the cost of inventory purchased as an asset and then the cost of goods sold as an expense.
   b. The *periodic inventory system* records the cost of inventory purchased as an expense (the Purchases account) and then records the cost of inventory on hand at the end of the period as an asset.

3. You should use the *perpetual inventory system* because it gives up-to-date inventory information that can be used to prepare the financial statements at any time.

Cost of Goods Sold (Cost of Sales) and Gross Margin (Gross Profit)

Exhibit 9-2 illustrates the measurement of cost of goods sold (cost of sales) in the two inventory systems. In a perpetual system, cost of sales is simply the sum of all the amounts posted to the Cost of Goods Sold account throughout the period (see Exhibit 9-2, Panel A, the left column). By contrast, the periodic system measures cost of sales only at the end of the period after a physical count of the inventory is done and the closing process is complete.

Using the periodic system, the cost-of-goods-sold computation from Exhibit 9-2 is as follows:

Cost of Goods Sold	
Beginning inventory	$100,000
+Purchases (including freight in)	560,000
=Cost of goods available for sale	660,000
−Ending inventory	(120,000)
=Cost of goods sold	$540,000

The business began the period with $100,000 of inventory. During the period, it purchased goods costing $560,000. The sum of the beginning inventory plus the purchases equals the **cost of goods available for sale** during the period, $660,000. Goods available are either in ending inventory, $120,000, or they were sold during the period. Cost of goods sold during the year was thus $660,000 − $120,000 = $540,000. Learn this model now because you will use it throughout your business career.

This computation of cost of goods sold is so important that all companies use it to bring together all the inventory data of an accounting period. Even companies that use the perpetual system often summarize their inventory data this way.

How Owners and Managers Use the Cost-of-Goods-Sold Model

Suppose you are the owner of CompuSave. You are planning for the next period and preparing a budget to guide your buying. You have examined the new lines of computers offered by IBM, Compaq, and Hewlett-Packard, your three main suppliers, and you've decided which PCs and lap-tops to purchase for the upcoming season. Now you must decide how much inventory to purchase.

How will you make the purchasing decision? The amount of inventory to purchase depends on three factors:

- budgeted cost of goods sold
- budgeted ending inventory
- the beginning inventory with which you started the period.

A rearrangement of the cost-of-goods-sold formula helps you decide how much to purchase for the coming year (all budgeted amounts for the next period are assumed):

Computation of Budgeted Purchases	
Cost of goods sold (based on budgeted sales for the next period)	$600,000
+Ending inventory (based on the budget for the next period)	150,000
=Cost of goods available for sale, as budgeted	750,000
−Beginning inventory (actual amount left over from the prior period)	(120,000)
=Purchases (how much inventory you need to buy to reach your goal)	$630,000

Business owners and managers use this formula to determine how much to spend on inventory, regardless of whether the business uses a perpetual or a periodic inventory system. The power of the cost-of-goods-sold model lies in the key information it captures: beginning and ending inventory levels, purchases, and cost of goods sold. The model works equally well for budgeting done in units.

Gross Margin (Gross Profit)

As we saw earlier, *gross margin*, or *gross profit*, is sales revenue minus cost of goods sold. A company's gross margin is one of its most important statistics. It reveals the company's success in selling its goods at a profit, before deducting operating expenses. "Gross" margin means *before operating expenses*. By contrast, "net" income means *after subtracting all expenses*.

Businesses must sell their merchandise at a profit, or they will go bankrupt. For this reason, owners and managers keep a close eye on the business's gross margin. Investors and creditors watch gross margin too. An increase in a company's gross margin means higher net income. A sharp downturn in the gross margin is cause for alarm.

Computing the Cost of Inventory

The CompuSave inventory record in Exhibit 9-1 follows the common practice of recording quantities only. The company can multiply the quantity of 8 RK42 calculators on hand at November 30 by the unit cost of each calculator to compute the value of the ending inventory for the balance sheet.

Quantity of Inventory on Hand	×	Unit Cost	=	Cost of Inventory on Hand
8 calculators	×	$20	=	$160

Determining the Quantity of Inventory   Many businesses—even those that use the perpetual system—physically count their inventory, on the last day of the fiscal year. If you have worked at a grocery store, or some other type of retail business, you will recall the process of "taking inventory." Some entities shut the business down to get a good count of inventory on hand.

Complications may arise in determining the inventory quantity. Suppose the business has purchased some goods that are in transit when the inventory is counted. Even though these items are not physically present, they should be included in the inventory count if legal title to the goods has passed to the purchaser. When title passes from seller to purchaser, the purchaser becomes the legal owner of the goods.

The FOB—free on board—terms of the transaction govern when title passes from the seller to the purchaser. Recall Chapter 5 (page 224), *FOB shipping point* indicates that title passes when the goods leave the seller's place of business and *FOB destination* means that title passes when the goods arrive at the purchaser's location. Therefore, goods in transit that a company has purchased FOB shipping point should be included in its inventory. Goods in transit that are bought FOB destination should not be included.

Another complication in counting inventory arises from consigned goods. In a **consignment** arrangement, the owner of the inventory (the *consignor*) transfers the goods to another business (the *consignee*). For a fee, the consignee sells the inventory for the owner. The consignee does *not* take title to the consigned goods and, therefore, should not include them in its own inventory. Consignments are common in retailing. Suppose CompuSave is the consignee for a line of notebook computers in its store. Should CompuSave include this consigned merchandise in its inventory count? No, because CompuSave does not own the goods. Instead, the computer manufacturer—the consignor—includes the consigned goods in its inventory. *A rule of thumb is to include in inventory only what the business owns.*

 **REAL WORLD EXAMPLE**

Typically, a business's year end coincides with the time of year when inventory is lowest, so that counting the inventory ("taking inventory") will be as simple as possible. Many retailers, such as Mark's Work Wearhouse, have a January 31 year end.

THINKING IT OVER

If you have participated in taking a physical inventory, how many times a year was the physical inventory taken? How did the company ensure the goods were not double counted? Was the business closed? (Depending on the type of merchandise, a physical inventory can be taken as often as weekly. Taking a physical inventory can be expensive if the business must be closed and additional workers hired.)

Determining the Unit Cost of Inventory   As we have seen, *inventory cost* is the price the business pays to acquire the inventory—not the selling price of the goods. Suppose CompuSave purchases boxes of computer disks for $5 and sells them for $10. The inventory is reported at its cost of $5 per unit, multiplied by the number of units owned, not at its selling price of $10.

Inventory cost includes its invoice price, less any purchase discounts or allowances, plus duty, exchange, tariffs, transportation charges, insurance while in transit, and all other costs incurred to make the goods ready for sale. *Net purchases* means the net cost of inventory acquired for resale, after subtracting any purchase discounts and purchase returns and allowances. As we stated earlier, in the remainder of this book, we use the term *purchases* and *net purchases* interchangeably.

While the retailer paid GST on the purchase, the GST was recorded in a separate account, *not* in the same account as other inventory costs. Separate accounts are used since the amount paid is recoverable as a deduction from the GST collected when the retailer sells the inventory. For example, CompuSave would pay $63 GST ($900 × 7 percent, the GST rate) on a purchase of a $900 home computer from the manufacturer. When CompuSave sells the computer the following month for $1,400, it would charge the purchaser GST of $98 ($1,400 × 0.07). Later, CompuSave would remit $35 ($98 − $63) to Canada Customs and Revenue Agency in connection with the purchase and sale.

Inventory Costing Methods

Determining the cost of inventory is easy when the unit cost remains constant during the period. But, the unit cost often changes. For example, during times of inflation, prices rise. The software package that cost CompuSave $100 in January may cost $115 in June and $122 in October. Suppose CompuSave sells 15 of the computer desks in November. How many of them cost $100, how many cost $115, and how many cost $122? To compute the cost of goods sold and cost of inventory on hand, the accountant must have some means of assigning the business's cost to each item sold. The four costing methods that GAAP allows are

1. Specific unit cost
2. Weighted-average cost (periodic inventory system) or moving weighted-average cost (perpetual inventory system)
3. First-in, first-out (FIFO) cost
4. Last-in, first-out (LIFO) cost

A company may use any of these methods. Many companies use several methods—different methods for different categories of inventory. Here we use the periodic inventory system to illustrate the four inventory costing methods. We illustrate the methods under the perpetual method later in this chapter.

Specific Unit Cost   Some businesses deal in inventory items that differ from unit to unit, such as automobiles, jewels, and real estate. These businesses usually cost their inventory at the specific unit cost of the particular unit. For instance, a Ford dealer may have two vehicles in the showroom, a "stripped-down" model that costs $16,000 and a "loaded" model that costs $21,000. If the dealer sells the loaded model for $23,700, cost of goods sold is $21,000, the cost of the specific unit. The gross margin on this sale is $2,700 ($23,700 − $21,000). If the stripped-down auto is the only unit left in inventory at the end of the period, ending inventory is $16,000, the cost to the retailer of the specific unit on hand.

The **specific-unit-cost method** is also called the **specific identification method.** This method is not practical for inventory items that appear identical, such as bushels of wheat, litres of paint, or boxes of laundry detergent.

Other Methods

The weighted-average cost, FIFO (first-in, first-out), and LIFO (last-in, first-out) methods are fundamentally different from the specific-unit-cost method. These methods do not assign to inventory the specific cost of particular units. Instead, they assume different flows of costs into and out of inventory, as illustrated in Exhibit 9-3. Panel A gives the illustrative data for all three inventory cost methods.

Weighted-Average Cost   The **weighted-average cost method**, often called the **average cost method**, is based on the weighted-average cost of inventory during the period. Under the periodic inventory system, weighted-average cost is determined as follows:

- Determine the weighted-average cost by dividing the cost of goods available for sale (beginning inventory plus purchases) by the number of units available for sale (beginning inventory plus purchases).
- Compute the ending inventory and cost of goods sold by multiplying the number of units by the weighted-average cost per unit.

To illustrate the costing methods, suppose the business has 60 units of inventory available for sale during the period.

- Ending inventory consists of 20 units.
- Cost of goods sold is based on 40 units.

Panel A of Exhibit 9-3 gives the data for computing ending inventory and cost of goods sold, and Panel B shows the weighted-average cost computations.

First-in, First-out (FIFO) Cost   Under the **first-in, first-out (FIFO) method**, the company must keep a record of the cost of each inventory unit purchased. The unit costs used in computing the ending inventory may be different from the unit costs used in computing the cost of goods sold. Under FIFO,

- The first costs into inventory are the first costs out to cost of goods sold—hence the name *first-in, first-out.*
- Ending inventory is based on the costs of the most recent purchases.

In our example in Exhibit 9-3, the FIFO cost of ending inventory is $360. Cost of goods sold is $540. Panel A gives the data, and Panel C shows the FIFO computations.

Last-in, First-out (LIFO) Cost   The **last-in, first-out (LIFO) method** also depends on the costs of particular inventory purchases. LIFO is the opposite of FIFO. Under LIFO,

- The last costs into inventory are the first costs out to cost of goods sold.
- Ending inventory is based on the oldest costs—those of beginning inventory plus the earliest purchases of the period.

Exhibit 9-3 shows that the LIFO cost of ending inventory is $240. Cost of goods sold is $660. Panel A gives the data, and Panel D shows the LIFO computations.

OBJECTIVE 3
Describe the income effects of the inventory costing methods

The Income Effects of FIFO, LIFO, and Weighted-Average Cost

In our example, the cost of inventory rose during the accounting period from $10 per unit to $14 and finally to $18 (Exhibit 9-3, Panel A). When inventory unit costs

Panel A: Illustrative Data

Beginning inventory (10 units @ $10 per unit)		$ 100
Purchases		
No. 1 (25 units @ $14 per unit)...	$ 350	
No. 2 (25 units @ $18 per unit)...	450	
Total		800
Cost of goods available for sale (60 units)		$ 900
Ending inventory (20 units @ $? per unit).........................		(?)
Cost of goods sold (40 units @ $? per unit)		$?

Panel B: Ending Inventory and Cost of Goods Sold

Weighted-Average Cost Method

Cost of goods available for sale—see Panel A		
(60 units @ average cost of $15* per unit)		$ 900
Ending inventory (20 units @ $15 per unit).........................		(300)
Cost of goods sold (40 units @ $15 per unit)		$ 600

*Cost of goods available for sale...		$ 900
Number of units available for sale...		÷ 60
Average cost per unit		$ 15

Panel C: Ending Inventory and Cost of Goods Sold

FIFO Cost Method

Cost of goods available for sale (60 units—see Panel A)		$ 900
Ending inventory (cost of the *last* 20 units available):		
20 units @ $18 per unit (from purchase No. 2)		(360)
Cost of goods sold (cost of the *first* 40 units available)		
10 units @ $10 per unit (all of beginning inventory)	$ 100	
25 units @ $14 per unit (all of purchase No. 1)..............	350	
5 units @ $18 per unit (from purchase No. 2)	90	
Cost of goods sold		$ 540

Panel D: Ending Inventory and Cost of Goods Sold

LIFO Cost Method

Cost of goods available for sale (60 units—see Panel A)		$ 900
Ending inventory (cost of the *first* 20 units available):		
10 units @ $10 per unit (all of beginning inventory)	$(100)	
10 units @ $14 per unit (from purchase No. 1)	(140)	
Ending inventory...		(240)
Cost of goods sold (cost of the last 40 units available):		
25 units @ $18 per unit (all of purchase No. 2)..............	$450	
15 units @ $14 per unit (from purchase No. 1)	210	
Cost of goods sold		$ 660

EXHIBIT 9-3

Inventory and Cost of Goods Sold under Three Costing Methods: Weighted-Average (Panel B), FIFO (Panel C), and LIFO (Panel D)

THINKING IT OVER

How does inventory usually physically flow in and out of a business such as a grocery store?

A: The first goods purchased are the first sold. This is essentially the FIFO method. However, remember that cost flow need not coincide with the physical flow of goods.

THINKING IT OVER

In a period of rising prices, which inventory costing method forces the highest inventory cost into COGS?

A: LIFO assigns the most recent unit costs to COGS. Because COGS is highest using LIFO, net income will be lowest.

LEARNING TIP

A sand company illustrates the LIFO concept. When a sand company dumps new sand on a pile, the new sand lies on the top. When the company needs sand, it takes the new sand off the top. Thus the last sand (the newest sand) on the pile is the first off the pile.

KEY POINT

Remember that the terms *FIFO* and *LIFO* do not describe which goods are left but rather which goods are sold. FIFO assumes that goods in first are sold first; therefore, the last goods purchased are left in ending inventory. LIFO assumes that the last goods in are sold first; therefore, the first goods purchased are left in ending inventory.

change, the different costing methods produce different cost of goods sold and ending inventory figures, as Exhibit 9-3 shows (Panels B, C, and D). When inventory unit costs are *increasing*,

- FIFO ending inventory is *highest* because it is priced at the most recent costs, which are the highest.

- LIFO ending inventory is *lowest* because it is priced at the oldest costs, which are the lowest.

	Units	Cost/ Unit	
Beg. Inventory	50	$ 8	$ 400
Purch. #1	90	9	810
Purch. #2	70	11	770
Purch. #3	30	12	360
	240		$2,340

Compute the cost of the ending inventory under (1) FIFO, (2) LIFO, and (3) weighted-average cost assuming 70 units were on hand.
A: 1. $800 [(30 @ $12) + (40 @ $11)]
2. $580 [(50 @ $8) + (20 @ $9)]
3. $682.50 [($2,340 ÷ 240) × 70]

When inventory unit costs are *decreasing*,

- FIFO ending inventory is lowest.
- LIFO ending inventory is highest.

Exhibit 9-4 summarizes the income effects of the three inventory methods under the periodic inventory system using the data from Exhibit 9-3. Study the exhibit carefully, focusing on ending inventory, cost of goods sold, and gross margin.

Remember that the terms *FIFO* and *LIFO* do not describe which goods are left but rather which goods are sold. FIFO assumes that goods purchased first are sold first; therefore, the last goods purchased are left in ending inventory. LIFO assumes that the last goods in are sold first; therefore, the first goods purchased are left in ending inventory.

GAAP and Practical Considerations: A Comparison of the Inventory Methods

To judge the three major inventory costing methods, ask two questions:

1. How well does each method match cost of goods sold to sales revenue on the income statement?
2. Which method reports the most up-to-date inventory amount on the balance sheet?

Matching of Expense With Revenue on the Income Statement LIFO better matches the current value of cost of goods sold with current revenue by assigning to this expense the most recent inventory costs. Therefore, LIFO produces the cost of goods sold figure that is closest to what it would cost the company to replace the goods that were sold. In this sense, LIFO produces the best measure of net income. In contrast, FIFO matches the oldest inventory costs against the period's revenue—a poor matching of current expense with current revenue.

Current Inventory Cost on the Balance Sheet FIFO reports the most current inventory costs on the balance sheet. LIFO can result in misleading inventory costs on the balance sheet because the oldest prices are left in ending inventory.

EXHIBIT 9-4

Income Effects of FIFO, LIFO, and Weighted-Average Cost Inventory Methods (Periodic Inventory System)

	FIFO		LIFO		Weighted-Average	
Sales revenue (assumed)		$1,000		$1,000		$1,000
Cost of goods sold						
Goods available for sale (from Exhibit 9-3)	$900		$ 900		$ 900	
Ending inventory	(360)		(240)		(300)	
Cost of goods sold		540		660		600
Gross margin		$ 460		$ 340		$ 400

Summary of Income Effects: When Inventory Unit Costs Are *Increasing*

FIFO—Highest ending inventory	LIFO—Lowest ending inventory	Weighted-average—Results fall
Lowest cost of goods sold	Highest cost of goods sold	between the extremes of
Highest gross margin	Lowest gross margin	FIFO and LIFO

Summary of Income Effects: When Inventory Unit Costs Are *Decreasing*

FIFO—Lowest ending inventory	LIFO—Highest ending inventory	Weighted-average—Results fall
Highest cost of goods sold	Lowest cost of goods sold	between the extremes of
Lowest gross margin	Highest gross margin	FIFO and LIFO

Accounting and the *e*-World

How Do E-tailers Manage Inventory?

Bricks-and-mortar retailers like Canadian Tire have large stores with thousands of items on hand so that shoppers can find whatever product they are looking for, from tires to plumbing and electrical fixtures to sporting goods. Each of the 432 Canadian Tire Associate Stores carries a large-dollar inventory to provide this selection. Shoppers at a Canadian Tire store select the items they want from the store's shelves, pay for the item on their way out of the store, take it home, and can use it instantly.

E-tailers, or online merchandisers, are very different from the bricks-and-mortar merchandisers. E-tailers have a large inventory of items for sale over the web but the company itself may not stock all the items it offers for sale. When a customer purchases an item over the web, the e-tailer must locate the item (it may be in a warehouse under the e-tailer's control, in a manufacturer's warehouse, or somewhere else) and arrange to have the item shipped to the customer.

E-tailers typically promise accurate orders and fast delivery, but many customers have had the opposite experience. Stories of late deliveries, receipt of incorrect orders, and billing problems are common. Bricks-and-mortar retailers advertise that if the product the customer selected is not what was needed, the customer can bring it back for a different product or a refund. Billing problems can be resolved quickly in person.

To combat order and delivery problems, e-tailers have developed relationships with trucking/warehouse companies to be responsible for warehousing and deliveries. The e-tailer takes the order and arranges for the trucking/warehouse company to deliver the product to the customer. The arrangement seems to be a win-win-win situation for the e-tailer, the trucking/warehouse company, and the e-tailer's customer. The e-tailer manages the product delivery arrangements and billing, the trucking/warehouse company expands its business using existing facilities, and the customer gets quicker, and probably more reliable, delivery of the product desired.

THINKING IT OVER

In a period of rising prices, which inventory method—LIFO or FIFO—best fits each of the following statements?

1. Results in the highest income.
A: FIFO
2. More realistic inventory cost.
A: FIFO
3. Creates inventory profit.
A: FIFO
4. Results in higher profits if inventory levels decline.
A: LIFO
5. Better matches costs with revenues.
A: LIFO

KEY POINT

During a period of rising prices—
Advantages of FIFO:
1. Always reports current cost for ending inventory
2. Reports higher income

Advantages of LIFO:
1. Always matches expenses and revenues

Disadvantages of FIFO:
1. Violates the matching principle (FIFO matches some of the previous year's inventory cost against current revenue)
2. Does not adjust cost of goods sold for the effects of inflation

Disadvantages of LIFO:
1. Reports lower income
2. Reports understated ending inventory
3. Can be used to manipulate income

FIFO Produces Inventory Profits FIFO is sometimes criticized because it overstates income by so-called inventory profit during periods of inflation. Briefly, **inventory profit** is the difference between gross margin computed on the FIFO basis and gross margin computed on the LIFO basis. Exhibit 9-4 illustrates inventory profit. The $120 difference between FIFO and LIFO gross margins ($460 – $340) results from the difference in cost of goods sold. This $120 amount is called *FIFO inventory profit*, *phantom profit*, or *illusory profit*. Why? Because to stay in business, the company must replace the inventory it has sold. The replacement cost of the merchandise is more closely approximated by the cost of goods sold under LIFO ($660) than by the FIFO amount ($540).

LIFO Allows Managers to Manipulate Reported Income—Up or Down LIFO is often criticized because it allows managers to manipulate net income when using the periodic inventory method. When inventory prices are rising rapidly, and a company wants to show less income for the year, managers can buy a large amount of inventory near the end of the year. Under LIFO these high inventory costs immediately become expense—as cost of goods sold. As a result, the income statement reports a lower net income.

Conversely, if the business is having a bad year, the owner may wish to increase reported income. To do so, she or he can delay a large purchase of high-cost inventory until the next period. This inventory is not expensed as cost of goods sold in the current year. Thus the owner avoids decreasing the current year's reported income. In the process, the company draws down inventory quantities, a practice known as *inventory liquidation.*

International Perspective   Many companies manufacture their inventory in foreign countries to decrease transportation costs and to break down trade barriers. Companies that value inventory by the LIFO method in one country often must use another accounting method for their inventories in another country.

LIFO is very popular in the United States where its use is permitted for tax purposes. As you can see in Exhibit 9-4, in a period of rising prices (such as we have had since World War II), LIFO leads to the lowest income of the three methods and, in the United States, to the lowest taxes.

LIFO is not allowed for income tax purposes in Canada, Australia, or the United Kingdom, but a company can use it for accounting purposes. That is probably why in Canada, as the opening story pointed out, very few companies use LIFO (2 percent); here the largest percentage uses average cost (40 percent), while the next largest number uses FIFO (33 percent). In other countries, such as Australia and Sweden, LIFO is not permitted. Virtually all countries permit FIFO and the average cost method.

Which Method to Use?   A company may want to report higher income, and FIFO meets this need when prices are rising. When prices are falling, LIFO reports the higher income. GAAP allows either method if used consistently.

Which inventory method is best? There is no single answer to this question. Different companies have different motives for the inventory method they choose. Leon's Furniture and Loblaws report that they use lower of cost (FIFO) and net realizable value less a normal profit margin. BCT.TELUS Communications and Canadian Utilities (the energy company) use lower of average cost and net realizable value. Inco uses lower of cost and net realizable value for supplies and average production or purchase cost for metals. Potash Corporation of Saskatchewan uses both FIFO and average cost in valuing inventories at the lower of cost or market. Sleeman Breweries Ltd. uses lower of cost and net realizable value. Shell Canada Ltd. is among the very few companies that use LIFO. The companies disclose the method used under the heading "Significant Accounting Policies" or "Summary of Significant Accounting Policies" in the notes to the financial statements. Bombardier Inc.'s specific disclosure in the 2000 financial statements is:

> (a) **Raw materials, work in process, and finished products**
> Raw materials, work in process, and finished products, other than those included in long-term contracts and aerospace programs, are valued at the lower of cost (specific cost, average cost, or first-in, first out depending on the [business] segment) and replacement cost (raw materials) or net realizable value. The cost of work in process and finished products includes the cost of raw materials, direct labour, and related overhead....

Ivaco Inc.'s disclosure is

> **Inventories**
>
> Inventories are stated at the lower of cost (determined substantially on the first-in, first-out method) and net realizable value.

Suppose a Nortel Networks division that handles telephone components has this inventory record for January 2002 for a particular component:

Date		Item	Quantity	Unit Cost	Selling Price
Jan.	1	Beginning inventory	100 units	$ 8	
	6	Purchase	60 units	9	
	13	Sale	70 units		$ 20
	21	Purchase	150 units	9	
	24	Sale	210 units		22
	27	Purchase	90 units	10	
	30	Sale	30 units		25

Company accounting records reveal that operating expenses relating to this component for January amounted to $1,900.

Required

1. Prepare the January income statement, showing amounts for FIFO, LIFO, and weighted-average cost. Label the bottom line "Operating Income." (Round the weighted-average cost per unit to three decimal places and all other figures to whole dollar amounts.) Show your computations and use the periodic inventory model in Exhibit 9-4 to compute cost of goods sold.

2. Suppose you are the financial vice-president of Nortel Networks. Which inventory method would you use if your motive is to
   a. Minimize income taxes?
   b. Report the highest operating income?
   c. Report operating income between the extremes of FIFO and LIFO?
   d. Report inventory on the balance sheet at the most current cost?
   e. Attain the best matching of current expense with current revenue on the income statement?

   State the reason for each of your answers.

Solution to Review Problem

Requirement 1

NORTEL NETWORKS (TELEPHONE COMPONENTS DIVISION)
Partial Income Statement
For the Month Ended January 31, 2002

	FIFO		LIFO		Weighted-Average
Sales revenue..............................		$6,770		$6,770	$6,770
Cost of goods sold:					
Beginning inventory	$ 800		$ 800		$ 800
Purchases..............................	2,790		2,790		2,790
Cost of goods					
available for sale..............	3,590		3,590		3,590
Ending inventory..................	(900)		(720)		(808)
Cost of goods sold		2,690		2,870	2,782
Gross margin.............................		4,080		3,900	3,988
Operating expenses..................		1,900		1,900	1,900
Operating income.....................		$2,180		$2,000	$2,088

Computations

Sales revenue .... $(70 \times \$20) + (210 \times \$22) + (30 \times \$25) = \$6,770$
Beginning inventory ...... $100 \times \$8$ $= \$800$
Purchases .... $(60 \times \$9) + (150 \times \$9) + (90 \times \$10) = \$2,790$
Ending inventory: FIFO .. $90^* \times \$10$ $= \$900$
                LIFO .. $90^* \times \$8$ $= \$720$
Weighted-average .... $90 \times \$8.975^{**}$ $= \$808$
.... (rounded from \$807.75)

---

*Number of units in ending inventory $= 100 + 60 - 70 + 150 - 210 + 90 - 30 = 90$
$^{**}\$3,590/400$ units $= \$8.975$ per unit
Number of units available $= 100 + 60 + 150 + 90 = 400$

Requirement 2

a. Use average cost to minimize income taxes. Operating income under LIFO is lowest when inventory unit costs are increasing, as they are in this case (from $8 to $10). Remember, LIFO cannot be used for income tax purposes in Canada.

   Average cost produces the next lowest income and, since it can be used for tax purposes, the lowest income taxes.

b. Use FIFO to report the highest operating income. Income under FIFO is highest when inventory unit costs are increasing, as in this situation.

c. Use weighted-average cost to report an operating income amount between the LIFO and FIFO extremes. This is true in this problem situation and in others whether inventory unit costs are increasing or decreasing.

d. Use FIFO to report inventory at the most current cost. The oldest inventory costs are expensed as cost of goods sold, leaving in ending inventory the most recent (most current) costs of the period.

e. Use LIFO to attain the best matching of current expense with current revenue. The most recent (most current) inventory costs are expensed as cost of goods sold.

The Perpetual Inventory System and Inventory Costing Methods

Many companies keep their perpetual inventory records in quantities only, as illustrated in Exhibit 9-1. Other companies keep perpetual records in both quantities and dollar costs. Here we show how the four inventory costing methods are applied in a *perpetual* inventory system.

FIFO

CompuSave uses the FIFO inventory method. Exhibit 9-5 shows CompuSave's perpetual inventory record for XL Computers in both quantities and dollar costs for the month of November.

To prepare financial statements at November 30, CompuSave can take the ending inventory cost ($3,280) straight to the balance sheet. Cost of goods sold for the November income statement is $18,560. Here is CompuSave's computation of cost of goods sold during November, with data taken from the perpetual record in Exhibit 9-5:

Cost of Goods Sold (XL Computers)—November		
	Beginning inventory	$8,000
+	Purchases	13,840
=	Cost of goods available for sale	21,840
–	Ending inventory	(3,280)
=	Cost of goods sold	$18,560

EXHIBIT 9-5

Perpetual Inventory Record—FIFO Cost for CompuSave

CompuSave									
Item: XL Computer									
	Received			**Sold**			**Balance**		
Date	Qty.	Unit Cost	Total	Qty.	Unit Cost	Total	Qty.	Unit Cost	Total
Nov. 1							10	$800	$8,000
8				6	$800	$4,800	4	800	3,200
10	10	$810	$8,100				4	800	3,200
							10	810	8,100
14				4	800	3,200			
				5	810	4,050	5	810	4,050
19	7	820	5,740				5	810	4,050
							7	820	5,740
27				5	810	4,050			
				3	820	2,460	4	820	3,280
Total	17		$13,840	23		$18,560	4	820	$3,280

Some companies combine elements of the perpetual and periodic inventory systems—the perpetual system for control and preparation of the financial statements, and the periodic system for analysis.

LIFO

Few companies keep perpetual inventory records at LIFO cost. The recordkeeping is expensive, and LIFO liquidations can occur during the year. LIFO liquidations occur when the LIFO method is used and inventory quantities fall below the level of the previous period. To compute cost of goods sold, the company must use inventory costs from a prior year. During a period of rising inventory unit costs, older, lower costs are used to compute cost of goods sold, resulting in higher net income than if no LIFO liquidation had occurred. To avoid these problems, LIFO companies can keep perpetual inventory records in terms of quantities only, as illustrated in Exhibit 9-1. For financial statements, they apply LIFO costs at the end of the period. Other LIFO companies maintain perpetual inventory records at FIFO cost and then convert the FIFO amounts to LIFO costs for the financial statements. This topic is covered in intermediate accounting courses.

Weighted-Average Cost

Perpetual inventory records can be kept at weighted-average cost. Some companies that use this method compute the weighted-average cost for the entire period. They apply this cost to both ending inventory and cost of goods sold. These procedures parallel those used in the periodic inventory system (Exhibit 9-3).

The use of computer software to account for inventory eases the computation of the average cost per unit each time additional goods are purchased. The new average unit cost is applied to each subsequent sale until more goods are purchased, at which time another new average cost is computed. This method gives the **moving weighted-average cost.** It is called "moving" because the unit cost is adjusted each time there is a purchase; it is called "weighted-average" because the units on hand and units purchased affect the cost proportionately, as discussed on page 464.

STOP & THINK

Examine Exhibit 9-5. What was CompuSave's moving weighted-average unit cost during November? How much were ending inventory and cost of goods sold at moving weighted-average unit cost? What was the cost of goods available for sale?

Answer:

Date	Received			Sold			Balance		
	Qty.	Unit Cost	Total	Qty.	Unit Cost	Total	Qty.	Unit Cost	Total
Nov. 1							10	$800.00	$8,000.00
8				6	$800.00	$4,800.00	4	800.00	3,200.00
10	10	$810.00	$8,100.00				14	807.14*	11,300.00
14				9	807.14	7,264.29	5	807.14	4,035.71
19	7	820.00	5,740.00				12	814.64**	9,775.71
27				8	814.64	6,517.14	4	814.64	3,258.57

*$11,300.00 ÷ 14 units = $807.14 per unit
**$9,775.71 ÷ 12 units = $814.64 per unit

Ending inventory = 4 units × $814.64 = $3,258.57
Cost of goods sold = $4,800.00 + $7,264.29 + $6,517.14 = $18,581.43
Cost of goods available for sale = $8,000.00 + $8,100.00 + $5,740.00 = $21,840.00

Accounting Principles and Their Relevance to Inventories

Several of the generally accepted accounting principles have special relevance to inventories. Among them are the consistency principle, the disclosure principle, the materiality concept, and accounting conservatism.

Consistency Principle

The **consistency principle** states that businesses should use the same accounting methods and procedures from period to period. Consistency makes it possible to compare a company's financial statements from one period to the next.

Suppose you are analyzing a company's net income pattern over a two-year period. The company switched from LIFO to FIFO during that time. Its net income has increased dramatically, but only as a result of the change in inventory method. If you did not know of the change, you might believe that the company's increased income arose from improved operations, which is not the case.

The consistency principle does not require that all companies within an industry use the same accounting method. Nor does it mean that a company may *never* change its accounting methods. However, a company making an accounting change must apply the change retroactively and must disclose the reason for the change and the effect of the change on net income and any other financial statement accounts. Sun Company, Inc., an oil company, disclosed the following in a note to its annual report:

> EXCERPT FROM NOTE 6 OF THE SUN COMPANY FINANCIAL STATEMENTS
>
> ... Sun changed its method of accounting for the cost of crude oil and refined product inventories at Sun from the FIFO method to the LIFO method. Sun believes that the use of the LIFO method better matches current costs with current revenues ... The change decreased the current year's net loss ... by $3 million ...

Disclosure Principle

The **disclosure principle** holds that a company's financial statements should report enough information for outsiders to make knowledgeable decisions about the company. In short, the company should report *relevant*, *reliable*, and *comparable* information about its economic affairs. With respect to inventories, the disclosure principle means to disclose the method or methods used to value inventories. For example, suppose a banker is comparing two companies—one using LIFO and the other, FIFO. The FIFO company reports higher net income in times of rising prices, but only because it uses a particular inventory method. Without knowledge of the accounting methods the companies are using, the banker could loan money to the wrong business or could refuse a loan to a promising customer. The major categories of inventory must also be disclosed, usually in the notes to the financial statements. For a manufacturer, major categories might include raw materials, goods in process, and finished goods. The valuation of inventory at the lower of cost or market should also be disclosed as discussed later in this chapter.

Materiality Concept

The **materiality concept** states that a company must perform strictly proper accounting *only* for items and transactions that are significant to the business's financial statements. Information is significant—or in accounting terminology, *material*—when its inclusion and correct presentation in the financial statements would cause a statement user to change a decision because of that information. Immaterial—nonsignificant—items justify less-than-perfect accounting. Their inclusion and proper presentation would not affect a statement user's decision. The materiality concept frees accountants from having to compute and report every last item in strict accordance with GAAP. Thus the materiality concept reduces the cost of recording accounting information.

How does a business decide where to draw the line between the material and the immaterial? This decision rests to a great degree on how large the business is. Westcoast Energy, for example, has close to $12 billion in assets. Management would likely treat as immaterial a $1,000 loss of inventory. A loss of this amount is immaterial to Westcoast Energy's total assets and net income, so company accountants may not report the loss separately. Will this accounting treatment affect anyone's decision about Westcoast Energy? Probably not, so it doesn't matter whether the loss is reported separately or simply embedded in cost of goods sold.

Accounting Conservatism

Conservatism in accounting means to report items in the financial statements at amounts that lead to the most cautious immediate financial results. Conservatism comes into play when there are alternative ways to account for an item. What advantage does conservatism give a business? Managers are often optimistic about being good leaders. This optimism sometimes causes them to look on the bright side of operations, and they may overstate a company's income and asset values. Many accountants regard conservatism as a counterbalance to management's optimistic tendencies. The goal is for financial statements to present realistic figures.

Conservatism appears in accounting guidelines such as

- "Anticipate no gains, but provide for all probable losses."
- "If in doubt, record an asset at the lowest reasonable amount and a liability at the highest reasonable amount."
- "When there's a question, debit an expense account rather than an asset."

Conservatism directs accountants to decrease the accounting value of an asset if it appears unrealistically high—even if no transaction occurs. Assume that a company paid $35,000 for inventory that has become obsolete, and its current value is only $12,000. Conservatism dictates that the inventory be *written down* (that is, decreased) to $12,000.

Lower-of-Cost-or-Market Rule

OBJECTIVE 4
Apply the lower-of-cost-or-market rule to inventory

······· **THINKING IT OVER**

In an inflationary period, most companies do not experience declining inventory prices. But in some cases inventory replacement cost is lower than historical cost. Give examples and reasons.

A: Due to technological advances, video recorders, compact disks, and computers have become cheaper. Fuel and some food products may decrease in cost due to changes in politics (affecting availability), weather, or consumer preference.

The **lower-of-cost-or-market rule** (abbreviated as **LCM**) shows accounting conservatism in action. LCM requires that an asset be reported in the financial statements at whichever is lower—its historical cost or its market value. Applied to inventories, *market value* may mean *current replacement cost* (that is, how much the business would have to pay in the market on that day to purchase the amount of inventory that it has on hand), or it may mean *net realizable value* (that is, the gross amount the business could get if it sold the inventory less the costs of selling it). If the replacement cost or net realizable value of inventory falls below its historical cost, the business must write down the value of its goods because of the likelihood of incurring a loss on the inventory in the future. GAAP requires this departure from historical cost accounting. The business reports ending inventory at its LCM value on the balance sheet. All this can be done automatically by a computerized accounting system. How is the write-down accomplished?

Suppose a business paid $3,000 for inventory on September 26. By December 31, its value has fallen. The inventory can now be replaced for $2,200 and the decline in value appears permanent. Market value, defined in this instance as current replacement cost, is below cost, and the December 31 balance sheet reports this inventory at its LCM value of $2,200.

Exhibit 9-6 presents the effects of LCM on the income statement and the balance sheet. The exhibit shows that the lower of (a) cost or (b) market value replacement cost is the relevant amount for valuing inventory on the balance sheet. Now examine

Income Statement

Sales revenue		$20,000
Cost of goods sold:		
Beginning inventory (LCM = Cost)	**$ 2,800**	
Net purchases	11,000	
Cost of goods available for sale................	13,800	
Ending inventory—		
Cost = $3,000*		
Replacement cost (market value) = $2,200*		
LCM = Market....................................	**2,200**	
Cost of goods sold		11,600
Gross margin...		$ 8,400

Balance Sheet

Current assets:		
Cash..	$ XXX	
Short-term investments	XXX	
Accounts receivable	XXX	
Inventories, at market (which is lower		
than $3,000 cost)..............................	2,200	
Prepaid expenses...................................	XXX	
Total current assets................................	$X,XXX	

*Note that this information does not normally appear on the income statement. It is shown here to demonstrate the effect on Cost of Goods Sold.

EXHIBIT 9-6

Lower-of-Cost-or-Market (LCM) Effects

LEARNING **TIP**

Note that the matching principle is applied to "Ending Inventory" in Exhibit 9-6. The reduction in the value of the inventory is shown in the year the inventory declines in value, *not* in the year the inventory is sold.

the income statement in Exhibit 9-6. What expense absorbs the impact of the $800 inventory write-down calculated as cost, $3,000 – market, $2,200? Cost of goods sold is debited when inventory is credited as follows in a perpetual inventory system:

Dec. 31	Costs of Goods Sold	800	
	Inventory		800

(It is also possible for an inventory write-down to be recorded and reported as a loss on write-down of inventory on the income statement. This is often done for large, one-time write-downs that are disclosed separately and not charged to cost of goods sold.)

Companies may use either net realizable value or replacement cost for market value, depending on which value is most appropriate. For example, net realizable value may be most appropriate for an inventory of equipment available for rent, while replacement cost may be more appropriate for raw materials. In 1998, 58 percent of 162 reporting companies used some form of net realizable value, 6 percent used replacement cost, and 36 percent used more than one method, according to *Financial Reporting in Canada*, 1999.[2]

Companies often disclose LCM in notes to their financial statements, as shown below for Spar Aerospace Limited:

FROM NOTE 1
(c) Inventories
Inventories of raw materials and finished goods are valued at the lower of cost ... and market value determined as the lesser of replacement cost or net realizable value.

Spar Aerospace Limited
www.spar.ca

---

[2] *Ibid.*, page 231.

IPSCO Inc., the steel products producer, states the following in the notes to the financial statements:

FROM NOTE 2—SIGNIFICANT ACCOUNTING POLICIES
Inventories
Inventories are valued at the lowest of cost, replacement cost and net realizable value.

OBJECTIVE 5
Determine the effects of inventory errors on cost of goods sold and net income

THINKING IT OVER

Suppose an error is made in computing the cost of inventory in 2002. What are the effects on the financial statements in 2002 and 2003?

A: In 2002: Ending inventory, total assets, COGS, gross margin, net income, and retained earnings are all affected. In 2003: COGS, gross margin, and net income are affected. Ending inventory, total assets, and retained earnings would all be correctly stated.

Effects of Inventory Errors

Businesses count their inventories at the end of the period in the case of the periodic system, and during or at the end of the period in the case of the perpetual system. In the process of counting the items, applying unit costs, and computing amounts, errors may arise. To highlight the effects of such errors, consider three identical, consecutive accounting periods, as shown in Exhibit 9-7. As the period 1 segment of Exhibit 9-7 shows, an error in the ending inventory amount creates errors in the amounts for cost of goods sold and gross margin. Compare period 1, when ending inventory is overstated, and cost of goods sold is understated, each by $5,000, with period 3, which is correct. Period 1 should look exactly like period 3.

Recall that one period's ending inventory is the next period's beginning inventory. Thus the error in ending inventory carries over into the next period. Note the highlighted amounts in Exhibit 9-7.

Because ending inventory is *subtracted* in computing cost of goods sold in one period and the same amount is *added* as beginning inventory to compute next period's cost of goods sold, the error's effect cancels out at the end of the second period. The overstatement of cost of goods sold in period 2 counterbalances the understatement in cost of goods sold in period 1. Thus the total gross margin amount for the two periods is the correct $100,000 figure, whether or not there is an error. As a result, owner's equity at the end of period 2 is correct. These effects are summarized in Exhibit 9-8.

Inventory errors cannot be ignored simply because they counterbalance. Suppose you are analyzing trends in the business's operations. Exhibit 9-7 shows a drop in gross margin from period 1 to period 2, followed by an increase in period 3. But that picture of operations is untrue because of the accounting error. The correct gross margin is $50,000 for each period. Providing accurate information for decision making requires that all inventory errors be corrected.

EXHIBIT 9-7

Inventory Errors: An Example

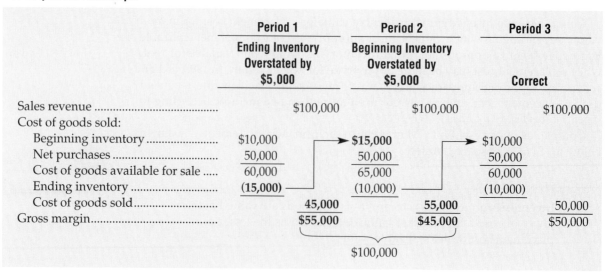

	Period 1	Period 2	Period 3
	Ending Inventory Overstated by $5,000	Beginning Inventory Overstated by $5,000	Correct
Sales revenue	$100,000	$100,000	$100,000
Cost of goods sold:			
Beginning inventory	$10,000	$15,000	$10,000
Net purchases	50,000	50,000	50,000
Cost of goods available for sale	60,000	65,000	60,000
Ending inventory	(15,000)	(10,000)	(10,000)
Cost of goods sold	45,000	55,000	50,000
Gross margin	$55,000	$45,000	$50,000

$100,000

Source: The authors thank Carl High for this example.

Inventory Error	Period 1			Period 2		
	Cost of Goods Sold	Gross Margin and Net Income	Ending Owner's Equity	Cost of Goods Sold	Gross Margin and Net Income	Ending Owner's Equity
Period 1 Ending inventory overstated	Understated	Overstated	Overstated	Overstated	Understated	Correct
Period 1 Ending inventory understated	Overstated	Understated	Understated	Understated	Overstated	Correct

EXHIBIT 9-8

Effects of Inventory Errors

Other Inventory Issues

Ethical Issues

No area of accounting has a deeper ethical dimension than inventory. Owners and managers of companies whose profits do not meet expectations are sometimes tempted to "cook the books" to increase reported income. The increase in reported income may lead investors and creditors into thinking the business is more successful than it really is.

What do managers hope to gain from the fraudulent accounting? In some cases, they are trying to keep their jobs. In other cases, their bonuses are tied to reported income. The higher the company's net income, the higher the managers' bonuses. In still other cases, the business may need a loan. Financial statements that report high profits and large inventory values are more likely to impress lenders than low net income and inventory accounts.

There are two main schemes for using inventory to increase reported income. The easier, and the most obvious, is simply to overstate ending inventory. (This is more easily done under the periodic inventory system.) In the preceding section on the effects of inventory errors, we saw how an error in ending inventory affects net income. A company can intentionally overstate its ending inventory. Such an error understates cost of goods sold and overstates net income and owner's equity, as shown in the accounting equation. The upward-pointing arrows indicate an overstatement—reporting more assets and equity than are actually present:

$$
\begin{array}{ccccc}
\text{Assets} & = & \text{Liabilities} & + & \text{Owner's Equity} \\
\hline
\uparrow & = & 0 & + & \uparrow
\end{array}
$$

The second way of using inventory to increase reported income involves sales. Sales schemes are more complex than simple inventory overstatements. Datapoint Corporation and MiniScribe, both computer-related companies, were charged with creating fictitious sales to boost their reported profits.

Datapoint Corporation is alleged to have hired drivers to transport its inventory around the city so that the goods could *not* be physically counted. Datapoint's logic seemed to be that excluding the goods from ending inventory would imply that the goods had been sold. The faulty reasoning broke down when the trucks returned the goods to Datapoint's warehouse. Datapoint had far too much in sales returns the following year. What would you think of a company with $10 million in sales if $4 million worth of the goods were returned by consumers?

MiniScribe is alleged to have "cooked its books" by shipping boxes of bricks labelled as computer parts to its distributors right before year end. The distributors refused to accept the goods and returned them to Mini-Scribe—but in the next accounting period. In the earlier period, MiniScribe recorded sales revenue and

WORKING IT OUT

The December 31 ending inventory and net income are $162,000 and $868,000, respectively. Inventory costing $2,000 shipped FOB shipping point was in transit on December 31 and not included in the ending inventory. However, the purchase was correctly recorded. What is the correct amount of inventory and net income for the year?

A: Inventory—$164,000. Net income—$870,000.

KEY POINT

Recognize that a dollar change in ending inventory means a dollar change in income. This is one reason auditors examine the ending inventory so carefully. An income statement may be manipulated by altering the amount of ending inventory.

Datapoint Corporation
www.datapoint.com

temporarily reported millions of dollars of sales and income that did not exist. Again, the offsetting effect occurred in the next period when MiniScribe had to record the sales returns. In virtually every area, accounting imposes a discipline that works to keep every business honest in its financial reporting.

OBJECTIVE 6
Estimate ending inventory by the gross margin method and the retail method

Estimating Inventory

Often a business must *estimate* the value of its inventory. Because of cost and inconvenience, few companies physically count and verify the accuracy of their inventories at the end of each month, yet they may need monthly financial statements for external users. If the company does not use the perpetual inventory system, it cannot determine inventory by looking at the Inventory account.

A fire or a flood may destroy inventory, and to file an insurance claim, the business must estimate the value of its loss. In both cases, the business needs to know the value of ending inventory without being able to count it. A widely used method for estimating ending inventory is the *gross margin method*. Another is the *retail method*.

Gross Margin (Gross Profit) Method   The **gross margin method** (also known as the **gross profit method**) is a way of estimating inventory based on the familiar cost of goods sold model (amounts assumed for illustration):

Beginning inventory	$10
+ Purchases	50
= Cost of goods available for sale	60
− **Ending inventory**	**(20)**
= **Cost of goods sold**	**$40**

Rearranging *ending inventory* and *cost of goods sold* makes the model useful for estimating ending inventory, and is illustrated in the following equation and in Exhibit 9-9 (amounts assumed for illustration):

Beginning inventory	$10
+ Purchases	50
= Cost of goods available for sale	60
− **Cost of goods sold**	**(40)**
= **Ending inventory**	**$20**

WORKING IT OUT

Beginning inventory is $100,000, net purchases total $500,000, and net sales are $800,000. With a normal gross margin rate of 32%, how much is ending inventory using the gross margin method?
A: $56,000 [$100,000 + $500,000 − (0.68 × $800,000)]

Suppose a fire destroys your business's inventory. To collect insurance, you must estimate the cost of the ending inventory. Beginning inventory and purchases amounts may be taken directly from the accounting records. Sales Revenue less Sales Returns and Allowances and Sales Discounts indicates net sales up to the date of the fire. Using the entity's normal *gross margin percent* (that is, gross margin divided by net sales revenue), you can estimate cost of goods sold. The last step is to subtract cost of goods sold from goods available to estimate ending inventory. Exhibit 9-9 illustrates the gross margin method.

Accountants, managers and auditors use the gross margin method to test the overall reasonableness of an ending inventory amount that has been determined by a physical count for all types of businesses. This method helps detect large errors.

Retail Method   The **retail method** of estimating the cost of ending inventory is often used by retail establishments that use the periodic system. This is because it is often easier for retail establishments to calculate the selling price, or retail price, of a wide range of items rather than to look at all the individual invoices to find the costs of each of those items.

Beginning inventory..	$16,000
Purchases	66,000
Cost of goods available for sale................................	82,000
Cost of goods sold:	
Net sales revenue.. $100,000	
Less estimated gross margin of 40%........................ (40,000)	
Estimated cost of goods sold	(60,000)
Estimated cost of *ending inventory*...............................	$22,000

EXHIBIT 9-9

Gross Margin Method of Estimating Inventory (amounts assumed)

LEARNING TIP

Remember that the gross margin % + the cost of goods sold % = 100%. If gross margin is 35% of sales, then cost of goods sold is 65% of sales.

Like the gross margin method, the retail method is based on the familiar cost of goods sold model, rearranged to calculate ending inventory:

Beginning inventory
+Net purchases
=Cost of goods available for sale
−Cost of goods sold
=Ending inventory

REAL WORLD EXAMPLE

The gross margin and retail methods are also used to estimate inventory for interim periods when it is impractical to take a physical inventory.

However, to use the retail method, a business must know both the total cost and the total selling price of its opening inventory, as well as both the total cost and total selling price of its net purchases. Total selling price is determined by counting each item of inventory and multiplying it by the item's retail selling price (the price given on the price tag). By summing the costs and selling prices of beginning inventory and net purchases, the business knows the cost and retail selling price of the goods it has available for sale.

The business can calculate the selling price of its sales because this is the sum of the amounts recorded on the cash register when sales are made. The total of sales at retail is deducted from the total selling price of the goods available for sale to give the total selling price of ending inventory. To convert ending inventory at selling price to ending inventory at cost, the business multiplies the ending inventory at selling price by the *retail ratio*. The retail ratio is the ratio of cost of goods available for sale at *cost* to the cost of goods available for sale at *selling price*. It is usually expressed as a percent. Exhibit 9-10 illustrates the retail method.

The retail method can be used to estimate inventory at any point in time, and it is acceptable to use the retail method to calculate year-end inventory cost for financial statement and income tax purposes, although an inventory count must be done at least once per year.

Internal Control over Inventory

Internal control over inventory is important because inventory is the lifeblood of a merchandiser. Successful companies take great care to protect their inventory. Elements of good internal control over inventory include

	Cost	Selling Price
Beginning inventory	$151,000	$216,000
Purchases	504,200	720,000
Goods available for sale	655,200	936,000
Net sales, at selling price (retail)		696,000
Ending inventory, at selling price (retail)		$240,000
Ending inventory, at cost ($240,000 × *70%)	$168,000	
*Retail ratio = ($655,200 ÷ 936,000) × 100 = 70%		

EXHIBIT 9-10

Retail Method of Estimating Inventory (amounts assumed)

1. Physically counting inventory at least once each year no matter which system is used.
2. Storing inventory to protect it against theft, damage, and decay.
3. Allowing access to inventory only to personnel who do *not* have access to the accounting records.
4. Keeping perpetual inventory records for high-unit-cost merchandise.
5. Keeping enough inventory on hand to prevent shortages, which lead to lost sales.
6. Not keeping too large an inventory stockpiled, thus avoiding the expense of tying up money in unneeded items and reducing the risk of obsolescence.
7. Purchasing inventory in economical quantities to reduce costs.

The annual physical count of inventory (item 1) is necessary because the only way to be certain of the amount and condition of inventory on hand is to count it. Errors arise in the best accounting systems, and the count is needed to establish the correct value of the inventory. When an error is detected, the records are brought into agreement with the physical count.

Keeping inventory handlers away from the accounting records (item 3) is an essential separation of duties, discussed in Chapter 7. An employee with access to inventory and the accounting records can steal the goods and make an entry to conceal the theft. For example, the employee could increase the amount of an inventory write-down to make it appear that goods decreased in value when in fact they were stolen.

Computerized inventory systems allow companies to minimize both the amount of inventory on hand and the chances of running out of stock (items 5 and 6). In an increasingly competitive business environment, companies cannot afford to have cash invested in too much inventory. Many manufacturing companies use *just-in-time (JIT) inventory systems*, which require suppliers to deliver materials just in time to be used in the production process. Just-in-time systems help minimize the amount of money a company has invested in inventory.

DECISION GUIDELINES — *Guidelines for Inventory Management*

Decision	Guidelines	System or Method
Which inventory system to use?	• Expensive merchandise • Cannot control inventory by visual inspection	⟶ Perpetual system
	• Can control inventory by visual inspection	⟶ Periodic system
Which costing method to use?	Unique Inventory Items	⟶ Specific unit cost
	• Most current cost in ending inventory • Maximizes reported income when costs are rising	⟶ FIFO
	• Most current measure of cost of goods sold and net income	⟶ LIFO
	• Middle-of-the-road approach for reported income	⟶ Weighted-average
How to estimate the cost of ending inventory?	• The cost-of-goods-sold model provides the framework	⟶ Gross margin (gross profit) method
	• Standard mark ups from cost price to selling price are used for all inventory items	⟶ Retail method

This chapter has discussed various aspects of controlling and accounting for inventory, cost of goods sold, and gross margin. The Decision Guidelines feature on page 480 summarizes some basic decision guidelines that are helpful in managing a business's inventory operations.

Summary Problem
for Your Review

Red Maple Hardware began 2003 with 60,000 units of inventory that cost $36,000. During 2003, Red Maple Hardware purchased merchandise on account for $352,500 as follows:

Purchase 1: 100,000 units, costing ....$ 65,000
Purchase 2: 270,000 units, costing 175,500
Purchase 3: 160,000 units, costing 112,000

Cash payments on account totalled $326,000 during the year.

Red Maple Hardware sales during 2003 consisted of 520,000 units of inventory for $660,000, all on account. The company uses the FIFO inventory method.

Cash collections from customers were $630,000. Operating expenses totalled $240,500, of which Red Maple Hardware paid $211,000 in cash. The company credited Accrued Liabilities for the remainder.

Required

1. Make summary journal entries to record Red Maple Hardware's transactions for the year, assuming the company uses a perpetual inventory system.

2. Determine the FIFO cost of Red Maple Hardware's ending inventory at December 31, 2003, two ways:
   a. Use a T-account.
   b. Multiply the number of units by the unit cost.

3. Use the cost-of-goods-sold model to show how Red Maple Hardware would compute cost of goods sold for 2003 under the periodic inventory system.

4. Prepare Red Maple Hardware's income statement for 2003. Show totals for the gross margin and net income.

Solution to Review Problem

Requirement 1

Inventory ($65,000 + $175,500 + $112,000)	352,500	
Accounts Payable		352,500
Accounts Payable...	326,000	
Cash..		326,000
Accounts Receivable...	660,000	
Sales Revenue		660,000
Cost of Goods Sold...	339,500	
Inventory		339,500

Cost of Goods Sold = $339,500 [$36,000 + $65,000 + $175,500 + $112,000 − 49,000 (calculated as $112,000/160,000 units = $0.70 × 70,000 units)]

Cash..	630,000	
Accounts Receivable		630,000
Operating Expenses		
(represents many individual expense accounts)	240,500	
Cash...		211,000
Accrued Liabilities		29,500

Requirement 2

a.

Inventory	
36,000	339,500
352,500	
49,000	

b. Number of units in ending inventory

(60,000 + 100,000 + 270,000 + 160,000 − 520,000)	70,000
Unit cost of ending inventory at FIFO ($112,000 ÷ 160,000)	× $ 0.70
FIFO cost of ending inventory............	$49,000

Requirement 3

Cost of goods sold (periodic inventory system):	
Beginning inventory	$ 36,000
Purchases..	352,500
Cost of goods available for sale......	388,500
Ending inventory	(49,000)
Cost of goods sold............................	$339,500

Requirement 4

RED MAPLE HARDWARE
Income Statement
For the Year Ended December 31, 2003

Sales revenue...	$660,000
Cost of goods sold	339,500
Gross margin..	320,500
Operating expenses.............................	240,500
Net income	$ 80,000

Cyber Coach

Visit the Student Resource area of the *Accounting* Companion Website for extra practice with the new material in Chapter 9.

www.pearsoned.ca/horngren

Summary

1. **Account for inventory by the perpetual and periodic systems.** Accounting for inventory plays an important part in merchandisers' accounting systems because selling inventory is the heart of their business. Inventory is generally the largest current asset on their balance sheet, and inventory expense—called *cost of goods sold*—is usually the largest expense on the income statement.

Merchandisers can choose between two inventory systems. In a *periodic inventory system*, the business does not keep a running record of the inventory on hand. Instead, at the end of the period, the business counts the inventory on hand and then updates its records. In a *perpetual inventory system*, the business keeps a continuous record for each inventory item to show the inventory on hand at all times. A physical count of inventory is needed in both systems for control purposes.

2. **Apply the inventory costing methods: specific unit cost, weighted-average cost, FIFO, and LIFO.** Businesses multiply the quantity of inventory items by their unit cost to determine inventory cost. There are four inventory costing methods : *specific unit cost*; *weighted-average cost*; *first-in, first-out (FIFO) cost*; and *last-in, first-out (LIFO) cost*. Only businesses that sell unique items, such as automobiles and jewels, use the specific-unit-cost method. Most other companies use the other methods. FIFO reports ending inventory at the most current cost. LIFO reports cost of goods sold at the most current cost. Weighted-average cost falls in the middle.

3. **Describe the income effects of the inventory costing methods.** When prices are rising, LIFO produces the highest cost of goods sold and the lowest income but may not be used in Canada for tax purposes. FIFO results in the highest income. The weighted-average cost method gives results between the extremes of FIFO and LIFO.

4. **Apply the lower-of-cost-or-market rule to inventory.** The *lower-of-cost-or-market (LCM) rule*—an example of accounting *conservatism*—requires that businesses report inventory on the balance sheet at the lower of its cost or current replacement or net realizable value. Companies disclose their definition of "market" for purposes of applying LCM in notes to their financial statements.

5. **Determine the effects of inventory errors on cost of goods sold and net income.** Although inventory overstatements in one period are counterbalanced by inventory understatements in the next period, effective decision making depends on accurate inventory information.

6. **Estimate ending inventory by the gross margin method and the retail method.** The *gross margin method* and the *retail method* are techniques for estimating the cost of ending inventory. They are useful for preparing interim financial statements and for estimating the cost of inventory destroyed by fire or other disasters.

Self-Study Questions

Test your understanding of the chapter by marking the correct answer to each of the following questions:

1. Which of the following items is the greatest in dollar amount? (*p. 461*)
   a. Beginning inventory   d. Ending inventory
   b. Purchases   e. Cost of goods sold
   c. Cost of goods available for sale

2. Sound Warehouse counts 6,000 compact discs, including 1,000 CDs held on consignment, in its Halifax store. The business has purchased an additional 2,000 CDs on FOB destination terms. These goods are still in transit. Each CD costs $3.40. The cost of the inventory to report on the balance sheet is (*p. 462*)
   a. $17,000   c. $23,800
   b. $20,400   d. $27,200

3. The inventory costing method that best matches current expense with current revenues is (*pp. 466–468*)
   a. Specific unit cost   e. FIFO or LIFO,
   b. Weighted-average   depending on whether
      cost   inventory costs are
   c. FIFO   increasing or
   d. LIFO   decreasing

4. Why do companies prefer the LIFO inventory method during a period of rising prices? (*p. 465*)
   a. Higher reported income
   b. Lower reported income
   c. Lower cost of goods sold
   d. Higher ending inventory

5. The consistency principle has the most direct impact on (*p. 473*)

   a. Whether to include or exclude an item in inventory
   b. Whether to change from one inventory method to another
   c. Whether to write inventory down to a market value below cost
   d. Whether to use the periodic or the perpetual inventory system

6. Application of the lower-of-cost-or-market rule often results in (*p. 474*)
   a. Higher ending inventory
   b. Lower ending inventory
   c. A counterbalancing error
   d. A change from one inventory method to another

7. An error understated ending inventory of 2002. This error will (*p. 476*)
   a. Overstate 2002 cost of sales
   b. Understate 2003 cost of sales
   c. Not affect owner's equity at the end of 2003
   d. All of the above

8. Beginning inventory was $35,000, purchases were $146,000, and sales totalled $240,000. With a normal gross margin rate of 35 percent, how much is ending inventory? (*p. 478*)
   a. $25,000   c. $97,000
   b. $35,000   d. $181,000

9. The year-end entry to close beginning inventory in a perpetual inventory system is (*p. 458*)
   a. Income Summary XXX
        Inventory   XXX
   b. Inventory XXX
        Income Summary   XXX

c. Either of the above, depending on whether inventory increased or decreased during the period

d. Not needed

10. Which of the following statements is true? (p. 457)
    a. Separation of duties is not an important element of internal control for inventories.

b. The perpetual system is used primarily for low-unit-cost inventory.

c. An annual physical count of inventory is needed regardless of the type of inventory system used.

d. All the above are true.

Answers to the Self-Study Questions follow the Similar Accounting Terms.

Accounting Vocabulary

Average-cost method (p. 464)
Conservatism (p. 474)
Consignment (p. 462)
Consistency principle (p. 473)
Cost of goods available for sale (p. 461)
Disclosure principle (p. 473)
First-in, first-out (FIFO) inventory costing method (p. 464)
Gross margin (p. 457)
Gross margin method (p. 478)
Gross profit (p. 457)
Gross profit method (p. 478)
Inventory profit (p. 467)

Last-in, first-out (LIFO) inventory costing method (p. 464)
Lower-of-cost-or-market (LCM) rule (p. 474)
Materiality concept (p. 473)
Merchandising company (p. 456)
Moving weighted-average cost method (p. 472)
Periodic inventory system (p. 457)
Perpetual inventory system (p. 457)
Retail method (p. 478)
Specific identification method (p. 464)
Specific-unit-cost method (p. 464)
Weighted-average cost method (p. 464)

Similar Accounting Terms

Cost of goods sold	Cost of sales
Gross margin method	Gross profit method
Inventory profit	FIFO inventory profit; phantom profit; illusory profit
Periodic inventory system	Physical inventory system
Weighted-average cost method	Average-cost method

Answers to Self-Study Questions

1. c
2. a $(6,000 - 1,000) \times \$3.40 = \$17,000$
3. d
4. b
5. b
6. b

7. d
8. a $\$35,000 + \$146,000 = \$181,000$
   $\$240,000 - (0.35 \times \$240,000) = \$156,000$
   $\$181,000 - \$156,000 = \$25,000$
9. d
10. c

Assignment Material

Questions

1. Why is merchandise inventory so important to a retailer or wholesaler?

2. Suppose your business deals in expensive jewellery. Which inventory system should you use to achieve good internal control over the inventory? If your business is a hardware store that sells low-cost goods, which inventory system would you be likely to use? Why would you choose this system?

3. Identify the accounts debited and credited in the standard purchase and sale entries under (a) the perpetual inventory system, and (b) the periodic inventory system.

4. What is the role of the physical count of inventory in (a) the perpetual inventory system and (b) the periodic inventory system?

5. If beginning inventory is $10,000, purchases total $85,000, and ending inventory is $12,700, how much is cost of goods sold?

6. If beginning inventory is $32,000, purchases total $119,000, and cost of goods sold is $127,000, how much is ending inventory?

7. What role does the cost principle play in accounting for inventory?

8. What two items determine the cost of ending inventory?

9. Briefly describe the four generally accepted inventory cost methods. During a period of rising prices, which method produces the highest reported income? Which produces the lowest reported income?

10. Which inventory costing method produces the ending inventory valued at the most current cost? Which method produces the cost-of-goods-sold amount valued at the most current cost?

11. Why is LIFO the most popular method in the United States? Why is it so little used in Canada? Do these reasons accord with the notion that the inventory costing method should produce the most accurate data on the income statement?

12. Which inventory costing method produces the most accurate data on the balance sheet? Why?

13. What is inventory profit? Which method produces it?

14. How does the consistency principle affect accounting for inventory?

15. Briefly describe the influence that the concept of conservatism has on accounting for inventory.

16. Manley Company's inventory has a cost of $48,000 at the end of the year, and the current replacement cost of the inventory is $51,000. At which amount should the company report the inventory on its balance sheet? Suppose the current replacement cost of the inventory is $45,000 instead of $51,000. At which amount should Manley Company report the inventory? What rule governs your answers to these questions?

17. Gabriel Products accidentally overstated its ending inventory by $10,000 at the end of period 1. Is gross margin of period 1 overstated or understated? Is gross margin of period 2 overstated, understated, or unaffected by the period 1 error? Is total gross margin for the two periods overstated, understated, or correct? Give the reason for your answers.

18. The market referred to in the lower-of-cost-or-market rule may have two meanings. Describe each of them.

19. Identify two important methods of estimating inventory amounts.

20. A fire destroyed the inventory of Olivera Supplies, but the accounting records were saved. The beginning inventory was $22,000, purchases for the period were $71,000, and sales were $140,000. Olivera's customary gross margin is 45 percent of sales. Use the gross margin method to estimate the cost of the inventory destroyed by the fire.

21. The retail method of estimating inventory seems simple but in reality can be difficult to apply. Why is this so?

22. True or false? A company that sells inventory of low unit cost needs no internal controls over the goods. Any inventory loss would probably be small.

Exercises

Exercise 9-1 *Recording and reporting transactions under the perpetual and periodic systems* **(Obj. 1)**

Active Sportswear's accounting records yield the following data for the year ended December 31, 2002 (amounts in thousands):

Inventory, January 1, 2002	39
Purchases of inventory (on account).....................	315
Sales of inventory—80 percent on account; 20 percent for cash (cost $282)	440
Inventory at FIFO cost December 31, 2002	?

Required

1. Journalize Active Sportswear's inventory transactions for the year—first under the perpetual system, then under the periodic system. Show all amounts in thousands. Use Exhibit 9-2 on page 459 as an example.

2. Report ending inventory, sales, cost of goods sold, and gross margin on the appropriate financial statement (amounts in thousands). Show the computation of cost of goods sold in the periodic system.

Exercise 9-2   *Budgeting inventory purchases*   *(Obj. 1)*

Suppose Toys "Я" Us is budgeting for the fiscal year ended January 31, 2002. During the preceding year ended January 31, 2001, sales totalled $9,427 million and cost of goods sold was $7,032 million. Inventory stood at $1,752 million at January 31, 2000, and at January 31, 2001, inventory stood at $1,999 million.

During the upcoming 2002 year, suppose Toys "Я" Us expects sales and cost of goods sold to increase by 10 percent. The company budgets next year's ending inventory at $2,110 million.

Required

How much inventory should Toys "Я" Us purchase during the upcoming year in order to reach its budgeted figures? Round to the nearest $1 million.

Exercise 9-3   *Computing ending inventory by applying four inventory costing methods*   *(Obj. 2)*

Tanco Electrical's inventory records for industrial switches indicate the following at November 30, 2003:

Nov.	1	Beginning inventory	7 units @ $160
	8	Purchase	4 units @ $160
	15	Purchase	11 units @ $170
	26	Purchase	5 units @ $176

The physical count of inventory at November 30, 2003 indicates that six units are on hand, and the company owns them.

Required

Compute ending inventory and cost of goods sold using each of the following methods, assuming the periodic inventory system:

1. Specific unit cost, assuming three $170 units and three $160 units are on hand
2. Weighted-average cost
3. First-in, first-out
4. Last-in, first-out

Exercise 9-4   *Recording inventory transactions*   *(Obj. 1, 2)*

Use the data in Exercise 9-3 to journalize, first for the perpetual inventory system, then for the periodic system:

1. Total November purchases in one summary entry. All purchases were on credit.
2. Total November sales in one summary entry. Assume the selling price was $280 per unit, and all sales were on credit. Tanco Electrical uses LIFO.
3. November 30 end-of-period entries for inventory in the periodic system. Tanco Electrical uses LIFO. Post to the Cost of Goods Sold T-account to show how this amount is determined. Label each item in the account. How does the balance of Cost of Goods Sold compare to the Cost of Goods Sold amount recorded under the perpetual system?

Exercise 9-5   *Applying the weighted-average, FIFO, and LIFO methods*   *(Obj. 2)*

Tsai Office Products markets the ink used in laser printers. Tsai started the year with 100 containers of ink (weighted-average cost of $9.14 each; FIFO cost of $9 each; LIFO cost of $8 each). During the year, Tsai purchased 800 containers of ink at

$12 and sold 700 units for $22 each, with all transactions on account. Tsai paid operating expenses throughout the year, a total of $4,700.

Journalize Tsai 's purchases, sales, and operating expense transactions under the following format. Tsai uses the perpetual inventory method to account for laser-printer ink.

	DEBIT/CREDIT AMOUNTS		
Accounts	Weighted-Average*	FIFO	LIFO

*Round weighted-average unit cost to the nearest cent.

Exercise 9-6   *Converting LIFO financial statements to the FIFO basis*   *(Obj. 3)*

Maria Calderone Designs reported:

Balance sheet	2002	2001
Inventories—note 4	$ 67,800	$ 59,300
Income statement		
Cost of goods sold	399,600	381,400

Note 4: The company determines inventory cost by the last-in, first-out method. If the first-in, first-out method were used, ending inventories would be $7,100 higher at year end 2002 and $4,500 higher at year end 2001.

Required

Show the cost-of-goods-sold computations for 2002 under LIFO and FIFO. Which method would result in higher reported income before taxes? Show the amount of the difference.

Exercise 9-7   *Note disclosure of a change in inventory method*   *(Obj. 3)*

Brubacher Plumbing Supplies has used the first-in, first-out inventory method for many years. At the start of the current year, Brubacher switched to the last-in, first-out method. This change decreased net income by $57,000. Write the note to disclose this accounting change in Brubacher Plumbing Supplies' financial statements.

Exercise 9-8   *Determining amounts for the income statement: periodic system*   *(Obj. 1)*

1. Supply the missing income statement amounts for each of the following companies for the year ended December 31, 2003:

Company	Net Sales	Beginning Inventory	Net Purchases	Ending Inventory	Cost of Goods Sold	Gross Margin
Arc Co.	$92,800	$12,500	$62,700	$19,400	(a)	$36,000
Bell Co.	(b)	27,450	93,000	(c)	$94,100	51,200
Court Co.	98,000	(d)	54,900	22,600	59,400	(e)
Dormer Co.	101,400	10,700	(f)	8,200	(g)	47,100

2. Prepare the income statement for Dormer Co., which uses the periodic inventory system. Dormer's operating expenses for the year were $32,100.

Exercise 9-9   *Measuring profitability*   *(Obj. 3)*

Link Back to Chapter 5 (Gross Margin Percentage and Inventory Turnover). Refer to the data in Exercise 9-8. Which business is likely to be the most profitable, based on its gross margin percentage and rate of inventory turnover? Why should the business with the fastest inventory turnover have the lowest operating expenses?

Suppose you are a financial analyst, and Tom O'Hara, a client, has asked you to recommend an investment in one of these businesses. Write a memo outlining which business you recommend, and explain your reasoning.

Exercise 9-10 *Computing ending inventory and cost of goods sold in a perpetual system*
(Obj. 1, 2)

Piazza Music World carries a large inventory of guitars, keyboards, and other musical instruments. Because each item is expensive, Piazza Music World uses a perpetual inventory system. Company records indicate the following for a particular line of Fender guitars:

Date		Item	Quantity	Unit Cost
May	1	Balance	5	$450
	6	Sale	3	
	8	Purchase	6	$480
	17	Sale	4	
	30	Sale	2	

Compute the amounts that Piazza Music World should report for ending inventory and cost of goods sold for Fender guitars by the FIFO method. Prepare the perpetual inventory record for Fender guitars, using Exhibit 9-5 as a model.

Exercise 9-11 *Change from LIFO to FIFO* *(Obj. 3)*

Leah Soffer's Girls' World is considering a change from the LIFO inventory method to the FIFO method. Leah Soffer, the owner, is concerned about the effects of this change on reported pretax income. If the change is made, it will become effective on March 1, 2002. Inventory on hand at February 28 is $63,000. During March, Soffer expects sales of $260,000, net purchases between $165,000 and $182,000, and operating expenses of $83,000. Inventories at March 31 are budgeted as follows: FIFO, $82,000; LIFO, $74,000.

Required

Create a spreadsheet model to compute estimated net income for March under FIFO and LIFO. Format your answer as follows:

	A	B	C	D	E
1		LEAH SOFFER'S GIRLS' WORLD			
2		Estimated Income under FIFO and LIFO			
3		For the Month Ended March 31, 2002			
4					
5		FIFO	LIFO	FIFO	LIFO
6					
7	Sales	$260,000	$260,000	$260,000	$260,000
8					
9	Cost of goods sold				
10	Beginning inventory	63,000	63,000	63,000	63,000
11	Net purchases	165,000	165,000	182,000	182,000
12					
13	Cost of goods available				
14	Ending inventory	82,000	74,000	82,000	74,000
15					
16	Cost of goods sold				
17					
18	Gross margin				
19	Operating expenses	83,000	83,000	83,000	83,000
20					
21	Net income before tax	$	$	$	$
22					

Exercise 9-12 *Identifying income and other effects of the inventory methods* **(Obj. 3)**

This exercise tests your understanding of the four inventory methods. In the space provided, write the name of the inventory method that best fits the description. Assume that the cost of inventory is rising.

_____ a. Enables a company to keep reported income from dropping lower by liquidating older layers of inventory.

_____ b. Matches the most current cost of goods sold against sales revenue.

_____ c. Results in an old measure of the cost of ending inventory.

_____ d. Results in a cost of ending inventory that is close to the current cost of replacing the inventory.

_____ e. Maximizes reported income.

_____ f. Enables a company to buy high-cost inventory at year end and thereby decrease reported income.

_____ g. Used to account for automobiles, jewellery, and art objects.

_____ h. Associated with inventory profits.

_____ i. Provides a middle-ground measure of ending inventory and cost of goods sold.

Exercise 9-13 *Applying the lower-of-cost-or-market rule to inventories: perpetual system* **(Obj. 1, 4)**

Walther Garden Supplies, which uses a perpetual inventory system, has these account balances at December 31, 2002, prior to releasing the financial statements for the year:

Inventory		Cost of Goods Sold		Sales Revenue	
Beg. bal. 12,489					
End. bal. 21,040		Bal. 118,003		Bal. 225,000	

A year ago, when Walther Garden Supplies prepared its 2001 financial statements, the replacement cost of ending inventory was $13,051. Enos Walther, the owner, has determined that the replacement cost of the December 31, 2002, ending inventory is $17,987.

Required

Prepare Walther Garden Supplies' 2002 income statement through gross margin to show how Walther would apply the lower-of-cost-or-market rule to its inventories. Include a complete heading for the statement.

Exercise 9-14 *Applying the lower-of-cost-or-market rule to inventories: periodic system* **(Obj. 1, 4)**

Baring Tool Company's income statement for the month ended August 31, 2003, reported the following data:

Income Statement		
Sales revenue		$89,000
Cost of goods sold		
Beginning inventory	$17,200	
Net purchases	67,700	
Cost of goods available for sale	84,900	
Ending inventory	23,800	
Cost of goods sold		61,100
Gross margin		$27,900

Before the financial statements were released, it was discovered that the current replacement cost of ending inventory was $17,800. Adjust the preceding income statement to apply the lower-of-cost-or-market rule to Baring Tool Company's inventory. Also, show the relevant portion of Baring Tool Company's balance sheet. The replacement cost of the beginning inventory was $18,600.

Exercise 9-15 *Correcting an inventory error* *(Obj. 5)*

Halcrow Marine Supply reported the comparative income statement for the years ended September 30, 2002 and 2001 shown below.

HALCROW MARINE SUPPLY
Income Statements
For the Years Ended September 30, 2002 and 2001

	2002		2001	
Sales revenue		$137,300		$121,700
Cost of goods sold:				
Beginning inventory	$14,000		$12,800	
Net purchases	76,000		65,000	
Cost of goods available	90,000		77,800	
Ending inventory	19,600		14,000	
Cost of goods sold.................		70,400		63,800
Gross margin..............................		66,900		57,900
Operating expenses		30,300		26,100
Net income before taxes............		$ 36,600		$ 31,800

During 2002, accountants for the company discovered that ending 2001 inventory was overstated by $3,000. Prepare the corrected comparative income statement for the two-year period complete with a heading for the statement. What was the effect of the error on net income for the two years combined? Explain your answer.

Exercise 9-16 *Assessing the effect of an inventory error on two years' statements* *(Obj. 5)*

Mary Putka, accountant of Now Electronics Ltd. learned that Now Electronics' $4 million cost of inventory at the end of last year was overstated by $1.2 million. She notified the company president of the accounting error and the need to alert the company's lenders that last year's reported net income was incorrect. Ed Hall, president of Now Electronics Ltd., explained to Putka that there is no need to report the error to lenders because the error will counterbalance this year. This year's error will affect this year's net income in the opposite direction of last year's error. Even with no correction, Hall reasons, net income for both years combined will be the same whether or not Now Electronics Ltd. corrects its errors.

Required

1. Was last year's reported net income of $6.0 million overstated, understated, or correct? What was the correct amount of net income last year?

2. Is this year's net income of $6.8 million overstated, understated, or correct? What is the correct amount of net income for the current year?

3. Whose perspective is better, Putka's or Hall's? Give your reason. Consider the trend of reported net income both without the correction and with the correction.

Exercise 9-17 *Ethical implications of inventory actions* *(Obj. 3, 4, 5)*

Determine whether each of the following actions in buying, selling, and accounting for inventories is ethical or unethical. Give your reason for each answer.

1. Duck River Corporation consciously overstated purchases to produce a high figure for cost of goods sold (low amount of net income). The real reason was to decrease the company's income tax payments to the government.

2. In applying the lower-of-cost-or-market rule to inventories, Wayne Industries recorded an excessively low market value for ending inventory. This allowed the company to pay no income tax for the year.

3. RNB Photo Film purchased lots of inventory shortly before year end to increase the LIFO cost of goods sold and decrease reported income for the year.

4. Edison Electrical Products delayed the purchase of inventory until after December 31, 2002, in order to keep 2002's cost of goods sold from growing too large. The delay in purchasing inventory helped net income of 2002 to reach the level of profit demanded by the company's investors.

5. Dover Sales Company deliberately overstated ending inventory in order to report higher profits (net income).

Exercise 9-18   *Estimating inventory by the gross margin method*   *(Obj. 6)*

Linklater Trailer Hitches began April with inventory of $35,000. The business made net purchases of $37,600 and had net sales of $60,000 before a fire destroyed the company's inventory. For the past several years, Linklater Trailer Hitches' gross margin on sales has been 45 percent. Estimate the cost of the inventory destroyed by the fire. Identify another reason owners and managers use the gross margin method to estimate inventory on a regular basis.

Exercise 9-19   *Estimating inventory by the retail method*   *(Obj. 6)*

Stephie's Fine Clothes has three lines of women's sportswear: Teenage, Young Woman, and Mature. The selling price of each item is double its cost price. On May 18, 2002, Stephie's Fine Clothes had a fire that destroyed all the inventory. Sales for the period January 1 to May 18 were: Teenage, $440,000; Young Woman, $540,000; and Mature, $720,000. Inventory at January 1, 2002, was: Teenage, $90,000; Young Woman, $120,000; and Mature, $150,000. Purchases made from January 1 to May 18, at cost, were: Teenage, $200,000; Young Woman, $200,000; and Mature, $300,000.

Required
Use the retail method to calculate the cost of the inventory lost in the fire.

Challenge Exercises

Exercise 9-20   *Inventory policy decisions*   *(Obj. 2, 3)*

For each of the following situations, identify the inventory method that you are using or would prefer to use, or, given the use of a particular method, state the strategy that you would follow to accomplish your goal.

a. Inventory costs are increasing. Your business uses LIFO and is having an unexpectedly good year. It is near year end, and you need to keep net income from increasing too much.

b. Inventory costs have been stable for several years, and you expect costs to remain stable for the indefinite future. (Give your reason for your choice of method.)

c. Suppliers of your inventory are threatening a labour strike, and it may be difficult for your business to obtain inventory.

d. Inventory costs are decreasing, and you want to maximize income.

e. Company management prefers a middle-of-the-road inventory policy that avoids extremes.

f. Your inventory turns over *very* rapidly, and the business uses a perpetual inventory system. Inventory costs are increasing, and the business prefers to report high income.

Exercise 9-21   *Evaluating a company's profitability*   *(Obj. 3)*

Canada Glass Products Ltd. is a leading provider of bottles for the brewing industry. Suppose the company recently reported these figures.

CANADA GLASS PRODUCTS LTD.
Income Statement
For the Years Ended July 31, 2002 and 2001

	2002	2001
Sales	$106,115,984	$81,685,715
Cost of sales	76,424,328	60,981,847
Gross Margin	29,691,656	20,703,868
Cost and expenses		
Selling, general and administrative	21,801,737	16,576,484
Amortization	2,169,196	918,693
Restructuring charges	7,096,774	—
	31,067,707	17,495,177
Operating income (loss)	(1,376,051)	3,208,691
Other items (summarized)	(635,153)	(1,315,490)
Net income (loss)	$(2,011,204)	$ 1,893,201

Required

Evaluate Canada Glass's operations during 2002 in comparison with 2001. Consider sales, gross margin, operating income, and net income. In the annual report, Canada Glass's management describes the restructuring charges in 2002 as a one-time event that is not expected to recur. How does this additional information affect your evaluation?

Beyond the Numbers

Assessing the impact of the inventory costing method on the financial statements (Obj. 2, 3, 4)

The inventory costing method chosen by a company can affect the financial statements and thus the decisions of the users of those statements.

Required

1. A leading accounting researcher stated that one inventory costing method reports the most recent costs in the income statement, while another method reports the most recent costs in the balance sheet. In this person's opinion, this results in one or the other of the statements being "inaccurate" when prices are rising. What did the researcher mean?

2. Conservatism is an accepted accounting concept. Would you want management to be conservative in accounting for inventory if you were (a) a shareholder, and (b) a prospective shareholder? Give your reason.

3. Duane's Cycle Shoppe follows conservative accounting and writes the value of its inventory of bicycles down to market, which has declined below cost. The following year, an unexpected cycling craze results in a demand for bicycles that far exceeds supply, and the market price increases well above the previous cost. What effect will conservatism have on the income of Duane's Cycle Shoppe over the two years?

Ethical Issue

During 2002, Favro Electronics changed to the LIFO method of accounting for inventory. Suppose that during 2003, Favro Electronics changes back to the FIFO method, and in the following year switches back to LIFO again.

Required

1. What would you think of a company's ethics if it changed accounting methods every year?
2. What accounting principle would changing methods every year violate?
3. Who can be harmed when a company changes its accounting methods too often? How?

Problems (Group A)

Problem 9-1A *Accounting for inventory: perpetual system* **(Obj. 1, 2)**

Zellers Inc. operates department stores across Canada. Assume you are dealing with one department in a Zellers store in Halifax, Nova Scotia. Assume the company's fiscal year ends each January 31. Also assume the department began fiscal year 2003 with an inventory of 50 toaster ovens that cost $1,500. During the year, the department purchased merchandise on account as follows:

March (60 units @ $32)...	$1,920
August (40 units @ $34)...	1,360
October (180 units @ $36).......................................	6,480
Total purchases..	$9,760

Cash payments on account during the year totalled $9,110.

During fiscal year 2003, the department sold 300 toaster ovens for $13,400, of which $2,100 was for cash and the balance was on account. Zellers Inc. uses the FIFO method for inventories.

Operating expenses for the year were $2,732. The department paid two-thirds of the operating expenses in cash and accrued the rest.

Required

1. Make summary journal entries to record the department's transactions for the year ended January 31, 2003. The company uses a perpetual inventory system.
2. Determine the FIFO cost of the department's ending inventory at January 31, 2003. Use a T-account.
3. Prepare the department's income statement for the year ended January 31, 2003. Show totals for the gross margin, and net income.

Problem 9-2A *Using the cost-of-goods-sold model to budget operations* **(Obj. 1)**

Condensed versions of Barney's Quick Trip's most recent income statement and balance sheet reported the following figures (on page 494). The business uses a periodic inventory system.

Barney Lewis, the owner, is budgeting for 2003. He expects sales to increase by 5% and the gross margin percentage to remain unchanged. To meet customer demand for the increase in sales, ending inventory will need to be $90 thousand at December 31, 2003. Barney can lower operating expenses by doing some of the work himself. He hopes to earn a net income of $110 thousand next year.

Required

1. A key variable Barney Lewis can control is the amount of inventory he purchases. Show how to determine the amount of purchases Barney should make in 2003.

2. Prepare the store's budgeted income statement for 2003 to reach the target net income of $110 thousand before taxes.

BARNEY'S QUICK TRIP
Income Statement
For the Year Ended Dec. 31, 2002

	Thousands
Sales..............................	$900
Cost of sales..................	675
Gross margin...............	225
Operating expenses.....	135
Net income	
before taxes...............	$ 90

BARNEY'S QUICK TRIP
Balance Sheet
December 31, 2002

Assets		Liabilities and Owner's Equity	
	Thousands		*Thousands*
Cash	$ 40	Accounts payable	$ 30
Inventories....................	70	Note payable	190
Land and buildings,		Total liabilities.................	220
net..............................	270	Owner's equity	160
		Total liabilities and	
Total assets	$380	owner's equity	$380

Problem 9-3A *Using the perpetual and periodic inventory systems* *(Obj. 1, 2)*

Lethbridge Tire began June with 50 units of inventory that cost $49 each. The sale price of each was $66. During June, Lethbridge Tire completed these inventory transactions:

			Units	Unit Cost	Unit Selling Price
June	2	Purchase...	12	$ 50	$ 67
	8	Sale..	27	49	66
	13	Sale..	23	49	66
		Sale..	3	50	67
	17	Purchase...	24	50	67
	22	Sale..	31	50	67
	29	Purchase...	24	51	69

Required

1. The above data are taken from Lethbridge Tire's perpetual inventory records. Which cost method does Lethbridge Tire use?

2. Compute Lethbridge Tire's cost of goods sold for June under the
   a. Perpetual inventory system
   b. Periodic inventory system

3. Compute gross margin for June.

Problem 9-4A *Computing inventory by three methods* *(Obj. 2, 3)*

Rudy's Skateboard Emporium began December with 120 units of inventory that cost $75 each. During December, Rudy's Skateboard Emporium made the following purchases:

Dec.	3...	217 @ $81
	12...	95 @ 82
	18...	210 @ 84
	24...	248 @ 87

The business uses the periodic inventory system, and the physical count at December 31 indicates that ending inventory consists of 176 units.

Required

Compute the ending inventory and cost of goods sold amounts under (1) weighted-average cost, (2) FIFO cost, and (3) LIFO cost. Round weighted-average cost per unit to five decimal places and round all other amounts to the nearest cent.

Problem 9-5A *Preparing an income statement directly from the accounts* *(Obj. 2, 3)*

The periodic inventory records of Malkani Office Products include the following accounts for one of its products at December 31, 2002:

Inventory

Jan.	1	Balance	{ 400 units @ $3.00 { 100 units @ 3.15 }	1,515	

Purchases

Feb.	6	800 units @ $3.15	2,520
May	19	600 units @ 3.35	2,010
Aug.	12	460 units @ 3.50	1,610
Oct.	4	700 units @ 3.70	2,590
Dec.	31 Balance		8,730

Sales Revenue

	Mar.	12	500 units @ $4.10	2,050
	June	9	1,100 units @ 4.10	4,510
	Aug.	21	300 units @ 4.50	1,350
	Nov.	2	600 units @ 4.50	2,700
	Dec.	18	100 units @ 4.80	480
	Dec.	31 Balance		11,090

Required

1. Compute the number of units in (a) ending inventory, and (b) cost of goods sold during the year.
2. Prepare a partial comparative income statement through gross margin under the weighted-average cost, FIFO cost, and LIFO cost methods. Round weighted-average cost to five decimal places and all other amounts to the nearest cent.

Problem 9-6A *Applying the lower-of-cost-or-market rule to inventories* *(Obj. 4)*

Kelly's Home Furniture has recently been plagued with lacklustre sales. The rate of inventory turnover has dropped, and some of the business's merchandise is gathering dust. At the same time, competition has forced some of the business's suppliers to lower the prices that Kelly's Home Furniture will pay when it replaces its inventory. It is now December 31, 2003. Assume the current replacement cost of a Kelly's Home Furniture store's ending inventory is $500,000 below what Kelly's Home Furniture paid for the goods, which was $4,100,000. Before any adjustments at the end of the period, assume the store's Cost of Goods Sold account has a balance of $22,730,000.

What action should Kelly's Home Furniture take in this situation, if any? Give any journal entry required. At what amount should Kelly's Home Furniture report Inventory on the balance sheet? At what amount should the business report Cost of Goods Sold on the income statement? Discuss the accounting principle or concept that is most relevant to this situation.

Problem 9-7A *Correcting inventory errors over a three-year period* *(Obj. 5)*

The accounting records of the Burger World restaurant chain show these data (in thousands):

	2002	2001	2000
Net sales revenue.............	$190	$165	$170
Cost of goods sold			
Beginning inventory........	$ 15	$ 25	$ 40
Net purchases..................	115	100	90
Cost of goods available....	130	125	130
Less ending inventory......	30	15	25
Cost of goods sold		100	110	105
Gross margin		90	55	65
Operating expenses..............		62	38	46
Net income........................		$ 28	$ 17	$ 19

In early 2003, a team of auditors discovered that the ending inventory of 2000 had been understated by $3 thousand. Also, the ending inventory for 2002 had been overstated by $4 thousand. The ending inventory at December 31, 2001, was correct.

Required

1. Show corrected comparative income statements for the three years.
2. State whether each year's net income as reported here and the related owner's equity amounts are understated or overstated. For each incorrect figure, indicate the amount of the understatement or overstatement.

 Problem 9-8A *Estimating inventory by the gross margin method; preparing the income statement* *(Obj. 6)*

Assume S&S Stores estimates its inventory by the gross margin method when preparing monthly financial statements (assume S&S Stores uses the periodic method otherwise). For the past two years, gross margin has averaged 30 percent of net sales. Assume further that the business's inventory records for stores in Nova Scotia and Prince Edward Island reveal the following data:

Inventory, July 1, 2002..	$ 304,000
Transactions during July:	
Purchases...	6,585,000
Purchase returns..	32,000
Sales..	9,375,000
Sales refunds	17,000

Required

1. Estimate the July 31, 2002 inventory using the gross margin method.
2. Prepare the July 2002 income statement through gross margin for the S&S Stores in Nova Scotia and Prince Edward Island.

Problem 9-9A *Accounting for inventory by the periodic and perpetual systems; estimating inventory by the gross margin method* *(Obj. 1, 6)*

The Grizzly Boot Company has a periodic inventory system and uses the gross margin method of estimating inventories for interim financial statements. The company had the following account balances for the fiscal year ended August 31, 2002:

Merchandise inventory—Sept. 1, 2001...................................	$ 43,000
Purchases..	246,000
Purchases returns and allowances...	8,000
Transportation-in...	1,600
Sales...	401,000
Sales returns and allowances..	13,000

Required

1. Use the gross margin method to estimate the cost of the business's ending inventory, assuming the business has an average gross profit margin of 35 percent.

2. The business has done a physical count of the inventory on hand on August 31, 2002. For convenience, this inventory was calculated based on the retail selling prices marked on the goods and amounted to $52,500. Use the information from Requirement 1 to calculate the cost of the inventory counted.

3. What is the cost of the business's estimated inventory overage?

4. Give the summary journal entries that would be appropriate if the business had used the perpetual inventory system. Also record any shortage or overage.

Problem 9-10A *Accounting for inventory by the periodic inventory system; applying the LIFO and FIFO costing methods; estimating inventory by the gross margin method.* **(Obj. 1, 2, 6)**

John's Hardware uses the periodic inventory system for the purchase and sale of inventory and had the following information available on May 31, 2003:

Purchases and Sales		Number of Units	Cost or Selling Price per Unit
May 1	Balance of inventory	2,600	$ 8
7	Purchased	4,000	$12
8	Sold	3,000	$17
12	Purchased	5,000	$11
16	Sold	6,000	$19
21	Purchased	3,000	$12
25	Purchased	7,000	$11
29	Sold	9,000	$19

Required

1. Calculate the cost of goods sold and the cost of the ending inventory for May under each of the following inventory costing methods: (a) the LIFO method, (b) the FIFO method.

2. Prepare the journal entries required to record the transactions using the periodic inventory system with FIFO costing.

3. An internal audit has discovered that a new employee—an accounting clerk—had been stealing merchandise and covering up the shortage by changing the inventory records. For example, if 120 units were purchased at $10 per unit, he would record it as 100 units purchased at $12 per unit and then take the other 20 units.

    The external auditors examined the accounting records prior to the employment of the individual and noted that the company has an average gross profit margin of 50%. They estimate that 95% of the incorrectly costed units have been sold.

    Use the gross profit method to estimate the cost of the inventory shortage (under the FIFO costing method) and give the journal entry required to correct it.

4. What would be the effect on the net income for the year ending May 31, 2003, if the inventory shortage had not been discovered? For the year ending May 31, 2004?

Problems (Group B)

Problem 9-1B *Accounting for inventory in a perpetual system* **(Obj. 1, 2)**

Home Depot purchases inventory in crates of merchandise, so each unit of inventory is a crate of tools or building supplies. Assume you are dealing with a single department in a Home Depot store in Winnipeg, Manitoba. The fiscal year of Home Depot ends each January 31.

Assume the department began fiscal year 2002 with an inventory of 20 units that cost a total of $1,200. During the year, the department purchased merchandise on account as follows:

April (30 units @ $65)	$ 1,950
August (50 units @ $65)..	3,250
November (100 units @ $70)	7,000
Total purchases	$12,200

Cash payments on account during the year totalled $11,390.

During fiscal year 2002, the department sold 190 units of merchandise for $19,200, of which $3,300 was for cash and the balance was on account. Assume Home Depot uses the LIFO method for inventories. Department operating expenses for the year were $5,630. The department paid two-thirds of the operating expenses in cash and accrued the rest.

Required

1. Make summary journal entries to record the department transactions for the year ended January 31, 2002. Home Depot uses a perpetual inventory system.

2. Determine the LIFO cost of the store's ending inventory at January 31, 2002. Use a T-account.

3. Prepare the department's income statement for the year ended January 31, 2002. Include a complete heading, and show totals for the gross margin and net income.

Problem 9-2B   *Using the cost-of-goods-sold model to budget operations*   (Obj. 1)

Condensed versions of Meg's Milk Marts' most recent income statement and balance sheet reported the following figures. The business uses a periodic inventory system.

MEG'S MILK MARTS
Balance Sheet
December 31, 2002

Assets		Liabilities and Owner's Equity	
	Thousands		*Thousands*
Cash	$ 70	Accounts payable	$ 35
Inventories.....................	35	Note payable	280
Land and buildings,		Total liabilities	315
net..............................	360	Owner's equity	150
		Total liabilities and	
Total assets	$465	Owner's equity	$465

MEG'S MILK MARTS
Income Statement
For the Year Ended Dec. 31, 2002

	Thousands
Sales	$800
Cost of sales.................	660
Gross margin	140
Operating expenses.....	80
Net income	
before taxes..............	$ 60

The owner is budgeting for 2003. She expects sales to increase by 15% and the gross margin percentage to remain unchanged. To meet customer demand for the increase in sales, ending inventory will need to be $42 thousand at December 31, 2003. The owner can lower operating expenses by doing some of the work herself. She hopes to earn a net income before taxes of $85 thousand next year.

Required

1. A key variable the owner can control is the amount of inventory she purchases. Show how to determine the amount of purchases she should make in 2003 (amounts in thousands).

2. Prepare the store's budgeted income statement for 2003 to reach the target net income of $85 thousand.

Problem 9-3B   *Using the perpetual and periodic inventory systems*   **(Obj. 1, 2)**

The Backpack Company (TBC) began May 2002 with 50 units of inventory that cost $40 each. The sale price of each was $71. During May, TBC completed these inventory transactions:

			Units	Unit Cost	Unit Sales Price
May	3	Sale	16	$40	$71
	8	Purchase	80	41	74
	11	Sale	34	40	71
	19	Sale	9	41	74
	24	Sale	35	41	74
	30	Purchase	18	42	75
	31	Sale	6	41	74

Required

1. The above data are taken from TBC's perpetual inventory records. Which cost method does the company use?
2. Compute TBC's cost of goods sold for May under the
   a. Perpetual inventory system
   b. Periodic inventory system
3. Compute gross margin for May.

Problem 9-4B   *Computing inventory by three methods*   **(Obj. 2, 3)**

Blanchet Office Supplies began March with 73 units of recordable compact disk inventory that cost $20 each. During the month Blanchet Office Supplies made the following purchases:

Mar.	4	113 @ $22
	12	81 @ 24
	19	167 @ 27
	25	44 @ 28

The company uses the periodic inventory system, and the physical count at March 31 indicates that ending inventory consists of 51 units.

Required

Compute the ending inventory and cost of goods sold amounts under (1) weighted-average cost, (2) FIFO cost, and (3) LIFO cost. Round weighted-average cost per unit to five decimal places, and round all other amounts to the nearest cent.

Problem 9-5B   *Preparing an income statement directly from the accounts*   **(Obj. 2, 3)**

The records of Bradshaw Sports Centre include the accounts shown below and on the next page for one of its products, CCM Pro hockey sticks, at December 31, 2003.

Inventory—Hockey Sticks (CCM Pro)

Jan.	1	Balance	{700 units @ $7.00}	4,900	

Purchases

Jan.	6		300 units @ $7.05	2,115	
Feb.	19		1,100 units @ 7.35	8,085	
Aug.	22		8,400 units @ 8.00	67,200	
Oct.	4		1,000 units @ 8.50	8,500	
Dec.	31	Balance		85,900	

Sales Revenue

Feb.	5	1,000 units @ $12.00	12,000
Mar.	10	700 units @ 12.10	8,470
Sept.	30	1,800 units @ 13.25	23,850
Oct.	4	3,500 units @ 13.50	47,250
Nov.	27	3,600 units @ 15.00	54,000
Dec.	31	Balance	145,570

Required

1. Compute the number of units in (a) ending inventory, and (b) cost of goods sold during 2003.

2. Prepare a partial comparative income statement through gross margin under the weighted-average cost, FIFO cost, and LIFO cost methods.

Problem 9-6B   *Applying the lower-of-cost-or-market rule to inventories*   *(Obj. 4)*

Builders' Supplies has recently been plagued with declining sales. The rate of inventory turnover has dropped, and some of the company's merchandise is gathering dust. At the same time, competition has forced Builders' Supplies' suppliers to lower the prices that the business will pay when it replaces its inventory. It is now December 31, 2002, and the current replacement cost of Builders' Supplies' ending inventory is $700,000 below what the business actually paid for the goods, which was $4,900,000. Before any adjustments at the end of the period, Builders' Supplies' Cost of Goods Sold account has a balance of $28,800,000.

What action should Builders' Supplies take in this situation, if any? Give any journal entry required. At what amount should Builders' Supplies report Inventory on the balance sheet? At what amount should the company report Cost of Goods Sold on the income statement? Discuss the accounting principle or concept that is most relevant to this situation.

Problem 9-7B   *Correcting inventory errors over a three-year period*   *(Obj. 6)*

The books of Waterloo Windows and Siding show these data (in thousands):

	2002		2001		2000	
Net sales revenue		$360		$275		$240
Cost of goods sold:						
Beginning inventory	$ 65		$ 55		$ 70	
Net purchases	195		135		130	
Cost of goods available	260		190		200	
Less ending inventory	70		65		55	
Cost of goods sold		190		125		145
Gross margin		170		150		95
Operating expenses		119		109		72
Net income		$ 51		$ 41		$ 23

In early 2003, a team of Canada Customs and Revenue Agency auditors discovered that the ending inventory of 2000 had been overstated by $12 thousand. Also, the ending inventory for 2002 had been understated by $6 thousand. The ending inventory at December 31, 2001 was correct.

Required

1. Show corrected comparative income statements for the three years.

2. State whether each year's net income and owner's equity amounts are understated or overstated. For each incorrect figure, indicate the amount of the understatement or overstatement.

Problem 9-8B *Estimating ending inventory by the gross margin method; preparing the income statement* *(Obj. 6)*

Assume Garden Furniture Stores estimates its inventory by the gross margin method when preparing monthly financial statements (it uses the periodic method otherwise). For the past two years, the gross margin has averaged 40 percent of net sales. Assume further that the company's inventory records for stores in Western Canada reveal the following data:

Inventory, June 1, 2002	$ 367,000
Transactions during June:	
Purchases	3,789,000
Sales	6,430,000

Required

1. Estimate the June 30, 2002 inventory using the gross margin method.

2. Prepare the June income statement through gross margin for the Garden Furniture Stores stores in the Western Canada region.

Problem 9-9B *Accounting for inventory by the periodic and perpetual systems; estimating inventory by the gross margin method* *(Obj. 1, 6)*

Doerr Mfg. has a periodic inventory system and uses the gross margin method of estimating inventories for interim financial statements. The business had the following account balances for the fiscal year ended August 31, 2003:

Merchandise inventory—Sept. 1, 2002	$ 38,000
Purchases	327,000
Purchases returns and allowances	47,000
Freight in	2,400
Sales	442,000
Sales returns and allowances	8,000

Required

1. Use the gross margin method to estimate the cost of the business's ending inventory, assuming the business has an average gross profit margin of 40 percent.

2. The business has done a physical count of the inventory on hand on August 31, 2003. For convenience, this inventory was calculated based on the retail selling prices marked on the goods and amounted to $81,300. Use the information from Requirement 1 to calculate the cost of the inventory counted.

3. What is the cost of the business's estimated inventory shortage?

4. Give the summary journal entries that would be appropriate if the business had used the perpetual inventory system, and the adjustment that would be required for the shortage.

5. Of what other use would the information in Requirement 4 be to the business?

Problem 9-10B *Accounting for inventory by the periodic inventory system, applying the LIFO and FIFO costing methods; estimating inventory by the gross margin method* *(Obj. 1, 2, 6)*

Phyldew Sales uses the periodic inventory system for the purchase and sale of inventory and had the following information available on August 31, 2002:

Purchases and Sales		Number of Units	Cost or Selling Price per Unit
Aug. 1	Balance of inventory	1,800	$12
7	Purchased	5,000	$11
8	Sold	4,000	$20
12	Purchased	3,500	$12
16	Sold	5,800	$21
21	Purchased	4,000	$13
25	Purchased	6,000	$15
29	Sold	8,000	$21

Required

1. Calculate the cost of goods sold and the cost of the ending inventory for August under each of the following inventory costing methods: (a) the LIFO method, (b) the FIFO method.

2. Prepare the journal entries required to record the August transactions using the periodic inventory system with FIFO costing.

3. An internal audit has discovered that two new employees—an accounting clerk and an employee from the purchasing department—had been stealing merchandise and covering up the shortage by changing the inventory records. For example, if 130 units were purchased at $10 per unit, they would record it as 100 units purchased at $13 per unit and then take the other 30 units.

   The external auditors examined the accounting records prior to the employment of the two individuals and noted that the company had an average gross profit margin of 48%. They estimate that 90% of the incorrectly costed units have been sold.

   Use the gross margin method to estimate the cost of the inventory shortage (under the FIFO costing method) and give the journal entry required to correct it.

4. What would be the effect on the net income for the year ending August 31, 2002, if the inventory shortage had not been discovered? For the year ending August 31, 2003?

Challenge Problems

Problem 9-1C *Inventory measurement and income* *(Obj. 3)*

An anonymous source advised Canada Customs and Revenue Agency that Don Rosset, owner of Rosset's Grocery Store, has been filing fraudulent tax returns for the past several years. You, a tax auditor with Canada Customs and Revenue Agency, are in the process of auditing Rosset's Grocery Store for the year ended December 31, 2001. Rosset's tax returns for the past five years show a decreasing value for ending inventory from 1996, when Rosset bought the business, to 2000; the return for 2001 shows the same sort of decrease. You have performed a quick survey of the large store and the attached warehouse and observed that both seemed very well stocked.

Required

Does the information set forth above suggest anything to you that might confirm the anonymous tip? What would you do to confirm or deny your suspicions?

Problem 9-2C *Estimating inventory from incomplete records* *(Obj. 6)*

It is Monday morning. You heard on the morning news that a client of your public accounting firm, Discount Stereo, had a fire the previous Friday night that destroyed its office and warehouse, and you concluded that inventory records as well as inventory probably perished in the fire. Since you had been at Discount Stereo on the previous Friday preparing the monthly income statement for the previous month that ended on Thursday, you realize you probably have the only current financial information available for Discount.

Upon arrival at your firm's office, you meet your partner who confirms your suspicions. Discount Stereo lost all its inventory and its records. She tells you that the company wants your firm to prepare information for a fire loss claim for Discount Stereo's insurance company for the inventory.

You know the audit file for the fiscal year that ended three months earlier contains a complete section dealing with inventory and the four product lines Discount Stereo carried, including the most recent gross margin rate for each line. The file will show total inventory and how much inventory there was by product line at the year end. You also recall that the file contains an analysis of sales by product line for the past several years and that Discount Stereo used a periodic inventory system.

Required

Explain how you would use the information available to you to calculate the fire loss by product line.

Extending Your Knowledge

Decision Problem

1. Assessing the impact of a year-end purchase of inventory (Obj. 2, 3)

Whitewater Camping Supplies is nearing the end of its first year of operations. The company uses the periodic inventory method and made inventory purchases of $74,500 during the year as follows:

January	100 units @ $100.00	=	$10,000
July	400 units @ 121.25	=	48,500
November	100 units @ 160.00	=	16,000
Totals	600		$74,500

Sales for the year will be 500 units for $125,000 revenue. Expenses other than cost of goods sold will be $22,000. The owner of the company is undecided about whether to adopt FIFO or LIFO.

The company has storage capacity for 400 additional units of inventory. Inventory prices are expected to stay at $160 per unit for the next few months. The president is considering purchasing 100 additional units of inventory at $160 each before the end of the year. He wishes to know how the purchase would affect net income before taxes under both FIFO and LIFO.

Required

1. To help the owner make the decision, prepare income statements under FIFO and under LIFO, both without and with the year-end purchase of 100 units of inventory at $160 per unit.

2. Compare net income before taxes under FIFO without and with the year-end purchase. Make the same comparison under LIFO. Under which method does the year-end purchase have the greater effect on net income before taxes?

3. Under which method can a year-end purchase be made in order to manipulate net income before taxes?

Financial Statement Problem

Inventories   (Obj. 2, 3)

The notes are an important part of a company's financial statements, giving valuable details that would clutter the tabular data presented in the statements. This problem will help you learn to use a company's inventory notes. Refer to the Intrawest Corporation statements and the related notes in Appendix A. Answer the following questions:

1. How much were Intrawest Corporation's ski and resort operations inventories at June 30, 2000? June 30, 1999?

2. How does Intrawest Corporation value its inventories?

3. Identify Intrawest Corporation's inventory other than that for ski and resort operations. (Hint: See Note 5.) What is the value of the other inventory?

4. What do the notes suggest the cost of the other inventory includes?

10

Capital Assets, Intangible Assets, and Related Expenses

CHAPTER OBJECTIVES

After studying this chapter, you should be able to

1 Measure the cost of a capital asset (property, plant, and equipment)

2 Account for amortization

3 Explain capital cost allowance, amortization for income tax purposes

4 Account for the disposal of a capital asset

5 Account for wasting assets and amortization

6 Account for intangible assets and amortization

PSCO Inc. is a steel producer whose head office is in Regina, Saskatchewan. The company has plants in Regina, Calgary, Edmonton, Red Deer, Surrey, and Toronto, and in the United States in Iowa, Alabama, Arkansas, Minnesota, Nebraska, and Texas.

IPSCO Inc.'s 1999 annual report describes the continuing acquisition and expansion of the company's capital assets involving the spending in 1999 of $118 million (U.S.). This includes new

equipment that is being installed at many of the company's plants. The annual report states spending is occuring on a number of minor projects and "IPSCO's major ongoing project, a new steelworks in Alabama."

As shown in the 1999 Annual Report, IPSCO Inc.'s policy of expansion and upgrading is reflected in growing sales and profits.

Source: IPSCO Inc. 1999 Annual Report.

IPSCO Inc.
www.ipsco.com

How is IPSCO Inc. able to increase tonnes of steel shipped, sales, and net income each year over the previous year? By continually expanding its facilities through acquisition of *capital assets*. IPSCO Inc.'s cash flow statement in Exhibit 10-1 shows the expenditures for capital assets for the years 1999, 1998, and 1997. We examine capital assets in this chapter. Capital assets were introduced in Chapter 3, page 116.

The IPSCO Inc. annual report mentioned *expenditures for capital assets* or *capital expenditures*, terms used often in the business press. These are the costs of acquiring and adding to buildings, automobiles, and other long-lived tangible assets used to operate a business and not held for sale. Capital expenditures are a major sign of growth in both business and nonprofit organizations such as churches, hospitals, and colleges and universities. Without capital expenditures, an organization falls behind its competitors. IPSCO Inc. and other leading companies work hard to keep that from happening.

This chapter also covers natural resource assets (such as oil, timber, and gravel). Finally, we discuss *intangible assets*, those assets without physical form, such as the cost in excess of the fair value of net assets acquired, better known as *goodwill*. The expense that relates to capital assets, natural resources, and intangible assets is *amortization*, but as Exhibit 10-2 shows, the terms *depreciation* and *depletion* are also used.

Chapter 10 concludes our coverage of assets, except for long-term investments, which we discuss in Chapter 16. After completing this chapter, you should understand the various assets of a business and how companies manage, control, and account for them.

EXHIBIT 10-1

IPSCO Inc. Cash Flow Statement (partial)

IPSCO Inc.
Cash Flow Statements (partial, adapted)
For the Years Ended December 31
(thousands of U.S. dollars)

	1999	1998	1997
Cash derived from (applied to) Investing Activities:			
Expenditures for capital assets	($118,740)	($105,410)	($148,776)

Measuring the Cost of a Capital Asset (Property, Plant, and Equipment)

OBJECTIVE 1
Measure the cost of a capital asset (property, plant, and equipment)

Long-lived assets used in the operation of the business and not held for sale as investments are termed **capital assets**. They can be divided into property, plant, and equipment, wasting assets—for example, natural resources such as mining properties and oil and gas properties—and intangibles. *Property*, *plant*, and *equipment* and *wasting assets* are those long-lived assets that are tangible. Their physical form provides their usefulness. Of the capital assets, land is unique. Its cost is not amortized—expensed over time—because its usefulness does not decrease like that of other assets. We introduced the concept of amortization in Chapter 3, page 116.

Intangible assets are useful not because of their physical characteristics, but because of the special rights they carry. Patents, copyrights, and trademarks are intangible assets. Accounting for intangibles is similar to accounting for property, plant, and equipment.

The accounting for capital assets has its own terminology. The *CICA Handbook* uses the term **amortization** to describe the allocating of the *cost of a capital asset* over its useful life; companies in Canada also use the terms shown in Exhibit 10-2 to describe amortization expenses with respect to the various capital assets listed, such as **depreciation**.

In the first half of the chapter we illustrate how to identify the cost of property, plant, and equipment, and how to expense its cost. In the second half, we discuss the disposal of property, plant, and equipment, and how to account for natural resources, intangible assets, and capital expenditures. Unless stated otherwise, we describe accounting in accordance with generally accepted accounting principles, as distinguished from reporting to Canada Customs and Revenue Agency for income tax purposes.

The *cost principle* directs a business to carry an asset on the balance sheet at the amount of consideration given in exchange for the asset. The general rule for measuring the cost of any asset (repeated from Chapter 9, page 458) is

> **The cost of an asset** = **The sum of all the costs incurred to bring the asset to its intended purpose, net of all discounts**

The *cost of property, plant, and equipment* is the purchase price, taxes, purchase commissions, and all other costs incurred to acquire the asset and to ready it for its intended use. In Chapter 9, we applied this principle to determine the cost of inventory. The types of cost differ for the various categories of property, plant, and equipment, so we discuss each asset individually.

Land and Land Improvements

The cost of land includes its purchase price (cash plus any note payable given), brokerage commission, survey fees, legal fees, and any property taxes in arrears

KEY POINT

Long-lived assets are classified as capital assets. They are often called long-term assets; property, plant, and equipment; or fixed assets.

KEY POINT

Land is not amortized because it does not wear out as do buildings and equipment.

LEARNING TIP

The cost of an asset includes all costs necessary to ready the asset for its intended use; "cost" will even include amounts not yet paid in cash, such as a note payable on the asset.

EXHIBIT 10-2

Terminology Used in Accounting for Capital Assets

Asset Account on the Balance Sheet	Related Expense Account on the Income Statement
Land	None
Buildings, Machinery and Equipment; Furniture and Fixtures; and Land Improvements	Amortization or Depreciation
Wasting Assets (Natural Resources)	Amortization or Depletion
Intangibles	Amortization

that the purchaser pays. Land cost also includes the cost for grading and clearing the land, and for demolishing or removing any unwanted buildings.

The cost of land does *not* include the cost of fencing, paving, sprinkler systems, and lighting. These separate capital assets—called *land improvements*—are subject to amortization.

Suppose IPSCO Inc. signs a $300,000 note payable to purchase 100 hectares of land for a new smelter. The company also pays $10,000 in brokerage commission, $8,000 in transfer taxes, $5,000 for removal of an old building, a $1,000 survey fee, and $26,000 for the construction of fences, all in cash. What is the cost of this land?

Purchase price of land..		$300,000
Add related costs:		
Brokerage commission	$10,000	
Transfer taxes...	8,000	
Removal of building	5,000	
Survey fee...	1,000	
Total incidental costs..		24,000
Total cost of land..		$324,000

Note that the cost of the fences, $26,000, is *not* included in the Land account. The fences are a land improvement that will be amortized over their useful life.

IPSCO Inc.'s entries to record the purchase of the land and the payment for the fences are as follows:

Land..	324,000	
Note Payable..		300,000
Cash..		24,000

We would say that IPSCO Inc. *capitalized* the cost of the land at $324,000. This means that the company debited an asset account (Land) for $324,000.

Land Improvements	26,000	
Cash..		26,000

Land and Land Improvements are two entirely separate asset accounts. Land improvements include lighting, signs, fences, paving, sprinkler systems, and landscaping. These costs are debited to the Land Improvements account and then amortized over their useful life.

Buildings

The cost of constructing a building includes architectural fees, building permits, contractors' charges, and payments for materials, labour, and overhead. The time to complete a new building can be many months, even years, and the number of separate expenditures can be numerous. If the company constructs its own assets, the cost of the building may include the cost of interest on money borrowed to finance the construction. (We discuss this topic in the next section of this chapter.)

When an existing building is purchased, its cost includes the purchase price, brokerage commission, sales and other taxes (but not GST), plus the cost to repair and renovate the building.

Machinery and Equipment

.... THINKING IT OVER

Which of the following would you include in the cost of machinery:
(1) installation charges;
(2) testing of the machine;
(3) repair to machinery due to installer's error;
(4) first-year maintenance cost?
A: Include 1 and 2, but not 3 or 4.

The cost of machinery and equipment includes its purchase price (less any discounts), plus transportation charges, insurance while in transit, provincial sales tax (PST), purchase commission, installation costs, and the cost of testing the asset before it is used. As soon as the asset is in use, we cease capitalizing these costs to the Machinery and Equipment account. Thereafter, insurance, taxes, and maintenance costs are recorded as expenses.

The goods and services tax (GST) paid on the purchase of an asset is recoverable if the acquired asset is used to earn income. Therefore, it would not be part of the capitalized cost of the asset. For example, a computer purchased for $2,000 in Ontario would incur PST of 8 percent ($160.00) and GST of 7% ($140.00) for a total cost of $2,300.00. Assuming the computer was to be used to earn revenue, the cost of the asset would be $2,160.00, not $2,300.00, since the GST would be recovered from the Canada Customs and Revenue Agency.

Leasehold Improvements

Leasehold improvements are similar to land improvements. *Leasehold improvements* are alterations to assets the company is leasing. For example, IPSCO Inc. leases some of its vehicles. The company also customizes some of these assets to meet its special needs. For example, IPSCO Inc. may paint its logo on a rental truck and install a special lift on the truck. These improvements are assets of IPSCO Inc. even though the company does not own the truck. The cost of improvements to leased assets appear on the company's balance sheet as *leasehold improvements*. The cost of leasehold improvements should be amortized over the term of the lease or the useful life of the leased asset, whichever is shorter.

Construction in Progress and Capital Leases

If you look at IPSCO Inc.'s financial statements, you will notice two additional categories of capital assets: Construction in progress and Capital leases.

Construction in Progress   *Construction in progress* is an asset, such as a warehouse, that the company is constructing for its own use. On the balance sheet date, the construction is incomplete and the warehouse is not ready for use. However, the construction costs are assets because IPSCO Inc. expects the warehouse, when completed, to render future benefits for the company.

Capital Leases   A *capital lease* is an arrangement where a capital asset is acquired by making regular periodic payments that are required in the lease contract. Companies report assets leased through capital leases on the balance sheet the same way as purchased assets. Why? Because their lease payments secure the use of the asset over the term of the lease. For example, IPSCO Inc. has long-term capital leases running until 2014. Chapter 15 on long-term liabilities goes into capital leases in more detail.

A capital lease is different from an *operating lease*, which is an ordinary rental agreement, such as an apartment lease or the rental of a Budget automobile or a photocopier. The lessee (the renter) records operating lease payments as Rent expense.

Capitalizing the Cost of Interest

IPSCO Inc. constructs some of its capital assets itself and contracts with others to construct other capital assets. Often the construction is financed with borrowed money, on which IPSCO Inc. must pay interest. The *CICA Handbook* Section 3060, "Capital Assets," permits a company to include interest costs up to the date the asset goes into service as part of the cost of the asset. The practice of including interest as part of an asset's cost is called *capitalizing interest*. To **capitalize a cost** means to debit an asset (versus an expense) account.

Capitalizing interest cost is an exception to the normal practice of recording interest as an expense. Ordinarily, a company that borrows money records interest expense. But on assets that the business builds for its own use, or has built, the company should, if it chooses, capitalize some of its interest cost. The reason is this: If IPSCO Inc. contracts Argo Construction Co. to build a building for it, the price of the building will include Argo's interest cost that was incurred to finance the construction. Since self-constructed assets and assets that are paid for during construction should be treated as equivalent assets, it makes sense to capitalize any interest incurred to finance the construction.

The amount of interest to capitalize is based on the average accumulated construction expenditures for the asset. The interest capitalized should not exceed the company's actual interest cost.

A Lump-Sum (or Basket) Purchase of Assets

Businesses often purchase several assets as a group, or in a "basket" for a single amount. For example, a company may pay one price for land and an office building. For accounting purposes, the company must identify the cost of each asset. The total cost is divided between the assets according to their relative sales (or market) values. This allocation technique is called the *relative-sales-value method*.

Suppose Magna International Inc. purchases land and a building in Saint John for an auto-parts plant. The combined purchase price of land and building is $280,000. An appraisal indicates that the land's market (sales) value is $30,000 and the building's market (sales) value is $270,000.

First, calculate the ratio of each asset's market price to the total market price of both assets combined. Total appraised value is $270,000 + $30,000 = $300,000. Thus the land, valued at $30,000, is 10 percent of the total market value. The building's appraised value is 90 percent of the total. The cost of each asset is determined as follows:

Asset	Market (Sales) Value	Percentage of Total Value		Total Purchase Price		Cost of Each Asset
Land	$ 30,000	$ 30,000 ÷ $300,000 = 10%	×	$280,000	=	$ 28,000
Building	$270,000	$270,000 ÷ $300,000 = 90%	×	$280,000	=	$252,000
Total	$300,000					$280,000

Assuming Magna pays cash, the entry to record the purchase of the land and building is

Land	28,000	
Building	252,000	
Cash		280,000

Betterments versus Repairs

When a company makes a capital asset expenditure on a capital asset it already owns, it must decide whether to debit an asset account or an expense account. In this context, *expenditure* refers to a cash or a credit purchase of goods or services related to the asset. Examples of these expenditures range from replacing the windshield on an Airways Limo Co. automobile to adding a wing to a building at Molson.

Expenditures that increase the capacity or efficiency of the asset or extend its useful life are called **betterments**. For example, the cost of a major overhaul that extends a taxi's useful life is a betterment. The amount of the expenditure, said to be *capitalized*, for a betterment is a debit to an asset account. For the cost of a betterment on the taxi, we would debit the asset account Automobile.

Other expenditures do not extend the asset's capacity or efficiency. Expenditures that merely maintain the asset in its existing condition or restore the asset to good working order are called **repairs.** These costs are matched against revenue. Examples include the following costs incurred after a period of use: repainting a taxi, repairing a dented fender, and replacing tires. Repairs are debited to an expense account. For these ordinary repairs on the taxi, we would debit Repair Expense.

The distinction between betterments and repairs is often a matter of opinion. Does the work extend the life of the asset (a betterment), or does it only maintain the asset in good order (a repair)? When doubt exists, companies tend to debit an expense, for two reasons. First, many expenditures are minor in amount, and most companies have a policy of debiting expense for all expenditures below a specified minimum, such as $1,000. Second, the income tax motive favours debiting all borderline expenditures to expense in order to create an immediate tax deduction. Higher expenses mean lower net income, which in turn means lower tax payments. Betterments do not result in immediate tax deductions.

Exhibit 10-3 illustrates the distinction between betterments (capital expenditures) and repairs (expenses) for several delivery truck expenditures.

Treating a betterment as a repair, or vice versa, creates errors in the financial statements. Suppose a company incurs the cost of a betterment to enhance the service potential of equipment and erroneously expenses this cost. A capital expenditure should have been debited to an asset account. This accounting error overstates expenses and understates net income on the income statement. On the balance sheet, the equipment account is understated, and so is owner's equity, as follows:

....
THINKING IT OVER

Basiden Company purchased a used truck. Identify the following truck-related expenditures as betterments or repairs (expenses):
1. Painting company logo on truck when purchased, $500
2. Gasoline for truck, $20
3. Hydraulic loader for truck, $1,500
4. 30,000-km inspection, $100

A: Betterments: 1, 3; Repairs (expenses): 2, 4

Income Statement

Revenues.....................	CORRECT
Expenses	OVERSTATED
Net income	UNDERSTATED

Balance Sheet

Current assets	CORRECT	Total liabilities..............	CORRECT
Capital assets	UNDERSTATED	Owner's equity	UNDERSTATED
		Total liabilities and owner's	
Total assets	UNDERSTATED	equity	UNDERSTATED

Capitalizing the cost of a repair creates the opposite error. Expenses are then understated and net income is overstated. And the balance sheet overstates assets and owner's equity.

Measuring the Amortization of Capital Assets

The allocation of a capital asset's cost to expense over the asset's useful life is called *amortization* in Section 3060 of the *CICA Handbook*. Another term used to describe the allocation of the cost when referring to capital assets such as property, plant, and equipment is *depreciation*. Amortization (see Chapter 3, page 116, for a discussion of the matching principle) is designed to match the expense of an asset against the revenue earned by the asset as the matching principle directs. Exhibit 10-4 shows this process for the purchase of a Boeing 757 jet by Air Canada. The

Debit an Asset Account for Betterments	Debit Repair and Maintenance Expense for Repairs
Betterments	**Repairs**
Major engine overhaul	Repair of transmission or other mechanism
Modification of body for new use of truck	Oil change, lubrication, and so on
Addition to storage capacity of truck	Replacement tires, windshield, and the like
	Paint job

EXHIBIT 10-3

Delivery Truck Expenditures—Betterment or Repair?

Exhibit 10-4

Amortization and the Matching of Expense to Revenue

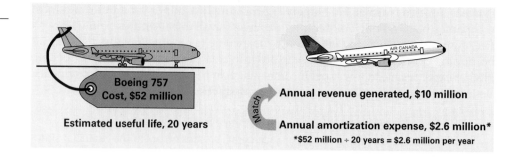

Boeing 757
Cost, $52 million

Estimated useful life, 20 years

Match

Annual revenue generated, $10 million

Annual amortization expense, $2.6 million*

*$52 million ÷ 20 years = $2.6 million per year

primary purpose of amortization accounting is to measure income. Of less importance is the need to account for the asset's decline in usefulness.

Suppose Mark's Work Wearhouse buys a computer to use in its accounting system. Mark's Work Wearhouse believes it will get four years of service from the computer, which will then be worthless. Using straight-line amortization, the business expenses one-quarter of the asset's cost in each of its four years of use.

Let's contrast what amortization accounting *is* with what it *is not*.

1. *Amortization is not a process of valuation.* Businesses do not record amortization based on appraisals of their capital assets made at the end of each period. Instead, businesses allocate the asset's cost to the periods of its useful life based on a specific amortization method. (We discuss these methods in this chapter.)

2. *Amortization does not mean that the business sets aside cash to replace assets as they become fully amortized.* Establishing a cash fund is a decision entirely separate from amortization. *Accumulated amortization* is that portion of the capital asset's cost that has already been recorded as an expense. Accumulated amortization does not represent a growing amount of cash. We learned in Chapter 3, page 117, that *accumulated amortization* is the cumulative sum of all amortization expense from the date a capital asset was acquired. *Amortization expense* is the amortization amount for the current period only.

Causes of Amortization

All assets except land wear out. For some property, plant, and equipment, physical *wear and tear* from operations and the elements may be the important cause of amortization. For example, physical deterioration wears out Intrawest's Bombardier snow-grooming machines and the golf carts on its golf courses. The same is true of Mark's Work Wearhouse's store fixtures.

Assets such as computers, other electronic equipment, and airplanes may become *obsolete* before they physically deteriorate. An asset is obsolete when another asset can do the job better or more efficiently. Thus an asset's useful life may be much shorter than its physical life. Accountants usually amortize computers over a short period of time—perhaps two to four years—even though they know the computers will remain in working condition much longer. Whether wear and tear or obsolescence causes amortization, the asset's cost is amortized over its expected useful life.

Measuring Amortization

Amortization for a capital asset, is based upon the asset's

1. Cost

2. Estimated useful life

3. Estimated residual value

We have already discussed cost, which is the purchase price of the asset. This is a known amount. The other two factors must be estimated.

Estimated useful life is the length of the service period expected from the asset—an estimate of how long the asset will be useful. Useful life may be expressed in years, units of output, kilometres, or other measures. For example, the useful life of a building is stated in years. The useful life of a bookbinding machine is the number of books the machine can bind—that is, its expected units of output. A reasonable measure of a delivery truck's useful life is the total number of kilometres the truck is expected to travel. Companies base such estimates on past experience, industry information, and government publications.

Estimated residual value—also called **salvage value** or **scrap value**—is the expected cash value of the asset at the end of its useful life. For example, a business may believe that a machine's useful life will be seven years. After that time, the company expects to sell the machine as scrap metal. The amount of cash the business believes it can sell the machine for is its estimated residual value. Estimated residual value is *not* amortized, because the business expects to receive this amount from disposing of the asset. If there is no residual value, then the company amortizes the full cost of the asset. The asset's cost minus its estimated residual value is called the **amortizable cost**.

Of the factors entering the computation of amortization, only one factor is known—cost. The other two factors— useful life and residual value—must be estimated. Amortization, then, is an estimated amount.

Amortization Methods

Three methods for computing amortization will be discussed in this text: straight-line, units-of-production, and declining-balance. These three methods allocate different amounts of amortization expense to different periods. However, they all result in the same total amount of amortization over the life of the asset. Exhibit 10-5 presents the data used to illustrate amortization computations by the three methods.

Straight-Line Method In the **straight-line method**, an equal amount of amortization expense is assigned to each year (or period) of asset use. Amortizable cost is divided by useful life in years to determine the annual amortization expense. The equation for straight-line amortization, applied to the truck data from Exhibit 10-5, is

$$\text{Straight-line amortization per year} = \frac{\text{Cost} - \text{Residual value}}{\text{Useful life in years}}$$

$$= \frac{\$55,000 - \$5,000}{5}$$

$$= \$10,000$$

The entry to record one year's amortization is

Amortization Expense	10,000	
Accumulated Amortization		10,000

Assume that the truck was purchased on January 1, 2001, and the business's fiscal year ends on December 31. A *straight-line amortization schedule* is presented in

KEY POINT

Note that the residual value is the portion of the asset's cost that will **not** be consumed or used; therefore it should **not** be amortized.

KEY POINT

The total amount of amortization recorded for an asset cannot exceed its amortizable cost. An asset can be used after it is fully amortized.

KEY POINT

It is impossible to quantify the exact amount that an asset has amortized during the period, but there is no doubt that a portion of the asset has been consumed. An estimate of the amount must be made using one of the amortization methods. Without this expense, there would be no *matching* of the cost of the asset with the revenues generated during the time the asset is used.

OBJECTIVE 2
Account for amortization

LEARNING TIP

The formula for the straight-line rate is: 1/useful life. If an asset has a 5-year useful life, then 1/5 of the asset is amortized each year. The straight-line rate is 1/5, or 20%.

Data Item	Amount
Cost of truck..	$55,000
Estimated residual value	5,000
Amortizable cost	$50,000
Estimated useful life	
Years	5 years
Units of production.......................................	400,000 units (kilometres)

EXHIBIT 10-5

Data for Amortization Computations for a Canadian Tire Truck

EXHIBIT 10-6

Straight-Line Amortization Schedule for a Canadian Tire Truck

Exhibit 10-6. The final column of Exhibit 10-6 shows the asset's *book value*, which is its cost less accumulated amortization. Book value is also called *carrying amount* or *carrying value*. We introduced book value in Chapter 3, page 118.

As an asset is used, accumulated amortization increases and the book value decreases. (Compare the Accumulated Amortization and the Book Value columns in Exhibit 10-6.) An asset's final book value is its *residual value* ($5,000 in Exhibit 10-6). At the end of its useful life, the asset is said to be *fully amortized*.

Units-of-Production Method In the **units-of-production** method, a fixed amount of amortization is assigned to each unit of output produced by the capital asset. Amortizable cost is divided by useful life in units of production to determine this amount. This per-unit amortization expense is multiplied by the number of units produced each period to compute amortization for that period. The units-of-production amortization equation for the truck data in Exhibit 10-5 is

$$\text{Units-of-production amortization per unit of output} = \frac{\text{Cost} - \text{Residual Value}}{\text{Useful life, in units of production}}$$

$$= \frac{\$55,000 - \$5,000}{400,000 \text{ kilometres}}$$

$$= \$0.125 \text{ per kilometre}$$

Assume the truck was driven 90,000 kilometres during the first year, 120,000 during the second, 100,000 during the third, 60,000 during the fourth, and 30,000 during the fifth. The units-of-production amortization schedule for this asset is shown in Exhibit 10-7.

The amount of units-of-production amortization per period varies with the number of units the asset produces. Note that the total number of units produced is 400,000—the measure of this asset's useful life. Therefore, units-of-production amortization does not depend directly on time as do the other methods.

Accelerated Methods There are two **accelerated-amortization methods**: a declining-balance method; and the sum-of-years-digits method, which is not widely used in Canada and so will not be discussed in this text. The most common declining-balance method is the double-declining-balance method; it is discussed below. An accelerated-amortization method writes off more of the asset's cost nearer the start of its useful life than does the straight-line method.

The **double-declining-balance amortization method** involves computing annual amortization by multiplying the asset's book value by a constant percentage, which is two times the straight-line amortization rate. Double-declining-balance rates are computed as follows:

1. Compute the straight-line amortization rate per year. For example, a five-year computer has a straight-line amortization rate of 100 percent divided by 5, or 20 percent per year. A ten-year asset, such as a desk, has a straight-line rate of 100 percent divided by 10, or 10 percent per year, and so on.

			Amortization for the Year				
Date	Asset Cost	Amortization Rate		Amortizable Cost		Amortization Amount	Accumulated Amortization	Asset Book Value
1-1-2001	$55,000							$55,000
31-12-2001		0.20	×	$50,000	=	$10,000	$ 10,000	45,000
31-12-2002		0.20	×	50,000	=	10,000	20,000	35,000
31-12-2003		0.20	×	50,000	=	10,000	30,000	25,000
31-12-2004		0.20	×	50,000	=	10,000	40,000	15,000
31-12-2005		0.20	×	50,000	=	10,000	50,000	5,000

		Amortization for the Year				
Date	Asset Cost	Amortization Per Unit	Number of Units	Amortization Amount	Accumulated Amortization	Asset Book Value
1-1-2001	$55,000					$55,000
31-12-2001		$0.125 ×	90,000 =	$11,250	$11,250	43,750
31-12-2002		0.125 ×	120,000 =	15,000	26,250	28,750
31-12-2003		0.125 ×	100,000 =	12,500	38,750	16,250
31-12-2004		0.125 ×	60,000 =	7,500	46,250	8,750
31-12-2005		0.125 ×	30,000 =	3,750	50,000	5,000

EXHIBIT 10-7

Units-of-Production Amortization Schedule for a Canadian Tire Truck

2. Compute the double-declining-balance rate: Multiply the straight-line rate by 2. The double-declining-balance rate for a ten-year asset is 20 percent per year ([100%/10] × 2 = 20%). For a five-year asset like the Canadian Tire truck in Exhibit 10-5, the double-declining-balance rate is 40 percent ([100%/5] × 2 = 40%).

3. Compute the year's double-declining-balance amortization. Multiply the asset's book value (cost less accumulated amortization) at the beginning of the year by the double-declining-balance rate. Ignore the asset's residual value in computing amortization except for the last year. The first year's amortization for the truck in Exhibit 10-5 is

$$\text{Double-declining-balance amortization for the first year} = \text{Asset book value at the beginning of the period} \times \text{Double-declining-balance rate}$$

$$= \$55,000 \times 0.40$$

$$= \$22,000$$

The same approach is used to compute double-declining-balance amortization for all later years, except for the final year, which is calculated as follows:

4. Determine the final year's amortization amount, which cannot exceed the amount needed to reduce the asset's book value to its residual value. In the double-declining-balance amortization schedule in Exhibit 10-8, the fifth and final year's amortization is $2,128—the $7,128 book value less the $5,000 residual value; 40 percent times the book value would be $2,851 (0.40 × $7,128), which is too much. The residual value should not be amortized but should remain on the books until the asset's disposal.

THINKING IT OVER

As Exhibit 10-7 shows, amortization by the units-of-production method varies proportionately to usage (kilometres driven). What is the disadvantage to using units-of-production?

A: Difficult to estimate the total number of units over the asset's life, so the units-of-production method may require frequent revisions; amortization may fluctuate causing net income to fluctuate.

EXHIBIT 10-8

Double-Declining-Balance Amortization Schedule for a Canadian Tire Truck

		Amortization for the Year				
Date	Asset Cost	Double-Declining-Balance Rate	Asset Book Value	Amortization Amount	Accumulated Amortization	Asset Book Value
1-1-2001	$55,000					$55,000
31-12-2001		0.40 ×	$55,000 =	$22,000	$22,000	33,000
31-12-2002		0.40 ×	33,000 =	13,200	35,200	19,800
31-12-2003		0.40 ×	19,800 =	7,920	43,120	11,880
31-12-2004		0.40 ×	11,880 =	4,752	47,872	7,128
31-12-2005				2,128*	50,000	5,000

* Amortization in year 2005 is the amount needed to reduce asset book value to the residual value ($7,128 – $5,000 = $2,128).

The double-declining-balance method differs from the other methods in two ways: (1) The asset's residual value is ignored initially. In the first year, amortization is calculated on the asset's full cost. (2) The final year's calculation is changed in order to bring the asset's book value to the residual value.

Most companies that use the double-declining-balance method do not calculate amortization on each capital asset separately, but rather they add the cost of each asset to a pool of similar assets and calculate amortization on the unamortized balance in the pool. This method is not as accurate as performing the individual calculations as illustrated in Exhibit 10-8, but it is much simpler and the degree of inaccuracy is small. (This text focuses on calculating amortization for individual assets, not pools of assets.)

Comparing Amortization Methods

Compare the three methods illustrated in Exhibits 10-6, 10-7, and 10-8 in terms of the yearly amount of amortization:

	Amount of Amortization per Year		
Year	Straight-Line	Units-of-Production	Double-Declining-Balance
1	$10,000	$11,250	$22,000
2	10,000	15,000	13,200
3	10,000	12,500	7,920
4	10,000	7,500	4,752
5	10,000	3,750	2,128
Total	$50,000	$50,000	$50,000

Annual amortization varies by method, but the total is the same for all methods—$50,000.

Straight-line method Generally accepted accounting principles (GAAP) direct a business to match the expense of an asset to the revenue that the asset produces. For a capital asset that generates revenue fairly evenly over time, the straight-line method follows the matching principle. During each period the asset is used, an equal amount of amortization is recorded.

Units-of-production method The units-of-production method best fits an asset that wears out because of physical use, rather than obsolescence. Amortization is recorded only when the asset is used, and the more units the asset produces, the greater the amortization expense.

Double-declining-balance method The double-declining-balance or accelerated method works best for assets that produce more revenue in their early years. The greater expense recorded in the early periods matches best against those periods' greater revenue.

Exhibit 10-9 graphs the relationship between annual amortization amounts for straight-line, units-of-production, and the double-declining-balance methods.

- The graph of straight-line amortization is flat because annual amortization is the same amount in each period.

- Units-of-production amortization follows no particular pattern because annual amortization varies depending on the use of the asset. The greater the use, the greater is the amount of amortization.

- Accelerated amortization is greatest in the asset's first year and less in the later years.

A recent survey indicated that over 91 percent of companies use the straight-line

Exhibit 10-9

Straight-Line	Units-of-Production	Declining-Balance
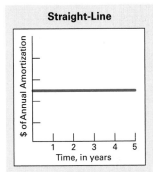	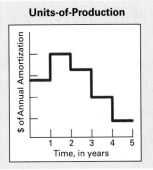	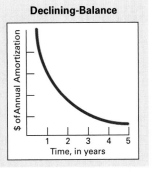

KEY POINT

The double-declining-balance method is an accelerated amortization method. An accelerated method expenses more asset cost in the early years of an asset's life than in the later years. This method assumes that an asset is more useful (productive) in its early years and therefore should be amortized more then.

method, approximately 19 percent use an accelerated method, and approximately 28 percent use the units-of-production method. (Some companies use more than one method for different kinds of capital assets, so the total exceeds 100 percent.)[1] For example, Schneider Corporation, the meat-packing and food-producing company, uses straight-line, while Inco Limited uses straight-line and units of production.

Mid-Chapter Summary Problem
for Your Review

Hubbard Company purchased equipment on January 1, 2002, for $44,000. The expected life of the equipment is ten years or 100,000 units of production, and its residual value is $4,000. Under three amortization methods, the annual amortization expense and the balance of accumulated amortization at the end of 2002 and 2003 are:

	Method A		Method B		Method C	
Year	Annual Amortization Expense	Accumulated Amortization	Annual Amortization Expense	Accumulated Amortization	Annual Amortization Expense	Accumulated Amortization
2002	$4,000	$4,000	$8,800	$ 8,800	$1,200	$1,200
2003	4,000	8,000	7,040	15,840	5,600	6,800

Required

1. Identify the amortization method used in each instance, and show the equation and computation for each. (Round off to the nearest dollar.)

2. Assume continued use of the same method through the year 2004. Determine the annual amortization expense, accumulated amortization, and book value of the equipment for 2002 through 2004 under each method, assuming 12,000 units of production in 2004.

---

[1] Byrd, C., I. Chen, and H. Chapman, *Financial Reporting in Canada, 1999,* Twenty-fourth edition. (Toronto: Canadian Institute of Chartered Accountants, 1999), p. 269.

Solution to Review Problem

Requirement 1

Method A: Straight-line method

Amortizable cost = $40,000 ($44,000 − $4,000)

Each year: $40,000/10 years = $4,000

Method B: Double-declining-balance method

$$\text{Rate} = \frac{100\%}{10 \text{ years}} \times 2 = 10\% \times 2 = 20\%$$

2002: 0.20 × $44,000 = $8,800

2003: 0.20 × ($44,000 − $8,800) = $7,040

Method C: Units-of-production method

$$\text{Amortization per unit} = \frac{\$44,000 - \$4,000}{100,000 \text{ units}} = \$0.40$$

2002: $0.40 × 3,000 units = $1,200
(since $1,200 ÷ $0.40 = 3,000 units)

2003: $0.40 × 14,000 units = $5,600
(since $5,600 ÷ $0.40 = 14,000 units)

Requirement 2

	Method A Straight-Line			Method B Double-Declining-Balance			Method C Units-of-Production		
Year	Annual Amortization Expense	Accumulated Amortization	Book Value	Annual Amortization Expense	Accumulated Amortization	Book Value	Annual Amortization Expense	Accumulated Amortization	Book Value
Start			$44,000			$44,000			$44,000
2002	$4,000	$ 4,000	40,000	$8,800	$ 8,800	35,200	$1,200	$ 1,200	42,800
2003	4,000	8,000	36,000	7,040	15,840	28,160	5,600	6,800	37,200
2004	4,000	12,000	32,000	5,632	21,472	22,528	4,800	11,600	32,400

Computations for 2004

Straight-line: $40,000/10 years = $4,000

Double-declining-balance: 0.20 × $28,160 = $5,632

Units-of-production: $0.40 × 12,000 units = $4,800

Cyber Coach

Visit the Student Resource area of the *Accounting* Companion Website for extra practice with the new material in Chapter 10.

www.pearsoned.ca/horngren

The Relationship between Amortization and Income Taxes

OBJECTIVE 3
Explain capital cost allowance, amortization for income tax purposes

The majority of businesses use the straight-line method for reporting capital asset values and amortization expense to their owners and creditors on their financial statements. But businesses must often keep a separate set of records for calculating the amortization they claim on their tax return. This is because, whatever amortization method a business uses, amortization expense on the income statement is often different from amortization deducted for income tax purposes. Canada Customs and Revenue Agency allows corporations, as well as individuals earning business or professional income, to deduct from income **capital cost allowance**, the term Canada Customs and Revenue Agency uses to describe amortization for tax purposes. Canada Customs and Revenue Agency specifies the *maximum* capital cost allowance rate a taxpayer may use. Different classes of assets have different capital cost allowance rates. The capital cost allowance rates published by Canada Customs and Revenue Agency are maximums. A taxpayer may claim from zero to the maximum capital cost allowance allowed in a year. Most taxpayers claim the maximum capital cost allowance since this provides the largest deduction from income as quickly as possible, thus decreasing the immediate tax payment. Claiming the maximum capital cost allowance leaves more cash available for investment or other business uses.

Capital cost allowance is discussed in more detail in the Appendix at the end of this chapter.

Amortization for Partial Years

Companies purchase capital assets whenever they need them. They do not wait until the beginning of a year or a month. Therefore, companies must develop policies to compute amortization for partial years. Suppose Falconbridge Limited, the mining company, purchases a building in Timmins, Ontario, as a maintenance shop on April 1, 2001, for $500,000. The building's estimated life is 20 years and its estimated residual value is $80,000. Falconbridge Limited's fiscal year ends on December 31. How does the company compute amortization for the year ended December 31?

Many companies compute partial-year amortization by first computing a full year's amortization. They then multiply the full-year amount by the fraction of the year they held the asset. Assuming the straight-line method, the year's amortization for the maintenance shop is $15,750, computed as follows:

$$\text{Full-year amortization: } \frac{\$500,000 - \$80,000}{20 \text{ years}} = \$21,000$$
$$\text{Partial-year amortization: } \$21,000 \times 9/12 = \$15,750$$

What if the company bought the asset on April 18? One widely used policy suggests businesses record no amortization on assets purchased after the 15th of the month and record a full month's amortization on an asset bought on or before the 15th. Thus the company would record no amortization for April for an April 18 purchase. In this case, the year's amortization would be $14,000 ($21,000 × 8/12).

How is partial-year amortization computed under the other amortization methods? Suppose Falconbridge acquired the building on October 4, and the company uses the double-declining-balance method. Since the straight-line rate is 5 percent (100%/20 years), the double-declining-balance rate is 10 percent (2 × 5%). The annual amortization computations for 2001, 2002, and 2003 are shown in Exhibit 10-10.

No special computation is needed for partial-year amortization under the units-of-production method. Simply use the number of units produced, regardless of the time period the asset is held.

Falconbridge Limited
www.falconbridge.com

WORKING IT OUT

On April 1, Year 1, Halifax Technologies Co. purchases a piece of robotic machinery with a 5-year useful life and no salvage value for $8,000. Compute straight-line amortization at December 31 for years 1 to 6.

A: Yr. 1: $1,200
([$8,000/5] × 9/12)
Yr. 2–5: $1,600 ($8,000/5)
Yr. 6: $400 ($1,600 × 3/12)

		Amortization for the Year						
Date	Asset Cost	DDB Rate	Asset Book Value— Beginning	Fraction of the Year		Amortization Amount	Accumulated Amortization	Asset Book Value— Ending
4-10-2001	$500,000							$500,000
31-12-2001		0.10 ×	$500,000 ×	3/12	=	$12,500	$12,500	487,500
31-12-2002		0.10 ×	487,500 ×	12/12	=	48,750	61,250	438,750
31-12-2003		0.10 ×	438,750 ×	12/12	=	43,875	105,125	394,875

EXHIBIT 10-10

Annual Double-Declining-Balance (DDB) Amortization for Partial Years

Most companies use computerized systems to account for capital assets. They identify each asset with a unique identification number and indicate the asset's cost, estimated life, residual value, and amortization method. The system will automatically calculate the amortization expense for each period. Both Accumulated Amortization and book value are automatically updated.

Change in the Useful Life of an Amortizable Asset

As previously discussed, a business must estimate the useful life of a capital asset to compute amortization on that asset. This prediction is the most difficult part of accounting for amortization. After the asset is put into use, the business is able to refine its estimate based on experience and new information. Such a change is called a change in accounting estimate. In an actual example, Precision Drilling Corporation included the following note in a recent financial statement:

Note 2 Property, Plant, and Equipment (in part)
... During 1998, the estimated life of drilling rig equipment was changed from 3,000 to 3,650 drilling days. The change resulted in a reduction of depreciation expense for 1998 of $5.7 million and an increase in net earnings after income taxes of $2.8 million ... from what otherwise would have been reported had the change not been made.

Accounting changes like these are common because no business has perfect foresight. Generally accepted accounting principles require the business to report the nature, reason, and effect of the change in estimate on net income, as the Precision Drilling Corporation example shows. To *record* a change in accounting estimate, the remaining book value of the asset is spread over its adjusted, or new, remaining useful life. The new useful life may be longer or shorter than the original useful life.

Assume that a Big Rock Brewery Ltd. machine cost $40,000, and the company originally believed the asset had an eight-year useful life with no residual value. Using the straight-line method, the company would record $5,000 amortization each year ($40,000/8 years = $5,000). Suppose Big Rock Brewery Ltd. used the asset for two years. Accumulated amortization reached $10,000, leaving a book value of $30,000 ($40,000 – $10,000). From its experience with the asset during the first two years, management believes the asset will remain useful for the next ten years. The company would compute a revised annual amortization amount and record it as follows:

Precision Drilling Corporation
www.precisiondrilling.com

WORKING IT OUT

In 1982, ABC Co. purchased for $600,000 a building that had an estimated residual value of $100,000 and a life of 40 years. In 2002, a $200,000 addition to the building increased its residual value by $50,000. The accumulated amortization on the building is $250,000. Calculate straight-line amortization expense for 2002.

A: Calculate book value:

Cost (new)	$800,000*
Acc. Amort.	250,000
Revised book value	$550,000

Revised straight-line amortization

$$= \frac{\$550,000 - \$150,000}{20}$$

$= \$20,000$ per year

*$600,000 + $200,000

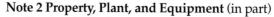

Asset's Remaining Amortizable Book Value		(New) Estimated Useful Life Remaining		(New) Annual Amortization Amount
$30,000	÷	10 years	=	$3,000

The yearly amortization entry based on new estimated useful life is

Amortization Expense—Machine 3,000
    Accumulated Amortization—Machine 3,000

The equation for revised straight-line amortization is

$$\text{Revised Straight-line Amortization} = \frac{\text{Cost} - \text{Accumulated Amortization} - \text{New Residual Value}}{\text{Estimated remaining useful life in years}}$$

STOP & THINK

1. Suppose Hi Value Stores was having a bad year—net income below expectations and lower than last year's income. For amortization purposes Hi Value Stores decided to extend the estimated useful lives of its amortizable assets. This decision was *not* based on any belief that the actual useful life was longer than originally thought. How would this accounting change affect Hi Value Stores' (a) amortization expense, (b) net income, and (c) owner's equity?

Answer: An accounting change that lengthens the estimated useful lives of amortizable assets (a) decreases amortization expense and (b, c) increases net income and owner's equity.

2. Suppose that the Hi Value Stores' accounting change turned a loss year into a profitable year. Without the accounting change, the company would have reported a net loss for the year. But the accounting change enabled the company to report net income. Under GAAP, Hi Value Stores' annual report must disclose the accounting change and its effect on net income. Would users of the financial statements, such as the bank, evaluate Hi Value Stores as better or worse in response to these disclosures?

Answer: Users' reactions are not always predictable. There is evidence, however, that businesses cannot fool users. If users have enough information—such as the knowledge of an accounting change disclosed in the annual report—they can process the information correctly. In this case, analysts would *probably* subtract from Hi Value Stores' reported net income the amount caused by the accounting change. Users could then use the remaining net *loss* figure to evaluate Hi Value Stores' lack of progress during the year. Users would probably view Hi Value Stores worse for having made this accounting change. For this reason, and because the ethics behind such an accounting change are questionable, many owners and managers would not engage in this type of income manipulation.

Using Fully Amortized Assets

A *fully amortized asset* is one that has reached the end of its *estimated* useful life. No more amortization is recorded for the asset. If the asset is no longer suitable for its purpose, the asset is disposed of, as discussed in the next section. However, the company may be unable to replace the asset. Or the asset's useful life may have been underestimated at the outset and the asset remains useful. In any event, companies sometimes continue using fully amortized assets. The asset account and its related accumulated amortization account remain in the ledger, even though no additional amortization is recorded for the asset.

> **THINKING IT OVER**
>
> A fully amortized asset has a cost of $80,000 and zero residual value. What is the asset's accumulated amortization?
>
> *A:* $80,000 (same as the asset's cost)
>
> Now suppose the asset's residual value is $10,000. How much is its accumulated amortization?
>
> *A:* $70,000 ($80,000 - $10,000).

Disposing of a Capital Asset (Property, Plant, and Equipment)

Eventually, a capital asset such as property, plant, or equipment ceases to serve its purpose. The asset may have become worn out, obsolete, or for some other reason, no longer useful to the business. In general, a company disposes of property, plant, and equipment by selling or exchanging it. If the asset cannot be sold or exchanged, then the asset is junked. Whatever the method of disposal, the business should bring amortization up to date to measure the asset's final book value properly.

To account for disposal, credit the asset account and debit its accumulated amortization account to remove these accounts from the accounting record. Suppose the final year's amortization expense has just been recorded for a machine that cost $6,000 with no residual value. The machine's accumulated amortization thus totals $6,000. Assume this asset cannot be sold or exchanged, so it is junked. The entry to record its disposal is

Accumulated Amortization—Machinery	6,000	
Machinery..		6,000
To dispose of a fully amortized machine.		

Now both accounts have a zero balance, as shown in the T-accounts below:

Machinery		Accumulated Amortization—Machinery	
6,000	6,000	6,000	6,000

If assets are junked before being fully amortized, the company records a loss equal to the asset's book value. Suppose Zellers' store fixtures that cost $4,000 are junked at a loss. Accumulated amortization is $3,000 and book value is therefore $1,000. Disposal of these store fixtures results in a loss equal to the book value of the asset, as follows:

Accumulated Amortization—Store Fixtures	3,000	
Loss on Disposal of Capital Assets...	1,000	
Store Fixtures		4,000
To dispose of store fixtures.		

All losses, including this Loss on Disposal of Capital Assets, decrease net income. Along with expenses, losses are reported on the income statement.

Selling a Capital Asset

Suppose a business sells furniture on September 30, 2003, for $5,000 cash. The furniture cost $10,000 when purchased on January 1, 2000, and has been amortized on a straight-line basis. Managers estimated a ten-year useful life and no residual value. Prior to recording the sale of the furniture, accountants must update its amortization. Since the business uses the calendar year as its accounting period, partial amortization must be recorded for the asset's expense from January 1, 2003, to the sale date of September 30. The straight-line amortization entry at September 30, 2003, is

Sept. 30	Amortization Expense	750	
	Accumulated Amortization—Furniture....................		750
	To update amortization ($10,000/10 years × $9/12$).		

After this entry is posted, the Furniture and the Accumulated Amortization—Furniture accounts appear as follows. The furniture book value is $6,250 ($10,000 – $3,750).

Furniture		Accumulated Amortization—Furniture	
Jan. 1, 2000 10,000		Dec. 31, 2000 1,000	
		Dec. 31, 2001 1,000	
		Dec. 31, 2002 1,000	
		Sept. 30, 2003 750	
		Balance 3,750	

Book value = $6,250

Suppose the business sells the furniture for $5,000 cash. The loss on the sale is $1,250, determined as follows:

Cash received from sale of the asset		$5,000
Book value of asset sold:		
Cost..	$10,000	
Accumulated amortization		
up to date of sale...	3,750	6,250
Gain (loss) on sale of the asset		($1,250)

The entry to record sale of the furniture for $5,000 cash is

Sept. 30	Cash..	5,000	
	Loss on Disposal of Capital Assets	1,250	
	Accumulated Amortization—Furniture.............	3,750	
	Furniture..		10,000
	To dispose of furniture.		

When recording the sale of property, plant, and equipment, the business must remove the balances in the asset account (Furniture, in this case) and its related accumulated amortization account, and also record a gain or a loss if the amount of cash received differs from the asset's book value. In our example, cash of $5,000 is less than the book value of the furniture, $6,250. The result is a loss of $1,250.

If the sale price had been $7,000, the business would have had a gain of $750 (Cash, $7,000 – asset book value, $6,250). The entry to record this transaction would be

Sept. 30	Cash...	7,000	
	Accumulated Amortization—Furniture.............	3,750	
	Furniture..		10,000
	Gain on Disposal of Capital Assets................		750
	To dispose of furniture.		

A gain is recorded when an asset is sold for a price greater than the asset's book value. A loss is recorded when the sale price is less than book value. Gains increase net income and losses decrease net income. All gains and losses are reported on the income statement.

Exchanging Capital Assets

When a business sells a capital asset it owns, the business may sell the asset for cash, or it may trade in the asset for a *similar* asset (an old truck for a newer truck) or for a *dissimilar* asset (an old tractor for a new truck). The accounting treatment differs depending on whether the assets are similar or dissimilar, and depending on the amount of cash involved in the exchange.

For example, Speedex Digging Company owns a 1996 Ford tractor that it purchased for $32,000 on January 2, 1996. The tractor was expected to last eight years and was amortized on a straight-line basis.

Equipment with original cost of $10,000, residual value of $2,000, and 5-year life was sold on March 31, 2002, for $6,400. Accumulated amortization (straight-line method) on the asset was $2,500 as of December 31, 2001. Record the sale.

A: First, calculate amortization from December 31, 2001, to March 31, 2002: ($10,000 – $2,000)/5 × 3/12 = $400. Add this figure to the $2,500 as of December 31, 2001, to bring accumulated amortization as of March 31, 2002, to $2,900.

Now, make the entry:

Cash.................	6,400	
Acc. Amort.	2,900	
Loss on Sale	700	
Equipment ...		10,000

LEARNING TIP

When an asset is sold, a gain or loss on the sale is determined by comparing the proceeds from the sale to the asset's book value:

- Proceeds > Book value
= **Gain**

- Proceeds < Book value
= **Loss**

Exchange of an asset for a dissimilar asset If an asset is exchanged for a dissimilar asset, the accounting treatment is similar to the sale of an asset for cash. Any gain or loss on the transaction must be recorded.

Assume, on January 2, 2001, Speedex Digging Company exchanged the tractor described above for a truck that had a list price of $24,000. Speedex Digging Company was allowed a trade-in of $5,000 for the tractor and paid the seller $19,000 cash. The entry to record the exchange of dissimilar assets would be:

Truck	24,000	
Loss on exchange of assets	7,000	
Accumulated Amortization—Tractor	20,000	
Cash		19,000
Tractor		32,000
To record exchange of the tractor and cash for a new truck.		

If the tractor was exchanged for the truck but trade-in allowed was $14,000 and cash payment was $10,000, the entry to record the exchange would be:

Truck	24,000	
Accumulated Amortization—Tractor	20,000	
Cash		10,000
Tractor		32,000
Gain on exchange of assets...		2,000
To record exchange of the tractor and cash for a new truck.		

....
      THINKING IT OVER

Why is the trade-in allowance usually different from the book value?

A: The book value depends on the asset's historical cost and on the amortization method used. The trade-in allowance is based on the market value of the asset being traded in (or may be an adjustment to the selling price).

Exchanges of Similar Assets Paragraph 3830.04 of the *CICA Handbook* states that in an exchange transaction where the cash paid is less than 10% of the value of the asset acquired, the exchange is *nonmonetary*. To illustrate, if a company exchanged its truck and $500 cash for another truck that had a market value of $8,000, the transaction would be nonmonetary, since the $500 cash is less than 10% of $8,000 ($8,000 × 10% = $800).

The reason that the classification of the transaction as *monetary* or *nonmonetary* is important is that gains (or losses) are recognized on monetary transactions (as was shown above) but they are not recognized on nonmonetary transactions. Instead, for nonmonetary exchanges of similar assets, the cost of the asset received is recorded as the book value of the asset traded in plus any cash paid or less any cash received. However, the recorded cost of the asset received can be no higher than its market value.

To illustrate, assume Speedex Digging Company owns a bulldozer that has an original cost of $200,000 and accumulated amortization of $110,000. The company exchanges this old bulldozer for a new one with a market value of $150,000. The company is allowed a trade-in of $140,000 and pays $10,000 cash. This is a nonmonetary transaction because the cash paid, $10,000, is less than 10% of the market value of the new bulldozer, $15,000 ($150,000 × 10% = $15,000).

The entry to record this nonmonetary exchange of similar assets would be:

Bulldozer (new)...	100,000	
Accumulated Amortization—Bulldozer (old)........................	110,000	
Cash		10,000
Bulldozer (old)		200,000
To record the nonmonetary exchange of an old bulldozer for a new bulldozer.		

Notice that the gain that would have been recognized in a monetary exchange of assets [(market value of new asset − (book value of old asset + cash)] is deducted from the cost of the new bulldozer, since no gain is recognized on a nonmonetary exchange of assets. Therefore, the new bulldozer's cost is $100,000 (calculated as $150,000 − [$200,000 − $110,000 + $10,000] = $50,000; $150,000 − $50,000 = $100,000).

The nonmonetary exchange of similar assets shown above would be recorded differently if the old asset's book value and cash given were greater than the market value of the new asset. Suppose all the details of the exchange of assets above were the same except that the accumulated amortization of the old bulldozer is only $50,000, not $110,000. The entry to record this nonmonetary exchange of similar assets would now be:

Bulldozer (new)...	150,000	
Accumulated Amortization—Bulldozer (old)........................	50,000	
Loss on the exchange of assets...	10,000	
Cash		10,000
Bulldozer (old)		200,000
To record the nonmonetary exchange of an old bulldozer for a new bulldozer.		

As was mentioned above, although the rule is that a gain or loss is not recognized on nonmonetary transactions, the cost of the new bulldozer must not be recorded at more than its market value of $150,000. Since the book value of the old bulldozer ($150,000) and the cash given ($10,000) is greater than the market value of the new bulldozer ($150,000), a loss of $10,000 must be recorded.[2]

STOP & THINK

Suppose Hudson's Bay Co.'s comparative income statement for two years included these items:

	2003	2002
	($ millions)	
Net sales..	$7,200	$6,800
Income from operations	$ 49	$ 65
Gain on sale of store facilities	28	—
Income before income taxes......................................	$ 67	$ 65

Which was a better year for The Bay—2003 or 2002?

Answer: From a *sales* standpoint 2003 was better because sales were higher. But from an *income* standpoint, 2002 was the better year. In 2002, merchandising operations—The Bay's main business—generated $65 million of income before taxes. In 2003, merchandising produced only $49 million of income before taxes. Part of the company's income in 2003 came from selling store facilities. A business cannot hope to continue on this path very long. This example illustrates why investors and creditors are interested in the sources of a company's profits, not just the final amount of net income.

Internal Control of Capital Assets (Property, Plant, and Equipment)

Internal control of capital assets (property, plant, and equipment) includes safeguarding them and having an adequate accounting system. Recall from Chapter 7 the importance of a strong system of internal controls within a business. To see the need for controlling capital assets, consider the following situation. The home office and top managers of Petrol Mfg. Ltd. are in Calgary. The company manufactures gas pumps in Michigan, then sells them in Europe. Top managers and owners of the company rarely see the manufacturing plant and therefore cannot control their capital assets by on-the-spot management. What features does their internal control system need?

---

[2] GAAP rules for exchanges may differ from income tax rules. In this discussion, we are concerned with the accounting rules.

Safeguarding capital assets (property, plant, and equipment) includes:

1. Assigning responsibility for custody of the assets.
2. Separating custody of assets from accounting for the assets. (This separation of duties is a cornerstone of internal control in almost every area.)
3. Setting up security measures—for instance, guards and restricted access to property, plant, and equipment—to prevent theft.
4. Protecting capital assets from the elements (rain, snow, and so on).
5. Having adequate insurance against fire, storm, and other casualty losses.
6. Training operating personnel in the proper use of the assets.
7. Checking capital assets regularly for existence and condition.
8. Keeping a regular maintenance schedule.

OBJECTIVE 5
Account for wasting assets and amortization

Accounting for Wasting Assets and Amortization

Wasting assets or *natural resources* such as iron ore, coal, oil, gas, and timber are capital assets of a special type. An investment in natural resources could be described as an investment in inventories in the ground (coal) or on top of the ground (timber). In the same way as capital assets (such as machines) are expensed through amortization, natural resource assets are also expensed. Some companies use the word **depletion** to describe amortization of wasting assets. **Amortization expense** is that portion of the cost of natural resources that is used up in a particular period. Amortization expense for wasting assets is computed in the same way as *units-of-production* amortization:

$$\text{Amortization per unit of natural resource} = \frac{\text{Cost} - \text{Residual value}}{\text{Estimated total units of natural resource}}$$

WORKING IT OUT

Pulp Products purchases for $500,000 land that contains an estimated 500,000 fbm (foot-board measure) of timber. The land can be sold for $100,000 after the timber has been cut. If Pulp Products harvests 200,000 fbm in the year of purchase, how much amortization should be recorded?

A: $160,000
[($500,000 − $100,000) ÷ 500,000 = $0.80/bfm.
$0.80 × 200,000 = $160,000]

An oil well may cost $100,000 and contain an estimated 10,000 barrels of oil. The amortization rate would be $10 per barrel ($100,000/10,000 barrels). If 3,000 barrels are extracted during the first year, amortization expense is $30,000 (3,000 barrels × $10 per barrel). The amortization entry for the year is

Amortization Expense...	30,000	
Accumulated Amortization—Oil		30,000

If 4,500 barrels are removed the second year, that period's amortization is $45,000 (4,500 barrels × $10 per barrel). Accumulated Amortization for wasting assets is a contra account similar to Accumulated Amortization for property, plant, and equipment.

Natural resource assets can be reported as follows:

Capital Assets:		
Property, plant, and equipment		
Land		$120,000
Buildings	$800,000	
Equipment..	160,000	
	960,000	
Less: Accumulated amortization	410,000	
Net property, plant, and equipment.............................		550,000
Oil and gas properties		
Oil	$340,000	
Less: Accumulated amortization*	90,000	
Net oil and gas properties		250,000
Total capital assets		$920,000

* Includes the $30,000 recorded above.

Future Removal and Site Restoration Costs

There is increasing concern by individuals and governments about the environment. Often, in the past, a company exploiting natural resources, such as a mining company, would simply abandon the site once the ore body was mined completely. Now, there is legislation in most jurisdictions requiring a natural resource company to remove buildings, equipment, and waste, and to restore the site once a location is to be dismantled and abandoned.

The costs of future removal and site restoration at a property are a charge against all revenues earned from that property; the matching principle suggests that such costs should be accumulated over the economic life of the location. The *CICA Handbook* in Section 3060 requires a natural resource company to accrue future removal and site restoration costs net of expected recoveries by charging income on a reasonable basis. The accrual should be shown as a liability on the balance sheet. When the costs cannot be reasonably determined, a contingent liability (a potential liability) should be disclosed in the notes to the financial statements.

Accounting for Intangible Assets and Amortization

OBJECTIVE 6
Account for intangible assets and amortization

As we saw earlier in this chapter, **intangible assets** are a class of long-lived assets that have no physical form. Instead, these assets consist of special rights to current and expected future benefits from patents, copyrights, trademarks, franchises, leaseholds, and goodwill.

In today's technology-driven economy, intangibles are surpassing tangible assets in value. The electronic economy rewards brand equity, knowledge capital, and customer loyalty. These intangibles create a global customer base. Consider online auctioneer eBay. The company has no physical products or equipment but it helps people buy and sell everything from toys to bathroom tiles. In 1999, eBay served 10 million customers and earned $225 billion in revenues (all amounts in U.S. dollars) with fewer than 150 employees.

Alas, accountants typically deal with historical costs rather than future value. Information about a company's intellectual capital is difficult to measure. But when one company buys another, we get a glimpse of the value of the acquired intellectual capital. For example, America Online (AOL) announced it would acquire Time Warner. AOL said it would exchange $146 billion worth of stock (all amounts in U.S. dollars) and agree to pay $38 billion of future liabilities for Time Warner's net tangible assets of only $9 billion. Why? Because Time Warner's identifiable intangible assets were worth $190 billion. Intangibles can account for as much as 85 percent of a company's perceived value, so companies must find ways to account for intangibles just as they do for their physical and financial assets.

The acquisition cost of an intangible asset is debited to an asset account. For example, the cost of a patent is debited to Patents, an asset account. The intangible is expensed as it expires through amortization. Amortization applies to intangible assets in the same way that it applies to property, plant, and equipment, and wasting assets.

Amortization is generally computed on a straight-line basis over the lesser of the asset's legal life or estimated useful life—up to a maximum of 40 years, according to GAAP. But, obsolescence often shortens an intangible asset's useful life. Amortization expense for intangibles can be written off directly against the intangible asset account rather than held in an accumulated amortization account. The residual value of most intangible assets is zero.

Assume that a business purchases a patent on a special manufacturing process. Legally, the patent may run for 20 years. However, the business realizes that new technologies will limit the patented process's life to four years. If the patent cost $80,000, each year's amortization expense is $20,000 ($80,000/4). The balance sheet reports the patent at its acquisition cost less the sum of all amortization expense to date. After one year, the patent has a $60,000 balance ($80,000 – $20,000), after two years a $40,000 balance, and so on.

Specific Intangibles

Patents Patents are federal government grants giving a holder the exclusive right for 20 years to produce and sell an invention. Patented products include Bombardier Skidoos and the Spar Aerospace "Canadarm" used on the NASA space shuttle flights. Like any other asset, a patent may be purchased. Suppose a company pays $170,000 to acquire a patent, and the company believes the expected useful life of the patent is only five years. Amortization expense is $34,000 per year ($170,000/5 years). The company's acquisition and amortization entries for this patent are

Jan.	1	Patent	170,000	
		Cash		170,000
		To acquire a patent.		
Dec.	31	Amortization Expense—Patent	34,000	
		Patent		34,000
		To amortize the cost of a patent ($170,000/5).		

Copyrights Copyrights are exclusive rights to reproduce and sell a book, musical composition, film, or other work of art. Issued by the federal government, copyrights extend 50 years beyond the author's, composer's, or artist's life. The cost of obtaining a copyright from the government is low, but a company may pay a large sum to purchase an existing copyright from the owner. For example, a publisher may pay the author of a popular novel $1 million or more for the book's copyright. The useful life of a copyright for a popular book may be usually no longer than two or three years, so that each period's amortization amount is a considerable portion of the copyright's cost; on the other hand, some copyrights, especially of musical compositions, such as works by the Beatles, seem to be popular over several decades.

Trademarks and Brand Names Trademarks and **trade names** (or **brand names**) are distinctive identifications of products or services. For example, The Sports Network has its distinctive logo of the yellow letters TSN on a black background shaped like a television screen; Apple Computer has the multi-colored apple with a bite out of it; and the Edmonton Oilers and Toronto Blue Jays have insignia that identify their respective teams. Molson Canadian, Swiss Chalet chicken, Petro-Canada, and Roots are everyday trade names. Advertising slogans such as Speedy Muffler's "At Speedy you're a somebody," or Shoppers Drug Mart's "Everything you want in a drugstore" are also legally protected.

The cost of a trademark or trade name is amortized over its useful life, not to exceed 40 years. The cost of advertising and promotions that use the trademark or trade name is *not* a part of the asset's cost but a debit to the advertising expense account.

Franchises and Licences Franchises and **licences** are privileges granted by a private business or a government to sell a product or service in accordance with specified conditions. The Vancouver Canucks hockey organization is a franchise granted to its owners by the National Hockey League. Tim Hortons and Re/Max Ltd. are well-known franchises. The acquisition costs of a franchise or licence is amortized over the lesser of its useful life and its legal life, subject to the 40-year maximum.

Leaseholds A **leasehold** is a prepayment that a lessee (renter) makes to secure the use of an asset from a lessor (landlord). For example, most malls lease the space to the mall stores and shops that you visit. Often leases require the lessee to make this prepayment in addition to monthly rental payments. The prepayment is a debit to an intangible asset account entitled Leaseholds. This amount is amortized over the life of the lease by debiting Rent Expense and crediting Leaseholds. Note that

Speedy Muffler
www.speedy.com

Re/Max Ltd.
www.remax.com

some leases stipulate that the last year's rent must be paid in advance when the lease is signed. This is Prepaid Rent, not a leasehold. The lessee debits the monthly lease payments to the Rent Expense account.

Sometimes lessees modify or improve the leased asset. For example, a lessee may construct a fence on leased land. The lessee debits the cost of the fence to a separate intangible asset account, Leasehold Improvements, and amortizes its cost over the lesser of the term of the lease and its useful life.

Goodwill   Goodwill in accounting is a more limited term than in everyday use, as in "goodwill among men." In accounting, **goodwill** is the excess of the cost to purchase a company over the market value of its net assets (assets minus liabilities). Suppose James Richardson & Sons Company acquires Manitoba Express at a cost of $10 million. The market value of Manitoba Express's assets is $9 million, and its liabilities total $1 million. In this case, James Richardson & Sons paid $2 million for goodwill, computed as follows:

Purchase price paid for Manitoba Express		$10 million
Sum of the market value of Manitoba Express's		
assets...	$9 million	
Less: Manitoba Express's liabilities	1 million	
Market value of Manitoba Express's net assets		8 million
Excess is called *goodwill*		$ 2 million

James Richardson & Sons' entry to record the acquisition of Manitoba Express, including its goodwill, would be

Assets (Cash, Receivables, Inventories,		
Capital Assets, all at market value)	9,000,000	
Goodwill	2,000,000	
Liabilities		1,000,000
Cash..		10,000,000
Purchased Manitoba Express.		

Goodwill has the following special features:

1. Goodwill is recorded, at its cost, only when it is purchased in the acquisition of another company. A company's favourable location, superior product, or outstanding reputation may create goodwill for a company, but it is never recorded by that entity. Instead, goodwill is recorded *only* by the acquiring entity when it buys another company. A purchase transaction provides objective evidence of the value of the goodwill.

2. According to generally accepted accounting principles, goodwill is amortized on a straight-line basis over a period of not less than two years and not to exceed 40 years. In reality, the goodwill of many entities increases in value. Nevertheless, the CICA's Accounting Standards Board specified in *CICA Handbook* Section 1580 that goodwill should be amortized to income on a straight-line basis over the goodwill's expected life. The section prohibits a lump-sum write-off of the cost of goodwill in the year of acquisition either on the income statement or to owner's equity.

Special Issues

International Accounting for Goodwill   Companies in The Netherlands (such as Royal Dutch Shell and Phillips), in Great Britain (such as British Petroleum and British Airways), and in most other European nations do not have to record goodwill when they purchase another business. Instead they may debit the cost of goodwill as a decrease in owners' equity. American GAAP allows purchases meeting certain criteria to use "pooling of interest" accounting, which does not result in the acquiring company having to record goodwill, although a proposed change to U.S. GAAP would prohibit pooling-of-interest accounting. These companies never have

to amortize the cost of goodwill, so their net income is higher than a Canadian company's net income would be. Canadian companies often cry "foul" when bidding against a European or American firm, in certain circumstances, to acquire another business. Why? Canadians claim the Europeans and Americans can pay higher prices because their income is often not reduced for amortization expense.

International Accounting for Research and Development Costs   Accounting for research and development (R&D) costs is one of the most difficult issues the accounting profession has faced. R&D is the lifeblood of companies such as Bombardier, Corel, and Nortel Networks because it is vital to the development of new products and processes. The cost of R&D activities is one of these companies' most valuable (intangible) assets.

Canada requires *development costs* meeting certain criteria to be capitalized, while other countries require such costs to be expensed in the year incurred. Canada and most other countries require *research costs* to be expensed as incurred.

Some critics argue that R&D costs represent future benefits and should be capitalized, others agree with the present accounting standards, and still others think all R&D costs should be expensed.

Research In Motion
www.rim.net

JDS Uniphase
www.jdsunph.com

Nortel Networks Corporation
www.nortel.com

Accounting and the *e*-World

How Do You Value Human Assets, the Drivers of the e-Economy?

The rules for valuing "hard" capital assets, such as computers, desks, trucks, buildings, mines, and copyrights, for financial reporting purposes are clear. The assets are valued at historical cost less accumulated amortization.

How do you value the programmers and systems designers at high-tech companies like Research in Motion (RIM), JDS Uniphase, and Nortel Networks? These companies are as dependent on their "human capital" as Bombardier and Air Canada are on their physical, non-human assets, yet RIM's and Nortel's financial statements show no value for these human assets.

This inability to capitalize the value of human assets and include them on the balance sheet can cause problems for high-tech companies. They tend not to have significant amounts of capital assets as would a manufacturing company like IPSCO, the steel producer, or Magna International, the auto parts manufacturer. Borrowing money can be a problem because high-tech companies do not have the hard assets that old-line companies, like Bombardier, IPSCO, and Magna, possess to secure a loan. Unsophisticated lenders and investors have difficulty valuing the human capital of high-tech companies.

Assigning a value to a programmer is very difficult. Should the future income of the programmer be calculated and discounted, then recorded as an intangible asset and amortized? Should the revenue the programmer will generate in the future for the company be calculated, discounted, and capitalized? Should a value be assigned to the cost of the programmer's education and experience? Should a programmer's hiring cost (for example, the fee paid to a search company who found the programmer for the company) be recorded and amortized?

If there was a method of assigning a cost to a programmer that was then amortized, should the cost of courses taken by the programmer be treated as "repairs" or "betterments"?

As you can see, there are many difficult and, so far, unanswered questions about valuing the employees of high-tech companies. Yet until such employees are valued, high-tech companies' financial statements will not reflect the full value of their assets.

How could companies around the world be placed on the same accounting basis?

Answer: If all companies worldwide followed the same accounting rules, they would be reporting income and other amounts computed similarly. But this is not the case. A company must follow the accounting rules of its own nation, and there are differences, as the goodwill situation illustrates. This is why international investors keep abreast of accounting methods used in different nations—much the same as a Canadian investor cares whether a company uses FIFO or average cost for inventories. An international body, the International Accounting Standards Committee, (IASC), part of the International Federation of Accountants (IFAC), discussed in Chapter 1, page 49, has set accounting standards, called *International Accounting Standards* or IAS. The Canadian Institute of Chartered Accountants' Accounting Standards Board (AcSB), discussed in Chapter 1 on page 48, is a member of IFAC and IASC. It is working with those bodies and accounting bodies around the world to harmonize accounting standards worldwide.

Ethical Issues in Accounting for Capital Assets and Intangibles

The main ethical issue in accounting for capital assets and intangibles is whether to capitalize or expense a particular cost. In this area, companies have split personalities. On the one hand, they all want to save on taxes. This motivates companies to expense all the costs Canada Customs and Revenue Agency allows in order to decrease their taxable income. On the other hand, most companies also want their financial statements to look as good as possible, with high net income and high reported amounts for assets.

In most cases, a cost that is capitalized or expensed for tax purposes must be treated the same way for reporting to owners, shareholders, and creditors in the financial statements. What, then, is the ethical path? Accountants should follow

DECISION GUIDELINES — Accounting for Capital Assets and Related Expenses

Decision	Guidelines
Capitalize or expense a cost?	General rule: Capitalize all costs that provide *future benefit* for the business. Expense all costs that provide *no future benefit*.
Capitalize or expense:	
• Cost associated with a new asset?	Capitalize all costs that bring the asset to its intended use.
• Cost associated with an existing asset?	Capitalize only those costs that add to the asset's usefulness or its useful life. Expense all other costs as maintenance or repairs.
• Interest cost incurred to finance the asset's acquisition?	Capitalize interest cost only on assets constructed by the business for its own use. Expense all other interest cost.
Which amortization method to use:	
• For financial reporting?	Use the method that best matches amortization expense against the revenues produced by the asset.
• For income tax?	Use the maximum capital cost allowance rates allowed by Canada Customs and Revenue Agency to produce the greatest tax deductions. A company can use different amortization methods for financial reporting and for income tax purposes. In Canada, this practice is considered both legal and ethical.

the general guidelines for capitalizing a cost: Capitalize all costs that provide a future benefit for the business, and expense all other costs, as outlined in the Decision Guidelines on page 531.

Many companies have gotten into trouble by capitalizing costs they should have expensed. They made their financial statements look better than the facts warranted. But there are few cases of companies getting into trouble by following the general guidelines, or even by erring on the side of expensing questionable costs. This is another example of accounting conservatism in action. It works. We discussed accounting conservatism in Chapter 9, page 474.

Summary Problem
for Your Review

Problem 1

The figures that follow appear in Requirement 2, Solution to Review Problem, on p. 518.

	Method A Straight-Line			Method B Double-Declining-Balance		
Year	Annual Amortization Expense	Accumulated Amortization	Book Value	Annual Amortization Expense	Accumulated Amortization	Book Value
Start			$44,000			$44,000
2002	$4,000	$ 4,000	40,000	$8,800	$ 8,800	35,200
2003	4,000	8,000	36,000	7,040	15,840	28,160
2004	4,000	12,000	32,000	5,632	21,472	22,528

Required

Both methods could be used for income tax purposes, since neither exceeds the allowable capital cost allowance (if the half-year rule is ignored). Which amortization method would you select for income tax purposes? Why?

Problem 2

SMJ Products purchased a building at a cost of $500,000 on January 1, 1998. The owner has amortized the building by using the straight-line method, a 35-year life, and a residual value of $150,000. On July 1, 2002, the business sold the building for $575,000 cash. The fiscal year of SMJ Products ends on December 31.

Required

Record amortization for 2002 and record the sale of the building on July 1, 2002.

Solution to Review Problem

Problem 1

Canada Customs and Revenue Agency will allow a company to use any amortization method it chooses as long as the amount of capital cost allowance claimed for tax purposes does not exceed the maximum amount allowed by Canada Customs and Revenue Agency. For tax purposes, most companies select the maximum amount allowed by Canada Customs and Revenue Agency, which results in accelerated amortization of the equipment. Accelerated amortization minimizes taxable income and income tax payments in the early years of the asset's life, thereby maximizing the business's cash at the earliest possible time. Straight-line amortization spreads amortization evenly over the life of the asset, which would *not* minimize income tax in the same way.

Problem 2

2002				
July 1	Amortization Expense—Building	5,000		
	Accumulated Amortization—Building		5,000	
	To update amortization—$5,000 expense			
	[(($500,000 – $150,000)/35 years) × $\frac{1}{2}$ year]			
July 1	Cash..	575,000		
	Accumulated Amortization—Building....................	45,000		
	Building		500,000	
	Gain on sale of building.......................................		120,000	
	To record sale of building.			
	Accumulated amortization is $45,000.			
	[(($500,000 – $150,000)/35 years) × $4\frac{1}{2}$ years]			

Cyber Coach

Visit the Student Resource area of the *Accounting* Companion Website for extra practice with the new material in Chapter 10.

www.pearsoned.ca/horngren

Summary

1. **Measure the cost of a capital asset (property, plant, and equipment).** *Capital assets,* of which property, plant, and equipment are a category, are long-lived assets that the business uses in its operations. The cost of a capital asset is the purchase price plus applicable taxes (but not GST), purchase commissions, and all other amounts incurred to acquire the asset and to prepare it for its intended use.

2. **Account for amortization.** The process of allocating a capital asset's cost to expense over the period the asset is used is called *amortization.* Businesses may account for the amortization of property, plant, and equipment by three methods: *straight-line, units-of-production,* and *declining-balance.* All these methods require accountants to estimate the asset's useful life and residual value.

3. **Explain capital cost allowance, amortization for income tax purposes.** Canada Customs and Revenue Agency allows companies and individuals to claim capital cost allowance (amortization) against taxable income but sets maximum rates that may be claimed for each class of capital assets. Many companies use the maximum rates allowed for tax purposes but lower rates (for example, straight-line) for income statement purposes.

4. **Account for the disposal of a capital asset.** Before disposing of, selling, or trading in a capital asset, the business updates the asset's amortization. Disposal is then recorded by removing the book balances from both the asset account and its related accumulated amortization account. Sales often result in a gain or a loss, which is reported on the income statement. Disposal may or may not result in a reported gain or loss, depending on the circumstances.

5. **Account for wasting assets and amortization.** The cost of natural resources, a special category of long-lived assets, is expensed through *amortization.* Amortization of natural resources is computed on a units-of-production basis.

6. **Account for intangible assets and amortization.** *Intangible assets* are assets that have no physical form. They give their owners a special right to current and expected future benefits. The major types of intangible assets are patents, copyrights, trademarks, franchises and licences, leaseholds, and goodwill. Amortization of intangibles is computed on a straight-line basis over the lesser of the legal life and useful life, to a maximum of 40 years.

Self-Study Questions

Test your understanding of the chapter by marking the correct answer for each of the following questions:

1. Which of the following payments is not included in the cost of land? (*p. 508*)
   a. Removal of old building
   b. Legal fees
   c. Property taxes in arrears paid at acquisition
   d. Cost of fencing and lighting

2. A business paid $120,000 for two machines valued at $90,000 and $60,000. The business will record these machines at (*p. 510*)
   a. $90,000 and $60,000   c. $72,000 and $48,000
   b. $60,000 each   d. $70,000 and $50,000

3. Which of the following items is a repair? (*pp. 510–511*)
   a. New brakes for delivery truck
   b. Paving of a company parking lot
   c. Cost of a new engine for a truck
   d. Building permit paid to construct an addition to an existing building

4. Which of the following definitions fits amortization? (*p. 511*)
   a. Allocation of the asset's market value to expense over its useful life
   b. Allocation of the asset's cost to expense over its useful life
   c. Decreases in the asset's market value over its useful life
   d. Increases in the fund set aside to replace the asset when it is worn out

5. Which amortization method's amounts are not computed based on time? (*pp. 512–516*)
   a. Straight-line
   b. Units-of-production
   c. Double-declining balance
   d. All are based on time

6. Which amortization method gives the largest amount of expense in the early years of using the asset and therefore is best for income tax purposes assuming the amount does not exceed the allowed capital cost allowance? (*p. 519*)
   a. Straight-line
   b. Units-of-production
   c. Double-declining balance
   d. All are equal

7. A company paid $450,000 for a building and was amortizing it by the straight-line method over a 40-year life with estimated residual value of $50,000. After ten years, it became evident that the building's remaining useful life would be 40 years. Amortization for the eleventh year is (*pp. 520–521*)
   a. $7,500   c. $10,000
   b. $8,750   d. $12,500

8. Labrador Stores scrapped an automobile that cost $14,000 and had a book value of $1,100. The entry to record this disposal is (*p. 522*)
   a. Loss on Disposal of Automobile   1,100
        Automobile   1,100
   b. Accumulated Amortization 14,000
        Automobile   14,000
   c. Accumulated Amortization 12,900
        Automobile   12,900
   d. Accumulated Amortization 12,900
      Loss on Disposal of Automobile   1,100
        Automobile   14,000

9. Amortization of a wasting asset is computed in the same manner as which amortization method? (*p. 526*)
   a. Straight-line
   b. Units-of-production
   c. Declining-balance

10. Lacy Company paid $550,000 to acquire Gentsch Systems. Gentsch's assets had a market value of $900,000 and its liabilities were $400,000. In recording the acquisition, Lacy will record goodwill of (*p. 529*)
    a. $50,000   c. $550,000
    b. $100,000   d. $0

Answers to the Self-Study Questions follow the Similar Accounting Terms.

Accounting Vocabulary

Accelerated-amortization method (*p. 514*)
Amortizable cost (*p. 513*)
Amortization (*p. 507*)
Amortization expense (*pp. 512, 526*)
Betterment (*p. 510*)
Brand name (*p. 528*)
Capital asset (*p. 507*)
Capital cost allowance (*p. 519*)
Capitalize (a cost) (*p. 509*)

Copyright (*p. 528*)
Depletion (*p. 526*)
Depreciation (*p. 507*)
Double-declining-balance amortization method (*p. 514*)
Estimated residual value (*p. 513*)
Estimated useful life (*p. 513*)
Franchise (*p. 528*)
Goodwill (*p. 529*)
Intangible asset (*p. 527*)

Leasehold *(p. 528)*
Licence *(p. 528)*
Patent *(p. 528)*
Repair *(p. 510)*
Salvage value *(p. 513)*
Scrap value *(p. 513)*

Straight-line amortization method
    (p. 513)
Trademark *(p. 528)*
Trade name *(p. 528)*
Units-of-production amortization method *(p. 514)*
Wasting asset *(p. 526)*

Similar Accounting Terms

Amortization   Depreciation (for capital assets); Depletion (for wasting assets)

Capital assets   Property, plant, and equipment; Fixed assets; Long-lived assets; Long-term assets

Wasting assets   Natural resources

Trade name   Brand name

Residual value   Salvage value; Scrap value

Answers to Self-Study Questions

1. d
2. c [($90,000/($90,000 + $60,000)) × $120,000 = $72,000;
   ($60,000/($90,000 + $60,000)) × $120,000 = $48,000]
3. a   4. b   5. b   6. c
7. a Amortizable cost = $450,000 – $50,000 = $400,000
   $400,000/40 years = $10,000 per year
   $400,000 – ($10,000 × 10 years) = $300,000
   $300,000/40 years = $7,500 per year
8. d   9. b
10. a [$550,000 – ($900,000 – $400,000) = $50,000]

Assignment Material

Questions

1. To what types of long-lived assets does amortization expense apply?

2. Describe how to measure the cost of a capital asset. Would an ordinary cost of repairing the asset after it is placed in service be included in the asset's cost?

3. Suppose land with a building on it is purchased for $100,000. How do you account for the $8,000 cost of removing this unwanted building?

4. When assets are purchased as a group for a single price and no individual asset cost is given, how is each asset's cost determined?

5. Distinguish a betterment from a repair. Why are they treated differently for accounting purposes?

6. Define amortization. Present the common misconceptions about amortization.

7. Which amortization method does each of the following graphs characterize: straight-line, units-of-production, or accelerated?

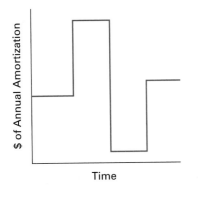

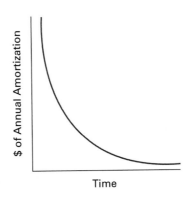

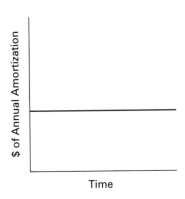

8. Explain the concept of accelerated amortization. Which of the three amortization methods results in the most amortization in the first year of the asset's life?

9. The level of business activity fluctuates widely for Harwood Delivery Service, reaching its peak around Christmas each year. At other times, business is slow. What amortization method is most appropriate for the company's fleet of Chevy Blazer trucks?

10. Oswalt Computer Service Centre uses the most advanced computers available to keep a competitive edge over other service centres. To maintain this advantage, the company usually replaces its computers before they are worn out. Describe the major factors affecting the useful life of a capital asset and indicate which seems more relevant to this company's computers.

11. Which amortization method does not consider estimated residual value in computing amortization during the early years of the asset's life?

12. What is capital cost allowance?

13. Does amortization affect income taxes? How does amortization affect cash provided by operations?

14. Describe how to compute amortization for less than a full year, and how to account for amortization for less than a full month.

15. Ragland Company paid $10,000 for office furniture. The company expected it to remain in service for six years and to have a $1,000 residual value. After two years' use, company accountants believe the furniture will last for the next six years. How much amortization will Ragland record for each of these last six years, assuming straight-line amortization and no change in the estimated residual value?

16. When a company sells a capital asset before the year's end, what must it record before accounting for the sale?

17. Describe how to determine whether a company experiences a gain or a loss when an old capital asset is exchanged for a similar new capital asset. Does GAAP favour the recognition of gains or losses? Which accounting concept underlies your answer?

18. Identify seven elements of internal control designed to safeguard capital assets.

19. What expense applies to wasting assets? By which amortization method is this expense computed?

20. How do intangible assets differ from most other assets? Why are they assets at all? What expense applies to intangible assets?

21. Why is the cost of patents and other intangible assets often expensed over a shorter period than the legal life of the asset?

22. Your company has just purchased another company for $400,000. The market value of the other company's net assets is $325,000. What is the $75,000 excess called? What type of asset is it? What is the maximum period over which its cost is amortized under generally accepted accounting principles?

23. Nortel Networks is recognized as a world leader in the manufacture and sale of communications equipment. The company's success has created vast amounts of business goodwill. Would you expect to see this goodwill reported on Nortel's financial statements? Why, or why not?

Exercises

Exercise 10-1 *Determining the cost of property, plant, and equipment* *(Obj. 1)*

Medical Associates purchased land, paying $70,000 cash as a down payment and signing a $120,000 note payable for the balance. In addition, the company paid delinquent property tax of $2,000, a legal fee of $500, and an $8,400 charge for levelling the land and removing an unwanted building. The company constructed an office building on the land at a cost of $610,000. It also paid $18,000 for a fence around the boundary of the property, $10,400 for the company sign near the entrance to the property, and $9,300 for special lighting of the grounds. Determine the cost of the company's land, land improvements, and building.

Exercise 10-2 *Measuring the cost of a capital asset* *(Obj. 1)*

Pages 507–508 of this chapter list the costs included for the acquisition of land. First is the purchase price of the land, which is obviously included in the cost of the land. The reasons for including the related costs are not so obvious. For example, property tax is ordinarily an expense, not part of the cost of an asset. State why the related costs listed on pages 507–508 are included as part of the cost of the land. After the land is ready for use, will these related costs be capitalized or expensed?

Exercise 10-3 *Allocating cost to assets acquired in a lump-sum purchase* **(Obj. 1)**

Sudbury Mfg. bought three used machines in a $40,000 purchase. An independent appraisal of the machines produced the following figures:

Machine No.	Appraised Value
1	$14,000
2	16,000
3	18,000

Sudbury Mfg. paid one-third in cash and signed a note for the remainder. Record the purchase in the journal, identifying each machine's individual cost in a separate Machine account. Round costs to two decimal places.

Exercise 10-4 *Distinguishing betterments from repairs* **(Obj. 1)**

Classify each of the following expenditures as a betterment or a repair (expense) related to a machine used to earn revenue: (a) purchase price; (b) sales tax paid on the purchase price; (c) transportation and insurance while the machine is in transport from seller to buyer; (d) installation; (e) training of personnel for initial operation of the machine; (f) special reinforcement to the machine platform; (g) income tax paid on income earned from the sale of products manufactured by the machine; (h) major overhaul to extend useful life by three years; (i) ordinary recurring repairs to keep the machine in good working order; (j) lubrication of the machine before it is placed in service; (k) periodic lubrication after the machine is placed in service; and (l) goods and services tax on the purchase price.

Exercise 10-5 *Explaining the concept of amortization* **(Obj. 2)**

John Fitzpatrick has just slept through the class in which Professor Russell explained the concept of amortization. Because the next test is scheduled for Wednesday, Fitzpatrick telephones Michelle White to get her notes from the lecture. White's notes are concise: "Amortization—Sounds like Greek to me." Fitzpatrick next tries Denise Hillier, who says she thinks amortization is what happens when an asset wears out. Orry Skrypec is confident that amortization is the process of building up a cash fund to replace an asset at the end of its useful life. Explain the concept of amortization for Fitzpatrick. Evaluate the explanations of Hillier and Skrypec. Be specific.

Exercise 10-6 *Determining amortization amounts by three methods* **(Obj. 3)**

JIT Delivery bought a delivery truck on January 2, 2002, for $27,000. The truck was expected to remain in service for four years and last 200,000 kilometres. At the end of its useful life, company officials estimated that the truck's residual value would be $3,000. The truck travelled 64,000 kilometres in the first year, 60,000 in the second year, 46,000 in the third year, and 38,000 in the fourth year.

Required

1. Prepare a schedule of *amortization expense* per year for the truck using the straight-line, units-of-production, and double-declining-balance amortization methods.
2. Which method tracks the wear and tear on the truck most closely? Why?
3. After two years under the double-declining-balance method, the company switched to the straight-line method. Prepare a schedule of amortization expense for this situation, showing all calculations.

Exercise 10-7 *Selecting the amortization method for income tax purposes* **(Obj. 3)**

In 2001, Joffre Products paid $140,000 for equipment that is expected to have a seven-year life. In this industry, the residual value is estimated to be 15 percent of the asset's cost. Joffre Products plans to use straight-line amortization for accounting purposes. What amortization method should Joffre Products use for income tax purposes?

Exercise 10-8 *Changing a capital asset's useful life* *(Obj. 2)*

Wicke Furniture purchased a building for $600,000 and amortized it on a straight-line basis over a 40-year period. The estimated residual value was $60,000. After using the building for 15 years, the company realized that wear and tear on the building would force the company to replace it before 40 years. Starting with the 16th year, the company began amortizing the building over a revised *total* life of 30 years, increasing the estimated residual value to $120,000. Record amortization expense on the building for years 15 and 16.

Exercise 10-9 *Analyzing the effect of a sale of a capital asset; double-declining-balance amortization* *(Obj. 4)*

On January 2, 2001, Somatic Bedding purchased store fixtures for $8,700 cash, expecting the fixtures to remain in service for five years. Somatic Bedding has amortized the fixtures on a double-declining-balance basis with an estimated residual value of $1,200. On September 30, 2002, Somatic Bedding sold the fixtures for $4,890 cash. Record both the amortization expense on the fixtures for 2002, and the sale of the fixtures on September 30, 2002. Somatic Bedding's year end is December 31.

Exercise 10-10 *Measuring a capital asset's cost, using units-of-production amortization, and trading in a used asset* *(Obj. 1, 2, 4)*

Atlantic Logistics, based in Halifax, Nova Scotia, is a large trucking company that operates throughout eastern Canada. Atlantic Logistics uses the units-of-production method to amortize its trucks because its managers believe units-of-production amortization best measures the wear and tear on the trucks. Atlantic Logistics trades in used trucks often to keep driver morale high and to maximize fuel efficiency. Consider these facts about one Mack truck in the company's fleet:

When acquired in 1998, the tractor/trailer rig cost $315,000 and was expected to remain in service for ten years, or 1,600,000 kilometres. Estimated residual value was $85,000. The truck was driven 120,000 kilometres in 1998, 192,000 kilometres in 1999, and 336,000 kilometres in 2000. After 64,000 kilometres in 2001, the company traded in the Mack truck for a less expensive Freightliner rig. Atlantic Logistics paid cash of $76,000. Determine Atlantic Logistics' cost of the new truck. Journal entries are not required.

Exercise 10-11 *Recording wasting assets and depletion* *(Obj. 5)*

Island Mining Company Ltd. paid $265,300 for the right to extract ore from a 200,000-tonne mineral deposit. In addition to the purchase price, the company also paid a $500 filing fee, a $1,000 licence fee to the province of British Columbia, and $47,000 for a geological survey. Because Island Mining Company Ltd. purchased the rights to the minerals only, the company expected the asset to have zero residual value when fully depleted. During the first year of production, the company removed 38,000 tonnes of ore. Make general journal entries to record (1) purchase of the mineral rights (debit Mineral Asset), (2) payment of fees and other costs, and (3) amortization for first-year production.

Exercise 10-12 *Recording intangibles, amortization, and a change in the asset's useful life* *(Obj. 6)*

Part 1 Karolyi Company manufactures high-speed printers and has recently purchased for $875,000 a patent for the design for a new laser printer. Although it gives legal protection for 20 years, the patent is expected to provide Karolyi Company with a competitive advantage for only seven years. Assuming the straight-line method of amortization, use general journal entries to record (1) the purchase of the patent, and (2) amortization for year 1.

Part 2 After using the patent for four years, Karolyi Company learns at an industry trade show that another company is designing a more efficient printer. Based on this new information, Karolyi Company decides to amortize the remaining cost of the patent over the current year, giving the patent a total useful life of five years. Record amortization for year 5.

Exercise 10-13 *Measuring goodwill* *(Obj. 6)*

Nortel Networks Corporation's annual report for the year ended December 31, 1999, indicated (in Note 4) that the company acquired two companies during the year. Nortel paid $340 million (all amounts in U.S. dollars) for Periphonics Corporation. The purchased assets included net tangible assets of $102 million and in-process research and development of $180 million.

Required

1. How was a value assigned to net tangible assets and in-process research and development?
2. What was the value assigned to goodwill?
3. The goodwill was to be written off over four years. Is that the normal period for writing off goodwill?

Exercise 10-14 *Accounting for goodwill* *(Obj. 6)*

Media-related companies such as newspapers and radio and television stations have little in the way of tangible capital assets. Instead, their main asset is goodwill. When one media company buys another, goodwill is often the most costly asset acquired. Fleming Newspapers paid $800,000 to acquire *The Thrifty Nickel*, an advertising paper headquartered in New Brunswick. At the time of the acquisition, *The Thrifty Nickel*'s balance sheet reported total assets of $1,300,000 and liabilities of $673,000. The fair market value of *The Thrifty Nickel*'s assets was $1,000,000.

Required

1. How much goodwill did Fleming Newspapers purchase as part of the acquisition of *The Thrifty Nickel*?
2. Make Fleming Newspapers' summary journal entry to record the acquisition of *The Thrifty Nickel*.
3. What is the maximum useful life of the goodwill under GAAP? If Fleming Newspapers amortizes the goodwill over the maximum useful life, how much amortization expense will Fleming Newspapers record each year?

Exercise 10-15 *Computing and recording goodwill* *(Obj. 6)*

Murphy's Chips Ltd. purchased Crunchee Chip Company, paying $1.3 million in a note payable. The market value of Crunchee Chip Company's assets was $1.4 million, and Crunchee Chip Company had liabilities of $1.2 million.

Required

1. Compute the cost of the goodwill purchased by Murphy's Chips Ltd.
2. Record the purchase by Murphy's Chips Ltd.
3. Record amortization of goodwill for year 1, assuming the straight-line method and a useful life of twenty years.

Challenge Exercises

Exercise 10-16   *Capitalizing versus expensing; measuring the effect of an error*   **(Obj. 1)**

Classic Sportswear is a catalogue merchant in Montreal. The company's assets consist mainly of inventory, a warehouse, and automated shipping equipment. Assume that early in year 1 Classic Sportswear purchased equipment at a cost of $800,000. Management expects the equipment to remain in service for five years. Because the equipment is so specialized, estimated residual value is negligible. Classic Sportswear uses the straight-line amortization method. Through an accounting error, Classic Sportswear accidentally expensed the entire cost of the equipment at the time of purchase. The company is family-owned and operated as a sole proprietorship, so it pays no corporate income tax.

Required

Prepare a schedule to show the overstatement or understatement in the following items at the end of each year over the five-year life of the equipment.

1. Total current assets
2. Equipment, net
3. Net income
4. Total owner's equity
5. Debt ratio

Exercise 10-17   *Reconstructing transactions from the financial statements*   **(Obj. 2, 4)**

Leon's Furniture Limited's 1999 annual report (adapted) reported these amounts (in thousands of dollars):

| | December 31 | | | |
| | 1999 | | 1998 | |
Properties	Cost	Accumulated Amortization	Cost	Accumulated Amortization
Land	$ 32,563	—	$ 31,540	—
Buildings	88,859	$40,525	84,397	$40,167
Equipment	12,469	8,204	12,271	8,121
Vehicles..	11,058	8,849	9,878	8,189
Computer hardware and software	5,547	3,537	5,469	3,043
Leasehold improvements	10,348	4,265	4,743	4,269
	$160,844	$65,380	$148,298	$63,789
Net book value		$95,464		$84,509

In the 1999 annual report, Leon's Furniture Limited reported amortization expense in 1999 of $6,401,000. In addition, the company reported it had disposed of certain capital assets and acquired others. The gain on disposal of capital assets was $5,726,000.

Required

1. What was the accumulated amortization of the assets disposed of during 1999?
2. Assume that Leon's Furniture Limited acquired assets costing $19,114,000 during 1999. What was the cost price of the assets sold during the year?
3. Write the journal entry to record the disposal of the assets during the year.

Beyond the Numbers

Beyond the Numbers 10-1

The following questions are unrelated except that they apply to capital assets:

1. Eric Hastings, the owner of Hasting's Hardware, regularly buys capital assets (property, plant, and equipment) and debits the cost to Repairs and Maintenance Expense. Why would he do that, since he knows this action violates GAAP?

2. Christie Ross, the owner of Christie's Dresses, regularly debits the cost of repairs and maintenance of capital assets to Plant and Equipment. Why would she do that, since she knows she is violating GAAP?

3. It has been suggested that, since many intangible assets have no value except to the company that owns them, they should be valued at $1.00 or zero on the balance sheet. Many accountants disagree with this view. Which view do you support? Why?

Ethical Issue

College Park Apartments purchased land and a building for a lump sum of $2.2 million. To get the maximum tax deduction, College Park Apartments' owner allocated 90 percent of the purchase price to the building and only 10 percent to the land. A more realistic allocation would have been 70 percent to the building and 30 percent to the land.

Required

1. Explain the tax advantage of allocating too much to the building and too little to the land.

2. Was College Park Apartment's allocation ethical? If so, state why. If not, why not? Identify who was harmed.

Problems (Group A)

Problem 10-1A   *Identifying the elements of a capital asset's cost (Obj. 1, 2)*

Boyle Financial Services incurred the following costs in acquiring land and a garage, making land improvements, and constructing and furnishing a home office building.

a. Purchase price of 3½ hectares of land, including an old building that will be used as a garage for company vehicles (land appraised market value is $700,000; building appraised market value is $100,000)...	$640,000
b. Real estate taxes in arrears on the land to be paid by Boyle Financial Services	3,700
c. Additional dirt and earth moving	3,550
d. Legal fees on the land acquisition..	2,000
e. Fence around the boundary of the land..	44,100
f. Building permit for the home office building	200
g. Architect fee for the design of the home office building	45,000
h. Company signs near front and rear approaches to the company property..	6,550
i. Renovation of the garage	23,800
j. Concrete, wood, steel girders, and other materials used in the construction of the home office building...	644,000
k. Masonry, carpentry, roofing, and other labour to construct home office building..	683,000
l. Parking lots and concrete walks on the property	17,450
m. Lights for the parking lot, walkways, and company signs	8,900
n. Supervisory salary of construction supervisor (96 percent to home office building and 4 percent to garage renovation)	55,000
o. Office furniture for the home office building...	137,000
p. Transportation of furniture from seller to the home office building..	1,300
q. Flowers and plants...	3,100

Boyle Financial Services amortizes buildings over 40 years, land improvements over 20 years, and furniture over eight years, all on a straight-line basis with zero residual value.

Required

1. Set up columns for Land, Land Improvements, Home Office Building, Garage, and Furniture. Show how to account for each of Boyle Financial Services' costs by listing the cost under the correct account. Determine the total cost of each asset.

2. Assuming that all construction was complete and the assets were placed in service on March 19, record amortization for the year ended December 31. Round figures to the nearest dollar.

Problem 10-2A *Recording capital asset transactions; exchanges; changes in useful life (Obj. 1, 2, 4)*

A. C. Nielsen Company of Canada Ltd. surveys Canadian viewing trends. The company's balance sheet reports the following assets under Property and Equipment: Land, Buildings, Office Furniture, Communication Equipment, and Televideo Equipment. The company has a separate accumulated amortization account for each of these assets except land. Assume that the company completed the following transactions:

Jan. 4 Traded in communication equipment with book value of $11,000 (cost of $96,000) for similar new equipment with a cash cost of $88,000. The seller gave Nielsen a trade-in allowance of $20,000 on the old equipment, and the company paid the remainder in cash.

Aug. 29 Sold a building that had cost $475,000 and had accumulated amortization of $353,500 through December 31 of the preceding year. Amortization is computed on a straight-line basis. The building has a 30-year useful life and a residual value of $47,500. Nielsen received $150,000 cash and a $600,000 note receivable.

Nov. 10 Purchased used communication and televideo equipment from the Decima Research polling organization. Total cost was $90,000 paid in cash. An independent appraisal valued the communication equipment at $75,000 and the televideo equipment at $37,500.

Dec. 31 Recorded amortization as follows:
Equipment is amortized by the double-declining-balance method over a five-year life. Record amortization on the equipment purchased on January 4 and on November 10 separately.
Amortization on buildings is computed by the straight-line method. The company had assigned buildings an estimated useful life of 30 years and a residual value that is 10 percent of cost. After using the buildings for 20 years, the company has come to believe that their *total* useful life will be 40 years. Residual value remains unchanged. The buildings cost $19,000,000.

Required

Record the transactions in the journal of A. C. Nielsen Company of Canada Ltd.

Problem 10-3A *Explaining the concept of amortization (Obj. 2)*

The board of directors of Saltspring Gymnastic Centre is having its regular quarterly meeting. Accounting policies are on the agenda, and amortization is being discussed. A new board member, a physician, has some strong opinions about two aspects of amortization policy. Dr. Lee argues that amortization must be coupled with a fund to replace company assets. Otherwise, he argues, there is no substance to amortization. He also challenges the five-year estimated life over which Saltspring Gymnastic Centre is amortizing centre computers. He notes that the computers will last much longer and should be amortized over at least 10 years.

Required

Write a paragraph or two to explain the concept of amortization to Dr. Lee and to answer his arguments.

Problem 10-4A   *Computing amortization by three methods*   **(Obj. 2, 3)**

On January 2, 2001, Sprattuli Haulage purchased a used dump truck at a total cost of $63,000. Before placing the truck in service, the company spent $2,200 painting it, $800 replacing tires, and $4,000 overhauling the engine. Jack Sprattuli, the owner, estimates that the truck will remain in service for six years and have a residual value of $16,000. The truck's annual usage is expected to be 28,000 kilometres in each of the first four years and 22,000 kilometres in each of the next two years. In trying to decide which amortization method to use, Judi Welsch, the accountant, requests an amortization schedule for each of the following generally accepted amortization methods: straight-line, units-of-production, and double-declining-balance.

Required

1. Assuming Sprattuli Haulage amortizes this dump truck individually, prepare an amortization schedule for each of the three generally accepted amortization methods, showing asset cost, amortization expense, accumulated amortization, and asset book value.

2. Sprattuli Haulage prepares for its bankers financial statements, using the amortization method that maximizes reported income in the early years of asset use. For income tax purposes, however, the company uses the amortization method that minimizes income tax payments in those early years. Identify the amortization methods that meet each of the company's objectives.

Problem 10-5A   *Journalizing capital asset transactions; betterments versus repairs*   **(Obj. 1, 2, 4)**

Assume that Baxter Plumbing completed the following transactions:

2002
Jan.   3   Paid $12,000 cash for a used service truck.
       5   Paid $1,200 to have the truck engine overhauled.
       7   Paid $850 to have the truck modified for business use.
Oct.   3   Paid $814 for transmission repair and oil change after truck was put into use.
Dec.   31 Used the double-declining-balance method to record amortization on the truck. (Assume a four-year life.)

2003
Mar.   13 Replaced the truck's broken windshield for $100 cash, the deductible on Baxter Plumbing's insurance.
June   26 Traded in the service truck for a new truck costing $23,000. The dealer granted a $4,000 allowance on the old truck, and Baxter Plumbing paid the balance in cash. Recorded 2003 amortization for the year to date and then recorded the exchange of trucks.
Dec.   31 Used the double-declining-balance method to record amortization on the new truck. (Assume a four-year life.)

Required

Record the transactions in the general journal, indicating whether each transaction amount should be capitalized as an asset or expensed.

Problem 10-6A   *Analyzing capital asset transactions from a company's financial statements*   **(Obj. 2, 4)**

Alberta Treasury Branches (ATB) is a regional bank based in Alberta. Assume the following excerpts from ATB's 2000 financial statements:

ALBERTA TREASURY BRANCHES
Consolidated Balance Sheet (adapted)

(Amounts in thousands)	March 31, 2000	March 31, 1999
Assets		
Current assets:		
Cash resources	$ 646,961	$ 595,092
Securities	630,224	468,479
Loans (net of allowances)	8,924,691	8,036,775
Total current assets	10,201,876	9,100,346
Property, plant, and equipment, at cost:		
Land	7,189	7,338
Buildings	61,590	60,719
Equipment and software	81,326	76,008
Leasehold improvements	41,773	37,375
	191,878	181,440
Accumulated amortization	128,262	127,269
Property, plant, and equipment, net	63,616	54,171
Other assets	166,451	127,182
Total assets	$10,431,943	$9,281,699

Required

1. At March 31, 2000, what was Alberta Treasury Branches' cost of its capital assets? What was the amount of accumulated amortization? What was the book value of the capital assets? Does book value measure how much the company could sell the assets for? Why or why not?

2. ATB's amortization expense for 2000 was $15,389,000. Why is the amount of amortization expense so different from accumulated amortization at March 31, 2000?

3. ATB paid $28,044,000 for capital assets during 2000. Prepare a T-account for Capital Assets at cost to determine whether the company bought more or sold more capital assets during the year.

Problem 10-7A *Recording intangibles and the related expenses (Obj. 5, 6)*

Part 1 TransCanada PipeLines Ltd. owns gas transmission facilities and other energy-related assets. The company's balance sheet includes the asset Oil Properties.

Suppose TransCanada Pipelines Ltd. paid $8 million cash for an oil lease that contained an estimated reserve of 725,000 barrels of oil. Assume that the company paid $350,000 for additional geological tests of the property and $110,000 to prepare the surface for drilling. Prior to production, the company signed a $65,000 note payable to have a building constructed on the property. Because the building provides on-site headquarters for the drilling effort and will be abandoned when the oil is depleted, its cost is debited to the Oil Properties account and included in amortization charges. During the first year of production, TransCanada Pipelines Ltd. removed 90,000 barrels of oil, which it sold on credit for $25 per barrel.

Required

Make general journal entries to record all transactions related to the oil and gas property, including amortization and sale of the first-year production.

Part 2 NewTel Communications provides telephone service to most of Newfoundland and Labrador. The company's balance sheet reports the asset Cost of Acquisitions in Excess of the Fair Market Value of the Net Assets of Subsidiaries.

Assume that NewTel Communications purchased this asset as part of the acquisition of another company, which carried these figures:

Book value of assets $780,000
Market value of assets 995,000
Liabilities 335,000

Required

1. What is another title for the asset Cost of Acquisitions in Excess of the Fair Market Value of the Net Assets of Subsidiaries?

2. Make the general journal entry to record NewTel Communications' purchase of the other company for $850,000 cash.

3. Assuming NewTel Communications amortizes Cost of Acquisitions in Excess of the Fair Market Value of the Net Assets of Subsidiaries over 20 years, record the straight-line amortization for one year.

Part 3 Suppose Nortel Networks purchased a patent for $520,000. Before using the patent, Nortel incurred an additional cost of $25,000 for a lawsuit to defend the company's right to purchase it. Even though the patent gives Nortel legal protection for 20 years, company management has decided to amortize its cost over an eight-year period because of the industry's fast-changing technologies.

Required

Make general journal entries to record the patent transactions, including straight-line amortization for one year.

Problem 10-8A   *Identifying the elements of property, plant, and equipment's cost; accounting for amortization by two methods; accounting for disposal of property, plant, and equipment; distinguishing betterments from repairs*
(Obj. 1, 2, 4)

Campanetta Printing Co. has a fiscal year ending September 30. The company completed the following capital asset transactions:

2002
Jan.   2   Paid $200,000 plus $5,000 in legal fees (pertaining to all assets purchased) to purchase the following assets from a competitor who was going out of business:

Asset	Appraised Value	Estimated Useful Life	Estimated Residual Value
Land......................	$100,000	—	—
Buildings...............	80,000	10 years	$4,000
Equipment.............	60,000	5 years	5,000

Campanetta Printing Co. plans to use the straight-line amortization method for the building and for the equipment.

July   2   Purchased a delivery truck with a list price of $25,000 for $23,000 cash. The truck is expected to be used for four years and driven a total of 100,000 kilometres; it is then expected to be sold for $4,000. It will be amortized using the units-of-production method.

July   3   Paid $1,000 to paint the truck with the company's colours and logo.

Sept.   30   Recorded amortization on the assets. The truck had been driven 16,000 kilometres since it was purchased.

2003
Jan.   4   Campanetta Printing Co. paid $3,500 to Fortin Services Ltd. for work done on the equipment. The job consisted of annual maintenance ($500) and the addition of automatic controls ($3,000), which will increase the expected useful life of the equipment to a total of six years and increase its expected residual value by $1,000.

July   1   Sold the truck for $15,000. The truck had an odometer reading of 65,000 kilometres.

Sept.   30   Recorded amortization on the assets.

Required

1. Record the above transactions of Campanetta Printing Co. Round all amounts to the nearest dollar.

2. Show the balance sheet presentation of the assets at September 30, 2003.

Problem 10-9A *Accounting for wasting assets, intangible assets, and related expenses (Obj. 3, 6, 7)*

On July 2, 2002, NWT Inc. acquired Yukon Exploration Ltd. for $6,000,000. At the time of the acquisition, Yukon's balance sheet contained the following items, which were transferred to NWT Inc.:

- Mining Equipment: original cost of $900,000 and a present market value of $660,000. The equipment is expected to last another 12 years and have a residual value of $20,000 at that time.

- Mineral Rights: the rights to mine property by Lake Lind. The mineral rights originally cost Yukon $1,000,000 but now have an appraised market value of $4,800,000. The mine is expected to produce 50,000,000 tonnes of ore over the next 12 years.

- Leasehold: the rights to rent office space in a nearby town for $6,000 per month for the next 12 years. The leasehold has a market value today of $50,000 because of high rental rates in the area.

- Mortgage Payable: a $640,000 mortgage is outstanding on the mining equipment with interest at current rates.

Required

1. Journalize the purchase of Yukon Exploration Ltd. by NWT Inc.

2. Journalize the adjusting entries required for the year ending June 30, 2003, to amortize the cost of the assets—assuming 2,000,000 tonnes of ore were taken out of the mine. Use the most appropriate methods and time frames from the data given.

3. Show how the assets would appear in the capital assets section of NWT Inc.'s balance sheet as of June 30, 2003.

Problems (Group B)

Problem 10-1B   *Identifying the elements of a capital asset's cost   (Obj. 1, 2)*

Jason Tang, the owner of Tang Properties, incurred the following costs in acquiring land, making land improvements, and constructing and furnishing his own office building in the year ended December 31, 2002.

a. Purchase price of four hectares of land, including an old building that will be used for a garage (land appraised market value is $280,000; building appraised market value is $40,000)	$300,000
b. Additional dirt and earth moving...	8,100
c. Fence around the boundary of the land	14,350
d. Legal fee for title search on the land	600
e. Real estate taxes in arrears on the land to be paid by Tang Properties	5,900
f. Company signs at front of the company property	2,500

g. Building permit for the office building 350

h. Architect fee for the design of the office building 19,800

i. Masonry, carpentry, roofing, and other labour to construct
   office building 709,000

j. Concrete, wood, steel girders, and other materials used in the
   construction of the office building 265,000

k. Renovation of the garage.. 41,800

l. Flowers and plants 6,400

m. Parking lot and concrete walks on the property 29,750

n. Lights for the parking lot, walkways, and company signs 7,300

o. Supervisory salary of construction supervisor (94 percent to
   office building and 6 percent to garage renovation) 40,000

p. Office furniture for the office building.. 107,100

q. Transportation and installation of office furniture 1,600

Tang Properties amortizes buildings over 40 years, land improvements over 20 years, and furniture over eight years, all on a straight-line basis with zero residual value.

Required

1. Set up columns for Land, Land Improvements, Office Building, Garage Building, and Furniture. Show how to account for each of Tang Properties' costs by listing the cost under the correct account. Determine the total cost of each asset.

2. Assuming that all construction was complete and the assets were placed in service on May 4, record amortization for the year ended December 31, 2002. Round off figures to the nearest dollar.

Problem 10-2B *Recording capital asset transactions; exchanges; changes in useful life* *(Obj. 1, 2, 4)*

Soldafi Freight provides nationwide general freight service in western and central Canada. The business's balance sheet includes the following assets under Capital Assets: Land, Buildings, and Motor Carrier Equipment. Soldafi Freight has a separate accumulated amortization account for each of these assets except land.

Assume that Soldafi Freight completed the following transactions:

Jan. 5 Traded in motor-carrier equipment with a book value of $47,000 (cost of $135,000) for similar new equipment with a cash cost of $176,000. Soldafi Freight received a trade-in allowance of $70,000 on the old equipment and paid the remainder in cash.

July 2 Sold a building that had cost $550,000 and had accumulated amortization of $247,500 through December 31 of the preceding year. Amortization is computed on a straight-line basis. The building has a 30-year useful life and a residual value of $55,000. Soldafi Freight received $200,000 cash and a $500,000 note receivable.

Oct. 26 Purchased land and a building for a single price of $330,000. An independent appraisal valued the land at $115,000, and the building at $230,000.

Dec. 31 Recorded amortization as follows:
      Motor-carrier equipment has an expected useful life of five years and an estimated residual value of 5 percent of cost. Amortization is computed using the double-declining-balance method.
      Amortization on buildings is computed by the straight-line method. The company had assigned to its older buildings, which cost $4,000,000, an estimated useful life of 30 years with a residual value equal to 10 percent of the asset cost. However, Enrico Soldafi, the owner of Soldafi Freight, has come to believe that the buildings will remain useful for a total of 40 years. Residual value remains unchanged. The company has used all its buildings, except for the one purchased on October 26, for ten years. The new

building carries a 40-year useful life and a residual value equal to 10 percent of its cost. Make separate entries for amortization on the building acquired on October 26 and the other buildings purchased in earlier years.

Required

Record the transactions in Soldafi Freight's general journal.

Problem 10-3B   *Explaining the concept of amortization*   *(Obj. 2)*

The board of directors of Markborough Properties Ltd. is reviewing the 2002 annual report. A new board member, a consulting psychologist with little business experience, questions the company accountant about the amortization amounts. The psychologist wonders why amortization expense has decreased from $200,000 in 2000, to $184,000 in 2001, and to $172,000 in 2002. She states that she could understand the decreasing annual amounts if the company had been disposing of properties each year, but that has not occurred. Further, she notes that growth in the city is increasing the values of company properties. Why is the company recording amortization when the property values are increasing?

Required

Write a paragraph or two to explain the concept of amortization to the psychologist and to answer her questions.

Problem 10-4B   *Computing amortization by three methods*   *(Obj. 2, 3)*

On January 9, 2001, RZ Technology paid $192,000 for equipment used in manufacturing automotive supplies. In addition to the basic purchase price, the business paid $700 transportation charges, $100 insurance for the goods in transit, $13,440 provincial sales tax, and $3,100 for a special platform on which to place the equipment in the plant. RZ Technology's owner estimates that the equipment will remain in service for five years and have a residual value of $20,000. The equipment will produce 60,000 units in the first year, with annual production decreasing by 10,000 units during each of the next four years (that is, 50,000 units in year 2, 40,000 units in year 3, and so on). In trying to decide which amortization method to use, owner Susan Racine has requested an amortization schedule for each of the three generally accepted amortization methods: straight-line, units-of-production, and double-declining-balance.

Required

1. For each of the generally accepted amortization methods, prepare an amortization schedule showing asset cost, amortization expense, accumulated amortization, and asset book value.

2. RZ Technology prepares for creditors financial statements, using the amortization method that maximizes reported income in the early years of asset use. For income tax purposes, however, the business uses the amortization method that minimizes income tax payments in those early years. Identify the amortization methods that meet each of the business's objectives.

Problem 10-5B   *Journalizing capital asset transactions; betterments versus repairs*   *(Obj. 1, 2, 4)*

Assume that Mannerowd Office Products completed the following transactions:

2002
Jan.   6   Paid $13,000 cash for a used delivery truck.
       7   Paid $960 to have the truck engine overhauled.
       8   Paid $200 to have the truck modified for business use.
Aug. 21   Paid $75 for a minor tuneup after truck was put into use.

Dec.	31	Recorded amortization on the truck by the double-declining-balance method. (Assume a four-year life.)

2003		
Feb.	8	Traded in the delivery truck for a new truck costing $16,000. The dealer granted a $5,000 allowance on the old truck, and the store paid the balance in cash. Recorded year 2003 amortization for the year to date and then recorded the exchange of trucks.
July	8	Repaired the new truck's damaged fender for $1,020 cash.
Dec.	31	Recorded amortization on the new truck by the double-declining-balance method. (Assume a four-year life and a residual value of $3,000.)

Required

Record the transactions in the general journal, indicating whether each transaction amount should be capitalized as an asset or expensed.

Problem 10-6B *Analyzing capital asset transactions from information taken from a company's financial statements* **(Obj. 2, 4)**

Bombardier Inc. is one of Canada's more successful companies, exporting its products all over the world and growing in size to assets of $17 billion in 2000. The following excerpts come from Bombardier Inc.'s 2000 financial statements:

BOMBARDIER INC.
Notes to the Financial Statements
For the Years Ended January 31, 2000, and 1999 (adapted)
(millions of dollars)

	2000		
	Cost	Accumulated amortization	Net book value
Land	$ 123	$ —	$ 123
Buildings	1,218	363	855
Equipment	1,696	1,005	691
Other	141	34	107
	3,178	1,402	1,776

	1999		
	Cost	Accumulated amortization	Net book value
Land	$ 139	$ —	$ 139
Buildings	1,185	376	809
Equipment	1,715	1,023	692
Other	148	41	107
	3,187	1,440	1,747

Required

1. At January 31, 2000, what was the cost of Bombardier Inc.'s capital assets? What was the amount of accumulated amortization?

2. Bombardier Inc.'s amortization expense was $227 million in 2000 and $232 million in 1999. Why did accumulated amortization increase from 1999 to 2000 by less than the 2000 amortization expense?

3. Bombardier Inc. paid $385 million for capital assets in 2000. Prepare a T-account for capital assets at cost to determine whether Bombardier Inc. bought or sold more capital assets during the year.

Problem 10-7B   *Accounting for wasting assets, intangibles, and the related expenses (Obj. 5, 6)*

Part 1   Inco Ltd. is one of Canada's largest mining companies.

Suppose Inco Ltd. paid $1.8 million cash for a lease giving the firm the right to work a mine that contained an estimated 150,000 tonnes of nickel-bearing ore. Assume that the company paid $10,000 to remove unwanted buildings from the land and $45,000 to prepare the surface for mining. Further assume that Inco Ltd. signed a $62,000 note payable to a landscaping company to return the land surface to its original condition after the lease ends. During the first year, Inco Ltd. removed 23,000 tonnes of nickel-bearing ore, which it sold on account for $17 per tonne.

Required

Make general journal entries to record all transactions related to the nickel-bearing ore, including amortization and sale of the first-year production.

Part 2   KFC Canada, a division of Tricon Global Restaurants (Canada) Inc., operates Kentucky Fried Chicken franchised restaurants. Suppose the KFC Canada company's balance sheet reports the asset Cost in Excess of Net Assets of Purchased Businesses. Assume that KFC Canada purchased this asset as part of the acquisition of another company, which carried these figures:

Book value of assets	$2.5 million
Market value of assets	2.9 million
Liabilities	2.2 million

Required

1. What is another title for the asset Cost in Excess of Net Assets of Purchased Businesses?
2. Make the general journal entry to record KFC Canada's purchase of the other company for $1.3 million cash.
3. Assuming KFC Canada amortizes Cost in Excess of Net Assets of Purchased Businesses over 20 years, record the straight-line amortization for one year.

Part 3   Suppose John Woo purchased a Kentucky Fried Chicken franchise licence for $340,000. In addition to the basic purchase price, Woo also paid a lawyer $8,000 for assistance with the negotiations. Woo believes the appropriate amortization period for its cost of the franchise licence is eight years.

Required

Make general journal entries to record the franchise transactions, including straight-line amortization for one year.

Problem 10-8B   *Identifying the elements of property, plant, and equipment's cost; accounting for amortization by two methods; accounting for disposal of property, plant, and equipment; distinguishing betterments from repairs (Obj. 1, 2, 4)*

Quik-Time Delivery's year end is September 30. The company completed the following capital asset transactions:

2002

Jan. 2 Paid $141,000 plus $4,000 in legal fees (pertaining to all assets purchased) to purchase the following assets from a competitor who was going out of business:

Asset	Appraised Value	Estimated Useful Life	Estimated Residual Value
Land	$80,000	—	—
Buildings	70,000	20 years	$3,000
Equipment	50,000	6 years	6,000

Quik-Time Delivery plans to use the straight-line amortization method for the building and for the equipment.

July 2 Purchased a delivery truck with a list price of $40,000 for $35,000 cash. The truck is expected to be used for five years and driven a total of 120,000 kilometres; it is then expected to be sold for $5,000. It will be amortized using the units-of-production method.

July 3 Paid $1,400 to paint the truck with the company's colours and logo.

Sept. 30 Recorded amortization on the assets. The truck had been driven 18,000 kilometres since it was purchased.

Dec. 30 Quik-Time Delivery paid $3,800 to De Rooy Repairs for work done on the equipment. The job consisted of annual maintenance ($400) and the addition of automatic controls ($3,000), which will increase the expected useful life of the equipment by one year (a total of seven years) and increase its expected residual value by $1,500.

2003
Sept. 1 Sold the truck for $18,000. The truck had an odometer reading of 72,000 kilometres.

Sept. 30 Recorded amortization on the assets.

Required

1. Record the above transactions of Quik-Time Delivery. Round all amounts to the nearest dollar.

2. Show the balance sheet presentation of the assets at September 30, 2003.

Problem 10-9B *Accounting for property, plant and equipment and amortization; accounting for wasting assets and amortization; accounting for intangible assets and amortization (Obj. 2, 5, 6)*

On July 2, 2002, Alco Mines Ltd. acquired Creek Explorations Ltd. for $3,500,000. At the time of the acquisition, Creek Explorations Ltd.'s balance sheet contained the following items, which were transferred to Alco Mines Ltd.:

- Mining Equipment: original cost of $800,000 and a present market value of $640,000. The equipment is expected to last another ten years and have a residual value of $60,000 at that time.

- Mineral Rights: the rights to mine property by Sydenham River. The mineral right originally cost Creek Explorations Ltd. $2,000,000 but now has an appraised market value of $3,000,000. The mine is expected to produce 40,000,000 tonnes of ore over the next 15 years.

- Leasehold: the rights to rent office space in a nearby town for $3,500 per month for the next ten years. The leasehold has a market value today of $19,000 because of high rental rates in the area.

- Mortgage Payable: a $510,000 mortgage is outstanding on the mining equipment with interest at current rates.

Required

1. Journalize the purchase of Creek Explorations Ltd. by Alco Mines Ltd.

2. Journalize the adjusting entries required for the year ending June 30, 2003, to amortize the cost of the assets—assuming 3,000,000 tonnes of ore were taken out of the mine. Use the most appropriate methods and time frames from the data given.

3. Show how the assets would appear in the capital assets section of Alco Mines Ltd.'s balance sheet as of June 30, 2003.

Challenge Problems

Problem 10-1C   *Understanding amortization and betterments and repairs   (Obj. 1, 2)*

The owner of newly formed Brown Flying Services, a friend of your family, knows you are taking an accounting course and asks for some advice. Mr. Brown tells you that he is pretty good at running the company but doesn't understand accounting. Specifically, he has two questions:

1. The company has just paid $1,000,000 for two used float planes. His accountants tell him that he should use accelerated amortization for his financial statements but he understands that straight-line amortization will result in lower charges to expense in the early years. He wants to use straight-line amortization.

2. A friend told him that Brown Flying Services should capitalize all repairs to the planes and "spread the cost out over the life of the planes." He wonders if there is anything wrong with this advice.

Required

Respond to Mr. Brown's questions using your understanding of amortization and betterments and repairs.

Problem 10-2C   *Accounting for wasting assets (Obj. 5)*

North Shore Mines Ltd. is a new company that has been formed to mine for nickel in Northern Ontario. The ore body is estimated to contain 100,000,000 kilograms of pure nickel for which the world price is $8,450 per tonne. The costs of mine development are estimated to be $80,000,000.

Required

Calculate the costs that would be charged against the nickel production in the form of amortization on a per-1,000-kilogram basis. Estimate any costs you think should also be included. Do not include the costs to mine and refine the ore, or shipping and selling costs.

Extending Your Knowledge

Decision Problem

Measuring profitability based on different inventory and amortization methods (Obj. 2)

Link Back to Chapter 9 (Inventory Methods). Suppose you are considering investing in two businesses, Smitjanic Co. and Rebkahn Co. The two companies are virtually identical, and both began operations at the beginning of 2002. During the year, each company purchased inventory as follows:

Jan.	4	10,000 units at $4	=	$ 40,000
Apr.	6	5,000 units at 5	=	25,000
Aug.	9	7,000 units at 6	=	42,000
Nov.	27	10,000 units at 7	=	70,000
Totals		32,000		$177,000

During 2002, both companies sold 25,000 units of inventory.

In early January, 2002, both companies purchased equipment costing $150,000 that had a five-year estimated useful life and a $20,000 residual value. Smitjanic Co. uses the first-in, first-out (FIFO) method for its inventory and straight-line amortization for its equipment. Rebkahn Co. uses last-in, first-out (LIFO) and double-declining-balance amortization. Both companies' trial balances at December 31, 2002 included the following:

Sales revenue	$440,000
Operating expenses	90,000

Required

1. Prepare both companies' income statements.

2. Write an investment newsletter to address the following questions for your clients: Which company appears to be more profitable? Which company has more cash to invest in promising projects? If prices continue rising in both companies' industries over the long term, which company would you prefer to invest in? Why?

Financial Statement Problem

Property, plant, and equipment, and intangible assets (Obj. 2, 4, 6)

Refer to the Intrawest Corporation's financial statements in Appendix A and answer the following questions.

1. With respect to ski and resort operations, which amortization method does Intrawest Corporation use for the purpose of reporting to shareholders and creditors in the financial statements? What type of amortization method does the company use for income tax purposes? Why is this method preferable for income tax purposes?

2. What was the amount of amortization expense for 2000?

3. Intrawest Corporation is really in two major lines of business and the capital assets reflect that fact. What are the two lines of business? Why are the two lines shown separately?

4. Intrawest Corporation classifies part of the assets relating to one of the lines of business as current assets and the balance as long-term. Why do you think this differentiation is done?

5. Does Intrawest Corporation capitalize interest costs? If so, how much was capitalized in 2000?

Appendix

Capital Cost Allowance

Canada Customs and Revenue Agency allows corporations as well as individuals with business or professional income to compute deductions from income to recognize the consumption or using up of capital assets. The deductions are called **capital cost allowance**. Canada Customs and Revenue Agency specifies the *maximum* rates allowed for each asset class, called *capital cost allowance rates*. Some typical Canada Customs and Revenue Agency rates and classes are:

	Rate	Class
Automobiles	30%	10
Brick, concrete, or stone buildings	4%	1
Computer software	100%	12
Office furniture and fixtures	20%	8
Computers	30%	10

Canada Customs and Revenue Agency allows the taxpayer to claim only 50 percent of the normal capital cost allowance rate in the year of acquisition. However, there are some exceptions and Class 12 is one of them. Class 12 assets have a full 100% capital cost allowance rate in the year of acquisition.

The capital cost allowance rate is applied to the undepreciated balance in the asset class at the end of the year (cost minus accumulated capital cost allowance claimed to date) in the same manner as with the double-declining-balance method discussed on pages 514 to 515.

To illustrate, during the year beginning January 2, 2001, Briana Weill, the entrepreneur from Chapter 1, bought a computer and an accounting software package to help her account for her business income. The computer cost $2,200 and the software cost $300. Briana decided to amortize the computer and the software on a straight-line basis over five years, and expects the computer and software to have no value at the end of five years. These assumptions lead to an amortization expense of $440 per year ($2,200/5 years) for the computer and an amortization expense of $60 per year ($300/5 years) for the software.

For income tax purposes, the computer is considered to be a Class 10 asset. The capital cost allowance rate for Class 10 assets is 30 percent. The software is considered to be a Class 12 asset. The capital cost allowance rate for Class 12 assets is 100 percent. Remember that a taxpayer can claim only 50 percent of normal capital cost allowance in the year of acquisition for most asset classes, which in Briana's case is the year 2001. In 2001, Briana could claim up to the maximum capital cost allowance of $330 ([$2,200 × 30%] × 50%) for the computer. However, she can claim up to the maximum capital cost allowance of $300 for the software in 2001. These are the only capital assets in these classes.

In 2002, Briana would apply the Class 10 rate of 30 percent to the cost of the computer remaining after the 2001 capital cost allowance is deducted. In 2002, Briana could claim up to the maximum capital cost allowance of $561 ([$2,200 − $330] × 30%) for the computer. Following the same process in 2003, Briana could claim up to the maximum capital cost allowance of $393 ([$2,200 − $330 − $561] × 30%) for the computer. The table below shows the maximum capital cost allowance Briana could deduct from her business income for the first six years:

	2001	2002	2003	2004	2005	2006
Computer	$330	$561	$393	$275	$192	$135
Software	$300	0	0	0	0	0

Notice that in 2006, the sixth year that Briana owned the computer, she is able to deduct capital cost allowance for income tax purposes. However, for accounting purposes, the computer would be fully amortized at the end of 2005, the fifth year, since Briana decided to amortize the computer on a straight-line basis over five years. This example shows that amortization expense deducted from income on the income statement often differs from the capital cost allowance claimed by a taxpayer on the tax return.

Capital cost allowance and amortization issues are quite complicated. These issues are studied more fully in advanced accounting courses and tax courses.

Current Liabilities and Payroll

CHAPTER OBJECTIVES

After studying this chapter, you should be able to

1 Account for current liabilities of known amount

2 Account for current liabilities that must be estimated

3 Identify and report contingent liabilities

4 Compute payroll amounts

5 Record basic payroll transactions

6 Use a payroll system

7 Report current liabilities on the balance sheet

"Airlines with frequent-flier programs must record as a current liability the cost of flying those who will use frequent-flyer miles over the next year," says Joseph D. Wesselkamper, CPA, President of Joseph D. Wesselkamper & Associates, Inc. "When the airline is in partnership with another organization (such as a hotel chain), the problem of determining the current liability becomes more complex."

First there were the frequent-flier programs of the airlines: Fly so many miles on a particular airline, and receive a free ticket to the destination of your choice. Now some hotels—Delta, Holiday Inn, and Marriott, among others—are offering their guests *airline* mileage that makes it easier for people to earn free travel on such airlines as Air Canada and several U.S. carriers.

Holiday Inn Hotels and Resorts, and Delta Hotels, for example, offer 500 Aeroplan (Air Canada) miles for each stay at a Holiday Inn or Delta Hotel. Why would these hotels make such offers? To encourage travellers to stay at Holiday Inn or Delta hotels. To the hotel, the cost is a promotion expense. Why would Air Canada allow the hotels to make this offer? To generate revenue: the airlines charge the hotels approximately $0.015 per mile credited to the customer's account (frequent flier rewards always seem to be measured in miles perhaps because the U.S. is the leader in the field).

This real example illustrates the challenge of accounting for liabilities. In this case the airlines have an obligation to provide travel paid for by the hotels.

A LIABILITY is an obligation to transfer assets or to provide services in the future. The obligation may arise from a transaction with an outside party. For example, a business incurs a liability when it purchases inventory on account or when it issues a note to borrow money.

An obligation may arise in the absence of individual transactions. For example, interest expense accrues with the passage of time. Until this interest is paid it is a liability. Income tax, a liability of corporations, accrues as income is earned. Proper accounting for liabilities is as important as proper accounting for assets. The failure to record an accrued liability causes the related expense to be understated on the balance sheet and, thus, owner's equity to be overstated.

The arrangement between hotels, such as Holiday Inn Hotels and Resorts, and the airlines illustrates the challenge of accounting for liabilities. In this case, the airlines have an obligation to provide travel that the hotels have paid for in advance. The airline receives cash in advance, which creates an obligation to provide future transportation. Suppose that a Holiday Inn grants 100,000 miles of Air Canada Aeroplan frequent-flier credit to its guests. Holiday Inn's cost is $1,500 (100,000 miles at $0.015 per mile). Assume that Holiday Inn pays Aeroplan $1,500. How would the airline account for these transactions?

Air Canada debits an expense and credits a liability when an Aeroplan member earns sufficient miles to redeem those miles for a ticket. When a partner, such as Delta Hotels and Holiday Inn, rewards a customer with Air Canada air miles, Air Canada debits amounts receivable and credits a deferred liability. The airline debits the deferred liability and credits revenue as frequent-flyer rewards are redeemed. Air Canada does not show a separate liability for Aeroplan rewards on its balance sheet. American Airlines, however, does show a separate liability, called Air Traffic Liability, for frequent-flier rewards on its balance sheet.

We discuss long-term liabilities in Chapter 15. We now turn to accounting for current liabilities, including those arising from payroll expenses.

Delta Hotels
www.deltahotels.com

Holiday Inn Hotels
www.basshotels.com/holiday-inn

Marriott Hotels, Resorts, and Suites
www.marriott.com

Air Canada—Aeroplan
www.aircanada.ca/aeroplan

American Airlines
www.aa.com

Current Liabilities of Known Amount

Recall that *current liabilities* are obligations due within one year or within the company's operating cycle if it is longer than one year. Obligations due beyond that period of time are classified as *long-term liabilities*. We discussed current liabilities and long-term liabilities in Chapter 4, page 175.

Current liabilities fall into one of two categories: liabilities of a known amount and liabilities that must be estimated. We look first at current liabilities of known amount.

Accounts Payable

Amounts owed to suppliers for products or services that are purchased on open account are *accounts payable*. We have seen many accounts payable examples in previous chapters. For example, a business may purchase inventories and office supplies on account. Air Canada reported accounts payable and accrued liabilities of $942 million at December 31, 1999 (see Exhibit 11-1).

Current liabilities arising from many similar transactions are well suited for computerized information systems. One of Air Canada's common transactions is the purchase of its inventory of food to be served on flights. Air Canada's accounts payable and perpetual inventory systems are integrated. When the food inventory dips below a predetermined level, the computer automatically prepares a purchase request for more food. After the order is placed and the goods are received, clerks enter inventory and accounts payable data into the system. Air Canada makes the following journal entry to purchase the inventory on account (amount assumed):

Inventory	600	
Accounts Payable		600
Purchase on account.		

The computer thus increases Inventory and Accounts Payable to account for the purchase. For payments, the computer debits Accounts Payable and credits Cash, as follows:

Accounts Payable	400	
Cash		400
Paid on account.		

The computer may also update account balances and print journals, ledger accounts, and the financial statements.

Air Canada completes thousand of transactions such as these. The sum of all the amounts Air Canada still owes on account is included in the $942 million balance of Accounts Payable and Accrued Liabilities shown in Exhibit 11-1.

WORKING IT OUT

After Air Canada buys inventory and pays the account payable in these two transactions, how much does Air Canada owe the other company? Stated differently, how much is Air Canada's account payable to the supplier?

A: $200 ($600 − $400)

EXHIBIT 11-1

How Air Canada Reports Its Current and Contingent Liabilities

AIR CANADA
Balance Sheet (partial, adapted)
December 31, 1999

Liabilities	(In millions)
Current	
Accounts payable and accrued liabilities	$ 942
Advance ticket sales	349
Current portion of long-term debt	114
	$1,405

Contingencies and commitments are described in the notes to the financial statements; no amounts appear on the balance sheet itself.

Short-Term Notes Payable

Short-term notes payable are a common form of financing. They are promissory notes that must be paid within one year. Companies often issue short-term notes payable to borrow cash or to purchase inventory. In addition to recording the note payable and its eventual payment, the business also pays interest expense and must accrue interest expense and interest payable at the end of the period. Recall from Chapter 3, page 119, that all adjusting entries for accrued expenses require a debit to an expense and a credit to a payable. The following entries are typical for a short-term note payable:

2002			
Sept. 30	Inventory..	16,000.00	
	Note Payable, Short-Term		16,000.00
	Purchase of inventory by issuing a one-year 10 percent note payable.		
Dec. 31	Interest Expense...	403.29	
	Interest Payable...		403.29
	Adjusting entry to accrue interest expense at year end ($8,000 × 0.10 × $^{92}/_{365}$).		

The balance sheet at December 31, 2002, will report the Note Payable of $16,000 and the related Interest Payable of $403 as current liabilities. The 2002 income statement will report interest expense of $403 ($403.29 rounded to the nearest dollar), as illustrated.

SAMPLE COMPANY
Balance Sheet
December 31, 2002

Assets		Liabilities	
		Current liabilities:	
Various......................	$XXX	Note payable, short-term....	$16,000
		Interest payable....................	403

SAMPLE COMPANY
Income Statement
For the Year Ended December 31, 2002

Revenues:....................	$XXX	
Expenses:		
Interest expense	$403	

The following entry records payment of the note at maturity:

2003			
Sept. 30	Note Payable, Short-Term	16,000.00	
	Interest Payable..	403.29	
	Interest Expense	1,196.71	
	Cash		17,600.00
	Payment of a note payable and interest at maturity. Interest expense is $1,196.71 ($16,000 × 0.10 × $^{273}/_{365}$). Cash paid is $17,600 [$16,000 + ($16,000 × 0.10)].		

The cash payment entry must split the total interest on the note between

- the interest expense of 2002 ($403.29)
- the interest expense of 2003 ($1,196.71).

This way, each year's financial statements report the correct amounts of interest expense for *that* year.

KEY POINT

The interest on a note is separate from the principal. The accrued interest should be credited to Interest Payable—*not* to Note Payable.

WORKING IT OUT

A $10,000, 11%, 90-day note was issued on Nov. 1, 2001. Record the accrual on Dec. 31, 2001 and the note payment on Jan. 30, 2002.

A:

Dec. 31, 2001
Interest Expense ($10,000 × 11% × 60/365)..... 181
   Interest Payable   181

Jan. 30, 2002
Note Payable 10,000
Interest Payable..... 181
Interest Expense.... 90
   Cash 10,271

LEARNING TIP

Interest Payable must have a zero balance after the September 30, 2003, note payment is recorded. After interest is paid, it is no longer a liability; the amount previously accrued must be reduced with a debit to Interest Payable.

The face amount of notes payable and their interest rates and payment dates can be stored for electronic data processing. Computer programs calculate interest, print the interest cheques, journalize the transactions, and update account balances.

Short-Term Notes Payable Issued at a Discount

There is another way to set up a borrowing arrangement. It is called **discounting a note payable**. The lender, usually a bank, subtracts the interest amount from the note's face value and the borrower receives the net amount. At maturity, the borrower pays back the full face value of the note, which includes all the interest.

Suppose Inco Ltd. discounts a $100,000, 60-day note payable to its bank at 12 percent. The company will receive $98,027, that is, the $100,000 face value less interest of $1,973 ($100,000 $\times$ 0.12 $\times$ $^{60}\!/_{365}$). Assume this transaction occurs on November 25, 2002. Inco Ltd.'s entries to record discounting the note follows:

2002			
Nov. 25	Cash	98,027	
	Discount on Note Payable	1,973	
	Note Payable, Short-Term		100,000
	Discounted a $100,000, 60-day, 12-percent note payable to borrow cash. The discount is $1,973 ($100,000 $\times$ 0.12 $\times$ $^{60}\!/_{365}$).		

Note Payable		Discount on Note Payable	
	Nov. 25 100,000	Nov. 25 1,973	

Net liability, $98,027

The T-accounts show that Discount on Note Payable is a contra account to the liability Note Payable, Short-Term. For this reason, Discount on Note Payable is journalized as a *debit*. A balance sheet prepared immediately after this transaction would report the note payable at its net amount of $98,027, as follows:

Balance Sheet	
Current liabilities	
Note payable, short-term...........................	$100,000
Less: Discount on note payable	(1,973)
Note payable, short-term, net	$ 98,027

Inco must record accrued interest at year end as it would for any note payable. The adjusting entry at December 31 records interest for 36 days as follows:

2002			
Dec. 31	Interest Expense	1,184	
	Discount on Note Payable		1,184
	Adjusting entry to accrue interest expense at year end ($100,000 $\times$ 0.12 $\times$ $^{36}\!/_{365}$).		

For a discounted note, this entry credits Discount on Note Payable instead of Interest Payable. Crediting the Discount on Note Payable reduces this contra account's balance and increases the net amount of the Note Payable. After the adjusting entry, only $789 of the Discount on Note Payable remains.

Note Payable		Discount on Note Payable			
	Nov. 25 100,000	Nov. 25 1,973	Dec. 31 1,184		
		Bal. 789			

Net liability, $99,211

The carrying amount of the note payable increases to $99,211, as follows:

Balance Sheet

Current liabilities	
Note payable, short-term.............................	$100,000
Less: Discount on note payable	
($1,973 – $1,184)................................	(789)
Note payable, short-term, net	$ 99,211

At maturity, the business records the final amount of interest expense and the payment of the note:

2003			
Jan. 24	Interest Expense..	789	
	Discount on Note Payable		789
	To record interest expense.		
Jan. 24	Note Payable, Short-Term	100,000	
	Cash..		100,000
	To pay note payable at maturity.		

After these entries, the balances in the note payable account and the discount account are zero.

Note Payable				**Discount on Note Payable**			
Jan. 24	100,000	Nov. 25	100,000	Nov. 25	1,973	Dec. 31	1,184
				Bal.	789	Jan. 24	789

In Chapter 8, we discussed discounting a note *receivable*, which means to sell the note receivable in order to receive the cash immediately. Here we are discounting a note *payable*, which means to borrow a lesser amount of money (a discounted amount) and pay back the face value of the note payable later.

Goods and Services Tax and Sales Tax Payable

There are two basic consumption taxes levied on purchases in Canada that are visible to the consumer: the goods and services tax (GST) levied by the federal government and provincial sales taxes (PST) levied by all the provinces except Alberta; there are, at present, no sales taxes in the Yukon, Nunavut, or the Northwest Territories. The goods and services tax was introduced in Chapter 5, page 228, and mentioned again in Chapter 9, page 463. There are also excise or luxury taxes, which are a form of sales tax levied by the federal and provincial governments on products such as cigarettes, jewellery, and alcoholic beverages; these taxes are hidden in that they are collected by the manufacturer. The focus of discussion in this section will be on the consumption or visible taxes; the goods and services tax and provincial sales taxes will be discussed in turn below. In order to simplify the discussion, the material concerning calculation and payment of the GST will exclude the PST and the material concerning calculation and payment of the PST will generally exclude the GST. Nova Scotia, New Brunswick, and Newfoundland and Labrador have harmonized the GST with their PST. Quebec has partially harmonized its sales tax (QST) with the GST. The Harmonized Sales Tax (HST) will be described below.

Goods and Services Tax   In 1991, the federal government passed legislation eliminating existing taxes imposed on manufactured and imported goods. At the same time, it implemented a goods and services tax (GST) that is collected from the ultimate consumer and includes most goods and services consumed in Canada. The tax and its application may be covered in an introductory tax course and is beyond the scope of this text; the ensuing discussion deals primarily with basic facts about the tax and how to account for it.

THINKING IT OVER

What is the difference between payment of interest on a loan and payment of interest on a discounted note?

A: On a loan, the interest is paid at maturity or during the term of the note. On a discounted note, the interest is deducted up front and therefore reduces the proceeds of the note. The dollar amount of the interest is the same, but the effective interest is higher on a discounted note than on a loan because you receive less cash.

LEARNING TIP

Discounted notes *receivable* are sometimes confused with discounted notes *payable*. Discounting a note *receivable* involves selling a note receivable (an asset) received from a third party. The interest on a discounted note receivable is deducted up front when the note is discounted. On the other hand, a discounted note *payable* is borrowing money using your own note payable (a liability). The interest on a discounted note payable is also deducted up front when the note is discounted.

GST/HST: Electronic Filing and Remitting
www.ccra-adrc.gc.ca/gsthst-edi

There are three categories of goods and services with respect to the GST:

1. Zero-rated supplies such as basic groceries, prescription drugs, and medical devices;
2. Exempt supplies such as educational services, health care services, and financial services; and
3. Taxable supplies, which basically includes everything that is not zero-rated or exempt.

The GST rate is 7 percent. The tax is collected by the individual or entity (called the *registrant*) supplying the taxable good or service (called *taxable supplies*) to the final consumer. The GST is remitted to the Receiver General. Suppliers of taxable goods and services have to pay tax on their purchases. However, they are able to deduct the amount of GST paid (called an *input tax credit*) from the GST they have collected from their sales of goods and services in calculating the amount due to the federal government. The GST Return and the net tax must be remitted to the Receiver General quarterly for most registrants and monthly for larger registrants.

For example, Mary Janicek purchased a power lawn mower on July 2, 2002, with the intention of earning money by cutting grass during the summer.[1] The lawn mower cost $250; the GST was $17.50. Because Mary is planning to use the mower exclusively to cut grass for a fee, she could recover the $17.50. However, assuming she were a registrant, she would have to charge all her customers the 7 percent GST on sales of her lawn-mowing services and remit it to the government. During the three-month first quarter, Mary earned revenue of $2,000.00, related GST of $140.00, and thus collected $2,140.00. She spent $107.00—$100.00 plus GST of $7.00—on gasoline for the mower. Her input tax credit of $24.50 included the $17.50 GST on the lawn mower and $7.00 GST on gasoline for the mower. The entries to record these transactions would be

2002
July 2

Equipment	250.00	
GST Receivable	17.50	
Cash		267.50
To record purchase of power mower.		

July–Sept.

Supplies Expense	100.00	
GST Receivable	7.00	
Cash		107.00
To record purchase of gasoline for power mower.		

July–Sept.

Cash	2,140.00	
Lawn-mowing Revenue		2,000.00
GST Payable		140.00
To record revenue from mowing lawns.		

Mary would be required to remit $115.50 ($140.00 − $17.50 − $7.00) as her first quarterly payment. Since Mary would be recovering the GST paid on the purchase of the mower and gasoline of $24.50 ($17.50 + $7.00), she would credit the recovery to the GST Receivable account, to bring its balance to zero. The entry would be as follows:

Oct. 31

GST Payable	140.00	
Cash		115.50
GST Receivable		24.50
To record payment of GST payable net of input tax credits to Receiver General.		

---

[1] If your business earns less than $30,000 per year, it does not have to be registered for GST purposes. In reality, Mary Janicek's business would be below the minimum threshold of $30,000, so Mary is unlikely to be a registrant. The scenario is illustrative. A business is only required to become a GST registrant if taxable supplies exceed $30,000 per year.

In the Mary Janicek example, we used two accounts—GST Receivable and GST Payable—to illustrate input tax credits and GST collections to be remitted to the Receiver General. Some registrants use only one account—GST Payable—to record input tax credits *and* GST collections. When the GST Return is sent to the Receiver General, the final account balance in the GST Payable account is remitted if the balance is a credit or a refund is requested if the balance is a debit. However, in the remainder of this chapter, we will continue to use the two-account approach to illustrate input tax credits and GST collections.

Because they collect the GST for the federal government, the registrants owe the Receiver General the net tax collected; the account Goods and Services Tax Payable is a current liability. Most companies include GST owing with Accounts Payable and Accrued Liabilities and GST receivable as a current asset on their balance sheets.

Provincial Sales Tax   As was mentioned above, all the provinces, except Alberta (as well as the Yukon, Nunavut, and the Northwest Territories), levy a sales tax on sales to the final consumers of products; they are not levied on sales to wholesalers or retailers. The final sellers charge their customers the sales tax in addition to the price of the item sold. The following provincial sales tax rates were in effect at the time of writing:

British Columbia	7%	
Saskatchewan	6%	
Manitoba	7%	
Ontario	8%	
Quebec	7.5%	(PST based on price including GST)
Prince Edward Island	10%	(PST based on price including GST)
New Brunswick	15%	(blended with GST)
Nova Scotia	15%	(blended with GST)
Newfoundland and Labrador	15%	(blended with GST)

As this list shows, four provinces charge PST and GST separately on the purchase price of a taxable good or service. Two provinces charge PST on the sum of the purchase price and the GST. Three provinces charge a combined GST and PST rate of 15 percent on the purchase price. This 15 percent rate is known as *Harmonized Sales Tax* (*HST*). By harmonizing their PST with the GST, New Brunswick, Nova Scotia, and Newfoundland and Labrador have reduced the cost of collecting and administering consumption taxes.

Consider a taxable item that costs $100 before tax. Ontario charges PST and GST separately; a taxable sale of $100.00 would have GST of $7.00 (0.07 × $100.00) and PST of $8.00 (0.08 × $100.00). Prince Edward Island charges PST on GST; a taxable sale of $100.00 would have GST of $7.00 (0.07 × $100.00) and PST of $10.70 [0.10 × ($100.00 + $7.00)]. Nova Scotia has harmonized the PST and the GST; a taxable sale of $100.00 would have PST and GST of $15.00 (0.15 × $100.00).

Consider Super Stereo Products, an electronics superstore located in Ottawa. Super Stereo does not pay provincial sales tax on its purchase of a TV set from Panasonic because it is inventory for resale, but you, as a consumer, would have to pay the province of Ontario's 8 percent provincial sales tax to Super Stereo when you buy a Panasonic TV from the store. Super Stereo pays the sales tax it collected from you to the provincial government. Panasonic, the manufacturer, would not have a sales tax liability at its year end, but Super Stereo probably would. (For purposes of the discussion of sales tax, we will ignore the GST.)

Suppose one Saturday's sales at the Super Stereo store totalled $20,000. The business would have collected an additional 8 percent in sales tax, which would equal $1,600 ($20,000 × 0.08). The business would record that day's sales as follows:

Cash	21,600	
Sales Revenue		20,000
Sales Tax Payable		1,600

To record cash sales of $20,000 subject to 8 percent sales tax.

Because the retailers owe to the province the sales tax collected, the account Sales Tax Payable is a current liability. Most companies include sales tax payable with Accounts Payable and Accrued Liabilities on their balance sheets.

Companies forward the collected sales tax to the taxing authority at regular intervals, at which time they debit Sales Tax Payable and credit Cash. Observe that Sales Tax Payable does not correspond to any sales tax expense that the business is incurring. Nor does this liability arise from the purchase of any asset. Rather, it is the cash that the business is collecting on behalf of the government.

Many companies consider it inefficient to credit Sales Tax Payable when recording each sale. Instead, they record sales revenue and sales tax together. Then, prior to paying tax to the province, they make a single entry for the entire period's transactions to bring Sales Revenue and Sales Tax Payable to their correct balances.

Suppose a company located in Vancouver had sales in July of $100,000, subject to the B.C. retail sales tax of 7 percent. Its summary entry to record the month's sales revenue could be

July 31	Cash..	107,000	
	Sales Revenue...		107,000
	To record sales for the month. Cash received is $107,000 ($100,000 × 1.07).		

The entry to adjust Sales Revenue and Sales Tax Payable to their correct balances would then be

July 31	Sales Revenue	7,000	
	Sales Tax Payable..		7,000
	To record sales tax. Sales tax payable is $7,000 [$107,000 − ($107,000 ÷ 1.07)].		

Companies that follow this procedure need to make an adjusting entry at the end of the period in order to report the correct amounts of revenue and liability on their financial statements.

Current Portion of Long-Term Debt

Some long-term notes payable and long-term bonds payable must be paid in instalments, which means that equal portions of the principal are repaid at specific time intervals. The **current portion of long-term debt**, or **current maturity**, is the amount of the principal that is payable within one year. At the end of each year, a company reclassifies (from long-term debt to a current liability) the amount of its long-term debt that must be paid during the upcoming year.

Air Canada's balance sheet (Exhibit 11-1, page 558) reports Current Portion of Long-Term Debt, the last current liability. On its full balance sheet, Air Canada

WORKING IT OUT

Record sales of $35,600 and the related 7% provincial sales tax if (1) the sales tax is recorded separately and (2) the sales tax is included in Sales. (Ignore GST.)

A: (1) Only one entry is required:

Cash.................	38,092	
Sales Revenue.........		35,600
Sales Tax Payable..........		2,492

(2) Two entries are required:

| Cash................. | 38,092 | |
| Sales Revenue......... | | 38,092 |

| Sales Revenue.......... | 2,492 | |
| Sales Tax Payable......... | | 2,492 |

$$\left(\$2{,}492 = \$38{,}092 - \frac{\$38{,}092}{1.07}\right)$$

LEARNING TIP

A current liability is due within one year or within the company's operating cycle if it is longer than one year. The portion of a long-term debt payable within the year is classified as a current liability. The interest payable is classified separately from the principal.

STOP & THINK

Suppose that Air Canada reported its full liability as long-term. Identify two ratios that would have been distorted by this accounting error. State whether the ratio values would be overstated or understated and whether they would report an overly positive or negative view of the company.

Answer: Reporting a liability as long-term could mislead external users because it understates current liabilities and has these effects:

Ratio	Overstated or Understated	View of the Company
Current ratio	Overstated	Overly positive
Acid-test ratio	Overstated	Overly positive

This example shows that accounting includes both *recording* transactions and *reporting* the information. Reporting is every bit as important as recording.

reports long-term debt immediately after total current liabilities. *Long-term debt* refers to the notes and bonds payable that are payable later than one year beyond the balance sheet date.

The liabilities for the current portion of long-term debt do *not* include any accrued interest payable. The account, Current Portion of Long-Term Debt, represents only the *principal amount owed*. Interest Payable is a separate account for a different liability—the interest that must be paid. Air Canada includes interest payable under the current liability caption Accounts Payable and Accrued Liabilities.

Accrued Expenses (Accrued Liabilities)

Every accrued expense (liability) involves a debit to an *expense* and a credit to a *liability*.

An **accrued expense** is an expense incurred but not yet paid by the company. Therefore, it is also a liability, which explains why accrued expenses are also called **accrued liabilities**. Accrued expenses typically occur with the passage of time, such as interest payable on long-term debt. By contrast, an account payable results from a particular transaction in which the company purchased a good or a service. We introduced accrued expenses in Chapter 3, page 119.

Some companies combine their accrued expenses as Air Canada did in Exhibit 11-1 on page 558, while other companies list each major current liability, as AS Products Company did in Chapter 4 on page 177. Salaries and wages payable are the company's accrued liabilities for salaries and wages payable at the end of the period. This caption also includes other payroll-related liabilities, such as taxes withheld from employee paycheques. Accrued liabilities payable includes the company's current liabilities for such items as interest payable and income tax payable. We illustrated the accounting for interest payable under the caption Short-term notes payable on page 561. The following section, plus the second half of this chapter, covers the accrued salaries and wages and other payroll liabilities.

Payroll Liabilities

Payroll liabilities are accrued liabilities. These liabilities are to various entities.

To the employee: For net wages, salaries, and bonuses

To the government: For income tax withheld, employment insurance, and Canada Pension

To outside providers of benefits: For insurance premiums, union dues, payroll savings plans

Payroll, also called **employee compensation**, is a major expense of many businesses. For service organizations—such as public accounting firms, real-estate brokers, and travel agents—payroll is *the* major expense. Service organizations sell their personnel's services, so employee compensation is their primary cost of doing business, just as cost of goods sold is the largest expense for a merchandising company.

Employee compensation takes different forms:

- *Salary* is pay stated at a yearly, monthly, or weekly rate.
- *Wages* are employee pay amounts that are stated at an hourly figure.
- *Commissions* are computed as a percentage of the sales the employee has made.
- *Bonus* is an amount over and above regular compensation.

Canada Pension Plan
www.cpp-rpc.gc.ca/

Accounting for all of these forms of compensation follows the same pattern, which is illustrated in Exhibit 11-2 (using assumed figures).

Salary (or other payroll) expense represents employees' *gross pay* (that is, pay before subtractions for taxes and other deductions). Salary expense creates several liabilities for the company.

The employer deducts income taxes and other withholdings, such as Canada Pension and employment insurance, from the employee's wages or salaries each pay period but does not have to remit this to the government immediately. The amounts withheld from the employee's pay are a liability until remitted.

- Salary payable to employees, which is their *net* (take-home) *pay*. This is the largest payroll liability.
- *Employee Income Tax Payable* is the employees' federal and provincial income tax that has been withheld from their paycheques.
- *Canada Pension Payable* (or, in Quebec, Quebec Pension Payable) includes Canada Pension Plan contributions withheld from the employees, as well as the employer's contribution.

- *Employment Insurance Payable* includes employment insurance contributions withheld from the employees, as well as the employer's contribution. The company owes the liabilities for these withholdings to the Canadian (or Quebec) government.
- In Exhibit 11-2, employees have authorized the company to withhold union dues, which are payable to the union.

In addition, the employer may have other expenses, such as Workers' Compensation premiums. Accounting for these payroll expenses is covered in more detail in the second half of this chapter.

Unearned Revenues

Maclean's Magazine
www.macleans.ca

Unearned revenues are also called *deferred revenues, revenues collected in advance,* and *customer prepayments.* As we saw in Chapter 3, page 121, an unearned revenue is a liability because it represents an obligation to provide a good or service. Each account title indicates that the business has received cash from its customers before it has earned the revenue. The company has an obligation to provide goods or services to the customer. Exhibit 11-1 shows Air Canada has received cash from customers for future flights of $349 million at December 31, 1999. Let's consider another example.

Maclean's may be purchased weekly or by means of a subscription. When subscribers pay in advance to have *Maclean's* delivered to their home or business, Maclean Hunter Publishing Limited incurs a liability to provide future service. The liability account is called Unearned Subscription Revenue (which could also be titled Unearned Subscription Income or Deferred Subscription Income).

Assume that Maclean Hunter Publishing Limited charges $154.47 for Mary Bish's three-year subscription to *Maclean's.* Maclean Hunter Publishing Limited's entries would be

```
2002
Jan. 2    Cash.............................................................................  $154.47
              Unearned Subscription Revenue.........................              $154.47
          To record receipt of cash at start of a three-year
          subscription.
```

After receiving the cash on January 2, 2002, Maclean Hunter Publishing Limited owes its customer magazines that Maclean Hunter Publishing Limited will provide over three years. Maclean Hunter Publishing Limited's liability is:

Unearned Subscription Revenue

	154.47

During 2002, Maclean Hunter Publishing Limited delivers one-third of the magazines and earns $51.49 ($ 154.47 × $\frac{1}{3}$) of the subscription revenue. At December 31, 2002, Maclean Hunter Publishing Limited makes the following adjusting entry to decrease (debit) the liability Unearned Subscription Revenue and increase (credit) Subscription Revenue:

EXHIBIT 11-2

Accounting for Payroll Expenses and Liabilities

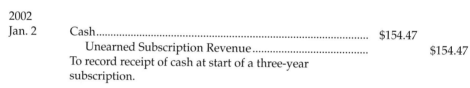

```
Salary Expense (or Wage Expense or Commission Expense)...   10,000
    Employee Income Tax Payable.................................             1,350
    Canada Pension Payable.........................................               320
    Employment Insurance Payable ............................               270
    Employee Union Dues Payable.............................               272
    Salary Payable to Employees (take-home pay).....................             7,788
To record salary expense.
```

2002
Dec. 31   Unearned Subscription Revenue...   51.49
                Subscription Revenue...   51.49
            Earned revenue that was collected in advance ($ 154.47 × ⅓).

After this entry is posted, the two accounts appear as follows:

Unearned Subscription Revenue				Subscription Revenue	
Dec. 31	51.49	Jan. 2	154.47	Dec. 31	51.49
		Bal.	102.98		

At December 31, 2002, Maclean Hunter Publishing Limited has earned $51.49 of the revenue. Maclean Hunter Publishing Limited still owes its customer $102.98 in total liabilities:

- $51.49 for the magazines Maclean Hunter Publishing Limited will deliver during 2003. This is a current liability.

- $51.49 for the magazines Maclean Hunter Publishing Limited will deliver during 2004. This is a long-term liability, but will likely be classed as current; most companies do not record unearned subscription revenue as long term.

Maclean Hunter Publishing Limited's financial statements would report this sequence:

		December 31	
Balance Sheet	2002	2003	2004
Current liabilities			
Unearned subscription revenue	$102.98	$51.49	$-0-

Income Statement	2002	2003	2004
Revenues			
Subscription revenue	$51.49	$51.49	$51.49

Customer Deposits Payable

Some companies require cash deposits from customers as security on borrowed assets. These amounts are called Customer Deposits Payable because the company must refund the cash to the customer under certain conditions.

For example, telephone companies may demand a cash deposit from a customer before installing a telephone. Utility companies and businesses that lend tools and appliances commonly demand a deposit as protection against damage and theft. When the customer ends the service or returns the borrowed asset, the company refunds the cash deposit—if the customer has paid all the bills and has not damaged the company's property. Because the company generally must return the cash deposit, that amount represents a liability. The uncertainty of when the deposits will be refunded and their relatively small amounts cause many companies to classify Customer Deposits Payable as current liabilities. This is consistent with the concept of conservatism.

Certain manufacturers of products sold through individual dealers, such as Avon or Mary Kay, require deposits from the dealers who sell their products; the deposit is usually equal to the cost of the sample kit provided to the merchandiser. Companies whose products are sold in returnable containers collect deposits on those containers. The most common example is the deposit on soft-drink and beer bottles. In both cases the deposits are shown as current liabilities by the manufacturers and the bottlers. The amounts are relatively small and so are included with accounts payable and accrued charges.

Current Liabilities That Must Be Estimated

A business may know that a liability exists but not know the exact amount. It cannot simply ignore the liability. The unknown amount of a liability must be estimated, recorded in the accounts, and reported on the balance sheet.

Estimated current liabilities vary among companies. As an example, let us look at Estimated Warranty Payable, a common liability account for merchandisers.

Estimated Warranty Payable

Many manufacturers and some merchandising companies guarantee their products against defects under *warranty* agreements. The warranty period may extend for any length of time. Ninety-day warranties and one-year warranties are common. Most automobile companies, such as General Motors and Chrysler have three-year, 60,000-kilometre warranties on new cars.

The matching principle demands that the company record the *warranty expense* in the same period that the business recognizes sales revenue, regardless of when the company pays warranty claims. For a review of the matching principle, see Chapter 3, page 111. Offering the warranty—and incurring warranty expense—is a part of generating revenue through sales. At the time of the sale, however, the company does not know which products are defective. The exact amount of warranty expense cannot be known with certainty, so the business must *estimate* its warranty expense and the related liability at the time of sale.

Assume that Inglis Ltd., which manufactures appliances sold under a number of brand names such as Kitchen Aid and Kenmore (Sears), made sales of $500 million that are subject to product warranties. Assume that in the past between 2 percent and 4 percent of products proved defective. Inglis Ltd. management could estimate that 3 percent of the products it sells this year will require repair or replacement during the one-year warranty period. The company would record the sales of $500,000,000 and the warranty expense of $15,000,000 ($500,000,000 × 0.03) in the same period as follows:

Accounts Receivable	500,000,000	
Sales Revenue		500,000,000
Sales on account.		

Warranty Expense	15,000,000	
Estimated Warranty Payable		15,000,000
To accrue warranty expense.		

Assume that defective merchandise totals $12,800,000. If Inglis repairs the defective appliances, Inglis makes this journal entry:

Estimated Warranty Payable	12,800,000	
Various Expenses		12,800,000
To *repair* defective products sold under warranty.		

If Inglis gives customers replacement appliances for the warranty claims, Inglis would instead make this entry:

Estimated Warranty Payable	12,800,000	
Inventory		12,800,000
To *replace* defective products sold under warranty.		

Student to Student

With so many different types of current liabilities ... I had difficulty remembering how to record journal entries for each type. The wide selection of Self-Study Questions and Exercises in the chapter allowed me to test my knowledge of each concept, and then apply that knowledge to the Problems. ... there is plenty of material to develop a solid understanding of each topic.

Bryan K., Waterloo

WORKING IT OUT

A company made sales of $400,000 and estimated warranty repairs at 5% of the sales. Actual warranty outlays were $19,000. Record the sales (ignore cost of goods sold), the warranty expense, and the warranty payments.

A:

Accounts Rec.	400,000	
Sales Revenue		400,000

Warranty Expense		
(400,000 × 5%)	20,000	
Est. Warr. Pay.		20,000

Est. Warr. Pay.	19,000	
Cash, Inventory,		
and so on		19,000

LEARNING TIP

A warrantied product may be sold in one year but repaired in another year. The dilemma in accounting is when the repair should be expensed—in the year the product is sold or in the year the product is repaired? The matching principle requires matching the warranty expense with the revenue from the sale.

Inglis Ltd.'s expense is $15,000,000 on the income statement in all cases. The amount of the cash payment or the cost of the replacement inventory has no bearing on the amount of warranty expense for the period. After paying these warranty claims, Inglis Ltd.'s Estimated Warranty Payable account appears as follows:

Estimated Warranty Payable

12,800,000	15,000,000
	Bal. 2,200,000

In future periods, the company may come to debit the liability Estimated Warranty Payable for the remaining $2,200,000. However, *when* the company repairs or replaces defective merchandise has no bearing on when the company records warranty expense. Inglis Ltd. records warranty expense in the same period as the sale. The company reports its Estimated Warranty Payable of $2,200,000 on the balance sheet under the current-liability caption Accrued Liabilities Payable.

Estimated Vacation Pay Liability

Most companies grant paid vacations to their employees. The employees receive this benefit when they take their vacation, but they earn the compensation by working the other days of the year. The law requires most employers to provide a minimum number of weeks holiday per year (usually two, but sometimes more based on number of years worked), although some employers provide longer holidays to employees who have worked for the company for a number of years. To match expense with revenue properly, the company accrues the vacation pay expense and liability for each of the 50 work weeks of the year. Then, the company records payment during the two-week vacation period. Employee turnover, terminations, and ineligibility (for example, no vacation allowed until one full year has been worked) force companies to estimate the vacation pay liability.

Suppose a company's January payroll is $100,000 and vacation pay adds 4 percent, or $4,000 (with the 4 percent calculated as two weeks of annual vacation divided by 50 work weeks each year). Experience indicates that only 90 percent of the available vacations will be taken. Therefore, the January vacation pay estimate is $3,600 ($4,000 × 0.90). In January, the company records the vacation pay accrual as follows:

Jan. 31	Vacation Pay Expense	3,600	
	Estimated Vacation Pay Liability		3,600

Each month thereafter, the company makes a similar entry.

If an employee takes a two-week vacation in August, his or her $2,000 monthly salary is recorded as follows:

Aug. 31	Estimated Vacation Pay Liability	2,000	
	Various Withholding Accounts and		
	Wages Payable[2]		2,000

Income Tax Payable (for a Corporation)

Corporations pay income tax in the same way that individual taxpayers do. Corporations file their income tax returns with Canada Customs and Revenue Agency (CCRA) and their provincial governments after the end of the fiscal year, so they must estimate their income tax payable for reporting on the balance sheet. During the year, corporations make monthly tax payments to the governments, based on their estimated tax for the year. A corporation with a December 31 year end would record the payment of $100,000 of income tax expense for September as follows:

Sept. 30	Income Tax Expense	100,000	
	Cash		100,000
	To pay monthly income tax instalment.		

---

[2]The various payroll accounts are discussed later in the chapter.

A Taxing Dilemma—Sales Tax Liability and the Internet

E-commerce continues to grow in popularity. It provides consumers with a convenient method for shopping and may help them save money in the process.

Suppose you decided to buy a friend a book as a birthday gift. The book sells for $26.59 at a local bookstore. In addition you will pay the Goods and Services Tax (GST) and provincial sales tax (PST)—unless you live in Alberta, the Northwest Territories and Nunavut—on the purchase price. If we assume that both GST and PST are 7%, you will pay $1.86 in GST and $1.86 in PST, for a total cost of $30.31 for the book.

How can buying a book online help you save money? If you buy a book or any other item online from Indigo.ca or another e-commerce bookseller, you will not have to pay PST. Why not? It appears that provincial-sales-tax legislation has not yet been changed to reflect this new form of retailing. If companies do not have a physical presence in a province, such as an office or a warehouse, they do not have to charge PST and so will not have a sales tax liability to the provincial government. While no dollar figures are available for Canada, in the United States, where similar state-sales-tax legislation exists, it is believed that sales tax revenue lost due to Internet sales will amount to $20 billion by 2003.

Consumers can voluntarily pay sales tax on products they purchase over the Internet, but most are not aware that they can and most do not want to pay more for a product than they have to. This issue of lost sales-tax revenue will become a growing concern to provincial governments because provincial sales tax is one of the provinces' largest sources of revenue. Expect to hear more on this issue, especially as e-commerce sales continue to increase.

At December 31, the corporation calculates actual tax expense for the year to be $1,240,000. Accordingly, the corporation pays the monthly instalment of $100,000 on December 30, and accrues the additional $40,000 at December 31. The entries are

Dec. 30	Income Tax Expense...	100,000	
	Cash...		100,000
	To pay quarterly income tax.		
Dec. 31	Income Tax Expense...	40,000	
	Income Tax Payable		40,000
	To accrue income tax at year end.		

The corporation will pay off this tax liability during the next year, when it files its tax returns with Canada Customs and Revenue Agency and its provincial government, so Income Tax Payable is a current liability.

OBJECTIVE 3
Identify and report contingent liabilities

Contingent Liabilities

A *contingent liability* is not an actual liability. Instead, it is a potential liability that depends on a *future* event arising out of past events. We introduced contingent liabilities in Chapter 8, page 452. For example, Packenham town council may sue North Ontario Electric Supply Ltd., the company that installed new street lights in Packenham, claiming that the electrical wiring is faulty. The past transaction is the street-light installation. The future event is the court case that will decide the suit. North Ontario Electric Supply Ltd. thus faces a contingent liability, which may or may not become an actual obligation.

It would be unethical for North Ontario Electric Supply Ltd. to withhold knowledge of the lawsuit from its creditors or from anyone considering investing in the business. A person or business could be misled into thinking the company is stronger financially than it really is. The *disclosure principle* of accounting (see Chapter 9, page 473) requires a company to report any information deemed relevant to outsiders to the business. The goal is to give people relevant, reliable information for decision making.

The Accounting Standards Board in *CICA Handbook* Section 3290 requires that *contingent losses* generally be accrued in the financial statements but bars *contingent gains* from being recognized *until* they are realized. This approach follows the principle of conservatism. The Section recognizes that there is always uncertainty underlying contingencies and has identified three levels of uncertainty:

likely:	the chance of the occurrence (or non-occurrence) of the future event is high. A hockey team promises a player a bonus for achieving a specified milestone.
unlikely:	the chance of the occurrence (or non-occurrence) of the future event is slight. A golf course promises to pay $25,000 to the first golfer to get a hole-in-one on a particular hole.
not determinable:	the chance of the occurrence (or non-occurrence) of the future event cannot be determined. A roofing company has guaranteed a new type of roofing for 25 years, with a promise to replace any roof that fails. The product is new, so the cost cannot be estimated.

It is up to management to assess how likely the contingent liability is and thus how, if at all, it should be disclosed.

Sometimes the contingent liability has a definite amount. Recall from Chapter 8 a contingent liability arises when one company *cosigns a note payable* for another company. In this case, Company A guarantees that Company B will pay a note payable owed to another party. This practice obligates Company A to pay the note and interest if Company B fails to pay. Thus Company A has a contingent liability until the note becomes due. If Company B pays off the note, Company A's contingent liability ceases to exist. If Company B does *not* pay off the note, Company A's contingent liability becomes an actual liability.

Sometimes the amount that will have to be paid, if the contingent liability becomes an actual liability, is not known at the balance sheet date. For example, companies face lawsuits, which may cause possible future obligations of amounts to be determined by the courts. In another case, Canada Customs and Revenue Agency (CCRA) may have indicated to the entity that a reassessment of its income and taxes has been made or is forthcoming but the company may not know the amount of its liability at the financial statement date.

Contingent liabilities are normally disclosed in the notes to the financial statements unless both the confirming future event is likely and the amount of the loss can be reasonably estimated, in which case the amount of the loss should be accrued in the financial statements. When the loss is both likely and estimable, then it is less a contingent loss than a real loss; that is why the loss is accrued or put through the books as of the statement date. For example, suppose CCRA had reassessed a company prior to its year end at December 31, 2002, disallowing expenses claimed by the company on its 2000 tax return. If the company decided to accept the reassessment (in which case the confirming future event is likely and the amount known), it should accrue the additional tax payable. If, on the other hand, the company had decided to appeal the reassessment based on the advice of a tax specialist (that is, neither condition is met), the reassessment should be treated as a contingent liability and shown in the notes.

Suncor Energy Inc., an integrated oil and gas company based in Calgary, reported the following in Note 12 in the Notes to the Consolidated Financial Statements for the year ended December 31, 1999:

Suncor Energy Inc.
www.suncor.com

(c) Contingencies

The company is subject to various regulatory and statutory requirements relating to the protection of the environment. These requirements, in addition to contractual agreements and management decisions, result in the accrual of estimated reclamation and environmental remediation costs. These costs are accrued at the company's exploration and production and oil sands operations on the unit of production basis. Estimated environmental remediation costs at service stations are also accrued upon completion of site investigations. These costs are reduced by any estimated gains likely to be realized on a sale of these sites. Any changes in these estimates will affect future earnings.

Under the company's business interruption insurance coverage, the company would bear the first $70 million of any loss arising from a future insured incident at its oil sands operations.

The company is defendant and plaintiff in a number of legal actions that arise in the normal course of business.

Costs attributable to these commitments and contingencies are expected to be incurred over an extended period of time and to be funded mainly from the company's cash provided from operating activities. Although the ultimate impact of these matters on net earnings cannot be determined at this time, it could be material for any one quarter or year. The company believes that any liabilities which might arise pertaining to such matters would not be expected to have a material effect on the company's consolidated financial position.

Ethical Issues in Accounting for Current and Contingent Liabilities

Accounting for current liabilities poses ethical and legal challenges. Business owners and managers want their company to look as successful as possible. They like to report high levels of net income on the income statement. Why? Because high net income makes the company look profitable and helps the company raise money from investors. And high net income leads to large bonuses for managers. Owners want their balance sheet to report high asset values and low liability amounts, which make the company look safe to lenders and help the company borrow at low interest rates. The following illustrates the relationships among expenses, net income, and liabilities:

- Low expenses → High net income
- Low accrued expenses → Low accrued liabilities
- Low liabilities → High owner's equity

Owners and managers may be tempted to overlook some accrued expenses at the end of the accounting period. For example, a company can fail to accrue warranty expense or employee vacation pay. This failure will cause total expenses to be understated and net income to be overstated on the income statement. It will also cause the balance sheet to understate total liabilities and overstate owner's equity.

Contingent liabilities also pose an ethical challenge. Because contingencies are not real liabilities, they are easy to overlook. But a contingent liability can be very important, especially if it threatens a company's existence. A business with a contingent liability walks a tightrope between (1) disclosing enough information to enable outsiders to evaluate the company realistically, and (2) not giving away too much information. For example, a company that is a defendant in a lawsuit may believe that it is 50 percent guilty. On the one hand, if this belief were disclosed in the financial statements, the lawsuit's outcome could be affected. On the other hand, suppose the company withheld the information and people invested in the company. If the company then loses the lawsuit and goes out of business, the investors are likely to lose all their money. In that case, they can blame the company's management for failing to give them enough information.

A basic element of an audit performed by independent public accountants is the search for unrecorded liabilities. Auditors perform extensive tests to ensure that a company's balance sheet reports the full amount of its actual liabilities. The audit also looks for contingent liabilities. The goal of the audit is to give outsiders the information they need to reach a reasonable conclusion about the company's operating performance, financial position, and cash flows.

Ethical business owners and managers do not play games with their accounting. Falsifying financial statements can ruin one's reputation. It can also lead to a prison term.

At this half-way point of the chapter, review what you have learned by studying the following Decision Guidelines.

DECISION GUIDELINES *Accounting for Current and Contingent Liabilities, Including Payroll*

Decision	Guidelines
What are the two main issues in accounting for current liabilities?	• *Recording* the liability and the asset acquired or the expense incurred • *Reporting* the liability on the balance sheet

What are the two basic categories of current liabilities?	• Current liabilities of *known amount*:
	  Accounts payable Accrued expenses (accrued liabilities)
	  Short-term notes payable Payroll liabilities
	  Sales tax payable Salary, wages, commission,
	  GST Payable and bonus payable
	  Current portion of long-term debt Unearned revenues

	• Current liabilities that *must be estimated*:
	  Estimated warranty payable
	  Estimated vacation pay liability
	  Income tax payable (for a corporation)

How to account for contingent (potential) liabilities?	• Report contingent liabilities with an explanatory note
What is the ethical and legal challenge in accounting for current and contingent liabilities?	• Ensure that the balance sheet (and the related notes) reports the *full amount* of *all* the business's current and contingent liabilities

---

Mid-Chapter Summary Problem
for Your Review

This problem consists of three independent parts:

1. Suppose a Harvey's hamburger restaurant in Charlottetown, PEI, made cash sales of $4,000 subject to the 7 percent GST and 10 percent provincial sales tax. Record the sales and the related consumption taxes (PEI charges PST on GST). Also record payment of the sales tax to the provincial government and the GST to the Receiver General (assume input tax credits amount to $109.00).

2. Suppose at June 30, 2002, McCain Foods Ltd. reported a 7 percent long-term debt as follows:

Current Liabilities (in part)	millions
Portion of long-term debt due within one year	$ 3.00
Interest payable*	0.36

Long-Term Debt and Other Liabilities (in part)	
Long-term debt	$17.50

*Calculated as $20.5 \times 0.07 \times \frac{3}{12}$

Assume the company pays interest on its long-term debt on March 31. Show how McCain Foods Ltd. would report its liabilities on the year-end balance sheet at June 30, 2003. Assume the current maturity of its long-term debt is $4 million and the long-term portion is $18 million on June 30, 2003.

3. What distinguishes a contingent liability from an actual liability?

Solution to Review Problem

1. Cash 4,708
    Sales Revenue 4,000
    GST Payable 280
    Sales Tax Payable 428

To record cash sales and related GST and provincial sales tax. Cash is $4,708 [($4,000 × 1.07) × 1.10]. GST Payable is $280 ($4,000 × 0.07). Sales Tax Payable is $428 ($4,280 × 0.10).

GST Payable 280
    Cash 171
    GST Receivable 109

To pay GST to the Receiver General, net of the input tax credit.

Sales Tax Payable 428
    Cash 428

To pay sales tax to the provincial government.

2. McCain Foods Ltd.'s balance sheet at June 30, 2003, would be as follows:

Current Liabilities (in part)	millions
Portion of long-term debt due within one year	$4.00
Interest payable*	0.39

Long-Term Debt and Other Liabilities (in part)	
Long-term debt	$18.0

*Calculated as $22 \times 0.07 \times \frac{3}{12}$

3. A contingent liability is a potential liability, which may or may not become an actual liability. It arises out of a past transaction and depends on a future event to determine if it will become an actual liability.

Cyber Coach

Visit the Student Resource area of the *Accounting* Companion Website for extra practice with the new material in Chapter 11.

www.pearsoned.ca/horngren

Accounting for Payroll

Payroll costs are so important to most businesses that they adopt special systems to account for their labour costs. This section covers the basics of accounting for payroll.

Businesses often pay employees at a base rate for a set number of hours—called *straight time*. For working any additional hours—called *overtime*—the employee receives a higher rate per hour.

Lucy Childres is an accountant for MicroAge Electronics Inc. Lucy earns $700 per week straight time. The company work week is 35 hours, so Lucy's hourly wage is $20 ($700/35). Her company pays her *time and a half* for overtime. The rate is 150 percent (1.5 times) the straight-time rate. Thus Lucy earns $30.00 for each hour of overtime she works ($20.00 × 1.5 = $30.00). For working 37 hours during a week, she earns $760, computed as follows:

Straight-time pay for 35 hours..	$700
Overtime pay for 2 overtime hours (2 × $30.00)	60
Total pay	$760

Gross Pay and Net Pay

Many years ago,[3] employees brought home all that they had earned. For example, Lucy Childres would have taken home the full $760 total that she made. Payroll accounting was straightforward. Those days are long past.

The federal government and most provincial governments demand that employers act as collection agents for employee taxes, which are deducted from employee paycheques. Insurance companies, labour unions, charitable organizations such as the United Way, and other organizations may also take portions of employees' pay. Amounts withheld from an employee's cheque are called *deductions*.

Gross pay is the total amount of salary, wages, commissions, or any other employee compensation before taxes and other deductions are subtracted. **Net pay**—or "take-home pay"—equals gross pay minus all deductions. As Exhibit 11-3 shows, net pay is the amount the employee actually takes home.

In addition to employee income taxes, Canada (or Quebec) Pension Plan contributions, and employment insurance premiums that employers must withhold from pay, employers themselves must pay some payroll expenses, such as the employer's share of Canada Pension Plan and employment insurance. Many companies also pay employee *fringe benefits*, such as medical and life insurance premiums and pension plan payments. Payroll accounting has become quite complex. Let's turn now to a discussion of payroll deductions.

Payroll Deductions

Payroll deductions that are *withheld* from employees' pay fall into two categories: (1) *required* (or *statutory*) *deductions*, which include employee income tax, employment insurance, and Canada Pension Plan or Quebec Pension Plan deductions; and (2) *optional deductions*, which include union dues (which may be automatic deductions for

Gross Pay − (Taxes + Other Deductions) = Net Pay

Exhibit 11-3

Gross Pay and Net Pay

---

[3] Income taxes were first imposed by the federal government in Canada in 1917 as a temporary measure to provide funds for the conduct of Canada's efforts in World War I.

all unionized employees), insurance premiums, charitable contributions, and other amounts that are withheld at the employee's request. After they are withheld, payroll deductions become the liability of the employer, who assumes responsibility for paying the outside party. For example, the employer pays the government the employee income tax withheld and pays the union the employee union dues withheld.

Required Payroll Deductions

Employee Withheld Income Tax Payable   The law requires most employers to withhold income tax from their employees' salaries and wages. The amount of income tax deducted from gross pay is called **withheld income tax**. For many employees, this deduction is the largest. The amount withheld depends on the employee's gross pay and on the number of non-refundable tax credits the employee claims.

Each employee files a Personal Tax Credits Return (Form TD1), shown in Exhibit 11-4 on pages 578 and 579. The TD1 is used by employers to determine how much income tax to withhold from an employee's gross pay. The amount of tax withheld is decreased if the employee expects to deduct particular items from her or his personal income tax return. These items include a spousal credit, tuition fees, a disability credit, and a caregiver credit, among others. These particular items are shown on pages 3 and 4 of the TD1. Employees can also choose, on page 1 of the TD1, to have extra tax withheld from their paycheque if they expect to earn income from other sources and want to avoid paying tax when they file their income tax return. The total amount of credits on the TD1 determines the employee's claim code number, which appears on page 2 of the TD1. Employers use the claim code number and tables issued by CCRA to compute the amount of income tax that should be withheld from an employee's gross pay.

The employer sends its employees' withheld income tax to the government. The amount of the income tax withheld determines how often the employer submits tax payments. Most employers must remit the taxes to the government at least monthly; larger employers must remit two or four times a month, depending on the total amounts withheld. Every business must account for payroll taxes on a calendar-year basis regardless of its fiscal year.

The employer accumulates taxes withheld in the Employees' Withheld Income Tax Payable account. The word *payable* indicates that the account is a liability of the employer, even though the employees are the people taxed.

Employee Withheld Canada (or Quebec) Pension Plan Contributions Payable   The **Canada (or Quebec) Pension Plan** (CPP or QPP) provides retirement, disability, and death benefits to employees who are covered by it. Employers are required to deduct premiums from each employee required to make a contribution (basically all employees between 18 and 70 years of age). The federal government, through CCRA, determines annually the maximum pensionable earnings level, the basic annual exemption, and the contribution rate. The contribution rate changes each year and has been steadily increasing. At the time of writing, the following information was applicable:

Maximum pensionable earnings	$37,600
Basic annual exemption	3,500
Maximum contributory earnings	34,100
Contribution rate	3.9%
Maximum employee contribution ($34,100 × 3.9 percent)	$1,329.90

CCRA provides tables that the employer uses to calculate the amount to deduct from each employee's pay each pay period; the tables take into account the basic exemption of $3,500 of income but also assume that the employee will be working for twelve months. For example, if your total employment income was earned when you worked for two months during the summer and earned $2,500 per month, the withholding would be $86.13 each month ($172.26 for two months), the normal

Finance Canada: Taxation Hotlinks
www.fin.gc.ca/links/taxe.html

Canada Customs and Revenue Agency (CCRA) Forms
www.ccra-adrc.gc.ca/formspubs/menu-e.html

deduction for an employee earning $2,500 per month. However, based on your total income of $5,000 (2 × $2,500) and the basic exemption of $3,500, CPP is $58.50 [($5,000 − $3,500) × 0.039] and your overpayment of $113.76 will be recovered when you file your income tax return.

Once the employee reaches the maximum contribution of $1,329.90, the employer stops deducting for that year. Some employees may have had more than one employer in a year; for example, you may have had a job for the summer and now have a part-time job while you are back at school. CCRA requires each employer to deduct Canada Pension Plan contributions; however, you recover the overpayment when you file your income tax return for the year. The employers do not recover any overpayment.

The employer must remit the Canada Pension Plan contributions withheld and the employer's share, discussed below, every month to CCRA. Larger employers must remit two or four times a month, depending on the amounts withheld.

Employee Withheld Employment Insurance Premiums Payable   The **Employment Insurance Act** requires employers to deduct employment insurance premiums from each employee each time that employee is paid. The purpose of the Employment Insurance Fund is to provide assistance to contributors to the fund who cannot work for a variety of reasons. The most common reason is that the employee has been laid off; another reason is maternity leave.

The federal government, through CCRA, establishes annually the maximum annual insurable earnings level and the Employment Insurance premium rate. The rate has been decreasing in recent years. At the time of writing, the following information was applicable:

Maximum insurable earnings	$39,000
Premium rate	2.4%
Maximum employee contribution ($39,000 × 2.4 percent)	$936.00

CCRA provides tables that the employer uses to calculate the amount to deduct from each employee's gross pay each pay period. For example, if you earned $2,000 per month, $48.00 ($2,000 × 2.4 percent) per month would be deducted for Employment Insurance.

As with the Canada Pension Plan, CCRA requires every employer to deduct Employment Insurance premiums from every eligible employee. Overpayments may be recovered when the employee files his or her income tax return.

The employer must remit the Employment Insurance premiums withheld and the employer's share, discussed below, to CCRA every month. Larger employers must remit two or four times a month depending on the amounts withheld.

Optional Payroll Deductions

As a convenience to their employees, many companies make payroll deductions and disburse cash according to employee instructions. Union dues, insurance payments, registered pension plan payments, payroll savings plans, and donations to charities such as the United Way are examples. The account Employees' Union Dues Payable holds employee deductions for union membership.

Employer Payroll Costs

Employers bear expenses for at least three payroll costs: (1) Canada Pension Plan contributions, (2) Employment Insurance Plan premiums, and (3) Workers' Compensation Plan premiums. In addition, Manitoba and Newfoundland levy a health and post-secondary education tax on employers, while Ontario and Quebec levy a health tax on employers in those provinces. As mentioned above, most employers must remit both employee and employer shares monthly. Larger employers must remit twice or four times monthly depending on the size of their payroll. Workers' Compensation payments are remitted quarterly.

Canada Customs and Revenue Agency — Agence des douanes et du revenu du Canada

PERSONAL TAX CREDITS RETURN

See the instructions on page 2 for completing this return.

Last name (capital letters)	Usual first name and initials	Employee number
Address	**For non-residents only –** country of permanent residence	Social insurance number
Postal code		Date of birth: Year, Month, Day

Basic personal amount – Everyone can claim $7,131 as the basic personal amount. If you choose not to claim this amount or if you are a non-resident, see section 1 on page 3.	$	1
Spousal amount – You may be able to claim an amount for supporting your spouse if you are married or have a common-law spouse. See section 2 on page 3.		2
Equivalent-to-spouse amount – You may be able to claim an equivalent-to-spouse amount if you are single, divorced, separated, or widowed. See section 3 on page 3.		3
Amount for infirm dependants age 18 or older – You may be able to claim an amount for infirm dependants age 18 or older if they are related to you. See section 4 on page 3.		4
Pension income amount – You can claim your eligible pension income or $1,000, whichever amount is less. See section 5 on page 4.		5
Age amount – You can claim an amount if you will be 65 or older at the end of the year and your estimated net income from all sources for the year will be $25,921 or less. See section 6 on page 4.		6
Tuition and education amounts (full-time) – You can claim your tuition fees and $200 for each month you are enrolled as a full-time student. See section 7 on page 4.		7
Tuition and education amounts (part-time) – You can claim your tuition fees and $60 for each month you are studying in a part-time course that qualifies for the education deduction. See section 8 on page 4.		8
Disability amount – You can claim $4,233 if you are claiming the disability amount by using Form T2201, *Disability Tax Credit Certificate*. See section 9 on page 4.		9
Caregiver amount – You may be able to claim an amount if you take care of your parent or grandparent age 65 or older or an infirm dependant age 18 or older who lives with you. See section 10 on page 4.		10
Amounts transferred from your spouse or dependants – You can transfer any of the following amounts that your spouse or dependants do not need to reduce their federal income tax to zero.		
Age amount – See item 11 on page 4.		11
Pension income amount – See item 12 on page 4.		12
Disability amount – See item 13 on page 4.		13
Tuition and education amounts – See item 14 on page 4.		14
Total personal tax credit amounts. Add lines 1 to 14.	$	

See the claim codes on page 2 to determine which claim code applies to you. Enter this code in box **A**. If the total of all your personal tax credit amounts is more than your total employment income from all sources for the year, your claim code is "E". **A**

Additional tax to be deducted – If you receive other income, you may want to have more tax deducted from each pay. By doing this, you may not have to pay as much tax when you file your income tax return. To choose this option, state the amount of additional tax you want to have deducted from each pay. To change this deduction later, you have to complete a new personal tax credits return. $

I certify that the information given in this return is, to the best of my knowledge, correct and complete.

Signature ______________ Date ______________

TD1 E (00) (Ce formulaire existe en français.) 0500 Canadä

Instructions for completing your personal tax credits return

page 2

Complete this return if you have a new employer or payer, and you will receive one or more of the following types of income:

- salary, wages, commissions, pensions, or any other remuneration; or
- Employment Insurance benefits.

You **do not** have to file a new return every year unless your marital status changes or you expect a change in your personal credits for that year. Complete a new return no later than seven days after the change.

If you make regular spousal support payments, or if you regularly contribute to a registered retirement savings plan (RRSP) during the year, you can reduce the amount of tax to be withheld from your income. To make this request, you have to write to any tax services office for a letter of authority. You do not need a letter of authority if your employer deducts RRSP contributions from your salary.

If you receive non-employment income, such as a pension or Old Age Security, and you want to have extra tax deducted at source, you can complete Form TD3, *Request for Income Tax Deduction on Non-Employment Income*, or complete the "Additional tax to be deducted" section on page 1.

If you need help, ask your employer or payer, or call your tax services office. You can find the telephone number in the Government of Canada section of your telephone book.

After you complete this return, give pages 1 and 2 to your employer. Keep the confidential calculations on pages 3 and 4 for your records.

It is an offence to file a false return.

Deduction for living in a prescribed zone (e.g., Yukon, Nunavut, or Northwest Territories)

If you live in **Yukon, Nunavut, the Northwest Territories**, or another prescribed zone for more than six months in a row, beginning or ending this year, you can claim:

- $7.50 for each day that you live in the prescribed zone; or
- $15 for each day that you live in the prescribed zone, if during that time you live in a dwelling that you maintain, and you are the only person living in that dwelling who is claiming this deduction. $

For more information, get Form T2222, *Northern Residents Deductions*, and the publication called *Northern Residents Deductions – Places in Prescribed Zones* from Internet at **www.ccra-adrc.gc.ca**, or by calling 1-800-959-2221.

Additional information for employers who use computer payroll programs. (Optional)

If you reside in one of the provinces indicated below and your employer uses a computer payroll program, the following information will be used to calculate your provincial tax and surtax reduction. If you do not reside in one of these provinces, you do not need to fill in this box.

If you reside in **Ontario, Manitoba, Saskatchewan**, or **British Columbia**, enter the number of dependants you have under 18 years old at the end of the year.

Notes

- For **Ontario, Manitoba**, and **Saskatchewan** residents, only the spouse with the higher net income can claim for a dependant.
- For **Ontario, Manitoba**, or **British Columbia** residents, do not include a child claimed for the equivalent-to-spouse amount on line 3 on page 1.

Claim codes

Total claim amount	Claim code	Total claim amount	Claim code
No claim amount	0	$13,458.01 – 15,039	6
Minimum $7,131	1	$15,039.01 – 16,621	7
$7,131.01 – 8,712	2	$16,621.01 – 18,202	8
$8,712.01 – 10,294	3	$18,202.01 – 19,784	9
$10,294.01 – 11,877	4	$19,784.01 – 21,368	10
$11,877.01 – 13,458	5	$21,368.01 and over (Manual calculation required by employer)	X

No tax withholding required E

Printed in Canada

Exhibit 11-4

2000 Personal Tax Credits Return (Form TD1)

Source: Canada Customs and Revenue Agency. Reproduced with permission of the Minister of Public Works and Government Services Canada, 2000

Employer Canada Pension Plan Contributions In addition to being responsible for deducting and remitting the employee contribution to the Canada Pension Plan, the employer must also pay into the program. The employer must match exactly the employee's contribution. Every employer must do so whether or not the employee also contributes elsewhere. Unlike the employee, the employer may not obtain a refund for overpayment.

Employer Employment Insurance Premiums The employer calculates the employee's premium and remits it together with the employer's share, which is generally 1.4 times the employee's premium, to CCRA. The maximum dollar amount of the employer's contribution would be 1.4 times the maximum employee's contribution of $936.00, which amounts to $1,310.40. Almost all employers and employees are covered by this program, unless you are self-employed.

Workers' Compensation Premiums Unlike the previous two programs, which are administered by the federal government, the **Workers' Compensation** plan is administered provincially. The purpose of the program is to provide financial support for workers injured on the job. The cost of the coverage is borne by the employer; the employee does not pay a premium to the fund.

In Manitoba, almost all employees are covered by the program. There are over 70 different categories that the Workers' Compensation Board uses to determine the cost of coverage. The category a group of workers is assigned to is based on the risk of injury to workers in that group, which is based on that group's and like groups' experience. The employer pays a premium equal to the rate assessed times the employer's gross payroll. Thus, in February 2001, the employer estimates gross payroll

page 3

1. Basic personal amount

Everyone can claim $7,131 as the basic personal amount.
- If you choose to claim this amount, **enter $7,131** on line 1 on page 1.
- If you choose not to claim this amount (e.g., when you have more than one employer or payer and you have already claimed the basic personal amount), **enter 0** in box **A** on page 1. Do not complete sections 2 to 14.

If you want additional tax to be deducted, complete the appropriate section on page 1.

If you are a non-resident, and you are including 90% or more of your annual world income when determining your taxable income in Canada, you can claim certain personal amounts. If you are including less than 90% of your annual world income, **enter 0** in box **A** on page 1. If you are not sure about your non-resident status, or need more information, call any tax services office or the International Tax Services Office.

2. Spousal amount

You may be able to claim an amount for supporting your spouse if you are **married** or have a **common-law spouse**.

Generally, a common-law spouse is a person of the opposite sex with whom you live in a common-law relationship for any continuous period of at least 12 months, including any period of separation (due to a breakdown in the relationship) of less than 90 days. It can also be a person of the opposite sex with whom you live in a common-law relationship and who is the natural or adoptive parent of your child. If you are not sure about your marital status, or need more information, call any tax services office.

If you marry during the year, your spouse's net income for the year includes the income earned before and during the marriage.

If your spouse's net income for the year will be:
- **$6,661** or more, you cannot make a claim; enter 0 on line 2 on page 1;
- **$606** or less, enter **$6,055** on line 2 on page 1; or
- more than **$606** but less than **$6,661**, complete the following calculation:

Base amount	**$6,661**
Minus: Spouse's net income	–
Enter this amount on line 2 on page 1.	=

3. Equivalent-to-spouse amount

You may be able to claim an equivalent-to-spouse amount if you are **single, divorced, separated,** or **widowed**, and you support a dependant who is:
- under 18, your parent or grandparent, or mentally or physically infirm;
- related to you by blood, marriage, or adoption; and
- living with you, in Canada, in a home that you maintain (a dependant may live away from home while attending school).

If your equivalent-to-spouse claim is for an infirm dependant age 18 or older, you may be able to claim an amount in section 4. Otherwise, any person you claim here cannot be claimed again in section 4.

If your dependant's net income for the year will be:
- **$6,661** or more, enter 0 on line 3 on page 1;
- **$606** or less, enter **$6,055** on line 3 on page 1; or
- more than **$606** but less than **$6,661**, complete the following calculation:

Base amount	**$6,661**
Minus: Dependant's net income	–
Enter this amount on line 3 on page 1.	=

4. Amount for infirm dependants age 18 or older

You may be able to claim an amount for each infirm dependant age 18 or older who has a physical or mental infirmity and who is your or your spouse's:
- child or grandchild; or
- parent, grandparent, brother, sister, aunt, uncle, niece, or nephew, who resides in Canada.

You have to complete a separate calculation for each infirm dependant you have.

If your dependant's net income for the year will be:
- **$7,131** or more, you cannot make a claim; enter 0 on line 4 on page 1; or
- less than **$7,131**, complete the following calculation:

Base amount	**$7,131**
Minus: Dependant's net income	–
If more than $2,353, enter $2,353.	
Minus: Equivalent-to-spouse amount claimed for this dependant in section 3	–
Enter this amount on line 4 on page 1.	=

5. Pension income amount

Eligible pension income includes pension payments received from a pension plan or fund as a life annuity, and foreign pension payments. It does not include payments from the Canada Pension Plan or Quebec Pension Plan, Old Age Security, guaranteed supplements, or lump-sum withdrawals from a pension fund.

If you receive an eligible pension income, you can claim your eligible pension income or $1,000, whichever amount is **less**.

Enter this amount on line 5 on page 1.

page 4

6. Age amount

If you will be 65 or older at the end of the year and your estimated net income from all sources for the year will be:
- **$49,134** or more, you cannot make a claim; enter 0 on line 6 on page 1;
- **$25,921** or less, enter **$3,482** on line 6 on page 1; or
- more than **$25,921**, but less than **$49,134**, complete the calculation.

Maximum age amount	**$3,482**	1
Annual estimated net income		2
Minus: Base amount	**$25,921**	3
Line 2 minus line 3		4
Multiply the amount on line 4 by 15%.	–	5
Line 1 minus line 5. (If negative, enter 0.) Enter this amount on line 6 on page 1.	=	6

7. Tuition and education amounts (full-time)

Enter your tuition fees for courses you will take in the year, to attend a university, college, or an institution that the Minister of Human Resources Development has certified.

Add $200 for each month in the year that you will be enrolled full-time in a qualifying educational program at a university, college, or a school offering job retraining courses or correspondence courses. **Subtotal**

Subtract any scholarships, fellowships, or bursaries you will receive in the year (do not report the first $500).
Enter the amount on line 7 on page 1. (If the amount is negative, **enter 0**.)

8. Tuition and education amounts (part-time)

Enter your tuition fees that are more than $100 in total for part-time courses you will take in the year at a designated educational institution.

Add $60 for each month in the year that you will be enrolled in a course that will last at least 3 consecutive weeks and involve a minimum of 12 hours of course time per month at a designated educational institution. You cannot claim both the part-time and full-time education tax credit in the same month.
Enter this amount on line 8 on page 1.

9. Disability amount

Enter **$4,233** if you are severely impaired, mentally or physically, and are claiming the disability amount by using Form T2201, *Disability Tax Credit Certificate*. Such an impairment has to markedly restrict your daily living activities. The impairment has to last, or be expected to last, for a continuous period of at least 12 months.
Enter this amount on line 9 on page 1.

10. Caregiver amount

If you take care of your parent or grandparent age 65 or older, or an infirm dependant age 18 or older, **who lives with you** in a home that you maintain, and your dependant's net income for the year will be:
- **$13,853** or more, you cannot make a claim; enter 0 on line 10 on page 1; or
- less than **$13,853**, complete the calculation.

You cannot claim this amount if you or anyone else is claiming an **infirm dependant amount** for the dependant.

You have to complete a separate calculation for each qualified dependant.

Base amount	**$13,853**	1
Minus: Dependant's net income	–	2
Line 1 minus line 2. If more than $2,353, enter $2,353.	=	3
Minus: equivalent-to-spouse amount claimed in section 3 for this dependent	–	4
Line 3 minus line 4. (If negative, enter 0.) Enter this amount on line 10 on page 1.	=	5

If any other person also contributes to the support of the dependant, the combined amount that you and that other person claim cannot be more than the amount on line 5.

Amounts transferred from your spouse or dependants

You can transfer any of the following amounts that your spouse or dependants do not need to reduce their federal income tax to zero.

11. Age amount – If your spouse will be 65 or older this year, you can claim any unused balance of the age amount, to a maximum of **$3,482**. Enter this amount on line 11 on page 1.

12. Pension income amount – If your spouse receives eligible pension income, you can claim any unused balance of the pension income amount, to a maximum of **$1,000**. Enter this amount on line 12 on page 1.

13. Disability amount – If your spouse or dependant qualifies for the disability amount, you can claim the unused balance of their disability amount, to a maximum of **$4,233** on line 13. Enter this amount on line 13 on page 1.

14. Tuition and education amounts (full or part-time) – If you are supporting a spouse, child, or grandchild attending a university, college, or certified educational institution, you can claim the unused balance of their tuition and education amounts, to a maximum of **$5,000** for each person. Enter this amount on line 14 on page 1.

Exhibit 11-4 (continued)

for 2001 and sends that information plus any premium owing from 2000 to the provincial government. Premiums, based on that estimated payroll, are remitted quarterly in most cases. In February 2002, the employer estimates gross payroll for 2002, calculates any premium owing for 2001 based on the excess of actual wages over estimated wages for 2001, and sends the estimate and premium owing to the provincial government.

Provincial Payroll Taxes   As was mentioned earlier, certain provinces levy taxes on employers to pay for provincial health care while others levy a combined health care and post-secondary education tax to pay for provincial health care and post-secondary education. Quebec and Newfoundland have fixed rates of tax while Ontario and Manitoba vary the rate employers are taxed. In Ontario, the rate of tax increases with the annual payroll amount, while it decreases in Manitoba.

Payroll Withholding Tables

We have discussed the tables that employers use in calculating the withholdings that must be made from employees' wages for income taxes, Canada (or Quebec) Pension Plan contributions and Employment Insurance premiums. Exhibit 11-5 provides illustrations of all three tables for a resident of British Columbia for 2000. Suppose an employee, Roberta Dean, is paid a salary of $2,000 twice a month (semi-monthly). Also suppose that her TD1 form indicated a net claim code of 3. From Panel A, you can see that, based on a net claim code of 3, she would have income tax of $484.95 withheld. Her Canada Pension Plan deduction, Panel B, would

**British Columbia
Federal and Provincial Tax Deductions
Semi-Monthly: 24 Pay Periods Per Year**

Pay	If the employee's claim code on the TD1(E) form is										
	0	1	2	3	4	5	6	7	8	9	10
From Less than	Deduct from each pay										
1950. – 1982.	575.45	499.95	491.60	474.85	458.10	441.35	424.60	407.85	391.10	374.35	357.60
1982. – 2008.	585.60	510.05	501.70	484.95	468.20	451.45	434.70	417.95	401.20	384.45	367.70
2008. – 2034.	595.70	520.15	511.80	495.05	478.30	461.55	444.80	428.05	411.30	394.55	377.80
2034. – 2060.	605.80	530.30	521.90	505.15	488.40	471.65	454.90	438.15	421.40	404.65	387.90
2060. – 2086.	615.90	540.40	532.00	515.25	498.50	481.75	465.00	448.25	431.50	414.75	398.00
2086. – 2112.	626.00	550.50	542.10	525.35	508.60	491.85	475.10	458.35	441.60	424.90	408.10
2112. – 2138.	636.10	560.60	552.20	535.50	518.70	501.95	485.20	468.50	451.75	435.00	418.20
2138. – 2164.	646.20	570.70	562.35	545.60	528.85	512.05	495.35	478.60	461.85	445.10	428.30
2164. – 2190.	656.30	580.80	572.45	555.70	538.95	522.20	505.45	488.70	471.95	455.20	438.45
2190. – 2216.	666.45	590.90	582.55	565.80	549.05	532.30	515.55	498.80	482.05	465.30	448.55

Panel B

Canada Pension Plan Contributions

Semi-Monthly (24 pay periods per year)

Pay		CPP
From	To	
1946.33 – 1956.72		70.43
1956.73 – 1966.72		70.82
1966.73 – 1976.72		71.21
1976.73 – 1986.72		71.60
1986.73 – 1996.72		71.99
1996.73 – 2006.72		72.38
2006.73 – 2016.72		72.77
2016.73 – 2026.72		73.16
2026.73 – 2036.72		73.55
2036.73 – 2046.72		73.94
2046.73 – 2056.72		74.33
2056.73 – 2066.72		74.72

Panel C

Employment Insurance Premiums

Semi-Monthly (24 pay periods per year)

Insurable Earnings		EI
From	To	Premium
1998.96 – 1999.37		47.98
1999.38 – 1999.79		47.99
1999.80 – 2000.20		48.00
2000.21 – 2000.62		48.01
2000.63 – 2001.04		48.02
2001.05 – 2001.45		48.03
2001.46 – 2001.87		48.04
2001.88 – 2002.29		48.05
2002.30 – 2002.70		48.06
2002.71 – 2003.12		48.07
2003.13 – 2003.54		48.08
2003.55 – 2003.95		48.09

EXHIBIT 11-5

Payroll Withholding Tables

be $72.38 and her Employment Insurance premium, Panel C, would be $48.00. Roberta Dean's employer would keep track, as we will demonstrate later in the chapter, of Dean's Canada Pension and Employment Insurance deductions and when they reached the maximums of $1,329.90 and $936.00 respectively, would stop deducting premiums from Dean's pay. The employer's share would be $72.38 for Canada Pension (matches employee's share), while the employer's share for Employment Insurance would be $67.20 (1.4 times employee share).

Exhibit 11-6 shows a typical disbursement of payroll costs by a British Columbia employer company for a single employee (claim code 1) who is paid $3,000 monthly.

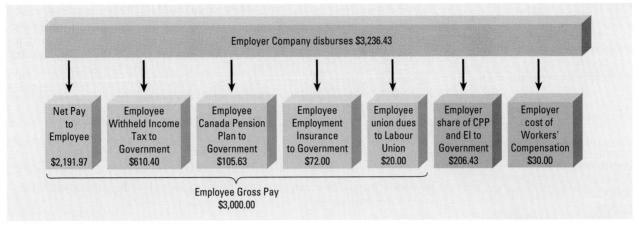

Employer Company disburses $3,236.43

| Net Pay to Employee $2,191.97 | Employee Withheld Income Tax to Government $610.40 | Employee Canada Pension Plan to Government $105.63 | Employee Employment Insurance to Government $72.00 | Employee union dues to Labour Union $20.00 | Employer share of CPP and EI to Government $206.43 | Employer cost of Workers' Compensation $30.00 |

Employee Gross Pay
$3,000.00

Exhibit 11-6

Typical Disbursement of Payroll Costs by an Employer Company (British Columbia)

Payroll Entries

OBJECTIVE 5
Record basic payroll transactions

Exhibit 11-7 summarizes an employer's entries to record a monthly payroll of $10,000 (all amounts are assumed for illustration only).

Entry A in Exhibit 11-7 records the employer's salary expense, which is the gross salary of all employees ($10,000) for a month. From this amount the employer collects for the federal government income tax, Canada Pension Plan amounts (except in Quebec where it is Quebec Pension), and Employment Insurance amounts. Union dues are also collected from gross salary by the employer on behalf of the union that represents the employees. The remaining amount is the employees' net (take-home) pay of $7,768. In this payroll transaction the employer acts as a collection agent for CCRA (income tax and Canada Pension), the provincial government (income tax), the Employment Insurance Commission, and the union, withholding the employees' contributions from their gross pay.

Entry B represents the employer's share of Canada Pension Plan and Employment Insurance. Remember, the employer's share is 1.0 times and 1.4 times the employee's share respectively for these two deductions.

Entry C records employee benefits paid by the employer. This company has a dental benefits plan for its employees for which it pays the premiums.

EXHIBIT 11-7

Payroll Accounting by the Employer

A.	Salary Expense (or Wage or Commission Expense)	10,000	
	Employee Withheld Income Tax Payable		1,350
	Canada Pension Plan Payable		370
	Employment Insurance Payable		240
	Employee Union Dues Payable		272
	Salaries Payable to Employees (net pay)		7,768
	To record salary expense and employee withholdings.		
B.	Canada Pension Plan and Employment Insurance Expense	706	
	Canada Pension Plan Payable		370
	Employment Insurance Payable		336
	To record employer's share of Canada Pension Plan (1.0 × $370) and Employment Insurance (1.4 × $240).		
C.	Employee Dental Benefits Expense	182	
	Employee Benefits Payable		182
	To record employee benefits payable by employer.		

WORKING IT OUT

Record the payroll, payroll deductions, and employer payroll costs, given the following information about an Ontario company:

Gross pay	$190,000
Employee withheld inc. tax	22,800
Employee withheld Can. Pen.	4,900
Employee withheld empl. ins.	4,560
Union dues	2,945
Employer cost Can. Pen.	1.0
Employer cost empl. ins.	1.4
Pension plan paid by employer only	1.0%

A:

Payroll entry:
Salary
  expense $190,000
    Emp. With. Inc.
      Tax Pay. 22,800
    Can. Pen. (CPP)
      Pay. 4,900
    Empl. Ins. (EI)
      Pay. 4,560
    Union Dues Pay. 2,945
    Salaries
      Payable 154,795

Employer payroll cost entry:
Can. Pen. and Emp.
  Ins. Exp. $11,284
    Can. Pen. (CPP)
      Pay. 4,900
    Emp. Ins. (EI)
      Pay. 6,384

Fringe benefits:
Pension Exp. 1,900
  Emp. Ben.
    Pay. 1,900

OBJECTIVE 6
Use a payroll system

In the exhibit, the total payroll expense for the month is made up of base salary ($10,000) plus the employer's share of Canada Pension Plan and Employment Insurance ($706) plus fringe benefits ($182) for a total of $10,888. There would also be Workers' Compensation, which, you will recall, is paid completely by the employer.

A company's payments to people who are not employees—outsiders called independent contractors—are *not* company payroll expenses. Consider two Chartered Accountants, Fermi and Scott. Fermi is the corporation's chief financial officer. Scott is the corporation's outside auditor. Fermi is an employee of the corporation, and his compensation is a debit to Salary Expense. Scott, however, performs auditing service for many clients, and the corporation debits Auditing Expense when it pays her. Any payment for services performed by a person outside the company is a debit to an expense account other than payroll.

The Payroll System

Good business means paying employees accurately and on time. Also, companies face the legal responsibility of remitting amounts withheld from employees and the corporation's matching amounts and employee benefits, as we have seen. These demands require companies to process a great deal of payroll data. To make payroll accounting accurate and timely, accountants have developed a *payroll system*.

The components of a typical payroll system are:

- A payroll register
- A special payroll bank account
- Payroll cheques
- An earnings record for each employee

In the discussion that follows, we will deal with each of the components and discuss how companies use variations of the four components listed above.

Payroll Register

Each pay period, the company organizes the payroll data in a special journal called the *payroll register* or *payroll journal*. This register lists each employee and the figures the business needs to record payroll amounts. The payroll register, which resembles the cash payments register, or cheque register, also serves as a cheque register by providing a column for recording each payroll cheque number. We introduced the cash payments journal in Chapter 6, page 310.

A payroll register similar to that in Exhibit 11-8 is used by companies such as Intrawest Corporation. The *Gross Pay* section has columns for straight-time pay, overtime pay, and total gross pay for each employee. The *Deductions* columns vary from company to company, but every employer must deduct federal and provincial (combined) income tax, Canada (or Quebec) Pension Plan contributions, and Employment Insurance premiums. Additional column headings depend on which optional deductions the business handles. In Exhibit 11-8, the employer, Global Company, deducts employee withholdings and donations to the United Way and then sends the amounts to the proper parties. The business may add deduction columns as needed. The *Net Pay* section lists each employee's net (take-home) pay and the number of the cheque issued to her or him. The last two columns indicate the *Account Debited* for the employee's gross pay. (The company has office workers and sales people.)

The payroll register in Exhibit 11-8 gives the employer the information needed to record salary expense for the pay period. Using the total amounts for columns (d) through (l), the employer records total salary expense as follows:

2001
Dec. 31   Office Salaries Expense 4,464.00
          Sales Salaries Expense 9,190.00
              Employee Withheld Income Tax Payable.........   3,167.76
              Employee Withheld Canada Pension
                  Plan Payable...   327.70
              Employee Withheld Employment
                  Insurance Payable 385.12
              Employee Gifts to United Way Payable 155.00
              Salaries Payable to Employees...........................   9,618.42
          To record payroll expenses for the week
          ended December 31, 2001.
2001
Dec. 31   Canada Pension Plan Expense 327.70
          Employment Insurance Expense 539.17
              Employer Canada Pension Plan Payable.........   327.70
              Employer Employment Insurance Payable 539.17
          To record the cost of employer's portion of
          payroll expenses for the week ended December 31, 2001.

Payroll Bank Account

After the payroll has been recorded, the company books include a credit balance in Salaries Payable to Employees for net pay of $9,618.42. (See column (i) in Exhibit 11-8.) How the business pays this liability depends on its payroll system. Many companies pay employees from a special *payroll bank account*. The employer transfers the net pay ($9,618.42 in our illustration) from its regular bank account into the special payroll bank account. Then the company writes paycheques to employees from the payroll account. When all the paycheques clear the bank, the payroll account has a zero balance, ready for the activity of the next pay period. Writing paycheques from a separate bank account isolates payroll amounts for analysis and control, as we discuss later in the chapter.

Other payroll-related payments—for withholdings, union dues, and so on—are neither as numerous nor as frequent as weekly or monthly paycheques. The employer pays withholdings, union dues, and donations to charities from its regular bank account.

Payroll Cheques

Most companies pay employees by cheque or by electronic funds transfer (EFT). A *payroll cheque* is like any other cheque except that its perforated attachment, or pay stub, lists the employee's gross pay, payroll deductions, and net pay. These amounts come from the payroll register. Exhibit 11-9 shows payroll cheque number 1622, issued to C.L. Drumm for net pay of $394.34 earned during the week ended December 31, 2001. To enhance your ability to use payroll data, trace all amounts on the cheque attachment to the payroll register in Exhibit 11-8.

Increasingly, companies are paying employees by electronic funds transfer. The employee can authorize the company to make all deposits directly to her or his bank. With no cheque to write and deliver to the employee, the company saves time and money. As evidence of the deposit, most companies issue to employees a pay summary slip showing the data for that pay period plus year-to-date data. The employee avoids having to receive, endorse, and deposit the paycheque.

Recording Cash Payments for Payroll

Most employers must record at least three cash payments: for payroll net payment to employees, payments of payroll withholdings to the government, and payments to third parties for employee fringe benefits.

REAL WORLD EXAMPLE

Even a small business with a manual bookkeeping system will find a computer to be a time-saving device for payrolls. The payroll report printed each pay period can serve as the payroll documentation required by law.

REAL WORLD EXAMPLE

Payroll for wages is typically paid several days after the end of the pay period. The wait allows time for the payroll information, such as hours worked, to be assembled.

EXHIBIT 11-8

Payroll Register for Global Company

Week ended December 31, 2001

| | | Gross Pay | | | Deductions | | | | | Net Pay | | Account Debited | |
Employee Name	Hours	a Straight time	b Overtime	c Total	d Federal Income Tax	e Canada Pension Plan	f Employment Insurance	g Winnipeg United Way	h Total	i (c–h) Amount	j Cheque No.	k Office Salaries Expense	l Sales Salaries Expense
Chen, W.L.*	40	500.00		500.00	84.10	13.85	13.50	2.00	113.45	386.55	1621	500.00	
Drumm, C.L.	46	400.00	90.00	490.00	66.90	13.53	13.23	2.00	95.66	394.34	1622		490.00
Ellis, M.	41	560.00	21.00	581.00	104.65	16.44	15.69		136.78	444.22	1623	581.00	
Trimble, E.A**	40	1,360.00		1,360.00	409.00			15.00	424.00	936.00	1641		1,360.00
Total		12,940.00	714.00	13,654.00	3,167.76	327.70	385.12	155.00	4,035.58	9,618.42		4,464.00	9,190.00

*W.L. Chen earned gross pay of $500. His net pay was $386.55, paid with cheque number 1621. Chen is an office worker, so his salary is debited to Office Salaries Expense.

**E.A. Trimble has exceeded maximum pensionable earnings of $37,600 and so has had the Canada Pension Plan maximum, $1,329.90, already deducted. Trimble has also exceeded the maximum insurable Employment Insurance earnings of $39,000 and so has already had the maximum, $936.00, deducted.

Exhibit 11-9

Payroll Cheque

Global Company									1622
Payroll Account									
Winnipeg, Manitoba									

January 2, 2002

Pay to the Order of _____ C.L. Drumm _____ $ 394.34

Three hundred and ninety-four & 34/100 ---------------------- Dollars

The Bank of Nova Scotia
Winnipeg,
Manitoba R2W 3Y1

Anna Figaro
Treasurer

⑆111900031⑆ 0787⑈500004 54⑈

Pay			Deductions					Net Pay	Cheque No.
Straight-time	Over-time	Gross	Income Tax	C.P.P.	Employ-ment Ins.	United Way	Total		
400.00	90.00	490.00	66.90	13.53	13.23	2.00	95.66	394.34	1622

Net Pay to Employees   When the employer pays employees, the company debits Salaries Payable to Employees and credits Cash. Using the data in Exhibit 11-8, the company would make the following entry to record the cash payment (column (i)) for the December 31 weekly payroll:

2001			
Dec. 31	Salaries Payable to Employees.................................	9,618.42	
	Cash..		9,618.42

Payroll Withholdings to the Government and Other Organizations   The employer must send income taxes withheld from employees' pay and the employee deductions and employer's share of Canada (or Quebec) Pension Plan contributions and Employment Insurance premiums to Canada Customs and Revenue Agency (CCRA). The payment for a given month is due on or before the 15th day of the following month. In addition, the employer has to remit any withholdings for union dues, charitable donations, etc.; the payment would probably be made in the following month. Assume federal income tax of $9,880.00, Canada Pension Plan contributions of $953.90, Employment Insurance premiums of $1,109.80, and United Way contributions of $465.00 were deducted in calculating the net pay for the employees of Global Company for the three weeks ended December 10, 17, and 24, 2001. Based on those amounts and columns (d) through (j) in Exhibit 11-8, the business would record payments to CCRA and Winnipeg United Way for the month of December 2001 as follows:

2002			
Jan. 3	Employee Withheld Income Tax		
	Payable ($9,880.00 + $3,167.76)..................................	13,047.76	
	Employee Withheld Canada Pension		
	Plan Payable ($953.90 + $327.70)...............................	1,281.60	
	Employee Withheld Employment		
	Insurance Payable ($1,109.80 + $385.12)	1,494.92	
	Canada Pension Plan Expense (1 × $1,281.60)...............	1,281.60	
	Employment Insurance Expense		
	(1.4 × $1,494.92)...	2,092.88	
	Cash		19,198.76
	To record payment to CCRA for		
	December 2001 withholdings.		

WORKING IT OUT

According to this journal entry, what is the total amount that the business will pay to the government on January 3, 2002, for taxes, Canada Pension Plan, and Employment Insurance withheld for the month of December 2001?

A: 13,047.76 + $1,281.60 + $1,494.92 = $15,824.28

```
2002
Jan. 3    Employee Donations to United Way Payable ...............    620.00
            Cash ..............................................................................                620.00
          To record payment to United Way for December
          2001 withholdings ($465.00 + $155.00).
```

Recall that Manitoba is one of the provinces that levies a tax on payroll to pay for health and post-secondary education in the province. There is no tax on the first $750,000 of payroll, 4.5 percent on the next $750,000, and 2.25 percent on payroll over $1,500,000. Assume that Global Company's payroll passed $750,000 with the November 12, 2001, payroll and that the payroll and benefits totalled $42,000 for the weeks of December 10, 17, and 24, 2001. Based on those amounts and the total payroll of December 31, 2001, from Exhibit 11-8, the journal entry to record payment to the Province of Manitoba is:

```
2002
Jan. 3    Health and Post-Secondary Education Tax
            Levy Expense.......................................................    2,504.43
            Cash..............................................................................                2,504.43
          To record payment to the Province of
          Manitoba for December 2001
          [($42,000.00 + $13,654.00) × 0.045].
```

Payments to Third Parties for Fringe Benefits   The employer sometimes pays for employees' dental benefits coverage and for a company pension plan. Assuming the total cash payment for these benefits is $1,927.14 and the payment is made to one company, this entry would be

```
2002
Jan. 10   Employee Benefits Payable—Dental Plan..............    600.14
          Employee Benefits Payable—Pension Plan ...........    1,327.00
            Cash..................................................................................              1,927.14
          To record payment for employee dental benefits
          coverage and company pension plan.
```

Earnings Record

The employer must file Summary of Remuneration Paid returns with Canada Customs and Revenue Agency (CCRA) and must provide the employee with a Statement of Remuneration Paid, Form T4, at the end of the year. Therefore, employers maintain an earnings record for each employee. (These earnings records are also used for Employment Insurance claims.) Exhibit 11-10 is a five-week excerpt from the earnings record of employee J.C. Jenkins.

The employee earnings record is not a journal or a ledger, and it is not required by law. It is an accounting tool—like the work sheet—that the employer uses to prepare payroll withholdings reports. The information provided on the earnings record with respect to year-to-date earnings also indicates when an employee has earned $37,600, the point at which the employer can stop withholding Canada Pension Plan contributions. The same is true for Employment Insurance deductions: the employer stops withholding Employment Insurance contributions after the employee has earned $39,000. There is no maximum income tax deduction.

Exhibit 11-11 is the Statement of Remuneration Paid, Form T4, for employee J.C. Jenkins. The employer prepares this form for each employee and a form called a T4 Summary, which summarizes the information on all the T4s issued by the employer for that year. The employer sends the T4 Summary and one copy of each T4 to CCRA by February 28 each year. CCRA uses the documents to ensure that the employer has correctly paid to the government all amounts withheld on its behalf from employees together with the employer's share. The employee gets two copies of the T4; one copy must be filed with the employee's income tax return, while the second copy is for the employee's records. CCRA matches the income on

EXHIBIT 11-10

Employee Earnings Record for 2001

Employee Name and Address:

Jenkins, J.C.
1400 Camousen Cres.
Victoria, BC V5J 5K9

Social Insurance No.: 978-010-789
Marital Status: Married
Net Claims Code: 4
Pay Rate: $700 per week; overtime $26.25 per hour.
Job Title: Salesperson

Week Ended	Hours	Gross Pay				Deductions					Net Pay	
		Straight time	Overtime	Total	To Date	Federal Income Tax	Canada Pension Plan	Employ-ment Insurance	United Way	Total	Amount	Cheque No.
Dec. 3	40	700.00		700.00	35,437.50	130.45	24.68	16.80	2.00	173.93	526.07	1525
Dec. 10	40	700.00		700.00	36,137.50	130.45	24.68	16.80	2.00	173.93	526.07	1548
Dec. 17	44	700.00	105.00	805.00	36,942.50	170.30	28.90	19.32	2.00	220.52	584.48	1574
Dec. 24	48	700.00	210.00	910.00	37,852.50	210.75	32.80	21.84	2.00	267.39	642.61	1598
Dec. 31	46	700.00	157.50	857.50	38,710.00	192.10	0	20.58	2.00	214.68	642.82	1622
Total		36,400.00	2,310.00	38,710.00	38,710.00	7,340.90	1,329.90	929.04	104.00	9,703.84	29,006.16	

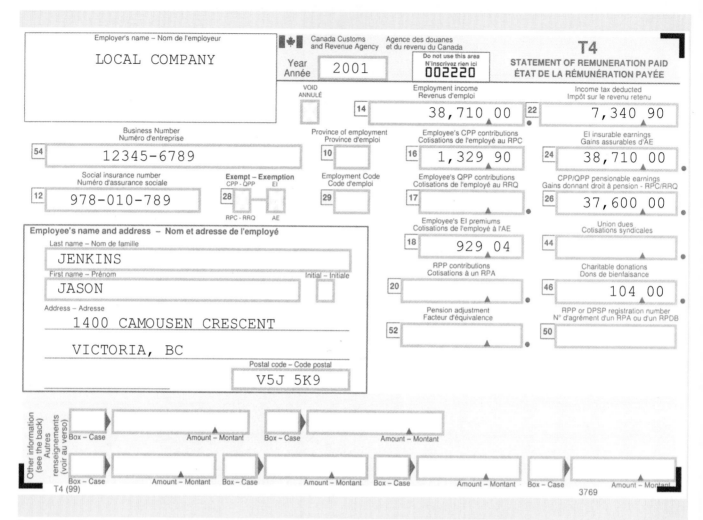

Source: Canada Customs and Revenue Agency. Reproduced with permission of the Minister of Public Works and Government Services Canada, 2000.

Exhibit 11-11

Employee Statement of Remuneration Paid (Form T4)

the T4 filed by the employer against the income reported on the employee's income tax return, filed by the employee, to ensure that the employee properly reported his or her income from employment.

Internal Control over Payroll

The internal controls over cash payments discussed in Chapter 7 apply to payroll. In addition, companies adopt special controls in payroll accounting. The large number of transactions and the complex arrangements increase the risk of a control failure. There are two main types of special controls for payroll: controls for efficiency and controls for safeguarding payroll disbursements.

Controls for Efficiency

For companies with many employees, reconciling the bank account can be time consuming because of the large number of paycheques. For example, a March 30 paycheque would probably not have time to clear the bank before a bank statement is created on March 31. This cheque and others in a March 30 payroll would be outstanding. A large number of outstanding cheques for the bank reconciliation increases accounting expense. To limit the number of outstanding paycheques, many companies use two payroll bank accounts. They pay the payroll from one payroll account one month and from the other payroll account the next month. This way they can reconcile each account every other month. In this system, a March 30 paycheque has until April 30 to clear the bank before the account is reconciled. Outstanding cheques are almost eliminated, the time it takes to prepare the bank reconciliation is reduced, and accounting expense is decreased. Also, many companies' cheques become void if not cashed within a certain period of time. This constraint also limits the number of outstanding cheques.

Payroll transactions are ideally suited for computer processing. Employee pay rates and withholding data are stored in a file. Each pay period, keyboarders enter the number of hours worked by each employee. The computer performs the calculations, prints the payroll register and the paycheques, and updates the employee earnings records. The program also computes payroll withholdings and prepares reports to government agencies. Expense and liability accounts are automatically updated for the payroll transactions. The payroll register is in a computer database form, which allows users to generate a wide variety of reports. At the end of an accounting period, the computerized payroll system automatically computes the amounts for the general ledger system, including any accruals of salary expense incurred but not paid.

Other payroll controls for efficiency include following established policies for hiring and terminating employees, and complying with government regulations. Hiring and termination policies provide guidelines for keeping a qualified, diligent work force dedicated to achieving the business's goals. Complying with government regulations helps companies avoid paying fines and penalties.

Controls for Safeguarding Payroll Disbursements

Owners and managers of small businesses can monitor their payrolls by personal contact with their employees. Large corporations cannot do so. These businesses must establish controls to ensure that paycheques go only to legitimate employees and for the correct amounts. A particular danger is that a paycheque may be written to a fictitious employee and cashed by a dishonest employee. To guard against this and other possible crimes, large businesses adopt strict internal control policies.

The duties of hiring and terminating employees should be separated from the duties of payroll accounting and distributing paycheques. Requiring an identification

REAL WORLD EXAMPLE

Another internal control feature is direct depositing of paycheques into employees' bank accounts (electronic funds transfer, or EFT). This eliminates the possibility of lost or stolen cheques and makes it difficult to distribute cheques to a fictitious employee. It is also useful to compare the current-employee list to a list of former employees to ensure that terminated employees are not still receiving paycheques.

STOP & THINK

Centurion Homes of Calgary, Alberta, builds houses and has four construction crews. The supervisors hire—and terminate—workers and keep their hourly records. Each Friday morning the supervisors telephone their workers' hours to the home office, where accountants prepare the weekly paycheques. Around noon the supervisors pick up the paycheques. They return to the construction site and pay the workers at day's end. What is the internal control weakness in this situation? Propose a way to improve the internal controls.

Answer: Construction workers often have limited contact with the home office. When the supervisors control most of the information used in the payroll system, they can forge the payroll records of fictitious employees and pocket their pay. To improve internal control, Centurion Homes could hire and terminate all workers through the home office. This practice would establish the identity of all workers listed in the payroll records. Another way to improve the internal controls would be to have a home-office employee distribute paycheques on a surprise basis. Any remaining cheques would arouse suspicion regarding the supervisor. This system would probably prevent supervisors from cheating the company.

badge bearing an employee's photograph helps internal control. Issuing paycheques only to employees with badges helps to ensure that only actual employees receive pay.

A formal time-keeping system helps ensure that employees actually worked the number of hours claimed. Having employees insert time cards into a time clock that "punches" the time at the start and end of the work day proves their attendance—as long as management makes sure that no employee punches in and out for others, too. Some companies have their workers fill in weekly or monthly time sheets.

Again we see that the key to good internal control is separation of duties. The responsibilities of the personnel department, payroll department, accounting department, time-card management, and paycheque distribution should be kept separate.

OBJECTIVE 7
Report current liabilities on the balance sheet

Reporting Payroll Expense and Liabilities

At the end of its fiscal year, the company reports the amount of *payroll liability* owed to all parties: employees, CCRA, provincial governments, unions, and so forth. Payroll liability is *not* the payroll expense for the year. The liability at year end is the amount that is still unpaid. Payroll expense appears on the income statement, payroll liability on the balance sheet.

Inco Limited reported accrued payrolls and benefits of approximately $118 million (Inco reports in U.S. funds in its financial statements) as a current liability on its December 31, 1999, balance sheet (Exhibit 11-12 on page 591). However, Inco Limited's payroll expense for the year far exceeded $118 million; total operating expenses exceeded $1.8 billion. Exhibit 11-12 also presents the other current liabilities that we have discussed in this chapter.

The following Decision Guidelines feature summarizes some of the more important payroll decisions that a business must consider.

DECISION GUIDELINES Accounting for Payroll

Decision	Guidelines
What are the key elements of a payroll accounting system?	• Personal Tax Credits Return, Form TD1(E) • Payroll register • Payroll bank account and payroll cheques • Employee earnings record • Employee wage and tax statement, Form T4
What are the key terms in the payroll area?	*Gross pay* (Total amount earned by the employee) − *Payroll deductions* a. Withheld income tax b. Withheld Canada (or Quebec) Pension Plan deductions—equal amount paid by employer c. Withheld Employment Insurance deductions—employer pays 1.4 times employee deduction d. Optional deductions (retirement savings plan, charitable contributions, union dues) = *Net (take-home) pay*
What is the employer's total payroll expense?	*Gross pay* + *Employer's payroll expenses* a. Canada (or Quebec) Pension Plan expense—equal amount also paid by employee b. Employment Insurance expense—employer pays 1.4 times amount employee pays

continued

Decision	Guidelines
	+ *Fringe benefits for employees* 　a. Insurance (dental, drug plan, and disability) 　b. Employer's share of retirement savings plan (and other retirement benefits) 　c. Club memberships and other benefits = *Employer's total payroll costs*
Where to report payroll amounts?	• Payroll expenses on the income statement • Payroll liabilities on the balance sheet

EXHIBIT 11-12

Partial Inco Limited Balance Sheet

Current Liabilities	(U.S. $ in millions)
Long-term debt due within one year.........	$190
Accounts payable	120
Accrued payrolls and benefits...................	118
Other accrued liabilities..............................	152
Total current liabilities...........................	$580

Summary Problem
for Your Review

Best Threads, a clothing store, employs one salesperson, Sheila Kingsley. Her straight-time pay is $420 per week. She earns time and a half for hours worked in excess of 35 per week. For Kingsley's wage rate and "net claim code" on her Personal Tax Credits Return (TD1), the income tax withholding rate is approximately 16 percent. Canada Pension is 3.9 percent on income until the maximum total contribution of $1,329.90 is reached, while Employment Insurance premiums are 2.4 percent. In addition, Best Threads pays Kingsley's Blue Cross supplemental health insurance premiums of $31.42 a month and dental insurance premiums of $18.50 a month.

During the week ended February 28, 2001, Kingsley worked 48 hours.

Required

1. Compute Sheila Kingsley's gross pay and net pay for the week.

2. Record the following payroll entries that Best Threads would make:
   a. Expense for Kingsley's wages including overtime pay
   b. Cost of employer's share of Kingsley's withholdings (ignore the basic Canada Pension Plan exemption)
   c. Expense for fringe benefits
   d. Payment of cash to Kingsley
   e. Payment Best Threads must make to Canada Customs and Revenue Agency (CCRA)
   f. Payment of fringe benefits for the month

3. How much total payroll expense did Best Threads incur for the week? How much cash did the business spend on its payroll?

Solution to Review Problem

Requirement 1

Gross pay:

Straight-time pay for 35 hours		$420.00
Overtime pay		
Rate per hour ($420/35 × 1.5)	$18.00	
Hours (48 – 35)	× 13	234.00
Total gross pay		$654.00

Net pay:

Gross pay		$654.00
Less: Withheld income tax ($654 × 0.16)	$104.64	
Withheld Canada Pension Plan ($654 × 0.039)	25.51	
Withheld Employment Insurance ($654 × 0.024)	15.70	145.85
Net pay		508.15

Requirement 2

a. Sales Salary Expense	654.00	
Employee Withheld Income Tax Payable		104.64
Employee Canada Pension Plan Payable		25.51
Employee Employment Insurance Payable		15.70
Wages payable		508.15
To record expense for S. Kingsley's wages.		
b. Canada Pension Plan Expense	25.51	
Employment Insurance Expense	21.98	
Employer Canada Pension Plan Payable		25.51
Employer Employment Insurance Payable		21.98
To record cost of employer's portion of S. Kingsley's wages.		
CPP is $25.51 ($25.51 × 1).		
EI is $21.98 ($15.70 × 1.4).		
c. Medical and Dental Expense	49.92	
Employee Benefits Payable		49.92
To record expense of fringe benefits ($31.42 + $18.50).		
d. Wages Payable to Employee	508.15	
Cash		508.15
To record payment of wages to S. Kingsley.		
e. Employee Withheld Income Tax Payable	104.64	
Employee Canada Pension Plan Payable	25.51	
Employee Employment Insurance Payable	15.70	
Employer Canada Pension Plan Payable	25.51	
Employer Employment Insurance Payable	21.98	
Cash		193.34
To record payment to CCRA.		
f. Employee Benefits Payable	49.92	
Cash		49.92
To record payment of monthly fringe benefits.		

Requirement 3

Best Threads incurred *total payroll expense* of $751.41 (gross salary of $654.00 + employer's cost of Canada Pension of $25.51 + employer's cost of Employment Insurance of $21.98 + fringe benefits of $49.92). See entries a to c.

Best Threads paid cash of $751.41 on payroll (Kingsley's net pay of $508.15 + payment to CCRA of $193.34 + fringe benefits of $49.92). See entries d to f.

Summary

1. **Account for current liabilities of known amount.** *Current liabilities* may be divided into those of *known amount* and those that must be *estimated*. Trade accounts payable, short-term notes payable, interest payable, GST payable, payroll, and unearned revenues are current liabilities of known amount.

2. **Account for current liabilities that must be estimated.** Current liabilities that must be estimated include warranties payable, vacation pay, and corporations' income tax payable.

3. **Identify and report contingent liabilities.** *Contingent liabilities* are not actual liabilities but potential liabilities that may arise in the future. Contingent liabilities, like current liabilities, may be of known amount or an indefinite amount. A business that faces a lawsuit not yet decided in court has a contingent liability of indefinite amount.

4. **Compute payroll amounts.** *Payroll* accounting handles the expenses and liabilities arising from compensating employees. Employers must withhold income taxes, Canada (or Quebec) Pension Plan contributions, and Employment Insurance premiums from employees' pay and send these *withholdings* together with the employer's share of the latter two to the government. In addition, many employers allow their employees to pay for insur-

ance and union dues and to make gifts to charities through payroll deductions. An employee's net pay is the gross pay less all withholdings and optional deductions.

5. **Record basic payroll transactions.** An *employer's* payroll expenses include the employer's share of Canada (or Quebec) Pension Plan contributions and Employment Insurance premiums; employers also pay provincial health and post-secondary education taxes in those provinces that levy them and Workers' Compensation. Also, employers may provide their employees with fringe benefits, such as life insurance coverage and retirement pensions.

6. **Use a payroll system.** A basic *payroll system* consists of a payroll register, a payroll bank account, payroll cheques, and an earnings record for each employee. Good *internal controls* over payroll help the business to achieve efficiency and to safeguard the company's cash. The cornerstone of internal control is the separation of duties.

7. **Report current liabilities on the balance sheet.** The company reports on the balance sheet all current liabilities that it owes: current liabilities of known amount, including payroll liabilities; and current liabilities that must be estimated.

Self-Study Questions

Test your understanding of the chapter by marking the correct answer for each of the following questions:

1. A $10,000, 9 percent, one-year note payable was issued on July 31. The balance sheet at December 31 will report interest payable of (*p. 559*)
   a. $0 because the interest is not due yet
   b. $453.70
   c. $377.26
   d. $900

2. If the note payable in the preceding question had been discounted, the cash proceeds from issuance would have been (*p. 560*)
   a. $9,100   c. $9,700
   b. $9,623   d. $10,000

3. Which of the following liabilities creates no expense for the company? (*p. 561*)
   a. Interest   c. Employment Insurance
   b. Sales tax   d. Warranty

4. Suppose Canadian Tire estimates that warranty costs will equal 1 percent of tire sales. Assume that November sales totalled $900,000, and the company's outlay in tires and cash to satisfy warranty claims was $7,400. How much warranty expense should the November income statement report? (*p. 568*)
   a. $1,600   c. $9,000
   b. $7,400   d. $16,400

5. Nu Systems Company is a defendant in a lawsuit that claims damages of $55,000. On the balance sheet date, it appears unlikely that the court will render a judgment against the company. How should Nu Systems Company report this event in its financial statements? (*p. 570*)
   a. Omit mention because no judgment has been rendered
   b. Disclose the contingent liability in a note

c. Report the loss on the income statement and the liability on the balance sheet.
d. Both b and c

6. Emilie Frontenac's weekly pay for 40 hours is $400, plus time and half for overtime. The tax rate, based on her income level and deductions, is 16 percent, the Quebec Pension Plan rate is 3.9 percent on her weekly earnings, and the Employment Insurance rate is 2.4 percent on her weekly earnings. What is Emilie's take-home pay for a week in which she works 50 hours? (*pp. 581–583*)
   a. $427.35   c. $460.80
   b. $436.80   d. $310.80

7. Which of the following represents a cost to the employer? (*p. 578*)
   a. Withheld income tax
   b. Canada Pension Plan
   c. Employment Insurance
   d. Both b and c

8. The main reason for using a separate payroll bank account is to (*p. 583*)

a. Safeguard cash by preventing the writing of payroll cheques to fictitious employees
b. Safeguard cash by limiting paycheques to amounts based on time cards
c. Increase efficiency by isolating payroll disbursements for analysis and control
d. All of the above

9. The key to good internal controls in the payroll area is (*pp. 588–590*)
   a. Using a payroll bank account
   b. Separating payroll duties
   c. Using a payroll register
   d. Using time cards

10. Which of the following items is reported as current liability on the balance sheet? (*p. 590*)
    a. Short-term notes payable
    b. Estimated warranties
    c. Accrued payroll withholdings
    d. All of the above

Answers to the Self-Study Questions follow the Similar Accounting Terms.

Accounting Vocabulary

Accrued expense (*p. 565*)
Accrued liability (*p. 565*)
Canada (or Quebec) Pension Plan (*p. 576*)
Current maturity (*p. 564*)
Current portion of long-term debt (*p. 564*)
Discounting a note payable (*p. 560*)
Employee compensation (*p. 565*)

Employment Insurance Act (*p. 577*)
Gross pay (*p. 575*)
Net pay (*p. 575*)
Payroll (*p. 565*)
Short-term note payable (*p. 559*)
Withheld income tax (*p. 576*)
Workers' Compensation (*p. 578*)

Similar Accounting Terms

Current portion of long-term debt	Current maturity
Unearned revenues	Deferred revenues; Revenues collected in advance; Customer prepayments
Payroll register	Payroll journal; Payroll record

Answers to Self-Study Questions

1. c $10,000 × 0.09 × $^{153}\!/_{365}$ = $377.26   7. d
2. a $10,000 – ($10,000 × 0.09) = $9,100   8. c
3. b   9. b
4. c $900,000 × 0.01 = $9,000   10. d
5. b
6. a Overtime pay: $400/40 = $10 × 1.5 = $15 per hour × 10 hours = $150
   Gross pay = $400 + $150 = $550
   Deductions = ($550 × 0.16) + ($550 × 0.039) + ($550 × 0.024)
            = $88.00 + $21.45 + $13.20 = $122.65
   Take-home pay = $550.00 – $122.65 = $427.35

Assignment Material

Questions

1. Give a more descriptive account title for each of the following current liabilities: Accrued Interest, Accrued Salaries, Accrued Income Tax.

2. What distinguishes a current liability from a long-term liability? What distinguishes a contingent liability from an actual liability?

3. A company purchases a machine by signing a $42,000, 10 percent, one-year note payable on July 31. Interest is to be paid at maturity. What two current liabilities related to this purchase does the company report on its December 31 balance sheet? What is the amount of each current liability?

4. A company borrowed cash by discounting a $45,000, 8 percent, six-month note payable to the bank, receiving cash of $43,200. (a) Show how the amount of cash was computed. Also, identify (b) the total amount of interest expense to be recognized on this note and (c) the amount of the borrower's cash payment at maturity.

5. Explain how GST that is paid by consumers is a liability of the store that sold the merchandise. To whom is it paid?

6. What is meant by the term *current portion of long-term debt*, and how is this item reported in the financial statements?

7. At the beginning of the school term, what type of account is the tuition that your college or university collects from students? What type of account is the tuition at the end of the school term?

8. Why is a customer deposit a liability? Give an example.

9. Patton Company warrants its products against defects for three years from date of sale. During the current year, the company made sales of $600,000. Store management estimated warranty costs on those sales would total $36,000 over the three-year warranty period. Ultimately, the company paid $44,000 cash on warranties. What is the company's warranty expense for the year? What accounting principle governs this answer?

10. Identify two contingent liabilities of a definite amount and two contingent liabilities of an indefinite amount.

11. Why is payroll expense relatively more important to a service business such as a public accounting firm than it is to a merchandising company such as Zellers?

12. Two persons are studying Allen Company's manufacturing process. One person is Allen Company's factory supervisor, and the other person is an outside consultant who is an expert in the industry. Which person's salary is the payroll expense of Allen Company? Identify the expense account that Allen Company would debit to record the pay of each person.

13. What are two elements of an employer's payroll expense in addition to salaries, wages, commissions, and overtime pay?

14. What determines the amount of income tax that is withheld from employee paycheques?

15. What is the Canada (or Quebec) Pension Plan? Who pays it? What are the funds used for?

16. Identify three required deductions and two optional deductions from employee paycheques.

17. Identify three employee benefit expenses an employer pays.

18. Who pays Employment Insurance premiums? What are these funds used for?

19. Briefly describe a basic payroll accounting system's components and their functions.

20. How much Employment Insurance has been withheld from the pay of an employee who has earned $52,288 during the current year? What is the employer's Employment Insurance expense for this employee?

21. Briefly describe the two principal categories of internal controls over payroll.

22. Why do some companies use two special payroll bank accounts?

23. Identify three internal controls designed to safeguard payroll cash.

Exercises

Exercise 11-1   *Recording sales tax and GST*   *(Obj. 1)*

Make general journal entries to record the following transactions of Madoc Products for a two-month period. Explanations are not required.

Mar. 31 Recorded cash sales of $187,200 for the month, plus provincial sales tax of 6 percent collected on behalf of the province of Saskatchewan and goods and services tax of 7 percent. Record the two taxes in separate accounts.

Apr. 6 Sent March provincial and goods and services taxes to appropriate authorities (Minister of Finance for PST and Receiver General for GST). Assume no GST input tax credits.

Exercise 11-2 *Accounting for warranty expense and the related liability* *(Obj.1)*

The accounting records of Chan Industries included the following balances at the end of the period:

Estimated Warranty Payable	Sales Revenue	Warranty Expense
Beg. bal. 9,300	483,000	

In the past, Chan Industries' warranty expense has been 5 percent of sales. During the current period, Chan Industries paid $31,200 to satisfy the warranty claims of customers.

Required

1. Record Chan Industries' warranty expense for the period and the company's cash payments during the period to satisfy warranty claims. Explanations are not required.

2. What ending balance of Estimated Warranty Payable will Chan Industries report on its balance sheet?

Exercise 11-3 *Recording note payable transactions* *(Obj. 1)*

Record the following note payable transactions of Vanderbilt Company in the company's general journal. Explanations are not required.

2003
Apr. 1 Purchased equipment costing $50,000 by issuing a one-year, 8 percent note payable.
Dec. 31 Accrued interest on the note payable.
2004
Apr. 1 Paid the note payable at maturity.

Exercise 11-4 *Discounting a note payable* *(Obj. 1)*

On September 1, 2002, Hart Supplies discounted a six-month, $120,000 note payable to the bank at 7 percent.

Required

1. Prepare general journal entries to record (a) issuance of the note, (b) accrual of interest at December 31, and (c) payment of the note at maturity in 2003. Explanations are not required.

2. Show how Hart Supplies would report the note on the December 31, 2002, balance sheet.

Exercise 11-5 *Accounting for unearned revenue* *(Obj. 1)*

The chapter-opening story describes the airlines' sale of frequent-flier miles to hotel chains such as Holiday Inn and Delta Hotels. Suppose Air Canada sells 1,000,000 Aeroplan frequent-flier miles to Delta for $0.015 per mile. During the next six months, Delta customers use 200,000 of the Aeroplan miles for free trips on Air Canada.

Required

1. Using Air Canada's (assumed) account title for the unearned revenue Unearned Air Traffic Revenue, journalize Air Canada's (a) receipt of cash from Delta, and (b) provision of transportation services for the Delta customers. Air Canada labels its revenue as Passenger Revenues.

2. Post to the unearned revenue (Unearned Air Traffic Revenue) T-account. How much does Air Canada owe the Delta customers after the preceding transactions?

Exercise 11-6 *Accounting for warranty expense and estimated warranty payable* *(Obj. 2)*

General Motors (G.M.), the automaker, warranties its automobiles for three years or 60,000 kilometres, whichever comes first. Suppose G.M.'s experience indicates that the company can expect warranty costs during the three-year period to add up to 5 percent of sales.

Assume that Prairie G.M. in Red Deer, Alberta, made sales of $1,000,000 during 2003, its first year of operations. Prairie G.M. received cash for 30 percent of the sales and notes receivable for the remainder. Payments to satisfy customer warranty claims totalled $44,000 during 2003.

Required

1. Record the sales, warranty expense, and warranty payments for Prairie G.M. Ignore any reimbursement Prairie G.M. may receive from G.M. Corporation.

2. Post to the Estimated Warranty Payable T-account. At the end of 2003, how much in estimated warranty payable does Prairie G.M. owe its customers? Why must the warranty payable amount be estimated?

Exercise 11-7 *Reporting a contingent liability* *(Obj. 3)*

Moncton Safety Products is a defendant in lawsuits brought against the marketing and distribution of its products. Damages of $340,000 are claimed against Moncton Safety Products but the company denies the charges and is vigourously defending itself. In a recent newspaper interview, the president of the company stated that she could not predict the outcome of the lawsuits. Nevertheless, she said management does not believe that any actual liabilities resulting from the lawsuits will significantly affect the company's financial position.

Required

Describe what, if any, disclosure Moncton Safety Products should provide of this contingent liability. Total liabilities are $1.8 million. If you believe note disclosure is required, write the note to describe the contingency.

Exercise 11-8 *Accruing a contingency* *(Obj. 3)*

Refer to the Moncton Safety Products situation in the preceding exercise. Suppose that Moncton Safety Products' lawyers advise that preliminary judgment of $100,000 has been rendered against the company.

Required

Describe how to report this situation in the Moncton Safety Products financial statements. Journalize any entry required under GAAP. Explanations are not required.

Exercise 11-9 *Interpreting a company's contingent liabilities* *(Obj. 3)*

Harley-Davidson, Inc., the motorcycle manufacturer, includes the following note in a recent annual report:

NOTES TO CONSOLIDATED FINANCIAL STATEMENTS

7 (In Part): Commitments And Contingencies

The Company self-insures its product liability losses in the United States up to $3 million (catastrophic coverage is maintained for individual claims in excess of $3 million up to $25 million). Outside the United States, the Company is insured for product liability up to $25 million per individual claim and in the aggregate.

Required

1. Why are these *contingent* (versus real) liabilities?
2. In the United States, how can the contingent liability become a real liability for Harley-Davidson? What are the limits to the company's product liabilities in the United States? Explain how these limits work.
3. How can a contingency outside the United States become a real liability for the company? How does Harley-Davidson's potential liability differ for claims outside the United States?

Exercise 11-10 *Reporting current liabilities* **(Obj. 7)**

Link Back to Chapter 4 (Current Ratio). The top management of Ontario Carbide examines the following company accounting records at December 29, immediately before the end of the year:

Total current assets.............................	$ 720,000
Capital assets	1,095,000
	$1,815,000
Total current liabilities.......................	$ 375,000
Long-term liabilities...........................	450,000
Owner's equity...................................	990,000
	$1,815,000

Ontario Carbide's borrowing agreements with creditors require the company to keep a current ratio of 2.0 or better. How much in current liabilities should Ontario Carbide pay off within the next two days in order to comply with its borrowing agreements?

Exercise 11-11 *Computing net pay* **(Obj. 4)**

Van Pringle is a salesclerk in the electronics department of Quality Furniture in Kelowna. He earns a base monthly salary of $1,800 plus a 6 percent commission on his sales. Through payroll deductions, Van donates $10 per month to a charitable organization and pays dental insurance premiums of $38.25. Compute Van's gross pay and net pay for December, assuming his sales for the month are $75,000. The income tax rate on his earnings is 30 percent, the Canada Pension Plan contribution is 3.9 percent, and the Employment Insurance Plan premium rate is 2.4 percent. Van has not yet reached the CPP or EI maximum earning levels

Exercise 11-12 *Computing and recording gross pay and net pay* **(Obj. 4, 5)**

Lucy Lee works for a Quik Trip convenience store for straight-time earnings of $10 per hour, with time and a half for hours in excess of 35 per week. Lucy's payroll deductions include income tax of 15 percent, Canada Pension of 3.9 percent on earnings and Employment Insurance of 2.4 percent on earnings. In addition, she contributes $2 per week to the United Way. Assuming Lucy worked 38 hours during the week, (1) compute her gross pay and net pay for the week, and (2) make a general journal entry to record the store's wage expense for Lucy's work, including her payroll deductions. Round all amounts to the nearest cent.

Exercise 11-13 *Recording a payroll* *(Obj. 4, 5)*

Summerside Department Store incurred salary expense of $82,000 for December. The store's payroll expense includes Canada Pension of 3.9 percent and Employment Insurance of 1.4 times the employee rate of 2.4 percent. Also the store provides the following fringe benefits for employees: dental insurance (cost to the store $2,632.07); life insurance (cost to the store $351.07); and pension benefits through a private plan (cost to the store $1,600.40). Record Summerside Department Store's payroll expenses for Canada Pension Plan and Employment Insurance and employee fringe benefits. Ignore the CPP basic exemption.

Exercise 11-14 *Using a payroll system to compute total payroll expense* *(Obj. 6)*

Study the Employee Earnings Record for J.C. Jenkins in Exhibit 11-10, page 587. In addition to the amounts shown in the exhibit, the employer also paid all employee benefits plus (a) an amount equal to 6 percent of gross pay into Jenkins' pension retirement account, and (b) dental insurance for Jenkins at a cost of $30 per month. Compute the employer's total payroll expense for employee J.C. Jenkins during 2001. Carry all amounts to the nearest cent.

Exercise 11-15 *Reporting current and long-term liabilities* *(Obj. 7)*

Suppose Ocean Outfitters borrowed $8,000,000 on December 31, 2001, by issuing 9 percent long-term debt that must be paid in four equal annual instalments plus interest each January 2, commencing in 2002. By inserting appropriate amounts in the following excerpts from the company's partial balance sheet, show how Ocean Outfitters would report its long-term debt.

	December 31,			
	2002	**2003**	**2004**	**2005**
Current liabilities:				
Current portion of long-term debt	$ _____	$ _____	$ _____	$ _____
Interest payable	$ _____	$ _____	$ _____	$ _____
Long-term liabilities:				
Long-term debt..	$ _____	$ _____	$ _____	$ _____

Exercise 11-16 *Reporting current and long-term liabilities* *(Obj. 7)*

Assume Watstar Sports completed these selected transactions during December 2002:

1. Sport Spectrum Inc., a chain of sporting goods stores, ordered $160,000 worth of hockey equipment. With its order, Sport Spectrum Inc. sent a cheque for $160,000. Watstar Sports will ship the goods on January 3, 2003.

2. The December payroll of $5,100,000 is subject to employee withheld income tax of 18 percent, Canada Pension Plan expenses of 3.9 percent for the employee and 3.9 percent for the employer, Employment Insurance deductions of 2.4 percent for the employee and 1.4 times the employee rate of 2.4 percent for the employer. On December 31, Watstar Sports pays employees but accrues all tax amounts.

3. Sales of $400,000,000 are subject to estimated warranty cost of 1.6 percent. This was the first year the company provided a warranty.

4. On December 2, Watstar Sports signed a $400,000 note payable that requires annual payments of $80,000 plus 9 percent interest on the unpaid balance each December 2.

Required

Report these items on Watstar's Sports' balance sheet at December 31, 2002.

Challenge Exercises

Exercise 11-17 *Accounting for and reporting current liabilities* **(Obj. 1, 7)**

Link Back to Chapter 4 (Current Ratio). Suppose the balance sheets of PepsiCo, Inc., parent company of Pepsi-Cola Canada Ltd., for two years reported these figures:

	Billions	
	2003	**2002**
Total current assets	$ 6.90	$ 6.15
Capital assets	21.30	19.50
	$28.20	$25.65
Total current liabilities	5.55	7.20
Long-term liabilities	14.25	11.10
Shareholders' equity	8.40	7.35
	$28.20	$25.65

The notes to PepsiCo, Inc.'s 2003 financial statements report that during 2002, because of some refinancing arrangements, PepsiCo, Inc. was able to reclassify $5.1 billion from current liabilities to long-term liabilities.

Required

1. Compute PepsiCo, Inc.'s current ratio at the end of each year. Describe the trend that you observe.

2. Assume that PepsiCo, Inc. had not refinanced and been able to reclassify the $5.1 billion of current liabilities as long-term during 2003. Recompute the current ratio for 2003. Why do you think PepsiCo, Inc. reclassified the liabilities as long-term?

Exercise 11-18 *Analyzing current liability accounts* **(Obj. 1, 7)**

Bentley Company recently reported notes payable and accrued payrolls and benefits as follows:

	December 31,	
	2003	**2002**
	(in millions of dollars)	
Current liabilities (partial):		
Notes payable	$ 9	$ 43
Accrued payrolls and benefits	137	154

Assume that during 2003, Bentley Company borrowed $2 million on notes payable. Also assume that Bentley paid $117 million for employee compensation and benefits during 2003.

Required

1. Compute Bentley Company's payment of notes payable during 2003.
2. Compute Bentley Company's employee compensation during 2003.

Beyond the Numbers

Beyond the Numbers 11-1

The Boeing Company, manufacturer of jet aircraft, is the defendant in numerous lawsuits claiming unfair trade practices. Boeing has strong incentives not to disclose these contingent liabilities. However, generally accepted accounting principles require companies to report their contingent liabilities.

Required

1. Why would a company prefer not to disclose its contingent liabilities?

2. Describe how a bank could be harmed if a company seeking a loan did not disclose its contingent liabilities.

3. What is the ethical tightrope that companies must walk when they report their contingent liabilities?

Beyond the Numbers 11-2

The following questions are not related.

a. A friend comments that he thought that liabilities represented amounts owed by a company. He asks why unearned revenues are shown as a current liability. How would you respond?

b. A warranty is like a contingent liability in that the amount to be paid is not known at year end. Why are warranties payable shown as a current liability, whereas contingent liabilities are reported in the notes to the financial statements?

c. Auditors have procedures for determining whether they have discovered all of a company's contingent liabilities. These procedures differ from the procedures used for determining that accounts payable are stated correctly. How would an auditor identify a client's contingent liabilities?

Ethical Issue

Many companies, such as Campeau Corporation, borrowed heavily during the 1970s and 1980s to exploit the advantage of financing operations with debt. At first, the companies were able to earn operating income much higher than their interest expense and were therefore quite profitable. However, when the business cycle turned down, their debt burdens pushed the companies to the brink of bankruptcy. Operating income was less than interest expense.

Required

Is it unethical for managers to commit a company to a high level of debt? Or is it just risky? Who could be hurt by a company's taking on too much debt? Discuss.

Problems (Group A)

Problem 11-1A *Journalizing liability-related transactions* *(Obj. 1, 2)*

The following selected transactions of Unique Medical Products, a Manitoba company, occurred during 2002 and 2003. The company's year end is December 31.

Required

Record the transactions in the company's general journal. Explanations are not required.

2002

Jan. 3 Purchased a machine at a cost of $100,000 plus 7 percent GST, signing an 8 percent, six-month note payable for that amount.

29 Recorded the month's sales of $611,000 (excludes PST and GST), three-quarters on credit and one-quarter for cash. Sales amounts are subject to Manitoba's 7 percent provincial sales tax plus 7 percent GST.

Feb. 5 Sent January's provincial sales tax and GST to the appropriate authorities.

28 Borrowed $1,000,000 on a 9 percent note payable that calls for annual instalment payments of $100,000 principal plus interest.

July 9 Paid the six-month, 8 percent note at maturity.

Nov. 30 Purchased inventory for $50,000 plus GST, signing a six-month, 10 percent note payable.

Dec. 31 Accrued warranty expense, which is estimated at 3 percent of annual sales of $5,000,000.

31 Accrued interest on all outstanding notes payable. Make a separate interest accrual entry for each note payable.

2003

Feb. 28 Paid the first instalment and interest for one year on the long-term note payable.

May 31 Paid off the 10 percent note plus interest at maturity.

Problem 11-2A   *Identifying contingent liabilities*   *(Obj. 3)*

Winnipeg Fine Cars is the only Rolls Royce and Jaguar dealer in South Winnipeg, and one of the largest imported car dealers in Manitoba. The dealership sells new and used cars and operates a body shop and a service department. Duke Covert, the general manager, is considering changing insurance companies because of a disagreement with Doug Stillwell, agent for the Dominion of Canada Insurance Company. Dominion is doubling Winnipeg Fine Cars' liability insurance cost for the next year. In discussing insurance coverage with you, a trusted business associate, Stillwell brings up the subject of contingent liabilities.

Required

Write a memorandum to inform Winnipeg Fine Cars of specific contingent liabilities arising from the business. In your discussion, define a contingent liability.

Problem 11-3A   *Computing and recording payroll amounts*   *(Obj. 4, 5)*

The partial monthly records of Armstrong Boat Company show the following figures:

Employee Earnings

(a) Regular employee earnings $24,646

(b) Overtime pay . . . .   ?

(c) Total employee earnings . . . .   ?

Deductions and Net Pay

(d) Withheld income tax   6,312

(e) Canada Pension Plan. . . . . . .   ?

(f) Employment Insurance . . . . $ 757

(g) Medical insurance 668

(h) Total deductions 8,831

(i) Net pay 22,728

Accounts Debited

(j) Salary Expense . . . .   ?

(k) Wage Expense 8,573

(l) Sales Commission Expense 2,077

Required

1. Determine the missing amounts on lines (b), (c), (e), and (j).

2. Prepare the general journal entry to record Armstrong Boat Company's payroll for the month. Credit Payrolls Payable for net pay. No explanation is required.

Problem 11-4A   *Computing and recording payroll amounts*   *(Obj. 4, 5)*

Assume that Tammie Jacobs is a Vice-President in the Bank of Nova Scotia's leasing operations. During 2001 she worked for the company all year at a $6,000 monthly salary. She also earned a year-end bonus equal to 10 percent of her salary.

Tammie's federal income tax withheld during 2001 was $1,919.00 per month. Also, there was a one-time federal withholding tax of $2,523.00 on her bonus cheque. She paid $221.00 per month into the Canada Pension Plan until she had paid the maximum of $1,329.90. In addition, Tammie paid $78 per month Employment Insurance through her employer until the maximum of $936.00 had been reached. She had authorized the bank to make the following payroll deductions: life insurance of $40 per month; United Way of Halifax of $35 per month.

The Bank of Nova Scotia incurred Canada Pension Plan expense equal to the amount deducted from Tammie's pay and Employment Insurance expense equal to 1.4 times the amount Tammie paid. In addition, the bank paid dental and drug insurance of $32 per month and pension benefits of 8 percent of her base salary.

Required

1. Compute Tammie Jacob's gross pay, payroll deductions, and net pay for the full year 2001. Round all amounts to the nearest cent.

2. Compute Bank of Nova Scotia's total 2001 payroll cost for Tammie.

3. Prepare the Bank of Nova Scotia's general journal entries to record its expense for
   a. Tammie's total earnings for the year, her payroll deductions, and her net pay. Debit Salary Expense and Executive Bonus Compensation as appropriate for salary and employee benefit expense. Credit liability accounts for the payroll deductions and Cash for net pay.
   b. Employer payroll expenses for Tammie. Credit the appropriate liability accounts.
   c. Fringe benefits provided to Tammie. Credit Health Insurance Payable and Company Pension Payable. Explanations are not required.

Problem 11-5A   *Journalizing, posting, and reporting liabilities*   **(Obj. 1, 2, 3, 4, 5, 7)**

The general ledger of Maxim Systems at June 30, 2001, the end of the company's fiscal year, includes the following account balances before adjusting entries. Parentheses indicate a debit balance.

Notes payable, short-term........	$ 30,000	Employee benefits	
Accounts payable	211,040	payable	_____
Current portion of long-		Estimated vacation pay	
term debt payable	_____	liability.................................	$ 15,240
Interest payable..........................	_____	Sales tax and GST payable.....	7,380
Salary payable............................	_____	Unearned rent revenue...........	12,000
Employee payroll		Long-term debt payable.........	200,000
withholdings payable..........	_____		
Payroll expense payable...........	_____		

The additional data needed to develop the adjusting entries at June 30 are as follows:

a. The $30,000 short-term note payable was issued on January 31. It matures six months from date of issuance and bears interest at 8 percent.

b. The long-term debt is payable in annual instalments of $40,000 with the next instalment due on July 31. On that date, Maxim Systems will also pay one year's interest at 7 percent. Interest was last paid on July 31 of the preceding year.

c. Gross salaries for the last payroll of the fiscal year were $10,088. Of this amount, employee payroll withholdings payable were $2,176, and salary payable was $7,912.

d. Employer payroll expense payable was $1,752, and Maxim's liability for employee health insurance was $2,092.

e. Maxim Systems estimates that vacation pay expense is 4 percent of gross salaries of $500,000 after adjustment for the last payroll of the fiscal year.

f. On February 1, the company collected one year's rent of $12,000 in advance.

g. At June 30, Maxim Systems is the defendant in a $300,000 lawsuit, which the company expects to win. However, the outcome is uncertain.

Required

1. Open T-accounts for the listed accounts, inserting their unadjusted June 30, 2001 balances.

2. Post the June 30, 2001 adjusting entries to the T-accounts opened.

3. Prepare the liability section of Maxim Systems' balance sheet at June 30, 2001.

Problem 11-6A   *Using payroll register; recording a payroll*   **(Obj. 6)**

Assume that the payroll records of a district sales office of Home Builders Company provided the following information for the weekly pay period ended December 21, 2001:

Employee	Hours Worked	Hourly Earnings Rate	Income Tax	Canada Pension	Employment Insurance	United Way	Year-to-date Earnings at the End of the Previous Week
Maria Aristotle	42	$28	$341.10	$ 0	$ 0	$20	$59,800
Louise Dufresne	40	11	54.10	13.13	9.70	2	10,300
James English	47	8	60.90	14.53	10.56	2	23,100
Robert LaFlair	41	22	218.70	0	0	3	49,450

Louise Dufresne and James English work in the office, and Maria Aristotle and Robert LaFlair work in sales. All employees are paid time and a half for hours worked in excess of 40 hours per week. Show computations.

Required

1. Enter the appropriate information in a payroll register similar to Exhibit 11-8.

2. Record the payroll information in the general journal, crediting net pay to Cash.

3. The employer's payroll costs include matching each employee's Canada Pension Plan contribution (employee rate 3.9 percent; maximum $1,329.90) and paying 1.4 times the employee's Employment Insurance premium (employee rate 2.4 percent; maximum $936.00). Record the employer's payroll costs in the general journal.

4. Why was no Canada Pension Plan or Employment Insurance deducted for Aristotle and LaFlair?

Problem 11-7A   *Reporting current liabilities   (Obj. 7)*

Following are six pertinent facts about events during the current year at Pacific Aquatics, a British Columbia company:

a. Sales of $860,000 were covered by Pacific Aquatics' product warranty. At January 1, estimated warranty payable was $16,200. During the year Pacific Aquatics recorded warranty expense of $44,600 and paid warranty claims of $47,200.

b. On September 30, Pacific Aquatics signed a six-month, 9 percent note payable to purchase inventory costing $60,000. The note requires payment of principal and interest at maturity.

c. On October 31, Pacific Aquatics discounted a $100,000 note payable to the Bank of Nova Scotia. The discount rate on the one-year note is 8 percent.

d. On November 30, Pacific Aquatics received rent of $10,200 in advance for a lease on a building. This rent will be earned evenly over three months.

e. December sales totalled $76,000 and Pacific Aquatics collected provincial sales tax of 7 percent plus goods and services tax of 7 percent on these sales. These taxes will be sent to the appropriate authorities early in January.

f. Pacific Aquatics owes $200,000 on a long-term note payable. At December 31, $40,000 of this principal plus 6 percent accrued interest since July 31 are payable within one year.

Required

For each item, indicate the account and the related amount to be reported as a current liability on Pacific Aquatics' December 31 (year end) balance sheet.

Problem 11-8A   *Accounting for current liabilities; making basic payroll entries; reporting current liabilities   (Obj. 1, 2, 5, 7)*

Atlantic Auto Supply of Halifax, Nova Scotia, operates an auto parts supply company with the following information available:

- 15 percent HST is applicable to all purchases and sales.

- Payroll costs—the employer's share of Canada Pension and Employment Insurance are 1.0 times and 1.4 times the employees' share, respectively. The company pays Workers' Compensation of 3 percent and estimates vacation pay at 4 percent of all earnings.

The company prepares quarterly financial statements and had the following transactions for the first three months of 2001:

Jan. 9 Discounted a $50,000, 60-day note payable to the bank using a discount rate of 8 percent.

31 Recorded the month's purchases of inventory, $800,000 (not including the HST). All purchases are on credit. The company uses the periodic inventory system.

31 Recorded the month's sales of $1,350,000 (not including the HST), of which 70 percent were on credit.

31 Recorded and paid the payroll for the month. Gross earnings were $300,000, with deductions of:
- Employee income taxes equal to 20 percent of gross earnings
- Canada Pension Plan deductions equal to 3.9 percent* of gross earnings (employees' share)
- Employment Insurance deductions equal to 2.4 percent of gross earnings (employees' share)
- Union dues deduction equal to $6,000.

Feb. 2 Borrowed $400,000 from the bank by signing a 9 percent, 30-day note payable with the principal and interest payable on the maturity date.

7 Paid the HST for the month of January.

15 Sent a cheque for all payroll deductions and contributions, including the employer's share, to the appropriate authorities.

28 Recorded the month's purchases of inventory, $1,075,000 (not including the HST). All purchases are on credit.

28 Recorded the month's sales of $1,700,000 (not including the HST), of which 80 percent were on credit.

28 Recorded and paid the payroll for the month. Gross earnings were $450,000, with deductions of:
- Employee income taxes equal to 20 percent of gross earnings
- Canada Pension Plan deductions equal to 3.9 percent* of gross earnings (employees' share)
- Employment Insurance deductions equal to 2.4 percent of gross earnings (employees' share)
- Union dues deduction equal to $7,500.

Mar. 4 Paid the note payable from February 2.

7 Paid the HST for the month of February.

10 Paid the note payable from January 9.

12 Discounted a $75,000, 10 percent, 90-day note payable to the bank, receiving the net amount in cash.

15 Sent a cheque for all payroll deductions and contributions, including the employer's share, to the appropriate authorities.

31 Recorded the month's purchases of $1,300,000 (not including the HST). All purchases are on credit.

31 Recorded the month's sales of $2,300,000 (not including the HST), of which 60 percent were on credit.

31 Recorded and paid the payroll for the month. Gross earnings were $600,000, with deductions of:
- Employee income taxes equal to 20 percent of gross earnings
- Canada Pension Plan deductions equal to 3.9 percent* of gross earnings (employees' share)
- Employment Insurance deductions equal to 2.4 percent of gross earnings (employees' share)
- Union dues deduction equal to $12,000.

*For purposes of this calculation, ignore the basic exemption of $3,500.

Required

1. Journalize all of the transactions, and any adjustments that would be required on March 31, 2001 (the end of the first quarter). Round all amounts to the nearest whole dollar. Use days, not months, to calculate interest amounts.

2. Show the current liability section of the balance sheet as of March 31, 2001. Assume there are nil balances in all accounts at January 1, 2001.

Problem 11-9A *Accounting for current liabilities, accounting for contingent liabilities, reporting current liabilities* *(Obj. 1, 2, 3, 7)*

Hibernia Drillers Company produces and sells customized mining equipment in Labrador. The company offers a 60-day, all parts and labour—and an extra 90-day, parts-only—warranty on all of its products. The company had the following transactions in 2003:

Jan.	31	Sales for the month totalled $60,000 (not including HST), of which 70 percent were on credit. The company collects 15 percent HST on all sales and estimates its warranty costs at 4 percent of sales.
	31	Based on last year's property tax assessment, estimated that the property taxes for the year would be $18,000 (1 percent of last year's $1,800,000 assessed value). Recorded the estimated property taxes for the month; credit Estimated Property Taxes Payable.
Feb.	4	Completed repair work for a customer. The parts ($1,000) and labour ($500) were all covered under the warranty.
	6	Sent a cheque for the appropriate HST for the month of January (the company had paid $1,900 of HST on purchases in January).
	28	Recorded the estimated property taxes for the month of February.
	28	Sales for the month totalled $75,000 (not including HST), of which 80 percent were on credit. The company estimates its warranty costs at 4 percent of sales.
Mar.	6	Sent a cheque for the appropriate HST for the month of February (the company had paid $2,300 of HST on purchases in February).
	8	Hibernia Drillers Company received notice that it was being sued by a customer for an accident resulting from the failure of its product. The company's lawyer was reluctant to estimate the likely outcome of the lawsuit, but another customer indicated that a similar case had resulted in a $180,000 settlement.
	15	Completed repair work for a customer. The parts ($3,000) and labour ($900) were all covered under the warranty.
	20	Completed repair work for a customer. The parts ($1,600) were covered by the warranty, but the labour ($700) was not. Payment from the customer is due for the labour in 30 days.
	31	Sales for the month totalled $50,000 (not including HST), of which 75 percent was on credit. The company estimates its warranty costs at 4 percent of sales.
	31	Received the property tax assessment for 2003. It showed the assessed value of the property to be $2,200,000 and a tax rate of 1.2 percent of the assessed value. The company made the appropriate adjustment and used the Property Taxes Payable account.

Required

1. Journalize the above transactions.
2. Show the appropriate financial statement presentation for all liabilities.

Problems (Group B)

Problem 11-1B *Journalizing liability-related transactions* *(Obj. 1, 2)*

The following transactions of Trent Construction Products of Edmonton, Alberta, occurred during 2002 and 2003. The company's year end is December 31.

2002

Feb. 3 Purchased a machine for $51,000, signing a six-month, 8 percent note payable.

28 Recorded the month's sales of $1,265,000, one-third for cash, and two-thirds on credit. All sales amounts are subject to the 7 percent goods and services tax, to be calculated on the sales of $ 1,265,000.

Mar. 7 Sent February's goods and services tax to the Receiver General.

Apr. 30 Borrowed $500,000 with a 9 percent note payable that calls for annual instalment payments of $125,000 principal plus interest.

Aug. 3 Paid the six-month, 8 percent note at maturity.

30 Purchased inventory at a cost of $36,000, signing a 9 percent, six-month note payable for that amount.

Dec. 31 Accrued warranty expense, which is estimated at 1 percent of annual sales of $13,350,000.

31 Accrued interest on all outstanding notes payable. Make a separate interest accrual entry for each note payable.

2003

Feb. 28 Paid off the 9 percent inventory note, plus interest, at maturity.

Apr. 30 Paid the first instalment and interest for one year on the long-term note payable.

Required

Record the transactions in the company's general journal. Explanations are not required.

Problem 11-2B   *Identifying contingent liabilities*   *(Obj. 3)*

King Farms provides riding lessons for children ages 8 through 15. Most students are beginners, and none of them own their own horse. Marg King, the owner of King Farms, uses horses stabled at her farm and owned by the Erbs. Most of the horses are for sale, but the economy has been down for several years and horse sales have been slow. The Erbs are happy that Marg uses their horses in exchange for rooming and boarding them. Because of a recent financial setback, Marg cannot afford insurance. She seeks your advice about her business exposure to liabilities.

Required

Write a memorandum to inform Marg King of specific contingent liabilities that could arise from the business. It will be necessary to define a contingent liability because she is a professional horse trainer, not a businessperson. Propose a way for Marg to limit her exposure to these possible liabilities.

Problem 11-3B   *Computing and reporting payroll amounts*   *(Obj. 4, 5)*

The partial monthly records of Estevan Products show the following figures:

Employee Earnings

(a) Regular earnings.................. ?

(b) Overtime pay........................ $5,109

(c) Total employee earnings..... ?

(g) Dental and drug insurance .... $ 806

(h) Total deductions..................... ?

(i) Net pay 64,813

Deductions and Net Pay

(d) Withheld income tax 16,787

(e) Canada Pension Plan 3,370

(f) Employment Insurance....... 2,109

Accounts Debited

(j) Salary Expense 31,278

(k) Wage Expense........................ ?

(l) Sales Commission Expense .. 27,931

Required

1. Determine the missing amounts on lines (a), (c), (h), and (k).

2. Prepare the general journal entry to record Estevan Products' payroll for the month. Credit Payrolls Payable for net pay. No explanation is required.

Problem 11-4B *Computing and recording payroll amounts* *(Obj. 4, 5)*

Assume that Nicole Leduc is a commercial lender in National Bank's mortgage department in Sherbrooke. During 2001, she worked for the bank all year at a $5,000.00 monthly salary. She also earned a year-end bonus equal to 12 percent of her salary.

Leduc's monthly income tax withholding for 2001 was $1,355.60. Also, she paid a one-time withholding tax of $2,521.70 on her bonus cheque. She paid $183.57 per month towards the Quebec Pension Plan until the maximum ($1,329.90) had been withheld. In addition, Leduc's employer deducted $135.00 per month for Employment Insurance until the maximum ($936.00) had been withheld. Leduc authorized the following deductions: 1 percent per month of her monthly pay to the National Bank's charitable donation fund and $28.00 per month for life insurance.

National Bank incurred Quebec Pension Plan expense equal to the amount deducted from Leduc's pay. Employment Insurance cost the bank 1.4 times the amount deducted from Leduc's pay. In addition, the bank provided Leduc with the following fringe benefits: dental and drug insurance at a cost of $52 per month, and pension benefits to be paid to Leduc upon retirement. The pension contribution is based on her income and was $4,114.00 in 2001.

Required

1. Compute Leduc's gross pay, payroll deductions, and net pay for the full year 2001. Round all amounts to the nearest cent.

2. Compute National Bank's total 2001 payroll cost for Leduc.

3. Prepare National Bank's summary general journal entries to record its expense for
   a. Leduc's total earnings for the year, her payroll deductions and her net pay. Debit Salary Expense and Executive Bonus Compensation as appropriate for sales and employee benefit expense. Credit liability accounts for the payroll deductions and Cash for net pay.
   b. Employer payroll expenses for Leduc. Credit the appropriate liability accounts.
   c. Fringe benefits provided to Leduc. Credit Health Insurance Payable and Company Pension Payable.
   Explanations are not required.

Problem 11-5B *Journalizing, posting, and reporting liabilities* *(Obj. 1, 2, 3, 4, 5, 7)*

Brandon Tire's general ledger at September 30, 2003, the end of the company's fiscal year, includes the following account balances before adjusting entries. Parentheses indicate a debit balance.

Note payable, short-term............	$ 42,000	Employee benefits payable	_____
Accounts payable........................	176,480	Estimated vacation pay	
Current portion of long-		liability....................................	$4,210
term debt payable..................	_____	GST payable	744
Interest payable...........................	_____	Property tax payable.................	2,866
Salary payable	_____	Unearned rent revenue.............	7,800
Employee payroll with-		Long-term debt payable...........	200,000
holding taxes payable	_____		
Payroll costs payable..................	_____		

The additional data needed to develop the adjusting entries at September 30 are as follows:

a. The $42,000 short-term note payable was issued on August 31, 2003, matures one year from date of issuance, and bears interest at 8 percent.

b. The long-term debt is payable in annual instalments of $50,000, with the next instalment due on January 31, 2004. On that date, Brandon Tire will also pay one year's interest at 6.5 percent. Interest was last paid on January 31, 2003.

c. Gross salaries for the last payroll of the fiscal year were $8,638. Of this amount, employee withholdings were $1,916, and salary payable was $6,722.

d. Employer payroll costs were $1,510, and Brandon Tire's liability for employee life insurance was $208.

e. Brandon Tire estimates that vacation pay is 4 percent of gross salaries of $108,000 after adjustment for the last payroll of the fiscal year.

f. On August 1, 2003, the company collected six months' rent of $7,800 in advance.

g. At June 30, 2003, Brandon Tire is the defendant in a $200,000 lawsuit, which the company expects to win. However, the outcome is uncertain.

Required

1. Open T-accounts for the listed accounts, inserting their unadjusted September 30, 2003 balances.

2. Post the September 30, 2003 adjusting entries to the accounts opened.

3. Prepare the liability section of Brandon Tire's balance sheet at September 30, 2003.

4. Is there a contingent liability? If yes, write the note and indicate where it should appear.

Problem 11-6B *Using a payroll register; recording a payroll* *(Obj. 6)*

Assume that payroll records of a branch of Purolator Courier provided the following information for the weekly pay period ended December 18, 2001:

Employee	Hours Worked	40-Hour Weekly Earnings	Income Tax	Canada Pension	Employ- ment Insurance	United Way	Year-to-date Earnings at the End of the Previous Week
Tina Albany	43	$400	$ 59.95	$14.73	$10.68	$3	$17,060.00
Maria Dixon	46	480	70.75	20.31	14.11	3	25,300.00
Karol Stastny	41	800	177.90	0	0	8	45,400.00
David Tsui	40	320	41.00	9.85	7.68	2	7,842.00

Tina Albany and David Tsui work in the office, and Maria Dixon and Karol Stastny are drivers. All employees are paid time and a half for hours worked in excess of 40 hours per week. Show computations.

Required

1. Enter the appropriate information in a payroll register similar to Exhibit 11-8.

2. Record the payroll information in the general journal, crediting net pay to Cash.

3. The employer's payroll costs are calculated by matching the employee's Canada Pension Plan contribution (employee rate 3.9 percent; maximum $1,329.90) and paying 1.4 times the employee's Employment Insurance premium (employee rate 2.4 percent; maximum $936.00). Record the employer's payroll costs in the general journal.

4. Why is no Canada Pension Plan or Employment Insurance deducted for Stastny?

Problem 11-7B *Reporting current liabilities* *(Obj. 7)*

Following are six pertinent facts about events during the year at Neil Tools Manufacturing, a New Brunswick company:

a. On August 31, Neil Tools Manufacturing signed a six-month, 7 percent note payable to purchase a machine costing $100,000. The note requires payment of principal and interest at maturity.

b. Sales of $1,818,000 were covered by Neil Tools' product warranty. At January 1, estimated warranty payable was $22,600. During the year, Neil Tools recorded warranty expense of $55,800 and paid warranty claims of $60,200.

c. On October 31, Neil Tools received rent of $4,800 in advance for a lease on a building. This rent will be earned evenly over four months.

d. On November 30, Neil Tools discounted a $20,000 note payable to St. Lawrence Trust. The discount rate on the one-year note is 8 percent.

e. December sales totalled $208,000 and Neil Tools collected harmonized sales taxes of 15 percent on these sales. This amount will be sent to the appropriate authority early in January.

f. Neil Tools owes $150,000 on a long-term note payable. At December 31, 6 percent interest for the year plus $50,000 of this principal are payable within one year.

Required

For each item, indicate the account and the related amount to be reported as a current liability on Neil Tools Manufacturing's December 31 (year end) balance sheet.

Problem 11-8B   *Accounting for current liabilities; making basic payroll entries; reporting current liabilities* **(Obj. 1, 2, 5, 7)**

Severn Boats, an Alberta company, is a marine parts supply company with the following information available:

- Goods and Services Tax: 7 percent GST is applicable to all purchases and sales.
- Employer Payroll Costs: the employer's share of Canada Pension and Employment Insurance is 1.0 times and 1.4 times the employees' share respectively. The company pays Workers' Compensation of 3 percent and estimates vacation pay at 4 percent of all earnings.

The company prepares quarterly financial statements and had the following transactions for the first three months of 2001:

Jan.	9	Discounted a $30,000, 60-day note payable to the bank, using a discount rate of 12 percent.
	31	Recorded the month's purchases of inventory, $225,000 (not including the GST). All purchases are on credit. The company uses the periodic inventory system.
	31	Recorded the month's sales of $375,000 (not including the GST), of which 80 percent were on credit.
	31	Recorded and paid the payroll for the month. Gross earnings were $105,000, with deductions of:

- Employee income taxes equal to 15 percent of gross earnings
- Canada Pension Plan deductions equal to 3.9 percent* of gross earnings (employees' share)
- Employment Insurance deductions equal to 2.4 percent of gross earnings (employees' share)
- Union dues deduction equal to $2,100.

Feb.	2	Borrowed $90,000 from the bank by signing a 10 percent, 30-day note payable with the principal and interest payable on the maturity date.
	7	Paid the GST for the month of January.
	15	Sent a cheque for all payroll deductions and contributions, including the employer's share, to the appropriate authorities.
	28	Recorded the month's purchases of inventory, $270,000 (not including the GST). All purchases are on credit.
	28	Recorded the month's sales of $420,000 (not including the GST), of which 80 percent were on credit.
	28	Recorded and paid the payroll for the month. Gross earnings were $120,000, with deductions of:

- Employee income taxes equal to 15 percent of gross earnings
- Canada Pension Plan deductions equal to 3.9 percent* of gross earnings (employees' share)

- Employment Insurance deductions equal to 2.4 percent of gross earnings (employees' share)
- Union dues deduction equal to $2,400.

Mar. 4 Paid the note payable from February 2.

7 Paid the GST for the month of February.

10 Paid the note payable from January 9.

12 Discounted a $37,500, 8 percent, 90-day note payable to the bank, receiving the net amount in cash.

15 Sent a cheque for all payroll deductions and contributions, including the employer's share, to the appropriate authorities.

31 Recorded the month's purchases of inventory, $420,000 (not including the GST). All purchases are on credit.

31 Recorded the month's sales of $585,000 (not including the GST), of which 60 percent were on credit.

31 Recorded and paid the payroll for the month. Gross earnings were $165,000, with deductions of:
- Employee income taxes equal to 15 percent of gross earnings
- Canada Pension Plan deductions equal to 3.9 percent* of gross earnings (employees' share)
- Employment Insurance deductions equal to 2.4 percent of gross earnings (employees' share)
- Union dues deduction equal to $3,150.

*For purposes of this calculation, ignore the basic exemption of $3,500.

Required

1. Journalize all of the transactions, and any adjustments that would be required on March 30, 2001 (the end of the first quarter). Round all amounts to the nearest whole dollar. Use days, not months, to calculate interest amounts.

2. Show the current liability section of the balance sheet as of March 30, 2001. Assume there are nil balances in all accounts at January 1, 2001.

Problem 11-9B *Accounting for current liabilities; accounting for contingent liabilities; reporting current liabilities* *(Obj. 1, 2, 3, 7)*

McLean Farm Equipment produces and sells customized farm equipment in Alberta. The company offers a 60-day, all parts and labour—and an extra 90-day, parts-only—warranty on all of its products. The company had the following transactions in 2003:

Jan. 31 Sales for the month totalled $270,000 (not including GST), of which 75 percent were on credit. The company collects 7 percent GST on all sales and estimates its warranty costs at 5 percent of sales.

31 Based on last year's property tax assessment, estimated that the property taxes for the year would be $24,000 (1 percent of last year's $2,400,000 assessed value). Recorded the estimated property taxes for the month; credit Estimated Property Taxes Payable.

Feb. 4 Completed repair work for a customer. The parts ($4,500) and labour ($2,100) were all covered under the warranty.

6 Remitted the appropriate GST for the month of January (the company had paid $10,200 GST on purchases in January).

28 Recorded the estimated property taxes for the month of February.

28 Sales for the month totalled $240,000 (not including GST), of which 70 percent were on credit. The company estimates its warranty costs at 4 percent of sales.

Mar. 6 Remitted the appropriate GST for the month of February (the company had paid $8,100 GST on purchases in February).

8 McLean Farm Equipment received notice that it was being sued by a customer for an accident resulting from the failure of its product. The company's lawyer was reluctant to estimate the likely outcome of the lawsuit, but another customer indicated that a similar case had resulted in a $180,000 settlement.

15 Completed repair work for a customer. The parts ($5,700) and labour ($1,200) were all covered under the warranty.

Mar. 20 Completed repair work for a customer. The parts ($5,400) were covered by the warranty, but the labour ($1,500) was not. Payment for the labour is due from the customer in 30 days.

31 Sales for the month totalled $210,000 (not including GST), of which 80 percent was on credit. The company estimates its warranty costs at 4 percent of sales.

31 Received the property tax assessment for 2003. It showed the assessed value of the property to be $2,600,000 and a tax rate of 1.2 percent of the assessed value. The company made the appropriate adjustment and used the Property Taxes Payable account.

Required

1. Journalize the above transactions.
2. Show the appropriate financial statement presentation for all liabilities.

Challenge Problems

Problem 11-1C   *Verifying the completeness of liabilities (Obj. 1)*

Public accounting firms acting as auditors of companies are very careful to ensure that all of the company's accounts payable are recorded in the proper period. In other words, they want to ensure that all payables relating to the year under review are recorded as a liability at year end.

Required

Explain why you think auditors are so concerned that all payables owing at year end be properly recorded in the right period.

Problem 11-2C   *Accounting for estimated liabilities (Obj. 1)*

There is no consensus on the proper amount for airlines to record with respect to frequent-flier expense. Two alternative scenarios are presented below:

a. The person claiming a ticket under the frequent-flier program would use a seat that otherwise would be empty.

b. The person claiming a ticket under the frequent-flier program would use a seat that otherwise would be used by a full-fare-paying passenger.

Required

1. Recommend to an airline how much it should record as a liability under each of the scenarios. Which amount would you suggest the airline record since it doesn't know which will occur?

2. Write a response to the person who states that, since it is not known if the frequent-flier miles will be used, the liability is contingent and need not be expensed until the passenger actually uses the frequent-flier miles. This person suggests that because the liability is contingent, not actual, it should be disclosed in the notes.

Extending Your Knowledge

Decision Problem

Identifying internal control weaknesses and their solution   (Obj. 6)

Matthews Custom Homes is a large home-building business in Saskatoon, Saskatchewan. The owner is Ed Matthews, who oversees all company operations. He employs 15 work crews, each made up of 6 to 10 members. Construction supervisors, who report directly to Matthews, lead the crews. Most supervisors are long-time employees, so Matthews trusts them to a great degree. The company's office staff consists of an accountant and an office manager.

Because employee turnover is rapid in the construction industry, supervisors hire and terminate their own crew members. Supervisors notify the office of all personnel changes. Also, supervisors forward to the office the employee TD1 forms, which the crew members fill out to claim tax-withholding exemptions. Each Thursday the supervisors submit weekly time sheets for their crews, and the accountant prepares the payroll. At noon on Friday the supervisors come to the office to get paycheques for distribution to the workers at 5 p.m.

Matthews Custom Homes' accountant prepares the payroll, including the payroll cheques, which are written on a single payroll bank account. Ed Matthews signs all payroll cheques after matching the employee name to the time sheets submitted by the supervisor. Often the construction workers wait several days to cash their paycheques. To verify that each construction worker is a bona fide employee, the accountant matches the employee's endorsement signature on the back of the cancelled payroll cheque with the signature on that employee's TD1 form.

Required

1. List one *efficiency* weakness in Matthews Custom Homes' payroll accounting system. How can the business correct this weakness?
2. Identify one way that a supervisor can defraud Matthews Custom Homes under the present system.
3. Discuss a control feature Matthews Custom Homes can use to *safeguard* against the fraud you identified in Requirement 2.

Financial Statement Problem

Current and contingent liabilities   *(Obj. 1, 2, 3)*

Details about a company's current and contingent liabilities appear in a number of places in the annual report. Use the Intrawest Corporation financial statements in Appendix A to answer the following questions.

1. Give the breakdown of Intrawest's current liabilities at June 30, 2000. Give the July 2000 entry to record the payment of accounts payable (amounts payable) and accrued liabilities at June 30, 2000.
2. How much was Intrawest's long-term debt and capital leases at June 30, 2000? Of this amount, how much was due in one year? Where did you find information about the composition of the long-term debt and capital leases ? When is the balance of the long-term debt and capital leases due?
3. Does Intrawest have any commitments coming due in the fiscal year ending in 2001? If so, where did you find information about them? Why are commitments not shown on the balance sheet as a liability?
4. Does Intrawest Corporation have any contingent liabilities at June 30, 2000? How do you know?

Comprehensive Problem

for Part Two

Comparing Two Businesses

Suppose you are the successful owner of an Internet service provider. You recently sold the business to a large company. Now you are ready to invest in a small resort property. Several locations look promising: Jekyll Island, Nova Scotia; Long Beach, Vancouver Island; and Kingsmere, Quebec. Each place has its appeal, but Jekyll Island wins out. The main allure is that prices there are low. Two small resorts are available. The property owners provide the following data:

	Jekyll Island Resort	Ocean Hideaway
Cash	$ 34,100	$ 63,800
Accounts receivable	20,500	18,300
Inventory	74,200	68,400
Land	270,600	669,200
Buildings	1,800,000	1,960,000
Accumulated amortization—buildings	(105,000)	(822,600)
Furniture and fixtures	750,000	933,000
Accumulated amortization— furniture and fixtures	(225,000)	(535,300)
Total assets	$2,619,400	$2,354,800
Total liabilities	$1,124,300	$1,008,500
Owner's equity	1,495,100	1,346,300
Total liabilities and owner's equity	$2,619,400	$2,354,800

Income statements for the last three years report total net income of $531,000 for Jekyll Island Resort and $283,000 for Ocean Hideaway.

Inventories   Jekyll Island Resort Ltd. uses the FIFO inventory method, and Ocean Hideaway uses the LIFO method. If Jekyll Island had used LIFO, its reported inventory would have been $7,000 lower. If Ocean Hideaway had used FIFO, its reported inventory would have been $6,000 higher. Three years ago there was little difference between LIFO and FIFO amounts for either company.

Capital Assets   Jekyll Island Resort uses the straight-line amortization method and an estimated useful life of 30 years for buildings and ten years for furniture and fixtures. Estimated residual values are $400,000 for buildings, and $0 for furniture and fixtures. Jekyll Island Resort's buildings and furniture and fixtures are three years old.

Ocean Hideaway uses the double-declining-balance method and amortizes buildings over 30 years with an estimated residual value of $460,000. The furniture and fixtures, now three years old, are being amortized over ten years with an estimated residual value of $85,000.

Accounts Receivable   Jekyll Island Resorts uses the direct write-off method for uncollectibles. Ocean Hideaway uses the allowance method. The Jekyll Island Resort owner estimates that $2,000 of the company's receivables are doubtful. Prior to the current year, uncollectibles were insignificant. Ocean Hideaway's receivables are already reported at net realizable value.

Required

1. Puzzled at first by how to compare the two resorts, you decide to convert Jekyll Island Resort's balance sheet to the accounting methods and the estimated useful lives used by Ocean Hideaway. Round all amortization amounts to the near-

est $100. The necessary revisions will not affect Jekyll Island Resort's total liabilities.

2. Convert Jekyll Island Resort's total net income for the last three years to reflect the accounting methods used by Ocean Hideaway. Round all amortization amounts to the nearest $100.

3. Compare the two resorts' finances after you have revised Jekyll Island Resort's figures, with the two resorts' finances beforehand. Which resort looked better at the outset? Which resort looks better when they are placed on equal footing?

Krave's Candy Co.: The Problems Faced by New and Growing Companies

Two boyhood friends, Chris Emery and Larry Finson, using a recipe developed by Chris's grandmother, have gone into the candy business in Winnipeg. The candy, which they call "Clodhoppers," is a Christmas candy, a seasonal purchase in competition with Turtles®, Toffifee®, and other Christmas candies.

The two partners started the business in 1995. They hope people will crave their candy and that is how the name, Krave's Candy Co., was developed.

The story on the videos begins in December 1998. The company's sales are $650,000 and its customers include Wal-Mart, Safeway, and Shoppers Drug Mart. The product has new eye-catching packaging. Krave's Candy Co. has just been voted the fastest-growing business in Manitoba; the company's business has grown by 938 percent in three years. But Chris and Larry realize that they must continue to grow if they are to be successful.

We learn in January 1999 that Krave's has a common problem—unsold inventory. The company manufactured 60,000 boxes of candy and still has 19,000 boxes on hand. The partners realize they must sell this inventory. In addition, they wish to increase their sales. Their goal is sales of $1,000,000 for 1999.

The two partners in Krave's use the spring and summer to develop sales for the following holiday season. Their efforts have paid off; they have received a significant re-order from Wal-Mart, and Zellers has elected to place an order for Christmas 1999. With orders in hand by April 1999 of $500,000, the partners seem well on their way to their goal. There is one problem—they need money to produce the product to deliver on the purchase commitments already received.

The bank is asking for more information and appears to be reluctant to lend more money. The partners decide to ask their suppliers to accept 120 days delay in being paid for raw materials.

Chris and Larry are successful in borrowing money from their families and mortgaging their houses. Their major supplier, Custom Food Processors, who sells them the basic ingredient for "Clodhoppers," offers to give Krave's financial assistance for 51 percent of the company's stock. A Manitoba venture capitalist (a company that advances money to start-up companies in exchange for shares), also agrees to provide funding in exchange for an interest in the company.

Projected sales are now $1,200,000. The company needs money for new equipment to produce the volume of product needed to meet the orders Chris and Larry have generate.

The new equipment is purchased and production is expanded to meet the expanded sales commitments. Chris and Larry are developing new products to spread Krave's business over the entire year and reduce the seasonality of "Clodhoppers." Their goal is now annual sales of $5,000,000. The company is on its way.

QUESTIONS

1. Why would inventory on hand at December 1998 be a problem?

2. Why would the company's suppliers not want to give the company more time to pay?

3. Why would the company gain from delaying payment to its suppliers?

4. Why do you think the partners are reluctant to give up part of the company in exchange for funding?

Turtles is a registered trademark of Société des Produits Nestlé S.A., Vevey, Switzerland. Toffifee is a registered trademark of August Storck KG, Germany

Appendix A

GREAT PLAYGROUNDS OF THE WESTERN WORLD

INTRAWEST ANNUAL REPORT 2000

CORPORATE PROFILE

Intrawest Corporation is the leading developer and operator of village-centered destination resorts across North America. It is redefining the resort world with its ten mountain resorts, one warm-weather resort, eighteen golf courses, a premier vacation ownership business—Club Intrawest—and five world-class resort villages at other locations, including one in France. In addition, Intrawest has a significant investment in Compagnie des Alpes, the largest ski company in the world in terms of skier visits, and Alpine Helicopters, owner of the largest heli-skiing operation in the world. The company has expertise in all aspects of resort living including lodging, food and beverage, themed retail, animated operations and real estate development. Its 16,000 employees are uniquely positioned to service the company's 6.2 million skier visits and 546,000 golf rounds, providing the best possible resort experience again and again. Intrawest Corporation's shares are listed on the New York (IDR) and Toronto (ITW) stock exchanges. The company is headquartered in Vancouver, British Columbia.

FIVE-YEAR HISTORICAL REVIEW

Years ended June 30	2000	1999	1998	1997	1996
Consolidated Operations		(in millions of U.S. dollars except per share amount			
Revenue					
Resort operations	$ 452.1	$ 382.5	$ 259.1	$ 192.7	$ 12:
Real estate (sales and rental)	348.4	221.2	162.8	88.8	8:
Other	14.8	5.9	2.5	3.2	⌐
Total revenue	815.3	609.6	424.4	284.7	20!
Expenses					
Resort operations	358.5	300.9	200.5	143.3	9:
Real estate costs	285.5	177.4	130.9	71.7	7(
Interest	35.2	24.8	16.1	15.3	1(
Depreciation and amortization	51.4	40.2	26.8	19.0	1:
General, administrative and other	32.6	27.7	19.8	14.7	!
Total expenses	763.2	571.0	394.1	264.0	19:
Income from continuing operations	$ 52.1	$ 38.6	$ 30.3	$ 20.7	$ 1⌐
Income per share from continuing operations	$ 1.20	$ 0.96	$ 0.88	$ 0.74	$ 0.
Weighted average number of shares (in thousands)	43,362	40,237	34,486	27,809	23,0
Total Company EBITDA*	$ 165.4	$ 128.8	$ 91.4	$ 64.8	$ 4:
Consolidated Balance Sheets					
Assets					
Resort operations	$ 784.7	$ 699.0	$ 471.5	$ 294.6	$ 18(
Properties – resort	569.3	460.9	296.9	233.6	15:
– discontinued operations	9.6	20.6	27.2	55.2	7!
Other	353.8	311.7	203.6	211.9	13!
Total assets	$ 1,717.4	$ 1,492.2	$ 999.2	$ 795.3	$ 55:
Liabilities and shareholders' equity					

KEY FINANCIAL OBJECTIVES

Over the past few years the Company has been acquiring and expanding its portfolio of assets and the focus has now changed from building the platform for future growth, to improving returns on the existing asset base. Fiscal 2000 was a transition year. Only one small acquisition was made – Swaneset, a golf and country club in metropolitan Vancouver. Capital expenditures were reduced by approximately 18% from last year and they will decline further in the future. On the real estate side of the business, the marketability of all of the Company's properties has now been proven with successful first-time sales launches during the year at Blue Mountain, Sandestin and Squaw Valley. The pace of investment in infrastructure is expected to decline over the next 24 months as the villages at the Company's resorts reach greater maturity.

The Company's key financial objectives over the next few years are clearly defined.

- Maintain earnings per share growth of at least 20% per annum.

- As resort villages are built out, increase operating profit margins as Intrawest's resort model takes effect.

- Focus on increasing free cash flow and maximizing returns on capital.

- Combine the capital of other parties with in-house expertise to carry out new business opportunities.

- Maintain a conservative risk profile in both the operations and real estate businesses.

- Sell non-core assets and redeploy capital in more profitable or higher-returning businesses.

CHANGE IN REPORTING CURRENCY

At the beginning of fiscal 2000, the Company changed its reporting currency from Canadian to U.S. dollars. This change was made in response to the recent growth in the Company's U.S. asset and revenue base (more than 60% of both assets and revenue was expected to be U.S.-based in fiscal 2000), the Company's increasing profile in the U.S. investment community and the Company's desire to gain closer comparability with other publicly traded leisure companies. **Unless otherwise stated, all dollar amounts in this Management's Discussion and Analysis and in the Consolidated Financial Statements that follow it are in U.S. dollars.**

OPERATING HIGHLIGHTS

The operating highlights for the year include:

- A 33.7% increase in total revenue from $609.6 million to $815.3 million, with ski and resort revenue increasing 18.2% and real estate sales revenue increasing 58.2%.

- A 34.9% increase in income from continuing operations to $52.1 million and a 25.0% increase in income per share from continuing operations to $1.20. The per share amount reflects a 7.8% increase in the weighted average number of shares outstanding in 2000.

- A 14.8% increase in operating profit from ski and resort operations and a 44.3% increase in operating profit from real estate sales.

- A 28.4% increase in Total Company EBITDA from $128.8 million to $165.4 million. Total Company EBITDA is computed as income before interest (including previously capitalized interest in real estate cost of sales), taxes, non-controlling interest, depreciation and amortization. It is not a term that has an established meaning under generally accepted accounting principles; however, management believes it is an important measure of operating performance.

REVIEW OF SKI AND RESORT OPERATIONS

The following table highlights the results of the ski and resort operations business.

	2000	1999	Change
Skier visits[1]	5,694,000	5,791,000	-1.7%
Revenue ($millions)	452.1	382.5	18.2%
EBITDA ($millions)	93.7	81.6	14.8%
Margin	20.7%	21.3%	

(1) All resorts are at 100% except Mammoth at 59% and Blue Mountain at 50%.

Revenue from ski and resort operations increased 18.2% from $382.5 million in 1999 to $452.1 million in 2000. Revenue from mountain resorts increased 16.0% from $340.2 million to $394.6 million while revenue from warm-weather resorts increased 35.9% from $42.3 million to $57.5 million.

Mountain resorts

The $54.4 million increase in mountain resort revenue was due to:

	($millions)
Timing of acquisitions in 1999	17.2
Reduction in skier visits	(7.6)
Increase in revenue per skier visit	36.5
Increase in non-skier visit revenue	8.3
	54.4

The Company acquired its 50% interest in Blue Mountain and its 45% interest in Alpine in the third quarter of 1999. Intrawest Vacations was purchased in the fourth quarter of 1999 and contributed no revenue in that year. The impact of including a full year of revenue for these businesses in 2000 versus a partial year of revenue in 1999 was $17.2 million.

Skier visits decreased 1.7% from 5,791,000 in 1999 to 5,694,000 in 2000. Skier visits declined 0.4% at the Company's Canadian resorts and 3.3% at its U.S. resorts. Weaker than expected millennium bookings and fears over possible repercussions from the Y2K problem impacted business across the entire travel sector during the important Christmas/New Year period and into January. The 1999/2000 winter season was also generally a difficult one for weather. In the northeast, the season started slowly and ended prematurely due to unusually warm weather, and the late timing of Easter impacted skier visits further in that region. Lack of snow at the start of the season in Colorado and California reduced skier visits at Copper and Mammoth. Mammoth had purchased skier visit insurance and collected $0.7 million under the policy. Skier visits at Copper were also impacted by construction of the central four buildings in the new village. Only Whistler/Blackcomb, Panorama and Snowshoe showed an increase in skier visits over 1999 with each resort registering all-time record skier visits. The impact of the reduction in skier visits in 2000 was estimated to decrease mountain resort revenue by $7.6 million.

Revenue per skier visit increased 12.1% from $51.89 in 1999 to $58.19 in 2000. Revenue per skier visit increased at every one of the Company's resorts ranging from 7% at Copper, Snowshoe and Mammoth to 32% at Mountain Creek. Revenue per skier visit is a function of ticket prices and ticket yields, and revenue from non-ticket sources includes retail

13

and rental stores, lodging, ski school and food services. Ticket yields reflect the mix of ticket types (e.g., adult, child, season pass and group), the proportion of day versus destination visitors (destination visitors tend to be less price sensitive), and the amount of discounting of full-price tickets. Revenue per visit from non-ticket sources is also influenced by the mix of day versus destination visitors, the affluence of the visitor base, and the quantity and type of amenities and services offered at the resort.

The Company's strategy at all of its resorts is to offer the highest quality product within its market area at a premium ticket price. In addition, the strong competitive position of each of the Company's resorts, created by the resort villages and the significant capital investments that have been made over the past few years, helps to attract destination visitors and reduces reliance on discounts to attract local visitors in favor of committed regional visitors. During 2000 the Company moved to a variable pricing policy at most of its resorts, adjusting ticket prices depending on peak or non-peak season and holidays. The effective ticket price (i.e., total ticket revenue divided by total skier visits) across all of the Company's resorts was 11.1% higher in 2000 than in 1999. On average, ticket prices increased by 3.3% and the balance of the increase in effective ticket price in 2000 was due to ticket mix and yield management. The impact of these factors was to increase revenue by $15.8 million.

Revenue per visit from non-ticket sources increased 13.3% in 2000. The strongest performance was in retail and rental, which increased 18.2% mainly because of new or renovated stores at Whistler/Blackcomb (including the acquisition of two Westbeach stores), Tremblant and Snowshoe. Lodging and property management revenue per visit increased 15.6% due both to growth in the inventory of managed properties and to yield improvements. The construction completion of several condo-hotel properties in advance of the ski season increased the available room inventory by 9.3% and revenue per available room (REVPAR)

increased by 7.6% across the mountain resorts. Revenue per visit from food and beverage increased 8.2% with improvements at Whistler/Blackcomb, Mountain Creek and Mammoth being partially offset by declines at Tremblant and Snowshoe. The overall impact of increases in revenue per visit from non-ticket sources was to increase revenue by $20.7 million.

For the purposes of this analysis, non-skier visit revenue comprises revenue from golf and other summer activities and revenue from businesses such as Alpine and Breeze which do not have skier visits. During 2000 the Company opened new golf courses at Mammoth and Panorama and revenue from existing mountain resort courses increased 20.4% compared with 1999. Revenue from other summer activities also increased at each of the mountain resorts as the Company's strategy to grow its revenue through all four seasons began to show positive results. Alpine experienced a strong winter season with year-over-year revenue growth of 11.1% while revenue at Breeze was approximately the same in 2000 as 1999 due primarily to weather factors in Colorado and to a significant decline in destination visitors to that state. Overall non-skier visit revenue increased by $8.3 million in 2000.

Warm-weather resorts

The $15.2 million increase in warm-weather resort revenue in 2000 was due to the acquisition of Swaneset, which added $3.9 million of revenue, and to increased revenue at both Sandestin and Raven. Revenue at Sandestin increased 32.9% with significant improvements in lodging, golf, and food and beverage revenue. A re-focused marketing program initiated last year resulted in a 16.5% increase in occupied room nights in 2000. This higher occupancy and the completion of the fourth golf course during the year generated a 58.9% increase in golf revenue. Revenue at Raven increased 6.9% in 2000. The number of rounds played was approximately the same in both years, with revenue per round higher in 2000.

The factors described above changed the composition of ski and resort operations revenue as follows:

	2000 Revenue (millions)	2000 Proportion (%)	1999 Revenue (millions)	1999 Proportion (%)	Increase in Revenue (millions)	Percentage Increase (%)
Mountain operations	$ 177.1	39.2	$ 155.6	40.7	$ 21.5	13.8
Retail and rental shops	72.8	16.1	65.0	17.0	7.8	12.0
Food and beverage	60.1	13.3	54.8	14.3	5.3	9.7
Lodging and property management	53.5	11.8	38.4	10.0	15.1	39.3
Ski school	25.8	5.7	22.2	5.8	3.6	16.2
Golf	30.9	6.8	21.3	5.6	9.6	45.1
Other	31.9	7.1	25.2	6.6	6.7	26.6
	$ 452.1	100.0	$ 382.5	100.0	$ 69.6	18.2

14

Since 1995 the proportion of revenue from mountain operations (i.e. lift tickets and heli-skiing) has fallen from 52.6% to 39.2%. This trend is likely to continue as the resort villages are built out, expanding the inventory of lodging units and changing the customer mix in favor of destination visitors who spend more on retail and rental, ski school, and food and beverage.

Ski and resort operations expenses increased from $300.9 million in 1999 to $358.5 million in 2000, in line with the increase in ski and resort operations revenue. EBITDA from ski and resort operations increased 14.8% from $81.6 million in 1999 to $93.7 million in 2000. The EBITDA margin was 20.7% in 2000 compared with 21.3% in 1999. The margin in 2000 was impacted by the weaker-than-expected millennium bookings and by the difficult weather conditions, which necessitated constant rebuilding of the snow base. Not only were visits reduced during the normally high-margin Christmas period, but the mix of visits was changed with relatively fewer destination visitors because people were not travelling. A significant decline in destination visitors to Colorado (mainly because of below-average snow conditions for the past two seasons) reduced EBITDA from Breeze. The moderate decline in EBITDA margin at the mountain resorts was partially offset by an increased margin at the warm-weather resorts from 13.2% in 1999 to 16.0% in 2000. The Company expects margins going forward to increase at both the mountain resorts and the warm-weather resorts as its villages mature, driving higher mid-week destination visits, and as it takes further advantage of economies of scale.

REVIEW OF RESORT REAL ESTATE OPERATIONS

The following table highlights the results of the real estate business.

	2000	1999	Change
Units delivered	1,317	1,126	17.0%
Revenue ($millions)	341.5	215.9	58.2%
Operating profit ($millions)	59.6	41.3	44.3%
Margin	17.5%	19.1%	

Revenue from the sale of real estate increased 58.2% from $215.9 million in 1999 to $341.5 million in 2000. The increase was due to volume and price increases in the traditional real estate business and to significantly higher revenue in the resort club (timeshare) business. Real estate revenue increased 8.0% at the Company's Canadian resorts and 84.6% at its U.S. resorts.

A total of 443 units were delivered at the Company's Canadian resorts in 2000 compared with 496 units last year. The average price per unit increased 20.9% from Cdn.$237,000 in 1999 to Cdn.$286,000 in 2000 due to the mix of resorts and product types. Comparatively more units were delivered at higher-priced Whistler/Blackcomb and comparatively less at Tremblant and Panorama in 2000 than in 1999. Furthermore the Company delivered more than twice as many townhouses and 43% fewer condo-hotel units in 2000 than in 1999. Condo-hotel units typically have a higher price per square foot than townhouses but a lower absolute price because of their smaller size.

The Company delivered 874 units at its U.S. resorts in 2000 compared with 630 units in 1999. Solitude and Three Peaks closed units for the first time in 2000 and significantly more units were closed at Copper and Mammoth than in 1999. The average price per unit was $285,000 in 2000 (after adjusting the number of units for the impact of joint ventures at Keystone and Sandestin), up from $267,000 in 1999. The mix of product types at U.S. resorts was similar in 2000 and 1999, approximately 70% condo-hotel, 10% townhouse and 20% single-family lots.

The Resort Club generated $29.2 million in sales revenue in 2000, up 87.2% from $15.6 million in 1999. The opening of the new club location at Palm Desert, California accounted for 22.6% of this increase. The balance of the increase was attributable to a 42.7% increase in the number of points sold at the Blackcomb and Tremblant club locations and two price increases during the year totaling approximately 10%. The significant improvement in sales at Blackcomb and Tremblant was due to the implementation of a variable pricing policy and changes within the sales and marketing organization. These changes included the establishment of a 100-seat call centre in Vancouver and a special team to handle referral and add-on point sales to existing members. Revenue from member referrals and add-on points increased 40% in 2000 to $2.6 million reflecting high member satisfaction and growing acceptance of the Resort Club's unique points system.

Standard real estate accounting practice requires that all costs in connection with the development of real estate be capitalized to properties under development and then expensed in the period when the properties are delivered and the revenue is recognized. Such costs include general and administrative costs of personnel directly involved in the development, construction and sale of real estate as well as interest on specific real estate debt and on the portion of general corporate debt used to fund real estate development expenditures. The amount of capitalized real estate costs has increased proportionately with the ramp-up in real estate production from approximately 500 units per year in 1996 to approximately 1,500 in 2000.

Operating profit from resort real estate sales increased 44.3% from $41.3 million in 1999 to $59.6 million in 2000. The profit margin was 17.5% in 2000 compared with 19.1% in 1999. The decline in margin in 2000 was due mainly to the mix of resorts and particularly the maturity of their villages. Normally margins are lower in the early years of development of a resort. There are a number of reasons for this.

- Land and infrastructure costs are estimated for the entire build-out of a resort and the resulting total cost is allocated to projects on the basis of buildable area. The land and infrastructure cost per buildable square foot is therefore relatively fixed for all the developable units at a resort. Since sales prices escalate over time, margins rise as villages mature.

- As the resort is built out, supply and demand factors tend to increase sales prices faster than project costs. In addition, enhancements to the resort during build-out (e.g., capital improvements on the mountain or reaching critical mass in the village) will increase demand for (and therefore the prices of) real estate.

Intrawest's historical real estate experience at Blackcomb, Tremblant and Keystone confirms this trend. At Tremblant, for example, margins realized on the first two condo-hotel projects built in the village in 1993 and 1994 were approximately half the margins on later and current condo-hotel projects.

The first condo-hotel projects in the new villages at Copper, Mammoth and Solitude completed construction during 2000. The villages at each of these resorts are in the early stage of development. Sales at these resorts accounted for 32.4% of the Company's total real estate sales in 2000 (compared with 6.6% in 1999) and the margin on these sales was 14.2%. This compares with an average margin of 22.4% in 2000 at Whistler/Blackcomb, Tremblant and Keystone.

As of August 31, 2000, the Company had pre-sold 1,158 units for approximately $390 million which it expects to close in fiscal 2001 and a further 425 units for approximately $190 million due to close in fiscal 2002. Intrawest follows a conservative accounting policy for real estate

15

sales whereby it does not recognize any revenue until title to a completed unit has been transferred to a purchaser and the Company has received the full cash proceeds. The Company's strategy of pre-selling real estate projects before the start of construction reduces market risk and helps to maintain margins since sales concessions are not required and holding costs are more readily determinable. Furthermore, pre-selling real estate increases the predictability of real estate earnings.

Rental Properties

The majority of the condo-hotel projects the Company develops contain ground-level retail space which is either leased to third-party operators or used by the Company for its own sports shops. At June 30, 2000, the Company owned 341,000 square feet of commercial space compared with 310,000 square feet at the end of the previous year. Rental revenue derived from third party operators increased from $5.4 million in 1999 to $6.9 million in 2000. The increase was due to additional leasing from recently completed condo-hotel properties at Tremblant, Keystone and Snowshoe. Operating profit from rental properties increased from $2.6 million in 1999 to $3.3 million in 2000, in line with the increase in rental revenue.

REVIEW OF CORPORATE OPERATIONS

Interest and Other Income

Interest and other income increased from $3.7 million in 1999 to $12.4 million in 2000. During 2000 the Company sold its investment in a property management business in Whistler/Blackcomb and recorded a gain of $5.2 million. The Company offers central reservations to many hotel and rental management partners at Whistler/Blackcomb through its division Resort Reservations Whistler, and ownership of a property management company was no longer considered necessary to the Company's success in the resort. The balance of the increase in interest and other income was due mainly to higher fee income and miscellaneous gains.

The Company's investment in Compagnie des Alpes generated $2.3 million of earnings in 2000 compared with $2.1 million in 1999. Compagnie des Alpes experienced record revenues and profits during 2000.

Interest Costs

The Company incurred total interest costs of $66.4 million in 2000 compared with $50.6 million in 1999. Interest on the $135 million debentures issued in January 2000 along with a full year of interest on the $200 million debentures issued in 1999 accounted for $11.2 million of the increase. Proceeds from the $135 million debentures were initially used to reduce the Company's revolving credit facility, a portion of which was subsequently redrawn and invested in the extensive real estate development program. The balance of the change in interest costs was mainly due to increased construction financing.

Interest incurred is either capitalized to real estate properties and resort assets under development or charged to income. Interest capitalized to real estate assets is subsequently expensed (as a component of real estate costs) in the period when those properties are delivered. During 2000 $46.6 million of interest incurred was charged to income – $35.2 million as interest expense, $10.9 million as a component of real estate costs, and $0.5 million in discontinued operations. By comparison, in 1999 a total of $31.7 million of interest incurred was charged to income. In addition, real estate costs for 2000 and 1999 included $5.9 million and $4.8 million, respectively, of interest that was incurred and capitalized to properties in prior years, principally 1999.

Depreciation and Amortization

Depreciation and amortization expense increased from $40.2 million in 1999 to $51.4 million in 2000. A full year of depreciation expense for the resorts and businesses acquired part way through 1999 accounted

for $1.7 million of the increase and the balance of the increase was due mainly to depreciation of capital expenditures made at the resorts during 2000. Capital expenditures are planned to decline by 20-25% in 2001 and 2002 and as a result the growth in depreciation and amortization will flatten out in the future.

General and Administrative Costs

All general and administrative costs incurred by the resorts are included in ski and resort operation expenses. Similarly, general and administrative costs incurred in the development of real estate are initially capitalized to properties, and then expensed to real estate costs in the period when the properties are delivered. Corporate general and administrative costs, which mainly comprise certain executive employee costs, public company costs, audit and legal fees, and capital taxes, increased from $7.4 million in 1999 to $8.0 million in 2000. As a percentage of revenues, corporate general and administrative costs declined from 1.2% in 1999 to 1.0% in 2000. The Company continually reviews its overhead costs and has instituted procedures to reduce or eliminate costs where appropriate.

Income Taxes

The Company provided for income taxes of $15.4 million in 2000 compared with $13.5 million in 1999. This equates to an effective tax rate of 20.1% in 2000, down from 22.9% in 1999. The lower rate was due mainly to a change in the Company's policy of accounting for income taxes.

The Canadian Institute of Chartered Accountants has changed the accounting standard related to income taxes from the deferred method to the asset and liability method. The differences between the two methods are explained in note 1(n) to the Consolidated Financial Statements. The adoption of the asset and liability method brings generally accepted accounting principles (GAAP) in Canada closer to GAAP in the United States.

The Company adopted the new standard retroactively to July 1, 1999 without restating the financial statements of any prior year. Due to the number of acquisitions that the Company has made over the past few years, the impact of the change on the Company's balance sheet was significant. The cumulative effect of differences between the accounting and tax bases of assets and liabilities, amounting to $57.5 million at July 1, 1999, was charged against retained earnings in 2000 with a corresponding increase mainly to future income taxes payable. The benefit of this charge to retained earnings will be felt in future years (as well as in 2000) through a somewhat lower income tax expense.

Non-Controlling Interest

The Company has a 23% limited partner in the two partnerships which own Whistler/Blackcomb and there is a 5% non-controlling interest in Sandestin. The results of all three entities are fully consolidated into the Company's financial statements with the outside partner's share of earnings shown as non-controlling interest. Non-controlling interest increased from $6.8 million in 1999 to $9.3 million in 2000. Approximately half of the increase was due to the gain on sale of the property management business referred to above in "Interest and Other Income" and the balance was due to increased operations and real estate earnings at both Whistler/Blackcomb and Sandestin.

DISCONTINUED OPERATIONS

The consolidated financial statements disclose the results of the Company's non-resort business as discontinued operations. The discontinued operations incurred a loss of $0.1 million in 2000 compared with a loss of $4.6 million (including $3.5 million of property write-downs) in 1999. During 2000 the Company sold $11.2 million of non-resort properties including Whitemud Crossing Shopping Centre in

16

Edmonton and the remaining units in the Coach Hill project in Calgary.

At June 30, 2000, the Company had $16.8 million of remaining non-resort assets, mainly comprising two properties—the AirCare vehicle emission testing centres and the Gateway commercial land site—and a receivable of $6.4 million related to an earlier sale of non-resort properties (see note 19 to the Consolidated Financial Statements). The liquidation of these remaining non-resort assets has no impact on the common shareholders. The net income or loss generated by the non-resort assets accrues to the holders of the non-resort preferred ("NRP") shares and the net cash flow from these assets can only be used to redeem NRP shares. During 2000 the Company used $19.5 million to redeem 9,246,000 NRP shares and a further $0.1 million to purchase 62,900 NRP shares under the Company's normal course issuer bid at an average cost of Cdn.$1.74.

Up to June 30, 1999, the results of discontinued operations were included in retained earnings. During 2000 the Company's shareholders passed a resolution to reduce the redemption price of the NRP shares from Cdn.$3.82 to Cdn.$2.65 per share. As a result, the cumulative loss from discontinued operations since the creation of the NRP shares, amounting to $7.6 million, was charged against NRP share capital and retained earnings was increased by the same amount.

LIQUIDITY AND CAPITAL RESOURCES

Analysis of Cash Flows

Intrawest generally funds its operating and capital requirements from cash flow from operations, bank and other indebtedness, and equity issues. Since 1996 the Company has been acquiring and upgrading its portfolio of resorts and ramping up its production of real estate units, and although cash flow from operations grew at an average annual rate of 47.5%, it has been insufficient to fund the Company's growth. During this period approximately one-quarter of the $1.2 billion increase in total assets has been funded by cash flow from operations and the balance from debt, equity and other sources. This trend is now changing and in 2000 only $70.9 million of net new financing was required to fund the Company's growth compared with $341.4 million in 1999.

The major sources and uses of cash in 2000 and 1999 were as follows.

($millions)	2000	1999	Change
Cash flow from continuing operations	122.5	90.6	31.9
Net new investment in real estate properties developed for sale	(83.4)	(86.9)	3.5
Expenditures on acquisitions	(19.3)	(181.8)	162.5
Expenditures on resort operations improvements	(118.6)	(144.2)	25.6
Other net receipts (expenditures)	24.4	(16.4)	40.8
Net cash outflows before financing inflows	(74.4)	(338.7)	264.3
Net proceeds from financing	70.9	341.4	(270.5)
Increase (decrease) in cash	(3.5)	2.7	(6.2)

In 2000 $122.5 million of cash flow was provided by continuing operations compared with $90.6 million in 1999. Cash flow from continuing operations comprises income from continuing operations adjusted for non-cash items, such as depreciation and amortization, and future income taxes. The components of, and year-over-year changes in, cash flow from continuing operations have been discussed earlier in the review of operations.

In the past few fiscal years the real estate business has been a net user of cash. In 2000 the Company spent $365.2 million on developing real estate properties and recovered $281.8 million of development costs from sales of properties, resulting in a net new investment in real estate properties of $83.4 million. This compares with a net new investment of $86.9 million in 1999. There are two main reasons why the real estate business has required net new investment. First, significant amounts have been expended on up-front infrastructure costs and second, the production of units has increased every year as development activity has taken place at recently acquired resorts.

Since 1996 the number of real estate units under construction each year has increased at an average annual rate of approximately 30%. During this period the first projects were built and sold at Stratton, Snowshoe, Copper, Mammoth, Sandestin and Solitude. The ramp-up in the production of real estate units is expected to continue in 2001, 2002 and 2003 as more units are built at these resorts and units are built for the first time at Blue Mountain, Squaw Valley, Mountain Creek and the recently announced Les Arcs and Lake Las Vegas properties. Between 2000 and 2003 it is expected that the annual production of units will increase by approximately 15% each year and then level off at about 2,100 units per year.

During the ramp-up stage, as production increases from 1,500 units per year to 2,100 units, it is likely that the Company's net new investment in real estate properties will increase. To some extent this will be offset by a decline in annual expenditures on infrastructure costs starting in 2002. When the increase in production levels off, the real estate business will become a significant generator of cash.

In 1999 the Company announced that it planned to spend less on acquisitions and capital improvements and focus on increasing returns from existing assets. The acquisition of Swaneset and buying out the Company's partner in the Lodestar lands at Mammoth used $19.3 million of cash in 2000. By comparison, in 1999 the Company invested a total of $181.8 million in new resorts and businesses, including Sandestin, Raven, Breeze, Alpine and Blue Mountain. Capital expenditures on ski and resort assets used $118.6 million of cash flow in 2000, down 17.8% from 1999. The Company estimates that it will make capital expenditures at its mountain and warm-weather resorts totaling approximately $90 million in fiscal 2001, comprising approximately $23 million of maintenance capital and $67 million of expansion capital. The expansion capital requirements are being driven mainly by the development of the villages at the Company's resorts. For example, planned expenditures for 2001 include $15 million to build out the retail store space in the base of new condo-hotels and $7 million for village infrastructure. Approximately $15 million of capital has been allocated to upgrading and enhancing information technology systems, including building e-commerce distribution and marketing capability and standardizing both customer interactive and back-of-the-house systems across resorts.

The Company expects to fund its real estate development and expenditures on resort operations improvements from cash flow from operations, construction financing and available lines of credit. It does not foresee a requirement to raise additional equity capital. Cash is also expected to be provided by the sale of certain non-core assets.

17

Management's Discussion and Analysis

Analysis of Debt

At June 30, 2000, total debt amounted to $833.2 million, an increase of $106.1 million from June 30, 1999. During the year the Company issued $135 million of 10.5% senior unsecured debentures due 2010. The proceeds were principally used to repay the Company's revolving credit facility. Since December 1997 the Company has issued $419.5 million of unsecured debentures in the public market. At year-end, this type of financing constituted 52.2% of total debt compared with 41.6% at the end of the previous year. The Company expects to continue to raise debt at the corporate level and to reduce its secured debt at the subsidiary level.

At June 30, 2000, 35.5% of total debt bore interest at floating rates, down from 43.3% at June 30, 1999. Intrawest has developed a hedging policy to manage its interest rate risk. Interim financing for real estate construction is normally arranged on a floating rate basis. Since the Company pre-sells its projects and mainly develops wood-frame buildings with a construction period of 9 to 18 months, exposure to higher interest rates on construction financing is not significant. Debt on defined-income stream properties (for example, commercial rental properties) is normally arranged on a longer-term, fixed-rate basis with the objective of matching the financing with the duration characteristics of the property. It is also the Company's policy to fix the interest on at least 50% of its general corporate and ski and resort operations debt, although a lower proportion may be hedged temporarily in anticipation of a refinancing. At year-end, 29.8% of such debt bore interest at floating rates. A 1% change in the rate of interest on this debt would impact annual earnings by approximately $2.1 million before income taxes.

The Company has various operating lines of credit totaling approximately $230 million, of which $61.4 million was drawn at June 30, 2000. These lines of credit are available to fund seasonal cash requirements and capital expenditures at the resorts, real estate development activity, and for general corporate purposes. In addition, the Company has three revolving credit facilities totaling approximately $185 million available for real estate construction, of which $87.6 million was drawn at June 30, 2000. Real estate projects must meet certain conditions (including pre-sales thresholds) in order to qualify for funding under these facilities. Once the conditions are satisfied, up to 85% of costs will be funded.

BUSINESS RISKS

Intrawest is subject to various risks and uncertainties that can cause volatility in its earnings. The Company's resort operations and resort real estate businesses are managed to deal with risks that are common to most companies, i.e., the risks of severe economic downturn, competition and currency fluctuations, and the more industry-specific risks of unfavorable weather conditions, seasonality of operations and construction overruns.

Economic Downturn

A severe economic downturn could reduce spending on resort vacations and weaken sales of recreational real estate. Although leisure and travel are discretionary activities that one might expect to be impacted by a significant economic slowdown, Intrawest's operating results have not historically shown this to be the case. Since the Company acquired Blackcomb in 1986, cash flow has increased every year at that resort despite widely varying economic conditions. Blackcomb, as well as Intrawest's other resorts, attracts customers who have incomes well above the national average and are therefore less likely to have their vacation plans impacted by an economic recession. In addition, Intrawest's resorts draw their visitors from a wide variety of locations and this diversity shelters these resorts somewhat from regional economic conditions.

Real estate developers face two major risks from an economic downturn: land risk and completed inventory risk. Land risk arises when land is purchased with debt and economic conditions deteriorate resulting in higher holding costs and reduced profitability, or worse, loan defaults and foreclosure. Intrawest has reduced its land risk by acquiring land at low cost with the purchase of a resort or by securing land through options and joint ventures. The extensive land holdings at Tremblant, Stratton, Snowshoe, Mountain Creek and Panorama were all low-cost acquisitions with the resort. At Blackcomb and Squaw Valley and the recently announced developments at Lake Las Vegas and Les Arcs, the Company secured its land holdings through a series of rolling options rather than outright purchases. Options are exercised for specific project sites only when permits are in place and construction is set to start. Similarly, at Whistler the land acquisition financing is repaid when building permits are issued, subject to minimum annual repayments. Intrawest secured its land holdings at Keystone by forming a joint venture with the land owner under which land is only paid for as completed units are sold and construction financing is repaid.

Completed inventory risk arises when completed units cannot be sold and construction financing cannot be repaid. Intrawest has mitigated this risk by pre-selling a significant portion of its units prior to commencement of, and during, construction. At June 30, 2000, the Company had 141 unsold units in its resort real estate inventory (representing 10.7% of the units delivered in 2000) and 80% of the approximately 1,500 resort units under construction on that date were pre-sold. Purchasers are required to make a significant non-refundable deposit (generally in the range of $50,000 – $60,000) prior to construction completion which has historically ensured that rescissions have been kept to an extremely low level. Furthermore, the Company generally has sufficient pre-sales in place to cover its construction and other real estate debt by 1.5 to 2 times. In the event of a severe economic downturn in the real estate business, the Company could complete construction of its pre-sold units, transfer title to purchasers and repay all of its real estate financing.

Competition

The mountain resort industry has significant barriers to entry (e.g., very high start-up costs and significant environmental hurdles) that prevent new resorts from being created. Competition therefore is essentially confined to existing resorts. Intrawest's resorts compete for destination visitors with other mountain resorts in Canada, the United States, Europe and Japan, and with other leisure industry companies, such as cruise lines. They also compete for day skiers with other ski areas within each resort's local market area. Skier visits in North America have been relatively flat over the past ten years, which has increased competition between resort owners. The Company's strategy is to acquire resorts that have natural competitive advantages (e.g., in terms of location, vertical drop and quality of terrain) and to enhance those advantages by investing in capital improvements on the mountain. Since 1997 the Company has invested a total of $390.8 million in such capital improvements. The Company's principal strength compared with its industry competitors is its ability to combine expertise in resort operations and real estate development, particularly in building master-planned resort villages. Increasingly the village has become the dominant attraction in generating visits to a resort.

The Company owns substantially all of the supply of developable land at the base of its resorts and hence competition in real estate is some-what restricted. Expertise in all aspects of the development process, including resort master-planning, project design, construction, sales and marketing, and property management also gives the Company a distinct competitive advantage. In the resort club business, the Company

18

has established a competitive position through its ownership of the mountain facilities, and by offering a high standard of accommodation and a flexible points-based system.

Currency Fluctuations
Over the past several years the Company's Canadian resort operations have benefited from the lower Canadian dollar relative to the U.S. dollar, the Japanese yen and European currencies. This has made the price of a ski lift ticket at Intrawest's Canadian resorts 70% or less of the price at comparable U.S. resorts when denominated in the same currency. Along with accommodation and food and beverage costs, this has made vacationing in Canada more affordable for foreign visitors and it has encouraged Canadians to vacation at home. A significant shift in the value of the Canadian dollar, particularly against its U.S. counterpart, could impact earnings at Canadian resorts.

Intrawest finances its U.S. assets with U.S. dollar debt and its Canadian assets with Canadian dollar debt. Generally the Company services its debt with revenue denominated in the same currency. In addition, cash flow generated by Canadian operations is generally retained in Canada and invested in expansion of Canadian assets. Similarly cash flow generated at the U.S. resorts is generally reinvested in the United States. Cross-border cash transactions and currency exchanges are kept to a minimum.

Since Intrawest reports its earnings in U.S. dollars but its income is derived from both Canadian and U.S. sources, the Company is exposed to foreign currency exchange risk in its reported earnings. Revenues and expenses of the Company's Canadian operations will be impacted by changes in exchange rates when such operations are reported in U.S. dollars. The impact of Canadian/U.S. dollar exchange rate changes on the balance sheet are reflected in the foreign currency translation amount included in shareholders' equity and does not affect reported earnings.

Unfavorable Weather Conditions
The Company's ability to attract visitors to its resorts is influenced by weather conditions and the amount of snowfall during the ski season. Intrawest manages its exposure to unfavorable weather in three ways: by being geographically diversified, by seeking to build its visits as evenly as possible through the seasons and by investing in snowmaking.

Geographically diversified companies like Intrawest can reduce the risk associated with a particular region's weather patterns. Every ski season since 1995, favorable and unfavorable weather conditions at different times across North America have offset one another, allowing the Company to come within 2% of its budgeted winter season ski and resort operations revenue on a same-resort basis. The more a resort can attract its visitors evenly through the season the less vulnerable it is to unfavorable weather at a particular time. In order to spread its visits, Intrawest attempts to increase traffic mid-week and at non-peak times by marketing to destination visitors who book in advance, stay several days and are less likely than day visitors to change their vacation plans. Investing in snowmaking can also mitigate the impact of poor natural snow conditions. Snowmaking is particularly important in eastern North America due to the number of competing resorts and less reliable snowfall. Intrawest has invested heavily in snowmaking at all of its resorts over the past few years.

Seasonality of Operations
Ski and resort operations are highly seasonal. In fiscal 2000 approximately 70% of the Company's ski and resort operations revenue was generated during the period from December to March. Furthermore, during this period a significant portion of ski and resort operations revenue is generated on certain holidays, particularly Christmas/New Year, Presidents' Day and school spring breaks, and on weekends. Conversely, Sandestin's peak operating season occurs during the summer months, partially offsetting the seasonality of the mountain resorts. The Company's real estate operations tend to be somewhat seasonal as well, with construction primarily taking place during the summer and the majority of sales closing in the December to June period. This seasonality of operations impacts reported quarterly earnings. The operating results for any particular quarter are not necessarily indicative of the operating results for a subsequent quarter or for the full fiscal year. The Company has taken steps to smooth its revenue and earnings throughout the year by investing in four-season amenities (e.g., golf) and growing its summer and shoulder-season businesses. As a result of these initiatives, the proportion of ski and resort operations revenue earned outside the historically strong third fiscal quarter has increased to 46.9% in 2000 from 32.7% three years ago.

Construction Overruns
Intrawest is not in the construction business but rather engages general contractors to construct its real estate projects. The Company's practice is to structure its construction contracts on a fixed-price basis so that cost overruns are at the contractor's risk. In addition construction contracts are priced only after the Company has completed full working drawings. The Company employs construction experts who oversee the general contractors and ensure that problems are properly and quickly resolved. The Company has also developed a comprehensive and sophisticated project reporting system, which helps to identify potential cost overruns early enough to permit corrective action.

OUTLOOK
The Company will continue to execute the same strategic plan in 2001 that guided its operations in 2000. The focus will be on increasing returns from the existing asset base by reducing capital spending, improving margins, and leveraging expertise to grow the business.

On the resort operations side of the business, the Company has a number of initiatives to increase revenue and limit cost growth at its resorts. These initiatives include the establishment of a national destination sales team to generate increased lodging bookings and higher occupancy, the roll-out of e-commerce sales and customer relationship systems, and plans to control labor costs (which account for more than 40% of total ski and resort operation costs). At the same time the Company expects to benefit from approximately 1,300 new units of accommodation across its resorts, access to the new village at Copper, and a return to more normal travel patterns during the important Christmas holiday period after the travel slowdown experienced in 2000 because of Y2K/millennium issues.

On the real estate side of the business, the Company has accelerated its development program. Incremental returns on these new projects are very high because of the speed that equity is rolled over, due to the Company's success in pre-selling. The accelerated expansion of the villages will also result in benefits to the operations by increasing the accommodation base for destination visitors and adding to the attractions at the resort. The Company has a record backlog of sales – approximately $580 million for delivery in 2001 and 2002 compared with $330 million this time last year.

Sales at the Resort Club continue to improve and margins are strengthening in this business. The Company expects to expand the Resort Club to new locations in 2001, including Sandestin, Blue Mountain and Vancouver.

19

Management's Responsibility

The consolidated financial statements of Intrawest Corporation have been prepared by management and approved by the Board of Directors of the Company. Management is responsible for the preparation and presentation of the information contained in the consolidated financial statements. The Company maintains appropriate systems of internal control, policies and procedures which provide management with reasonable assurance that assets are safeguarded and that financial records are reliable and form a proper basis for preparation of financial statements.

The Company's independent auditors, KPMG LLP, have been appointed by the shareholders to express their professional opinion on the fairness of the consolidated financial statements. Their report is included below.

The Board of Directors ensures that management fulfills its responsibilities for financial reporting and internal control through an Audit Committee which is composed entirely of outside directors. This committee reviews the consolidated financial statements and reports to the Board of Directors. The auditors have full and direct access to the Audit Committee.

Joe S. Houssian
Chairman, President and Chief Executive Officer

Daniel O. Jarvis
Executive Vice President and Chief Financial Officer
September 5, 2000

Auditors' Report to the Shareholders

We have audited the consolidated balance sheets of Intrawest Corporation as at June 30, 2000 and 1999 and the consolidated statements of operations, retained earnings, and cash flows for the years then ended. These financial statements are the responsibility of the Company's management. Our responsibility is to express an opinion on these financial statements based on our audits.

We conducted our audits in accordance with Canadian generally accepted auditing standards. Those standards require that we plan and perform an audit to obtain reasonable assurance whether the financial statements are free of material misstatement. An audit includes examining, on a test basis, evidence supporting the amounts and disclosures in the financial statements. An audit also includes assessing the accounting principles used and significant estimates made by management, as well as evaluating the overall financial statement presentation.

In our opinion, these consolidated financial statements present fairly, in all material respects, the financial position of the Company as at June 30, 2000 and 1999 and the results of its operations and its cash flows for the years then ended in accordance with Canadian generally accepted accounting principles. As required by the Company Act (British Columbia), we report that, in our opinion, these principles have been applied on a consistent basis except for the change in the method of accounting for income taxes and employee future benefits as explained in notes 1(n) and 1(t) to the consolidated financial statements.

Significant differences between Canadian and United States accounting principles as they affect these consolidated financial statements are explained and quantified in note 21.

KPMG LLP

Chartered Accountants
Vancouver, British Columbia
September 5, 2000

20

Consolidated Statements of Operations

(expressed in U.S. dollars)

For the years ended June 30, 2000 and 1999
(in thousands of dollars except per share amounts)

	2000	1999
Revenue:		
Ski and resort operations	$ 452,141	$ 382,525
Real estate sales	341,455	215,867
Rental properties	6,905	5,368
Interest and other income	12,449	3,720
Income from equity accounted investment	2,333	2,145
	815,283	609,625
Expenses:		
Ski and resort operations	358,453	300,942
Real estate costs	281,845	174,598
Rental properties	3,641	2,771
Interest (note 15)	35,217	24,813
Depreciation and amortization	51,399	40,199
General and administrative	7,985	7,384
	738,540	550,707
Income before undernoted	76,743	58,918
Provision for income taxes (note 12)	15,394	13,473
Income before non-controlling interest and discontinued operations	61,349	45,445
Non-controlling interest	9,258	6,817
Income from continuing operations	52,091	38,628
Results of discontinued operations (note 3)	(99)	(4,565)
Net income	$ 51,992	$ 34,063
Income per common share:		
Income from continuing operations	$ 1.20	$ 0.96
Net income	1.20	0.96
Weighted average number of common shares outstanding (in thousands)	43,362	40,237

See accompanying notes to consolidated financial statements.

21

Consolidated Balance Sheets

(expressed in U.S. dollars)

June 30, 2000 and 1999
(in thousands of dollars)

	2000	1999
Assets		
Current assets:		
Cash and cash equivalents	$ 78,985	$ 82,457
Amounts receivable (note 6)	72,233	79,453
Other assets (note 7(a))	78,966	46,059
Properties (note 5):		
Resort	254,801	175,710
Discontinued operations	103	10,129
Future income taxes (note 12)	4,445	–
	489,533	393,808
Ski and resort operations (note 4)	784,725	698,958
Properties (note 5):		
Resort	314,481	285,193
Discontinued operations	9,521	10,504
	324,002	295,697
Amounts receivable (note 6)	35,262	28,009
Other assets (note 7(b))	67,999	56,565
Goodwill	15,834	19,147
	$ 1,717,355	$ 1,492,184

22

Consolidated Balance Sheets

(expressed in U.S. dollars)

June 30, 2000 and 1999
(in thousands of dollars)

	2000	1999
Liabilities and Shareholders' Equity		
Current liabilities:		
Amounts payable	$ 146,648	$ 119,069
Deferred revenue (note 9)	70,832	38,314
Bank and other indebtedness, current portion (note 8):		
Resort	158,144	148,758
Discontinued operations	84	5,526
	375,708	311,667
Bank and other indebtedness (note 8):		
Resort	670,539	568,651
Discontinued operations	4,394	4,137
	674,933	572,788
Due to joint venture partners (note 13)	16,963	11,411
Deferred revenue (note 9)	26,974	20,398
Future income taxes (note 12)	82,522	–
Deferred income taxes	–	14,493
Non-controlling interest in subsidiaries	28,983	22,959
	1,206,083	953,716
Shareholders' equity:		
Capital stock (note 11)	413,719	437,938
Retained earnings	131,953	136,288
Foreign currency translation adjustment	(34,400)	(35,758)
	511,272	538,468
Contingencies and commitments (note 14)		
	$ 1,717,355	$ 1,492,184

Approved on behalf of the Board:

Joe S. Houssian
Director

R. Thomas M. Allan
Director

See accompanying notes to consolidated financial statements.

2 3

Consolidated Statements of Retained Earnings

(expressed in U.S. dollars)

For the years ended June 30, 2000 and 1999
(in thousands of dollars)

	2000	1999
Opening retained earnings:		
As previously reported	$ 136,288	$ 106,607
Adjustment to reflect change in accounting for income taxes (note 1(n))	(57,457)	–
Adjustment to reflect change in accounting for employee future benefits (note 1(t))	(1,743)	–
As restated	77,088	106,607
Net income	51,992	34,063
Reduction in redemption price of non-resort preferred shares (note 11(a))	7,588	–
Dividends	(4,715)	(4,382)
Retained earnings, end of year	$ 131,953	$ 136,288

See accompanying notes to consolidated financial statements.

24

Consolidated Statements of Cash Flows (expressed in U.S. dollars)

For the years ended June 30, 2000 and 1999
(in thousands of dollars)

	2000	1999
Cash provided by (used in):		
Operations:		
Income from continuing operations	$ 52,091	$ 38,628
Items not affecting cash:		
Depreciation and amortization	51,399	40,199
Future income taxes	12,109	7,075
Income from equity accounted investment	(2,333)	(2,145)
Non-controlling interest	9,258	6,817
Cash flow from continuing operations	122,524	90,574
Recovery of costs through real estate sales	281,845	174,598
Increase in amounts receivable, net	(8,890)	(1,993)
Acquisition and development of properties for sale	(365,249)	(261,530)
Changes in non-cash operating working capital (note 20)	32,332	12,373
Cash provided by continuing operating activities	62,562	14,022
Cash provided by discontinued operations (note 3)	10,699	5,845
	73,261	19,867
Financing:		
Proceeds from bank and other borrowings	341,373	466,559
Repayments on bank and other borrowings	(244,285)	(193,292)
Issue of capital stock for cash, net of issuance costs	1,254	79,209
Redemption of non-resort preferred shares	(19,520)	(13,621)
Proceeds on dilution of partnership interest	–	9,714
Dividends paid	(4,715)	(4,382)
Distributions to non-controlling interests	(3,234)	(2,805)
	70,873	341,382
Investments:		
Expenditures on:		
Revenue-producing properties	1,315	(3,868)
Ski and resort operation assets	(118,614)	(144,195)
Other assets	(11,026)	(28,639)
Business acquisitions, net of cash acquired of $207 (1999 – $8,597)	(19,281)	(181,826)
	(147,606)	(358,528)
Increase (decrease) in cash and cash equivalents	(3,472)	2,721
Cash and cash equivalents, beginning of year	82,457	79,736
Cash and cash equivalents, end of year	$ 78,985	$ 82,457

Supplementary information (note 20)

See accompanying notes to consolidated financial statements.

25

Intrawest Corporation is incorporated under the Company Act (British Columbia) and, through its subsidiaries, is engaged in the development and operation of mountain and golf resorts principally throughout North America.

1. SIGNIFICANT ACCOUNTING POLICIES:

(a) Basis of presentation:

The consolidated financial statements are prepared in accordance with generally accepted accounting principles in Canada as prescribed by The Canadian Institute of Chartered Accountants ("CICA"). Information regarding United States generally accepted accounting principles as it affects the Company's consolidated financial statements is presented in note 21.

(b) Principles of consolidation:

The consolidated financial statements include:

(i) the accounts of the Company and its subsidiaries;

(ii) the accounts of all incorporated and unincorporated joint ventures to the extent of the Company's interest in their respective assets, liabilities, revenues and expenses.

The Company's principal subsidiaries and joint ventures are as follows:

	Percentage interest held by the Company
Blackcomb Skiing Enterprises Limited Partnership	77%
Whistler Mountain Resort Limited Partnership	77%
Blue Mountain Resorts Limited (note 2)	50%
Alpine Helicopters Ltd. (note 2)	45%
Mont Tremblant Resorts and Company, Limited Partnership	100%
IW Resorts Limited Partnership	100%
Swaneset Bay Golf Course Ltd. (note 2)	100%
Intrawest Resort Ownership Corporation	100%
The Stratton Corporation	100%
Snowshoe Resort, Inc.	100%
Copper Mountain, Inc.	100%
Mountain Creek Resort, Inc.	100%
Mammoth Mountain Ski Area	59.5%
Keystone/Intrawest L.L.C.	50%
Intrawest Retail Group, Inc. (note 2)	100%
Intrawest Sandestin Company, L.L.C. (note 2)	100%
Intrawest Golf Holdings, Inc. (note 2)	100%
Intrawest/Lodestar Limited Partnership (note 2)	100%
Mt. Tremblant Reservations Inc. (note 2)	100%
Whistler Blackcomb Resorts Inc. (note 2)	100%

All significant intercompany balances and transactions have been eliminated.

(c) Accounting for investments:

The Company accounts for investments in which it is able to exercise significant influence in accordance with the equity method. Under the equity method, the original cost of the shares is adjusted for the Company's share of post-acquisition earnings or losses, less dividends.

(d) Measurement uncertainty:

The preparation of financial statements in conformity with generally accepted accounting principles requires management to make estimates and assumptions that affect the reported amounts of assets and liabilities and disclosure of contingent assets and liabilities at the date of the financial statements and the reported amounts of revenues and expenses during the reporting period. Actual results could differ from those estimates.

The significant areas requiring management estimates include useful lives for depreciation, the impairment of ski and resort operations and properties, and the recoverability of amounts receivable.

(e) Cash equivalents:

The Company considers all highly liquid investments with terms to maturity of three months or less when acquired to be cash equivalents.

(f) Properties:

(i) Properties under development and held for sale:

Properties under development and held for sale are recorded at the lower of cost and net realizable value. Cost includes all expenditures incurred in connection with the acquisition, development and construction of these properties. These expenditures consist of all direct costs, interest on general and specific debt, and general and administrative expenses. Incidental operations related specifically to such properties are treated as an increase in or a reduction of costs.

Costs associated with the development of sales locations of the vacation ownership business, including operating and general and administrative costs incurred until a location is fully operational, are capitalized. Incidental operations related specifically to a location are treated as an increase in or a reduction of costs during the start-up period. These net costs are amortized on a straight-line basis over seven years.

The Company provides for write-downs where the carrying value of a particular property exceeds its net realizable value.

(ii) Revenue-producing properties:

Revenue-producing properties are stated at the lower of cost, net of accumulated depreciation, and net recoverable amount. Buildings are depreciated using the declining balance method at annual rates of 3.3% to 5%. Leasehold improvements and other tenant inducements are amortized using the straight-line method over the lease term. Furniture and equipment are depreciated on a declining balance basis at 20% per annum.

(iii) Classification:

Properties that are currently under development for sale and properties available for sale are classified as current assets. Related bank and other indebtedness is classified as a current liability.

(g) Ski and resort operations:

The assets of the ski and resort operations are stated at cost less accumulated depreciation. Costs of ski lifts, area improvements and buildings are capitalized. Certain buildings, area improvements and equipment are located on leased or licensed land. Depreciation is provided over the estimated useful lives of each asset category using the declining balance method as follows:

Buildings	3.3% to 5.0%
Ski lifts	5.0% to 8.0%
Golf courses	2.0% to 3.3%
Area improvements	2.0% to 3.3%
Automotive, helicopters and other equipment	10.0% to 50.0%
Leased vehicles	20.0% to 25.0%

2 6

Inventories are recorded at the lower of cost and net realizable value, and consist primarily of retail goods, food and beverage products, and mountain operating supplies.

(h) Administrative furniture, equipment and leasehold improvements:

Administrative furniture and equipment are stated at cost less accumulated depreciation. Depreciation is provided using the declining balance method at annual rates of 20% and 30%, respectively.

Leasehold improvements are stated at cost less accumulated amortization. Amortization is provided using the straight-line method over the lease term.

(i) Deferred financing costs:

Deferred financing costs consist of legal and other fees related to the financing of the Company's ski and resort operations. These costs are amortized over the term of the related financing.

(j) Goodwill:

Goodwill is amortized on the straight-line basis over a period of 10 to 40 years based on the nature of the acquired business. In determining whether there is a permanent impairment in value, recoverability is based on undiscounted estimated future cash flows.

(k) Deferred revenue:

Deferred revenue mainly comprises real estate deposits, season pass revenue, golf club initiation deposits, government grants and the exchange gains arising on the translation of long-term monetary items that are denominated in foreign currencies (note 1(o)). Deferred revenue which relates to the sale of season passes is recognized throughout the season based on the number of skier visits. Deferred revenue which relates to golf club initiation deposits is recognized on a straight-line basis over the estimated membership terms. Deferred revenue which relates to government grants for ski and resort operation assets is recognized on the same basis as the related assets are amortized. Deferred revenue which relates to government grants for properties under development is recognized as the properties are sold.

(l) Government assistance:

The Company periodically applies for financial assistance under available government incentive programs. Non-repayable government assistance relating to capital expenditures is reflected as a reduction of the cost of such assets.

(m) Revenue recognition:

(i) Ski and resort revenue from ski and resort operations is recognized as the service is provided.

(ii) Revenue from the sale of properties is recorded when title to the completed unit is conveyed to the purchaser and the purchaser becomes entitled to occupancy.

(iii) Points revenue associated with membership in the vacation ownership business of Club Intrawest (which revenue is included in real estate sales) is recognized when the purchaser has paid the amount due on closing, all contract documentation has been executed and all other significant conditions of sale are met.

(iv) Revenue from revenue-producing properties is recognized upon the earlier of attaining break-even cash flow after debt servicing or the expiration of a reasonable period of time following substantial completion. Prior to this time, the properties are categorized as

properties under development, and incidental operations related to such properties are applied to development costs.

(n) Future income taxes:

During fiscal 2000 the Company has adopted the provisions of Section 3465 of the CICA Handbook, Income Taxes ("Section 3465") which requires a change from the deferred method of accounting for income taxes to the asset and liability method of accounting for income taxes.

Under the asset and liability method of Section 3465, future tax assets and liabilities are recognized for future tax consequences attributable to differences between the financial statement carrying amounts of existing assets and liabilities and their respective tax bases.

Future tax assets and liabilities are measured using enacted or substantively enacted tax rates expected to apply to taxable income in the years in which those temporary differences are expected to be recovered or settled. Under Section 3465, the effect on future tax assets and liabilities of a change in tax rates is recognized in income in the period that includes the enactment date.

Pursuant to the deferral method, which was applied in prior years, deferred income taxes were recognized for income and expense items that were reported in different years for financial reporting purposes and income tax purposes using the tax rate applicable for the year of the calculation. Under the deferral method, deferred taxes were not adjusted for subsequent changes in tax rates.

The Company has calculated the effect of adopting the provisions of Section 3465 retroactively to July 1, 1999. The cumulative effect of this change in accounting for income taxes of $57,457,000 is reported separately in the fiscal 2000 consolidated statement of retained earnings as an adjustment to the opening balance of retained earnings for the year ended June 30, 2000. This charge represents the cumulative effect to July 1, 1999 of differences between accounting and tax bases of assets and liabilities principally due to differences arising on acquisition of ski and resort operations.

The financial statements for the year ended June 30, 1999 have not been restated to reflect the provisions of Section 3465.

(o) Foreign currency translation:

These consolidated financial statements are presented in U.S. dollars. The majority of the Company's operations are located in the United States and are conducted in U.S. dollars. The Company's Canadian operations use the Canadian dollar as their functional currency. The Canadian entities' financial statements have been translated into U.S. dollars using the exchange rate in effect at the balance sheet date for asset and liability amounts and at the average rate for the period for amounts included in the determination of income.

Cumulative unrealized gains or losses arising from the translation of the assets and liabilities of these operations are recorded as a separate component of shareholders' equity.

Exchange gains or losses arising on the translation of long-term monetary items that are denominated in foreign currencies to the applicable currency of measurement are deferred and amortized on a straight-line basis over the remaining terms of the related monetary item. Other exchange gains or losses are included in income as realized.

Prior to the year ended June 30, 2000, these consolidated financial statements were presented in Canadian dollars. Fiscal 1999's

27

comparative figures have been restated into U.S. dollars using exchange rates consistent with those in effect at the dates of the underlying transactions to the financial statements. The consolidated statement of operations for the year ended June 30, 1999 has been restated into U.S. dollars using an average exchange rate of 1.5103.

(p) Interest allocated to discontinued operations:
Interest allocated to discontinued operations is the total of interest on debt directly attributable to the discontinued operations and an allocation of interest on general corporate debt not directly attributable to continuing operations.

(q) Per share calculations:
Income per common share has been calculated using the weighted average number of common shares outstanding during the year. Fully diluted per common share amounts have not been presented as the effect of outstanding options is not materially dilutive.

(r) Cash flow from continuing operations:
Cash flow from continuing operations is computed as income from continuing operations adjusted for future income taxes, depreciation and amortization of capital items, non-controlling interest, income from equity accounted investment and other non-cash items. Cash flow from continuing operations is different from cash flow from continuing operating activities since it excludes the cash provided by or used for non-cash operating working capital accounts such as real estate inventory, amounts receivable and amounts payable.

(s) Stock options:
The Company has a stock option plan as described in note 11(c). No compensation expense is recognized when shares or stock options are issued. Any consideration paid on the exercise of options or purchase of shares is credited to capital stock.

(t) Employee future benefits:
During fiscal 2000 the Company has adopted the provisions of Section 3461 of the CICA Handbook, Employee Future Benefits ("Section 3461") which requires that the Company accrue its obligations under employee benefit plans and the related costs, net of plan assets as the underlying services are provided. The Company has adopted the following policies:

- The cost of pensions and other retirement benefits earned by employees is actuarially determined using the projected benefit method pro rated on service and management's best estimate of expected plan investment performance, salary escalation, retirement ages of employees and expected health care costs.

- For the purpose of calculating the expected return on plan assets, those assets are valued at fair value.

- Past service costs from plan amendments are amortized on a straight-line basis over the average remaining service period of employees active at the date of amendment.

- Experience gains and losses are amortized into pension expense over the plan membership's expected average remaining service lifetime using the straight-line amortization method.

The Company has calculated the effect of adopting the provisions of Section 3461 retroactively to July 1, 1999. The cumulative effect of this change in accounting for employee future benefits of $1,743,000 is reported separately in the fiscal 2000 consolidated statement of retained earnings as an adjustment to

the opening balance of retained earnings for the year ended June 30, 2000. This change represents the cumulative obligation at July 1, 1999 of employee future benefits previously calculated under different methods. The financial statements for the year ended June 30, 1999 have not been restated to reflect the provisions of Section 3461.

(u) Comparative figures:
Certain comparative figures for 1999 have been reclassified to conform with the financial presentation adopted in the current year.

2. ACQUISITIONS:
During the year ended June 30, 2000, the Company completed the following acquisitions each of which was accounted for by the purchase method with effect from the date of acquisition:

(a) On January 17, 2000, the Company acquired the assets of Swaneset Bay Resort & Country Club ("Swaneset"), including two golf courses and developable real estate in British Columbia. The purchase price of the assets acquired was as follows:

Net assets acquired at assigned values:	
Ski and resort operations	$ 9,486
Property under development	5,348
Net working capital	263
Other amounts	648
Assumption of debt	(4,253)
	11,492
Cash	207
	$ 11,699
Financed by:	
Cash	$ 5,988
Bank and other indebtedness	5,711
	$ 11,699

(b) During fiscal 2000 the Company increased its interest in Intrawest/Lodestar Limited Partnership ("Lodestar") in California from 60% to 100% through the acquisition of the other partner's interest for cash of $13,500,000. Effective from November 1, 1999, the Company has consolidated the results of Lodestar with the operations of the Company. Prior to this date the operations were proportionately consolidated as the partners shared joint control. The net assets acquired at assigned values consisted primarily of land and properties under development.

During the year ended June 30, 1999, the Company completed the following acquisitions each of which was accounted for by the purchase method with effect from the date of acquisition:

(a) Effective July 13, 1998, the Company acquired 100% of the shares of Sandestin Resort & Club, Inc. ("Sandestin"), owner of Sandestin Resort, a golf, tourist and retirement destination in northwestern Florida. The purchase price of the shares acquired was $127,455,000 for which the Company paid cash. Concurrent with the acquisition, the Company sold, at assigned cost, 50% of specific real estate assets and 5% of all other assets.

(b) Effective July 23, 1998, the Company acquired the assets of the Raven Golf Group ("Raven"), including two golf courses in Arizona, U.S.A. The purchase price of the assets acquired was $30,613,000, including costs, which was settled by the issuance of 125,000 common shares of the Company, the issuance of a promissory note payable in the amount of $4,711,000 and by the payment of cash.

28

(c) Effective September 3, 1998, the Company acquired all of the shares of Breeze, Inc. ("Breeze") and Max Snowboard, Inc. ("Max") (now named Intrawest Retail Group, Inc.). Intrawest Retail Group, Inc. rents ski and snowboard equipment and also owns sports retail stores in the western United States. The purchase price of the shares acquired was $15,160,000, including costs, which was settled through the payment of cash.

(d) Effective December 27, 1998, the Company acquired a 45% equity interest in Alpine Helicopters Ltd. ("Alpine"), parent company of Canadian Mountain Holidays Inc., which provides helicopter skiing, mountaineering and hiking services in southeastern British Columbia. The purchase price of the shares acquired was $14,729,000, including costs. The purchase price was settled by the issuance of 200,000 common shares of the Company and the balance was paid in cash.

(e) Effective January 27, 1999, the Company acquired a 50% equity interest in Blue Mountain Resorts Limited ("Blue"), owner and operator of a mountain resort in Ontario. The purchase price of the shares acquired of $10,159,000, including costs, was settled through the payment of cash.

(f) Effective March 31, 1999, the Company acquired 100% of the shares of Mt. Tremblant Reservations Inc. and 100% of the shares of Whistler Blackcomb Resorts Inc. ("MTR/WBR"). Both companies are engaged in the business of providing vacation rental, real estate and property management services at the Company's resorts in Mont Tremblant, Quebec and Whistler, British Columbia. The purchase price of the shares acquired was $4,202,000, including costs, and was settled through the payment of cash and the issuance of 74,458 common shares of the Company subsequent to year end.

The assignment of the purchase prices for the above acquisitions is as follows:

	Sandestin	Raven	Breeze/Max	Alpine	Blue	MTR/WBR	Total
Net assets acquired at assigned values:							
Ski and resort operations	$ 51,964	$ 31,102	$ 2,590	$ 24,197	$ 12,231	$ 161	$ 122,245
Properties under development	75,304	–	–	–	–	–	75,304
Goodwill	–	–	15,329	–	–	3,644	18,973
Net working capital	(14,111)	(262)	(391)	(2,461)	1,849	(404)	(15,780)
Other amounts	15,242	–	–	(1,965)	(1,069)	(11)	12,197
Assumption of debt	(6,252)	(681)	(2,667)	(6,182)	(3,421)	(15)	(19,218)
	122,147	30,159	14,861	13,589	9,590	3,375	193,721
Cash	5,308	454	299	1,140	569	827	8,597
	$ 127,455	$ 30,613	$ 15,160	$ 14,729	$ 10,159	$ 4,202	$ 202,318
Financed by:							
Cash	$ 127,455	$ 23,480	$ 15,160	$ 11,190	$ 10,159	$ 2,979	$ 190,423
Bank and other indebtedness	–	4,711	–	–	–	1,223	5,934
Issue of common shares (note 11(b))	–	2,422	–	3,539	–	–	5,961
	$ 127,455	$ 30,613	$ 15,160	$ 14,729	$ 10,159	$ 4,202	$ 202,318

2 9

3. DISCONTINUED OPERATIONS:

For reporting purposes, the results of operations and cash flow from operating activities of the non-resort real estate business have been disclosed separately from those of continuing operations for the periods presented.

The results of discontinued operations are as follows:

	2000	1999
Revenue	$ 13,148	$ 11,694
Loss before current income taxes	$ (99)	$ (4,565)
Provision for current income taxes	–	–
Loss from discontinued operations	$ (99)	$ (4,565)

Assets and liabilities presented in the consolidated balance sheets include the following assets and liabilities of discontinued operations:

	2000	1999
Current assets:		
Properties	$ 103	$ 10,129
Other current assets, excluding cash	2,845	10,038
Properties	9,521	10,504
Other non-current assets	4,331	6,753
Current liabilities	(602)	(8,003)
Non-current liabilities	(4,317)	(4,861)

The cash flows from discontinued operations are as follows:

	2000	1999
Cash provided by (used in):		
Operations	$ 10,699	$ 5,845
Financing	(24,458)	(14,348)
Investments	6,989	1,398
Decrease in cash and cash equivalents	$ (6,770)	$ (7,105)

The cash flow used for financing activities in fiscal 2000 includes a $19,520,000 (1999 – $13,621,000) redemption of non-resort preferred ("NRP") shares (note 11(a)). The Company has the right to apply the net cash flow from the discontinued operations from January 1, 1997 to the redemption of NRP shares. The shares are redeemable quarterly at Cdn.$2.65 per share, except for the final redemption which shall be subject to a premium or discount based on available cash flow relating to the non-resort assets.

4. SKI AND RESORT OPERATIONS:

2000	Cost	Accumulated depreciation	Net book value
Ski operations:			
Land	$ 49,752	$ –	$ 49,752
Buildings	205,832	34,765	171,067
Ski lifts and area improvements	386,708	85,974	300,734
Automotive, helicopters and other equipment	94,411	60,538	33,873
Leased vehicles	5,681	2,388	3,293
	742,384	183,665	558,719
Resort operations:			
Land	21,579	–	21,579
Buildings	55,183	7,062	48,121
Golf courses	108,963	6,517	102,446
Area improvements	65,012	11,152	53,860
	250,737	24,731	226,006
	$ 993,121	$ 208,396	$ 784,725

1999	Cost	Accumulated depreciation	Net book value
Ski operations:			
Land	$ 48,028	$ –	$ 48,028
Buildings	182,400	29,979	152,421
Ski lifts and area improvements	351,911	75,257	276,654
Automotive, helicopters and other equipment	84,005	51,303	32,702
Leased vehicles	4,783	1,700	3,083
	671,127	158,239	512,888
Resort operations:			
Land	20,275	–	20,275
Buildings	50,744	5,537	45,207
Golf courses	74,627	3,169	71,458
Area improvements	56,393	7,263	49,130
	202,039	15,969	186,070
	$ 873,166	$ 174,208	$ 698,958

The ski and resort operations have been pledged as security for certain of the Company's bank and other indebtedness (note 8).

30

5. PROPERTIES:

	2000	1999
Properties under development and held for sale:		
Acquisition costs	$ 167,119	$ 187,598
Interest	46,427	35,733
Development costs	298,415	176,887
Administrative	30,786	25,075
	$ 542,747	$ 425,293

			2000
	Cost	Accumulated depreciation	Net book value
Revenue-producing properties:			
Land	$ 6,062	$ –	$ 6,062
Buildings	33,472	5,478	27,994
Leasehold improvements and equipment	3,410	1,307	2,103
	$ 42,944	$ 6,785	$ 36,159

			1999
	Cost	Accumulated depreciation	Net book value
Revenue-producing properties:			
Land	$ 6,816	$ –	$ 6,816
Buildings	53,865	7,120	46,745
Leasehold improvements and equipment	5,108	2,426	2,682
	$ 65,789	$ 9,546	$ 56,243

Summary of properties:

	2000	1999
Properties under development and held for sale	$ 542,747	$ 425,293
Revenue-producing properties	36,159	56,243
	$ 578,906	$ 481,536

Properties are classified for balance sheet purposes as follows:

	2000	1999
Current assets:		
Resort	$ 254,801	$ 175,710
Discontinued operations	103	10,129
Long-term assets:		
Resort	314,481	285,193
Discontinued operations	9,521	10,504
	$ 578,906	$ 481,536

During the year ended June 30, 2000, the Company capitalized interest of $30,004,000 (1999 – $22,979,000) (note 15), and administrative expenses of $20,418,000 (1999 – $18,939,000) to properties.

Properties have been pledged as security for certain of the Company's bank and other indebtedness (note 8).

6. AMOUNTS RECEIVABLE:

	2000	1999
Receivable from sales of real estate	$ 19,672	$ 26,881
Ski and resort operation receivables	29,485	25,630
Loans, mortgages and notes receivable (note 19)	37,020	39,897
Funded senior employee share purchase plan (note 11(e))	560	677
Other accounts receivable	20,758	14,377
	107,495	107,462
Less: current portion	72,233	79,453
	$ 35,262	$ 28,009

Receivables are due approximately as follows:

Year ending June 30, 2001	$ 72,233
2002	6,543
2003	3,094
2004	3,394
2005	2,777
Subsequent to 2005	19,454
	$ 107,495

The loans, mortgages and notes receivable bear interest at both fixed and floating rates which averaged 11.69% per annum as at June 30, 2000 (1999 – 11.15%). These amounts have been pledged as security for certain of the Company's bank and other indebtedness (note 8).

7. OTHER ASSETS:

(a) Current:

	2000	1999
Ski and resort operation inventories	$ 23,828	$ 18,207
Restricted cash deposits	41,952	17,064
Prepaid expenses and other	13,186	10,788
	$ 78,966	$ 46,059

(b) Long-term:

	2000	1999
Investment in Compagnie des Alpes, at equity	$ 30,741	$ 26,422
Deferred financing costs	14,526	14,377
Administrative furniture, equipment and leasehold improvements, net of accumulated depreciation of $6,651,000 (1999 – $3,141,000)	7,598	5,085
Other	15,134	10,681
	$ 67,999	$ 56,565

31

8. BANK AND OTHER INDEBTEDNESS:

The Company has obtained financing for its ski and resort operations and properties from various financial institutions by pledging individual assets as security for such financing. Security for general corporate debt is provided by general security which includes a floating charge on the Company's assets and undertakings, fixed charges on real estate properties, and assignment of mortgages and notes receivable. The following table summarizes the primary security provided by the Company, where appropriate, and indicates the applicable type of financing, maturity dates and the weighted average interest rate at June 30, 2000:

	Maturity dates	Weighted average interest rate	2000	1999
Ski and resort operations:				
Mortgages and bank loans	Demand-2017	6.73%	$ 211,561	$ 229,595
Obligations under capital leases	2001-2005	8.28%	3,771	4,306
			215,332	233,901
Properties				
Interim financing on properties under development and held for resale	2001-2019	8.12%	111,609	116,545
Mortgages on revenue-producing properties	2001-2015	8.57%	12,425	15,739
			124,034	132,284
General corporate debt	2001	8.01%	59,210	58,076
Unsecured debentures	2002-2010	9.35%	434,585	302,811
			833,161	727,072
Less: current portion			158,228	154,284
			$ 674,933	$ 572,788

Principal repayments and the components related to either floating or fixed interest rates are as follows:

	Interest rates Floating	Interest rates Fixed	Total Repayments
Year ending June 30, 2001	$ 127,967	$ 30,261	$ 158,228
2002	5,127	117,017	122,144
2003	141,706	26,525	168,231
2004	3,794	339,374	343,168
2005	1,166	7,934	9,100
Subsequent to 2005	16,185	16,105	32,290
	$ 295,945	$ 537,216	$ 833,161

The Company has entered into a swap agreement to fix the interest rate on a portion of its floating rate debt denominated in Canadian dollars. The Company had Cdn.$30,000,000 (1999 – Cdn.$30,000,000) of bank loans swapped against debt with a fixed interest rate of 6.5% (1999 – 6.5%) per annum, excluding applicable stamping fees, under an agreement expiring in 2001 (note 16(a)).

Bank and other indebtedness includes indebtedness in the amount of $349,277,000 (1999 – $369,616,000), which is repayable in Canadian dollars of $517,140,000 (1999 – $540,748,000).

The Company is subject to certain covenants in respect of some of the bank and other indebtedness which require the Company to maintain certain financial ratios. The Company is in compliance with these covenants at June 30, 2000.

9. DEFERRED REVENUE:

	2000	1999
Deposits on real estate sales	$ 51,200	$ 21,114
Government assistance (note 10)	8,917	8,724
Exchange gains	3,309	8,025
Golf club initiation deposits	15,463	6,780
Season pass revenue	11,236	5,881
Other deferred amounts	7,681	8,188
	97,806	58,712
Less: current portion	70,832	38,314
	$ 26,974	$ 20,398

10. GOVERNMENT ASSISTANCE:

The federal government and the Province of Quebec have granted financial assistance to the Company in the form of interest-free loans and grants for the construction of specified four-season tourist facilities at Mont Tremblant. The loans, which are fully advanced, totaled $9,658,000 and are repayable over 17 years starting in 2000. The grants, which will total $37,156,000 (1999 – $39,608,000) when they are fully advanced, amounted to $18,925,000 at June 30, 2000 (1999 – $19,578,000). During the year ended June 30, 2000, grants received of $1,289,000 (1999 – $2,874,000) were credited as follows: $359,000 (1999 – $322,000) to ski and resort operation assets, $930,000 (1999 – $2,552,000) to properties.

11. CAPITAL STOCK:

(a) Share capital reorganization:

Effective March 14, 1997, the Company completed a reorganization of its share capital designed to separate the remaining non-resort real estate assets from the rest of the Company's business. Under the reorganization, each existing common share was exchanged for one new common share and one non-resort preferred ("NRP") share. The new common shares have the same attributes as the old common shares.

The NRP shares were initially recorded at a value of $64,545,000 (Cdn.$3.82 per share) before deduction of issue costs of $240,000, equal to the book value of the net equity of the non-resort assets at December 31, 1996, and the value assigned to the common shares was reduced by the same amount. The Company expects that the non-resort assets will be disposed of in an orderly manner and the net cash flow from these assets distributed to the NRP shareholders, primarily by way of redemption of their shares as described in note 3. The amount ultimately realized by the Company and distributed to the NRP shareholders will be subject to prevailing real estate market conditions. As at June 30, 2000, the book value of the net equity of the remaining non-resort assets was $14,206,000 (1999– $33,655,000).

On November 15, 1999, the shareholders of the Company passed a resolution reducing the redemption price of the NRP shares from Cdn.$3.82 to Cdn.$2.65 per share. As a result, the carrying value of the NRP shares has been reduced by $7,588,000 and retained earnings has been increased by the same amount.

3 2

(b) Capital stock:

The Company's capital stock comprises the following:

	2000	1999
Common shares	$ 395,795	$ 393,153
NRP shares	17,924	44,785
	$ 413,719	$ 437,938

(i) Common shares:
Authorized:
200,000,000 without par value
Issued:

	Number of common shares	2000 amount	Number of common shares	1999 amount
Balance, beginning of year	43,254,386	$ 393,153	38,359,786	$ 308,303
Issued for cash, net of issue cost	–	–	4,450,000	77,902
Issued for settlement of bank and other indebtedness	74,458	1,236	–	–
Issued on acquisitions	–	–	325,000	5,961
Stock option plan	134,450	1,007	119,600	987
Future income tax adjustment	–	399	–	–
Balance, end of year	43,463,294	$ 395,795	43,254,386	$ 393,153

(ii) NRP shares:
Authorized:
50,000,000 without par value
Issued:

	Number of NRP shares	2000 amount	Number of NRP shares	1999 amount
Balance, beginning of year	16,726,586	$ 44,785	21,811,911	$ 58,086
Stock option plan	343,275	321	374,675	320
Purchased for cancellation	(62,900)	(74)	–	–
Redemption	(9,246,000)	(19,520)	(5,460,000)	(13,621)
Reduction in redemption price	–	(7,588)	–	–
Balance, end of year	7,760,961	$ 17,924	16,726,586	$ 44,785

(iii) Preferred shares:
Authorized:
20,000,000 without par value
Issued – nil

(c) Stock options:

The Company has a stock option plan which provides for grants to officers and employees of the Company and its subsidiaries of options to purchase common shares and NRP shares of the Company. Options granted under the stock option plan may not be exercised except in accordance with such limitations as the Company's Human Resources Committee may determine.

The following table summarizes the status of options outstanding under the Plan:

	2000 share options outstanding	Weighted average price	1999 share options outstanding	Weighted average price
Outstanding, beginning of year	3,257,850	$ 14.44	2,894,650 $	13.36
Granted	255,500	17.09	542,500	19.30
Exercised	(134,450)	9.20	(119,600)	9.55
Forfeited	(157,300)	18.38	(59,700)	16.00
Outstanding, end of year	3,221,600	$ 14.68	3,257,850 $	14.44
Exercisable, end of year	1,758,650	$ 11.94	1,369,350 $	9.37

The following table provides details of options outstanding at June 30, 2000:

Range of exercise prices	Number outstanding June 30, 2000	Weighted average life remaining (years)	Weighted average price	Number exercisable June 30, 2000	Weighted average price
$7.64-$11.72	1,248,100	3.1	$ 9.43	1,206,900 $	9.40
$14.96-$19.77	1,973,500	7.7	18.00	551,750	17.50
	3,221,600	5.9	$ 14.68	1,758,650 $	11.94

(d) Employee share purchase plan:

The employee share purchase plan permits certain full-time employees of the Company and its subsidiaries and limited partnerships to purchase common shares through payroll deductions. The Company contributes $1 for every $3 contributed by an employee. To June 30, 2000, a total of 65,809 (1999 – 65,809) common shares have been issued from treasury under this plan. A further 100,000 common shares have been authorized and reserved for issuance under this plan.

(e) Funded senior employee share purchase plan:

The Company has a funded senior employee share purchase plan which provides for loans to be made to designated eligible employees to be used to subscribe for common shares. At June 30, 2000, loans to employees under the funded senior employee share purchase plan amounted to $560,000 with respect to 131,150 common shares and 37,272 NRP shares (1999 – $677,000 with respect to 131,150 common shares and 83,160 NRP shares). The loans are interest-free, secured by a promissory note and a pledge of the shares and mature by 2005. A further 96,400 common shares have been authorized and reserved for issuance under this plan.

12. INCOME TAXES:

(a) Provision for income taxes:

	2000	1999
Current	$ 3,285	$ 6,398
Future	12,109	7,075
	$ 15,394	$ 13,473

33

The reconciliation of income taxes calculated at the statutory rate to the actual income tax provision is as follows:

	2000	1999
Statutory rate	45.58%	45.58%
Income tax charge at statutory rate	$ 34,934	$ 24,775
Non-deductible depreciation and amortization	825	3,329
Large corporations tax	373	1,616
Taxes related to non-controlling interest share of earnings	(4,220)	(3,107)
Taxes related to equity accounted investment	(1,063)	(978)
Foreign taxes different from statutory rate	(15,754)	(13,278)
Other	299	1,116
Provision for income taxes	$ 15,394	$ 13,473

(b) The tax effects of temporary differences that give rise to significant portions of the future tax assets and future tax liabilities at June 30, 2000 are presented below:

	2000
Future tax assets:	
Non-capital loss carry forwards	$ 25,573
Share issue and financing costs	708
Differences in working capital deductions for tax and accounting purposes	1,854
Other	1,321
Total gross future tax assets	29,456
Less: valuation allowance	(6,910)
Net future tax assets	22,546
Future tax liabilities:	
Differences in depreciation and undepreciated capital cost:	
Ski and resort assets	93,472
Properties	6,287
Other	864
Total gross future tax liabilities	100,623
Net future tax liabilities	$ 78,077

(c) At June 30, 2000, the Company has non-capital loss carryforwards for income tax purposes of approximately $86,049,000 that are available to offset future taxable income through 2015.

13. JOINT VENTURES:

The following amounts represent the Company's proportionate interest in joint ventures and non-controlled partnerships including Mammoth, Alpine, Blue and Keystone/Intrawest L.L.C.:

	2000	1999
Properties, current	$ 40,977	$ 46,472
Other current assets	26,638	18,609
	67,615	65,081
Current liabilities	(53,927)	(34,383)
Working capital	13,688	30,698
Ski and resort operations	132,589	104,238
Properties, non-current	78,699	90,716
Bank and other indebtedness, non-current	(41,498)	(58,042)
Other, net	(14,760)	7,826
	$ 168,718	$ 175,436

	2000	1999
Revenue	$ 136,557	$ 123,282
Expenses	127,496	110,563
Income for continuing operations before income taxes	9,061	12,719
Results of discontinued operations	97	444
	$ 9,158	$ 13,163

	2000	1999
Cash provided by (used in):		
Operations	$ 26,107	$ 23,562
Financing	483	4,009
Investments	(28,720)	(26,213)
Increase (decrease) in cash and cash equivalents	$ (2,130)	$ 1,358

Due to joint venture partners is the amount payable to the Company's joint venture partners in various properties for costs they have incurred on the Company's behalf. Payments to the joint venture partners are governed by the terms of the respective joint venture agreement.

14. CONTINGENCIES AND COMMITMENTS:

(a) The Company holds licenses and land leases with respect to certain of its ski operations. These leases expire at various times between 2032 and 2051 and provide for annual payments generally in the range of 2% of defined gross revenues.

(b) The Company has estimated costs to complete ski and resort operation assets and properties currently under construction and held for sale amounting to $327,788,000 at June 30, 2000 (1999 – $250,323,000). These costs are substantially covered by existing financing commitments.

(c) The Company has entered into various operating lease commitments, payable as follows:

Year ending June 30,		
2001	$	4,953
2002		3,863
2003		3,421
2004		2,223
2005		2,112
Subsequent to 2005		3,483
	$	20,055

(d) The Company is contingently liable for indebtedness at June 30, 2000 of $8,698,000 (1999 – $13,722,000) which relates to certain non-resort properties under development sold during the year ended September 30, 1994 (note 19). The purchasers of these properties have provided guarantees to the Company in respect of the indebtedness and have indemnified the Company for any potential losses resulting from the contingent liability.

(e) The Company is contingently liable for the obligations of certain joint ventures and limited partnerships. The assets of these joint ventures and limited partnerships, which in all cases exceed the obligations, are available to satisfy such obligations.

34

15. INTEREST EXPENSE:

	2000	1999
Total interest incurred	$ 66,426	$ 50,552
Less:		
Interest capitalized to ski and resort operation assets	721	1,883
Interest capitalized to properties, net of capitalized interest included in real estate cost of sales of $10,875,000 (1999 – $6,004,000)	19,129	16,975
	$ 46,576	$ 31,694

	2000	1999
Interest was charged to income as follows:		
Real estate costs	$ 10,875	$ 6,004
Interest expense	35,217	24,813
Discontinued operations	484	877
	$ 46,576	$ 31,694

Real estate costs and discontinued operations also include $5,892,000 (1999 – $4,746,000) and $nil (1999 – $605,000), respectively, of interest incurred in prior years.

16. FINANCIAL INSTRUMENTS:

(a) Fair value:

The Company has various financial instruments including cash and cash equivalents, amounts receivable, certain amounts payable and accrued liabilities. Due to their short-term maturity or, in the case of amounts receivable, their market comparable interest rates, the instruments' book value approximates their fair value. Debt and interest swap agreements are also financial instruments. The fair values at June 30, 2000 and 1999 were estimated by discounting future cash flows at estimated market rates and are summarized as follows:

	2000		1999	
	Book value	Fair value	Book value	Fair value
Bank and other indebtedness including the effect of interest swap agreements	$ 833,161	$ 1,022,700	$ 727,072	$ 721,612

(b) Interest rate risk:

As described in note 8, $295,945,000 of the Company's debt instruments bear interest at floating rates. Fluctuations in these rates will impact the cost of financing incurred in the future.

(c) Credit risk:

The Company's products and services are purchased by a wide range of customers in different regions of North America and elsewhere. Due to the nature of its operations, the Company has no concentrations of credit risk.

17. EMPLOYEE BENEFITS:

The Company has two defined benefit pension plans for certain of its senior executives. Information about these defined benefit plans is as follows:

	2000	1999
Accrued benefit obligation:		
Balance at beginning of year	$ 3,810	$ 3,435
Current service cost	208	203
Interest cost	231	172
Balance at end of year	4,249	3,810
Plan assets:		
Fair value at beginning of year	2,016	1,454
Contributions	231	214
Actual return on plan assets	68	92
Contribution receivable	242	256
Balance at end of year	2,557	2,016
Plan deficit	(1,692)	(1,794)
Unamortized past service costs	–	1,814
Accrued benefit asset (liability)	$ (1,692)	$ 20

The significant actuarial assumptions adopted in measuring the Company's accrued benefit obligations are as follows (weighted-average assumptions as of June 30):

	2000	1999
Discount rate	7%	3.5%
Expected long-term rate of return on plan assets	8%	3.5%
Rate of compensation increase	6%	4%

The company's net benefit plan expense is as follows:

	2000	1999
Current service costs	$ 208	$ 203
Interest cost	231	172
Expected return on plan assets	(68)	(92)
Amortized past service costs	–	159
	$ 371	$ 442

35

18. SEGMENTED INFORMATION:

The Company has four reportable segments: ski and resort operations, real estate operations, warm-weather operations, and corporate and all other. The ski and resort segment includes all of the Company's mountain resorts and associated activities. The real estate segment includes all of the Company's real estate activities. The warm-weather operations include all of the Company's stand-alone golf courses that are not located at mountain resorts.

The Company evaluates performance based on profit or loss from operations before interest, depreciation and amortization, and income taxes. Intersegment sales and transfers are accounted for as if the sales or transfers were to third parties.

The Company's reportable segments are strategic business units that offer distinct products and services, and that have their own identifiable marketing strategies. Each of the reportable segments has senior level executives responsible for the performance of the segment.

The following table presents the Company's results from continuing operations by reportable segment:

	2000	1999
Revenue:		
Ski and resort	$ 394,630	$ 340,205
Real estate	348,360	221,235
Warm-weather	57,511	42,320
Corporate and all other	14,782	5,865
	$ 815,283	$ 609,625

	2000	1999
Operating profit before interest, depreciation and amortization, and income taxes:		
Ski and resort	$ 85,136	$ 75,947
Real estate	62,874	43,865
Warm-weather	8,552	5,637
Corporate and all other	14,782	5,865
	171,344	131,314
Less:		
Interest	(35,217)	(24,813)
Depreciation and amortization	(51,399)	(40,199)
General and administrative	(7,985)	(7,384)
	(94,601)	(72,396)
	$ 76,743	$ 58,918

	2000	1999
Segment assets:		
Ski and resort	$ 696,406	$ 633,487
Real estate	578,915	460,903
Warm-weather	104,153	84,618
Corporate and all other	321,081	266,655
Discontinued operations	16,800	46,521
	$ 1,717,355	$ 1,492,184

	2000	1999
Capital acquisitions:		
Ski and resort	$ 103,303	$ 138,660
Real estate	–	3,858
Warm-weather	15,311	5,535
Corporate and all other	6,501	5,476
	$ 125,115	$ 153,529

Geographic information:

	2000	1999
Revenue:		
Canada	$ 336,320	$ 260,415
United States	478,963	349,210
	$ 815,283	$ 609,625

	2000	1999
Operating income before income taxes, non-controlling interest and results of discontinued operations:		
Canada	$ 52,520	$ 40,718
United States	24,223	18,200
	$ 76,743	$ 58,918

	2000	1999
Identifiable assets:		
Canada	$ 777,762	$ 658,714
United States	922,793	786,949
Discontinued operations	16,800	46,521
	$ 1,717,355	$ 1,492,184

36

19. RELATED PARTY TRANSACTIONS:

Effective April 1, 1994, the Company sold substantially all of its industrial and non-resort residential properties under development in British Columbia and Washington State to two partnerships formed by a group of investors. An officer and a director of the Company is the majority shareholder of corporations that invested in a 20% interest in the partnerships. Such corporations are also the managing general partners of the partnerships.

The consideration for the sale included a vendor take-back note originally for $22,926,000, of which $8,230,000 was outstanding at June 30, 1999. During the year ended June 30, 2000, the partnerships repaid $6,663,000 leaving $1,567,000 outstanding at June 30, 2000. This amount is due, with interest at 10 % per annum, in two installments: $892,000 on July 31, 2000 (paid) and $675,000 on January 31, 2001.

The Company committed to provide the partnerships various credit facilities, including a $4,728,000 revolving line of credit until January 31, 2001, reducing to $4,052,000 until July 31, 2001 and thereafter to $2,702,000 until the availability terminates on January 31, 2002. The line of credit earns interest at prime plus 2% per annum. At June 30, 2000, $4,708,000 (1999 – $4,765,000) was advanced under these facilities and accrued and unpaid interest amounted to $142,000 (1999 – $480,000). In addition, the Company agreed to provide financial assistance by way of continuing liability in respect of certain indebtedness and liabilities of the partnerships. The Company earns fees in consideration for this financial assistance. The partnerships have guaranteed repayment of these facilities and indemnified the Company for any losses under them.

20. CASH FLOW INFORMATION:

The changes in non-cash operating working capital balance consist of the following:

	2000	1999
Cash provided by (used in):		
Amounts receivable	$ 531	$ (33,683)
Other assets	(32,837)	(8,334)
Amounts payable	23,365	22,862
Due to joint venture partner	5,736	13,806
Deferred revenue	35,537	17,722
	$ 32,332	$ 12,373
Supplemental information:		
Interest paid	$ 63,789	$ 39,323
Taxes paid	2,575	1,176
Non-cash investing and financing activities		
Capital stock issued on acquisitions	$ –	$ 5,961
Capital stock issued for settlement of bank and other indebtedness	1,236	–
Bank and other indebtedness incurred on acquisitions	5,711	5,934

21. DIFFERENCES BETWEEN CANADIAN AND UNITED STATES GENERALLY ACCEPTED ACCOUNTING PRINCIPLES:

The consolidated financial statements have been prepared in accordance with generally accepted accounting principles ("GAAP") in Canada. The principles adopted in these financial statements conform in all material respects to those generally accepted in the United States and the rules and regulations promulgated by the Securities and Exchange Commission ("SEC") except as summarized below:

	2000	1999
Income from continuing operations in accordance with Canadian GAAP	$ 52,091	$ 38,628
Effects of differences in accounting for:		
Cost of sales pursuant to SFAS 109 (d)	–	(942)
Depreciation pursuant to SFAS 109 (d)	(549)	(1,776)
Provision for future taxes pursuant to SFAS 109 (d)	–	1,073
Foreign exchange pursuant to FAS 52 (g)	(4,716)	8,025
Income from continuing operations in accordance with United States GAAP	46,826	45,008
Results of discontinued operations in accordance with Canadian and United States GAAP	(99)	(4,565)
Net income in accordance with United States GAAP	46,727	40,443
Opening retained earnings in accordance with United States GAAP (b)	127,645	91,584
Reduction in redemption price of non-resort preferred shares	7,588	–
Common share dividends	(4,715)	(4,382)
Closing retained earnings in accordance with United States GAAP	$ 177,245	$ 127,645
Weighted average number of shares outstanding (in thousands)	43,362	40,237
Income per common share (basic and diluted; in dollars)		
Income from continuing operations	$ 1.08	$ 1.12
Net income	$ 1.08	$ 1.12

	2000	1999
Comprehensive income		
Net income in accordance with United States GAAP	$ 46,727	$ 40,443
Other comprehensive income (loss)	1,358	(8,010)
	$ 48,085	$ 32,433

37

	2000	1999
Total assets in accordance with Canadian GAAP	$ 1,717,355	$ 1,492,184
Effects of differences in accounting for:		
Shareholder loans (c)	(560)	(677)
Ski and resort assets (d)	4,893	4,231
Goodwill (d)	37,943	39,156
Properties (d)	710	710
Total assets in accordance with United States GAAP	$ 1,760,341	$ 1,535,604

	2000	1999
Total liabilities in accordance with Canadian GAAP	$ 1,206,083	$ 953,716
Effects of differences in accounting for:		
Future income taxes (d)	–	56,381
Employee future benefits (i)	–	1,743
Foreign exchange (g)	(3,309)	(8,025)
Total liabilities in accordance with United States GAAP	$ 1,202,774	$ 1,003,815

	2000	1999
Capital stock in accordance with Canadian GAAP	$ 413,719	$ 437,938
Effects of differences in accounting for:		
Extinguishment of options and warrants (a)	1,563	1,563
Future income taxes (d)	–	399
Shareholder loans (c)	(560)	(677)
Capital stock in accordance with United States GAAP	414,722	439,223
Closing retained earnings in accordance with United States GAAP	177,245	127,645
Accumulated other comprehensive income (h)	(34,400)	(35,758)
Shareholders' equity in accordance with United States GAAP	$ 557,567	$ 531,110

(a) Extinguishment of options and warrants:

Payments made to extinguish options and warrants can be treated as capital items under Canadian GAAP. These payments would be treated as income items under United States GAAP. As a result, payments made to extinguish options in prior years impact the current year's capital stock and retained earnings. No payments were made during the years ended June 30, 2000 and 1999.

(b) Retained earnings:

Opening retained earnings in accordance with United States GAAP for the year ended June 30, 1999 includes the effects of:

(i) adopting SFAS 109 as described in (d). The net decrease in retained earnings was $11,717,000.

(ii) treating payments made to extinguish options and warrants as income items as described in (a). The net decrease in retained earnings was $1,563,000.

(iii) recognizing post employment benefits as described in (i). The net decrease in retained earnings was $1,743,000.

(c) Shareholder loans:

The Company accounts for loans provided to senior employees for the purchase of shares as amounts receivable. Under the rules of the SEC, these loans, totaling $560,000 and $677,000 as at June 30, 2000 and 1999, respectively, would be deducted from share capital.

(d) Income taxes:

As described in note 1(n), the Company adopted Section 3465 in its year ended June 30, 2000 and has calculated the provisions of Section 3465 retroactively to July 1, 1999. Prior to this date, the Company had adopted the Statement of Financial Accounting Standards ("SFAS") 109, "Accounting for Income Taxes", for the financial statement amounts presented under United States GAAP. SFAS 109 requires that future tax liabilities or assets be recognized for the difference between assigned values and tax bases of assets and liabilities acquired pursuant to a business combination except for non tax-deductible goodwill and unallocated negative goodwill, effective from the Company's year ended September 30, 1994. The effect of adopting SFAS 109 increases the carrying values of certain balance sheet amounts at June 30, 2000 and 1999 as follows:

	2000	1999
Ski and resort assets	$ 4,893	$ 4,231
Goodwill	37,943	39,156
Properties	710	710
Capital stock	–	399
Future income tax liability	–	56,381

38

The tax effects of temporary differences that give rise to significant portions of the future tax assets and future tax liabilities at June 30, 1999 are presented below:

	1999
Future tax assets:	
Non-capital loss carry forwards	$ 24,711
Share issue and financing costs	1,861
Other	911
Total gross future tax assets	27,483
Less: valuation allowance	(11,323)
Net future tax assets	16,160
Future tax liabilities:	
Differences in depreciation and undepreciated capital cost:	
Ski and resort assets	77,704
Properties	6,417
Differences in working capital deductions for tax and accounting purposes	479
Other	2,434
Total gross future tax liabilities	87,034
Net future tax liabilities	$ 70,874

(e) Joint ventures:

In accordance with Canadian GAAP, joint ventures are required to be proportionately consolidated regardless of the legal form of the entity. Under United States GAAP, incorporated joint ventures are required to be accounted for by the equity method. However, in accordance with practices provided for by the SEC, the Company has elected for the purpose of this reconciliation to account for incorporated joint ventures by the proportionate consolidation method (note 13).

(f) Stock compensation:

Statement of Financial Accounting Standards No. 123 ("FAS 123"), Accounting for Stock-Based Compensation, requires that stock-based compensation be accounted for based on a fair value methodology, although it allows an entity to elect to continue to measure stock-based compensation costs using the intrinsic value based method of accounting proscribed by Accounting Principles Board Opinion No. 25, "Accounting for Stock Issued to Employees" ("APB 25"). The Company has elected to account for stock-based compensation in accordance with APB 25 for purposes of this United States GAAP reconciliation. Accordingly, no compensation expense has been recognized for the years presented.

Had compensation expense been determined in accordance with the provisions of FAS 123 using the Black-Scholes option pricing model at the date of the grant, the following weighted average assumptions would be used for option grants in:

	2000	1999
Dividend yield	0.6%	0.7%
Risk-free interest rate	6.25%	5.0%
Expected option life	7 years	5 years
Expected volatility	69%	39%

Using the above assumptions, the Company's net income under United States GAAP would have been reduced to the pro forma amounts indicated below:

	2000	1999
Net income in accordance with United States GAAP:		
As reported	$ 46,727	$ 40,443
Estimated fair value of option grants	(2,894)	(2,403)
Pro forma	$ 43,833	$ 38,040

Pro forma net income reflects only options granted since June 30, 1996. Therefore, the full impact of calculating compensation costs for stock options under FAS 123 is not reflected in the pro forma net income amounts presented above because compensation cost is reflected over the options' vesting period of 7 years (1999 – 5 years) and compensation cost for options granted prior to July 1, 1996 is not considered.

(g) Foreign exchange on bank and other indebtedness:

Under Canadian GAAP the Company defers and amortizes foreign exchange gains and losses on bank and other indebtedness denominated in foreign currencies over the remaining term of the debt. Under United States GAAP, foreign exchange gains and losses are included in income in the period in which the exchange rate fluctuates.

(h) Other comprehensive income:

Statement of Financial Accounting Standards No. 130, Reporting Comprehensive Income ("FAS 130") requires that a company classify items of other comprehensive income by their nature in a financial statement and display the accumulated balance of other comprehensive income separately from retained earnings and capital stock in the equity section of the balance sheet.

The foreign currency translation adjustment in the amount of $34,400,000 (1999 – $35,758,000) presented in shareholders' equity under Canadian GAAP would be considered accumulated other comprehensive income under United States GAAP. The change in the balance of $1,358,000 would be other comprehensive income for the year (1999 – loss of $8,010,000).

(i) Employee future benefits:

As discussed in note 1(t), the Company has adopted new requirements in Canada for the recognition of post employment benefits. This adoption eliminates a previously existing Canada – United States GAAP difference. The application of these principles to the fiscal 1999 income reported under United States GAAP was not material.

(j) Comparative figures:

Certain comparative figures for 1999 have been reclassified to conform with the financial presentation adopted in the current year.

39

Appendix B

Summary of Generally Accepted Accounting Principles (GAAP)

Every technical area has professional associations and regulatory bodies that govern the practice of the profession. Accounting is no exception. In Canada, the Canadian Institute of Chartered Accountants (CICA) has the responsibility for issuing accounting standards that form the basis of generally accepted accounting principles (GAAP). The authority for setting GAAP was delegated to the CICA by the federal and provincial governments and the Canadian Securities Administrators in the 1970s.

The CICA's pronouncements, called *Recommendations,* are collected in Volume I of the *CICA Handbook.* The Recommendations specify how to account for particular business transactions and must be followed, except in those rare cases where a particular Recommendation or Recommendations would not lead to fair presentation. In those cases, the accountant should, using professional judgment, select the appropriate accounting principles. An accountant who determines that the *CICA Handbook* is not appropriate and selects some other basis of accounting must be prepared to defend that decision.

Each new Recommendation issued by the CICA becomes part of GAAP, the "accounting law of the land." In the same way that our laws draw authority from their acceptance by the people, GAAP depends on general acceptance by the business community. Throughout this book, we refer to GAAP as the proper way to do financial accounting.

The Objective of Financial Reporting

The basic objective of financial reporting is to provide information that is useful in making investment and lending decisions. Accounting information can be useful in decision making only if it is *understandable, relevant, reliable, comparable,* and *consistent.*

Accounting information must be *understandable* to users if they are to be able to use it. *Relevant* information is useful in making predictions and for evaluating past performance—that is, the information has feedback value. For example, Canadian Tire Corporation, Limited's disclosure of the profitability of each of its lines of business is relevant for investor evaluations of the company. To be relevant, information must be timely. *Reliable* information is free from significant error—that is, it has validity. Also, it is free from the bias of a particular viewpoint—that is, it is verifiable and neutral. *Comparable* and *consistent* information can be compared from period to period to help investors and creditors assess the entity's progress through time. These characteristics combine to shape the concepts and principles that comprise GAAP. Exhibit B-1 on page 647 summarizes the concepts and principles that accounting has developed to provide useful information for decision making.

Exhibit B-1

Summary of Important Accounting Concepts, Principles, and Financial Statements

Concepts, Principles, and Financial Statements	Quick Summary	Text Reference
Concepts		
Entity Concept	Accounting draws a boundary around each organization to be accounted for.	Chapter 1
Going-concern concept	Accountants assume the business will continue operating for the foreseeable future.	Chapter 1
Stable-monetary-unit concept	Accounting information is expressed primarily in monetary terms.	Chapter 1
Time-period concept	Ensures that accounting information is reported at regular intervals.	Chapter 3
Conservatism concept	Accountants report items in the financial statements in a way that avoids overstating assets, shareholders' equity, and revenues and avoids understating liabilities and expenses.	Chapter 9
Materiality concept	Accountans consider the4 materiality of an amount when making disclosure dicisions.	Chapter 9
Principles		
Reliability (objectivity) principle	Accounting records and statements are based on the most reliable data available	Chapter 1
Cost principle	Assets and services, revenues and expenses are recorded at their actual historical cost.	Chapter 1
Revenue principle	Tells accountants when to record revenue (only after it has been earned) and the amount of revenue to record (the cash value of what has been received).	Chapter 3
Matching principle	Directs accountants to (1) identify all expenses incurred during the period, (2) measure the expenses, and (3) match the expenses against the revenues earned during the period. The goal is to measure net income.	Chapter 3
Consistency principle	Businesses should use the same accounting methods from period to period.	Chapter 9
Disclosure principle	A company's financial statements should report enough information for outsiders to make informed decisions about the company.	Chapter 9
Financial Statements		
Balance sheet	Assets = Liabilities + Owners' Equity at a point in time (for proprietorships and partnerships). Assets = Liabilities + Shareholders' Equity at a point in time (for corporations).	Chapters 1 and 13
Income statement	Revenues and gains –Expenses and losses =Net income or net loss for the period.	Chapters 1 and 14
Cash flow statement	Cash receipts –Cash disbursements =Increase or decrease in cash during the period, grouped under operating, investing, and financing activities.	Chapters 1 and 17
Statement of retained earnings	Beginning retained earnings +Net income (or – Net loss) –Dividends =Ending retained earnings	Chapter 1
Statement of shareholders' equity	Shows the reason for the change in each shareholders' equity account, including retained earnings.	Chapter 14

Appendix C

Typical Charts of Accounts for Different Types of Businesses
(For Businesses Discussed in Chapters 1–12)

SERVICE PROPRIETORSHIP

ASSETS	LIABILITIES	OWNER'S EQUITY
Cash	Accounts Payable	Owner, Capital
Accounts Receivable	Notes Payable, Short-Term	Owner, Withdrawals
Allowance for Uncollectible Accounts	Salary Payable	**Revenues and Gains**
Notes Receivable, Short-Term	Wages Payable	Service Revenue
GST Receivable	Goods and Services Tax Payable	Interest Revenue
Interest Receivable	Employee Income Tax Payable	Gain on Sale of Land (or Furniture, Equipment, or Building)
Supplies	Employment Insurance Payable	**Expenses and Losses**
Prepaid Rent	Canada Pension Plan Payable	Salary Expense
Prepaid Insurance	Quebec Pension Plan Payable	Wages Expense
Notes Receivable, Long-Term	Employee Benefits Payable	Payroll Benefits Expense
Land	Interest Payable	Insurance Expense for Employees
Furniture	Unearned Service Revenue	Rent Expense
Accumulated Amortization—Furniture	Notes Payable, Long-Term	Insurance Expense
Equipment		Supplies Expense
Accumulated Amortization—Equipment		Uncollectible Account Expense
Building		Amortization Expense—Furniture
Accumulated Amortization—Building		Amortization Expense—Equipment
		Amortization Expense—Building
		Property Tax Expense
		Interest Expense
		Miscellaneous Expense
		Loss on Sale (or Exchange) of Land (Furniture, Equipment, or Buildings)

SERVICE PARTNERSHIP

Same as Service Proprietorship, except for Owners' Equity:

OWNER'S EQUITY

Partner 1, Capital
Partner 2, Capital
Partner N, Capital
Partner 1, Withdrawals
Partner 2, Withdrawals
Partner N, Withdrawals

Merchandising Corporation

ASSETS	LIABILITIES	SHAREHOLDERS' EQUITY

SHAREHOLDERS' EQUITY

Common Stock
Retained Earnings
Dividends

ASSETS

Cash
Short-Term Investments
(Trading Securities)
Accounts Receivable
Allowance for Uncollectible
Accounts
Notes Receivable, Short-
Term
Goods and Services Tax
Receivable
Interest Receivable
Inventory
Supplies
Prepaid Rent
Prepaid Insurance
Notes Receivable, Long-
Term
Investments in Subsidiaries
Investments in Stock
Investments in Bonds
Other Receivables, Long-
Term
Land
Land Improvements
Accumulated
Amortization—Land
Improvements
Furniture and Fixtures
Accumulated
Amortization—Furniture
and Fixtures
Equipment
Accumulated
Amortization—
Equipment
Buildings
Accumulated
Amortization—Buildings
Organization Cost
Franchises
Patents
Leaseholds
Goodwill

LIABILITIES

Accounts Payable
Notes Payable, Short-Term
Current Portion of Bonds
Payable
Salary Payable
Wages Payable
Goods and Services Tax
Payable
Employee Income Tax
Payable
Employment Insurance
Payable
Canada Pension Plan
Payable
Quebec Pension Plan
Payable
Employee Benefits Payable
Interest Payable
Income Tax Payable
Unearned Service Revenue
Notes Payable, Long-Term
Bonds Payable
Lease Liability

Revenues and Gains

Sales Revenue
Interest Revenue
Dividend Revenue
Equity-Method Investment
Revenue
Gain on Sale of Investments
Gain on Sale of Land
(Furniture and Fixtures,
Equipment, or Building)
Discontinued Operations—
Gain
Extraordinary Gains

Expenses and Losses

Cost of Goods Sold
Salary Expense
Wages Expense
Commission Expense
Payroll Benefits Expense
Insurance Expense for
Employees
Rent Expense
Insurance Expense
Supplies Expense
Uncollectible Accounts
Expense
Amortization Expense—
Land Improvements
Amortization Expense—
Furniture and Fixtures
Amortization Expense—
Equipment
Amortization Expense—
Buildings
Incorporation Expense
Amortization Expense—
Franchises
Amortization Expense—
Leaseholds
Amortization Expense—
Goodwill
Income Tax Expense
Loss on Sale of Investments
Loss on Sale (or Exchange)
of Land (or Furniture
and Fixtures, Equipment,
or Buildings)
Discontinued Operations—
Loss
Extraordinary Losses

Manufacturing Corporation

Same as Merchandising Corporation, except for Assets and Certain Expenses:

ASSETS

Inventories:
Materials Inventory
Work in Progress Inventory
Finished Goods Inventory
Factory Wages
Factory Overhead

EXPENSES (CONTRA EXPENSES IF CREDIT BALANCE)

Direct Materials Price Variance
Direct Materials Efficiency Variance
Direct Labour Price Variance
Direct Labour Efficiency Variance
Overhead Flexible Budget Variance
Overhead Production Volume Variance

Glossary

Accelerated amortization method See declining-balance method (p. 514).

Account The detailed record of the changes that have occurred in a particular asset, liability, or owner's equity during a period (p. 52).

Account payable A liability that is backed by the general reputation and credit standing of the debtor (p. 12).

Account receivable An asset, a promise to receive cash from customers to whom the business has sold goods or services (p. 12).

Accounting The system that measures business activities, processes that information into reports and financial statements, and communicates the findings to decision makers (p. 2).

Accounting cycle Process by which accountants produce an entity's financial statements for a specific period (p. 163).

Accounting equation The most basic tool of accounting: Assets = Liabilities + Owner's Equity (proprietorship) or Assets = Liabilities + Shareholders' Equity (corporation) (p. 11).

Accounting information system The combination of personnel, records, and procedures that a business uses to meet its need for financial data (p. 293).

Accrual-basis accounting Accounting that recognizes (records) the impact of a business event as it occurs, regardless of whether the transaction affected cash (p. 109).

Accrued expense An expense that has been incurred but not yet paid in cash (pp. 119, 65).

Accrued liability Another name for an accrued expense (p. 565).

Accrued revenue A revenue that has been earned but not yet received in cash (p. 120).

Accumulated amortization The cumulative sum of all amortization expense from the date of acquiring a capital asset (p. 117).

Acid-test ratio Ratio of the sum of cash plus short-term investments plus net current receivables to current liabilities. Tells whether the entity could pay all its current liabilities if they came due immediately. Also called the quick ratio (p. 425).

Adjusted trial balance A list of all the ledger accounts with their adjusted balances (p. 125).

Adjusting entry Entry made at the end of the period to assign revenues to the period in which they are earned and expenses to the period in which they are incurred. Adjusting entries help measure the period's income and bring the related asset and liability accounts to correct balances for the financial statements (p. 113).

Aging of accounts receivable A way to estimate bad debts by analyzing individual accounts receivable according to the length of time they have been due (p. 413).

Allowance for Doubtful Accounts A contra account, related to accounts receivable, that holds the estimated amount of collection losses. Also called allowance for uncollectible accounts (p. 411).

Allowance for Uncollectible Accounts Another name for allowance for doubtful accounts (p. 411).

Allowance method A method of recording collection losses based on estimates made prior to determining that the business will not collect from specific customers (p. 411).

Amortizable cost The asset's cost minus its estimated residual value (p. 513).

Amortization The term the CICA Handbook uses to describe the systematic changing of the cost of a capital asset; it is often called depletion when applied to wasting assets. The term is also used to describe the writing off to expense of capital assets (pp. 116, 507).

Amortization expense That portion of the cost of capital assets or natural resources used up in a particular period (p. 526).

Asset An economic resource a business owns that is expected to be of benefit in the future (p. 12).

Auditing or Audit The examination of financial statements by outside accountants, the most significant service that public accountants perform. The conclusion of an audit is the accountant's professional opinion about the financial statements (p. 352).

Average-cost method Another name for the weighted-average cost method (p. 464).

Bad-debt expense Another name for uncollectible-account expense (p. 411).

Balance sheet List of an entity's assets, liabilities and owner equity (proprietorship) or shareholder equity (corporation) as of a specific date. Also called the statement of financial position (p. 20).

Balance-sheet approach Another name for the aging of accounts receivable method of estimating uncollectibles (p. 413).

Bank collection Collection of money by the bank on behalf of a depositor (p. 360).

Bank reconciliation Process of explaining the reasons for the difference between a depositor's records and the bank's records about the depositor's bank account (p. 360).

Bank statement Document for a particular bank account showing its beginning and ending balances and listing the month's transactions that affected the account (p. 356).

Batch processing Computerized accounting for similar transactions in a group or batch (p. 295).

Betterment Expenditure that increases the capacity or efficiency of an asset or extends its useful life. Capital expenditures are debited to an asset account (p. 539).

Brand name Distinctive identification of a product or service (p. 528).

Budget Quantitative expression of a plan of action that helps managers to coordinate and implement the plan (p. 374).

Canada (or Quebec) Pension Plan All employees and self-employed persons in Canada (except in Quebec where the pension plan is the Quebec Pension Plan) between 18 and 70 years of age are required to contribute to the Canada Pension Plan administered by the Government of Canada (p. 576).

Capital Another name for the owner's equity of a business (p. 12).

Capital asset Long-lived asset, like property, plant and equipment, wasting asset, and intangible asset used in the operation of a business. Its value is in use (pp. 116, 175, 507).

Capital cost allowance Amortization allowed for income tax purposes by Canada Customs and Revenue Agency; the rates allowed are called capital cost allowance rates (p. 519).

Capitalize a cost To record a cost as part of an asset's cost, rather than as an expense (p. 509).

Carrying value of a capital asset The asset's cost less accumulated amortization (p. 118).

Cash-basis accounting Accounting that records only transactions in which cash is received or paid (p. 109).

Cash flow statement Reports cash receipts and cash disbursements classified according to the entity's major activities: operating, investing, and financing (p. 20).

Cash payments journal Special journal used to record cash payments by cheque (p. 310).

Cash receipts journal Special journal used to record cash receipts (p. 306).

Chart of accounts List of all the accounts and their account numbers in the ledger (p. 70).

Cheque Document that instructs the bank to pay the designated person or business the specified amount of money (p. 356).

Closing entries Entries that transfer the revenue, expense, and owner withdrawal balances from these respective accounts to the capital account (p. 170).

Closing the accounts Step in the accounting cycle at the end of the period that prepares the accounts for recording the transactions of the next period. Closing the accounts consists of journalizing and posting the closing entries to set the balances of the revenue, expense, and owner withdrawal accounts to zero (p. 168).

Collection period Another name for the days' sales in receivables (p. 426).

Computer virus A malicious computer program that reproduces itself, gets included in program code without consent, and destroys program code (p. 354).

Conservatism Concept by which the least favourable figures are presented in the financial statements (p. 474).

Consignment Transfer of goods by the owner (consignor) to another business (consignee) who, for a fee, sells the inventory on the owner's behalf. The consignee does not take title to the consigned goods (p. 462).

Consistency principle A business must use the same accounting methods and procedures from period to period or disclose a change in method (p. 473).

Contingent liability A potential liability that will become an actual liability only if a future event does occur (p. 452).

Contra account An account that always has a companion account and whose normal balance is opposite that of the companion account (p. 117).

Control account An account whose balance equals the sum of the balances in a group of related accounts in a subsidiary ledger (p. 305).

Controller The chief accounting officer of a company (p. 350).

Copyright Exclusive right to reproduce and sell a book, musical composition, film, or other work of art. Issued by the federal government, copyrights extend 50 years beyond the author's life (p. 528).

Corporation A business owned by shareholders that begins when the federal government or provincial government approves its articles of incorporation. A corporation is a legal entity, an "artificial person," in the eyes of the law (p. 6).

Cost of goods available for sale Beginning inventory plus purchases during a period (p. 461).

Cost of goods sold The cost of the inventory that the business has sold to customers, the largest single expense of most merchandising businesses. Also called cost of sales (p. 217).

Cost of sales Another name for cost of goods sold (p. 231).

Cost principle States that assets and services are recorded at their purchase cost and that the accounting record of the asset continues to be based on cost rather than current market value (p. 10).

Credit The right side of an account (p. 55).

Credit memorandum (credit memo) The document issued by a seller for a credit to a customer's Account Receivable (p. 313).

Creditor The party to a credit transaction who sells a service or merchandise and obtains a receivable (pp. 407, 420).

Current asset An asset that is expected to be converted to cash, sold, or consumed during the next 12 months, or within the business's normal operating cycle if longer than a year (p. 174).

Current liability A debt due to be paid within one year or one of the entity's operating cycles if the cycle is longer than a year (p. 175).

Current maturity Another name for the current portion of long-term debt (p. 564).

Current portion of long-term debt Amount of the principal that is payable within one year (p. 564).

Current ratio Current assets divided by current liabilities. Measures the ability to pay current liabilities from current assets (p. 178).

Database Computerized storehouse of information that can be systematically assessed in a variety of report forms (p. 294).

Days' sales in receivables Ratio of average net accounts receivable to one day's sales. Indicates how many days' sales remain in Accounts Receivable awaiting collection (p. 426).

Debit The left side of an account (p. 55).

Debit memorandum (debit memo) The document issued by a buyer to reduce the buyer's Account Payable to a seller (p. 314).

Debt ratio Ratio of total liabilities to total assets. Gives the proportion of a company's assets that it has financed with debt (p. 179).

Debtor The party to a credit transaction who makes a purchase and creates a payable (pp. 407, 420).

Default on a note Failure of the maker of a note to pay at maturity. Also called dishonour of a note (p. 424).

Deferred revenue Another name for unearned revenue (p. 121).

Depletion Another word to describe the amortization of wasting assets (p. 526).

Deposit in transit A deposit recorded by the company but not yet by its bank (p. 360).

Depreciation Another name for amortization (p. 507).

Direct write-off method A method of accounting for bad debts by which the company waits until the credit department decides that a customer's account receivable is uncollectible and then debits Uncollectible-Account Expense and credits the customer's Account Receivable (p. 415).

Disclosure principle A business's financial statements must report enough information for outsiders to make knowledgeable decisions about the business (p. 473).

Discounting a note payable A borrowing arrangement in which the bank subtracts the interest amount from the note's face value. The borrower receives the net amount (p. 560).

Discounting a note receivable Selling a note receivable before its maturity (p. 451).

Dishonour of a note Failure of the maker of a note to pay a note receivable at maturity. Also called default on a note (p. 424).

Double-declining-balance amortization method A type of amortization method that expenses a relatively larger amount of an asset's cost nearer the start of its useful life than does the straight-line method (p. 514).

Doubtful-account expense Another name for the uncollectible-account expense (p. 411).

Due date The date on which the final payment of a note is due. Also called the maturity date (p. 421).

Electronic funds transfer (EFT) System that transfers cash by digital communication rather than paper documents (p. 357).

Employee compensation Payroll, a major expense of many businesses (p. 565).

Employment Insurance Act All employees and employers in Canada must contribute to the Employment Insurance Fund, which provides assistance to unemployed workers (p. 577).

Encrypting The process of rearranging plain-text messages by some mathematical formula to achieve confidentiality (p. 354).

Entity An organization or a section of an organization that, for accounting purposes, stands apart from other organizations and individuals as a separate economic unit. This is the most basic concept in accounting (p. 9).

Estimated residual value Expected cash value of an asset at the end of its useful life. Also called residual value, scrap value, and salvage value (p. 513).

Estimated useful life Length of the service that a business expects to get from an asset; may be expressed in years, units of output, kilometres, or other measures (p. 513).

Expense Decrease in owner's equity (proprietorship) or shareholders' equity (corporation) that occurs in the course of delivering goods or services to customers or clients (p. 12).

Financial accounting The branch of accounting that provides information to people outside the business (p. 4).

Financial statements Business documents that report financial information about an entity to persons and organizations outside the business (p. 3).

Financing activity Activity that obtains the funds from investors and creditors needed to launch and sustain the business; a section of the cash flow statement (p. 447).

Firewall Barriers used to prevent entry into a computer network or a part of a network. Examples include passwords, personal identification numbers (PINs), and fingerprints (p. 355).

First-in, first-out (FIFO) inventory costing method Inventory costing method by which the first costs into inventory are the first costs out to cost of goods sold. Ending inventory is based on the costs of the most recent purchases (p. 464).

Franchise Privileges granted by a private business or a government to sell a product or service in accordance with specified conditions (p. 528).

General journal Journal used to record all transactions that do not fit one of the special journals (p. 301).

General ledger Ledger of accounts that are reported in the financial statements (p. 304).

Generally accepted accounting principles (GAAP) Accounting guidelines, formulated by the CICA's Accounting Standards Committee, that govern how businesses report their results in financial statements to the public (pp. 7, 47).

Going-concern or continuity concept Accountants' assumption that the business will continue operating in the foreseeable future (p. 11).

Goodwill Excess of the cost of an acquired company over the sum of the market values of its net assets (assets minus liabilities) (p. 529).

Gross margin Excess of sales revenue over cost of goods sold. Also called gross profit (pp. 218, 457).

Gross margin method A way to estimate inventory based on a rearrangement of the cost of goods sold model: Beginning inventory + Net purchases = Cost of goods available for sale. Cost of goods available for sale – Cost of goods sold = Ending inventory. Also called the gross profit method (p. 478).

Gross margin percentage Gross margin divided by net sales revenue. A measure of profitability (p. 239).

Gross pay Total amount of salary, wages, commissions, or any other employee compensation before taxes and other deductions are taken out (p. 575).

Gross profit Another name for gross margin (pp. 218, 457).

Gross profit method Another name for the gross margin method (p. 478).

Hardware Electronic equipment that includes computers, disk drives, monitors, printers, and the network that connects them (p. 294).

Imprest system A way to account for petty cash by maintaining a constant balance in the petty cash account, supported by the fund (cash plus disbursement tickets) totalling the same amount (p. 373).

Income from operations Another name for operating income (p. 236).

Income statement List of an entity's revenues, expenses, and net income or net loss for a specific period. Also called the statement of operations (p. 20).

Income-statement approach Another name for the percent of sales method of estimating uncollectibles (p. 412).

Income summary A temporary "holding tank" account into which the revenues and expenses are transferred prior to their final transfer to the Capital account (p. 171).

Intangible asset An asset with no physical form, a special right to current and expected future benefits (p. 527).

Interest The revenue to the payee for loaning out the principal, and the expense to the maker for borrowing the principal (p. 438).

Interest period The period of time during which interest is to be computed, extending from the original date of the note to the maturity date (p. 421).

Interest rate The percentage rate that is multiplied by the principal amount to compute the amount of interest on a note (p. 421).

Internal control Organizational plan and all the related measures adopted by an entity to meet management's objectives of discharging statutory responsibilities, profitability, prevention and detection of fraud and error, safeguarding of assets, reliability of accounting records, and timely preparation of reliable financial information (p. 349).

Inventory All goods that company owns and expects to sell in the normal course of operation (p. 216).

Inventory profit Difference between gross margin costed on the FIFO basis and gross margin costed on the LIFO basis (p. 467).

Inventory turnover Ratio of cost of goods sold to average inventory. Measures the number of times a company sells its average level of inventory during a year (pp. 239, 929).

Investing activity Activity that increases and decreases the long-term assets available to the business; a section of the cash flow statement (p. 447).

Invoice A seller's request for cash from the purchaser (p. 2121).

Journal The chronological accounting record of an entity's transactions (p. 58).

Last-in, first-out (LIFO) inventory costing method Inventory costing method by which the last costs into inventory are the first costs out to cost of goods sold. This method leaves the oldest costs—those of beginning inventory and the earliest purchases of the period—in ending inventory (p. 464).

Leasehold Prepayment that a lessee (renter) makes to secure the use of an asset from a lessor (landlord) (p. 528).

Ledger The book of accounts (p. 52).

Liability An economic obligation (a debt) payable to an individual or an organization outside the business (p. 12).

Licence Privileges granted by a private business or a government to sell a product or service in accordance with special conditions (p. 528).

Liquidity Measure of how quickly an item may be converted to cash (p. 174).

Long-term asset An asset other than a current asset (p. 175).

Long-term liability A liability other than a current liability (p. 175).

Lower-of-cost-or-market (LCM) rule Requires that an asset be reported in the financial statements at the lower of its historical cost or its market value (current replacement cost for inventory) (p. 474).

Maker of a note The person or business that signs the note and promises to pay the amount required by the note agreement. The maker is the debtor (p. 420).

Management accounting The branch of accounting that generates information for internal decision makers of a business, such as top executives (p. 4).

Matching principle The basis for recording expenses. Directs accountants to identify all expenses incurred during the period, measure the expenses, and match them against the revenues earned during that same span of time (p. 123).

Materiality concept A company must perform strictly proper accounting only for items and transactions that are significant to the business's financial statements (p. 473).

Maturity date The date on which the final payment of a note is due. Also called the due date (p. 421).

Maturity value The sum of the principal and interest due at the maturity date of a note (p. 421).

Menu A list of options for choosing computer functions (p. 297).

Merchandising company A company that buys ready-made inventory for resale to customers (p. 456).

Module Separate compatible units of an accounting package that are integrated to function together (p. 300).

Moving weighted-average cost method A weighted-average cost method where unit cost is changed to reflect each new purchase of inventory (p. 472).

Multi-step income statement Format that contains subtotals to highlight significant relationships. In addition to net income, it also presents gross margin and income from operations (p. 238).

Net earnings Another name for net income or net profit (p. 17).

Net income Excess of total revenues over total expenses. Also called net earnings or net profit (p. 17).

Net loss Excess of total expenses over total revenues (p. 17).

Net pay Gross pay minus all deductions; the amount of employee compensation that the employee actually takes home (p. 575).

Net profit Another name for net income or net earnings (p. 17).

Net purchases Purchases less purchase discounts and purchase returns and allowances (p. 241).

Net sales Sales revenue less sales discounts and sales returns and allowances (p. 217).

Network The system of electronic linkages that allow different computers to share the same information (p. 294).

Nominal account Another name for a temporary account (p. 169).

Nonsufficient funds (NSF) cheque A "bounced" cheque, one for which the maker's bank account has insufficient money to pay the cheque (p. 360).

Note payable A liability evidenced by a written promise to make a future payment (p. 12).

Note period Another name for the interest period of a note (p. 421).

Note receivable An asset evidenced by another party's written promise that entitles you to receive cash in the future (p. 12).

Note term Another name for the interest period of a note (p. 421).

Objectivity principle Another name for the reliability principle (p. 10).

On-line processing Computerized processing of related functions, such as the recording and posting of transactions, on a continuous basis (p. 298).

Operating cycle The time span during which cash is paid for goods and services that are sold to customers who then pay the business in cash (p. 175).

Operating expense Expense, other than cost of goods sold, that is incurred in the entity's major line of business: rent, amortization, salaries, wages, utilities, property tax, and supplies expense (p. 234).

Operating income Gross margin minus operating expenses plus any other operating revenues. Also called income from operations (p. 236).

Other expense Expense that is outside the main operations of a business, such as a loss on the sale of capital assets (p. 236).

Other revenue Revenue that is outside the main operations of a business, such as a gain on the sale of capital assets (p. 236).

Outstanding cheque A cheque issued by the company and recorded on its books but not yet paid by its bank (p. 360).

Owner's equity In a proprietorship, the claim of an owner of a business to the assets of the business. Also called capital (p. 12).

Owner withdrawals Amounts removed from the business by an owner (p. 12).

Partnership An unincorporated business with two or more owners (p. 6).

Patent A federal government grant giving the holder the exclusive right for 20 years to produce and sell an invention (p. 528).

Payee of a note The person or business to whom the maker of a note promises future payment. The payee is the creditor (p. 420).

Payroll Employee compensation, a major expense of many businesses (p. 565).

Percent of sales method A method of estimating uncollectible receivables as a percent of the net credit sales (or net sales) (p. 412).

Periodic inventory system Type of inventory accounting system in which the business does not keep a continuous record of the inventory on hand. Instead, at the end of the period the business makes a physical count of the on-hand inventory and applies the appropriate unit costs to determine the cost of the ending inventory (pp. 220, 457).

Permanent account Another name for a real account—asset, liability, or owner's equity—that is not closed at the end of the period (p. 169).

Perpetual inventory system Type of accounting inventory system in which the business keeps a continuous record for each inventory item to show the inventory on hand at all times *(pp. 220, 457)*.

Petty cash Fund containing a small amount of cash that is used to pay minor expenditures *(p. 372)*.

Postclosing trial balance List of the ledger accounts and their balances at the end of the period after the journalizing and posting of the closing entries. The last step of the accounting cycle, the postclosing trial balance ensures that the ledger is in balance for the start of the next accounting period *(p. 173)*.

Posting Transferring of amounts from the journal to the ledger *(p. 60)*.

Prepaid expense A category of miscellaneous assets that typically expire or get used up in the near future. Examples include prepaid rent, prepaid insurance, and supplies *(p. 114)*.

Principal The amount loaned out by the payee and borrowed by the maker of a note *(p. 420)*.

Principal amount Another name for the principal *(p. 420)*.

Promissory note A written promise to pay a specified amount of money at a particular future date *(p. 420)*.

Proprietorship An unincorporated business with a single owner *(p. 6)*.

Purchases journal Special journal used to record all purchases of inventory, supplies and other assets on account *(p. 308)*.

Quick ratio Another name for the acid-test ratio *(p. 425)*.

Real account Another name for a permanent account *(p. 169)*.

Real-time processing Computerized processing of related functions, such as the recording and posting of transactions, on a continuous basis. Also called on-line processing *(p. 298)*.

Receivable A monetary claim against a business or an individual, acquired mainly by selling goods and services and by lending money *(p. 407)*.

Reliability principle Requires that accounting information be dependable (free from error and bias). Also called the Objectivity principle *(p. 10)*.

Repair Expenditure that merely maintains an asset in its existing condition or restores the asset to good working order. Repairs are expensed (matched against revenue) *(p. 510)*.

Retail method A method of estimating ending inventory based on the total cost and total selling price of opening inventory and net purchases *(p. 478)*.

Revenue Increase in owner's equity (proprietorship) or shareholders' equity (corporation) that is earned by delivering goods or services to customers or clients *(p. 12)*.

Revenue principle The basis for recording revenues; tells accountants when to record revenue and the amount of revenue to record *(p. 110)*.

Reversing entry An entry that switches the debit and the credit of a previous adjusting entry. The reversing entry is dated the first day of the period following the adjusting entry *(p. 212)*.

Sales Another name for sales revenue *(p. 217)*.

Sales discount Reduction in the amount receivable from a customer, offered by the seller as an incentive for the customer to pay promptly. A contra account to sales revenue *(p. 227)*.

Sales journal Special journal used to record credit sales *(p. 302)*.

Sales returns and allowances Decrease in the seller's receivable from a customer's return of merchandise or from granting the customer an allowance from the amount the customer owes the seller. A contra account to sales revenue *(p. 227)*.

Sales revenue Amount that a merchandiser earns from selling inventory before subtracting expenses Also called sales *(p. 217)*.

Salvage value Another name for estimated residual value *(p. 513)*.

Scrap value Another name for estimated residual value *(p. 513)*.

Server The main computer in a network, where the program and data are stored *(p. 294)*.

Shareholder A person who owns stock in a corporation *(p. 6)*.

Short-term note payable Note payable due within one year, a common form of financing *(p. 559)*.

Single-step income statement Format that groups all revenues together and then lists and deducts all expenses together without drawing any subtotals *(p. 238)*.

Software Set of programs or instructions that cause the computer to perform the work desired *(p. 294)*.

Special journal An accounting journal designed to record one specific type of transaction *(p. 301)*.

Specific identification method Another name for the specific-unit-cost method *(p. 464)*.

Specific-unit-cost method Inventory cost method based on the specific cost of particular units of inventory *(p. 464)*.

Spreadsheet A computer program that links data by means of formulas and functions; an electronic work sheet *(p. 300)*.

Stable-monetary-unit concept Accountants' basis for ignoring the effect of inflation and making no adjustments for the changing value of the dollar *(p. 11)*.

Statement of earnings Another name for the income statement *(p. 20)*.

Statement of financial position Another name for the balance sheet *(p. 20)*.

Statement of operations Another name for the income statement. Also called the statement of earnings *(p. 20)*.

Statement of owner's equity Summary of the changes in an entity's owner's equity during a specific period *(p. 20)*.

Straight-line (SL) amortization method Amortization method in which an equal amount of amortization expense is assigned to each year (or period) of asset use *(p. 513)*.

Subsidiary ledger Book of accounts that provides supporting details on individual balances, the total of which appears in a general ledger account *(p. 304)*.

Temporary account Another name for a nominal account. The revenue and expense accounts that relate to a particular accounting period and are closed at the end of the period are temporary accounts. For a proprietorship, the owner withdrawal account is also temporary *(p. 169)*.

Time-period concept Ensures that accounting information is reported at regular intervals *(p. 112)*.

Time Another name for the interest period *(p. 421)*.

Trademarks and trade names or brand names Distinctive identifications of a product or service *(p. 528)*.

Transaction An event that affects the financial position of a particular entity and may be reliably recorded *(p. 13)*.

Trial balance A list of all the ledger accounts with their balances *(p. 72)*.

Trojan horse A computer virus that does not reproduce but gets included into program code without consent and performs actions that can be destructive *(p. 354)*.

Uncollectible-account expense Cost to the seller of extending credit. Arises from the failure to collect from credit customers. Also called doubtful-account expense or bad-debt expense *(p. 411)*.

Unearned revenue A liability created when a business collects cash from customers in advance of doing work for the customer. The obligation is to provide a product or a service in the future. Also called deferred revenue *(p. 121)*.

Units-of-production (UOP) amortization method Amortization method by which a fixed amount of amortization is assigned to each unit of output produced by the capital asset *(p. 514)*.

Wasting assets or natural resources Capital assets that are natural resources *(p. 526)*.

Weighted-average cost method Inventory costing method based on the weighted-average cost of inventory during the period. Weighted average cost is determined by dividing the cost of goods available for sale by the number of units available. Also called the average cost method *(p. 464)*.

Withheld income tax Income tax deducted from employees' gross pay *(p. 576)*.

Work sheet A columnar document designed to help move data from the trial balance to the financial statements *(p. 164)*.

Workers' Compensation A provincially administered plan that is funded by contributions by employers and that provides financial support for workers injured on the job *(p. 578)*.

Index

Check Figures

P1-1A	Total assets, $80,800
P1-2A	Total assets, $80,000
P1-3A	Total assets, $160,000
P1-4A	No check figure
P1-5A	Net income, $70,000; total assets, $335,000
P1-6A	Net income, $7,900; total assets, $35,650
P1-7A	No check figure
P1-8A	Total assets, $122,000; net income, $50,000
P1-1B	Total assets, $107,000
P1-2B	Total assets, $49,000
P1-3B	Total assets, $110,000
P1-4B	No check figure
P1-5B	Net income, $40,000; total assets, $126,000
P1-6B	Net income, $5,240; total assets, $41,220
P1-7B	No check figure
P1-8B	Total assets, $93,850; net income, $7,350
P1-1C	No check figure
P1-2C	No check figure
DP 1	No check figure
DP 2	No check figure
FSP 1	No check figure

P2-1A	Net income, $70,000
P2-2A	No check figure
P2-3A	Trial balance total, $43,500
P2-4A	Trial balance total, $39,700
P2-5A	Trial balance total, $70,000; net income, $5,870
P2-6A	Trial balance total, $119,200
P2-7A	Net income, $1,400; total assets, $111,400
P2-8A	No check figure
P2-9A	No check figure
P2-1B	Net loss, $7,000
P2-2B	No check figure
P2-3B	Trial balance total, $45,500
P2-4B	Trial balance total, $53,700
P2-5B	Trial balance total, $61,900; net income, $7,640
P2-6B	Trial balance total, $60,500
P2-7B	Net income, $1,400; total assets, $53,600
P2-8B	No check figure
P2-9B	No check figure
P2-1C	No check figure
P2-2C	No check figure
DP 1	Trial balance total, $21,800; net income, $5,200
DP 2	No check figure
FSP 1	No check figure

P3-1A	Cash net loss, $2,475; accrual net income, $1,350
P3-2A	No check figure
P3-3A	No check figure
P3-4A	No check figure
P3-5A	Adjusted trial balance total, $99,750
P3-6A	Net income, $138,940; total assets, $240,060
P3-7A	Net income, $11,175; total assets, $64,575
P3-8A	Trial balance total, $356,400; net income, $68,400
P3-1B	Cash net loss, $5,400; accrual net income, $1,600
P3-2B	No check figure
P3-3B	No check figure
P3-4B	No check figure
P3-5B	Adjusted trial balance total, $76,095
P3-6B	Net income, $92,060; total assets, $125,620
P3-7B	Net income, $11,400; total assets, $68,850
P3-8B	Trial balance total, $231,000; net income, $64,600
P3-1C	No check figure
P3-2C	No check figure
DP 1	Ending adjusted owner's equity, $83,100
DP 2	No check figure
FSP 1	Ending balance (thousands): Prepaid expenses and other, $13,186
P3A-1	Ending balances: Unearned service revenue, $2,400; Service revenue, $800
P3A-2	Total liabilities and owner's equity, $900

P4-1A	Net income, $33,920
P4-2A	Net income, $50,778; total assets, $148,608
P4-3A	Net income, $114,000; total assets, $196,000
P4-4A	Postclosing trial balance total, $286,000
P4-5A	Net income, $38,625; total assets, $156,480
P4-6A	Total assets, $257,600
P4-7A	Net income understated by $920
P4-8A	Net income, $30,600
P4-9A	Net income, $75,200; total assets, $263,600
P4-1B	Net income, $29,640
P4-2B	Net income, $59,480; total assets, $325,320
P4-3B	Net income, $144,000; total assets, $238,000
P4-4B	Postclosing trial balance total, $272,000
P4-5B	Net income, $11,985; total assets, $178,620
P4-6B	Total assets, $44,100
P4-7B	Net income overstated by $1,960
P4-8B	Net income, $138,000
P4-9B	Net income, $14,450; total assets, $63,050
P4-1C	No check figure
P4-2C	No check figure
DP 1	Net income, $107,080; total assets, $116,780; total owner's equity, $70,240
DP 2	No check figure
FSP 1	Current ratio, 2000, 1.30; debt ratio, 2000, 0.70
P4A-1	Ending balances: Salary payable, $0; Salary expense, $180

P5-1A	No check figure
P5-2A	No check figure
P5-3A	No check figure
P5-4A	Net income, $100,780
P5-5A	Ending capital balance, $133,520
P5-6A	Net income, $105,200; total assets, $236,400
P5-7A	Net income, $105,400; total assets, $336,400
P5-8A	Net income, $65,250
P5-9A	Gross margin, $28,500
P5-10A	Gross margin, $14,860
P5-11A	Net loss, $7,050; total assets, $18,300
P5-1B	No check figure
P5-2B	No check figure
P5-3B	Receivable amount, $2,400; no discount
P5-4B	Net income, $72,480
P5-5B	Ending capital balance, $126,120
P5-6B	Net loss, $8,550; total assets, $172,350
P5-7B	Net loss, $8,400; total assets, $172,350
P5-8B	Net income, $54,300
P5-9B	Gross margin, $34,300
P5-10B	Gross margin, $10,968
P5-11B	Net loss, $12,540; total assets, $123,060
P5-1C	No check figure
P5-2C	No check figure
DP 1	Net income, $60,170; total assets, $105,630
DP 2	No check figure
DP 3	No check figure
FSP 1	Closed to Retained earnings, $76,493,000
P5S-1	No check figure
P5S-2	No check figure
P5S-3	Receivable balance, $2,400; no discount
P5S-4	Gross margin, $196,160; net income, $88,050; total assets, $218,110

P6-1A	No check figure
P6-2A	Total cash, $69,906
P6-3A	Total cash, $5,929
P6-4A	Total accounts payable, $21,500; total cash, $28,372
P6-5A	Total cash, $29,160
P6-6A	Total cash, $25,440
P6-1B	No check figure
P6-2B	Total cash, $72,007
P6-3B	Total cash, $26,380
P6-4B	Total accounts payable, $4,577; total cash, $6,326
P6-5B	Total cash, $27,170